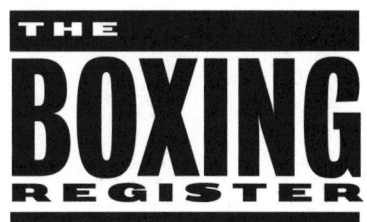

THE
BOXING
REGISTER

THE
BOXING
REGISTER

INTERNATIONAL BOXING HALL OF FAME
Official Record Book

4TH EDITION

By James B. Roberts and Alexander G. Skutt

McBooks Press, Inc.
Ithaca, New York

Book and cover design by Rider Design
Cover Photo: Willie Pep retains World Featherweight title over Ray Famechon, Johnny Addie refereed (3/17/50). AP Images.

Library of Congress Cataloging-in-Publication Data

Roberts, James B., 1962-
   The boxing register : international boxing hall of fame official record book / by James B. Roberts and Alexander G. Skutt.—4th ed.
       p. cm.
   ISBN-13: 978-1-59013-121-3 (trade pbk. : alk. paper)
   ISBN-10: 1-59013-121-5
   1. Boxing—Records. 2. Boxers (Sports)—Biography. 3. Boxing—History.
4. International Boxing Hall of Fame. I. Skutt, Alexander G., 1948-
   II. International Boxing Hall of Fame. III. Title.
   GV1137.R63 2006
   796.83—dc22
                           2006007850

Additional copies of this book may be ordered from any bookstore or directly from McBooks Press, Inc., ID Booth Building, 520 North Meadow Street, Ithaca, NY 14850. Please include $5.00 postage and handling with mail orders. New York State residents must add sales tax to total remittance (books and shipping). All McBooks Press publications can also be ordered by calling toll-free 1-888-BOOKS11 (1-888-266-5711).

The Boxing Register and other boxing books and memorabilia are available from the International Boxing Hall of Fame, One Hall of Fame Drive, Canastota, NY 13032, 1-315-697-7095.

Visit the McBooks Press website at
www.mcbooks.com

Printed in the United States of America

9 8 7 6 5 4 3 2 1

CONTENTS

FOREWORD

I GREW UP WITH BOXING. I must have been seven or eight years old when I had a kind of vision—boxing gloves flashed through my mind—that let me know that the sport was going to play a big part in my life. Of course, living in Canastota, New York, may have had something to do with that. I was born and raised in this village of 5,000 people. It has produced two world champions as well as a number of trainers, managers, boxing writers, and other participants of the sport. Canastota loves boxing and has supported it for a long time.

I was born in 1956, the year Canastota's Carmen Basilio lost the world welterweight title to Johnny Saxton and then won it back again. As I grew up, I heard stories about Carmen from my father and other townspeople. By the time I was ten or eleven, I was mowing lawns and doing odd jobs to earn enough money for my subscription to *The Ring* and the boxing books I wanted, like Nat Fleischer's series on how to box, how to train, and how to manage a fighter.

You can imagine my excitement when up-and-coming Canastota boxer Billy Backus moved in next door. Billy was fighting top-ten opponents in the welterweight division. I often went to Syracuse to watch his bouts, and at the age of 14, I sat in his corner for his victorious championship fight against Jose Napoles. After that, I accompanied Billy to subsequent fights. I spent time in the dressing room, I watched him train in the gym, and I paid attention to everything that went on around me. I even got in the ring a few times myself, mostly for the experience. I knew trying out the boxer's role would give me more insight into the sport.

By the time I was in my late teens, I had started training some amateurs, and I learned as much as I could about what it was like to run a gym. I was interested in the concept of inspiring troubled youth to direct their energies toward learning to box. I was able to follow my interest in promotion in my early twenties, when I rented the Syracuse War Memorial several times and put on boxing shows. I dealt with the matchmakers, and I saw firsthand what happens when a match falls apart 48 hours before the show and how you put it back together again.

If you add to this background my interest as a fan, historian, and collector, I've been very fortunate in seeing and experiencing just about every aspect of the sport. As executive director of the International Boxing Hall of Fame, I now help to preserve the history of boxing.

IN 1984, THE HALL OF FAME WAS JUST AN IDEA, operating out of a borrowed office with a desk, a phone, a pencil, and a pad of paper. From finding out what a "feasibility study" was, to having one done, to the first Induction Weekend, and now plans for expansion, the Hall has fulfilled many purposes. It's a place where the rich history of boxing can be maintained and where visitors can develop a deeper understanding of the world's oldest sport. It's also a place where mottos like Willie Pep's "keep on punchin'" or Muhammad Ali's "dare to be great" continue to inspire.

The Hall of Fame is also a way for Canastota to say thank you to the sport and to those who have kept it alive. The village has become a second hometown to many in the boxing world. Canastota has an appreciation of the sport, and the Hall is a way of getting boxers to come here and be thanked for everything they have given us. Friendships among townspeople and international boxers have developed, and as Canastota continues to extend its hospitality, more and more boxers feel comfortable coming here.

The International Boxing Hall of Fame is proud to now have its own official record book, *The Boxing Register*, which gives boxing fans, as well as newcomers to the sport, something to study and enjoy long after their visit to the Hall of Fame. Those who have boxing in their blood will appreciate it as a way to keep memories alive. Those who are just learning about boxing will be exposed to the excitement of the sport's unparalleled competition. The book also touches on the cultural and social significance of boxing, and through the life stories of many of the boxers in this book, it will be obvious that the sport has provided many young people with a way to turn their lives around. And it still continues to do so today.

Boxing is an international, equal-opportunity sport that transcends borders and ethnic differences. Controlled boxing, with judges and referees and gloves, is a healthy outgrowth of humankind's natural instinct to fight. It is both an art and a science, and it is very much about personal achievement. *The Boxing Register* offers a look into the lives and careers of the best in this unique sport.

EDWARD BROPHY
Canastota, New York

ACKNOWLEDGMENTS

THE AUTHORS RECEIVED A GREAT DEAL OF HELP FROM THE BOXING COMMUNITY in creating this updated fourth edition of *The Boxing Register*. First, we want to thank Executive Director Edward Brophy, Historian Jeff Brophy, the Board of Directors, and the rest of the IBHOF staff for their help. They warmly welcomed us to their exciting museum and gave us access to their excellent library. Jeff Brophy is a knowledgeable and meticulous researcher who demonstrated an endless willingness to review our work, answer our questions, and locate invaluable news clippings and magazine articles in the Hall of Fame's extensive files.

We are extremely grateful for the generosity of Anibal Miramontes of Fight Fax, Inc., and his predecessor Phill Marder, who gave us fight-by-fight records of all the Modern Era boxers. The information we present on fighters' weigh-in weights was initially based on the data they provided. Fight Fax publishes the mammoth annual, *The Boxing Record Book,* which contains the complete records of all contemporary boxers. When we were well along in producing the fourth edition of *The Boxing Register,* we received the extremely kind help of Deepak Nahar. Mr. Nahar shared the fruits of his extensive research on historical fight-by-fight records—in particular, weigh-in weight information—which he painstakingly gleaned from original sources.

The Ring magazine has been a vitally important part of boxing since 1922. It is now published by London Publishing Co., 7002 West Butler Pike, Ambler, PA 19002, which also publishes several other boxing magazines. We want to thank publisher Stuart Saks for giving us access to *The Ring*'s amazing archive of boxing photographs. Editor-in-chief Nigel Collins and the rest of London's sports staff were very hospitable and informative.

Any boxing record book owes a huge debt to the long series of boxing annuals that were published from 1941 to 1987: *The Ring Record Book and Boxing Encyclopedia*. These volumes were edited for many years by *The Ring* founder Nat Fleischer and, for the last few years of their existence, by the distinguished boxing historian, Herbert G. Goldman. Recently, the Internet revolutionized boxing scholarship. Collecting and verifying records of early fights used to require trips to the distant libraries or archives and mind-numbing searches through stacks of dusty newspapers, magazines, boxing commission minutes, or through endless rolls of microfilmed newspapers. Some of this work has been made much easier by the power of the computer and the availability of such on-line research services as ProQuest and newspaperarchives.com.

Much of the boxing community is cooperating on the wonderful (and gargantuan) record keeping effort at www.boxrec.com. This Internet boxing database project is an invaluable source to the serious boxing fan and was a great aid in researching many additions and corrections to the fourth edition of *The Boxing Register.* The discussion forum editors and participants usually had speedy responses to our questions.

Many boxing experts have provided information and advice for this and earlier editions of this book. We would like to especially thank Herbert G. Goldman, Don Majeski, Mike DeLisa, Tracy Callis, Laurence Fielding, and Ed Maloney.

Wendy Skinner of McBooks Press, original editor of *The Boxing Register,* is a fine writer who truly appreciates the terrible allure of boxing. The authors thank her for her Herculean efforts in bringing the first edition of this book into existence. We also want to acknowledge the outstanding editorial work of Jackie Swift, Jameson Romeo-Hall, Ellen Potter, Devon Stout, Patricia Zafiriadis, S.K. List, Romana Mancini, and Corinne Wright.

Michael Rider of Rider Design created the striking design for *The Boxing Register*. Panda Musgrove skillfully produced this extensively revised edition. Judith Kip compiled the excellent index.

ABBREVIATIONS

Opponents' Designation

♛   World Champion
⑩   Top Ten Contender
★   Member, International Boxing Hall of Fame

Ring Records

TB	Total Bouts
KO	Knockouts
W	Wins by Decision
WF	Wins by Foul or Disqualification
KO'd	Knocked Out ("KO by")
L	Losses by Decision
LF	Losses by Foul or Disqualification
ND	No-Decision Bouts

Results

KO	Knock-out Win
TKO	Technical Knock-out Win
W	Win by Decision
WF	Win by Foul or Disqualification
TW	Technical Win
D	Draw
KO'd	Knock-out Loss ("KO by")
TKO'd	Technical Knock-out Loss
L	Loss by Decision
LF	Loss by Foul or Disqualification
TL	Technical Loss
TD	Technical Draw
ND	No-Decision Bout
ND-W	No-Decision Bout with "Newspaper-Win"
ND-L	No-Decision Bout with "Newspaper-Loss"
ND-D	No-Decision Bout with "Newspaper-Draw"
NC	No Contest
Exh	Exhibition

NO-DECISION BOUTS

The authors have provided, where possible, the "newspaper result" of no-decision bouts—early 20th century fights where by state law or other rule judges did not render official decisions when the bout went the distance. However, because of their unofficial nature, these newspaper results have not been included in the totals of wins, losses, and draws listed at the top of each boxer's record.

Title Bouts

BK	Bare-knuckle title
For	Fought for a title and lost
Lost	Lost a title
Reg	Regained a title formerly held
Ret	Retained a title by winning or drawing
Won	Won a title for the first time
Vac	Fought for a vacant title (no current titleholder)

Weight Divisions

symbol	division	modern weight limits	contested since
H	Heavyweight*	Over 190 lbs.	1719
C	Cruiserweight	176-190	1979
LH	Light Heavyweight*	169-175	1903
SM	Super Middleweight	161-168	1984
M	Middleweight*	155-160	1853
JM	Junior Middleweight	148-154	1962
W	Welterweight*	141-147	1888
JW	Junior Welterweight~	136-140	1922 (except 1935–1946)
L	Lightweight*	131-135	1896
JL	Junior Lightweight+	127-130	1921 (except 1934–1949)
FE	Featherweight*	123-126	1890
JFE	Junior Featherweight✓	119-122	1922 (except 1924–1976)
B	Bantamweight*	116-118	1887
JB	Junior Bantamweight	113-115	1980
FL	Flyweight*	109-112	1913
JFL	Junior Flyweight	106-108	1975
S	Strawweight	105 and under	1988

* Long-contested titles, historically the most widely recognized and prestigious
~ Called Super Lightweight by the WBC
+ Called Super Featherweight by the WBC
✓ Called Super Bantamweight by the WBC

Sanctioning Bodies

EBU	European Boxing Union
IBF	International Boxing Federation
NABF	North American Boxing Federation
NBA	National Boxing Association
NYSAC	New York State Athletic Commission
USBA	United States Boxing Association
WBA	World Boxing Association
WBC	World Boxing Council
WBO	World Boxing Organization

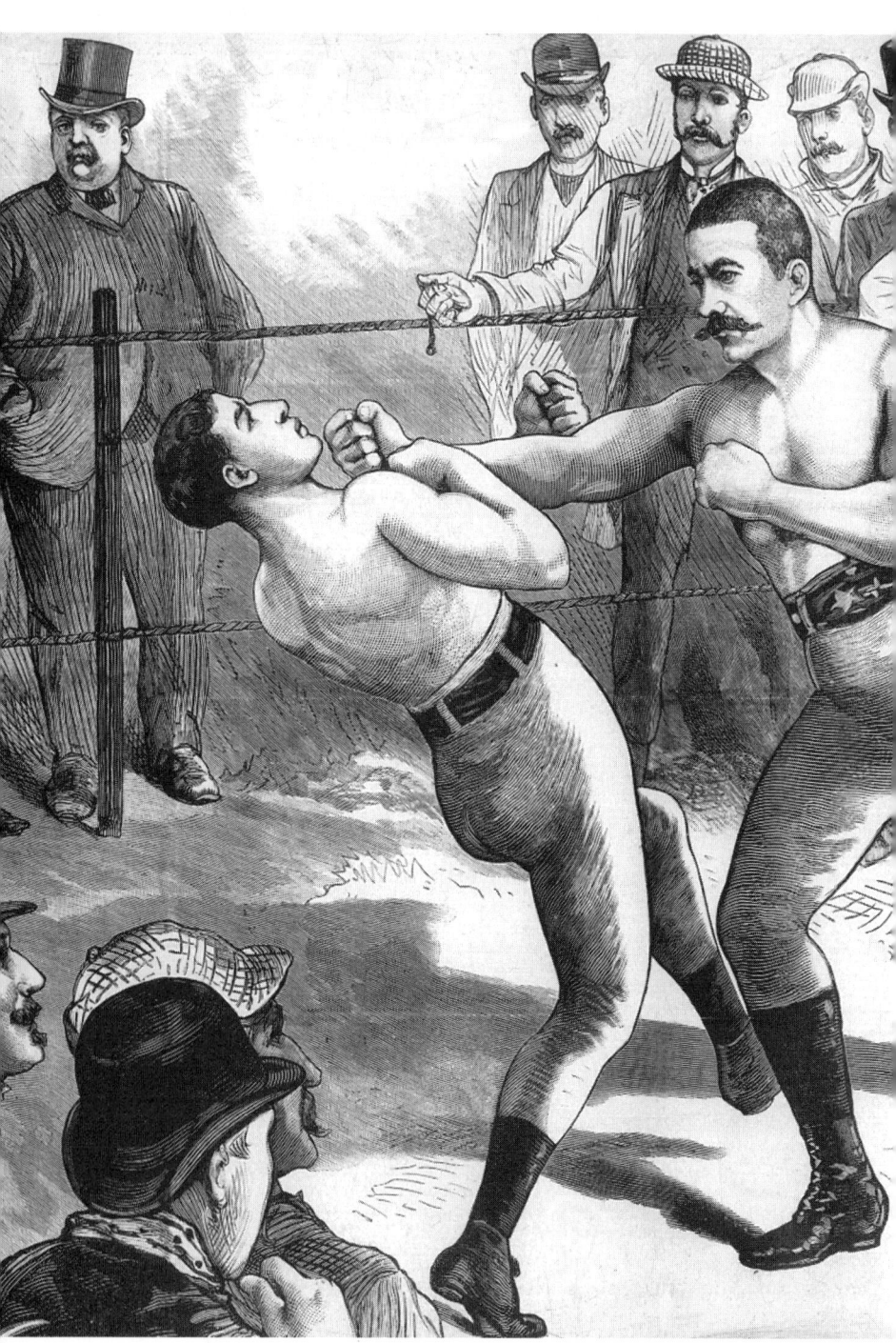

THE
PIONEERS

From Bare-Knuckle Brawlers to The Boston Strong Boy

WHILE THE ANCIENT CIVILIZATIONS of Egypt, and later Greece and Rome, provide the first recorded history of hand-to-hand combat as an organized public spectacle, the origins of modern boxing are to be found in eighteenth-century England, where the first bare-knuckle champions were recognized. The Pioneers inducted into the International Boxing Hall of Fame all fought in the bare-knuckle era. Now largely forgotten by all but boxing historians, these early fighters laid the foundations of boxing as we know it today.

The typical early contest was an un-regulated, no-holds-barred battle. The "ring" was defined by the circle of spectators. There was no referee, nor any rounds or time limits. Gloves had yet to be introduced and, beyond the fighters' personal sense of sportsmanship, there were no rules. The object was to fight until one man could no longer go on. Bouts routinely lasted for hours, and while fists were considered the primary weapon, no tactic—including strangling, gouging, throwing, kicking, sometimes even using a small cudgel—was forbidden. For many decades, no consideration was given to the relative weight of the opponents, and no organization existed to give official recognition to champions or

Daniel Mendoza's three bouts with Richard Humphries captured England's imagination.

challengers. To set up a title bout, a fighter would issue, often in writing, a challenge or response to the champion's open invitation to take on worthy contenders.

Fisticuffs as a sport first arose in the working class, sometimes as the result of a grudge or dispute, but as bare-knuckle fights gained popularity, the upper classes—even royalty—took notice. Wealthy patrons sponsored fighters, arenas, and schools where "the noble art of self-defense" was taught. The ring soon became a square, permanently enclosed with wooden rails or heavy rope.

Boxing's first recognized champion was Hall of Famer James Figg, who claimed and wore the crown from 1719 until his death in 1740. He operated Figg's Amphitheatre in London and did much to establish boxing as a popular sport. In 1743, a subsequent champion, Jack Broughton, wrote a set

of rudimentary rules for governing behavior in the ring. Broughton's Rules stood until 1838, when the more detailed London Prize Ring Rules were introduced.

Until the appearance of Daniel Mendoza, English champion from 1791 to 1795, fisticuffs was largely a contest of brawn. Stamina and sheer brute strength often determined the winner of a marathon bout. Mendoza, a middleweight by modern standards, introduced a wider range of ring skills and strategies for overcoming an opponent, and the anything-goes crudity of the early fights began to give way to the science of boxing.

Americans invaded the English boxing scene when black freemen Bill Richmond and Tom Molineaux arrived in the early 1800s to challenge English fighters. Molineaux became the first African-American to fight in a title bout when he met Tom Cribb in 1810. The first organized bout in the United States took place in 1816 in New York when Americans Jacob Hyer and Tom Beasley fought under English rules. In 1836, English champion James ("Deaf") Burke followed Irish title-holder Sam O'Rourke to New Orleans for a rowdy set-to that ended when spectators rushed the ring. Five years later, Hyer's son Tom and a fighter called Yankee Sullivan met in the first recognized American championship fight. In 1860, American John Heenan ("The Benica Boy") travelled to England to face English champion Tom Sayers in the first transatlantic title fight to be well-publicized on both sides of the ocean.

Boxing began to resemble its modern-day form more closely when Englishman John Graham Chambers,

A CHRONOLOGY OF PIONEER HALL OF FAMERS

Name	Birth	Death	Nationality	Weight	Approx. Reign	Page
James Figg	1695	1734	British	Heavyweight	1719–1734	28
Jack Broughton	1704	1789	British	Heavyweight	1738–1750	18
Tom Johnson	1750	1797	British	Heavyweight	1784–1791	32
Benjamin Brain	1753	1794	British	Heavyweight	1791–1794	17
Bill Richmond	1763	1829	American	Heavyweight	—	41
Daniel Mendoza	1764	1836	British	Heavyweight	1794–1795	36
Caleb Baldwin	1769	1827	British	Lightweight	circa 1800	15
John Jackson	1769	1845	British	Heavyweight	1795	31
Dutch Sam	1775	1816	British	Lightweight	—	25
Henry ("Hen") Pearce	1777	1809	British	Heavyweight	1805	39
Jem Belcher	1781	1811	British	Heavyweight	1800–1803	16
Tom Cribb	1781	1848	British	Heavyweight	1809–1822	22
Tom Molineaux	1784	1818	American	Heavyweight	—	37
Jack Randall	1794	1828	British	Middleweight	—	40
Tom Spring	1795	1851	British	Heavyweight	1823–1824	43
Barney Aaron	1800	1850	British	Lightweight	—	14
Jem Ward	1800	1884	British	Heavyweight	1825–1831	47
Young Dutch Sam	1808	1843	British	Lightweight	—	26
James Burke	1809	1845	British	Heavyweight	1833–1839	19
William Thompson	1811	1880	British	Heavyweight	1839–40, 1845–50	46
Nat Langham	1820	1871	British	Middleweight	1843–1853	34
Tom Sayers	1826	1865	British	Middle/Heavy	1857–1860	42
John Morrissey	1831	1878	American	Heavyweight	1858	38
Jem Mace	1831	1910	British	Heavyweight	1866–1871	35
John C. Heenan	1835	1873	American	Heavyweight	—	30
Tom King	1835	1888	British	Heavyweight	1862–1863	33
Joe Goss	1838	1885	British	Middle/Heavy	1876–1880	29
Billy Edwards	1844	1907	British	Lightweight	1868–1872	27
Arthur Chambers	1847	1925	British	Lightweight	1872–1877, 1879	21
Mike Donovan	1847	1918	American	Middleweight	—	23
Jem Carney	1857	1941	British	Lightweight	1884–1891	20
Paddy Duffy	1864	1890	American	Welterweight	1888–1889	24
John L. Sullivan	1858	1918	American	Heavyweight	1882–1892	44–45

under the sponsorship of the Marquess of Queensberry, devised a new set of rules in 1867. The Queensberry Rules, as they came to be known, established three-minute rounds with a minute's rest in between and called for the use of protective gloves. The new rules were universally adopted, and John L. Sullivan ("The Boston Strong Boy"), who was American champion from 1882 to 1892, was both the last bare-knuckle titleholder and the first heavyweight to be crowned under the Queensberry Rules.

While boxing in England had become an acceptable pastime, with many boxers touring in circuses or performing at fairs, it was illegal in much of the United States, and most early fights were held in out-of-the-way places to avoid police intervention. By the time the enormously popular Sullivan came along, police often looked the other way. Boxing exhibitions were often staged in vaudeville theatres, and audiences expanded to include ladies and top-hatted gentlemen.

BARNEY AARON
The Star of the East

Right-handed; 5'8"; 138 lbs.
Hall of Fame Induction: 2001
Born: 11/21/1800, Aldgate, England
Died: 1850

One of the top lighter-weight fighters of early nineteenth-century England, Barney Aaron enjoyed boxing even as a young boy. Aaron's first recorded fight was in 1819 when he was challenged by William Connelly, known as the Rosemary Lane Champion. Aaron beat the more experienced Connelly in sixteen rounds over 33 minutes. In his next fight Aaron suffered defeat at the fists of the heavier Manny Lyons. Worn out after 75 minutes of battle, Aaron was unable to continue. He avenged this loss in a 50-minute rematch victory.

With a few more wins, Aaron established a solid reputation as one of the best lightweights of that era. On March 19, 1823, he attended the fights at Moulsey Hurst. A third bout was added to the bill when a purse was offered, and Tom Collins and Aaron rose to the challenge. Aaron dominated the fight until an injury to his left hand forced him to quit. His performance attracted notice, however, and he now began to fight on a more regular basis. Aaron's 1823 and 1824 victories over Ned Stockman, Lenney (twice), Frank Redmond, and Peter Warren, earned him a reputation as one of the best lightweights in England. Called The Star of the East, Aaron was considered the greatest Jewish fighter since Hall of Famer Dutch Sam.

Aaron next challenged Arthur Matthewson, who was undefeated and known as one of the top small fighters of his day. The two battled through 57 rounds until Matthewson caught Aaron with a shot to the throat, knocking him out. A blow to the throat also spelled defeat for Aaron in a match against Dick Curtis on February 27, 1827, though the match was considered a great exhibition of fighting skill on the part of both combatants.

Aaron continued to fight until April 1, 1834, when he lost to Tom Smith, the East End Sailor Boy, seven years his junior. While he met with defeat in some of his toughest battles, Aaron left behind a sterling reputation in the prize ring. In retirement, he served as an attendant at ringside for important fights, while making his living as a fishmonger. His namesake son immigrated to America in 1855 and soon began to box as Young Aaron. Young Aaron twice held the American lightweight championship, in 1857–58 and in 1867.

SELECTED BOUTS

Date	Year	Opponent	Location	Result / Duration	Title
—	1819	William Connelly	—	W 16 rounds	—
Mar 19	1823	Tom Collins	Moulsey Hurst, Surrey, Eng.	L stopped by injury 30 min.	—
May 6	1823	Ned Stockton	Blindlow Heath, Sussex, Eng.	W 40 rounds	—
Aug 5	1823	Lenney	Harpenden Common, Eng.	W 11 rounds	—
Nov 11	1823	Lenney	Moulsey Hurst	W 21 rounds	—
Dec 30	1823	Frank Redmond	Moulsey Hurst	W 29 rounds	—
Apr 6	1824	Peter Warren	Colbrook, England	W 29 rounds	—
June 21	1824	Arthur Matthewson	—	L 57 rounds	—
Feb 27	1827	Dick Curtis	Andover, England	L 50 min.	—
Oct 23	1827	Frank Redmond	near St. Albans, England	W 42 rounds	—
Apr 1	1834	Tom Smith	Greenstreet Green, Kent, Eng.	L 20 rounds	—

CALEB BALDWIN
The Pride of Westminster, The Westminster Costermonger

Considered by some to be the first lightweight champion in boxing, Caleb Baldwin is known to have lost only one fight. Baldwin was born in the Lambeth area of Westminster, England, on April 22, 1769, and named Caleb Stephen Ramsbottom. His father was a costermonger, or fruit seller. Baldwin was forced to fend for himself at an early age. Each day Baldwin went to the markets to buy goods to sell and then peddled them all over London. In the course of his daily trade, there would often be disputes that were settled with fisticuffs.

Right-handed; 5'6½"; 133–135 lbs.
Hall of Fame Induction: 2003
Born: 4/22/1769, Westminster, London, England
Named: Caleb Stephen Ramsbottom
Died: 11/8/1827

In his first recorded fight, the seventeen-year-old Baldwin defeated Jim Gregory, a porkpickler, in twenty rounds. In his next bout, he defeated Jem Jones, a chimney sweep. Tom Johnson, then the English champion, witnessed the Jones fight and was very impressed. Johnson backed Baldwin in a match against Arthur ("The Gypsy") Smith. Baldwin won a convincing victory.

There is no record of Baldwin having lost a fight until he met Hall of Famer Dutch Sam on August 7, 1804, at Woodford Green. By this point the 5'6½"-135 pound Baldwin was in some circles considered the lightweight champion. Baldwin was more experienced than Sam and did better in the early going. He attempted to control the action on the inside to utilize his somewhat superior size, while Sam countered with uppercuts to the face. For the first twenty rounds Baldwin dominated, but by the 26th both fighters were near exhaustion. Sam then took command and stopped Baldwin in the 37th round.

Baldwin fought a draw the next year with Bill Ryan. There is no record of him fighting again until May 1816, when he met Young Massa Bristow. Baldwin, then 47, was serving as master of ceremonies at a prizefight. He struck about with a riding whip to clear the inner ring for the contest. Young Massa Bristow, a black servant, took umbrage at being struck and punched Baldwin to the ground. The two parties agreed to immediately enter the ring. The aging Baldwin was no match for Bristow. Bristow threw him with a cross-buttock hold and then pointed his finger derisively at the veteran. Bristow was paid 30 pounds after the thirteenth round to call the fight off. Baldwin died in London at the age of 58.

SELECTED BOUTS

Date	Year	Opponent	Location	Result / Duration		Title
—	1786	Jim Gregory	London	W	20 rds	—
—	1786	Jem Jones	Wimbledon, England	W	15 min	—
—	—	Arthur ("The Gypsy") Smith	Kelsey Green, England	W	25 min	—
May 14	1792	Tom ("Paddington") Jones	Hurley Bottom, Berkshire, England	D	30 min	—
July 3	1792	Jem Jones	East London, England	W	40 min	—
Dec 22	1800	James Kelly	Wimbledon	W	12 rds	—
Nov 25	1801	Jack ("Butcher") Lee	Hurley Bottom	W	21 rds	—
Oct 21	1803	Jack O'Donnell	Wimbledon	W	8 rds	—
Aug 7	1804	Dutch Sam★	Woodford Green, Essex, England	L	37 rds	—
Aug 6	1805	Bill Ryan	Blackheath, London	D	26 rds	—
May	1816	Young Massa Bristow	England	D	13 rds	—

JEM BELCHER

Right-handed; 5'11½"; 166–182 lbs.
English Champion 1800–05
Hall of Fame Induction: 1992
Born: 4/15/1781, Bristol, England
Died: 7/30/1811

A very agile, quick-hitting fighter, Jem Belcher held the English prize ring title for five years at the beginning of the nineteenth century. Born in Bristol, the home of many of boxing's early champions, Belcher first fought professionally in his hometown in 1798 when he defeated Jack Britton. A year later, Belcher fought Jack Bartholomew to a 51-round draw. At the time, Bartholomew was considered the champion in many quarters because he had beaten title-claimant Tom Owen. When Belcher triumphed over Bartholomew in a seventeen-round rematch in 1800, he was hailed as the new champion.

In 1803, Belcher lost sight in one eye when he was struck by the ball in a game of racquets. Half-blind, Belcher avoided defending his title for two years, fighting exhibition bouts only. In 1805, Belcher's former protégé, Henry Pearce, made a claim to the championship because of Belcher's inactivity. The weakened Belcher agreed to fight but, hurt by the loss of the eye and his intemperate lifestyle, he could not stand up to the aggressive, slugging Pearce. Belcher submitted after eighteen rounds.

Perhaps Belcher should have retired to his pub, The Jolly Brewer, after the Pearce defeat. Instead, he agreed in 1807 to fight Hall of Famer Tom Cribb, a champion in the making. The fight attracted a large crowd. For the first twenty rounds, Belcher dominated. Then Cribb hit Belcher over his good eye, nearly closing it. Belcher's hands were seriously injured and his punches were weak. Finally, after 41 rounds, the incapacitated Belcher could not go on. In a rematch two years later, Cribb outclassed Belcher again and won in 31 rounds. The defeat was particularly painful for Belcher because he had wagered his entire fortune on his own victory. He served four weeks in prison for starting a fracas after the fight and, while there, became seriously ill. A ruined man, Belcher died in 1811 and was honored at a well-attended funeral.

SELECTED BOUTS

Date	Year	Opponent	Location	Result / Duration		Title
Mar 16	1798	Jack Britton	Bristol, England	W	33 min.	—
Apr 15	1799	Paddington Jones	Wormwood Scrubbs, England	W	33 min.	—
Aug 15	1799	♛ Jack Bartholomew	Uxbridge, England	D	51 rounds	For-England-H
May 15	1800	♛ Jack Bartholomew	Finchley, England	W	17 rounds	Won-England-H
Dec 22	1800	Andrew Gamble	Wimbledon, England	W	5 rounds	Ret-England-H
Mar 16	1801	Joe Berks	Camberwell, England	W	14 rounds	Ret-England-H
Nov 25	1801	Joe Berks	Hurley, England	W	16 rounds	Ret-England-H
Aug 20	1802	Joe Berks	London	W	14 rounds	Ret-England-H
Apr 12	1803	Jack Firley	Linton, England	W	11 rounds	Ret-England-H
Dec 6	1805	Henry ("Hen") Pearce ★	Near Doncaster, England	L	18 rounds	Lost-England-H
Apr 8	1807	Tom Cribb ★	Moulsey Hurst, England	L	41 rounds	—
Feb 1	1809	Tom Cribb ★	Epsom Downs, England	L	31 rounds	—

BENJAMIN BRAIN
Big Ben

Benjamin ("Big Ben") Brain outweighed most men and even most professional fighters in the England of the 1780s. A coal miner by trade, Brain was a valiant fighter whose career spanned twenty years. Brain was born in the port city of Bristol, in southwestern England. His first recorded fight took place in 1774, when he defeated Jack Clayton, the champion of Kingswood.

In 1786, when Brain battled John Boone ("The Fighting Grenadier"), toughs broke into the ring and ganged up on Brain. In the resulting melee, Brain suffered a beating that almost closed his eyes. When order was restored and a surgeon had lanced the swelling around Brain's eyes, Big Ben resumed fighting. Within ten minutes, he forced Boone to quit in defeat.

In 1789, Brain was scheduled to fight the English champion, Hall of Famer Tom Johnson. When Brain fell ill and cancelled the bout, he forfeited the large sum of money he had put up for the fight. Two years later, Brain got his chance to fight Johnson for the title at Wrotham-in-Kent. Brain battered Johnson's nose effectively, and Johnson broke a finger in the course of the eighteen-round battle. Brain, then 37, prevailed, to take the title from the 40-year-old Johnson.

Right-handed; 5'10"; 196 lbs.
English Champion 1791–94
Hall of Fame Induction: 1994
Born: 1753, Bristol, England
Died: 4/8/1794

Brain's toppling of Johnson is sometimes seen to mark the end of the first era of boxing, when men stood toe-to-toe and punched and grappled until one of them could no longer go on. There is no question that the early brawlers were courageous, but the boxers who came after Brain began to rely on more than just strength and stamina.

Soon after winning the championship in 1791, and with no challengers coming forward, Brain retired from boxing. The title was then declared vacant. Three years later, there was still no champion, although a suitable challenger had come forward. Brain agreed to return to the ring as the acknowledged titleholder and was scheduled to fight Will Wood in February of 1794 in a comeback bout. However, Brain was stricken with an illness and was unable to fight. He died in April 1794, still considered the champion.

SELECTED BOUTS

Date	Year	Opponent	Location	Result / Duration		Title
—	1774	Jack Clayton	England	W	—	—
Oct 31	1786	John Boone	Bloomsbury, England	W	app. 40 min.	—
Oct 31	1788	W. Corbally	Navestock, England	W	20 min.	—
Oct 23	1789	Jack Jacombs	Banbury, England	W	2 hrs. 5 min.	—
—	1789	Tom Tring	Dartford, England	W	12 rounds	—
Aug 30	1790	William Hooper	Chapel Row Level, Eng.	D	180 rounds	—
Jan 17	1791	♛ Tom Johnson★	Wrotham, England	W	18 rounds	Won-England-H

JACK BROUGHTON
The Father of Boxing

Right-handed; 5'11"; 196–200 lbs.
English Champion 1738–50
Hall of Fame Induction: 1990
Born: 1704, Cirencester, England
Died: 1/8/1789

Jack Broughton is remembered both for his skill as a fighter and for the innovations he brought to the free-for-all fist-icuffs that preceded modern boxing. In Broughton's time, there were few standards of fair play. Bare-handed combat between two men was seen as a civilized advance over dueling with swords or guns, but "the manly art of boxing" was an anything-goes sport with no written code. Broughton came to realize, however, that a well-placed punch could often do more damage than some of the less refined gambits. More than any other fighter before him, Broughton saw the advantage of sizing up a rival and adjusting his methods to overcome a perceived weakness. In 1738, Broughton defeated George Taylor, a student of England's first champion, James Figg, to win the title.

Broughton devised "Broughton's Rules" in 1743, two years after he unintentionally killed ring opponent George Stevenson. While still allowing many avenues of attack, Broughton's Rules introduced the now-familiar prohibition against hitting an adversary "when he is down," banned all but the fighters and their seconds from the ring, and gave a downed man half a minute to get up. Broughton also invented "mufflers," forerunners of modern boxing gloves, for use in training and exhibition matches.

Boxing was a popular diversion of the aristocratic class in the early eighteenth century, and like many early fighters, Broughton had a patron, the Duke of Cumberland. Cumberland abruptly withdrew his support, however, when Broughton lost the title to Jack Slack, Figg's grandson and a butcher by trade, in 1750. The bout with Slack lasted only fourteen minutes because Broughton could not recover from a blinding punch. Boxing historian Pierce Egan reported that Cumberland had thousands of pounds riding on the match and pushed Broughton to fight on even after his eyes had swollen shut. He shouted accusatorially at his fighter, "What are you about, Broughton? You can't fight! You're beat!" According to Egan, the courageous Broughton replied, "I can't see my man, your Highness; I am blind, but not beat; only let me be placed before my antagonist, and he shall not gain the day yet." After this defeat, Broughton never fought again, and he turned his academy, a popular boxing arena, into a profitable antique shop.

Broughton, who lived to be 85 years old, was buried in Westminster Abbey in remembrance of his contribution to English boxing. He earned lasting recognition as "The Father of the English School of Boxing" and as the "Father of the Science of the Art of Self-Defense." His Rules survived for almost 100 years, to be superceded by the London Prize Ring Rules in 1838.

SELECTED BOUTS

Date	Year	Opponent	Location	Result / Duration		Title
Circa	1733	Tom Pipes	England	W	—	—
Circa	1733	Bill Gretting	England	W	—	—
—	1738	George Taylor	England	W	—	Won-England-H
Feb 17	1741	♛ George Stevenson	London	W	40 min.	—
Apr 10	1750	Jack Slack	England	L	14 min.	Lost-England-H

JAMES BURKE
The Deaf 'Un

James ("Deaf") Burke was the first British champion to fight on American soil. He was also the most active champion of his day, fighting twenty bouts, some of gruelling duration. Burke learned to box while working as a waterman on the Thames River. An older boxer gave Burke instruction and put him in the ring against Ned Murphy in 1828. The two battled for 50 rounds, until the match was called a draw because of darkness. Burke fought more marathon bouts in the next few years, including a three-hour victory over Bill Fitzmaurice and a two-hour-and-fifty-minute loss to Bill Cousens.

Burke was unsuccessful in attempts to be matched against champion Jem Ward, but when Ward retired, Burke fought Harry Macone for the title. In a brutal match, Burke triumphed in 59 rounds. The next year, Burke battled challenger Simon Byrne. By the nineteenth round, Burke was on the ground and his ear had been bitten through. The two men fought doggedly for more than three hours, however. Burke finally tapped an exhausted Byrne to the ground in the 99th round. Byrne died three days after the fight. Burke was not blamed, but he avoided competitions and fought only exhibitions for a time.

Right-handed; 5'8½"; 175–178 lbs.

English Champion 1833–39

Hall of Fame Induction: 1992

Born: 12/8/1809, St. Giles, London, England

Died: 1/8/1845

The Irish champion Sam O'Rourke challenged Burke for the title, but Burke declined when O'Rourke insisted that the fight be held in Ireland. O'Rourke then travelled to America, where he constantly denigrated Burke's abilities and courage. On hearing of the insults, Burke decided to meet his challenger in New Orleans in 1836. In the first round, Burke threw O'Rourke to the ground with a cross-buttock hold. In the next round, one of O'Rourke's seconds threw Burke into O'Rourke's grasp. By the third round, the fight had degenerated into a violent free-for-all. The crowd surged into the ring, and Burke was forced to flee the scene on horseback in fear for his life.

On his return to England, Burke faced Bendigo Thompson in the first championship match conducted under the more stringent London Prize Ring Rules, adopted in 1838. Thompson won on a foul in the tenth round. Burke fought twice more before retiring in 1843. Penniless, he died of tuberculosis less than two years later.

SELECTED BOUTS

Date	Year	Opponent	Location	Result / Rounds		Title
Feb 4	1828	Ned Murphy	England	D	50	—
Aug 6	1828	Thomas ("Bull") Hands	England	W	12	—
Jun 9	1829	Bill Fitzmaurice	Herpenden Cmn., Eng.	W	166	—
—	1832	Harry Macone	Lockington Bottom, Eng.	W	59	Won-Vac England-H
May 30	1833	Simon Byrne	near London	W	99	Ret-England-H
May 6	1836	Samuel O'Rourke	New Orleans	NC	3	—
Aug 21	1837	Tom O'Connell	Harts Island, NY	W	10	—
Feb 12	1839	Bendigo Thompson ★	Heather, England	LF	10	Lost-England-H
Jun 13	1843	Bob Castles	Rainham Ferry, England	W	37	—

JEM CARNEY

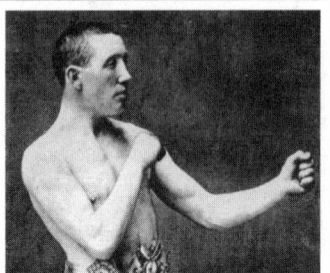

Right-handed; 5'4½"; 127–154 lbs.

English Lightweight Champion 1884–91

Hall of Fame Induction: 2006

Born: 11/5/1857, Birmingham, England

Named: James Carney

Died: 9/11/1941

One of the top lightweight fighters of the nineteenth century, Jem Carney fought both in his native England and in the US. Carney started his boxing career in 1878, when he won all of his three recorded bouts.

In April 1881, Carney journeyed to the United States along with fellow English fighters Sam Breeze, Charles Hopkin, and Jim Walder. He demonstrated his skill at Owney Goeghegan's in the Bowery and also gave exhibitions in Boston and Philadelphia.

After he returned to England, he faced Jimmy Highland. Carney weighed in at 128 pounds and they fought for £25 a side. The pair met near Farnsworth and battled for 43 rounds before the police appeared and broke up the bout. Though the fight was a draw, Carney had by far the better of the action. Highland suffered broken ribs, and he died four days later. Carney was arrested and charged with manslaughter. He was acquitted of that crime but served six months in jail for prizefighting.

On December 20, 1884, Carney defeated Jake Hyams in 45 rounds to take the lightweight championship of England. Carney's next recorded fight was in June 1887 when he met Jimmy Mitchell in eleven rounds on a barge on Long Island Sound. In the eleventh, Carney dealt Mitchell a left to the mouth, and a right and a left to the face and body. He then shoved Mitchell to the ground and finished him with a left hand to the right cheek bone.

On November 16, 1887, Carney faced Hall of Famer Jack McAuliffe for the world lightweight championship in a stable in Revere, Massachusetts. The fight did not start until midnight to avoid the attention of the police. McAuliffe bloodied Carney's nose in the tenth and worked on Carney's eye from the twentieth to the 30th. In the 68th round, the fighters fell to the ground in a clinch. McAuliffe accused Carney of head butting him below the belt while the two were on the stable floor. In the 74th, a Carney right to the jaw sent McAuliffe sprawling. Carney fell on McAuliffe. Just then, some fans entered the ring and the ensuing confusion made it impossible for the fight to continue. It was a draw.

Carney used every means at his disposal while in the ring as when he fought Dick Burge on May 25, 1891. He was disqualified after Burge's seconds called for a foul and the referee heeded their pleas. Carney retired after the Burge fight. In retirement he served as the bodyguard for George Alexander Baird, a colorful figure in English boxing. After Baird's death, Carney enjoyed going to the racetrack. He died in London on September 11, 1941.

SELECTED BOUTS

Date	Year	Opponent	Location	Result / Duration		Title
—	1878	Paddy Giblin	Bromford, England	W	11 min.	
Jul 21	1880	George ("Punch") Callow	London	D	74 rds.	—
Oct 7	1881	James Highland	Wishaw, England	D	43 rds.	For-England BK-128 lbs.
Dec 20	1884	Young Jacob Hyams	London	W	45 rds.	Won-England BK-L
June 17	1887	Jimmy Mitchell	Barge on Long Island Sound	KO	11 rds.	Won-World-136 lbs.
Nov 16	1887	Jack McAuliffe★	Revere, MA	D	74 rds.	For-World-L
May 25	1891	Dick Burge	London	LF	11 rds.	For-England-L

ARTHUR CHAMBERS

Arthur Chambers began fighting at the age of sixteen after a brief stint in the Royal Navy. His first fight on October 1, 1864, was a triumph, a twenty-round victory over his hometown opponent, Arthur Webber. Over the next eight years, Chambers won eight recorded bouts and drew four times. His lone defeat was at the hands of Jem Brady in a fight that lasted one hour and twenty minutes, until it was interrupted by police, then continued the next day for another three and one quarter hours before Brady's eventual victory.

Chambers next travelled to New York. In the manner of the day, he issued public challenges to fighters under 120 pounds, but found no takers. Finally, he was paired with a fellow Englishman, the American lightweight champion, Billy Edwards. Each side put up $2000, the money and championship to go to the victor. The fight—held on Squirrel Island, Canada, north of Detroit, on September 4, 1872—proved more difficult than Chambers anticipated. He absorbed a solid beating for 25 rounds. After coming to scratch for the 26th, Chambers clinched with Edwards and immediately claimed that Edwards had bitten him. The referee examined Chambers, found tooth marks, and awarded Chambers the victory on a foul. Rumors circulated that Chambers's second—not Edwards—had bitten him prior to the start of the 26th round to dupe the referee.

Right-handed; 5'4½"; 115–125 lbs.

American Lightweight Champion 1872–77, 1879

Hall of Fame Induction: 2000

Born: 12/3/1847, Salford, Lancashire, England

Died: 5/25/1925

The next year, Chambers defeated the highly regarded George Seddons. In 1877, he was forced to retire after the middle finger of his left hand was amputated, but two years later he returned to answer the challenge of Professor Johnny Clark, who claimed the lightweight title. Chambers proved his fighting mettle in a marathon 136-round, two-hour-and-twenty-minute victory over Clark and then retired for good.

In retirement, Chambers remained active in the boxing world, serving as advisor and backer of John L. Sullivan, and also opened a bar in Philadelphia.

SELECTED BOUTS

Date	Year	Opponent	Location	Result / Rounds		Title
Oct 1	1864	Arthur Webber	Mode Wheel, near Manchester, England	W	20	—
Nov 15	1864	Fred Finch	London	W	64	—
Nov 8	1865	Ned Evans	Hazlehead Bridge, England	W	44	—
Aug 7	1866	Jem Brady	Southport Place, England	NC	28	—
Aug 8	1866	Jem Brady	Barton Moss, England	L	63	—
Feb 19	1867	Dick Goodwin	Acton, Cheshire, England	D	105	—
Sep 29	1868	Tom Scattergood	Manchester	W	40	—
Oct 6	1870	George Fletcher	Manchester	W	56	—
Sep 4	1872	Billy Edwards	Squirrel Island, Canada	WF	26	Won-Amer-L
Aug 3	1873	George Seddons	Long Island, NY	W	39	Ret-Amer-L
Mar 27	1879	Johnny Clark	Chippewa Falls, Canada	W	136	Won-Amer-L

TOM CRIBB

Right-handed; 5'10"; 196–199 lbs.

English Champion 1809–1822

Hall of Fame Induction: 1991

Born: 7/8/1781, Hanaham, Gloucestershire, England

Died: 5/11/1848

One of the first fighters to actually train for bouts, Tom Cribb is remembered as the master of milling on the retreat, or attacking and then stepping away. He held the championship for thirteen years and defeated the first fighters to arrive from America. Cribb worked for a time on the wharves of London, where he survived a couple of near-fatal accidents. Once he was crushed between two coal barges. Another time a 500-pound load of oranges fell on his chest.

Cribb's first recorded fight was a victory over George Maddox. He then defeated the black American fighter Bill Richmond in a 90-minute bout before facing former champion Jem Belcher in 1807. Belcher came close to winning at one point, but Cribb's second initiated a discussion concerning bets which lasted long enough to allow Cribb to get back on his feet. Cribb was able to close Belcher's one good eye to gain the victory. In a rematch in 1809, Cribb won easily and was generally considered to be the champion.

In 1810, Cribb fought Tom Molineaux, a former American slave and the first black to fight for a championship. On an extremely cold day in December, the fighters battered each other mercilessly. In the nineteenth round, Molineaux held Cribb so that Cribb could neither hit him nor fall down. A crowd of spectators rushed the ring, and Molineaux suffered a broken finger in the unruly scene. When the fight resumed, Molineaux seized control for the next several rounds, but eventually Cribb managed to close both of the challenger's eyes. Molineaux also began shivering from the weather and, after 33 rounds, could not continue.

Before a rematch with Molineaux, Cribb went to Scotland to train. Using runs and long walks, Cribb reduced his weight and improved his stamina. He also stayed away from alcohol, reportedly no small sacrifice. The fight was short, for those days, and brutal. Molineaux dominated the early rounds until Cribb—with nose and mouth bleeding and both eyes swollen—turned to body punching. In the ninth round, Cribb knocked his opponent down with a left to the jaw. Molineaux did not get up in time, but Cribb, wanting to prove his worth, allowed the fight to continue. In the eleventh, he knocked Molineaux unconscious.

Cribb then retired except for one comeback bout, a victory over Jack Carter in 1820. He went on to own a public house and became a coal merchant, but these careers did not bring him lasting success. Cribb died at age 68.

SELECTED BOUTS

Date	Year	Opponent	Location	Result / Duration		Title
Jan 7	1805	George Maddox	Hailsham, Sussex, Eng.	W	90 min.	—
Oct 8	1805	Bill Richmond★	Wood Green, England	W	76 rds	—
Apr 8	1807	Jem Belcher★	Moulsey Hurst, England	W	41 rds	—
Feb 1	1809	Jem Belcher★	Epsom Downs, England	W	31 rds	Won-England-H
Dec 18	1810	Tom Molineaux★	Copthall Common, England	W	33 rds	Ret-England-H
Sep 28	1811	Tom Molineaux★	Thistleton, England	W	11 rds	Ret-England-H

MIKE DONOVAN
Professor

Mike Donovan, who came to be known as "Professor" in honor of his long career as boxing instructor at the New York Athletic Club, was born in Chicago on September 27, 1847. While still a teenager, he enlisted with the Union Army and served in the Civil War.

After the war, Donovan went to New Orleans where he trained under veteran boxer Frank Kendrick. He then traveled up the Mississippi to St. Louis. In July 1866, in a 92-round fight, Donovan lost on a foul to Billy Crowley.

By 1872, Donovan had moved his base of operations to New York City. He became a popular attraction at Harry Hill's, the legendary fight club and tavern. The next year, he fought the toughest bout of his career against Jim Murray. The pair battled for 44 bloody rounds until police intervened.

Right-handed; 5'9½"; 148 lbs.
Hall of Fame Induction: 1998
Born: 9/27/1847, Chicago, IL
Died: 3/24/1918

In April 1878, Donovan faced William McClellan for the American middleweight crown but lost on a foul in fourteen rounds. In 1881, Donovan gained some recognition as the American middleweight champion when he battered title claimant George Rooke for two rounds before police stopped the fight.

In 1880 and 1881, Donovan fought two exhibitions with the up-and-coming John L. Sullivan. Though Donovan's great defensive skills enabled him to survive both these fights with draws, Sullivan's punching power convinced Donovan that the heavyweight crown was beyond his reach.

Donovan retired after defeating 180-pound Walter Watson in October 1884. In addition to a purse, he was awarded the position of boxing instructor at the New York Athletic Club. Donovan worked at the club for over 30 years. One of his pupils was Theodore Roosevelt, who later invited Donovan to the White House to spar.

In 1888, Donovan came out of his ring retirement to fight middleweight champion Jack Dempsey ("The Nonpareil"). Though Donovan had not fought in four years and was 41 years old, he forced the action from the start. Dempsey had to flee along the ropes to escape Donovan's attack. After six rounds, the referee called the fight a draw.

When World War I started, Donovan served as a boxing instructor for recruits in the New York area. He died of pneumonia on March 24, 1918. Donovan's son, referee Arthur Donovan, is also a member of the International Boxing Hall of Fame, and his grandson, Art, is a member of the Pro Football Hall of Fame.

SELECTED BOUTS

Date	Year	Opponent	Location	Result / Duration		Title
Jul	1866	Billy Crowley	St. Louis	LF	92 rounds	—
Jun	1873	Jim Murray	Philadelphia	D	44 rounds	—
Apr 5	1878	William McClellan	San Francisco	LF	14 rounds	For-Amer-M
May 18	1878	William McClellan	—	W	7 rounds	—
Feb	1880	John L. Sullivan★	Boston	Exh	4 rounds	—
Apr 25	1881	George Rooke	New York	W	2 rounds	—
Mar 21	1881	John L. Sullivan★	Boston	Exh	4 rounds	—
Oct 17	1884	Walter Watson	New York	W	7 rounds	—
Nov 15	1888	Jack Dempsey ("The Nonpareil")★	Brooklyn	D	6 rounds	—
May	1891	William McClellan	New York	W	48 seconds	—

PADDY DUFFY

Right-handed; 5'7"; 135–142 lbs.
Welterweight Champion 1888–89
Hall of Fame Induction: 1994
Born: 11/12/1864, Boston, MA
Died: 7/10/1890

Considered the first welterweight champion, Paddy Duffy, like John L. Sullivan, was an Irish-American from Boston. His first fight, at age nineteen, was a knockout victory over Skin Doherty in 1884.

Duffy won his first four bouts before fighting three draws with Paddy Sullivan. After one loss in a bout with Jack C. McGee, Duffy never lost again. He fought in Baltimore, Washington, and Philadelphia in 1886 and 1887 before returning to Boston, where he entered a four-fight series with Jack McGinty. Their first two fights ended in draws. Duffy won a six-round decision in the third fight and solidified his reputation by knocking out McGinty in the ninth round of the fourth fight.

At this point, Duffy sported a record of 21-1-11, which earned him the right to face William McMillan, the English welterweight champ. Fighting at Fort Foote in Vancouver, Canada, Duffy knocked McMillan out in seventeen rounds to claim the world title.

In Duffy's next fight, he faced Tom Meadows, the Australian champion, in San Francisco. At the time, the welterweight division had an upper weight limit of 142 pounds. Duffy tipped the scales for this bout at 140 while Meadows came in at 143. The two battled for 45 rounds before Duffy won on a foul. Duffy never fought again and died in 1890 at the age of 25.

SELECTED BOUTS

Date	Year	Opponent	Location	Result / Rounds		Title
Feb	1884	Skin Doherty	Boston	KO	3	—
May	1884	Paddy Sullivan	Gloucester, MA	D	6	—
Jun	1884	Paddy Sullivan	Lowell, MA	D	6	—
Jun	1884	Paddy Sullivan	Boston	D	6	—
Dec 19	1884	Jack C. McGee	Boston	KO'd	2	—
Jan 28	1886	Bill Young	Baltimore	D	6	—
Mar	1886	Bill Young	Baltimore	KO	2	—
Apr 22	1886	Bill Nally	Washington, DC	KO	4	—
May	1886	Danny Shea	Baltimore	KO	7	—
June	1886	Charles Gleason	Philadelphia	W	4	—
June	1886	Butler's Unknown	Philadelphia	W	4	—
Oct	1886	Charles Gleason	Philadelphia	D	4	—
May	1887	Jack McGinty	Boston	D	6	—
Jun	1887	Jack McGinty	Boston	D	6	—
Oct	1887	Jack McGinty	Boston	W	6	—
Feb 9	1888	Jack McGinty	Boston	KO	9	—
Oct 30	1888	William McMillan	Vancouver, B.C.	KO	17	Won-Vac World-W
Mar 29	1889	Tom Meadows	San Francisco	WF	45	Ret-World-W

DUTCH SAM
The Terrible Jew

Dutch Sam (born Samuel Elias) never fought at more than 134 pounds, but he often defeated men more than 30 pounds heavier. Sam came from the Whitechapel area of London that would later produce Jackie ("Kid") Berg and Ted ("Kid") Lewis.

As legend has it, Sam first began to box formally after Harry Lee, a man active in the fight game, noticed Sam in a fight and taught him the basics of boxing. Fighting Lee himself, Sam recorded his first victory on October 12, 1801. Sam impressed ring observers with his extremely well-muscled physique although he stood only 5'6½". Despite his lack of size, Sam was known as the hardest hitter of his era and earned the nickname, "The Man with the Iron Hand."

In 1804 Sam fought his first major battle, facing the "Pride of Westminster," Caleb Baldwin, a bigger and more experienced pugilist. For twenty rounds Baldwin dominated, attempting to fight inside to utilize his superior size. Sam held Baldwin at bay by firing uppercuts to his face, then began to gain strength and hammered away at Baldwin until he knocked him out in the 37th round.

Right-handed; 5'6½"; 133 lbs.
Hall of Fame Induction: 1997
Born: 4/4/1775, London, England
Named: Samuel Elias
Died: 7/3/1816

Sam's most important fights were with Tom Belcher. When they first met in 1806, Belcher, the brother of Hall of Famer Jem Belcher, was considered England's top boxer at the 140-pound level. The two engaged in a hard-fought battle that lasted 57 rounds before Belcher succumbed. In the rematch Sam had the edge. The fight ended in controversy when a wild swing by Sam hit Belcher in the face while Belcher was on his way to the ground. Belcher's supporters argued that Sam had committed a foul. Ring officials could not agree on the proper ruling, so the fight ended without a winner. In their final meeting, Sam defeated Belcher in 36 rounds. Daniel Mendoza seconded Sam in this battle.

After defeating Ben Medley in 1810, Sam announced his retirement. A man who had always boasted that he could train on gin, Sam drank heavily. He fought once more in 1814 against William Nosworthy, with whom he had gotten into a dispute while drunk. The years of drinking and lack of training had rendered Sam a much less physically impressive version of his former self. Nosworthy easily defeated him in nine rounds.

This defeat did not tarnish Sam's overall reputation as a scientific fighter with incredibly strong hands and a hard punch. Sam and Mendoza rank as the two greatest Jewish fighters of the Pioneer era, and historians believe Sam was the first boxer to use the uppercut. Sam died in 1816. His son, Young Dutch Sam, followed in his father's footsteps and had a very successful ring career.

SELECTED BOUTS

Date	Year	Opponent	Location	Result / Duration		Title
Oct 12	1801	Harry Lee	—	W	—	—
Aug 7	1804	Caleb Baldwin★	Woodford Green, England	W	37 rounds	—
Apr 27	1805	Bill Britton	Shepperton, England	W	30 rounds	—
Feb 8	1806	Tom Belcher	Virginia Water, England	W	57 rounds	—
Jul 28	1807	Tom Belcher	Moulsey Hurst, England	ND	34 rounds	—
Aug 21	1807	Tom Belcher	Crawley Common, England	W	36 rounds	—
May 10	1808	Bill Cropley	—	W	25 min.	—
May 10	1810	Ben Medley	Moulsey Hurst	W	49 rounds	—
Dec 8	1814	Bill Nosworthy	Moulsey Hurst	L	9 rounds	—

YOUNG DUTCH SAM

Right-handed; 5'9"; 137 lbs.

Hall of Fame Induction: 2002

Born 1/30/1808, London, England

Named: Samuel Evans

Died: 11/4/1843

With Young Dutch Sam's 2002 induction, he and his father, Dutch Sam, join referee Arthur Donovan and Professor Mike Donovan as the only father-son combinations in the International Boxing Hall of Fame. His father was still an active fighter when Young Dutch Sam (Samuel Evans) was born in London on January 30, 1808. Like his father, Young Dutch Sam was not a heavyweight. He stood about 5'9" and never weighed more than 145 pounds.

As a youngster, Young Dutch Sam gained employment with Pierce Egan—Hall of Famer, early boxing journalist, and publisher. Evans worked as a "runner" for Egan's weekly newspaper, *Pierce Egan's Life in London*. The runner's job was to distribute the paper to pubs frequented by "the Fancy" (as sports fans were then termed). Through Egan, Sam met Hall of Famer Gentleman Jackson, who—years before—had defeated Mendoza for the heavyweight championship. Soon after meeting Jackson, Sam abandoned the newspaper business for the prize ring.

In his first recorded fight, when he was only fifteen, he defeated Bill Dean. Young Dutch displayed a mixture of power and speed in the ring. His movements were very graceful, and yet he had the ability to inflict great punishment with his left hand as he did when he cut Gypsy Cooper to ribbons with his left jab in 1826 at Gravesend. Hughes Ball, a wealthy and socially prominent member of the Fancy, became Sam's patron. In one of Sam's best-remembered bouts, it took a total of 3 hours and 35 minutes for Sam to finally vanquish Dick Davis on June 19, 1827, at Haversham.

Surviving records of Young Dutch's career show only victories in his sixteen battles between 1823 and 1834. He may also have had a few losses, however. A quote by one of his contemporaries, Charles Knight, in his autobiography recounts a match in which he "saw Young Dutch Sam fall across the ropes with a broken arm."

Tragedy struck on March 13, 1838, while Sam was acting as a second to Owen Swift in his bout with Brighton Bikl. Bikl died in the ring and Swift, Sam, and all the other participants were arrested and tried. Some of the defendants were sentenced to prison, but all were soon released. Sam retired from the ring and opened a public house or "pub." Young Dutch Sam died at the age of 35.

SELECTED BOUTS

Date	Year	Opponent	Location	Result / Duration	Title
—	1823	Bill Dean	England	W 45 min.	—
Oct 18	1825	Harry Jones	Shere Mere, England	W 18 rounds	—
Apr 25	1826	Gypsy Cooper	Gravesend, England	W 18 rounds	—
Jun 8	1826	Bill Carroll	Ascot, England	W 16 rounds	—
Apr 27	1827	Jack Cooper	Andover, England	W 9 rounds	—
Jun 19	1827	Dick Davis	Haversham, England	W 30 rounds	—
Apr 7	1829	Ned Neale	Ludlow, England	W 78 rounds	—
Jun 24	1834	Tom Gaynor	Andover, England	W 17 rounds	—

BILLY EDWARDS

One of the best of the early lightweight fighters, Englishman Billy Edwards achieved his greatest fame in the United States. William H. Edwards was born on December 21, 1844, in Birmingham, England. He began fighting at the age of fourteen and quickly achieved success. At most, he stood 5'5" tall and weighed about 125 pounds. Still, his diminutive size did not prevent Edwards from taking on much larger men. Once Edwards fought the German-born heavyweight Ben Hogan. Though Hogan outweighed him by 67 pounds, Edwards emerged the victor.

In 1865, Edwards came to the United States because restrictive laws against prizefighting had been enacted in England. As in his home country, Edwards gained a reputation as a hard hitter and a skillful boxer. On August 24, 1868, Edwards was matched with Sam Collyer, the American lightweight champion, for the title. The match was set for Cherry Point on the Eastern shore of Virginia. The pair battled for 47 rounds before Edwards emerged victorious. Edwards also won two subsequent meetings with Collyer.

Right-handed; 5'4 1/2"; 123 1/2–140 lbs.

Hall of Fame Induction: 2005

Born: 12/21/1844, Birmingham, England

Named: William H. Edwards

Died: 8/12/1907

Hall of Famer Arthur Chambers, like Edwards a transplanted English boxer, issued a challenge to Edwards, which the champion accepted. Each side put up $2,000 with the money and championship to go to the victor. The fighters squared off on Squirrel Island, Canada, north of Detroit on September 4, 1872. Edwards pummeled Chambers for 25 rounds. After coming to scratch for the 26th round, Chambers and Edwards clinched. Chambers immediately claimed that Edwards had bitten him. When the referee examined Chambers, he found tooth marks and awarded Chambers the victory on a foul. After the bout, rumors circulated that Chambers's second—not Edwards—had bitten the challenger prior to the start of the 26th round to trick the referee.

After the loss to Chambers, Edwards defeated Will Fawcett and Collyer. After his boxing career ended, Edwards had a long stint as a house detective and bouncer at Hoffman House, a New York hotel. His reputation was usually enough to maintain order. He also served as a private boxing instructor to prominent New Yorkers such as George J. Gould, E.H. Harriman, August Belmont, and Harry Payne Whitney. Edwards held an annual boxing benefit show at Madison Square Garden where he and Professor Mike Donovan would finish the event by facing each other in the ring. Unlike many fighters who end up penniless, Edwards successfully invested in real estate and died a wealthy man.

SELECTED BOUTS

Date	Year	Opponent	Location	Result / Rounds		Title
Aug 24	1868	♔ Sam Collyer	Cherry Point, VA	W	47	Won-Amer-L
March 2	1870	Sam Collyer	Mystic Island, CT	W	40	Ret-Amer-L
Sept 4	1872	Arthur Chambers ★	Squirrel Island, Canada	LF	26	Lost-Amer-L
Mar 11	1874	Will Fawcett	Manchester, England	W	45	—
Aug 1	1874	Sam Collyer	Mill Creek, Line Island, VA	W	11	—
May 12	1884	Charlie Mitchell ★	New York	L	3	—

JAMES FIGG

Right-handed; 6'; 185 lbs.
First English Champion 1719–34
Hall of Fame Induction: 1992
Born: 1695, Thame, Oxfordshire, England
Died: 12/8/1734

Although fisticuffs as a sport started in England about 40 years before his rise to prominence, James Figg is considered to have been the first heavyweight boxing champion. He was also the first to teach and promote boxing both as a skill and a competitive sport.

Six feet tall and a multi-talented athlete, Figg was an expert fencer and was a popular performer in fairs. He gained fame for his skill in exhibitions with the sword and the cudgel before adding bare-knuckle fighting to his repertoire. By 1719, Figg's claim to the bare-knuckle championship was secure. He fended off several challengers, including three-time opponent Ned Sutton. Figg defeated Sutton with his fists, sword, and cudgel.

With the backing of a patron, the Earl of Peterborough, Figg opened a fighting academy in London on what is now known as Tottenham Court Road. His advertising card, designed for him by the artist William Hogarth, proclaimed him "master of the noble science of defence" and offered to teach gentlemen in the use of "the small backsword and quarterstaff at home and abroad." Hogarth was a great friend of Figg's and also painted a portrait showing the fighter in a lace shirt and wig, holding his clenched fists before him.

Figg later established Figg's Amphitheatre in Oxford Road, one of several London arenas devoted to staging matches in the growing sport of prizefighting. In these permanent venues, the "ring" that had originally been formed by spectators, sometimes holding a rope in their hands, became an elevated square platform, enclosed with wooden rails. Figg popularized sparring as an public entertainment, and his school was frequented by the upper classes, with noblemen often arriving in groups to try their hand at boxing or fencing.

Since bare-knuckle exhibitions were also tremendously popular with the working classes, Figg continued to make appearances in public, often at London's Southwark Fair, in a boxing booth where he would take on all comers. Fighting infrequently in formal matches, Figg retained the championship until his retirement in 1734 when his premier student, George Taylor, declared himself successor to the title.

Figg, who socialized with the Prince of Wales and other members of the royal family, died in 1734, leaving a wife and several children. Although some considered him a better swordsman than boxer, Figg is called "The Father of Boxing" for his role in popularizing and teaching the sport.

SELECTED BOUTS

Date	Year	Opponent	Location	Result / Duration		Title
Circa	1720	Timothy Buck	England	W	—	—
Circa	1720	Tom Stokes	England	W	—	—
Circa	1720	Bill Flanders	England	W	—	—
—	1723	Chris Clarkson	England	W	30 min.	—
—	—	Ned Sutton (3 bouts)	England	W	—	—

JOE GOSS

Like many English fighters from the mid-nineteenth century, Joe Goss traveled to the United States seeking fame and a championship. He achieved both, though his popularity was soon dwarfed by that of his friend John L. Sullivan. Goss was born in Northampton, England, on November 5, 1838. He grew up admiring fighters and decided to be one himself. Although he was of average size, he often fought much bigger men.

Right-handed; 5′8¹/₂″; 150 lbs.

American Bare-knuckle Champion 1876–80

Hall of Fame Induction: 2003

Born: 11/5/1838, Northampton, England

Died: 3/24/1885

Goss fought Jack Rooke on September 20, 1859, winning a marathon contest that lasted 64 rounds and one hour 40 minutes. Goss's next match, with Tom Price, failed to occur on schedule. Goss's father, disapproving of his son's pugilistic aspirations, had him arrested at the weigh-in on November 9, 1859. The bout took place the following February.

Goss faced Jem Mace in what some historians consider a middleweight title fight on September 1, 1863, but lost in a one-hour-55-minute battle. Goss proved unable to beat Mace in two subsequent contests.

Goss came to the United States in 1876 and issued a challenge to Tom Allen, considered the champion in the United States. Each side put up $2,500. On September 7, 1876, the match commenced in Kenton County, Kentucky, but had to be moved in the middle of the bout to Boone County, Kentucky, due to interference from the authorities. After 21 rounds, Allen, who was ahead, punched Goss in the face while Goss knelt on one knee. This was a blatant foul and Goss was awarded the title.

Goss did not defend his championship until May 30, 1880, when he faced Paddy Ryan at Collier's Station, West Virginia. The 42-year-old Goss did not enter the ring in top condition. He cut the larger Ryan numerous times but could not put him away. As the fight wore on, Goss wore out. After 87 rounds, Goss turned to his second, Hall of Famer Arthur Chambers, and told him that he could not continue. Chambers threw in the sponge.

Except for some exhibitions with his good friend John L. Sullivan, whom Goss probably helped train, Goss did not fight again. He operated a tavern, "Saracen's Head," in Boston. Goss died of Bright's disease on March 24, 1885, in Boston.

SELECTED BOUTS

Date	Year	Opponent	Location	Result / Duration		Title
—	1857	George Ayres	—		1 hr. 20 min.	—
Sept 20	1859	Jack Rooke	Leaseford, England	W	64 rounds	—
July 17	1860	Bodger Crutchley	Oxford, England	W	120 rounds	—
Nov 25	1862	John ("Posh") Price	Stonebridge, England	W	66 rounds	—
Sept 1	1863	Jem Mace★	London	L	19 rounds	—
Dec 16	1863	Ike Baker	London	W	27 rounds	—
May 24	1866 ♛	Jem Mace★	Kent, England	D	1 round	For-England-H
Aug 6	1866 ♛	Jem Mace★	London	L	21 rounds	For-England-H
Mar 5	1867	Tom Allen	Bristol, England	D	34 rounds	—
Sept 7	1876 ♛	Tom Allen	Kenton & Boone Counties	WF	21 rounds	Won-BK Amer-H
May 30	1880	Paddy Ryan	Collier's Station, WV	L	87 rounds	Lost-BK Amer-H

JOHN C. HEENAN
The Benicia Boy

Right-handed; 6'2"; 182–195 lbs.
Hall of Fame Induction: 2002
Born: 5/2/1835, Troy, NY
Named: John Carmel Heenan
Died: 10/28/1873

The son of Irish immigrant parents, John Heenan worked as an unskilled laborer before moving to California in 1852, where he swung a hammer in the workshops of the Pacific Mail Steamship Company in Benicia. The 6'2", 200-pound Heenan was very muscular and earned a reputation for toughness.

Heenan returned to the East and obtained a position in the New York Customs House. Soon after, he began to issue challenges to American heavyweight champion John Morrissey through the *New York Sun*. On July 3, 1858, Heenan published a card issuing a formal challenge, and Morrissey agreed to fight.

In order to avoid police interference, the fight took place in Canada. Held on October 20, 1858, with stakes of $5,000 a side, the match drew bets from around the country. Heenan entered the ring suffering from an abscess in his leg, and though he got off to a strong start, the veteran Morrissey began to dominate as the bout continued. By the eleventh round, Heenan, weakened by the abscess, collapsed. The victorious Morrissey refused Heenan a rematch and never fought again.

Unable to fight Morrissey, Heenan set his sights on Tom Sayers, who, as the British champion, was the de facto champion of the world. Enthusiasm in the U.S. about that meeting surpassed even the excitement over the Morrissey fight, and many believe that no sporting event between the years 1825 and 1875 attracted as much attention.

On April 17, 1860, Heenan met Sayers in a field at Farnborough, England. Heenan was eight years younger, five inches taller, and much heavier, but Sayers was favored. The pair battled for more than two hours, neither gaining a decisive upper hand. In the 37th round, constables attempted to push through the crowd to the ring to stop the fight. According to some accounts, Heenan thrust Sayers's throat against the ropes, which were then cut. The referee called the fight a draw, but the timekeeper called the fighters back for another five rounds before the confusion in and around the ring forced the end of the match. Again, the match was ruled a draw.

Heenan had only one more major fight, facing champion Tom King at Wadhurst, England, on December 10, 1863. Relying on superior strength and wrestling tactics, Heenan ignored defense and was soundly defeated in 24 rounds, although controversy surrounded the bout.

Plagued by consumption and pneumonia, Heenan never fought again. His health had long been in decline, and at Green Run Station, Wyoming, he was forced by illness to leave the train in which he was travelling. Heenan died shortly thereafter.

SELECTED BOUTS

Date	Year		Opponent	Location	Result / Rounds		Title
Oct 20	1858		John Morrissey ★	Long Pt. Island, Canada	L	11	For-Vac America-H
Apr 17	1860	♛	Tom Sayers ★	Farnborough, England	D	42	For-England-H
Dec 10	1863	♛	Tom King ★	Wadhurst, Kent, England	L	24	For-England-H

JOHN JACKSON
Gentleman Jackson

Winning England's prize ring championship in the third and final fight of his sparse career, John Jackson exemplified the "gentleman boxer." The son of a builder, Jackson was of a higher socioeconomic status than his predecessors, and he hobnobbed successfully with the nobility. He dressed well and behaved in a polite manner, and so brought an often-missing gentility to the sport.

A great athlete, Jackson was also an accomplished sprinter and long jumper. He first fought professionally in 1788 when he defeated the more experienced and previously unbeaten William Fewterel. Jackson proved himself to be a fine two-handed puncher, using his left more than most fighters of his time. Jackson next fought George Ingelston. Jackson won the first two rounds, but in the third, as he was attempting to finish Ingelston, Jackson skidded on the slippery ring surface. Historians disagree as to whether Jackson turned his ankle or broke his leg, but in any case, he was down, and Ingelston was declared the winner.

The loss stung Jackson badly and he retired from the ring, having only fought twice. Not until six years later, in 1795, did the chance to fight the highly skilled Daniel Mendoza for the title finally motivate Jackson to return. Jackson scored an easy victory in nine rounds totaling eleven minutes, although he prevailed through the use of a questionable tactic. Jackson grabbed Mendoza's long hair with one hand. With Mendoza held before him, Jackson slugged him mercilessly with his free hand. This maneuver was not against the rules of the time, and Jackson won the fight without penalty.

Right-handed; 5'11"; 202 lbs.

English Champion 1795

Hall of Fame Induction: 1992

Born: 9/25/1769, London, England

Died: 10/7/1845

Content in the knowledge that he had at last won the title, Jackson retired again. He turned his attention to operating his London boxing academy, where he instructed many members of the nobility, including Lord Byron. Jackson encouraged fighters at his academy to use "mufflers," the hand covering that Hall of Famer Jack Broughton invented for training and sparring.

During King George IV's coronation, Jackson was recruited to assemble guards to keep order. He assembled a complement of eighteen prizefighters. A popular sports celebrity of his day, Jackson was a favorite of the more common people as well as the aristocrats. He died at the age of 76, and at his grave, a statue of a crouching lion was erected to symbolize his great skill and strength.

SELECTED BOUTS

Date	Year	Opponent	Location	Result / Duration		Title
Jun 9	1788	William Fewterel	Smitham Bottom, Eng.	W	1 hr. 7 min.	—
Mar 12	1789	George Ingelston	England	L	20 min.	—
Apr 15	1795	♔ Daniel Mendoza★	Hornchurch, England	W	9 rounds	Won-England-H

TOM JOHNSON

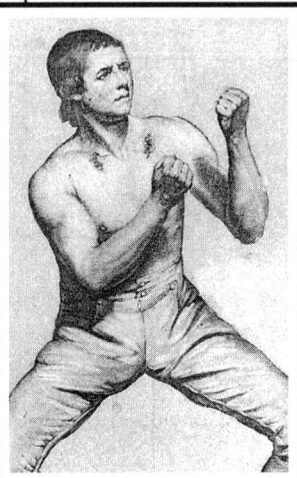

Right-handed; 5'10"; 202 lbs.
English Champion 1784–91
Hall of Fame Induction: 1995
Born: 1750, Derby, England
Named: Thomas Jackling
Died: 1/21/1797

Tom Johnson restored to boxing a modicum of credibility and public respect—lost since the days of Hall of Famer Jack Broughton. After Broughton's demise in 1750, the title was held for ten years by Jack Slack, inventor of the paralyzing rabbit punch and accused fixer of fights. By the time Slack was defeated, crooked fights were common. The championship bounced from one fighter to another, and by the 1780s, no one had a firm hold on it.

Born in Derby, Johnson worked for many years as a stevedore on London's wharves. In 1783, he became champion almost by chance when he offended a fighter named Jack Jarvis. This led to a challenge and a boxing match in which Johnson convincingly defeated Jarvis in just fifteen minutes. After this victory, some acclaimed Johnson as the champion. No one had held the title since Irishman Duggan Fearns defeated Harry Sellers in a 90-second fight, reputed to have been fixed. When Fearns abruptly disappeared from the scene, the title became vacant.

Johnson defeated the Croydon Drover in 1784, and later that year, triumphed over Stephen ("Death") Oliver. At this point, Johnson declared himself champion. In 1786, Johnson whipped four more opponents easily, then faced the Irish champion Michael Ryan the next year. The two champions fought ferociously. When Ryan landed a hard punch to Johnson's temple, sending him reeling against the ropes, Johnson's second entered the ring and grabbed Ryan. Ryan could have claimed victory on the foul but did not. Given time to recover, Johnson came back to defeat Ryan ten minutes later. He also won a rematch.

Johnson's next fight was a grueling 62-round battle with Isaac Perrins. Though he suffered several knockdowns, Johnson hung on to win. In 1791, the aging Johnson lost his title to Ben Brain in eighteen rounds.

By the time he retired, Johnson had amassed a small fortune, but within a year, he had spent and gambled it all away. He then taught boxing in Ireland until his death in 1797. Johnson's refusal to engage in "crosses," as fixed fights were called, rekindled the public's interest in boxing and restored much-needed integrity to the sport.

SELECTED BOUTS

Date	Year	Opponent	Location	Result / Duration		Title
Jun	1783	Jack Jarvis	Walworth, England	W	15 min.	—
Mar	1784	Croydon Drover	England	W	27 min.	—
Jun	1784	Stephen ("Death") Oliver	England	W	35 min.	Won-Vac England-H
Jan 18	1787	Bill Warr	Okingham, England	W	1 hr. 40 min.	Ret-England-H
Dec 19	1787	Michael Ryan	England	W	30 min.	Ret-England-H
Feb 11	1789	Michael Ryan	Rickmansworth, Eng	W	33 min.	Ret-England-H
Nov 22	1789	Isaac Perrins	Banbury, England	W	62 rounds	Ret-England-H
Jan 17	1791	Benjamin Brain★	England	L	18 rounds	Lost-England-H

TOM KING
The Fighting Sailor

Born on England's seacoast, Tom King became a sailor at an early age and travelled to Africa, among other ports. He learned to box in the British Royal Navy where he fought both bare-fisted and with gloves. He later worked as a foreman on the London docks. After King defeated a bully known as Brighton Bill, Hall of Famer Jem Ward took an interest in King and began to train him. King scored a one-round victory over a top dockyard fighter, Bill Clamp, in his first professional bout.

King defeated Tom Truckle and Young Broome before taking a shot at the championship, held by Hall of Famer Jem Mace, in 1862. For the first half of the 43-round match, King dominated Mace, nearly closing both of his eyes. Mace recovered, however, and took control from the 30th round until the end of the fight. A knockdown blow to the throat put King out of commission.

In a rematch less than a year later, Mace again appeared to be getting the better of King, whose face was badly battered. In the nineteenth round, Mace went in for the kill, but left himself open for a right cross to the face from King.

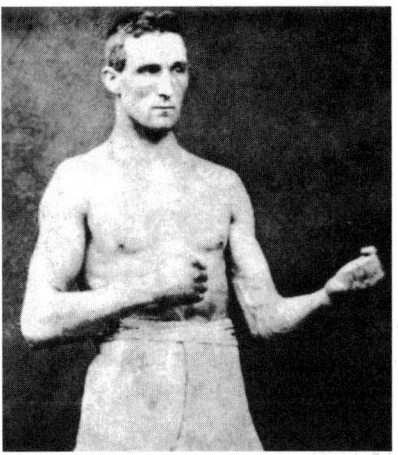

Right-handed; 6'2"; 175 lbs.

English Champion 1862–63

Hall of Fame Induction: 1992

Born: 8/14/1835, Stepney, London, England

Died: 10/3/1888

Mace was knocked down, and only frantic efforts by his seconds enabled him to start the next round. Mace struggled into the 21st round when King simply pushed him down. Mace's seconds then threw in the sponge, and King was the champion.

Although King refused to fight Mace again, he did agree to a match with John Heenan, the American known as the Benicia Boy, who had earlier fought Tom Sayers to a draw. Heenan relied on his superior strength and wrestling tactics, foolishly ignoring defensive fighting. The more accomplished King easily took the measure of Heenan and won a 24-round fight, absorbing very little punishment himself.

After successfully defending the English boxing crown against Heenan, King retired. Unlike many professional fighters of his time—and many since—King did not live out his remaining days in poverty. He became an accomplished oarsman and a very successful bookmaker. He married the daughter of a ship owner and amassed considerable wealth before his death.

SELECTED BOUTS

Date	Year	Opponent	Location	Result / Rounds		Title
—	1859	Bill Clamp	—	W	1	—
Nov 27	1860	Tom Truckle	Kentish Marshes, England	W	49	—
Oct 21	1861	Young Broome	Farnborough, England	W	43	—
Jan 28	1862	♛ Jem Mace★	Godstone, England	L	43	For-England-H
Nov 26	1862	♛ Jem Mace★	Medway, England	W	21	Won-England-H
Dec 10	1863	John C. Heenan★	Wadhurst, England	W	24	Ret-England-H

NAT LANGHAM

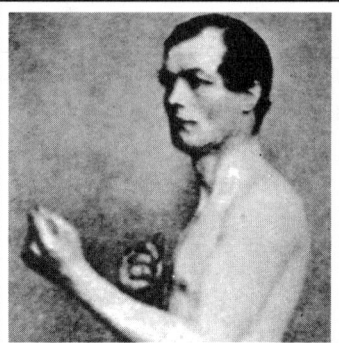

Right-handed; 5'10"; 152–156 lbs.

Middleweight Champion 1843–53

Hall of Fame Induction: 1992

Born: May 1820, Hinckley, Leicestershire, England

Died: 9/1/1871

Considered the best middleweight of his day, Nat Langham compiled a fine record which included a victory over Hall of Famer Tom Sayers. Born in Hinckley, England, Langham worked as a farm laborer before moving to London to work briefly as a delivery man. Langham's earliest recorded bouts took place in Hinckley, but he honed his skills in London where he came under the direction of former heavyweight champion Ben Caunt. Using sharp, well-timed blows—especially with his left, which Tom Sayers called the "Pickaxe"—Langham carved out several impressive victories. A win over William Ellis in 1843 gave Langham the middleweight title.

In 1851, Langham suffered the only defeat of his career, at the hands of Harry Orme. The battle raged for 117 rounds. Langham cut Orme's mouth and nose in the first round. Langham's shots raised a mouse under each eye but an Orme hip-toss dazed Langham in the eleventh. The fighting continued for two hours and forty-six minutes. Finally, Langham gave up the struggle after Orme threw him again, and Orme had the victory.

When Langham faced the highly respected George Guttridge, the two fought for an hour and 25 minutes. In the first ten rounds, Langham had the advantage. For the next 40, Guttridge appeared to improve. From the 51st until the 93rd, Langham took control until Guttridge finally conceded.

Langham also fought the up-and-coming Tom Sayers. In the 61st round, Langham closed both of Sayers's eyes and knocked him to the ground, ending the fight. After this grueling fight, Sayers attempted to secure a rematch but none was forthcoming. Langham then retired to open the Cambrian Stores, a tavern. He also owned a boxing booth and founded the Rum-Rum-Pas Club for aristocratic ring patrons. He remained active in boxing and as a tavern owner for many years. He did come out of retirement once, in part to settle a family dispute with his former mentor, Caunt, who was also his wife's uncle. The two fought to a 60-round draw in 1857.

SELECTED BOUTS

Date	Year	Opponent	Location	Result / Rounds		Title
—	1842	Bill Croazier	England	W	8	—
—	1842	Ned Ellis	England	W	8	—
Feb 9	1843	William Ellis	—	W	8	Won-England-M
May 7	1844	Tom Lowe	England	W	43	—
Jun 12	1845	Doc Campbell	—	W	27	—
Jun 9	1846	George Guttridge	Bourne, England	W	93	Ret-England-M
May 4	1847	William Sparks	—	W	67	—
May	1851	Harry Orme	—	L	117	—
Oct 18	1853	Tom Sayers ★	Lakenheath, England	W	61	Ret-England-M
Sep 9	1857	Ben Caunt	—	D	60	—

JEM MACE
The Gypsy

Jem Mace brought a more scientific style of fighting to the ring than did most of his predecessors. Before making fighting his career, Mace worked as an apprentice cabinet-maker and as a fiddler. He defeated Slasher Slack in his first professional fight in 1855.

Mace's success brought him the attention of Nat Langham, who hired him to man his touring boxing booth, taking on all comers. In 1861, Mace agreed to fight Sam Hurst, considered the champion by virtue of his victory over title-claimant Tom Paddock. Hurst, a noted wrestler, outweighed Mace by about 100 pounds. Mace eluded Hurst's rushes and in the eighth round, knocked him unconscious.

As champion, Mace toured the country in a circus before facing Tom King in 1862. Mace had taken notes on King's style, an unusual practice in those days. On a cold, rainy January day, Mace struggled for 22 rounds with the larger King, who outweighed him by about 25 pounds. King's punches closed Mace's left eye and almost closed his right. In the 30th round, Mace backheeled King, who fell on his head. In the 43rd, a left to the throat and a throw to the ground ended it for King.

In the rematch, King upset Mace to win the championship. When King refused to fight Mace again, Mace picked a fight with him on the street. When King retired, Mace was again considered the champion. With boxing in a decline in England, Mace travelled to the United States. In 1870 and 1871, he fought the American champion Joe Coburn. Police stopped the first bout, held in Port Ryeson, Canada, before a winner was determined. In the second fight, in Bay St. Louis, Mississippi, the two fought to a draw. Mace continued to fight sporadically until he was in his sixties.

Mace also helped foster the growth of boxing in Australia when he toured there. He taught Australia's top trainer, Larry Foley, many fine points of the sport which Foley later imparted to such notables as Bob Fitzsimmons, Peter Jackson, and Young Griffo. Mace spent the last years of his life back in England, where he died at the age of 79.

Right-handed; 5'9½"; 144–168 lbs.

English Welterweight Champ 1860
English Heavyweight Champion 1861-62, 1866-70
English Middleweight Champ 1863
World Heavywt Champ 1870-71

Hall of Fame Induction: 1990

Born: 4/8/1831, Beeston, Norwich, England

Died: 3/3/1910

SELECTED BOUTS

Date	Year	Opponent	Location	Result / Rounds		Title
Oct 2	1855	Slasher Slack	Mildenhall, England	W	9	—
Sep 21	1858	Bob Brettle	Near Thames Haven, England	L	2	For-England-W
Sep 20	1860	Bob Brettle	Near Foolness Island, England	W	5	Won-England-W
Jun 18	1861	♔ Sam Hurst	Medway Island, England	W	8	Won-England-H
Jan 28	1862	Tom King★	Godstone, England	W	43	Ret-England-H
Nov 26	1862	Tom King★	Near Thames Haven	L	21	Lost-England-H
Sep 1	1863	Joe Goss★	London	W	19	Won-England-M
Aug 6	1866	Joe Goss★	London	W	21	Reg-England-H
May 10	1870	Tom Allen	Kennerville, LA	W	10	Won-World-H
Nov 30	1871	Joe Coburn	Bay St. Louis, MS	D	12	Ret-World-H
Feb 7	1890	Charlie Mitchell★	Glasgow	L	4	For-Vac-England-H

DANIEL MENDOZA

Right-handed; 5'7"; 160–168 lbs.
English Champion 1794–95
Hall of Fame Induction: 1990
Born: 7/5/1764, London, England
Died: 9/3/1836

Daniel Mendoza was the first to truly put the "science" in the Sweet Science. More than any previous fighter, Mendoza relied on footwork, jabs, and defense rather than pure brute force. Although relatively small at 5'7" and 160 pounds, Mendoza's speed and agility allowed him to triumph over larger, slower opponents. Lauded by early boxing historian Pierce Egan as "a complete artist" and "a star of the first brilliancy," Mendoza was a very popular fighter who enjoyed a short reign as England's champion.

Of Spanish heritage, Mendoza was the first Jewish fighter to gain prominence. He grew up in London's East End in poor surroundings and worked as a glass cutter, laborer, assistant to a green grocer, and an actor before making a career of fighting. His first recorded fight was a victory over Harry the Coalheaver. After he defeated Sam Martin ("The Bath Butcher") in 1787, Mendoza established a reputation as a fighter of the first rank.

In 1788, Mendoza embarked on a bitter three-fight series with Richard Humphries. Mendoza lost the first fight when he suffered a leg injury and threw in the towel after 29 minutes. In the rematch the following year, Mendoza thoroughly dominated Humphries to win in 52 minutes. Mendoza also won the third encounter in fifteen minutes.

With the retirement of Ben Brain, Mendoza claimed the championship. His grip on the title was solidified with a victory over Bill Warr in 1794. As champion, Mendoza toured England, Scotland, and Ireland demonstrating his skills as part of the Aston Circus. While in Ireland, Mendoza thrashed Squire Fitzgerald, who had made derogatory remarks about Mendoza's skills and ethnicity.

Mendoza held the title until 1795 when John Jackson rather easily knocked him out in nine rounds. Mendoza retired only to return, for financial reasons, at the age of 41 with a victory over Harry Lee in 1806. He even fought one losing effort in 1820. He ran boxing schools and owned a tavern in retirement. Mendoza's contributions to boxing had a lasting impact. His impressive ring displays further popularized boxing, and by teaching and example, he advanced the use of more sophisticated tactics in the ring.

SELECTED BOUTS

Date	Year	Opponent	Location	Result / Duration		Title
—	—	Harry the Coalheaver	England	W	40 min.	—
—	1787	Bill Warr	England	W	23 rounds	—
Jan 9	1788	Richard Humphries	Odiham, England	L	29 min.	—
May 6	1789	Richard Humphries	Stilton, England	W	52 min.	—
Sep 29	1790	Richard Humphries	Doncaster, England	W	15 min.	—
May 14	1792	Bill Warr	Croyden, England	W	23 rounds	—
Nov 12	1794	Bill Warr	Bexley Common, Eng.	W	15 min.	Won-England-H
Apr 15	1795	John Jackson ★	Hornchurch, England	L	9 rounds	Lost-England-H
Jul 4	1820	Tom Owen	Banstead Downs, Eng.	L	12 rounds	

TOM MOLINEAUX
The Virginia Slave

Tom Molineaux was the first American to fight in England for the heavyweight title. Born a slave, he was raised on a plantation in Virginia owned by Algernon Molineaux. He participated in fights with slaves from neighboring plantations as arranged by the plantation owners. Before one of these bouts, Algernon Molineaux promised his fighter freedom should he win. Molineaux won the fight and was granted his freedom. He traveled to New York, where he worked as a porter and a laborer on the docks.

Hearing of better opportunities for fighters in England, Molineaux joined a ship as a deckhand and set sail for England. In London, he declared himself to be the American champion even though no such title existed. Molineaux further boasted that he could beat anyone, including the retired champion, Hall of Famer Tom Cribb. Eager to prove the superiority of British fighters, Cribb arranged for his protégé, Bill Burrows ("The British Unknown"), to fight Molineaux. Seconded and trained by Bill Richmond, another African-American fighter, Molineaux overpowered "The Unknown" with short arm jolts and blows to the head. Richmond, a free New Yorker, had fought Cribb several years earlier.

Right-handed; 5'8½"; 185–198 lbs.
Hall of Fame Induction: 1997
Born: 3/23/1784, Georgetown, MD
Died: 8/4/1818

Cribb came out of retirement to face Molineaux on December 18, 1810, on a cold, rainy day. Molineaux drew first blood in the second round. In the 28th, Molineaux floored Cribb, who failed to come to scratch within thirty seconds. Under the rules, Molineaux should have been declared the winner. However, Cribb's second accused Molineaux of hiding bullets in his hands to give his punches more power. The referee searched Molineaux, found no foreign objects, and then let the revived Cribb continue. By the 33rd round, Molineaux was exhausted, shivering from the cold, and dazed from hitting his head on a ring post. He fell to the ground, unable to continue.

Molineaux immediately challenged Cribb for a rematch. While Cribb trained arduously, Molineaux, now estranged from Richmond, preferred carousing. Molineaux dominated for five rounds. A Cribb right knocked the wind out of him in the sixth. Molineaux never recovered and was knocked out in the eleventh when a Cribb right broke his jaw.

Molineaux never again fought for the title. Beset by problems with alcohol, Molineaux toured rural areas of England, Ireland, and Scotland in a traveling boxing and wrestling show. While in Ireland, he fell ill, possibly with tuberculosis, and died at the age of 34.

SELECTED BOUTS

Date	Year	Opponent	Location	Result / Duration		Title
Jul 14	1810	Bill Burrows	England	W	1 hr.	—
Aug 21	1810	Tom Blake	England	W	8 rounds	—
Dec 18	1810	Tom Cribb★	Copthall Common, England	L	33 rounds	—
May 21	1811	Jim Rimmer	England	W	21 rounds	—
Sep 28	1811	Tom Cribb★	Thistleton Gap, England	L	11 rounds	—
Apr 2	1813	Jack Carter	England	WF	25 rounds	—
—	1813	George Cooper	Scotland	D	10 rounds	—
May 31	1814	Bill Fuller	Auchineaux, Scotland	WF	2 rounds	—
Mar 10	1815	George Cooper	Edinburgh, Scotland	L	14 rounds	—

JOHN MORRISSEY
Old Smoke

Right-handed; 5'11"; 175 lbs.
American Heavywt. Champ 1858
Hall of Fame Induction: 1996
Born: 2/12/1831, Templemore, Ireland
Died: 5/1/1878

A poor Irish immigrant, John Morrissey grew up in Troy, New York. He was allowed one year of school before becoming a manual laborer. Head of a gang of young toughs, Morrissey had frequent run-ins with the police—an inauspicious start for a man who later became a U.S. congressman.

After Morrissey took a bartending job in Troy, his boss tried to arrange a boxing match between Morrissey and "Dutch" Charlie Duane. When the young fighter went to New York City to challenge Duane at a Tammany Hall hangout, he was badly beaten by the unfriendly crowd. Morrissey stayed in the city, however, as a hired bully, enforcing the political loyalty of recent immigrants. Morrissey was dubbed "Old Smoke" when he and another "immigrant runner" knocked over a coal stove in a saloon fight and Morrissey was pinned to the burning embers before going on to win.

In 1851, Morrissey made his way to California as a stowaway in search of gold. His first organized prizefight took place in 1852 when he challenged Englishman George Thompson, then the California champion. Thompson had the upper hand, but when Morrissey's supporters brandished weapons, he fouled Morrissey in the twelfth round to forfeit the match.

Morrissey then returned to New York to challenge veteran fighter Yankee Sullivan. The fight was held at Boston Corners where New York, Connecticut, and Massachusetts meet, to stymie state authorities who might try to halt the match. Sullivan was 41, and Morrissey just 22, but for 37 rounds, the quicker and more scientific Sullivan thrashed Morrissey, who displayed his great ability to absorb a beating. Then onlookers stormed the ring. When the fighters were called to come to scratch for the 38th round, Sullivan was fending off Morrissey's second, Orville ("Awful") Gardner. The referee gave Morrissey the fight, in violation of a rule of that day which stated a fight must be stopped until the ring was clear. Morrissey parlayed his "win" into starting a bar and a gambling house. He used his connections to avoid convictions for shooting two waiters, three separate charges of assault with intent to kill, and possible involvement in the murder of a political foe.

In 1858, Morrissey faced another Troy native son, John C. ("Benicia Boy") Heenan, for what was considered the American heavyweight championship. Heenan fought well but was suffering from an earlier leg injury, and also broke his hand on a corner post during the fight. He collapsed in the eleventh round.

Morrissey then retired from the ring. He opened a gambling house and then a racetrack in Saratoga Springs, New York, helping to establish the town as a popular resort and horse racing center. He later testified against Tammany Hall political leader, Boss Tweed, which helped speed the breakup of his organization. Morrissey was elected to two terms in Congress and two in the New York State Senate before his death in 1878.

SELECTED BOUTS

Date	Year	Opponent	Location	Result / Rounds		Title
Aug 31	1852	George Thompson	California	WF	12	—
Oct 12	1853	Yankee Sullivan	Boston Corners, NY	W	38	—
Oct 20	1858	♛ John C. Heenan★	Long Pt. Island, Canada	W	11	Won-Amer-H

HENRY ("HEN") PEARCE
The Game Chicken

Although he did not possess the boxing skill of his immediate predecessor, Jem Belcher, Henry Pearce used his great strength and slugging ability to take the championship. Like Belcher, Pearce hailed from Bristol, England. Pearce started fighting in and around Bristol, although his first recorded bout is listed as having taken place in London in 1803 when he beat Jack Firley.

In 1805, he fought a memorable battle with his friend John Gully, an inmate of debtors' prison. The two staged a bout on the prison grounds with Gully getting the best of Pearce by a small margin. Impressed with his opponent's showing, Pearce arranged for a sponsor to pay Gully's debts so that he could be released from prison. The two then met in Hailsham for a public battle. Pearce dominated Gully early in the fight, knocking him down in each of the first seven rounds. In the eighteenth round, Gully came back to bloody Pearce badly. Two rounds later, one of Pearce's eyes was almost swollen shut. The two fighters battled on, both bruised and bleeding. From the 33rd round until the end of the fight, Pearce controlled the action. After an hour and ten minutes, Pearce's persistent attack sufficiently weakened Gully so that he could not continue.

Pearce laid full claim to the title in his next fight, when he battled Jem Belcher. Although blind in one eye from an accident, Belcher agreed to the challenge. The slugging Pearce outfought Belcher for eighteen rounds to win the undisputed championship. Pearce never fought again. He toured the country after the Belcher victory, celebrating in high fashion. According to contemporary accounts, Pearce was drunk more often than sober. He contracted tuberculosis and other ailments and died in 1809, only four years after winning the championship.

Right-handed; 5'9"; 175 lbs.
English Champion 1805
Hall of Fame Induction: 1993
Born: 1777, Bristol, England
Died: 4/30/1809

SELECTED BOUTS

Date	Year	Opponent	Location	Result / Rounds		Title
Jun 3	1803	Jack Firley	London	W	10	—
Aug 12	1803	Joe Berks	London	W	15	—
Jan 23	1804	Joe Berks	Wimbledon, England	W	24	—
Mar 11	1805	Elias Spray	Hampton, England	W	29	—
Apr 27	1805	Stephen Carte	Shepperton, England	W	25	—
Oct 8	1805	John Gully	Hailsham, England	W	64	—
Dec 6	1805	♛ Jem Belcher★	near Doncaster, England	W	18	Won-England-H

BOXING GLOVES While it may seem to the uninitiated that boxing gloves were introduced to lessen injury to an opponent's face and body, in fact, they were invented to protect the attacker's hands. Many an early bare-fisted fight was lost because of hand injuries. Over the years, gloves evolved from the early "mufflers" used in training to the padded mittens now in use. To inflict injury to the opponent and not to one's hands is still the object, although modern gloves are a far cry from those used in Greek and Roman times. In the fights to the death of ancient times, gloves were often studded or covered with spikes.

RINGFACT

JACK RANDALL
The [Original] Nonpareil, The Prime Irish Lad

Right-handed; 5'6"; 136–146 lbs.

Hall of Fame Induction: 2005

Born: 11/25/1794, St. Giles, London, England

Died: 3/12/1828

Jack Randall was the first great fighter in history to retire undefeated. He was the second boxer with the nickname "The Nonpareil" to be inducted into the Hall of Fame—following the "first" Jack Dempsey (the US middleweight of the late nineteenth century). Randall was the original Nonpareil from whom Dempsey borrowed the moniker.

Randall was born in London, England, on November 25, 1794. Randall's first recorded bouts were in 1815. He won four and fought to a draw with Jack Henshaw who outweighed him by 40 pounds. On September 30, 1817, he faced Abby Belasco in a fight of huge popular interest. Randall worked Belasco's body and stopped him in a masterful performance of 54½ minutes.

Randall faced another tough opponent, Ned Turner, on December 5, 1818, at Crawley Downs. Though evenly matched in terms of height, weight, and age, the popular Randall was the betting favorite. Neither man landed a punch for the first five minutes. Randall knocked Turner down with a pair of hard lefts in the thirteenth. Turner threw Randall out of the ring in the seventeenth. After 24 rounds, Randall was in command. By the end of the 32nd, some of the spectators urged Turner to give up to avoid further damage. Randall put him out of his misery with a knockout in the 34th round.

In his next fight on May 4, 1819, before a crowd of 25,000 at Crawley Downs, Randall faced Jack Martin. Martin's long reach proved troublesome for Randall. However, Randall went inside and worked the ribs and stomach until the weakened Martin dropped his guard and exposed his head. Randall emerged victorious in 49 minutes, 10 seconds. After this fight Randall retired and opened a tavern, "The Hole in the Wall."

Randall did fight once more, however. Martin boasted that he could beat Randall, and urged on by his fans, Randall agreed to a rematch. The fight was held on September 16, 1821, at East Grimstead before a crowd of 20,000. Randall battered the boastful Martin for eight minutes until Martin dropped to the ground, bleeding and unable to continue.

As a fighter, Randall was credited with originating the "one-two" punch (the classic combination of a left jab followed quickly by a right cross) and was considered a skillful boxer. He may also have been the first fighter whose popularity led him to the stage. He appeared weekly at the Regency—shadowboxing and staging exhibitions. Like many fighters, Randall had a problem with alcohol. He died in 1828, at the young age of 33.

SELECTED BOUTS

Date	Year	Opponent	Location	Result / Duration	Title
—	1815	Jack ("The Butcher") Payne	Marylebone Lane, England	W 20 min	—
—	1815	Jack Henshaw	Marylebone Lane	D 25 min	—
May 28	1816	Ikey ("Ugly") Borrock	Combe Wood, England	W 6 rds	—
Sep 30	1817	Abey Belasco	Shepperton Range, England	W 7 rds	—
Nov 27	1817	Joe ("The Waterman") Parish	Hayes Common, Kent, England	W 11 rds	—
Dec 5	1818	Ned Turner	Crawley Downs, England	W 34 rds	—
May 4	1819	Jack Martin	Crawley Downs	W 19 rds	—
Sep 16	1821	Jack Martin	Crawley Downs	W 1 rd	—

BILL RICHMOND
The Black Terror

Bill Richmond, the first African-American fighter to gain prominence in British boxing, was born to slaves belonging to Dr. George C. Charlton, a minister. Not much is known about Richmond's youth, but at the start of the Revolutionary War Dr. Charlton left New York for England, leaving his slaves behind. Richmond, the story goes, occupied his time sparring with British soldiers under the command of General Earl Percy, later the Duke of Northumberland, and because of his fistic prowess and his good character was made Percy's valet and accompanied him to England in 1777. Percy paid for Richmond to serve as an apprentice cabinet-maker, and Richmond learned the trade well, working as a journeyman in both York and London.

Right-handed; 5'9"; 152–175 lbs.

Hall of Fame Induction: 1999

Born: 8/5/1763, Cuckold's Town, Richmond (Staten Island), NY

Died: 12/29/1829

Richmond's first recorded fight was on August 25, 1791. Richmond was part of a large crowd at the racetrack in York, when George Moore insulted him and challenged him to a fight. Onlookers formed a ring on the spot and offered a purse to the winner. Though Moore outweighed him by approximately 50 pounds, Richmond easily dispensed with him.

Despite this success, Richmond declined offers to become a prizefighter and continued as a cabinetmaker for the next seven years, fighting only in response to insults and personal affronts. After thrashing Frank ("The York Bully") Meyers in an impromptu match, reportedly over a woman, Richmond decided to turn to fighting on a full-time basis.

His early career saw a loss to George Maddox and wins over Youssop ("The Jew") and Jack Holmes, also known as Tom Tough. But Richmond faced a sterner test of his abilities when he fought future champion and Hall of Famer Tom Cribb on October 8, 1805. Giving away almost 30 pounds, Richmond displayed a knack for avoiding Cribb's heavy blows, and landed some of his own. He struggled gamely, but clearly took the worst of the fighting before succumbing in the 25th round of a 90-minute fight.

Though he never again contended for the championship, Richmond continued to box for the next five years. He then opened a public house and taught boxing, holding lessons at the Royal Tennis Court in London. In his sixth decade, he fought twice more, scoring victories, and then continued to fight exhibitions and impromptu battles for another six years. Richmond frequently served as a second and trainer, as he did for Tom Molineaux, another African-American, in his unsuccessful title fight against Tom Cribb.

SELECTED BOUTS

Date	Year	Opponent	Location	Result / Duration	Title
Aug 25	1791	George ("Dockey") Moore	York, England	W	25 min.	—
—	—	Frank Meyers	York	W	—	—
—	—	Whipmaker Green	London	W	10 min.	—
Jan 23	1804	George Maddox	Wimbledon Commons, Eng.	L	3 rounds	—
May 21	1805	Youssop ("The Jew")	Blackheath, England	W	6 rounds	—
Jul 8	1805	Jack Holmes	Cricklewood Green, Eng.	W	26 rounds	—
Oct 8	1805	Tom Cribb ★	Hailsham, Sussex, Eng.	L	90 min.	—
Aug 9	1809	George Maddox	Near Margate, Kent, Eng.	W	52 rounds	—
Nov 12	1818	Jack Carter	—	W	3 rounds	—

TOM SAYERS
The Napoleon of the Prize Ring

Right-handed; 5'8½"; 152 lbs.

English Champion 1857–60

Hall of Fame Induction: 1990

Born: 5/25/1826, Brighton, Sussex, England

Died: 11/8/1865

Although a middleweight or lighter by modern standards, Tom Sayers fought in the first great international heavyweight championship match against American John C. Heenan. Sayers, who never topped 152 pounds, routinely took on opponents of all sizes.

In 1849, Sayers defeated Abe Couch in his first professional fight. His next fight was broken up by the police after nine rounds, then later reconvened to end in a 39-round draw when darkness fell. In 1853, Sayers met the acknowledged middleweight champion, Nat Langham. By the 61st round, Sayers's eyes had swollen shut and his seconds threw in the towel.

After an impressive victory over Harry Poulson, Sayers fought a tough draw with Aaron Jones and whipped him soundly in the rematch. Sayers then met Bill Perry, who at that time called himself the heavyweight champion. Perry outweighed Sayers by 50 pounds and won the early rounds of the match, but in the tenth, Sayers split Perry's lip and his seconds called an end to the fight. Although his evasive tactics led some to accuse Sayers of cowardice, he had fought a very smart fight that won him the heavyweight championship.

Sayers mounted four successful defenses before facing Heenan, a claimant to the American heavyweight title. For the first time, a match in England aroused interest on both sides of the Atlantic, and was well-reported in the newspapers. Heenan outweighed Sayers by 46 pounds and towered five inches above him. The fight was bloody from the beginning, and in the sixth round, Sayers broke his right arm blocking a punch. In the eighth, Heenan broke his left hand. Sayers then targeted Heenan's eyes, and although the American dominated the fight, he was rapidly becoming blinded. In the 37th, Heenan held Sayers helpless against the ropes, which someone suddenly cut. The crowd surged inside the ring and the referee deserted, but the two bloody battlers continued for five rounds until the match ended in a draw. The courage of both competitors was much admired, and boxing interest in the U.S. soared. Sayers retired after the fight and died of tuberculosis and diabetes six years later.

SELECTED BOUTS

Date	Year	Opponent	Location	Result / Rounds		Title
Mar 19	1849	Abe Couch	Greenhithe, England	W	6	—
Oct 18	1853	♛ Nat Langham ★	Lakenheath, England	L	61	For-England-M
Jan 29	1856	Harry Poulson	Appledore, England	W	109	—
Jun 16	1857	♛ Bill Perry	Down R. Thames, Eng.	W	10	Won-England-H
Sep 21	1857	Bob Brett	Leashford, England	W	7	—
Jan 5	1858	Bill Benjamin	Isle of Grain, England	W	3	—
Jun 15	1858	Tom Paddock	Kent, England	W	21	Ret-England-H
Apr 5	1859	Bill Benjamin	near Ashford, England	W	11	—
Apr 17	1860	John C. Heenan ★	Farnborough, England	D	42	Ret-England-H

TOM SPRING

One of the most scientific of the early fighters, Tom Spring possessed a style that distinguished him from most of his contemporaries. Not known for his punching power and troubled by bad hands, Spring had good defense, fine footwork, and a solid left. Spring first fought at the age of seventeen while working as a butcher in Hereford. His first recorded professional bout was a win over the towering John Hollands.

In 1818, Spring twice faced Ned Painter, a more experienced fighter, for a win and a loss. As the first bout began, Spring hit Painter on the side of the throat, sending him down. When Painter toppled to the ground, his head and shoulder struck a stake holding the ring together. Badly injured, Painter nevertheless fought through the 31st round before succumbing. In the rematch, Painter opened a gash over Spring's right eye with a hard right. Spring continued to bleed but hung on for 42 rounds before quitting.

Right-handed; 5'11½"; 186 lbs.
English Champion 1823–24
Hall of Fame Induction: 1992
Born: 2/22/1795, Townhope, Herefordshire, England
Named: Thomas Winter
Died: 8/20/1851

After defeating Jack Carter in 1819, Spring went on an exhibition tour of England, sparring with the champion, Tom Cribb. When Cribb retired in 1821, he handed the title to Spring. Challengers were slow to take Spring up on his offer to fight anyone in England until Spring signed to fight Bill Neat in 1823. Though denigrated as a "lady's maid fighter" for his lack of punching power, Spring scored a knockdown in the first round and cut Neat in the next. The fight ended in 37 minutes with Spring the winner.

Spring next fought two tough battles with the Irish fighter Jack Langan. The fights presented a great contrast in styles—Spring was quick and athletic and Langan was big, slow, and ponderous. Spring won both marathon battles against Langan. He was forced to retire largely because of his ruined hands, a common hazard for bare-knuckle fighters. Except for one fight with Painter, Spring's ability to avoid punishment and hit often, though without much power, enabled him to triumph over his opponents. His "Spring's Harlequin Step," in which he feinted briefly into his opponent's range, evaded the reactive punch, and then scored a hit himself, was an especially effective move.

Well-respected for his kindness and gentlemanly demeanor outside of the ring, Spring became a prosperous innkeeper upon his retirement.

SELECTED BOUTS

Date	Year	Opponent	Location	Result / Rounds		Title
—	c.1814	John Hollands	England	W	—	—
Sep 9	1817	Jack Stringer	Moulsey, England	W	29	—
Apr 1	1818	Ned Painter	Mickleham Downs, England	W	31	—
Aug 7	1818	Ned Painter	Russia Farm, England	L	42	—
May 4	1819	Jack Carter	Crawley Downs, England	W	71	—
Dec 20	1819	Ben Burn	England	W	11	—
Feb 20	1821	Tom Oliver	Arlington Corners, England	W	25	—
May 17	1823	Bill Neat	Hinckley Downs, England	W	8	Won-Vac England-H
Jan 7	1824	Jack Langan	Worcester, England	W	77	Ret-England-H
Jun 8	1824	Jack Langan	Warwick, England	W	76	Ret-England-H

JOHN L. SULLIVAN
The Boston Strong Boy

Right-handed; 5'10½"; 190 lbs.

Hvywt Bare-Knuckle Champion 1882–89
Heavyweight (Queensberry Rules) Champion
1885–92

Hall of Fame Induction: 1990

Born: 10/15/1858, Roxbury, MA

Named: John Lawrence Sullivan

Died: 2/2/1918

John L. Sullivan was an extraordinarily popular figure in the late nineteenth century, a living hero whose prowess in the ring brought him lasting fame. Sullivan remains well known even today, over 100 years after his last fight. Born to Irish immigrant parents in the town of Roxbury, neighboring Boston, Sullivan apparently inherited his solid physique—he was 5'10" tall and weighed 190 pounds—from his mother, who equalled her grown son's stature. Sullivan's father, although an aggressive scrapper himself, was barely 5'3".

Sullivan briefly attended Boston College in an effort to satisfy his mother's desire to have him become a priest. He worked for a short time as a hod carrier, his father's profession, before becoming an assistant plumber, and then attempting to learn the tinsmith trade. His stint as a plumber reportedly ended when he broke his employer's jaw in a dispute about the proper pipe to use on a job. A versatile athlete, Sullivan played semi-pro baseball in the Boston area. The Cincinnati Red Stockings offered him a contract, which he declined.

From an early age, Sullivan showed great proficiency with his fists. As a teenager, he would fight in Boston barrooms, issuing a challenge that he "could lick any man in the house." He also engaged in weightlifting exhibitions, hefting and sometimes throwing kegs of beer. Sullivan turned to fighting more seriously at the age of eighteen when he engaged in three- and four-round amateur bouts. Sullivan's big break came when he went to the Dudley Street Opera House in Boston in 1877. One of the acts featured heavyweight boxer Tom Scannel, who skipped rope, shadowboxed, and sparred with partners chosen from the audience. Often, the sparring partner was in on the act and would box two furious rounds before succumbing in the third. This night, Sullivan, urged on by the crowd, climbed the stage to face Scannel. Scannel, offering to shake hands, suddenly slugged Sullivan instead. In return, Sullivan blasted Scannel with a half-dozen rapid blows and knocked him into the orchestra pit.

The scene at the opera house launched young Sullivan on his professional career. In 1879, he knocked out Cockey Woods in Boston. In 1880, he boxed exhibitions with noted scientific boxer Professor Mike Donovan and former champion Joe Goss. Sullivan outclassed them both. The next year he scored an eight-round knockout over John Flood, known as the Bull's Head Terror. Fighting on a barge in the Hudson River to evade the authorities, Sullivan made short work of Flood, knocking him down eight times. Both fighters wore tight, unpadded gloves.

The next year Sullivan met Paddy Ryan, the heavyweight champion—at least in

American eyes—in Mississippi City, Mississippi. It was a bare-knuckle contest, and basically one-sided. Sullivan dominated the fight and knocked Ryan out in the eighth round with a right to the jaw. Sullivan was now considered the world champion although there was some disagreement among British and Australian followers of the sport. In addition to his regular bouts, Sullivan went on an American tour, challenging anyone to stay in the ring with him for four rounds for a $1,000 prize. He took on all comers. Only Tug Wilson, an English fighter, went the distance.

In 1883, Sullivan faced British Empire champion, Charlie Mitchell, in a gloved bout. Although Sullivan was winning the fight when the police stepped in to prevent the battered Mitchell from absorbing more punishment, Mitchell had shocked Sullivan and his fans by knocking him down in the first round. Five years later, the two met at the estate of Baron Rothschild in France. They battled in a rain-soaked ring for 39 rounds to a draw.

In 1889, Sullivan fought one of his most famous bouts with Jake Kilrain in the last significant bare-knuckle bout in boxing. Kilrain was hailed by Richard Fox, the publisher of the *Police Gazette*, as the new champion. Fox disliked Sullivan for a perceived slight in a bar and had long searched for an opponent to topple him. Sullivan's weight had ballooned to 240 flabby pounds, and he went into extensive training with champion wrestler William Muldoon to trim down to 205. In the fight, Sullivan got off to a good start by tripping and hip-tossing Kilrain to win the first two rounds. Sullivan was thrown in the third. From then on, Kilrain fought on gamely, but Sullivan had the better of it. Beaten and battered, Kilrain could not come to scratch for the 76th round.

Sullivan did not fight for three years after the Kilrain match and instead toured as the hero in a mawkish play called *Honest Hearts and Willing Hands*. He continued to box in exhibitions and to carouse. In one exhibition, against Gentleman Jim Corbett, both fighters sparred in full evening attire.

In 1892, Sullivan faced Corbett in earnest in New Orleans as part of the Carnival of Champions, fought under the Queensberry Rules. The fighters wore five-ounce gloves. The contrast in styles was obvious. The powerful, steadfast Sullivan had little use for ring trickery or defense, while Corbett was known for his peerless boxing ability. Young and agile, Corbett outboxed Sullivan, who was out of condition as a result of his indulgent lifestyle. Corbett stayed clear of the champion for twelve rounds. By the seventeenth, Corbett's forays were wearing Sullivan down, and he had a clear advantage. Corbett knocked out Sullivan in the 21st round.

Sullivan never fought again. He did some acting and, surprisingly, swore off alcohol. Previously known for his prodigious drinking, Sullivan became a temperance lecturer. He retired to a Massachusetts farm, having depleted most of the $1 million he had earned in his public career. Sullivan's vast renown and charismatic style did much to advance the sport of boxing in America.

SELECTED BOUTS

Date	Year	Opponent	Location	Result / Rounds		Title
Mar 14	1879	Cockey Woods	Boston	TKO	5	—
Feb 7	1882	♛ Paddy Ryan	Mississippi City, MS	KO	9	Won-BK World-H
May 14	1883	Charlie Mitchell★	New York	W	3	—
Oct 17	1883	James McCoy	McKeesport, PA	TKO	1	—
Jan 19	1885	Paddy Ryan	New York	TKO	1	—
Aug 29	1885	Dominick McCaffrey	Cincinnati	W	6	Won-Vac M of Q World-H
Nov 13	1886	Paddy Ryan	San Francisco	KO	3	—
Mar 10	1888	Charlie Mitchell★	Chantilly, France	D	39	Ret-BK World-H
Jul 8	1889	Jake Kilrain	Richburg, MS	TKO	75	Ret-BK World-H
Sep 7	1892	James J. Corbett★	New Orleans	KO'd	21	Lost-M of Q World-H

WILLIAM THOMPSON
Bendigo

Left-handed; 5'9½"; 165 lbs.

English Champion: 1839–40, 1845–50

Hall of Fame Induction: 1991

Born: 10/11/1811, ottingham, England

Died: 8/23/1880

The name of William ("Bendigo") Thompson is inextricably linked with that of Ben Caunt by their three epic battles. Thompson, one of a set of triplets, was called Abednego, later shortened to Bendigo. As a boxer, he was often known by his nickname alone.

Thompson started fighting professionally in 1832 with a victory over Joe Hanley, and in 1835, he faced Caunt for the first time. According to contemporary reports, Caunt was incensed by Thompson's tactic of falling to the ground when in difficulty. In the 22nd round, Caunt hit the kneeling Thompson and lost the fight on a foul.

Thompson won his next three fights before facing Caunt again. Caunt came into the ring in less than the best fighting condition. A great athlete, Thompson easily eluded Caunt's clumsy attacks. However, in the fifth round Caunt caught Bendigo against the ropes and nearly strangled him. Thompson continuously peppered Caunt with shots to the body. In the thirteenth, Caunt again nearly strangled Thompson. In the 50th round, Caunt alleged that Thompson had illegally kicked him, but the claim was disallowed. In the 75th round, Thompson lost on a foul when he slipped to the ground without having been hit. Some observers believed that Thompson intentionally fell to avoid further punishment, while others believed that Thompson had the fight well in hand and would have won.

In his next battle, Thompson faced the champion James ("Deaf") Burke. Fighting under the new London Prize Ring Rules, Thompson dominated the fight. In the tenth, a badly beaten Burke head-butted Thompson and was disqualified. In 1840, the new champion, after watching some steeplechase races, exuberantly tried to turn a somersault and fell, seriously injuring his leg. He did not fight for six years until he faced Caunt for the third time. Thompson entered this bout crouching to make himself less of a target and eluded many of Caunt's thrusts. Thompson dominated the fight and earned the victory when Caunt sat down in the 93rd round without getting hit.

Thompson then retired only to return for one fight in 1850, a victory over Tom Paddock. A hard drinker and an innkeeper, Thompson turned to preaching in his later years, especially concerning himself with temperance issues. Although some questioned his sincerity, he continued his ministry for many years.

SELECTED BOUTS

Date	Year	Opponent	Location	Result / Rounds		Title
Oct	1832	Joe Hanley	England	W	16	—
Jul 21	1835	Ben Caunt	Nottingham, England	WF	22	—
Jun 13	1837	Bill Looney	Chapel-en-le-Frith, Eng.	W	99	—
Apr 3	1838	Ben Caunt	Shelby, England	LF	75	—
Feb 12	1839	♛ James ("Deaf") Burke★	Heather, England	WF	10	Won-England-H
Sep 9	1845	♛ Ben Caunt	Stoney Stratford, England	WF	93	Reg-England-H
Jun 5	1850	Tom Paddock	Mildenhall, England	WF	49	Ret-England-H

JEM WARD
The Black Diamond

Although an excellent fighter, Jem Ward—English champion for most of the period from 1825 to 1831—was the first boxer to be disciplined by a governing body for throwing a fight. Ward turned professional at the age of fifteen with a victory over George Robinson. He remained unbeaten until 1822 when he lost to Bill Abbott, a fighter most observers considered to be far inferior to Ward. After many rounds, Ward shouted to Abbott loud enough that those at ringside could hear, "Now, Bill, look sharp, hit me and I'll go down." When Abbott then hit Ward, he collapsed. The Pugilistic Society conducted an inquiry into the match. Ward confessed that he had been paid 100 pounds to lose. The Pugilistic Society expelled Ward and barred him from fighting in any ring under its control.

Right-handed; 5'10"; 175 lbs.

English Champion: 1825–31

Hall of Fame Induction: 1995

Born: 12/26/1800, Ratcliff Hwy., England

Died: 4/3/1884

The next year Ward was attending a bout and, when the main event ended quickly, he was called upon to enter the ring against Ned Baldwin, whom he easily defeated. Still unable to clear his name, Ward toured England with other boxers. He defeated Joe Rickens while pretending to be an unschooled farm boy named Sawney Wilson, so as to get better betting odds.

In 1823, the Pugilistic Society reinstated Ward. He lost his next bout to Josh Hudson. In 1825, he challenged the champion Tom Cannon, who was seconded by Hall of Famers Tom Spring and Tom Cribb. On an intensely hot day, Ward won easily. He very briefly lost the title when Peter Crawley defeated him in 1827. Crawley retired within days, and Ward reclaimed the championship. He held it until 1831 when he retired.

A fine fighter and powerfully built man, Ward received criticism for refusing to face the younger challenger, James Burke. Ward had some success as an artist, and his paintings were displayed in London and Liverpool. He also enjoyed playing the violin and flute. Among his retirement ventures, he sang in concerts and operated a tavern.

SELECTED BOUTS

Date	Year	Opponent	Location	Result / Duration		Title
May 6	1816	George Robinson	Stepney, England	W	45 min.	—
Jun 18	1816	Bill Wall	Limehouse Fields, England	W	2 hrs.	—
Jul 27	1817	George Webb	Limehouse Fields	W	3 min.	—
Jul 4	1819	Nick Murphy	Barking, England	W	35 min.	—
Sep 29	1820	Mike Hayes	Isle of Dogs, England	W	40 min.	—
Nov 11	1823	Josh Hudson	Moulsey Hurst, England	L	15 rounds	—
Jun 21	1824	Phil Sampson	Colnbrook, England	W	26 rounds	—
Dec 28	1824	Phil Sampson	Stony Stratford, England	W	27 rounds	—
Jul 19	1825	♛ Tom Cannon	Warwick, England	W	10 rounds	Won-England-H
Jan 2	1827	Peter Crawley	Royston, England	L	11 rounds	Lost-England-H
May 27	1828	Jack Carter	Shepperton, England	W	17 rounds	Ret-England-H
Jul 12	1831	Simon Byrne	Willeycutt, England	W	33 rounds	Ret-England-H

WHO RULES?

Boxing's Governing Bodies

WHEN BOXING WAS A GROWING SPORT in England, it produced one champion at a time. A man achieved acclaim by defeating the current champion or, if no champion existed, through other accomplishments in the ring. There were no organizations to supervise the conduct of boxing and boxers, but fans and historians could follow a fairly cohesive lineage of champions. By the early twentieth century, when eight weight classes were established, each division had its own champion.

Today, the potential exists for 68 champions to hold titles offered by four dominant boxing organizations. The World Boxing Association (WBA), the World Boxing Council (WBC), the International Boxing Federation (IBF), and the World Boxing Organization (WBO) each has its own version of seventeen weight-division titles. Several other organizations also offer titles, with the result that one can no longer get a simple answer to the question: Who's the heavyweight (or any weight) champ?

The history of boxing's governing bodies reaches back to England where the sport was largely unregulated until 1891 when Hall of Famer Lord Lonsdale helped establish the National Sporting Club. This club regulated English boxing for 38 years, during which time it formally defined and standardized the eight recognized weight classes and presented Lonsdale Belts to British champions. The British Boxing Board of Control was established around 1930 and continues to regulate boxing in the United Kingdom. The British board is affiliated with the European Boxing Union (EBU), which in 1946 replaced the International Boxing Union (IBU), first formed in 1911 in Paris. The EBU continues to administer boxing through its affiliate members in European countries.

Meanwhile, the United States was slower to organize any type of regulation for the sport. Richard K. Fox, publisher of the popular *Police Gazette,* instituted the practice of distributing championship belts in the U.S. in the late 1880s, when he presented a belt to Jake Kilrain, who was perhaps less deserving of the honor than John L. Sullivan, the more widely accepted champion. Fox continued to present belts to fighters he deemed worthy, but the *Police Gazette* had no function as an official sanctioning body.

With passage of the Walker Law in 1920, boxing became legal in the state of New York under the purview of the New York State Athletic Commission (NYSAC). New York quickly became the center of boxing, and served as a model for other states interested in legalizing the sport. In February 1921, representatives of fifteen state athletic commissions met in Manhattan's Flatiron Building to form the National Boxing Association (NBA). The group's stated objective was to standardize rules and regulations in the sport. Of equal concern, particularly to Abe J. Greene, the New Jersey state boxing commissioner, was finding a way to keep boxing's growing profits from concentrating solely in New York.

However, even though it was founded in New York City, the NBA failed to capture NYSAC as a member. The state commission refused to join, citing a prohibition in state law. In reality, New York did not wish to share its power or potential revenue.

Lennox Lewis held four major heavyweight championships (WBC, WBA, IBF, and IBO) although never more than three simultaneously.

The state's refusal to join the fledgling NBA created, in effect, two sanctioning bodies and, often, the NBA and NYSAC crowned different champions in the same weight class. New York maintained its considerable power in boxing through the 1960s, when other venues for headline fights—especially rapidly proliferating casinos—began to dominate.

In the ongoing conflict between the NBA and NYSAC, disputes over the real champion in a given weight class were often settled by Nat Fleischer, editor of *The Ring* magazine. Under Fleischer's authority, the magazine issued monthly rankings of contenders and awarded championship belts.

Following World War II, boxing gained considerable ground in Mexico, South America, Australia, Asia, and Africa. In response to this expansion, the NBA changed its name to the World Boxing Association (WBA) in 1962. Nevertheless, the WBA remained primarily a U.S. organization because of its voting scheme: Each state commission was granted one vote, while each foreign country also had only a single vote, regardless of its level of boxing activity. This imbalance gave a boxing-poor state like New Hampshire, for instance, an equal vote with countries like Argentina or Mexico, which were home to hundreds of bouts each year.

Disputes were often settled by Nat Fleischer, editor of The Ring.

American domination of the WBA led promoter and matchmaker George Parnassus and others to form the World Boxing Council (WBC) in 1963. Parnassus, who often showcased lighter-weight Latin American contenders, believed these fighters were not accurately or fairly represented in the WBA's rankings. As originally established, the World Boxing Council (WBC) consisted of eleven countries organized into continental federations with two votes granted to each federation.

Predictably, the WBA and WBC often had different champions in the same weight classes. In the 1970s and '80s, both sanctioning bodies doubled the number of weight classes, adding to the panoply of champions.

In 1976, fight manager Jose ("Pepe") Cordero of Puerto Rico engineered changes in the WBA which ended its control by United States interests. Under the rules of the organization, Cordero realized that if each state had a vote then, by rights, so should the provincial boxing commissions in other nations. That year, representatives of provincial commissions appeared at the WBA convention, seized control of the organization from the Americans and have retained it ever since.

In 1983, a third major sanctioning body formed when Bob Lee, head of the United States Boxing Association (USBA), attempted to gain the presidency of the

WBA. When his attempt failed, he took the USBA from under the WBA umbrella and formed the International Boxing Federation (IBF), a body that now offers its own array of seventeen titles.

The World Boxing Organization (WBO), yet another outgrowth of the WBA, was formed when a disgruntled Latin American contingent and some Americans bolted from the WBA. The WBO, of course, supports its own titles and champions. Other sanctioning bodies have been formed in recent years, including the International Boxing Association (IBA), the International Boxing Organization (IBO), the World Boxing Union (WBU), the World Boxing Federation (WBF), and the International Boxing Council (IBC), but the four described here—the WBA, WBC, IBF, and WBO—are generally considered to have the most clout by the boxing media.

The multiplication of sanctioning bodies has drawn some criticism from the public and the boxing media. Fans must puzzle out which "world champion" is really the best, or why the boxer who is apparently the best in a particular weight class may not hold a championship belt. A second and more serious charge leveled at the sanctioning bodies is that the rating systems are at best inaccurate and at worst corrupt. Rankings have reportedly been purchased, and often, one organization's rankings bear little resemblance to those of another, or to the independent rankings of The Ring.

Despite these problems, some proponents of boxing's growth and renewed popularity support the proliferation of titles. More boxers can compete for titles, adding excitement to the sport and possibly enhancing the quality of the fights. Since title fights tend to carry higher purses, more boxers are allowed opportunities to gain financial reward. Television producers and advertisers tend to be more attracted to bouts they can bill as title fights, and the economic benefit for arenas, casinos, and tourism must be considered as well.

Fans would undoubtedly appreciate more guidance in interpreting the tangle of titles. The governing bodies have begun to recognize the public's distaste for anything less than fairness in rankings, as well as the great value of having tournaments that would produce "super-champions" in each of the weight classes. The interest generated in seeing belt holders fight each other to become true world champions does much to justify the existence of many titles.

OLD-TIMERS

The Sweet Science Becomes an American Passion

BOXING WAS BORN IN ENGLAND, but it grew up in America. The sport was embraced by the growing nation, and by the time the last of the bare-knuckle fighters had faded into history, the United States was the principal proving ground for ring hopefuls. In the early twentieth century, boxing as a crowd-pleasing, money-making endeavor flourished first in the American West, then moved east to capture the attention of the entire country. While Britain, Australia, and the West Indies produced occasional champions, with Europe, Asia, South America, and Africa joining in later, nowhere was the sport as popular as in the United States.

Until the 1920s, public prizefighting was illegal in most states, and matches often had to be conducted in secret locations, or as so-called "sparring sessions" in private clubs. Police intervention was still a hazard, and it was not uncommon for boxers to find themselves confined to a local jail for several days following a raided fight. Fixed bouts were not uncommon, and it could be as dangerous to be a spectator as it was to be a boxer because of the police raids or eruptions of violence among spectators.

Legal attempts to clean up the sport sometimes backfired. The Frawley Law, passed in 1911, ended a ten-year period when authorities tried to ban boxing completely. It was decided that fixes would be less likely to occur if only a knockout could be recognized as a win. If both men were still on their feet at the end of a match, it was called a no-decision bout, with no official winner. The no-decision regulation was

intended to foil crooked gamblers by making it harder to influence the boxers, referees, or judges. However, the newspaper reporters—who often identified the supposed winners of no-decision bouts—were still vulnerable to payoffs. The arrival of the Walker Law in New York State in 1920 put an end to the no-decision era when it set up more stringent regulations as well as an athletic commission to oversee the sport. The Walker Law was quickly emulated by other states.

Because the West had fewer restrictions, it dominated boxing in the early part of the century. Operating in California, James Coffroth became the nation's first great boxing promoter, and in 1910 Tex Rickard arranged what was probably the most anticipated clash up to that time—the Jack Johnson–James J. Jeffries heavyweight championship match in Reno, Nevada.

Boxing began to shed its unsavory reputation when influential people like former President Theodore Roosevelt recommended controlled fisticuffs to promote health and fitness. This view, as well as a growing public acceptance of the sport as conducted on a professional level, led to its legalization in many states.

With the passage of the Walker Law, the center of boxing activity shifted to New York City and environs. Boxing came to be seen as a legitimate, major athletic pursuit, and when the first million-dollar gate was realized, promoters set up other high-profit matches. Boxing produced larger-than-life heroes like Jack Dempsey and Gene Tunney, acknowledged pillars of "The Golden Age of Sport," along with such stars as baseball's Babe Ruth and tennis player Bill Tilden. Boxer celebrities like Max Baer mixed show business into their careers, and several boxers retired to become film or stage actors.

This period of growth also saw formal establishment of the traditional eight weight classes: heavyweight, light heavyweight, middleweight, welterweight, lightweight, featherweight, bantamweight, and flyweight. Reports of fights were brought to a much wider audience through films, radio broadcasts, increased newspaper coverage, and the establishment of the seminal boxing publication, The Ring.

Although the era grappled with racism as increasing numbers of African-American boxers entered the ring, many fighters—including blacks—built substantial careers, fighting frequently and over long periods of time. Unlike the earliest pugilists, who may have fought only a dozen recorded bouts, or later boxers, for whom 40 fights could make an entire career, it was not unusual for fighters in the Old-Timers era to record 200 or more encounters.

LOU AMBERS
The Herkimer Hurricane

LIGHTWEIGHT

Right-handed; 5'6"; 131–140 lbs.

104 bouts, 6/16/1932 to 2/28/1941

Managers: Nicanor Rafael 1932–33,
Dave Steinberg 1933–34,
Al Weill 1934–41

Lightweight Champion 1936–38,
1939–40

Hall of Fame Induction: 1992

Born: 11/8/1913, Herkimer, NY

Named: Luigi Guiseppe D'Ambrosio

Died: 4/24/1995

One of the top lightweights of the 1930s, Lou Ambers built a reputation as a clever, aggressive boxer. Ambers first picked up the rudiments of boxing in a church basement gym in his native Herkimer, New York. When the Great Depression forced his family's restaurant to close and Ambers ended up working in a furniture factory, he decided to try boxing as a career. After fighting in amateur "bootleg" bouts for a few dollars a fight, Ambers entered the professional ranks with a second-round knockout of Frankie Curry in 1932. Ambers continued his winning ways as a pro, going undefeated in his first 32 fights. He earned the attention of *The Ring* and was named its ninth-best lightweight contender in the 1933 annual rankings.

In 1935, Ambers fought his idol, Tony Canzoneri, for the world lightweight title vacated by Barney Ross. Ambers had previously been Canzoneri's sparring partner. Canzoneri quite easily dispatched Ambers, winning a fifteen-round decision. The next year Ambers faced Canzoneri for the title again. Fighting in Madison Square Garden before a crowd of 18,026, Ambers avenged the earlier defeat to claim the title. He scored with straight lefts—cutting Canzoneri under the eye—and with right uppercuts. Ambers maintained a healthy respect for Canzoneri's slugging ability and avoided serious damage while earning a unanimous decision. Ambers faced the sternest

Ambers (L) engages in some relaxed sparring with boyish Marty Servo who later beat Freddie Cochrane for the welterweight crown.

IN THE RING	WON 90	LOST 8	DRAWS 6	TB 104	KO 30	W 60	WF 0	D 6	KO'd 2	L 6	LF 0

Date	Year	Opponent	Site	Result / Rounds		Title
SELECTED BOUTS						
Jun 9	1932	Frankie Curry	Brooklyn, NY	KO	2	—
Sep 26	1932	Ray Meyers	New York	W	5	—
Jan 11	1935	⑩ Harry Dublinsky	New York	W	10	—
Mar 1	1935	⑩ Sammy Fuller	New York	W	15	—
Apr 24	1935	Harold Hughes	Providence, RI	KO	5	—
May 10	1935	⑩ Tony Canzoneri★	New York	L	15	For-Vac World-L
Jul 1	1935	Fritzie Zivic★	Pittsburgh	W	10	—
Jan 3	1936	⑩ Frankie Klick	New York	W	10	—
Feb 7	1936	⑩ Baby Arizmendi★	New York	W	10	—
Sep 3	1936	♛ Tony Canzoneri★	New York	W	15	Won-World-L
Oct 28	1936	⑩ Eddie Cool	Philadelphia	L	10	—
Nov 20	1936	⑩ Jimmy McLarnin★	New York	L	10	—
Dec 29	1936	Stumpy Jacobs	Rochester, NY	TKO	7	—
Feb 10	1937	⑩ Davey Day	New York	W	10	—
Apr 5	1937	⑩ Pedro Montanez	New York	L	10	—
Apr 18	1937	Phil Baker	New Haven, CT	W	10	—
May 7	1937	⑩ Tony Canzoneri★	New York	W	15	Ret-World-L
Sep 23	1937	⑩ Pedro Montanez	New York	W	15	Ret-World-L
Jun 7	1938	⑩ Baby Arizmendi★	Los Angeles	W	10	—
Jul 17	1938	Henry Armstrong★	New York	L	15	Lost-World-L
Feb 24	1939	⑩ Baby Arizmendi★	New York	TKO	11	—
May 26	1939	Paul Junior	Boston	TKO	8	—
Aug 22	1939	♛ Henry Armstrong★	New York	W	15	Reg-World-L
Apr 25	1940	Norment Quarles	Charleston, SC	W	10	—
May 10	1940	⑩ Lew Jenkins★	New York	TKO'd	3	Lost-NY World-L
Feb 14	1941	Norment Quarles	Hartford, CT	W	10	—
Feb 28	1941	♛ Lew Jenkins★	New York	TKO'd	7	—

challenge to his title when he met the feather- and welterweight champion, Henry Armstrong, in Madison Square Garden in 1938. Armstrong knocked Ambers down in the fifth and sixth rounds. Although Ambers recovered sufficiently to gash Armstrong's left eye and mouth, Armstrong continued to fight, swallowing blood so that the damage to his mouth would not be apparent enough to force the referee to stop the fight. Armstrong won a split decision to take the lightweight title. Ambers won the title back in a rematch in Yankee Stadium the next year. It was a vicious fight in which Armstrong lost five rounds because of his low blows. Ambers delivered several telling punches to Armstrong's face and closed one of his eyes to win a split decision. A proposed third fight between these two well-matched fighters never took place.

In 1940, Ambers lost the title when Lew Jenkins stopped him in three rounds. After losing the rematch to Jenkins in seven rounds, Ambers retired. He operated a restaurant and was involved in public relations after leaving the ring.

BABY ARIZMENDI

FEATHERWEIGHT

Right-handed; 5'5"; 118–147 lbs.

109 bouts, 10/11/1927 to 8/21/1942

Manager: Cal Working

California/Mexico World Featherweight Champion 1935–36

Hall of Fame Induction: 2004

Born: 3/17/1914, Torreon, Coahuila, Mexico

Named: Alberto Arizmendi

Died: 12/31/1963

Alberto ("Baby") Arizmendi was the first world champion from Mexico. He suffered a bout of infantile paralysis as a small boy, and his doctor advised that he take up boxing as therapy. He first boxed publicly at the age of seven in a "fleaweight" bout on a Mexican boxing card.

Arizmendi's first professional bout came on October 11, 1927, when he drew with Kid Laredo in San Antonio. Arizmendi was only thirteen, and by all accounts he had been fighting professionally for some time.

After winning nine more fights in Texas over the next nine months, Arizmendi returned to Mexico. He continued his winning ways there. His record was blemished only by two decision losses to Babe Colima and Chito Laredo. On November 14, 1931, he decisioned Kid Pancho to take the Mexican bantamweight title. He first attracted the attention of American fight fans when he scored a surprising decision over Hall of Famer Fidel LaBarba on New Year's Day, 1932, in Mexico City.

Arizmendi moved his base of operations to Los Angeles, where he quickly became a fan favorite. His first fight in Los Angeles was a victory over Speedy Dado on February 9, 1932. The California Boxing Commission declared Arizmendi as its world featherweight champion on October 14, 1932, based on Arizmendi's previous-month's win over Tommy Paul. This recognition did not extend beyond the borders of California and Mexico.

In February 1933, Arizmendi faced Hall of Famer Freddie Miller at the Olympic Auditorium in Los Angeles with the latter's NBA world featherweight title and Arizmendi's California/Mexico world featherweight title at stake. Miller dominated the fight. He won seven of ten rounds with one even.

Arizmendi fought seven different Hall of Famers. His record against Henry Armstrong was two wins and three losses.

IN THE RING	WON 70	LOST 26	DRAWS 13	TB 109	KO 12	W 58	WF 0	D 13	KO'd 3	L 23	LF 0

Date	Year	Opponent	Site	Result / Rounds		Title

SELECTED BOUTS

Date	Year	Opponent	Site	Result	Rounds	Title
Oct 11	1927	Kid Laredo	San Antonio, TX	D	10	—
Nov 14	1931	Kid Pancho	Mexico City	W	12	Won-Mexico-B
Jan 1	1932	ⓦ Fidel LaBarba★	Mexico City	W	10	—
Feb 9	1932	ⓦ Speedy Dado	Los Angeles	W	10	—
Oct 18	1932	ⓦ Newsboy Brown	Los Angeles	W	10	Ret-CA World-FE
Nov 22	1932	ⓦ Varias Milling	Los Angeles	D	10	Ret-CA World-FE
Jan 24	1933	ⓦ Speedy Dado	Los Angeles	W	10	Ret-CA World-FE
Feb 28	1933	♛ Freddie Miller★	Los Angeles	L	10	For-NBA-FE
Jun 12	1933	♛ Freddie Miller★	San Francisco	W	10	—
Mar 13	1934	ⓦ Tony Canzoneri★	Los Angeles	L	10	—
Nov 3	1934	ⓦ Henry Armstrong★	Mexico City	W	10	—
Jan 1	1935	ⓦ Henry Armstrong★	Mexico City	W	12	Reg-Vac CA Mex World-FE
Feb 2	1935	Albert ("Chalky") Wright★	Mexico City	KO	4	—
Feb 7	1936	ⓦ Lou Ambers★	New York	L	10	—
Aug 4	1936	ⓦ Henry Armstrong★	Los Angeles	L	10	Lost-CA Mex World-FE
Oct 5	1937	ⓦ Albert ("Chalky") Wright★	Los Angeles	W	10	—
Mar 15	1938	♛ Henry Armstrong★	Los Angeles	L	10	—
Jun 7	1938	ⓦ Lou Ambers★	Los Angeles	D	10	—
Jan 10	1939	♛ Henry Armstrong★	Los Angeles	L	10	For-World-W
Feb 24	1939	♛ Lou Ambers★	New York	TKO'd	11	—
Nov 3	1939	ⓦ Sammy Angott★	Chicago	L	10	—
Jun 25	1940	ⓦ Sammy Angott★	Los Angeles	D	10	—
Aug 21	1942	Roman Alvarez	Hollywood	L	10	—

In 1934, Arizmendi faced Henry Armstrong in Mexico City. Though Arizmendi injured his left hand in the second round, he won six of the ten rounds to gain the decision. In their rematch on January 2, 1935, Arizmendi again beat Armstrong by decision to regain California and Mexico world featherweight honors.

While he still retained a featherweight title, Arizmendi decided to campaign as a lightweight as well. On February 7, 1936, he faced another Hall of Famer, Lou Ambers. Arizmendi was beaten by Ambers who won all ten rounds of the fight at Madison Square Garden. On August 4, 1936, Arizmendi lost any claim to the featherweight crown when Armstrong beat him in a ten-round decision to take the California/Mexico world featherweight title.

On February 24, 1939, when he faced Ambers again, Arizmendi was stopped short of the distance for the first time in his career. Although he remained on his feet, the ringside doctor halted the bout after Arizmendi suffered a bad cut.

The long years in the ring had begun to take their toll on young Arizmendi. He retired after a loss to Roman Alvarez on August 21, 1942. Arizmendi served in the U.S. Navy in World War II. After that he managed some fighters and operated restaurants in Los Angeles. He died on December 31, 1963. Though he was not a knockout artist, Arizmendi was a very popular figure in Los Angeles boxing in the 1930s because of his courage and aggressive style.

ABE ATTELL
The Little Hebrew

FEATHERWEIGHT

Right-handed; 5'4"; 118–130 lbs.

171 bouts, 8/19/1900 to 1/8/1917

Managers: Al Lippe, Jack McKenna, Tim McGrath, Zeke Abrams, Ike Bloom, Lob Kohn, Billy Nolan, George Weedon, Jack Kearns, Dan Morgan, John Reisler

Featherweight Champion 1901–12

Hall of Fame Induction: 1990

Born: 2/22/1884, San Francisco, CA

Named: Abraham Washington Attell

Died: 2/7/1970

Long-reigning featherweight champion Abe Attell defended the title fourteen times over nine years, although at times his claim to the championship was disputed. A small, quick, and clever boxer, Attell learned to fight in the streets of San Francisco as a Jewish boy growing up in an Irish neighborhood. He quickly found boxing success at the amateur level, then turned professional in 1900 at age sixteen, knocking Kid Lennett out in two rounds. Later, Attell confided that Lennett had been one of the neighborhood toughs who had given him a thrashing in the street.

Although eventually known more for his skillful boxing than his punching ability, Attell scored knockouts in fifteen of his first sixteen fights, and 21 of his first 25. Attell credited Hall of Famer George Dixon, whom he fought three times in 1901, with inspiring him to develop an easier, more graceful style. Between Attell's first and second fights—both draws—with the aging Dixon, he worked to emulate Dixon's apparently effortless movements. He beat Dixon in the third match, a fifteen-round bout advertised by Attell's manager, Jack McKenna, as a fight for the vacant featherweight championship.

Although Attell claimed the title, which then had a 122 lb limit, others asserted that Young Corbett's victory over Terry McGovern later that year made Corbett the featherweight champ. Attell's hold on the title was strengthened in 1903, when he beat Johnny Reagan in twenty rounds. He was generally accepted as the champion until he faced Tommy Sullivan in St. Louis the next year. Sullivan scored a knockout over Attell in five rounds, but Attell discounted

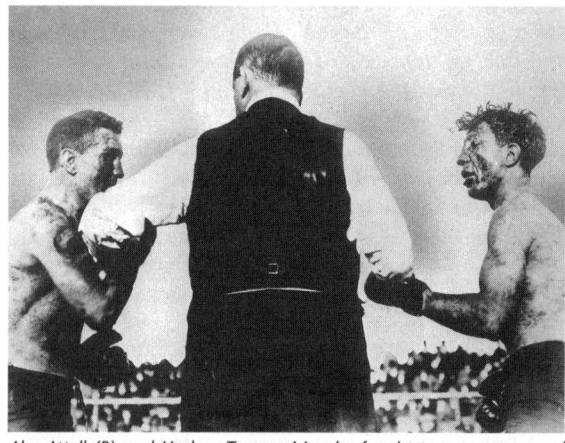

Abe Attell (R) and Harlem Tommy Murphy fought to a twenty-round draw in a long, bloody war in Daly City, CA, on August 3, 1912.

IN THE RING	WON 91	LOST 9	DRAWS 18	TB 171	KO 53	W 36	WF 2	D 18	KO'd 4	L 5	LF 0	ND 51	NC 2

Date	Year	Opponent	Site	Result / Rounds		Title

SELECTED BOUTS

Date	Year	Opponent	Site	Result	Rounds	Title
Aug 19	1900	Kid Lennett	San Francisco	KO	2	—
Aug 24	1901	George Dixon★	Denver	D	10	—
Oct 20	1901	George Dixon★	Cripple Creek, CO	D	20	—
Oct 28	1901	George Dixon★	St. Louis	W	15	—
Sep 3	1903	Johnny Reagan	St. Louis	W	20	Won-Vac-World-FE
Feb 1	1904	Harry Forbes	St. Louis	KO	5	Ret-World-FE
Feb 22	1906	♛ Jimmy Walsh	Chelsea, MA	W	15	Ret-World-FE
Jul 4	1906	Frankie Neil	Los Angeles	W	20	Ret-World-FE
Oct 30	1906	Harry Baker	Los Angeles	W	20	Ret-World-FE
Dec 7	1906	Jimmy Walsh	Los Angeles	KO	8	Ret-World-FE
May 24	1907	Kid Solomon	Los Angeles	W	20	Ret-World-FE
Jan 1	1908	♛ Owen Moran★	San Francisco	D	25	Ret-World-FE
Feb 28	1908	Eddie Kelly	San Francisco	KO	7	Ret-World-FE
Mar 31	1908	♛ Battling Nelson★	San Francisco	D	15	—
Apr 30	1908	Tommy Sullivan	San Francisco	KO	4	Ret-World-FE
Nov 25	1908	Freddie Welsh★	Vernon, CA	L	15	—
Dec 11	1908	Ad Wolgast★	Los Angeles	ND-W	10	—
Jan 14	1909	Freddie Weeks	Goldfield, NV	KO	10	Ret-World-FE
Feb 19	1909	Jim Driscoll★	New York	ND-L	10	—
Oct 24	1910	Johnny Kilbane★	Kansas City, MO	W	10	Ret-World-FE
Nov 13	1910	Frankie Conley	New Orleans	D	15	Ret-World-FE
Feb 22	1912	Johnny Kilbane★	Vernon, CA	L	20	Lost-USA-World-FE
Jan 8	1917	Phil Virgets	New Orleans	KO'd	4	—

the win, alleging that Sullivan had been over the weight limit. Most boxing experts agreed. When Attell knocked Sullivan out in four rounds in 1908, this dispute was settled. Attell tried to move up to the lightweight class in 1908. He fought Hall of Famer and future champion, Battling Nelson, to a draw in a fight Attell claimed to have won.

Attell lost his title in 1912 to Johnny Kilbane in Vernon, California, in a twenty-round decision. The two fighters had split two previous meetings. Kilbane earned the lasting enmity of Attell by claiming that Attell had coated his back with chloroform. Attell insisted the substance was a cooling slather of cocoa butter.

Attell continued to fight for another year before retiring. His one-fight comeback was a knock-out loss to Phil Virgets. In retirement, Attell operated a succession of bars. He was involved in baseball's 1919 Black Sox Scandal—when gamblers bribed eight players on the Chicago team to throw the World Series—although he was not actually convicted of any crime.

By his own admission, Attell did not always perform at his best. Sometimes his goal was to get a lucrative return match with the same opponent. Nevertheless, he only lost nine times in his 171-fight career.

MAX BAER
The Livermore Larruper

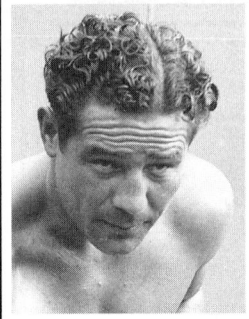

HEAVYWEIGHT

Right-handed; 6'2½"; 205–215 lbs.
84 bouts, 5/16/1929 to 4/4/1941
Manager: Ancil Hoffman
Heavyweight Champion 1934–35
Hall of Fame Induction: 1995
Born: 2/11/1909, Omaha, NE
Named: Maximillian Adalbert Baer
Died: 11/21/1959

Possessing perhaps the most powerful right hand in heavyweight history, Max Baer was a flashy performer who wisecracked and clowned his way through his career. Although he never fully realized his tremendous potential, Baer won the heavyweight title, and his showmanship entertained an America rocked by the Great Depression. Born in Omaha, Baer moved with his family to Colorado and then to California. He dropped out of school after eighth grade to work with his father on a cattle ranch, where he built his great physical strength doing range work.

Early in his career, Baer trained with a zeal he did not demonstrate later. He turned pro in 1929 and won 22 of his first 24 fights, nine with first-round knockouts. Baer was in supreme condition and dangerous in the ring. In 1930, he was charged with manslaughter when Frankie Campbell, brother of baseball player Dolph Camilli, died as a result of a Baer knockout. Ultimately cleared of criminal charges, Baer was suspended from fighting in California for a year.

Baer quit boxing for several months after Campbell's death, then lost four of his next six fights, partly because of his reluctance to go on the attack. One victor, Tommy Loughran, told Baer that he was looping and telegraphing his punches. Jack Dempsey helped Baer shorten his punches and took an interest in him for the rest of his career. In 1932, Baer knocked Ernie Schmeling unconscious at the bell in the tenth round of what had been a fairly even fight. Not long after, Schaaf died following a bout with Primo Carnera. The death was attributed in part to the beating administered by Baer.

In 1933, in the best fight of his career, Baer beat Max Schmeling at Yankee Stadium before 60,000 fans. Baer hammered Schmeling so thoroughly, referee Arthur Donovan stopped the fight in the tenth round. Now in line

Tony ("Two Ton") Galento hugs Baer in an effort to postpone his fate—an eighth-round KO in Jersey City in July 1940.

IN THE RING	WON 72	LOST 12	DRAWS 0	TB 84	KO 53	W 19	WF 0	D 0	KO'd 3	L 7	LF 2

Date	Year		Opponent	Site	Result / Rounds		Title
SELECTED BOUTS							
May 16	1929		Chief Caribou	Stockton, CA	KO	2	—
Apr 22	1930		Ernie Owens	Los Angeles	W	10	—
Jun 25	1930		Ernie Owens	Oakland	KO	5	—
Jul 15	1930		Les Kennedy	Los Angeles	L	10	—
Dec 19	1930	⑩	Ernie Schaaf	New York	L	10	—
Jan 16	1931		Tom Heeney	New York	KO	3	—
Feb 6	1931	⑩	Tommy Loughran★	New York	L	10	—
Apr 7	1931		Ernie Owens	Portland, OR	KO	2	—
May 5	1931	⑩	Johnny Risko	Cleveland	L	10	—
Jul 4	1931		Paolino Uzcudun	Reno, NV	L	20	—
Nov 9	1931	⑩	Johnny Risko	San Francisco	W	10	—
Nov 23	1931		Les Kennedy	Oakland	KO	3	—
Jan 29	1932	⑩	King Levinsky	New York	W	10	—
Feb 22	1932		Tom Heeney	San Francisco	W	10	—
Jul 4	1932	⑩	King Levinsky	Reno	W	20	—
Aug 31	1932	⑩	Ernie Schaaf	Chicago	W	10	—
Sep 26	1932	⑩	Tuffy Griffiths	Chicago	KO	10	—
Jun 8	1933	⑩	Max Schmeling★	New York	KO	10	—
Jun 14	1934	♛	Primo Carnera	Long Island City, NY	TKO	11	Won-World-H
Jun 13	1935	⑩	Jim Braddock★	Long Island City	L	15	Lost-World-H
Sep 24	1935	⑩	Joe Louis★	New York	KO'd	4	—
Apr 15	1937	⑩	Tommy Farr	London	L	12	—
Mar 11	1938	⑩	Tommy Farr	New York	W	15	—
Jun 1	1939	⑩	Lou Nova	New York	TKO'd	11	—
Jul 2	1940	⑩	Tony Galento	Jersey City, NJ	KO	8	—
Apr 4	1941	⑩	Lou Nova	New York	TKO'd	8	—

for the world heavyweight title, Baer fought Primo Carnera in 1934. At the Madison Square Garden Bowl, before a throng of 50,000, Baer knocked the giant Carnera down eleven times in eleven rounds.

Baer was now at the height of his fame. He starred in a movie, *The Prizefighter and the Lady* (banned in Germany because Baer's grandfather was Jewish), and lived the high life. He was romantically linked to innumerable starlets, socialites, chorus girls, and Broadway actresses before marrying in 1935.

Baer frittered away the title to James J. Braddock in his first defense. He fought with an injured right hand, and his half-hearted, joking effort lost him the fifteen-round decision. He had been champion for a year. Three months later, Joe Louis demolished Baer in four rounds.

Baer continued to fight for another six years, compiling a record of 30-4 in that time. In retirement, Baer acted, had a successful nightclub act both individually and with Slapsie Maxie Rosenbloom, and refereed boxing and wrestling matches. Baer's son, Max Jr., became famous in his own right for playing the role of Jethro Bodine in the long-running television comedy series, *The Beverly Hillbillies*.

JIMMY BARRY
The Little Tiger

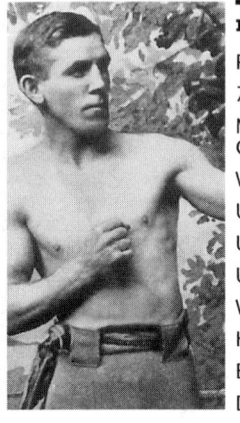

F L Y W E I G H T

Right-handed; 5'2"; 95–115 lbs.

70 bouts, 1891 to 9/1/1899

Managers: Dominick O'Malley, Charles E. ("Parson") Davies

World 100 lbs Champ 1893

USA World 102 lbs Champ 1894

USA World 105 lbs Champ 1894–95

USA World 110 lbs Champ 1895–99

World 108 lbs Champ 1897–99

Hall of Fame Induction: 2000

Born: 3/7/1870, Chicago, IL

Died: 4/5/1943

A flyweight fighter in the early days of gloved boxing, before the division was established, Jimmy Barry is one of a select few Hall of Famers who never lost a match. He was born in Chicago of Irish parents and fought in rough and tumble schoolboy bouts. The diminutive Barry came under the tutelage of former lightweight boxer Harry Gilmore, impressing him with his two-handed power. Barry's first match was against Jack Larson at McGurn's Handball Court in Chicago, and though Larson was more experienced and outweighed the newcomer by ten pounds, Barry knocked him out in the first.

Barry became a regular at McGurn's, then ventured out of Illinois to the Columbian Athletic Club in Roby, Indiana, to face the well-regarded "Portland Cyclone" Jimmy Shea on July 10, 1893. Though he once again gave away a considerable amount of weight—fourteen pounds—Shea's handlers threw in the towel after only three rounds. Later that year in Roby, Barry knocked out touring Londoner Jack Levy in seventeen rounds to win what was billed as the "World 100-lb Championship," and on June 2, 1894, he defeated Jim Gorman in eleven rounds at the famed Olympic Club in New Orleans to claim the world 102-lb title.

Next, "The Little Tiger" faced his greatest rival, Casper Leon, for the American paperweight title, contested at 105 pounds. Barry, a clever boxer and two-handed puncher, was considered the premier small man in the Midwest, while Leon was top in the East. The fight went twenty rounds before a Barry right turned the tide, leading to a knockout victory in the 28th. In a rematch on March 30, 1895, in Chicago, the

A Sicilian by birth, but fighting out of New York, Casper Leon was Barry's most frequent opponent.

IN THE RING	WON 59	LOST 0	DRAWS 9	TB 70	KO 39	W 20	WF 0	D 9	KO'd 0	L 0	LF 0	NC 2

Date	Year	Opponent	Site	Result / Rounds		Title
SELECTED BOUTS						
—	1891	Jack Larson	Chicago	KO	1	—
—	1891	Barney McCall	Chicago	W	4	—
Sep 3	1892	Frank Murphy	Springfield, IL	KO	7	—
Feb 12	1893	Billy Murphy	Chicago	KO	1	—
Jul 10	1893	Jimmy Shea	Roby, IN	TKO	4	—
Dec 5	1893	Jack Levy	Roby	KO	17	Won-World-100 lbs
Jun 2	1894	♛ Jimmy Gorman	New Orleans	W	11	Won-USA World-102 lbs
Sep 15	1894	Casper Leon	Lamont, IL	KO	28	Won-USA World-105 lbs
Mar 30	1895	Casper Leon	Chicago	D	14	Ret-USA World-105 lbs
Oct 21	1895	Jack Madden	Maspeth, NY	KO	4	Ret-USA World-105 lbs
Feb 18	1896	Young Spitz	Chicago	KO	8	—
Jul 24	1896	Casper Leon	Elmira, NY	NC	6	—
Jan 10	1897	Harry Dally	Chicago	KO	2	—
Jan 30	1897	Sammy Kelly	New York	D	20	—
Mar 1	1897	Jack Ward	New York	W	20	—
Apr 23	1897	Jimmy Anthony	San Francisco	W	20	—
Dec 6	1897	Walter Croot	London	KO	20	Won-Vac World-110 lbs
May 30	1898	Casper Leon	New York	D	20	Ret-USA World-110 lbs
Jun 3	1898	Steve Flanagan	Philadelphia	D	6	—
Nov 21	1898	Casper Leon	Chicago	D	6	—
Dec 29	1898	Casper Leon	Davenport, IA	D	20	Ret-USA World-110 lbs
Sep 1	1899	Harry Harris ★	Chicago	D	6	—

police intervened and stopped the bout in the fourteenth round. Though the fight was called a draw, Barry was generally considered the winner. Leon fought him four more times, all either draws or no decisions.

Barry next faced Walter Croot at the National Sporting Club in London, seeking acknowledgment as the world paperweight champion. For the first sixteen rounds, the fight was fairly even, but in the seventeenth, Barry's attack began to wear on Croot. In the twentieth, an exhausted Croot attempted to launch one last barrage in hopes of a victory, but Barry landed a right which dazed Croot and then knocked him out with a left to the head and a right to the jaw. Croot never regained consciousness and died the next morning. Charged with manslaughter, Barry was exonerated when it was determined that Croot died of a skull fracture sustained when his head hit the unpadded wooden floor.

Though cleared of wrongdoing in Croot's death, Barry was deeply affected by the incident and immediately announced his retirement. After his return to the United States, he came out of retirement and fought nine more times, with two wins, seven draws, and no knockouts. Before the fatality, Barry generally won by knockout, and he admitted that Croot's death affected his fighting style. In his last fight against future bantam champ and Hall of Famer Harry Harris, on September 1, 1899, most observers believed that Harris won but that the referee called the match a draw to enable Barry to again retire undefeated.

BENNY BASS
The Little Fish

FEATHERWEIGHT

Right-handed; 5'1½"; 120–135 lbs.
239 bouts, 1/29/1921 to 5/7/1940
Manager: Phil Glassman
Featherweight Champion 1927–28
Junior Lightweight Champion 1929–31
Hall of Fame Induction: 2002
Born: 12/4/1904, Kiev, Ukraine, Russia
Died: 6/25/1975

Another of the many great fighters who earned their stripes in Philadelphia, Benny Bass arrived at the City of Brotherly Love by a circuitous route.

Bass was born in Kiev, at a time when Russian Jews were the victims of frequent pogroms. His father immigrated to the U.S. in 1907, and three years later, he sent for his wife and five sons. They survived a shipwreck near Ireland and reached America.

As a boy, Bass developed a keen interest in boxing, fighting his first amateur match when he was twelve. A scheduled fighter, Young Smithy, fell ill before his bout at the Gayety Theater and allowed Bass to fight in his place. Bass knocked out his opponent in the first round.

For the next few years, Bass boxed regularly as an amateur while holding a day job. It was during this time that he came to the attention of Harry McGrath, the head of the AAU boxing program in Philadelphia. Under McGrath's guidance, the sixteen-year-old Bass turned professional on January 29, 1921, in a no-decision bout against Matty Dechter. He fought frequently over the next few years in the Philadelphia area, then took Phil Glassman as his manager in 1923. By 1924, Bass was a main event fighter in small clubs along the East Coast.

In 1926, Kid Kaplan vacated the featherweight title and Bass, as the next ranked contender, signed to face Red Chapman for the NBA championship in Philadelphia on September 12, 1927. The match was a ten-round slugfest, high-lighted by a double knock-down. At its conclusion, Bass was awarded the decision and the title.

He did not hold the title for long. His first defense came on February 10, 1928, in Madison Square Garden, against Hall of Famer Tony Canzoneri. Bass suffered a broken collarbone in the third, but battled back courageously. While he lasted the full fifteen rounds, he lost a unanimous decision

Benny Bass won a unanimous, bloody ten-round decision from Red Chapman at Municipal Stadium in Philadelphia on September 12, 1927, to claim the NBA version of the Featherweight Championship. The fighters rose from a double knockdown in the ninth to finish the legendary battle. Frank McCracken refereed.

IN THE RING	WON 152	LOST 28	DRAWS 5	TB 239	KO 69	W 80	WF 3	D 5	KO'd 3	L 14	LF 11	ND NC 52 2

Date	Year	Opponent	Site	Result / Rounds	Title

SELECTED BOUTS

Date	Year	Opponent	Site	Result / Rounds	Title
Jan 29	1921	Matty Dechter	Philadelphia	ND-W 6	—
Apr 29	1924	⑩ Johnny Brown	Philadelphia	KO 3	—
Sep 24	1925	⑩ Eddie Anderson	Philadelphia	W 10	—
Nov 2	1925	⑩ Lew Mayrs	Philadelphia	KO 2	—
Jan 11	1926	⑩ Leo ("Kid") Roy	Philadelphia	W 10	—
Jun 8	1926	⑩ Andy Martin	Providence, RI	L 12	—
Jul 29	1926	⑩ Johnny Farr	New York	W 10	—
Oct 1	1926	⑩ Babe Herman	Philadelphia	W 10	—
May 2	1927	⑩ Chick Suggs	Philadelphia	W 10	—
Aug 10	1927	⑩ Johnny Farr	Cleveland	W 10	—
Sep 12	1927	⑩ Red Chapman	Philadelphia	W 10	Won-Vac NBA-FE
Jan 2	1928	⑩ Pete Nebo	Philadelphia	W 10	—
Feb 10	1928	♛ Tony Canzoneri★	New York	L 15	For-World-FE, Lost-NBA-FE
Jun 18	1928	♛ Pete Nebo	Philadelphia	L 10	—
Sep 10	1928	⑩ Harry Blitman	Philadelphia	KO 6	—
Jan 14	1929	⑩ Davey Abad	Philadelphia	W 10	—
Jan 28	1929	Red Chapman	Philadelphia	KO 1	—
Dec 20	1929	♛ Tod Morgan	New York	KO 2	Won-World-JL
Jul 21	1930	⑩ Tony Canzoneri★	Philadelphia	L 10	—
Jan 5	1931	⑩ Lew Massey	Philadelphia	W 10	Ret-World-JL
Jul 15	1931	⑩ Kid Chocolate★	Philadelphia	TKO'd 7	Lost-World-JL
Mar 8	1933	⑩ Joe Ghnouly	St. Louis	W 10	—
Dec 27	1933	⑩ Eddie Cool	Philadelphia	W 10	—
Apr 30	1934	⑩ Anacleto ("Cleto") Locatelli	Philadelphia	L 10	—
Jul 31	1934	⑩ Johnny Jadick	Philadelphia	W 10	—
Jul 27	1937	⑩ Henry Armstrong★	Philadelphia	KO'd 4	—
May 7	1940	⑩ Tommy Spiegel	Philadelphia	L 10	—

and his crown. Over the next year and a half, Bass fought frequently, recording wins over Harry Blitman, Chapman, and others.

On December 20, 1929, Bass fought for a new title—this time the junior lightweight belt held by Tod Morgan. Though he was not known as a knockout artist, Bass stopped Morgan in just two rounds at Madison Square Garden.

Bass fought Canzoneri again in a non-title bout on July 21, 1930, but lost the ten-round decision. The champ successfully defended his title on January 5, 1931, with a decision over Lew Massey, and on July 15 of that same year, Bass put his belt on the line against Hall of Famer Kid Chocolate. "The Cuban Bon Bon" proved to be too much for Bass, who was stopped short in the seventh round.

While Bass never had a chance to claim another championship, he was nowhere near retiring from the ring. He moved up to lightweight as a ranked contender in 1932 and 1933, and continued to fight in and around Philadelphia until Tommy Spiegel gained a ten-round decision over him on May 7, 1940.

In retirement, Bass was very active in the Veteran Boxers Association, and he enjoyed attending fights and other boxing functions.

BATTLING BATTALINO
Bat

FEATHERWEIGHT
Right-handed; 5'5"; 123–145 lbs.
87 bouts, 6/6/1927 to 1/30/1940
Managers: Hy Malley, Lenny Marello, Pete Reilly
Featherweight Champ 1929–32
Hall of Fame Induction: 2003
Born: 2/18/1908, Hartford, CT
Named: Christopher Battaglia
Died: 7/25/1977

Christopher ("Battling") Battalino earned his place in boxing history for his toughness in winning the world featherweight title with two broken hands. Battalino was born in Hartford, Connecticut, on February 18, 1908. The son of Italian immigrants, he didn't attend high school, working in a typewriter factory and laboring in the tobacco fields outside Hartford, among other jobs.

Battalino had always liked to fight and idolized Johnny Dundee. Over the objections of his father, he began spending time in a local gym in 1925. Hy Malley, the owner of the gym, and his friend, Lenny Marello, oversaw Battalino's development, and the fighter quickly found success in the amateur ranks. He won the Connecticut featherweight title in both 1926 and 1927. Emboldened by his success in 1927, Battalino entered the National AAU tournament in Boston and won the title, knocking out four opponents in eight minutes over two days.

At Malley's urging, Battalino turned pro on June 6, 1927, and knocked out Archie Rosenberg in Hartford in two rounds. Battalino became popular in Connecticut, posting a record of 16-2-2 in two years of fighting. On July 26, 1929, Battalino faced Hall of Famer and Bantamweight Champion of the World Panama Al Brown in a non-title fight. Battalino knocked down Brown en route to a ten-round decision.

Battalino's performance in the Brown fight earned him an opportunity to fight for the world featherweight title held by Andre Routis before 25,000 fans in Hartford on September 23, 1929. Battalino, blessed with great speed and, at the time, great punching power, dominated the first four rounds. In the fourth round Battalino broke both his hands. He refused to give in to the pain though it

In the Garden, referee Patsy Haley calls a halt to this December 11, 1931, contest. Battalino (R) is the second-round-TKO victor over Al Singer.

IN THE RING	WON 57	LOST 26	DRAWS 3	TB 87	KO 23	W 34	WF 0	D 3	KO'd 1	L 24	LF 1	NC 1

Date	Year	Opponent	Site	Result / Rounds		Title
SELECTED BOUTS						
Jun 6	1927	Archie Rosenberg	Hartford, CT	KO	2	—
Jul 26	1929	♛ Panama Al Brown★	Hartford	W	10	—
Sep 23	1929	♛ Andre Routis	Hartford	W	15	Won-World-FE
Mar 20	1930	⑩ Charles ("Bud") Taylor★	Detroit	L	10	—
Aug 18	1930	⑩ Charles ("Bud") Taylor★	Hartford	W	10	—
Sep 24	1930	⑩ Louis ("Kid") Kaplan★	Hartford	L	10	—
Dec 12	1930	⑩ Kid Chocolate★	New York	W	15	Ret-World-FE
Jan 23	1931	⑩ Eddie Shea	Chicago	L	10	—
May 22	1931	⑩ Fidel LaBarba★	New York	W	15	Ret-World-FE
Jul 23	1931	⑩ Freddie Miller★	Cincinnati	W	10	Ret-World-FE
Sep 15	1931	⑩ Eddie Shea	Hartford	W	10	—
Nov 4	1931	⑩ Earl Mastro	Chicago	W	10	Ret-World-FE
Nov 19	1931	⑩ Bushy Graham	New York	KO	1	—
Jan 27	1932	⑩ Freddie Miller★	Cincinnati	NC	3	Strip-World-FE
Mar 24	1932	⑩ Billy Petrolle★	New York	TKO'd	12	—
May 20	1932	⑩ Billy Petrolle★	Chicago	L	10	—
Oct 21	1932	⑩ Barney Ross★	Chicago	L	10	—
Jan 30	1940	Dick Turcotte	Hartford	L	10	—

was excruciating. From the tenth round on, Battalino put on such a great display of boxing that Routis did not land a clean shot while Battalino continued to score points. When the fight was over, Battalino was declared the winner by a decision. With the victory Battalino almost fainted with pain. Amazingly, Battalino had won every round.

When he faced Kid Chocolate in Madison Square Garden on December 12, 1930, Kid surprised Battalino and knocked him down with the first punch of the fight. Battalino got up and began a relentless pursuit of Kid. Battalino worked the body while Kid countered to the head. Though the fight was close, Battalino took the decision and earned $25,000, his biggest payday.

His next two title defenses came against Hall of Famers as well, Fidel LaBarba and Freddie Miller. Battalino won both by decision. His rematch with Miller on January 27, 1932, in Cincinnati sullied the reputations of both fighters. Before the fight, Battalino and his manager, Pete Reilly, took over Miller's contract for $3,500 dollars. It was arranged that Battalino would take a dive. He performed this charade so artlessly that the referee declared the fight no contest. Battalino voluntarily relinquished the title to move up to lightweight.

As a lightweight, Battalino fought two stirring battles with Hall of Famer Billy Petrolle. In the first bout, Petrolle knocked Battalino out—the only time Battalino was counted out in his career. Petrolle decisioned Battalino in the second contest. After a loss to Hall of Famer Barney Ross, Battalino's career began to wind down. He retired only to return to the ring in 1939. After Dick Turcotte beat him on January 30, 1940, Battalino retired for good. He worked in construction in Hartford for many years. Battalino died in his hometown at the age of 69.

PAUL BERLENBACH
The Astoria Assassin

LIGHT HEAVYWEIGHT

Right-handed; 5'10½"; 165–180 lbs.
52 bouts, 10/4/1923 to 9/28/1933
Manager: Dan Hickey
Light Heavyweight Champ 1925–26
Hall of Fame Induction: 2001
Born: 2/18/1901, New York, NY
Died: 9/30/1985

Paul Berlenbach was the only man to ever win both an AAU national wrestling championship and a world boxing title. Left deaf and mute by scarlet fever at age two, the accidental touch of a downed electrical wire when he was fifteen miraculously restored Berlenbach's hearing and speech.

Berlenbach first became interested in wrestling at a local gymnastics club, where he came to the attention of Nat Pendleton, himself a national wrestling champion. Pendleton got Berlenbach a membership at the New York Athletic Club, and the latter went on to great success, as an amateur free-style wrestler.

While campaigning as a wrestler, Berlenbach began boxing lessons with Dan Hickey at the New York Athletic Club. Though an ungainly fighter, Berlenbach's left hand packed tremendous punching power. Hickey changed him to a right-hander to bring his powerful left closer to his opponent, taught him the rudiments of boxing, and became his manager. Meanwhile, Berlenbach continued to star as a wrestler, winning the 1922 and 1923 AAU national championships.

On October 4, 1923, Berlenbach launched his pro-boxing career with a first-round knockout of Jimmy Roberts and went on to win his next eight fights with KOs, four in the first round. On March 14, 1924, he faced future champion and Hall of Famer Jack Delaney. The more experienced Delaney knocked Berlenbach down three times in the fourth, and the referee stopped the fight.

Berlenbach shrugged off the loss and won fourteen of his next seventeen bouts with no losses, including a knockout of former light heavyweight champ Battling Siki. Then, on May 30, 1925, in front of 45,000 fans at Yankee Stadium, Berlenbach abandoned his puncher style and boxed light heavyweight champion Mike McTigue to a fifteen-round decision to win the light heavyweight

Referee Patsy Haley sends Berlenbach (L) to a neutral corner while Jimmy Slattery takes the count in their September 11, 1925, title bout in Yankee Stadium.

IN THE RING	WON 39	LOST 8	DRAWS 3	TB 52	KO 33	W 6	WF 0	D 3	KO'd 3	L 4	LF 1	ND 1	NC 1

Date	Year	Opponent	Site	Result / Rounds		Title
SELECTED BOUTS						
Oct 4	1923	Jimmy Roberts	New York	KO	1	—
Mar 14	1924	Jack Delaney★	New York	KO'd	4	—
Aug 15	1924	Joe ("Hambone") Kelly	Boston	KO	5	—
Aug 27	1924	⑩ Young Stribling★	New York	D	6	—
Oct 1	1924	Johnny Gill	Jersey City, NJ	ND-W	10	—
Jan 30	1925	Young Tony Marullo	New York	W	12	—
Mar 13	1925	Battling Siki	New York	TKO	10	—
May 30	1925	♛ Mike McTigue	New York	W	15	Won-World-LH
Sep 11	1925	⑩ Jimmy Slattery★	New York	TKO	11	Ret-World-LH
Dec 11	1925	⑩ Jack Delaney★	New York	W	15	Ret-World-LH
Mar 19	1926	⑩ Johnny Risko	New York	L	10	—
Jun 10	1926	⑩ Young Stribling★	New York	W	15	Ret-World-LH
Jul 16	1926	⑩ Jack Delaney★	Brooklyn	L	15	Lost-World-LH
Jan 28	1927	⑩ Mike McTigue	New York	TKO'd	4	—
Nov 25	1927	♛ Mickey Walker★	Chicago	L	10	—
Dec 9	1927	⑩ Jack Delaney★	Chicago	KO'd	6	—
May 22	1928	Larry Estridge	New York	TKO	8	—
Mar 31	1931	Eddie Clark	Brooklyn	KO	3	—
Sep 28	1933	Carl Knowles	Atlanta, GA	L	10	—

title, which he then successfully defended against Jimmy Slattery before facing Delaney again. Tex Rickard paired the two for the opening bout at the newly built third Madison Square Garden on December 11, 1925: Berlenbach won a fifteen-round decision.

Like most light heavyweights, Berlenbach wanted the fatter purses and greater attention of the top heavyweights, but his attempt to move up in 1926 ended in a loss to Johnny Risko. After winning a decision over Hall of Famer Young Stribling, Berlenbach again faced Delaney, this time in front of a crowd of 49,000 at Ebbets Field. Delaney outboxed Berlenbach and took the championship.

After the loss of his title, Berlenbach's fortune seemed to change. He broke with Hickey, and on January 28, 1927, he was TKO'd in four rounds by McTigue. After that fight, he briefly retired, disillusioned with boxing and its fans. He returned to the ring later that year but lost to Hall of Famer Mickey Walker and again to Delaney, who knocked him out in the sixth round. After winning two fights in 1928, he retired again, returned to wrestling in 1929, and came back briefly for five boxing matches in '31 and one in '33. By this time, however, the Astoria Assassin's skills had faded.

Berlenbach's real estate investments soured during the Great Depression, and he was forced to turn to a succession of odd jobs, such as bartending, refereeing, and selling newspapers. Later, he was hired by Jacob Ruppert, owner of the New York Yankees and Ruppert Breweries, as a goodwill ambassador.

JAMES J. BRADDOCK
The Cinderella Man

HEAVYWEIGHT

Right-handed; 6'2½"; 162–199½ lbs.

86 bouts, 4/14/1926 to 1/21/1938

Manager: Joe Gould

World Heavyweight Champion 1935–37

Hall of Fame Induction: 2001

Born: 6/7/1905, New York, NY

Named: James Walter Braddock

Died: 11/29/1974

James J. Braddock's "rags to riches" story captured the nation's attention during his brief reign as heavyweight champion of the world and inspired Hollywood to make a movie about his life in 2005.

Braddock grew up in Northern New Jersey and had a notable amateur career, winning New Jersey's state light heavyweight and heavyweight amateur titles. Braddock turned professional on April 14, 1926, with a four-round, no-decision bout against Al Settle. Campaigning as a light heavyweight, Braddock knocked out his next eleven opponents, eight of them in the first round, and on January 28, 1927, made his Madison Square Garden debut with a one-round knockout of George LaRocco.

A decision against Pete Latzo and knockout victories over Tuffy Griffith and Jimmy Slattery earned Braddock a shot at the light heavyweight title held by Hall of Famer Tommy Loughran on July 18, 1929. Though a solid boxer-puncher, Braddock was outfought by the gifted Loughran in a fifteen round decision.

The loss, coupled with a broken knuckle that required medical care Braddock could not afford, derailed the fighter's promising career. Over the next five years, Braddock fought 33 times but won just eleven bouts.

In 1934, Braddock's manager, Joe Gould, got Braddock a fight against Corn Griffin on the undercard of the Max Baer–Primo Carnera heavyweight championship fight. Braddock, now a heavyweight, was viewed as a mere "opponent" for the up-and-coming Griffin, yet he surprised everyone with a third-round knockout. Propelled by a victory over Hall of Famer John Henry Lewis, Braddock next fought top contender Art Lasky, and decisioned him at Madison Square Garden to earn a shot against Max Baer for the heavyweight title.

Braddock was given no chance against the hard-hitting, though light-training,

Champion Max Baer's (R) hands are low as Braddock hones in on his target during their June 13, 1935, heavyweight championship bout in Long Island City, NY.

IN THE RING	WON 46	LOST 23	DRAWS 4	TB 86	KO 27	W 19	WF 0	D 4	KO'd 2	L 20	LF 1	ND 11	NC 2

Date	Year	Opponent	Site	Result / Rounds		Title

SELECTED BOUTS

Date	Year	Opponent	Site	Result	Rounds	Title
Apr 14	1926	Al Settle	West Hoboken, NJ	ND-D	4	—
Jan 28	1927	George LaRocco	New York	KO	1	—
Feb 1	1927	Johnny Alberts	Wilkes Barre, PA	KO	4	—
Oct 17	1928	⑩ Pete Latzo	Newark, NJ	W	10	—
Nov 30	1928	⑩ Gerald ("Tuffy") Griffith	New York	KO	2	—
Jan 18	1929	⑩ Leo Lomski	New York	L	10	—
Mar 11	1929	⑩ Jimmy Slattery ★	New York	TKO	9	—
Jul 18	1929	♛ Tommy Loughran ★	New York	L	15	For-World-LH
Nov 15	1929	⑩ Maxie Rosenbloom ★	New York	L	10	—
Jan 17	1930	⑩ Leo Lomski	Chicago	L	10	—
Jan 23	1931	⑩ Ernie Schaaf	New York	L	10	—
Nov 10	1931	⑩ Maxie Rosenbloom ★	Minneapolis	NC	2	—
Dec 4	1931	⑩ Al Gainer	New Haven, CT	L	10	—
May 13	1932	Charley Retzlaff	Boston	L	10	—
Sep 21	1932	⑩ John Henry Lewis ★	San Francisco	L	10	—
Nov 9	1932	⑩ Lou Scozza	San Francisco	TKO'd	6	—
Jun 14	1934	John ("Corn") Griffin	New York	TKO	3	—
Nov 16	1934	⑩ John Henry Lewis ★	New York	W	10	—
Mar 22	1935	⑩ Art Lasky	New York	W	15	—
Jun 13	1935	♛ Max Baer ★	Long Island City, NY	W	15	Won-World-H
Jun 22	1937	⑩ Joe Louis ★	Chicago	KO'd	8	Lost-World-H
Jan 21	1938	⑩ Tommy Farr	New York	W	10	—

Baer. But if Baer did not take the fight seriously, Braddock did. He scored effectively with both hands to take command of the battle by the eighth round, and continued to pepper Baer with jabs to win the championship on a fifteen-round decision. Journalist Damon Runyon christened the upset winner "The Cinderella Man."

Braddock signed on to defend his title against Max Schmeling in the summer of 1936, but arthritis in his right hand forced the fight's postponement. Braddock's manager, Gould, then broke his contract with Madison Square Garden, ostensibly because of opposition to the German Schmeling by the Non-Sectarian Anti-Nazi League. It is likely, however, that the real reason Braddock bypassed the Schmeling fight was an amazing offer from promoter Mike Jacobs of $500,000 or half the gate and radio revenues (whichever was greater), plus ten percent of Jacobs's profits from all his heavyweight title promotions for the next ten years, should Braddock fight and lose to a different opponent: Joe Louis. On June 22, 1937, in Comiskey Park, Chicago, in front of 45,000 fans, Braddock came out strong in the first round, knocking down Louis with a right uppercut, but the more talented Louis quickly asserted his dominance and knocked Braddock out in the eighth. Braddock would fight just one more time.

In retirement, Braddock was in the military surplus business, and operated electrical generators and welding equipment.

JACK BRITTON

WELTERWEIGHT

Right-handed; 5'8"; 118–150 lbs.

342 bouts, 11/11/1904 to Aug. 1930

Managers: G.F. Thiel 1906, Marcus Williams 1906–10, Charlie Redman 1910–11, Jack Costello 1911–12, Dan Morgan 1912–25

Welterweight Champion 1915, 1916–17, 1919–22

Hall of Fame Induction: 1990

Born: 10/14/1885, Clinton, NY

Named: William J. Breslin

Died: 3/27/1962

Jack Britton was a masterful boxer whose career spanned 25 years. He was 37 when Mickey Walker took the welterweight title from him, and he continued to fight top contenders until his retirement at age 44. An Irish street scrapper from Clinton, New York, Britton's earliest professional bouts took place in 1904 and 1905 at small boxing clubs in Milwaukee and Chicago. Although he was a talented fighter, Britton languished in the lower ranks until he teamed up with manager Dan Morgan, who insisted his boxers live clean and train hard. Under Morgan's guidance, Britton's career took off.

Britton fought three times against Hall of Famer Packey McFarland. Their first match was a draw and the next two were no-decisions, but all were memorable for the ring artistry displayed by the two fighters. In 1915, Britton won a twelve-round decision over Mike Glover to stake a claim as the welterweight champion. After Ted ("Kid") Lewis also defeated Glover, the stage was set for Lewis and Britton to meet, with the winner to be acclaimed as champion. The bout became the first in a twenty-fight rivalry between Britton and the closely matched Lewis. Enemies from the onset, Britton and Lewis exchanged threats and then refused to speak to each other. In the ring, both spurned the customary handshake. In a wild bout, the hard-hitting Lewis won the decision and the championship.

Most of the Britton–Lewis matches were officially no-decision bouts, but in 1916, Britton won a decision over Lewis to take the welterweight title. For the next six years, the two fighters monopolized the championship. Lewis regained it in a twenty-round decision in 1917. In 1919, Britton knocked out Lewis in the ninth round to

Welterweight champ Jack Britton fought many top contenders in his 25-year career. He was 44 before he finally quit the ring.

IN THE RING	WON 104	LOST 27	DRAWS 21	TB 344	KO 28	W 72	WF 4	D 21	KO'd 1	L 24	LF 2	ND 190	NC 2

Date	Year	Opponent	Site	Result / Rounds		Title
SELECTED BOUTS						
Nov 11	1904	Jack Nelson	Milwaukee	W	6	—
Oct 7	1905	Tommy Shea	Chicago	L	6	—
Jan 30	1911	Packey McFarland★	Memphis, TN	D	8	—
Mar 7	1913	Packey McFarland★	New York	ND-L	10	—
Dec 8	1913	Packey McFarland★	Milwaukee	ND-L	10	—
Mar 26	1915	Ted ("Kid") Lewis★	New York	ND-L	10	—
Jun 22	1915	♛ Mike Glover	Boston	W	12	Won-World-W
Aug 31	1915	Ted ("Kid") Lewis★	Boston	L	12	Lost-World-W
Sep 27	1915	♛ Ted ("Kid") Lewis★	Boston	L	12	For-World-W
Jan 20	1916	♛ Ted ("Kid") Lewis★	Buffalo	ND-W	10	—
Feb 15	1916	♛ Ted ("Kid") Lewis★	Brooklyn	ND-W	10	—
Apr 24	1916	♛ Ted ("Kid") Lewis★	New Orleans	W	20	Reg-World-W
Oct 17	1916	Ted ("Kid") Lewis★	Boston	W	12	—
Nov 14	1916	Ted ("Kid") Lewis★	Boston	D	12	—
Mar 26	1917	Ted ("Kid") Lewis★	Cleveland	ND-L	10	—
May 19	1917	Ted ("Kid") Lewis★	Toronto	ND-L	10	—
Jun 6	1917	Ted ("Kid") Lewis★	St. Louis	ND-D	12	—
Jun 14	1917	Ted ("Kid") Lewis★	New York	ND-D	10	—
Jun 25	1917	Ted ("Kid") Lewis★	Dayton, OH	L	20	Lost-World-W
Mar 6	1918	♛ Ted ("Kid") Lewis★	Atlanta	ND-D	10	—
May 2	1918	♛ Ted ("Kid") Lewis★	Scranton, PA	ND-D	10	—
May 24	1918	♛ Ted ("Kid") Lewis★	New York	ND-W	6	—
Jun 20	1918	♛ Ted ("Kid") Lewis★	New York	ND-W	6	—
Mar 17	1919	♛ Ted ("Kid") Lewis★	Canton, OH	KO	9	Reg-World-W
Jul 28	1919	Ted ("Kid") Lewis★	Jersey City, NJ	ND-W	8	—
Aug 23	1920	Lou Bogash	Bridgeport, CT	D	12	Ret-World-W
Feb 7	1921	Ted ("Kid") Lewis★	New York	W	15	Ret-World-W
Feb 17	1922	Dave Shade	New York	D	15	Ret-World-W
Jun 13	1922	Benny Leonard★	New York	WF	13	Ret-World-W
Nov 1	1922	Mickey Walker★	New York	L	15	Lost-World-W
Aug	1930	Rudy Marshall	Stamford, CT	L	10	—

take it back. Britton remained the champion until 1922. In his last successful title defense, Britton fought lightweight champion Benny Leonard at the New York Velodrome before approximately 18,000 fans. Leonard knocked Britton down in the thirteenth round, then hit him again before he got up, giving Britton the victory on the foul. Some ringside observers believed that Leonard deliberately went for the foul because he didn't want to hold two titles.

Britton lost the welterweight belt in Madison Square Garden later that year to the much younger Mickey Walker, who floored Britton three times. Though he never again contended for the title, Britton continued to fight for seven more years, pushed beyond his prime when he lost his ring earnings in failed Florida land investments. He left the ring to become a boxing instructor and mentor to young athletes in New York City, where he and Morgan continued the close association that had built one of boxing's strongest careers.

LOU BROUILLARD

MIDDLEWEIGHT

Left-handed; 5'7"; 144–170 lbs.

140 bouts, 1928 to 1/12/1940

Managers: Maurice Lemoine, Johnny Buckley

Welterweight Champion 1931–32
NBA World Middleweight Champion 1933

Born: 5/23/1911, Saint Eugene, Quebec, Canada

Named: Lucien Pierre Brouillard

Died: 9/14/1984

Lou Brouillard was an outstanding fighter who captured both the world welterweight and middleweight titles—in a span of less than two years. Brouillard was born in St. Eugene, Quebec, on May 23, 1911. His family moved twice, finally settling in Worcester, Massachusetts. Brouillard quit school when he was fifteen and worked in a mill. He trained at night. As an amateur, he recorded an outstanding record of 37-2. Despite his dedication to training, Brouillard was not a picture-perfect fighter. He was only about 5'6" with big shoulders, thick arms, and virtually no neck. He employed an aggressive if somewhat graceless style. He liked to bull forward and attack.

Brouillard turned professional in 1928 under the direction of Maurice Lemoine. He was an active fighter in New England. In three years he accumulated 58 wins—43 by knockout.

On July 23, 1931, he met welterweight champion Young Jack Thompson in a non-title event and took a ten-round decision. On October 23, 1931, the pair met again—this time for the title—in Boston Garden. It was a match of contrasting styles: Thompson was a very skilled boxer; Brouillard was a raw aggressor from the start, working the body with hard rights and then going upstairs with lefts to the jaw. In the sixth, Brouillard scored with a stinging right, though Thompson claimed he was fouled. Brouillard knocked Thompson down with a left cross to the chin in the tenth and floored him again in the same round with a right jab. Brouillard earned a win by decision and was the world welterweight champion at the age of twenty.

One writer called Brouillard "two parts stampeding buffalo, one part maniac." He usually fought as a lefty which accentuated his unusual style.

IN THE RING	WON 107	LOST 29	DRAWS 2	TB 140	KO 66	W 40	WF 1	D 2	KO'd 1	L 25	LF 3	ND 2

Date	Year	Opponent	Site	Result / Rounds		Title
SELECTED BOUTS						
1928		Billy Krake	Willimantic, CT	KO	2	—
Mar 6	1931	⑩ Baby Joe Gans	Worcester, MA	W	10	—
Jul 23	1931	♔ Young Jack Thompson	Boston	W	10	—
Oct 23	1931	♔ Young Jack Thompson	Boston	W	15	Won-World-W
Jan 28	1932	⑩ Jackie Fields ★	Chicago	L	10	Lost-World-W
Aug 4	1932	⑩ Jimmy McLarnin ★	New York	W	10	—
Jul 6	1933	⑩ Mickey Walker ★	Boston	W	10	—
Aug 9	1933	♔ Ben Jeby	New York	KO	7	Won-NBA World-M
Oct 30	1933	⑩ Vince Dundee	Boston	L	15	Lost-NBA World-M
Nov 23	1934	⑩ Al Gainer	New York	W	10	—
Jul 4	1935	Young Corbett III ★	San Francisco	W	10	—
Nov 25	1935	♔ Marcel Thil ★	Paris	L	12	
Jan 20	1936	♔ Marcel Thil ★	Paris	LF	4	For-IBU World-M
Oct 9	1936	⑩ Fred Apostoli ★	San Francisco	L	10	—
Feb 15	1937	♔ Marcel Thil ★	Paris	LF	6	For-IBU World-M
May 7	1937	⑩ Teddy Yarosz ★	Boston	L	10	—
Jan 12	1940	Henry Chmielewski	Worcester	L	10	—

After losing his title to Jackie Fields, Brouillard moved up to middleweight. He faced Ben Jeby, the New York world middleweight champion, on August 9, 1933, in the Polo Grounds. Brouillard put together a masterful attack, using his great strength and aggressiveness to take the fight to Jeby. He rocked Jeby in the sixth. In the seventh, he knocked out Jeby with a left hook to the jaw and became a world champion for the second time.

Brouillard lost his title to Vince Dundee in his first defense. Brouillard was favored, but Dundee managed to sidestep his bull rushes and made contact with looping rights. He never hurt Brouillard, yet he won eight of fifteen rounds.

On January 20, 1936, Brouillard fought European world champion Marcel Thil with the IBU title at stake. In the third round, Brouillard was warned twice for head butting. In the fourth, he knocked Thil down with a punch that the referee immediately called a low blow. Brouillard was disqualified.

A return match took place over a year later on February 15, 1937. This time Brouillard was clearly the aggressor. In the sixth, Brouillard scored with a hard right, which appeared to land on Thil's jaw. Thil fell to one knee, clutching his abdomen. The referee first counted Thil out but, after discussing the matter with the judges, determined that Thil had been fouled and awarded him the bout.

Returning to the United States, Brouillard lost a decision to Teddy Yarosz. Though he was only 25, Brouillard's career was in decline. He suffered his only knockout on February 18, 1938, from tough light heavy Tiger Jack Fox. After a loss to Henry Chmielewski on January 12, 1940, the 28-year-old Brouillard retired. He served as a physical training instructor in the Army and later worked in a shipyard until an injury forced him to retire. He died on September 14, 1984.

PANAMA AL BROWN
The Elongated Panamanian

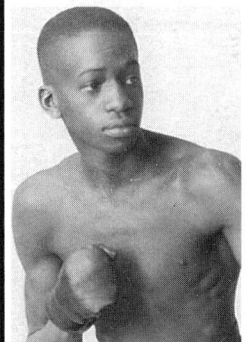

BANTAMWEIGHT

Right-handed; 5'11"; 112–126 lbs.

155 bouts, 1922 to 12/4/1942

Manager: Dave Lumiansky

Bantamweight Champion 1929–35

Hall of Fame Induction: 1992

Born: 7/5/1902, Colon, Panama

Named: Alfonso Teofilo Brown

Died: 4/11/1951

Tall, thin, and all muscle, Panama Al Brown held the world bantamweight title for six years. He was born in Panama's Canal Zone and as a young man was employed as a clerk with the United States Shipping Board. He became interested in boxing while watching bouts between U.S. military personnel and, when encouraged by his boss, gave the ring a try.

Brown had surprising punching power and an incredible 76" reach. He turned professional at age twenty and won the Isthmus flyweight title in his third fight, with a decision over Sailor Patchett. Brown's performance caught the attention of fight manager Dave Lumiansky, who took him to New York. Brown was un-

beaten in his first seventeen bouts in the U.S. and was ranked as the third-best flyweight in the 1924 annual rankings of *The Ring*. By 1926, Brown had moved up to the bantamweight level and was ranked sixth by *The Ring*. He then spent a year in Paris, where he was a favorite of French fight fans, compiling a 6-2-1 record in nine bouts.

In 1929, Brown challenged Vidal Gregorio for the vacant world bantamweight title. The fight took place in Queensboro Stadium in Long Island City, with 15,000 looking on. Brown dominated the fight and

Brown (L) uses his long reach to dig into Baltazar Sangchili's ribs on his way to a fifteen-round win in this 1938 bout in Paris.

IN THE RING	WON 123	LOST 18	DRAWS 10	TB 155	KO 55	W 64	WF 4	D 10	KO'd 0	L 16	LF 2	ND 4

Date	Year	Opponent	Site	Result / Rounds		Title
SELECTED BOUTS						
Mar 19	1922	Jose Moreno	Colon, Panama	W	6	—
Aug 22	1923	Johnny Breslin	New York	D	4	—
Oct 16	1925	⑩ Johnny Breslin	New York	W	10	—
Nov 10	1926	Antoine Merlo	Paris	KO	2	—
Apr 2	1927	Eugene Criqui★	Paris	W	10	—
Sep 13	1928	⑩ Kid Francis	New York	W	12	—
Oct 23	1928	⑩ Alf ("Kid") Pattenden	Paris	D	15	—
Apr 9	1929	Joe Cadman	Paris	TKO	3	—
Jun 18	1929	⑩ Vidal Gregorio	Long Island City, NY	W	15	Won-Vac World-B
Jul 26	1929	⑩ Battling Battalino★	Hartford, CT	L	10	—
Feb 8	1930	Johnny Erickson	New York	WF	4	Ret-World-B
Jul 23	1930	⑩ Domenico Bernasconi	Brooklyn	W	10	—
Oct 4	1930	Eugene Huat	Paris	W	15	Ret-World-B
Aug 15	1931	⑩ Pete Sanstol	Montreal	W	15	Ret-World-B
Oct 27	1931	⑩ Eugene Huat	Montreal	W	15	Ret-World-B
Dec 15	1931	⑩ Newsboy Brown	Los Angeles	L	10	—
Jan 18	1932	⑩ Eugene Huat	Paris	W	10	—
Jul 10	1932	Kid Francis	Marseilles, France	W	15	Ret-World-B
Sep 19	1932	⑩ Emile Pladner	Toronto	KO	1	Ret-World-B
Mar 19	1933	Domenico Bernasconi	Milan	W	12	Ret-World-B
Jul 3	1933	⑩ Johnny King	London	W	15	Ret-World-B
Oct 1	1933	Georges LePerson	Algiers, Algeria	W	10	—
Nov 12	1933	Alfredo Magnolfi	Casablanca, Morocco	W	10	—
Dec 9	1933	Luigi Quadrini	Oran, Algeria	W	10	—
Feb 19	1934	Young Perez	Paris	W	15	Ret-World-B
Nov 1	1934	Young Perez	Tunis, Tunisia	KO	10	Ret-World-B
Dec 24	1934	♛ Freddie Miller★	Paris	L	10	—
Mar 18	1935	⑩ Baltazar Sangchili	Valencia, Spain	L	10	—
Jun 1	1935	⑩ Baltazar Sangchili	Valencia	L	15	Lost-World-B
Sep 11	1935	Pete Sanstol	Oslo, Norway	L	10	—

easily won the decision. Over the next six years, Brown, a true world champion, defended his title in New York, Paris, Montreal, Marseilles, Toronto, Milan, London, and Tunis, and fought non-title bouts in many other cities around the world.

The merry-go-round stopped in Valencia, Spain, in 1935, when Baltazar Sangchili beat Brown in a fifteen-round decision and walked off with the title. Brown kept fighting, mostly in Paris and New York, and finally back home in Panama. He twice retired and twice came back, until he at last quit the ring in 1942. Although the money had poured in during his globe-trotting days, Brown died penniless in New York in 1951, after a bout with tuberculosis.

TOMMY BURNS
Tiny

HEAVYWEIGHT

Right-handed; 5′7″; 158–184 lbs.
60 bouts, 1900 to 7/16/1920
Heavyweight Champion 1906–1908
Hall of Fame Induction: 1996
Born: 6/17/1881, Chesley, Ontario, Canada
Named: Noah Brusso
Died: 5/10/1955

A largely forgotten and sometimes belittled champion, Tommy Burns held the heavyweight title for nearly three years and set a record for the most consecutive defenses by knockout. Burns, who acted as his own manager, also made a lot of money, an accomplishment that distinguishes him from many top fighters. When, badly overmatched, he finally fell to Jack Johnson, there was no question that he displayed great courage.

Burns was a French-Canadian who excelled as a lacrosse and hockey player in his youth. He polished his boxing skills in mining camps and turned professional in 1900, first fighting as a lightweight. Two years later he won the Michigan state middleweight title, which he successfully defended three times. Burns was small and fast, holding his hands low and darting in and out to score punches. It was a technique that often worked against larger, slower men. He had a fairly long reach for his height—he was only 5′7″—and preferred to score on the inside, especially with left hooks.

In a light heavyweight match in 1904, Hall of Famer Philadelphia Jack O'Brien proved too much for him, but Burns continued to beef up, heading for the heavyweight division. In 1905, when he knocked out Dave Barry in San Francisco, promoter Tom McCarey proposed matching him with heavyweight champ Marvin Hart. Although Johnson and some other black fighters may have been better qualified, the color bar was still very strong, and McCarey was looking for white contenders. The fight with Hart took place in Los Angeles in 1906, with retired heavyweight champ James J. Jeffries refereeing. Burns outboxed Hart in twenty rounds and took the championship and a purse of $15,000.

Burns then launched his series of defenses. He KO'd Fireman Jim Flynn, then fought O'Brien to a draw before winning a twenty-round decision in the rematch. He scored a one-round knockout of Australian contender Bill Squires, then added Squires to his camp as a sparring partner. With Johnson

Burns (R) was the first true world champion, defending his title in England, Ireland, France, Australia, and the U.S. He knocked out sometime sparring partner Bill Squires in all three of their meetings.

IN THE RING	WON 46	LOST 5	DRAWS 8	TB 60	KO 37	W 9	WF 0	D 8	KO'd 2	L 3	LF 0	ND 1

Date	Year		Opponent	Site	Result / Rounds		Title

SELECTED BOUTS

Date	Year		Opponent	Site	Result	Rounds	Title
—	1900		Fred Thornton	Detroit	KO	5	—
Dec 26	1902		Tom McCune	Detroit	KO	7	Won-Mich. State-M
Sep 25	1903		Jimmy Duggan	Houghton, MI	KO	9	Ret-Mich. State-M
Oct 12	1903		Jack Hammond	Sioux Ste. Marie, MI	KO	3	Ret-Mich. State-M
Dec 31	1903		Tom McCune	Detroit	W	10	Ret-Mich. State-M
Oct 7	1904		Phila. Jack O'Brien★	Milwaukee	L	6	—
Aug 31	1905		Dave Barry	San Francisco	KO	20	—
Oct 17	1905		Jack (Twin) Sullivan	Los Angeles	L	20	—
Feb 23	1906	♛	Marvin Hart	Los Angeles	W	20	Won-World-H
Oct 2	1906		Fireman Jim Flynn	Los Angeles	KO	15	Ret-World-H
Nov 28	1906		Phila. Jack O'Brien★	Los Angeles	D	20	Ret-World-H
May 8	1907		Phila. Jack O'Brien★	Los Angeles	W	20	Ret-World-H
Jul 4	1907		Bill Squires	Colma, CA	KO	1	Ret-World-H
Dec 2	1907		James ("Gunner") Moir	London	TKO	10	Ret-World-H
Feb 10	1908		Jack Palmer	London	KO	4	Ret-World-H
Mar 17	1908		Jem Roche	Dublin	KO	1	Ret-World-H
Apr 18	1908		Jewey Smith	Paris	KO	5	Ret-World-H
Jun 13	1908		Bill Squires	Paris	TKO	8	Ret-World-H
Aug 24	1908		Bill Squires	Sydney	KO	13	Ret-World-H
Sep 2	1908		Bill Lang	Melbourne	KO	6	Ret-World-H
Dec 26	1908		Jack Johnson★	Sydney	TKO'd	14	Lost-World-H
Apr 7	1910		Bill Lang	Sydney	W	20	Won-Vac Brit Emp-H
Jan 26	1914		Battling Brant	Taft, CA	KO	4	—
Jul 16	1920		Joe Beckett	London	TKO'd	7	For-Brit Emp-H

on his heels, Burns took his title on a world tour, recording knockout victories in London, Dublin, Paris, Sydney, and Melbourne. Three times, he put Squires in the ring as his opponent.

Johnson, who had followed Burns to London and Paris, finally secured a title bout in Sydney the day after Christmas, 1908. Promoted by canny Australian entrepreneur Hugh D. ("Huge Deal") McIntosh, the fight was timed to coincide with the arrival in Sydney of the American fleet. Johnson was to receive $5,000 and Burns $30,000, the largest amount ever earned by a boxer for a single fight up to that time. Burns was the three-to-one favorite, but Johnson was unquestionably the superior fighter. He was bigger, faster, stronger, and more skilled as a boxer. He took revenge for the racist insults he had endured, battering and taunting Burns, who, though bloodied and bruised, hung on for fourteen rounds. When police finally entered the ring, McIntosh, who was refereeing, conceded that Johnson had won.

Burns took a year off, then beat Bill Lang for the vacant British Empire heavyweight title, which he relinquished the next year. He fought only five more times, ending his career with a failed comeback effort against Joe Beckett in London in 1920. In retirement, Burns owned a tavern in Bremerton, Washington, before becoming an evangelist. He died of a heart attack in 1955.

TONY CANZONERI

LIGHTWEIGHT

Right-handed; 5'5"; 118–140 lbs.

175 bouts, 7/24/1925 to 11/1/1939

Manager: Sammy Goldman

Featherweight Champion 1927–28

Lightweight Champion 1930–33, 1935–36

Junior Wltrwt Champ 1931-32, 1933

Hall of Fame Induction: 1990

Born: 11/6/1908, Slidell, LA

Died: 12/9/1959

One of the best in an era of excellent fighters, Tony Canzoneri was an aggressive combatant who lit into his opponents with zeal and power. He was knocked out only once, in the final fight of his career. Canzoneri bounced in and out of titleholder status in three weight classes, and he fought in 22 championship bouts in the ten years he stayed at his peak.

Louisiana-born Canzoneri started boxing as an amateur in New Orleans and continued the pursuit after moving to New York City with his family. He won New York State's amateur bantamweight title in 1924 and turned professional the next year at age sixteen. Within two years, Canzoneri was ready to challenge Bud Taylor for the vacant NBA bantamweight title. The results of the heated battles with Taylor were a draw and a loss for Canzoneri. Soon afterward, Canzoneri abandoned the bantamweight class and moved to featherweight, going for the vacant world featherweight title against Hall of Famer Johnny Dundee. Canzoneri outboxed the aging Dundee to win the belt, then went after NBA featherweight champ Benny Bass to unify the title. Canzoneri won a decision over Bass, but lost the title to French boxer Andre Routis seven months later.

In 1929, Canzoneri moved up to lightweight but failed to snare the title from champion Sammy Mandell in a ten-round decision. The years 1930 and '31 saw three furious battles between Canzoneri and Jackie ("Kid") Berg, a gutsy, aggressive fighter well-prepared to meet Canzoneri's attacks. Canzoneri lost to Berg on points in a non-title bout, but stunned the boxing world later in 1930 by knocking out lightweight champ Al Singer in 66 seconds at New York's Polo Grounds to gain the world lightweight crown.

Canzoneri floors Joe Glick in this 1930 bout in Brooklyn. Glick got up, but Canzoneri won the decision.

IN THE RING	WON 137	LOST 24	DRAWS 10	TB 175	KO 44	W 93	WF 0	D 10	KO'd 1	L 22	LF 1	ND 4

Date	Year	Opponent	Site	Result / Rounds		Title
SELECTED BOUTS						
Jul 24	1925	Jack Gardner	Rockaway, NY	KO	1	—
Mar 26	1927	⑩ Charles("Bud")Taylor★	Chicago	D	10	For-Vac NBA-B
Jun 24	1927	⑩ Charles("Bud")Taylor★	Chicago	L	10	For-Vac NBA-B
Oct 24	1927	Johnny Dundee★	New York	W	15	Won-Vac World-FE
Feb 10	1928	♛ Benny Bass★	New York	W	15	Ret-World-FE
Sep 28	1928	⑩ Andre Routis	New York	L	15	Lost-World-FE
Aug 2	1929	♛ Sammy Mandell★	Chicago	L	10	For-World-L
Jan 17	1930	⑩ Jackie ("Kid") Berg★	New York	L	10	—
Sept 11	1930	⑩ Billy Petrolle★	Chicago	L	10	—
Nov 14	1930	♛ Al Singer	New York	KO	1	Won-World-L
Apr 24	1931	♛ Jackie ("Kid") Berg★	Chicago	KO	3	Ret-World-L & Won-World-JW
Jul 13	1931	Cecil Payne	Los Angeles	W	10	Ret-World-JW
Sep 10	1931	⑩ Jackie ("Kid") Berg★	New York	W	15	Ret-World-L & JW
Oct 29	1931	Phillie Griffin	Newark	W	10	Ret-World-JW
Nov 20	1931	⑩ Kid Chocolate★	New York	W	15	Ret-World-L & JW
Jan 18	1932	⑩ Jackie Jadick	Philadelphia	L	10	Lost-World-JW
Jul 18	1932	♛ Jackie Jadick	Philadelphia	L	10	For-World-JW
Nov 4	1932	⑩ Billy Petrolle★	New York	W	15	Ret-World-L
May 21	1933	♛ Battling Shaw	New Orleans	W	10	Reg-World-JW
Jun 23	1933	♛ Barney Ross★	Chicago	L	10	Lost-World-L & JW
Sep 12	1933	♛ Barney Ross★	New York	L	15	For-World-L & JW
May 10	1935	⑩ Lou Ambers★	New York	W	15	Won-Vac World-L
Oct 4	1935	⑩ Al Roth	New York	W	15	Ret-World-L
May 8	1936	⑩ Jimmy McLarnin★	New York	W	10	—
Sep 3	1936	⑩ Lou Ambers★	New York	L	15	Lost-World-L
Oct 5	1936	⑩ Jimmy McLarnin★	New York	L	10	—
May 7	1937	♛ Lou Ambers★	New York	L	15	For-World-L

The next year Canzoneri avenged his earlier loss to Berg, knocking him out in the third round and taking the junior welterweight title in the process. Canzoneri won the fifteen-round rematch, then added to his winning streak with a decision over the great boxer Kid Chocolate.

Canzoneri lost the junior welterweight title in 1932 and won it back in 1933. He lost both his lightweight and junior welterweight titles to Barney Ross in Chicago Stadium on a decision and also lost a rematch with Ross several months later.

In 1935, Canzoneri won his last championship when he decisioned Hall of Famer Lou Ambers for the lightweight title vacated by Ross. In two subsequent rematches, Ambers defeated Canzoneri to take and retain the title. Canzoneri fought until 1939 when Al ("Bummy") Davis knocked him out in the third round—the first time Canzoneri had been on the short end of a fight that did not go the distance. He quit the ring and in retirement backed Broadway shows, had a nightclub act, and operated a restaurant.

GEORGES CARPENTIER
The Orchid Man

LIGHT HEAVYWEIGHT

Right-handed; 5'11½"; 126–175 lbs.

109 bouts, 11/1/1908 to 9/15/1926

Manager: Francois Descamps

Light Heavyweight Champ 1920–22

Hall of Fame Induction: 1991

Born: 1/12/1894, Lens, France

Died: 10/28/1975

Perhaps the greatest European fighter of all time, Georges Carpentier competed in virtually every weight class. He started fighting in the *savatte* style—in which the use of the feet was allowed—but his manager, Francois Descamps, quickly switched him to conventional boxing. Carpentier's formidable skills allowed him to become a professional in 1908 at just fourteen years old, fighting as either a flyweight or a bantamweight.

In 1911, Carpentier knocked out Robert Eustache to win the French welterweight title. He also triumphed over Young Joseph in a knock-out win for the European welterweight title. The next year he added the European middleweight title. Carpentier's collection of titles grew in 1913 when he claimed the European light heavyweight title with a second-round knockout of Bandsman Rice and the European heavyweight title with a fourth-round knockout of Bombardier Billy Wells.

Carpentier had great success against bigger men. He won a victory on a foul over Gunboat Smith in 1914 to claim the so-called white heavyweight championship, which was contested during Jack Johnson's reign as true world champion. The advent of World War I interrupted Carpentier's boxing career. He served in the French military as an observation pilot and was decorated twice. Already popular, Carpentier was hailed as a true hero in France.

In 1920, Carpentier came to the United States and became a favorite of

An enormous throng of over 80,000 fans saw Carpentier fall to champ Jack Dempsey in a fourth-round knockout in this July 2, 1921, heavyweight title fight at Boyle's Thirty Acres in Jersey City, NJ.

IN THE RING	WON **88**	LOST **14**	DRAWS **6**	TB 109	KO 56	W 28	WF 4	D 6	KO'd 8	L 4	LF 2	ND 1

Date	Year	Opponent	Site	Result / Rounds		Title

SELECTED BOUTS

Date	Year	Opponent	Site	Result	Rounds	Title
Nov 1	1908	Ed Salmon	Mais-Laffitte, France	WF	13	—
Feb 19	1909	George Gloria	Paris	KO'd	6	—
Jun 15	1911	Robert Eustache	Paris	TKO	16	Won-France-W
Aug 29	1911	Dixie Kid★	Trouville, France	TKO'd	5	—
Oct 23	1911	Young Joseph	London	KO	10	Won-Europe-W
Feb 29	1912	Jim Sullivan	Monte Carlo	KO	2	Won-Vac Eur-M
Apr 4	1912	George Gunther	Paris	W	20	Ret-Europe-M
May 23	1912	Willie Lewis	Paris	W	20	Ret-Europe-M
Oct 23	1912	Billy Papke★	Paris	LF	17	—
Feb 12	1913	Bandsman Rice	Paris	KO	2	Won-Vac Eur-LH
Jun 1	1913	Bomb. Billy Wells	Ghent, Belgium	KO	4	Won-Vac Eur-H
Dec 8	1913	Bomb. Billy Wells	London	KO	1	Ret-Europe-H
Mar 21	1914	Joe Jeannette★	Paris	L	15	—
Jul 16	1914	Ed ("Gunboat") Smith	London	WF	6	Won-White-H
Jul 19	1919	Dick Smith	Paris	KO	8	Ret-Europe-H
Dec 4	1919	Joe Beckett	London	KO	1	Ret-Europe-H
Oct 12	1920	♛ Battling Levinsky★	Jersey City, NJ	KO	4	Won-World-LH
Jul 2	1921	♛ Jack Dempsey★	Jersey City	KO'd	4	For-World-H
May 11	1922	Ted ("Kid") Lewis★	London	KO	1	Ret-World-LH
Sep 24	1922	Battling Siki	Paris	KO'd	6	Lost-World-LH
May 6	1923	Marcel Nilles	Paris	KO	1	Won-France-H
May 31	1924	⑩ Tommy Gibbons★	Michigan City, IN	ND	10	—
Jul 24	1924	⑩ Gene Tunney★	New York	TKO'd	15	—
Jun 17	1926	⑩ Tommy Loughran★	Philadelphia	L	10	—
Sep 15	1926	Rocco Stramaglia	Coeur d'Alene, ID	KO	3	—

American fans as well. He knocked out Battling Levinsky in four rounds in Jersey City to claim the world light heavyweight title. The next year, master promoter Tex Rickard paired Carpentier with Jack Dempsey for the heavyweight championship of the world. Over 80,000 people paid $1,789,238 to attend the match at Boyle's Thirty Acres in Jersey City. Blessed with extremely quick hands and feet and a strong right, Carpentier believed that he had a good chance to defeat Dempsey, even though the champion outweighed him by twenty pounds. In the second round, Carpentier broke his thumb with a punch that sent Dempsey reeling into the ropes. In the fourth, Dempsey knocked Carpentier down. Carpentier rose at the count of nine, but a left to the face and a right to the heart sent him down again, this time for the knockout.

In 1922, Carpentier defended his light heavyweight title with a one-round knockout of Hall of Famer Ted ("Kid") Lewis but then lost it to Battling Siki, who knocked him out in six. Carpentier lost to the future heavyweight champion Gene Tunney in the fifteenth when his corner threw in the towel to protect him from further punishment. Carpentier remained active through 1926. In retirement, he acted in French movies and music hall shows and operated a restaurant.

JOE CHOYNSKI
Chrysanthemum, The California Terror

LIGHT HEAVYWEIGHT

Right-handed; 5'10"; 168–172 lbs.
79 bouts, 11/14/1888 to 11/24/1904
Hall of Fame Induction: 1998
Born: 11/8/1868, San Francisco, CA
Named: Joseph Bartlett Choynski
(coy-EN-ski)
Died: 1/24/1943

Although never a titleholder, San Francisco's "Chrysanthemum" Joe Choynski fought many of the most famous boxers of the late nineteenth and early twentieth centuries.

Despite his father's intellectual life—Yale graduate Isadore Choynski was a writer who eventually published a San Francisco newspaper focused on exposing municipal corruption and anti-Semitism—the younger Choynski followed a decidedly different career path. Choynski dropped out of high school and worked in a succession of jobs, among them blacksmith and candy puller, before becoming a professional boxer in 1888.

Although not an overly large man at 170 pounds, Choynski made a name for himself fighting top heavyweights. Early in his pro career, Choynski fought three wars with his neighbor, fellow San Franciscan and future heavyweight champion, Jim Corbett. Among fight fans, their rivalry was intensified because Choynski was a Jewish laborer while Corbett was a Gentile who worked in a bank. The first bout between the two was held on May 30, 1889, in rural San Anselmo, California, and was stopped by the local sheriff in the fourth round. The next week Corbett and Choynski met again on a barge off Benicia in San Francisco Bay. Boxing historian Frank Menke described this fight as "one of the epics of pugilism, for [its] duration of savagery." Choynski donned a spectator's driving gloves when Corbett refused to fight bare-knuckled. The seams of the gloves created welts on Corbett's face and body, while Corbett's punches left Choynski's face badly bruised and bloody. In the third round, Corbett broke two knuckles on his left hand; then he broke his right thumb in the fourteenth. Finally, in the 27th round,

Choynski (R) poses with the much larger Jim Jeffries before their November 30, 1897, meeting in San Francisco. The twenty-round fight ended in a draw. Jeffries, less than two years later, would take the heavyweight championship from Bob Fitzsimmons.

IN THE RING	WON 50	LOST 14	DRAWS 6	TB 79	KO 25	W 22	WF 3	D 6	KO'd 10	L 4	LF 0	ND 8	NC 1

Date	Year	Opponent	Site	Result / Rounds		Title
SELECTED BOUTS						
Nov 14	1888	George Bush	San Francisco	KO	2	—
May 30	1889	Jim Corbett★	San Anselmo, CA	NC	4	—
Jun 5	1889	Jim Corbett★	Benicia, CA	KO'd	27	—
Jul 15	1889	Jim Corbett★	San Francisco	L	4	—
Feb 10	1891	Joe Goddard	Sydney	KO'd	4	—
Jul 20	1891	Joe Goddard	Melbourne	KO'd	4	—
Dec 17	1891	Billy Woods	San Francisco	KO	34	—
Dec 20	1891	♛ John L. Sullivan★	San Francisco	Exh	3	—
Jun 17	1894	♛ Bob Fitzsimmons★	Boston	D	5	—
Mar 21	1896	Kid McCoy★	New York	ND	4	—
Apr 16	1896	Tom Sharkey★	San Francisco	L	8	—
Nov 30	1897	Jim Jeffries★	San Francisco	D	20	—
Mar 11	1898	Tom Sharkey★	San Francisco	D	8	—
Mar 24	1899	♛ Kid McCoy★	San Francisco	L	20	—
Oct 6	1899	♛ Kid McCoy★	Chicago	D	8	—
Jan 12	1900	♛ Kid McCoy★	New York	KO'd	4	—
Feb 23	1900	Joe Walcott★	New York	KO'd	7	—
May 8	1900	Tom Sharkey★	Chicago	KO'd	2	—
Feb 25	1901	Jack Johnson★	Galveston, TX	KO	3	—
Sep 29	1902	Jack O'Brien★	Chicago	L	6	—
Mar 30	1903	Jack O'Brien★	Philadelphia	ND-L	6	—
Nov 24	1904	Jack Williams	Philadelphia	ND	6	—

Corbett knocked out the barely conscious Choynski. Six weeks later the pair fought for a third time with Corbett winning a four-round decision.

In 1890, Choynski traveled to Australia where he twice lost to the Australian champion, Joe Goddard. On June 17, 1894, Choynski fought a five-round draw with future heavyweight champion Bob Fitzsimmons in a Boston bout which was stopped by police. On November 30, 1897, Choynski fought to a draw with another future champion, young Jim Jeffries, who outweighed him by approximately fifty pounds.

In 1901, Choynski faced a third future heavyweight champion, Jack Johnson. Choynski knocked Johnson out in the third round. Johnson would not suffer another knockout for fourteen years. After the fight, Choynski and Johnson were arrested for participating in a mixed-race match. In jail for four weeks, the two were allowed to box to entertain their fellow inmates, providing excellent training for Johnson. In a 1940 interview, Johnson called Choynski "the hardest puncher in the last fifty years."

Choynski remained in fine physical condition after his 1904 retirement. For ten years, he was the boxing and athletic instructor for the Pittsburgh Athletic Club. He later became a chiropractor, worked in the insurance business, and served as a consultant for the movie "Gentleman Jim." He died on January 24, 1943, in Cincinnati.

JAMES J. CORBETT
Gentleman Jim

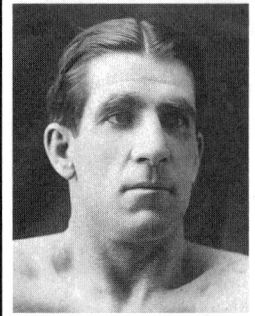

HEAVYWEIGHT

Right-handed; 6'1"; 178–190 lbs.
19 bouts, 1884 to 8/14/1903
Manager: William A. Brady
Heavyweight Champion 1892–97
Hall of Fame Induction: 1990
Born: 9/1/1866, San Francisco, CA
Named: James John Corbett
Died: 2/18/1933

James J. Corbett gained lasting fame when he knocked out the hugely popular John L. Sullivan to take the heavyweight title in 1892. The first heavyweight to win a championship under the Marquess of Queensberry Rules, Gentleman Jim was a masterful boxer who also prided himself on his social respectability. Although grieving fans of Sullivan were slow to accept Corbett, the new champ's decent lifestyle attracted a better sort of audience for the fights.

Corbett grew up in a large Irish family in San Francisco, where his father owned a livery stable. A street fighter as a boy, Corbett completed high school and took a job as a bank clerk. He led another life outside the bank, however, sharpening his pugilistic skills by taking on all comers on saloon stages. Corbett's formal training began when—with the blessing of the bank's president—he was taken under the wing of English boxing instructor Walter Watson at San Francisco's Olympic Club. He fought his first professional bout, a knockout, at age eighteen.

Corbett's career took off when he faced Joe Choynski for a three-fight series in 1889. Choynski, who went on to defeat Jack Johnson, was an extremely hard puncher. The first fight was stopped by police after just four rounds, but six days later the two met again on the blistering hot deck of a barge in San Francisco Bay. It was a bloody fight. The seams on Choynski's gloves cut Corbett, and in the third round, Corbett broke his left hand with a punch to Choynski's head. Finally, in the 27th round, a battered Corbett knocked out Choynski with a left hook.

Corbett won a rematch with Choyn-ski and the next year deci-sioned Jake Kilrain who had earlier fought an epic, though losing,

Relentlessly banging at the champion, Corbett (R) dropped John L. Sullivan in the 21st round of their 1892 title bout in New Orleans.

IN THE RING	WON **11**	LOST **4**	DRAWS **3**	TB 19	KO 7	W 4	WF 0	D 3	KO'd 3	L 0	LF 1	NC 1

Date	Year	Opponent	Site	Result / Rounds		Title
SELECTED BOUTS						
—	1884	Frank Smith	Salt Lake City	KO	2	—
—	—	Duncan McDonald	Evanston, WY	D	8	—
May 30	1889	Joe Choynski★	San Anselmo, CA	NC	4	—
Jun 5	1889	Joe Choynski★	Benicia, CA	KO	27	—
Jul 15	1889	Joe Choynski★	San Francisco	W	4	—
Jul 29	1889	Dave Campbell	Portland, OR	D	10	—
Feb 18	1890	Jake Kilrain	New Orleans	W	6	—
Apr 14	1890	Dominick McCaffrey	Brooklyn	W	4	—
May 21	1891	Peter Jackson★	San Francisco	D	61	—
Jun 26	1891	♛ John L. Sullivan★	San Francisco	Exh	4	—
Oct 8	1891	Ed Kinney	Milwaukee	W	4	—
Feb 16	1892	Bill Spilling	—	KO	1	—
—	1892	Bob Caffrey	—	KO	1	—
Sep 7	1892	♛ John L. Sullivan★	New Orleans	KO	21	Won-World-H
Jan 25	1894	Charlie Mitchell★	Jacksonville, FL	KO	3	Ret-World-H
Mar 17	1897	Bob Fitzsimmons★	Carson City, NV	KO'd	14	Lost-World-H
Nov 22	1898	Tom Sharkey★	New York	LF	9	—
May 11	1900	♛ James J. Jeffries★	Coney Island	KO'd	23	For-World-H
Aug 30	1900	Charles ("Kid") McCoy★	New York	KO	5	—
Aug 14	1903	♛ James J. Jeffries★	San Francisco	KO'd	10	For-World-H

battle with Sullivan. Corbett then faced Hall of Famer Peter Jackson, a black fighter with whom Sullivan had refused to tangle. The two great boxers battled for 61 rounds until the fight was stopped and declared a draw.

Corbett was slowly gaining on Sullivan, first meeting him in a high society exhibition where both men wore evening clothes. The theatrical Corbett, who would later have a lengthy career in movies, plays, and vaudeville, did not strike many blows but he did not allow Sullivan to hit him either.

In 1892 in New Orleans, Corbett and Sullivan met in earnest, with the heavyweight title at stake. Under the Queensberry Rules, the fighters wore light gloves. Throughout the fight, Corbett made Sullivan chase him to land a punch. Sullivan finally knocked Corbett down with a hard right in the seventeenth, but in round 21, Corbett shot a left hook to Sullivan's jaw, followed it up with a flurry of punches, and finished Sullivan with a right.

Corbett lost the title in 1897 when the lighter Bob Fitzsimmons knocked him out in fourteen rounds. Corbett tried to regain his title from his former sparring partner, James J. Jeffries, in 1900. Although he still displayed great boxing skills, Corbett was knocked out in the 23rd round. Three years later, Jeffries knocked him out again, and Corbett quit. In retirement, he continued his stage career.

YOUNG CORBETT III

WELTERWEIGHT

Left-handed; 5'7½"; 137–163 lbs.

151 bouts, 10/3/1919 to 8/20/1940

Managers: Ralph Manfredo, Larry White

Welterweight Champ 1933
California World Middleweight Champion 1938

Hall of Fame Induction: 2004

Born: 5/27/1905, Protenza, Italy

Named: Raffaele Capabianca Giordano

Died: 7/15/1993

Born Raffaele Capabianca Giordano in Protenza, Italy, on May 27, 1905, Corbett left Italy with his family when he was a baby. After a four-year stop in Pittsburgh, the family settled in California. Corbett picked grapes before beginning to box for "the fun of it" when he was thirteen. Corbett fought his first recorded fight when he was fourteen: a decision over Young Terry McGovern on September 28, 1919.

Once, Corbett and a friend hopped a freight train and headed for Sacramento in hopes of getting a match there. The pair leapt from the train only to realize that they were in Marysville rather than Sacramento. Corbett and his friend came upon an ad for a boxing show that night. Corbett convinced the promoter that he was a fighter and was given a bout against a much more experienced pugilist, Eddie Morris. Morris knocked Corbett out in the third round. Corbett, however, earned $7.50 for his efforts. After graduating from Edison Junior High School in Fresno in 1920, Corbett began to take boxing more seriously.

Corbett was unrelated to Hall of Famer James J. Corbett, to George Green who was the original Young Corbett, or to William Rothwell who was known as Young Corbett II. Corbett got his name early in his career when a ring announcer told him he would not announce him as Ralph Giordano and dubbed him "Young Corbett III." Corbett suffered only five defeats in his first 75 recorded bouts. Fighting from a left-handed stance, he did not have great punching power. He could hit, though, and was gifted with great speed. Corbett's primary weapon was a left to the body.

As time went on, Corbett began to face a better class of opponent. He split two bouts with ranked contender Sergeant Sammy Baker in 1928. By 1929, Corbett was beginning to earn national acclaim.

Finally, on February 22, 1933, Corbett met welterweight champ Jackie Fields for the title in San Francisco. Corbett

Young Corbett III (R) twice bested ranked-contender Bep Van Klaveren (L) in San Francisco in 1935.

IN THE RING	WON 124	LOST 12	DRAWS 15	TB 151	KO 32	W 91	WF 1	D 15	KO'd 4	L 8	LF 0

Date	Year	Opponent	Site	Result / Rounds		Title

SELECTED BOUTS

Date	Year	Opponent	Site	Result	Rounds	Title
Oct 3	1919	Kid Jeffries	Fresno, CA	D	4	—
Jun 24	1927	⑩ Young Jack Thompson	San Francisco	W	10	—
Feb 13	1928	⑩ Young Jack Thompson	San Francisco	W	10	—
Sep 13	1928	⑩ Sgt. Sammy Baker	New York	W	10	—
Sep 26	1928	⑩ Sgt. Sammy Baker	Brooklyn	L	12	—
Feb 22	1930	♛ Jackie Fields ★	San Francisco	W	10	—
Jul 4	1930	♛ Young Jack Thompson	San Francisco	W	10	—
Oct 1	1930	⑩ Sammy Jackson	Los Angeles	W	10	—
Feb 20	1931	⑩ Paulie Walker	Los Angeles	W	10	—
Mar 20	1931	⑩ Paul Pirrone	San Francisco	W	10	—
Feb 22	1933	♛ Jackie Fields ★	San Francisco	W	10	Won-World-W
May 29	1933	⑩ Jimmy McLarnin ★	Los Angeles	KO'd	1	Lost-World-W
Aug 14	1934	Mickey Walker ★	San Francisco	W	10	—
Jan 20	1935	⑩ Bep Van Klaveren	San Francisco	W	10	—
Feb 22	1935	⑩ Bep Van Klaveren	San Francisco	W	10	—
Jul 4	1935	⑩ Lou Brouillard ★	San Francisco	L	10	—
Mar 12	1937	⑩ Gus Lesnevich	San Francisco	KO	5	—
Aug 13	1937	⑩ Billy Conn ★	San Francisco	W	10	—
Nov 8	1937	⑩ Billy Conn ★	Pittsburgh	L	10	—
Feb 22	1938	♛ Fred Apostoli ★	San Francisco	W	10	—
May 25	1938	Jack Burke	Salt Lake City	W	10	Ret-Cal World-M
Nov 18	1938	♛ Fred Apostoli ★	New York	TKO'd	8	For-NY World-M
Aug 20	1940	Richard ("Sheik") Rangel	Fresno	W	10	—

took the first five rounds in a closely contested battle. He hurt his left thumb in the fifth but continued to fight on. The referee, Lieutenant Jack Kennedy, later described Corbett as "vicious in those first five rounds. He ripped in like a tiger. Fields could not protect himself."

Corbett's reign as welterweight champion was short-lived. In his very next fight on May 29, 1933, in Los Angeles, Corbett faced Hall of Famer Jimmy McLarnin. Within seconds, McLarnin floored Corbett with a right to the chin, and then knocked him down again with three lefts. Two more blows sent Corbett to the canvas. The fight was over before the bell sounded to end the first round.

Corbett continued to fight for another six years. On February 22, 1938, five years to the day after he won the welterweight championship, Corbett defeated Hall of Famer—and then middleweight champion—Fred Apostoli in a non-title bout in San Francisco. Corbett had earned a title shot and faced Apostoli in New York on November 18, 1938, but he was knocked out in eight rounds.

Corbett won four more fights before retiring. He then sold insurance—a trade he began while still an active fighter. Like many boxers of the era, Corbett lost much of his ring earnings in the Depression. He later operated a bar in Fresno. On October 2, 1945, Corbett was nearly killed in an automobile accident. He suffered a fractured skull and other injuries. He died in 1993.

JOHNNY COULON
The Chicago Spider, The Cherry Picker from Logan Square

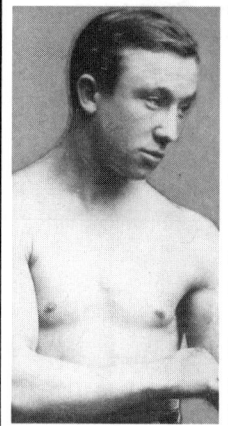

B A N T A M W E I G H T

Right-handed; 5'0"; 102–117 lbs.

93 bouts, 1/18/1905 to 3/16/1920

Managers: E.E. ("Pop") Coulon 1905–11, Emil Thierry 1911–14

USA World 105 lbs Champ 1908–09

USA World 108 lbs Champ 1909

USA World 112 lbs Champ 1910

USA World Bantamweight Champ 1910–14

Hall of Fame Induction: 1999

Born: 2/12/1889, Toronto, Canada

Died: 10/29/1973

Coulon's father, a piano manufacturer and fight manager, instructed him in the fine points of boxing from a very young age. When he was fifteen, he was sent to New York to study boxing with his cousin, George ("Elbows") McFadden, who had previously knocked out Hall of Famer Joe Gans.

Coulon turned pro when he KO'd Young Bennie in Chicago on January 18, 1905. He won his first 26 fights, twelve of them by knockout, before facing Kid Murphy in Milwaukee on March 1, 1907. Murphy won the ten-round decision and claimed the American version of the world paperweight title. Coulon avenged his defeat in a rematch on January 8, 1908, with a decision in ten, and claimed the world title. This was an era of conflicting title claims and championship fights made at two, or three, pound intervals; most British observers considered ten-round fights inadequate to decide championships.

On February 19, 1910, Coulon decisioned English contender Jim Kendrick, and two weeks later he faced Kendrick again in a widely recognized bantamweight championship fight. Coulon outlasted Kendrick and knocked him out in the nineteenth round. Coulon successfully defended his title numerous times at a weight limit of either 115 or 116 lbs. However, in a rematch with Kid Williams in Vernon, California, the challenger quickly fractured two of Coulon's ribs, knocked him out in the third, and took his title.

Coulon stayed out of the ring for two years after this loss, and never received another title shot. He served in the army during World War I as a physical instructor, and after the war fought twice in Paris. After European standout Charles Ledoux knocked him out in six rounds, Coulon retired.

After his fighting days, Johnny Coulon (L) still had a few tricks up his sleeve. A finger placed on Joe Louis's neck makes the 120-pound Coulon unliftable!

IN THE RING	WON 52	LOST 6	DRAWS 4	TB 93	KO 30	W 22	WF 0	D 4	KO'd 3	L 3	LF 0	ND 30	NC 1

Date	Year	Opponent	Site	Result / Rounds		Title

SELECTED BOUTS

Date	Year	Opponent	Site	Result	Rounds	Title
Jan 18	1905	Young Bennie	Chicago	KO	6	—
Mar 1	1907	Kid Murphy	Milwaukee	L	10	For-USA World-105 lbs
Jan 8	1908	Kid Murphy	Peoria, IL	W	10	Won-USA World-105 lbs
Jan 29	1908	Kid Murphy	Peoria	W	10	Ret-USA World-105 lbs
Feb 20	1908	Cooney Kelley	Peoria	KO	9	Ret-USA World-105 lbs
Mar 13	1908	Young Terry McGovern	Los Angeles	W	10	Ret-USA World-105 lbs
Feb 11	1909	Kid Murphy	New York	TKO	5	Ret-USA World-105 lbs
May 28	1909	Tibby Watson	Dayton, OH	KO	10	Won-USA World-108 lbs
Jan 29	1910	Earl Denning	New Orleans	KO	9	Won-USA World-112 lbs
Feb 19	1910	Jim Kendrick	New Orleans	W	10	Ret-USA World-112 lbs
Mar 6	1910	Jim Kendrick	New Orleans	KO	19	Won-USA World-B (115 lbs)
Apr 11	1910	Young O'Leary	New York	ND-D	10	Ret-USA World-B (115 lbs)
Apr 25	1910	Frankie Burns	Brooklyn	ND-L	10	Ret-USA World-B (115 lbs)
May 12	1910	Phil McGovern	New York	ND-W	10	Ret-USA World-B (115 lbs)
Jun 8	1910	Frankie Burns	New York	ND	10	Ret-USA World-B (115 lbs)
Dec 3	1910	Charlie Harvey	New Orleans	W	10	Ret-USA World-B (115 lbs)
Jan 19	1911	Terry Moran	Memphis, TN	KO	2	Ret-USA World-B (115 lbs)
Feb 26	1911	Frankie Conley	New Orleans	W	20	Ret-USA World-B (116 lbs)
Mar 22	1911	George Kitson	Akron, OH	TKO	5	Ret-USA World-B (116 lbs)
Mar 28	1911	Harry Forbes	Kenosha, WI	ND-W	10	Ret-USA World-B (116 lbs)
Apr 20	1911	Phil McGovern	Kenosha	ND-W	10	Ret-USA World-B (116 lbs)
Jan 11	1912	George Kitson	South Bend, IN	KO	3	Ret-USA World-B (116 lbs)
Feb 3	1912	Frankie Conley	Vernon, CA	W	20	Ret-USA World-B (116 lbs)
Feb 18	1912	Frankie Burns	New Orleans	W	20	Ret-USA World-B (116 lbs)
Oct 18	1912	Kid Williams★	New York	ND-L	10	—
Nov 20	1912	Charley Goldman★	Brooklyn	ND-W	10	—
Jun 9	1914	♛ Kid Williams★	Vernon	KO'd	3	Lost-USA World-B (116 lbs)
May 14	1917	♛ Pete Herman★	Racine, WI	TKO'd	3	—
Mar 16	1920	Charles Ledoux	Paris	KO'd	6	—

The end of his fighting career did not lead to the end of his productive life. Coulon toured with vaudeville groups and made many friends in his travels, including European heads of state, actors, and even Ernest Hemingway. During his travels he devised a popular trick: he would ask someone to lift him and usually—since he weighed only 120 pounds—they were successful. Coulon would then place a finger on the lifter's neck and ask them to try again, whereupon they would inevitably fail. Such luminaries as Jack Dempsey, Primo Carnera, and Joe Louis fell victim to this stunt.

Returning to Chicago, Coulon and his wife, Marie, opened a gym in 1923. Heavyweight champs, from Dempsey to Ali, trained there when in the Chicago area, and countless amateur boxers learned to fight under Coulon's direction. Coulon always had an interest in the underprivileged in his neighborhood and helped many poor youngsters, once saving a community youth center that was on the brink of closing its doors. He briefly appeared in the 1969 movie *Medium Cool*, which contains scenes filmed in his gym.

EUGENE CRIQUI
Gégène, Roi du KO (KO King)

FEATHERWEIGHT

Right-handed; 5'4";
112–126 lbs.

125 bouts, 10/10/1910 to
3/19/1928

Manager: Robert Eudeline

Featherweight Champ 1923

Hall of Fame Induction: 2005

Born: 8/15/1893, Belleville,
France

Died: 3/7/1977

Eugene Criqui overcame a serious injury in World War I to win the featherweight championship of the world. He was born on August 15, 1893, in Belleville, France, a suburb of Paris. He turned professional at seventeen, winning a four-round decision over Gouguillon in Paris on October 10, 1910. Criqui quickly made a name for himself as he won the French flyweight title with a tenth-round knockout of Voirin on February 14, 1912. In 1913, Criqui faced former British flyweight champion Sid Smith for the vacant European and world flyweight titles but lost a twenty-round decision. In 1914, he lost his second bid for the European version of the world flyweight title with another twenty-round loss, this time to Percy Jones. Then Charles Ledoux stopped him in the twelfth to take Criqui's French title.

With the outbreak of World War I, Criqui joined the French army and served in the trenches until a bullet shattered his jaw. Doctors repaired it with wire and metal plates. Criqui could not speak for several months.

Determined to resume his boxing career, Criqui announced his return to the ring with a fifth-round knockout of George Dravin in Paris on September 26, 1917. Primarily a boxer before the war, Criqui developed increased punching power during this second phase of his career. He knocked out only twelve of his 59 pre-War opponents but then proceeded to knock out 44 of his 66 post-War combatants.

In 1920, Criqui embarked on an extended boxing visit to Sydney, Australia. He returned to France to score a first-round knockout over Auguste Grassi on September 27, 1921, to win the French featherweight title. He retained the title the next year with a first-round knockout of Ledoux. On July 7, 1922, Criqui knocked out Arthur Wyns in the twelfth round to take the European featherweight title.

Criqui's status as the European feather-

After World War I, Criqui fought in England, Australia, Spain, and America as well as in his native France.

IN THE RING	WON 98	LOST 16	DRAWS 11	TB 125	KO 56	W 40	WF 2	D 11	KO'd 5	L 10	LF 1

Date	Year	Opponent	Site	Result / Rounds		Title
SELECTED BOUTS						
Oct 10	1910	Gouguillon	Paris	W	4	—
Feb 14	1912	Voirin	Paris	KO	10	Won-France-FL
Aug 9	1912	Marcel Lepreux	Paris	TKO	13	Ret-France-FL
Feb 15	1913	Bombardier Rousseau	Bordeaux, France	W	10	—
Apr 11	1913	Sid Smith	Paris	L	20	For-Vac GB/IBU World-FL
Feb 15	1914	Percy Jones	Liverpool, England	W	15	—
Mar 26	1914 ♛	Percy Jones	Liverpool	L	20	For-GB/IBU World-FL
Jul 10	1914	Charles Ledoux	Paris	TKO'd	12	Lost-France-FL
Jan 23	1918	Bombardier Rousseau	Bordeaux	W	12	—
Apr 10	1919	Tommy Noble	London	TKO'd	19	—
Dec 26	1919	Memphis Pal Moore	Paris	TKO'd	14	—
Feb 19	1921	Silvino Jamito	Sydney	W	20	—
Sep 27	1921	Auguste Grassi	Paris	KO	1	Won-France-FE
Feb 4	1922	Charles Ledoux	Paris	KO	1	Ret-France-FE
Jun 16	1922	Joseph Youyou	Barcelona	KO	2	—
Jul 7	1922	Arthur Wyns	Paris	KO	12	Won-Europe-FE
Sep 10	1922	Arthur Wyns	Paris	TKO	6	Ret-Europe-FE
Nov 4	1922	Walter Rossi	Paris	KO	1	Ret-Europe-FE
Dec 2	1922	Billy Matthews	Paris	TKO	17	Ret-Europe-FE
Jun 2	1923 ♛	Johnny Kilbane ★	New York	KO	6	Won-World-FE
Jul 26	1923	Johnny Dundee ★	New York	L	15	Lost-World-FE
Dec 20	1923	Edouard Mascart	Paris	L	20	Lost-Europe-FE
Apr 2	1927	Panama Al Brown ★	Paris	L	10	—
Dec 20	1927	Gustav ("Tiger") Humery	Paris	TKO'd	6	For-France-FE
Mar 19	1928	Benny ("Kid") Carter	Paris	W	10	—

weight champ earned him a shot at the world featherweight title held by Hall of Famer Johnny Kilbane. The title bout was held in New York's Polo Grounds on June 2, 1923. Babe Ruth, who hurried over from Yankee Stadium, was in attendance. Kilbane took the first round, but Criqui pressed the action in the second. In the fourth, Kilbane scored with rights to the jaw while Criqui worked the body and responded with lefts to the jaw. In general, Kilbane did better at long range, while Criqui fought better inside. In the fifth, Criqui opened a cut to Kilbane's mouth. In the sixth, he staggered Kilbane with a right that landed just below the heart. He then finished off Kilbane with a "half swing, half hook" right to the jaw.

Criqui did not have time to enjoy the title. Fifty-four days after he won it, he faced Hall of Famer Johnny Dundee again at the Polo Grounds, this time before a crowd of 40,000. Criqui was knocked down three times in the early rounds. In the eighth, blood streamed from his nose and mouth. By the fifteenth, Criqui lay helpless on the ropes as Dundee pummeled him. Dundee deserved the decision.

Later that year, back in Paris, Criqui lost his European title in a twenty-round decision to Edouard Mascart. He fought five times over the next five years, losing four of the fights. After winning a ten-round decision over Benny Carter on March 19, 1928, Criqui retired. He died at age 83 in Villepinte, France.

LES DARCY
The Maitland Wonder

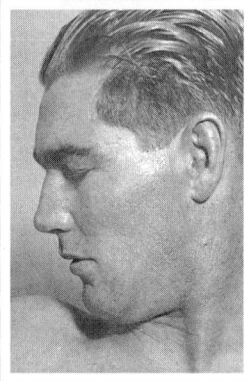

MIDDLEWEIGHT

Right-handed; 5'6"; 147–165 lbs.

49 bouts, 1910 to 9/30/1916

Manager: Tim O'Sullivan

Australian World Middleweight Champion 1915–16

Hall of Fame Induction: 1993

Born: 10/31/1895, East Maitland, NSW, Australia

Named: James Leslie Darcy

Died: 5/24/1917

Les Darcy had a short but brilliant fighting career that came to an unglamorous end when the young boxer died far from home. Considered one of the greatest middleweights of all time, Darcy proved his mettle in his native Australia. Born in New South Wales, he started boxing as an amateur at age fifteen and quickly turned professional. He won his first sixteen fights before challenging the veteran Bob Whitelaw for the Australian welterweight title. Darcy lost the twenty-round decision but, in a rematch, knocked Whitelaw out in five.

Darcy graduated from regional bouts to fighting in Sydney Stadium, and promoters began to import talent to challenge him. He lost his first two fights in Sydney, one by decision and one by foul, to American Fritz Holland. The next year Darcy faced another American, Jeff Smith, in what was considered a contest for the Australian world middleweight title. When Darcy complained of a low blow at the end of the fifth round, the referee believed that Darcy did not want to continue and awarded the decision to Smith. In a rematch, Darcy was awarded the victory when Smith punched him in the groin.

As Australian world middleweight champ, Darcy defeated such top-flight visiting Americans as Eddie McGoorty, Billy Murray, Jimmy Clabby, George Chip, George ("K.O.") Brown, and Buck Crouse, as well as knocking out Smith and Holland in rematches.

American Jimmy Clabby bends to avoid punishment from Darcy (R) in one of two meetings in Sydney. Darcy took twenty-round decisions both times.

IN THE RING	WON 45	LOST 4	DRAWS 0	TB 49	KO 29	W 15	WF 1	D 0	KO'd 0	L 2	LF 2

Date	Year	Opponent	Site	Result / Rounds		Title
SELECTED BOUTS						
—	1910	Sid Pasco	Maitland, Australia	KO	2	—
Nov 3	1913	Bob Whitelaw	Newcastle, Australia	L	20	For-Australia-W
Mar 21	1914	Bob Whitelaw	Maitland	KO	5	—
Jul 18	1914	Fritz Holland	Sydney	L	20	—
Sep 12	1914	Fritz Holland	Sydney	LF	18	—
Jan 23	1915 ♛	Jeff Smith	Sydney	LF	5	For-Australia World-M
Mar 13	1915	Fritz Holland	Sydney	W	20	—
May 1	1915	Fritz Holland	Melbourne	KO	13	—
May 22	1915 ♛	Jeff Smith	Sydney	WF	2	Won-Australia World-M
Jun 12	1915	Mick King	Sydney	TKO	10	Won-Australia-M & Ret-Australia World-M
Jul 31	1915	Eddie McGoorty	Sydney	TKO	15	Ret-Australia World-M
Sep 4	1915	Billy Murray	Sydney	W	20	Ret-Australia World-M
Oct 9	1915	Fred Dyer	Sydney	TKO	6	Ret-Australia World-M
Oct 23	1915	Jimmy Clabby	Sydney	W	20	Ret-Australia World-M
Nov 1	1915	Billy Murray	Melbourne	KO	6	—
Dec 27	1915	Eddie McGoorty	Sydney	KO	8	—
Jan 15	1916	George ("K.O.") Brown	Sydney	W	20	—
Feb 19	1916	Harold Hardwick	Sydney	KO	7	Won-Australia-H
Mar 25	1916	Les O'Donnell	Sydney	KO	7	Ret-Australia-H
Apr 8	1916	George ("K.O.") Brown	Sydney	W	20	—
May 13	1916	Alex Costica	Sydney	TKO	5	Ret-Australia World-M
Jun 3	1916	Buck Crouse	Sydney	KO	2	—
Jun 24	1916	Dave Smith	Sydney	KO	12	Ret-Australia-H
Aug 16	1916	Dave Smith	Brisbane, Australia	KO	11	Ret-Australia-H
Sep 9	1916	Jimmy Clabby	Sydney	W	20	Ret-Australia World-M
Sep 30	1916	George Chip	Sydney	KO	9	Ret-Australia World-M

Darcy's opponents are said to have admired his courage, stamina, and punching power. In 1916, Darcy KO'd Harold Hardwick to capture the Australian heavyweight title.

Darcy was Australia's best known sportsman at the time his country mobilized to join the Allied cause in World War I. Because he failed to enlist in the military, public opinion turned against him. He escaped the mounting controversy by stowing away on an oil tanker, the S.S. *Cushing,* bound for New York. In America he was vilified by the press and labeled a "slacker." New York's governor refused to issue a license for a fight involving Darcy. Other states' governors followed suit and a six-month tour, promoted by Tex Rickard, failed to materialize. To regain favor, Darcy signed an oath of allegiance to the U.S. and joined the armed services (with the understanding that he would be given furloughs to fight). However, he collapsed a few days later and died in Memphis of blood poisoning from an infected tooth. His body was shipped home, where he was mourned as a hero.

JACK DELANEY
Bright Eyes

LIGHT HEAVYWEIGHT

Right-handed; 5'11½"; 158–178 lbs.

93 bouts, 10/1919 to 4/21/1932

Managers: Al Jennings 1919–1922,
Pete Reilly 1923–1928,
Billy Prince 1932

Light Heavyweight Champion
1926–1927

Hall of Fame Induction: 1996

Born: 3/18/1900, St. Francis du
Lac, Quebec, Canada

Named: Ovila Chapdelaine

Died: 11/27/1948

Jack Delaney was one of the most popular fighters of the 1920s. A French-Canadian born in Quebec, Delaney moved with his parents to Holyoke, Massachusetts, and then Bridgeport, Connecticut. He started to fight professionally in 1919. In his first three years, he compiled a record that included a regional title win and only three losses in nearly 30 fights.

In 1924, under the direction of Pete Reilly, Delaney decisioned future light heavyweight champion Tommy Loughran. Less than a month later, in Madison Square Garden, Delaney had his first clash with former AAU wrestling champion Paul Berlenbach. The fight, billed as "The Wrestler versus The Boxer," pulled in $50,000, a new record for the Garden. In the first round, Delaney, who had a smooth, graceful style, eluded Berlenbach's crude rushes and peppered him with punishing left jabs. Berlenbach knocked Delaney down in the second round. When Delaney saw Berlenbach before him, he dropped back to the canvas to get a new count, a move that would disqualify him today. The two fighters traded knockdowns in the third, but then Delaney took control so completely that Berlenbach had difficulty finding his corner. Delaney knocked the wrestler down twice in the fourth round before the referee ended the fight. Berlenbach went on to become light heavyweight champion when he defeated Mike McTigue in 1925.

Delaney scored two knockouts over Tiger Flowers before facing Berlenbach again. He lost to the champ in a fifteen-round decision, but then embarked on an eleven-fight winning streak that led to a rematch. The fight was held in Brooklyn's Ebbets Field and drew a crowd of 41,000 and a gate of $450,000. Delaney was the popular favorite and was loudly cheered by female fans known as "Delaney's screaming mamies." Delaney fought as Reilly had directed,

Delaney (seated) won this heavyweight fight against Paolino Uzcudun by foul in the seventh round on August 11, 1927. Trainer Pete Reilly is reaching through the ropes displaying Delaney's dented protective cup.

IN THE RING	WON 77	LOST 10	DRAWS 2	TB 93	KO 44	W 31	WF 2	D 2	KO'd 3	L 7	LF 0	ND 2	NC 2

Date	Year	Opponent	Site	Result / Rounds		Title
SELECTED BOUTS						
Oct	1919	Steve August	Bridgeport, CT	W	4	—
Feb 13	1922	Lou Bogash	Bridgeport	W	15	—
Aug 31	1923	Jimmy Darcy	New York	W	10	—
Feb 19	1924	⑩ Tommy Loughran ★	Boston	W	10	—
Mar 14	1924	⑩ Paul Berlenbach ★	New York	KO	4	—
Oct 3	1924	⑩ Jimmy Slattery ★	New York	L	6	—
Jan 16	1925	⑩ Tiger Flowers ★	New York	KO	2	—
Feb 13	1925	⑩ Jimmy Slattery ★	New York	L	6	—
Feb 26	1925	⑩ Tiger Flowers ★	New York	KO	4	—
Jul 16	1925	⑩ Tommy Loughran ★	Philadelphia	D	10	—
Dec 11	1925	♛ Paul Berlenbach ★	New York	L	15	For-World-LH
Feb 5	1926	Johnny Risko	New York	W	10	—
Mar 15	1926	⑩ Mike McTigue	New York	KO	4	—
Mar 22	1926	⑩ Maxie Rosenbloom ★	Philadelphia	W	10	—
Jun 3	1926	Tommy Burns ★	Brooklyn	TKO	2	—
Jul 16	1926	♛ Paul Berlenbach ★	Brooklyn	W	15	Won-World-LH
Dec 10	1926	Jamaica Kid	Waterbury, CT	KO	3	—
Feb 18	1927	Jimmy Maloney	New York	L	10	—
Aug 11	1927	Paolino Uzcudun	New York	WF	7	—
Sep 14	1927	Johnny Risko	Cleveland	L	10	—
Dec 9	1927	⑩ Paul Berlenbach ★	Chicago	KO	6	—
Mar 1	1928	Tom Heeney	New York	L	15	—
Apr 30	1928	Jack Sharkey ★	New York	KO'd	1	—
Mar 3	1932	Phil Johnson	Bridgeport	KO	2	—
Mar 29	1932	Frank Willis	Stamford, CT	KO	3	—
Apr 21	1932	Leo Williams	Hartford, CT	KO	1	—

looking to pile up points rather than try for a knockout. He staggered Berlenbach in the first round with a right cross to the jaw. In the fifth, a left hook dropped Berlenbach to one knee. Delaney controlled the remaining rounds and won the light heavyweight title.

Early in 1927, Delaney relinquished his championship in order to pursue the heavyweight crown. He was matched against Jimmy Maloney, as a step to a challenge of then-heavyweight champion Gene Tunney. Delaney lost to Maloney, in part because of an injured hand—reportedly the result of a misplaced punch intended for a porter on a train. The loss sidetracked Delaney's quest. He defeated Paolino Uzcudun on a questionable foul before ending the year with a knockout of Berlenbach in their last meeting.

In his last important fight, Delaney suffered a one-round knockout by future heavyweight champion Jack Sharkey. Delaney never threw a punch and it was speculated that he may have been intoxicated. After one more fight, Delaney retired, although he made a brief three-fight comeback in 1932. Delaney returned to Bridgeport where he operated a number of businesses. He also ran a tavern in New York and refereed. He died of cancer in 1948.

JACK DEMPSEY
The Nonpareil

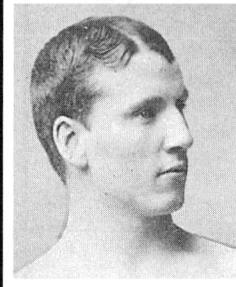

MIDDLEWEIGHT

Right-handed; 5'8"; 140–148 lbs.
64 bouts, 4/7/1883 to 1/18/1895
Middleweight Champion 1884–91
Hall of Fame Induction: 1992
Born: 12/15/1862, County Kildare, Ireland
Named: John Kelly
Died: 11/2/1895

Now largely overshadowed by his namesake, the heavyweight champion Jack Dempsey, the original Jack Dempsey was a boxer of enormous talent. At the peak of his career, he was the best around, which earned him the nickname "The Nonpareil" (without equal). Born in Ireland, Dempsey came to New York as a child and worked in a Brooklyn barrel factory before venturing into wrestling and then boxing. He turned professional as a lightweight in 1883, at the age of twenty.

Dempsey was unbeaten in his first fourteen fights. In 1884, he earned a chance to battle George Fulljames, who had recently claimed the middleweight championship. Dempsey knocked Fulljames out in the 22nd round to become the American—some said world—middleweight champion.

Fighting on both coasts, Dempsey remained undefeated until 1889 when he fought George LaBlanche in San Francisco. In their first encounter, three years before, Dempsey had knocked LaBlanche out in thirteen rounds. This time the two battled for 32 rounds. Dempsey was getting the better of LaBlanche when

Police intervened in the eleventh round to end the 1883 Coney Island, NY, bout between Jack Dempsey and Harry Force held in the shadow of the elevated train tracks. This was Dempsey's third recorded fight.

IN THE RING	WON 50	LOST 3	DRAWS 8	TB 64	KO 26	W 24	WF 0	D 8	KO'd 3	L 0	LF 0	NC 3

Date	Year	Opponent	Site	Result / Rounds		Title
SELECTED BOUTS						
Apr 7	1883	Ed McDonald	Maspeth, NY	KO	21	—
Aug 14	1883	Jack Boylan	Flushing, NY	KO	23	—
Sep 17	1883	Soap McAlpine	New York	D	4	—
Feb 28	1884	Jim Barry	New York	KO	3	—
Mar 2	1884	Joe Hennessey	New York	KO	4	—
Mar 4	1884	Tom Sullivan	New York	KO	2	—
Mar 6	1884	Bill Dacey	Coney Island, NY	KO	9	—
May 1	1884	Jack Bowles	New York	W	6	—
Jul 9	1884	Tom Henry	Rockaway, NY	NC	3	—
Jul 30	1884	George Fulljames	Great Kills, NY	KO	22	Won-Vac Amer-M
Sep 4	1884	Mike Dempsey	Rockaway	KO	7	—
Nov 30	1884	Mike Malone	Philadelphia	KO	2	—
Mar 19	1885	Charles Bixamos	New Orleans	KO	5	—
May 4	1885	Tom Barry	San Francisco	KO	5	—
Feb 3	1886	Jack Fogarty	New York	KO	27	Ret-Amer-M
Mar 14	1886	George LaBlanche	Larchmont, NY	KO	13	Ret-Amer-M
Dec 13	1887	Johnny Reagan	Manhasset, NY	TKO	45	Ret-Amer-M
Nov 15	1888	Mike Donovan ★	Brooklyn	D	6	—
Aug 22	1889	Mike Dempsey	San Francisco	KO	7	—
Aug 27	1889	George LaBlanche	San Francisco	KO'd	32	—
Feb 18	1890	Aus. Billy McCarthy	San Francisco	TKO	28	Won-World-M
Jan 14	1891	Bob Fitzsimmons ★	New Orleans	TKO'd	13	Lost-World-M
Mar 2	1893	Mike Keogh	Portland, OR	W	4	—
Sep 6	1894	Aus. Billy McCarthy	New Orleans	D	20	—
Jan 18	1895	♛ Tommy Ryan ★	Coney Island	TKO'd	3	For-World-W

the challenger executed a pivot punch which dropped Dempsey in his tracks. The pivot punch was thrown using a backhand motion so that the puncher's elbow, forearm, or fist would connect with the victim's head. This move was declared illegal, and though Dempsey lost the fight, he was permitted to retain the title.

Dempsey became undisputed middleweight champion with his victory over Australian Billy McCarthy. In 1891, he faced Hall of Famer Bob Fitzsimmons in New Orleans. Fitzsimmons, who would later go on to take the heavyweight championship, dominated the fight. He knocked Dempsey down thirteen times in thirteen rounds and pleaded with him to give up. Dempsey refused, reportedly saying, "A champion never quits." Finally, Dempsey went down in the thirteenth for the knockout defeat. A punch to the throat in this fight affected Dempsey's speech for the remainder of his life.

Though only 28 at the time of the Fitzsimmons fight, Dempsey fought only three more times. Hall of Famer Tommy Ryan stopped him in the third round in his final fight in 1895. By this time, Dempsey was already weakened by the tuberculosis which would claim his life later that year.

JACK DEMPSEY
The Manassa Mauler

HEAVYWEIGHT

Right-handed; 6'¾"; 170–195 lbs.

81 bouts, 8/17/1914 to 9/22/1927

Managers: Jack Kearns 1917–23, Leo P. Flynn 1927

Heavyweight Champion 1919–26

Hall of Fame Induction: 1990

Born: 6/24/1895, Manassa, CO

Named: William Harrison Dempsey

Died: 5/31/1983

A ferocious fighter and one of the Roaring Twenties' most famous personalities, Jack Dempsey embodied the spirit of a brash America that still had frontiers and believed anything was possible. From beginnings as an itinerant miner and fruit picker, Dempsey became a roughneck Adonis who ruled the ring as heavyweight champ. He married a Hollywood actress, cared enough about his appearance to have his flattened nose rebuilt, and always gave fight fans a show to remember.

Born in Manassa, Colorado, Dempsey came from a large, poor family. He managed to get through eighth grade before setting out on his own, following rumors of work from town to town. Like his two older brothers—professional boxers who both called themselves "Jack" Dempsey in honor of Jack Dempsey, The Nonpareil—Dempsey frequently tested his mettle in bars and saloons, challenging

Snarling with a terrible ferocity, Dempsey (R) follows a series of crushing uppercuts with left hooks to the face to take the heavyweight championship title from Jess Willard on Independence Day 1919.

IN THE RING	WON 61	LOST 6	DRAWS 8	TB 81	KO 50	W 10	WF 1	D 8	KO'd 1	L 5	LF 0	ND 6

Date	Year	Opponent	Site	Result / Rounds		Title

SELECTED BOUTS

Date	Year	Opponent	Site	Result	Rounds	Title
Aug 17	1914	Young Herman	Ramona, CO	D	6	—
Nov 2	1914	Young Hancock	Salt Lake City	KO	1	—
Jun 24	1916	Andre Anderson	New York	ND-W	10	—
Jul 8	1916	Wild Burt Kenny	New York	ND-W	10	—
Jul 14	1916	John Lester Johnson	New York	ND-D	10	—
Feb 13	1917	Jim Flynn	Murray, UT	KO'd	1	—
Mar 28	1917	Willie Meehan	Oakland	L	4	—
Aug 10	1917	Willie Meehan	San Francisco	D	4	—
Sep 7	1917	Willie Meehan	San Francisco	D	4	—
Oct 2	1917	Ed ("Gunboat") Smith	San Francisco	W	4	—
Feb 14	1918	Jim Flynn	Ft. Sheridan, IL	KO	1	—
May 3	1918	Billy Miske	St. Paul, MN	ND-W	10	—
Jul 27	1918	Fred Fulton	Harrison, NJ	KO	1	—
Sep 13	1918	Willie Meehan	San Francisco	L	4	—
Nov 6	1918	♛ Battling Levinsky	Philadelphia	KO	3	—
Nov 28	1918	Billy Miske	Philadelphia	ND-W	6	—
Dec 30	1918	Ed ("Gunboat") Smith	Buffalo, NY	KO	2	—
Jul 4	1919	♛ Jess Willard★	Toledo, OH	TKO	3	Won-World-H
Sep 6	1920	Billy Miske	Benton Harbor, MI	KO	3	Ret-World-H
Dec 14	1920	Bill Brennan	New York	KO	12	Ret-World-H
Jul 2	1921	Georges Carpentier★	Jersey City, NJ	KO	4	Ret-World-H
Jul 4	1923	Tommy Gibbons★	Shelby, MT	W	15	Ret-World-H
Sep 14	1923	Luis Angel Firpo	New York	KO	2	Ret-World-H
Sep 23	1926	⑩ Gene Tunney★	Philadelphia	L	10	Lost-World-H
Jul 21	1927	⑩ Jack Sharkey★	New York	KO	7	—
Sep 22	1927	♛ Gene Tunney★	Chicago	L	10	For-World-H

any man to beat him. He first fought professionally in 1914 and adopted the name "Jack" when his brothers retired.

At the start of his career, Dempsey fought mostly in the West. In 1917, he suffered his only knock-out loss when Fireman Jim Flynn leveled him in one round. Shortly afterward, Dempsey linked up with manager Jack Kearns, who guided him to the heavyweight title. Dempsey's record for the rest of 1917 and 1918 included fourteen one-round knockouts. Beautiful to watch in the ring, the great Western brawler's bobbing, weaving style inspired more than one writer to compare him to a coiled cobra.

In 1919, Dempsey took the heavyweight crown from Jess Willard, who out-weighed him by 58 pounds but fell victim to Dempsey's crouching, weaving attacks. Dempsey knocked Willard down seven times in the first round, then worried the exhausted champ through two more rounds for a TKO. Dempsey defended the title twice in 1920. The next year, promotional genius Tex Rickard set up a bout between Dempsey, an alleged draft-dodger, and French war hero Georges Carpentier. The title fight at Boyle's Thirty Acres in Jersey City broke all

Dempsey might have regained the championship in this 1927 fight in Chicago but was slow to go to a neutral corner after downing Gene Tunney. Tunney benefited from the "long count" and won in ten.

previous records for gate earnings. A throng of 80,000 paid nearly $1.8 million to see Dempsey knock out Carpentier in the fourth round.

Dempsey defended his title twice more in the next five years, earning a decision over Tommy Gibbons and knocking out Argentinian Luis Firpo in a topsy-turvy contest at New York's Polo Grounds. In the first round, Dempsey knocked Firpo down seven times, and Firpo knocked Dempsey down twice, once sending him through the ropes onto the press tables. The knockout came in the second round.

Dempsey never fought Hall of Famer Harry Wills, a top contender, because Rickard refused to arrange a mixed-race title bout. When the New York State Athletic Commission reacted by cancelling Dempsey's license to fight in that state, Rickard signed his star to fight Gene Tunney in Philadelphia in 1926. Tunney triumphed in a ten-round decision and took Dempsey's title.

A crowd of 102,000 filed into Soldier Field in Chicago to watch the championship rematch a year later. The match became famous as "The Battle of the Long

Count." Dempsey knocked down Tunney in the seventh, but the start of the count was delayed because Dempsey was unaware of Illinois boxing rules and was slow in going to a neutral corner. Tunney rose at the count of nine—although he had really been down for about fourteen seconds—and recovered to win a decision. Dempsey supporters believed that the fight turned on the referee's action, while Tunney partisans maintained that Tunney would have gotten up and won the fight anyway.

A few months later, Dempsey retired. He boxed exhibitions, managed and promoted fighters, and officiated at boxing and wrestling matches. Dempsey also served as a Commander in the Coast Guard in World War II and owned a popular New York City restaurant.

Luis Angel Firpo knocks Dempsey through the ropes and onto the press tables in New York's Polo Grounds in 1923. The champ scrambled back into the ring and knocked out Firpo in the second round.

JACK DILLON
The Hoosier Bearcat

LIGHT HEAVYWEIGHT

Right-handed; 5'7½"; 140–175 lbs.

245 bouts, 4/18/1908 to 1/12/1923

Managers: Sam Marburger 1912–20, Al Harter 1920–23

Light Heavyweight Champ 1914–16

Hall of Fame Induction: 1995

Born: 2/2/1891, Frankfort, IN

Named: Ernest Cutler Price

Died: 8/7/1942

Some called light heavyweight Jack Dillon "Jack the Giant Killer" for his ability to handle the most unstoppable heavyweights of the day. A prolific fighter who travelled the U.S. and Canada setting up fights as often as he could, Dillon had stamina, strength, and intelligence. He turned welterweight pro in his native Indiana at the age of seventeen, but soon moved up to the middleweight division and fought for two years before being handed his first loss, a ten-rounder with Eddie McGoorty.

In 1912, Dillon scored a third-round knockout against Hugo Kelly, and promptly claimed the world light heavyweight title, uncontested since Philadelphia Jack O'Brien had won it some years earlier. By 1914, Dillon was officially recognized as champion when he won a decision over Battling Levinsky. Later that year, a referee cut short a Dillon–K.O. Brown meeting after three rounds, saying the fighters were just going through the motions.

Dillon, who did sometimes carry weaker fighters, was apparently affected by the criticism that followed that bout and began to fight heavyweights who were invariably larger. He defeated such big men as Al Weinert, Tom Cowler, and Fireman Jim

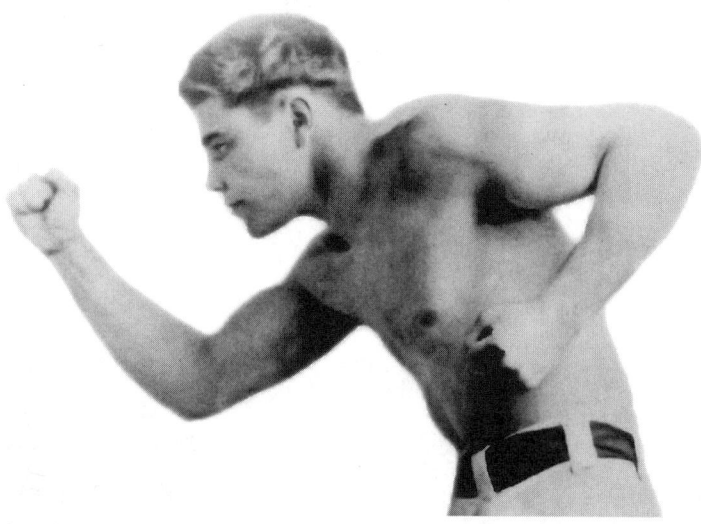

Dillon, here demonstrating his dangerous right uppercut, felled many a larger fighter. He first claimed the light heavyweight crown with his victories over Hugo Kelly in 1912 and Al Norton in 1914.

IN THE RING	WON 94	LOST 7	DRAWS 14	TB 245	KO 64	W 30	WF 0	D 14	KO'd 2	L 5	LF 0	ND 129	NC 1

Date	Year	Opponent	Site	Result / Rounds		Title
SELECTED BOUTS						
Apr 18	1908	Kid Brown	Indianapolis	D	6	—
Oct 21	1910	George Chip	Pittsburgh	ND-W	6	—
Jan 24	1911	George Chip	Dayton, OH	W	15	—
Apr 28	1911	George Chip	Terre Haute, IN	ND	10	—
Oct 23	1911	Battling Levinsky★	Philadelphia	ND-W	6	—
Feb 10	1912	George Chip	Pittsburgh	ND-W	6	—
Mar 23	1912	Frank Klaus	San Francisco	L	20	—
May 3	1912	Frank Klaus	New York	ND-L	10	—
May 28	1912	Hugo Kelly	Indianapolis	KO	3	—
Jul 25	1912	George Chip	Indianapolis	ND	10	—
Oct 19	1912	George Chip	Pittsburgh	ND-D	6	—
Apr 14	1913	George Chip	Youngstown, OH	ND-W	12	—
Apr 17	1913	Battling Levinsky★	Rochester, NY	ND-D	10	—
Apr 14	1914	Battling Levinsky★	Butte, MT	W	12	Won-Vac World-LH
May 29	1914	Battling Levinsky★	Indianapolis	ND-W	10	—
Jun 15	1914	Bob Moha	Butte	W	12	Ret-World-LH
Mar 16	1915	Ed ("Gunboat") Smith	Milwaukee	ND-W	10	—
Jul 5	1915	George Chip	Kansas City, MO	D	10	—
Jul 16	1915	Zulu Kid	Far Rockaway, NY	ND-W	10	—
Feb 8	1916	Battling Levinsky★	Brooklyn	ND-D	10	—
Mar 14	1916	Ed ("Gunboat") Smith	Brooklyn	ND-W	10	—
Apr 25	1916	Battling Levinsky★	Kansas City, MO	W	15	Ret-World-LH
Jul 13	1916	Battling Levinsky★	Baltimore	ND-L	10	—
Sep 12	1916	Battling Levinsky★	Memphis, TN	D	8	—
Oct 24	1916	Battling Levinsky★	Boston	L	12	Lost-World-LH
Nov 19	1916	Mike Gibbons★	St. Paul, MN	ND-L	10	—
Feb 16	1917	Ed ("Gunboat") Smith	New Orleans	W	20	—
Jul 30	1917	Harry Greb★	Pittsburgh	ND-L	10	—
Sep 3	1917	Mike Gibbons★	Terre Haute	ND-L	10	—
Oct 17	1917	Zulu Kid	Montreal	ND-W	10	—
Mar 4	1918	Harry Greb★	Toledo, OH	ND-L	12	—
Jan 12	1923	Joe Walters	Bicknell, IN	ND	10	—

Flynn. Dillon defeated Flynn twice, knocking him out in 1916 only a year after Flynn had defeated Jack Dempsey.

Dillon lost the world light heavyweight title to Battling Levinsky in 1916 in their ninth meeting. Levinsky employed ring science to avoid Dillon's still powerful punches and won on points. Dillon continued to fight for seven years after losing the title. A workmanlike fighter who did not vigorously seek the spotlight, Dillon's aggressive attacking style against bigger men won him a place in ring history. Dillon left boxing in 1923 not much richer than when he started. He retired to Florida where he lived next door to a small restaurant he owned and ran. He died in 1942.

DIXIE KID

WELTERWEIGHT

Right-handed; 5'8"; 138–155 lbs.

154 bouts, 3/2/1900 to 3/14/1920

Managers: Bill Jacobs, Charlie Gavin

Welterweight Championship Claims 1904–1912

Hall of Fame Induction: 2002

Born: 12/23/1883, Fulton, MO

Named: Aaron Lister Brown

Died: 4/6/1934

The Dixie Kid was born in Fulton, Missouri, and fought locally as an amateur with four bouts at age fifteen. By 1900, he had moved to California where he fought seventeen pro bouts in 1900 and 1901, compiling a record of 10–5–2. With age came more skill and power, and 1902 and 1903 saw the Kid win thirteen fights, twelve of them by knockout.

After recording knockouts over Al Neil and John Solomon in 1904, the Kid earned the chance to face Joe Walcott, the welterweight champion of the world. This meeting, on April 29, 1904, in San Francisco, was a rare championship bout in which both fighters were blacks. The more experienced Walcott—who had won the title from Jim ("Rube") Ferns two and one-half years earlier—held the advantage in the first nineteen rounds. In the twentieth, referee James ("Duck") Sullivan stopped the fight and awarded the title to the Kid on a foul. Walcott's manager, Hall of Famer Tom O'Rourke, stormed into the ring and punched Sullivan in the mouth; the promoter and fans who'd bet on Walcott stormed the ring. Sullivan escaped, but he never officiated another title bout. Later it was discovered that the referee had bet on the Kid.

No matter the controversy, the Kid claimed the championship. He fought non-title bouts in 1904 and 1905, including a six-round no-decision bout with Hall of Famer Philadelphia Jack O'Brien.

There are no recorded Dixie Kid fights from 1907 to 1908, while the Kid served a prison sentence for assault. Returning to the ring, the Kid's championship status was in doubt, and most boxing groups thought his title forfeit. He fought frequently in the next two years—primarily in no-decision bouts in Philly—but also in New York and Memphis. In a foray into Boston, he was knocked out by Hall of Famer Sam Langford and again the next time the pair met, in Memphis on January 10, 1910.

In 1911, the Kid left the U.S. to fight the rest of his career in England,

The Dixie Kid (C) is nicely turned out to watch the 1914 Jockeys and Variety Artists Football Match.

IN THE RING	WON **80**	LOST **29**	DRAWS **12**	TB 154	KO 58	W 19	WF 3	D 12	KO'd 6	L 20	LF 3	ND 30	NC 3

Date	Year	Opponent	Site	Result / Rounds		Title
SELECTED BOUTS						
Mar 2	1900	Cuter Kid	Los Angeles	D	3	—
Feb 14	1901	Henry Lewis	Stockton, CA	KO'd	4	—
Feb 9	1904	Al Neil	Oakland	KO	1	—
Feb 26	1904	John Solomon	Fresno, CA	KO	11	—
Apr 29	1904 ♛	Joe Walcott★	San Francisco	WF	20	Won-World-W*
Nov 12	1904	Philadelphia Jack O'Brien★	Philadelphia	ND-L	6	—
Dec 26	1904	Young Peter Jackson	Baltimore	D	15	—
Sep 28	1909	Sam Langford★	Boston	TKO'd	5	—
Jan 10	1910	Sam Langford★	Memphis, TN	KO'd	3	—
Nov 24	1910	Frank Mantell	Waterbury, CT	NC	4	—
Jan 17	1911	Mike ("Twin") Sullivan	Buffalo, NY	ND-D	10	—
Aug 29	1911	Georges Carpentier★	Trouville, France	TKO	5	—
Nov 9	1911	Johnny Summers	Liverpool, England	KO	2	Won-Vac GB World-W
Jan 18	1912 ♛	Harry Lewis	Liverpool	TKO'd	8	—
Apr 24	1912	George Bernard	Paris	KO	10	Ret-GB & France World-W
Oct 4	1912	Marcel Thomas	Paris	L	15	Lost-IBU World-W
Mar 14	1920	Paul Buisson	Marseille, France	L	12	—

*Result was suspect.

France, and Ireland. He knocked out Hall of Famer Georges Carpentier in Trouville, France, on August 29, 1911. When Harry Lewis, who had claimed the welterweight title in 1908, stopped the Kid in eight rounds on January 18, 1912, all doubt ended about the Kid's title contention.

In Paris on April 24, 1912, the Kid regained another welterweight title in a most unusual way when he met George Bernard of France in a twenty-rounder recognized by Britain and France as a championship bout. Late in the tenth, Bernard dropped to the canvas writhing from a claimed low blow. Referee Willie Lewis waited until after the start of the eleventh round to award the match to Bernard as a win by foul, but three doctors who examined him later were unconvinced. The decision was reversed, and the Dixie Kid was declared the winner.

The Kid continued to be a very active fighter for some four years after the Bernard fight, but his long career had taken its toll and his record was just 23-17-6. On March 14, 1920, he returned for one last fight, and lost a twelve-round decision to Paul Buisson in Marseille, France.

The Kid is often remembered for his unique fighting style—his hands at his sides, and his chin jutting towards his opponent, daring him to strike. Very fast and a master counterpuncher, his favorite move was a right uppercut, followed by a left hook to the head.

Extremely inventive outside the ring, the Kid was granted a number of patents in the 1920s, but as time passed he sank into a world of drug abuse and squandered his ring earnings. On April 6, 1934, the penniless Kid fell from a tenement window in Los Angeles, by accident or by design, and died.

GEORGE DIXON
Little Chocolate

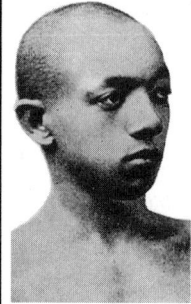

FEATHERWEIGHT

Right-handed; 5'3½"; 101–126 lbs.

130 bouts, 11/1/1886 to 12/10/1906

Manager: Tom O'Rourke

Bantamweight Champion 1890-92

Featherweight Champion 1893–96, 1897, 1898–1900

Hall of Fame Induction: 1990

Born: 7/29/1870, Halifax, Nova Scotia, Canada

George Dixon became the first black man to win a world boxing title when he captured the bantamweight crown in England and then successfully defended it in America. He later added the world featherweight title, which he held for a total of eight years. Considered to be one of the finest small boxers ever, Dixon was well-respected for both his grace and power. He became interested in fighting while assisting a photographer who took posed boxing pictures. Dixon entered the pro ring in his native Halifax, Nova Scotia, in 1886 at the age of sixteen.

Under the guidance of manager Tom O'Rourke, Dixon fought Cal McCarthy at the Union Athletic Club in Boston in 1890 for the American version of the featherweight title. Wearing two-ounce gloves, Dixon and McCarthy battled for 70 rounds, only to have the exhausting fight called a draw. That same year Dixon travelled to England to face Nunc Wallace, the holder of the British version of the world bantamweight title. Dixon easily vanquished Wallace, scoring a knockout in the eighteenth round.

Dixon returned to America to lay further claim to the title by knocking out bantamweight challenger Johnny Murphy. Dixon also knocked out McCarthy in a rematch in 1891. By 1892, he had outgrown the bantamweight division and began competing solely as a featherweight. With a fourteenth-round knockout of Fred Johnson in Coney Island in 1892, Dixon asserted his claim to the featherweight title.

Dixon participated in the three-day Carnival of Champions at the Olympia Club in New Orleans, where most of boxing's top contenders met. Dixon was matched against the amateur champion Jack Skelly,

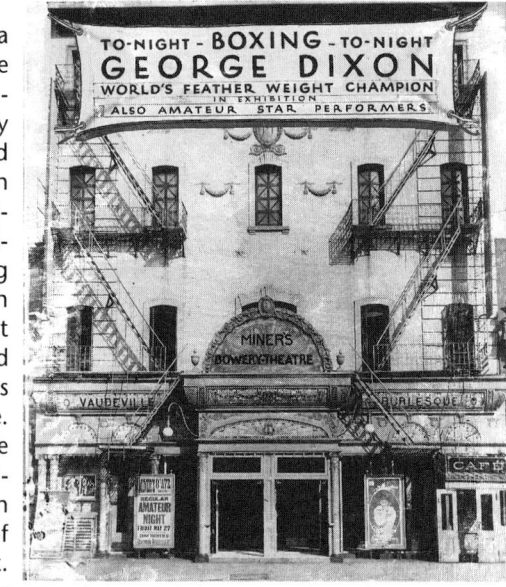

Including the hundreds of unrecorded exhibitions in vaudeville halls, Dixon may have fought as many as 800 times.

IN THE RING	WON 50	LOST 26	DRAWS 44	TB 130	KO 27	W 22	WF 1	D 44	KO'd 5	L 20	LF 1	ND 7	NC 3

Date	Year	Opponent	Site	Result / Rounds		Title
SELECTED BOUTS						
Nov 1	1886	Young Johnson	Halifax, N.S.	KO	3	—
Feb 7	1890	Cal McCarthy	Boston	D	70	For-Amer-115 lbs
Jun 27	1890	♛ Nunc Wallace	London	KO	18	Won-Vac World-114 lbs
Oct 23	1890	Johnny Murphy	Providence, RI	KO	40	Ret-World-114 lbs
Mar 31	1891	Cal McCarthy	Troy, NY	KO	22	Won-World-115 lbs
Jul 28	1891	Abe Willis	San Francisco	KO	5	Ret-World-115 lbs
Jun 27	1892	Fred Johnson	Coney Island, NY	KO	14	Won-World-118 lbs
Sep 6	1892	Jack Skelly	New Orleans	KO	8	Ret-World-118 lbs
Aug 7	1893	Eddie Pierce	Coney Island	KO	3	Won-World-120 lbs
Sep 25	1893	Solly Smith	Coney Island	KO	7	Ret-World-120 lbs
Jun 29	1894	Young Griffo★	Boston	D	20	—
Jan 19	1895	Young Griffo★	Coney Island	D	25	—
Aug 27	1895	Johnny Griffin	Boston	W	25	Won-World-126 lbs
Oct 28	1895	Young Griffo★	New York	D	10	—
Nov 27	1896	Frank Erne	New York	L	20	For-World-122 lbs
Mar 24	1897	Frank Erne	New York	W	25	Won-World-122 lbs
Oct 4	1897	Solly Smith	San Francisco	L	20	Lost-World-120 lbs
Jun 6	1898	Eddie Santry	New York	W	20	Ret-World-122 lbs
Jul 1	1898	Ben Jordan	New York	L	25	Lost-World-122 lbs
Nov 11	1898	♛ Dave Sullivan	New York	WD	10	Reg-World-122 lbs
Nov 29	1898	Oscar Gardner	New York	W	25	Ret-World-122 lbs
Jan 17	1899	Young Pluto	New York	KO	10	—
May 15	1899	Kid Broad	Buffalo, NY	W	20	Won-World-124 lbs
Jun 2	1899	Joe Bernstein	New York	W	25	Ret-World-124 lbs
Jul 11	1899	Tommy White	Denver	W	20	Won-World-125 lbs
Aug 11	1899	Eddie Santry	New York	D	20	Ret-World-125 lbs
Nov 2	1899	Will Curley	New York	W	25	Ret-World-FE
Nov 21	1899	Eddie Lenny	New York	W	25	Ret-World-FE
Jan 9	1900	Terry McGovern★	New York	TKO'd	8	Lost-World-118 lbs
Jun 23	1900	♛ Terry McGovern★	Chicago	L	6	—
Aug 24	1901	Abe Attell★	Denver	D	10	—
Oct 20	1901	Abe Attell★	Cripple Creek, CO	D	20	—
Oct 28	1901	Abe Attell★	St. Louis	L	15	—
Jan 24	1903	Jim Driscoll★	London	D	6	—
Dec 10	1906	Monk the Newsboy	Providence	L	15	—

who was white. Dixon controlled the action from the start, broke Skelly's nose, and knocked him out in the eighth. White fans at the match reacted with shock and disgust, and to keep peace, the Olympia Club decided not to conduct any more mixed-race matches. The racist reaction to this fight led to limited black access to other matches, including heavyweight championships.

A long string of title defenses was interrupted by only a few quickly-avenged defeats. Terry McGovern finally bested Dixon in 1900 to take the crown away. Dixon lost a non-title rematch with McGovern and never again contended for the title, though he continued to fight until 1906. Dixon died, penniless, two years after retiring.

JIM DRISCOLL
Peerless Jim

FEATHERWEIGHT

Right-handed; 5'6"; 122–126 lbs.
69 bouts, 1901 to 10/20/1919
Manager: Charles Harvey
British World Featherweight
Champion 1912–13
Hall of Fame Induction: 1990
Born: 12/15/1880, Cardiff, Wales
Died: 1/31/1925

Like Jimmy Wilde before him, Welshman Jim Driscoll (also known as Jem Driscoll) got his start fighting in the boxing booths of the British Isles. There a fighter offered all comers a chance to beat him. After fighting hundreds of bouts in the booths, Driscoll turned professional in 1901 at the age of eighteen and promptly won his first ten fights by knockout. In his next fight, he decisioned Joe Ross to win the Welsh featherweight title. Driscoll was quick and elusive in the ring. He had great hand speed, which he combined with enough power to rack up 35 knockouts in 69 fights.

In 1907, Driscoll won the vacant British featherweight title with a seventeenth-round knockout of Joe Bowker. After adding the British Empire featherweight title in 1908, Driscoll avenged one of the few defeats of his career by beating Harry Mansfield in a rematch. He next travelled to the United States, where he won a newspaper decision over the tough Leach Cross. Driscoll fought a no-decision match with world featherweight champ Abe Attell at the National Athletic Club

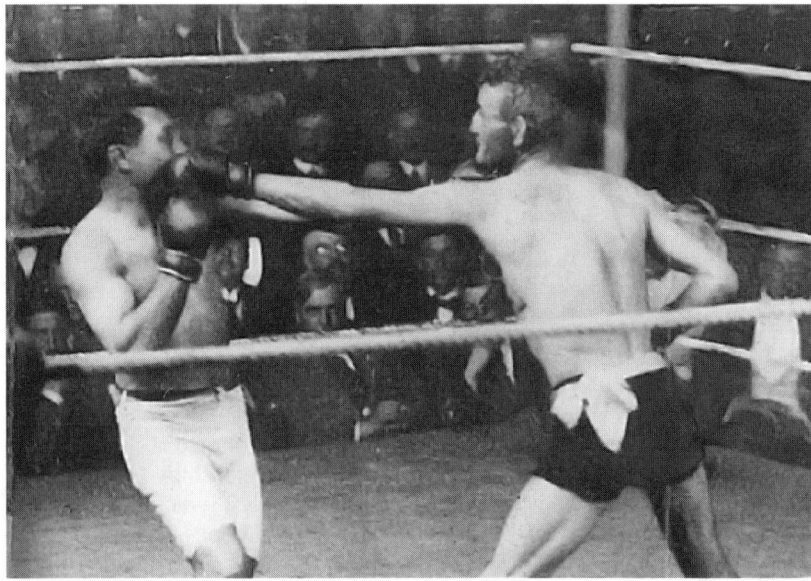

Charles Ledoux (L) handed Driscoll his only knock-out loss, in the last fight of Driscoll's career, at the National Sporting Club of London, in 1919. Here Driscoll holds Ledoux at bay with his jab.

IN THE RING	WON 52	LOST 3	DRAWS 6	TB 69	KO 35	W 15	WF 2	D 6	KO'd 1	L 1	LF 1	ND 8

Date	Year	Opponent	Site	Result / Rounds		Title
SELECTED BOUTS						
—	1901	Bill Radford	Cardiff, Wales	KO	2	—
Dec 24	1901	Joe Ross	Cardiff	W	10	Won-Wales-FE
Sep 29	1902	Harry Mansfield	Cardiff	D	10	—
Jan 24	1903	George Dixon★	London	W	6	—
—	1903	Harry Mansfield	Cardiff	W	10	—
—	1903	Harry Mansfield	Cardiff	W	6	—
Aug 29	1904	Harry Mansfield	Cardiff	L	10	—
Dec 26	1905	Harry Mansfield	Wednesbury, Eng.	TKO	15	—
May 28	1906	Joe Bowker	London	W	15	—
Jun 3	1907	Joe Bowker	London	KO	17	Won-Vac Britain-FE
Feb 24	1908	Charlie Griffin	London	WF	15	Won-Vac Brit Emp-FE
Aug 17	1908	Harry Mansfield	Cardiff	W	6	—
Nov 13	1908	Matty Baldwin	New York	ND-W	6	—
Dec 29	1908	Matty Baldwin	Boston	W	12	—
Feb 10	1909	Leach Cross	New York	ND-W	10	—
Feb 19	1909	♛ Abe Attell★	New York	ND-W	10	—
Feb 14	1910	Seaman Arthur Hayes	London	TKO	6	Ret-Britain-FE
Apr 18	1910	Spike Robson	London	KO	15	Ret-Britain-FE
May 25	1910	Pal Moore	Philadelphia	ND-D	6	—
Dec 20	1910	Freddie Welsh★	Cardiff	LF	10	—
Jan 30	1911	Spike Robson	London	TKO	11	Ret-Britain-FE
Jun 3	1912	Jean Poesy	London	KO	12	Won-Vac Eur & Vac Brit World-FE
Jan 27	1913	Owen Moran★	London	D	20	Ret-Brit, Eur & Brit World-FE
Mar 10	1919	Pedlar Palmer	London	TKO	4	—
Oct 20	1919	Charles Ledoux	London	TKO'd	16	—

in New York. Though Driscoll failed to knock Attell out, he completely dominated the fight. Driscoll left the ring unmarked, but Attell had one eye closed and a badly swollen nose. Driscoll later claimed that he and Attell had agreed that the title would change hands based on the newspaper decision, the unofficial vote by ringside reporters. Attell, who had clearly been outboxed, did not acknowledge that such an agreement had been made.

After the Attell fight, Driscoll went back to Britain, returning to the United States only once more, to fight Pal Moore in Philadelphia. In 1912, Driscoll knocked out Jean Poesy in twelve rounds to win the vacant British and European world featherweight titles. The next year, Driscoll retired undefeated. He served in the British military during World War I, then attempted a comeback in 1919. He fought twice before losing to Charles Ledoux by a technical knockout. Driscoll was ahead in the Ledoux fight but became exhausted by the sixteenth round. After this defeat, Driscoll quit the ring for good. He was suffering from tuberculosis, and six years later died of pneumonia after a long stretch of ill health.

JOHNNY DUNDEE
The Scotch Wop

FEATHERWEIGHT

Right-handed; 5'4½"; 120–130 lbs.

335 bouts, 8/10/1910 to 12/5/1932

Managers: Scotty Monteith 1910–20, Jimmy Johnston 1920–29

Jr Lightwt Champ 1921–23, 1923–24
NY World Featherwt Champ 1922–23
Featherweight Champion 1923–24

Hall of Fame Induction: 1991

Born: 11/22/1893, Sciacca, Sicily, Italy

Named: Giuseppe Carrora

Died: 4/22/1965

Johnny Dundee fought an amazing 335 times from 1910 until 1932. In 1911 alone, he entered the ring 47 times, enough to equal an entire career for many fighters. A master of ring trickery and dazzling footwork, Dundee presented a variety of styles which opponents found very difficult to decipher. He was especially adept at launching punches while bouncing off the ropes. Not much of a knockout artist, Dundee nevertheless outboxed the best fighters of his era.

Born in Italy as Giuseppe Carrora, Dundee was brought to New York as an infant and grew up in "Hell's Kitchen," where his family ran a fish market. Dundee was a street brawler who caught the attention of manager Scotty Monteith. Monteith gave his young charge a new name and shaped his early career. Dundee never fought as an amateur, but went right into professional boxing at age sixteen. More than half of his bouts were no-decisions, although newspaper reporters at ringside declared him the winner of a majority of these matches.

In 1913, Dundee travelled to California to face world featherweight champion Johnny Kilbane, another boxer with an inscrutable style. The referee stopped the match in the twentieth round and declared it a draw, but most observers thought Dundee appeared to be winning. Dundee fought eight no-decision bouts against Hall

Dundee might have enjoyed a better record if he had always fought as a featherweight. He was less successful as a lightweight.

IN THE RING	WON 90	LOST 31	DRAWS 19	TB 335	KO 22	W 67	WF 1	D 19	KO'd 2	L 29	LF 0	ND 194	NC 1

Date	Year		Opponent	Site	Result / Rounds		Title
SELECTED BOUTS							
Aug 10	1910		Skinny Bob	New York	ND-L	4	—
Sep 4	1912	♛	Johnny Kilbane ★	New York	ND-L	10	—
Apr 29	1913	♛	Johnny Kilbane ★	Vernon, CA	D	20	For-World-FE
Jan 1	1914		Freddie Welsh ★	New Orleans	ND-L	10	—
Mar 2	1915		Benny Leonard ★	New York	ND-W	10	—
Mar 8	1916		Benny Leonard ★	New York	ND-L	10	—
Jun 12	1916		Benny Leonard ★	New York	ND-W	10	—
Nov 15	1916		Benny Leonard ★	Philadelphia	ND-W	6	—
Mar 26	1917		Lew Tendler ★	Philadelphia	ND	6	—
Oct 1	1917		Lew Tendler ★	Philadelphia	ND	6	—
Jan 20	1919	♛	Benny Leonard ★	Newark	ND-L	8	—
Jun 16	1919	♛	Benny Leonard ★	Philadelphia	ND-D	6	—
Sep 17	1919	♛	Benny Leonard ★	Newark, NJ	ND-D	8	—
Feb 9	1920	♛	Benny Leonard ★	Jersey City, NJ	ND-L	8	—
Nov 18	1921		George ("K.O.") Chaney	New York	WF	5	Won-Vac World-JL
May 5	1922		Lew Tendler ★	Philadelphia	L	15	—
Jul 6	1922		Jack Sharkey ★	New York	W	15	Ret-World-JL
Aug 15	1922		Danny Frush	Brooklyn	KO	9	Won-Vac NY World-FE
Aug 28	1922		Pepper Martin	New York	W	15	Ret-World-JL
Feb 2	1923		Elino Flores	New York	W	15	Ret-World-JL
May 30	1923		Jack Bernstein	New York	L	15	Lost-World-JL
Jul 26	1923	♛	Eugene Criqui ★	New York	W	15	Won-World-FE
Dec 17	1923	♛	Jack Bernstein	New York	W	15	Reg-World-JL
Jun 20	1924	⑩	Kid Sullivan	Brooklyn	L	10	Lost-World-JL
Oct 24	1927	⑩	Tony Canzoneri ★	New York	L	15	For-Vac World-FE
Dec 5	1932		Mickey Greb	Orange, NJ	W	6	—

of Famer Benny Leonard between 1915 and 1920. Though Leonard generally had the edge, newspaper accounts gave Dundee three of these battles. In 1921, Dundee faced George ("K.O.") Chaney for the vacant world junior lightweight title and won on a foul in the fifth round. While still holding that title, Dundee faced Danny Frush for what was, in some circles, considered to be the world featherweight title. Dundee knocked Frush out in the ninth round, for the last knockout of his career.

In 1923, Dundee lost the junior lightweight title to Jack Bernstein, but regained it in their rematch. Then Dundee conquered Eugene Criqui, the generally accepted featherweight champion, in a bout at New York's Polo Grounds. With 40,000 fans watching, Dundee dominated the fight and won the championship. In 1924, he lost the junior lightweight title and gave up the featherweight title because he could no longer make the weight. Dundee continued to fight until 1932 but his best days were clearly behind him. He lost most of his ring earnings investing in a mediocre stable of race horses.

SIXTO ESCOBAR

BANTAMWEIGHT

Right-handed; 5'4"; 115–121 lbs.

72 bouts, 9/1/1930 to 12/2/1940

Managers: Arturo Gigante 1930–34, Lou Brix 1934–40

NBA Bantamweight Champion 1934–35, 1935–1936

Bantamweight Champion 1936–37, 1938–39

Hall of Fame Induction: 2002

Born: 3/23/1913, Barceloneta, Puerto Rico

Died: 11/17/1979

Sixto Escobar was the first world champion to come from Puerto Rico. He was the sixth child of a labor boss in the sugar cane fields in Barceloneta, a small town west of San Juan. Though his father was massively built, Sixto never grew taller than 5'4".

Escobar fought 23 times as an amateur, winning all but three. He turned professional at seventeen in a six-round decision over Luis Perez in September 1930. Though the earliest fights were in San Juan, he soon moved to Venezuela, where he lost a bid for that country's lightweight title on March 19, 1932.

In 1934, Escobar exploded onto the world boxing stage in Holyoke, Massachusetts, where he knocked out bantamweight contender Bobby Leitham in the seventh round. Two weeks later he defeated future featherweight champion Joey Archibald in a ten-round decision. After knocking out Leitham yet again, Escobar faced Baby Casanova in Montreal on June 26, 1934, for the vacant NBA bantamweight title. Escobar knocked Casanova out in nine rounds to win NBA recognition as the bantamweight titleholder.

On August 7, 1935, he fought Pete Sanstol in a bout at the Montreal Forum in front of 10,000 fans. Escobar started out strong, and by the end of the ninth, Sanstol's face was so swollen that his left eye was completely closed. Escobar won the twelve-round decision.

In his next fight on August 26, Escobar put his title on the line against Lou Salica in Madison Square Garden. Salica won the fifteen-round decision, but in the rematch, less than three months later, Escobar regained the NBA crown, again by decision. On August 31, 1936, Escobar met Tony Marino, the acknowledged world title-holder. Escobar knocked

"On your mark!" Escobar poses for a photo with some young female sprinters.

IN THE RING	WON 46	LOST 23	DRAWS 3	TB 72	KO 22	W 24	WF 0	D 3	KO'd 0	L 23	LF 0

Date	Year	Opponent	Site	Result / Rounds		Title
SELECTED BOUTS						
Sep 1	1930	Luis Perez	San Juan, PR	W	6	—
Nov 15	1931	Enrique Chafferdet	Caracas	L	10	—
Mar 19	1932	Jose T. Rosales	Caracas	L	12	For-Venezuela-FE
Jan 9	1933	Enrique Chafferdet	Caracas	D	10	—
Feb 11	1933	Enrique Chafferdet	Caracas	L	10	—
May 7	1934	⑩ Bobby Leitham	Holyoke, MA	KO	7	—
Jun 5	1934	⑩ Bobby Leitham	Montreal	TKO	5	—
Jun 26	1934	⑩ Baby Casanova	Montreal	KO	9	Won-Vac NBA-B
Aug 8	1934	Eugene Huat	Montreal	W	15	Ret-NBA-B
May 28	1935	⑩ Joey Archibald	New York	KO	6	—
Aug 7	1935	Pete Sanstol	Montreal	W	12	—
Aug 26	1935	⑩ Lou Salica	New York	L	15	Lost-NBA-B
Nov 15	1935	♛ Lou Salica	New York	W	15	Reg-NBA-B
Aug 31	1936	♛ Tony Marino	New York	TKO	13	Won-World-B
Oct 5	1936	⑩ Harry Jeffra	Baltimore	L	10	—
Oct 13	1936	Carlos ("Indian") Quintana	New York	TKO	1	Ret-World-B
Dec 9	1936	⑩ Harry Jeffra	New York	L	10	—
Feb 21	1937	⑩ Lou Salica	San Juan	W	15	Ret-World-B
Sep 23	1937	⑩ Harry Jeffra	New York	L	15	Lost-World-B
Feb 20	1938	♛ Harry Jeffra	San Juan	W	15	Reg-World-B
Apr 19	1938	⑩ K.O. Morgan	Detroit	L	10	—
Nov 1	1938	⑩ Henry Hook	Toronto	L	10	—
Apr 2	1939	⑩ K.O. Morgan	San Juan	W	15	Ret-World-B
Aug 14	1939	Jimmy Perrin	New Orleans	L	10	—
Oct 4	1939	⑩ Tony Olivera	Oakland	L	10	—

Marino out in thirteen rounds to become the undisputed bantamweight champion of the world.

Later that year, Escobar lost two non-title fights to Harry Jeffra. After another successful defense in San Juan against Salica, Escobar put up his belt against Jeffra on September 23, 1937, at the Polo Grounds in a fight night dubbed "The Carnival of Champions." Escobar lost his crown in a fifteen-round decision.

In the rematch on February 20, 1938, at Escambron Beach Park in San Juan stadium which was named in his honor, Escobar delighted his fans when he decisioned Jeffra to retake the title, but after this fight his career quickly deteriorated. When Jeffra defeated him on December 2, 1940, Escobar retired, though he was only 27.

In the ring, Escobar became best known for a lethal right cross and for his great stamina. He was never knocked out. Escobar moved forward, throwing left jabs and hooks to create an opening for his magnificent right. In retirement, he served in the U.S. Army in World War II, owned real estate in Puerto Rico, and worked in public relations.

JACKIE FIELDS

WELTERWEIGHT

Right-handed; 5'7½"; 135–153 lbs.

86 bouts, 2/6/1925 to 5/2/1933

Managers: Willis ("Gig") Rooney 1924–28, Jack Kearns 1929–32

1924 Olympic Featherweight Gold Medalist

Welterweight Champ 1929–30, 1932–33

Hall of Fame Induction: 2004

Born: 2/9/1908, Chicago, IL

Named: Jacob Finkelstein

Died: 6/3/1987

Jackie Fields rose to boxing prominence at the young age of sixteen when he won the gold medal in the featherweight division at the 1924 Olympic Games in Paris. Fields was born Jacob Finkelstein in Chicago on February 9, 1908. When he was fourteen, he moved with his family to Los Angeles.

A friend encouraged Fields to go to the Los Angeles Athletic Club and ask George Blake to teach him how to box. Blake was impressed with Fields's potential and began to train the young boxer. In 1924, he lost in the semi-finals of the qualifying tournament for berths in the featherweight division on the U.S. Olympic boxing team. At the time the United States could send two fighters in each weight class. Fields and Patsy Ruffalo, the other semi-final loser, were chosen as alternates. Fields, however, so impressed the coaches in training that he was chosen to represent the United States along with fellow Californian Joe Salas. The Americans both won all their matches until they met in the finals. Fields decisioned Salas to win the gold medal.

Even though he was only sixteen, Fields turned professional. On November 12, 1925, he had his first fight with a name opponent, Hall of Famer Jimmy McLarnin, who at the time was the third-ranked featherweight. The more experienced McLarnin had little trouble with Fields, knocking him out in the second round. Fields's jaw was broken, and he did not fight for four months. This was the only time that he was knocked out.

In 1928, Fields defeated such highly rated fighters as Vince Dundee (twice), Farmer Joe Cooper, Young Jack Thompson, and Sergeant Sammy Baker. *The Ring* rated him as the top contender for the welterweight crown held by Joe Dundee, but Dundee was unwilling to risk his championship. As a result, the National Boxing Association stripped Dundee of the title and sanctioned a bout for its welterweight crown between Fields and Young Jack

Jackie Fields faced the leading featherweights, lightweights, and welterweights of his day.

IN THE RING	WON 72	LOST 9	DRAWS 2	TB 86	KO 31	W 40	WF 1	D 2	KO'd 1	L 8	LF 0	ND 2	NC 1

Date	Year	Opponent	Site	Result / Rounds		Title
SELECTED BOUTS						
Feb 6	1925	Benny Pascal	Pasadena, CA	W	6	—
Nov 12	1925	⓾ Jimmy McLarnin ★	Los Angeles	KO'd	2	—
Apr 4	1927	♛ Sammy Mandell ★	Los Angeles	ND-D	12	—
Jun 15	1927	⓾ Louis ("Kid") Kaplan ★	New York	L	10	—
Feb 23	1928	♛ Sammy Mandell ★	Chicago	L	10	—
Jul 13	1928	⓾ Farmer Joe Cooper	San Francisco	W	10	—
Oct 1	1928	⓾ Young Jack Thompson	San Francisco	W	10	—
Oct 30	1928	⓾ Sammy Baker	San Francisco	KO	2	—
Mar 25	1929	⓾ Young Jack Thompson	Chicago	W	10	Won-Vac NBA-W
Jul 25	1929	♛ Joe Dundee	Detroit	WF	2	Won-World-W
Oct 2	1929	⓾ Vince Dundee	Chicago	W	10	—
Oct 21	1929	⓾ Gorilla Jones	San Francisco	W	10	—
Feb 22	1930	⓾ Young Corbett III ★	San Francisco	L	10	—
May 9	1930	⓾ Young Jack Thompson	Detroit	L	15	Lost-World-W
Jan 28	1932	♛ Lou Brouillard ★	Chicago	W	10	Reg-World-W
Feb 22	1933	Young Corbett III ★	San Francisco	L	10	Lost-World-W
May 2	1933	Young Peter Jackson	Los Angeles	W	10	—

Thompson in Chicago on March 25, 1929. Fields dominated the action at the Coliseum, winning a ten-round decision.

Some still considered Dundee the welterweight champion. On July 25, 1929, Fields met Dundee to unify the title. Fields knocked Dundee down five times in the first two rounds. After the last knockdown, Dundee crawled across the ring and punched Fields below the belt. Fields flopped to the canvas—losing consciousness from the pain. Dundee was disqualified on the foul, and Fields was champion. Reportedly, Dundee and his handlers had a large sum of money riding on the fight—but all bets were off if the fight ended on a foul. When it was clear to Dundee that he wouldn't win, he fouled Fields.

Defending the title in a rematch with Thompson, Fields lost a fifteen-round decision. Fields considered retirement, but his new manager, Doc Kearns, promised to get him a shot at the title. Kearns got Fields an opportunity against the new welterweight champ, Lou Brouillard, on January 28, 1932. Fields knocked Brouillard down in the eighth en route to winning back the crown by decision.

In an automobile accident later that year, Fields suffered an eye injury that surgery failed to correct. The tough Fields, a consummate ring technician though not a knockout artist, refused to retire. On February 22, 1933, he gave Corbett a chance at his title. Corbett took a close ten-round decision. Fields soon retired.

Fields suffered financial reverses in the Depression. Following his ring career, he worked as an assistant unit manager for Twentieth Century Fox, a film editor for MGM, a distributor for Wurlitzer juke boxes, a salesman for J & B Scotch, and as public relations director of the Tropicana Hotel in Las Vegas. He was also Vice Chairman of the Nevada State Athletic Commission. Fields died on June 3, 1987.

BOB FITZSIMMONS
Ruby Robert

HEAVYWEIGHT

Right-handed; 5'11¾"; 150–175 lbs.

115 bouts, 1883 to 2/20/1914

Manager: Martin Julian

Middleweight Champion 1891–97
Heavyweight Champion 1897–99
Light Heavywt. Champion 1903–05

Hall of Fame Induction: 1990

Born: 5/26/1863, Helston, Cornwall, England

Named: Robert James Fitzsimmons

Died: 10/22/1917

The first triple titleholder in history, Bob Fitzsimmons won the world middleweight, heavyweight, and light heavyweight championships in a career that spanned 27 years. As a young man, Fitzsimmons worked as a blacksmith, and his punches held the power of an iron hammer hitting an anvil. He defied age, consistently fought larger men, and was crafty and resilient in the ring.

Born in England, Fitzsimmons moved to New Zealand with his family as a small boy. School was a luxury and, before long, Fitzsimmons went to work as a carriage painter and in a foundry. His interest in boxing heated up when he entered an amateur boxing tournament supervised by visiting Hall of Famer Jem Mace. Weighing just 140 pounds, Fitzsimmons knocked out four larger opponents and won the heavyweight division of the contest.

In 1885, Fitzsimmons moved to Australia, where most of his early professional bouts took place. Over the next seven years, he posted a record of 21-2, with 24 no-decisions. In 1890, he travelled to America where three knockout bouts earned him a chance to fight world middleweight champion Jack Dempsey ("The Nonpareil"). Fitzsimmons proved to be more than Dempsey's equal and, after a vicious battle, he knocked the champion out in the thirteenth round.

Fitzsimmons defended his middleweight crown just once before aiming at the heavyweight title. He knocked out fellow contender Peter Maher in one round in 1896 and, later that year, delivered an eighth-round wallop that floored heavyweight Tom Sharkey. Referee Wyatt Earp, the former lawman, called the punch a low blow and disqualified Fitzsimmons, to the dismay of most observers, who thought the punch was fair.

In 1897, Fitzsimmons faced heavyweight champion James J. Corbett in Carson City, Nevada for the title. The balding, spindly

Fitzsimmons (L) parries a blow from the scantily-clad James J. Corbett, as he heads toward a 14th-round knockout and the title.

IN THE RING	WON **74**	LOST **8**	DRAWS **3**	TB 115	KO 67	W 7	WF 0	D 3	KO'd 7	L 0	LF 1	ND 30

Date	Year	Opponent	Site	Result / Rounds		Title
SELECTED BOUTS						
—	1883	Arthur Cooper	Timaru, NZ	KO	3	—
Feb 11	1888	Billy McCarthy	Sydney	ND	4	—
Nov 10	1888	Jim Hall	Sydney	ND	4	—
Nov 24	1888	Jim Hall	Sydney	ND	4	—
Nov 30	1889	Professor West	Sydney	KO	1	—
Feb 10	1890	Jim Hall	Sydney	KO'd	4	For-Australia-M
May 17	1890	Frank Allen	San Francisco	TKO	1	—
May 29	1890	Aus. Billy McCarthy	San Francisco	KO	5	—
Jan 14	1891	♛ Jack Dempsey (Nonpareil)★	New Orleans	TKO	13	Won-World-M
Mar 2	1892	Peter Maher	New Orleans	KO	12	—
Mar 8	1893	Jim Hall	New Orleans	KO	4	—
Jun 17	1894	Joe Choynski★	Boston	D	5	—
Sep 26	1894	Dan Creedon	New Orleans	KO	2	Ret-World-M
Feb 21	1896	Peter Maher	Langtry, TX	KO	1	—
Dec 2	1896	Tom Sharkey★	San Francisco	LF	8	—
Mar 17	1897	♛ James J. Corbett★	Carson City, NV	KO	14	Won-World-H
Jun 9	1899	James J. Jeffries★	Coney Island, NY	KO'd	11	Lost-World-H
Apr 30	1900	Ed Dunkhorst	Brooklyn	KO	2	—
Aug 10	1900	Gus Ruhlin	New York	KO	6	—
Aug 24	1900	Tom Sharkey★	Coney Island	KO	2	—
Jul 25	1902	♛ James J. Jeffries★	San Francisco	KO'd	8	For-World-H
Nov 25	1903	♛ George Gardner	San Francisco	W	20	Won-World-LH
Jul 23	1904	Phila. Jack O'Brien★	Philadelphia	ND-L	6	—
Dec 20	1905	Phila. Jack O'Brien★	San Francisco	TKO'd	13	Lost-World-LH
Jul 17	1907	Jack Johnson★	Philadelphia	KO'd	2	—
Dec 27	1909	Bill Lang	Sydney	KO'd	12	For-Australia-H
Feb 20	1914	Jersey Bellew	Bethlehem, PA	ND-W	6	—

legged Fitzsimmons (John L. Sullivan called him "a fighting machine on stilts") did not look like a potential heavyweight champion. He was 34 years old, to Corbett's 30, and weighed sixteen pounds less. Corbett landed seriously damaging blows for most of the fight. Fitzsimmons was bleeding badly, but his blacksmith's arm won him the fight in the fourteenth round when he slammed a paralyzing blow into Corbett's solar plexis, the nerve center just below the breastbone. Corbett went down with a horrified gasp, and Fitzsimmons took the title. He wore the crown for two uncontested years before losing it to James J. Jeffries, who knocked him out in the eleventh round.

Fitzsimmons continued boxing and in 1903, at 40 years old, he knocked George Gardner down four times in twenty rounds to win the light heavyweight title. He lost the title to Philadelphia Jack O'Brien in 1905 but continued to fight on and off for the next nine years. He lost a two-round knockout to Jack Johnson in one of his last fights. In retirement, Fitzsimmons toured the vaudeville circuit before becoming an evangelist.

TIGER FLOWERS
The Georgia Deacon

MIDDLEWEIGHT

Left-handed; 5'10"; 157–169 lbs.
157 bouts, 1918 to 11/12/1927
Manager: Walk Miller
Middleweight Champion 1926
Hall of Fame Induction: 1993
Born: 8/5/1895, Camille, GA
Named: Theodore Flowers
Died: 11/16/1927

Tiger Flowers was the first African-American to become a world middleweight champion. Born in Georgia, Flowers began fighting in 1918, when he was working in a Philadelphia shipbuilding plant. He started his professional boxing career at the age of 23, much later than most who plan to reach the top. A southpaw, Flowers was sometimes called a "left-handed Harry Greb," because of the way he hit opponents with the side of his fist. Flowers was a deeply religious man who recited a passage from Psalm 144 before every bout.

Flowers won his first 25 fights before experiencing a knockout at the hands of Panama Joe Gans. In 1922 and 1923, Flowers racked up several wins, interrupted by knockout losses to Kid Norfolk, Sam Langford, and the Jamaica Kid. In 1924, *The Ring* magazine rated Flowers the top contender for champion Harry Greb's middleweight title. Flowers earned a title shot after losing a controversial decision to light heavyweight Mike McTigue. The judges for this special holiday-time bout, held December 23 in New York, were Bernard Gimbel, the department store magnate; and Peter J. Brady, a banker. These unqualified judges gave the decision to McTigue, although nearly all expert observers thought the fight

The high point of Flowers's (R) career was this fifteen-round decision over Harry Greb to take the middleweight title on February 26, 1926, in New York. Flowers died within two years of this triumph.

IN THE RING	WON 115	LOST 14	DRAWS 6	TB 157	KO 53	W 56	WF 6	D 6	KO'd 9	L 3	LF 2	ND 21	NC 1

Date	Year		Opponent	Site	Result / Rounds		Title
SELECTED BOUTS							
—	1918		Bill Hooper	Brunswick, GA	KO	11	—
—	1922		Kid Norfolk	—	KO'd	3	—
Feb 21	1922		Gorilla Jones	Juarez, Mexico	KO	4	—
Jun 5	1922		Sam Langford★	Atlanta	KO'd	2	—
Jul 26	1922		Jamaica Kid	Covington, KY	TKO'd	2	—
Apr 20	1923		Jamaica Kid	Toledo, OH	ND-W	12	—
May 8	1923		Kid Norfolk	Springfield, OH	KO'd	1	—
May 15	1923		Tom King	Juarez	W	15	—
Sep 3	1923		Jamaica Kid	Atlanta	W	10	—
Mar 3	1924		Jamaica Kid	Fremont, OH	ND-W	12	—
Mar 29	1924		Lee Anderson	New York	W	12	—
Jun 27	1924		Jamaica Kid	Grand Rapids, MI	ND-W	10	—
Jul 21	1924		Jamaica Kid	Covington	WF	3	—
Aug 21	1924	♛	Harry Greb★	Fremont	ND-L	10	—
Sep 15	1924		Jamaica Kid	Columbus, OH	ND-W	12	—
Oct 11	1924		Jamaica Kid	New York	TKO	9	—
Feb 5	1925		Jamaica Kid	Dayton, OH	KO	10	—
Mar 20	1925		Lou Bogash	Boston	W	10	—
Dec 23	1925	⑩	Mike McTigue	New York	L	10	—
Feb 26	1926	♛	Harry Greb★	New York	W	15	Won-World-M
Aug 19	1926	⑩	Harry Greb★	New York	W	15	Ret-World-M
Oct 15	1926	⑩	Maxie Rosenbloom★	Boston	LF	9	—
Dec 3	1926	⑩	Mickey Walker★	Chicago	L	10	Lost-World-M
Feb 18	1927		Lou Bogash	Boston	W	10	—
Jul 4	1927	⑩	Maxie Rosenbloom★	Chicago	D	10	—
Nov 9	1927	⑩	Maxie Rosenbloom★	Detroit	D	10	—
Nov 12	1927		Leo Gates	New York	TKO	4	—

belonged to Flowers. The crowd of 12,000 rose to their feet and shouted their disapproval when the verdict was announced.

In February of 1926, Flowers met Greb for the title in Madison Square Garden in front of a crowd of 16,311. Flowers got off to a good start and staggered Greb in the first round. Greb cut Flowers in the second and the fourth. As the fight went on, the battle degenerated into a wrestling match with considerable holding, gouging, and low blows. Flowers won a unanimous decision to capture the title. He also won an August rematch with Greb. Just four months later, Flowers lost his title to Mickey Walker in Chicago, even though Flowers had dominated the fight. The referee's questionable decision was investigated by the Illinois State Athletic Commission, but Walker still held the title.

Flowers tried for most of the next year to obtain a rematch with Walker. Still a top contender, he twice fought to a draw with Hall of Famer Maxie Rosenbloom. In November of 1927, Flowers was hospitalized for an operation to remove scar tissue from around his eyes. He died as a result of the procedure, which was similar to the surgery that had claimed the life of Harry Greb the previous year.

JOE GANS
The Old Master

LIGHTWEIGHT

Right-handed; 5'6¼"; 131–137 lbs.
155 bouts, 1891 to 3/12/1909
Manager: Al Herford
Lightwt. Champ 1902–04, 1906–08
Hall of Fame Induction: 1990
Born: 11/25/1874, Baltimore, MD
Named: Joseph Gaines
Died: 8/10/1910

The first native-born black American to win a world title, Joe Gans impressed the boxing community with his scientific approach to the sport. Gans never moved more than a few inches to avoid a punch, studied his opponents' strengths and weaknesses much more intently than other fighters of the time, and directed his punches with pinpoint accuracy to key points of weakness.

Gans's first-known boxing experience took place at the Monumental Theater in Baltimore when he won a "battle royal," a wild contest in which several black fighters entered the ring at once to fight until one remained. Gans's superiority in this brutal exhibition attracted the interest of boxing manager Al Herford, who directed Gans to a professional career. Gans started boxing professionally in 1891 in Baltimore. Over the rest of the decade, he compiled an enviable record of 58-3-6 with two no-decisions.

In 1900, Gans, then 26 years old, faced Frank Erne for the world lightweight title. Erne peppered Gans with a blistering left jab throughout the fight, seriously cutting Gans's left eyelid. Realizing that to continue would risk blindness, Gans asked that the fight be stopped in the twelfth round. Gans spent hours analyzing Erne's style until he developed a strategy to counteract that murderous left. In their rematch two years later, Gans executed his plan perfectly and knocked Erne out in one round to recapture the lightweight title.

Also in 1900, Gans met Hall of Famer Terry McGovern, who knocked him out in the second round after four earlier knockdowns. This match raised eyebrows as few believed Gans would fall to the wildly swinging McGovern. Later, Gans regretfully admitted to taking a dive in this fight.

Never weighing more than 137 pounds, Gans

Gans (R) shakes hands with champ Battling Nelson before the start of their marathon 1906 title fight in Goldfield, NV.

IN THE RING	WON 120	LOST 8	DRAWS 9	TB 155	KO 85	W 30	WF 5	D 9	KO'd 5	L 3	LF 0	ND 18

Date	Year	Opponent	Site	Result / Rounds		Title

SELECTED BOUTS

Date	Year	Opponent	Site	Result	Rounds	Title
—	1891	Dave Armstrong	Baltimore	KO	12	—
Nov 18	1895	Young Griffo ★	Baltimore	D	10	—
Sep 21	1897	Young Griffo ★	Philadelphia	D	15	—
Mar 23	1900	♛ Frank Erne	New York	TKO'd	12	For-World-L
Dec 13	1900	Terry McGovern ★	Chicago	KO'd	2	—
May 12	1902	♛ Frank Erne	Fort Erie, Ont.	KO	1	Won-World-L
Jun 27	1902	George McFadden	San Francisco	KO	3	Ret-World-L
Jul 24	1902	Rufe Turner	Oakland	KO	15	Ret-World-L
Sep 17	1902	Gus Gardner	Baltimore	KO	5	Ret-World-L
Oct 13	1902	Kid McPartland	Fort Erie	KO	5	Ret-World-L
Jan 1	1903	Gus Gardner	New Britain, CT	WF	11	Ret-World-L
Mar 11	1903	Steve Crosby	Hot Springs, AR	KO	11	Ret-World-L
May 29	1903	Willie Fitzgerald	San Francisco	KO	10	Ret-World-L
Jul 4	1903	Buddy King	Butte, MT	KO	4	Ret-World-L
Nov 2	1903	Jack Blackburn ★	Philadelphia	ND-D	6	—
Dec 8	1903	Sam Langford ★	Boston	L	15	—
Mar 25	1904	Jack Blackburn ★	Baltimore	W	15	—
Sep 30	1904	♛ Joe Walcott(Barbados) ★	San Francisco	D	20	For-World-W
Oct 31	1904	Jimmy Britt	San Francisco	WF	5	Ret-World-L
Jun 29	1906	Jack Blackburn ★	Philadelphia	ND-D	6	—
Sep 3	1906	♛ Battling Nelson ★	Goldfield, NV	WF	42	Ret-World-L
Jan 1	1907	Kid Herman	Tonopah, NV	KO	8	Ret-World-L
Sep 9	1907	Jimmy Britt	San Francisco	TKO	6	Ret-World-L
Sep 27	1907	George Memsic	Los Angeles	W	20	Ret-World-L
May 14	1908	Rudy Unholz	San Francisco	KO	11	Ret-World-L
Jul 4	1908	Battling Nelson ★	Colma, CA	KO'd	17	Lost-World-L
Sep 9	1908	♛ Battling Nelson ★	Colma	KO'd	21	For-World-L
Mar 12	1909	Jabez White	New York	ND-W	10	—

often fought heavier men. He lost a fifteen-round decision to Hall of Famer Sam Langford in 1903 and fought to a draw with Joe Walcott in an attempt to take the welterweight title in 1904. Gans relinquished the lightweight title to fight Walcott, though in some quarters he still was considered the titleholder.

In 1906, Gans met Battling Nelson in Goldfield, Nevada, in a fight arranged by Tex Rickard. Neither Nelson nor Rickard had much regard for black fighters. Gans, although he was the defending champion, was offered only one-third of the purse, and Nelson insisted that Gans make the 133-pound weight limit, rigidly enforced with three weigh-ins on the day of the fight. Gans knocked Nelson down a couple of times and each time helped him up. In the 42nd round, Nelson felled Gans with a low blow. The referee called the punch a foul and declared Gans the winner. Nelson knocked Gans out in the rematch to take the title, and then knocked Gans out again in their third meeting. At the time of his last two fights with Nelson, Gans already had begun to feel the effects of tuberculosis. He died from the disease in 1910.

FRANKIE GENARO

F L Y W E I G H T

Right-handed; 5′2½″; 110–116 lbs.

130 bouts, 10/15/1920 to 3/3/1934

Managers: Harry Garsh, Phil Bernstein, Joe Jacobs, Billy McCarney

American Flyweight Champion 1923–25

NBA Flyweight Champion 1928–29

NBA-IBU Champion 1929–31

Hall of Fame Induction: 1998

Born: 08/26/1901, New York, NY

Named: Frank DiGennaro

Died: 12/27/1966

Frankie Genaro was one of the top flyweights in an era that included Hall of Famers Pancho Villa, Fidel LaBarba, Jimmy Wilde, and Benny Lynch. A popular fighter, Genaro used speed and science in the ring as he took on fly-, bantam-, and featherweights.

Born Frank DiGennaro in New York City, Genaro started boxing as a teenager under the name of a cousin, Al DeVito. In 1919, Genaro won the New York State, Metropolitan Association, and National AAU flyweight titles and capped his stunning amateur career by winning a gold medal in the 1920 Olympic Games in Antwerp. Genaro turned professional later that year.

Fighting primarily in New York, Genaro twice defeated Charley Phil Rosenberg and suffered his first loss at the hands of Harry Leonard in a twelve-round decision. He took on future flyweight champ Pancho Villa twice, for a no-decision and a win.

On March 1, 1923, Genaro met Villa, then owner of the American flyweight title, for the third time. Throughout most of the fight, Villa was the aggressor. However, Genaro scored often enough to earn the judges' approval and with it, the title. The booing crowd thought neither fighter had worked hard enough, but gave the edge to Villa.

Genaro then set his sights on the world flyweight title held by Jimmy Wilde. Wilde had virtually retired but agreed to come to the United States for one last title bout. However, when Genaro's manager could not reach an agreement with Wilde, the champ fought Villa. Villa knocked out Wilde in the seventh round to take the world title. When Villa died on July 14, 1925, Genaro became the "uncrowned" champion.

Genaro defended his American title on August 22, 1925, against 1924 Olympic gold medalist Fidel LaBarba, who took the title with a decision. In 1927, Genaro unsuccessfully challenged for the vacant NBA world flyweight title against Frenchy Belanger in

The diminutive Genaro clowns with Charly Kranchi, middleweight champ of Switzerland.

IN THE RING	WON 82	LOST 21	DRAWS 8	TB 130	KO 19	W 58	WF 5	D 8	KO'd 5	L 13	LF 3	ND 19

Date	Year	Opponent	Site	Result / Rounds		Title

SELECTED BOUTS

Date	Year	Opponent	Site	Result	Rounds	Title
Oct 15	1920	Joe Colletti	New York	WF	3	—
Feb 16	1921	Joe Colletti	Poughkeespie, NY	D	12	—
Apr 9	1921	Joe Colletti	Brooklyn	W	10	—
Aug 12	1921	Joe Colletti	Saratoga, NY	W	12	—
May 24	1922	Charley Phil Rosenberg	New York	W	12	—
Jul 6	1922	Pancho Villa ★	Jersey City, NJ	ND-W	12	—
Aug 18	1922	Harry Leonard	New York	L	12	—
Aug 22	1922	Pancho Villa ★	Brooklyn	W	10	—
Mar 1	1923	⑩ Pancho Villa ★	New York	W	15	Won-American-FL
Jun 26	1925	Kid Williams ★	Baltimore	W	12	—
Aug 22	1925	⑩ Fidel La Barba ★	Los Angeles	L	10	Lost-American-FL
Nov 28	1927	⑩ Albert Belanger	Toronto	L	10	For-Vac-NBA-FL
Feb 6	1928	⑩ Albert Belanger	Toronto	W	10	Won-NBA-FL
Mar 2	1929	⑩ Emile Pladner	Paris	KO'd	1	Lost-NBA-FL
Apr 18	1929	⑩ Emile Pladner	Paris	WF	5	Reg-NBA-IBU-FL
Oct 17	1929	Ernie Jarvis	London	W	15	Ret-NBA-IBU-FL
Jun 10	1930	Albert Belanger	Toronto	W	10	Ret-NBA-IBU-FL
Dec 26	1930	⑩ Midget Wolgast★	New York	D	15	For-Vac-World-FL
Mar 25	1931	Victor Ferrand	Madrid	D	15	Ret-NBA-IBU-FL
Jul 30	1931	Jackie Harmon	Waterbury, CT	KO	6	Ret-NBA-IBU-FL
Oct 3	1931	⑩ Valentin Angelmann	Paris	W	15	Ret-NBA-IBU-FL
Oct 27	1931	Victor ("Young") Perez	Paris	KO'd	2	Lost-NBA-IBU-FL
Apr 5	1933	Joey Archibald	Fall River, MA	W	10	—
Mar 3	1934	Little Pancho	Oakland, CA	KO'd	9	—

Toronto. In the rematch less than two months later, Genaro outpunched and outboxed Belanger. In contrast to the Villa title fight, Genaro fought furiously and clearly won the decision.

In 1929, Genaro took his title to Europe to face highly regarded Emile ("Spider") Pladner in Paris. Pladner knocked Genaro out in the first round. In the rematch six weeks later, Genaro regained the title on a foul. Genaro fought in England, France, Germany, and Italy before returning to New York to face the New York world flyweight champ Midget Wolgast on December 26, 1930, in Madison Square Garden. After fifteen rounds the fight was called a draw with each fighter retaining his title.

The next year, Genaro lost his title when Victor ("Young") Perez knocked him out in the second round. At thirty, Genaro did not have much left. He compiled a record of 6-5, including a victory over future featherweight champ Joey Archibald. Age and an aggressive career had taken its toll on this fine fighter. He retired after Little Pancho knocked him out in 1934. In retirement Genaro was involved in sales and real estate. He owned lakefront property in Cochecton, New York, where he planned to open a resort. He also worked for the Department of Marine Aviation in New York for fifteen years. Genaro died on December 27, 1966.

MIKE GIBBONS
St. Paul Phantom

MIDDLEWEIGHT

Right-handed; 5'9"; 148 lbs.
127 bouts, 1/11/1908 to 5/16/1922
Manager: George Barton
Hall of Fame Induction: 1992
Born: 7/20/1887, St. Paul, MN
Named: Mike J. Gibbons
Died: 8/31/1956

Although he never became a champion, Mike Gibbons is considered by many boxing historians to be one of the top ten middleweights of all time. Gibbons learned to box at the YMCA in his native St. Paul. He turned professional at the age of nineteen with a third-round knockout of Roy Moore and was unbeaten in his first fourteen fights before losing a decision to Jimmy Clabby. A footwork wizard who could wear an opponent out with his defensive maneuvers, Gibbons could punch hard, too. As a young fighter, he built a reputation that put him in line for the middleweight championship.

In 1912, the middleweight division had no recognized champion. More than half a dozen fighters, including Gibbons and Eddie McGoorty, claimed a right to the title. Gibbons signed to fight McGoorty with the winner to be declared champion. The heavier McGoorty was the favorite by far, and Gibbons employed his ring choreography not to beat McGoorty but to keep him from winning. Gibbons constantly backpedaled and put on a great display of footwork, but he

Mike Gibbons (R) spars with his brother, Hall of Famer Tommy Gibbons atop the American Building in New York City on March 12, 1917. Tommy, who fought both Dempsey and Tunney, outweighed Mike by 24 lbs.

IN THE RING	WON 62	LOST 3	DRAWS 4	TB 127	KO 38	W 23	WF 1	D 4	KO'd 0	L 3	LF 0	ND 58

Date	Year	Opponent	Site	Result / Rounds		Title
SELECTED BOUTS						
Jan 11	1908	Roy Moore	St. Paul, MN	KO	3	—
Mar 12	1910	Jimmy Clabby	St. Paul	L	10	—
Apr 17	1911	Gus Christie	Milwaukee	ND	8	—
May 5	1911	Gus Christie	Milwaukee	ND	10	—
Sep 1	1911	Jimmy Clabby	Milwaukee	ND	10	—
Nov 10	1911	Young Sherman	New York	KO	4	—
Dec 4	1912	Eddie McGoorty	New York	ND	10	—
May 13	1913	Gus Christie	Boston	W	12	—
Jan 21	1915	Jimmy Clabby	Milwaukee	ND	10	—
Mar 2	1915	Eddie McGoorty	Hudson, WI	ND	10	—
May 31	1915	Soldier Bartfield	Brooklyn	ND	10	—
Sep 11	1915	Packey McFarland★	Brooklyn	ND	10	—
May 18	1916	Ted ("Kid") Lewis★	New York	ND	10	—
Nov 10	1916	Jack Dillon★	St. Paul	ND	10	—
Feb 10	1917	Harry Greb★	Philadelphia	ND	6	—
Jul 4	1917	George Chip	Youngstown, OH	ND	12	—
Sep 3	1917	Jack Dillon★	Terre Haute, IN	ND	10	—
Apr 26	1918	Packey McFarland★	Camp Dodge, IA	Exh	6	—
Jan 31	1919	George Chip	Duluth, MN	ND	10	—
Mar 4	1919	Soldier Bartfield	St. Paul	ND	10	—
Apr 22	1919	Soldier Bartfield	San Francisco	W	4	—
May 19	1919	George ("K.O.") Brown	Memphis, TN	ND	8	—
Jun 12	1919	George Chip	Terre Haute	ND	10	—
Jun 23	1919	Harry Greb★	Pittsburgh	ND	10	—
May 16	1922	Danny Fagan	Winnipeg, Man.	KO	2	—

did not really fight. The newspapers awarded McGoorty the decision, but the fight's lack of action kept him from gaining general acclaim as the titleholder. Asked by a reporter why he had not fought more vigorously, Gibbons replied, "Because you and every other writer said that McGoorty would beat me, simply because he was ten pounds heavier than me. I decided to prove you were wrong, and that he couldn't lay a glove on me. And he didn't. That's all I cared about."

Gibbons continued to fight successfully after the McGoorty fight and proved his mettle in a 1916 match with Hall of Famer Jack Dillon. At the time, Dillon was reputed to have the best punch in all of boxing. For ten rounds, Gibbons eluded Dillon's attack and countered beautifully when Dillon missed him. Gibbons won every round of the fight, according to those at ringside.

Gibbons fought for another six years, taking on Harry Greb, among others. Even the blurringly fast Greb was confused by Gibbons, by then known as the "Phantom of St. Paul." Greb shouted to his manager, "From now on, match me with one guy at a time." Gibbons was a member of the Minnesota state boxing commission at the time of his death at age 69. He suffered a fatal heart attack at home while playing cards with his wife.

TOMMY GIBBONS

HEAVYWEIGHT

Right-handed; 5'9½"; 172 lbs.

106 bouts, 9/5/1911 to 6/5/1925

Manager: Eddie Kane

Hall of Fame Induction: 1993

Born: 3/22/1891, St. Paul, MN

Died: 11/19/1960

Like his older brother Mike, Tommy Gibbons is best remembered for a fight in which he kept a champion at bay. Widely acknowledged as a stellar fighter in several weight classes, Gibbons held his own with heavyweight king Jack Dempsey and was knocked out only once in his career.

Gibbons learned to box at the YMCA in his hometown of St. Paul. He turned professional at the age of twenty and recorded knockouts in his first three fights. At the start of his career, Gibbons fought as a welterweight. As he added weight, he moved up in class until he eventually contended for the heavyweight title. Gibbons battled Hall of Famer Harry Greb four times from 1915 to 1922, losing the only one of the four bouts in which a decision was rendered. He also fought multiple bouts with George ("K.O.") Brown, Joe Herrick, George Chip, Gus Christie, Silent Martin, Billy Miske, Clay Turner, Burt Kenny, and Chuck Wiggins. Only Miske beat Gibbons, and he won on a foul.

Initially, Gibbons was famed for his speed and boxing ability. However, as he gained weight, he developed a more powerful punch. In 1921, Gibbons won 21 fights by knockouts, with ten of them coming in the first round. Although not all of the victories were against top competition, Gibbons succeeded in making enough of a name for himself to earn a shot at Dempsey's heavyweight title.

The title fight took place in Shelby, Montana. The city fathers wanted to put the town on the map by hosting a heavyweight championship bout. Jack Kearns, Dempsey's manager, agreed to have his fighter perform there if Dempsey were paid $310,000. Kearns also insisted on using his own referee, James Dougherty. Gibbons, hungry for the championship, agreed to

Gibbons floors Georges Carpentier in the seventh round of a ten-round no-decision bout before a huge throng in Michigan City, IN, on May 31, 1924.

IN THE RING	WON 57	LOST 4	DRAWS 1	TB 106	KO 47	W 10	WF 0	D 1	KO'd 1	L 2	LF 1	ND 43	NC 1

Date	Year	Opponent	Site	Result / Rounds		Title
SELECTED BOUTS						
Sep 5	1911	Oscar Kelly	Minneapolis	KO	5	—
Jul 12	1912	Tommy Nelson	New York	KO	1	—
Feb 9	1914	George ("K.O.") Brown	Hudson, WI	ND	10	—
Mar 24	1914	Billy Miske	Hudson	ND	3	—
Apr 20	1914	George ("K.O.") Brown	Superior, WI	ND	10	—
Jul 12	1915	Billy Miske	St. Paul, MN	ND	10	—
Nov 16	1915	Harry Greb★	St. Paul	ND	10	—
Mar 23	1917	♛ Battling Levinsky★	St. Paul	ND	10	—
Aug 22	1917	George Chip	St. Paul	ND	10	—
Sep 3	1917	Gus Christie	Dayton, OH	W	15	—
Apr 26	1918	Gus Christie	Terre Haute, IN	W	10	—
May 3	1918	George Chip	Des Moines, IA	W	12	—
Apr 11	1919	George Chip	Denver	W	10	—
Jun 19	1919	Billy Miske	Minneapolis	ND	10	—
Jul 4	1919	George ("K.O.") Brown	Denver	ND	12	—
Feb 3	1920	George ("K.O.") Brown	Peoria, IL	ND	10	—
May 15	1920	Harry Greb★	Pittsburgh	ND	10	—
Jul 31	1920	Harry Greb★	Pittsburgh	ND	10	—
Mar 13	1922	Harry Greb★	New York	L	15	—
Oct 13	1922	Billy Miske	New York	LF	10	—
Nov 13	1922	George Ashe	Detroit	KO	1	—
Dec 15	1922	Billy Miske	St. Paul	W	10	—
Apr 30	1923	Chuck Wiggins	New Orleans	KO	10	—
Jul 4	1923	♛ Jack Dempsey★	Shelby, MT	L	15	For-World-H
May 31	1924	Georges Carpentier★	Michigan City, IN	ND	10	—
Jun 5	1925	⑩ Gene Tunney★	New York	KO'd	12	—

be paid beyond expenses only if there were money left over after Dempsey's cut. Dempsey got paid, but because the fight drew only about 7,000 spectators, Gibbons received nothing. In fact, the fight was a financial disaster for Shelby, and three banks failed as a result of backing the fiasco.

Still, it was a good fight. Dempsey hit Gibbons with some solid shots, notably in the eleventh and fifteenth rounds, but Gibbons parried and slipped away from punches that would have scored against a less-accomplished fighter. It was later rumored that Kearns told Dempsey to be sure to go a full fifteen rounds so that his agent could get out of town with Dempsey's purse before the local promoters reconsidered. The stories surrounding the fight do little to diminish Gibbons's achievement; most observers believed that he could not have been knocked out under any circumstances.

It took Dempsey's nemesis, Gene Tunney, to finally stop Gibbons. In a fight in 1925, Tunney dropped Gibbons in the twelfth round. It was the first and only time he was knocked out. Gibbons then retired, never having won a championship. In retirement, he sold insurance and served four terms as sheriff of St. Paul.

HARRY GREB
The Pittsburgh Windmill

MIDDLEWEIGHT

Right-handed; 5'8"; 142–170 lbs.

299 bouts, 5/29/1913 to 8/19/1926

Managers: James M. ("Red") Mason 1913–20, 1923–26; George Engel 1921–22

Middleweight Champion 1923–26

Hall of Fame Induction: 1990

Born: 6/6/1894, Pittsburgh, PA

Named: Edward Henry Greb

Died: 10/22/1926

Possibly the most fearless fighter ever to enter the ring, Harry Greb is remembered both for the frequency with which he fought and for the great ferocity he displayed. He came up against the best fighters of his day, demolishing many of them with bloodthirsty enthusiasm. He often challenged Jack Dempsey, but the two never fought. In a career which spanned thirteen years, Greb fought 299 times, and won 264, including so-called newspaper decisions. He was only knocked out twice, once in his first year of fighting, and once when he broke his arm throwing a punch.

Greb began his pro career at the age of eighteen in his native Pittsburgh, fighting mostly in and around his hometown for the first few years. Rising through the ranks, he triumphed over the likes of George ("K.O.") Brown, Jack Dillon, Eddie McGoorty, Gunboat Smith, and Tommy Gibbons. In 1922, Greb faced the unbeaten Gene Tunney in Madison Square Garden for the American light heavyweight title. Greb immediately swarmed all over Tunney, relentlessly attacking him from every angle. In a gory battle, Tunney's nose splashed

Harry Greb (R) poses with Johnny Wilson, referee Jack O'Sullivan, and announcer Joe Humphrys before contesting the title on August 31, 1923, in New York.

IN THE RING	WON 105	LOST 8	DRAWS 3	TB 299	KO 48	W 55	WF 2	D 3	KO'd 2	L 5	LF 1	ND 183

Date	Year	Opponent	Site	Result / Rounds		Title
SELECTED BOUTS						
May 29	1913	Frank Kirkwood	Pittsburgh	ND-W	6	—
Nov 16	1915	Tommy Gibbons★	St. Paul, MN	ND-L	10	—
Feb 10	1917	Mike Gibbons★	Philadelphia	ND-L	6	—
Sept 6	1917	Battling Levinsky★	Pittsburgh	ND-W	10	—
Mar 4	1918	Jack Dillon★	Toledo, OH	ND-W	12	—
Apr 28	1919	Battling Levinsky★	Canton. OH	ND-W	12	—
Jun 23	1919	Mike Gibbons★	Pittsburgh	ND-W	10	—
Jul 31	1920	Tommy Gibbons★	Pittsburgh	ND-W	10	—
May 23	1922	Gene Tunney★	New York	W	15	Won-USA-LH
Jan 30	1923	Tommy Loughran★	New York	W	15	Ret-USA-LH
Feb 23	1923	Gene Tunney★	New York	L	15	Lost-USA-LH
Aug 31	1923	♛ Johnny Wilson	New York	W	15	Won-World-M
Dec 3	1923	Bryan Downey	Pittsburgh	W	10	Ret-World-M
Dec 10	1923	Gene Tunney★	New York	L	15	For-USA-LH
Dec 25	1923	Tommy Loughran★	Pittsburgh	W	10	—
Jan 18	1924	⑩ Johnny Wilson	New York	W	15	Ret-World-M
Mar 24	1924	Fay Keiser	Baltimore	TKO	12	Ret-World-M
Jun 26	1924	⑩ Ted Moore	New York	W	15	Ret-World-M
Aug 21	1924	⑩ Tiger Flowers★	Fremont, OH	ND-W	10	—
Sep 17	1924	⑩ Gene Tunney★	Cleveland	ND-D	10	—
Mar 27	1925	⑩ Gene Tunney★	St. Paul	ND-L	10	—
Jul 2	1925	Mickey Walker★	New York	W	15	Ret-World-M
Jul 16	1925	⑩ Maxie Rosenbloom★	Cleveland	ND-W	10	—
Nov 13	1925	⑩ Tony Marullo	New Orleans	W	15	Ret-World M
Feb 26	1926	⑩ Tiger Flowers★	New York	L	15	Lost-World-M
Aug 19	1926	♛ Tiger Flowers★	New York	L	15	For-World-M

blood from 40 seconds into the first round; Greb soon reopened scars on Tunney's forehead. The lighter, faster, more experienced Greb overwhelmed the "Fighting Marine" and took the fifteen-round decision. Although he was denied a chance to face the world titleholder, Georges Carpentier, Greb successfully defended his American title against Hall of Famer Tommy Loughran before facing Tunney in a rematch. This time Tunney won a controversial decision. Referee Patsy Haley apparently penalized Greb for holding and hitting and other roughhouse tactics in awarding Tunney the fight. The two would battle three more times with Tunney winning one and with two no-decisions.

In his first bout after the second Tunney fight, Greb dropped to middleweight and captured the world title with a fifteen-round decision over Johnny Wilson. Greb held the title until 1926 when Tiger Flowers dethroned him. Greb failed to reclaim the title in a return bout.

A remarkably tough competitor, Greb had suffered a detached retina in a fight in 1921 against Kid Norfolk. A month later, Greb was back in the ring, and he continued to fight for five years, half-blind. Greb's life came to an untimely end in 1926 when he died while undergoing surgery to repair facial injuries caused by boxing and an auto accident.

YOUNG GRIFFO

FEATHERWEIGHT

Right-handed; 5'4"; 122–135 lbs.
219 bouts, 1886 to 9/25/1911
Featherweight Champ 1890–93
Hall of Fame Induction: 1991
Born: 4/15/1869, Sofala, NSW, Australia
Named: Albert Griffiths
Died: 12/7/1927

One of the greatest defensive fighters of all time, Young Griffo compiled an outstanding record while eschewing traditional training methods. Born in Australia, the illiterate Griffo got his first experience fighting while selling newspapers on the docks of Sydney. When noted Australian boxer Larry Foley saw him in a street fight, Foley added Griffo to his stable of fighters. Griffo first started boxing under the old London Prize Ring Rules in 1886.

In 1889, Griffo won an eight-round decision over Nipper Peakes to take the Australian featherweight title. The next year, he scored a fifteenth-round knockout of Torpedo Billy Murphy in Sydney to win a version of the world featherweight title. Though Griffo successfully defended this title once, he did not gain widespread acclaim as the title holder.

In 1893, Griffo journeyed to the United States and dazzled fans with his incredible ability to avoid getting hit. He used to boast that he could stand on a

Griffo ducks out of danger in the last stanza of his twelve-round decision victory over Horace Leeds at the Seaside Athletic Club of Coney Island, NY, on March 4, 1895. Insets 1 and 2 show other bouts that day.

IN THE RING	WON 63	LOST 9	DRAWS 37	TB 219	KO 32	W 28	WF 3	D 37	KO'd 4	L 4	LF 1	ND 110

Date	Year	Opponent	Site	Result / Rounds		Title
SELECTED BOUTS						
—	1886	Joe Francis	Sydney	KO	3	—
May 1	1888	Joe Pluto	Melbourne	D	8	—
Sep 1	1888	Joe Pluto	Melbourne	D	4	—
Dec 12	1889	Joe Pluto	Melbourne	D	70	—
Dec 27	1889	Nipper Peakes	Melbourne	W	8	Won-Australia-FE
Mar 29	1890	Chiddy Ryan	Sydney	W	4	—
Sep 2	1890 ♕	Billy Murphy	Sydney	TKO	15	Won-World-126 lbs
Mar 12	1891	George Powell	Sydney	WD	20	Ret-World-126 lbs
Jul 25	1892	Jim Barron	Darlinghurst, Australia	D	22	For-Australia-L
—	1892	Chiddy Ryan	Sydney	D	45	—
Nov 13	1893	Young Scotty	Chicago	W	6	—
Feb 10	1894	Kid Lavigne★	New York	D	8	—
May 5	1894	Billy Murphy	Boston	W	8	—
Jun 29	1894 ♕	George Dixon★	Boston	D	20	—
Aug 27	1894	Jack McAuliffe★	New York	L	10	—
Jan 19	1895 ♕	George Dixon★	Coney Island, NY	D	25	—
Oct 12	1895	Kid Lavigne★	Maspeth, NY	D	20	—
Oct 28	1895 ♕	George Dixon★	New York	D	10	—
Nov 18	1895	Joe Gans★	Baltimore	D	10	—
Feb 3	1896	Hugh Behan	New York	KO'd	1	—
Sep 21	1897	Joe Gans★	Philadelphia	D	15	—
Jul 10	1900	Joe Gans★	New York	KO'd	8	—
Feb 10	1904	Tommy White	Chicago	KO'd	1	—
Sep 25	1911	Honey Mellody	Philadelphia	ND	6	—

handkerchief and dodge punches without taking a step in any direction. Griffo fought a host of notables, usually competing as a lightweight, although he did not earn a title shot. He fought three draws with George Dixon, which could have gone Griffo's way had the rules allowed the rendering of a decision. He also lost a controversial decision to Hall of Famer Jack McAuliffe, who barely touched Griffo in ten rounds.

Griffo did not treat his boxing career seriously. Usually, he did not train at all for his fights. If legend is to believed, he often arrived in the ring drunk or hung over. Even so, he was able to win more than his share of fights while absorbing only a minimal amount of punishment. By 1900, the years of hard living had slowed Griffo, and he suffered a knockout by Joe Gans. Griffo continued to fight until 1904 and made an abortive comeback in 1911. In retirement, the hard-drinking, wise-cracking Griffo used up his fame and money until he was reduced to panhandling in Times Square. He became a familiar figure, spending his days perched on the steps of the Rialto Theater. When Griffo died in 1927, promoter Tex Rickard reportedly paid for the funeral.

HARRY HARRIS
Human Scissors, Human Hairpin

BANTAMWEIGHT

Right-handed; 5'7¾"; 115 lbs.

52 bouts, 4/5/1896 to 6/3/1907

British World Bantamweight (115 lbs.) Champion 1901

Hall of Fame Induction: 2002

Born: 11/18/1880; Chicago, IL

Died: 6/5/1959

Unlike many boxing greats, Harry Harris's productive career did not end with his last ring battle.

As a 90-pound teenager, Harris, along with his twin brother Sam, began taking boxing lessons at the Bill O'Connell gym in Chicago. It was O'Connell who recommended the Harris boys to Chicago newspaper artist Ed Carey—also a local amateur bantamweight—as sparring partners. Gaining experience with Carey, Harry Harris decided to try his hand as a professional and debuted at fifteen in a five-round decision over Dennis Mahoney on April 5, 1896.

After turning pro, Harris formed a friendship with Hall of Famer Kid McCoy. The two sparred together in Chicago and toured in a traveling show, taking on all comers. McCoy was a mentor to Harris and taught him many tricks of the trade, including his famed "Corkscrew Punch." Lean and lanky, Harris cut an unlikely figure as a boxer. But with his extraordinarily long reach, long, thin legs, and surprising power, he handled both boxers and sluggers with equal panache.

In 1898, Harris first became known to the New York fight crowd when he fought and won a five-bout series there, three by knockout. He suffered his first loss the next year, a six-round decision to Steve Flanagan. Also in 1899, Harris fought one of the defining matches of his career when he faced undefeated Hall of Famer and bantamweight champion Jimmy Barry. Though Harris dominated the six-round battle, the referee called the fight a draw out of respect for Barry's record.

When Terry McGovern vacated the bantamweight title in 1900, Harris was viewed as the successor to the title. He defeated future welterweight champ Buddy Ryan and Casper Leon in

Hall of Fame middleweight Charles ("Kid") McCoy (L) was a friend and mentor to the younger (and lighter) Harris (R).

IN THE RING	WON 38	LOST 2	DRAWS 7	TB 52	KO 14	W 23	WF 1	D 7	KO'd 0	L 2	LF 0	ND 5

Date	Year	Opponent	Site	Result / Rounds		Title
SELECTED BOUTS						
Apr 5	1896	Dennis Mahoney	Chicago	W	5	—
Sep 9	1898	George Ross	New York	W	10	—
Feb 7	1899	Steve Flanagan	Chicago	L	6	—
May 19	1899	Torpedo Billy Murphy	Chicago	KO	4	—
Sep 1	1899	Jimmy Barry ★	Chicago	D	6	—
Sep 22	1899	Steve Flanagan	Chicago	D	6	—
Oct 14	1899	Steve Flanagan	Chicago	D	6	—
Jan 20	1900	Barney ("Kid") Abel	Chicago	KO	3	—
Oct 16	1900	Casper Leon	Chicago	W	6	—
Oct 26	1900	Johnny Reagan	Chicago	W	6	—
Oct 30	1900	Kid McFadden	Chicago	W	6	—
Nov 27	1900	Clarence Forbes	Chicago	L	6	—
Mar 18	1901	Thomas ("Pedlar") Palmer	London	W	15	Won-British World-B (115 lbs)
Feb 27	1902	Austin Rice	Chicago	D	6	—
Mar 26	1902	Danny Dougherty	Philadelphia	ND	6	—
Mar 31	1906	Jack Goodman	New York	ND	3	—
Jun 3	1907	Harlem Tommy Murphy	New York	WF	8	—

that same year, then sailed to England in hopes of meeting Harry Ware— Britain's top bantam. The fight never materialized.

Instead, Harris signed to meet Pedlar Palmer on March 18, 1901, at London's National Sporting Club. In contrast to Harris's unusually long, thin physique, Palmer was a compact 5'3". He started out strong, moving inside and working the body while avoiding Harris's left. Harris was too skilled to be baffled by Palmer for long. In the fifth round, instead of jabbing with a straight left, he turned his throw into a part hook, part uppercut that connected with Palmer's jaw, knocking him down. Harris won an easy decision and claimed the world 115 lbs. title.

When he returned to the U.S., the top bantamweights avoided him. Around this time, he met A. L. Erlanger, of Klaw and Erlanger, a New York theatrical firm. Harris impressed Erlanger, who employed him as treasurer and theater manager until 1916.

Harris did not retire entirely from the ring. He tried unsuccessfully to land a fight with featherweight champion Abe Attell. After fighting a no-decision match with Barney ("Kid") Abel in 1905, and three no-decision bouts with Jack Goodman in 1906 and 1907, Harris, now fighting as a lightweight, defeated Harlem Tommy Murphy on a foul on June 3, 1907, and then retired.

Harris continued to box for fun at the City Athletic Club, where he gave instruction to future heavyweight champion Gene Tunney. He also sparred with financier J. Robinson Duff, who persuaded him to leave Broadway for Wall Street. Harris became a member of the New York Curb Exchange, later known as the American Stock Exchange. He continued there until his retirement.

PETE ("KID") HERMAN

BANTAMWEIGHT
Right-handed; 5'2"; 105–125 lbs.
144 bouts, 9/30/1912 to 4/24/1922
Managers: Jerome Gargano, Doc Cutch,
Sammy Goldman, Red Walsh
Bantamweight Champ 1917–20, 1921
Hall of Fame Induction: 1997
Born: 2/12/1896, New Orleans, LA
Named: Peter Gulotta
Died: 4/13/1973

One of the toughest competitors ever to hold the bantamweight title, Pete Herman was a fast, durable fighter with two-fisted punching power that was especially effective at close range.

Born Peter Gulotta, Herman went to work as a shoeshine boy in New Orleans at the age of twelve. He and his friend, Eddie Coulon, went to a gym to box during their lunch hours. When Coulon began fighting professionally, Herman decided to turn pro as well. In his first bout, at age sixteen, he fought to a draw with Coulon. He quickly became a formidable opponent for any bantamweight.

In 1914, Herman fought well in a no-decision, non-title bout with bantam champ Kid Williams. Less than two years later, he again faced Williams, this time with the title on the line. Under the terms of the contract, the champion had his choice of referee. Williams named his friend Billy Rocap. The fight went twenty rounds, a heated contest all the way, with much of the fighting conducted in close. According to most ringside observers, Herman had won, but Rocap gave the fight to Williams.

Herman fought Williams again on January 9, 1917. This time, Herman chose Rocap to officiate, convinced the referee would not risk his reputation by making another questionable decision. The battle raged for the full twenty rounds. Herman knocked Williams down twice. Rocap awarded the fight and the championship to Herman, who was just twenty years old. On April 27, 1917, Herman fought the other bantamweight who campaigned with a similar name. He engaged in a ten-round no-decision bout with "Pekin" Kid Herman of Pekin, Illinois.

For close to four years, Herman met a wide range of opponents, including Williams in a no-decision fourth match, but only defended the title once. In this period, Herman suffered an injury that would dramatically change his life. In a charity benefit match, his right eye was permanently damaged.

On December 22, 1920, Herman fought Joe Lynch in a title match in New York. His declining vision made worse by the thick tobacco smoke in the hall, Herman lost to Lynch. He

Herman (L) sends bantam champ Jimmy Wilde through the ropes in their London, January 13, 1921, non-title battle. The stunned Wilde failed to hear the bell to begin the 14th round. The referee finally called a halt to the bout after 17 rounds.

IN THE RING	WON 67	LOST 12	DRAWS 8	TB 144	KO 21	W 46	WF 0	D 8	KO'd 1	L 10	LF 1	ND 57

Date	Year	Opponent	Site	Result / Rounds		Title
SELECTED BOUTS						
Sep 30	1912	Eddie Coulon	New Orleans	D	6	—
Jun 30	1914	♛ Kid Williams★	New Orleans	ND-D	10	—
May 1	1915	Young Zulu Kid	New Orleans	D	10	—
Nov 6	1915	Young Zulu Kid	New Orleans	W	15	—
Nov 15	1915	Memphis Pal Moore	Memphis, TN	L	8	—
Feb 7	1916	♛ Kid Williams★	New Orleans	D	20	For-World-B
Feb 28	1916	Lou Tendler★	Philadelphia	ND-L	6	—
Jan 9	1917	♛ Kid Williams★	New Orleans	W	20	Won-World-B
Feb 16	1917	Johnny Ertle	Milwaukee	ND-W	10	—
Apr 27	1917	Pekin Kid Herman	Peoria, IL	ND	10	—
May 14	1917	Johnny Coulon★	Racine, WI	TKO	3	—
Jun 13	1917	Kid Williams★	Philadelphia	ND-L	6	—
Nov 5	1917	Frankie Burns	New Orleans	W	20	Ret-World-B
May 4	1918	Jack Sharkey	Philadelphia	ND	6	—
Sep 6	1918	Young Zulu Kid	Jersey City, NJ	ND-W	8	—
Mar 24	1919	Memphis Pal Moore	Memphis	ND-L	8	—
May 23	1919	Johnny Ertle	Minneapolis	KO	5	—
Sep 1	1919	Joe Lynch★	Waterbury, CT	ND-L	10	—
Sep 15	1919	Jack Sharkey	Detroit	ND-D	10	—
Nov 12	1919	Joe Lynch★	Philadelphia	ND-W	6	—
Jan 7	1920	Johnny Ritchie	New Orleans	KO	8	—
Dec 22	1920	Joe Lynch★	New York	L	15	Lost-World-B
Jan 13	1921	♛ Jimmy Wilde★	London	TKO	17	—
Jul 25	1921	♛ Joe Lynch★	Brooklyn	W	15	Reg-World-B
Sep 23	1921	Johnny Buff	New York	L	15	Lost-World-B
Dec 9	1921	Packy O'Gatty	Brooklyn	KO	1	—
Apr 24	1922	Roy Moore	Boston	W	10	—

then went to England to face Hall of Famer Jimmy Wilde. Wilde balked at going into the ring because of a dispute over Herman's weight. The Prince of Wales, who was in attendance, went to Wilde's dressing room and persuaded him to compete. When the fight finally took place, Herman scored a TKO over the lighter Wilde in seventeen rounds. The Prince, later King Edward VII, became friendly with Herman and remained in contact with him over the years.

At Brooklyn's Ebbets Field, on July 25, 1921, with poor vision in both eyes, Herman used an effective body attack to decision Lynch and regain the title. He was able to hold it just two months before losing to Johnny Buff. In his last fight, against Roy Moore, Herman could not see his opponent and could only hit him when they clinched. Despite this handicap, Herman won the decision.

Herman retired at age 26. Shortly thereafter, he became totally blind. He opened a cafe, Pete Herman's, in the French Quarter in New Orleans and received a lifetime appointment to the Louisiana State Athletic Commission. Nat Fleischer, the founder of *The Ring*, ranked Herman as the second-greatest bantamweight of all time.

PETER JACKSON
The Black Prince

HEAVYWEIGHT

Right-handed; 6'1½"; 192 lbs.

85 bouts, 1882 to 12/2/1899

Hall of Fame Induction: 1990

Born: 7/3/1861, St. Croix, West Indies

Died: 7/13/1901

Racial prejudice was the only thing that kept Peter Jackson from his chance to win the world heavyweight crown. A world-class fighter, Jackson was not always granted the kind of competition he deserved. Born in the Virgin Islands, Jackson moved with his family to Australia when he was six years old. When his parents returned to the Caribbean, Jackson stayed in his new homeland. He became an excellent swimmer and diver and found work on ships at the age of fourteen. As a young man, Jackson used his fists to help quell a mutiny, and the incident received attention in the Australian press. Larry Foley, who had also handled Young Griffo, sought Jackson out and started him on his professional career.

Jackson won the Australian heavyweight title in 1886 with a knockout of Tom Leeds in the 30th round. Having difficulty securing bouts in Australia and eager to prove his worth, Jackson travelled to the United States in 1888. However, most top fighters shunned him for racial or competitive reasons. John L. Sullivan, the heavyweight champion and the most famous American boxer, stated, "I will not fight a Negro. I never have, and I never shall." Although Sullivan had actually faced a black opponent previously, he would not change his stance regarding Jackson.

Jackson knocked out George Godfrey, another black fighter, and several white opponents who agreed to fight him as he travelled across the country. He then journeyed

Jackson (L) outboxed Gus Lambert in Troy, NY, on March 5, 1890. After four rounds, police called a halt to the bout, which is officially recorded as a "no-contest." Starting in 1892, Jackson virtually abandoned the ring for nearly six years, touring as an actor in Uncle Tom's Cabin *and other plays.*

IN THE RING	WON 45	LOST 4	DRAWS 5	TB 85	KO 30	W 12	WF 3	D 5	KO'd 3	L 1	LF 0	ND 31

Date	Year	Opponent	Site	Result / Rounds		Title

SELECTED BOUTS

Date	Year	Opponent	Site	Result / Rounds		Title
—	1882	Jack Hayes	Sydney	D	5	—
Jul 26	1884	Bill Farnan	Melbourne	KO'd	3	For-Australia-H
Oct 4	1884	Bill Farnan	Melbourne	D	6	—
Sep 25	1886	Tom Leeds	Sydney	KO	30	Won-Australia-H
Aug 24	1888	George Godfrey	San Francisco	KO	10	—
Dec 27	1888	Joe McAuliffe	San Francisco	KO	24	—
Apr 26	1889	Patsy Cardiff	San Francisco	W	10	—
May 1	1889	Shorty Kincaid	Virginia City, NV	W	2	—
Jul 11	1889	Sailor Brown	Chicago	KO	4	—
Jul 30	1889	Mile Lynch	Buffalo, NY	KO	2	—
Aug 5	1889	Paddy Brennan	Buffalo	KO	1	—
Nov 11	1889	Jem Smith	London	WF	3	—
Dec 25	1889	Peter Maher	Dublin	KO	2	—
Mar 5	1890	Gus Lambert	Troy, NY	ND	4	—
Apr	1890	Dick Keating	Louisville, KY	KO	1	—
May 19	1890	Ed Smith	Chicago	W	5	—
Jul 23	1890	Tom Johnson	Maryville, CA	W	4	—
Oct 21	1890	Joe Goddard	Melbourne	D	3	—
May 21	1891	James J. Corbett★	San Francisco	D	61	—
Jan 12	1892	Al Fish	Chicago	W	2	—
Jan 12	1892	Jack Dalton	Chicago	KO	3	—
—	1892	Jem Smith	London	KO	2	Won-Brit Emp-H
May 30	1892	Frank Slavin	London	KO	10	Ret-Brit Emp-H
Mar 22	1898	James J. Jeffries★	San Francisco	KO'd	3	—
Aug 24	1899	Jim Jeffords	Vancouver, B.C.	KO'd	4	—
Dec 2	1899	Billy Warren	Melbourne	D	25	—

to England where he beat Jem Smith in two rounds to claim the championship of the British Empire. Jackson dominated the fight and forced Smith to resort to wrestling to avoid a knockout.

Back in the U.S., Jackson found an adequate foe in future heavyweight champion James J. Corbett. In 1891, at the California Athletic Club in San Francisco, the two battled to a 61-round draw. Jackson displayed great boxing ability, although some observers believed that the 30-year-old fighter's punches were not the incredibly powerful weapons they had once been. Corbett later stated in his autobiography that Jackson could have beaten any heavyweight Corbett ever saw.

Over the next several years, Jackson fought when he could obtain a match, acted, and ran a boxing school in London. In 1898, an over-the-hill Jackson lost to future champion James J. Jeffries on a third-round knockout. Shortly thereafter, Jackson returned to Australia to fight the tuberculosis which ultimately killed him.

JOE JEANNETTE

HEAVYWEIGHT

Right-handed; 5'10"; 185–205 lbs.

157 bouts, 11/11/1904 to 11/11/1919

Manager: Dan McKetrick

Hall of Fame Induction: 1997

Born: 8/26/1879, North Bergen, NJ

Named: Joseph Jennette

Died: 7/2/1958

Like Sam Langford, the fighter he most admired, Joe Jeannette was barred from fighting for the heavyweight championship not for lack of skill but because of the color of his skin. Racism, promoters' fear of riots, and economic considerations made it nearly impossible for black boxers to get bouts against top whites.

Born in New Jersey, Jeannette learned to fight in street brawls as a youth. On a dare, he became a professional fighter at the age of 25. Jeannette quickly moved into the first rank of black heavyweights. Within two years of turning pro, Jeannette had fought Hall of Famer Jack Johnson seven times, with one win, one loss, one draw, and four no-decisions.

Because most of the white heavyweights of the day refused to face black fighters, black heavyweights were repeatedly matched against each other. Jeannette fought Langford fifteen times, resulting in a record of 3–6–2 with four no-decisions. He fought Sam McVey five times, with a record of 1–1–2 with one no-decision. Jeannette also fought multiple battles with Morris Harris (4), Black Bill (10), Battling Jim Johnson (9), and Hall of Famer Harry Wills (three no-decisions). Because the records for early black fighters are often incomplete or contradictory, it is quite possible that Jeannette actually faced these opponents many more times.

Jeannette's most famous fight occurred on April 17, 1909, when he met Hall of Famer McVey in Paris. The pair had fought a lackluster bout there two months before. The dissatisfied crowd had showered the ring with programs and other debris, and rumors began to circulate that the two had treated the fight as a mere exhibition. Eager to dispel that notion, Jeannette and McVey agreed to fight to the finish with no round limit. The resulting battle was one of the greatest marathons in boxing history. McVey scored the first of his 27 knockdowns in the first round. In the sixteenth McVey countered a Jeannette uppercut with a right to the jaw that most likely would have finished Jeannette—had he not been saved by the bell. Jeannette went down in the next round, the 21st time in seventeen rounds that he had hit the canvas. Looking beaten after nineteen rounds, Jeannette miraculously revived

Jeannette rests against the ropes as Englishman Ben Taylor receives the ten count in the third round of their January 23, 1909, Paris bout.

IN THE RING	WON **79**	LOST **9**	DRAWS **6**	TB 157	KO 66	W 8	WF 5	D 6	KO'd 2	L 7	LF 0	ND 62	NC 1

Date	Year	Opponent	Site	Result / Rounds		Title
SELECTED BOUTS						
Nov 11	1904	Morris Harris	Philadelphia	ND-L	6	—
May 19	1905	Jack Johnson★	Philadelphia	ND-L	6	For-Black-H
Nov 25	1905	Jack Johnson★	Philadelphia	WF	2	—
Dec 2	1905	Jack Johnson★	Philadelphia	ND-L	6	For-Black-H
Dec 25	1905	Sam Langford★	Lawrence, MA	TKO	8	—
Jan 16	1906	Jack Johnson★	New York	ND-L	3	—
Mar 14	1906	Jack Johnson★	Baltimore	L	15	For-Black-H
Apr 5	1906	Sam Langford★	Chelsea, MA	L	15	—
Sep 20	1906	Jack Johnson★	Philadelphia	ND-D	6	For-Black-H
Nov 26	1906	Jack Johnson★	Portland, ME	D	10	For-Black-H
Jan 11	1907	Sam Langford★	Lawrence	D	12	—
Apr 15	1907	Sam McVey★	New York	ND-W	10	—
Mar 3	1908	Sam Langford★	Boston	D	12	—
Sep 1	1908	Sam Langford★	New York	ND-L	6	—
Feb 20	1909	Sam McVey★	Paris	L	20	For-VacBlk-H
Apr 17	1909	Sam McVey★	Paris	TKO	50	Won-Black-H
Sep 6	1910	Sam Langford★	Boston	L	15	Lost-Black-H
Sep 5	1911	Sam Langford★	New York	ND-D	10	For-Black-H
Jul 1	1913	Harry Wills★	New Orleans	ND	10	—
Dec 20	1913	Sam Langford★	Paris	L	20	For-Black-H
Mar 21	1914	Georges Carpentier★	Paris	W	15	—
Jun 9	1914	Harry Wills★	New Orleans	ND-D	10	—
Apr 13	1915	Sam Langford★	Boston	W	12	Reg-Black-H
May 12	1916	Sam Langford★	Syracuse, NY	KO'd	7	Lost-Black-H
Sep 14	1917	Sam Langford★	Toledo, OH	ND-W	12	For-Black-H
Oct 20	1919	Harry Wills★	Jersey City, NJ	ND-L	8	For-Black-H
Nov 11	1919	Barley Madden	Bayonne, NJ	WF	4	—

and seized control of the fight. As the bout moved past the 40-round mark, Jeannette began to floor McVey with regularity, but still could not put him away. In the 42nd, Jeannette dropped McVey seven times. Finally, after 49 rounds, McVey could not continue. Despite having been knocked down 27 times, Jeannette had triumphed in this unbelievable test of endurance, courage, and boxing ability. This fight underscores Jeannette's indomitable will.

In one of his few bouts against a top-quality white opponent, Jeannette decisioned Hall of Famer Georges Carpentier in 1914 when the young European champ was only twenty. In later years, Jeannette lamented the fact that champion Jack Johnson refused to give him a title bout, saying, "Jack forgot about his old friends after he became champion and drew the color line against his own people."

Jeannette continued to fight until his retirement in 1919 at the age of 40. While existing records credit him with slightly over 150 fights, Jeannette believed that he had actually fought about 400 times. After leaving the ring, he worked as a referee, operated a gym, and ran a limousine rental company.

JAMES J. JEFFRIES
The Boilermaker

HEAVYWEIGHT

Right-handed; 6'2½"; 206–227 lbs.

21 bouts, 1896 to 7/4/1910

Manager: William A. Brady

Heavyweight Champ 1899–1905

Hall of Fame Induction: 1990

Born: 4/15/1875, Carroll, Ohio

Named: James Jackson Jeffries

Died: 3/3/1953

One of the finest heavyweights in history, James J. Jeffries retired undefeated but, six years later, was coaxed into an ill-fated comeback fight with Jack Johnson.

Jeffries moved with his family from Ohio to a Los Angeles–area farm at the age of seven. As a youth, he was a great athlete who distinguished himself in boxing, wrestling, and track. While working as a boilermaker and for a meat packing company, among other jobs, Jeffries boxed at the East Side Athletic Club. In his first professional fight, he knocked out Hank Griffin in the fourteenth round. Nineteen at the time, Jeffries waited until he was 21 to box professionally fulltime, honoring a promise to his parents.

Jeffries fought draws with Gus Ruhlin and Joe Choynski in 1897. The next year, he won five fights, including a knockout victory over Peter Jackson and a decision over Tom Sharkey, whom Jeffries would later call his toughest opponent. He also went to New York, where he agreed to fight twice in one night. He won a decision over Bob Armstrong, but broke his thumb and had to cancel the second bout. Jeffries was shaken by the crowd's boos and returned to California.

Jeffries then came under the direction of a new manager, William A. Brady, who was able to sign his man for a match with the world heavyweight champion, Bob Fitzsimmons, at the Coney Island Athletic Club. Jeffries embarked on an arduous training regimen for this bout. With the help of middleweight Tommy Ryan he devised a new fighting style which he intended to try out against the lanky Fitzsimmons. Jeffries fought in a crouch with his left arm extended and his face protected by his right forearm. He developed a terrific left hook, as well as a straight left he could throw out of the crouch, often at short range and with great effect. In the championship

Author Jack London led the chorus that urged Jeffries (L) out of retirement to face Jack Johnson in Reno, NV, on July 4, 1910.

IN THE RING	WON 18	LOST 1	DRAWS 2	TB 21	KO 15	W 3	WF 0	D 2	KO'd 1	L 0	LF 0

Date	Year	Opponent	Site	Result / Rounds		Title
SELECTED BOUTS						
—	1896	Hank Griffin	Los Angeles	KO	14	—
—	1896	Jim Barber	Los Angeles	KO	2	—
Jul 2	1896	Dan Long	San Francisco	KO	2	—
Apr 9	1897	T. Van Buskirk	San Francisco	KO	2	—
May 19	1897	Henry Baker	San Francisco	KO	9	—
Jul 17	1897	Gus Ruhlin	San Francisco	D	20	—
Nov 30	1897	Joe Choynski★	San Francisco	D	20	—
Feb 28	1898	Joe Goddard	Los Angeles	KO	4	—
Mar 22	1898	Peter Jackson★	San Francisco	KO	3	—
Apr 22	1898	Pete Everett	San Francisco	KO	3	—
May 6	1898	Tom Sharkey ★	San Francisco	W	20	—
Aug 5	1898	Bob Armstrong	New York	W	10	—
Jun 9	1899	♛ Bob Fitzsimmons★	Coney Island, NY	KO	11	Won-World-H
Nov 3	1899	Tom Sharkey ★	Coney Island	W	25	Ret-World-H
Apr 6	1900	Jack Finnegan	Detroit	KO	1	Ret-World-H
May 11	1900	James J. Corbett★	Coney Island	KO	23	Ret-World-H
Nov 15	1901	Gus Ruhlin	San Francisco	TKO	5	Ret-World-H
Jul 25	1902	Bob Fitzsimmons★	San Francisco	KO	8	Ret-World-H
Aug 14	1903	James J. Corbett★	San Francisco	KO	10	Ret-World-H
Aug 26	1904	Jack Munroe	San Francisco	TKO	2	Ret-World-H
Jul 4	1910	♛ Jack Johnson★	Reno, NV	KO'd	15	For-World-H

bout, Jeffries knocked Fitzsimmons down in the second round. Early in the fight, Fitzsimmons landed some hard punches, but Jeffries's blows were more effective. In the tenth, Jeffries knocked the champion down twice with powerful lefts. In the eleventh, he finished off Fitzsimmons with a left hook and a right uppercut.

The new champion then won a very tough 25-round decision over Sharkey before facing the former champion James J. Corbett. Jeffries had previously served as Corbett's sparring partner and welcomed the chance to best him in the ring. Corbett had the advantage in the first ten rounds and, after twenty rounds, still had a clear lead. But in the 23rd, Jeffries knocked Corbett out with a straight left and then a left hook to the jaw.

Jeffries defended his title four more times with four knockout victories before retiring. Included among his victims were Fitzsimmons, Corbett, and Ruhlin. After six years of retirement, at age 35, Jeffries returned to the ring in an attempt to wrest the championship from Jack Johnson. Though out of shape at the time he signed for the match, Jeffries brought himself into condition. Touted as a "Great White Hope," Jeffries was nevertheless no match for Johnson, who knocked him out in the fifteenth round.

In retirement, Jeffries owned a bar and a farm where he bred prize cattle, although a series of poor investments forced him to declare bankruptcy in the 1920s. He also performed in boxing exhibitions in vaudeville and acted in movies.

JACK JOHNSON
The Galveston Giant, Li'l Arthur

H E A V Y W E I G H T

Right-handed; 6'¼"; 185–221 lbs.

123 bouts, 1897 to 5/15/1928

Managers: Morris Hart, Johnny Connors, Alec McLean, Sam Fitzpatrick, Abe Arends, George Little, Tom Flanagan, Sig Hart

Heavyweight Champion 1908–15

Hall of Fame Induction: 1990

Born: 3/31/1878, Galveston, TX

Named: John Arthur Johnson

Died: 6/10/1946

The first African-American heavyweight champion, Jack Johnson dared to crash through the color bar that had created two classes of boxers since the sport's beginnings. A gaudy, bold character who lived just as he wanted, Johnson enraged the defenders of white supremacy with his refusal to accept anything less than equality. He was beloved by blacks and some whites, but thoroughly hated and eventually conquered by those who saw him as a threat to America's divided society.

The son of a former slave, Johnson grew up poor in Galveston, Texas, where at that time, blacks were forbidden to use the same sidewalks as whites. He got a little schooling, then went to work on the docks and elsewhere. Johnson honed his fighting skills in "battle royals," racist spectacles in which several black men

Johnson (R) and champion Tommy Burns met for the title in Rushcutter's Bay Arena, Sydney, on December 26, 1908. After Burns was thoroughly battered, police stepped in, and the referee declared Johnson the victor.

IN THE RING	WON 77	LOST 13	DRAWS 14	TB 123	KO 48	W 26	WF 3	D 14	KO'd 7	L 5	LF 1	ND 19

Date	Year		Opponent	Site	Result / Rounds		Title
SELECTED BOUTS							
—	1897		Jim Rocks	Galveston, TX	KO	4	—
Feb 25	1901		Joe Choynski ★	Galveston	KO'd	3	—
Nov 4	1901		Hank Griffin	Bakersfield, CA	L	20	—
Dec 27	1901		Hank Griffin	Oakland	D	15	—
Oct 31	1902		George Gardner	San Francisco	W	20	—
Feb 3	1903		Denver Ed Martin	Los Angeles	W	20	Won-Black-H
Feb 27	1903		Sam McVey ★	Los Angeles	W	20	Ret-Black-H
Oct 27	1903		Sam McVey ★	Los Angeles	W	20	Ret-Black-H
Apr 22	1904		Sam McVey ★	San Francisco	KO	20	Ret-Black-H
Oct 18	1904		Denver Ed Martin	Los Angeles	KO	2	Ret-Black-H
Mar 28	1905		Marvin Hart	San Francisco	L	20	—
May 9	1905		Joe Jeannette ★	Philadelphia	ND-W	6	Ret-Black-H
Mar 14	1906		Joe Jeannette ★	Baltimore	W	15	Ret-Black-H
Apr 26	1906		Sam Langford ★	Chelsea, MA	W	15	Ret-Black-H
Jul 17	1907		Bob Fitzsimmons ★	Philadelphia	KO	2	—
Nov 2	1907		Jim Flynn	San Francisco	KO	11	—
Dec 26	1908	♛	Tommy Burns ★	Sydney	TKO	14	Won-World-H
May 19	1909		Phila. Jack O'Brien ★	Philadelphia	ND-D	6	—
Sep 9	1909		Al Kaufman	San Francisco	ND-W	10	Ret-World-H
Oct 16	1909		Stanley Ketchel ★	Colma, CA	KO	12	Ret-World-H
Jul 4	1910		James J. Jeffries ★	Reno, NV	KO	15	Ret-World-H
Jul 4	1912		Jim Flynn	Las Vegas, NM	WD	9	Ret-World-H
Dec 19	1913		Jim Johnson	Paris	D	10	Ret-World-H
Jun 27	1914		Frank Moran	Paris	W	20	Ret-World-H
Apr 5	1915		Jess Willard ★	Havana, Cuba	KO'd	26	Lost-World-H
Apr 23	1916		Arthur Craven	Barcelona, Spain	KO	1	—
Apr 3	1918		Blink McCloskey	Madrid	W	4	—
May 17	1920		George Roberts	Tijuana, Mexico	KO	3	—
Feb 22	1923		Homer Smith	Montreal	W	10	—
May 2	1926		Pat Lester	Nogales, Mexico	W	15	—
May 15	1928		Bill Hartwell	Kansas City, KS	KO'd	7	—

fought at once until the last man standing was declared the winner. White audiences then tossed coins to the victor. These crude free-for-alls were often the only venues available to black fighters, and only the very best emerged victorious.

Johnson turned professional in 1897 with a knockout victory over Jim Rocks. West Coast champion Joe Choynski took Johnson down in 1901, then taught him ring tactics when both were jailed after police raided the fight. In 1903, Johnson won a twenty-round decision over Denver Ed Martin for the black heavyweight title, which he defended four times in the next two years. In 1905, he lost a decision to future heavyweight champion Marvin Hart. Two years later, Johnson scored a second-round knockout of former heavyweight champion Bob Fitzsimmons.

Even though he was an obvious contender for the crown, Johnson was

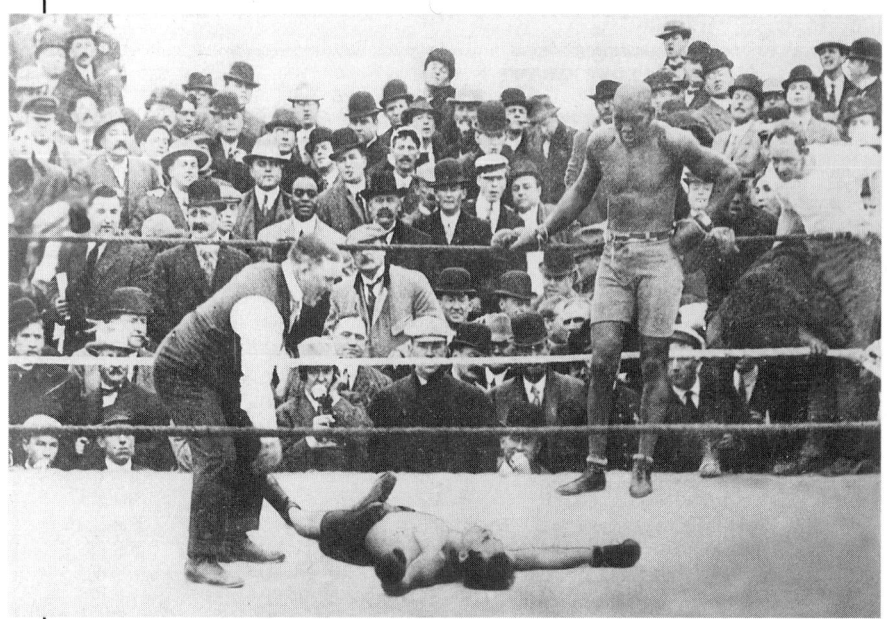

Outweighed by 35 pounds, Stanley Ketchel survived twelve rounds before succumbing to Johnson's knockout punch on October 16, 1909, in Colma, CA. Ketchel floored Johnson earlier in that same twelfth round.

repeatedly refused a shot at the heavyweight title because of his race. He was finally given his chance in 1908 when he faced champion Tommy Burns in Australia in a stadium erected especially for the fight, in Rushcutter's Bay near Sydney. Johnson won on a technical knockout in the fourteenth round to become the first black heavyweight champion of the world.

White society was outraged, and Johnson rubbed salt in the wound by flaunting his fame and wealth. The search was already on for a "Great White Hope" to reclaim the crown. In 1909, middleweight champion Stanley Ketchel tried to topple Johnson. When Ketchel floored Johnson in the twelfth, the champion rose and knocked Ketchel out with one vicious punch. After the match, Johnson claimed that he had agreed to carry Ketchel and had become outraged when Ketchel knocked him down.

Finally, white hopes were pinned to former champion James J. Jeffries, who was persuaded to come out of retirement to face Johnson on July 4, 1910, in Reno, Nevada. Jeffries, who hadn't been in the ring for six years, trained hard for the fight. Movie cameras recorded the battle, which Johnson clearly dominated. Jeffries was totally defenseless by the fifteenth, when Johnson went for the easy knockout. Blacks in cities across the country burst into an extended celebration, starting race riots in which several people died. The films of Jeffries's demolition by the black champ were never shown.

Meanwhile, Johnson's bi-racial love life sent his enemies scurrying for revenge, and eventually he was convicted of transporting a woman across state lines for immoral purposes. Johnson, who often befriended prostitutes, had given money to his friend Belle Screiber to fund her trip from Pittsburgh to Chicago to establish a brothel there. Johnson did not expect to benefit from the enterprise. However, after his conviction he avoided prison by fleeing to Canada and then Europe, where he twice defended his title in Paris.

In 1915, Johnson was persuaded to fight the huge 6'6" Jess Willard in a title bout in Havana. By then 37 years old, Johnson tired as the fight passed the twenty-round mark. In the 26th, Willard knocked Johnson out with a left to the body and a jab to the head. A promise from the fight's promoter to get Johnson a pardon in the U.S. failed to materialize, and the fighter continued to live in exile. In 1920, Johnson surrendered to federal authorities and served eight months in Kansas's Leavenworth prison. After his release, he fought sporadically until 1928 when he retired at the age of 50. Johnson also acted in Hollywood movies, owned a Chicago nightclub, and fought bulls in Spain during his long career. He was working as an amusement arcade entertainer when he died in a car accident in 1946. Sports historian Arthur Ashe later called Johnson the most significant black athlete in history.

Jess Willard and Johnson exchange blows in the April 5, 1915, fight in Havana that resulted in the loss of Johnson's crown. Referee Jack Welch counted the supine, glassy-eyed Johnson out in the 26th round.

LOUIS ("KID") KAPLAN
Meriden Buzzsaw

FEATHERWEIGHT

Right-handed; 5'4"; 119–138 lbs.

153 bouts, 9/1919 to 2/20/1933

Managers: Joe Beasley, Dinny McMahon, Billy Gibson

Featherweight Champion 1925–27

Hall of Fame Induction: 2003

Born: 10/15/1901, Kiev, Russia

Named: Gershon Mendeloff

Died: 10/26/1970

A tough, aggressive featherweight and lightweight, Louis ("Kid") Kaplan was born in Kiev, Russia, on October 15, 1901. He came to the United States and settled in Meriden, Connecticut, with his family when he was five years old. He learned to fight in the streets and once ran away to New York City briefly when he was eleven.

Kaplan turned professional in September 1919 with a no-decision bout versus Young Dempsey in Jersey City. After four fights in Jersey City, Kaplan returned to Connecticut. He tirelessly worked in the gym to build his strength and stamina, endlessly pounding the heavy bag. Though the 5'4" Kaplan campaigned as a featherweight , he had a thickly muscled upper body. He was neither a graceful boxer nor a powerful puncher, but he was a relentless fighter. He plowed straight ahead, throwing a barrage of punches. His opponents had to be especially wary of his left hook. Kaplan could absorb punishment as well.

Like many fighters of his era, Kaplan kept very busy. In his first four pro years he compiled an excellent record of 31-6-5, plus eleven no-decision bouts. When Johnny Dundee vacated his featherweight title, the New York State Athletic Commission set up an elimination tournament to crown a new champ. Kaplan participated. In his first bout, he won a hard-fought decision over Bobby Garcia. In the second, Kaplan knocked out Jose Lombardo.

On January 2, 1925, Kaplan faced Danny Kramer for the title. There were rumors that Kaplan would have to win by knockout because the "fix" was in for Kramer if the fight went the distance. From the opening bell Kaplan attacked. In the second, Kaplan fired a left hook to the neck, catching Kramer off guard and sending him to the canvas. Kaplan won every round as he pursued Kramer with rights and lefts to the jaw. By the end of the seventh round, Kramer's right eye was almost closed. Kaplan pummelled Kramer's bleeding face until Kramer's corner threw in the towel approximately one minute and ten seconds into the ninth round.

On August 27, 1925, Kaplan defended his

In Hartford, on August 24, 1931, Kaplan (L) squares off against former lightweight champ Sammy Mandell.

IN THE RING	WON 104	LOST 18	DRAWS 12	TB 153	KO 25	W 76	WF 3	D 12	KO'd 3	L 14	LF 1	ND 19

Date	Year	Opponent	Site	Result / Rounds		Title
SELECTED BOUTS						
Sep	1919	Young Dempsey	Jersey City, NJ	ND	4	—
Dec 18	1922	⑩ Babe Herman	Meriden, CT	L	12	—
Mar 8	1923	⑩ Babe Herman	Meriden	D	12	—
Mar 20	1924	⑩ Bobby Garcia	Waterbury, CT	W	12	—
Dec 12	1924	⑩ Jose Lombardo	New York	KO	4	—
Jan 2	1925	⑩ Danny Kramer	New York	TKO	9	Won-Vac World-FE
Aug 27	1925	⑩ Babe Herman	Waterbury	D	15	Ret-World-FE
Dec 18	1925	⑩ Babe Herman	New York	W	15	Ret-World-FE
Mar 1	1926	⑩ Billy Petrolle★	Hartford, CT	W	12	—
Jun 28	1926	Bobby Garcia	Hartford	W	10	Ret-World-FE
May 9	1927	⑩ Al Foreman	Philadelphia	W	10	—
Oct 18	1927	⑩ Jimmy McLarnin★	Chicago	KO'd	8	—
May 31	1928	⑩ Manuel Quintero	New Haven	L	10	—
Jan 11	1929	⑩ Johnny Jadick	Boston	KO	7	—
Apr 2	1929	⑩ Joe Glick	New Haven	W	10	—
May 10	1929	⑩ Billy Wallace	New York	W	10	—
Dec 13	1929	⑩ Andy Callahan	New York	W	10	—
Jun 2	1930	⑩ Joey Medill	Hartford	W	10	—
Sep 24	1930	♛ Battling Battalino★	Hartford	W	10	—
Feb 4	1931	⑩ Jack Portney	New Haven	W	10	—
Aug 24	1931	Sammy Mandell★	Hartford	W	10	—
Feb 20	1933	Cocoa Kid	New Haven	L	10	—

title against Babe Herman in Waterbury, Connecticut, before 20,000 fans who paid $59,000 for their ducats. Both the attendance and the gate established new state records. This was the sixth of seven Kaplan–Herman bouts; it ended in a draw. In their final meeting on December 18, 1925, Kaplan floored Herman four times en route to a decision win.

In 1927, Kaplan decided he could not keep making weight and relinquished his featherweight title. When word got out that Kaplan was considering giving up the championship, Kramer's manager, Boo Boo Hoff, and Philadelphia gamblers offered Kaplan $50,000 to lose his title to Kramer in the ring. Kaplan refused the offer. On October 18, 1927, Kaplan faced Hall of Famer Jimmy McLarnin, then the top-rated lightweight contender. Kaplan started out like a ball of fire. He broke McLarnin's jaw in the first round and knocked him down four times in the first two rounds. However, by the fourth round Kaplan began to tire. In the eighth, McLarnin knocked Kaplan out with a straight right to the jaw.

Although still a highly ranked contender for several years, Kaplan received no more title shots. He retired after losing a ten-round decision to Cocoa Kid on February 20, 1933. At the time of his retirement, Kaplan revealed that he was blind in his right eye. In retirement, Kaplan sold insurance, operated a restaurant, refereed, and worked for the Connecticut Department of Motor Vehicles and the Connecticut Department of Public Works before his death on October 26, 1970.

STANLEY KETCHEL
The Michigan Assassin

MIDDLEWEIGHT

Right-handed; 5′9″; 142–170 lbs.

64 bouts, 5/2/1904 to 6/10/1910

Managers: Joe O'Connor 1904–09, Willus Britt 1909–10

Middleweight Champion 1908–10

Hall of Fame Induction: 1990

Born: 9/14/1886, Grand Rapids, MI

Named: Stanislaus Kiecal

Died: 10/15/1910

Stanley Ketchel is considered by some to be the greatest middleweight of all time. A natural fighter who was never formally trained, Ketchel propelled himself to fame and the middleweight championship in just six years. Sadly, his career ended when he was murdered at age 24. Ketchel's life often resembled a torrid movie script. Orphaned at fourteen, he ran away from his adoptive home and lived as a hobo, travelling through the Canadian and American West. In Butte, Montana, he worked as a bouncer and also took on all comers in fights at a local theatre. He fought his first recorded professional bout—a one-round knockout—in 1903.

Ketchel lost only twice in his first 42 matches, all fought in Montana. In 1907, he went to California, where he won matches with several well-respected fighters, and by 1908, he had achieved national prominence. His twentieth-round knockout of Jack (Twin) Sullivan earned him the vacant world middleweight title. In his first three months as champion, Ketchel decisioned Billy Papke, and knocked out Hugo Kelly and Joe Thomas. In the rematch with Papke, the challenger punched Ketchel in the head as the fighters were meeting in the center of the ring to shake hands. The referee merely chided Papke, and the fight commenced. Still dazed by the illegal punch, Ketchel never seized control of the fight and was knocked out in the twelfth round. Eleven weeks later, Ketchel fought Papke with a savage fury and knocked him out in the eleventh, becoming the first middleweight champion to regain a lost title.

In 1909, Ketchel fought some of the most memorable battles of his career. In a no-decision bout against light heavyweight champion Philadelphia Jack O'Brien, Ketchel absorbed a solid beating for six rounds, but came back to knock O'Brien down four times in the ninth and tenth rounds. The fight would have been a knockout if O'Brien hadn't been saved by the bell. In their rematch, Ketchel demolished O'Brien in three rounds.

Feeling bold after his

World champion boxers visit Ketchel's grave—Jimmy Clabby (#2 from left), Johnny Kilbane (3), Johnny Coulon (4), and Luther McCarthy (5).

IN THE RING	WON 52	LOST 4	DRAWS 4	TB 64	KO 49	W 3	WF 0	D 4	KO'd 2	L 2	LF 0	ND 4

Date	Year	Opponent	Site	Result / Rounds		Title

SELECTED BOUTS

Date	Year	Opponent	Site	Result	Rounds	Title
May 2	1903	Kid Tracy	Butte, MT	KO	1	—
May 11	1904	Maurice Thompson	Butte	L	6	—
Oct 21	1904	Maurice Thompson	Butte	L	10	—
Mar 23	1907	Mike McClure	Redding, CA	KO	7	—
May 3	1907	Benny Hart	Marysville, CA	KO	8	—
May 23	1907	George Brown	Sacramento	KO	3	—
Sep 2	1907	Joe Thomas	Colma, CA	KO	32	—
Dec 12	1907	Joe Thomas	San Francisco	W	20	—
Feb 22	1908	♛ Mike (Twin) Sullivan	Colma	KO	1	—
May 9	1908	Jack (Twin) Sullivan	Colma	KO	20	Won-Vac World-M
Jun 4	1908	Billy Papke ★	Milwaukee	W	10	Ret-World-M
Jul 31	1908	Hugo Kelly	San Francisco	KO	3	Ret-World-M
Aug 18	1908	Joe Thomas	San Francisco	KO	2	Ret-World-M
Sep 7	1908	Billy Papke ★	Vernon, CA	TKO'd	12	Lost-World-M
Nov 26	1908	♛ Billy Papke ★	Colma	KO	11	Reg-World-M
Mar 26	1909	♛ Phila. Jack O'Brien ★	New York	ND-W	10	—
Jun 2	1909	Tony Caponi	Schenectady, NY	KO	4	—
Jun 9	1909	♛ Phila. Jack O'Brien ★	Philadelphia	KO	3	—
Jul 5	1909	Billy Papke ★	Colma	W	20	Ret-World-M
Oct 16	1909	♛ Jack Johnson ★	Colma	KO'd	12	For-World-H
Apr 27	1910	Sam Langford ★	Philadelphia	ND-W	6	—
Jun 10	1910	Jim Smith	New York	KO	5	—

Feeling bold after his strong performances, Ketchel agreed to challenge Jack Johnson for the heavyweight championship. The champ far outweighed Ketchel and was at the peak of his career. For the first six rounds, Ketchel stayed out of Johnson's way. In the seventh, Ketchel caught Johnson with a stinging left to the jaw. Ketchel went on the attack in the eighth and on into the tenth round. Meanwhile, Johnson landed enough punches to bloody Ketchel's face. The moment of truth came in the twelfth round, when Ketchel pounded a right into Johnson's jaw that threw the champ off balance. To the roaring of the crowd, Johnson briefly sat down on the canvas but rose up enraged and blasted Ketchel with a right to the jaw. Ketchel, his mouth a ruin, fell and stayed down for the count.

After the loss to Johnson, Ketchel continued to rack up victories. In 1910, determined to get another shot at the championship, he went to a ranch in Conway, Missouri, to train. In this remote locale, the melodrama of Ketchel's life caught up with him. He died with a bullet in his lung, shot by a jealous hired hand who claimed the handsome prizefighter tried to steal his ladyfriend. The killer, Walter Dipley, was convicted of first-degree murder and served 23 years in prison.

Had he not died, Ketchel might have accomplished much more, perhaps even winning the heavyweight championship. As it was, he built a great record as middleweight champion and recorded 49 knockouts in 64 fights.

KID CHOCOLATE
The Cuban Bon Bon

FEATHERWEIGHT

Right-handed; 5'6"; 120–132 lbs.
146 bouts, 2/10/1928 to 12/18/1938
Manager: Luis Gutierrez
Jr. Lightweight Champ 1931–33
NY World Featherwt. Champ 1932–34
Hall of Fame Induction: 1991
Born: 1/6/1910, Cerro, Cuba
Named: Eligio Sardinias-Montalbo
Died: 8/8/1988

One of the most popular fighters in New York from the late 1920s to the late 1930s, Kid Chocolate dazzled fans with his speed and two-handed punching ability. The Kid, a Cuban whose birth name was Eligio Sardinias-Montalbo, first started fighting as a newspaper boy in Havana, defending his sales turf. After he won an amateur boxing tournament sponsored by the newspaper *La Noche*, the Kid came under the guidance of the newspaper's sports editor, Luis Gutierrez. Neither Gutierrez nor the Kid knew a lot about boxing at that point and part of the Kid's training was to watch films of famous fights.

The Kid never lost a fight as an amateur and racked up 21 knockouts in 21 bouts as a pro before taking on New York in 1928 at the age of eighteen. The Kid quickly made a name for himself, and his fights moved from small clubs to Madison Square Garden. By 1929, he was ranked the top featherweight contender in the annual ratings by *The Ring*. In 1930, the Kid faced his stiffest challenge when he met Hall of Famer Jackie ("Kid") Berg at the Polo Grounds with 40,000 fans watching. Berg outweighed the Kid by almost ten pounds. The Kid's best round of the fight was the third, when he pounded Berg with jarring uppercuts to the head. As the fight went on, however, Berg's relentless attack tired the Kid. Berg won a fairly close decision, handing the Kid the first defeat of his career.

Later that same year, the Kid lost decisions to Fidel LaBarba and featherweight champion Battling Battalino. Ringside observers said the Kid appeared slightly listless. The Kid was back

Kid Chocolate, here posing in bag gloves, first saw pro boxing in films shown in Havana theatres.

IN THE RING	WON 131	LOST 9	DRAWS 6	TB 146	KO 50	W 80	WF 1	D 6	KO'd 2	L 7	LF 0

Date	Year		Opponent	Site	Result / Rounds		Title

SELECTED BOUTS

Date	Year		Opponent	Site	Result / Rounds		Title
Feb 10	1928		Kid Sotolongo	Havana, Cuba	KO	5	—
Aug 25	1928		Nick Mercer	Brooklyn	KO	3	—
Sep 17	1928		Sammy Tisch	New York	W	10	—
May 22	1929	⑩	Fidel LaBarba★	New York	W	10	—
Aug 29	1929		Al Singer	New York	W	12	—
Aug 7	1930	♛	Jackie ("Kid") Berg★	New York	L	10	—
Nov 3	1930	⓪	Fidel LaBarba★	New York	L	10	—
Dec 12	1930	♛	Battling Battalino★	New York	L	15	For-World-FE
Jul 15	1931	♛	Benny Bass★	Philadelphia	TKO	7	Won-World-JL
Nov 20	1931	♛	Tony Canzoneri★	New York	L	15	For-World-L
Apr 10	1932		Davey Abad	Havana	W	15	Ret-World-JL
Jun 22	1932		Johnny Farr	Pittsburgh	W	10	—
Jul 18	1932	⑩	Jackie ("Kid") Berg★	Long Island City, NY	L	15	—
Aug 4	1932	⑩	Eddie Shea	Chicago	W	10	Ret-World-JL
Aug 10	1932		Johnny Farr	Cincinnati	W	10	—
Oct 4	1932		Johnny Farr	Detroit	W	10	—
Oct 13	1932	⑩	Lew Feldman	New York	TKO	12	Won-Vac NY World-FE
Dec 9	1932	⑩	Fidel LaBarba★	New York	W	15	Ret-NY World-FE
May 1	1933		Johnny Farr	Philadelphia	W	10	Ret-World-JL
May 19	1933	⑩	Seaman Watson	New York	W	15	Ret-NY World-FE
Jul 15	1933		Nic Bensa	Madrid	W	10	—
Nov 24	1933	⑩	Tony Canzoneri★	New York	KO'd	2	—
Dec 4	1933	⑩	Frankie Wallace	Cleveland	W	10	—
Dec 25	1933	⑩	Frankie Klick	Philadelphia	TKO'd	7	Lost-World-JL
Apr 16	1934	⑩	Frankie Wallace	San Francisco	W	10	—
Dec 18	1938		Nicky Jerome	Havana	D	10	—

in top form by July of 1931, when he won his first title with a technical knockout over junior lightweight champion Benny Bass. The same year, the Kid attempted to add the lightweight title to his holdings, but fell victim to the blistering attack of champion Tony Canzoneri, who won by decision.

In 1932, the Kid lost a rematch with Berg but claimed New York's world featherweight title when he TKO'd Lew Feldman at Madison Square Garden. The Kid defended this particular title twice before relinquishing it, allegedly for failing to make the weight.

By 1933, the Kid clearly was on the downside of his career. Canzoneri knocked him out in two rounds, and he lost his junior lightweight championship when Frankie Klick scored a technical knockout over him in seven. He continued to fight until 1938 against second-rate competition.

Although he was sometimes criticized for not training seriously enough for important bouts, the Kid was recognized as a consummate ring artist: skillful, quick, and powerful. His ring earnings spent on New York night life and grand good times, the Kid retired to Cuba, where he operated a gym.

JOHNNY KILBANE

FEATHERWEIGHT

Right-handed; 5'5"; 122–126 lbs.
142 bouts, 12/2/1907 to 6/2/1923
Manager: Jimmy Dunn
Featherweight Champion 1912–23
Hall of Fame Induction: 1995
Born: 4/18/1889, Cleveland, OH
Named: John Patrick Kilbane
Died: 5/31/1957

The man who ended the featherweight championship reign of Abe Attell, Johnny Kilbane spent much of his life in the public eye. Kilbane defended the featherweight title for eleven years and, in retirement, became a senator in the Ohio state legislature. A Cleveland native, Kilbane started fighting professionally in the Ohio area in 1907 with three victories, according to the somewhat spotty records of his early career.

Kilbane was a good scientific boxer who could also punch. He fought Attell three times, twice in championship bouts. In 1910, he lost a decision to Attell. Two years later, on a extremely hot night in Vernon, California, Kilbane took the crown from Attell with a twenty-round decision. Kilbane scored frequently with his left jab, while Attell resorted to heeling, butting, and elbowing. After the fight, Kilbane claimed that Attell had coated his back with chloroform in an attempt to daze his opponent. Attell said it was cooling cocoa butter and, for many years, bore ill will towards Kilbane for this charge, which Kilbane often repeated. Through five title bouts, including one in 1913, in which he fought Hall of Famer Johnny Dundee to a draw, Kilbane defended his crown until 1923.

In 1917, Kilbane attempted to move up in class and faced the lightweight

On February 22, 1912, in Vernon, CA, Kilbane triumphs over Abe Attell, ending Attell's eleven-year grip on the featherweight crown.

IN THE RING	WON 51	LOST 4	DRAWS 7	TB 142	KO 25	W 25	WF 1	D 7	KO'd 2	L 2	LF 0	ND 78	NC 2

Date	Year	Opponent	Site	Result / Rounds		Title
SELECTED BOUTS						
Dec 2	1907	Tom Mangan	Cleveland	W	3	—
Jan 1	1908	Tommy Kilbane	Lorain, OH	W	3	—
Feb 10	1908	Tommy Kilbane	Cleveland	D	4	—
Nov 25	1908	Tommy Kilbane	Cleveland	W	25	—
Dec 31	1909	Tommy Kilbane	Canton, OH	W	15	—
Oct 24	1910	♛ Abe Attell★	Kansas City, MO	L	10	For-World-FE
Jan 31	1911	♛ Abe Attell★	Cleveland	NC	4	—
May 6	1911	Joe Rivers	Vernon, CA	L	20	—
May 30	1911	Jimmy Walsh	Canton	ND-W	12	—
Sep 16	1911	Joe Rivers	Vernon	KO	16	—
Dec 23	1911	Charley White	Cleveland	ND-W	12	—
Feb 22	1912	♛ Abe Attell★	Vernon	W	20	Won-World-FE
May 21	1912	Jimmy Walsh	Boston	D	12	Ret-World-FE
Sep 4	1912	Johnny Dundee★	New York	ND-D	10	—
Apr 29	1913	Johnny Dundee★	Vernon	D	20	Ret-World-FE
Jun 10	1913	Jimmy Fox	Oakland	TKO	6	Ret-World-FE
Sep 16	1913	Jimmy Walsh	Boston	W	12	Ret-World-FE
Mar 17	1915	Kid Williams★	Philadelphia	ND-W	6	—
Apr 29	1915	Benny Leonard★	New York	ND-W	10	
Sep 4	1916	George ("K.O.") Chaney	Cedar Point, OH	KO	3	Ret-World-FE
Mar 26	1917	Eddie Wallace	Bridgeport, CT	D	12	Ret-World-FE
May 1	1917	Freddie Welsh★	New York	ND-W	10	—
Jul 25	1917	♛ Benny Leonard★	Philadelphia	KO'd	3	—
Apr 21	1920	Alvie Miller	Lorain	KO	7	Ret-World-FE
May 25	1921	Freddy Jacks	Cleveland	ND-W	10	—
Sep 17	1921	Danny Frush	Cleveland	KO	7	Ret-World-FE
Jun 2	1923	Eugene Criqui★	New York	KO'd	6	Lost-World-FE

champion Benny Leonard in a non-title fight. Kilbane could not handle the heavier Leonard and was knocked out in three rounds. World War I put Kilbane's professional boxing career on hold while he served as a boxing instructor at Camp Sherman.

In 1921, Kilbane again defended his title in Cleveland with a knockout of Danny Frush. In 1923, at age 34, he returned to the ring after almost two years of inactivity to face Eugene Criqui at New York's Polo Grounds. Reportedly, Kilbane received $75,000 to come back. At the time, Criqui was the European champion. Past his prime, Kilbane could not handle the punching power of Criqui, who had the champ sagging on the ropes and knocked him out in the sixth.

Never known for his knock-out power, Kilbane knew how to put forth just enough effort to win. If necessary, he could throw a mean punch, but for the most part, he was content to outbox an opponent and avoid getting hit.

In retirement, Kilbane refereed and operated a gym as well as serving in the state senate. He was clerk of the Cleveland Municipal Court when he died in 1957.

FIDEL LABARBA

F L Y W E I G H T

Right-handed; 5'3"; 112–124 lbs.
95 bouts, 9/18/1924 to 2/13/33
Manager: George Blake
1924 Olympic Flyweight Gold Medalist
Flyweight Champion 1927
Hall of Fame Induction: 1996
Born: 9/29/1905, New York, NY
Died: 10/3/1981

A championship boxer who gave up his title to attend Stanford University, Fidel LaBarba was one of the first fighters to parlay an Olympic gold medal into a professional career. A converted lefty, LaBarba was a great defensive fighter whose weaving style often kept him from getting hit. He was never knocked out.

LaBarba was the son of Italian immigrants. He grew up in Los Angeles where he became a paperboy, often using his fists to claim a busy street corner. At age fourteen, he came under the direction of manager George Blake. He fought successfully as an amateur, and in 1924, won top flyweight honors at the national Amateur Athletic Union tournament in Boston, then went on to Paris to win a gold medal at the Olympics. He turned pro later that year while still attending high school.

LaBarba's third professional fight was against Hall of Famer Jimmy McLarnin, a far more experienced fighter. When the referee gave McLarnin the decision in the four-round bout, Blake and LaBarba grabbed the judges' slips from the referee's hand. Two of the three judges had awarded LaBarba the fight, but the referee's decision stood. In two rematches, LaBarba held McLarnin to a four-round draw but lost on points in his first ten-rounder.

In 1925, LaBarba challenged Frankie Genaro for the American flyweight title. LaBarba won a convincing ten-round decision. That year, *The Ring* placed LaBarba at the top of its flyweight rankings. In 1927, LaBarba faced Elky Clark for the world flyweight title, vacant since the death of Pancho Villa. LaBarba outboxed Clark in every round and knocked him down—but not out—five times to win the championship.

In 1928, never having defended his title, LaBarba announced he was leaving boxing to attend Stanford. A year later, he was back in the ring, this time campaigning as a bantamweight. LaBarba won all five of his fights that year. Over the next two years, LaBarba compiled a strong record. He split two decisions with Kid

LaBarba was undefeated when he retired as flyweight champion in 1927 to enter Stanford and study journalism. One year later he returned to the ring as a bantamweight.

IN THE RING	WON 70	LOST 15	DRAWS 6	TB 95	KO 16	W 53	WF 1	D 6	KO'd 0	L 15	LF 0	ND 4

Date	Year	Opponent	Site	Result / Rounds		Title
SELECTED BOUTS						
Sep 18	1924	Pat Pringle	Los Angeles	KO	1	—
Oct 28	1924	Jimmy McLarnin★	Vernon, CA	L	4	—
Nov 11	1924	Jimmy McLarnin★	Vernon	D	4	—
Jan 13	1925	Jimmy McLarnin★	Vernon	L	10	—
Aug 22	1925	♛ Frankie Genaro★	Los Angeles	W	10	Won-Amer-FL
Jul 8	1926	Georgie Rivers	Los Angeles	W	10	Ret-Amer -FL
Oct 5	1926	⑩ Newsboy Brown	Vernon	D	10	—
Jan 21	1927	⑩ Elky Clark	New York	W	12	Won-Vac World-FL
Feb 14	1927	⑩ Johnny Vacca	Boston	L	10	—
Mar 22	1927	⑩ Johnny Vacca	Boston	L	10	—
Jul 12	1927	Memphis Pal Moore	Chicago	W	10	—
Aug 23	1927	⑩ Johnny Vacca	Los Angeles	W	10	—
Nov 23	1928	Ray Ravini	San Francisco	KO	8	—
Jan 26	1929	Billy McAllister	Sydney	KO	9	—
Mar 16	1929	Willie Smith	Sydney	TKO	12	—
May 22	1929	⑩ Kid Chocolate★	New York	L	10	—
Aug 30	1929	Jackie Mandell	Hollywood	TKO	8	—
Oct 12	1929	Kid Francis	Paris	L	12	—
Mar 4	1930	Santiago Zorilla	Los Angeles	W	10	—
Nov 3	1930	⑩ Kid Chocolate★	New York	W	10	—
May 22	1931	♛ Battling Battalino★	New York	L	15	For-World-FE
Jul 20	1931	Jackie Mandell	Stockton, CA	KO	1	—
Nov 27	1931	Santiago Zorilla	Hollywood	KO	6	—
Jan 1	1932	⑩ Baby Arizmendi★	Mexico City	L	10	—
Mar 11	1932	⑩ Varias Milling	Hollywood	W	10	—
Apr 22	1932	⑩ Petey Sarron	Detroit	W	10	—
Jun 28	1932	Bobby Gray	San Jose, CA	KO	8	—
Dec 9	1932	♛ Kid Chocolate★	New York	L	15	For-NY World-FE
Dec 29	1932	♛ Tommy Paul	Chicago	L	10	—
Jan 27	1933	⑩ Seaman Watson	New York	L	12	—
Feb 13	1933	Mose Butch	Pittsburgh	W	10	—

Chocolate, then in 1931, moved up to featherweight to challenge Battling Battalino for the world featherweight title. Battalino took the decision in fifteen hard-fought rounds.

In 1932, while training for a challenge to Kid Chocolate for the New York featherweight title, LaBarba seriously injured his eye. He fought Chocolate anyway but, hampered by obscured vision, narrowly lost the decision. LaBarba fought three more times, losing twice, before retiring from the ring. Later, his injured eye was removed.

LaBarba returned to Stanford, where he earned a degree in journalism. He worked as a sportswriter before entering the army in World War II. He later worked in public relations, and was a screenwriter and technical advisor for boxing movies, until a series of heart attacks forced his retirement. LaBarba died in 1981 in Los Angeles.

SAM LANGFORD
The Boston Tar Baby

HEAVYWEIGHT

Right-handed; 5'8"; 139–204 lbs.
291 bouts, 4/11/1902 to 8/2/1926
Manager: Joe Woodman
Hall of Fame Induction: 1990
Born: 3/4/1883, Weymouth, Nova Scotia, Canada
Named: Samuel E. Langford
Died: 1/12/1956

One of many top black boxers denied a chance to fight for a championship largely because of racial discrimination, Sam Langford took on every fighter he could, from lightweight to heavyweight, in his 24-year career. He combined great punching power and agility with intelligence and courage. Those who agreed to face Langford often considered him so dangerous they would request assurances that he be merciful in the ring. Because the pool of his potential opponents was so limited, Langford at times held back in hopes of a rematch.

Born in Canada, Langford began his professional boxing career in 1902 at the age of nineteen with a knockout victory over Jack McVicker in Boston. Quickly rising to prominence, Langford defeated Joe Gans in 1903. The next year, he fought to a draw with Joe Walcott. In 1906, though he was outweighed by at least twenty pounds, Langford faced the future heavyweight champion of the world, Jack Johnson. Langford lost the fifteen-round decision and never really had Johnson in trouble although, years later, exaggerated accounts circulated that Langford had nearly beaten Johnson. Once he was champion, Johnson refused to give Langford a title shot.

In 1910, Langford fought a very tough, six-round no-decision bout against the aggressive middleweight champion, Stanley Ketchel. Langford scored well in the early rounds, but Ketchel took control towards the end of the fight. Newspaper accounts generally awarded the decision to Ketchel, although the verdict could have gone either way. Langford was never

Langford finishes Ian Hague in four rounds on May 24, 1909, in London. Some of the best boxers spurned Langford's challenges.

IN THE RING	WON 167	LOST 38	DRAWS 37	TB 293	KO 117	W 48	WF 2	D 37	KO'd 9	L 29	LF 0	ND 48	NC 3

Date	Year	Opponent	Site	Result / Rounds		Title
SELECTED BOUTS						
Apr 11	1902	Jack McVicker	Boston	KO	6	—
Dec 8	1903	♛ Joe Gans ★	Boston	W	15	—
Sep 5	1904	Joe Walcott (Barbados) ★	Manchester, NH	D	15	—
Apr 5	1906	Joe Jeannette ★	Chelsea, MA	W	15	—
Apr 26	1906	Jack Johnson ★	Chelsea	L	15	For-Black-H
Jan 11	1907	Joe Jeannette ★	Lawrence, MA	D	12	—
Dec 21	1908	Jim Flynn	San Francisco	KO	1	—
Apr 27	1910	♛ Stanley Ketchel ★	Philadelphia	ND-L	6	—
Sep 6	1910	Joe Jeannette ★	Boston	W	15	Won-Black-H
Aug 15	1911	♛ Phila. Jack O'Brien ★	New York	KO	5	—
Apr 8	1912	Sam McVey ★	Sydney	W	20	Ret-Black-H
Dec 20	1913	Joe Jeannette ★	Paris	W	20	—
May 1	1914	Harry Wills ★	New Orleans	L	10	Lost-Black-H
Oct 1	1914	Joe Jeannette ★	New York	ND-W	10	—
Nov 26	1914	Harry Wills ★	Los Angeles	KO	14	Reg-Black-H
Apr 13	1915	Joe Jeannette ★	Boston	L	12	Lost-Black-H
Jan 3	1916	Harry Wills ★	New Orleans	L	20	For-Black-H
Feb 11	1916	Harry Wills ★	New Orleans	KO	19	Reg-Black-H
Apr 7	1916	Sam McVey ★	Syracuse, NY	ND-W	10	Ret-Black-H
Apr 25	1916	Harry Wills ★	St. Louis	ND-L	8	Ret-Black-H
May 12	1916	Joe Jeannette ★	Syracuse	KO	7	Ret-Black-H
Apr 14	1918	Harry Wills ★	Panama City	KO'd	6	Lost-Black-H
Jul 4	1919	Harry Wills ★	St. Louis	L	8	For-Black-H
Sep 30	1919	Harry Wills ★	Syracuse	ND-L	10	—
Apr 19	1920	Harry Wills ★	Denver	L	15	For-Black-H
Aug 14	1920	Sam McVey ★	East Chicago, IN	ND-D	10	—
Jan 17	1922	Harry Wills ★	Portland, OR	L	10	For-Black-H
Jun 5	1922	Tiger Flowers ★	Atlanta	KO	2	—
Aug 2	1926	Brad Simmons	Drumright, OK	TKO'd	1	—

given an opportunity to fight for Ketchel's title. In 1911, Langford made short work of former light heavyweight champion Philadelphia Jack O'Brien with a fifth-round knockout.

Because of his difficulty in finding matches, Langford often fought the same opponents—especially other black fighters in a similar predicament—over and over. Langford and Harry Wills tangled eighteen times. Wills knocked Langford out twice and generally had the better of the series, although it must be noted that the first meeting occurred when Langford was 31 years old. Langford had more than ten fights each against Sam McVey, Joe Jeannette, Jim Barry, Jeff Clarke, and Bill Tate.

After almost three hundred recorded bouts, Langford retired at the age of 43. In his last years in the ring, he was troubled by eye problems which eventually resulted in blindness. When he retired at last, he struggled to live comfortably until a sportswriters' fund for his care was established.

GEORGE ("KID") LAVIGNE
The Saginaw Kid

L I G H T W E I G H T

Right-handed; 5'3½"; 128–140 lbs.
56 bouts, 9/7/1886 to 12/25/1909
Manager: Sam Fitzpatrick
Lightweight Champion 1896–99
Hall of Fame Induction: 1998
Born: 12/6/1869, Bay City, MI
Named: George Henry Lavigne
(luh VEEN)
Died: 3/9/1928

John L. Sullivan said of George ("Kid") Lavigne, "Of all the fighters of the present day, Kid Lavigne is the one I most admire. He is the grandest little man of our time." At his peak the slim, fair-haired Lavigne displayed tremendous stamina, heart, and punching power.

Lavigne was born in Bay City, Michigan, to French-Canadian parents. He turned professional in Saginaw in 1886 with a one-round knockout at age seventeen. In 1887, Lavigne took on the far more experienced George Siddons. The pair battled for 77 rounds in Saginaw before the fight was called a draw. They fought to a 55-round draw in the rematch.

After continued success in Michigan, Lavigne traveled to California. In 1894, he fought to a draw with master stylist Young Griffo. Later that year, Lavigne administered such a beating to Andy Bowen, a fighter of some renown, that Bowen died after the fight.

Another draw with Griffo set the stage for Lavigne's greatest fight ever, against Joe Walcott on December 2, 1895, in Maspeth, New York. Under the terms of a special advance agreement, Walcott had to knock Lavigne out in fifteen rounds or less in order to win. In one of the most grueling fights in boxing history, Walcott attacked Lavigne relentlessly. Lavigne, an ear torn, one eye closed, and his mouth bloody, but showing an incredible will to win, took control in the fourteenth. By the close of the fifteenth, the great Walcott refused to quit but clearly had nothing left. Lavigne was awarded the victory, although many believed the brutal battle should have ended in a draw.

Lavigne then journeyed to England to challenge Dick Burge in a twenty-round bout for the vacant world lightweight title. British boxing fans were amazed that the angelic-looking, boyish man who stood only 5'3" was the ferocious Kid Lavigne. Although Burge was the larger fighter, at the end of the sixteenth he had

Lavigne (C) trained in London prior to his June 1, 1896, fight with Dick Burge. A victory gave Lavigne the vacant world lightweight championship. Here, he is flanked by Sam Fitzpatrick (L), his manager, and Michael ("Dad") Butler (R), his trainer.

IN THE RING	WON 35	LOST 6	DRAWS 10	TB 56	KO 19	W 16	WF 0	D 10	KO'd 4	L 2	LF 0	ND 5

Date	Year	Opponent	Site	Result / Rounds		Title
SELECTED BOUTS						
Sep 7	1886	Morris McNally	Saginaw, MI	KO	1	—
Mar 1	1887	George Siddons	Saginaw	D	77	—
Apr 26	1887	George Siddons	Grand Rapids, MI	D	55	—
Nov 20	1891	Joe Soto	San Francisco	W	30	—
Aug 10	1892	Jim Burge	San Francisco	D	50	—
Feb 10	1894	Young Griffo ★	New York	D	8	—
Oct 12	1895	Young Griffo ★	Maspeth, NY	D	20	—
Dec 2	1895	Joe Walcott ★	Maspeth	W	15	—
Jun 1	1896	Dick Burge	London	KO	17	Won-Vac-World-L
Oct 27	1896	Jack Everhardt	New York	TKO	24	Ret-World-L
Feb 8	1897	Kid McPartland	New York	W	25	Ret-World-L
Apr 30	1897	Eddie Connolly	New York	TKO	11	Ret-World-L
Oct 29	1897	Joe Walcott ★	San Francisco	TKO	12	Ret-World-L
Mar 17	1898	Jack Daly	Cleveland	D	20	Ret-World-L
Apr 11	1898	Jack Daly	Philadelphia	ND	6	—
Sep 28	1898	Frank Erne	Coney Island, NY	D	20	Ret-World-L
Nov 25	1898	Tom Tracy	San Francisco	W	20	—
Mar 10	1899	♛ Mysterious Billy Smith	San Francisco	TKO'd	14	For-World-W
Apr 25	1899	Andy Davy	Berlin, NH	D	10	—
Jul 3	1899	Frank Erne	Buffalo, NY	L	20	Lost-World-L
May 25	1902	Jimmy Britt	San Francisco	KO'd	8	—
Dec 25	1909	Dick Nelson	Detroit	L	6	—

to be helped to his corner after Lavigne landed a savage right hook. In the seventeenth, Lavigne fired a right to the jaw which knocked Burge out and gave Lavigne the championship.

Returning home, Lavigne won his first six title defenses, but many speculated that his disdain for training and excessive consumption of alcohol were taking their toll. His trainer, Biddy Bishop, once said, "Keeping Lavigne sober between fights was a tremendous achievement, and it is with great pride that I look back at the masterpiece of my career in training, keeping the Kid away from the bottle for eleven whole days." On March 10, 1899, Lavigne attempted to add the welterweight title to his list of honors when he faced Mysterious Billy Smith in San Francisco. Lavigne had trained diligently for this fight, and the press marveled at his physical condition. However, Smith's rights to Lavigne's left side fractured a rib, and in the fourteenth another right staggered Lavigne, who fell against the ropes. Five more rights to the jaw rendered him helpless. Lavigne's brother rushed into the ring claiming foul, but referee Jim McDonald stopped the fight and declared Smith the winner.

Lavigne lost the lightweight title to Frank Erne in 1899. In his next fight, Lavigne was knocked out by George McFadden. Lavigne fought very little over the next ten years before officially retiring in 1909. Outside the ring he held a variety of odd jobs until becoming a night watchman at the Ford Motor Company plant in Detroit in the 1920s. He died March 9, 1928.

BENNY LEONARD
The Ghetto Wizard

LIGHTWEIGHT

Right-handed; 5'5"; 123–153 lbs.

212 bouts, 1911 to 10/7/1932

Managers: Buck Areton 1911–14, Louis Wallach 1914, Billy Gibson 1914–25, Jack Kearns and Joey Leonard 1931–32

Lightweight Champion 1917–25

Hall of Fame Induction: 1990

Born: 4/7/1896, New York, NY

Named: Benjamin Leiner

Died: 4/18/1947

Perhaps the greatest lightweight of all time, Benny Leonard possessed superb boxing skills as well as potent punching power. He fought over two hundred times and suffered only four knockouts: three early in his career and the fourth in his final fight. Born on the East Side of New York, Leonard learned to fight in neighborhood battles and turned pro in 1911 at just fifteen years of age. In his inaugural bout he was knocked out in the third round.

By 1915, Leonard was working his way to the top of the lightweight ranks. A scientific boxer whose poise in the ring led observers to say fighting scarcely even mussed his hair, Leonard fought a series of no-decision bouts with Hall of Famer Johnny Dundee. He also performed well in no-decision matches with Hall of Famer Johnny Kilbane and lightweight champion Freddie Welsh. In 1917, Leonard challenged Welsh for the title. He skillfully hammered away at Welsh, knocking him out in the ninth round.

Leonard held the lightweight title for eight years. In his first defense, he knocked out Kilbane, then featherweight champ, in three rounds. Leonard also successfully held several other challengers at bay. In 1922, Leonard set his sights on the welterweight crown and challenged champion

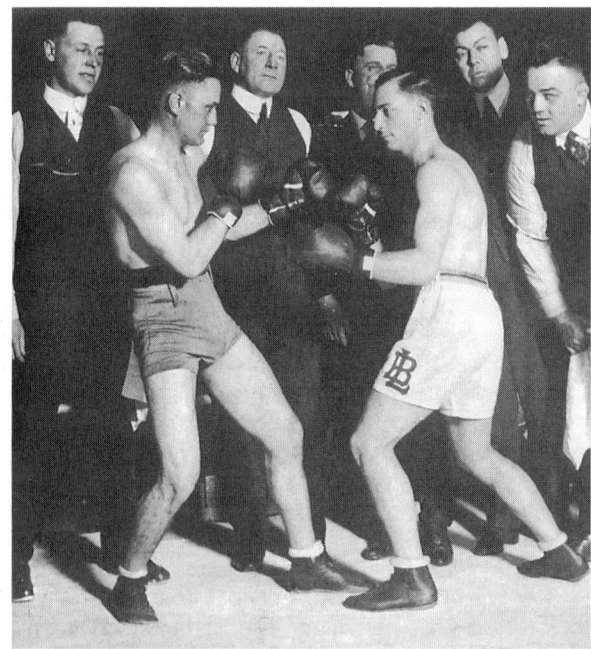

Leonard, sporting monogrammed trunks, squares off with Richie Mitchell. After trading knockdowns, a shaken Leonard ended it with a sixth-round TKO.

IN THE RING	WON 85	LOST 5	DRAWS 1	TB 212	KO 69	W 15	WF 1	D 1	KO'd 4	L 0	LF 1	ND 121

Date	Year	Opponent	Site	Result / Rounds		Title

SELECTED BOUTS

Date	Year	Opponent	Site	Result / Rounds		Title
—	1911	Mickey Finnegan	New York	TKO'd	3	—
Nov 2	1912	Special Delivery Hirsch	New York	ND-L	10	—
Feb 18	1914	Irish Patsy Cline	New York	ND-W	10	—
Mar 2	1915	Johnny Dundee ★	New York	ND-L	10	—
Apr 29	1915	♛ Johnny Kilbane ★	New York	ND-L	10	—
Mar 8	1916	Johnny Dundee ★	New York	ND-W	15	—
Mar 31	1916	♛ Freddie Welsh ★	New York	ND-W	10	—
Jun 12	1916	Johnny Dundee ★	New York	ND-L	10	—
Jul 28	1916	♛ Freddie Welsh ★	Brooklyn	ND-L	10	—
May 28	1917	♛ Freddie Welsh ★	New York	TKO	9	Won-World-L
Jul 25	1917	Johnny Kilbane ★	Philadelphia	TKO	3	Ret-World-L
Oct 19	1917	Jack Britton ★	New York	ND-W	10	—
Jun 25	1918	Jack Britton ★	Philadelphia	ND-W	6	—
Sep 23	1918	♛ Ted ("Kid") Lewis ★	Newark, NJ	ND-L	8	—
Jan 20	1919	Johnny Dundee ★	Newark	ND-W	8	—
Jun 16	1919	Johnny Dundee ★	Philadelphia	ND-D	6	—
Sep 4	1919	Soldier Bartfield	Philadelphia	ND-W	6	—
Feb 9	1920	Johnny Dundee ★	Jersey City, NJ	ND-W	8	—
Jul 5	1920	Charlie White	Benton Harbor, MI	KO	9	Ret-World-L
Nov 26	1920	Joe Welling	New York	TKO	14	Ret-World-L
Jan 14	1921	Richie Mitchell	New York	TKO	6	Ret-World-L
Feb 10	1922	Rocky Kansas	New York	W	15	Ret-World-L
Jun 26	1922	♛ Jack Britton ★	New York	LF	13	For-World-W
Jul 27	1922	Lew Tendler ★	Jersey City	ND-W	12	—
Jul 23	1923	Lew Tendler ★	New York	W	15	Ret-World-L
Aug 1	1924	Pal Moran	Cleveland	ND-W	10	—
Oct 6	1931	Pat Silvers	Long Island City, NY	KO	2	—
Nov 23	1931	Buster Brown	Baltimore	W	10	—
Apr 11	1932	Buster Brown	New York	W	10	—
May 16	1932	Marty Goldman	Newark	KO	2	—
Oct 7	1932	⑩ Jimmy McLarnin ★	New York	TKO'd	6	—

Jack Britton. In a well-attended fight at New York's Velodrome, Leonard knocked Britton down in the thirteenth round, then in an uncharacteristic move, hit Britton again during the referee's count. Britton was given the win because of Leonard's foul. Leonard fought left-hander Lew Tendler twice. A no-decision twelve-rounder in Jersey City was very close and earned Tendler the right to try for the title. The two met in 1923 in Yankee Stadium with nearly 60,000 fans looking on. Leonard outboxed his closely matched rival to win in fifteen rounds.

Leonard retired in 1925, but hard times brought him back to the ring in 1931. He won the first nineteen fights of his comeback before Jimmy McLarnin knocked him out in six rounds. Leonard then retired for good. In 1947, he died of a heart attack in the ring at St. Nicholas Arena in New York while refereeing a match.

BATTLING LEVINSKY

LIGHT HEAVYWEIGHT

Right-handed; 5'11"; 162–199½ lbs.

289 bouts, 1909 to 10/21/1930

Managers: Fred Douglas 1910–13, Dan Morgan 1913–22, Al Lippe 1926–29

World Light Heavyweight Champ 1916–20

Hall of Fame Induction: 2000

Born: 6/10/1891, Philadelphia, PA

Named: Barney Lebrowitz

Also Fought as: Barney Williams

Died: 2/12/1949

Battling Levinsky—never reluctant to enter the ring—fought at least 289 times. While the exact total is unknown and some fights remain unrecorded, his bouts may exceed 500.

Levinsky began fighting as Barney Williams at the age of seventeen or eighteen. His career took off under the managerial aegis of Hall of Famer Dumb Dan Morgan. According to Morgan, Levinsky appeared at Morgan's New York office and said, "I think I'm a fighter. I want a chance." He got it as a substitute heavyweight on that night's card at St. Nicholas Arena, pitted against the 40-pounds-heavier Porky Flynn in a no-decision bout. At the close of the fight, Morgan had ring announcer Joe Humphreys proclaim, "Morgan's new find is now named 'Battling Levinksy,' and he defies any Irishman in the country to lick him."

Levinsky was a supreme defensive fighter, who scored enough points to win "newspaper decisions" in the no-decision bouts that comprised more than half his career totals. No knock-out artist, he stopped his opponent short of the distance in less than twelve percent of his fights.

Dan Morgan touted Levinsky's durability with a tale of New Year's Day 1915. Levinsky supposedly fought a ten-round, no-decision bout with Bartley Madden in the morning in Brooklyn, followed by another ten-round, no-decision in the afternoon with Soldier Kearns in Manhattan, and then took a train ride to Waterbury, Connecticut, where he faced Gunboat Smith in a twelve-round, no-decision contest to close the day. Only the last fight actually happened!

Though Levinsky often fought heavyweights, he was a lighter man himself, and he and Morgan set their sights on the light heavyweight title held by Hall of Famer Jack Dillon. On April 25, 1916, in Kansas City, Dillon won the fifteen-round decision. When Dillon put the title on the line again on October 24 in Boston, the pair's ninth

Former Heavyweight Champ Gentleman Jim Corbett (L) and Battling Levinsky exchange a handshake.

IN THE RING	WON 77	LOST 19	DRAWS 15	TB 289	KO 34	W 42	WF 1	D 15	KO'd 3	L 13	LF 3	ND 178

Date	Year	Opponent	Site	Result / Rounds		Title
SELECTED BOUTS						
—	1909	Paddy Burns	Pottsville, PA	ND	6	—
Oct 23	1911	Jack Dillon ★	Philadelphia	ND-L	6	—
Apr 17	1913	Jack Dillon ★	Rochester, NY	ND-D	10	—
Jul 20	1913	Dan ("Porky") Flynn	New York	ND-D	10	—
Jan 27	1914	Alfred ("Soldier") Kearns	New York	ND-D	10	—
Apr 14	1914	Jack Dillon ★	Butte, MT	L	12	For-Vac World-LH
May 29	1914	♛ Jack Dillon ★	Indianapolis, IN	ND-L	10	—
Feb 8	1916	♛ Jack Dillon ★	Brooklyn	ND-D	10	—
Apr 25	1916	♛ Jack Dillon ★	Kansas City, MO	L	15	For-World-LH
Jul 13	1916	♛ Jack Dillon ★	Baltimore	W	10	—
Sep 12	1916	♛ Jack Dillon ★	Memphis, TN	D	8	—
Oct 24	1916	♛ Jack Dillon ★	Boston	W	12	Won-World-LH
Mar 23	1917	Tommy Gibbons ★	St. Paul, MN	ND-L	10	—
Sep 6	1917	Harry Greb ★	Pittsburgh	ND-L	10	—
Nov 6	1918	Jack Dempsey ★	Philadelphia	KO'd	3	—
Feb 17	1919	Harry Greb ★	Buffalo, NY	ND-L	10	—
Jul 14	1919	Harry Greb ★	Philadelphia	ND-L	6	—
Oct 12	1920	Georges Carpentier ★	Jersey City, NJ	KO'd	4	Lost-World-LH
Jan 13	1922	Gene Tunney ★	New York	L	12	For-USA-LH
Nov 11	1926	Young Stribling ★	Des Moines, IA	ND-L	10	—
Jan 15	1929	Herman Weiner	Hagerstown, MD	KO'd	1	—
Oct 21	1930	Joe Sims	Brooklyn	KO	3	—

meeting, most ring pundits did not give Levinsky much of a chance, nor did Dillon. Yet Levinsky handled Dillon's pressing attack and scored enough with a left jab and left hook to win the twelve-round match.

Levinsky was in no hurry to defend his title and spent the next four years fighting non-title bouts, including six no-decisions against Harry Greb and a three-round knockout loss to a young Jack Dempsey. On October 12, 1920, he finally put the title up for grabs against Georges Carpentier in Jersey City, and was knocked out in four rounds. In 1922, Levinsky faced Gene Tunney for the American light heavyweight title, and lost a twelve-round decision in a rather lackluster fight. Actually, few of Levinsky's fights were ever exciting. Sportswriter Damon Runyon noted, "If you have seen one of Levinsky's fights, you have seen them all. They are of a piece. There is rarely any prospect of the unexpected occurring in his battles. He will be there at the finish, but so will the other fellow."

After the loss to Tunney, Levinsky retired, but was lured back to the ring four years later. Following a first-round knockout loss to Herman Weiner on January 15, 1929, Levinsky again retired. Nearly two years later, he fought one more bout. During the Depression he worked for the WPA. He died at age 59 after an illness of several months aggravated by a car accident.

JOHN HENRY LEWIS

LIGHT HEAVYWEIGHT

Right-handed; 5'11"; 140–181 lbs.

117 bouts, 1928 to 1/25/1939

Managers: Ernie Lira, Larry White, Frank Schuler, Gus Greenlee

Light Heavyweight Champ 1935–39

Hall of Fame Induction: 1994

Born: 5/1/1914, Los Angeles, CA

Died: 4/18/1974

John Henry Lewis was the first black American to win the light heavyweight championship, a title he held for four years. And as with many light heavyweights, Lewis often fought larger heavyweights to gain more attention and bigger purses. Lewis was not the first fighter in his family. His great-great uncle was Tom Molineaux, an early bare-knuckle heavyweight who travelled to England to challenge for the title.

Born in California, Lewis moved to Arizona when his father got a job as trainer for the University of Arizona athletic teams. Lewis's father also opened a gym in Phoenix. At a very early age, Lewis and his brother Christy were put to work at the gym, fighting "midget boxing" exhibitions. Later, the Lewises toured the Southwest in such exhibitions.

Given this early training, Lewis was well-prepared to turn professional at the age of fourteen as a welterweight. Three years later Lewis won a decision over Lloyd Phelps to take what was considered to be the Arizona middleweight championship. In 1932, Lewis received wide attention when

Lewis (L) traps Len Harvey in the corner during a successful title defense in Wembley Stadium on November 9, 1936.

IN THE RING	WON 103	LOST 8	DRAWS 6	TB 117	KO 60	W 43	WF 0	D 6	KO'd 1	L 7	LF 0

Date	Year	Opponent	Site	Result / Rounds		Title
SELECTED BOUTS						
—	1928	Buster Grant	Phoenix	W	4	—
Sep 21	1932	Jim Braddock★	San Francisco	W	10	—
Oct 26	1932	Lou Scozza	San Francisco	W	10	—
Nov 16	1932	♛ Maxie Rosenbloom★	San Francisco	L	10	—
Jul 10	1933	♛ Maxie Rosenbloom★	San Francisco	W	10	—
Jul 31	1933	♛ Maxie Rosenbloom★	San Francisco	W	10	—
Nov 16	1934	James J. Braddock★	New York	L	10	—
Mar 13	1935	Emilio Martinez	Denver	W	10	—
Apr 12	1935	♛ Bob Olin	San Francisco	W	10	—
Jul 17	1935	⑩ Maxie Rosenbloom★	Oakland	L	10	—
Jul 24	1935	Abe Feldman	New York	L	10	—
Oct 31	1935	♛ Bob Olin	St. Louis	W	15	Won-World-LH
Nov 29	1935	⑩ Maxie Rosenbloom★	San Francisco	L	10	—
Jan 29	1936	Emilio Martinez	Denver	L	10	—
Mar 13	1936	⑩ Jock McAvoy	New York	W	15	Ret-World-LH
Nov 9	1936	Len Harvey	London	W	15	Ret-World-LH
May 4	1937	Emilio Martinez	St. Louis	W	10	—
Jun 3	1937	Bob Olin	St. Louis	TKO	8	Ret-World-LH
Apr 25	1938	Emilio Martinez	Minneapolis	KO	4	Ret-World-LH
Oct 28	1938	Al Gainer	New Haven, CT	W	15	Ret-World-LH
Jan 25	1939	♛ Joe Louis★	New York	KO'd	1	For-World-H

he decisioned future heavyweight champion James J. Braddock in San Francisco and lost a close decision in a non-title bout with light heavyweight champion Maxie Rosenbloom.

The next year, Lewis scored two victories over Rosenbloom, a closely matched rival who came back to defeat Lewis twice. Lewis lost a rematch with Braddock in his first New York appearance in 1934. Managed by the owner of the Pittsburgh Crawfords Negro League baseball team, Gus Greenlee, Lewis fought as often as possible in an attempt to secure a shot at the title. In 1935, he got his chance, fighting for the light heavyweight belt against Bob Olin in St. Louis. But being champ apparently didn't mean being paid. Under the terms of his contract, Lewis forfeited his purse when the sparse crowd failed to provide the minimum expected gate.

Lewis possessed all of the attributes of a great boxer. He had the speed of a welterweight, was aggressive, skilled at defense, and a master puncher. The lack of financial reward was a problem, however. In 1939, Lewis signed for a heavyweight title fight against his friend, Joe Louis. Although it was not widely known, Lewis was almost blind in one eye and had been for some years. Joe Louis gave his friend a chance for a big payday before the eye problem forced him to retire. Louis made short work of the challenger, knocking him out in one round. This fight was the only knockout Lewis suffered in 117 fights. Lewis retired after this defeat.

TED ("KID") LEWIS

WELTERWEIGHT

Right-handed; 5'8½"; 116–166 lbs.

282 bouts, 9/13/1909 to 12/13/1929

Managers: Charles Rose, Freeman Bernstein, Jimmy Johnston, Charles Harvey

Welterweight Champion 1915–16, 1917–19

Hall of Fame Induction: 1992

Born: 10/24/1894, London, England

Named: Gershon Mendeloff

Died: 10/20/1970

Perhaps the best pound-for-pound boxer England has ever produced, Ted ("Kid") Lewis began fighting as a flyweight and battled in every division, including heavyweight, during his lengthy career. He won numerous British and European titles and was twice welterweight champion of the world.

Born in London's East End, Lewis was attracted as a boy to boxing matches in a neighborhood theatre. He first fought professionally at the age of fourteen, when he earned sixpence for defeating another youngster. Fighting frequently and for little reward, Lewis became an excellent boxer. In 1913, he won the British featherweight title with a knock-out victory over Alec Lambert, and he added the European featherweight title the next year.

In 1914, Lewis travelled to the United States with his sights set on the world welterweight title. In 1915, he faced Hall of Famer Jack Britton in the first of many battles between the two well-matched boxers. The fight was a no-decision bout in which Lewis was generally acknowledged to be the winner. A few months later, Lewis took the welterweight crown from Britton with a twelve-round decision in Boston. For the next six years, Lewis and Britton fought bitterly in rematch after

Tom Gummer is on the receiving end of a left on the way to a first-round knockout by Lewis (R) in Brighton, England on February 16, 1922.

IN THE RING	WON 173	LOST 30	DRAWS 14	TB 282	KO 71	W 99	WF 3	D 14	KO'd 7	L 18	LF 5	ND 65

Date	Year	Opponent	Site	Result / Rounds		Title

SELECTED BOUTS

Date	Year	Opponent	Site	Result	Rounds	Title
Sep 13	1909	Johnny Sharpe	London	L	6	—
Oct 6	1913	Alec Lambert	London	TKO	17	Won-Britain-FE
Feb 2	1914	Paul Til	London	WF	12	Won-Vac Eur-FE
Mar 26	1915	Jack Britton ★	New York	ND-W	10	—
Aug 31	1915 ♛	Jack Britton ★	Boston	W	12	Won-World-W
Apr 24	1916	Jack Britton ★	New Orleans	L	20	Lost-World-W
May 18	1916	Mike Gibbons ★	New York	ND-L	10	—
Jun 25	1917 ♛	Jack Britton ★	Dayton, OH	W	20	Reg-World-W
May 17	1918	Johnny Tillman	Denver	W	20	Ret-World-W
Mar 17	1919	Jack Britton ★	Canton, OH	KO'd	9	Lost-World-W
Mar 11	1920	Johnny Bee	London	KO	4	Won-Britain-W
Jun 9	1920	Johnny Basham	London	KO	9	Ret-Brit-W & Won-Eur-W
Nov 19	1920	Johnny Basham	London	KO	19	Ret-Brit & Eur-W
Feb 7	1921	Jack Britton ★	New York	L	15	For-World-W
Jun 27	1921	Jack Bloomfield	London	W	20	Won-Britain-M
Oct 14	1921	Johnny Basham	London	KO	12	Ret-Brit-M & Won-Eur-M
Nov 17	1921	Boy McCormick	London	TKO	14	Won-Britain-LH
May 11	1922 ♛	Georges Carpentier ★	London	KO'd	1	For-World-LH
Jun 19	1922	Frankie Burns	London	KO	11	Won-Brit Emp-M
Nov 20	1922	Roland Todd	London	W	20	Ret-Brit, Brit Emp & Eur-M
Feb 15	1923	Roland Todd	London	L	20	Lost-Brit, Brit Emp & Eur-M
Jul 3	1923	Johnny Brown	London	W	20	Ret-Brit-W & Won-Brit Emp-W
Nov 26	1923	Tommy Milligan	Edinburgh	L	20	Lost-Brit & Brit Emp-W
Dec 13	1929	Johnny Basham	London	TKO	3	—

rematch. In 1916, Britton reclaimed the welterweight title with a twenty-round decision. Lewis took back the crown in 1917 and held it until Britton knocked Lewis out in the ninth round in 1919. Altogether, Britton and Lewis met at least twenty times, although Lewis later claimed that the two had battled even more frequently.

Lewis returned to England in 1919 and over the next three years won British welterweight, middleweight, and light heavyweight titles, and the European middleweight and British Empire middleweight titles. He KO'd the skillful Johnny Basham three times, and overwhelmed middleweight Jack Bloomfield in a fierce twenty-round bout.

In 1922, Lewis challenged Hall of Famer Georges Carpentier for the world light heavyweight title but was knocked out in one round. The knock-out punch took Lewis by surprise, when he turned his head to catch a comment from the referee.

Lewis continued to fight for the next seven years in Europe, the United States, and South Africa. He fought 282 bouts officially, though he estimated that he actually fought many more. Known as one of the first combination punchers, Lewis attacked relentlessly and with great stamina. Lewis fought until he was 35. In retirement, he was involved in several businesses, including a nightclub.

TOMMY LOUGHRAN

LIGHT HEAVYWEIGHT

Right-handed; 5'11"; 140–192 lbs.
172 bouts, 12/9/1919 to 1/18/1937
Manager: Joe Smith
Light Heavyweight Champ 1927–29
Hall of Fame Induction: 1991
Born: 11/29/1902, Philadelphia, PA
Named: Thomas Patrick Loughran
Died: 7/7/1982

A gifted boxer with one of the greatest left hands in history, Tommy Loughran started his career as a middleweight, then went on to dominate the light heavyweight ranks in the late 1920s. Later, he jumped to the heavyweight division where he also compiled a solid record.

Manager Joe Smith handled Loughran from the start of his career. Fighting in the Philadelphia area, Loughran was undefeated in his first 43 bouts. In 1922, he faced ferocious Harry Greb in the first of six meetings. In this no-decision bout, Greb was generally credited with the victory. In the same year, Loughran took on the then-unbeatable Gene Tunney. Tunney knocked Loughran down in the first round, but Loughran held his own in the fairly even match. In 1923, Loughran fought Greb again, for one win, two losses, and a no-decision. Their final meeting in 1924 was a draw.

Loughran broke his right hand early in his career and as time went on, relied almost exclusively on his powerful left. His finely-honed boxing skills caught the public's attention when he served as a sparring partner for Jack Dempsey before the first Dempsey–Tunney fight. Loughran's ability to handle the powerful Dempsey won him many admirers. In 1927, Loughran faced

Known as one of the cleverest boxers in history, Loughran was a sugar broker after his fight career. He also refereed several important bouts.

IN THE RING	WON 94	LOST 23	DRAWS 9	TB 172	KO 17	W 76	WF 1	D 9	KO'd 2	L 21	LF 0	ND 45	NC 1

Date	Year		Opponent	Site	Result / Rounds		Title

SELECTED BOUTS

Date	Year		Opponent	Site	Result	Rounds	Title
Dec 9	1919		Eddie Carter	Philadelphia	KO	2	—
Jul 10	1922		Harry Greb ★	Philadelphia	ND-L	8	—
Aug 24	1922		Gene Tunney ★	Philadelphia	ND-L	8	—
Jan 15	1923		Harry Greb ★	Pittsburgh	ND-L	10	—
Jan 30	1923		Harry Greb ★	New York	L	15	For-USA-LH
Oct 11	1923	♛	Harry Greb ★	Boston	W	10	—
Dec 25	1923	♛	Harry Greb ★	Pittsburgh	L	10	—
Oct 13	1924	♛	Harry Greb ★	Philadelphia	D	10	—
Jun 17	1926		Georges Carpentier ★	Philadelphia	W	10	—
Oct 7	1927	⑩	Mike McTigue	New York	W	15	Won-Vac NY World-LH
Dec 12	1927		Jimmy Slattery ★	New York	W	15	Won-World-LH
Jan 6	1928	⑩	Leo Lomski	New York	W	15	Ret-World-LH
Jun 1	1928	⑩	Pete Latzo	Brooklyn	W	15	Ret-World-LH
Jul 16	1928	⑩	Pete Latzo	Wilkes-Barre, PA	W	10	Ret-World-LH
Mar 28	1929	♛	Mickey Walker ★	Chicago	W	10	Ret-World-LH
Jul 18	1929		Jim Braddock ★	New York	W	15	Ret-World-LH
Sep 26	1929	⑩	Jack Sharkey ★	New York	KO'd	3	—
Feb 6	1931	⑩	Max Baer ★	New York	W	10	—
Dec 18	1931		King Levinsky	New York	L	10	—
Jan 10	1933	⑩	King Levinsky	Philadelphia	W	10	—
Sep 27	1933		Jack Sharkey ★	Philadelphia	W	15	—
Mar 1	1934	♛	Primo Carnera	Miami	L	15	For-World-H
Jan 18	1937	⑩	Sonny Boy Walker	Philadelphia	W	10	—

Mike McTigue for the vacant world light heavyweight title. For fourteen rounds, Loughran dominated the fight. McTigue rallied in the fifteenth, but Loughran hung on to win a convincing victory. He defended the title five times before he gave it up to seek the heavyweight crown. In 1929, he faced Jack Sharkey as part of a series of bouts which would determine the successor to retired heavyweight champion Tunney. Fighting in Yankee Stadium before approximately 45,000 fans, Loughran scored with hard jabs in the first round, but in the third, Sharkey landed a right to the temple which sent Loughran to the canvas. Though he got up, Loughran was out on his feet, and referee Louie Magnolia stopped the fight.

Loughran continued to fight over the next four years and beat many top heavyweights such as Max Baer and Sharkey (in a rematch). In 1934, he got another shot at the title, then held by the lumbering Primo Carnera. Carnera outweighed Loughran by 86 pounds, the biggest weight differential for any title fight in history. En route to a decision in fifteen rounds, Carnera stepped on Loughran's foot, breaking a toe. Loughran never again challenged for the title. He continued to fight for three years before retiring, still acclaimed as a master of footwork and boxing skill.

BENNY LYNCH
The Kid from the Gorbals

FLYWEIGHT

Right-handed; 5'5"; 109–119 lbs.

111 bouts, 4/24/1931 to 10/3/1938

NBA-IBU Flyweight Champion 1935–38

World Flyweight Champion 1937–38

Hall of Fame Induction: 1998

Born: 4/2/1913, Clydesdale, Scotland

Named: Samuel Benjamin John Lynch

Died: 8/6/1946

Scottish champion Benny Lynch earned a reputation as one of the greatest and most popular flyweights of all time. Although he rarely fought outside the Glasgow area and never traveled beyond the British Isles, Lynch gained national and international recognition.

Born in Clydesdale, Scotland, Lynch fought as a boy in amateur competitions. He also toured Scotland with boxing booths, taking on all comers, before turning professional at age eighteen.

On May 16, 1934, he won a close fifteen-round decision over Jim Campbell to capture the Scottish flyweight title. In the rematch six weeks later, Lynch won again. Also that year he defeated Italian champion Carlo Cavagnoli, French champion Valentin Angelmann, and Spanish champion Pedrito Ruiz.

Lynch then persuaded Jackie Brown, NBA, British, and International Boxing Union (IBU) flyweight champion, to come to Scotland for a non-title match. Lynch outboxed Brown but came away with only a draw. On September 9, 1935, Lynch met Brown again. This time the fight, at Manchester's Belle Vue Stadium, was for Brown's titles. Using superior foot speed and an awe-inspiring left hook, Lynch knocked down Brown ten times in less than two rounds before the champion surrendered. The first Scots world champion, Lynch was literally the toast of the country, feted in many taverns and pubs.

On January 19, 1937, Lynch met Small Montana, who held the New York State version of the world flyweight title, to unify the crown in London's Wembley Arena. Although Montana started fast, Lynch weathered his attacks and won a fifteen-round decision to become the undisputed world champion at the age of 23. Few observers would have guessed that Lynch would retire from boxing in less than two years and that he would be dead in nine.

In his first title defense, against nineteen-year-old former blacksmith Peter Kane, Lynch dominated. He knocked Kane down several times, but at one point when the challenger slipped and fell, Lynch offered him a hand to

Hands still wrapped, Lynch (L) accepts the flyweight belt from Hall of Famer Lord Lonsdale.

IN THE RING	WON 83	LOST 13	DRAWS 15	TB 111	KO 34	W 48	WF 1	D 15	KO'd 1	L 11	LF 1

Date	Year		Opponent	Site	Result / Rounds		Title

SELECTED BOUTS

Date	Year		Opponent	Site	Result	Rounds	Title
Apr 24	1931		Young Bryce	Glasgow, Scotland	KO	2	—
May 23	1931		Packy Boyle	Glasgow	L	6	—
Mar 25	1933		Jim Brady	Glasgow	W	12	—
May 2	1933		Jim Brady	Dundee, Scotland	D	12	—
Oct 10	1933		Willie Vogan	Edinburgh	KO	2	—
Nov 9	1933		Bob Fielding	Liverpool, England	D	10	—
Feb 1	1934		Jim Brady	Edinburgh	W	12	—
Mar 21	1934		Carlo Cavagnoli	Glasgow	W	12	—
May 16	1934		Jim Campbell	Glasgow	W	15	Won-Scottish-FL
Jun 27	1934		Jim Campbell	Glasgow	W	15	Ret-Scottish-FL
Sep 26	1934	⑩	Valentin Angelmann	Glasgow	W	12	—
Nov 7	1934		Pedrito Ruiz	Glasgow	W	12	—
Mar 4	1935	♛	Jackie Brown	Glasgow	D	12	—
Sep 9	1935	♛	Jackie Brown	Manchester, England	TKO	2	Won-NBA-IBU-FL
Mar 2	1936	⑩	Jimmy Warnock	Belfast	L	12	—
Sep 16	1936	⑩	Pat Palmer	Glasgow	KO	8	Ret-NBA-IBU-FL
Jan 19	1937	♛	Small Montana	London	W	15	Won-Vac-World-FL
Mar 1	1937		Len Hampston	Manchester	LW	5	—
Mar 22	1937		Len Hampston	Leeds, England	TKO	10	—
Jun 2	1937	⑩	Jimmy Warnock	Glasgow	L	10	—
Oct 13	1937	♛	Peter Kane	Glasgow	KO	13	Ret-NBA-IBU-FL
Mar 24	1938	♛	Peter Kane	Liverpool	D	15	Ret-NBA-IBU-FL
Jun 29	1938	⑩	Jackie Jurich	Paisley, Scotland	KO	12	—
Sep 28	1938		Kayo Morgan	Glasgow	L	12	—
Oct 3	1938		Aurel Toma	London	KO'd	3	—

help him up. In the thirteenth, however, Lynch dropped Kane twice more to end the fight. Their rematch was a draw.

Lynch was next scheduled to defend his title against American Jackie Jurich. The fight, postponed twice because Lynch was injured, finally took place on June 29, 1938. Lynch weighed in 6½ pounds over the flyweight limit so the fight had to be held as a non-title event. Lynch knocked Jurich down six times before scoring a twelfth-round knockout. After the fight, Lynch received a stiff fine for not making weight and was stripped of the title.

Lynch moved up to bantamweight and, after suffering the first knockout of his career at the hands of Aurel Toma on October 3, 1938, he retired. Lynch returned to the boxing booths and held a variety of jobs. Although he continued to be very popular in Scotland, he drank excessively.

On the morning of August 6, 1946, a policeman found him lying ill. He was taken to a hospital where it was determined that he was suffering from pneumonia brought on by malnutrition and alcoholism. He died later that day. Knowledgeable fight fans remember Lynch for his brief dominance of the flyweight division, surprising power for his size, fine footwork, boxing ability, and sportsmanship.

JOE LYNCH

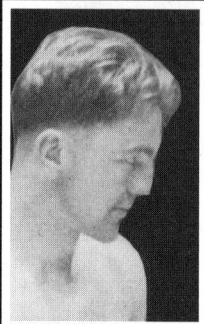

BANTAMWEIGHT

Right-handed; 5'7½"; 116–124 lbs.
157 bouts, 8/21/1915 to 9/22/1926
Manager: Eddie Mead
Bantamweight Champ 1920–21, 1922–24
Hall of Fame Induction: 2005
Born: 11/30/1898, New York, NY
Named: Joseph Aloysius Lynch
Died: 8/1/1965

Joe Lynch was a two-time holder of the world bantamweight championship. He was born in New York on November 30, 1898, and grew up in the tough Hell's Kitchen area.

Lynch's career began when he entered a tournament sponsored by a newspaper to find the newsboy champion of the Times Square District. Six months later Lynch turned pro and fought a no-decision bout on August 21, 1915, with Jack Wagner. In 1916, Lynch fought 24 times. The next year, he fought no-decision bouts with Kid Williams and Pete Herman. In a rematch with Williams in 1918, Lynch knocked him out in four rounds.

Lynch's career was briefly interrupted when he served with the U.S. Navy in World War I. While still in the military, he competed in the King's Trophy tournament in London, but lost a three-round decision to Hall of Famer and world flyweight champion Jimmy Wilde. After he mustered out of the service, Lynch fought a rematch with Wilde, who won a hotly disputed fifteen-round decision.

Back in the States, Lynch won the newspaper decision in a ten-round bout with Herman who was then the world bantamweight champ. Unfortunately for Lynch, the fight was not for the title, and it was mired in controversy because Herman's manager, Sammy Goldstein, accused Lynch's manager, Eddie Mead, of planting an iron bar in Lynch's glove. Journalist Dan Parker said he saw the slug fall from the glove.

After another no-decision bout with Herman, Lynch earned a chance at the world title on December 22, 1920, in Madison Square Garden. The 5'8" Lynch battered the 5'2" Herman to win a clear decision. In a July 1921 return match, Herman worked Lynch's body effectively to regain the crown.

Less than a year later, Lynch received another opportunity to fight for the bantamweight crown—then held by Johnny Buff. Lynch pounded Buff's face

Joe Lynch built up the muscles in his arms and shoulders while working in his father's moving business

IN THE RING	WON 52	LOST 12	DRAWS 10	TB 157	KO 38	W 14	WF 0	D 10	KO'd 0	L 12	LF 0	ND 83

Date	Year	Opponent	Site	Result / Rounds		Title
SELECTED BOUTS						
Aug 21	1915	Jack Wagner	New York	ND-W	10	—
Oct 10	1916	♛ Johnny Ertle	New York	ND	10	—
Mar 13	1917	Kid Williams ★	New York	ND-L	10	—
Jun 1	1917	♛ Pete Herman ★	New York	ND-L	10	—
Jan 29	1918	Kid Williams ★	Philadelphia	TKO	4	—
Feb 3	1919	Tommy Noble	London	W	25	—
Mar 31	1919	Jimmy Wilde ★	London	L	15	—
Sep 1	1919	♛ Pete Herman ★	Waterbury, CT	ND-W	10	—
Nov 12	1919	♛ Pete Herman ★	Philadelphia	ND-L	6	—
May 24	1920	Memphis Pal Moore	Jersey City, NJ	ND-L	12	—
Dec 22	1920	♛ Pete Herman ★	New York	W	15	Won-World-B
May 6	1921	Memphis Pal Moore	Louisville, KY	ND-L	10	—
Jul 25	1921	Pete Herman ★	New York	L	15	Lost-World-B
Jun 1	1922	Midget Smith	New York	W	15	—
Jul 10	1922	♛ Johnny Buff	New York	TKO	14	Reg-World-B
Aug 21	1922	Frankie Murray	Shreveport, LA	KO	6	Ret-World-B
Sep 4	1922	Memphis Pal Moore	Michigan City, IN	ND-W	10	—
Sep 21	1922	Jack ("Kid") Wolfe	New York	L	15	For-Vac World-JFE
Dec 22	1922	Midget Smith	New York	W	15	Ret-World-B
Apr 4	1923	Midget Smith	Chicago	ND-W	10	—
Mar 21	1924	Abe Goldstein	New York	L	15	Lost-World-B
Sep 22	1926	Frankie Murray	Mineola, NY	KO	3	—

into rivers of blood. In the fourteenth, Lynch knocked Buff down with a right to the jaw. Buff somehow staggered to his feet, but the referee stopped the fight. Lynch then went on a barnstorming tour with Jack Dempsey.

He was scheduled to defend his championship against Joe Burman on October 19, 1923, at Madison Square Garden, but on the day of the bout, he claimed that he was unable to fight because of a shoulder injury from an accident. Skeptical officials stripped Lynch of his title and awarded it to Burman—who lost it that very evening when Abe Goldstein, who substituted for Lynch, defeated Burman, to end the shortest reign in boxing history! New York boxing officials later restored the title to Lynch. Confusion about the legitimate champion was settled when Lynch met Goldstein in March 1924 and was out-boxed in a fifteen-round battle. Lynch fought for another two years but never again for a title.

Lynch is remembered for his ability to take a punch (he was never knocked out), for his stiff jab followed by a right, and for his crowd-pleasing style. In retirement, he moved to a farm he owned near New City, New York. He served as postmaster and also judged many championship fights for the NYSAC. Lynch owned New York City real estate, which he had inherited from his parents. On one of his trips to New York to collect rents, Lynch visited his brother-in-law. He was not seen again until his body was found in Sheepshead Bay. Police determined that Lynch had died by accidental drowning on August 1, 1965.

SAMMY MANDELL
The Rockford Sheik, The Boxing Beau Brummel

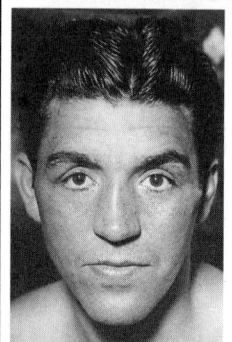

LIGHTWEIGHT

Right-handed; 5'8"; 110–146 lbs.

187 bouts, 1/14/1920 to 6/27/1934

Managers: Eddie Long 1920–1924, Eddie Kane 1920–1931, Hugh Shannon 1933

Lightweight Champion 1926–1930

Hall of Fame Induction: 1998

Born: 2/2/1904, Piana dei Greci, Sicily

Named: Salvador Mandala

Died: 11/7/1967

A Midwest favorite, Sammy Mandell outboxed two great Hall of Famers, Jimmy McLarnin and Tony Canzoneri. He held the world lightweight title for four years.

Of Italian-Albanian descent, Mandell came to the United States with his father at the age of three and settled in Rockford, Illinois. Mandell's two older brothers boxed, and he followed them into the sport, turning professional in 1920 at the age of fifteen. Most of his early fights were no-decision bouts. His modified ring name was designed to boost his appeal to Jewish boxing fans.

In 1924, Mandell fought tough junior lightweight Jack Bernstein three times, scoring one win, one draw, and one no-decision. Dubbed "The Rockford Sheik" by a Chicago sportswriter because of his good looks, Mandell also scored a newspaper victory in a no-decision bout with Hall of Famer Johnny Dundee. In its inaugural annual rankings, The Ring rated Mandell as the third-best lightweight.

With champion Benny Leonard's retirement in January 1925, the division title became vacant. Mandell won a twelve-round decision over the highly-rated Sid Terris on February 6, which Mandell thought should have earned him recognition as the titleholder. When the recognition was not forthcoming, Mandell entered the New York State Athletic Commission's eight-man elimination tournament to determine a new champion. But Mandell lost on a foul to Jimmy Goodrich in the first round of the tournament, and Rocky Kansas became champion after defeating tournament-winner Goodrich.

On July 3, 1926, Mandell met Kansas for the title in Chicago's Comiskey Park. Rain fell throughout the fight and soaked the ring. Kansas, 35, had the edge in strength and experience, but the light-hitting Mandell was a quicker and

Lightweight champion Rocky Kansas lost a 1926 ten-round decision and the title in Chicago's Comiskey Park to 22-year-old Mandell (R), who was thirteen years his junior.

IN THE RING	WON 82	LOST 21	DRAWS 9	TB 187	KO 32	W 49	WF 1	D 9	KO'd 6	L 14	LF 1	ND 73	NC 2

Date	Year		Opponent	Site	Result / Rounds		Title
SELECTED BOUTS							
Jan 14	1920		Stub Lowery	Camp Grant, IL	ND-W	4	—
Jul 31	1923		Sailor Larson	Peoria, IL	ND-W	8	—
Dec 17	1923	⑩	Sid Terris	New York	D	10	—
Jan 11	1924	⑩	Jack Bernstein	New York	D	15	—
May 15	1924	⑩	Jack Bernstein	Louisville, KY	ND-W	12	—
Jun 9	1924	⑩	Johnny Dundee ★	East Chicago, IN	ND-W	10	—
Sep 12	1924		Dick Hoppe	Los Angeles	W	4	—
Nov 7	1924		Jack Bernstein	New York	W	12	—
Feb 6	1925	⑩	Sid Terris	New York	W	12	—
May 8	1925	⑩	Jimmy Goodrich	Long Island City, NY	LF	6	—
Jul 3	1926	♛	Rocky Kansas	Chicago	W	10	Won-World-L
Apr 4	1927	⑩	Jackie Fields ★	Los Angeles	ND-D	12	—
Nov 15	1927	⑩	Spug Meyers	Chicago	W	10	—
Jan 13	1928	⑩	Billy Petrolle ★	Minneapolis	ND-W	10	—
Feb 23	1928		Jackie Fields ★	Chicago	W	10	—
May 21	1928	⑩	Jimmy McLarnin ★	New York	W	15	Ret-World-L
Jun 26	1928		Jack Zivic	Los Angeles	TKO	7	—
Aug 2	1929	⑩	Tony Canzoneri ★	Chicago	W	10	Ret-World-L
Aug 28	1929		Frankie Frisco	Petoskey, MI	TKO	3	—
Nov 4	1929	⑩	Jimmy McLarnin ★	Chicago	L	10	—
Mar 1	1930	⑩	Jimmy McLarnin ★	Chicago	L	10	—
Jul 17	1930	⑩	Al Singer	New York	KO'd	1	Lost-World-L
Oct 2	1930		Spug Meyers	Cedar Rapids, IA	ND-W	10	—
Jun 27	1934		Joe Bernal	Oakland	KO'd	6	—

better boxer. He fought a methodical, systematic fight and took the ten-round decision.

Mandell fought 23 non-title fights before meeting top contender and future Hall of Famer Jimmy McLarnin on May 21, 1928. Fighting for his title in the Polo Grounds before a paid crowd of 20,290, Mandell put on, in the words of *New York Times* writer James P. Dawson, "an exhibition of ring wizardry which stamps him as a worthy successor to the great boxers of the ring who have held the lightweight title." Although the hard-hitting McLarnin took several rounds, the fight was Mandell's. Later, in two non-title rematches, McLarnin beat Mandell by decision.

The next year Mandell successfully defended his title against Tony Canzoneri in Chicago Stadium with a split decision. Mandell held the title until July 17, 1930, when Al Singer surprised the boxing world with a stunning first-round knockout of the champ. Never before had Mandell received the count of ten. Mandell continued to box for four more years but never again contended for the title.

In retirement, Mandell kept his hand in boxing as a promoter and manager for a time. He then worked as a security guard in a Chicago bank before a stroke in 1957 left him incapacitated until his death ten years later.

JACK McAULIFFE
The Napoleon of the Prize Ring

L I G H T W E I G H T

Right-handed; 5'6"; 128–141 lbs.

36 bouts, 10/19/1884 to 9/30/1897

Manager: Billy Madden

Lightweight Champion 1886–94

Hall of Fame Induction: 1995

Born: 3/24/1866, Cork, Ireland

Died: 11/5/1937

Jack McAuliffe, lightweight champion for eight years, is one of only a handful of fighters to have retired undefeated. Born in Ireland, McAuliffe moved with his family to Bangor, Maine, as a child. Like many top boxers of the period, he learned to fight in the streets. At sixteen, he became convinced that he could become a boxer when he defeated an English sailor in a bare-knuckle bout in the basement of a Bangor storehouse.

According to legend, McAuliffe later worked in a Williamsburg, New York, cooperage where fellow employee Jack Dempsey (The Nonpareil) gave the younger fighter boxing lessons and advice. McAuliffe turned professional in 1884 with a knock-out victory over Jake Karcher and, two years later, knocked out Jack Hopper to win the American lightweight title.

McAuliffe further asserted his claim to the title when Jimmy Mitchen, a top contender, refused to face him. When he knocked out Billy Frazier, McAuliffe's grip on the world lightweight title was solidified, although McAuliffe reportedly was five pounds over the weight limit, and Frazier complained of a fast count in the 21st and final round.

In 1887 in Revere, Massachusetts, McAuliffe met British titleholder Jem

McAuliffe (L) defended his world lightweight title in an eleven-round victory over Billy Dacey on October 10, 1888, at Dover, NJ.

IN THE RING	WON 30	LOST 0	DRAWS 5*	TB 36	KO 22	W 8	WF 0	D 5*	KO'd 0	L 0	LF 0	ND 1

*includes 1 technical draw

Date	Year	Opponent	Site	Result / Rounds		Title
SELECTED BOUTS						
Oct 19	1884	Jake Karcher	Brooklyn	KO	17	—
Jan 13	1886	Jack Hopper	New York	W	6	—
Feb 27	1886	Jack Hopper	Cedarhurst, NY	KO	17	Won-Amer-L
Apr 21	1886	Joe Heiser	New York	W	4	—
Jul 24	1886	Ed Carroll	Philadelphia	TKO	1	—
Jul 31	1886	Charles McCarthy	Philadelphia	KO	3	—
Oct 29	1886	Billy Frazier	Boston	KO	21	Won-Vac World-L
Jan 14	1887	Harry Gilmore	Lawrence, MA	KO	28	Ret-World-L
Nov 16	1887	Jem Carney★	Revere, MA	D	74	Ret-World-L
Oct 10	1888	Billy Dacey	Dover, NJ	KO	11	Ret-World-L
Dec 17	1888	Sam Collyer	Brooklyn	KO	2	—
Dec 26	1888	Jake Hyams	Brooklyn	KO	9	—
Feb 23	1889	Billy Myer	Judson, IN	D	64	Ret-World-L
Feb 28	1889	Billy Boltz	Elgin, IL	KO	1	—
Mar 21	1890	Jimmy Carroll	San Francisco	KO	47	Ret-World-L
Sep 11	1891	Austin Gibbons	Hoboken, NJ	TKO	6	—
Jun 22	1892	Billy Frazier	New York	KO	3	—
Sep 5	1892	Billy Myer	New Orleans	KO	15	Ret-World-L
Dec 16	1892	Billy Myer	Chicago	W	6	—
Jan 16	1894	Jem Ryan	San Francisco	W	6	—
Aug 27	1894	Young Griffo★	Coney Island, NY	W	10	—
Nov 20	1896	Jimmy Carroll	San Francisco	W	10	—
Sep 30	1897	Phila. Tommy Ryan	Scranton, PA	W	10	—

Carney in a long, bloody, and disorderly match held after dark at a secret location, in an attempt to forestall police interference. Spectators were advised to arrive in small groups at a nearby hotel where they were carefully screened for several hours before the fight. Later, they were escorted by lantern light to the site, a barn where, as the story goes, a Salvation Army band was practicing. Finally, all was ready and the long fight started. McAuliffe was knocked down in the seventh round but got up without a problem. The two then went round after round. By the 60th, McAuliffe was visibly tiring, and his backers were getting nervous. In the 70th round, Carney knocked McAuliffe down again and probably would have won had McAuliffe's friends not rushed into the ring to help their man. Four rounds later, Carney again knocked McAuliffe down, and McAuliffe's supporters again interfered. The referee declared the match a draw to stop the unruly behavior before the police arrived. Twenty-seven years later in London, Carney and McAuliffe re-enacted their epic fight.

In 1892, McAuliffe won a rematch with Frazier and knocked out Billy Myer in the famous Carnival of Champions in New Orleans. Two years later, McAuliffe was awarded a questionable decision over Hall of Famer Young Griffo. McAuliffe retired in 1894 but came back to fight four more times in 1896 and 1897.

CHARLES ("KID") McCOY
The Corkscrew Kid

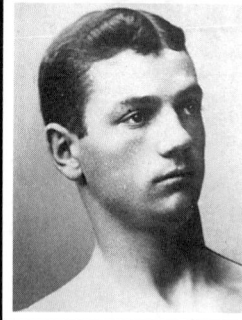

MIDDLEWEIGHT

Right-handed; 5'11"; 142–173 lbs.
107 bouts, 6/2/1891 to 8/4/1916
Manager: Ben Benton
Middleweight Champion 1897
Hall of Fame Induction: 1991
Born: 10/13/1872, Rush County, IN
Named: Norman Selby
Died: 4/18/1940

One of the most controversial figures in boxing history, Charles ("Kid") McCoy was also one of the best and most popular fighters of the 1890s. Inventor of the damaging "corkscrew" punch, which added a twist at the moment of impact, McCoy slashed and mauled opponents, sometimes to excess. He delighted in such ring tactics as pointing excitedly into the crowd and then slugging the unwary opponent who was gullible enough to look away.

McCoy's difficult life was marked by violence outside the ring and ended tragically. Born in rural Indiana as Norman Selby, McCoy reportedly adopted his ring name when he ran away from home as a youth. He began fighting professionally in 1891 at the age of seventeen and scored knockouts in twelve of his first eighteen fights.

In 1896, McCoy faced welterweight champion Tommy Ryan in a non-title event. A one-time sparring partner for Ryan, McCoy pretended to be weak and ill-trained for the fight. He asked Ryan to take it easy on him because he was only fighting for the loser's purse. Ryan was taken by surprise when McCoy turned tiger and battered him badly before knocking him out in the fifteenth round.

In 1897, McCoy knocked out Dan Creedon to win the world middleweight title. McCoy never defended this title but sought instead to move up to the heavyweight division. He earned a decision over tough Gus Ruhlin in 1898, suffered a loss to Tom Sharkey, and decisioned Joe Choynski in San Francisco in 1899. McCoy's performance overshadowed a lesser boxer named Peter McCoy, who had fought in San Francisco days earlier, and inspired the newspaper headline,

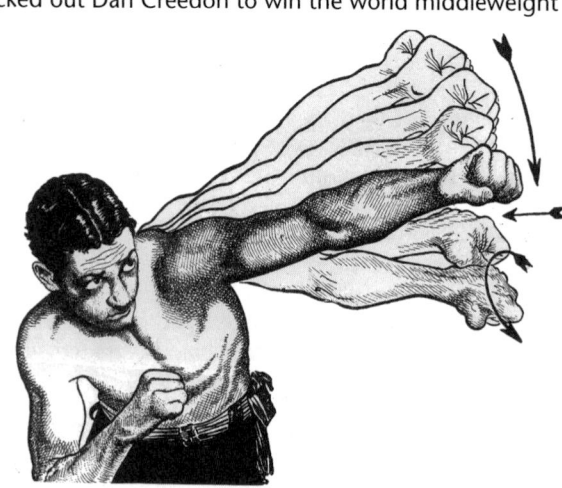

Kid McCoy's trademarked weapon was the "corkscrew" punch— delivered with a final punishing twist that could tear an opponent's skin.

IN THE RING	WON 86	LOST 6	DRAWS 6	TB 107	KO 64	W 20	WF 2	D 6	KO'd 4	L 2	LF 0	ND 6	NC 3

Date	Year	Opponent	Site	Result / Rounds		Title
SELECTED BOUTS						
Jun 2	1891	Pete Jenkins	St. Paul, MN	W	4	—
Nov 25	1895	Ted White	London	L	10	—
Mar 2	1896	♛ Tommy Ryan★	Maspeth, NY	KO	15	—
Mar 21	1896	Joe Choynski★	New York	ND	4	—
May 18	1896	Mysterious Billy Smith	Boston	WF	6	—
Sep 8	1897	♛ Tommy Ryan★	Syracuse, NY	NC	5	—
Nov 12	1897	George LaBlanche	Dayton, OH	KO	1	—
Nov 12	1897	Beach Ruble	Dayton	KO	1	—
Dec 17	1897	Dan Creedon	Long Island City, NY	TKO	15	Won-Vac World-M
May 20	1898	Gus Ruhlin	Syracuse	W	20	—
Jan 10	1899	Tom Sharkey★	New York	KO'd	10	—
Mar 24	1899	Joe Choynski★	San Francisco	W	20	—
Oct 6	1899	Joe Choynski★	Chicago	D	8	—
Jan 1	1900	Peter Maher	Coney Island, NY	KO	5	—
Jan 12	1900	Joe Choynski★	New York	KO	4	—
May 29	1900	♛ Tommy Ryan★	Chicago	W	6	—
Aug 30	1900	James J. Corbett★	New York	KO'd	5	—
Apr 22	1903	Jack Root	Detroit	L	10	For-Vac World-LH
May 14	1904	Phila. Jack O'Brien★	Philadelphia	ND-D	6	—
Jul 25	1908	Peter Maher	New York	KO	2	—
Aug 4	1916	Artie Sheridan	Mission, TX	W	4	—

"Choynski is Beaten by the Real McCoy," which coined a lasting phrase.

McCoy continued his quest for the heavyweight title in 1900 with knock-out victories over Peter Maher, Choynski, and Jack Bonner, and decisions over Ryan and Creedon. He then faced James J. Corbett. McCoy did not perform well, and when Corbett knocked him out in the fifth round, rumors flew that the fight was fixed. Corbett left for Europe immediately afterward, adding fuel to the mystery. When Vice President Theodore Roosevelt, a proponent of boxing, declared that both fighters were honest, the story died. McCoy lost a decision to Jack Root in 1903 for the newly created light heavyweight title. He continued to fight off and on until 1916, when he retired at the age of 43.

McCoy led a stormy life outside the ring. He was married eight times to six different women. He owned a tavern, a gym, appeared in early movies, and worked as a salesman and a detective. In 1924, he was convicted of manslaughter for shooting and killing Theresa Moers, a woman with whom he was living. He also wounded three other people in the course of the incident. McCoy's melodramatic courtroom re-enactment of what he claimed was Moers's suicide probably saved him from the death penalty. Sentenced to 24 years in prison, he served seven before he was released on parole. He married again and worked for the Ford Motor Company for several years following his parole. McCoy committed suicide in 1940.

PACKEY McFARLAND
The Pride of the Stockyards; The Chicago Flash

LIGHTWEIGHT

Right-handed; 5'8"; 130–140 lbs.

104 bouts, 1904 to 9/11/1915

Manager: Emil Theiry

Hall of Fame Induction: 1992

Born: 11/1/1888, Chicago, IL

Named: Patrick McFarland

Died: 9/23/1936

One of several excellent World War I–era fighters who never won titles, Packey McFarland held his own with the very best. Not a brawler by nature, McFarland gained experience fighting in the Chicago stockyards. When he knocked out a fellow employee in a lunch-hour match, McFarland decided to adopt boxing as his vocation. Turning pro at the age of sixteen, McFarland initially fought on handball courts in the Irish neighborhoods of Chicago.

Because the crowds demanded it, McFarland employed a fine knock-out punch in his early encounters. Later, as his career developed, McFarland became better known for his boxing skill. In fact, he expressed a distinct lack of interest in knocking out opponents, preferring to win by decision. Going east for the first time, McFarland decisioned highly touted Bert Keyes in Boston in 1908. He then

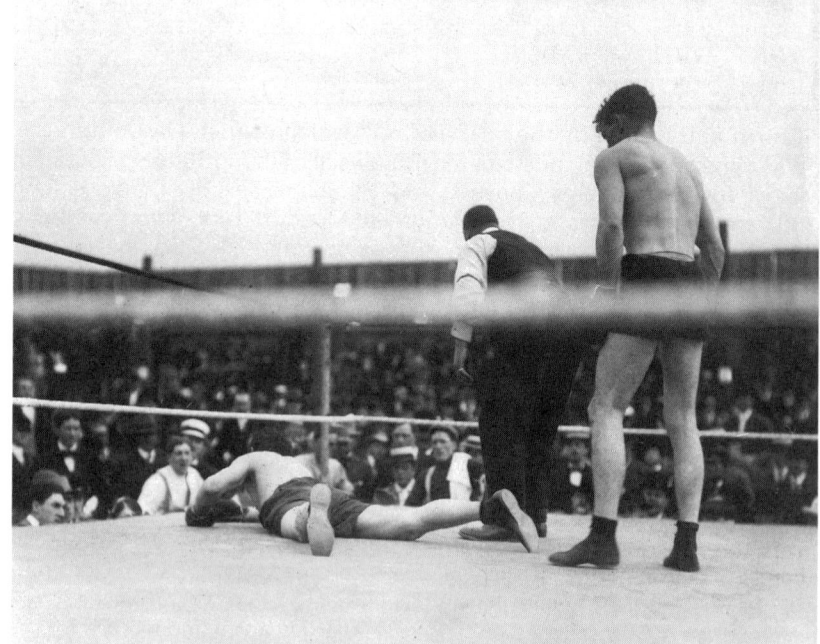

Jimmy Britt was a skillful fighter, but on April 11, 1908, in Colma, CA, he couldn't withstand Packey McFarland's greater punching power. He was knocked out in the sixth round.

IN THE RING	WON 64	LOST 1	DRAWS 5	TB 104	KO 47	W 17	WF 0	D 5	KO'd 1	L 0	LF 0	ND 34

Date	Year	Opponent	Site	Result / Rounds		Title
SELECTED BOUTS						
—	1904	Dusty Miller	—	KO'd	5	—
Jan 24	1905	Jack Walker	Chicago	KO	4	—
Feb 10	1905	Jack Meyers	South Bend, IN	KO	3	—
Nov 21	1907	Kid Herman	Davenport, IA	ND	15	—
Jan 14	1908	Bert Keyes	Boston	W	12	—
Jan 28	1908	Young Loughrey	Philadelphia	ND	6	—
Feb 21	1908	Freddie Welsh★	Milwaukee	W	10	—
Apr 11	1908	Jimmy Britt	Colma, CA	KO	6	—
Jul 4	1908	Freddie Welsh★	Los Angeles	D	25	—
Aug 7	1908	Phil Brock	Los Angeles	KO	7	—
Nov 18	1908	Tommy Murphy	Philadelphia	ND	6	—
Sep 19	1909	Ray Bronson	New Orleans	D	20	—
Apr 1	1910	Dick Lee	Plymouth, England	KO	9	—
May 30	1910	Freddie Welsh★	London	D	20	—
Jun 18	1910	Jack Goldswain	London	KO	3	—
Jan 9	1911	Johnny McCarthy	Kansas City, MO	W	10	—
Jan 30	1911	Jack Britton★	Memphis, TN	D	8	—
Mar 20	1911	Billy Ryan	Oswego, NY	KO	4	—
May 12	1911	Tommy Kilbane	Buffalo, NY	ND	10	—
Jul 3	1911	Young Ahearn	Albany, NY	KO	8	—
Nov 30	1911	Tommy Murphy	San Francisco	W	20	—
Apr 26	1912	Matt Wells	New York	ND	10	—
Oct 11	1912	Tommy Kilbane	Winnipeg, Alb.	KO	10	—
Mar 7	1913	Jack Britton★	New York	ND	10	—
Oct 17	1913	Tommy Murphy	New York	ND	10	—
Nov 20	1913	Kid Alberts	Waterbury, CT	ND	10	—
Dec 8	1913	Jack Britton★	Milwaukee	ND	10	—
Sep 11	1915	Mike Gibbons★	Brooklyn	ND	10	—

won a decision over Freddie Welsh before fighting him to a 25-round draw in a rematch in Los Angeles. A third bout with Welsh in London also resulted in a draw.

Though McFarland was highly regarded, he was never given a shot at the lightweight title held by Battling Nelson. In 1908, the two nearly came to blows outside the Hotel Astoria in New York. In fairness to Nelson, McFarland usually fought above the lightweight limit, which was then 133 pounds.

McFarland fought Jack Britton three times. The first bout, held in Memphis, was called a draw, although Chicago newspapers declared Britton the winner. In two no-decision rematches, Britton and McFarland fought very evenly. McFarland closed his career by fighting in a much ballyhooed contest with the clever Hall of Famer Mike Gibbons, but the ten-round fight was a flop with neither fighter landing any significant punches.

In retirement, McFarland managed his sizable investments, was director of two banks, and also served on the Illinois State Athletic Commission.

TERRY McGOVERN
Terrible Terry

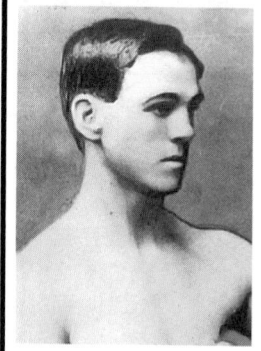

FEATHERWEIGHT

Right-handed; 5'4"; 112–127 lbs.
78 bouts, 4/3/1897 to 5/27/1908

Managers: Sam Harris, Joe Humphreys

Bantamwt. Champ 1899–1900
Featherweight Champ 1900–01

Hall of Fame Induction: 1990

Born: 3/9/1880, Johnstown, PA

Named: John Terrence McGovern

Died: 2/26/1918

One of the hardest hitters in the history of the featherweight division, Terry McGovern captured both the bantamweight and featherweight titles. In his prime, McGovern was a fearless, powerful puncher who recorded 38 knockouts in his first 62 fights. Not much for fancy maneuvers, McGovern simply went after his opponents with a ferocious will to win.

McGovern, who grew up in Brooklyn, never went to school. He was a newsboy and later worked at a variety of jobs. As a laborer in a lumber yard, McGovern handled himself well in the occasional fights there, and his boss encouraged him to become a fighter. He turned pro in 1897 at the age of seventeen.

Within two years, McGovern was a contender for the vacant world bantamweight title. He faced British bantamweight champ Tom ("Pedlar") Palmer for the crown in 1899. Though previously unbeaten, Palmer could not last one round with the solid-punching McGovern, who knocked him out in less than two minutes. The next year McGovern took the world featherweight title from a declining George Dixon with an eighth-round knockout in Madison Square Garden.

McGovern (L) shakes hands with Young Corbett II before one of their battles. Corbett was the only opponent to ever knock out McGovern. He KO'd him twice.

IN THE RING	WON 60	LOST 4	DRAWS 4	TB 78	KO 42	W 17	WF 1	D 4	KO'd 2	L 1	LF 1	ND 10

Date	Year	Opponent	Site	Result / Rounds		Title
SELECTED BOUTS						
Apr 3	1897	Jack Shea	Brooklyn	KO	1	—
May 5	1898	George Munroe	Yonkers, NY	D	20	—
Jun 11	1898	George Munroe	Coney Island, NY	KO	24	—
Aug 4	1898	George Munroe	Brooklyn	WF	7	—
Apr 28	1899	Joe Bernstein	New York	W	25	—
Jul 1	1899	Johnny Ritchie	Tuckahoe, NY	KO	3	—
Sep 12	1899	♛ Tom ("Pedlar") Palmer	Tuckahoe	KO	1	Won-World-B
Jan 9	1900	♛ George Dixon★	New York	TKO	8	Won-World-FE
Feb 1	1900	♛ Eddie Santry	Chicago	KO	5	Ret-World-FE
Mar 9	1900	Oscar Gardner	New York	KO	3	Ret-World-FE
Jun 12	1900	Tommy White	Coney Island	KO	3	Ret-World-FE
Jun 23	1900	George Dixon★	Chicago	W	6	—
Jul 16	1900	♛ Frank Erne	New York	KO	3	—
Nov 2	1900	Joe Bernstein	Louisville, KY	KO	7	Ret-World-FE
Dec 13	1900	Joe Gans★	Chicago	KO	2	—
Apr 30	1901	Oscar Gardner	San Francisco	KO	4	Ret-World-FE
May 29	1901	Aurelio Herrera	San Francisco	KO	5	Ret-World-FE
Nov 28	1901	Young Corbett II	Hartford, CT	KO'd	2	Lost-World-FE
Mar 31	1903	♛ Young Corbett II	San Francisco	KO'd	11	For-World-FE
Mar 14	1906	Battling Nelson★	Philadelphia	ND-L	6	—
Oct 17	1906	♛ Young Corbett II	Philadelphia	ND-W	6	—
May 27	1908	Spike Robson	New York	ND-L	6	—

McGovern successfully defended his featherweight title several times in 1900 and 1901. He also scored a third-round knockout over the world lightweight champion Frank Erne in a non-title bout. He beat Hall of Famer Joe Gans in two rounds in 1900, although Gans later admitted to throwing the fight.

McGovern's toughest opponent was Young Corbett, a fighter from Denver whose fierce attitude rivaled the ruthlessness that McGovern exhibited. A fight between the two, who were only seven months apart in age, was set up in 1901 in Hartford, with McGovern's title at stake. Observors have said that Corbett unnerved the champion by not showing any fear or deference toward him. Passing by McGovern's dressing room on his way to the ring, Corbett shouted, "Come on out, you Irish rat, and take the licking of your life." Corbett and McGovern each scored a knockdown in the first round, but in the second, Corbett handed McGovern the first knockout of his career. McGovern tried to win back the title from Corbett in 1903 but was knocked out again.

McGovern fought infrequently for the next five years, never regaining his earlier skill. In the latter stages of his career, McGovern's behavior became erratic, and he spent time in various sanitariums. He collapsed while serving as a referee at an Army camp during World War I and died soon after.

JIMMY McLARNIN
Baby Face

WELTERWEIGHT

Right-handed; 5'6"; 112–147 lbs.
77 bouts, 1923 to 11/20/1936
Manager: Pop Foster
Welterwt. Champ 1933–34, 1934–35
Hall of Fame Induction: 1991
Born: 12/19/1907, Hillsborough, Ireland
Named: James Archibald McLarnin
Died: 10/28/2004

Jimmy McLarnin was a hard hitter who could target a punch with devastating accuracy. His bouts with Hall of Famer Barney Ross are remembered as some of the very best contests in any weight class or era. Born in Ireland, McLarnin grew up in Vancouver, Canada. Fight manager Pop Foster took McLarnin under his wing at an early age and trained him for the professional ranks. Foster debuted McLarnin in Canada at age sixteen as a flyweight, then took his young star to California, pitting him against increasingly tough opponents. In 1925, McLarnin decisioned Hall of Famer Pancho Villa in the Filipino's last fight.

In 1928, McLarnin challenged Sammy Mandell for the world lightweight championship. Mandell won a convincing decision over the young McLarnin, who nevertheless was lauded for his courage and willingness to fight. Later, in two non-title bouts, McLarnin won decisions over Mandell. McLarnin defeated

McLarnin (R) won his last fight, decisioning Lou Ambers in ten on November 20, 1936, in New York. Ambers had won the lightweight crown just two months earlier, but this meeting was a non-title bout.

IN THE RING	WON 62	LOST 11	DRAWS 3	TB 77	KO 20	W 41	WF 1	D 3	KO'd 1	L 10	LF 0	ND 1

Date	Year	Opponent	Site	Result / Rounds		Title
SELECTED BOUTS						
Dec 28	1923	Mickey Gill	Vancouver, Canada	W	6	—
Feb 22	1924	Eddie Collins	Oakland	KO	3	—
Oct 28	1924	Fidel LaBarba ★	Vernon, CA	W	4	—
Nov 11	1924	Fidel LaBarba ★	Vernon	D	4	—
Jan 13	1925	⑩ Fidel LaBarba ★	Vernon	W	10	—
Jul 4	1925	♛ Pancho Villa ★	Oakland	W	10	—
Feb 24	1928	Sid Terris	New York	KO	1	—
May 21	1928	♛ Sammy Mandell ★	New York	L	15	For-World-L
Nov 4	1929	♛ Sammy Mandell ★	Chicago	W	10	—
Dec 13	1929	⑩ Ruby Goldstein ★	New York	KO	2	—
Mar 1	1930	♛ Sammy Mandell ★	Chicago	W	10	—
Sep 11	1930	♛ Al Singer	New York	KO	3	—
Nov 21	1930	⑩ Billy Petrolle ★	New York	L	10	—
May 27	1931	⑩ Billy Petrolle ★	New York	W	10	—
Aug 20	1931	⑩ Billy Petrolle ★	New York	W	10	—
Aug 4	1932	⑩ Lou Brouillard ★	New York	L	10	—
Oct 7	1932	Benny Leonard ★	New York	TKO	6	—
Dec 16	1932	⑩ Sammy Fuller	New York	KO	8	—
May 29	1933	♛ Young Corbett III ★	Los Angeles	KO	1	Won-World-W
May 28	1934	⑩ Barney Ross ★	Long Island City, NY	L	15	Lost-World-W
Sep 17	1934	⑩ Barney Ross ★	Long Island City, NY	W	15	Reg-World-W
May 28	1935	⑩ Barney Ross ★	New York	L	15	Lost-World-W
May 8	1936	♛ Tony Canzoneri ★	New York	L	10	—
Oct 5	1936	⑩ Tony Canzoneri ★	New York	W	10	—
Nov 20	1936	♛ Lou Ambers ★	New York	W	10	—

Billy Petrolle, Benny Leonard, and others to earn a shot at the welterweight title held by Young Corbett III. The fight was held in Los Angeles in 1933. McLarnin was on fire. Within seconds, he floored the champ with a right to the chin, then knocked him down again with three lefts. Two more blows sent Corbett sprawling and it was all over before the bell sounded to end the first round.

The next year, McLarnin defended his title against Ross, the lightweight and junior welterweight champ, in the Madison Square Garden Bowl before a crowd of 65,000. In a split decision, Ross won the championship. In the rematch four months later, Ross fought in furious flurries and McLarnin boxed magnificently, even with one eye completely closed from the twelfth round on. This time, McLarnin won and reclaimed his title. McLarnin faced Ross for a third time at the Polo Grounds in 1935 with 40,000 fans looking on. Jack Dempsey refereed. The two champions went at each other relentlessly for fifteen rounds, and Ross was declared the winner on a unanimous decision. McLarnin then split two fights with Tony Canzoneri and defeated Lou Ambers before leaving the ring. In retirement, McLarnin pursued a business career and also acted, golfed, and lectured.

SAM McVEY

HEAVYWEIGHT

Right handed; 5'10½"; 200–215 lbs.

97 bouts, 4/12/1902 to 8/2/1921

Manager: Billy Roche 1902–03, Spider Kelly 1904, Frank Carillo 1906–07, Frank Bernard 1907, Cal McClain 1912

Unofficial Black Heavyweight Champ 1909, 1915

Hall of Fame Induction: 1999

Born: 5/17/1884, Waelder, TX

Named: Samuel E. MacVea

Died: 12/23/1921

Like fellow black Hall of Famers Sam Langford and Joe Jeannette, Sam McVey never fought for the heavyweight title. McVey grew up in California. As a youth he worked in an Oxnard livery stable, where he joined in occasional informal boxing matches. His success in these bouts drew the attention of the stable's owner, Billy Roche, who quickly arranged to manage McVey. His first recorded fight was a six-round knock-out victory over George Sullivan on April 12, 1902, in Oxnard.

McVey won his first seven fights by knockout before he was paired with Hall of Famer and future heavyweight champion Jack Johnson in a bout advertised as for "The Negro Heavyweight Title." The inexperienced McVey was no match for Johnson, and he lost. When the rematch ended in another twenty-round decision for Johnson, Roche severed his connection with McVey. In the third McVey–Johnson fight, McVey was KO'd in the twentieth round.

In 1907, McVey left California for the first time, fighting Joe Jeannette in a no-decision battle in New York. Then McVey set sail for Europe, fighting once in England before moving on to France, where black heavyweights were generally well accepted. On February 20, 1909, McVey won a twenty-round decision over Jeannette in a particularly lackluster bout. Rumors circulated that the two combatants had treated the fight merely as an exhibition. A rematch on April 17, 1909, turned out to be one of the greatest displays of endurance in ring history. The powerful McVey, who often charged opponents with his left arm extended, knocked Jeannette down 27 times and nearly finished him with a right to the jaw in the sixteenth round. Jeannette was

McVey (L) met "Chicago Jim" Barry in Sydney, Australia, on March 16, 1912. Barry (not to be confused with Hall of Famer Jimmy Barry, also from Chicago) lasted a full twenty rounds and lost on points.

IN THE RING	WON 63	LOST 12	DRAWS 7	TB 97	KO 48	W 14	WF 1	D 7	KO'd 5	L 7	LF 0	ND 13	NC 2

Date	Year	Opponent	Site	Result / Rounds		Title
SELECTED BOUTS						
Apr 12	1902	George Sullivan	Oxnard, CA	KO	6	—
Feb 26	1903	Jack Johnson ★	Los Angeles	L	20	For-Black-H
Oct 27	1903	Jack Johnson ★	Los Angeles	L	20	For-Black-H
Apr 22	1904	Jack Johnson ★	San Francisco	KO'd	20	For-Black-H
Feb 20	1909	Joe Jeannette ★	Paris	W	20	Won-Vac Black-H
Apr 9	1909	Cyclone Billy Warren	Paris	KO	2	Ret-Black-H
Apr 17	1909	Joe Jeannette ★	Paris	TKO'd	49	Lost-Black-H
Jul 20	1911	George ("The Boer") Rodel	Liverpool, England	KO	1	—
Apr 11	1912	Sam Langford ★	Sydney	L	20	For Black-H
Aug 3	1912	Sam Langford ★	Sydney	L	20	For-Black-H
Oct 10	1912	Sam Langford ★	Perth, Australia	TKO'd	11	For-Black-H
Dec 26	1912	Sam Langford ★	Sydney	KO'd	13	For-Black-H
Dec 20	1914	Harry Wills ★	New Orleans	W	20	—
Jun 29	1915	Sam Langford ★	Boston	W	12	Won-Black-H
Sep 7	1915	Harry Wills ★	Boston	L	12	Lost-Black-H
Apr 7	1916	Sam Langford ★	Syracuse, NY	ND-W	10	For-Black-H
Aug 12	1916	Sam Langford ★	Buenos Aires	D	20	For-Black-H
Feb 17	1918	Harry Wills ★	Panama City	KO'd	5	—
Sep 8	1920	Harry Wills ★	Philadelphia	NC	6	For-Black-H
Aug 2	1921	Jeff Clark	Lancaster, PA	ND-D	10	—

saved by the bell, and in the later rounds began to take control of the fight, knocking McVey down seven times in the 42nd. After 49 rounds, McVey could not continue. Though he suffered defeat, his tremendous performance showcased his slugging power and fighting spirit.

On April 1, 1911, McVey met Sam Langford for the first time in a fight that ended in a twenty-round draw. In the course of his career, McVey would fight Langford fifteen times; Jeannette five; another black heavyweight, Battling Jim Johnson, seven times; and Hall of Famer Harry Wills five. Unable to secure bouts with top white opponents—or with Jack Johnson when he was champion—the top black fighters were forced to face each other repeatedly. In Liverpool, England, on July 20, 1911, McVey scored a first-round knockout over George ("The Boer") Rodel, a rare white adversary.

Later that year, the globe-trotting McVey next moved his operations to Australia, campaigning there for three years. He faced Langford six times Down Under. McVey returned to the United States from 1914 to 1916, then embarked on a Latin American tour, which ended when Wills knocked him out in Panama City. By this time, McVey's career was winding down. He did not fight for over two and a half years before making a brief eight-fight comeback before retiring.

Unfortunately, McVey's retirement did not last long. In 1921, he contracted pneumonia and died. Jack Johnson paid for the funeral and for the debts of his one-time rival.

FREDDIE MILLER

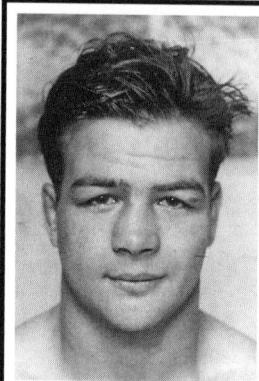

FEATHERWEIGHT

Left-handed; 5'5"; 122–132 lbs.

248 bouts, 4/4/1927 to 4/1/1940

Managers: Danny Davis 1927–31, Pete Reilly 1931–37, Dom and Tony Vairo 1938

NBA Featherweight Champ 1933–34

World Fthrwt Champ 1934–36

Hall of Fame Induction: 1997

Born: 4/3/1911, Cincinnati, OH

Died: 5/8/1962

Although Freddie Miller rarely strayed far from his hometown of Cincinnati for his first 95 fights, by the end of his career few fighters could claim to have fought in as many places as the diminutive southpaw. Miller donned the gloves in virtually every major city in the United States. Abroad, he campaigned in England, Scotland, Spain, France, Ireland, Mexico, Cuba, Belgium, South Africa, Wales, and Venezuela. Through all his travels, Miller impressed observers as one of the greatest left-handers in boxing history.

Miller turned professional at the age of sixteen with a third-round knockout of Billy Barnes in Fort Thomas, Kentucky. A knock-out victory would prove to be somewhat unusual for Miller, who recorded knockouts in fewer than twenty percent of his fights. Miller won 71 of his first 75 fights which led *The Ring* to recognize him as the third-best featherweight contender in its annual rankings for 1929. It is astonishing that Miller was a veteran of 75 pro bouts at the age of eighteen.

In 1930 and 1931, Miller was ranked by *The Ring* as a junior lightweight even though he managed to make weight as a featherweight in a bout with Battling Battalino for his world title. Battalino decisioned Miller in ten rounds. In their rematch six months later, Miller and Battalino engaged in a shameful performance. At the time both fighters were managed by Pete Reilly. Beforehand, the fighters agreed that Miller could win the title. However, Miller and Battalino performed this charade so artlessly that the referee declared the fight no contest. In 1932, Miller was dropped from *The Ring*'s annual rankings.

Miller rebounded on January 13, 1933, in Chicago, when he faced NBA world featherweight champion Tommy Paul. In this battle, their fourth meeting, Miller took the decision in ten rounds. The next year, Miller gained recognition as the undisputed featherweight champion when he decisioned Nel Tarleton in Liverpool, England. Also in 1934, Miller earned decisions over Hall of Famers Chalky Wright and Panama Al

Miller sends IBU featherweight champion Nel Tarleton to his knees. In their September 20, 1934, Liverpool meeting, Miller gained a unified world title.

IN THE RING	WON 208	LOST 28	DRAWS 7	TB 248	KO 42	W 163	WF 3	D 7	KO'd 1	L 25	LF 2	ND 1	NC 4

Date	Year	Opponent	Site	Result / Rounds		Title
SELECTED BOUTS						
Apr 4	1927	Billy Barnes	Ft. Thomas, KY	KO	3	—
Jan 1	1929	⑩ Cecil Payne	Cincinnati	W	10	—
Jan 29	1930	⑩ Bushy Graham	Cincinnati	D	10	—
Oct 2	1930	⑩ Johnny Farr	Cincinnati	W	10	—
Nov 13	1930	⑩ Johnny Farr	Cincinnati	L	10	—
Jun 11	1931	⑩ Eddie Shea	Cincinnati	W	10	—
Jul 23	1931	♛ Battling Battalino ★	Cincinnati	L	10	For-World-FE
Jan 27	1932	♛ Battling Battalino ★	Cincinnati	NC	3	For-World-FE
Jan 13	1933	⑩ Tommy Paul	Chicago	W	10	Won-NBA-FE
Feb 28	1933	⑩ Baby Arizmendi ★	Los Angeles	W	10	Ret-NBA-FE
Mar 21	1933	⑩ Speedy Dado	Los Angeles	W	10	Ret-NBA-FE
Jun 12	1933	⑩ Baby Arizmendi ★	San Francisco	L	10	—
Jan 1	1934	Jackie Sharkey	Cincinnati	W	10	Ret-NBA-FE
Feb 7	1934	⑩ Petey Sarron	Cincinnati	W	10	—
Jun 8	1934	Albert ("Chalky") Wright ★	El Centro, CA	W	10	—
Sep 20	1934	⑩ Nel Tarleton	Liverpool, England	W	15	Won-Vac World-FE
Dec 24	1934	♛ Panama Al Brown ★	Paris	W	10	—
Feb 17	1935	Jose Girones	Barcelona	KO	1	Ret-World-FE
Jun 12	1935	⑩ Nel Tarleton	Liverpool	W	15	Ret-World-FE
Oct 22	1935	⑩ Vernon Cormier	Boston	W	15	Ret-World-FE
Feb 18	1936	Johnny Pena	Seattle	W	12	Ret-World-FE
Mar 2	1936	⑩ Petey Sarron	Coral Gables, FL	W	15	Ret-World-FE
May 11	1936	⑩ Petey Sarron	Washington, DC	L	15	Lost-World-FE
Feb 9	1937	⑩ Jackie Wilson	Pittsburgh	L	10	—
Apr 26	1937	⑩ Jackie Wilson	Cincinnati	L	10	—
Jul 31	1937	⑩ Petey Sarron	Johannesburg, South Africa	W	10	—
Sep 4	1937	⑩ Petey Sarron	Johannesburg	L	12	For-World-FE
Oct 24	1938	⑩ Leo Rodak	Washington, DC	L	15	For-MD World-FE
Dec 5	1938	⑩ Sammy Angott ★	Louisville, KY	L	10	—
Apr 1	1940	Herschel Joiner	Cincinnati	TKO'd	8	—

Brown. As champion, Miller took on all comers in a wide range of venues. He defended the world featherweight title successfully five times in three years and fought 48 non-title fights, winning 41.

On May 11, 1936, Miller put his title on the line against Petey Sarron. Miller had previously defeated Sarron three times, with the most recent victory coming only two months before. However, Sarron decisioned Miller to take the title. Miller defeated Sarron in a non-title bout in the rematch, but when they fought for the title in Johannesburg, South Africa, Sarron retained the crown. This was the first time that two Americans ever fought for a world title on foreign soil.

Miller did not get another chance at Sarron but did unsuccessfully battle Leo Rodak for the Maryland version of the world featherweight title in 1938. After suffering the only knock-out defeat of his career, at the hands of Herschel Joiner, Miller retired. Though only 28, Miller had fought 248 times in thirteen years.

CHARLIE MITCHELL

HEAVYWEIGHT

Right-handed; 5'9"; 130–175 lbs.

47 bouts, 1878 to 1/25/1894

Managers: George ("Pony") Moore, Billy Thompson

Hall of Fame Induction: 2002

Born: 11/24/1861, Birmingham, England

Named: Charles Watson Mitchell

Died: 4/3/1918

Though no bigger than a modern-day middleweight, Charlie Mitchell took on the top heavyweights of his day and floored the great champion he most yearned to beat—John L. Sullivan.

A game, scientific fighter, who was skillful with both gloves and bare knuckles, Mitchell started fighting as a bare-knuckle lightweight at sixteen. The next year, he fought English lightweight champ Billy Kennedy to a draw in a gloved match. Mitchell held court at a series of taverns in England from 1878 through 1880, where he took on all comers.

In 1881, Mitchell's pugilistic career began to take off. He fought a draw with Jack Burke for the welterweight championship of England. In April, 1882, Mitchell beat Ned Harnatty in a middleweight competition, and later that year he defeated six opponents—some much bigger than he—to win the heavyweight championship of England in a tournament staged to find a challenger for John Sullivan. As the winner, Mitchell came to the United States in 1883.

Sullivan agreed to fight Mitchell on May 14, 1883, in Madison Square Garden. The fight received a great deal of attention, and *Police Gazette* publisher Richard K. Fox touted the chances of the smaller Mitchell. At the start of the match, Sullivan charged Mitchell, firing lefts and rights, but the challenger used his superior speed to avoid many wild blows. Sullivan, who outweighed Mitchell by 40 pounds, landed enough punches to knock Mitchell down several times and dominate the action. Police stopped the fight after three rounds, but in the first, a quick left by Mitchell had knocked Sullivan down for the first time in his career.

Mitchell fought exhibitions for the next year or so, both in the U.S. and in England. On March 26, 1884, a fight with Jake Kilrain in Boston was called a draw after the police intervened. Next up was a Sullivan rematch. On the day of the fight, June 30, 1884, there were rumors that Mitchell had malaria and that Sullivan was on a binge, and indeed the latter arrived at Madison Square Garden so drunk that he announced he was sick and unable to fight.

ROUND 9.—MITCHELL LANDED WELL.

Mitchell (R) connects to the mouth in a solid ninth round in his uphill bare-knuckle battle to defeat heavyweight champion of the world, John L. Sullivan. Several times both fighters tumbled to the grass in an exhausted heap.

IN THE RING	WON 31	LOST 3	DRAWS 12	TB 47	KO 7	W 24	WF 0	D 12	KO'd 1	L 2	LF 0	NC 1

Date	Year	Opponent	Site	Result / Rounds		Title
SELECTED BOUTS						
Jan 11	1878	Bob Cunningham	Birmingham, England	W	50 min.	—
—	1879	Billy Kennedy	London	D	4	For-England-L
Jun 16	1881	Jack Burke	Winkfield, England	D	25	For-England-W
Apr 4	1882	Ned Harnatty	Chelsea Baths, England	W	3	—
Feb 17	1883	Jack Clarke	Newcastle, England	TKO	1	Won-North England-H
May 14	1883	John L. Sullivan ★	New York	L	3	—
Jun	1883	Garrett	Syracuse, NY	W	1	—
Oct 2	1883	William Sheriff	Flushing, NY	D	7	—
Mar 20	1884	Joe Denning	New York	W	4	—
Mar 26	1884	Jake Kilrain	Boston	D	4	—
May 12	1884	Billy Edwards ★	New York	KO	3	—
Oct 13	1884	Dominick McCaffrey	New York	L	4	—
Oct 21	1884	Jack Burke	New York	D	4	—
Nov 24	1884	Jack Burke	New York	D	3	—
Feb 23	1885	John F. Scholes	Toronto	W	4	—
May 22	1885	Mike Cleary	San Francisco	D	4	—
Jun 29	1885	Jack Burke	Chicago	D	6	—
May 16	1886	Jack Burke	Chicago	D	10	—
Jun 11	1886	Patsy Cardiff	Minneapolis	W	6	—
Mar 10	1888	♛ John L. Sullivan ★	Chantilly, France	D	39	For-BK World-H
Feb 7	1890	Jem Mace ★	Glasgow, Scotland	W	4	Won-Vac England-H
Mar 2	1892	Arthur Upham	New Orleans	TKO	3	—
Jan 25	1894	♛ Jim Corbett ★	Jacksonville, FL	KO'd	3	For-World-H

Mitchell continued his ambitious fight schedule. When Sullivan toured England, his manager arranged another fight with Mitchell at the estate of Baron Alphonse Rothschild in Chantilly, France, the parties agreeing to fight for $2,500 a side. Sullivan knocked Mitchell down in the first, second, and third rounds, but Mitchell kept moving, trying to wear down his big opponent. In the seventh, Mitchell threw Sullivan to the turf for the first time. The ninth round was also a good one for Mitchell; he connected with Sullivan's jaw. For a total of 39 rounds, the fighting continued, Sullivan attacking and Mitchell dodging. Finally, with both fighters moving as though in slow motion, they agreed to a draw.

Though he was unsuccessful in his title bid, Mitchell remained active in boxing both as a fighter and as a second for Jake Kilrain in his famous battle with Sullivan. On February 7, 1890, Mitchell met 58-year-old Hall of Famer Jem Mace in a fight billed as the heavyweight championship of England. Police broke up the match with Mitchell leading.

On January 25, 1894, Mitchell once again fought for the world heavyweight title, now held by Jim Corbett. The younger Corbett proved to be too much for Mitchell, knocking him out in three rounds. Though Mitchell continued to fight exhibitions, he would never again fight for the championship.

OWEN MORAN
The Fearless

BANTAMWEIGHT

Right-handed; 5'4"; 102–130 lbs.
107 bouts, 1900 to 8/21/1916
Manager: Charley Harvey
Brit World Bantam Champ 1907
Hall of Fame Induction: 2002
Born: 11/4/1884, Birmingham, England
Died: 3/17/1949

Though he was never widely acclaimed as a champion, Owen Moran is considered one of the greatest British fighters of all time.

Moran started boxing in carnival booths around 1900, adeptly taking on all comers. He was spotted by Captain Cleveland, a former amateur boxer and "man of means," who was impressed by Moran's skill. In his first major bout, Moran lost a tough, twenty-round decision to ring veteran Digger Stanley on June 17, 1901. Shortly after the Stanley fight, Cleveland arranged for Charley Harvey to manage Moran.

Harvey quickly signed Moran to fight Harry Slough at Leicester's Mafeking Gymnasium. At first, Slough pushed the less experienced Moran around the ring, but the challenger went the full fifteen rounds to be declared the winner. In 1904, he earned a six-round decision over Hall of Famer George Dixon.

Moran then went to the United States, where he debuted in a six-round, no-decision bout with Danny Dougherty. The 5'4" Moran impressed observers with his speed and double-fisted attack. A Philadelphia sportswriter reported, "I can't believe this Moran is an Englishman. He fights like an American." Moran faced another fine fighter in Abe Attell's brother, Monte, beating him in an easy twenty-round bout.

In 1907, Harvey brought Moran to the U.S. for an extended stay. In Philadelphia, on October 19, 1907, Moran battered Tommy O'Toole in a six-round, no-decision bout. Harvey then took Moran to the West Coast, where he arranged a fight for Moran with Frankie Neil, considered the lightweight champion of California. He pounded Neil to the verge of collapse, eased up to let him recover, then hammered him again, knocking him out in the sixteenth round.

Outraged California fight fans persuaded featherweight champion Abe Attell to put his

In San Francisco, on November 26, 1910, Battling Nelson "The Durable Dane" suffers the second knockout of his distinguished career at the hands of Owen Moran. Referee Ben Selig administers the ten-count.

IN THE RING	WON 67	LOST 16	DRAWS 5	TB 107	KO 34	W 33	WF 0	D 5	KO'd 2	L 9	LF 5	ND 19

Date	Year		Opponent	Site	Result / Rounds		Title

SELECTED BOUTS

Date	Year		Opponent	Site	Result	Rounds	Title
—	1900		Bill Lovesey	Birmingham, Eng.	KO	2	—
Jun 17	1901		Digger Stanley	Birmingham	L	20	—
Oct 9	1901		Harry Slough	Leicester, Eng.	W	15	—
May 30	1904		Joe Bowker	London	L	20	For-English-B (116 lbs)
Oct 17	1904		George Dixon ★	London	W	6	—
Oct 29	1904		Harry Ware	Newcastle, Eng.	TKO	3	Won-English-B (116 lbs)
Jan 23	1905		Digger Stanley	London	W	20	—
Mar 12	1905		Danny Dougherty	Philadelphia	ND-W	6	—
May 15	1905		Monte Attell	New York	W	20	—
Apr 22	1907		Al Delmont	London	W	20	Won-Brit World-B (116 lbs)
Jul 22	1907		Young Pierce	Liverpool	KO	18	—
Nov 22	1907		Frankie Neil	San Francisco	TKO	16	—
Jan 1	1908	♛	Abe Attell ★	San Francisco	D	25	For-World-FE
Apr 7	1908		Ad Wolgast ★	New York	ND-W	6	—
Sep 7	1908	♛	Abe Attell ★	Colma, CA	D	23	For-World-FE
Apr 1	1910	♛	Abe Attell ★	New York	ND-D	10	—
Jun 24	1910		Abe Attell ★	Los Angeles	ND-L	10	—
Nov 9	1910	♛	Abe Attell ★	Philadelphia	ND-D	6	—
Nov 26	1910		Battling Nelson ★	San Francisco	KO	11	—
Mar 14	1911		Packey McFarland ★	New York	ND-L	10	—
Jul 4	1911		Ad Wolgast ★	San Francisco	KO'd	13	For-World-L
Jan 27	1913	♛	Jem Driscoll ★	London	D	20	For-British World-FE
May 31	1915		Llew Edwards	London	LF	11	For-Vac British-FE
Aug 21	1916		Billy Marchant	Liverpool	LF	2	—

title on the line against Moran on New Year's Day, 1908, in San Francisco. Moran had to slim down to 120 pounds. The fight was called a draw and a return battle was scheduled for 23 rounds in Colma, California, on September 7, 1908. Once again, the two Hall of Famers battled to a draw.

On November 26, 1910, Moran faced Battling Nelson. Early in the fight, Nelson winked at friends at ringside to show that Moran would be an easy opponent, but by the eleventh round, Nelson was visibly weakened. Although Moran was bleeding profusely from his nose and eyes, a right to the side of the neck knocked the Durable Dane unconscious.

On July 4, 1911, Moran returned to San Francisco to challenge for the lightweight title held by Wolgast. Throughout the fight, Moran complained of Wolgast's butts and low blows. A punch to Moran's midsection doubled him over in the thirteenth, and Wolgast then fired a right behind Moran's ear to knock him out. To his death, Moran claimed the body blow was low.

Moran continued to fight for another five years, winning only three of his last fifteen bouts. A twenty-round draw with Jem Driscoll for the British featherweight title was the final highlight of Moran's distinguished career.

BATTLING NELSON
The Durable Dane

LIGHTWEIGHT

Right-handed; 5'7½"; 120–140 lbs.

131 bouts, 9/3/1896 to 4/17/1917

Managers: John Robinson,
Ted Murphy, Billy Nolan

Lightwt Champ 1905-06, 1908–10

Hall of Fame Induction: 1992

Born: 6/5/1882, Copenhagen,
Denmark

Named: Oscar Matthew Nielson

Died: 2/7/1954

One of the toughest boxers in ring history, Battling Nelson twice held the world lightweight title. Slight of build but relentless in both delivering and enduring beatings, Nelson spooked more than one opponent with his unblinking resistance. His trademark punch was a short left hook aimed at the liver, with thumb and forefinger extended to provide greater penetration. A Dane by birth, Nelson grew up in a suburb of Chicago. He fought professionally for the first time against a fighter in a travelling circus. Challenged to last three rounds, the fourteen-year-old Nelson knocked Wallace's Kid out in one.

Nelson's career blossomed in 1904. He knocked out Martin Canole, Eddie Hanlon, and Young Corbett and won a decision against the hard-hitting Aurelio Herrera, who once flipped Nelson into an involuntary somersault with a powerful punch. In December 1904, Nelson lost to Jimmy Britt in a fight for a lightweight title claim. The next year Britt and Nelson again squared off. In the eighteenth round, Nelson caught Britt with a flurry of punches and knocked him out. In 1906, Nelson met black champion Joe Gans in Nevada, in a Tex Rickard promotion. Gans had won the lightweight title in 1904 but relinquished it to fight for (and win) the welterweight title. Gans knocked Nelson

In Washington, DC, Nelson poses with Captain J.W. Thompson, Company M of the 14th Infantry, and a special patriotic punching bag.

IN THE RING	WON 59	LOST 19	DRAWS 19	TB 131	KO 38	W 20	WF 1	D 19	KO'd 3	L 14	LF 2	ND 33	NC 1

Date	Year	Opponent	Site	Result / Rounds		Title
SELECTED BOUTS						
Sep 3	1896	Wallace's Kid	Hammond, IN	KO	1	—
Apr 6	1899	Eddie Penny	Chicago	KO	1	—
Apr 6	1904	Spider Welsh	Salt Lake City	KO	16	—
Nov 29	1904	Young Corbett	San Francisco	KO	10	—
Dec 20	1904	Jimmy Britt	San Francisco	L	20	For-Vac World-L
Feb 28	1905	Young Corbett	San Francisco	TKO	9	—
May 22	1905	♛ Abe Attell★	Philadelphia	ND-L	6	—
Jun 6	1905	Jack O'Neil	Philadelphia	ND-W	6	—
Sep 9	1905	♛ Jimmy Britt	Colma, CA	KO	18	Won-World-L
Mar 14	1906	Terry McGovern★	Philadelphia	ND-W	6	—
Sep 3	1906	Joe Gans★	Goldfield, NV	LF	42	Lost-World-L
Jul 31	1907	Jimmy Britt	San Francisco	L	20	—
Mar 31	1908	♛ Abe Attell★	San Francisco	D	15	—
Jul 4	1908	♛ Joe Gans★	Colma	KO	17	Won-World-L
Sep 9	1908	Joe Gans★	Colma	KO	21	Ret-World-L
May 29	1909	Dick Hyland	Colma	KO	23	Ret-World-L
Jun 22	1909	Jack Clifford	Oklahoma City	TKO	5	Ret-World-L
Jul 13	1909	Ad Wolgast★	Los Angeles	ND-L	10	—
Jan 21	1910	Eddie Lang	Memphis, TN	KO	8	Ret-World-L
Feb 22	1910	Ad Wolgast★	Richmond, CA	TKO'd	40	Lost-World-L
Nov 26	1910	Owen Moran★	San Francisco	KO	11	—
Nov 28	1912	Leach Cross	New York	ND-L	10	—
Oct 13	1913	Ad Wolgast★	Milwaukee	ND-L	10	—
Apr 17	1917	♛ Freddie Welsh★	St. Louis	ND-L	12	—

down several times but could not knock him out. In the 33rd round, Gans broke his hand but continued to fight. Finally, in the 42nd round, Nelson hit Gans with a low blow and lost on the foul. Two years later, Nelson reclaimed the title with a seventeenth-round knockout of Gans. In their third meeting, Nelson again recorded a knock-out victory.

In 1909, Nelson met his fiercest opponent, Ad Wolgast, in a bloody no-decision fight that newspaper reporters gave to Wolgast. The next year the two fought in a brutally wild brawl for the title. In the 22nd round, Nelson knocked Wolgast down hard, but Wolgast surprised the crowd by getting up before the ten count. Both of Nelson's eyes swelled shut, and by the start of the 40th round, he was so nearly blind that he took his fighting stance opposite one of the ring posts. At that point, the referee stopped the fight, and Wolgast was the champion.

Nelson continued to fight for seven more years but never again contended for the championship. He lost the newspaper decision in a return match with Wolgast in 1913 when both men were past their primes. Nelson lost his career earnings and died in poverty.

PHILADELPHIA JACK O'BRIEN

LIGHT HEAVYWEIGHT

Right-handed; 5'10½"; 155–165 lbs.

179 bouts, 12/12/1896 to 6/17/1912

Light Heavyweight Champ 1905–12

Hall of Fame Induction: 1994

Born: 1/17/1878, Philadelphia, PA

Named: James Francis Hagen

Died: 11/12/1942

Philadelphia Jack O'Brien was one of the most colorful fighters of the early twentieth century. A showman and a shrewd self-publicist, O'Brien was a great boxer as well. His strong left jab and solid right were complemented by his skill at blocking punches and countering attacks. Debuting as a lightweight, O'Brien turned professional at age eighteen in 1896 in his native Philadelphia. As he matured, O'Brien moved into the welterweight and then middleweight classes. Ultimately he fought light heavyweights and heavyweights, even though he never weighed more than 165 pounds.

In 1901 O'Brien sailed for England, where he hoped to build up his record. He won all nineteen of his fights there, fifteen by knockout. Not all of his opponents were of the first rank, but O'Brien nevertheless sent reports of his victories to the Associated Press, which alerted American fans to his success. Returning to the United States in glory (and reportedly with eighteen trunks of new clothes), he was greeted at the dock by the mayor of Philadelphia and a crowd of 10,000 fans. O'Brien hit the lecture circuit with Major Anthony J. Drexel Biddle, a prominent Philadelphian and avid boxing fan who encouraged young men to emulate O'Brien's "muscular Christianity."

O'Brien prepares for a violin performance. After he retired from the ring, O'Brien stayed close to the world of boxing and often attended important bouts.

IN THE RING	WON 100	LOST 6	DRAWS 16	TB 179	KO 51	W 41	WF 8	D 16	KO'd 3	L 3	LF 0	ND 57

Date	Year	Opponent	Site	Result / Rounds		Title
SELECTED BOUTS						
Dec 12	1896	Isadore Strauss	Philadelphia	D	6	—
Feb 14	1900	Young Peter Jackson	San Francisco	TKO'd	13	—
Feb 25	1901	Harry Smith	Newcastle, England	TKO	4	—
Mar 3	1902	Andy Walsh	Philadelphia	TKO	3	—
Apr 11	1902	♛ Joe Walcott (The Barbados Demon) ★	Philadelphia	ND-W	6	—
Sep 29	1902	Joe Choynski ★	Chicago	W	6	—
Nov 19	1902	Marvin Hart	Philadelphia	ND-D	6	—
Mar 30	1903	Joe Choynski ★	Philadelphia	ND-W	6	—
Apr 20	1903	♛ Joe Walcott (The Barbados Demon) ★	Boston	D	10	—
May 5	1903	Marvin Hart	Philadelphia	ND-L	6	—
Jan 27	1904	♛ Tommy Ryan ★	Philadelphia	ND-W	6	—
May 14	1904	Charles ("Kid") McCoy ★	Philadelphia	ND-D	6	—
Jul 23	1904	♛ Bob Fitzsimmons ★	Philadelphia	ND-W	6	—
Nov 12	1904	Dixie Kid ★	Philadelphia	ND-W	6	—
Mar 24	1905	Young Peter Jackson	Baltimore	WF	2	—
Apr 7	1905	Young Peter Jackson	Baltimore	W	10	—
Dec 20	1905	♛ Bob Fitzsimmons ★	San Francisco	TKO	13	Won-World-LH
Nov 28	1906	♛ Tommy Burns ★	Los Angeles	D	20	For-World-H
May 8	1907	♛ Tommy Burns ★	Los Angeles	L	20	For-World-H
Jun 10	1908	Jack Blackburn ★	Philadelphia	ND-W	6	—
Mar 26	1909	♛ Stanley Ketchel ★	New York	ND-L	10	—
May 19	1909	♛ Jack Johnson ★	Philadelphia	ND-D	6	—
Jun 9	1909	♛ Stanley Ketchel ★	Philadelphia	TKO'd	3	—
Aug 15	1911	Sam Langford ★	New York	TKO'd	5	—
Jun 17	1912	Ben Koch	Philadelphia	ND-L	6	—

Over the next few years, O'Brien fought such notables as Joe Choynski, Joe Walcott ("The Barbados Demon"), and Young Peter Jackson. By 1905, his string of successes allowed him to challenge Bob Fitzsimmons, the recognized world light heavyweight titleholder. Fitzsimmons, then 44, also claimed the heavyweight title, vacant since the retirement of James J. Jeffries. Fitzsimmons collapsed after thirteen rounds with O'Brien. Now acknowledged as the light heavyweight champ and, in some quarters, as the heavyweight champ, O'Brien embarked on a vaudeville tour to capitalize on his fame.

In 1906, O'Brien fought to a draw with the more widely recognized heavyweight titleholder, Tommy Burns, in Los Angeles. In a rematch, Burns won the twenty-round decision. In 1909, Stanley Ketchel made his eastern debut against O'Brien at the National Athletic Club in New York. O'Brien dominated the first six rounds, but in the ninth, Ketchel knocked him down. In the tenth, O'Brien was decked twice and only the bell saved him from a knockout. O'Brien retired in 1912, never having defended his light heavyweight title.

After a financial reversal resulting in bankruptcy, O'Brien operated a successful gym in New York.

BILLY PAPKE
The Illinois Thunderbolt

MIDDLEWEIGHT

Right handed; 5'8¾"; 150–162 lbs.
62 bouts, 3/24/1906 to 4/8/1919
Managers: Tom Jones and Al Lippe
Middleweight Champion 1908
Hall of Fame Induction: 2001
Born: 9/17/1886, Spring Valley, IL
Named: William Herman Papke
Died: 11/26/1936

Billy Papke's violent life led to the middleweight championship of the world, but also to a tragic and untimely demise. Papke became known for his fistic prowess at age six. His youth was spent fighting, working, and playing baseball, and he soon followed his father to the local mines, where workers staged impromptu boxing matches.

Papke turned pro on March 24, 1906, outpointing the "Mexican Wonder" over four rounds in LaSalle, Illinois. In the next eighteen months, fighting mostly in Illinois, he accrued a record of seventeen wins and three draws before his first big fight—at age 21—a newspaper decision over former British champion Pat O'Keefe in Philadelphia.

After beating Hugo Kelly on March 6, 1908, Papke earned a title shot against one of the greatest fighters ever, Hall of Famer Stanley Ketchel. Ketchel opened the June 4, 1908, match in Milwaukee with a quick left hook, downing Papke. Though Papke shook it off and fought for another ten rounds, he complained that Ketchel had hit him when he was reaching out to shake hands. Ketchel won the decision and retained his title, but Papke served notice that he would not be duped again.

The rematch was held on Labor Day, September 7, 1908, at the James J. Jeffries Athletic Club in Vernon, California, with Jeffries himself serving as referee. At the start of the fight, Papke stunned Ketchel with a right to the face when Ketchel extended *his* arm to shake hands, and proceeded to knock him down five times in the first round. By the ninth, Papke had closed

Referee Jim Jeffries restarts the action in the brutal September 7, 1908, bout in which Papke (L) took the title from the battered Stanley Ketchel.

IN THE RING	WON 37	LOST 11	DRAWS 6	TB 62	KO 30	W 6	WF 1	D 6	KO'd 1	L 8	LF 2	ND 8

Date	Year	Opponent	Site	Result / Rounds		Title

SELECTED BOUTS

Date	Year	Opponent	Site	Result	Rounds	Title
Mar 24	1906	Mexican Wonder	LaSalle, IL	W	4	—
Mar 6	1908	Hugo Kelly	Milwaukee	W	10	—
Jun 4	1908	♛ Stanley Ketchel ★	Milwaukee	L	10	For-World-M
Aug 13	1908	Frank Mantell	Boston	KO	1	—
Sep 7	1908	♛ Stanley Ketchel ★	Vernon, CA	TKO	12	Won-World-M
Nov 26	1908	Stanley Ketchel ★	Colma, CA	KO'd	11	Lost-World-M
Mar 19	1909	Fireman Jim Flynn	Los Angeles	L	10	—
Jul 5	1909	♛ Stanley Ketchel ★	Colma	L	20	For-World-M
Jun 21	1910	Jack ("Twin") Sullivan	Boston	W	12	—
Feb 11	1911	Cyclone Johnny Thompson	Sydney	L	20	—
Jun 8	1911	Jim Sullivan	London	KO	9	—
Oct 31	1911	Bob Moha	Boston	L	12	—
Jun 29	1912	Marcel Moreau	Paris	KO	16	Won-French-M
Oct 23	1912	Georges Carpentier ★	Paris	WF	17	—
Mar 5	1913	Frank Klaus	Paris	LF	15	For-Vac-World-M
Apr 8	1919	Soldier Jacob Bartfield	San Francisco	L	4	—

both of Ketchel's eyes. In the eleventh round, he knocked Ketchel through the ropes. Finally, in the twelfth, Papke, covered with the other man's gore from wrist to shoulder, knocked Ketchel down twice. Jeffries stopped the fight, one of the bloodiest matches in history. Papke won the middleweight championship, believing that his own sneak attack repaid Ketchel for his previous early blow.

Papke soon faced Ketchel for a third time on Thanksgiving Day, 1908, in Colma, California. Hoping to lull Papke, now called the "Illinois Thunderbolt," into a false sense of security, Ketchel's camp spread rumors that he was drinking heavily, while he actually trained vigorously for the match. He knocked Papke out in the eleventh round. Ketchel won their fourth battle, July 5, 1909, with a twenty-round decision.

Ketchel was murdered in October of 1910, and Papke claimed his title, yet losses hurt his reputation. He travelled to London and knocked out the British champ, Jim Sullivan, for what some considered the middleweight title. After an extremely lackluster fight against Bob Moha in 1911, Papke briefly retired.

Soon he was back, and on June 29, 1912, Papke knocked out Marcel Moreau in Paris to win the French crown. Finally he faced Frank Klaus in Paris on March 5, 1913, in a fight universally recognized as for the middleweight championship. Papke was knocked down twice and then was disqualified for butting in the fifteenth round. He fought twice more before leaving the sport.

In retirement, Papke owned real estate and trained his son, Billy Jr., who tried his hand at boxing. Papke's later life was marred by conflict with his estranged wife, Edna. On Thanksgiving Day, 1936, he left his job as a greeter at ex-boxer Fireman Jim Flynn's tavern in Los Angeles and went to Edna's apartment with his .38 revolver. Papke killed her and then turned the gun on himself.

BILLY PETROLLE
The Fargo Express

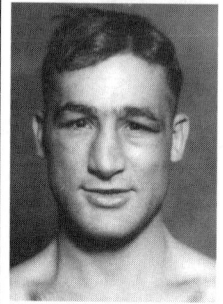

LIGHTWEIGHT

Right-handed; 5'7"; 130–144 lbs.

160 bouts, 10/27/1922 to 1/24/1934

Manager: Jack Hurley

Hall of Fame Induction: 2000

Born: 1/10/1905, Berwick, PA

Named: William Michael Petrolle

Died: 5/14/1983

A tough crowd-pleaser, Billy Petrolle defeated three Hall of Famers, yet was never a champion himself. Petrolle's family moved to Fargo, North Dakota, when he was a small boy. His father was a laborer for the Northern Pacific Railroad, and Petrolle left school in seventh grade to join him in the shops. Lured by the $60 offered for bouts at the Elks Club of Fargo, Petrolle entered a match. He later explained, "I would have fought Jack Dempsey for sixty bucks. It was more than I made for two weeks in the shops. I knocked the kid out in the second round, and when they counted ten over him, I knew I was never going back." After two more bouts at the Elks Club, promoter/manager Jack Hurley began training Petrolle, teaching him to both jab and hook with his left.

Petrolle is credited with 160 fights during his career, though his total may have exceeded 250. Dubbed "The Fargo Express" after a cartoonist pictured him as a runaway locomotive, Petrolle was always ready to fight, entering the ring for at least 76 bouts in his first four years as a boxer. Petrolle went the distance against champion and Hall of Famer Sammy Mandell on January 13, 1928, in a non-title, no-decision bout, but later that year he knocked out Hall of Famer Kid Berg. Then a beating at the hands of King Tut in a no-decision fight in October, 1928, kept him out of the ring for four months. Though 1929 brought a "newspaper" victory over former lightweight champ Jimmy Goodrich, a loss to King Tut in Detroit sent Petrolle into retirement.

Patsy Haley counts out Eddie Ran in Madison Square Garden on January 22, 1932. Petrolle scores a sixth-round knockout.

IN THE RING	WON 83	LOST 21	DRAWS 10	TB 160	KO 62	W 17	WF 4	D 10	KO'd 3	L 17	LF 1	ND 45	NC 1

Date	Year	Opponent	Site	Result / Rounds		Title
SELECTED BOUTS						
Oct 27	1922	Kid Fogarty	Fargo, ND	KO	2	—
Mar 1	1926	⑩ Louis ("Kid") Kaplan ★	Hartford, CT	L	12	—
Jun 15	1927	⑩ Billy Wallace	New York	L	10	—
Jan 13	1928	♛ Sammy Mandell ★	Minneapolis	ND-L	10	—
Jun 21	1928	⑩ Bruce Flowers	Detroit	W	10	—
Jul 26	1928	⑩ Jackie ("Kid") Berg ★	Chicago	D	10	—
Aug 24	1928	⑩ Jackie ("Kid") Berg ★	Chicago	TKO	5	—
Oct 16	1928	⑩ King Tut	Minneapolis	ND-L	10	—
Sep 12	1929	⑩ King Tut	Detroit	L	10	—
Sep 11	1930	⑩ Tony Canzoneri ★	Chicago	W	10	—
Oct 10	1930	♛ Jackie ("Kid") Berg ★	New York	L	10	—
Nov 21	1930	⑩ Jimmy McLarnin ★	New York	W	10	—
Feb 27	1931	⑩ King Tut	New York	KO	4	—
May 27	1931	⑩ Jimmy McLarnin ★	New York	L	10	—
Aug 20	1931	⑩ Jimmy McLarnin ★	New York	L	10	—
Dec 30	1931	⑩ Billy Townsend	New York	KO	7	—
Mar 24	1932	⑩ Battling Battalino ★	New York	TKO	12	—
Nov 4	1932	⑩ Tony Canzoneri ★	New York	L	15	For-World-L
Mar 22	1933	⑩ Barney Ross ★	Chicago	L	10	—
Jul 12	1933	⑩ Bep Van Klaveren	New York	TKO	4	—
Sep 8	1933	⑩ Sammy Fuller	Boston	D	10	—
Oct 21	1933	⑩ Sammy Fuller	Brooklyn	W	10	—
Jan 24	1934	♛ Barney Ross ★	New York	L	10	—

Petrolle launched a comeback four months later, scoring a decision against Hall of Famer Tony Canzoneri on September 11, 1930. On November 21, he faced Hall of Famer Jimmy McLarnin, and though McLarnin was heavily favored, Petrolle emerged victorious.

Petrolle's star dimmed the next year as he faced two defeats at the hands of McLarnin. He rebounded with a knockout victory over former champion Battling Battalino in a ferocious twelve-round battle on March 24, 1932, winning with a left jab followed by a right under the heart. Unfortunately, Petrolle injured his left arm, which had become his biggest weapon in the ring. Nevertheless, he won the rematch and earned a title shot against Canzoneri. Petrolle had trouble making weight for the fight, and though only 27, he was past his prime. He lost a fifteen-round decision to Canzoneri, and after two losses to Hall of Famer Barney Ross in 1933 and '34, Petrolle again retired.

Petrolle was an aggressive fighter who favored a crouched stance, his head bobbing from side to side. He attacked the body more than most boxers, and his left hook was a devastating weapon. As a good-luck charm, Petrolle always entered the ring wrapped in a red and green Navajo blanket. He fought ten current or former champions and defeated five of them, yet he lost his one title shot. In retirement, Petrolle operated a foundry, then a religious goods shop.

WILLIE RITCHIE

LIGHTWEIGHT

Right-handed; 5'7½"; 133–147 lbs.

76 bouts, 1/13/1907 to 8/29/1927

Manager: Emil Thiery 1911–12, 1913; Billy Nolan 1912–13; Harry Foley 1913–14; Tom Jones 1914

Lightweight Champion 1912–14

Hall of Fame Induction: 2004

Born: 2/13/1891, San Francisco, CA

Named: Gerhardt Anthony Steffen

Died: 3/24/1975

Ritchie was born Gerhardt Anthony Steffen on February 13, 1891, in San Francisco. Ritchie idolized a fighter prominent in the Bay Area, Oakland Frankie Edwards. On January 13, 1907, Ritchie had the opportunity to carry the water bucket for Edwards in his fight that night. When one of the preliminary fighters didn't show up, the promoter sought someone to take his place at the last minute. Edwards volunteered Ritchie—though Ritchie was initially reluctant, fearing his mother's reaction. When Edwards told him he couldn't carry the water bucket for him unless he fought, Ritchie relented. The fighter who had backed out was named Willie Richards or Willie Richardson. The ring announcer introduced Ritchie with that name. In the newspaper the next day, the name read "Willie Ritchie"—a monicker that stuck with the fifteen-year-old for the rest of his life. Ritchie was knocked out in the second round.

After his initial knock-out defeat, Ritchie won eighteen of his next 28 fights with three losses and seven draws over the next four and one-half years. On October 6, 1911, he scored a four-round decision over Hall of Famer Jack Britton.

Once he became established, Ritchie hounded lightweight champ and Hall of Famer Ad Wolgast for a fight. He called the champion names, mocked his fighting ability, and challenged him to a fight for the title anywhere, anytime.

On Thanksgiving Day 1912, Ritchie got the chance to fight for the title in Colma, California. By the fourteenth round, the effect of Wolgast's punches around the eyes began to show as Ritchie's eyes swelled almost closed. By the fifteenth, Ritchie could only see out of one eye but still managed to win the round. In the sixteenth, he knocked Wolgast down with a right. Then he knocked

Ritchie knocks out Mexican Joe Rivers in the eleventh round of a scheduled twenty-round lightweight title bout on Independence Day 1913. Ritchie threw a right and left to the body followed by a right to the jaw.

IN THE RING	WON 37	LOST 8	DRAWS 12	TB 76	KO 9	W 27	WF 1	D 12	KO'd 2	L 6	LF 0	ND 19

Date	Year	Opponent	Site	Result / Rounds		Title
SELECTED BOUTS						
Jan 13	1907	Eddie Steele	Oakland	KO'd	2	—
Oct 6	1911	Jack Britton ★	San Francisco	W	4	—
Nov 30	1911	Freddie Welsh ★	Los Angeles	L	20	—
May 11	1912	Ad Wolgast ★	San Francisco	ND-D	4	—
Nov 28	1912	Ad Wolgast ★	Colma, CA	WF	16	Won-World-L
Jul 4	1913	Mexican Joe Rivers	San Francisco	KO	11	Ret-World-L
Mar 12	1914	Ad Wolgast ★	Milwaukee	ND-W	10	—
Apr 17	1914	Tommy Murphy	San Francisco	W	20	Ret-World-L
Jul 7	1914	Freddie Welsh ★	London	L	20	Lost-World-L
Oct 23	1914	Johnny Dundee ★	San Francisco	D	4	—
Mar 11	1915	♛ Freddie Welsh ★	New York	ND-W	10	For-World-L
Oct 26	1915	Johnny Dundee ★	New York	ND-W	10	—
Dec 28	1915	♛ Ted ("Kid") Lewis ★	New York	ND-L	10	For-World-W
Feb 21	1919	Benny Leonard ★	San Francisco	ND-W	4	—
Apr 28	1919	Benny Leonard ★	Newark, NJ	TKO'd	8	—
Aug 29	1927	Dick Hoppe	Los Angeles	W	6	—

Wolgast against the ropes. Wolgast hit Ritchie with a left to the groin. Referee Jim Griffin warned Wolgast, but when he punched Ritchie below the belt again Griffin disqualified him, and Ritchie became the champion.

Once Ritchie was champion, he refused to make weight at the then lightweight limit of 133 pounds and came in at 135, which became the weight limit in that class to this day. He eventually accepted an offer of $25,000 and traveling expenses to go to England to face Freddie Welsh for the world lightweight title. Welsh fought in a very defensive posture while at times scoring inside. Ritchie fought in more of an erect style. Ritchie achieved the fight's only knockdown in the twelfth. Referee Eugene Corri scored the first nineteen rounds even but gave Welsh the twentieth round and the championship. Ritchie believed that he deserved the decision.

Ritchie fought Welsh again and won a no-decision bout. He fought a couple of draws with Johnny Dundee and suffered a newspaper loss to Ted ("Kid") Lewis. In 1917–1918, Ritchie served as a physical instructor for the U.S. Army. He returned to the ring and won a newspaper decision over the great Hall of Famer Benny Leonard. In the rematch, Leonard avenged the defeat with a TKO. After that, Ritchie fought sporadically. Though he only recorded nine knockouts in his 75 fights, he was a skillful, fearless boxer.

Later Ritchie owned a Chevrolet dealership, a tire franchise, and an apartment building. He also refereed and promoted. In 1934, he became assistant chief inspector of the California Athletic Commission. In 1937, he was appointed chief inspector, a position he held until his retirement in 1962. He was credited with limiting corruption in California boxing. Ritchie died on March 24, 1975, in Millbrae, California.

MAXIE ROSENBLOOM
Slapsie Maxie

LIGHT HEAVYWEIGHT

Right-handed; 5'11"; 160–188 lbs.
299 bouts, 9/24/1923 to 6/26/1939
Manager: Frank Bachman
Light Heavyweight Champ 1930–34
Hall of Fame Induction: 1993
Born: 9/6/1904, Leonard's Bridge, CT
Died: 3/6/1976

Few fighters stepped into the ring more often than Maxie Rosenbloom, who fought 299 times in sixteen years. Raised on the Lower East Side of New York, Rosenbloom left school after third grade and later served time in reform school. Reportedly, actor George Raft spotted the young Rosenbloom in a street brawl and advised him to become a boxer. Rosenbloom had an unusual style. He was a weak puncher and often slapped at his opponents with an open hand—earning him the nickname "Slapsie"—but he was a consummate defensive fighter and did whatever was necessary to avoid getting hit. He won the vast majority of his fights, although he only recorded nineteen knockouts in his entire professional career.

Rosenbloom turned pro at the age of nineteen and quickly became ranked as a contender, placing tenth in the 1925 annual rankings by *The Ring*. In 1927, Rosenbloom faced Jimmy Slattery—who had already beaten him twice—for the vacant NBA light heavyweight title. Slattery again won the decision. Over the next couple of years, Rosenbloom kept up a rigorous schedule, battling 46 times in 1928 and 1929.

In 1930, Rosenbloom again faced Slattery in a title fight. Rosenbloom took the decision in fifteen rounds and won the world light heavyweight championship, as recognized by the New York State Athletic Commission. Most ring experts considered Rosenbloom the best light heavyweight in the game, and he was acclaimed as the undisputed champion when he defeated Lou Scozza in July of 1932.

Rosenbloom held the title until

Toward the end of his career, Rosenbloom fought mostly on the West Coast, where the popular fighter operated two restaurants.

IN THE RING	WON 210	LOST 38	DRAWS 26	TB 299	KO 19	W 186	WF 5	D 26	KO'd 2	L 36	LF 0	ND 23	NC 2

Date	Year	Opponent	Site	Result / Rounds		Title
SELECTED BOUTS						
Sep 24	1923	Nick Scanlon	New York	W	6	—
Mar 3	1925	Hambone Kelly	New York	W	6	—
Jul 16	1925	♛ Harry Greb ★	Cleveland	ND-L	10	—
Aug 22	1925	⑩ Jimmy Slattery ★	Brooklyn	L	6	—
Jan 1	1926	⑩ Jimmy Slattery ★	Buffalo, NY	L	10	—
Jan 11	1926	⑩ Art Wiegand	Buffalo	L	6	—
Oct 15	1926	♛ Tiger Flowers ★	Boston	WF	9	—
Mar 17	1927	⑩ Young Stribling ★	Boston	L	10	—
Jun 21	1927	⑩ Leo Lomski	New York	L	12	—
Jul 4	1927	⑩ Tiger Flowers ★	Chicago	D	10	—
Aug 30	1927	⑩ Jimmy Slattery ★	Hartford, CT	L	10	For-Vac NBA-LH
Nov 9	1927	⑩ Tiger Flowers ★	Detroit	D	10	—
Mar 5	1928	⑩ Cuban Bobby Brown	Pittsburgh	W	10	—
Jul 31	1928	Ted ("Kid") Lewis ★	New York	WF	6	—
Aug 24	1928	⑩ Leo Lomski	Long Branch, NJ	D	10	—
Nov 22	1928	⑩ Cuban Bobby Brown	Jersey City, NJ	W	10	—
Nov 15	1929	⑩ Jim Braddock ★	New York	W	10	—
Jun 25	1930	♛ Jimmy Slattery ★	Buffalo	W	15	Won-World-LH
Oct 22	1930	Abie Bain	New York	TKO	11	Ret-World-LH
Aug 5	1931	⑩ Jimmy Slattery ★	Brooklyn	W	15	Ret-World-LH
Nov 10	1931	Jim Braddock ★	Minneapolis	NC	2	—
Jul 14	1932	⑩ Lou Scozza	Buffalo	W	15	Ret-World-LH
Nov 16	1932	⑩ John Henry Lewis ★	San Francisco	W	10	—
Mar 10	1933	⑩ Adolf Heuser	New York	W	15	Ret-World-LH
Mar 24	1933	⑩ Bob Godwin	New York	TKO	4	Ret-World-LH
Jul 10	1933	⑩ John Henry Lewis ★	San Francisco	L	10	—
Jul 31	1933	⑩ John Henry Lewis ★	San Francisco	L	10	—
Nov 3	1933	⑩ Mickey Walker ★	New York	W	15	Ret-World-LH
Feb 5	1934	⑩ Joe Knight	Miami	D	15	Ret-World-LH
May 8	1934	⑩ Mickey Walker ★	Los Angeles	L	10	—
Nov 16	1934	⑩ Bob Olin	New York	L	15	Lost-World-LH
Jul 17	1935	⑩ John Henry Lewis ★	Oakland	W	10	—
Nov 29	1935	♛ John Henry Lewis ★	Chicago	W	10	—
Jun 26	1939	Al Ettore	Hollywood	KO	3	—

1934, when he lost a decision to Bob Olin, although many sports writers at ringside believed Rosenbloom had won. Along the way, Rosenbloom fought John Henry Lewis, winning three of their five matches. Rosenbloom had a reputation of fighting just about anyone who would get in the ring with him. He once asked for a match with Joe Louis. As the story goes, Louis was confident of winning but declined because he feared Rosenbloom would make him look bad.

A lively character, Rosenbloom didn't devote much time to training. Although he stayed away from alcohol, he enjoyed gambling, the company of women, and late night celebrations. Rosenbloom parlayed his colorful reputation into a successful acting and night club career, often portraying a punch-drunk fighter.

BARNEY ROSS
The Pride of the Ghetto

WELTERWEIGHT

Right-handed; 5'7"; 130–145 lbs.

81 bouts, 8/31/1929 to 5/31/1938

Managers: Willis ("Gig") Rooney 1929–30, Sam Pian and Art Winch 1930–38

Lightweight Champ 1933–35
Jr. Welterweight Champ 1933–35
Welterwt. Champ 1934, 1935–38

Hall of Fame Induction: 1990

Born: 12/23/1909, New York, NY

Named: Beryl David Rosofsky

Died: 1/17/1967

Barney Ross was a tough fighter whose excellent physical fitness and stamina made him a champion three times over. He held world titles in the lightweight, junior welterweight, and welterweight classes. Ross grew up in Chicago, where he was raised by Orthodox Jewish parents who wanted him to become a Hebrew teacher. His family was opposed to fighting of any kind, but after his father was killed in a hold-up and Ross became the breadwinner, he convinced his mother he could make money in the ring. A fast, clever, and hard-hitting boxer, Ross won the 1929 Inter-City Golden Gloves Championship and turned pro later that year.

Fighting mostly in the Chicago area as a lightweight, Ross compiled a record of 40-2-2 and in 1932 was ranked as the third-best lightweight contender by *The Ring*. In 1933, Ross won a ten-round decision over Tony Canzoneri at Chicago Stadium for both the lightweight and the junior welterweight championships. Canzoneri and his manager, Sammy Goldman, disputed the decision. To silence

Ross (L) is about to connect with a left cross in one of his series of bouts with welterweight contender Filipino Ceferino Garcia, who, in 1939, took the world middleweight title from Fred Apostoli.

IN THE RING	WON 72	LOST 4	DRAWS 3	TB 81	KO 22	W 50	WF 0	D 3	KO'd 0	L 4	LF 0	ND 2

Date	Year	Opponent	Site	Result / Rounds		Title

SELECTED BOUTS

Date	Year		Opponent	Site	Result / Rounds		Title
Aug 31	1929		Ramon Lugo	Los Angeles	W	6	—
Oct 21	1929		Virgil Tobin	San Francisco	KO	2	—
Nov 19	1929		Joey Barth	Chicago	W	5	—
Oct 21	1932	⑩	Battling Battalino ★	Chicago	W	10	—
Mar 22	1933	⑩	Billy Petrolle ★	Chicago	W	10	—
May 4	1933	⑩	Joe Ghnouly	St. Louis	W	10	—
Jun 23	1933	♛	Tony Canzoneri ★	Chicago	W	10	Won-World-L & JW
Jul 26	1933		Johnny Farr	Kansas City, MO	KO	6	Ret-World-JW
Sep 12	1933	⑩	Tony Canzoneri ★	New York	W	15	Ret-World-L & JW
Nov 17	1933	♛	Sammy Fuller	Chicago	W	10	Ret-World-JW
Jan 24	1934	⑩	Billy Petrolle ★	New York	W	10	—
Feb 7	1934		Pete Nebo	Kansas City, MO	W	12	Ret-World-JW
Mar 5	1934	⑩	Frankie Klick	San Francisco	D	10	Ret-World-JW
Mar 27	1934	⑩	Bobby Pacho	Los Angeles	W	10	Ret-World-JW
May 28	1934	♛	Jimmy McLarnin ★	Long Island City, NY	W	15	Won-World-W
Sep 17	1934	⑩	Jimmy McLarnin ★	Long Island City	L	15	Lost-World-W
Dec 10	1934	⑩	Bobby Pacho	Cleveland	W	12	Ret-World-JW
Jan 28	1935	⑩	Frankie Klick	Miami	W	10	Ret-World-JW
Apr 9	1935		Henry Woods	Seattle	W	12	Ret-World-JW
May 28	1935	♛	Jimmy McLarnin ★	New York	W	15	Reg-World-W
Sep 13	1935	⑩	Ceferino Garcia	San Francisco	W	10	—
Nov 29	1935	⑩	Ceferino Garcia	Chicago	W	10	—
Nov 27	1936	⑩	Izzy Jannazzo	New York	W	15	Ret-World-W
Sep 23	1937	⑩	Ceferino Garcia	New York	W	15	Ret-World-W
May 31	1938		Henry Armstrong ★	Long Island City	L	15	Lost-World-W

any thought that he had been the beneficiary of a hometown bias, Ross made sure a rematch was promptly scheduled on Canzoneri's home turf at the Polo Grounds in New York. In the bloody fifteen-rounder, Ross was again the victor by decision.

In 1934 and '35 Ross engaged in three title fights with welterweight champion Jimmy McLarnin. Ross and McLarnin traded knockdowns in the first fight, which Ross won by decision, becoming the new champion. In a rematch held at the Madison Square Garden Bowl, McLarnin decisioned Ross to reclaim the title. In the third fight, however, Ross outlasted McLarnin to win by a unanimous decision. Again welterweight champ, Ross had by this time relinquished his lightweight and junior welterweight titles. Ross lost the welterweight title in 1938. He was so thoroughly battered by Henry Armstrong that fans shouted for the referee to stop the action, but Ross refused to go down in what was to be his last fight.

Ross enlisted in the Marines in World War II and was decorated for his bravery at Guadalcanal, but he became addicted to the morphine used to ease the pain from his war injuries. Eventually he overcame his addiction and wrote an autobiography, *Monkey on My Back*, later made into a motion picture starring Cameron Mitchell.

TOMMY RYAN

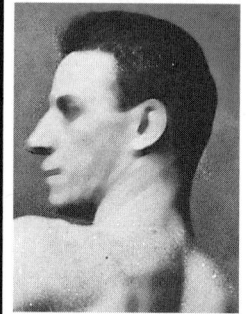

MIDDLEWEIGHT

Right-handed; 5'7¾"; 142–158 lbs.

105 bouts, 1887 to 3/4/1907

Welterweight Champ 1894–98
Middleweight Champ 1898–1907

Hall of Fame Induction: 1991

Born: 3/31/1870, Redwood, NY

Named: Joseph Youngs

Died: 8/3/1948

An intelligent, adaptable fighter, Tommy Ryan held world titles in both the welterweight and middleweight divisions. He also schooled several of his contemporaries, including champions James J. Jeffries and Gentleman Jim Corbett, in some of the finer points of boxing. Ryan helped Jeffries develop the crouch he used when he wrested the heavyweight title from Bob Fitzsimmons, and later he showed Corbett how to counteract the same maneuver.

Born Joseph Youngs, Ryan changed his name after he ran away from home. He honed his boxing skills in lumber camps then turned professional in 1887 as a lightweight. He scored knockouts in seventeen of his first eighteen bouts, the exception being a 57-rounder with Jimmy Murphy that ended without a decision.

In 1893, Ryan began a five-battle series (not counting an exhibition) with the brawling Mysterious Billy Smith. The first two contests were draws. The third, held

1) Ryan floors Jack Dempsey ("The Nonpareil") in the third at Coney Island on January 18, 1895.
2) Referee Hurst calls the fight a TKO. 3) Dempsey pleads in vain for Police Captain Clayton to intercede.

IN THE RING	WON 86	LOST 3	DRAWS 6	TB 105	KO 68	W 17	WF 1	D 6	KO'd 1	L 1	LF 1	ND 4	NC 6

Date	Year	Opponent	Site	Result / Rounds		Title

SELECTED BOUTS

Date	Year	Opponent	Site	Result / Rounds		Title
—	1887	John Case	—	KO	5	—
Apr 30	1889	M. Shaughnessy	Detroit	KO	23	—
Jun 18	1889	M. Shaughnessy	Detroit	KO	46	—
Aug 10	1889	Jimmy Murphy	Grand Rapids, MI	NC	57	—
Aug 29	1893	Mysterious Billy Smith	Coney Island, NY	D	6	—
Jan 9	1894	Mysterious Billy Smith	Boston	D	6	—
Jun 1	1894	Jack Pitts	Minneapolis	KO	3	—
Jul 26	1894 ♛	Mysterious Billy Smith	Minneapolis	W	20	Won-World-W
Jan 18	1895	Jack Dempsey ★	Coney Island	TKO	3	Ret-World-W
May 27	1895	Mysterious Billy Smith	Coney Island	NC	18	Ret-World-W
Mar 2	1896	Charles ("Kid") McCoy ★	Maspeth, NY	KO'd	15	—
Nov 25	1896	Mysterious Billy Smith	Maspeth	WF	9	Ret-World-W
Dec 23	1896	Bill Payne	Syracuse, NY	KO	4	Ret-World-W
Feb 24	1897	Tom Tracy	Syracuse	TKO	9	Ret-World-W
Sep 8	1897	Charles ("Kid") McCoy ★	Syracuse	NC	5	—
Jun 13	1898	Tommy West	New York	TKO	14	Ret-World-W
Oct 24	1898	Jack Bonner	Coney Island	W	20	Won-Vac World-M
Sep 18	1899	Frank Craig	Coney Island	TKO	10	Ret-World-M
May 29	1900	Charles ("Kid") McCoy ★	Chicago	L	6	—
Mar 4	1901	Tommy West	Louisville, KY	TKO	17	Ret-World-M
Mar 14	1902	Mysterious Billy Smith	Kansas City, MO	KO	4	—
Jun 24	1902	Johnny Gorman	London	KO	3	Ret-World-M
Sep 15	1902	Kid Carter	Fort Erie, Ont.	KO	6	Ret-World-M
Jan 27	1904	Phila. Jack O'Brien ★	Philadelphia	ND-L	6	—
Mar 4	1907	Hugo Kelly	Rochester, NY	D	6	—

in Minneapolis, was a challenge for Smith's welterweight title. After twenty rounds, the Minneapolis police interrupted the fight. Ryan, judged to be in the lead at that point, was awarded the championship.

Ryan easily resisted an attempt by Jack Dempsey ("The Nonpareil") to take the title in 1895, stopping the older boxer in the third round. The next year, Ryan faced his former sparring partner Kid McCoy in a non-title match. Ryan trained lightly for this bout and lost by knockout in the fifteenth round. Supposedly, McCoy tricked Ryan by telling him that he was not in shape.

In 1898, after triumphing in a brutal brawl with Tommy West, Ryan turned his attention to the middleweight ranks. He captured the championship with a twenty-round decision over Jack Bonner. Ryan never relinquished this title, holding it until his retirement in 1907. This ten-year hold on the middleweight crown is unrivaled.

Following his retirement, Ryan travelled the vaudeville circuit and performed in boxing exhibitions with Fitzsimmons. He also managed boxers, ran a gym in Syracuse, New York, and invested in several businesses in California, where he eventually settled.

JACK SHARKEY
The Boston Gob

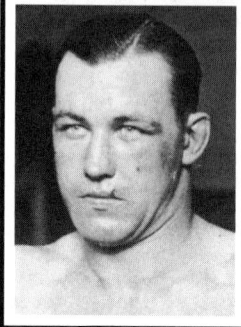

HEAVYWEIGHT

Right-handed; 6'; 188–205 lbs.

55 bouts, 1/29/1924 to 8/18/1936

Manager: Johnny Buckley

Heavyweight Champion 1932–33

Hall of Fame Induction: 1994

Born: 10/26/1902, Binghamton, NY

Named: Joseph Paul Cukoschay

Died: 8/17/1994

Although he held the heavyweight championship for barely a year, Jack Sharkey was a well-respected boxer with great ring skills and an arsenal of punches. Over the years, he faced eleven opponents who either were or had been world champions, and he was the only man to fight both Joe Louis and Jack Dempsey. Sharkey learned to box in the navy, where he became champion of the Atlantic Fleet. He turned pro in 1924, adopting his ring name in imitation of Jack Dempsey and Sailor Tom Sharkey. At the beginning of his career, Sharkey was a hard hitter, knocking out four of his first five opponents. Later, several hand injuries required him to evolve into more of a boxer, although he could still command a variety of punches, including a devastating left hook.

By 1925, *The Ring* ranked Sharkey as the seventh top contender for Jack Dempsey's heavyweight title. By the next year, he had risen to the number two spot in the same listing. Sharkey helped pave the way to a title challenge by defeating the formidable Harry Wills in 1926 at Brooklyn's Ebbets Field with 42,000 fans looking on. Wills gave away the win with a foul in the thirteenth, but the fight had been Sharkey's all the way.

In 1927, Sharkey faced Dempsey, who had lost the championship to Gene

Sharkey (L) takes a ten-round decision from the tough Young Stribling on February 27, 1929, at Flamingo Park in Miami. Official attendance was 30,102 and Sharkey's share of the receipts was $100,000.

IN THE RING	WON 38	LOST 13	DRAWS 3	TB 55	KO 14	W 21	WF 3	D 3	KO'd 4	L 8	LF 1	ND 1

Date	Year	Opponent	Site	Result / Rounds		Title
SELECTED BOUTS						
Jan 29	1924	Billy Muldoon	Boston	KO	1	—
Mar 18	1924	Eddie Record	Boston	L	10	—
Apr 25	1924	Eddie Record	Boston	KO	7	—
Sep 17	1925	⑩ Johnny Risko	Boston	W	10	—
Oct 12	1926	⑩ Harry Wills ★	Brooklyn	WF	13	—
Mar 3	1927	⑩ Mike McTigue	New York	TKO	12	—
Jul 21	1927	⑩ Jack Dempsey ★	New York	KO'd	7	—
Jan 13	1928	⑩ Tom Heeney	New York	D	12	—
Mar 12	1928	⑩ Johnny Risko	New York	L	15	—
Apr 30	1928	⑩ Jack Delaney ★	New York	KO	1	—
Jun 21	1928	Leo Gates	St. Louis	KO	3	—
Dec 10	1928	⑩ Arthur DeKuh	Boston	W	10	—
Jan 25	1929	K.O. Christner	New York	W	10	—
Feb 27	1929	Young Stribling ★	Miami	W	10	—
Sep 26	1929	⑩ Tommy Loughran ★	New York	KO	3	—
Feb 27	1930	⑩ Phil Scott	Miami	KO	3	—
Jun 12	1930	⑩ Max Schmeling ★	New York	LF	4	For-Vac World-H
Jul 22	1931	⑩ Mickey Walker ★	Brooklyn	D	15	—
Oct 12	1931	⑩ Primo Carnera	Brooklyn	W	15	—
Jun 21	1932	♛ Max Schmeling ★	Long Island City, NY	W	15	Won-World-H
Jun 29	1933	⑩ Primo Carnera	Long Island City	KO'd	6	Lost-World-H
Sep 18	1933	King Levinsky	Chicago	L	10	—
Sep 27	1933	⑩ Tommy Loughran ★	Philadelphia	L	15	—
Aug 18	1936	⑩ Joe Louis ★	New York	KO'd	3	—

Tunney just the year before, in Yankee Stadium. More than 72,000 fans paid $1.8 million to be there, a record gate for a non-title fight. Sharkey dominated the early going and came close to knocking Dempsey out. In the seventh, Dempsey peppered Sharkey with low blows. When Sharkey, grimacing in pain, turned to the referee to protest, Dempsey caught him with a left hook and knocked him out.

In 1930, Sharkey fought Max Schmeling for the vacant heavyweight title in Yankee Stadium before another huge crowd. Sharkey won the first three rounds but was disqualified in the fourth when Schmeling fell to the canvas, claiming a foul. In the rematch two years later, Sharkey won the decision and the world championship. He lost the title in his first defense to the ungainly giant, Primo Carnera. Sharkey dominated for the first five rounds. In the sixth, Carnera caught Sharkey with a wild right uppercut which knocked him out. Carnera was rumored to be under the control of mobsters, and noted writers such as Dan Parker and Paul Gallico believed underworld money had convinced Sharkey to take a fall. Sharkey vehemently denied the charge.

Sharkey lost his final fight on a third-round knockout to Joe Louis. In retirement, he operated a bar, refereed, made personal appearances at sportsmen's shows, and fished.

Sailor Tom Sharkey

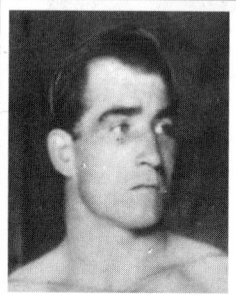

HEAVYWEIGHT

Right-handed; 5'8½"; 172–186 lbs.

54 bouts, 3/17/1893 to 2/27/1904

Managers: Dan Lynch, Tom O'Rourke

Hall of Fame Induction: 2003

Born: 11/26/1873, Dundalk, Ireland

Named: Thomas J. Sharkey

Died: 4/17/1953

Sharkey was born in Dundalk, an Irish seaport, on November 26, 1873. When he was fourteen, he ran away to sea as a cabin boy. Life at sea was not easy, since cabin boys were often subjected to beatings by the other crewmembers. Sharkey usually stood his ground against his tormentors. After he defeated a big Swedish sailor, the captain promoted him from cabin boy to seaman.

In 1892, he decided to join the United States Navy. In the Navy, Sharkey fought with gloves for the first time and picked up the basics of boxing. He was not known as a stylist, but his training in the Navy helped initiate him into prizefighting rather than the simple brawling to which he was accustomed.

Sharkey served on the USS *Philadelphia* and sailed to Hawaii to protect American interests there. In Hawaii, Sharkey first boxed in a ring. He faced fellow sailors as well as some British who served on ships stationed in the islands. The British fleet sent their champion, Jim Gardner, to Hawaii just to take on Sharkey. Gardner was bigger than the 5'8½" Sharkey and more experienced. Nevertheless, Sharkey knocked Gardner out in four rounds.

Sharkey eventually left the Navy and devoted himself to boxing fulltime. California promoters brought him to their state for a series of fights. On July 25, 1895, he knocked out the veteran Australian Billy Smith in seven rounds.

Hall of Famer Joe Choynski challenged Sharkey to a match in which Choynski had to knock out Sharkey within eight rounds or Sharkey would be the victor. Immediately, Sharkey rushed at Choynski, and hit him in the jaw with a left that sent Choynski through the ropes headfirst. Chastened by Sharkey's punch, Choynski kept him at bay but did not come close to a KO.

The Operation.

SHARKEY'S EAR

Sharkey suffered from the same unsightly malady as many early fighters: cauliflower ears. A cauliflower ear can be caused by blood clots or by damaged cartilage that is separated from the skin covering the ear. Sharkey's condition was surgically corrected.

IN THE RING	WON 40	LOST 6	DRAWS 5	TB 54	KO 37	W 1	WF 2	D 5	KO'd 2	L 3	LF 1	ND 1	NC 2

Date	Year	Opponent	Site	Result / Rounds		Title
SELECTED BOUTS						
Mar 17	1893	J Gardner	Honolulu	KO	4	—
Jul 25	1895	Australian Billy Smith	Colma, CA	KO	7	—
Mar 12	1896	Alec Greggains	San Francisco	D	8	—
Apr 16	1896	Joe Choynski★	San Francisco	W	8	—
Jun 24	1896	James J. Corbett★	San Francisco	D	4	—
Dec 2	1896	Bob Fitzsimmons★	San Francisco	WF	8	—
Aug 7	1897	Pat McCourt	Dundalk, Ireland	KO	2	—
Mar 11	1898	Joe Choynski★	San Francisco	D	8	—
May 6	1898	James J. Jeffries★	San Francisco	L	20	—
Nov 22	1898	Jim Corbett★	San Francisco	WF	9	—
Jan 10	1899	Charles ("Kid") McCoy★	New York	KO	10	—
Nov 3	1899	♛ James J. Jeffries★	Coney Island, NY	L	25	For-World-H
May 8	1900	Joe Choynski★	Chicago	TKO	3	—
Jun 26	1900	Gus Ruhlin	Coney Island	KO'd	15	—
Aug 24	1900	Bob Fitzsimmons★	Coney Island	KO'd	2	—
Feb 27	1904	Jack Munroe	Philadelphia	ND-L	6	—

Later that year, Sharkey met Heavyweight Champion James Corbett in a non-title fight. Corbett was not in top physical condition. Their bout was officially called a draw, but most onlookers believed that Sharkey had won.

Sharkey's next match came against another Hall of Famer, Bob Fitzsimmons. In the eighth round, Fitzsimmons landed a hard right to the chin and followed with a "solar plexus punch" which sent Sharkey to the canvas. Referee Wyatt Earp, the Western sheriff and gunfighter, counted Sharkey out but raised his hand at the conclusion of the count and announced that Fitzsimmons had fouled Sharkey with a low blow. He declared Sharkey the winner.

On November 3, 1899, Sharkey finally received a chance to fight for the world heavyweight title now held by Jeffries. As usual Sharkey attacked his opponent aggressively. In the sixth round, a Sharkey left hook shook Jeffries, who finished that round with cuts around the mouth and ear. Also, at some point in the fight, a Jeffries punch broke two of Sharkey's ribs. Through twenty rounds Sharkey appeared to be in control. From the 21st through the 25th rounds, though, Sharkey tired badly. At the end of the bout, referee George Siler awarded the decision to Jeffries, angering Sharkey partisans.

Sharkey won his next six bouts by KO but was then, in turn, knocked out by underdog Gus Ruhlin—whom he had beaten in one round during their previous meeting. Next, Bob Fitzsimmons knocked Sharkey out in two rounds. After fighting a no-decision bout with Jack Munroe on February 27, 1904, Sharkey retired.

Sharkey operated a tavern in New York for a time. He also dabbled in harness racing. He toured in vaudeville and made personal appearances with Jeffries, appeared in a motion picture comedy with Jack Johnson, and worked as a guard at California racetracks before his death on April 17, 1953, in San Francisco.

JIMMY SLATTERY

LIGHT HEAVYWEIGHT

Right-handed; 5'11", 144–176 lbs.

129 bouts, 11/28/1921 to 6/19/1934

Manager: Paul ("Red") Carr

NBA World Light Hvywt. Champ. 1927

NY World Light Hvywt. Champ. 1930

Hall of Fame Induction: 2006

Born: 8/24/1904, Buffalo, NY

Named: James Patrick Slattery

Died 8/30/1960

Slattery was born in Buffalo, New York, on August 25, 1904. His father was a fireman who taught Slattery to box. When Slattery was eleven, he attended a smoker where one of his friends was scheduled to fight. When his friend didn't appear, Slattery got in the ring with a boxer named Art Colpoys who battered the inexperienced youngster. Slattery begged for a rematch and scored a knockout. Fueled by this experience, he and his father took to holding spirited battles in their backyard that attracted many onlookers. Slattery received formal instruction in fisticuffs from Red Carr who later became his manager. Eventually Slattery quit school when he was fourteen and ended up selling newspapers and working on the docks on Buffalo's busy waterfront.

Slattery turned pro in 1921 at the age of seventeen. After that, he quickly became a fan favorite in Buffalo. He was a graceful, crowd-pleasing fighter who was handsome and affable. He won his first 36 bouts, including a victory over Soldier Bartfield, a veteran campaigner. Bartfield told the Buffalo press, "If that kid is only nineteen and still growing, he'll be heavyweight champion someday."

Slattery did not suffer his first defeat until veteran Joe Eagan scored a six-round victory on January 14, 1924. Slattery did not properly prepare for the wily Eagan and was beaten soundly by decision. Five weeks later, he faced Hall of Famer Young Stribling at the Broadway Auditorium in Buffalo. This fight was another six-round affair. (Since Slattery was under twenty years old he was restricted to a maximum of six rounds pursuant to a NYSAC rule.) In the sixth, two hard hooks by Slattery to Stribling's jaw weakened Stribling. He then pounded Stribling's body, forcing him to clinch before the bell sounded. Slattery won the decision in impressive fashion.

After a knock-out loss to Hall of Famer Paul Berlenbach, Slattery's drinking increased while his training decreased. He

Slattery (R) gained the vacant NBA light heavyweight title in the Velodrome of Hartford, CT, on August 30, 1927, over Maxie Rosenbloom.

IN THE RING	WON **113**	LOST **12**	DRAWS **0**	TB 129	KO 50	W 61	WF 2	D 0	KO'd 3	L 9	LF 0	ND 4

Date	Year	Opponent	Site	Result / Rounds		Title
SELECTED BOUTS						
Nov 28	1921	Jack Casey	Buffalo, NY	W	4	—
Apr 23	1923	Soldier Bartfield	Buffalo	W	6	—
Feb 25	1924	⑩ Young Stribling ★	Buffalo	W	6	—
Sep 3	1924	♛ Harry Greb ★	Buffalo	L	6	—
Oct 3	1924	⑩ Jack Delaney ★	New York	W	6	—
Feb 13	1925	⑩ Jack Delaney ★	New York	W	6	—
Jul 2	1925	⑩ Dave Shade	New York	KO'd	3	—
Aug 22	1925	⑩ Maxie Rosenbloom ★	Brooklyn	W	6	—
Sep 11	1925	♛ Paul Berlenbach ★	New York	KO'd	11	For-World-LH
Jan 1	1926	⑩ Maxie Rosenbloom ★	Buffalo	W	10	—
Mar 25	1926	⑩ Young Stribling ★	New York	L	10	—
Aug 30	1927	⑩ Maxie Rosenbloom ★	Hartford, CT	W	10	Won-Vac NBA World-LH
Dec 12	1927	⑩ Tommy Loughran ★	New York	L	15	Lost-World-LH
Mar 11	1929	⑩ James J. Braddock ★	New York	KO'd	9	—
Oct 14	1929	⑩ Maxie Rosenbloom ★	Philadelphia	L	10	—
Nov 25	1929	⑩ Maxie Rosenbloom ★	Buffalo	W	10	—
Feb 10	1930	♛ Lou Scozza	Buffalo	W	15	Won-NY World-LH
Jun 25	1930	⑩ Maxie Rosenbloom ★	Buffalo	L	15	Lost-NY World-LH
Aug 5	1931	♛ Maxie Rosenbloom ★	Brooklyn	L	15	For-NY World-LH
Oct 30	1931	⑩ King Levinsky ★	Detroit	L	10	—
Jun 19	1934	Eddie Kaminski	Buffalo	WF	5	—

went on drinking binges from which it took days to recover. After the deaths of his father and brother from TB, he believed he would die young as well.

On August 30, 1927, Slattery faced Hall of Famer Maxie Rosenbloom for the vacant NBA light heavyweight belt. Slattery won seven of the ten rounds before 9,000 in Hartford to earn the decision. His title reign was short-lived, however. On December 12, 1927, he lost the title in a fifteen-round decision to Hall of Famer Tommy Loughran. James P. Dawson of the *New York Times* called the fight a "brilliant, dazzling, impressive exhibition of the best in boxing." On February 10, 1930, Slattery received another title shot—getting a chance at the vacant New York world light heavyweight crown. He faced Buffalo native Lou Scozza in their hometown. Slattery won a split decision.

Once again, Slattery's title reign was brief. On June 25, 1930, he faced old foe Rosenbloom. Rosenbloom took the title on a split decision. In their meeting the next year in Ebbets Field, Rosenbloom slapped, cuffed, and wrestled his way to a unanimous decision.

In 1934, Slattery quit boxing, but retirement was not kind to him. He worked a Buffalo relief job for $18 a week and lived in a four-dollar-a-week flophouse. His worst fear was realized when he contracted tuberculosis in 1940. A benefit held for him raised $10,000 to send him to Arizona for his health. He returned to Buffalo two years later and was given a job caring for flowers in Buffalo city parks. Slattery died on August 30, 1960—in Buffalo.

FREDDIE STEELE

MIDDLEWEIGHT

Right handed; 5'10"; 127–162 lbs.

134 bouts, 1/12/1928 to 5/23/1941

Manager: Dave Miller

NY/NBA Middleweight Champion 1936–38

Hall of Fame Induction: 1999

Born: 12/18/1912, Tacoma, WA

Named: Frederick Earle Steele

Died: 8/23/1984

Perhaps the finest American middleweight of the 1930s, Freddie Steele—who grew up far from America's major boxing centers—decided to become a boxer at age six, when he watched pro Tod Morgan train. Morgan, another product of Washington State, went on to become world junior lightweight champion.

Steele began training at a local gym when he was twelve. The owner, Dave Miller, was so impressed with Steele's dedication and slugging ability that he soon had the young fighter sparring with pros and ultimately became his manager. Steele himself turned pro at age fifteen when he decisioned Hermosa Villa in four rounds in Tacoma, Washington, and by age eighteen he had fought professionally at least 39 times, winning 32; the remaining bouts were draws.

In 1932, Steele knocked out future champion Ceferino Garcia twice, and the next year beat Leonard Bennett, despite suffering a broken jaw. In 1935, he defeated such impressive opponents as Baby Joe Gans, future champion Fred Apostoli, and former champions Gorilla Jones and Vince Dundee, breaking Dundee's jaw in three places in a fight punctuated with at least eleven knockdowns.

On July 11, 1936, Steele defeated Babe Risko in Seattle in a fifteen-round decision to win recognition from both the NBA and New York Athletic Commission as the world middleweight champion. Steele was an active champion, defending his title four times during the next fifteen months, with points wins over Risko and Jones and knockout victories over Frankie Battaglia and Ken Overlin. He also won eight non-title bouts in the same period.

Boxing fans were now

Vince Dundee, former middleweight champ from Baltimore, suffered a savage body attack, eleven knockdowns, a broken jaw, and a possible concussion at the hands of Freddie Steele before their July 30, 1935, fight was stopped in the third round.

IN THE RING	WON 120	LOST 4	DRAWS 9	TB 134	KO 60	W 60	WF 0	D 9	KO'd 3	L 1	LF 0	NC 1

Date	Year	Opponent	Site	Result / Rounds		Title

SELECTED BOUTS

Date	Year	Opponent	Site	Result / Rounds		Title
Jan 12	1928	Hermosa Villa	Tacoma, WA	W	4	—
May 18	1932	Ceferino Garcia	Seattle	KO	2	—
Sep 20	1932	Ceferino Garcia	Los Angeles	KO	2	—
Jan 17	1933	Leonard Bennett	Seattle	W	6	—
May 22	1934	⑩ William ("Gorilla") Jones	Seattle	D	10	—
Jan 24	1935	⑩ Baby Joe Gans	Tacoma	KO	3	—
Apr 1	1935	⑩ Fred Apostoli★	San Francisco	KO	10	—
Jul 30	1935	⑩ Vince Dundee	Seattle	TKO	3	—
Sep 17	1935	William ("Gorilla") Jones	Seattle	W	10	—
Mar 24	1936	⑩ Eddie ("Babe") Risko	Seattle	W	10	—
Jul 11	1936	⑩ Eddie ("Babe") Risko	Seattle	W	15	Won-NY/NBA World-M
Nov 17	1936	⑩ Gus Lesnevich	Los Angeles	KO	2	—
Jan 1	1937	William ("Gorilla") Jones	Milwaukee	W	10	Ret-NY/NBA World-M
Feb 10	1937	⑩ Eddie ("Babe") Risko	New York	W	15	Ret-NY/NBA World-M
May 11	1937	⑩ Frank Battaglia	Seattle	KO	3	NY/NBA World-M
Sep 11	1937	Ken Overlin	Seattle	KO	4	NY/NBA World-M
Jan 7	1938	♛ Fred Apostoli★	New York	KO'd	9	—
Feb 19	1938	Carmen Barth	Cleveland	TKO	7	Ret-NY/NBA World-M
Jul 28	1938	⑩ Al Hostak	Seattle	KO'd	1	Lost-NBA World-M
May 23	1941	Jimmy Casino	Hollywood	TKO'd	5	—

clamoring for a unification bout between Steele and IBU World champion Fred Apostoli. Negotiations broke down due to a disagreement over money, but Steele agreed to meet Apostoli in a non-title bout. In a prior fight, Steele had knocked out a then-inexperienced Apostoli, but this time Apostoli battered Steele in a brutal bout until the referee stopped the contest in the ninth round. Steele defended his championship once more with a seventh-round knockout of Carmen Barth, but was stripped of the New York crown for not agreeing to a title match with Apostoli.

Steele still reigned as the NBA world middleweight champion, but he put that belt on the line on July 28, 1938, against Al Hostak at Civic Stadium in Seattle. For the first time, Steele entered the ring without the support of manager Dave Miller, who had died suddenly at age 36. Hostak launched an impressive first-round flurry and knocked Steele out at one minute and 43 seconds of the first round. After this defeat, Steele, only 25, retired from the ring. A brief comeback attempt three years later ended with a knockout by Jimmy Casino.

After his boxing career, Steele made a living as a Hollywood actor, capitalizing on a golfing friendship with Bing Crosby. He appeared in such films as *Gentleman Jim*, *G.I. Joe*, *Hail the Conquering Hero*, and *Deep Purple*, but his acting career didn't last long. Steele later became a longshoreman then operated a restaurant in Westport, Washington.

YOUNG STRIBLING
King of the Canebrakes

HEAVYWEIGHT

Right-handed; 5'11½"; 172 lbs.

285 bouts, 1/17/1921 to 9/22/1933

Manager: W. L. Stribling

Hall of Fame Induction: 1996

Born: 12/26/1904, Bainbridge, GA

Named: William Lawrence Stribling, Jr.

Died: 10/2/1933

Young Stribling knocked out 125 opponents, setting a record that only Archie Moore topped. Stribling failed to win a championship, but his career was still going strong when he died in a motorcycle accident at the age of 28.

Stribling's mother, a vaudeville acrobat, claimed she wanted him to be a boxer from the time he was a baby. "When he was six weeks old, I started rolling him around the bed just as you would a lump of dough. When he was two years old, I started him on leg and arm exercises," she later told an interviewer. Stribling's parents put him and his kid brother in their vaudeville act as juvenile boxers. When the family retired from the stage, they settled in Macon, where Stribling got formal boxing instruction at the YMCA. His first professional bout was a four-round decision in 1921 over a tough Atlanta newsboy named Kid Domb.

A bantamweight at age sixteen, Stribling added bulk steadily. He fought successfully as a middleweight in the Atlanta area and then, in 1923, gained national attention when he was matched in a non-title bout with light heavyweight champion Mike McTigue. Their first fight ended in a hotly contested draw. When the two met again six months later, Stribling knocked McTigue down in the tenth round, but New Jersey boxing regulations stipulated that only a knockout could be counted as a victory. Stribling had to be content with a "newspaper win," granted by ringside reporters.

For all but a brief period, Stribling was managed by his father; his mother, "Ma" Stribling, handled much of her son's training. Stribling beat Hall of Famer Tommy Loughran in 1924, and was second in *The Ring*'s rankings of light heavyweight contenders that year. He would remain in *The Ring*'s top ten rankings, as either a light heavy- or a heavyweight, through 1931. The magazine ranked him as the top heavyweight in 1928.

A 1926 title bout with light heavy-

Stribling (C) poses with his parents. W.L. Stribling was his son's manager; "Ma" Stribling, a powerful athlete herself, served as Young Stribling's trainer.

IN THE RING	WON 221	LOST 12	DRAWS 14	TB 285	KO 125	W 93	WF 3	D 14	KO'd 1	L 9	LF 2	ND 36	NC 2

Date	Year	Opponent	Site	Result / Rounds		Title
SELECTED BOUTS						
Jan 17	1921	Kid Domb	Atlanta	W	4	—
Oct 4	1923	♛ Mike McTigue	Columbus, GA	D	10	—
Mar 31	1924	♛ Mike McTigue	Newark, NJ	ND-W	12	—
May 2	1924	Tommy Burns★	Toronto	W	10	—
Jun 26	1924	⑩ Tommy Loughran★	New York	W	6	—
Aug 27	1924	⑩ Paul Berlenbach★	New York	D	6	—
Mar 28	1925	⑩ Tommy Loughran★	San Francisco	W	10	—
Mar 25	1926	⑩ Jimmy Slattery★	New York	W	10	—
Jun 10	1926	♛ Paul Berlenbach★	New York	L	15	For-World-LH
Nov 11	1926	Battling Levinski★	Des Moines, IA	ND-W	10	—
Jan 23	1928	⑩ Martin Burke	Miami	KO	1	—
Aug 13	1928	⑩ Martin Burke	Mobile, AL	KO	1	—
Jan 21	1929	Sully Montgomery	Memphis	KO	2	—
Feb 27	1929	⑩ Jack Sharkey★	Miami	L	10	—
Nov 4	1929	Maurice Grizelle	Paris	W	10	—
Nov 18	1929	⑩ Primo Carnera	London	LF	4	—
Dec 7	1929	⑩ Primo Carnera	Paris	WF	7	—
May 8	1930	Hans Schoenrath	London	KO	3	—
Dec 12	1930	⑩ Tuffy Griffiths	Chicago	W	10	—
Jul 3	1931	♛ Max Schmeling★	Cleveland	KO'd	15	For-World-H
Feb 26	1932	⑩ Ernie Schaaf	Chicago	L	10	—
Nov 5	1932	Tony Gora	Adelaide, Australia	KO	6	—
Dec 17	1932	Don McCorkindale	Johannesburg	W	12	—
Mar 6	1933	Pierre Charles	Paris	L	5	—
Aug 2	1933	Benny O'Dell	Rome	KO	2	—
Sep 22	1933	♛ Maxie Rosenbloom★	Houston	W	10	—

weight champion Paul Berlenbach was a disappointment for Stribling, who had overtrained and tired badly in the later rounds. He scored a string of knockouts in 1928, however, and the next year faced heavyweight Jack Sharkey. Sharkey was staggered by a right to the heart, but when Stribling failed to follow up with more punches, Sharkey recovered. Later Sharkey said, "Had our positions been reversed, I could—in fact, I would—have murdered him." Jim Corbett considered Stribling the best feinter he ever saw but lamented Stribling's unwillingness to follow up with a solid punch. However, Stribling recorded over 100 knockouts using his "buckshot" punch, a right to the jaw following a right-left feint.

Stribling got another chance at a title when he fought heavyweight champion Max Schmeling in 1931. Stribling was reeling by the tenth round and was knocked down in the fifteenth. Referee George Blake stopped the fight with just fourteen seconds left in the final round. Again, it was speculated that Stribling had overtrained.

Stribling's last fight was a win over Maxie Rosenbloom in 1933. In October of that year, Stribling was struck by a car while riding his motorcycle home from a round of golf. He died in a hospital two days later.

CHARLES ("BUD") TAYLOR
The Blond Terror of Terre Haute

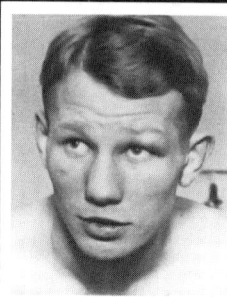

BANTAMWEIGHT

Right-handed; 5'6"; 117–131 lbs.
163 bouts, 1920 to 3/16/1931
Manager: Eddie Long
NBA Bantamweight Champ 1927–28
Hall of Fame Induction: 2005
Born: 7/22/1903, Terre Haute, IN
Died: 3/8/1962

Born on July 22, 1903, Taylor grew up in an area of Terre Haute where boys frequently fought. Taylor proved adept and set his sights on boxing.

Taylor turned professional on New Year's Day, 1920, with a third-round knockout of Walter Gorring. Taylor fought thirteen times his first year. He did not suffer a clear defeat until February 10, 1922, when Jimmy Kelly knocked him out in the sixth.

Taylor received national attention when he battled Hall of Famer and flyweight champion Pancho Villa in a non-title tilt in Chicago on September 8, 1923. Though Villa won the newspaper decision, Taylor greatly impressed ringside observers.

On January 11, 1924, Taylor knocked out Frankie Jerome at Madison Square Garden. Jerome keeled over in the twelfth and had to be carried out of the ring. Taylor spoke to Jerome the next day when he visited him in the hospital. Jerome died the day after that. Though Taylor was cleared of any wrongdoing, he was troubled by Jerome's death and considered retirement. However, in the end he kept boxing.

Taylor then won a newspaper decision over Villa before losing a twelve-round decision to him. In 1926, Taylor beat McLarnin in a ten-round decision and defeated contender Tommy Ryan. Then he earned a ten-round newspaper decision over Clever Sencio, who died afterward from his injuries. Once again, the death of an opponent had a great impact on Taylor. He asked, "Why couldn't he have knocked me out with the first punch he threw?"

With an eleventh-round left hook to the chin, Taylor (L) floors Frankie Jerome who strikes his head and suffers a skull fracture. Jerome died two days after the January 11, 1924, Madison Square Garden bout.

IN THE RING	WON **71**	LOST **23**	DRAWS **6**	TB 163	KO 37	W 33	WF 1	D 6	KO'd 4	L 16	LF 3	ND 63

Date	Year	Opponent	Site	Result / Rounds		Title
SELECTED BOUTS						
—	1920	Walter Gorring	Indiana	KO	3	—
Apr 4	1923	⑩ Frankie Genaro★	Chicago	ND-L	10	—
Sep 8	1923	♛ Pancho Villa★	Chicago	ND-L	10	—
Jan 7	1924	⑩ Johnny Brown	Indianapolis, IN	KO	3	—
Mar 6	1924	♛ Pancho Villa★	Milwaukee	ND-W	10	—
Jun 10	1924	♛ Pancho Villa★	Brooklyn	L	12	—
Jun 2	1925	⑩ Jimmy McLarnin★	Vernon, CA	W	10	—
Dec 8	1925	⑩ Jimmy McLarnin★	Vernon	LF	2	—
Jan 12	1926	⑩ Jimmy McLarnin★	Vernon	W	10	—
Mar 26	1927	⑩ Tony Canzoneri★	Chicago	D	10	For-Vac NBA World-B
Jun 24	1927	⑩ Tony Canzoneri★	Chicago	W	10	Won-NBA World-B
Dec 30	1927	♛ Tony Canzoneri★	New York	L	10	—
Apr 3	1928	⑩ Santiago Zorrilla	Los Angeles	W	10	—
Feb 8	1929	⑩ Al Singer	New York	LF	4	—
Mar 15	1929	⑩ Al Singer	New York	L	10	—
Mar 20	1930	♛ Battling Battalino★	Detroit	W	10	—
Apr 21	1930	⑩ Fidel La Barba★	Chicago	L	10	—
Aug 18	1930	♛ Battling Battalino★	Hartford, CT	L	10	—
Nov 28	1930	⑩ Fidel La Barba★	New York	L	10	—
Feb 16	1931	⑩ Benny Bass★	Philadelphia	TKO'd	2	—
Mar 16	1931	⑩ Lew Massey	Philadelphia	LF	8	—

Once again Taylor was cleared of responsibility for an opponent's death. Later, on October 18, 1926, the NBA awarded Taylor the bantamweight title after the Illinois Boxing Commission suspended its champion, Charley Phil Rosenberg, because he failed to post a forfeit deposit prior to a scheduled bout with Taylor.

On March 26, 1927, Taylor fought Tony Canzoneri with the title on the line. In a great fight, the two Hall of Famers battled to a draw. Canzoneri connected with more clean punches, but Taylor was the more aggressive. In the rematch at Wrigley Field on June 24, 1927, before 18,000, Taylor won a decision in a lively fight. *The Chicago Tribune* scored the fight three rounds for Taylor, two for Canzoneri, and five even. A couple of weeks later, Taylor had a bone fragment removed from over his eye. In the third fight between the two, Canzoneri, by this time the featherweight champion, won a twelve-round decision.

In 1928, the NBA withdrew bantamweight title recognition from Taylor because of his failure to defend his belt. On July 27, 1928, Taylor lost to Santiago Zorrilla, whom he had defeated twice previously. Due to injuries suffered in that fight and cumulative career damage, Taylor had five operations: to restore his nose to its original location and shape, to repair his lips, to realign his brow, and to reduce his cauliflower ears.

After losing two fights in 1931 Taylor retired. He was working in public relations for a freight company when he died of a heart attack on March 8, 1962.

LEW TENDLER

LIGHTWEIGHT

Left-handed; 5'6"; 118–147 lbs.

169 bouts, 1913 to 6/18/1928

Manager: Phil Glassman

Hall of Fame Induction: 1999

Born: 9/28/1898, Philadelphia, PA

Died: 11/5/1970

Though never a champion, Lew Tendler is considered one of the greatest left-handed fighters of all time. Tendler learned to fight on the streets as a boy, and after his father's death in 1908, he used his fists to gain and keep the most lucrative newspaper-selling corner in Philadelphia.

Encouraged to become a prizefighter, Tendler sought the advice of Phil Glassman, head of the Philadelphia Newsboys' Association and manager of several local boxers. Glassman managed Tendler for his whole career, starting with a fight at the Broadway Athletic Club, where Tendler fought a six-round, no-decision bout with Mickey Brown, the champion of the newsboys. Tendler earned $17.50 for the fight, based on his own ticket sales, and when his mother learned what he could get paid for boxing, she recanted her disapproval.

Tendler's early career consisted mainly of local no-decision bouts, fighting 96 no-decisions overall. At sixteen, he received a chance to fight Johnny Kilbane for the featherweight title, but Glassman turned it down because he felt Tendler was not yet ready. In 1916, Tendler performed well in a no-decision bout with Hall of Famer Pete Herman—who had fought to a draw for the bantamweight title three weeks earlier—and the next year fought two no-decision bouts against Hall of Famer Johnny Dundee. In 1919, he knocked out George ("K.O.") Chaney in one round. However, Tendler lost to Rocky Kansas on points in 1921.

A victory over Johnny Dundee on May 5, 1922, established Tendler as the top contender for Hall of Famer Benny Leonard's lightweight title. Tex Rickard paired the two at Boyle's Thirty Acres near Jersey City—where, the previous year, Jack Dempsey had fought Georges Carpentier in boxing's first million-

Lew Tendler works out on the speed bag.

IN THE RING	WON 59	LOST 11	DRAWS 2	TB 169	KO 38	W 21	WF 0	D 2	KO'd 1	L 7	LF 3	ND 96	NC 1

Date	Year	Opponent	Site	Result / Rounds		Title
SELECTED BOUTS						
Nov 6	1913	Mickey Brown	Philadelphia	ND	6	—
Feb 28	1916	Pete Herman★	Philadelphia	ND-W	6	—
Mar 26	1917	Johnny Dundee★	Philadelphia	ND-L	6	—
Oct 1	1917	Johnny Dundee★	Philadelphia	ND-W	6	—
Oct 29	1917	Rocky Kansas	Philadelphia	ND-W	6	—
Sep 18	1918	George ("K.O.") Chaney	Philadelphia	ND	6	—
Jan 1	1919	Rocky Kansas	Buffalo, NY	ND-W	10	—
Jun 4	1919	George ("K.O.") Chaney	Philadelphia	KO	1	—
Jun 13	1919	Packey Hommey	Newark, NJ	ND-W	8	—
Nov 8	1919	George Erne	Philadelphia	KO	2	—
May 19	1920	Pinky Mitchell	Milwaukee	ND-W	10	—
Oct 21	1921	Rocky Kansas	New York	L	15	—
May 5	1922	♛ Johnny Dundee★	New York	W	15	—
Jul 27	1922	♛ Benny Leonard★	Jersey City, NJ	ND-L	12	For-World-L
Jul 24	1923	♛ Benny Leonard★	New York	L	15	For-World-L
Jan 1	1924	Nate Goldman	Philadelphia	L	10	—
Jun 2	1924	♛ Mickey Walker★	Philadelphia	L	10	For-NBA World-W
Jan 19	1925	Jack Zivic	Pittsburgh	KO'd	5	—
Mar 16	1925	Nate Goldman	Philadelphia	W	10	—
Jun 8	1925	Jack Zivic	Philadelphia	W	10	—
Mar 15	1927	Young Harry Wills	Los Angeles	KO	8	—
Jan 2	1928	Jack McFarland	Philadelphia	KO	8	—
Jun 18	1928	Nate Goldman	Philadelphia	KO	5	—

dollar gate. Fifty-five thousand fans paid a total of $367,862 to see the July 27, 1922, fight. Tendler cut Leonard's eye in the first, nearly knocked him down in the fourth, and in the eighth hit him with a right and a left to the face and another left to the chin. Leonard looked as though he might fall, but he pulled through and the fight went to its twelve-round conclusion. Officially a no-decision contest, the bout did not lead to the title changing hands. Despite his troubles in the fourth and eighth, Leonard won the newspaper decision.

The Cromwell Athletic Club and matchmaker Jimmy Johnston staged a rematch at Yankee Stadium on July 24, 1923. A crowd of 58,519 paid $452,648 to see the fight, a tremendous figure for the lightweight class. Leonard outboxed Tendler and won the fifteen-round decision. Tendler then moved up to welterweight and fought champion and Hall of Famer Mickey Walker on June 2, 1924, but he lost the ten-round decision. Tendler retired in 1928 after knocking out Nate Goldman.

Tendler was a somewhat unorthodox fighter. He was one of the few lefties who could jab and hook effectively with his right hand, though his most effective punch was a straight left to the body. In retirement, he operated successful restaurants in Philadelphia and Atlantic City.

MARCEL THIL

MIDDLEWEIGHT

Right-handed; 5'10"; 157–175 lbs.
148 bouts, 7/9/1920 to 9/23/1937
Manager: Alex Taitard
IBU Middleweight Champ 1932–37
Hall of Fame Induction: 2005
Born: 5/25/1904, Saint-Dizier, France
Died: 8/14/1968

Marcel Thil was truly a standout middleweight of the 1930s. He was born in Saint-Dizier, France, in 1904.

Thil was only sixteen years old at the time of his first professional fight. His early fistic career gave little indication that he would, one day, merit enshrinement in the Hall of Fame. His career record through 1927 stood at 44-18-13. He lost four of his last five fights that year in England and Italy, when he made a rare foray away from French soil.

In 1928, Thil knocked out seven of his first eight opponents and won the other fight by decision. His improved record earned him a chance at the French middleweight title, which he seized with a first-round technical knockout of Marcel Thuru. The next year, he acquired the European middleweight belt when he decisioned Leone Jacovacci in fifteen rounds in Paris on March 27, 1929. Thil subsequently lost the European title to Mario Bosisio in a fifteen-round decision.

After the Bosisio loss, Thil embarked on a long winning streak as he triumphed in his next 21 fights. On June 11, 1932, he faced Gorilla Jones, then the NBA/IBU world middleweight champion for the title before a crowd of 60,000—the largest at that time ever to watch a fight in France. Through the first four rounds, Thil was unable to penetrate Jones's defense. In the fifth round, he began to take charge, concentrating on Jones's body. In the ninth round, he had Jones in trouble. At the start of the eleventh round, Thil was clearly ahead on points. Early in that round, Jones hit Thil below the belt and received a warning from the referee. Shortly thereafter, Jones fired another low blow and was disqualified. While Thil received acclaim as the European and International Boxing Union world champion, he was not recognized as such by the NYSAC or the NBA.

Thil successfully defended his title three times before he moved up in class and won the European light heavyweight title. After three more title defenses of his middleweight crown, he won a non-title match with Lou Brouillard by decision.

Thil had the ignominious distinction of winning several of his biggest fights by foul. Here he visibly reacts to a low blow.

IN THE RING	WON 112	LOST 22	DRAWS 14	TB 148	KO 53	W 54	WF 5	D 14	KO'd 3	L 19	LF 0

Date	Year	Opponent	Site	Result / Rounds		Title
SELECTED BOUTS						
Jul 9	1920	Leon Patoux	Nancy, France	W	4	—
Oct 12	1928	Marcel Thuru	Paris	TKO	1	Won-France-M
Mar 27	1929	Leone Jacovacci	Paris	W	15	Won-Europe-M
Mar 17	1930	Alfredo Pegazzano	Paris	W	15	Ret-Europe-M
Nov 23	1930	Mario Bosisio	Milan	L	15	Lost-Europe-M
Jun 11	1932 ♔	Gorilla Jones	Paris	WF	1	Won-NBA/IBU World-M
Jul 4	1932	Len Harvey	London	W	15	Ret-NBA/IBU World-M
Oct 2	1933	Kid Tunero	Paris	W	15	Ret-IBU World-M
Feb 26	1934	Ignacio Ara	Paris	W	15	Ret-IBU World-M
Mar 26	1934	Martinez De Alfara	Paris	WF	13	Won-Europe-LH
May 3	1934	Gustave Roth	Paris	W	15	Ret-IBU World-M
Jun 6	1934	Adolf Witt	Paris	TKO	8	Ret-Europe-LH
Oct 15	1934	Carmelo Candel	Paris	D	15	Ret-IBU World-M
Jan 14	1935	Jock McAvoy	Paris	W	15	Ret-Europe-LH
May 4	1935	Vilda ("Kid") Jaks	Paris	TKO	14	Ret-IBU World-M
Jun 1	1935	Ignacio Ara	Madrid	W	15	Ret-IBU World-M
Nov 25	1935	Lou Brouillard ★	Paris	W	12	—
Jan 20	1936	Lou Brouillard ★	Paris	WF	4	Ret-IBU World-M
Feb 15	1937	Lou Brouillard ★	Paris	WF	6	Ret-IBU World-M
Sep 23	1937	Fred Apostoli ★	New York	TKO'd	10	—

Less than two months later, on January 20, 1936, Thil fought Brouillard with the title at stake. In the third round, Brouillard was warned twice for headbutting. In the fourth, he knocked Thil down with a punch that the referee called a low blow. Brouillard was disqualified. Many in the crowd booed the decision.

The return match took place over a year later on February 15, 1937. Once again, Brouillard was the aggressor. In the sixth round, Brouillard scored with a hard right, which appeared to land on Thil's jaw. Thil fell to one knee, clutching his stomach. The referee first counted Thil out but, after discussing the matter with the judges, determined that Thil had been fouled and awarded him the bout. Once again, the crowd met the decision with derision.

Thil fought just once more. He made his only trip to the United States to fight Fred Apostoli as part of Mike Jacobs's Carnival of Champions. New York State would only sanction the bout if Thil agreed that his title would not be at issue. In the ninth, an Apostoli left opened a gash above Thil's right eye. Apostoli focused on the gash until the referee stopped the fight in the tenth.

Thil then retired. Though he was only 33, he looked much older. He was bald, his face was scarred, and he had a cauliflower ear. At his peak, he had been an intimidating fighter who liked to work inside.

During World War II, Thil worked for the French Resistance. He was captured by the Germans and tortured. He lived in France until his death on August 14, 1968, from complications resulting from two automobile accidents.

GENE TUNNEY
The Fighting Marine

HEAVYWEIGHT

Right-handed; 6'½"; 155–192 lbs.

83 bouts, 7/3/1915 to 7/26/1928

Managers: Bill Jacob 1915–18, Billy Roche and Sammy Kelly 1919–20, Frank ("Doc") Bagley 1920–22, Billy Gibson 1923–28

Heavyweight Champion 1926–28

Hall of Fame Induction: 1990

Born: 5/25/1897, New York, NY

Named: James Joseph Tunney

Died: 11/7/1978

Gene Tunney—bright, good-looking, and an acknowledged pillar of the 1920s' "Golden Age of Sports"—was never as popular among boxing fans as the man he defeated to become heavyweight champion of the world. Tunney outfought Jack Dempsey in 1926, and he retained the title in the famous "long count" rematch a year later. Tunney's relative intellectualism, reticence in public, and scientific boxing style distanced him from fight fans and the press. Despite this lack of contemporary acclaim, Tunney is remembered as a great fighter who lost only once in his career and was the first heavyweight champion to retire—and stay retired—as the titleholder.

Although he later found his way into high society, Tunney's origins were strictly working class. He grew up in New York, where his father was a longshoreman. He learned to fight in the streets, and the gift of a pair of boxing gloves when he was ten is often cited as significant to his development. Still, Tunney did not pursue boxing in earnest until his teens, when he frequented the Greenwich Village Athletic Club at night after working all day as a typist for a steamship company.

Twenty-nine-year-old Gene Tunney signs a contract to meet Jack Dempsey for the heavyweight championship on September 23, 1926. Tunney is flanked by his manager Billy Gibson (R) and promoter Tex Rickard.

IN THE RING	WON 61	LOST 1	DRAWS 1	TB 83	KO 45	W 16	WF 0	D 1	KO'd 0	L 1	LF 0	ND 19	NC 1

Date	Year	Opponent	Site	Result / Rounds		Title

SELECTED BOUTS

Date	Year	Opponent	Site	Result	Rounds	Title
Jul 3	1915	Bobby Dawson	New York	TKO	9	—
Aug	1915	Battling Genrimo	New York	KO	3	—
Dec 5	1918	Victor Marchand	Paris	KO	2	—
Dec	1918	Howard Morrow	Romorantin, France	KO	6	—
Dec	1918	Tommy Gavigan	Romorantin	D	12	—
Apr 26	1919	Ted Jamieson	Paris	W	10	—
Nov 14	1919	Dan O'Dowd	Bayonne, NJ	ND-W	8	—
Jun 28	1920	Ole Anderson	Jersey City, NJ	TKO	3	—
Jul 2	1921	Soldier Jones	Jersey City	TKO	7	—
Oct 14	1921	Jack Burke	New York	TKO	3	—
Jan 13	1922	Battling Levinsky ★	New York	W	12	Won-Vac Amer-LH
Apr 10	1922	Jack Burke	Pittsburgh	TKO	9	—
May 23	1922	Harry Greb ★	New York	L	15	Lost-Amer-LH
Aug 24	1922	Tommy Loughran ★	Philadelphia	ND-W	8	—
Feb 23	1923	Harry Greb ★	New York	W	15	Reg-Amer-LH
Jul 31	1923	Dan O'Dowd	Long Island City, NY	W	12	—
Dec 10	1923 ♛	Harry Greb ★	New York	W	15	Ret-Amer-LH
Jul 24	1924	Georges Carpentier ★	New York	TKO	15	—
Sep 17	1924	Harry Greb ★	Cleveland	ND-D	10	—
Mar 27	1925	Harry Greb ★	St. Paul, MN	ND-W	10	—
Jun 5	1925 ⑩	Tommy Gibbons ★	New York	KO	12	—
Nov 18	1925 ⑩	Johnny Risko	Cleveland	ND-W	12	—
Dec 29	1925 ⑩	Dan O'Dowd	St. Petersburg, FL	KO	2	—
Sep 23	1926 ♛	Jack Dempsey ★	Philadelphia	W	10	Won-World-H
Sep 22	1927 ⑩	Jack Dempsey ★	Chicago	W	10	Ret-World-H
Jul 26	1928 ⑩	Tom Heeney	New York	TKO	11	Ret-World-H

He turned pro in 1915 with a TKO over Bobby Dawson, a far more experienced boxer.

When World War I erupted, Tunney joined the Marines. While stationed in France, he won the American Expeditionary Force light heavyweight championship. Back in the United States, Tunney continued his ring success. In 1921, he stopped Soldier Jones on the undercard of the Dempsey–Carpentier fight in Jersey City. The next year, Tunney decisioned Battling Levinsky to win the American light heavyweight title. Tunney's first defense came just months later against Hall of Famer Harry Greb, a fighter whose tornado-like attacks were feared by many fighters. In a brutal match, Greb used a variety of tactics—some of questionable legality. It was Tunney's only loss. His nose was broken by a headbutt, his eyes were nearly swollen shut and his face was covered in blood, but Greb couldn't knock him out. The fight went the full fifteen and Greb won the decision. In a rematch the next year, Tunney avenged the loss. He won a fifteen-round decision over Greb by slamming him with a series of body punches on the advice of master ring technician, Benny Leonard.

Tunney fought in eleven professional bouts before he joined the Marines in 1917, when the U.S. entered World War I.

Tunney's (R) only loss came at the hands of Harry Greb on May 23, 1922. Tunney avenged the defeat the next year.

Tunney then turned his attention to his longtime goal, the heavyweight title held by Jack Dempsey. In 1926, Tunney signed to face Dempsey in Philadelphia at the Sesquicentennial Stadium. The match could not be held in New York because that state's athletic commission banned Dempsey for refusing to defend his title against African-American contender, Harry Wills. Tunney trained purposefully. He studied films of Dempsey, and he brought many former Dempsey opponents or sparring partners to his camp to learn as much about the champ's style as possible. In interviews, he exuded confidence (although he was belittled by the press for reading a book while in training). Thanks to the promotional genius of Tex Rickard, the fight attracted 120,757 fans who paid almost $2 million in hopes of seeing Tunney get his comeuppance. In the first round, Tunney countered a left hook with a chopping right to the cheek which staggered Dempsey. Tunney then out-boxed the Manassa Mauler for the remaining nine rounds of the fight to win the decision and the championship.

Dempsey demanded a rematch and the two met in 1927 at Soldier Field in Chicago. Over 100 thousand fans showed up, and the $2.6 million gate set a record. Through the first six rounds, Tunney was leading the fight, although neither fighter had seriously damaged the other. In the seventh, Dempsey stunned Tunney with a right cross to the temple, then followed it up

A barrage from Jack Dempsey felled Tunney in the seventh round of their September 22, 1927, rematch in Chicago. When Dempsey delayed in retreating to a neutral corner, Tunney had time to recover.

with six more strong blows, knocking Tunney down. Under Illinois boxing rules, Dempsey had to go to a neutral corner before the count could begin. Instead, Dempsey went to Tunney's corner, an action that would have been legal in New York. By the time referee Dave Barry got Dempsey to the neutral corner, Tunney had been down for at least four seconds. Tunney rose at the delayed ten count and continued the battle. Tunney won the decision, although the "long count" tainted the fight in the minds of many fans.

Tunney fought one more time, scoring an eleventh-round TKO over title challenger Tom Heeney, before retiring. He married a steel heiress and, interrupted by a stint in the Navy in World War II, had a very successful business career. An object of interest to literary sportsmen, Tunney counted Ernest Hemingway and George Bernard Shaw among his friends. One of his four children, John, became a United States Senator.

PANCHO VILLA

F L Y W E I G H T

Right-handed; 5'1"; 109–115 lbs.
105 bouts, 1919 to 7/4/1925
Manager: Frank A. Churchill
Flyweight Champion 1923–25
Hall of Fame Induction: 1994
Born: 8/1/1901, Iloilo, Philippines
Named: Francisco Guilledo
Died: 7/14/1925

Pancho Villa is considered by many to be the greatest Asian fighter in boxing history. Just over five feet tall, Villa was explosive and unrelenting in the ring. He had fought 105 times, sometimes with as little as a week between bouts, by the time of his death at age 24. Born Francisco Guilledo on the island of Panay in the Philippines, Villa often fought with other boys in his village. His reputation with his fists brought him to the attention of promoter Frank Churchill in Manila. Impressed with the then-80-pound fighter, Churchill began handling Villa and, reportedly, named him after the famous Mexican bandit.

Villa fought exclusively in the Philippines from 1919 through April 1922, often facing much larger men. In that time, he lost only three fights and captured two Filipino titles. In 1922, Churchill took Villa to the United States. The young Filipino fought two no-decision bouts in New Jersey, losing—according to the newspapers—to Abe Goldstein and Frankie Genaro. The America press and public were at first slow to take notice of Villa. Churchill had difficulty arranging fights in major venues until, for almost no money, he got Villa and another Filipino, Elino Flores, on a card at Ebbets Field, home of the Brooklyn Dodgers. Each fighter won his bout, and the crowd gave Villa a standing ovation.

Three months after his arrival in the U.S., Villa knocked out Johnny Buff in

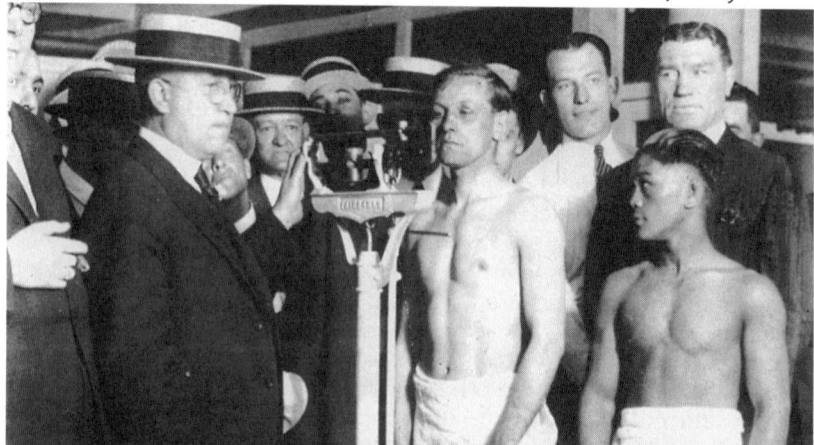

Philadelphia Jack O'Brien stands directly behind Villa as towel-wrapped Jimmy Wilde is weighed in for the defense of his flyweight title. Villa triumphed with a seven-round knockout of the aging star.

IN THE RING	WON 73	LOST 5	DRAWS 4	TB 105	KO 22	W 51	WF 0	D 4	KO'd 0	L 4	LF 1	ND 23

Date	Year	Opponent	Site	Result / Rounds		Title

SELECTED BOUTS

Date	Year	Opponent	Site	Result / Rounds		Title
—	1919	Kid Castro	Manila	W	4	—
Jun 7	1922	Abe Goldstein	Jersey City, NJ	ND-L	12	—
Jul 6	1922	Frankie Genaro ★	Jersey City	ND-L	12	—
Jul 19	1922	Battling Murray	Averne, NY	W	6	—
Jul 29	1922	Terry Miller	Asbury Park, NJ	ND-W	12	—
Aug 2	1922	Johnny Hepburn	New York	W	6	—
Aug 22	1922	Frankie Genaro ★	New York	L	10	—
Sep 14	1922	Johnny Buff	New York	KO	11	Won-Amer-FL
Nov 17	1922	Abe Goldstein	New York	W	15	Ret-Amer-FL
Dec 29	1922	Terry Martin	New York	W	15	Ret-Amer-FL
Jan 1	1923	Battling Murray	Philadelphia	ND-W	8	—
Mar 1	1923	Frankie Genaro ★	New York	L	15	Lost-Amer-FL
May 11	1923	Battling Murray	Chicago	ND-W	10	—
May 24	1923	Bobby Wolgast	Philadelphia	ND-L	8	—
Jun 18	1923	♛ Jimmy Wilde ★	New York	KO	7	Won-World-FL
Jul 31	1923	Kid Williams ★	Philadelphia	ND-L	8	—
Oct 13	1923	Benny Schwartz	Baltimore	W	15	Ret-World-FL
Dec 10	1923	Patsy Wallace	Philadelphia	ND-W	8	—
Feb 8	1924	Georgie Marks	New York	W	15	Ret-World-FL
May 30	1924	Frankie Ash	Brooklyn	W	15	Ret-World-FL
Jul 28	1924	Battling Murray	Atlantic City	ND-W	6	—
Mar 9	1925	Francisco Pilapel	Manila	KO	8	—
May 1	1925	Clever Sencio	Manila	W	15	Ret-World-FL
Jul 4	1925	Jimmy McLarnin ★	Oakland	L	10	—

eleven rounds to win the American flyweight title. Genaro took the title back in 1923 in a fifteen-round decision that most observers believed belonged to Villa. Meanwhile, British flyweight champion Jimmy Wilde had come to New York seeking the world title. Although Genaro was a likely opponent, the now wildly popular Villa was considered a better draw. In the match at New York's Polo Grounds, Villa displayed his relentless attacking style, peppering Wilde with punches from both hands. In the seventh round, Villa battered Wilde to a state of helplessness, ending the fight and Wilde's career.

Although a proposed rematch with Genaro never took place, Villa defended his title several times in the U.S. and the Philippines. Villa fought in a non-title bout with Jimmy McLarnin on July 4, 1925, in Oakland. Weak from the recent extraction of a wisdom tooth, Villa lost the decision. It was to be his last fight. Another visit to the dentist resulted in the discovery of an infection and the extraction of three more teeth. Villa ignored the dentist's instructions to rest and return for a follow-up visit, and instead indulged in a week-long party. The infection worsened, and by the time Villa's trainer, Whitey Ekwert, discovered the fighter's distress and rushed him to the hospital, it was too late. Villa died in the hospital of Ludwig's Angina, an infection of the throat cavity.

JOE WALCOTT
The Barbados Demon

WELTERWEIGHT

Right-handed; 5'1½"; 133–148 lbs.
164 bouts, 2/28/1890 to 11/13/1911
Manager: Tom O'Rourke
Welterweight Champion 1901–04
Hall of Fame Induction: 1991
Born: 3/13/1873, Barbados, British West Indies
Died: 10/4/1935

In 1950, when Nat Fleischer published his listings of the all-time best fighters in each weight class, he ranked Joe Walcott as the greatest of the welterweights. Walcott was a tough, skillful fighter willing to take on all comers from welterweight to heavyweight. Not quite 5'2", Walcott was nevertheless powerfully built and had a long reach that allowed him to compete with much larger men. He had great stamina and withstood beatings that would have finished most fighters.

Born in Barbados, Walcott grew up in his family's adopted home of Massachusetts. Although not a street brawler, Walcott excelled in both boxing and wrestling. While working as an elevator operator in a Boston hotel, Walcott began his professional career under the direction of promoter Tom O'Rourke. He won his first fight with a second-round knockout of Tom Powers.

After tallying a 46-4-8 record, including 30 wins by knockout, Walcott faced Kid Lavigne in San Francisco in 1897 for the world lightweight title. A natural welterweight, Walcott was weakened by the necessity of making the lower weight limit. Lavigne retained the title with a twelve-round decision. Walcott scrapped with Mysterious Billy Smith for the welterweight title in 1898. Smith and Walcott always put on a good show and they fought for 20 anything-goes rounds with the win going to Smith. In 1900, Walcott knocked out Joe Choynski, the heavyweight who went on to vanquish Jack Johnson the next year.

A few times in his long career, Walcott was forced to throw a fight. In a bout with Tommy West, Walcott, who was boxing well, simply quit at the end of the eleventh round. O'Rourke later told Fleischer, "Walcott didn't dare to win that night. I got the

George ("Kid") Lavigne gets the worst of it from Walcott, but was credited with the December 2, 1895, victory in Maspeth, NY. The combatants had agreed beforehand that Walcott could only win by knockout.

IN THE RING	WON 92	LOST 25	DRAWS 24	TB 164	KO 58	W 34	WF 0	D 24	KO'd 9	L 12	LF 4	ND 21	NC 2

Date	Year	Opponent	Site	Result / Rounds		Title
SELECTED BOUTS						
Feb 28	1890	Tom Powers	Boston	KO	2	—
Jun 5	1893	Paddy McGuigan	Newark, NJ	W	10	—
Mar 1	1895	Mysterious Billy Smith	Boston	D	15	—
Dec 2	1895	George ("Kid") Lavigne★	Maspeth, NY	L	15	—
Oct 29	1897 ♕	George ("Kid") Lavigne★	San Francisco	TKO'd	12	For-World-L
Apr 4	1898	Mysterious Billy Smith	Bridgeport, CT	D	25	—
Dec 6	1898 ♕	Mysterious Billy Smith	New York	L	20	For-World-W
Apr 25	1899	Dan Creedon	New York	KO	1	—
Nov 25	1899	Dan Creedon	Chicago	W	6	—
Nov 29	1899	Dan Creedon	Utica, NY	W	20	—
Feb 23	1900	Joe Choynski★	New York	TKO	7	—
May 4	1900	Mysterious Billy Smith	New York	W	25	—
Sep 24	1900	Mysterious Billy Smith	Hartford, CT	TKO	10	—
Sep 27	1901	George Gardner	San Francisco	W	20	—
Dec 15	1901 ♕	Jim ("Rube") Ferns	Fort Erie, Ont.	TKO	5	Won-World-W
Apr 11	1902	Phila. Jack O'Brien★	Philadelphia	ND-L	6	—
Apr 25	1902	George Gardner	San Francisco	L	20	—
Jun 23	1902	Tommy West	London	W	15	Ret-World-W
Apr 1	1903	Billy Woods	Los Angeles	D	20	Ret-World-W
Apr 20	1903	Phila. Jack O'Brien★	Boston	D	10	—
Apr 29	1904	Dixie Kid★	San Francisco	LF	20	Lost-World-W
Sep 5	1904	Sam Langford★	Manchester, NH	D	15	—
Sep 30	1904 ♕	Joe Gans★	San Francisco	D	20	—
Oct 16	1906	Billy ("Honey") Mellody	Chelsea, MA	L	15	For-Vac World-W
Nov 29	1906 ♕	Billy ("Honey") Mellody	Chelsea	TKO'd	12	For-World-W
Nov 13	1911	Henry Hall	Eastport, ME	ND	6	—

tip . . . he must lose . . . If West had been stopped in that twelfth round. . . I'd probably have been laying nice, peaceful and natural on the next slab."

Walcott was given another shot at the welterweight title in 1901 when he fought Jim ("Rube") Ferns. Walcott won easily with a fifth-round knockout. He retained his title until 1904, when he lost on a foul in the twentieth round to the Dixie Kid in the first world title match between two blacks. When the Dixie Kid outgrew the welterweight class later that year, Walcott was unofficially considered to have reclaimed the title. In 1906, Honey Mellody won a fifteen-round decision over Walcott to become the new welterweight champ.

Walcott held his own against much larger fighters, such as Sam Langford and Philadelphia Jack O'Brien. In addition to his recorded bouts, Walcott is reputed to have fought many other times. He retired in 1911 at the age of 38. In retirement, he worked as a fireman, a porter on a freighter, and as a handyman at Madison Square Garden. Jimmy Walker, then Mayor of New York, is said to have interceded with Garden officials to obtain this job for the down-and-out fighter who had once been a star. Walcott died in 1935 when struck by a car in Massillon, Ohio.

MICKEY WALKER
The Toy Bulldog

MIDDLEWEIGHT

Right-handed; 5'7"; 140–170 lbs.

163 bouts, 2/10/1919 to 12/1/1935

Managers: Johnny Anthes 1919–20, Jack Bulger 1920–23, Joe Diegnan 1923–25, Jack Kearns 1925–34, Bill Duffy 1934–35

Welterweight Champion 1922–26
Middleweight Champion 1926–31

Hall of Fame Induction: 1990

Born: 7/13/1901, Elizabeth, NJ

Named: Edward Patrick Walker

Died: 4/28/1981

Hard hitting, hard drinking Mickey Walker was a classic brawler who loved fighting for its own sake. He ran through millions of dollars during his lucrative career, living the life of a playboy whose off-hours carousing did little to affect his prowess in the ring. Compact and heavily-muscled, Walker had a repertoire of punches to mince the opposition, no matter what their weight class. He was a champion for nine years, holding the welterweight and middleweight titles successively.

Walker began his ring career at age seventeen in his native Elizabeth, New Jersey. He built a good record in the New Jersey area from 1919 to 1921, then in 1922, battered an aging Jack Britton in Madison Square Garden to take the world welterweight crown. At the top of the heap, Walker attracted Jack Dempsey's estranged manager Jack Kearns, and in 1925 the two formed a longtime partnership that included indulging in the flashy lifestyle Walker enjoyed.

Walker defended his welterweight title several times before challenging Harry Greb for the middleweight championship in 1925. A crowd of 65,000 filled New York's Polo Grounds to see these two aggressive fighters meet. Walker opened up early to try to wear down the champ, but Greb's speed was too much for him. Greb hung on to his title, winning the fifteen-round decision.

In 1926, Walker lost the welterweight title to Pete Latzo in a ten-round decision in Scranton, Pennsylvania, Latzo's home turf. Still title-hungry, Walker went after

Walker (L) held the welterweight title on July 2, 1925, when he moved up to middleweight to challenge Harry Greb.

IN THE RING	WON 93	LOST 19	DRAWS 4	TB 163	KO 60	W 33	WF 0	D 4	KO'd 5	L 11	LF 3	ND 46	NC 1

Date	Year	Opponent	Site	Result / Rounds		Title

SELECTED BOUTS

Date	Year	Opponent	Site	Result	Rounds	Title
Feb 10	1919	Dominic Orsini	Elizabeth, NJ	ND	4	—
Sep 14	1922	Artie Bird	New York	KO	8	—
Nov 1	1922	♛ Jack Britton★	New York	W	15	Won-World-W
Mar 22	1923	Pete Latzo	Newark, NJ	ND-W	12	Ret-World-W
Oct 8	1923	Jimmy Jones	Newark	NC	9	Ret-World-W
Jun 2	1924	⑩ Lew Tendler★	Philadelphia	W	10	Ret-World-W
Oct 1	1924	Bobby Barrett	Philadelphia	KO	6	Ret-World-W
Jul 2	1925	♛ Harry Greb★	New York	L	15	For-World-M
Sep 21	1925	⑩ Dave Shade	New York	W	15	Ret-World-W
May 20	1926	⑩ Pete Latzo	Scranton, PA	L	10	Lost-World-W
Dec 3	1926	♛ Tiger Flowers★	Chicago	W	10	Won-World-M
Jun 21	1927	Ace Hudkins	Chicago	W	10	Ret-World-M
Jun 30	1927	⑩ Tommy Milligan	London	KO	10	Ret-World-M
Nov 25	1927	⑩ Paul Berlenbach★	Chicago	W	10	—
Mar 28	1929	♛ Tommy Loughran★	Chicago	L	10	For-World-LH
Oct 29	1929	⑩ Ace Hudkins	Los Angeles	W	10	Ret-World-M
Feb 25	1931	Johnny Risko	Miami	W	10	—
Apr 10	1931	Bearcat Wright	Omaha, NE	W	10	—
Jul 22	1931	⑩ Jack Sharkey★	Brooklyn	D	15	—
Apr 29	1932	⑩ King Levinsky	Chicago	W	10	
Jun 24	1932	⑩ Johnny Risko	Cleveland	L	12	—
Sep 26	1932	⑩ Max Schmeling★	Long Island City, NY	TKO'd	8	—
Nov 3	1933	♛ Maxie Rosenbloom★	New York	L	15	For-World-LH
May 8	1934	♛ Maxie Rosenbloom★	Los Angeles	W	10	—
Dec 1	1935	Eric Seelig	New York	TKO'd	7	—

Tiger Flowers's middleweight crown, which he took in a controversial decision. In 1929, Walker attempted to add the light heavyweight title to his list of laurels but lost a ten-round decision to Hall of Famer Tommy Loughran.

After defeating Ace Hudkins in October of 1929, Walker did not again defend the middleweight title, formally relinquishing it in 1931. That year, with his sights on the heavyweight belt, Walker battled future heavyweight champion Jack Sharkey to a draw (though a majority of the reporters at ringside believed that Walker won the fight). He also took on and conquered Bearcat Wright, a fighter who outweighed him by 100 pounds and stood almost a foot taller. After suffering a beating at the hands of Max Schmeling, Walker returned to the light heavyweight ranks. He lost a fifteen-round decision in a title fight with Maxie Rosenbloom, although he beat Rosenbloom in a non-title rematch.

After losing to Eric Seelig on a seventh-round TKO in 1935, Walker retired. His ring earnings largely spent, Walker did some acting, operated a tavern, and worked as a salesman for a distillery. He later became an artist whose primitive-style paintings earned critical acclaim and also worked as sports editor of the *Police Gazette*.

FREDDIE WELSH
The Welsh Wizard

LIGHTWEIGHT

Right-handed; 5'7"; 130–140 lbs.
168 bouts, 12/21/1905 to 4/15/1922
Managers: Jack Clancy 1905–13,
Harry Pollock 1913–22
British Lightweight Champ 1909–11,
1912–14
World Lightweight Champ 1914–17
Hall of Fame Induction: 1997
Born: 3/5/1886, Pontypridd, Wales
Named: Frederick Hall Thomas
Died: 7/29/1927

Considered one of the greatest defensive fighters in boxing history, Freddy Welsh parlayed excellent boxing skills, fantastic footwork, and expert use of his left jab into the lightweight championship of the world. Born in Wales, in the same region that produced Hall of Famer Jimmy Wilde, Welsh learned the basics of boxing in his homeland. He competed in amateur tournaments in Scotland under the name Freddy Welsh so that his mother would not know that her son, Frederick Hall Thomas, was a fighter.

When he was sixteen, Welsh ran away to the United States with three other boys. After a year he came back to Wales but soon returned to America. Looking for work, Welsh rode the rails to the Dakotas to labor in the farm fields. He eventually got a job in a New York gymnasium where he honed his boxing skills.

Welsh turned professional at the age of eighteen with a knockout victory over Young Williams in Philadelphia. He fought 25 times in 1906 with all but three of those fights no-decision bouts. He then returned to the British Isles where he won thirteen fights in a row, including ten by knockout. Not known as a slugger, Welsh would only record twenty more knockouts during the remainder of his career.

Back in the United States, in 1908, Welsh lost a close decision and then fought to a draw with Packey McFarland. Then, frustrated at his inability to land a title shot against lightweight champion Battling Nelson, Welsh returned to England to contend for the first Lonsdale Belt offered by the National Sporting Club. He won a fairly easy twenty-round decision over Johnny Summers to take the belt. Welsh beat Hall of Famer Jim Driscoll on a foul to retain the belt before losing to Matt Wells, but he defeated Wells in the rematch. Still, Welsh could not get a shot at the world title. Nelson's

In Cardiff, Wales, two Welshmen, both Hall of Famers, vie for the Lonsdale belt, symbolic of British lightweight supremacy. Welsh (L) beat Jim Driscoll by disqualification on December 20, 1910.

IN THE RING	WON 76	LOST 4	DRAWS 6	TB 168	KO 32	W 40	WF 4	D 6	KO'd 1	L 3	LF 0	ND 82

Date	Year	Opponent	Site	Result / Rounds		Title
SELECTED BOUTS						
Dec 21	1905	Young Williams	Philadelphia	KO	3	—
Feb 18	1907	Seaman Hayes	London	W	6	—
Feb 21	1908	Packey McFarland ★	Milwaukee	L	10	—
Jul 4	1908	Packey McFarland ★	Los Angeles	D	25	—
Nov 25	1908	Abe Attell ★	Vernon, CA	W	15	—
Nov 8	1909	Johnny Summers	London	W	20	Won-Britain-L
May 30	1910	Packey McFarland ★	London	D	20	—
Dec 20	1910	Jim Driscoll ★	Cardiff, Wales	WF	10	Ret-Britain-L
Feb 27	1911	Matt Wells	London	L	20	Lost-Britain-L
Nov 11	1912	Matt Wells	London	W	20	Reg-Britain-L
Dec 16	1912	Hugh Mehegan	London	W	20	Ret-Britain-L
Jan 1	1914	Johnny Dundee ★	New Orleans	ND-W	10	—
Apr 28	1914	Leach Cross	Los Angeles	W	20	—
Jul 7	1914	♛ Willie Ritchie ★	London	W	20	Won-World-L
Nov 2	1914	Ad Wolgast ★	New York	TKO	8	—
Mar 6	1916	Ad Wolgast ★	Milwaukee	ND-W	10	—
Mar 31	1916	Benny Leonard ★	New York	ND-L	10	
Jul 4	1916	Ad Wolgast ★	Denver	WF	11	Ret-World-L
Jul 28	1916	Benny Leonard ★	Brooklyn	ND-W	10	—
Sep 4	1916	Charley White	Colorado Springs, CO	W	20	Ret-World-L
Apr 17	1917	Battling Nelson ★	St. Louis	ND-W	12	—
Apr 20	1917	Rocky Kansas	Buffalo, NY	ND-L	10	—
May 1	1917	Johnny Kilbane ★	New York	ND-L	10	—
May 28	1917	Benny Leonard ★	New York	TKO'd	9	Lost-World-L
Apr 15	1922	Archie Walker	Brooklyn	L	10	—

vanquisher, the new champ Ad Wolgast, signed for a fight with Welsh that was canceled when Wolgast was stricken with appendicitis.

Finally, Welsh met world lightweight champion Willie Ritchie in London for the title. In a very close fight, Welsh adopted a defensive posture which allowed Ritchie few clear shots at him. From time to time Welsh scored in close. Ritchie recorded the only knockdown of the fight in the twelfth round. The referee, the sole judge in the fight, scored the first nineteen rounds even and gave the twentieth and final round to Welsh.

Welsh defended his title twice and fought a host of no-decision bouts before facing Benny Leonard in a title contest on May 28, 1917. The great Leonard broke through Welsh's usually impenetrable defenses to knock him down three times in the ninth round before the referee stopped the fight. This bout was the only time in Welsh's career that he was stopped before the final bell.

Welsh served as a captain in the U.S. Army during World War I. After the war he fought five times before retiring, after a loss to Archie Walker. For some years Welsh operated a health farm in New Jersey before he lost it to foreclosure. He died in a New York hotel room in 1927 at the age of 41, unemployed and nearly penniless.

JIMMY WILDE
Ghost with a Hammer in His Hand; Mighty Atom

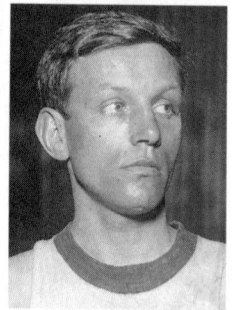

F L Y W E I G H T

Right-handed; 5'2½"; 94–109 lbs.

149 bouts, 12/26/1910 to 6/18/1923

Manager: Teddy Lewis

Flyweight Champion 1916–23

Hall of Fame Induction: 1990

Born: 5/15/1892, Tylorstown, Glamorganshire, Wales

Died: 3/10/1969

Heavyweight champion Gene Tunney lauded Jimmy Wilde as "the greatest fighter I ever saw." The frail-looking Wilde, whose skinny limbs and protruding ribs belied the power of his punches, became the first flyweight champion to be recognized in the United States as well as in Britain. The flyweight class was established in England in 1909 by the National Sporting Club, but American recognition of the division did not come until 1916, the year Wilde took the world title.

Wilde was born in Wales in the same area that produced Freddie Welsh and Jim Driscoll. The son of a poor coal miner, Wilde worked as a pit boy as a child, hacking coal from channels too narrow for a grown man. When he began boxing in 1908 at the age of sixteen, he weighed just 74 pounds. He competed in boxing booth tournaments in his home of Tylorstown, taking on all comers. His first recorded professional match was a knockout of Ted Roberts in 1911.

Wilde won the British 98-pound title in 1913 when he recorded an eighteen-round technical knockout over Billy Padden. In 1915, he failed in his bid to win the British and European flyweight championships in the first loss of his career when Tancy Lee stopped him in seventeen. The next year, however, Wilde won wide acclaim as flyweight champion when he defeated Joe Symonds in London with a TKO in twelve. He also trounced Lee in a rematch in 1916

Wilde's (R) June 18, 1923, meeting with Pancho Villa was his last bout. After his knock-out loss, Wilde turned to sports writing.

Date	Year	Opponent	Site	Result / Rounds		Title
SELECTED BOUTS						
Dec 26	1910	Les Williams	Pontypridd, Wales	ND	3	—
Jan 20	1912	Matt Wells' Nipper	London	KO	1	—
Jan 1	1913	Billy Padden	Glasgow, Scotland	TKO	18	Won-Britain-98 lbs.
Jul 19	1913	Young Dando	Tonypandy, Wales	W	15	—
Sep 23	1913	Young Dando	Cardiff, Wales	W	20	—
Dec 6	1913	Young Dando	Merthyr, Wales	WF	10	—
Apr 27	1914	Alf Mansfield	Leeds, England	W	20	—
Sep 28	1914	Alf Mansfield	London	TKO	10	—
Jan 25	1915	Tancy Lee	London	TKO'd	17	For-Britain & Europe-FL
Jan 24	1916	Tommy Noble	London	TKO	11	—
Jan 27	1916	Jimmy Morton	Liverpool, England	KO	2	—
Feb 14	1916	Joe Symonds	London	TKO	12	Won-Britain-FL
Apr 24	1916	Johnny Rosner	Liverpool	TKO	11	Ret-Britain-FL
May 29	1916	Tommy Harrison	London	TKO	8	—
Jun 26	1916	Tancy Lee	London	TKO	11	Won-Eur-FL & Ret-Britain-FL
Nov 9	1916	Tommy Noble	Liverpool	TKO	15	—
Dec 18	1916	Young Zulu Kid	London	KO	11	Won-World-FL
Mar 12	1917	George Clark	London	TKO	4	Ret-Brit, Eur & World-FL
May 16	1919	Alf Mansfield	London	TKO	13	—
Jul 17	1919	Memphis Pal Moore	London	W	20	—
Dec 6	1919	Jackie Sharkey	Milwaukee	ND-L	10	—
Apr 12	1920	Young Zulu Kid	Windsor, Ont.	ND-W	10	—
Jan 13	1921	Pete Herman★	London	TKO'd	17	—
Jun 18	1923	Pancho Villa★	New York	KO'd	7	Lost-World-FL

to unify the British and European flyweight titles. Later the same year, Wilde knocked out Young Zulu Kid of the U.S. to gain universal acceptance as the world champion.

Wilde kept fighting and winning until former bantamweight champ Pete Herman hammered him for seventeen rounds in 1921 in London, and Wilde collapsed from exhaustion. Still considered the flyweight champion, Wilde did not fight for over two years until he put his title on the line against the very hot Pancho Villa at the Polo Grounds in New York in 1923. In the first two rounds, Wilde fought well, but a hard right from Villa at the end of the second dazed him. Villa then pounded the champ at will until the fight ended in the seventh.

Wilde retired after the fight with Villa, putting his amazing seven-year career to bed. Veteran ring observers marveled for years at Wilde's power. He punched harder and more accurately than many men who outweighed him by 30 or 40 pounds. His scrawny physical appearance remained a source of scrutiny throughout his career, and once he became champion, several doctors studied him, trying to determine the unique source of his strength. During World War II he was seriously injured in a German air raid on southeastern England. He later returned to Wales and lived in a small cottage by the sea until his death.

JESS WILLARD
The Pottawatomie Giant

HEAVYWEIGHT

Right-handed; 6'6½"; 214–265 lbs.
36 bouts, 2/15/1911 to 7/12/1923
Manager: Tom Jones
Heavyweight Champ 1915–19
Hall of Fame Induction: 2003
Born: 12/29/1881, St. Clere,
Pottawatomie County, KS
Died: 12/15/1968

Willard was born in Pottawatomie County, Kansas, on December 29, 1881. His father, who operated a grocery store, died two months before Willard was born. He quit school at the age of eleven. When he was twelve, he started horse-trading with the Pottawatomie Indians. Willard would acquire wild ponies in exchange for whiskey. He would then break the ponies and sell them. Later, he operated a livery stable and married his childhood sweetheart.

Willard didn't decide to become a fighter because he liked boxing or enjoyed the idea of fame, but rather to provide a better life for himself and his family. In Willard's first bout on February 15, 1911, in Sapulpa, Oklahoma, he lost when he fouled Louis Fink in the tenth round. Six weeks later, he knocked out Fink in the third. He had won seven fights in a row when he faced Joe Cox in Springfield, Missouri. When Cox scored with a hard right, Willard walked out of the ring.

Willard journeyed to Chicago where he came under the influence of Charles ("Kid") Cutler, a former John L. Sullivan sparring partner who taught Willard how to box. Three knock-out victories brought Willard to the attention of Tom Jones, a manager who had worked with Ad Wolgast. Jones persuaded Willard to travel with him to New York where he might earn a shot at Jack Johnson's title. In New York Willard earned newspaper decisions over Arthur Pelkey and Luther McCarty, but Willard was cited for lack of aggression.

Tragedy struck when Willard faced William ("Bull") Young in Vernon, California. In the eleventh round, an uppercut from Willard caused a fatal brain hemorrhage. Willard was troubled by Young's death and became reluctant to use his power in the ring.

Promoter Jack Curley managed to get champion Jack Johnson to agree to fight Willard, April 5, 1915, in Havana, Cuba. The title bout was held on a blistering

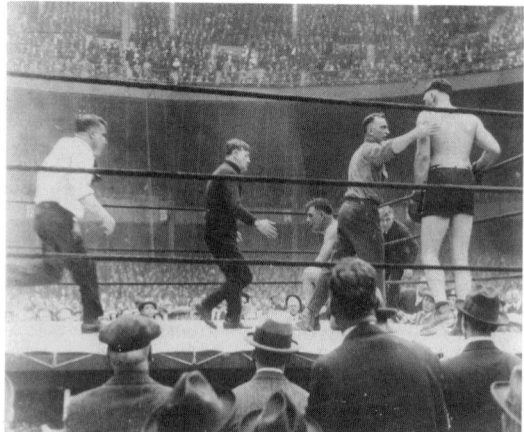

Referee Jack Appell calls a halt to the fight as Jess Willard (R) is TKO winner over Floyd Johnson in this comeback bout in Yankee Stadium on May 12, 1923. Willard hadn't fought in four years.

IN THE RING	WON 24	LOST 6	DRAWS 1	TB 36	KO 21	W 3	WF 0	D 1	KO'd 3	L 2	LF 1	ND 5

Date	Year	Opponent	Site	Result / Rounds		Title
SELECTED BOUTS						
Feb 15	1911	Louis Fink	Sapulpa, OK	LF	1	—
Mar 28	1911	Louis Fink	Oklahoma City, OK	KO	3	—
Dec 27	1912	Alfred ("Soldier") Kearns	New York	KO	8	—
May 20	1913	Ed ("Gunboat") Smith	San Francisco	L	20	—
Aug 22	1913	William ("Bull") Young	Vernon, CA	KO	11	—
Dec 29	1913	George ("Boer") Rodel	New Haven, IN	KO	9	—
Apr 28	1914	George ("Boer") Rodel	Atlanta	KO	6	—
Apr 5	1915	♛ Jack Johnson ★	Havana, Cuba	KO	26	Won-World-H
Mar 25	1916	Frank Moran	New York	ND-W	10	Ret-World-H
Jul 4	1919	Jack Dempsey ★	Toledo, OH	TKO'd	3	Lost-World-H
May 12	1923	Floyd Johnson	New York	TKO	11	—
Jul 12	1923	Luis Firpo	Jersey City, NJ	KO'd	8	—

day with a temperature of 105°. Johnson showed his skills in the first few rounds and seemed to confuse Willard. In the seventh round, Johnson cut Willard's lip and cheek. In the eighth and ninth, Willard was the aggressor. Johnson's punches seemed to have lost their effect. By the tenth, Johnson's mouth was bloody. As the fight went on, a combination of Johnson's age, his lack of conditioning, Willard's size, and the intense heat began to wear on the champion. In the 26th, Willard scored with a long left to the face and a right to the stomach. Johnson clinched. Then a left to the body shook him. Finally, with an overhand right to the jaw, Willard knocked Johnson out. Johnson later claimed that he took a dive. Geoffrey C. Ward, author of the fine Johnson biography *Unforgivable Blackness: The Rise and Fall of Jack Johnson*, does not believe there was a fix.

As champion, Willard showed little inclination to defend his title. He purchased a ranch in Lawrence, Kansas, toured in Buffalo Bill's Wild West Show, and starred in his own wild west show and circus. Tex Rickard finally lured Willard into a title match with Jack Dempsey on July 4, 1919, in Toledo, Ohio. Though Willard outweighed Dempsey by 58 pounds, Dempsey knocked the champion down seven times in the first round and eventually won when a beaten Willard could not answer the bell for the fourth round. Willard later claimed that Dempsey's hands were coated in plaster of Paris—a charge discounted by most historians.

Willard retired after losing the title. He attempted a comeback four years later. However, Willard lost his chance for a rematch with Dempsey when Luis Firpo knocked Willard out in the eighth round of their bout.

"I never liked it," Willard said of boxing. "In fact, I hated it as I never hated a thing previously, but there was money in it. I needed the money and decided to go after it." Despite his reluctance to box, he used his long left and strong right along with his size and strength to win the heavyweight championship. Willard sold his ranch in 1921. He later worked in real estate and opened a large supermarket in Hollywood. He died on December 15, 1968, in Los Angeles.

KID WILLIAMS

BANTAMWEIGHT

Right-handed; 5'1"; 110–124 lbs.

202 bouts, 7/18/1910 to 9/3/1929

Managers: Sam H. Harris, Dave Warnick, Max Waxman

Bantamweight Champ 1914–17

Hall of Fame Induction: 1996

Born: 12/5/1893, Copenhagen, Denmark

Named: John Gutenko

Died: 10/18/1963

Kid Williams, who fought for nineteen years, is considered one of the top bantamweights of all time. Born in Denmark, Williams came to the United States with his parents in 1904. The family settled in a poor section of Baltimore, where Williams found work as a newsboy, often fighting for the choicest spots to sell papers.

Williams's skill with his fists attracted the attention of Baltimore matchmaker John Barrett, who persuaded the sixteen-year-old to enter his first professional match. The fight was held at Baltimore's Gayety Theatre in 1910. Williams attacked his opponent, Shep Farren, in an all-out fury and knocked him out in the fifth round. After this victory Barrett gave Gutenko a more "American-sounding" name to use in the ring.

Flamboyant manager Sam Harris soon latched onto Williams and controlled him—and his earnings—until the end of the fighter's career. Williams churned through a succession of opponents until he was matched against the more experienced George ("K.O.") Chaney, who handed him his first loss in 1911.

In 1912, Williams fought bantamweight champion Johnny Coulon in a nontitle bout. The no-decision fight was deemed Williams's win by the newspapers, and the fans agreed, loudly cheering as he dominated Coulon in eight of the ten rounds. In 1914, Williams KO'd European bantamweight champ Eddie Campi. Five months later, he met Coulon again—this time for the world title—in Vernon, California, then a hotbed of boxing. The match was slated to go 20 rounds if necessary, but Williams wasted little time in vanquishing Coulon. By the third round, bleeding and with two fractured ribs, Coulon fell to a right cross to the chin.

Williams, at 21, was bantamweight champion of the

Dave Warnick (L) was one of Kid Williams's managers. In his long career, the short, solidly-built Williams fought over 200 battles.

IN THE RING	WON 104	LOST 17	DRAWS 9	TB 202	KO 55	W 43	WF 6	D 9	KO'd 3	L 9	LF 5	ND 71	NC 1

Date	Year	Opponent	Site	Result / Rounds		Title
SELECTED BOUTS						
Jul 18	1910	Shep Farren	Baltimore	KO	5	—
Jul 10	1911	George ("K.O.") Chaney	Baltimore	L	20	—
Jul 27	1911	Young McFarland	New York	KO	5	—
Sep 14	1912	Mickey Brown	New York	TKO	8	—
Oct 18	1912	♛ Johnny Coulon ★	New York	ND-W	10	—
Dec 11	1912	♛ Charles Ledoux	Philadelphia	ND-W	6	—
Feb 12	1913	Eddie Campi	Los Angeles	W	20	—
Jul 15	1913	♛ Charles Ledoux	Los Angeles	TKO	15	—
Jan 31	1914	♛ Eddie Campi	Los Angeles	KO	12	Won-Brit World-B
Jun 9	1914	♛ Johnny Coulon ★	Vernon, CA	KO	3	Won-World-B
Jun 30	1914	Pete Herman ★	New Orleans	ND-D	10	—
Dec 19	1914	Joe O'Donnell	Philadelphia	TKO	3	—
Mar 17	1915	♛ Johnny Kilbane	Philadelphia	ND-L	6	—
Sep 10	1915	Johnny Ertle	St. Paul, MN	LF	5	—
Oct 28	1915	Memphis Pal Moore	Memphis, TN	L	8	—
Dec 6	1915	Frankie Burns	New Orleans	D	20	Ret-World-B
Feb 7	1916	Pete Herman ★	New Orleans	D	20	Ret-World-B
Sep 4	1916	Frankie Burns	Baltimore	ND-W	10	—
Jan 9	1917	Pete Herman ★	New Orleans	L	20	Lost-World-B
Jan 29	1918	Joe Lynch	Philadelphia	TKO'd	4	—
Mar 2	1921	Tommy Ryan ★	Pittsburgh	ND-W	10	—
Jul 31	1923	Pancho Villa ★	Philadelphia	ND-W	8	—
Dec 22	1923	Danny Lee	New York	KO	1	—
Jun 26	1925	Frankie Genaro ★	Baltimore	L	12	—
Dec 14	1928	Willie Parrish	Baltimore	TKO	5	—
Sep 3	1929	Bobby Burns	Baltimore	KO'd	2	—

world. He went on to face some top talent, fighting a tough ten-round draw with Pete Herman in New Orleans in his first fight after winning the championship. He lost a no-decision bout to featherweight champ Johnny Kilbane in 1915 and later that year, in St. Paul, lost on a controversial foul to Johnny Ertle.

Williams met Herman again in New Orleans in 1916, this time for the title. Herman clearly had the best of the fight, which was nevertheless declared a draw by referee Billy Rocap, a friend of Williams's. A year later, the two were back in New Orleans for another title challenge by Herman, who won the twenty-round decision.

Williams continued to fight for another twelve years. A tiny powerhouse at 5'1", Williams had an aggressive, attacking style which made him a formidable opponent to the end of his career. A profligate spender, Williams was also often bilked out of a fair share of his purses. He left the ring almost as poor as he entered it. He held jobs as a taxi driver, salesman, and steel worker. In 1934, he was sentenced to a year in jail for failure to support his wife and children. He tried, at the age of 42, to make a comeback as a boxer, but the Maryland State Athletic Commission refused to issue him a license. In 1957, Williams was arrested for drunkenness. He died in Baltimore in 1963.

HARRY WILLS
The Black Panther

HEAVYWEIGHT

Right-handed; 6'4"; 220 lbs.

103 bouts, 1910 to 8/4/1932

Managers: Jim Buckley, Paddy Mullins

Hall of Fame Induction: 1992

Born: 5/15/1889, New Orleans, LA

Died: 12/21/1958

One of the greatest heavyweights to never fight for a championship, Harry Wills was hampered during his entire career by the color bar that limited opportunities for black fighters. An undeniable rival for Jack Dempsey's crown, Wills was nevertheless shut out of a chance at the title. The race barrier may also have provided a convenient way for white boxers, wary of Wills's extraordinary size and power, to avoid facing him in the ring.

Wills worked as a longshoreman before turning to pro boxing in 1910. Initially he relied almost entirely on his bulk to win fights, but with time, Wills developed fine boxing skills and speed in the ring. Wills found several worthy opponents among a growing class of black heavyweights. He fought Hall of Famer Sam Langford eighteen times and got the better of the series. He also battled Sam McVey, Joe Jeannette, Jeff Clarke, Kid Cotton and Roughhouse Ware. Wills travelled around the country and to Panama to participate in these fights, which were often held in less than ideal conditions.

Wills floors Luis Angel Firpo before a crowd of 80,000 people at Boyle's Thirty Acres on September 1, 1924. The twelve-round bout was officially a no-decision contest, but the result was clear.

IN THE RING	WON 65	LOST 8	DRAWS 2	TB 103	KO 47	W 18	WF 0	D 2	KO'd 4	L 1	LF 3	ND 25	NC 3

Date	Year	Opponent	Site	Result / Rounds		Title
SELECTED BOUTS						
—	1910	Kid Ravarro	New Orleans	KO	1	—
May 1	1914	Sam Langford ★	New Orleans	W	10	Won-Black-H
Nov 26	1914	Sam Langford ★	Vernon, CA	KO'd	14	Lost-Black-H
Dec 20	1914	Sam McVey ★	New Orleans	L	20	—
Sep 7	1915	Sam McVey ★	Boston	W	12	Reg-Black-H
Jan 3	1916	Sam Langford ★	New Orleans	W	20	Ret-Black-H
Feb 11	1916	Sam Langford ★	New Orleans	KO'd	19	Lost-Black-H
Feb 7	1917	Jim Johnson	St. Louis	KO'd	2	—
Apr 14	1918	Sam Langford ★	Panama City	KO	6	Reg-Black-H
May 19	1918	Sam Langford ★	Panama City	KO	7	Ret-Black-H
Sep 30	1919	Sam Langford ★	Syracuse, NY	ND	10	Ret-Black-H
Nov 5	1919	Sam Langford ★	Tulsa, OK	W	15	Ret-Black-H
Apr 19	1920	Sam Langford ★	Denver	W	15	Ret-Black-H
Jul 26	1920	Fred Fulton	Newark, NJ	KO	3	—
Oct 10	1921	Ed ("Gunboat") Smith	Havana, Cuba	KO	1	—
Nov 18	1921	Ed Martin	Portland, OR	KO	1	Ret-Black-H
Jan 17	1922	Sam Langford ★	Portland, OR	W	10	Ret-Black-H
Sep 1	1924	⑩ Luis Angel Firpo	Jersey City, NJ	ND-W	12	—
Oct 12	1926	⑩ Jack Sharkey ★	Brooklyn	LF	13	—
Jul 13	1927	⑩ Paolino Uzcudun	Brooklyn	KO'd	4	—
Aug 4	1932	Vinko Jankassa	Brooklyn	KO	1	—

Wills demonstrated his prowess to white audiences in 1920 when he knocked out white contender Fred Fulton in the third round at the First Regiment Armory in Newark, New Jersey. Fulton fell victim to Wills's tremendous strength and body punching. Although this victory thrust Wills into the status of top contender for Jack Dempsey's heavyweight crown, promoter Tex Rickard balked at holding a mixed-race title bout. In 1924, James A. Farley, chairman of the New York State Athletic Commission, announced the commission would not sanction a title match for Dempsey unless Wills was the opponent. Dempsey gave up his license to fight in New York, and Rickard instead signed Gene Tunney to fight Dempsey in Philadelphia. Reportedly, rival promoter Floyd Fitzsimmons attempted to arrange a Dempsey–Wills bout and paid Wills $50,000 in advance, which Wills could keep if the fight did not take place. As a result of Rickard's interference, the fight never happened. Some charged that Dempsey was afraid to fight Wills, but Wills never publicly made that assertion.

Wills fought Luis Angel Firpo in 1924 and was generally acclaimed the winner in a no-decision bout. In 1926 and past his prime, Wills fought future champion Jack Sharkey and was behind on points when he fouled Sharkey and was disqualified. Wills continued to fight until 1932. Had history been different, he could well have been heavyweight champion of the world. After his retirement, Wills prospered managing his New York real estate interests.

AD WOLGAST
The Michigan Wildcat

LIGHTWEIGHT

Right-handed; 5'4¼"; 118–133 lbs.

134 bouts, 6/10/1906 to 9/6/1920

Managers: Frank Mulkern 1906–08, Tom Jones 1908–15, Larney Lichtenstein 1915–17

World Lightweight Champ 1910–12

Hall of Fame Induction: 2000

Born: 2/8/1888, Cadillac, MI

Named: Adolphus Wolgast

Died: 4/14/1955

Extremely aggressive, Ad Wolgast rose to the top of the lightweight ranks with little concern for defense and a great ability to take a punch. Tragically, he paid a terrible price for too many blows to the head. After an undistinguished stint in school, Wolgast got a job as a bootblack in a barber shop. He purchased a pair of boxing gloves, although his parents objected, and began to learn the fight game. He first saw a pro fight in Petoskey, Michigan. When he didn't have enough money for a ticket, Wolgast told the promoter he was a promising young amateur and found himself being matched with Kid Moore. Wolgast won the fight in a six-round decision—though Moore outweighed him by 27 pounds.

Wolgast fought his first two years as a pro primarily in Grand Rapids and Milwaukee before moving on to fight in California. There, he knocked out two opponents, but largely fought no-decision bouts. On July 13, 1909, Wolgast, now dubbed "The Michigan Wildcat," met Hall of Famer and lightweight champion Battling Nelson in Los Angeles for a no-decision, non-title fight. The newspaper decision in the bloody brawl went to Wolgast.

On February 22, 1910, Wolgast and Nelson met again in a "distance" title fight scheduled for 45 rounds. Nelson had the advantage in the early rounds, but by the 40th his vision was so impaired that he took his fighting stance opposite one of the ring posts, and the referee stopped the fight. Wolgast was the new world lightweight champion.

Wolgast made his fifth title defense against Mexican Joe Rivers. He managed to force Rivers into accepting as referee Jack Welch, who was known to encourage the wild brawling-style fight that favored Wolgast. Rivers began well, and a discouraged Wolgast nearly did not answer the bell for the thirteenth, coming out only when his cornerman threatened him with a bottle. Wolgast unleashed a hard left to Rivers's groin, while Rivers smashed him with a right-left

Referee Ed W. Smith is about to step in and stop this brutal fight in the 40th round. Battling Nelson (L) is blinded by Ad Wolgast's attack in Richmond, CA, on February 22, 1910.

IN THE RING	WON 60	LOST 12	DRAWS 13	TB 134	KO 40	W 19	WF 1	D 13	KO'd 4	L 4	LF 4	ND 49

Date	Year	Opponent	Site	Result / Rounds		Title
SELECTED BOUTS						
Jun 10	1906	Kid Moore	Petoskey, MI	W	6	—
Dec 11	1908	Abe Attell★	Los Angeles	ND-L	10	—
Jul 13	1909	Battling Nelson★	Los Angeles	ND-W	10	—
Feb 22	1910	♛ Battling Nelson★	Richmond, CA	TKO	40	Won-World-L
Jun 10	1910	Jack Redmond	Milwaukee	ND-L	10	—
Feb 8	1911	K.O. Brown	Philadelphia	ND-L	6	—
Mar 17	1911	George Memsic	Vernon, CA	TKO	9	Ret-World-L
Mar 31	1911	Anton LaGrave	San Francisco	TKO	5	Ret-World-L
May 27	1911	California Frankie Burns	San Francisco	TKO	17	Ret-World-L
Jul 4	1911	Owen Moran★	San Francisco	KO	13	Ret-World-L
May 11	1912	Willie Ritchie★	San Francisco	ND-D	4	—
Jul 4	1912	Mexican Joe Rivers	Vernon	TKO	13	Ret-World-L
Nov 28	1912	Willie Ritchie★	Daly City, CA	LF	16	Lost-World-L
Oct 13	1913	Battling Nelson★	Milwaukee	ND-W	10	—
Jan 23	1914	Mexican Joe Rivers	Milwaukee	ND-W	10	—
Nov 2	1914	♛ Freddie Welsh★	New York	TKO'd	8	—
Mar 6	1916	♛ Freddie Welsh★	Milwaukee	ND-L	10	—
Jul 4	1916	♛ Freddie Welsh★	Denver	LF	11	For-World-L
Sep 6	1920	Lee Morrissey	San Bernardino, CA	D	4	—

combination to the jaw. Both fighters fell, Wolgast on top of Rivers, and Welch started a count on Rivers while helping Wolgast back to his feet. When his count reached ten, Welch raised Wolgast's arm in victory, then hurriedly fled as a mob rushed the ring. Wolgast retained his title in this notorious "double knockout" fight.

His next title defense came against Willie Ritchie on November 28, 1912. Wolgast came out fighting, but in the sixteenth Ritchie landed a long, wild right to the jaw, spinning Wolgast around and nearly sending him down. Braced with one fist on the canvas, Wolgast launched two low blows at Ritchie, and referee Jim Griffen stopped the fight, awarding the victory to Ritchie on a foul.

After losing two fights in a row in 1913, Wolgast spoke of retirement, yet later that year he scored a newspaper victory in a no-decision fight with Nelson in Milwaukee. His retirement put on hold, he next challenged Freddy Welsh in a bout billed as the lightweight championship, but the fight was stopped in the eighth round when Wolgast's arm was broken. (Technically, the 1914 match wasn't for the belt—both fighters weighed in over the 135 lbs. limit.) Two years later, Wolgast and Welsh met twice more. Wolgast lost both: once by a newspaper decision, and once by a foul.

Wolgast's all-attack fighting style resulted in numerous injuries, including broken arms, hands, and ribs; cauliflowered ears; and extensive brain damage. In 1917, Wolgast fought just once and was knocked out in the second round. He fought only one more bout, in 1920. Jack Doyle, a boxing promoter in Vernon, California, was appointed as Wolgast's guardian and allowed him to "train" for nonexistent fights. By 1927, Wolgast was institutionalized and remained so for the rest of his life.

MIDGET WOLGAST
Greased Lightning

FLYWEIGHT

Right-handed; 5'3½"; 107–135 lbs.

212 bouts, 10/8/1925 to 3/14/1940

Managers: Jimmy Coster and Chris Dundee, Johnny Keyes, Al Ketchel, Al Lippe, Eddie Walker

New York World Flyweight Champion 1930–35

Hall of Fame Induction: 2001

Born: 7/18/1910, Philadelphia, PA

Named: Joseph Robert Loscalzo

Died: 10/19/1955

Midget Wolgast made a meteoric rise to the top of the flyweight division, winning a world title at the age of nineteen. Wolgast enjoyed fighting as a boy and engaged in many schoolyard brawls, often with bigger kids. Unfortunately, his fighting instinct also led to his expulsion from public school for striking a teacher, but he returned after six weeks of reform school.

After he left school, Wolgast got a job installing hardwood floors. To learn more about fighting, he also became a janitor at a local boxing gym. The lure of the ring proved strong, and Wolgast began to train in secret. He caught the eye of trainer/manager Jimmy Coster, who coached him for six months before putting him in the ring for the first time. The fifteen-year-old Wolgast decisioned Al Ketchel in the October 8, 1925, match and earned $12 for his efforts. He adopted the name Wolgast in honor of popular Philadelphia boxer Bobby Wolgast, and "Midget," obviously, because of his size. By 1928, he was ranked as the ninth-best flyweight in *The Ring*'s annual ratings.

In 1929, Wolgast compiled a record of 16-0-1 (plus two NDs), including victories over ranked contenders Phil Tobias and Ruby Bradley, and his ranking rose to number two. In late 1929, the New York State Athletic Commission declared Willie La Morte's flyweight title vacant, and Wolgast, now jointly managed and trained by Hall of Famer Chris Dundee and Jimmy Coster, was paired with Black Bill on March 21, 1930, for the New York version of the world title. Wolgast scored consistently with left hooks in the second, third, and fourth rounds, but Bill battled back with body shots in the fifth and sixth. The fight again went Wolgast's way in the seventh, and though Bill fought back desperately, opening a cut over Wolgast's eye in the final round, the decision and the title went to Wolgast.

Only two months later, Wolgast

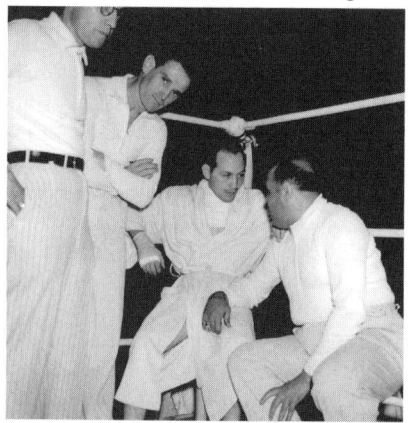

Midget Wolgast is surrounded by his nattily attired brain trust. Wolgast held the New York–version of the flyweight title during a period when there was no universally recognized champion.

IN THE RING	WON 149	LOST 35	DRAWS 16	TB 212	KO 16	W 133	WF 0	D 16	KO'd 6	L 28	LF 1	ND 12

Date	Year	Opponent	Site	Result / Rounds		Title

SELECTED BOUTS

Date	Year	Opponent	Site	Result	Rounds	Title
Oct 8	1925	Al Ketchel	Philadelphia	W	6	—
Nov 5	1926	Jimmy Britt	Philadelphia	W	6	—
Nov 3	1927	⑩ Willie Davies	New York	W	10	—
Jan 23	1928	⑩ Billy Kelly	Scranton, PA	L	10	—
Jan 26	1929	⑩ Phil Tobias	Philadelphia	W	10	—
Mar 21	1930	⑩ Black Bill	New York	W	15	Won-Vac NY World-F
May 16	1930	⑩ Willie La Morte	New York	TKO	6	Ret-NY World-F
Dec 19	1930	⑩ Willie Davies	Toronto	W	10	—
Dec 26	1930	♛ Frankie Genaro ★	New York	D	15	For-World-F
Feb 23	1931	⑩ Ruby Bradley	Holyoke, MA	W	10	—
Jul 13	1931	⑩ Ruby Bradley	Brooklyn	W	15	Ret-NY World-F
Sep 8	1931	⑩ Happy Atherton	Indianapolis	W	10	—
Dec 2	1931	⑩ Speedy Dado	Oakland	W	10	—
Mar 18	1932	⑩ Little Pancho	Honolulu	W	10	—
Jul 13	1933	⑩ Lew Farber	Brooklyn	L	10	—
Sep 27	1933	⑩ Bobby Leitham	Montreal	L	10	—
Oct 30	1933	⑩ Jackie Brown	London	W	12	—
Nov 13	1933	⑩ Valentin Angelmann	Paris	D	10	—
Sep 4	1934	⑩ Henry Moreno	New Orleans	L	10	—
Nov 9	1934	⑩ Pablo Dano	Hollywood	L	10	—
Jan 25	1935	⑩ Young Tommy	Hollywood	W	10	—
Jul 3	1935	⑩ Small Montana	Sacramento, CA	L	10	—
Sep 16	1935	⑩ Small Montana	Oakland	L	10	Lost-NY World-F
Nov 5	1935	♛ Small Montana	Los Angeles	W	10	—
Nov 27	1935	⑩ Henry Armstrong ★	Oakland	L	10	—
Mar 14	1940	Bill Morris	Lancaster, PA	L	6	—

successfully defended the title against Willie La Morte, winning with one of his infrequent knockouts in the sixth round. On December 26, 1930, Wolgast met NBA and International Boxing Union champion Frankie Genaro in Madison Square Garden for a unification bout, but the fight ended in a draw and both men retained their titles.

Though he fought frequently over the next four years, Wolgast made only one title defense, a victory over Ruby Bradley. His skills declined; his wondrous speed did not seem quite so fast; his difficult-to-defend-against style—which featured Wolgast switching from conventional to southpaw and back—no longer seemed so confusing. In his personal life, Wolgast's marriage collapsed. The diminutive Romeo was romantically linked to Mae West—amongst others. He spent considerably more time inside barrooms than in the practice ring. On September 16, 1935, he lost his title to Small Montana in a ten-round decision.

Though he was only 25 years old, Wolgast was finished as a serious title contender. He continued to box for another four and a half years with a record of 15-19-3, and was knocked out five times. In retirement, he trained young boxers. Wolgast died of a heart attack in a Philadelphia bar in 1955.

TEDDY YAROSZ

MIDDLEWEIGHT

Right-handed; 5'10"; 144–176 lbs.
128 bouts, 6/13/1929 to 2/12/1942
Manager: Ray Foutts
NBA/NY World Middleweight
Champion 1934–35
Hall of Fame Induction: 2006
Born: 6/24/1910, Pittsburgh, PA
Named: Thaddeus Yarosz
Died: 3/29/1974

Teddy Yarosz used great boxing ability, including superb defensive skills, to become middleweight champion. Yarosz was born in Pittsburgh in 1910. When he was ten, he moved with his family to Monaca, PA. Yarosz and his brothers loved to spar and scrap—much to their father's chagrin. Once Mr. Yarosz used a hatchet to chop up the boys' boxing gloves. When Yarosz was sixteen, his father died. Yarosz and his older brother, Eddie, quit school to support their large family. Eddie started boxing on amateur cards; Teddy followed suit.

Yarosz turned professional on June 13, 1929, when he won a four-round decision over Jackie King in New Brighton, Pennsylvania. The promoter of the card, Ray Foutts, was very impressed with Yarosz, despite his lack of polish, and became his manager. Fighting primarily in the Pittsburgh area, Yarosz won his first 59 fights before he lost to Eddie ("Kid") Wolfe in a decision in Pittsburgh on January 23, 1933. He cemented his reputation among middleweights when he posted two decisions over contender Vince Dundee in 1933.

On February 12, 1934, Yarosz went fifteen rounds for the first time to decision Jimmy Smith and earn the vacant Pennsylvania world middleweight title. He defended the title against former middleweight champion Ben Jeby and emerged victorious in the twelve-round battle. He then scored a rare knockout victory when he stopped his idol, former welterweight champ Pete Latzo, in four rounds. In 128 career fights, the stylish Yarosz only recorded seventeen knockouts.

On September 11, 1934, Yarosz again faced Dundee. The NBA and New York middleweight titles held by Dundee were on the line. In the sixth, Yarosz put together a series of hard rights to the jaw and grabbed the offense for the rest of the round. Yarosz used his left jab to great advantage, sending Dundee to the ropes six times. In the last round, Yarosz put together a two-fisted attack. He won unanimously.

On January 1, 1935, Yarosz faced Babe Risko in a non-title bout. Risko

Teddy Yarosz (L) wins the NY/NBA World Middleweight title from Vince Dundee September 11, 1934, in Forbes Field, Pittsburgh. Here, Yarosz is about to deliver a left hook.

IN THE RING	WON 107	LOST 18	DRAWS 3	TB 128	KO 17	W 90	WF 0	D 3	KO'd 1	L 17	LF 0

Date	Year	Opponent	Site	Result / Rounds		Title
SELECTED BOUTS						
Jun 13	1929	Jackie King	New Brighton, PA	W	4	—
Jan 23	1933	⑩ Eddie ("Kid") Wolfe	Pittsburgh	L	10	—
Jun 20	1933	⑩ Sammy Slaughter	Cleveland	W	10	—
Aug 21	1933	⑩ Vince Dundee	Pittsburgh	W	10	Won-Vac PA World-M
Oct 25	1933	⑩ Young Terry	Newark	L	10	—
Feb 12	1934	⑩ Jimmy Smith	Pittsburgh	W	15	Ret-PA World-M
Apr 6	1934	⑩ Ben Jeby	Pittsburgh	W	12	Ret-PA World-M
Sep 11	1934	⑩ Vince Dundee	Pittsburgh	W	15	Won-NBA/NY-M
Sep 19	1935	⑩ Eddie ("Babe") Risko	Pittsburgh	L	15	Lost-NBA/NY-M
May 7	1937	⑩ Lou Brouillard★	Boston	W	10	—
Jun 30	1937	⑩ Billy Conn★	Pittsburgh	L	12	—
Sep 30	1937	⑩ Billy Conn★	Pittsburgh	L	15	—
Dec 9	1937	⑩ Carmelo Candel	Paris	L	10	—
Jul 25	1938	⑩ Billy Conn★	Pittsburgh	W	12	—
Apr 20	1939	Archie Moore★	St. Louis	W	10	—
Apr 15	1940	⑩ Jimmy Reeves	Cleveland	W	10	—
Mar 5	1941	Jimmy Bivins★	Cleveland	L	10	—
Nov 17	1941	⑩ Ezzard Charles★	Cincinnati	L	10	—
Feb 12	1942	Joe Muscato	Rochester	L	8	—

knocked Yarosz down three times in the first round, and Yarosz tore the cartilage in his right leg. He continued to fight although he was barely able to defend himself. The fight was stopped in the seventh round—the only time in his career that Yarosz was stopped short of the distance. He required knee surgery and a lengthy rehabilitation. After two tune-up fights, Yarosz risked his title in a rematch with Risko on September 19, 1935, in Pittsburgh's Forbes Field before 30,000. Risko knocked Yarosz down in the fourth, and Yarosz again injured his knee. Although he managed to last the full fifteen rounds, Yarosz lost the decision and the title.

Yarosz again had surgery; his doctor placed a brace on his leg, and Yarosz came back about eight months later. However, his comeback was derailed when he dropped two decisions to fellow Pittsburgher Billy Conn. He avenged the Conn losses when he decisioned Conn in twelve rounds on July 25, 1938. Though Yarosz was known for his graceful boxing skill and strong defense, he employed a much rougher style in this fight. Four times the boxers continued to fight after the bell. Once, police were called into the ring to stop the brutal brawling.

Yarosz retired after losing an eight-round decision to Joe Muscato on February 12, 1942. In retirement he worked as a policeman, operated a tavern, and toiled as a caster in a steel mill. Yarosz was not the only member of his family to make a name for himself in the prize ring. Brothers Eddie and Victor fought professionally, his younger brother Tommy was a ranked light heavyweight, and his brother Joe won an all-service welterweight title in an Army–Navy tournament of champions during World War II. His youngest brother, Johnny, had some ring success before he was killed in a bomber crash. Yarosz died on March 29, 1974.

FIXES
AND FALLEN HEROES

The Seamy Side of Boxing

Throughout its colorful history, boxing has had more than its share of scandal, both inside and outside the ring. The sport is inherently very dangerous, and death and chronic injury often are mixed with the laurels that boxers receive. Almost from its very beginnings, the sport has attracted a criminal element, and many fighters and non-combatants have risen from environments where obeying the law is less relevant than economic or physical survival. The violence that is prized in the ring has at times erupted in boxers' private lives, and stints in reform school or prison are woven into many champions' histories.

TAKING A DIVE

A continuing theme in boxing's checkered history is the fixing of fights. The sport is very susceptible to rigging. First, a bout involves only two active participants, and only one needs to be convinced to throw a fight. Fixing team sports, in which there are many players and where events can occur more haphazardly, is much less practical. Furthermore, boxing is essentially an entrepreneurial endeavor in which individual fighters must guard their own financial interests. Lacking the kind of central authority established in other professional sports, boxing does not have rigorous procedures for self-regulation. Certain boxers, with the control of their careers in the hands of trainers and managers and perhaps living from purse to purse, have been vulnerable to manipulation.

While no one can say for certain when the first fight was thrown, the first known fix by a Hall of Famer took place in 1822 when Englishman Jem Ward threw his fight with Bill Abbott. In more modern times, allegations of fixed fights have arisen many times, although the charges have rarely been proven. For instance, it was rumored that Stanley Ketchel was to allow the great black heavyweight Jack Johnson to beat him, and in return, Johnson would take it easy on the lighter Ketchel. When Ketchel knocked Johnson down, some say Johnson was outraged at the betrayal. In any case, he responded with a ferocious attack, which ended the fight quickly.

Action in other heavyweight boxing matches has raised cries of "fix" as well. Many suspected Hall of Famer Jack Sharkey of giving less than his best effort when he lost the heavyweight championship to the ungainly giant, Primo Carnera. Sharkey vehemently denied the charges for the rest of his life, but Carnera had known underworld connections and won other fights in which his opponents took dives. Reportedly, Carnera's handlers arranged the fixes without his knowledge.

In the sixties, the two Muhammad Ali–Sonny Liston title fights raised some eyebrows. In the first, then-champion Liston quit between rounds, refusing to get up from his stool because of an injured shoulder. Although an examination after the fight did reveal an injury, the seeming invincibility of Liston and the shady figures with whom he associated cast doubt on the legitimacy of the fight's outcome. In the second fight, Ali floored Liston with a short right which Ali dubbed the "anchor punch." But some at ringside called it the "phantom punch" because they never saw it. Confusion over the count by referee Jersey Joe Walcott contributed to the perception that the fight was not on the level. As with most boxing fix stories, the charges were never substantiated. It was never implied that Ali himself was knowingly involved.

Shown here in happier times, Alicia Muñiz strolls along with her common-law husband middleweight Carlos Monzon. Muñiz's life came to an end in 1988 when Monzon threw her to her death from a balcony.

Publicly confirmed fixes include middleweight Jake LaMotta's admitted fall to Billy Fox in return for a promised title shot. Rocky Graziano was suspended by the New York State Athletic Commission for not reporting a bribe offer, and Harold Johnson had his license suspended for collapsing against Julio Mederos without being hit. Fans and boxing commissions alike have undoubtedly been duped at other times by unscrupulous figures whose influence on boxing has diminished the sport's integrity.

BEHIND BARS

With some notable exceptions, boxing has always tended to draw its participants from the lower socioeconomic strata. The streets of urban neighborhoods have been a wellspring of aspiring boxers. Historically, youngsters particularly adept with their fists have been urged to channel their aggressiveness through formal boxing instruction.

Unavoidably, the type of environment which fosters a career in boxing may also lead to tangles with the law. Several great boxers served time in youth detention centers or prison. In his autobiography, *Somebody Up There Likes Me,* Rocky Graziano details the many youthful misdeeds that landed him in reform school. Former heavyweight champion Sonny Liston learned to box in prison, and the young Mike Tyson was discovered by trainer Cus D'Amato while serving time in an Upstate New York detention center. Even fighters who came to be highly respected for strength of character, such as Archie Moore and Floyd Patterson—both former chairmen of the New York State Athletic Commission—served time in reform schools.

Some boxers have been involved in criminal activities in their adult lives as well. Liston, who was strongly linked to St. Louis racketeer John Vitale, was arrested numerous times, although sometimes he may have been a victim of police harassment. Hall of Famer Kid McCoy, whose gradual decline ended with suicide, was convicted of killing a woman with whom he lived and shooting three other people. Carlos Monzon, former middleweight champion and a national hero to Argentinians, was convicted of killing the mother of his youngest child by throwing her off a second-story balcony, and Hall of Fame trainer Jack Blackburn killed his wife and shot two others. More recently, in a case which received national attention, Tyson was convicted of rape and served over three years in prison before his release in 1995.

Criminality is by no means the norm for successful boxers—many have had stable home lives or followed their boxing careers with public service or youth work—but for some, the violence that defines the sport is not confined to the squared circle.

CORRUPTION AND CONTROL

Boxing has been tainted with widespread corruption at various times in its history. During the period from the late 1940s to the early 1960s, the New York City–based International Boxing Club (IBC) dominated the promotion of boxing. Though owned primarily by James Norris (a member of the family which owned the Detroit Red Wings in the National Hockey League) and Arthur Wirtz (who had ties to the NHL Chicago Blackhawks), the IBC fell under the influence of mobster Frankie Carbo. Carbo and his associates also controlled the Boxing Managers Guild of New York and the International Boxing Managers Guild, which gave them strong influence over two aspects of the fight game: staging fights and controlling fighters.

Interestingly, a plan by declining champion Joe Louis to maintain an interest in heavyweight championship fights coincided with the IBC's early activities. Louis, who realized his reign as champ would soon come to an end, set up a corporation in hopes of getting exclusive management contracts with top heavyweights. Promoters would have to go through Joe Louis Enterprises, Inc., to sign the fighters. Norris bought Louis out for $150,000 and a twenty percent share of IBC's stock in return for the contracts Louis had landed with Ezzard Charles, Jersey Joe Walcott, Lee Savold, and Gus Lesnevich. Although ostensibly employed by the IBC, Louis quickly faded from the scene.

Norris then arranged for Madison Square Garden to buy out its promoter, Mike Jacobs, and also to buy out the only major competitor, the Tournament of Champions. These purchases gave Norris and the IBC a virtual monopoly on boxing promotion in the U.S. Norris controlled the Garden and owned Chicago Stadium, the Detroit Olympia, and the St. Louis Arena. The IBC promoted 36 of 44 championship fights held between May 1949 and May 1953.

Norris assured the IBC of obtaining quality fighters by making payments to the Boxing Managers Guild, and Carbo helped Norris line up fighters for IBC promotions. Although the very wealthy Norris had the arenas and promotional contracts, he needed Carbo to provide fighters through his links to managers such as Frank ("Blinky") Palermo.

Carbo's behind-the-scenes machinations dominated boxing for several years. Although Floyd Patterson, the heavyweight champion of the late 1950s and early '60s, resisted the IBC, the organization still wielded an incredible amount of influence over the sport. Lightweight champion Ike Williams fell under IBC control and later testified that, although he did not succumb, he had often been pressured by Palermo to throw fights. Williams also said he was sometimes cheated out of purses. The mob's influence on boxing also extended to deciding who got title shots based on which fighters were under their control. Patterson's manager, Cus D'Amato, refused to allow him to fight IBC fighters. While this stand helped somewhat in diminishing the importance of the corrupt IBC, the competitive aspect of the sport suffered as Patterson faced less than top contenders.

The mob's influence extended to deciding who got title shots.

Trainer Ray Arcel apparently ran afoul of the IBC when he began promoting fights for the ABC television network. Arcel's matches competed with those run by the IBC. Following threats to get out of television, Arcel was struck on the head with a lead pipe in 1953. Arcel recovered, but while the assault was never officially linked to the IBC, he nevertheless ended his association with the network and, in fact, stayed away from boxing for almost twenty years.

A significant factor in the demise of the IBC was the action of the Justice Department to prosecute for anti-trust violations. In 1959, the U.S. Supreme Court upheld a lower court decision which ordered Norris and Wirtz to sell their holdings in Madison Square Garden, dissolved the IBC in Illinois and New York, and set a limit on the number of championship fights which could be held in IBC venues.

In a New York State criminal prosecution, Carbo was sentenced to two years in prison for undercover matchmaking and managing. However, Carbo's conviction and the breakup of the IBC did not end the criminal influence on boxing. Carbo and Palermo were eventually convicted of trying to extort money from California promoter Jackie Leonard after the Don Jordan–Virgil Akins welterweight championship fight. Carbo was sentenced to 25 years in prison, and Palermo received a 15-year sentence. With the decline of Norris, Wirtz, Carbo, and Palermo, the influence of organized crime greatly diminished in boxing, although some assert that the criminal element still has a presence in the sport.

The reputation of premier fight promoter Don King, a hugely successful figure in today's boxing scene, makes many observers uneasy. King, convicted of manslaughter in 1967 in connection with the death of a rival in the Cleveland numbers racket, has since survived numerous scrapes with law enforcement authorities. An FBI sting operation, three grand jury probes, an income tax evasion case, and prosecution for insurance fraud all failed to prove King guilty of wrongdoing.

Many questions about King's complex dealings seem to arise from an apparent conflict of interest when he acts as both promoter and manager. According to a 1991 *Sports Illustrated* article by a former FBI agent who had investigated King's alleged mob connections, then-heavyweight champion Larry Holmes, managed by King, said in private that he feared for his safety if he cooperated with the government. Former heavyweight champion Buster Douglas reportedly paid $7 million in a lawsuit settlement to get out from under King's influence. Former Junior Welterweight WBC titleholder Julio Cesar Chavez has spoken against King. At King's 1995 insurance fraud trial, Chavez testified that he never saw $350,000 in training expenses that King attempted to recover from Lloyd's of London when a Chavez fight was canceled due to injury.

STAYING ALIVE

At its best, boxing is an unparalleled physical art. At its worst, it is a killer and maimer of good men. Blindness, hearing loss, mental impairment, respiratory or speech difficulties, paralysis, and death are among the possibilities that lurk just behind the glory of being a star in satin trunks. While serious injuries and deaths do occur in other sports—skiing and auto racing, for instance—boxing is perhaps the only sport where death and injuries are viewed as "part of the game." Financial or other pressures have led more than one hurt or sick boxer to fight at extreme risk to his health.

According to the 1982 *Ring Record Book*, between 1918 and 1981 over 400 amateur and professional fighters died as a result of injuries suffered in the ring.

In 2005, the boxing world experienced the death of a reigning champion as a result of ring trauma. Veteran fighter Leavander Johnson had finally won a world title—the IBF lightweight belt—after sixteen years as a pro. His first title defense, in Las Vegas, was his biggest payday ever—$150,000. The fight wasn't close. Johnson absorbed a total of 409 punches from his opponent, Jesus Chavez. After ten rounds, Johnson's father and trainer, Bill Johnson, considered throwing in the towel but let his son reenter the ring after a quick check by the ringside physician. Referee Tony Weeks stopped the bout just 38 seconds into the eleventh, after twenty unanswered blows from Chavez. It was too late. Forty minutes later Johnson was in surgery, but even the removal of part of Johnson's skull couldn't relieve the pressure caused by brain damage. Six days later Johnson died.

Chronic injuries can result from the cumulative effect on the brain of numerous blows to the head. The once-comic image of a punch-drunk boxer is a tragic reality for many ring veterans. One-time heavyweight contender Jerry Quarry died at age 53 after suffering from the form of dementia pugilistica that resembles Alzheimer's disease. Sports fans are familiar with the transformation of Muhammad Ali from a quick-witted, swaggering champion to a soft-spoken, slow-moving figure because of Parkinson's syndrome, probably a result of his ring career.

A disturbing article by Dr. Ira Casson written for the National Parkinson's Foundation summarizes recent research about the brain damage that boxers often sustain during their ring careers.

Dr. Casson's own studies, as well as work by other researchers, indicate that "15–40 percent of ex-boxers have been found to have symptoms of chronic brain injury. Recent work, employing detailed psychological testing and MRI scanning, has shown that most professional boxers (even those without symptoms) have some degree of brain damage." Fortunately, "today's boxers have fewer bouts and shorter careers, resulting in fewer blows to the head and less cumulative brain injury."

Examinations of hundreds of former boxers reveal that "symptoms usually begin near or shortly after the end of a boxer's career. On occasion they are first noticed after a particularly hard bout. Symptoms develop an average of 16 years after beginning the sport, although some cases have occurred as early as 6 years after becoming a boxer. [Brain disorders] can occur in all weight classes but [are] seen most often in the heavier divisions, and champion boxers run as much risk of sustaining chronic brain injury as less skilled journeymen."

Casson's findings are that "while boxers with less than 20–30 professional bouts usually do not have any symptoms of brain injury those with 25–50 bouts often show MRI and psychological test abnormalities without obvious symptoms. Boxers with more than 50 professional bouts often have obvious symptoms of brain injury as well as MRI and psychological test abnormalities."

The dangerous nature of boxing has periodically led to calls for reforms, ranging from more thorough and frequent medical examinations to protective headgear. At various times, Congress has held hearings to discuss federal control of boxing and, from time to time, movements to ban the sport have arisen.

Boxing has been a part of human history for centuries, however, and it may never be "civilized" out of existence. The promise of prize money, as well as the possibility of being the very best at something excruciatingly difficult, is a timeless lure to talented young men. And for some who love the sport, the real-life metaphor of rise and decline, of glorious win and devastating loss, stands as an elemental human truth that must be acted out regardless of the risks involved.

Being the best at something excruciatingly difficult is a timeless lure.

THE MODERN ERA

Boxing Waxes and Wanes but the Great Stars Shine

BOXING'S MODERN PERIOD is perhaps best defined by the stars it produced. Names like Joe Louis, Archie Moore, Rocky Marciano, Sugar Ray Robinson, Joe Frazier, George Foreman, and of course Muhammad Ali are indelibly etched into our collective memory of an era that saw boxing wax and wane. International champions arrived to challenge American dominance as boxing flourished in Japan, the Philippines, Thailand, Mexico, Puerto Rico, Latin America, and elsewhere. Champions such as Alexis Arguello of Nicaragua, Japan's Fighting Harada, and Filipino Gabriel ("Flash") Elorde built careers in their home countries, then went abroad to continue their winning ways. (In order to be classified as modern-era boxers, Hall of Fame inductees must have ended their careers after 1942.)

Racism as a deterrent to non-white fighters was largely overcome in the modern era of boxing. The door Joe Louis opened was flung wide with the emergence of a pantheon of great black fighters from the 1950s on. The careers of headliners like Floyd Patterson and Sonny Liston were still largely handled by whites, however. The next transition came when blacks took positions as trainers, managers, and promoters. With the appearance in the 1970s of powerful and controversial promoter Don King, African-American influence in boxing continued to strengthen. The broadening international scope of boxing, with more fighters coming from countries beyond the United States, especially in the lower weight classes, has also populated the sport with many different ethnic groups.

Television coverage had a great effect on boxing. Evolving from novelty broadcasts in the 1940s to extensive network exposure in the 1950s, televised bouts brought boxing many new fans but also seriously damaged the gate for live fights. This likewise contributed to the decline of small boxing venues where neophyte boxers typically started their careers. Then other broadcast entertainment crowded out coverage of boxing, and the public shifted its attention away from the fights.

Public wariness was aroused when the 1950s and '60s saw the exposure of corruption and organized crime in boxing. Mobster Frankie Carbo was shown to exert considerable influence on the International Boxing Club, the dominant promoter for Madison Square Garden and other major venues. Blinky Palermo, manager for many fighters during this period, was closely associated with Carbo.

Meanwhile, interest in amateur boxing as an Olympic sport was keen. During this era, success in the Olympics became an important springboard to a successful professional career in the ring. Americans Floyd Patterson, Muhammad Ali, Joe Frazier, George Foreman, Sugar Ray Leonard, Leon Spinks, Michael Spinks, and Oscar de la Hoya; Italian Nino Benvenuti; and Pascual Perez of Argentina are all fine boxers whose Olympic laurels preceded world titles.

Among the many forces that have shaped boxing's modern era, perhaps none has been more influential than the career and personality of heavyweight Muhammad Ali. Olympic gold medal winner in 1960, Ali was brash, flamboyant, and extremely talented. His star-wattage persona sold out his 1963 Madison Square Garden bout with Doug Jones despite the fact that it took place during a New York City newspaper strike, and his fame never stopped growing. He outraged both the boxing organizations and the U.S. government by becoming a Black Muslim and protesting the Vietnam War. Temporarily stripped of his heavyweight championship title, Ali was nevertheless hailed as "The People's Champion."

Another change in boxing in the modern era has been the rise of some important new boxing venues. Manhattan's Madison Square Garden is still regarded as the "Mecca of Boxing." However, many high-profile bouts now take place at gambling casinos in Las Vegas, Atlantic City, Connecticut, and elsewhere throughout the U.S.

As in earlier eras, some of the wealthiest individuals in the fight game are the promoters. Don King emerged as the most influential man in boxing. His promotional accomplishments are unprecedented. His mega-promotion of the 1974 "Rumble in the Jungle" between Muhammad Ali and George Foreman paid a then-unheard-of $10 million in purses and drew an estimated one billion television viewers worldwide. He produced the HBO elimination series that resulted in explosive Mike Tyson being crowned the undisputed heavyweight champion. In 1994, King promoted a record 47 world title bouts. After Mike Tyson's release from prison, King carefully directed Tyson's comeback attempt until Tyson's career was again derailed—this time by his suspension for biting Evander Holyfield's ears.

Another very important promoter of the modern era is Bob Arum, head of Top Rank. He organized the widely watched boxing series on ESPN and countless other major bouts over the last 40 years. He promoted the November 5, 1994, fight in which George Foreman beat Michael Moorer to regain the world championship that he had lost in 1974 to Muhammad Ali. Recently, Arum promoted the Hasim Rahman–James ("Lights Out") Toney WBC heavyweight championship fight on March 18, 2006, at Boardwalk Hall in Atlantic City.

Oscar de la Hoya expanded his role in the boxing world remarkably when, at age 29, the six-time world championship fighter formed Golden Boy Promotions. Golden Boy is the first major Hispanic-owned promotional company, and it quickly achieved great success in organizing profitable boxing events. Ironically, among the fighters that the firm promotes are some stars who fought de la Hoya in the ring, such as Shane Mosely and Bernard Hopkins.

The modern era of boxing has seen fragmentation of the direct lineage of champions with a proliferation of weight classes and titles. The number of fully contested weight divisions has more than doubled, from eight to seventeen, and the number of sanctioning bodies has grown dramatically.

As the new century began, some highly skilled boxers were already claiming their places in history. Roy Jones Jr. thoroughly dominated the light heavyweight class for years until the inevitable changing of the guard occurred with his two defeats at the hands of Antonio Tarver. Sugar Shane Mosley, Bernard Hopkins, Erik Morales, and Felix Trinidad are now winding down their impressive careers. In 2006, some of the best pound-for-pound boxers are middleweights Winky Wright and Jermain Taylor, welterweight Floyd Mayweather Jr., junior welterweights Ricky Hatton and Jose Luis Castillo, and super featherweights Manny Pacquiao and Marco Antonio Barrera.

While interest in boxing may now be at a relatively low point, the success and critical acclaim of the motion pictures *Million Dollar Baby* and *Cinderella Man*, as well as the popularity of the boxing television show *The Contender*, may point to an increase in boxing fans in the near future. It is also possible that some of the current interest in ultimate fighting contests will translate into increased interest in the true sport of boxing. Similarly, it is likely that women's boxing will attract new fans with such competitors as Laila Ali, Alicia Ashley, and Ann Wolfe.

Like so many other fields of interest, boxing benefits immeasurably from the power of the Internet. Many excellent boxing websites provide a wealth of easily accessible information and opinion for fight fans. Noteworthy examples include www.fightnews.com, www.boxingtalk.com, www.maxboxing.com, www.secondsout.com, www.doghouseboxing.com, www.boxingtimes.com, and www.cyberboxingzone.com. Especially impressive is the huge boxing information database that is being created at www.boxrec.com.

MUHAMMAD ALI
The Louisville Lip; The Greatest

HEAVYWEIGHT

Right-handed; 6'3"; 186–236 lbs.

61 bouts, 10/29/1960 to 12/11/1981

Managers: Bill Faversham, Angelo Dundee, Herbert Muhammad

1960 Olympic Light Heavyweight Gold Medalist

Heavyweight Champion 1964–67, 1974–78, 1978–79

Hall of Fame Induction: 1990

Born: 1/17/1942, Louisville, KY

Named: Cassius Marcellus Clay, Jr.

In all of boxing history, Muhammad Ali stands alone. In early boasts, he called himself "The Greatest," and by the time his storied career came to an end, most fight fans agreed. Ali had also become the best-known athlete in the world and, very possibly, the best-loved as well.

Cassius Clay—who used his birth name until he became a Black Muslim in 1964—grew up in a quiet black neighborhood of Louisville, Kentucky. He was a popular student in high school, where his stunning self-confidence made him noteworthy even then. He had been focussed on boxing since he was twelve and trained with the single-mindedness of a future champion. He started boxing at the amateur level in his

Ali (R) springs from the ropes to knock out George Foreman and regain the heavyweight championship in the eighth round of the 1974 "Rumble in the Jungle." Foreman recovered the crown twenty years later.

IN THE RING	WON 56	LOST 5	DRAWS 0	TB 61	KO 37	W 19	WF 0	D 0	KO'd 1	L 4	LF 0

Date	Opponent	Site	Result / Rounds		Title	Wt.
1960						
Oct 29	Tunney Hunsaker	Louisville, KY	W	6	—	192
Dec 27	Herbert Siler	Miami	KO	4	—	190
1961						
Jan 17	Anthony Sperti	Miami	TKO	3	—	195
Feb 7	Jimmy Robinson	Miami	TKO	1	—	193
Feb 21	Donnie Fleeman	Miami	TKO	7	—	190
Apr 19	Lamar Clark	Louisville	KO	2	—	192
Jun 26	Duke Sabwedong	Las Vegas	W	10	—	194
Jul 22	Alonzo Johnson	Louisville	W	10	—	192
Oct 7	⑩ Alex Miteff	Louisville	TKO	6	—	188
Nov 29	Willi Besmanoff	Louisville	TKO	7	—	193
1962						
Feb 10	Lucian Banks	New York	TKO	4	—	194
Feb 28	Jack Wagner	Miami	TKO	4	—	195
Apr 23	George Logan	Miami	TKO	4	—	196
May 19	⑩ Billy Daniels	New York	TKO	7	—	196
Jul 20	⑩ Alejandro Lavorante	Los Angeles	KO	5	—	199
Nov 15	⑩ Archie Moore★	Los Angeles	TKO	4	—	204
1963						
Jan 24	Charles Powell	Pittsburgh	KO	3	—	205
Mar 13	⑩ Doug Jones	New York	W	10	—	202
Jun 18	Henry Cooper	London	TKO	5	—	207
1964						
Feb 25	♛ Sonny Liston★	Miami	TKO	7	Won-World-H	210
1965						
May 25	⑩ Sonny Liston★	Lewiston, ME	KO	1	Ret-World-H	206
Nov 22	⑩ Floyd Patterson★	Las Vegas	TKO	12	Ret-World-H	210
1966						
Mar 29	⑩ George Chuvalo	Toronto	W	15	Ret-World-H	214
May 21	Henry Cooper	London	TKO	6	Ret-World-H	201
Aug 6	⑩ Brian London	London	TKO	3	Ret-World-H	209
Sep 10	⑩ Karl Mildenberger	Frankfurt, Germany	TKO	12	Ret-World-H	203
Nov 14	Cleveland Williams	Houston	TKO	3	Ret-World-H	210
1967						
Feb 6	♛ Ernie Terrell	New York	W	15	Ret-World-H	212
Mar 22	⑩ Zora Folley	New York	TKO	7	Ret-World-H	211
1970						
Oct 26	⑩ Jerry Quarry	Atlanta	TKO	3	—	213
Dec 7	⑩ Oscar Bonavena	New York	TKO	15	—	212
1971						
Mar 8	♛ Joe Frazier★	New York	L	15	For-World-H	215
Jul 26	⑩ Jimmy Ellis	Houston	TKO	12	Won-Vac NABF-H	220
Nov 17	Buster Mathis	Houston	W	12	Ret-NABF-H	227
Dec 26	Jurgen Blin	Zurich, Switzerland	KO	7	—	226
1972						
Apr 1	⑩ McArthur Foster	Tokyo	W	15	—	226
May 1	George Chuvalo	Vancouver, B.C.	W	12	Ret-NABF-H	217
Jun 27	⑩ Jerry Quarry	Las Vegas	TKO	7	Ret-NABF-H	216

Date		Opponent	Location	Result	Round	Title	Weight
Jul 19		Alvin Lewis	Dublin	TKO	11	—	217
Sep 20	⑩	Floyd Patterson ★	New York	TKO	7	Ret-NABF-H	218
Nov 21	♛	Bob Foster ★	Stateline, NV	KO	8	Ret-NABF-H	221
1973							
Feb 14	⑩	Joe Bugner	Las Vegas	W	12	—	217
Mar 31	⑩	Ken Norton ★	San Diego	L	12	Lost-NABF-H	221
Sep 10	⑩	Ken Norton ★	Inglewood, CA	W	12	Reg-NABF-H	212
Oct 20		Rudy Lubbers	Jakarta, Indonesia	W	12	—	217
1974							
Jan 28	⑩	Joe Frazier ★	New York	W	12	Ret-NABF-H	215
Oct 30	♛	George Foreman ★	Kinshasa, Zaire	KO	8	Reg-World-H	216
1975							
Mar 24	⑩	Chuck Wepner	Cleveland	TKO	15	Ret-World-H	223
May 16	⑩	Ron Lyle	Las Vegas	TKO	11	Ret-World-H	224
Jul 1	⑩	Joe Bugner	Kuala Lumpur, Malaysia	W	15	Ret-World-H	224
Oct 1	⑩	Joe Frazier ★	Quezon, Philippines	TKO	14	Ret-World-H	224
1976							
Feb 20		Jean Coopman	San Juan, PR	KO	5	Ret-World-H	226
Apr 30	⑩	Jimmy Young	Landover, MD	W	15	Ret-World-H	230
May 24		Richard Dunn	Munich, Germany	TKO	5	Ret-World-H	220
Sep 28	⑩	Ken Norton ★	New York	W	15	Ret-World-H	221
1977							
May 16	⑩	Alfredo Evangelista	Landover	W	15	Ret-World-H	221
Sep 29	⑩	Ernie Shavers	New York	W	15	Ret-World-H	225
1978							
Feb 15	⑩	Leon Spinks	Las Vegas	L	15	Lost-World-H	225
Sep 15	♛	Leon Spinks	New Orleans	W	15	Reg-World (WBA)-H	221
1980							
Oct 2	♛	Larry Holmes	Las Vegas	TKO'd	11	For-Vac World (WBC)-H	217
1981							
Dec 11	⑩	Trevor Berbick	Nassau, Bahamas	L	10	—	236

hometown and captured the AAU and Golden Gloves titles in 1959 and 1960. He competed in the 1960 Olympics in Rome, where he won a gold medal in the light heavyweight division.

Ali first boxed professionally in 1960, at age eighteen, with a win over a boxer named Tunney Hunsaker. In subsequent early bouts, it was quickly apparent that Ali possessed unbelievable hand and foot speed for someone his size. As he developed, he displayed a stinging jab and a strong right hand. Ali liked to hold his hands low and evade punches to the head by simply bobbing out of harm's way.

The brash young fighter's knack for self-promotion nearly rivalled his ring skills. He mugged for the cameras, talked in rhymes, and boasted that he was not only the greatest, but also the prettiest of all time. He began to predict, with unnerving accuracy, the round in which he would stop opponents ("They all fall/In the round I call"). In a time when interest in boxing had waned, Ali dramatically revitalized the sport. He was a one-man show, full of swagger and contempt, and the press and public embraced him.

Ali proved over and over, with great talent and boxing intelligence, that he was much more than an entertaining huckster. In 1961, he knocked out Alex Miteff, who had been considered a top contender the previous year. In 1962 and

A vital aspect of Ali's speed, besides his fancy footwork, was his remarkable ability to dodge punches by bending and twisting his torso. Here he eludes the mighty Sonny Liston en route to taking the title.

1963, he defeated such daunting adversaries as George Logan, Billy Daniels, Archie Moore, Doug Jones, and Henry Cooper.

Having emerged as the top heavyweight contender, Ali faced the formidable Sonny Liston for the world championship in 1964. Many observers gave Ali little chance against big, bad Liston. But Ali dominated the fight and, though nearly blinded for two rounds by a foreign substance used by Liston's corner (perhaps liniment or a coagulant applied to a cut and then transferred to Liston's gloves), he won when Liston refused to answer the bell for the seventh round, claiming an injured shoulder. After the victory, Ali announced that he had become a member of the Nation of Islam, the Black Muslim religion, and had changed his name.

Ali's conversion upset some fans. The jokester had gotten serious about race and politics. It cost him some popularity and probably, though never acknowledged, influenced his future as a titleholder. When Ali agreed to give Liston a return match, the WBA took the title away—ostensibly because the rematch contract was a violation of WBA rules. Ali continued to be outspoken, particularly in statements against the Vietnam War. It wasn't until his February, 6, 1967, victory over WBA pretender to the throne Ernie Terrell that Ali was again universally recognized as heavyweight champion.

In his second fight with Liston, Ali triumphed in one round, apparently using his famed "anchor punch." As with the first Liston fight, this rematch was shrouded in controversy. Some thought that Liston took a dive. After flooring Liston, Ali did not immediately move to a neutral corner. Liston eventually rose from the can-

vas and the fight resumed. It was only when Nat Fleischer, editor of *The Ring,* shouted from ringside that Liston had been down for at least a count of ten, that referee Jersey Joe Walcott stopped the fight.

Ali's refusal, on religious grounds, to accept induction into the armed forces caused him to be stripped of his undisputed world title in 1967. Furthermore, Ali faced imprisonment for his action and was barred from

People around the world responded positively to Muhammad Ali's expressive face, charismatic personality, and shameless self-promotion.

boxing while his case was litigated. He called himself "The People's Champion" and continued to be recognized as the world heavyweight titleholder in Great Britain and Japan. Ultimately, in June 1971, the U.S. Supreme Court ruled in Ali's favor, after he returned to the ring in an October 1970 conquest over Jerry Quarry.

In his last fights before his banishment, Ali had combined stylish footwork with great punching power. Most experts concede that upon his return, the older, slightly heavier fighter was not quite the equal of the 1967 Ali. Ali met the new champion, Joe Frazier, in the "Fight of the Century" in Madison Square Garden in 1971. In an extremely hard-fought battle, Frazier won the decision, handing Ali his first defeat. In one of the greatest series in ring history, the two met twice more in battles of strength, skill, and courage, with Ali emerging as the victor both times. Ali scored a technical knockout over Frazier in their final bout, called the "Thrilla in Manila" and considered by many to be one of the greatest fights of all time.

Ali reclaimed the heavyweight championship in 1974 when he knocked out the previously unbeaten George Foreman. Dubbed the "Rumble in the Jungle," the match was held in Kinshasa, Zaire. Ali used his "rope-a-dope" strategy in which he leaned against the ropes and allowed Foreman to punch himself out. After Foreman tired, Ali knocked him out.

Ali lost his title to the unproven Leon Spinks in 1978, but reclaimed it in the rematch later that same year. He then announced his retirement only to make ill-fated comeback attempts against Larry Holmes and Trevor Berbick. Plagued by ill health in retirement, Ali remains a respected public figure.

Ali courageously fought for eleven rounds with a broken jaw on March 31, 1973, in San Diego, when Ken Norton handed him his second career loss. Ali won their rematch six months later.

SAMMY ANGOTT
The Clutch

LIGHTWEIGHT

Right-handed; 5'8"; 128–155 lbs.
133 bouts, 3/9/1935 to 8/8/1950
Manager: Charlie Jones
Lightweight Champion 1941–42
NBA Lightweight Champion
1940–41, 1943–44
Hall of Fame Induction: 1998
Born: 1/17/1915, Washington, PA
Named: Salvatore Engotti
Died: 10/22/1980

A tough, scrappy fighter who held his own with Hall of Famers Willie Pep, Henry Armstrong, and Beau Jack, Sammy Angott seldom scored knockouts but twice captured the lightweight title.

Reared in Washington, Pennsylvania, as Salvatore Engotti, Angott won his first professional bout in 1935 at the age of twenty. By 1938 he was ready to challenge Leo Rodak, the top-ranked featherweight. In the first of three matches held in Pittsburgh, Rodak outfought Angott to take a ten-round decision. In the rematch, Angott dramatically avenged his defeat with a first-round knockout and, in the third match, Angott won a ten-round decision. As 1940 dawned, Angott's career was solidly established and *The Ring* rated him the second-best lightweight contender.

The next year, Angott met Davey Day for the vacant NBA lightweight title, previously held by Lou Ambers. The fight was in Angott's adopted home base of Louisville the night before the Kentucky Derby. Former heavyweight champ Jack Dempsey, the referee and sole judge of the fight, awarded the decision to Angott.

The new champion fought only non-title fights for the next year and a half. In his most notable battles, he defeated Bob Montgomery but lost to the heavier Fritzie Zivic and a young Sugar Ray Robinson. In late 1941, Angott successfully defended his title against Lew Jenkins in New York before 11,346 fans. Jenkins, who had defeated Ambers, held the New York version of the world title. Angott dominated with ease but never went for the knockout. The crowd, disappointed in both fighters, booed constantly from the sixth round on.

Angott started 1942 with a non-title decision over Montgomery in Madison Square Garden. Uncharacteristically, Angott abandoned his cautious approach and slugged it out with Montgomery, knocking him down in the ninth. Four months later, the pair met again at Shibe Park in Philadelphia, before a crowd of 16,000. Angott started fast and held off a furious rally by Montgomery to win a narrow split decision.

Between the Montgomery bouts, Angott fended off Allie Stolz, winning a hotly contested split decision. After another loss to Robinson and a win over Aldo Spoldi, Angott surprised the boxing world by announcing his retirement, at the age of 27, to work in a steel mill to support the war effort. Angott also told reporters that his right hand was injured and had not responded to treatment.

Even so, Angott returned to the ring on March 19, 1943, with a non-title win over the previously undefeated featherweight champion Willie Pep. Later that

IN THE RING	WON 98	LOST 27	DRAWS 8	TB 134	KO 23	W 75	WF 0	D 8	KO'd 1	L 27	LF 0

Date	Opponent	Site	Result / Rounds		Title	Wt.
1935						
Mar 9	Tony Marengo	New York	W	4	—	130
Apr 23	Long SinQue	New York	KO	2	—	129
Apr 30	Charlie Vaughn	New York	W	6	—	128
May 14	Al Gillette	New York	W	6	—	129
Jun 26	Jimmy Ferry	Washington, PA	KO	1	—	—
Jul 22	Jackie Wilson	Pittsburgh	L	6	—	131
Nov 25	Al Farone	Pittsburgh	W	6	—	—
Dec 31	Dick Cabello	New York	W	6	—	137
1936						
Jan 14	Eddie Hannon	New York	W	6	—	130
Mar 11	Solly Ambrosso	New York	W	6	—	132
Mar 25	Leonard Del Genio	New York	L	8	—	130
May 5	Johnny Morro	New York	D	8	—	132
May 14	Bobby Dean	Washington, DC	L	6	—	128
Jun 2	Joe Boscarino	New York	W	10	—	130
Jun 17	Lee Sheppard	Pittsburgh	L	10	—	—
Jun 22	Eddie McGeever	New York	L	8	—	130
Jul 14	Victor Vallee	New York	W	6	—	126
Jul 30	Billy Miller	Pittsburgh	W	6	—	127
Aug 10	Harry Krause	Pittsburgh	W	10	—	—
Aug 24	Tommy Spiegal	Millvale, PA	L	8	—	129
Sep 10	Harry Krause	Pittsburgh	W	10	—	128
Sep 14	Lee Sheppard	Millvale, PA	KO	4	—	—
Sep 29	Lee Sheppard	Pittsburgh	KO	4	—	128
Oct 12	Lee Sheppard	Pittsburgh	L	10	—	130
Nov 23	Harry Krause	Pittsburgh	L	8	—	133
Dec 7	Lloyd Pine	Louisville, KY	W	10	—	127
1937						
Feb 22	Johnny Hutchinson	Pittsburgh	L	8	—	—
Mar 8	Lloyd Pine	Louisville	D	10	—	128
Mar 22	Dave Barry	Louisville	W	10	—	129
Apr 18	Jimmy Buckler	Louisville	W	10	—	—
May 10	Louis Gallop	Chicago	TKO	4	—	130
May 17	George Feist	Chicago	W	6	—	127
Jun 3	Pete Lello	Chicago	TKO	5	—	—
Jun 14	Lloyd Pine	Chicago	W	10	—	129
Jun 18	Roger Bernard	Milwaukee	W	10	—	128
Jul 12	Jimmy Christy	Chicago	W	10	—	131
Aug 12	Everett Rightmire	Milwaukee	W	10	—	130
Aug 23	Jimmy Christy	Chicago	W	10	—	132
Sep 20	Billy Marquart	Chicago	L	8	—	131
Oct 18	Johnny Pena	Chicago	W	10	—	131
Oct 25	Jimmy Vaughn	Louisville	W	10	—	130
Nov 8	Wishy Jones	Louisville	W	10	—	132
Nov 16	Billy Marquart	Chicago	L	8	—	128
Dec 6	Lew Massey	Louisville	W	10	—	133
1938						
Feb 7	Harvey Woods	Chicago	W	8	—	133
Feb 25	Everett Simmington	Chicago	W	8	—	—

Date		Opponent	Location	Result	Rounds	Notes	Weight
Mar 22		Jackie Wilson	Milwaukee	W	10	—	132
May 6	⑩	Wesley Ramey	Louisville	W	10	—	—
May 23		Frankie Covelli	Chicago	W	10	—	135
Jun 1		Irving Eldridge	Pittsburgh	W	10	—	133
Jun 28		Tommy Spiegal	Pittsburgh	W	10	—	132
Jul 25		Leo Rodak	Pittsburgh	L	10	—	130
Aug 8		Nick Camarata	Chicago	W	10	—	132
Aug 15		Leo Rodak	Pittsburgh	KO	1	—	130
Sep 2		Wishy Jones	Louisville	W	10	—	—
Sep 16	⑩	Wesley Ramey	Dallas	W	10	—	133
Sep 27		Leo Rodak	Pittsburgh	W	10	—	132
Oct 7		Lloyd Pine	Louisville	W	10	—	—
Nov 14		Norment Quarles	New Orleans	W	10	—	135
Dec 5		Freddie Miller★	Louisville	W	10	—	133
1939							
Jan 23		Joey Ferrando	Pittsburgh	KO	10	—	133
Jan 30		Eddie Brink	Pittsburgh	KO	5	—	135
Apr 14	⑩	Aldo Spoldi	York, PA	W	10	—	134
May 3		Milton Aron	Chicago	W	10	—	135
Jun 26		Howard Scott	Louisville	W	10	—	136
Jul 17	⑩	Petey Sarron	Pittsburgh	W	10	—	137
Aug 28		Billy Marquart	Pittsburgh	W	10	—	133
Oct 6	⑩	Davey Day	Chicago	W	10	—	135
Nov 3	⑩	Baby Arizmendi★	Chicago	W	10	—	135
Dec 8	⑩	Davey Day	Chicago	L	12	—	134
1940							
Feb 2	⑩	Pete Lello	New York	D	10	—	134
Mar 1		Baby Boy Breese	Milwaukee	W	10	—	138
May 3	⑩	Davey Day	Louisville	W	15	Won-Vac NBA-L	134
Jun 25		Baby Arizmendi★	Los Angeles	D	10	—	139
Jul 24		Nick Castiglione	Chicago	W	10	—	135
Aug 28		Fritzie Zivic★	Pittsburgh	L	10	—	137
Nov 4		George Latka	San Francisco	D	10	—	140
Nov 25	⑩	Bob Montgomery★	Philadelphia	W	10	—	137
Dec 18		Don Eddy	Miami	W	10	—	140
1941							
May 2		Dave Castilloux	Louisville	W	12	—	137
May 19		Lenny Mancini	Cleveland	W	10	—	138
Jun 1		Lloyd Pine	Chicago	W	10	—	—
Jun 24		Henry Hurst	Toronto	W	10	—	137
Jul 21		Sugar Ray Robinson★	Philadelphia	L	10	—	136
Aug 12		Jimmy Tygh	Pittsburgh	KO	3	—	136
Sep 8		Pete Galiano	Washington, PA	KO	6	—	135
Sep 19		Lee Sheppard	Akron, OH	KO	1	—	138
Oct 30		Chino Lopez	Pittsburgh	KO	6	—	138
Dec 19	♛	Lew Jenkins★	New York	W	15	Won-World-L	133
1942							
Mar 6	⑩	Bob Montgomery★	New York	W	12	—	139
May 15		Allie Stolz	New York	W	15	Ret-World-L	134
Jul 7	⑩	Bob Montgomery★	Philadelphia	W	12	—	139
Jul 31	⑩	Sugar Ray Robinson★	New York	L	10	—	139
Sep 28		Aldo Spoldi	New Orleans	W	10	—	139
1943							
Mar 19	♛	Willie Pep★	New York	W	10	—	134
Jun 11	⑩	Henry Armstrong★	New York	L	10	—	138

Date		Opponent	Location	Result	Rounds		Weight
Oct 1	⑩	Joey Peralta	Detroit	W	10	—	138
Oct 27	⑩	Luther White	Los Angeles	W	15	Won-Vac-NBA-L	134
Dec 17		Bobby Ruffin	New York	W	10	—	137
1944							
Jan 28	⑩	Beau Jack★	New York	D	10	—	140
Mar 8	⑩	Juan Zurita	Hollywood	L	15	Lost-NBA-L	135
Apr 4		Aaron Perry	Washington, DC	W	10	—	141
Jun 7	⑩	Ike Williams★	Philadelphia	L	10	—	140
Aug 1		Aaron Perry	Washington, DC	W	12	—	143
Sep 6	⑩	Ike Williams★	Philadelphia	L	10	—	140
Nov 10		Jimmy McDaniels	New York	L	10	—	144
1945							
Aug 20		Gene Burton	Pittsburgh	D	10	—	142
Sep 19	⑩	Ike Williams★	Pittsburgh	KO	6	—	140
Oct 24		Danny Kapilow	Washington, DC	W	10	—	143
Dec 10		Danny Kapilow	Pittsburgh	W	10	—	142
1946							
Mar 4	⑩	Sugar Ray Robinson★	Pittsburgh	L	10	—	143
Jul 8	⑩	Beau Jack★	Washington, DC	KO'd	7	—	143
1947							
Feb 17		George Dixon	Wheeling, OH	TKO	1	—	144
Feb 24		John Bryant	Canton, OH	KO	5	—	145
Feb 27		Jackie McFarland	Mansfield, OH	KO	2	—	146
Mar 14		Nick Castiglione	Chicago	KO	4	—	143
Mar 24		Teddy Davis	Wheeling, OH	TKO	3	—	144
Apr 9		Cal Elphante	Zanesville, OH	KO	3	—	145
May 16	⑩	Johnny Bratton	Chicago	W	10	—	143
1948							
Feb 17		Eddie Pusey	Louisville	KO	2	—	145
Mar 15		Rudy Zadell	Cumberland, KY	W	10	—	140
Jun 11		Buster Miles	Huntington, WV	W	10	—	145
1949							
Mar 3		Johnny Bryant	Clarksburg, VA	KO	2	—	147
Aug 5		Billy Suddeth	Topeka, KS	W	10	—	142
Oct 19		Don Williams	Worcester, MA	L	10	—	143
Dec 12		Tony Riccio	Newark, NJ	L	10	—	146
1950							
Jan 2	⑩	Sonny West	Baltimore	D	10	—	139
Jan 23		Clem Custer	Baltimore	KO	8	—	143
Feb 20		Ralph Zanelli	Providence, RI	W	10	—	145
Mar 20	⑩	Sonny West	Baltimore	L	10	—	144
May 10		John Davis	Oakland, CA	L	10	—	144
Jun 22		Tim Dalton	Davenport, IA	W	10	—	143
Jun 26		Kid Azteca	El Paso, TX	W	10	—	—
Aug 8	⑩	Sonny West	Detroit	L	10	—	—

year Angott reclaimed the vacant NBA lightweight title with a decision over Slugger White in the baseball stadium of the Pacific Coast League Hollywood Stars. The next year, Angott lost his title in a fifteen-round decision to Juan Zurita. This was Angott's last title bout.

Angott moved up to welterweight and was a ranked contender in that class in 1944 and 1945. He continued to fight through 1950. In retirement, Angott lent his fame to many charitable activities and worked for a manufacturing plant in Canton, Ohio. He died in 1980 after suffering a blood clot on the brain.

FRED APOSTOLI
Boxing Bellhop

MIDDLEWEIGHT

Right-handed; 5'9½"; 154–170 lbs.

72 bouts, 10/8/1934 to 12/1/1948

Managers: Joe Niderost, Larry White, Whitey Bimstein

NY World Middleweight Champion 1938–39

Hall of Fame Induction: 2003

Born: 2/2/1913, San Francisco, CA

Named: Dan Apostoli

Died: 11/29/1973

Apostoli was born in San Francisco on February 2, 1913. He had a hard childhood: his mother died when he was seven, and his father could not care for Apostoli and his three siblings. The children first went to live with their grandmother, and subsequently to orphanages, where Apostoli first boxed.

When he was fifteen, he left the orphanage to live on a chicken ranch in Occidental, California. After a year at the ranch, Apostoli moved back to San Francisco to live with his father who had remarried. Apostoli attended school and worked as a hod carrier. In 1931, he quit school. He worked as a plasterer and then for a jeweler. When the jeweler learned that Apostoli was interested in boxing, he put his employee in touch with another jeweler, Joe Niderost. Niderost was commissioner of the Olympic Boxing Club. He helped Apostoli obtain a membership in the club where he joined the boxing team. Apostoli received formal boxing instruction from the club's coach, Spider Roche, but he didn't have much success initially in the ring and left the club after a year.

Jobless, Apostoli then signed up for the National Guard. At camp he joined the boxing and baseball teams. He tasted his first success in the ring when he won the 139-pound camp championship. After leaving the Guard, Apostoli got a job as freight elevator operator at the St. Francis Hotel in San Francisco through the efforts of Niderost. He later was promoted to bellhop, leading to his nickname "The Boxing Bellhop." In 1933, Apostoli, once again a member of the Olympic Club, won the amateur welterweight championship of the Pacific Coast. The next year, he won the Golden Gloves middleweight championship. That title enabled him to fight in the AAU Nationals, where he also triumphed. As a reward for winning this title, the hotel promoted him to bell captain!

Apostoli turned professional on October 8, 1934, with a third-round knockout over a veteran fighter, Gilbert Attell. Apostoli won his next five fights before Niderost, his advisor, and Roche, his trainer,

In July and August 1947, Apostoli (L) twice defeated Cowboy Reuben Shank in bouts at San Francisco's Civic Auditorium—once by TKO and once by decision.

IN THE RING	WON 61	LOST 10	DRAWS 1	TB 72	KO 31	W 30	WF 0	D 1	KO'd 4	L 6	LF 0

Date		Opponent	Site	Result / Rounds		Title	Wt.
1934							
Oct 8		Gilbert Attell	San Francisco	KO	3		157
Nov 12		Jackie Riley	San Francisco	KO	1		157
Nov 30		Eddie Daniels	San Francisco	KO	2		158
1935							
Jan 7		Eddie Fox	San Francisco	KO	5		158
Jan 28		Andy Di Vodi	San Francisco	W	6		155
Feb 22		Newsboy Millich	San Francisco	KO	4		156
Apr 1	ⓦ	Freddie Steele★	San Francisco	KO'd	10		157
May 31		Indian Mike Payan	San Francisco	W	10		157
Jul 17		Eddie Schneider	San Francisco	KO	1		157
Jul 31		Dick Foster	San Francisco	KO	6		157
Aug 14		Rudy Mendez	San Francisco	W	8		157
Oct 4		Young Stuhley	San Francisco	W	10		157
Oct 25		Babe Marino	San Francisco	W	10		155
Nov 27		Swede Berglund	San Francisco	W	10		160
1936							
Jan 20		Frankie Britt	San Francisco	W	10		154
Feb 28	ⓦ	Paul Pirrone	San Francisco	KO	7		161
Apr 6		Young Stuhley	San Francisco	W	10		160
May 8	ⓦ	Eddie ("Babe") Risko	San Francisco	W	10		162
Aug 21		Marty Simmons	San Francisco	W	10		160
Oct 9	ⓦ	Lou Brouillard	San Francisco	W	10		157
Dec 14		Babe Marino	San Francisco	W	10		155
1937							
Jan 27	ⓦ	Ken Overlin	New York	L	10		155
Feb 17	ⓦ	Solly Krieger	New York	W	10		160
Mar 15		Joe Lynch	Newark, NJ	TKO	9		160
Apr 14	ⓦ	Solly Krieger	New York	TKO	5		159
Jun 11		Dale Sparr	San Francisco	W	10		157
Jun 22		Tommy Jones	Portland, OR	KO	2		159
Sep 23	♛	Marcel Thil★	New York	TKO	10		159
Oct 25		Tony Celli	Philadelphia	TKO	2		162
1938							
Jan 7	♛	Freddie Steele★	New York	KO	9		161
Feb 4	ⓦ	Glen Lee	New York	W	12		158
Feb 22	ⓦ	Young Corbett III★	San Francisco	L	10		159
Apr 1	ⓦ	Glen Lee	New York	W	15		160
Sep 6		Indian Mike Payan	San Francisco	KO	2		160
Sep 16		Joe Lynch	San Francisco	KO	2		161
Nov 18	♛	Young Corbett III★	New York	TKO	8	Won-Vac NY World-M	159
Dec 20		Al Cocozza	New Haven, CT	KO	4		161
1939							
Jan 6	ⓦ	Billy Conn★	New York	L	10		160
Feb 10	ⓦ	Billy Conn★	New York	L	15		161
Apr 17		George Nichols	Houston	KO	2		162
May 1		Erich Seelig	Cleveland	W	10		159
Aug 7		Mohammed Fahmy	Springfield, MA	TKO	3		164
Aug 28		Glen Lee	Pittsburgh	W	10		160

Date		Opponent	Location	Result	Rounds	Notes	Weight
Oct 2	Ⓦ	Ceferino Garcia	New York	KO'd	7	Lost-NY World-M	160
1940							
Jan 5	Ⓦ	Melio Bettina	New York	W	12		169
Feb 2	Ⓦ	Melio Bettina	New York	TKO'	12		170
Jul 22		Dale Sparr	San Francisco	KO	5		162
Aug 19		Willard Hogue	San Francisco	W	10		160
Sep 16		Bobby Pacho	San Francisco	W	10		162
Nov 19	♔	Tony Zale★	Seattle	L	10		163
1941							
Aug 21		Bill McDowell	Norfolk, VA	KO	2		158
Sep 15		Joey Spangler	Norfolk	KO	5		156
Oct 14		Ed Brookman	Washington, DC	TKO	6		159
1942							
Mar 7		Augie Arellano	Brooklyn, NY	TKO	5		160
Apr 4		Joe Mulli	Brooklyn	TKO	1		160
Jun 6	Ⓦ	Ken Overlin	Norfolk	D	10		160
Aug 24		Saverio Turiello	Norfolk	W	10		157
1946							
Aug 12		Pedro Jimenez	San Francisco	KO	4		158
Aug 27		Richard Rangel	Sacramento, CA	W	10		157
Sep 9		Dencio Cabanella	San Francisco	KO	7		159
Sep 20		George Duke	San Francisco	KO	9		157
Oct 21		Tommy Egan	San Francisco	W	10		155
Nov 18		Frank Angustain	San Francisco	W	10		160
Dec 11		Paul Lewis	Oakland	W	10		159
1947							
Feb 28		Bobby Volk	San Francisco	TKO'	1		156
Apr 7		Bobby Volk	San Francisco	KO	3		160
May 2		George Duke	Las Manos, CA	W	10		157
May 21		Earl Turner	Oakland	W	10		157
Jul 14		Reuben Shank	San Francisco	TKO	8		161
Aug 25		Reuben Shank	San Francisco	W	10		160
Nov 17		Georgie Abrams	San Francisco	W	10		162
1948							
Dec 1		Earl Turner	Oakland	L	10		159

made a poor decision to put Apostoli in the ring with Freddie Steele. Experienced Steele had 53 pro bouts, including some against very tough fighters. For the first six rounds the fight was even. Then Apostoli, who had never gone more than six rounds, started to wilt. In the ninth round, he fell to the canvas twice without being hit. The referee stopped the fight in the tenth for Apostoli's first career loss.

Larry White, who previously had managed Young Corbett III, soon replaced Niderost as Apostoli's manager. Apostoli won his remaining seven fights in 1935. In 1936, he won all seven of his fights, including victories over formidable contenders Paul Pirrone, Babe Risko, and Lou Brouillard.

On January 27, 1937, Apostoli fought outside his hometown for the first time when he went to New York to meet Ken Overlin, a future middleweight champion. Overlin upset Apostoli to earn a majority decision, though the fight could have gone either way. Staying in New York, Apostoli rebounded to beat another future middleweight champion, Solly Krieger, on February 17, 1937. The two fighters went toe to toe with Apostoli showing that he was the better, sharper, and faster puncher. Apostoli earned a unanimous decision.

On September 23, 1937, Apostoli earned a place on the famed Carnival of Champions card staged by Mike Jacobs at the Polo Grounds in which four champions fought. Apostoli faced European world middleweight champion Marcel Thil. New York would only sanction the bout if Thil agreed that his title would not be at issue. Jacobs made sure of that by prevailing upon both Thil and Apostoli to come in over the weight limit. In the ninth round, an Apostoli left opened an inch-long gash above Thil's right eye. Apostoli focused on the gash until the referee stopped the fight in the tenth. By this point, *The Ring* considered Apostoli the best middleweight in the world, though he did not have a title.

On January 7, 1938, Apostoli fought a non-title rematch with Steele who was now the NBA and New York middleweight champion. Before 10,000 in Madison Square Garden, Apostoli took the action to Steele. In an exciting fight, Apostoli triumphed in the ninth round when he unleashed an estimated 165 punches, forcing the referee to call a halt to the action. The New York State Athletic Commission ordered Steele to defend his title against Apostoli. When Steele refused, he was stripped of the title. Apostoli decisioned Glen Lee in his next bout and then dropped a decision to Hall of Famer Young Corbett III back home in San Francisco in the Seals baseball stadium before approximately 15,000 spectators.

After Apostoli again defeated Lee, he earned recognition as the world middleweight champion in Europe, in New York, and in some other states. In his rematch with Corbett for the title, Apostoli knocked Corbett down three times before the fight was stopped in the eighth. On January 6, 1939, Hall of Famer Billy Conn, who outweighed Apostoli by seven and one-half pounds, scored an upset in a fast-moving non-title bout that lasted the ten-round distance. In the rematch one month later before a capacity crowd of 18,988 in Madison Square Garden, Conn again took the decision in a non-title bout.

On October 2, 1939, Apostoli lost any claim to the middleweight title when Ceferino Garcia knocked him out in the seventh round with a barrage of rights and lefts to the head, culminating with a right to the jaw that put Apostoli down for the count. Apostoli would never again challenge for a championship belt.

Apostoli saw combat in World War II and was honored by *The Ring* as Boxing's Man of the Year for 1943. After the war, Apostoli resumed his boxing career back in his native California. He won thirteen of fourteen fights before he lost a decision to Earl Turner on December 1, 1948. Apostoli had a successful career in retirement. He worked as a referee and as an advertising executive. He died of a heart attack on November 29, 1973. He left his mark as a courageous fighter who could take a punch as well as deliver punishment.

Apostoli served in the Navy in World War II, first as a physical instructor and then as a gun captain in the Pacific

ALEXIS ARGUELLO
Flaco de Explosivo

LIGHTWEIGHT

Right-handed; 5'10"; 122–143 lbs.
88 bouts, 8/1/1968 to 1/21/1995
Manager: Bill Miller
WBA Featherwt. Champ 1974–77
WBC Super Featherwt. Champ 1978–80
WBC Lightwt. Champ 1981–83
Hall of Fame Induction: 1992
Born: 4/19/1952, Managua,

The first Nicaraguan to be inducted into the Hall of Fame, Alexis Arguello transcended poverty and political strife in his home country to hold titles in three different weight classes during his long career. Arguello was a master offensive boxer and tactician who could adapt his fighting to take advantage of his opponents' weaknesses. He would wait patiently for an opening and then strike with damaging accuracy. Of his 80 professional victories, 64 were knockouts.

A street fighter as a youth, Arguello learned ring basics from a brother-in-law in Managua and quickly parlayed his skills into an escape from his hardscrabble life. When his family's poverty forced him to leave school at fourteen to work on a dairy farm, Arguello dedicated himself to boxing. After a year of amateur fighting, he turned pro in 1968 at age sixteen. Fighting exclusively in Nicaragua in the early stages of his career, Arguello racked up 34 wins, many by knockout, and only two losses.

By 1974, Arguello's world was expanding. *The Ring* ranked him the second-best contender for the featherweight title, and in February, Arguello fought outside Nicaragua for the first time, travelling to Panama to challenge Ernesto Marcel for the WBA featherweight belt. Marcel squeaked by Arguello on a fifteen-round decision. Marcel retired in June, and in July, Ruben Olivares KO'd Japanese fighter Zensuke Utagawa to take the vacant title. Arguello then went after Olivares. The two met in November of 1974, at the Fabulous Forum in Inglewood, California, before a crowd of 14,313. It was Arguello's first fight in the United States. Both boxers were in top condition, and the fight was close. Arguello narrowly won the first five rounds, then Olivares came back to take control. He hurt Arguello in the eighth, ninth, and tenth rounds. In the thirteenth, Arguello saw his opening and knocked Olivares down

Arguello (L) staggers Ray ("Boom Boom") Mancini with a left on the way to a fourteen-round KO in their October 1981 bout in Atlantic City.

IN THE RING	WON 82	LOST 8	DRAWS 0	TB 90	KO 65	W 17	WF 0	D 0	KO'd 4	L 4	LF 0

Date	Opponent	Site	Result / Rounds	Title	Wt.
1968					
Aug 1	Cachorro Amaya	Managua, Nicaragua	TKO'd 1	—	—
Nov 18	Israel Medina	Managua	W 4	—	—
Dec 14	Alacran Espinoza	Managua	W 4	—	—
1969					
Jan 23	Burrito Martinez	Managua	KO 3	—	—
Apr 26	Alacran Espinoza	Managua	L 6	—	—
1970					
Jul 29	Carlos Huete	Managua	W 8	—	—
Aug 12	Ricardo Donoso	Managua	KO 2	—	—
Sep 7	Marcelino Beckles	Managua	TKO 8	—	—
Oct 17	Mario Bojorge	Managua	KO 3	—	—
Nov 14	Jose Urbina	Managua	KO 1	—	—
Dec 5	Julio Morales	Managua	KO 3	—	—
Dec 19	Armando Figueroa	Managua	TKO 1	—	—
1971					
Feb 12	Tony Quiroz	Managua	KO 6	—	—
Mar 13	Raton Hernandez	Managua	W 10	—	—
Apr 17	Raton Hernandez	Managua	W 10	—	—
May 1	Mauricio Buitrago	Managua	KO 7	—	—
Jun 5	Kid Chapula	Managua	KO 1	—	—
Jun 26	Marcial Loyola	Managua	TKO 2	—	—
Jul 17	Hurricane Clay	Managua	TKO 5	—	—
Aug 14	Catalino Alvarado	Managua	KO 1	—	—
Sep 4	Ray Mendoza	Managua	TKO 4	—	—
Oct 2	Hurricane Clay	Managua	W 10	—	—
Nov 18	Vicente Worrel	Managua	KO 2	—	—
1972					
Feb 8	Guillermo Barrera	Managua	KO 1	—	—
Apr 11	Tanquecito Gonzalez	Managua	KO 2	—	—
Jun 22	Jorge Reyes	Managua	TKO'd 6	—	—
Aug 16	Fernando Fernandez	Managua	KO 1	—	—
Sep 23	Jorge Benitez	Managua	KO 1	—	—
Oct 22	Memo Barrera	Managua	KO 2	—	—
Nov 17	Guillermo Ortiz	Managua	KO 2	—	—
Dec 12	Rafael Gonzalez	Managua	TKO 7	—	—
1973					
Mar 30	Fernando Fernandez	Managua	TKO 2	—	—
Apr 22	Magalio Lozada	Managua	W 10	—	—
May 26	Kid Pascualito	Managua	KO 3	—	—
Jun 30	Octavio Gomez	Managua	KO 2	—	—
Aug 25	Ignacio Lomeli	Masaya, Nicaragua	KO 1	—	—
Oct 17	Sigfredo Rodriguez	Managua	TKO 9	—	—
Nov 27	⑩ Jose Legra	Masaya	KO 1	—	—
1974					
Jan 8	Raul Martinez	Managua	KO 1	—	—
Feb 16	♛ Ernesto Marcel	Panama City	L 15	For-WBA-FE	123
Apr 27	Enrique Garcia	Masaya	KO 3	—	—
May 20	⑩ Art Hafey	Masaya	KO 5	—	—
Aug 29	Oscar Aparicio	Masaya	W 12	Won-Cent Am-FE	—
Sep 21	Otoniel Martinez	Masaya	KO 1	—	—
Nov 23	♛ Ruben Olivares★	Inglewood, CA	KO 13	Won-WBA-FE	124

1975							
Feb 8		Oscar Aparicio	San Salvador, El Salvador	W	10	—	—
Mar 15	⑩	Leonel Hernandez	Caracas	TKO	8	Ret-WBA-FE	126
May 31		Rigoberto Riasco	Managua	TKO	2	Ret-WBA-FE	126
Jul 18		Rosalio Muro	San Francisco	TKO	2	—	128
Oct 12	⑩	Royal Kobayashi	Tokyo	KO	5	Ret-WBA-FE	125
Dec 20		Saul Montano	Managua	KO	3	—	—
1976							
Feb 1		Jose Torres	Mexicali, Mexico	W	10	—	127
Apr 10		Modesto Concepcion	Managua	KO	2	—	—
Jun 19		Salvador Torres	Inglewood	KO	3	Ret-WBA-FE	125
1977							
Feb 19		Godfrey Stevens	Managua	KO	2	—	—
May 14		Alberto Herrera	Managua	KO	1	—	—
Jun 22		Cocoa Sanchez	New York	TKO	4	—	132
Aug 3		Jose Fernandez	New York	TKO	1	—	131
Aug 27		Benjamin Ortiz	San Juan, PR	W	10	—	—
Sep 29		Jerome Artis	New York	TKO	2	—	134
Dec 18	⑩	Enrique Solis	Managua	KO	5	—	—
1978							
Jan 28	♛	Alfredo Escalera	Bayamon, PR	TKO	13	Won-WBC-JL (SFE)	129
Mar 25		Mario Mendez	Las Vegas	TKO	3	—	134
Apr 29		Rey Tam	Inglewood	TKO	5	Ret-WBC-JL (SFE)	129
Jun 3		Diego Alcala	San Juan	KO	1	Ret-WBC-JL (SFE)	129
Jul 26	⑩	Vilomar Fernandez	New York	L	10	—	135
Nov 10	⑩	Arturo Leon	Las Vegas	W	15	Ret-WBC-JL (SFE)	130
1979							
Feb 4	⑩	Alfredo Escalera	Rimini, Italy	KO	13	Ret-WBC-JL (SFE)	129
Jul 8	⑩	Rafael Limon	New York	TKO	11	Ret-WBC-JL (SFE)	130
Nov 16	⑩	Bobby Chacon★	Inglewood	TKO	7	Ret-WBC-JL (SFE)	129
1980							
Jan 20	⑩	Ruben Castillo	Tucson, AZ	TKO	11	Ret-WBC-JL (SFE)	130
Mar 31		Gerald Hayes	Las Vegas	W	10		131
Apr 27		Rolando Navarrete	San Juan	TKO	5	Ret-WBC-JL (SFE)	130
Aug 9		Cornelius Boza-Edwards	Atlantic City	TKO	8	—	135
Nov 14		Jose Ramirez	Miami	W	10	—	136
1981							
Feb 7		Robert Vasquez	Miami	TKO	3	—	136
Jun 20	♛	Jim Watt	London	W	15	Won-WBC-L	134
Oct 3	⑩	Ray ("Boom Boom") Mancini	Atlantic City	TKO	14	Ret-WBC-L	135
Nov 21		Roberto Elizondo	Las Vegas	KO	7	Ret-WBC-L	135
1982							
Feb 13		James Busceme	Beaumont, TX	KO	6	Ret-WBC-L	135
May 22	⑩	Andy Ganigan	Las Vegas	KO	5	Won-Vac World (WBC)-L	133
Jul 31		Kevin Rooney	Atlantic City	KO	2	—	140
Nov 12	♛	Aaron Pryor★	Miami	KO'd	14	For-WBA-JW	138
1983							
Feb 26		Vilomar Fernandez	San Antonio, TX	W	10	—	140
Apr 24		Claude Noel	Atlantic City	TKO	3	—	140
Sep 9	♛	Aaron Pryor★	Las Vegas	KO'd	10	For-WBA-JW	139
1985							
Oct 25		Pat Jefferson	Anchorage, AK	KO	5	—	142
1986							
Feb 9		Billy Costello	Reno, NV	TKO	4	—	143
1994							
Aug 27		Jorge Palomares	Miami Beach	W	10	—	142
1995							
Jan 21		Scott Walker	Las Vegas	L	10	—	142

with a short left hook. Olivares got up but fell later in the same round to a flurry of punches from which he could not recover.

Arguello kept his WBA featherweight title until 1977 when he relinquished it because he could no longer comfortably make the weight. In 1978 in Puerto Rico, Arguello faced Alfredo Escalera for the WBC super featherweight title. Arguello scored a thirteenth-round knockout. He defended this belt several times over the next two years before he gave it up and set his sights on the lightweight title.

In 1981, Arguello won his third title with a decision over WBC lightweight champ Jim Watt. Later that year, future WBA champ, Ray ("Boom Boom") Mancini put Arguello to the test in a hard-fought battle which Arguello won with a TKO in the

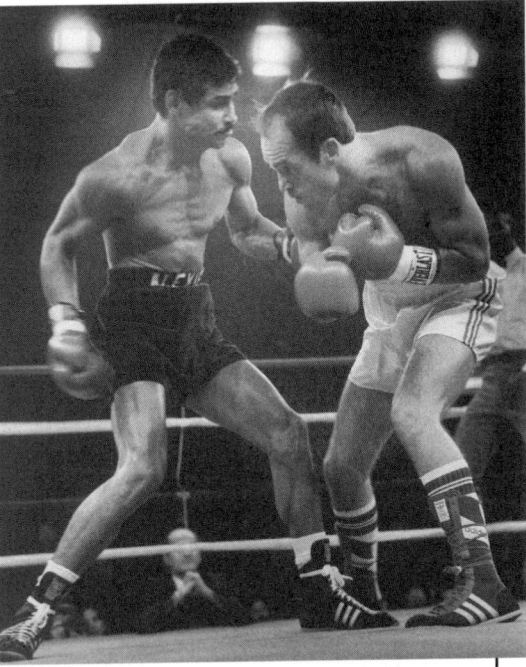

Sinewy Arguello knocked out future Tyson trainer Kevin Rooney (R) in two rounds on July 31, 1982, in Atlantic City.

fourteenth. The next year, his knockout victory over Andy Ganigan, titleholder in the short-lived WAA, led to Arguello's acclaim as world lightweight champion. Trying for a fourth belt, Arguello challenged Aaron Pryor for the WBA junior welterweight title. Pryor was 27 and in top condition. Arguello, at 31, was still fit, but fighting the younger man took all his strength. In the first five rounds, Arguello carefully probed the tireless Pryor. In the middle rounds, Arguello dominated, inflicting serious damage. But Pryor withstood Arguello's attacks and, in the fourteenth round, came back to pound Arguello so effectively that the referee stopped the fight. Rumors that Pryor's turnaround was boosted by an illegal substance in his water bottle or by less than the required padding in his gloves were never substantiated. In the rematch less than a year later, Arguello was knocked out in the tenth. He then retired for two years before making a two-fight comeback. After another stretch of retirement, during which he was elected to the Hall of Fame, Arguello again returned to the ring for one win in 1994 and one loss in 1995.

After a period of living abroad, Arguello returned to Nicaragua in 1990 when the Sandinistas left power. Although initially a Sandinista supporter, Arguello had switched his allegiance when the Sandinista government seized his property and bank account. He fought briefly as a Contra in the early 1980s after a brother was killed in the conflict. A national hero who still loves his country passionately, Arguello works with amateur boxers in Nicaragua.

HENRY ARMSTRONG
Homicide Hank, Hammerin' Hank

WELTERWEIGHT

Right-handed; 5'5½"; 120–147 lbs.

181 bouts, 7/27/1931 to 2/14/1945

Managers: Wirt Ross 1932–36, Eddie Mead 1936–41, George Moore 1942–45

Featherweight Champion 1937–38
Lightweight Champion 1938–39
Welterweight Champion 1938–40

Hall of Fame Induction: 1990

Born: 12/12/1912, Columbus, MS

Named: Henry Jackson

At a time when boxing had only eight weight classes, Henry Armstrong simultaneously held world titles in three of them. Armstrong collected everything but money in his impressive career. He was a knockout artist with a killer punch and a killer attitude in the ring. His incessant windmill style dazed his opponents, and he was extraordinarily resistant to battering. Poorly paid or cheated out of most of his ring earnings, Armstrong could rarely afford the high life of a champion, but prizefighting has never seen a more deserving bearer of its top honors.

Born in Mississippi as Henry Jackson, Armstrong moved to St. Louis with his family when he was four. As a boy, he joined in neighborhood street brawls, and soon decided he wanted to become a fighter. He finished high school (where he read an original poem at graduation) before briefly appearing in the amateur ranks as Melody Jackson. His first professional bouts, one win and one loss, took place in the Pittsburgh area, where Armstrong lived for a short time. He then moved to Los Angeles, where he resumed his amateur status, fighting as Henry Armstrong. He won his next 85 fights while making a living operating a shoeshine parlor. Armstrong officially turned pro after failing to make the 1932 Olympic boxing team.

Lou Ambers (R) got a beating and the win in his 1939 rematch with Armstrong. The referee took five rounds from Hank for low blows.

IN THE RING	WON 152	LOST 21	DRAWS 10	TB 183	KO 102	W 50	WF 0	D 9	KO'd 2	L 17	LF 2

Date	Opponent	Site	Result / Rounds		Title	Wt.
1931						
Jul 27	Al Iovino	North Braddock, PA	KO'd	3	—	120
Jul 31	Sammy Burns	Millville, PA	W	6	—	124
1932						
Aug 30	Eddie Trujillo	Los Angeles	L	4	—	—
Sep 27	Al Greenfield	Los Angeles	L	4	—	128
Oct	Max Tarley	Los Angeles	W	4	—	—
Dec	Vince Trujillo	Los Angeles	KO	2	—	—
Dec 13	Gene Espinosa	Los Angeles	W	4	—	123
Dec 31	Young Corpus	Los Angeles	W	4	—	—
1933						
Jan	Steve Harkey	Los Angeles	W	4	—	—
Feb 3	Johnny Ryan	Ventura, CA	W	6	—	—
Feb 17	George Dundee	Ventura	W	6	—	—
Mar 21	Paul Wangley	Los Angeles	KO	4	—	130
Apr 28	Perfecto Lopez	Ventura	W	6	—	—
May 24	Young Bud Taylor	Los Angeles	W	4	—	129
May 31	Max Tarley	Los Angeles	KO	3	—	—
Jun 7	Ricky Hall	Pismo Beach, CA	TKO	3	—	—
Jul 11	Baby Manuel	Los Angeles	L	6	—	126
Aug 8	Bobby Calmes	Los Angeles	KO	5	—	127
Aug 30	Hoyt Jones	Los Angeles	D	4	—	—
Sep 5	Perfecto Lopez	Los Angeles	D	4	—	—
Sep 7	Joe Sanchez	Ventura	KO	4	—	—
Sep 28	Perfecto Lopez	Ventura	W	8	—	—
Oct 11	Perfecto Lopez	Los Angeles	D	4	—	128
Oct 19	Johnny Granone	Sacramento, CA	TKO	6	—	—
Nov 3	Kid Moro	Pismo Beach	W	10	—	130
Nov 23	Kid Moro	Stockton, CA	D	10	—	131
Dec 14	Gene Espinosa	Sacramento	KO	7	—	125
1934						
Jan 26	Baby Manuel	Sacramento	W	10	—	131
Feb 13	Benny Pelz	Los Angeles	W	6	—	130
Mar 8	Perfecto Lopez	Bakersfield, CA	W	8	—	—
Mar 17	Young Danny	Los Angeles	KO	1	—	131
May 4	Kid Moro	Watsonville, CA	D	10	—	—
May 10	Mark Diaz	Ventura	W	8	—	—
May 22	Johnny DeFoe	Los Angeles	KO	5	—	—
Jun 5	Vicente Torres	Los Angeles	W	4	—	—
Jun 14	Davey Abad	Sacramento	W	10	—	130
Jul 17	Perfecto Lopez	Los Angeles	W	6	—	128
Aug 28	Perfecto Lopez	Los Angeles	KO	5	—	128
Sep 7	Joe Sanchez	Ventura	KO	4	—	—
Sep 13	Max Tarley	Sacramento	KO	3	—	—
Nov 3	⑩ Baby Arizmendi★	Mexico City	L	10	—	—
Dec 2	Joe Conde	Mexico City	KO	7	—	—
Dec 15	Ventura Arana	Mexico City	TKO	5	—	—
1935						
Jan 1	⑩ Baby Arizmendi★	Mexico City	L	12	For-Vac CA-Mex World-FE	126

Date		Opponent	Location	Result	Rnds	Notes	Wt
Feb 15	⑩	Baby Casanova	Mexico City	LF	4	—	—
Mar 19		Sal Hernandez	Los Angeles	KO	2	—	128
Mar 31		Davey Abad	Mexico City	L	10	—	128
Apr 6		Tully Corvo	Sacramento	KO	5	—	—
Apr 16		Frankie Covelli	Los Angeles	W	8	—	128
May 28		Davey Abad	Los Angeles	W	10	—	129
Jun 25		Varias Milling	Los Angeles	W	10	—	126
Sep 13		Alton Black	Reno, NV	TKO	8	—	125
Sep 18		Perfecto Lopez	San Francisco	D	8	—	128
Oct 21		Lester Marston	Oakland	KO	7	—	127
Nov 12		Leo Lomelli	Oakland	TKO	6	—	129
Nov 27	⑩	Midget Wolgast★	Oakland	W	10	—	125
Dec 6		Alton Black	Reno	KO	8	—	126

1936

Date		Opponent	Location	Result	Rnds	Notes	Wt
Jan 1		Joe Conde	Mexico City	L	10	—	—
Feb 26		Ritchie Fontaine	Oakland	L	10	—	125
Mar 31		Ritchie Fontaine	Los Angeles	W	10	—	127
Apr 17		Alton Black	Reno	TKO	8	—	—
May 19	⑩	Bobby Leyvas	Los Angeles	KO	4	—	126
Jun 22		Johnny DeFoe	Butte, MT	W	10	—	127
Aug 4	⑩	Baby Arizmendi★	Los Angeles	W	10	Won-CA-Mex World-FE	125
Aug 28		Juan Zurita	Los Angeles	KO	4	—	128
Sep 3		Buzz Brown	Portland, OR	W	10	—	127
Sep 8		Dommy Ganzon	Sacramento	KO	1	—	126
Oct 27	♛	Mike Belloise	Los Angeles	W	10	—	125
Nov 2		Gene Espinosa	Los Angeles	KO	1	—	127
Nov 17		Joey Alcanter	St. Louis	TKO	6	—	130
Dec 3	⑩	Tony Chavez	St. Louis	LF	8	—	131

1937

Date		Opponent	Location	Result	Rnds	Notes	Wt
Jan 1		Baby Casanova	Mexico City	KO	3	—	127
Jan 19	⑩	Tony Chavez	Los Angeles	KO	10	—	131
Feb 2		Moon Mullins	Los Angeles	TKO	2	—	130
Feb 19		Varias Milling	San Diego	KO	4	—	130
Mar 2		Joe Rivers	Los Angeles	KO	4	—	130
Mar 12	⑩	Mike Belloise	New York	KO	4	—	128
Mar 19		Aldo Spoldi	New York	W	10	—	126
Apr 6	⑩	Pete DeGrasse	Los Angeles	KO	10	—	129
May 4		Frankie Klick	Los Angeles	KO	4	—	131
May 28		Wally Hally	Los Angeles	KO	4	—	131
Jun 9		Mark Diaz	Pasadena, CA	KO	4	—	128
Jun 15		Jackie Carter	Los Angeles	KO	4	—	132
Jul 8		Alf Blatch	New York	TKO	3	—	132
Jul 19		Lew Massey	Brooklyn	TKO	4	—	131
Jul 27		Benny Bass★	Philadelphia	KO	4	—	130
Aug 13		Eddie Brink	New York	KO	3	—	133
Aug 16		Johnny Cabello	Washington, DC	TKO	2	—	131
Aug 31		Orville Drouillard	Detroit	TKO	5	—	131
Sep 9		Charley Burns	Pittsburgh	KO	4	—	131
Sep 16		Johnny DeFoe	New York	TKO	4	—	132
Sep 21		Bobby Dean	Youngstown, PA	KO	1	—	131
Oct 18		Joe Marciente	Philadelphia	KO	3	—	131
Oct 29	♛	Petey Sarron	New York	KO	6	Won-World-FE	124
Nov 19	⑩	Billy Beauhuld	New York	TKO	5	—	132
Nov 23		Joey Brown	Buffalo, NY	KO	2	—	130
Dec 6	⑩	Tony Chavez	Cleveland	TKO	1	—	134

Campaigning as a featherweight, Armstrong fought often—his bouts were sometimes only days apart—and with great success. In 1934, *The Ring* ranked him as the sixth-best featherweight contender in its annual rankings. In 1936, Armstrong won a ten-round decision over Baby Arizmendi for the California-Mexico version of the world featherweight title. By 1937, Armstrong was unstoppable. He fought 27 times and won 27 times, 26 by knockout. Among his victims was Petey Sarron, acclaimed as the world featherweight titleholder. Armstrong knocked Sarron out in six to lay undisputed claim to the championship.

But 1938 was the greatest year of Armstrong's career. In May, he challenged Barney Ross for the welterweight title. The fight was held in the open-air Madison Square Garden Bowl in front of 28,290 fans. Although Armstrong struggled to make the maximum weight, the end was near for Ross, who was unaware that his career had peaked. For fifteen rounds, Armstrong gave the champ a merciless shellacking that had the crowd calling for the fight to be stopped.

With the featherweight and welterweight titles firmly in hand, Armstrong then faced Lou Ambers for the lightweight championship. In a very fierce fight, Armstrong knocked Ambers down in the fifth and sixth rounds, but Ambers cut Armstrong's mouth and eyes so seriously that the referee considered stopping the fight. Fighting without a mouthpiece so that he could swallow the blood

Armstrong (R) took the title from Lou Ambers on August 17, 1938. Armstrong scored knockdowns in the fifth and sixth. However, Amber's late comeback made the split-decision victory controversial.

Date		Opponent	Location	Result	Rds	Title	Wt
Dec 12		Johnny Jones	New Orleans	KO	2	—	130

1938

Date		Opponent	Location	Result	Rds	Title	Wt
Jan 12		Enrico Venturi	New York	KO	6	—	134
Jan 21		Frankie Castillo	Phoenix	TKO	3	—	129
Jan 22		Tommy Brown	Tucson, AZ	KO	2	—	129
Feb 1	⑩	Albert ("Chalky") Wright★	Los Angeles	TKO	3	—	133
Feb 9		Al Citrino	San Francisco	TKO	4	—	133
Feb 25	⑩	Everett Rightmire	Chicago	TKO	3	—	132
Feb 28		Charley Burns	Minneapolis	TKO	2	—	133
Mar 15	⑩	Baby Arizmendi★	Los Angeles	W	10	—	130
Mar 25		Eddie Zivic	Detroit	TKO	4	—	135
Mar 30		Lew Feldman	New York	KO	5	—	133
May 31	♛	Barney Ross★	Long Island City, NY	W	15	Won-World-W	134
Aug 17	♛	Lou Ambers★	New York	W	15	Won-World-L	134
Nov 25	⑩	Ceferino Garcia	New York	W	15	Ret-World-W	134
Dec 5		Al Manfredo	Cleveland	TKO	3	Ret-World-W	134

1939

Date		Opponent	Location	Result	Rds	Title	Wt
Jan 10	⑩	Baby Arizmendi★	Los Angeles	W	10	Ret-World-W	134
Mar 4		Bobby Pacho	Havana, Cuba	TKO	4	Ret-World-W	134
Mar 16		Lew Feldman	St. Louis	KO	1	Ret-World-W	135
Mar 31	⑩	Davey Day	New York	KO	12	Ret-World-W	135
May 25	⑩	Ernie Roderick	London	W	15	Ret-World-W	135
Aug 22	⑩	Lou Ambers★	New York	L	15	Lost-World-L	135
Oct 9		Al Manfredo	Des Moines, IA	TKO	4	Ret-World-W	141
Oct 13		Howard Scott	Minneapolis	KO	2	Ret-World-W	141
Oct 20		Ritchie Fontaine	Seattle	KO	3	Ret-World-W	139
Oct 24		Jimmy Garrison	Los Angeles	W	10	Ret-World-W	138
Oct 30		Bobby Pacho	Denver	TKO	4	Ret-World-W	140
Dec 11		Jimmy Garrison	Cleveland	KO	7	Ret-World-W	138

1940

Date		Opponent	Location	Result	Rds	Title	Wt
Jan 4		Joe Ghnouly	St. Louis	KO	5	Ret-World-W	136
Jan 24		Pedro Montanez	New York	TKO	9	Ret-World-W	139
Mar 1	♛	Ceferino Garcia	Los Angeles	D	10	For-World-M	142
Apr 26		Paul Junior	Boston	TKO	7	Ret-World-W	139
May 24		Ralph Zanelli	Boston	TKO	5	Ret-World-W	140
Jun 21		Paul Junior	Portland, ME	TKO	3	Ret-World-W	144
Jul 17		Lew Jenkins★	New York	TKO	6	—	139
Sep 23		Phil Furr	Washington, DC	KO	4	Ret-World-W	146
Oct 4	⑩	Fritzie Zivic★	New York	L	15	Lost-World-W	142

1941

Date		Opponent	Location	Result	Rds	Title	Wt
Jan 17	♛	Fritzie Zivic★	New York	TKO'd	12	For-World-W	140

1942

Date		Opponent	Location	Result	Rds	Title	Wt
Jun 1		Johnny Taylor	San Jose, CA	KO	4	—	148
Jun 24	⑩	Richard ("Sheik") Rangel	Oakland	W	10	—	145
Jul 3		Reuben Shank	Denver	L	10	—	145
Jul 20		Joe Ibarra	Sacramento	TKO	3	—	144
Aug 3		Aldo Spoldi	San Francisco	TKO	7	—	143
Aug 13		Jackie Burke	Ogden, UT	W	10	—	143
Aug 26		Rodolfo Ramirez	Oakland	KO	8	—	144
Sep 7		Johnny Taylor	Pittman, NV	KO	3	—	—
Sep 14		Leo Rodak	San Francisco	KO	4	—	145
Sep 30		Earl Turner	Oakland	KO	4	—	142
Oct 13	⑩	Juan Zurita	Los Angeles	KO	2	—	142
Oct 26	⑩	Fritzie Zivic★	San Francisco	W	10	—	142
Dec 4		Lew Jenkins★	Portland, OR	KO	8	—	144

Date		Opponent	Location	Result	Rounds		Weight
Dec 14		Saverio Turiello	San Francisco	KO	4	—	144
1943							
Jan 5		Jimmy McDaniels	Los Angeles	W	10	—	140
Mar 2	⑩	Willie Joyce	Los Angeles	L	10	—	137
Mar 8	⑩	Tippy Larkin	San Francisco	KO	2	—	139
Mar 22		Al Tribuani	Philadelphia	W	10	—	138
Apr 2	♛	Beau Jack★	New York	L	10	—	138
Apr 30		Saverio Turiello	Washington, DC	TKO	5	—	142
May 7		Tommy Jessup	Boston	KO	1	—	140
May 24	⑩	Maxie Shapiro	Philadelphia	KO	7	—	140
Jun 11	⑩	Sammy Angott★	New York	W	10	—	140
Jul 24	⑩	Willie Joyce	Hollywood	W	10	—	140
Aug 6		Jimmy Garrison	Portland, OR	W	10	—	140
Aug 14		Joey Silva	Spokane, WA	W	10	—	140
Aug 27	⑩	Sugar Ray Robinson★	New York	L	10	—	140
1944							
Jan 14		Aldo Spoldi	Portland, OR	KO	3	—	141
Jan 26		Saverio Turiello	Kansas City, MO	KO	7	—	144
Feb 7		Lew Hanbury	Washington, DC	KO	3	—	139
Feb 23		Jimmy Garrison	Kansas City, MO	TKO	5	—	145
Feb 29		Jackie Byrd	Des Moines	KO	4	—	142
Mar 14		Johnny Jones	Miami	KO	5	—	145
Mar 20	⑩	Frankie Wills	Washington, DC	W	10	—	142
Mar 24	⑩	Ralph Zanelli	Boston	W	10	—	142
Apr 25	⑩	John Thomas	Los Angeles	W	10	—	140
May 16	⑩	Ralph Zanelli	Boston	W	10	—	143
May 22		Aaron Perry	Washington, DC	TKO	6	—	140
Jun 2	⑩	Willie Joyce	Chicago	L	10	—	140
Jun 15	⑩	Al Davis	New York	KO	2	—	141
Jun 21		Nick Latsios	Washington, DC	W	10	—	142
Jul 4	⑩	John Thomas	Los Angeles	L	10	—	139
Jul 14	⑩	Luther ("Slugger") White	Hollywood	D	10	—	137
Aug 21	⑩	Willie Joyce	San Francisco	W	10	—	139
Sep 15		Aldo Spoldi	St. Louis	KO	2	—	141
Nov 4	⑩	Mike Belloise	Portland, OR	KO	4	—	140
1945							
Jan 17		Chester Slider	Oakland	D	10	—	140
Feb 6		Genaro Rojo	Los Angeles	W	10	—	140
Feb 14		Chester Slider	Oakland	L	10	—	141

flowing in his mouth, Armstrong went the distance and won a split decision to become boxing's first simultaneous triple titleholder.

Armstrong voluntarily relinquished the featherweight title in 1938. In 1939, Ambers took the lightweight title back in a rematch in which Armstrong was severely penalized for low blows. Armstrong failed to attain the middleweight title in 1940 when he fought hard-hitting Ceferino Garcia to a draw. That same year, he lost the welterweight belt, the last of his titles, to Fritzie Zivic. Zivic repeatedly worked Armstrong's eyes, which were scarred and vulnerable to cutting. Armstrong, who considered Zivic a dirty fighter, could not beat him in the rematch. When they met a third time, Armstrong won, but Zivic was no longer champion. Armstrong continued to box into 1945, though the days of his unbeatable rapid-fire attack were behind him. In retirement, Armstrong overcame alcoholism and became an ordained Baptist minister.

CARMEN BASILIO
The Upstate Onion Farmer

MIDDLEWEIGHT

Right-handed; 5'6½"; 143–155 lbs.

79 bouts, 11/24/1948 to 4/22/1961

Managers: Johnny DeJohn,
Joe Netro

Welterwt Champ 1955–56, 1956–57

Middleweight Champion 1957–58

Hall of Fame Induction: 1990

Born: 4/2/1927, Canastota, NY

From the farm country around Canastota, New York sprang one of boxing's toughest heroes, Carmen Basilio. Twice welterweight champ, Basilio had the nerve to challenge—and beat— middleweight king Sugar Ray Robinson in one of the most brutal matches of ring history. An all-out fighter who took as many punches as he delivered, Basilio bore the badges of his profession on his angular face—flattened nose, scarred cheeks, and split eyebrow. Built low to the ground, Basilio was a game fighter who looked mean and who fought with great courage.

Basilio's father, Joseph, an onion farmer, was a boxing fan who inspired his son's early interest in the sport. Basilio fought some bouts in the Marine Corps before turning professional in 1948, at the age of 21. In 1953, he decisioned Hall of Famer Ike Williams and then defeated Billy Graham to win the New York State welterweight championship. After fighting Graham to a draw in a rematch the same year, Basilio faced Kid Gavilan for the welterweight championship of the world. Fighting in the War Memorial Auditorium in Syracuse, New York, before 6,803 fans, Basilio came close to knocking Gavilan out in the second round. Gavilan, however, rose at the count of nine and prevailed in a fifteen-round decision.

Basilio got another chance to fight for the welterweight title when he faced the new champion, Tony DeMarco, in the Syracuse War Memorial in 1955. In a wild, bloody brawl, DeMarco

At Yankee Stadium in September 1957, Basilio (R) relentlessly battered away at Sugar Ray Robinson and took his crown.

led through eight rounds. In the tenth, Basilio floored DeMarco twice. DeMarco managed to avoid a knockout but succumbed in the twelfth when the referee stopped the fight. Basilio lost his title to Johnny Saxton in 1956. Basilio had Saxton seriously shaken up, but the challenger's corner reportedly fabricated a delay in replacing a damaged glove, giving Saxton time to recover sufficiently to win a decision. Basilio won the rematch six months later to reclaim the title.

In 1957, Basilio fought what many consider to be the finest battle of his career. He moved up to middleweight in a bid to topple the enduring Sugar Ray

IN THE RING	WON 56	LOST 16	DRAWS 7	TB 79	KO 27	W 29	WF 0	D 7	KO'd 2	L 14	LF 0

Date	Opponent	Site	Result / Rounds		Title	Wt.
1948						
Nov 24	Jimmy Evans	Binghamton, NY	KO	3	—	145
Nov 29	Bruce Walters	Syracuse, NY	KO	1	—	145
Dec 8	Eddie Thomas	Binghamton	KO	2	—	—
Dec 16	Rollie Johns	Syracuse	W	6	—	142
1949						
Jan 5	Johnny Cunningham	Binghamton	D	6	—	145
Jan 19	Jay Parlin	Binghamton	D	6	—	141
Jan 25	Ernie Hall	Syracuse	KO	2	—	141
Feb 19	Luke Jordan	Rochester, NY	W	6	—	142
Apr 20	Elliott Throop	Syracuse	KO	1	—	143
May 2	Connie Thies	Rochester	L	6	—	146
May 8	Jerry Drain	Syracuse	KO	3	—	143
May 18	Johnny Clemons	Syracuse	KO	3	—	145
Jun 7	Johnny Cunningham	Syracuse	KO	2	—	146
Jul 12	Jesse Bradshaw	Syracuse	TKO	2	—	147
Jul 21	Sammy Daniels	Utica, NY	W	8	—	146
Aug 2	Johnny Cunningham	Utica	L	8	—	145
Aug 17	Johnny Cunningham	Syracuse	W	8	—	145
Sep 7	Tony DiPelino	Rochester	W	8	—	147
Sep 30	Jackie Parker	Syracuse	TKO	3	—	147
1950						
Jan 10	Sonny Hampton	Buffalo, NY	W	8	—	149
Jan 24	Cassill Tate	Buffalo	W	8	—	148
Feb 7	Adrien Mourguiart	Buffalo	KO	7	—	144
Mar 6	Lew Jenkins ★	Syracuse	W	10	—	142
Mar 27	Mike Koballa	Brooklyn	L	8	—	145
Apr 12	Gaby Ferland	New Orleans	D	10	—	142
May 8	Gaby Ferland	New Orleans	KO	1	—	144
Jun 21	Guillermo Giminez	New Orleans	TKO	8	—	140
Jul 31	Guillermo Giminez	New Orleans	TKO	9	—	140
Aug 28	Eddie Giosa	New Orleans	L	10	—	145
Dec 15	Vic Cardell	New York	L	10	—	145
1951						
Mar 9	Floro Hita	Syracuse	W	8	—	145
Apr 12	Eddie Giosa	Syracuse	W	10	—	145
May 29	Lester Felton	Syracuse	L	10	—	145
Jun 18	Johnny Cesario	Utica	L	10	—	143

Date		Opponent	Location	Result	Rounds	Notes	Weight
Sep 17		Shamus McCray	Syracuse	W	8	—	146
Sep 26		Ross Virgo	New Orleans	L	10	—	142
1952							
Feb 4		Emmett Norris	Wilkes-Barre, PA	W	10	—	148
Feb 28		Jimmy Cousins	Akron, OH	W	8	—	152
Mar 31		Jackie O'Brien	Wilkes-Barre	W	10	—	149
May 29	⑩	Chuck Davey	Syracuse	D	10	—	146
Jul 16	⑩	Chuck Davey	Chicago	L	10	—	145
Aug 20	⑩	Billy Graham★	Chicago	L	10	—	146
Sep 22		Baby Williams	Miami	W	10	—	149
Oct 20		Sammy Giuliani	Syracuse	KO	3	—	150
Nov 18		Chuck Foster	Buffalo	TKO	5	—	150
1953							
Jan 12		Ike Williams★	Syracuse	W	10	—	147
Feb 28		Vic Cardell	Toledo, OH	W	10	—	149
Apr 11		Carmine Fiore	Syracuse	TKO	9	—	150
Jun 6	⑩	Billy Graham★	Syracuse	W	12	Won-NY State-W	145
Jul 25	⑩	Billy Graham★	Syracuse	D	12	Ret-NY State-W	147
Sep 18	♛	Kid Gavilan★	Syracuse	L	15	For-World-W	147
Nov 28		Johnny Cunningham	Toledo	TKO	4	—	150
Dec 19	⑩	Pierre Langlois	Syracuse	D	10	—	148
1954							
Jan 16		Italo Scortichini	Miami	D	10	—	149
Apr 17	⑩	Pierre Langlois	Syracuse	W	10	—	151
May 15		Italo Scortichini	Syracuse	W	10	—	150
Jun 26		Al Andrews	Syracuse	W	10	—	148
Aug 17		Ronnie Harper	Fort Wayne, IN	TKO	2	—	150
Sep 10		Carmine Fiore	New York	W	10	—	147
Oct 15		Allie Gronik	Syracuse	W	10	—	151
Dec 16		Ronnie Harper	Akron	TKO	4	—	150
1955							
Jan 21		Peter Muller	Syracuse	W	10	—	152
Jun 10	♛	Tony DeMarco	Syracuse	TKO	12	Won-World-W	145
Aug 10		Italo Scortichini	New York	W	10	—	150
Sep 7		Gil Turner	Syracuse	W	10	—	150
Nov 30	⑩	Tony DeMarco	Boston	TKO	12	Ret-World-W	145
1956							
Mar 14	⑩	Johnny Saxton	Chicago	L	15	Lost-World-W	146
Sep 12	♛	Johnny Saxton	Syracuse	TKO	9	Reg-World-W	146
1957							
Feb 22	⑩	Johnny Saxton	Cleveland	KO	2	Ret-World-W	147
May 16		Harold Jones	Portland, OR	TKO	4	—	150
Sep 23	♛	Sugar Ray Robinson★	New York	W	15	Won-World-M	153
1958							
Mar 25	⑩	Sugar Ray Robinson★	Chicago	L	15	Lost-World-M	159
Sep 5		Art Aragon	Los Angeles	TKO	8	—	155
1959							
Apr 1		Arley Selfer	Augusta, GA	TKO	3	—	155
Aug 28	⑩	Gene Fullmer★	San Francisco	TKO'd	14	For-Vac NBA-M	156
1960							
Jun 29	♛	Gene Fullmer★	Salt Lake City	TKO'd	12	For-NBA-M	156
1961							
Jan 7	⑩	Gaspar Ortega	New York	W	10	—	159
Mar 11		Don Jordan	Syracuse	W	10	—	156
Apr 22	♛	Paul Pender	Boston	L	15	For-World-M	159

Basilio (R) is on the home turf of Syracuse's War Memorial Auditorium when he takes out Johnny Saxton in the ninth with a booming right to regain the world welterweight title on September 12, 1956.

Robinson. Robinson had lost and regained the title four times, and had recently come out of a short retirement. He was 37; Basilio was 30. The contest, later ranked the twelfth greatest fight of all time by *The Ring*, took place in Yankee Stadium before a crowd of 38,000. At the start of the fight, Robinson jabbed Basilio persistently and effectively. He bloodied Basilio's nose in the third round and cut his left eye in the fourth. Basilio dominated in the fifth and continued to press Robinson in the following rounds. There was no holding back as each fighter felt the effect of many resounding, jarring punches. At times, each man appeared dazed and ready to drop. After fifteen rounds had finally gone by, the bloody and exhausted Basilio went down on one knee to pray. A few moments later, it was announced that he had won the split decision to take the middleweight title. The rematch six months later was just as gruesome, with Basilio fighting one-eyed from the sixth round on. This time, Robinson won the decision. In three later bids, Basilio failed to claim the middleweight title from subsequent champions Gene Fullmer and Paul Pender.

Basilio's aggressive, charging style and powerful left hook enabled him to win championships in two weight classes and to have a long and memorable career. In retirement, he worked as a physical education instructor at LeMoyne College in Syracuse and as a Genesee Brewery representative. Basilio's hometown of Canastota is also the site of the International Boxing Hall of Fame. Basilio is a frequent visitor to the shrine that honors him and other great boxers of the past.

WILFRED BENITEZ

JUNIOR MIDDLEWEIGHT

Right-handed; 5'10"; 140–160 lbs.

62 bouts, 11/22/1973 to 9/18/1990

Manager: Jimmy Jacobs

Junior Welterweight Champ 1976–79
Welterweight Champion 1979
WBC Junior Middleweight
(Super Welterweight) Champ 1981–82

Hall of Fame Induction: 1996

Born: 9/12/1958, Bronx, NY

A talented fighter who sometimes got away with perfunctory preparation for formidable opponents, Wilfred Benitez became a triple title-holder at the age of 22. Born in New York the youngest of eight children, Benitez was brought up on boxing. His father, Gregorio ("Goyo"), had boxed as a boy in Puerto Rico and often set up playground matches for his sons in the Bronx, charging passersby a quarter to watch.

At seven, Benitez moved with his family to Puerto Rico where he fought in the regional Golden Gloves tournament and turned professional at the age of fifteen. Winning his first eleven fights, he returned to New York in 1974 to face Al Hughes in Madison Square Garden's Felt Forum. Barely sixteen, Benitez was legally too young to fight in New York but carried a baptismal certificate showing he was older.

A year later in San Juan, he challenged Antonio ("Kid Pambele") Cervantes, the WBA junior welterweight champion. Training seriously for this fight, Benitez

Benitez's right shakes welterweight champion Carlos Palomino (L). Benitez took the title in a 15-round decision on January 14, 1979, in an outdoor arena in San Juan.

IN THE RING	WON 53	LOST 8	DRAWS 1	TB 62	KO 31	W 22	WF 0	D 1	KO'd 4	L 4	LF 0

Date	Opponent	Site	Result / Rounds		Title	Wt.
1973						
Nov 22	Hiram Santiago	San Juan, PR	KO	1	—	—
Nov 30	Jesse Torres	St. Martin, VI	KO	2	—	—
1974						
Jan 7	Hector Amadia	San Juan	KO	4	—	—
Jan 26	Joe ("Hawk") York	St. Martin	KO	2	—	—
Feb 18	Roberto Flanders	San Juan	TKO	4	—	142
Apr 1	Victor Mangual	San Juan	W	8	—	141
Apr 30	Juan Disla	San Juan	TKO	3	—	143
May 11	Sonny Lake	St. Martin	KO	1	—	—
Jun 21	Ives St. Jean	St. Martin	KO	1	—	—
Jun 26	Carlos Crispin	San Juan	TKO	3	—	—
Aug 31	Sonny Lake	St. Martin	TKO	5	—	—
Sep 16	Al Hughes	New York	TKO	5	—	138
Oct 25	Terry Summerhayes	New York	TKO	6	—	144
Dec 2	Lawrence Hafey	New York	W	8	—	145
1975						
Jan 4	Francisco Rodriguez	San Juan	TKO	7	—	142
Feb 8	Santiago Rosa	San Juan	KO	4	—	143
Mar 31	Wilbur Seales	San Juan	TKO	4	—	—
May 5	Santos Solis	San Juan	W	10	—	—
Jun 9	Angel R. Garcia	San Juan	W	10	—	145
Jun 28	Joe Henry	San Juan	TKO	8	—	—
Aug 1	Eyue Jeudy	St. Martin	KO	4	—	—
Aug 19	Young Woodall	St. Martin	KO	4	—	—
Sep 1	Marcelino Alicea	San Juan	TKO	2	—	140
Oct 20	Omar Piton	New York	TKO	6	—	143
Dec 13	Chris Fernandez	San Juan	W	10	—	—
1976						
Mar 6 ♛	Antonio Cervantes ★	San Juan	W	15	Won-World-JW	138
May 31	Emiliano Villa	San Juan	W	15	Ret-World-JW	140
Oct 16 ⑩	Tony Petronelli	San Juan	TKO	3	Ret-World-JW	140
1977						
Feb 2 ⑩	Harold Weston	New York	D	10	—	144
Mar 6 ⑩	Mel Dennis	Marion, OH	W	8	—	146
Jun 2	Roberto Gonzalez	St. Thomas, VI	KO	1	—	—
Jul 1	Easy Boy Lake	St. Thomas	KO	1	—	—
Aug 3	Ray Guerrero	New York	TKO	15	Ret-World-JW	139
Nov 18 ⑩	Bruce Curry	New York	W	10	—	144
1978						
Feb 4 ⑩	Bruce Curry	New York	W	10	—	145
Aug 25 ⑩	Randy Shields	New York	TKO	6	—	145
Dec 5	Vernon Lewis	New York	W	10	—	147
1979						
Jan 14 ♛	Carlos Palomino ★	San Juan	W	15	Won-World-W	146
Mar 25 ⑩	Harold Weston	San Juan	W	15	Ret-World-W	147

Date		Opponent	Location	Result		Title	Weight
Nov 30	⑩	Sugar Ray Leonard ★	Las Vegas	TKO'd	15	Lost-World-W	144
1980							
Mar 9		Johnny Turner	Miami Beach	TKO	9	—	150
Aug 1	⑩	Tony Chiaverini	Las Vegas	TKO	8	—	154
Dec 12	⑩	Pete Ranzany	Sacramento, CA	W	10	—	150
1981							
May 23	♛	Maurice Hope	Las Vegas	TKO	12	Won-WBC-JM (SW)	153
Nov 13		Carlos Santos	Las Vegas	W	15	Ret-WBC-JM (SW)	153
1982							
Jan 30	⑩	Roberto Duran	Las Vegas	W	15	Ret-WBC-JM (SW)	152
Dec 3	⑩	Thomas Hearns	New Orleans	L	15	Lost-WBC-JM (SW)	152
1983							
May 18		Tony Cerda	Las Vegas	W	10	—	158
Jul 16	⑩	Mustafa Hamsho	Las Vegas	L	12	—	157
1984							
Feb 11		Stacy McSwain	Detroit	W	10	—	154
Jul 14	⑩	Davey Moore	Monte Carlo	TKO'd	2	—	154
1985							
Mar 30		Mauricio Bravo	Oranjestad, Aruba	KO	2	—	155
Jul 6		Danny Chapman	Washington, DC	TKO	7	—	153
Aug 21		Kevin Moley	New York	W	10	—	154
1986							
Feb 15	⑩	Matthew Hilton	Montreal	KO'd	9	—	152
Jul 2		Paul Whittaker	New Orleans	W	10	—	158
Sep 17		Harry Daniels	Baltimore, MD	W	10	—	164
Nov 28		Carlos Herrera	Salta, Argentina	TKO'd	7	—	155
1990							
Mar 8		Ariel Conde	Phoenix	KO	7	—	158
May 23		Pat Lawlor	Tucson, AZ	L	10	—	158
Aug 24		Sam Wilson	Denver	W	10	—	160
Sep 18		Scott Papsadora	Winnipeg, Man.	L	10	—	159

outboxed the champ and won a decision to become the youngest boxer ever to win a world title. He defended his belt three times, but a scheduled rematch with Cervantes was postponed after Benitez crashed his car. When he failed to reschedule quickly enough, the WBA stripped him of the title.

In the meantime, Benitez's chronic habit of lax preparation had begun to surface. After just twelve days of training to fight Harold Weston, he clowned around in the ring and only managed to score a draw. Fighting Bruce Curry with barely a week's training, he was knocked down three times and just squeaked out a split decision.

As he matured physically, Benitez moved up to welterweight and faced champion Carlos Palomino in San Juan in 1979. Although contracted to Hall of Famer Jimmy Jacobs, Benitez was still trained by his father and, at Jacobs's direction, by another Hall of Famer, Emile Griffith, as well. Nearing the Palomino fight, Griffith and Goyo Benitez clashed over the tactical approach Wilfred should use, but Griffith prevailed. Benitez scored a split decision and won his second world title.

In many of Benitez's best performances, he employed an unusual defensive tactic. He spread his legs wide while keeping his feet flat on the floor. From this position, he quickly moved his upper body, dodging his opponents' punches.

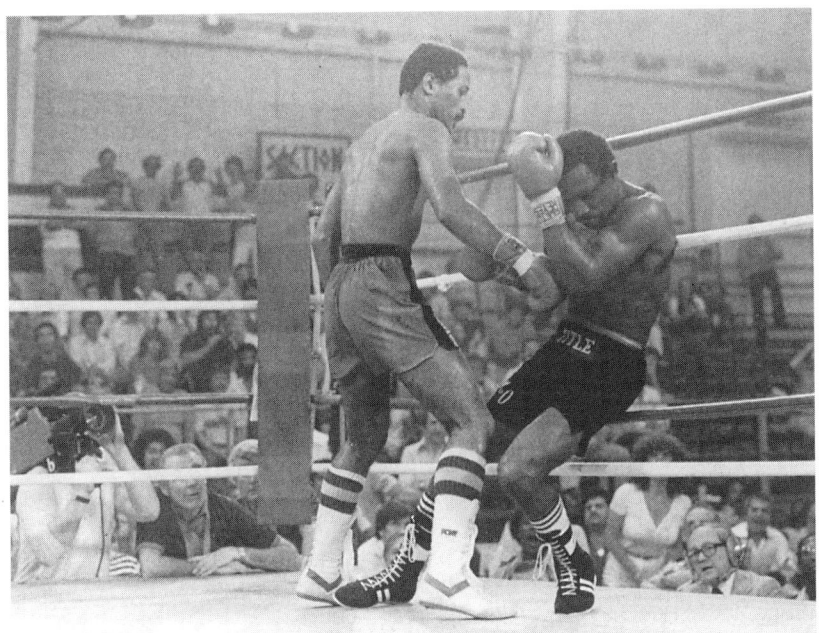

In 1981 Benitez moved up to junior middleweight and attempted to gain his third world crown. Here he crumples Maurice Hope against the ropes for a twelve-round TKO victory and the WBC belt.

Later in 1979, Benitez took on Sugar Ray Leonard, his stiffest challenge to date, with minimal preparation estimated at something between two and nine days. Nevertheless, Benitez nearly went the distance, until the fight was stopped in the final seconds. Even though Leonard knocked Benitez down twice and won, Sugar Ray openly admired his opponent's ring skills.

In 1981, Benitez moved up to junior middleweight and faced WBC champion Maurice Hope. Jacobs had turned down a bigger paycheck for a potential match with Thomas Hearns and had Benitez fight Hope for a third world title instead. In the ring, Hope did some damage, but Benitez did much more, knocking out two of Hope's teeth and, in the twelfth round, the fighter himself.

This bout may have marked the high point of Benitez's career. A year later he defeated Roberto Duran but lost his very next fight by decision to Hearns. An attempt to move up to middleweight under the training of Victor Machado and Cus D'Amato failed with a loss by decision to Mustafa Hamsho. Back under the direction of his father, Benitez broke his ankle in a fight with Davey Moore. He continued to fight but never again contended for a title.

By the age of 37, Benitez had squandered his ring earnings and suffered from chronic traumatic encephalopathy. He was recently awarded a newly instituted boxer's pension by the Puerto Rican government. Benitez is remembered for his remarkable defensive skills in the ring and his facility for fighting both right- and left-handed. "At one time," observed promoter Teddy Brenner, "he was the best fighter in the world."

GIOVANNI ("NINO") BENVENUTI

MIDDLEWEIGHT

Right-handed; 5'11"; 153–164 lbs.

90 bouts, 1/20/1961 to 5/9/1971

Manager: Bruno Amaduzzi

1960 Olympic Welterweight
Gold Medalist

Jr. Middlewt. Champion 1965–66
Middlewt. Champion 1967, 1968–70

Hall of Fame Induction: 1992

Born: 4/26/1938, Trieste, Italy

Name: Carmine Tilelli

A handsome idol of the Italian public as well as many fans around the world, Giovanni ("Nino") Benvenuti moved from Olympic stardom to the professional ring with great ease. He is best remembered for three bitter fights in 1967 and 1968 with Hall of Famer Emile Griffith, for the middleweight championship.

Born the son of a fisherman in Trieste, Benvenuti was one of four boys in the family who all aspired to boxing careers. He began boxing as an amateur in his native Italy, where he won 120 fights and lost none. An all-round athlete, he engaged in some unconventional training methods, such as swimming, to stay in top form. He had a wide repertoire of punches, as well as speed and good defensive moves. Benvenuti capped his amateur career by earning a gold medal in the welterweight division

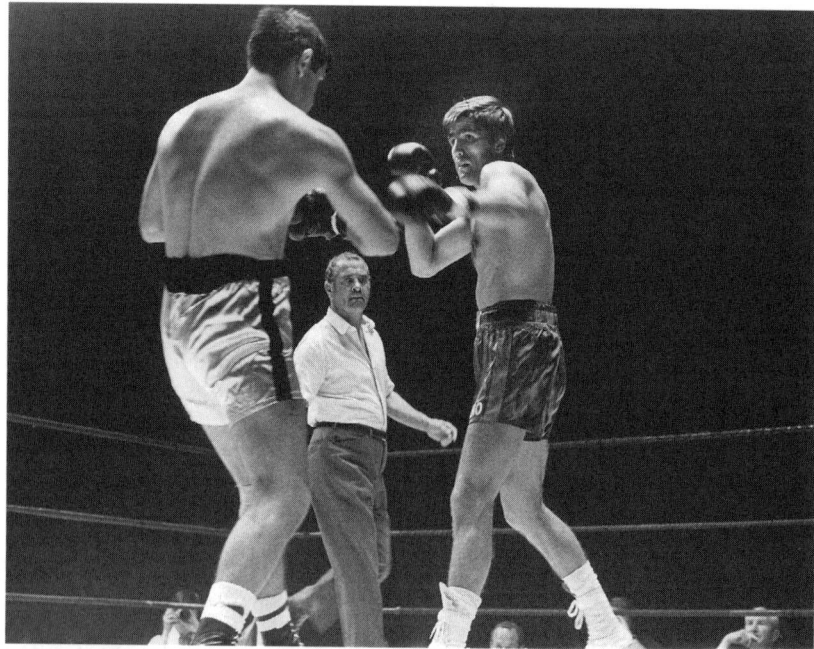

Benvenuti (R) measures Art Hernandez with a short jab. This September 17, 1968, non-title bout was a ten-round victory for Benvenuti. Earlier in 1968, he had regained the middleweight title.

IN THE RING	WON 82	LOST 7	DRAWS 1	TB 90	KO 35	W 42	WF 5	D 1	KO'd 3	L 4	LF 0

Date	Opponent	Site	Result / Rounds		Title	Wt.
1961						
Jan 20	Ali Allala	Trieste, Italy	W	6	—	—
Feb 10	Nicola Sanmartino	Rome	TKO	3	—	—
Feb 27	Ali Allala	Naples, Italy	KO	1	—	—
Mar 14	Sahib Mosri	Bologna, Italy	TKO	3	—	—
Apr 7	Nick Maric	Milan	W	6	—	—
Apr 21	Pierre Mondino	Florence, Italy	W	6	—	—
May 3	Daniel Brunet	Naples	WD	3	—	—
May 16	Michel Francois	Turin, Italy	KO	4	—	—
Jun 7	Henri Cabelduc	Bologna	W	6	—	—
Jun 17	Marc Desforneaux	Trieste	W	6	—	—
Oct 2	Retmia Mahrez	Bologna	TKO	3	—	—
Nov 1	Angelo Brisci	Trieste	KO	1	—	—
Nov 9	Jesse Jones	Rome	WD	6	—	—
Dec 20	Giuseppe Catalano	Rome	W	8	—	—
1962						
Jan 19	George Aldridge	Rome	KO	6	—	—
Feb 19	Jose Riquelme	Bologna	W	8	—	—
Mar 8	Manfred Haas	Turin	W	8	—	—
Mar 17	Gianni Lommi	Milan	TKO	5	—	—
Apr 1	Jim Hegerle	Rome	TKO	4	—	154
May 1	Hector Constance	Trieste	W	10	—	—
Jun 2	Jean Ruellet	Cagliari, Italy	W	8	—	—
Jun 22	Heini Freytag	Rome	W	8	—	—
Jul 12	Gino Rossi	Trieste	W	10	—	—
Aug 2	Mahmout Le Noir	Lignano, Italy	W	8	—	—
Aug 30	Giuseppe Gentiletti	Senigallia, Italy	TKO	2	—	—
Sep 28	Diego Infantes	Rome	W	8	—	—
Oct 18	Daniel Leullier	Padua, Italy	W	10	—	—
Nov 30	Isaac Logart	Rome	W	10	—	155
Dec 26	Giampaolo Melis	Bologna	TKO	2	—	—
1963						
Mar 1	Tomasso Truppi	Rome	KO	11	Won-Vac Italy-M	160
Apr 5	Georges Estatoff	Turin	KO	6	—	—
Apr 24	Jean Ruellet	Alejandria, Italy	W	10	—	—
May 23	Jimmy Beecham	Rome	W	10	—	159
Jun 7	Tony Montano	Rome	W	10	—	—
Aug 31	Francesco Fiori	Priverno, Italy	KO	3	Ret-Italy-M	160
Sep 16	Willy Niederau	Prato, Italy	TKO	6	—	—
Sep 27	Victor Zalazar	Rome	TKO	2	—	—
Oct 18 ⑩	Gaspar Ortega	Rome	W	10	—	156
Nov 7	Jackie Cailleau	Prato	W	10	—	159
Nov 15	Lou Gutierrez	Rome	TKO	7	—	160
Dec 13 ⑩	Teddy Wright	Rome	W	10	—	160
1964						
Feb 28	Memo Ayon	Rome	KO	5	—	160
Mar 18	Michel Diouf	Bologna	W	10	—	160
Apr 10	Sugar Boy Nando	Rome	W	10	—	159

Date		Opponent	Location	Result	Rounds		Weight
May 28		Jimmy Beechman	Bologna	TKO	2	—	160
Jul 30		Fabio Bettini	San Remo, Italy	W	12	Ret-Italy-M	160
Sep 18		Denny Moyer	Rome	W	10	—	156
Oct 9		Abrao DeSouza	Rome	WD	7	—	158
Nov 27		Aristeo Chavarin	Rome	KO	4	—	—
Dec 19		Juan Duran	Milan	W	10	—	158
1965							
Jan 22		Art Hernandez	Rome	TKO	3	—	157
Feb 12		Tommaso Truppi	Bologna	TKO	5	Ret-Italy-M	160
Feb 26		Mick Lehaly	Milan	W	10	—	157
Mar 18		Dick Knight	Bologna	KO	6	—	158
Apr 2		Rip Randall	Rome	W	10	—	157
Apr 30		Milo Calhoun	Genoa, Italy	W	10	—	156
Jun 18	♕	Sandro Mazzinghi	Milan	KO	6	Won-World-JM	153
Aug 15		Daniel Leullier	Senigallia	TKO	7	—	154
Oct 15	⑩	Luis Folledo	Rome	TKO	6	Won-Vac Europe-M	160
Nov 5		Johnny Torres	Turin	WD	7	—	157
Nov 15		James Shelton	Bologna	W	10	—	155
Dec 17	⑩	Sandro Mazzinghi	Rome	W	15	Ret-World-JM	153
1966							
Feb 4	⑩	Don Fullmer	Rome	W	12	—	160
Mar 11		Clarence James	Turin	W	10	—	157
May 14		Jupp Elze	Berlin	KO	14	Ret-Europe-M	158
Jun 25	⑩	Ki-Soo Kim	Seoul	L	15	Lost-World-JM	153
Sep 23		Harry Scott	Rome	W	10	—	157
Oct 21		Pascal Di Benedetto	Rome	TKO	11	Ret-Europe-M	159
Dec 2		Ferd Hernandez	Rome	W	10	—	163
Dec 23		Renato Moares	Rome	KO	9	—	161
1967							
Jan 19		Manfred Graus	Bologna	KO	2	—	162
Mar 3		Milo Calhoun	Rome	W	10	—	161
Apr 17	♕	Emile Griffith★	New York	W	15	Won-World-M	159
Sep 29	⑩	Emile Griffith★	New York	L	15	Lost-World-M	159
1968							
Jan 19		Charley Austin	Rome	W	10	—	159
Mar 4	♕	Emile Griffith★	New York	W	15	Reg-World-M	160
Jun 7		Yoshiaki Akasaka	Rome	KO	2	—	161
Jul 5		Jimmy Ramos	Turin	TKO	4	—	162
Sep 17		Art Hernandez	Toronto	W	10	—	163
Oct 14	⑩	Doyle Baird	Akron, OH	D	10	—	162
Dec 14	⑩	Don Fullmer	San Remo	W	15	Ret-World-M	160
1969							
May 26	⑩	Dick Tiger★	New York	L	10	—	164
Oct 4	⑩	Fraser Scott	Naples	WD	7	Ret-World-M	160
Nov 22	⑩	Luis Rodriguez★	Rome	KO	11	Ret-World-M	159
1970							
Mar 13		Tom Bethea	Melbourne	TKO'd	8	—	163
May 23		Tom Bethea	Umag, Yugoslavia	KO	8	Ret-World-M	160
Sep 12	⑩	Doyle Baird	Bari, Italy	KO	10	—	—
Nov 7	⑩	Carlos Monzon★	Rome	KO'd	12	Lost-World-M	159
1971							
Mar 17		Jose Chirino	Bologna	L	10	—	163
May 9	♕	Carlos Monzon★	Monte Carlo	TKO'd	3	For-World-M	160

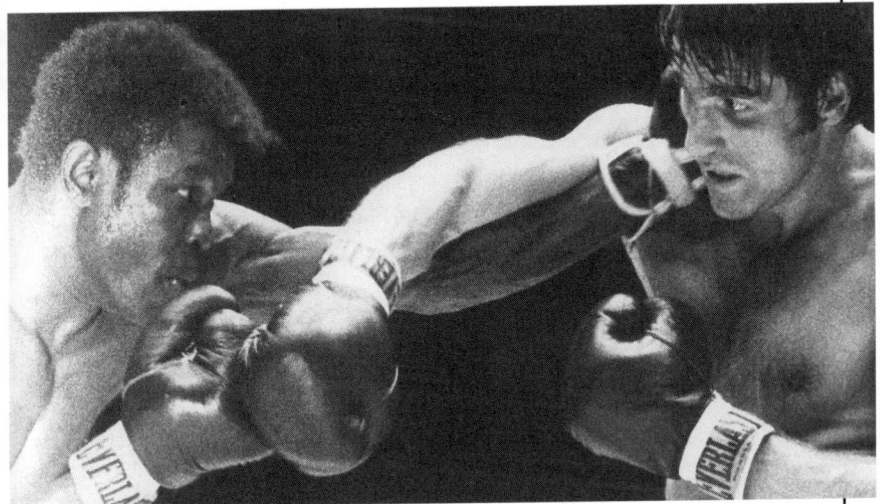

Within a twelve-month stretch, Nino Benvenuti (R) and Emile Griffith met three times in New York for the middleweight championship. Each fight went the distance. Benvenuti won two; Griffth one.

in the 1960 Olympics, the same year Muhammad Ali participated in the games. Looking back on his entire boxing career, Benvenuti commented, "Winning the Olympic medal was my biggest thrill."

The following year, Benvenuti turned professional and continued to win. He triumphed in his first 65 professional fights—along the way winning the Italian and European middleweight titles, as well as the world junior middleweight title. Although the junior middleweight division was not well established in 1965, when Benvenuti defeated countryman Sandro Mazzinghi in Milan, he was recognized as a world champion. But a year later, Benvenuti lost that title when he suffered his first loss, to Korean Ki-Soo Kim.

As early as 1963, Benvenuti had been placed among the top ten middleweights in the annual rankings by *The Ring*. In 1967, he had his first opportunity to fight for the world middleweight championship when he travelled to the United States to face Emile Griffith in Madison Square Garden. Over 18,000 fans had come to watch the former Olympian scrap with Griffith. Although Griffith knocked the Italian challenger down in the fourth round, Benvenuti used his superior size and reach to keep Griffith away with jabs and hooks. When Griffith did venture inside, Benvenuti traded punches with the champion on an equal basis. Benvenuti won the title in a fifteen-round decision.

In their rematch in New York's Shea Stadium, Griffith used an effective attack to Benvenuti's body to regain the championship. The two foes met a third time in a bout which helped open the new Madison Square Garden, with Benvenuti regaining the championship by decision. He held the belt until 1970 when Carlos Monzon knocked him out in the twelfth round. After losing to Monzon again, Benvenuti retired to the business world. His suave manner and good looks later led to appearances in Italian movies.

JACKIE ("KID") BERG
The Whitechapel Whirlwind

JR. WELTERWEIGHT

Right-handed; 5'9"; 134–153 lbs.

192 bouts, 6/8/1924 to 5/19/1945

Managers: Harry Levene (England), Frank Jacobs, Sol Gold

Jr. Welterweight Champion 1930–31

Hall of Fame Induction: 1994

Born: 6/28/1909, London, England

Named: Judah Bergman

Died: 4/22/1991

Trained by Hall of Famer Ray Arcel, Jackie ("Kid") Berg boxed professionally for over two decades, during which time he recorded 157 wins. Like many fighters of his time, he fought frequently, sometimes with as little as a week between bouts. Berg is the first modern-era Hall of Fame inductee from England, the cradle of prizefighting.

Born Judah Bergman in Whitechapel in London's East End, Berg was an early devotee of the boxing matches staged at a theatre in his district. In 1924, when he was just fourteen, he convinced the show promoters to let him compete. Berg's energetic, attacking style was an instant success with the fans. He fought exclusively in London until 1928 with a record of 53 wins, three losses, and three draws. Ready to challenge a broader field of opponents, Berg arrived in the United States early in 1928. He fought primarily in Chicago before moving on to New York the following year.

Berg performed well in New York and quickly became a favorite in Madison Square Garden. His swarming, continuous attack earned him the nickname "The Whitechapel Whirlwind." His handlers played up his Jewish ethnicity by having him enter the ring wearing a tallis (prayer shawl) and tefilin (small leather box containing sacred scripture). In 1928, Berg was ranked as the ninth-best lightweight by *The Ring*. In 1929, he advanced to second top contender in the magazine's annual rankings. In

When Berg won the junior welterweight title in 1930, that division had only been contested for five years.

IN THE RING	WON 157	LOST 26	DRAWS 9	TB 192	KO 57	W 87	WF 13	D 9	KO'd 8	L 18	LF 0

Date	Opponent	Site	Result / Rounds		Title	Wt.
1924						
Jun 8	Young Johnny Gordon	London	TKO	8	—	—
Jul 7	Charley Harwood	London	TKO	7	—	—
Jul 20	Syd Lyons	London	TKO	3	—	—
Aug 3	Billy Clarke	London	D	10	—	—
Aug 21	Billy Clarke	London	W	10	—	—
Sep 21	Teddy Pullen	London	KO	1	—	—
Oct 2	Jimmy Wooder	London	D	10	—	—
Oct 16	Albert Hicks	London	W	10	—	—
Nov 3	Young Clancy	London	W	15	—	—
Nov 10	Jimmy Wooder	London	W	10	—	—
Nov 20	Harry Miller	London	TKO	6	—	—
Nov 27	Fred Patten	London	W	15	—	—
Dec 7	Teddy Sheperd	London	TKO	9	—	—
Dec 11	Fred Saunders	London	TKO	14	—	—
Dec 15	Arthur Lloyd	London	W	10	—	—
Dec 26	Billy Colebourne	London	TKO	6	—	—
1925						
Jan 8	Albert Colcombe	London	TKO	13	—	—
Jan 26	Billy Streets	London	W	15	—	—
Feb 9	Arthur Lloyd	London	W	15	—	—
Feb 26	Billy Streets	London	TKO	9	—	—
Mar 12	Johnny Cuthbert	London	L	15	—	—
Apr 6	Sid Carter	London	W	15	—	—
Apr 19	George Davis	London	WF	6	—	—
May 21	Ted ("Kid") Lewis★	London	TKO	10	—	—
Jun 7	Billy Shepherd	London	TKO	13	—	—
Jun 18	Johnny Cuthbert	London	L	15	—	—
Jun 28	Jack Slattery	London	TKO	9	—	—
Jul 16	Joe Samuels	London	TKO	15	—	—
Jul 26	George Green	London	TKO	11	—	—
Aug 6	Fred Green	London	W	15	—	—
Aug 20	Fred Green	London	W	15	—	—
Aug 30	Johnny Britton	London	W	15	—	—
Sep 10	Norman Radford	London	KO	14	—	—
Oct 15	Johnny Cuthbert	London	TKO	11	—	—
Oct 29	Johnny Curley	London	W	15	—	—
Nov 12	Ernie Swash	London	WF	2	—	—
Nov 26	Battling Van Dyke	London	W	15	—	—
1926						
Feb 11	Harry Corbett	London	L	15	—	—
Mar 18	Andre Routis	London	W	15	—	—
Apr 26	Harry Corbett	London	D	15	—	—
May 16	Mick Hill	London	W	15	—	—
Jun 21	Andre Routis	London	WF	3	—	—
Jul 8	Henry Hebrans	London	TKO	5	—	—
Jul 29	Paul Gay	London	TKO	6	—	—
Aug 29	Harry Corbett	London	W	15	—	—
Oct 10	Phil Bond	London	W	16	—	—

Date		Opponent	Location	Result	Rounds	Title	Weight
Nov 21		Billy Gilmore	London	TKO	8	—	—
Dec 19		Omer Saerens	London	WF	9	—	—
1927							
Jan 13		Walter Wright	London	TKO	2	—	—
Jan 23		Joe Claes	London	W	15	—	—
Feb 27		Paul Fritsch	London	TKO	8	—	—
Apr 21		Alf Simmons	London	WF	8	—	—
May 29		Bob Miller	London	TKO	6	—	—
Sep 18		Robert Sirvain	London	TKO	6	—	—
Sep 29		Jack Kirk	London	KO	13	—	—
Oct 11		Raymond Jansin	London	WF	7	—	—
Nov 7		Vittorio Venturi	London	W	10	—	—
Dec 4		Lucien Vinez	London	W	15	—	—
1928							
Feb 27		Jack Donn	London	WF	10	—	—
May 31	⑩	Pedro Amador	Chicago	W	10	—	134
Jun 7		Johnny Mellow	Detroit	W	10	—	—
Jun 14	⑩	Freddie Mueller	Chicago	W	10	—	134
Jul 12		Mike Watters	Chicago	TKO	9	—	134
Jul 26	⑩	Billy Petrolle★	Chicago	D	10	—	133
Aug 24	⑩	Billy Petrolle★	Chicago	TKO'd	5	—	—
Oct 8		Spug Meyers	Chicago	WF	3	—	137
Dec 6		Alf Mancini	London	W	15	—	—
1929							
Jan 12		Lucien Vinez	London	W	15	—	—
May 10	⑩	Bruce Flowers	New York	W	10	—	138
May 23	⑩	Bruce Flowers	New York	W	10	—	137
Jun 11	⑩	Estanislao Loayza	New York	D	10	—	136
Jul 12		Herman Perlick	Chicago	W	10	—	138
Jul 24	♛	Mushy Callahan	Brooklyn	W	10	—	143
Aug 5		Joe Trabon	New York	TKO	5	—	140
Aug 19		Harry Wallace	New York	TKO	9	—	138
Aug 29		Spug Meyers	New York	W	10	—	137
Sep 16		Georgie Balduc	Brooklyn	WF	2	—	138
Sep 30		Phil McGraw	New York	W	10	—	139
Oct 21	⑩	Bruce Flowers	New York	W	10	—	137
Nov 2		Tommy Gerval	New York	KO	2	—	138
Nov 18		Eddie Elkins	New York	W	10	—	137
Nov 30		Artie DeLuca	New York	W	6	—	137
Dec 18		Tony Caragliano	New York	WF	2	—	134
1930							
Jan 16	⑩	Tony Canzoneri★	New York	W	10	—	134
Feb 18	♛	Mushy Callahan	London	TKO	10	Won-World-JW	137
Apr 4	⑩	Joe Glick	New York	W	10	Ret-World-JW	139
Apr 7		Jackie Philips	Toronto	W	10	—	139
May 29		Al Delmont	Newark, NJ	TKO	4	Ret-World-JW	139
Jun 11		Herman Perlick	Long Island City, NY	W	10	—	138
Jul 10		Henry Perlick	Newark	W	10	—	139
Aug 7	⑩	Kid Chocolate★	New York	W	10	—	133
Sep 3		Buster Brown	Newark	W	10	Ret-World-JW	136
Sep 18	⑩	Joe Glick	Long Island City	W	10	Ret-World-JW	136
Oct 10	⑩	Billy Petrolle	New York	W	10	Ret-World-JW	135
1931							
Jan 23		Goldie Hess	Chicago	W	10	Ret-World-JW	138
Jan 30		Herman Perlick	New York	W	10	Ret-World-JW	138

Date		Opponent	Location	Result	Rds	Notes	Wt
Apr 10	⑩	Billy Wallace	Detroit	W	10	Ret-World-JW	138
Apr 24	♛	Tony Canzoneri★	Chicago	KO'd	3	For-World-L & Lost-World-JW	134
May 8	⑩	Tony Herrera	New York	W	10	—	137
May 18		Ray Kiser	Pittsburgh	W	10	—	137
Jun 22		Tony Lambert	Newark	TKO	8	—	139
Jul 24		Teddy Watson	Jersey City, NJ	KO	7	—	139
Jul 27		Phillie Griffin	Newark	W	10	—	138
Aug 4		Jimmy McNamara	New York	W	10	—	137
Sep 10	♛	Tony Canzoneri★	New York	L	15	For-World-L & For-World-JW	134
Dec 14		Maurius Baudry	London	TKO	5	—	—
1932							
Mar 21		Buster Brown	New York	W	10	—	140
Apr 1	⑩	Sammy Fuller	New York	D	10	—	133
May 20	♛	Sammy Fuller	New York	L	12	—	138
Jun 29		Mike Sarko	New York	W	6	—	140
Jul 18	♛	Kid Chocolate★	New York	W	15	—	137
1933							
Apr 27		Cleto Locatelli	London	L	10	—	—
May 28		Louis Saerens	London	KO	4	—	—
Jul 8		George Rose	Cardiff, Wales	TKO	5	—	—
Jul 14		Eugene Drouhin	London	TKO	8	—	—
Sep 30		Harry Wallace	New York	TKO	4	—	142
Oct 19		Tony Falco	New York	L	10	—	140
1934							
Jan 12		Cleto Locatelli	New York	L	10	—	139
Apr 14		Jackie Flynn	London	W	10	—	—
May 12		Len Wickwar	Leicester, England	WF	6	—	—
May 29		Jimmy Stewart	Liverpool, England	TKO'd	3	—	—
Jul 10		Joe Kerr	Liverpool	TKO	6	—	—
Aug 19		Nicholas Wilke	London	TKO	9	—	—
Oct 29		Harry Mizler	London	TKO	10	Won-Britain-L	135
Dec 2		Alfred Bastin	London	TKO	4	—	—
1935							
Jan 21		Gustave Humery	London	TKO	8	—	—
Feb 25		Gustave Humery	Paris	L	10	—	134
Apr 1		Gustave Humery	London	L	10	—	—
May 19		Harry Brown	London	KO	3	—	—
Oct 21		Peter McKinley	London	W	10	—	—
Nov 14		Pat Butler	London	TKO	4	—	—
1936							
Jan 11	⑩	Laurie Stevens	Johannesburg	L	12	For-Brit Emp-L	134
Apr 24	⑩	Jimmy Walsh	Liverpool	TKO'd	9	Lost-Britain-L	—
Jul 22	⑩	Aldo Spoldi	Brooklyn	TKO'd	2	—	141
1937							
Jan 24		Ivor Pikens	London	W	10	—	—
Feb 7		Pat Haley	London	WF	10	—	—
Feb 11		George ("Panther") Purchase	West Ham, England	TKO	12	—	—
Feb 21		Harry Mason	London	TKO	5	—	—
Mar 22		Louis Saerens	Bristol, England	D	10	—	—
Apr 11		Pat Haley	Cricklewood, England	TKO	9	—	—
May 6		Alby Day	London	W	10	—	—
Aug 14		Jack Lewis	Poole, England	D	10	—	—
Oct 4		Jake Kilrain	London	TKO	6	—	—
Nov 1		George Odwell	London	TKO'd	10	—	—
Dec 6		Charlie Chetwynd	Manchester, England	TKO	5	—	—

Date		Opponent	Location	Result	Rounds		
Dec 13		Leo Phillips	Birmingham, England	W	10	—	—

1938

Date		Opponent	Location	Result	Rounds		
Feb 10		Silvio Zangrillo	Brooklyn	KO	8	—	146
Mar 5		Larry Anzalone	Brooklyn	W	8	—	146
Mar 15		Vincent Pimpinella	Brooklyn	W	10	—	145
Mar 29	⑩	Frankie Wallace	Brooklyn	W	8	—	145
Apr 9		Johnny Horstman	Brooklyn	W	8	—	145
May 3		Ray Napolitano	Brooklyn	W	8	—	145
Jun 7		Johnny McHale	Brooklyn	W	8	—	146
Jun 15		Augie Arellano	Long Island City	D	8	—	146
Jun 30		Johnny Horstman	Brooklyn	W	8	—	144
Jul 12		Johnny McHale	Brooklyn	W	8	—	145
Jul 25		Freddie ("Red") Cochrane	Newark	L	10	—	146
Aug 5		Pete Cara	Brooklyn	W	8	—	144
Oct 11		Johnny McHale	Brooklyn	W	8	—	147
Oct 25		Joey Greb	New York	W	8	—	147
Nov 22		Frankie Cavanna	Brooklyn	W	8	—	146

1939

Date		Opponent	Location	Result	Rounds		
Feb 3		Baby Breese	Hollywood, FL	L	10	—	144
Mar 10	⑩	Pedro Montanez	New York	KO'd	5	—	146
Apr 4		Pete Galiano	Brooklyn	W	8	—	147
Apr 11		Marine Bunker	Bermuda	KO	8	—	—
Jun 6		Tippy Larkin	Garfield, NJ	W	10	—	143
Jun 26	⑩	Milt Aron	Chicago	TKO'd	6	—	145
Jun 30		Mike Piskin	Long Branch, NJ	L	10	—	145
Jul 11		Johnny Rohrig	Garfield	W	10	—	143
Aug 1		Joey Greb	Garfield	W	8	—	144
Oct 12		Paddy Roche	Southampton, England	W	10	—	—
Nov 30		Paddy Roche	Nottingham, England	TKO	5	—	—

1940

Date		Opponent	Location	Result	Rounds		
Jan 25		Harry Davis	Hackney, England	W	10	—	—
Feb 5		George Reynolds	Bristol, England	W	10	—	—
Feb 29		Eddie Ryan	London	WF	6	—	—
Mar 8		Paddy Roche	Dublin	TKO	4	—	—
Mar 10		Dick Bradshaw	Hackney	TKO	3	—	—
Apr 4		Harry Davis	Hackney	TKO	8	—	—

1941

Date		Opponent	Location	Result	Rounds		
Jan 20		Harry Craster	London	W	10	—	—
Feb 20		Harry Charman	London	W	6	—	153
Feb 27		Harry Mizler	London	W	10	—	—
Apr 21		Eric Boon	London	WF	2	—	—
May 30		Ernie Roderick	London	L	10	—	—
Jul 24		Arthur Danahar	London	TKO'd	5	—	—
Nov 2		George Odwell	Stoke Newington, England	L	10	—	—
Nov 24		Joe Connolly	Leeds, England	TKO	8	—	—

1942

Date		Opponent	Location	Result	Rounds		
Feb 5		Paddy Roche	Newcastle, England	TKO	4	—	—
Mar 12		Joe Connolly	Glasgow, Scotland	TKO	4	—	—

1943

Date		Opponent	Location	Result	Rounds		
May 22		Gordon Woodhouse	Handcross, England	L	6	—	—

1945

Date		Opponent	Location	Result	Rounds		
Mar 1		Eric Dolby	London	KO	4	—	—
Mar 8		Jimmy Brunt	London	W	8	—	—
May 19		Johnny McDonald	Coventry, England	KO	5	—	—

those years, Berg was 4-0-1 against lightweight and junior welterweight contenders.

In 1930, Berg faced Hall of Famer Tony Canzoneri, who would soon become lightweight champ. In the first two rounds, Berg attempted a stand-up boxing style, which wasn't successful. From the third round until the end of the fight, Berg went back to his typical style and won the decision. In his next fight, held in London, Berg knocked out American Mushy Callahan to win the world junior welterweight title. Later that year in a non-title fight, Berg won a split decision over the previously unbeaten Kid Chocolate—a natural featherweight. Berg forced the action and chased Chocolate all over the ring.

The next year he again faced Canzoneri, this time for the lightweight title. Berg could not handle Canzoneri and was knocked out in the third round. In the rematch, Berg performed well but lost the fifteen-round decision. Most of the boxing world believed that Canzoneri had taken the junior welterweight belt from Berg, while simultaneously successfully defending his own lightweight crown. But Berg still asserted the belt was his. Berg's disputed claim

Jackie ("Kid") Berg handed the brilliant Cuban, Kid Chocolate, his first defeat in 161 fights. Berg outweighed Chocolate by nearly ten pounds.

to the junior welterweight title ended when he lost to Sammy Fuller in 1932. That same year, he won another decision over Chocolate.

Though Berg continued to fight in the U.S., Britain, and elsewhere, he never again challenged for a world title. He held the British lightweight title for two years before losing it to Jimmy Walsh in 1936. Berg retired in 1945, after 21 years as a fighter, then worked as a movie stunt man in England.

JIMMY BIVINS

HEAVYWEIGHT

Right-handed; 5'10"; 157–195 lbs.

112 bouts, 1/15/1940 to 10/28/1955

Managers: Wilfred ("Whizbang") Carter 1940–42, Claude Shane, Jr. 1942–53

Hall of Fame Induction: 1999

Born: 12/6/1919, Dry Branch, GA

Named: James Louis Bivins

Not so long ago, when there were just eight weight classes and one champion in each, even fighters considered all-time greats in the sport were not guaranteed a chance at a championship belt. Jimmy Bivins is one such boxer. Few fighters have maintained as high a level of excellence as Bivins for such a long time, or fought so many quality opponents.

Bivins's family moved to Cleveland when he was two. He worked an assortment of jobs while in school, and he was a good student. After graduation, Bivins began visiting local gyms. In his first fight against a more experienced boxer, Bivins easily dominated his opponent. His performance attracted the attention of Wilfred ("Whizbang") Carter, an amateur trainer who entered Bivins in the Golden Gloves competition, where he won the 126-pound novice title. The next year Bivins won the 147-pound open division title, finished second in the nationals, then turned professional.

Carter continued as Bivins's trainer and Charles ("Claude") Shane, Jr. became Bivins's manager. On January 15, 1940, Bivins made his pro debut as a welterweight with a one-round triumph against Emory ("KO") Morgan. Bivins soon moved to middleweight and quickly faced top competition. On April 8, 1940, Bivins won an eight-round decision over Nate Bolden, and in September decisioned Hall of Famer Charley Burley. Bivins closed 1940 splitting two decisions with Anton Christoforidis, who would win the NBA light heavyweight title in his next fight. In his incredible debut year, Bivins won nineteen of twenty fights against some excellent opponents.

While Bivins continued to face very high-quality opponents, his chances for a title shot in 1942 were hurt when titles were frozen for the duration of WWII. He started the year with a punishing ten-round decision over former middleweight champion Billy Soose, who retired after the fight. Bivins

After suffering three losses in a row, Bivins (L) still had enough left for a ten-round decision over seventh-ranked light heavyweight contender Doc Williams on November 21, 1951, in New York. Here Bivins connects to the belt.

IN THE RING	WON 86	LOST 25	DRAWS 1	TB 112	KO 31	W 55	WF 0	D 1	KO'd 5	L 20	LF 0

Date		Opponent	Site	Result / Rounds		Title	Wt.
1940							
Jan 15		Emory Morgan	Cleveland	TKO	1	—	147
Feb 12		Tito Taylor	Chicago	W	6	—	—
Feb 26		Joe Sutka	Chicago	W	8	—	154
Mar 18		Joe Sutka	Chicago	W	8	—	158
Mar 27		Young Flowers	Cleveland	KO	3	—	—
Apr 8		Nate Bolden	Chicago	W	8	—	—
Apr 15		Johnny Dean	Cleveland	KO	3	—	159
Apr 25		Enzo Ionozzi	Cleveland	KO	1	—	158
May 13		Paul Frazier	Chicago	KO	1	—	157
Jun 13		Homer Jackson	Pittsburgh	TKO	1	—	160
Jun 24		Frankie Hughes	Chicago	W	8	—	—
Jul 1		Mose Brown	Pittsburgh	W	6	—	161
Jul 15		Paul Frazier	Chicago	W	8	—	160
Aug 5		Johnny Barbara	Chicago	KO	2	—	158
Sep 3	⑩	Charley Burley★	Pittsburgh	W	10	—	160
Sep 9		Johnny Barbara	Chicago	TKO	7	—	158
Sep 23		Larry Kellum	Pittsburgh	KO	1	—	162
Oct 22		Vincent Pimpinella	Cleveland	W	10	—	160
Nov 15	⑩	Anton Christoforidis	Cleveland	W	10	—	161
Dec 2	⑩	Anton Christoforidis	Cleveland	L	10	—	159
1941							
Feb 9		Pete Tamalonis	Cleveland	TKO	1	—	174
Mar 5	⑩	Teddy Yarosz★	Cleveland	W	10	—	174
Apr 2		Buddy Knox	Cleveland	W	10	—	172
Jul 2		Curtis Sheppard	Pittsburgh	W	10	—	176
Jul 14		Lem Franklin	Chicago	TKO'd	9	—	173
Sep 11		Tony Musto	Cleveland	L	10	—	180
Oct 20	⑩	Nate Bolden	Chicago	W	10	—	—
Nov 17	⑩	Melio Bettina	Cleveland	L	10	—	173
1942							
Jan 13	⑩	Billy Soose	Cleveland	W	10	—	176
Mar 11	♛	Gus Lesnevich	Cleveland	W	10	—	176
Apr 17	⑩	Bob Pastor	Cleveland	L	10	—	176
Jun 22	⑩	Joey Maxim★	Cleveland	W	10	—	176
Jul 23		Joe Muscato	Cleveland	KO	5	—	176
Sep 15		Tami Mauriello	Cleveland	W	10	—	177
Oct 20	⑩	Bob Pastor	Cleveland	W	10	—	177
Nov 27		Lee Savold	New York	W	10	—	175
1943							
Jan 7		Ezzard Charles★	Cleveland	W	10	—	174
Feb 26	⑩	Anton Christoforidis	Cleveland	W	15	—	174
Mar 12	⑩	Tami Mauriello	New York	W	10	—	177
Apr 6		Watson Jones	Los Angeles	W	10	—	179
Apr 26		Pat Valentino	San Francisco	W	10	—	176
Jul 8	⑩	Lloyd Marshall	Cleveland	KO	13	—	174
Aug 24		Herbert Marshall	Washington, DC	KO	6	—	179
Sep 15	⑩	Melio Bettina	Cleveland	W	10	—	182
Dec 1		Lee Q. Murray	Cleveland	W	10	—	187
1944							
Feb 29	⑩	Lee Q. Murray	Cleveland	W	10	—	191

1945

Date		Opponent	Location	Result	Rounds		
Feb 5		George Parks	Washington, DC	TKO	4	—	188
Feb 19		Buddy Walker	Baltimore	KO	2	—	188
Feb 27		Johnny Flynn	Cleveland	W	10	—	188
Mar 16	⑩	Melio Bettina	New York	D	10	—	185
Jun 12		Buddy Scott	Washington, DC	KO	4	—	188
Jul 26	⑩	Curtis Sheppard	Pittsburgh	W	10	—	190
Aug 22	⑩	Archie Moore★	Cleveland	KO	6	—	186
Sep 26		Yancey Henry	Washington, DC	W	10	—	185

1946

Date		Opponent	Location	Result	Rounds		
Jan 7		Watson Jones	San Francisco	TKO	6	—	187
Jan 22		Johnny Haynes	Los Angeles	KO	2	—	187
Jan 29	⑩	Billy Smith	Oakland	W	10	—	186
Feb 10		Yancey Henry	Baltimore	KO	10	—	186
Feb 25	⑩	Jersey Joe Walcott★	Cleveland	L	10	—	182
Jun 20	⑩	Lee Q. Murray	Cleveland	L	10	—	190
Nov 12	⑩	Ezzard Charles★	Pittsburgh	L	10	—	186
Dec 5		Colion Chaney	Akron, OH	KO	5	—	187

1947

Date		Opponent	Location	Result	Rounds		
Jan 16		Johnny Flynn	Washington, DC	W	10	—	190
Feb 3		Booker Beckworth	Chicago	KO	4	—	187
Feb 17	⑩	Curtis Sheppard	Pittsburgh	W	10	—	185
Mar 10	⑩	Ezzard Charles★	Cleveland	KO'd	4	—	184
Apr 21	⑩	Curtis Sheppard	Baltimore	W	10	—	185
May 9	⑩	Lee Q. Murray	Detroit	L	10	—	185
Jun 2		Omelio Agramonte	Baltimore	KO	2	—	182
Jun 9	⑩	Lee Q. Murray	Baltimore	W	10	—	183
Jul 1		Bobby Zander	Los Angeles	W	10	—	181
Sep 8	⑩	Archie Moore★	Baltimore	TKO'd	9	—	184
Nov 12		Sid Peaks	Chicago	W	10	—	185

1948

Date		Opponent	Location	Result	Rounds		
Jan 13		Johnny Shkor	Buffalo, NY	W	10	—	185
Mar 1		Johnny Haynes	Baltimore	KO	4	—	185
Mar 9	⑩	Turkey Thompson	Los Angeles	W	10	—	185
Apr 12	⑩	Billy Thompson	Philadelphia	TKO	7	—	185
Apr 20		Pat Valentino	Cleveland	W	10	—	186
Aug 28	⑩	Archie Moore★	Baltimore	L	10	—	187
Sep 13	⑩	Ezzard Charles★	Washington, DC	L	10	—	178
Oct 11	⑩	Johnny Flynn	Philadelphia	W	10	—	179
Nov 17	⑩	Joe Louis★	Cleveland	Exh	6	—	—
Dec 7	⑩	Joey Maxim★	Cleveland	L	10	—	178

1949

Date		Opponent	Location	Result	Rounds		
Mar 21	⑩	Rusty Payne	Pittsburgh	W	10	—	185
Apr 11	⑩	Archie Moore★	Toledo, OH	KO'd	8	—	185
Jun 20		Willie Bean	Cleveland	W	10	—	186
Jul 5	⑩	Leonard Morrow	Los Angeles	L	10	—	182
Jul 15		Watson Jones	Las Vegas	KO	2	—	182
Sep 21	⑩	Leonard Morrow	Oakland	W	10	—	183
Sep 27		Clarence Henry	Los Angeles	TKO	8	—	183
Oct 26	⑩	Harold Johnson★	Philadelphia	L	10	—	180

1950

Date		Opponent	Location	Result	Rounds		
Feb 1		Willis Applegate	Miami	W	10	—	180
Feb 6		Sid Peaks	Newark, NJ	L	10	—	188

1951

Date		Opponent	Location	Result	Rounds		
Jan 22		Young Harry Wills	Baltimore	KO	4	—	184
Feb 12		Ted Lowry	Baltimore	W	10	—	180

Date		Opponent	Location	Result				Weight
Feb 21	⑩	Archie Moore ★	New York	TKO'd	9		—	180
May 4		Willie Bean	Hollywood	W	10		—	184
May 18		Bobby Mitchell	Phoenix	W	10		—	182
May 29		Willie Bean	Los Angeles	W	10		—	179
Jun 26	⑩	Clarence Henry	Los Angeles	L	10		—	177
Aug 15	⑩	Joe Louis ★	Baltimore	L	10		—	180
Nov 5	⑩	Bob Baker	Pittsburgh	L	10		—	186
Nov 21	⑩	Charley ("Doc") Williams	New York	W	10		—	184
1952								
Mar 31		Aaron Wilson	Baltimore	TKO	3		—	184
Sep 19		Coley Wallace	New York	KO	9		—	184
Oct 22		Wesbury Bascom	St. Louis	W	10		—	183
Nov 3	⑩	Tommy Harrison	Providence, RI	L	10		—	185
Nov 26	⑩	Ezzard Charles ★	Chicago	L	10		—	183
1953								
Apr 6		Tommy Harrison	Miami	L	10		—	192
Apr 24		Claude Rolfe	Tampa	W	10		—	182
Jun 9		Chubby Wright	Huntington, WV	W	10		—	186
1955								
Aug 31		Dan Moray	Cleveland	KO	3		—	190
Oct 28		Mike DeJohn	Cleveland	W	6		—	195

next defeated light heavyweight champion Gus Lesnevich in a non-title bout in Cleveland, but the win hurt his chances for a title match. After the fight, Lesnevich's manager said, "This guy is too good for us—now or ever." Bivins did lose to heavyweight Bob Pastor in his next fight, but he avenged that defeat later in the year. He also decisioned Hall of Famer Joey Maxim and top heavyweight contenders Tami Mauriello and Lee Savold.

The next year opened with a decision over Hall of Famer Ezzard Charles, whom he knocked down four times. The next month, Bivins decisioned Christoforidis for the "duration" light heavyweight title. On March 12, 1943, Bivins won eight of ten rounds for an easy decision against Mauriello for the "duration" heavyweight title. Bivins fought only once in 1944 before he was inducted into the army, but he returned from the service as strong as before with a sixth-round knockout of Hall of Famer Archie Moore. On February 25, 1946, Bivins lost a disputed split decision to Hall of Famer and future heavyweight champion, Jersey Joe Walcott. Had Bivins won, he might have received the title shot against Louis instead of Walcott.

Bivins bounced in and out of top-ten-contender status in the late '40s. Though he beat heavyweight contender Rusty Payne and light heavyweight contender Leonard Morrow, in 1949, he lost decisions to Morrow and to Hall of Famer Harold Johnson. In 1951, he was knocked out by Archie Moore shortly after returning from a one-year boxing hiatus. Bivins fought his last bout on October 28, 1955, when he decisioned up-and-coming Mike DeJohn.

In retirement, Bivins worked for a Cleveland bakery and as a trainer of amateurs, a gym owner, and a boxing commissioner. Sadly, in 1998 Bivins was found imprisoned by his son-in-law and daughter in a dirty attic. He was in terrible health when he was rescued, and after hospitalization he came under the care of family and friends, while his son-in-law pleaded guilty to elder abuse.

JOE BROWN
Old Bones

LIGHTWEIGHT

Right-handed; 5'7½"; 126–144 lbs.
161 bouts, 9/3/1946 to 4/24/1970

Managers: Lester Majoue and
Louis Chattard 1946–1955,
Lou Viscusi 1955–1970

Lightweight Champion 1956–1962
Hall of Fame Induction: 1996
Born: 5/18/1926, New Orleans, LA
Died: 11/21/1997

Known for a strong right as well as his fine left jabs and hooks, Joe ("Old Bones") Brown was born in New Orleans and brought up in Baton Rouge. A carpenter like his father, he honed his boxing skills with the navy in the Pacific, although he had a single pro bout in 1943.

After the war, Brown resumed his professional career with a series of fights in New Orleans. In spite of an out-of-the-gate loss to Melvin Bartholomew in 1946 he established a 5-2-1 record, with all his wins by decision. Over the next two years, Brown maintained

In a close match between two veterans, Joe Brown (R) wrests the lightweight crown from Wallace ("Bud") Smith in New Orleans on August 24, 1956.

IN THE RING	WON 104	LOST 44	DRAWS 13	TB 162	KO 47	W 57	WF 0	D 13	KO'd 9	L 33	LF 2	NC 1

Date	Opponent	Site	Result / Rounds		Title	Wt.
1943						
Sep 3	Leonard Ceasar	New Orleans	W	4	—	133
1945						
Jul 9	Melvin Bartholomew	New Orleans	KO'd	3	—	139
1946						
Jan 13	Leonard Ceasar	New Orleans	L	5	—	143
Jan 20	Johnny Monroe	New Orleans	W	6	—	142
Mar 22	Leonard Ceasar	New Orleans	D	6	—	141
Mar 29	Leonard Ceasar	New Orleans	W	8	—	136
Apr 5	Frankie Adams	New Orleans	W	6	—	140
Jun 28	Herbert Jones	New Orleans	W	8	—	138
Jul 26	Buster Tyler	New Orleans	L	10	—	139
Oct 18	Bob Weatherley	New Orleans	W	8	—	139
1947						
Mar 7	Buster Tyler	New Orleans	D	10	—	142
Mar 28	Melvin Bartholomew	New Orleans	L	10	—	140
Apr 18	Jimmy Carter★	New Orleans	W	10	—	137
May 2	⑩ Sandy Saddler★	New Orleans	KO'd	3	—	136
Jul 4	Melvin Bartholomew	New Orleans	W	10	—	137
Jul 23	Freddie Latson	Norwalk, CT	W	6	—	126
Aug 6	Danny Webb	Montreal	W	10	—	130
Sep 24	Dan Robinson	Jersey City, NJ	W	8	—	138
Oct 6	Ernie Butler	Newark, NJ	KO	5	—	138
Oct 21	⑩ Arthur King	Toronto	W	8	—	134
Nov 10	⑩ Arthur King	Toronto	L	8	—	134
Dec 15	Joey Bagnato	Toronto	KO	1	—	134
1948						
Feb 29	Bobby McQuillar	New Orleans	D	10	—	134
May 7	Bobby McQuillar	New Orleans	L	10	—	135
Jul 25	Luther Burgess	New Orleans	D	10	—	130
Oct 1	⑩ Freddie Dawson	New Orleans	L	10	—	135
Oct 26	Frank Cockrell	San Antonio, TX	KO	5	—	—
Oct 31	Arthur Persley	New Orleans	W	10	—	136
Dec 3	⑩ Johnny Bratton	New Orleans	KO'd	4	—	136
1949						
Mar 22	Booker Ellis	St. Paul, MN	W	6	—	140
Mar 28	Luther Rawlings	Chicago	W	10	—	139
Apr 25	Joe Sgro	Chicago	W	8	—	141
May 10	Hugh Sublett	South Bend, IN	W	8	—	—
May 23	John LaBroi	Chicago	D	8	—	137
May 27	Leroy Willis	New Orleans	W	10	—	135
Jun 6	Willie Russell	Cincinnati	W	10	—	137
Dec 5	Ike Jenkins	Philadelphia	W	6	—	136
1950						
Jan 20	Milton Scott	Chicago	KO	2	—	—
Feb 6	Danny Womber	Chicago	W	8	—	137
Feb 22	Dave Marsh	Chicago	W	4	—	—
Jun 16	⑩ John L. Davis	Hollywood	L	10	—	134

Date		Opponent	Location	Result	Rounds		Weight
Sep 22		Jack Hassen	Melbourne	KO	8	—	136
Oct 30		Charley Williams	Sydney	KO	1	—	139
Nov 27		Howell Steen	Sydney	NC	10	—	138
Dec 14		Bernie Hall	Broken Hill, Australia	TKO	11	—	138
1951							
Feb 20	Ⓝ	Tommy Campbell	Los Angeles	L	10	—	136
Mar 10		Baby Ortiz	Ocean Park, CA	KO	2	—	137
Apr 13		Teddy Davis	New Orleans	W	10	—	133
Apr 27		Lester Felton	New Orleans	W	10	—	136
May 11		Clarence Johnson	New Orleans	W	10	—	139
May 25	Ⓝ	Virgil Akins	New Orleans	W	10	—	136
Jul 6	Ⓝ	Virgil Akins	New Orleans	W	10	—	135
Aug 31	Ⓝ	Tommy Campbell	New Orleans	KO	1	—	134
Sep 28		Stonewall Jackson	New Orleans	TKO	5	—	137
Dec 6	Ⓝ	Virgil Akins	St. Louis	L	10	—	137
1952							
Feb 4		Walter Haines	Miami	D	6	—	141
Feb 15		Walter Haines	New Orleans	D	10	—	138
Mar 14		Walter Haines	New Orleans	W	10	—	137
Mar 28		Calvin Smith	New Orleans	TKO	7	—	137
Jun 10		Jerry Turner	Tampa	TKO	5	—	135
Jul 11		Melvin Bartholomew	New Orleans	W	10	—	138
Jul 18		Marshall Clayton	New Orleans	TKO	9	—	136
Aug 22		Jimmy Taylor	New Orleans	W	10	—	136
Oct 10	Ⓝ	George Araujo	New York	KO'd	7	—	134
Dec 10		Don Bowman	Cleveland	KO	1	—	137
1953							
Jan 7		Joey Greenwood	Cleveland	W	8	—	138
Apr 22	Ⓝ	Orlando Zulueta	Baltimore	D	10	—	135
Jun 9		Luther Rawlings	Miami Beach	D	10	—	137
Dec 29		Cliff Dyes	Miami Beach	TKO	9	—	—
1954							
Feb 8		Charlie Smith	Providence, RI	LD	6	—	134
Mar 24		Isaac Logart	Miami Beach	W	10	—	135
Jun 20		Federico Plummer	Colon, Panama	TKO	9	—	—
Jul 25		Wilfredo Brown	Colon	KO	4	—	—
Aug 31		Nat Jackson	New Orleans	KO	4	—	135
Sep 28		Carl Coates	New Orleans	L	10	—	138
Dec 29		Antonio Armenteros	Miami	L	6	—	—
1955							
Jan 18		Antonio Armenteros	New Orleans	TKO	7	—	137
Jan 30		Tito Despaigne	Colon	KO	4	—	—
Mar 6		Bobby Rosado	Colon	W	10	—	—
Mar 20		Antonio Armenteros	Colon	W	10	—	—
Jun 16		Junius West	Colon	KO	3	—	—
Aug 1	Ⓝ	Arthur Persley	New Orleans	L	12	—	135
Oct 31		Jimmy Hackney	New Orleans	W	10	—	137
Nov 8		Ray Rojas	Houston	TKO	7	—	135
Dec 13		Ray Portilla	Houston	TKO	5	—	136
1956							
Feb 6		Arthur Persley	New Orleans	TKO	9	—	136
May 2	♔	Wallace ("Bud") Smith	Houston	W	10	—	139

Jun 5		Eddie Brant	Beaumont, TX	TKO	3	—	136
Aug 24	♛	Wallace ("Bud") Smith	New Orleans	W	15	Won-World-L	133

1957

Feb 13	⑩	Wallace ("Bud") Smith	Miami Beach	TKO	11	Ret-World-L	134
Mar 12		Armand Savoie	Houston	W	10	—	138
Jun 19	⑩	Orlando Zulueta	Denver	TKO	15	Ret-World-L	134
Jul 30		Gilberto Holguin	San Antonio	W	10	—	139
Aug 21	⑩	Joey Lopes	Chicago	D	10	—	139
Nov 12		Kid Centella	Houston	W	10	—	140
Dec 4	⑩	Joey Lopes	Chicago	TKO	11	Ret-World-L	133

1958

Jan 24		Ernie Williams	Washington, DC	TKO	5	—	137
Feb 26		Orlando Echevarria	Havana, Cuba	KO	1	—	136
May 7	⑩	Ralph Dupas	Houston	TKO	8	Ret-World-L	134
Jul 23	⑩	Kenny Lane	Houston	W	15	Ret-World-L	134
Nov 5	⑩	Johnny Busso	Miami Beach	L	10	—	140

1959

Feb 11	⑩	Johnny Busso	Houston	W	15	Ret-World-L	134
Jun 3	⑩	Paolo Rosi	Washington, DC	TKO	9	Ret-World-L	132
Aug 27		Santiago Ramirez	Baton Rouge, LA	KO	8	—	138
Sep 9		Gale Kerwin	Columbus, OH	TKO	4	—	140
Sep 26		Joey Parks	Albuquerque, NM	D	10	—	139
Dec 2	⑩	Dave Charnley	Houston	TKO	6	Ret-World-L	134
Dec 14		Joey Parks	New Orleans	W	10	—	139

1960

Mar 21		Ray Portilla	San Antonio	TKO'd	6	—	136
Aug 25		Harlow Irwin	Minneapolis	TKO	5	—	136
Oct 4	⑩	Battling Torres	Houston	KO	4	—	137
Oct 28	⑩	Cisco Andrade	Los Angeles	W	15	Ret-World-L	134
Dec 7		Giordano Campari	Milan	L	10	—	136

1961

Mar 7		Joey Parks	Houston	W	10	—	138
Apr 18	⑩	Dave Charnley	London	W	15	Ret-World-L	134
Oct 28	⑩	Bert Somodio	Quezon, Philippines	W	15	Ret-World-L	135

1962

Apr 21	⑩	Carlos Ortiz★	Las Vegas	L	15	Lost-World-L	134
Aug 24	⑩	Luis Molina	San Jose, CA	L	10	—	138

1963

Jan 22		Tony Noriega	Houston	KO	6	—	137
Feb 25	⑩	Dave Charnley	Manchester, England	KO'd	6	—	134
Apr 20	⑩	Manuel Alvarez	Monterrey, Mexico	KO	8	—	—
May 21		Joey Lopes	Sacramento, CA	TKO	8	—	136
Jun 22	⑩	Alfredo Urbina	Monterrey	L	10	—	134
Aug 10	⑩	Nicolino Locche★	Buenos Aires	L	10	—	134
Sep 14		Pedro Galasso	Rio de Janeiro	TKO	5	—	138
Nov 11	⑩	Carlos Hernandez	Maracaibo, Venezuela	KO'd	3	—	136

1964

Apr 2	⑩	Manuel Gonzalez	Odessa, TX	L	10	—	138
Apr 28	⑩	Paul Armstead	Sacramento	L	10	—	138
May 5		Tony Perez	San Jose	W	10	—	138
May 25	⑩	Paul Armstead	San Francisco	L	10	—	137
Jun 21		Esteban Santamaria	Colon	W	10	—	135

Aug 25	Ricardo Medrano	Austin, TX	LD	10	—	134
Sep 14	Hector (Chino) Diaz	Omaha, NE	KO	8	—	135
Oct 3	Percy Hayles	Kingston, Jamaica	L	10	—	136
Nov 21	Levi Madi	Johannesburg	W	10	—	135
Dec 19	Joas (Kangaroo) Maoto	Johannesburg	KO	6	—	134
1965						
Feb 9	Levi Madi	Cape Town, S. Africa	W	10	—	136
Feb 27	Joe N'Gidi	Johannesburg	L	10	—	—
Mar 9	Vic Andretti	London	TKO'd 5		—	138
May 18	Joey Olguin	Sacramento	L	10	—	138
Jun 29	Porfirio Zamora	Corpus Christi, TX	W	10	—	—
Aug 27	Antonio Herrera	Cali, Columbia	L	10	—	135
Oct 2	Mario Rossito	Barranquilla, Colombia	L	10	—	—
Nov 13	❿ Frankie Narvaez	San Juan, PR	L	10	—	—
1966						
Mar 11	Bruno Arcari	Turin, Italy	L	10	—	137
Apr 15	Jarmo Bergloef	Helsinki, Finland	D	10	—	133
May 14	Josiah Nakedi	Bloemfontein, S. Africa	KO	9	—	—
Jun 4	Enoch Nhlapo	Johannesburg	W	10	—	138
Jun 25	Joe N'Gidi	Durban, South Africa	L	10	—	—
Jul 30	Joe N'Gidi	Johannesburg	L	10	—	—
Aug 30	Rodwell LeKay	Lourenco Marques, Mozambique	W	10	—	—
1967						
Jun 16	Porfirio Zamora	Baton Rouge	TKO	8	—	139
Jun 26	Joe Barrientes	New Orleans	W	10	—	139
Aug 1	❿ Percy Pugh	New Orleans	L	10	—	138
Sep 11	Benito Juarez	New Orleans	W	10	—	139
Dec 23	Nathaniel Jackson	Pensacola, FL	KO	5	—	—
1968						
Apr 23	Vic Graffio	Beaumont, TX	TKO	8	—	140
Jun 9	❿ Chango Carmona	Mexico City	TKO'd 4		—	134
Sep 11	Ricardo Medrano	Beaumont	L	10	—	137
Nov 6	Jose Garcia	Beaumont	KO'd	9	—	137
1969						
Aug 12	Steve Freeman	Houston	D	10	—	135
1970						
Apr 24	Ramon Flores	Tucson, AZ	W	10	—	136
Aug 24	Dave Oropeza	Phoenix	L	10	—	144

a modest record of 15-8-4, winning a decision over future lightweight champion Jimmy Carter but losing by knockout to Hall of Fame featherweight Sandy Saddler and the formidable welterweight Johnny Bratton.

In the early 1950s, Brown's career ran hot and cold, as did his ranking. But by 1955, ready to improve on his erratic record and overcome general dismissal as a "fancy Dan" (a fine defensive fighter with little power), he began working with trainer Bill Gore. Almost immediately, he racked up knockouts in consecutive fights with Ray Rioja, Ray Portilla, and Arthur Persley.

A non-title decision over lightweight champion Wallace ("Bud") Smith set the stage for a title-making rematch. On August 24, 1956, a partisan crowd jammed New Orleans's Municipal Auditorium, hoping to see the hometown Brown beat

Brown (R) defended his lightweight title twelve times including two rough wins against Britisher Dave Charnley. In their second meeting in London on April 18, 1961, Charnley bulls in while sustaining damage.

Smith. Starting off quickly in the first, Brown led the scoring with both rights and lefts. Sustaining a broken hand in the second round, Brown nevertheless resourcefully outboxed his opponent for much of the fight. Hurt in the twelfth, he used both hands to knock Smith down in the fourteenth and, by the final round, had claimed a split decision and the title. In the rematch, Brown won by knockout.

Over the next six years, Brown defended his title successfully eleven times, twice knocking out Ralph Dupas and winning a close decision over tough southpaw Kenny Lane. On April 21, 1962, he faced Hall of Famer Carlos Ortiz in the Las Vegas Convention Center. Much younger and quicker, Ortiz used snapping left jabs to keep Brown from mounting an effective attack and won an easy decision. Brown's manager, Lou Viscusi, blamed his fighter's loss on tonsillitis, although he'd been cleared ahead of time by the state's physician.

Brown lost his next fight—and thus a shot at a rematch with Ortiz—and never again challenged for the title. He continued to box for another eight years until the age of 44, often in such far-flung venues as South America, South Africa, and Finland. Brown died at age 72, just one year after his induction into the Hall of Fame.

KEN BUCHANAN

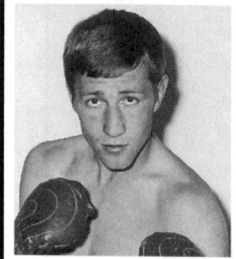

LIGHTWEIGHT

Right-handed; 5'7½"; 126–138 lbs.
69 bouts, 9/20/1965 to 1/25/1982
Manager: Eddie Thomas, 1965–71
Lightweight Champion 1970–1972
Hall of Fame Induction: 2000
Born: 6/28/1945, Edinburgh, Scotland

One of the top Scots fighters of all time, Buchanan yearned to be a boxer from the time he was a small boy. He cajoled his father into letting him join a boxing club when he was only eight, and although younger than the minimum age of nine, he won a medal in his first year.

An accomplished amateur fighter, Buchanan participated in the European championships in Moscow in 1963 and in Berlin in 1965. That year he also won the British Amateur Boxing Association featherweight title.

After his ABA title win, Buchanan turned professional and signed with manager Eddie Thomas. Thomas, who also managed Howard Winstone, a top featherweight, decided that Buchanan would be most successful as a lightweight. Buchanan's first professional fight was on September 20, 1965, when he knocked out Brian Tonks in the second round. Buchanan won his first sixteen bouts before winning the vacant Scottish lightweight title on January 23, 1967, with a ten-round decision over John McMillan. On February 19, 1968, Buchanan knocked out Maurice Cullen in eleven rounds to win the British lightweight title.

Buchanan started off 1969 with a decision over contender Frank Narvaez and won his next three fights before abruptly announcing his retirement at only 24. The impetus for this shocking announcement was an attempt to sever his contract in a dispute with Thomas, his manager. When the British Boxing Board of Control ruled in Thomas's favor, Buchanan did retire, only to return on November 11, 1969, with a second-round knockout of Vincenzo Pitardi.

On January 29, 1970, Buchanan left Britain for the first time to fight Miguel Velazquez for the vacant European lightweight title in Madrid. Though much favored, Buchanan lost a fifteen-round decision. Later that year, he faced lightweight champion Ismael Laguna in San Juan, Puerto

A tired Ken Buchanan wins a Lonsdale Belt, emblematic of the British championship, with his lightweight knockout victory over Maurice Cullen. Because Buchanan won a total of three British championships, he was given permanent possession of his belt.

IN THE RING	WON 61	LOST 8	DRAWS 0	TB 69	KO 27	W 34	WF 0	D 0	KO'd 1	L 7	LF 0

Date	Opponent	Site	Result / Rounds		Title	Wt.
1965						
Sep 20	Brian Tonks	London	TKO	2	—	126
Oct 18	Vic Woodhall	Manchester, England	TKO	2	—	—
Nov 1	Billy Williams	London	TKO	3	—	—
Nov 22	Joe Okezie	London	TKO	3	—	—
Dec 13	Junior Cassidy	London	W	8	—	—
1966						
Jan 24	Tommy Tiger	London	W	8	—	—
Mar 7	Manley Brown	London	TKO	4	—	—
Apr 4	Tommy Tiger	London	W	8	—	—
Apr 19	Chris Elliot	Manchester	W	8	—	—
May 11	Junior Cassidy	Manchester	W	8	—	—
Jul 12	Brian Smith	Aberavon, England	TKO	1	—	—
Aug 6	Ivan Whiter	London	W	8	—	131
Sep 6	Mick Laud	London	W	8	—	—
Oct 17	Antonio Paiva	London	W	10	—	—
Nov 29	Al Keen	Leeds, England	W	8	—	134
Dec 19	Phil Lundgren	London	W	10	—	—
1967						
Jan 23	John McMillan	Glasgow, Scotland	W	10	Won-Scots-L	—
Feb 14	Tommy Garrison	London	W	10	—	133
May 11	Franco Brondi	Paisley, Scotland	TKO	3	—	—
Jun 28	Winston Laud	London	W	8	—	134
Jul 26	Rene Roque	Aberavon	W	10	—	—
Sep 14	Al Rocca	London	TKO	7	—	—
Oct 30	Jim ("Spike") McCormack	London	W	12	—	134
1968						
Feb 19	Maurice Cullen	London	KO	11	Won-British-L	131
Apr 22	Leonard Tavarez	London	W	8	—	—
Jun 10	Ivan Whiter	London	W	8	—	—
Oct 23	Angel Robinson Garcia	Mayfair, England	W	10	—	131
Dec 11	Ameur Lamine	Hamilton, Scotland	TKO	3	—	—
1969						
Jan 2 ⑩	Frank Narvaez	Piccadilly, England	W	10	—	131
Feb 17	Mike Cruz	Mayfair	TKO	5	—	132
Mar 5	Jose Luis Torcida	Solihull, England	W	10	—	—
Jul 14	Jerry Gracy	Nottingham, England	TKO	1	—	—
Nov 11	Vincenzo Pitardi	Mayfair	TKO	2	—	137
1970						
Jan 29 ⑩	Miguel Velazquez	Madrid	L	15	For-Vac Eur-L	130
Feb 23	Leonard Tavarez	Piccadilly	W	10	—	134
Apr 6	Chris Fernandez	Nottingham	W	10	—	—
May 12	Brian Hudson	London	KO	5	Ret-Brit-L	134
Sep 26 ♛	Ismael Laguna★	San Juan, PR	W	15	Won-WBA-L	134
Dec 7	Donato Paduano	New York	W	10		136
1971						
Feb 12 ⑩	Ruben Navarro	Los Angeles	W	15	Won-World-L	134
May 10 ⑩	Carlos Hernandez	London	TKO	8	Won-WBC-L	135
Sep 13 ⑩	Ismael Laguna★	New York	W	15	Ret-WBA-L	133

1972							
Mar 28	Ⓦ	Al Ford	London	W	10	—	—
Apr 29		Andries Steyn	Johannesburg	TKO	3	—	136
Jun 26	Ⓦ	Roberto Duran	New York	TKO'd	14	Lost-WBA-L	133
Sep 20		Carlos Ortiz★	New York	TKO	7	—	134
Dec 4		Chang-Kil Lee	New York	TKO	2	—	135
1973							
Jan 29		Jim Watt	Glasgow	W	15	Reg-Brit-L	133
Mar 27		Hector Matta	London	W	10	—	136
May 29		Frankie Otero	Miami Beach	W	10	—	132
Sep 1		Edwin ("Chuchu") Malave	New York	TKO	7	—	137
Oct 11	Ⓦ	Frankie Otero	Toronto	TKO	6	—	134
Dec 6		Miguel Araujo	Copenhagen	KO	1	—	—
1974							
Feb 7		Jose Peterson	Copenhagen	W	10	—	—
Apr 4		Joe Tetteh	Copenhagen	KO	3	—	—
May 1		Antonio Puddu	Cagliari, Italy	KO	6	Won-Eur-L	134
Nov 21		Winston Noel	Copenhagen	TKO	2	—	—
Dec 16		Leonard Tavarez	Paris	TKO	14	Ret-Eur-L	134
1975							
Feb 27	♛	Ishimatsu Suzuki	Tokyo	L	15	For-WBC-L	133
Jul 25		Giancarlo Usai	Cagliari	TKO	12	Ret-Eur-L	133
1979							
Jun 28		Benny Benitez	Randers, Denmark	W	8	—	—
Sep 6		Eloi De Souza	Randers	W	8	—	—
Dec 6		Charlie Nash	Copenhagen	L	12	For-Eur-L	—
1980							
May 15		Najib Daho	London	KO	7	—	135
Oct 20		Des Gwilliam	Birmingham, England	W	8	—	136
1981							
Jan 26		Steve Early	Edgebaston, Scotland	L	12	—	137
Apr 4		Langton Tinago	Salisbury, England	L	10	—	—
Nov 24		Lawrence Williams	London	L	8	—	—
1982							
Jan 25		George Feeney	Piccadilly	L	8	—	138
1983							
*Mar 8		Johnny Claydon	London	KO	7	—	—

Unsanctioned bout, not included in totals

Rico. The fight was held on September 26, 1970, at Hiram Bithorn Stadium, and temperatures soared over 100 degrees. Buchanan started off well against the favored Laguna, but in the fourth and fifth, Laguna frequently connected with Buchanan's body and head. The challenger recovered in the sixth, and while the champ again took charge in the seventh, Laguna soon appeared to be faring worse than his opponent from the intense heat. Buchanan pinned Laguna against the ropes in the twelfth, then got the better of him over the next three rounds to earn a split decision, winning on two cards, 145-144 and 144-143, and losing on one, 143-144.

Buchanan had won, but the WBC refused to recognize him as champion—the California Athletic Commission had previously suspended Laguna for breaking a contract to defend his title. The Laguna fight marked the end of Buchanan's association with Thomas. Buchanan then managed his own career. For his efforts, in 1970 the Boxing Writers Association of America awarded Buchanan the Edward J. Neil Trophy for Fighter of the Year.

In his first bout after winning the WBA title, Buchanan fought in Madison Square Garden on the undercard of the Ali–Bonavena fight, easily defeating Donato Paduano and winning over the New York fans. He traveled to California for his next fight and decisioned Ruben Navarro, a late substitute for Mando Ramos, on February 12, 1971, before 10,360 spectators at the L.A. Sports Arena. It was after this bout that Buchanan finally received official WBC recognition of his championship.

He did not maintain the WBC title for long. After defeating Laguna in a rematch in Madison Square Garden on September 13, 1971, Buchanan was stripped of the title for fighting Laguna instead of the WBC's top contender, Pedro Carrasco.

On June 26, 1972, in Madison Square Garden, Buchanan's WBA championship reign came to an end when he faced the brawling Roberto Duran. Duran attacked Buchanan from every angle, even using his head as a weapon. Though Buchanan fought well, Duran had the edge as the fight wore on. Duran received a warning for hitting below the belt in the thirteenth, and the fight ended with a blow (perhaps from Duran's knee) to Buchanan's groin that floored the champion. He could not continue, the punch was ruled legal, and Buchanan lost the WBA title.

Buchanan knocked out fading Hall of Famer Carlos Ortiz in his next fight, and on January 29, 1973, he won a Lonsdale Belt when he decisioned Jim Watt in Glasgow for the British lightweight title. On May 1, 1974, he knocked out Antonio Puddu to win the European championship, and the next year he trav-

Ken Buchanan batters Ruben Navarro against the ropes in Buchanan's first world lightweight title defense, before a large crowd in Los Angeles on February 12, 1971.

eled to Tokyo to face WBC lightweight champion Ishimatsu Suzuki for a world title. Buchanan lost a close split decision. After one more fight, a defense of his European belt, he retired.

Four years later, financial reverses forced Buchanan back into the ring. While he won four of his first five fights, he dropped his last four against fighters who would once have presented no challenge to him. He officially retired after losing to George Feeney on January 25, 1982, though he did continue to fight in unlicensed bouts. After further financial setbacks, Buchanan was forced to work as a carpenter and, for a time, lived in a one-room apartment in Glasgow, claiming unemployment benefits. Buchanan has written two autobiographies, *High Life and Hard Times* and *The Tartan Legend*.

CHARLEY BURLEY

MIDDLEWEIGHT

Right-handed; 5'9½"; 145–166 lbs.

98 bouts, 9/29/1936 to 7/22/1950

Managers: Phil Goldstein 1936–42, Tommy O'Loughlin 1942–50

Hall of Fame Induction: 1992

Born: 9/6/1917, Bessemer, PA

Named: Charles Duane Burley

Died: 10/16/1992

Charley Burley had an excellent, if frustrating, career as a black fighter up against the color bar. Part of an outstanding crop of boxers to come out of the Pittsburgh area in the late 1930s and early '40s, Burley entered the pro ranks in his hometown in 1936. In his first eighteen months of fighting, he compiled an outstanding record of 16 wins and one loss and was given a chance to fight a prominent local fighter, Hall of Famer Fritzie Zivic. Burley lost a decision to the far more experienced Zivic, but he later beat Zivic twice.

Despite his success, or perhaps because of it, Burley had great difficulty getting matches with the top fighters. Normally a middleweight , Burley faced heavyweights who sometimes outweighed him by as much as 50 pounds. Not all prizefighting greats refused to face him. He lost two decisions to a much heavier Ezzard Charles and defeated the great Archie Moore. However, proposed fights against Billy Conn, Sugar Ray Robinson, a fourth fight against Zivic, and bouts with other champions never materialized.

Though unable to gain a title shot as a welterweight, middleweight, or light heavyweight, Burley did receive

Burley was a careful tactician in the ring. He was sparing with his punches and was remarkable in his ability to avoid opponents' shots.

	WON	LOST	DRAWS	TB	KO	W	WF	D	KO'd	L	LF	NC
IN THE RING	**83**	**12**	**2**	98	50	33	0	2	0	12	0	1

Date		Opponent	Site	Result / Rounds		Title	Wt.
1936							
Sep 29		George Leggins	Pittsburgh	KO	4	—	150
Oct 22		Ralph Gizzy	Pittsburgh	W	6	—	147
Nov 9		Eddie Wirko	Pittsburgh	TKO	5	—	150
1937							
Jan 22		Ralph Gizzy	Oil City, PA	KO	2	—	148
Feb 8		Ray Collins	Oil City	TKO	5	—	147
Apr 15		Johnny Folio	McKeesport, PA	TKO	5	—	149
Apr 19		Ray Gray	Pittsburgh	W	6	—	148
May 3		Sammy Grippe	Pittsburgh	W	6	—	147
May 27		Keith Goodballet	Pittsburgh	TKO	2	—	148
Jun 24		Mickey O'Brien	Pittsburgh	W	10	—	146
Aug 9		Remo Fernandez	Pittsburgh	TKO	7	—	148
Aug 16		Sammy Grippe	Millvale, PA	TKO	6	—	145
Sep 9		Eddie Dolan	Pittsburgh	L	8	—	148
1938							
Jan 27		Tiger Jackson	Pittsburgh	KO	2	—	—
Feb 3		Johnny Folio	Pittsburgh	W	4	—	148
Feb 10		Carl Turner	Pittsburgh	W	4	—	147
Mar 3		Art Tate	Pittsburgh	KO	2	—	149
Mar 21	⑩	Fritzie Zivic★	Pittsburgh	L	10	—	147
Jun 1		Mike Barto	Millvale	KO	4	—	147
Jun 13	⑩	Fritzie Zivic★	Millvale	W	10	—	149
Aug 2		Leon Zorrita	Millvale	TKO	6	—	148
Aug 22	⑩	Cocoa Kid	Millvale	W	16	—	145
Nov 3		Werther Arcelli	Pittsburgh	KO	1	—	151
Nov 21		Billy Soose	Pittsburgh	W	10	—	152
1939							
Jan 10		Sonny Jones	Pittsburgh	TKO	7	—	148
Jun 20	⑩	Jimmy Leto	Millvale	L	10	—	147
Jul 17	⑩	Fritzie Zivic★	Pittsburgh	W	10	—	149
Aug 28	⑩	Jimmy Leto	Pittsburgh	W	10	—	146
Oct 23		Mickey Makar	Pittsburgh	KO	1	—	149
Dec 1	⑩	Holman Williams	New Orleans	L	15	—	155
1940							
Feb 12	⑩	Nate Bolden	Pittsburgh	W	10	—	155
Apr 12		Baby Kid Chocolate	New Orleans	KO	5	—	149
Apr 26		Sammy Edwards	New Orleans	KO	2	—	151
Jun 17		Carl Dell	Holyoke, MA	W	10	—	147
Jul 29	⑩	Georgie Abrams	Millvale	D	10	—	156
Aug 19		Kenny LaSalle	Millvale	W	10	—	149
Sep 3	⑩	Jimmy Bivins★	Millvale	L	10	—	153
Oct 18		Eddie Peirce	Pittsburgh	W	10	—	150
Nov 11		Vincent Pimpinella	Washington, DC	W	10	—	151
1941							
Mar 31		Babe Synnott	Pittsburgh	TKO	5	—	149

Date		Opponent	Location	Result	Rounds		Weight
Apr 18		Eddie Ellis	Boston	TKO	5	—	149
Jun 2		Ossie Harris	Millvale	TKO	9	—	150
Jul 14		Gene Buffalo	Philadelphia	KO	5	—	152
Aug 25		Otto Blackwell	Millvale	W	8	—	153
Sep 25	⑩	Antonio Fernandez	Philadelphia	W	10	—	149
Dec 12		Ted Morrison	Minneapolis	KO	2	—	153
Dec 23		Jerry Hayes	Eau Claire, WI	KO	4	—	155
1942							
Jan 9		Shorty Hogue	Minneapolis	KO	10	—	155
Jan 23		Jackie Burke	Minneapolis	TKO	5	—	150
Feb 6		Milo Theodorescu	San Diego	TKO	4	—	—
Feb 13		Willard ("Big Boy") Hogue	San Diego	TKO	6	—	151
Feb 26	⑩	Holman Williams	Minneapolis	W	10	—	148
Mar 13		J.D.Turner	Minneapolis	TKO	6	—	151
Apr 10		Cleo McNeal	Minneapolis	KO	5	—	150
Apr 20		Phil McQuillan	New York	TKO	1	—	154
Apr 24		Joe Sutka	Chicago	TKO	4	—	152
Apr 30		Sonny Wilson	Minneapolis	TKO	2	—	153
May 25	⑩	Ezzard Charles★	Pittsburgh	L	10	—	155
Jun 23	⑩	Holman Williams	Cincinnati	W	10	—	157
Jun 29	⑩	Ezzard Charles★	Pittsburgh	L	10	—	151
Aug 14	⑩	Holman Williams	New Orleans	TKO	9	—	160
Oct 16	⑩	Holman Williams	New Orleans	L	15	—	157
Nov 13		Cecilio Lozada	San Diego	TKO	2	—	156
Dec 13	⑩	Lloyd Marshall	Los Angeles	L	10	—	158
1943							
Feb 3		Harvey Massey	Oakland	KO	9	—	158
Feb 19	⑩	Jack Chase	Hollywood	W	10	—	152
Mar 3		Aaron Wade	Oakland	W	10	—	153
Apr 19	⑩	Cocoa Kid	New Orleans	D	10	—	152
May 14	⑩	Holman Williams	Hollywood	NC	10	—	154
Jun 26		Bobby Birch	San Diego	W	10	—	158
1944							
Mar 3		Bobby Berger	San Diego	KO	5	—	151
Mar 20		Aaron Wade	San Diego	W	10	—	153
Apr 3	⑩	Jack Chase	Hollywood	KO	9	Won-CA-M	153
Apr 21	⑩	Archie Moore★	Hollywood	W	10	—	155
May 12		Al Gilbert	San Diego	TKO	4	—	158
Jun 23		Frankie Nelson	Hollywood	TKO	6	—	160
Aug 28		Gene Buffalo	San Francisco	TKO	5	—	158
Sep 11	⑩	Jack Chase	San Francisco	TKO	12	Ret-CA-M	157
1945							
Mar 12	⑩	Joe Carter	San Francisco	W	10	—	166
Jul 11	⑩	Holman Williams	Buffalo, NY	L	12	—	161
Jul 26		Oscar Boyd	Pittsburgh	KO	2	—	156
Aug 20	⑩	Aaron Wade	Pittsburgh	W	10	—	158
Sep 4		Dave Clark	Cincinnati	KO	1	—	160
Sep 28		Walter Duval	New Orleans	TKO	4	—	156
Oct 8	⑩	Billy Smith	San Francisco	W	10	—	160
1946							
Mar 14		Charley Dotson	Pittsburgh	TKO	3	—	157
Apr 8		Paul Peters	San Francisco	TKO	1	—	158

Apr 24	⑩	Billy Smith	Oakland	W	10	—	160
Jul 16		Charley Banks	Pittsburgh	W	10	—	158
Aug 5	⑩	Bert Lytell	Pittsburgh	W	10	—	157
1947							
Feb 17	⑩	Bert Lytell	Baltimore	L	10	—	160
Aug 8		Larry Cartwright	Huntington, WV	TKO	7	—	158
1948							
Mar 24		Battling Blackjack	Phoenix	KO	3	—	165
1949							
Apr 3	⑩	Charley Williams	New Orleans	L	10	—	160
Jul 25		Willie Wright	Pittsburgh	W	8	—	160
1950							
Feb 2		Chuck Higgins	Pittsburgh	KO	1	—	162
Mar 2		Buddy Hodnett	Pittsburgh	TKO	7	—	159
Jul 22		Pilar Bastidas	Lima, Peru	W	10	—	—

recognition in *The Ring*'s annual ratings of fighters. From 1939 through 1941, he was considered among the top five welterweight contenders. In 1942 and from 1944 through 1946, Burley was judged at least the third-best middleweight contender.

Racism was an undeniable force in preventing this talented fighter from receiving an opportunity to fight for a title. Ineffective management and Burley's unwillingness to take a dive probably also contributed. Burley asserted that he could have had a bout with Robinson, but he would have had to throw the first of a scheduled three-fight series deliberately. And, as with many strong African-American fighters, the question of whether white fighters were afraid to face him is unresolved. For a short time, Zivic became Burley's manager, perhaps so he would not have to fight him.

As with the Negro League diamond stars active before the integration of major league baseball, the descriptions of Burley's skills by his contemporaries are more indicative of his quality than is his record. Archie Moore called Burley the toughest man he fought in 234 fights. Trainer Eddie Futch said, "Charley Burley was the finest all-around fighter I ever saw." Futch added that Burley could do it all, box and punch.

Burley continued to fight until 1950. After retiring from the ring, he worked for the City of Pittsburgh.

STARE-DOWN

Sonny Liston intimidated his opponents, even before punches flew, with a steady menacing stare during the referee's instructions. Joe Frazier and Mike Tyson also were disconcerting starers. Shirley Povich, long-time sportswriter for the *Washington Post* credits Jack Sharkey with originating the tactic at the weigh-in for his July 1927 fight with Jack Dempsey. Dempsey seemed shaken by the stare, asking his seconds, "What's he doing?"

RINGFACT

MIGUEL CANTO
El Maestro

FLYWEIGHT

Right-handed; 5'1"; 105–113 lbs.

74 bouts, 2/5/1969–7/24/1982

Manager: Jesus Rivero

WBC Flyweight Champion 1975–79

Hall of Fame Induction: 1998

Born: 1/30/49, Merida, Mexico

Named: Miguel Angel Canto Solis

Mexico's Miguel Canto was known for his superb speed, footwork, counterpunching ability, and stamina. Despite a lack of knock-out power, he was an active champion who held the WBC flyweight belt for over four years.

Born in Merida, in the Yucatan Peninsula, Canto learned to fight in the streets. He began formal training as a boxer at the age of thirteen. Four years later, he won the Yucatan amateur flyweight title. Canto turned professional in 1969 after his father's death.

Canto quickly developed a rivalry with future-ranked flyweight Vicente Pool, whom he defeated three times in less than six months. Their final battle gave Canto the Yucatan State flyweight title. Canto's manager, Jesus Rivero, who would later handle Oscar de la Hoya, brought Tarcisio Gomez from Mexico City to Merida to face Canto. The undersized Canto, weighing less than the flyweight limit of 112 pounds, lost to the bigger and more experienced Gomez.

The fight with Gomez became a turning point for Canto, who trained hard

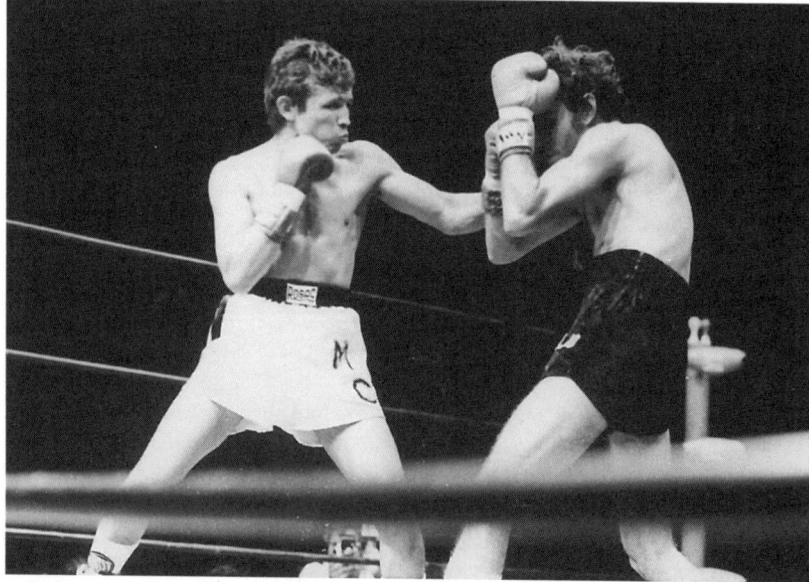

After taking the title belt, Canto (L) avenged his 1973 loss to Betulio Gonzalez with two successful title defenses in 1975 and 1976.

IN THE RING	WON 61	LOST 9	DRAWS 4	TB 74	KO 15	W 45	WF 1	D 4	KO'd 5	L 4	LF 0

Date	Opponent	Site	Result / Rounds		Title	Wt.
1969						
Feb 5	Raul Hernandez	Merida, Mexico	TKO'd	3	—	—
May 5	Pedro Martinez	Merida	W	4	—	—
Aug 13	Pedro Carrillo	Mexico City	TKO'd	4	—	—
Dec 6	Vicente Pool	Chetumal, Mexico	W	8	—	—
1970						
Jan 21	Rudy Granados	Merida	W	10	—	105
Feb 4	Joe Calvario	Merida	D	10	—	—
Mar 4	Vicente Pool	Merida	W	10	—	—
Mar 21	Baby Albornoz	Chetumal	TKO	9	—	—
Apr 8	Alex Basilio	Merida	TKO	6	—	—
Apr 29	Ranita Torres	Merida	D	8	—	110
May 27	Vicente Pool	Merida	W	12	Won-State-FL	112
Jun 24	Jose Cetina	Merida	W	12	Ret-State-FL	110
Oct 14	Tarcisio Gomez	Merida	L	10	—	109
Nov 11	Arturo Velazquez	Merida	W	10	—	109
Dec 9	Jose Medrano	Merida	W	10	—	109
1971						
Jan 21	Pedro Martinez	Cansahcab, Mexico	KO	2	—	—
Feb 14	Francisco Montalvo	Cansahcab	TKO	6	—	—
Mar 17	Marcus Gomez	Merida	TKO	6	—	110
Apr 4	Tigre Bracamontes	Merida	W	8	—	—
Apr 29	Jose Cetina	Merida	W	10	—	—
May 14	Gavilan Martinez	Tekax, Mexico	W	10	—	111
Jun 2	Mario Garcia	Merida	TKO	10	—	111
Jul 14	Pedro Lopez	Merida	KO	3	—	111
Jul 28	Domingo Ledesma	Merida	W	10	—	111
Sep 1	Roberto Alvarez	Merida	W	10	—	110
Oct 20	Alberto Morales	Merida	W	10	—	111
Dec 1	Luis Urrunaga	Merida	W	10	—	—
1972						
Jan 22	Constancio Garcia	Merida	W	12	Won-Mexican-FL	112
Mar 15	Jose Vargas	Merida	W	10	—	112
Apr 5	Armando Villa	Merida	TKO	4	—	113
May 20	Ricardo Delgado	Merida	W	12	Ret-Mexican-FL	110
Jul 26	Jose Valencia	Merida	W	10	—	110
Sep 27	Jose Corral	Merida	TKO	3	—	112
Nov 18	Alberto Morales	Merida	W	12	Ret-Mexican-FL	111
1973						
Jan 31	Ignacio Espinal	Merida	D	10	—	112
Mar 24	Tarcisio Gomez	Merida	TKO	2	Ret Mexican-FL	110
May 2	Rudy Billones	Merida	W	10	—	111
May 26	Luis Garcia	Tenosique, Mexico	TKO	7	—	111
Jun 29	Alfredo Rodriguez	Chetumal	KO	5	—	111
Aug 4 ⑩	Betulio Gonzalez	Caracas, Venezuela	L	15	For-Vac-WBC-FL	111
Nov 17	Lupe Hernandez	Merida	W	12	Ret-Mexican-FL	112
1974						
Feb 13 ⑩	Tony Moreno	Merida	TKO	5	—	—
Apr 27	Manuel Montiel	Merida	W	12	Ret-Mexican-FL	110
Jun 8	Pablito Jimenez	Merida	W	10	—	112

Date		Opponent	Location	Result	Rounds	Title	Weight
Aug 17		Alberto Morales	Mexico City	W	10	—	111
Oct 25		Ricardo Delgado	Valladolid, Mexico	W	10	—	112
1975							
Jan 8	♛	Shoji Oguma	Sendai, Japan	W	15	Won-WBC-FL	111
Mar 8	⑩	Ignacio Espinal	Merida	W	10	—	113
May 24	⑩	Betulio Gonalez	Monterrey, Mexico	W	15	Ret-WBC-FL	111
Jul 18		Lupe Madera	Cozumel, Mexico	TKO	9	—	115
Aug 23		Jiro Takada	Merida	TKO	11	Ret-WBC-FL	111
Dec 13	⑩	Ignacio Espinal	Merida	W	15	Ret-WBC-FL	112
1976							
Mar 13		Francisco Marquez	Mexico City	W	10	—	—
May 15		Susumu Hanagata	Merida	W	15	Ret-WBC-FL	111
Oct 3	⑩	Betulio Gonzalez	Caracas	W	15	Ret-WBC-FL	111
Nov 20		Orlando Javierto	Los Angeles	W	15	Ret-WBC-FL	112
1977							
Apr 24		Reyes Arnal	Caracas	W	15	Ret-WBC-FL	111
Jun 15		Kimio Furesawa	Tokyo	W	15	Ret-WBC-FL	112
Sep 17		Martin Vargas	Merida	W	15	Ret-WBC-FL	112
Nov 30		Martin Vargas	Santiago, Chile	W	15	Ret-WBC-FL	112
1978							
Jan 4	⑩	Shoji Oguma	Tokyo	W	15	Ret-WBC-FL	111
Apr 18	⑩	Shoji Oguma	Tokyo	W	15	Ret-WBC-FL	112
Nov 20		Tacomron Vibonchai	Houston	W	15	Ret-WBC-FL	111
1979							
Feb 10		Antonio Avelar	Merida	W	15	Ret-WBC-FL	111
Mar 18		Chan-Hee Park	Pusan, Korea	L	15	Lost-WBC-FL	111
Sep 9	♛	Chan-Hee Park	Seoul	D	15	For-WBC-FL	112
1980							
Aug 16		Alfredo Hernandez	Merida	W	10	—	112
Oct 18		Orlando Maldonado	Guadalajara, Mexico	WF	6	—	113
1981							
Feb 22	⑩	Sung-Jun Kim	Merida	W	10	—	113
Mar 29		Gabriel Bernal	Villahermosa, Mexico	L	10	—	112
Jun 6		Gabriel Bernal	Merida	W	10	—	113
Aug 29	⑩	Candido Tellez	Villahermosa	TKO'd	4	—	113
Oct 31		Alfredo Hernandez	Torreon, Mexico	TKO'd	7	—	113
1982							
Jul 24		Rodolfo Ortega	Merida	TKO'd	9	—	—

to gain needed strength. He went on to win his next fourteen bouts and, on January 22, 1972, he took the Mexican flyweight title from Constancio ("Rocky") Garcia. Fighting exclusively in Merida, Canto successfully defended the title twice in 1972.

In 1973, Canto traveled to Caracas, Venezuela, to challenge Betulio Gonzalez for the vacant WBC flyweight title. Although he lost to Gonzalez, Canto moved up to third in *The Ring's* flyweight rankings for 1973. Five more victories in 1974 gave Canto the top spot on *The Ring* list.

On January 8, 1975, Canto again challenged for the WBC title, then held by Shoji Oguma of Japan. Canto was the aggressor in the bout and used his unusually long reach to fire rights and lefts to his opponent's body. He earned a majority decision to take the title.

After eleven successful title defenses, Canto met Oguma in a rematch in 1978 in Tokyo. Canto won a hotly contested split decision. He won on two scorecards—147-146 by the United States judge and 147-145 by the Mexican judge. Oguma came out ahead on the Japanese judge's card by a score of 148-145. When the decision was announced, the overwhelmingly Japanese crowd threw debris into the ring. In the rematch, again held in Tokyo, Canto retained his title with a fifteen-round decision.

After decisioning future champion Antonio Avelar on February 10, 1979, Canto held a flyweight record of fourteen successful title defenses. There would not be a fifteenth. On March 18, 1979, Canto met Chan-Hee Park in Pusan, South Korea. Park built up a significant lead in the early rounds. Although Canto made a spirited comeback starting in the eleventh round, he could not overcome Park's early lead. Canto's career weakness, the lack of real knock-out power, kept him from ending the fight. Although it was close on two of the three cards, the challenger earned a unanimous decision. In the rematch six months later, Canto was knocked down in the fifth round but seized control in the later rounds. Again the fight went the full fifteen rounds. This time, however, it was ruled a draw. The Mexican judge favored Canto; the Korean judge favored Park; and the Italian referee called it even.

Canto briefly retired in 1979 following the draw in South Korea. He became involved in a wide variety of business ventures, including a restaurant and a hotel, but he returned to boxing in 1980. He won four of his first five comeback fights but was stopped in the next three in less than regulation. In a fight against Candido Tellez, he suffered his first knockout since 1969. After Rodolfo Ortega stopped him in the ninth round on July 24, 1982, Canto retired for good.

Like his idol and stylistic model, Willie Pep, Canto is remembered as a classy ring general with fourteen successful title defenses to his credit.

Demonstrating his signature speed and balance, Canto (L) avoids a blow by Ignacio Espinal. They met three times: Canto won twice; one fight was a draw.

MICHAEL CARBAJAL
Manitas De Piedra (Little Hands of Stone)

JUNIOR FLYWEIGHT

Right-handed; 5'5½"; 106–113 lbs.

53 bouts, 2/24/1989 to 7/31/1999

Manager: Danny Carbajal

IBF Jr Flyweight Champion 1990–94, 1996–97

WBC Jr Flyweight Champ 1993–94

WBO Jr Flyweight Champ 1994, 1999

Hall of Fame Induction: 2006

Born: 9/17/1967, Phoenix, AZ

Michael Carbajal's popularity made the diminutive junior flyweight class attractive to network television and pay-per-view providers. Carbajal was born in Phoenix, Arizona, on September 17, 1967. He was exposed to boxing at a young age. His two older brothers, Danny and Alex, boxed as amateurs. His father, Manuel Carbajal, an Arizona Golden Gloves champion in the 1940s, took Carbajal to watch local boxing matches when he was only six years old. Carbajal loved the spectacle right from the start. When he was nine, he drew pictures of championship belts on paper, cut out the belts, and then wore them, pretending to be a champion.

When he was fourteen, Carbajal, then tipping the scales at 65 pounds, had his first amateur bout. Though he lost, he fought with such fervor that older brother Danny was inspired to turn the family garage into a gym for Carbajal to train. Carbajal went on to have a very successful amateur career. He won a silver medal in the 1987 Pan American Games and a silver medal in the 1988 Olympics in Seoul, South Korea.

Carbajal turned pro on February 24, 1989, fighting on the undercard of the Roberto Duran–Iran Barkley middleweight championship fight. Carbajal won a four-round decision over Will Grigsby, but was not particularly impressive. Danny Carbajal, who trained and managed his brother, attributed his slow start to the adjustment from amateur boxing. In amateur matches, the goal is to make contact regardless of how much power is behind the punches. In professional boxing, power counts more than the sheer number of punches. Whatever the reason for his modest debut, Carbajal scored knockouts in his next six fights with two going only one round, three two

The initial meeting of Michael Carbajal and Humberto ("Chiquita") Gonzalez was a title unification bout. Gonzalez scored the first knockdown, but Carbajal (light trunks) triumphed with a seventh-round KO.

IN THE RING	WON 49	LOST 4	DRAWS 0	TB 53	KO 33	W 16	WF 0	D 0	KO'd 1	L 3	LF 0

Date	Opponent	Site	Result / Rounds		Title	Wt.
1989						
Feb 24	Will Grigsby	Atlantic City	W	4	—	106
Apr 4	Silviano Perez	Phoenix	TKO	1	—	107
May 2	Camerino Rojas	Stateline, NV	KO	2	—	109
May 21	Pedro Espinoza	Phoenix	TKO	1	—	108
Jun 12	Eduardo Nunez	Las Vegas	KO	4	—	109
Jul 15	Francisco Luevanos	Atlantic City	TKO	2	—	108
Aug 14	Prudencio De Jesus	Reno, NV	KO	2	—	108
Sep 5	Jose Luis Herrera	Stateline, NV	W	8	—	108
Oct 17	Jose Manuel Diaz	Phoenix	TKO	3	—	108
Nov 17	Pedro Feliciano	Phoenix	W	10	—	108
1990						
Jan 12	Miguel Banda	Atlantic City	W	8	—	109
Feb 18	Tony DeLuca	Las Vegas	W	12	Won-NABF-JFL	108
Apr 1	Raul Acosta	Stateline	W	10	—	109
Jun 14	Fernando Martinez	Las Vegas	TKO	9	Ret-NABF-JFL	108
Jul 29	♛ Muangchai Kittikasem	Phoenix	TKO	7	Won-IBF-JFL	108
Sep 20	Oscar Calzada	Las Vegas	TKO	3	—	109
Oct 25	Luis Monzote	Phoenix	KO	5	—	109
Dec 8	Leon Salazar	Scottsdale, AZ	KO	4	Ret-IBF-JFL	108
1991						
Feb 17	Macario Santos	Las Vegas	KO	2	Ret-IBF-JFL	108
Mar 17	Javier Varguez	Las Vegas	W	12	Ret-IBF-JFL	107
May 10	Hector Patri	Davenport, IA	W	12	Ret-IBF-JFL	106
Oct 18	Jesus Chong	Atlantic City	W	10	—	109
1992						
Feb 15	Marcos Pacheco	Phoenix	W	12	Ret-IBF-JFL	107
Apr 30	Jose Luis Velarde	Albuquerque, NM	W	10	—	110
Aug 13	Jorge Luis Roman	Phoenix	W	10	—	109
Oct 14	Jose Manuel Diaz	Rosemont, IL	TKO	8	—	111
Dec 12	⑩ Robinson Cuesta	Phoenix	KO	8	Ret-IBF-JFL	108
1993						
Mar 13	♛ Humberto Gonzalez★	Las Vegas	KO	7	Won-WBC/IBF-JFL	107
Jul 17	⑩ Kwang-Sun Kim	Las Vegas	TKO	7	Ret-WBC/IBF-JFL	108
Oct 30	⑩ Domingo Sosa	Phoenix	TKO	5	Ret-WBC/IBF-JFL	108
1994						
Feb 19	⑩ Humberto Gonzalez★	Inglewood, CA	L	12	Lost-WBC/IBF-JFL	108
Apr 8	Abner Barajas	Laughlin, NV	TKO	3	—	112
Jul 15	Josue Camacho	Phoenix	W	12	Won-WBO-JFL	106
Nov 12	♛ Humberto Gonzalez★	Mexico City	L	12	For-WBC/IBF-JFL	108
1995						
Apr 1	Armando Diaz	Stateline	W	10	—	110
May 24	Francisco Carrasco	Bakersfield, CA	KO	4	—	111
Jun 20	Andres Cazares	Bakersfield	TKO	10	—	113
Aug 12	Jose Quirino	Las Vegas	KO	1	—	110
Sep 16	Gregorio Goyo Garcia	Las Vegas	KO	3	—	109
Nov 16	Francisco Montiel	Phoenix	TKO	3	—	111
1996						
Feb 19	Mauro Diaz	Tempe, AZ	TKO	7	—	111
Mar 16	Melchor Cob Castro	Las Vegas	W	12	Reg-Vac IBF-JFL	107

Date	Opponent	Location	Result	Round		
Jul 14	Manuel Serabia	Denver	KO	1	—	109
Sep 13	Julio Coronell	Des Moines, IA	TKO	8	Ret-IBF-JFL	107
Oct 12	Tomas Rivera	Anaheim, CA	KO	5	Ret-IBF-JFL	108
Dec 10	Tomas Cordoba	Corpus Christi, TX	TKO	3	—	111
1997						
Jan 18	Mauricio Pastrana	Las Vegas	L	12	Lost-IBF-JFL	108
Mar 22	Scotty Olson	Corpus Christi	KO	10	—	107
Jul 18	⑩ Jacob Matlala	Las Vegas	TKO'd	9	—	107
1999						
Feb 27	Jose Luis De Jesus Lopez Zatarain	Tampa	TKO	7	—	113
May 8	Oscar Andrade	Miami	W	10	—	—
Jul 2	Oscar Calzada	Tucson, AZ	TKO	4	—	113
Jul 31	♛ Jorge Arce	Tijuana, Mexico	TKO	11	Won-WBO-JFL	108

rounds, and one four rounds. His May 21, 1989, first-round knockout of Pedro Espinoza was televised on ABC. That was only the second junior flyweight bout ever shown on network television and the first since the Hilario Zapata–Joey Olivo WBC title fight in 1981. Carbajal signed a three-bout $700,000 contract with NBC in November 1989.

On February 18, 1990, fighting at home in Phoenix, Carbajal went twelve rounds for the first time when he decisioned Tony ("Bazooka") DeLuca to win the North American Boxing Federation junior, or light flyweight, title. Later that same year, Carbajal fought for a world title for the first time, taking on IBF junior flyweight champion Muangchai Kittikasem in Phoenix. "Little Hands of Stone"—as Carbajal became known after his idol Roberto Duran—easily won the bout, stopping Kittikasem in the seventh round.

Carbajal made short work of his next four opponents—with none lasting longer than five rounds. Though there was concern that he had lost his knockout power when he went six straight fights without a knockdown, those fears were unfounded. He silenced skeptics when he defended his title and knocked out Robinson Cuesta in the eighth round on December 12, 1992.

The victory over Cuesta set the stage for the most important fight of Carbajal's career: a bout with Hall of Famer and WBC junior flyweight champion Humberto Gonzalez at the Las Vegas Hilton on March 13, 1993. Their meeting was the first time that two fighters in that weight class were guaranteed $1,000,000 each. It was also the first junior flyweight bout to headline a pay-per-view card. At 5'5½", Carbajal towered over the 5'1" Gonzalez. Curiously, Carbajal never had trouble making weight even though he was exceedingly tall for a junior flyweight. The Carbajal–Gonzalez fight was an exceptional one which surpassed the high expectations. Gonzalez knocked Carbajal down in the second and fifth rounds and built a 58-54 lead after six rounds on all three judges' cards. Carbajal surprised experts by fighting in close with the powerful Gonzalez. Gonzalez's tactic of switching from orthodox to southpaw confused Carbajal. In the seventh round, Carbajal staggered Gonzalez with a hook to the chin and a right to the forehead. Gonzalez handled a Carbajal flurry along the ropes but was hurt by a right to the side of the head. Late in the round, Carbajal unleashed a sweeping left hook that knocked Gonzalez flat where he was counted out by referee Mills Lane at 2:59 of the seventh. The fight was declared Fight of the Year by *The Ring*.

Not content to rest on his laurels, Carbajal met and knocked out Olympic gold medalist Kwang-Sun Kim on July 17, 1993, at the Caesars Palace Sports Pavilion in Las Vegas. Kim's punches caused a lump to form under Carbajal's left eye. In the seventh, a straight right from Carbajal hurt Kim who dropped his guard. Carbajal ended it with a left hook which knocked Kim down. Though he attempted to rise, the fight was stopped.

In yet another defense of his title on October 30, 1993, Carbajal gave his hometown Phoenix fans something to cheer about. Fighting at the America West Arena before 15,800 fans, Carbajal faced previously unbeaten Domingo Sosa. Carbajal knocked Sosa down in the first, but suffered a wide cut to the forehead in the second due to an accidental headbutt. Carbajal inflicted a great deal of punishment in the next two rounds and continued the assault in the fifth. The fight was stopped 48 seconds into the round. For these three performances, Carbajal was named 1993 Fighter of the Year by *The Ring*.

For his next bout, Carbajal faced Gonzalez in a rematch on February 19, 1994, at the Great Western Forum before 10,333 spectators. Gonzalez changed his style from their first bout, employing a great deal of lateral movement and footwork. Early in the bout, Gonzalez suffered a cut over his left eye which bled profusely. In the sixth, Carbajal backed Gonzalez up with a big right hand. In the seventh round, the pair started slugging away. In the eighth, Gonzalez scored with a left uppercut/right uppercut combination, but Carbajal nevertheless won the round on two cards. Over the last four rounds, Gonzalez dominated. He was awarded a unanimous decision and was the junior flyweight champion for the third time.

Carbajal regained a version of the junior flyweight title when he decisioned Josue Camacho to win the WBO title on July 15, 1994. A third fight with Gonzalez followed. This time Gonzalez prevailed with a majority decision.

Carbajal won his next seven fights to set up a bout with Melchor Cob Castro for the vacant IBF junior flyweight title. Carbajal won a unanimous decision. He defended the title twice before losing it in a split decision to Mauricio Pastrana on January 18, 1997. After Jacob Matlala stopped him in the ninth round on July 18, 1997—the first time he had lost by knockout—Carbajal retired. He returned to the ring on February 27, 1999, with a knockout of Jose De Jesus. On July 31, 1999, he fought Jorge Arce for the WBO junior flyweight title. Arce was leading comfortably through ten rounds when Carbajal turned the fight around in the eleventh. After a left sent Arce into the ropes and a series of rights again sent him reeling backwards, the fight was stopped. Carbajal, satisfied that he had again won a title, retired— this time for good. The charismatic Carbajal now operates a gym in Phoenix.

Long-serving WBC chairman Jose Sulaiman was among the first to congratulate Carbajal after he unified the junior flyweight title with a victory over Humberto Gonzalez.

JIMMY CARTER

LIGHTWEIGHT

Right-handed; 5'6"; 129–145 lbs.
119 bouts, 3/14/1946 to 4/1/1960
Manager: Willie Ketchum
Lightweight Champion 1951–52, 1952–54, 1954–55
Hall of Fame Induction: 2000
Born: 12/15/1923, Aiken, SC
Named: James Walter Carter
Died: 9/21/1994

The first three-time lightweight champion, Jimmy Carter received neither the publicity nor the accolades normally accorded to world title holders. Carter once remarked, "I know it sounds strange, but I don't care what they say about me. I win most of my fights."

Carter moved from South Carolina to Harlem when he was nine. As a member of the Army Corps of Engineers during WWII, Carter boxed while serving in France, England, and the Pacific.

After his discharge, Carter turned professional on March 14, 1946, with a four-round decision over Clifton Bordies in Newark. The following year, he faced two future Hall of Famers, dropping a ten-round decision to Joe Brown in New Orleans and battling Sandy Saddler to a ten-round draw. By 1949, Carter was discouraged by his lack of progress, but his manager, Willie Ketchum, persuaded him to keep at it. That year, he traveled extensively for the first time, scoring wins in New York, Detroit, and California, and two wins out of three fights in Australia.

In 1950, Carter began to attract national attention. He decisioned future champion Wallace ("Bud") Smith, defeated veteran Jesse Underwood, and closed the year with a draw against third-rated contender Tommy Campbell.

Carter earned his first shot at the lightweight title of Hall of Famer Ike Williams. Perhaps because the fight was televised, it attracted only 3,594 fans to Madison Square Garden on May 25, 1951.

Williams had great difficulty making weight. Carter dominated the fight, knocking Williams down four times before referee Petey Scalzo stopped the contest in the fourteenth round with Williams pinned against the ropes. Carter, the new title holder, got only about $4,000 for his efforts.

On April 1, 1952, Carter successfully defended his title against Lauro Salas. In a rematch on May 14, Salas—ranked by some oddsmakers as the 15-1 underdog—shocked the boxing world when he captured the

Kid Gavilan's (L) reign as welterweight champion began exactly one week before Jimmy Carter's (R) first term as lightweight champ.

IN THE RING	WON 81	LOST 31	DRAWS 9	TB 120	KO 32	W 49	WF 0	D 9	KO'd 3	L 28	LF 0

Date	Opponent	Site	Result / Rounds		Title	Wt.
1946						
Mar 14	Clifton Bordies	Newark, NJ	W	4	—	130
Apr 5	Joe Krikis	New York	W	4	—	130
Apr 8	Ray Morris	Newark	KO	5	—	—
Apr 16	Clifton Bordies	New York	KO	1	—	132
Apr 19	George Wright	New York	W	6	—	130
May 1	Johnny LaRusso	Long Island City, NY	W	6	—	130
May 7	Lou Daniels	New York	KO	3	—	131
May 28	Leo LeBrun	New York	W	6	—	131
May 31	Johnny LaRusso	New York	L	4	—	130
Jun 12	Lou Langley	New York	KO	1	—	132
Jul 9	Joey Monterio	Norwalk, CT	W	6	—	130
Jul 29	Paul Midiri	New York	D	6	—	130
Aug 12	Ray Lewis	New York	L	6	—	132
Aug 26	Al Turner	Brooklyn	KO	5	—	—
Sep 5	Johnny Johnson	New York	KO	4	—	129
Sep 16	Danny Carabella	Brooklyn	L	8	—	130
Oct 2	Paul Midiri	Long Island City	W	8	—	130
Oct 19	Charley Noel	New York	W	8	—	131
Nov 5	Bill Williams	New York	KO	7	—	134
Dec 2	Eddie Smith	New York	W	8	—	131
Dec 17	Ruby Garcia	New York	KO	3	—	133
1947						
Jan 7	Walter Keene	New York	W	8	—	134
Feb 24	Walter Lewis	New York	W	8	—	135
Mar 18	Eddie White	New York	TKO	4	—	133
Mar 28	Walter Stevens	New York	W	6	—	134
Apr 18	Joe Brown★	New Orleans	L	10	—	136
May 12	Johnny Johnson	New York	W	8	—	135
May 27	Chico Morales	New York	KO	7	—	131
Jun 3 ⑩	Sandy Saddler★	Washington, DC	D	10	—	132
Jul 22	Thompson Harmon	New York	KO	5	—	133
Sep 8	Henry Polowitzer	New Haven, CT	W	8	—	—
Sep 16	Patsy Spataro	New York	KO	7	—	135
Sep 29	Dave Williams	New Haven	D	8	—	134
Oct 27	Dave Williams	New Haven	D	8	—	132
Nov 18 ⑩	Charles ("Cabey") Lewis	Hartford, CT	KO'd	7	—	132
Dec 9	Al Pennino	New York	D	8	—	133
1948						
Jan 27	Thompson Harmon	New York	W	8	—	134
Mar 9	Charley ("Cabey") Lewis	New York	W	10	—	132
Mar 29	Cal Smith	Boston	W	8	—	133
Apr 18	Willie Russell	Cincinnati	W	10	—	—
May 21	Bobby McQuillar	New Orleans	L	10	—	—
Jun 29	Phil Burton	Springfield, IL	W	10	—	139
Jul 12	Wilfredo Miro	Springfield	W	10	—	136
Jul 20	Woody Winslow	New York	D	8	—	133
Jul 26	Julie Kogan	Springfield	KO	8	—	135
Aug 9	George Smith	Springfield	W	10	—	134

Date		Opponent	Location	Result	Rounds		Weight
Aug 30		Joey Angelo	Springfield	W	10	—	135
Sep 27		Isaac Jenkins	New Haven	W	8	—	134
Nov 1	⑩	Sonny Boy West	Baltimore	L	10	—	134
Dec 6		Louis Joyce	Holyoke, MA	W	10	—	136
1949							
Jan 17		Harold Jones	New York	W	10	—	134
Jan 31		Talmadge Bussey	Detroit	W	10	—	134
Apr 4		Nick Diaz	Ocean Park, CA	TKO	6	—	135
Apr 22		Archie Whitewater	San Francisco	KO	6	—	134
May 23		Mario Trigo	Ocean Park	TKO	8	—	134
Sep 16		Norman Gent	Melbourne	L	12	—	134
Oct 4		Charlie Ashenden	Sydney	KO	4	—	134
Oct 28		Bernie Hall	Melbourne	W	12	—	—
Nov 29	⑩	Rudy Cruz	Los Angeles	L	10	—	135
1950							
Mar 28	⑩	Wallace ("Bud") Smith	Cincinnati	W	10	—	136
Jul 25		Jesse Underwood	Cincinnati	W	10	—	133
Oct 6	⑩	Tommy Campbell	New Orleans	D	10	—	133
1951							
Jan 30		Calvin Smith	Philadelphia	L	10	—	—
Feb 7		Percy Bassett	New York	W	10	—	135
Mar 5		Percy Bassett	Philadelpia	L	10	—	132
May 25	♛	Ike Williams ★	New York	TKO	14	Won-World-L	133
Jun 18		Chick Boucher	Fall River, MA	KO	4	—	140
Jul 2		Ronnie Harper	Flint, MI	KO	5	—	135
Jul 10		Enrique Bolanos	Los Angeles	TKO	7	—	135
Aug 2	⑩	Del Flanagan	Minneapolis	TKO	7	—	135
Aug 14		Mario Trigo	Los Angeles	W	10	—	135
Aug 28	⑩	Art Aragon	Los Angeles	L	10	—	135
Nov 14	⑩	Art Aragon	Los Angeles	W	15	Ret-World-L	134
1952							
Jan 21		Mario Trigo	Philadelphia	W	10	—	138
Feb 5		Alan McFater	Toronto	W	9	—	136
Mar 12		Luther Rawlings	Chicago	W	10	—	136
Apr 1	⑩	Lauro Salas	Los Angeles	W	15	Ret-World-L	134
May 14	⑩	Lauro Salas	Los Angeles	L	15	Lost-World-L	134
Sep 1		Basil Marie	Dartmouth, NS, Canada	W	10	—	138
Oct 15	♛	Lauro Salas	Chicago	W	15	Reg-World-L	135
Dec 9		Archie Whitewater	Oakland	W	10	—	136
Dec 16		Freddie ("Babe") Herman	Sacramento, CA	D	10	—	136
1953							
Jan 12	⑩	Eddie Chavez	San Francisco	L	10	—	136
Feb 16		Armand Savoie	Montreal	L	10	—	136
Apr 24		Tommy Collins	Boston	TKO	4	Ret-World-L	134
Jun 12	⑩	George Araujo	New York	TKO	13	Ret-World-L	135
Sep 12		Johnny Cunningham	Miami	L	10	—	139
Sep 28		Ben Miloud	Johnstown, PA	KO	8	—	138
Oct 15		Carlos Chavez	Los Angeles	KO	6	—	136
Nov 11		Armond Savoie	Montreal	KO	5	Ret-World-L	133
1954							
Feb 8		Billy Lauderdale	Nassau, Bahamas	W	10	—	137
Mar 5	⑩	Paddy DeMarco	New York	L	15	Lost-World-L	135
Jun 2		Charley Riley	St. Louis	KO	2	—	137
Aug 4		Glen Flanagan	Chicago	W	10	—	138
Sep 22		Freddie Herman	San Francisco	W	10	—	137
Nov 17	♛	Paddy DeMarco	San Francisco	KO	15	Reg-World-L	135

1955							
Jan 26		Bobby Woods	Spokane, WA	W	10	—	137
Feb 11	Ⓣ	Tony DeMarco	Boston	D	10	—	138
Apr 20		Orlando Zulueta	Washington, DC	L	10	—	137
Jun 29	Ⓣ	Wallace ("Bud") Smith	Boston	L	15	Lost-World-L	134
Oct 19	♛	Wallace ("Bud") Smith	Cincinnati	L	15	For-World-L	135
1956							
Feb 1	Ⓣ	Cisco Andrade	Chicago	L	10	—	140
Mar 5		Phil Burton	Quebec City, Quebec, Canada	W	10	—	141
Mar 29		Don Jordan	Los Angeles	W	10	—	138
May 3	Ⓣ	Art Aragon	Los Angeles	L	10	—	139
Jun 21		Lauro Salas	Los Angeles	W	10	—	136
Sep 11	Ⓣ	Larry Boardman	Boston	KO'd	8	—	139
1957							
May 23		Buddy McDonald	Spokane	W	10	—	141
Sep 7		Mickey Northup	Hollywood	W	10	—	137
Oct 8	Ⓣ	Willie Toweel	London	L	10	—	137
1958							
Jan 14	Ⓣ	Joey Lopes	Sacramento	L	10	—	138
Mar 11	Ⓣ	Joey Lopes	Sacramento	L	10	—	139
Jul 19		Jimmy Grow	Hollywood	KO	7	—	138
Sep 9	Ⓣ	Al Nevarez	Ciudad Juarez, Mexico	L	10	—	139
Sep 23		Rudy Jordan	Fresno, CA	KO'd	6	—	141
1959							
Aug 11		Kildo Nunez	San Jose, CA	W	10	—	138
Oct 13		Jimmy Smith	Richmond, CA	KO	3	—	140
Nov 10		Kildo Nunez	Richmond	KO	4	—	139
Nov 24		Art Ramponi	Oakland	L	10	—	138
1960							
Feb 25		Jimmy Grow	Boise, ID	L	10	—	138
Apr 1		Luis Garduno	Mesa, AZ	L	10	—	145

lightweight title in a split decision. On October 15, a mere five months later, Carter decisioned Salas to regain the crown.

Carter's second stint as champion ended when he lost on points to Paddy DeMarco on March 5, 1954. Once again he regained his title in a rematch, stopping DeMarco in the fifteenth round. Carter thus became the first fighter to win the lightweight belt three times. A solid, if unspectacular and methodical fighter, Carter combined good boxing skills with a decent punch that brought him many victories.

Carter's third championship reign proved to be his shortest, as Wallace ("Bud") Smith decisioned him seven months later. Smith won their rematch as well.

In retirement, Carter worked for fifteen years in a Ford assembly plant, then as a teacher's aide.

Then-Vice President Richard Nixon (L) meets Jimmy Carter in Washington, DC.

MARCEL CERDAN
The Casablanca Clouter

MIDDLEWEIGHT

Right-handed; 5'8"; 143–163 lbs.

110 bouts, 11/4/1934 to 6/16/1949

Managers: Lucien Roupp, Jo Longman

Middleweight Champ 1948–49

Hall of Fame Induction: 1991

Born: 7/22/1916, Sidi Bel-Abbes, Algeria

Died: 10/27/1949

One of the most popular boxers in the era immediately after World War II, Marcel Cerdan died tragically in a plane crash as he was flying back to the United States from Paris to attempt to reclaim the world middleweight title.

Cerdan was born into a boxing family in Algeria, then a French possession. His father, a butcher by trade, promoted amateur bouts in Casablanca, and two of his brothers preceded him into the professional prize ring. Cerdan quit school at the age of eleven to work along the waterfront. At eighteen, he started fighting professionally under the guidance of manager Lucien Roupp. Cerdan won his first 34 fights before facing Omar Kouidri in Casablanca for the French welterweight title. Cerdan took the decision

A right cross rocks the already-battered Tony Zale (L) as Cerdan inflicts more damage. Zale couldn't answer the bell for the twelfth round, and Cerdan took the middleweight belt on September 21, 1948.

IN THE RING	WON 107	LOST 4	DRAWS 0	TB 111	KO 62	W 45	WF 0	D 0	KO'd 1	L 1	LF 2

Date	Opponent	Site	Result / Rounds		Title	Wt.
1934						
Nov 4	Marcel Bucchianer	Meknes, Morocco	W	6	—	—
Nov 12	Benazra	Meknes	TKO	5	—	—
1935						
Feb 16	Perez Tercero	Casablanca, Morocco	W	10	—	—
Apr 13	Privat	Casablanca	TKO	5	—	—
Apr 13	Benazra	Casablanca	W	10	—	—
Jul 5	Mac Perez	Casablanca	TKO	2	—	—
Jul 19	Joseph Sarfati	Casablanca	W	10	—	—
Aug 8	Mestre	Casablanca	W	10	—	—
Nov 23	Mac Perez	Casablanca	W	10	—	—
Dec 14	Mac Perez	Casablanca	W	10	—	—
1936						
Mar 4	Antoine Abad	Casablanca	W	10	—	—
Apr 7	M. Hergane	Casablanca	W	10	—	—
Apr 11	Joseph Martinez	Taza, Morocco	TKO	9	—	—
May 23	M. Ricardo	Casablanca	KO	5	—	—
May 27	Kid Abadie	Casablanca	KO	3	—	—
Jun 6	M. Castillanos	Casablanca	W	10	—	—
Jul 19	Joseph Sarfati	Casablanca	W	10	—	—
Aug 2	Al Francis	Oran, Algeria	KO	6	—	—
Oct 17	Primo Rubio	Casablanca	W	10	—	—
Nov 2	Aisa Attaf	Casablanca	KO	1	—	—
Nov 21	Jean Debeaumont	Casablanca	W	10	—	—
1937						
Jan 16	Aisa Attaf	Algiers, Algeria	KO	8	—	—
Jan 30	Maurice Naudin	Algiers	KO	3	—	—
Mar 2	Omar Kouidri	Rabat, Morroco	W	10	—	—
Apr 3	Omar Kouidri	Algiers	W	10	—	—
Jul 3	Ali Omar	Algiers	KO	5	—	—
Aug 2	Kid Marcel	Oran	W	10	—	—
Sep 13	Eddy Rabak	Casablanca	KO	6	—	—
Oct 7	Louis Jampton	Paris	W	10	—	—
Oct 21	Jean Morin	Paris	W	10	—	—
Dec 18	Ifergane	Rabat	W	10	—	—
1938						
Jan 6	Charles Feodorowich	Paris	KO	2	—	—
Jan 13	Eddie Ran	Paris	KO	2	—	—
Jan 20	Jean Zides	Paris	KO	9	—	—
Feb 21	Omar Kouidri	Casablanca	W	12	Won-France-W	—
Mar 12	Charles Pernot	Algiers	W	10	—	—
Mar 25	Lucien Krawsyck	Paris	W	10	—	—
Apr 13	Eddy Rabak	Paris	W	10	—	—
May 5	Anacleto Locatelli	Paris	W	12	—	—
May 20	Gustave Humery	Paris	KO	6	—	—
Jun 4	Jean Morin	Algiers	W	10	—	—
Jul 3	Victor Deckmyn	Oran	W	10	—	—
Sep 15	Al Baker	Paris	W	10	—	—

Oct 27		Amadeo Deyana	Paris	W	10	—	—
Nov 10		Alfredo Katter	Paris	KO	4	—	—
Nov 24		Omar Kouidri	Paris	W	12	Ret-France-W	—
1939							
Jan 9		Harry Craster	London	LF	5	—	—
Jan 21		Ercole Buratti	Algiers	W	10	—	—
Feb 4		Al Baker	Brussels	KO	7	—	—
Feb 20	⑩	Saverio Turiello	Paris	W	12		
Mar 22		Felix Wouters	Brussels	W	12	—	—
May 21		Roger Cadot	Marseilles, France	KO	6	—	—
Jun 3	⑩	Saverio Turiello	Milan	W	15	Won-Europe-W	—
Jun 18		Anacleto Locatelli	Marseilles	W	10	—	—
1941							
Jan 19		Young Raymond	Algiers	KO	1	—	—
Feb 2		Victor Fortes	Casablanca	TKO	7	—	—
Mar 9		Victor Janas	Casablanca	W	10	—	—
Apr 13		Victor Fortes	Oran	TKO	2	—	—
May 4		Omar Kouidri	Oran	TKO	6	—	—
Jun 22		Francois Blanchard	Marseilles	KO	6	—	—
Jul 20		Joe Brun	Oran	TKO	2	—	—
Sep 13		Roland Coureau	Algiers	TKO	9	—	—
Nov 6		Young Raymond	Casablanca	TKO	6	—	—
Dec 31		Robert Seidel	Vichy, France	KO	3	—	—
1942							
Feb 21		Fred Flury	Nice, France	KO	7	—	—
Apr 26		Gustave Humery	Paris	KO	1	—	—
May 17		Fernand Viez	Paris	W	10	—	—
Jun 28		Gaspard de Ridder	Paris	KO	1	—	—
Jul 25		Victor Janas	Algiers	TKO	2	—	—
Aug 2		Ben Frely	Marseilles	KO	3	—	—
Aug 15		Victor Buttin	Algiers	LF	8	—	—
Sep 30		Jose Ferrer	Paris	TKO	1	Ret-Europe-W	—
1943							
Aug 8		John McCoy	Oran	KO	2	—	—
Sep 12		Omar Kouidri	Algiers	W	10	—	—
Oct ?		Omar Kouidri	Algiers	KO	1	—	—
Oct 13		Larry Cisneros	Oran	KO	6	—	—
Oct 31		Bulldog Milano	Casablanca	KO	2	—	—
Dec 26		James Toney	Oran	KO	2	—	—
Dec 29		Larry Cisneros	Algiers	KO	2	—	—
1944							
Jan 30		Willie Sampson	Casablanca	KO	2	—	—
Oct 21		Bouaya	Casablanca	KO	1	—	—
1945							
Mar 9		Joe Brun	Paris	TKO	7		
May 13		Jean Despeaux	Paris	KO	5	—	—
Jun 3		Oscar Menozzi	Marseilles	KO	3	—	—
Jun 24		Edouard Tenet	Croix de Berny, France	W	10	—	—
Oct 19		Tommy Davies	Paris	KO	1	—	—
Nov 30		Assane Diouf	Paris	KO	3	Won-France-M	—
Dec 8		Victor Buttin	St. Etienne, France	KO	3	—	—
1946							
Jan 13		Agustin Guedes	Lisbon, Portugal	KO	1	—	—
Jan 18		Edouard Tenet	Paris	W	12	Ret-France-M	—
Feb 24		Jose Ferrer	Barcelona, Spain	KO	4	—	—

Date		Opponent	Location	Result	Rounds	Title	Weight
Apr 14		Joe Brun	Nice	KO	2	—	—
May 25		Robert Charron	Paris	W	12	Ret-France-M	157
Jul 7	⑩	Holman Williams	Paris	W	10	—	157
Oct 20		Jean Pankowiak	Paris	KO	5	—	—
Dec 6	⑩	Georgie Abrams	New York	W	10	—	159
1947							
Feb 2		Leon Foquet	Paris	KO	1	Won-Vac Europe-M	158
Feb 11		Bert Gilroy	London	KO	4	—	161
Mar 28		Harold Green	New York	KO	2	—	159
Oct 7		Billy Walker	Montreal	TKO	1	—	161
Oct 31	⑩	Anton Raadik	Chicago	W	10	—	160
1948							
Jan 26		Giovanni Manca	Paris	KO	2	Ret-Europe-M	—
Feb 9		Jean Walzack	Paris	KO	4	Ret-Europe-M	—
Mar 12		Lavern Roach	New York	TKO	8	—	156
Mar 25		Lucien Krawsyck	Paris	W	10	—	157
May 23	⑩	Cyrille Delannoit	Brussels	L	15	Lost-Europe-M	160
Jul 10	⑩	Cyrille Delannoit	Brussels	W	15	Reg-Europe-M	159
Sep 21	♛	Tony Zale ★	Jersey City, NJ	TKO	12	Won-World-M	158
1949							
Mar 29	⑩	Dick Turpin	London	KO	7	—	163
May 8		Lucien Krawsyck	Casablanca	KO	4	—	164
Jun 16	⑩	Jake LaMotta ★	Detroit	TKO'd	10	Lost-World-M	159

in twelve rounds. In 1939, he added the European welterweight crown with a victory over Saverio Turiello.

With the outbreak of World War II, Cerdan served in the French Navy before his artillery unit was disbanded by the Germans. He boxed several times in occupied Paris after France fell to the Nazi invasion. A meeting with Spanish middleweight champion Jose Ferrer, whom Cerdan knocked out in one round, irritated the Germans, and Cerdan wisely fled, using forged travel permits. He then joined the Free French Navy. Cerdan first became known to American audiences when he won two major Inter-Allied boxing tournaments in 1944. American fans liked him, even when he beat American boxers.

After the war, Cerdan won the French and European middleweight titles. In 1946, he traveled to the United States to face the tough Georgie Abrams. Cerdan won a ten-round decision and, at the close of that year, was rated the fourth-top contender for the middleweight title by *The Ring* in its annual rankings. He finally fought Tony Zale for the world championship in 1948 at Roosevelt Stadium in Jersey City. Cerdan used his superior speed, quickness, and punching accuracy to pile up a lead over Zale before knocking him down with a left hook at the end of the eleventh round. Zale could not come out for the twelfth round, and Cerdan was the champion.

The next year Cerdan defended his title against Hall of Famer Jake LaMotta. In the first round, LaMotta wrestled Cerdan to the canvas, damaging the champ's shoulder. Cerdan, who once knocked an opponent out with a broken hand, fought one-armed until he could not continue. In the tenth round, he conceded defeat. The rematch was postponed when LaMotta claimed an injury.

Cerdan's plane crashed on its way to the United States for the LaMotta rematch. The entire boxing community mourned the French fighter's passing.

ANTONIO CERVANTES
Kid Pambele

JUNIOR WELTERWEIGHT

Right-handed; 5'10"; 121–143 lbs.

79 bouts, 1/31/1964 to 12/9/1983

Manager: Ramiro Machado

Junior Welterweight Champion
1972–76, 1977–80

Hall of Fame Induction: 1998

Born: 12/23/1945, San Basilio de
Palenque, Colombia

Cervantes has an unusual heritage. While approximately 90 percent of Colombians are either white or Indian, Cervantes hails from the all-black San Basilio de Palenque, a town with a population of about 3,000. The founders of the town were slaves who rebelled against their Spanish masters in the late 1500s. Using guerrilla warfare, the former slaves maintained their forest settlement and their freedom.

Ultimately, Palenque became part of Colombia, but certain vestiges of its origin remained. For instance, young boys and girls in Palenque were traditionally trained in the arts of war, including fist fighting. Today, the town's children still engage in organized fighting, seen as a noble pastime. Often, boys become members of a "cuadro," fighting each other and the members of other cuadros. In addition to Cervantes, tiny Palenque has since produced three other champions: middleweight Rodrigo Valdez, junior featherweight Ricardo Cardona, and flyweight Prudencio Cardona.

Cervantes had three formal amateur bouts before turning professional at the age of eighteen in 1964. Venezuelan Ramiro Machado, who believed that the raw Cervantes could develop into a fine fighter, purchased Cervantes's contract and moved him to Venezuela. Cervantes's uncle nicknamed his nephew "Kid Pambele" after a favorite Nicaraguan fighter.

In 1970, Cervantes outfought his first ranked opponent, Enrique Jana. The next year, Cervantes challenged for the world junior welterweight title held by Nicolino Locche. Fighting gamely on Locche's home turf, Luna Park in Buenos Aires, Cervantes lost by decision.

After Locche lost the title to Alfonso ("Peppermint") Frazer, Cervantes faced Frazer in the champion's native Panama on October 28, 1972. Cervantes knocked Frazer down three times before

Hard-hitting Cervantes leaves Alfonso Frazer spread-eagled on the canvas and takes the junior welterweight title in Panama City on October 28, 1972.

IN THE RING	WON 90	LOST 12	DRAWS 3	TB 105	KO 44	W 46	WF· 0	D 3	KO'd 2	L 10	LF 0

Date	Opponent	Site	Result / Rounds		Title	Wt.
1964						
Jan 31	Juan Martinez	Cerete, Colombia	W	6	—	—
Feb 28	Rodolfo Marquez	Valledupar, Colombia	W	4	—	—
Apr 21	Rodolfo Marquez	Maria La Baja, Colombia	KO	3	—	—
May 5	Oscar Gonzalez	Medellin, Colombia	W	8	—	—
Jun 20	Felix Salgado	Barranquilla, Colombia	W	4	—	—
1965						
Oct 2	Antonio Yi	Barranquilla	W	6		
1966						
Jan 7	Oscar Gonzalez	Cartegena, Colombia	W	4	—	—
Jan 19	Rafael Donado	Cartegena	KO	2	—	—
Feb 2	Rodolfo Marquez	Cartegena	W	4	—	—
Feb 27	Rodolfo Marquez	Baranquilla	KO	2	—	—
Mar 19	Antonio Yi	Cartegena	W	6	—	—
Mar 28	Eliodoro Pitalua	Cartegena	W	10	—	—
Apr 29	Jose Godoy	Cartegena	W	6	—	—
May 10	Jesus Cardenas	Turbaco, Colombia	KO	7	—	—
May 24	Jose Godoy	Calamar, Colombia	W	6	—	—
Jun 21	Rafael Donado	Cartegena	W	10	—	—
Jun 24	Jose Zuniga	Cartegena	W	6	—	—
Jul 29	Reynaldo Lopez	Cartegena	D	8	—	123
Aug 20	Eliodoro Pitalua	Cartegena	KO	2	—	—
Sep 23	Cipriano ("Barbulito") Zuluaga	Monteria, Colombia	L	10	—	—
Oct 1	Jose Godoy	Cartegena	W	10	—	—
Nov 6	Cipriano ("Barbulito") Zuluaga	Monteria	L	10	—	—
Nov 16	Antonio Yi	Baranquilla	KO	6	—	—
1967						
Feb 3	Victor Cano	Bogota, Colombia	L	8	—	—
Feb 8	Jose Godoy	Cartegena	W	10	—	—
Mar 1	Antonio Yi	Cartegena	W	10	—	—
Apr 2	Eliodoro Pitalua	Cartegena	L	8	—	—
May 20	Eliodoro Pitalua	San Andres, Colombia	W	10	—	—
May 30	Jose Godoy	Cartegena	W	10	—.	—
Jun 3	Reynaldo Lopez	San Andres	W	10	—	—
Jun 14	Antonio Yi	Cartegena	W	10	—	—
Jul 14	Nestor Rojas	Caracas, Venezuela	L	8	—	—
Jul 28	Rala Rojas	Cartegena	KO	5	—	—
Aug 5	Rafael Rojas	Barranquilla	KO	5	—	—
Sep 30	Jesus Gonzalez	Cartegena	KO	3	—	—
Oct 15	Reynaldo Lopez	Cartegena	D	10	—	—
Nov 16	Reynaldo Lopez	Cartegena	W	10	—	—
Nov 21	Eliodoro Pitalua	Cartegena	W	10	—	—
Dec 7	Milton Mendez	Bogota	D	10	—	—
Dec 21	Victor Cano	Cartegena	KO	8	—	—
1968						
Jan 21	Eliodoro Pitalua	Cartegena	W	10	—	—
Mar 3	Milton Mendez	Cartegena	W	10	—	—
Jun 14	Cipriano ("Barbulito") Zuluaga	Cartegena	W	10	—	—
Aug 29	Cipriano ("Barbulito") Zuluaga	Cartegena	W	10	—	—
Aug 31	Jose Godoy	Bogota	W	8	—	—

Oct 7		Juan Martinez	Cartegena	KO	7	—	—
Nov 25		Orlando Ruiz	Caracas	KO	1	—	—
Nov 28		Nestor Rojas	Caracas	W	10	—	—
Dec 14		Orlando Rivas	Caracas	W	10	—	—
Dec 20		Cruz Marcano	Caracas	KO'd	4	—	—
1969							
Feb 9		Jesus Gonzalez	Cartagena	TKO	2	—	—
Apr 15		Frank Leroy	Caracas	KO	2	—	—
May 15		Jose Torres	Cartegena	KO	2	—	—
Jun 4		Milton Mendez	Cartegena	W	10	—	—
Aug 15		Francisco Bolivar	Caracas	L	10	—	—
Aug 16		Orlando Rivas	Caracas	KO	2	—	—
Nov 10		Antonio Gomez	Caracas	L	10	—	—
1970							
Feb 20		Pedro Chirinos	Caracas	W	10	—	—
Mar 12		Diego Tovar	Caracas	KO	1	—	—
Nov 6		Jorge Rodriguez	San Jose, CA	KO	8	—	—
Dec 10		Rodolfo Gonzalez	Los Angeles	TKO	8	—	135
1971							
Feb 18	⑩	Enrique Jana	Los Angeles	TKO	8	—	137
May 28		Lupe Ramirez	Caracas	W	10	—	—
Jul 10		Gerardo Ferrat	Valencia, Venezuela	W	10	—	—
Oct 18		Julio Viera	Caracas	W	10	—	—
Dec 11	♛	Nicolino Locche★	Buenos Aires	L	15	For-World-JW	138
1972							
Mar 10		Jose Escudero	Barranquilla	KO	1	—	—
Apr 26		Frank Medina	Barranquilla	KO	8	—	141
Aug 19		Lupe Ramirez	Maracay, Venezuela	W	10	—	—
Oct 28	⑩	Alfonso Frazer	Panama City	TKO	10	Won-World-JW	139
1973							
Feb 16		Josue Marquez	Hato Rey, PR	W	15	Ret-World-JW	140
Mar 17		Nicolino Locche★	Maracay	TKO	10	Ret-World-JW	139
Apr 28		Benny Huertas	Cali, Colombia	KO	1	—	—
May 19	⑩	Alfonso Frazer	Panama City	TKO	5	Ret-World-JW	139
Jul 20		Ray Mercado	Barranquilla	TKO	5	—	—
Sep 8	⑩	Carlos Gimenez	Bogota	TKO	5	Ret-World-JW	139
Dec 5		Lion Furuyama	Panama City	W	15	Ret-World-JW	139
1974							
Mar 20		Chang-Kil Lee	Cartagena	KO	6	Ret-World-JW	140
Jun 8		Pedro Adigue	Maracay	KO	5	—	—
Jul 28	⑩	Victor Ortiz	Cartagena	KO	2	Ret-World-JW	139
Oct 26		Shinichi Kadoto	Tokyo	KO	8	Ret-World-JW	140
1975							
Mar 15		Ray Guerrero	Caracas	TKO	2	—	—
May 17	⑩	Esteban De Jesus	Panama City	W	15	Ret-World-JW	139
Sep 20		Kiyoshi Kazama	Caracas	TKO	6	—	—
Nov 15	⑩	Hector Thompson	Panama City	TKO	8	Ret-World-JW	139
1976							
Mar 6		Wilfred Benitez★	San Juan, PR	L	15	Lost-World-JW	140
May 22		Javier Ayala	Maracay	KO	1	—	—
Jul 17		Beau Jaynes	Maracay	W	10	—	—
Oct 16		Ariel Maciel	Maracay	KO	2	—	—
Nov 13	⑩	Saoul Mamby	Maracay	W	10	—	—

1977							
Mar 19		Adriano Marrero	Maracay	W	10	—	—
Jun 25		Carlos Gimenez	Maracaibo, Venezuela	TKO	6	Won-Vac-World-JW	139
Nov 5		Adriano Marrero	Maracay	W	15	Ret-World-JW	139
1978							
Mar 10		Johnny Copeland	Caracas	TKO	3	—	—
Apr 28		Tongta Kiatvayupak	Udon Thani, Thailand	KO	6	Ret-World-JW	140
Aug 26		Norman Sekgapane	Mmabatho, South Africa	TKO	9	Ret-World-JW	139
1979							
Jan 18	⑩	Miguel Montilla	New York	W	15	Ret-World-JW	140
Aug 25	⑩	Kwang-Min Kim	Seoul	W	15	Ret-World-JW	139
1980							
Mar 29	⑩	Miguel Montilla	Cartagena	TKO	7	Ret-World-JW	139
Aug 2	⑩	Aaron Pryor★	Cincinnati	KO'd	4	Lost-World-JW	139
1981							
Dec 4	⑩	Lennox Blackmoore	Bogota	KO	9	—	—
1982							
Apr 2		Jerome Artis	Cartagena	W	10	—	—
1983							
Mar 26		Amancio Castro	Cartagena	W	12	Won-Vac-CenAm-JW	140
Jul 30		Sergio Alvarez	Cartagena	TKO	11	Ret-CenAm-JW	140
Dec 9		Danny Sanchez	Miami	L	10	—	140

the fight was stopped in the tenth round. The first world champion in Colombian history, Cervantes became a national hero. He met with national political leaders and, through his influence, electricity was first brought to Palenque.

Cervantes defended his title successfully ten times, recording seven knockouts. His reign came to an end in 1976 when he lost a split decision to Hall of Famer Wilfred Benitez. Benitez, just seventeen, became the youngest-ever world champion. On June 25, 1977, in Maracaibo, Venezuela, Cervantes fought Carlos Gimenez to determine a new WBA junior welterweight champion. Cervantes stopped Gimenez in the sixth round.

Cervantes defended his title six times over the next three years until another Hall of Famer dethroned him. Aaron Pryor scored a TKO in the fourth round of their August 2, 1980, bout. Cervantes won the Central American and Caribbean super lightweight titles before retiring.

Cervantes invested in real estate and boxing promotions. He had several brushes with the law. Hospitalized for drug and alcohol addiction in Colombia, Cervantes was sent to a Cuban hospital. After his release, he worked as a trainer in Cartagena, Colombia, not far from Palenque.

In Independence Stadium, Mmabatho, Bophuthatswana, South Africa, on August 26, 1978, Cervantes (R) successfully defends his WBA junior welterweight belt with a nine-round TKO of Norman ("Panga-man") Sekgapane.

BOBBY CHACON
Schoolboy

LIGHTWEIGHT

Right-handed; 5'5½"; 124–137 lbs.
67 bouts, 4/17/1972 to 6/2/1988
Managers: Joe Ponce 1972–75,
1975–76; Red Tracton and Jackie
Barnett 1977; Jackie Barnett 1978–79
WBC Featherweight Champ 1974–75
WBC Super Featherweight Champ
1982–83
Hall of Fame Induction: 2005
Born: 11/28/1951, Sylmar, CA

The tragedy and tumult that has surrounded Bobby Chacon's life outside the ring shouldn't obscure the fact that he was truly a fine-caliber fighter. Chacon was born in Sylmar, California, on November 28, 1951. He was the first of his mother's seven children. His father soon disappeared from his life. Before he was eighteen, Chacon had been placed on probation twice and had run away from home several times.

He frequently engaged in street fights. His girlfriend, Valerie—who would later become his first wife—encouraged him to take his fighting to a gym. Chacon heeded the advice and started visiting a gym in Pacoima. Joe Ponce, a boxing manager, encouraged Chacon, though he doubted the young man would ever be a serious fighter when he saw his shoulder-length hair. For six months, Chacon worked a full eight-hour shift at a Lockheed plant, worked out in the gym, and ran at night. In November 1970, he fought his first amateur bout. With only seven fights under his belt, he went to the National Golden Gloves where he lost a close decision in his first match. Chacon made it to the quarterfinals the next year.

Chacon started his pro career off with a fifth-round knockout of José Antonio Rosa on April 17, 1972. Chacon fought frequently, winning all fifteen of his 1972 fights—fourteen by knockout. Chacon knocked out former bantam champ Chucho Castillo and earned a chance at the North American Boxing Federation featherweight title. Chacon faced former bantamweight world champ Ruben Olivares. The fight, held at the Forum in Los Angeles, was a huge gate attraction with 15,100 attending. Chacon was much less experienced than Olivares, but he packed knockout power in each hand. Chacon was the aggressor for the first two rounds. In the third, the superior boxing ability and ring saavy of Olivares took over. In the ninth, an Olivares right to the chin knocked Chacon down. He finished the round but did not answer the bell for the next stanza.

Chacon turned professional rather than trying for a shot at the 1972 United States Olympic team.

IN THE RING	WON 59	LOST 7	DRAWS 1	TB 67	KO 47	W 12	WF 0	D 1	KO'd 5	L 2	LF 0

Date	Opponent	Site	Result / Rounds		Title	Wt.
1972						
Apr 17	José Antonio Rosa	Los Angeles	KO	5	—	126
Apr 19	Limon Salas	Inglewood, CA	KO	1	—	125
May 8	Ruben Coria	Inglewood	KO	2	—	125
May 15	Moises Felix Sanchez	Inglewood	KO	1	—	125
May 23	Luis Robles	Inglewood	KO	1	—	126
Jun 5	Ray Llamas	Inglewood	KO	1	—	126
Jun 19	Alfredo de la Rosa	Inglewood	W	6	—	125
Jun 30	Jesus Robles	Inglewood	KO	2	—	127
Jul 17	Alberto Perez	Inglewood	KO	5	—	127
Jul 31	Alfredo de la Rosa	Inglewood	KO	4	—	126
Aug 11	Modesto Dayaganon	Maui, HI	KO	2	—	126
Aug 21	Juan Montoya	Inglewood	TKO	8	—	127
Sep 11	Valente Vera	Anaheim, CA	KO	5	—	127
Oct 16	Albert Reyes	Woodland Hills, CA	TKO	9	—	126
Nov 9	Ray Echeverria	Woodland Hills	TKO	1	—	128
1973						
Feb 15	Arturo Pineda	Los Angeles	KO	5	—	127
Feb 28	Jose Del Campo	Inglewood	TKO	3	—	127
Mar 30	Frankie Crawford	Anaheim	W	10	—	127
Apr 28	Chucho Castillo	Inglewood	TKO	10	—	126
Jun 23 ⑩	Ruben Olivares★	Inglewood	TKO'd	9	For-NABF-FE	126
Sep 28	Jorge Ramos	San Diego	TKO	10	—	128
Oct 13	Jose Del Campo	Inglewood	KO	9	—	128
1974						
Feb 1	Jorge Ramos	San Diego	KO	5	—	128
Mar 4	Genzo Kurozawa	Inglewood	TKO	5	—	—
May 24	Danny ("Little Red") Lopez	Los Angeles	TKO	9	—	126
Sep 7 ⑩	Alfredo Marcano	Los Angeles	TKO	9	Won-Vac WBC-FE	125
1975						
Mar 1	Jesus Estrada	Los Angeles	KO	2	Ret-WBC-FE	126
Jun 20 ⑩	Ruben Olivares★	Inglewood	TKO'd	2	Lost-WBC-FE	124
Nov 18	Fel Clemente	Honolulu	TKO	5	—	—
Dec 7	Rafael ("Bazooka") Limon	Mexicali, Mexico	L	10	—	—
1976						
Jan 27	Gene Prado	Fresno, CA	KO	5	—	133
Feb 17	Modesto Concepcion Martinez	San Jose, CA	TKO	10	—	—
Feb 25	David Sotelo	Inglewood	W	10	—	132
Nov 10	Bonnie Necessario	Stockton, CA	TKO	2	—	132
Dec 16	Miguel Meza	Los Angeles	TKO	3	—	132
1977						
Jan 13	Julio Leal	Los Angeles	TKO	7	—	131
May 19	Ramon Contreras	Los Angeles	TKO	8	—	133
Jun 9	Miguel Estrada	Los Angeles	TKO	2	—	—
Jul 15	Alejandro Lopez	San Diego	TKO	7	—	133
Aug 20	Ruben Olivares★	Inglewood	W	10	—	131
Nov 18	Arturo Leon	Anaheim	L	10	—	134
1978						
May 12	Ignacio Campos	San Diego	KO	7	—	130

Date		Opponent	Location	Result	Round	Title	Weight
Sep 27		Augie Pantellas	Philadelphia	TKO	7	—	130
Dec 6		Gerald Hayes	Stockton	W	10	—	131
1979							
Feb 26		Shig Fukuyama	Los Angeles	TKO	5	—	130
Apr 9	⑩	Rafael ("Bazooka") Limon	Los Angeles	TD	7	For-NABF-JL	130
Jun 18		Jose Torres	Los Angeles	W	10	—	130
Nov 16	♛	Alexis Arguello ★	Inglewood	TKO'd	7	For-WBC-JL	129
1980							
Mar 21	⑩	Rafael ("Bazooka") Limon	Inglewood	W	10	—	130
1981							
Feb 5		Roberto Garcia	Los Angeles	TKO	10	—	131
Mar 12		Leon Smith	Los Angeles	TKO	3	—	131
May 30	♛	Cornelius Boza-Edwards	Las Vegas	TKO'd	13	For-WBC-JL	130
Nov 7		Augustine Rivera	Los Angeles	TKO	6	—	131
1982							
Feb 23		Renan Marota	Sacramento, CA	KO	8	—	132
Mar 16		Salvador Ugalde	Sacramento	KO	3	—	133
May 4		Rosendo Ramirez	Sacramento	KO	8	—	131
Jun 15		Arturo Leon	Sacramento	W	10	—	133
Dec 11	♛	Rafael ("Bazooka") Limon	Sacramento	W	15	Won-WBC-JL	130
1983							
May 15	⑩	Cornelius Boza-Edwards	Las Vegas	W	12	Ret-WBC-JL	129
1984							
Jan 14	♛	Ray ("Boom Boom") Mancini	Reno, NV	TKO'd	3	For-WBA-L	133
Jun 12		Carlton Sparrow	Sacramento	KO	5	—	136
1985							
Mar 5		Freddie Roach	Sacramento	W	10	—	134
May 20		Davey Montana	Reno	KO	8	—	133
Aug 15		Arturo Frias	Sacramento	KO	7	—	135
Oct 4	⑩	Rafael Solis	Sacramento	KO	5	—	133
1987							
Jun 23		Martin ("Chiva") Guevara	Tucson, AZ	TKO	3	—	137
1988							
Jun 2		Bobby Jones	Orlando, FL	W	10	—	134

On May 24, 1974, Chacon faced an old friend from his amateur days, Danny ("Little Red") Lopez, an undefeated future featherweight champ. A capacity crowd of 16,080 turned out at the L.A. Sports Arena. Chacon out-boxed Lopez and seemed to be in command for most of the fight. In the ninth round, Chacon unleashed a flurry that knocked Lopez down. A groggy Lopez made it to his feet but was helpless along the ropes when the referee stopped the fight.

In his next fight, Chacon met Alfredo Marcano for the vacant WBC featherweight title. Chacon took control of the action in the second round, using jabs and combinations. Marcano took the sixth and seventh rounds. In the ninth, the pair battled furiously until Chacon knocked Marcano down with a devastating right uppercut. Marcano, a former world junior lightweight champion, rose at the count of eight with glassy eyes. The referee saw he was not fit to continue and stopped the fight. Chacon was now WBC featherweight champion.

He soon signed to defend his title against the only fighter ever to beat him: Ruben Olivares. The fight was highly anticipated by the crowd of 18,770—who paid a record California gate of $410,150 at the Forum on June 20, 1975.

Chacon was forced to lose sixteen pounds within a week of the fight to make the featherweight limit. In the second round, Olivares staggered Chacon with an overhand right and then knocked him down with a left-right combination. Chacon got up only to be sent down again by Olivares's blistering attack. Again Chacon arose, but Olivares trapped him in a corner and pummeled the champion once more. The fight was then stopped at 2:29 of the second round.

After being floored twice by Dave Sotelo on February 25, 1976—in a fight that Chacon won by decision—he followed his wife's wishes and retired. He did not stay away from boxing for long, however. Nine months later, he returned to the ring and won six matches before facing Olivares for the third time on August 20, 1977. Chacon knocked Olivares down in the second round en route to a close, but unanimous, decision.

Chacon received a shot at the WBC super featherweight title held by Alexis Arguello on November 16, 1979. Chacon used jabs to Arguello's ribs and got inside the taller fighter to land short punches. Chacon led through six rounds. In the seventh, Arguello staggered him with a right uppercut. Chacon was knocked to a neutral corner where he crouched down to take a count. Arguello then blasted Chacon for the remainder of the round and opened a cut under his eye. The fight was stopped at the end of the seventh.

In March 1982, Chacon was preparing for a fight with Salvador Ugalde when Chacon's wife, Valerie, committed suicide. The fight went on as scheduled the next night, and Chacon scored a third-round knockout.

On December 11, 1982, Chacon made his third attempt to win the WBC super featherweight title. This time his opponent was Rafael ("Bazooka") Limon. Chacon and Limon engaged in a wild brawl. Limon knocked Chacon down in the third and the tenth rounds. In the last round, Chacon caught Limon near the ropes with a right and then knocked him down with two more rights. As the referee was counting, the bell sounded to end the fight. Chacon won a unanimous decision by a narrow margin. He dedicated the victory to his late wife.

Chacon then successfully defended his title against Cornelius Boza-Edwards—angering the WBC who wanted Chacon to honor a disputed contract with Don King to fight Hector ("Macho") Camacho. In a real slugfest, Chacon—his face flowing with blood—knocked Boza-Edwards down three times and won a unanimous decision. Afterwards, the WBC stripped Chacon of his title. He moved up to lightweight and challenged Ray ("Boom Boom") Mancini for the WBA lightweight title but was stopped in three rounds. Chacon went 6-0-1 in his next seven bouts before retiring after decisioning Bobby Jones on June 2, 1988.

Outside of the ring, Chacon's life often was in turmoil. He had his boxing license suspended in 1985 after he was charged with drug possession. He was later sentenced to six months in jail for a probation violation. In 1986, he served time in jail after a conviction for domestic abuse. His son was killed in a gang shooting. Years later, Chacon pleaded no contest to selling drugs but was placed in a treatment program in lieu of serving time because he was suffering from dementia. Then he was divorced from his fourth wife. He later subsisted on a disability pension and served as a boxing coach at a small gym in a poor area of Los Angeles. His dementia worsened, and he is now unable to work.

JEFF CHANDLER
Joltin' Jeff

BANTAMWEIGHT

Right-handed; 5'7"; 113–121 lbs.

37 bouts, 2/25/1976 to 4/7/1984

Manager: "KO" Becky O'Neill

WBA Bantamweight Champion
1980–1984

Hall of Fame Induction: 2000

Born: 9/3/1956, Philadelphia, PA

In 1980, Jeff Chandler became the first American in 30 years—since the championship reign of Manuel Ortiz—to hold the world bantamweight title.

Unlike many boxers, Chandler had not set his sights on boxing at an early age. Chandler did not box formally until he was nineteen, but he learned a good bit about fighting on the streets of South Philly. The son of a construction worker, he joined street gangs while attending Bartlett Junior High at the same time as fellow Hall of Famer Matthew Saad Muhammad.

After high school, Chandler worked in construction, but a trip to a local gym with one of his friends galvanized his interest in boxing. After only two months of training, Chandler won his first amateur fight. His next bout was less successful—a loss to the more experienced Johnny Carter—but shortly thereafter Chandler turned professional.

On February 25, 1976, Chandler fought a four-round draw with lefty Mike Dowling, and less than two months later he recorded his first victory in a four-round decision over Chico Vivas. At that point in his career, Chandler had not yet developed the punching power that would be central to his success, yet he went undefeated through his next seven fights of which six were decision victories.

In 1978, "KO" Becky O'Neill and her husband, Willie, took Chandler under their wings. The O'Neills were long-time Philadelphia fight fans who took a liking to Chandler after watching some of his early fights. A former vaudevillian and national jitterbug champion, the diminutive Mrs. O'Neill became Chandler's manager, while her husband trained him. The pair developed a close bond with Chandler, regarding him as one

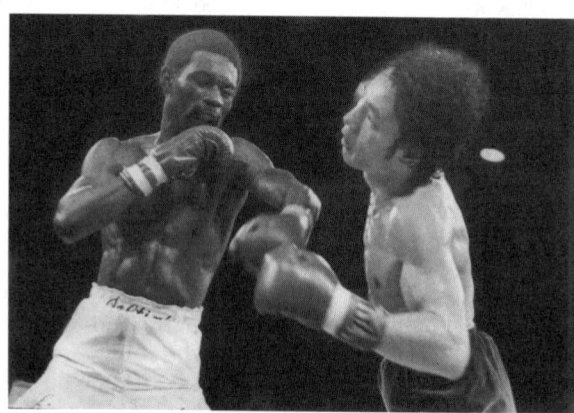

Chandler's (L) first meeting with tough Japanese bantamweight Eijiro Murata ended in a draw, but his next two title defenses were knockout victories. Chandler sends a stunned Murata to the canvas with a left hook.

IN THE RING	WON 33	LOST 2	DRAWS 2	TB 37	KO 18	W 15	WF 0	D 2	KO'd 1	L 1	LF 0

Date		Opponent	Site	Result / Rounds		Title	Wt.
1976							
Feb 25		Mike Dowling	Scranton, PA	D	4	—	117
Apr 13		Chico Vivas	Philadelphia	W	4	—	118
Jun 8		Mike Frazier	Philadelphia	W	4	—	116
Aug 6		John Glover	Philadelphia	W	4	—	116
Oct 14		Larry Huffin	Wilmington, DE	KO	3	—	116
Nov 30		Tony ("Pee Wee") Stokes	Philadelphia	W	4	—	115
1977							
Feb 21		Fernando Sanchez	Philadelphia	W	6	—	117
Jun 15		John Glover	Philadelphia	W	6	—	116
Oct 25		Tony Reed	Philadelphia	W	8	—	115
1978							
Mar 14		Tony Hernandez	Philadelphia	KO	2	—	117
May 24		Jose Luis Garcia	Philadelphia	KO	5	—	116
Jun 19		Roque Moreno	Philadelphia	KO	5	—	117
Aug 24		Sergio Reyes	Philadelphia	W	8	—	116
Oct 24		Andres Torres	Philadelphia	W	10	—	117
Dec 5		Rafael Gandarilla	Philadelphia	KO	9	—	116
1979							
Apr 3		Davey Vasquez	Philadelphia	W	10	—	118
May 14		Justo Garcia	Philadelphia	W	10	—	118
Jul 31		Alberto Cruz	Atlantic City	KO	3	—	114
Sep 26		Baby Kid Chocolate	Upper Darby, CT	KO	9	Won-Vac-USBA-B	117
Dec 4		Francisco Alvarado	Upper Darby	KO	7	—	118
1980							
Feb 1		Javier Flores	Philadelphia	KO	10	Won-Vac-NABF-B	118
Mar 29		Andres Hernandez	Atlantic City	W	12	—	116
Jul 12		Gilberto Villacana	Atlantic City	KO	4	—	117
Jul 31		Gustavo Martinez	Atlantic City	KO	8	—	118
Nov 14	♛	Julian Solis	Miami	KO	14	Won-World-B	118
1981							
Jan 31	⑩	Jorge Lujan	Philadelphia	W	15	Ret-World-B	113
Apr 4	⑩	Eijiro Murata	Tokyo	D	15	Ret-World-B	115
Jul 25	⑩	Julian Solis	Atlantic City	KO	7	Ret-World-B	115
Dec 10	⑩	Eijiro Murata	Atlantic City	KO	13	Ret-World-B	117
1982							
Mar 27	⑩	Johnny Carter	Philadelphia	KO	6	Ret-World-B	117
Oct 27		Miguel Iriarte	Atlantic City	KO	9	Ret-World-B	117
1983							
Mar 13	⑩	Gaby Canizales	Atlantic City	W	15	Ret-World-B	118
May 22		Hector Cortez	Atlantic City	W	10	—	121
Jul 23	⑩	Oscar Muniz	Atlantic City	L	10	—	121
Sep 10		Eijiro Murata	Tokyo	KO	10	Ret-World-B	118
Dec 17	⑩	Oscar Muniz	Atlantic City	KO	6	Ret-World-B	116
1984							
Apr 7	⑩	Richard Sandoval	Atlantic City	KO'd	15	Lost-World-B	118

of their family. Meanwhile, promoter Russell Peltz also became a part of the growing Chandler team.

For his part, Chandler continued to rack up victories. On September 26, 1979, Chandler knocked out Baby Kid Chocolate in nine rounds to win the vacant USBA bantamweight title. Two fights later, Chandler added the vacant North American Boxing Federation bantamweight title, stopping Javier Flores in ten rounds. He was subsequently offered a title shot against WBC super bantamweight champ Wilfredo Gomez. Knowing that Chandler had difficulty bulking up to the 118-pound bantamweight limit, let alone the 122-pound super bantamweight level, O'Neill turned down the fight. She and Chandler also rejected an offer to fight WBC bantamweight champion Lupe Pintor in a non-title match, not wanting to have to defeat him twice to win the championship.

In 1980, it appeared that Chandler was in line for a fight against Pinter, but on July 31 of that year, he fought Pinter's sparring partner, Gustavo Martinez, in Atlantic City. He easily defeated Martinez with an eight-round knockout, and the proposed Pinter title fight never materialized. Martinez had reportedly warned Pinter away from "Joltin' Jeff."

Instead, Chandler signed on to face WBA bantamweight champion Julian Solis—as yet undefeated—on November 14, 1980. The fight was held at the Miami Jai-Alai Fronton before a crowd of over 5,000 fans, many of whom taunted Chandler as he waited in his corner for the opening bell. They were forced to eat their words as Chandler took command from the start. He spun Solis away from

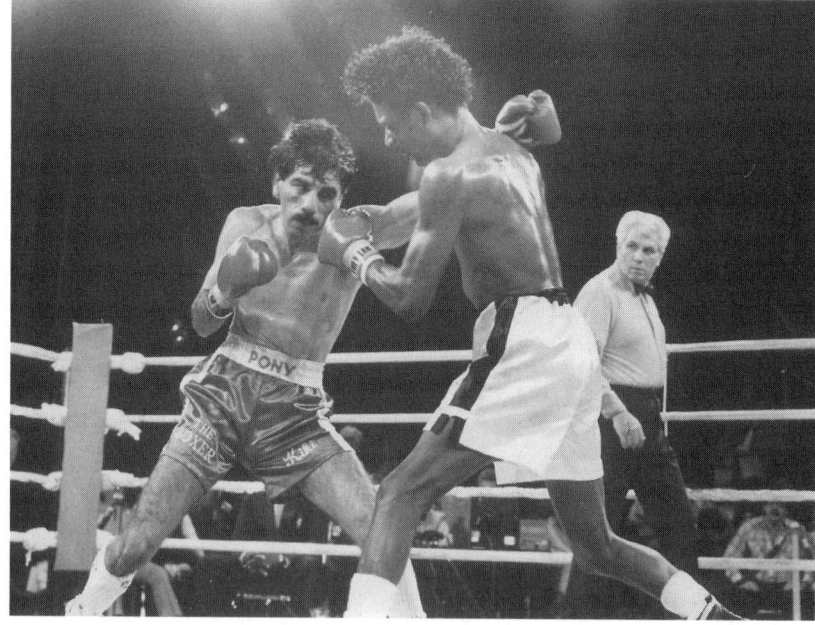

Chandler (R) is on his way to a six-round successful title defense when he lands this counterpunch to the left cheek of Oscar Muniz in Atlantic City on December 17, 1983.

him after a clinch and followed with a left hook that knocked the champ to the canvas. When Solis made a move to get inside, Chandler warded him off with right uppercuts and cut Solis's right eye in the third. He continued to hold firm as Solis annoyed him with a lunging left hook, followed by clutching and grabbing. Chandler landed a left hook in the eighth that hurt the champ. Though Solis rallied towards the end of each of the next few rounds, he never hurt Chandler. Finally, Chandler drove Solis against the ropes with a succession of potent rights, continuing the barrage until the referee stopped the fight at 1:05 of the fourteenth round.

Chandler's first title defense came less than three months later on January 31, 1981, when he faced former champion Jorge Lujan in the ballroom of a Philadelphia hotel before a national television audience. Lujan's side-to-side movement allowed him to slip many of Chandler's shots. However, the champion landed enough left hooks and hard, straight rights to win a unanimous decision.

In his next defense, Chandler managed a draw against Eijiro Murata in Tokyo. He followed this fight with three against old opponents, knocking out Solis and Murata, and then his old amateur foe, Carter. Yet outside the ring Chandler began to run into problems. He was charged with possession of cocaine and marijuana. Though he claimed he was set up, he received six months probation. Then, two months before his scheduled fight with Miguel Iriarte, Chandler was stabbed in the back with a broken bottle after an altercation with a motorist that quickly escalated into a large brawl. He did not postpone the upcoming fight, and managed to stop Iriarte in the ninth.

In a non-title fight on July 23, 1983, Chandler suffered his first defeat at the hands of Oscar Muniz. Chandler accepted the fight on short notice and didn't take his opponent seriously. In their rematch, this time with the title at stake, Chandler opened a cut over Muniz's left eye in the second round and continued to administer punishment into the seventh round, when the fight was stopped with Chandler the victor.

Chandler's title reign came to an abrupt end on April 7, 1984, when Richie Sandoval dominated him over fifteen rounds to win an easy decision. Though only 27, Chandler retired after undergoing cataract surgery later that year. He considered returning to the ring, but he never did. In his relatively short career, Chandler had become known as a stylish fighter, and a hard-hitting boxer. In retirement, he works as a trainer.

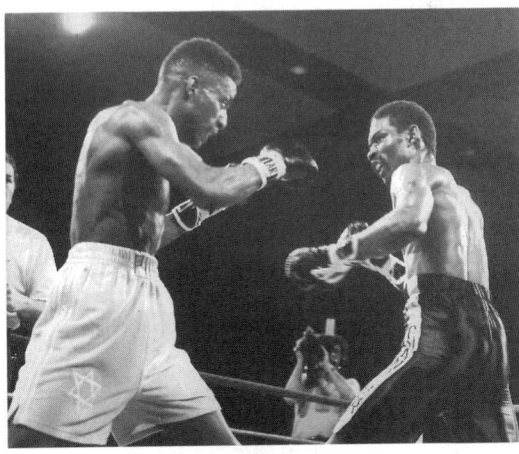

Chandler's (R) title proved unattainable for world-ranked fellow Philadelphian Johnny Carter. Carter succumbed in six on March 27, 1982.

EZZARD CHARLES
The Cincinnati Cobra

HEAVYWEIGHT

Right-handed; 6'; 160–204 lbs.

122 bouts, 3/27/1940 to 9/1/1959

Managers: George W. Rhein; Jake Mintz and Tom Tannas

NBA Heavywt. Champ 1949–50
World Heavywt. Champ 1950–51

Hall of Fame Induction: 1990

Born: 7/7/1921, Lawrenceville, GA

Named: Ezzard Mack Charles

Died: 5/27/1975

One of the most underrated of the former heavyweight champions, Ezzard Charles compiled an outstanding record in his nineteen-year professional career. He fought in thirteen championship bouts and triumphed over some of the best boxers of his day.

Charles was born in Georgia but grew up in Cincinnati. As an amateur, he was unbeatable, winning 42 consecutive fights, including Golden Gloves and other tournament championships. He turned professional in 1940 after winning the 1939 National Amateur Athletic Union middleweight title. Charles started fighting as a middleweight before moving up to light heavyweight and, ultimately, to the heavyweight division. He earned a reputation as both a clever boxer and a hard puncher. Among those vanquished early in his career are Hall of Famers Charley Burley, Joey Maxim, and Archie Moore.

The death of an opponent shocked Charles in 1948. He was fresh from his third victory over Moore, when he faced Sam Baroudi in Chicago. In the final round of this fight, Charles unleashed a devastating knockout attack. Baroudi never recovered and died a few days after the fight. Baroudi's death affected Charles deeply, and observers saw a change in his style from that point on. Although he was criticized for being too conservative, Charles no longer possessed the desire to finish his opponents off in the manner which had earned him the nickname "The Cincinnati Cobra."

In 1949, Charles

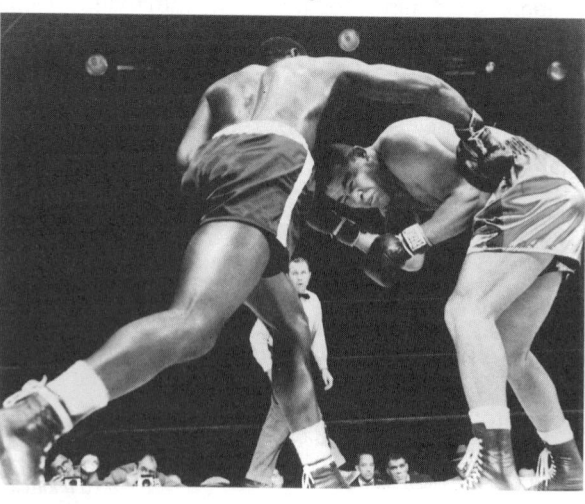

An over-the-hill Joe Louis (R) grimaces from a blow to his side by Charles on September 27, 1950. Charles won the vacant heavyweight championship.

Date		Opponent	Site	Result / Rounds		Title	Wt.
1940							
Mar 27		John Reeves	Cincinnati	W	6	—	—
Apr 3		Remo Fernandez	Cincinnati	KO	6	—	—
May 20		Charley Banks	Cincinnati	W	6	—	—
Jun 3		Charley Banks	Cincinnati	KO	1	—	—
Jun 13		Frankie Williams	Cincinnati	KO	7	—	—
Sep 23		Billy Hood	Cincinnati	KO	2	—	—
Oct 1		Marty Simmons	Cincinnati	W	10	—	162
Dec 2		Charley Jerome	Cincinnati	KO	2	—	—
1941							
Feb 10		Billy Bengal	Cincinnati	W	10	—	162
Feb 22		Slaka Cavrich	Cincinnati	KO	2	—	164
Mar 10		Floyd Howard	Cincinnati	KO	7	—	164
Mar 31		Joe Sutka	Cincinnati	W	10	—	164
May 12		Rudy Kozole	Cincinnati	W	10	—	164
Jun 9	⑩	Ken Overlin	Cincinnati	L	10	—	161
Jul 21		Al Gilbert	Cincinnati	KO	6	—	162
Oct 13		Pat Mangini	Cincinnati	KO	1	—	162
Nov 17	⑩	Teddy Yarosz★	Cincinnati	W	10	—	163
1942							
Jan 12	⑩	Anton Christoforidis	Cincinnati	KO	3	—	161
Mar 2	⑩	Ken Overlin	Cincinnati	D	10	—	162
Apr 8		Billy Pryor	Cincinnati	W	10	—	—
May 13	⑩	Kid Tunero	Cincinnati	L	10	—	162
May 25	⑩	Charley Burley★	Pittsburgh	W	10	—	161
Jun 29	⑩	Charley Burley★	Pittsburgh	W	10	—	160
Jul 14		Steve Mamakos	Cincinnati	KO	1	—	163
Jul 27	⑩	Booker Beckwith	Pittsburgh	KO	9	—	163
Aug 17	⑩	Jose Basora	Pittsburgh	KO	5	—	161
Sep 15	⑩	Mose Brown	Pittsburgh	KO	6	—	166
Oct 27	⑩	Joey Maxim★	Pittsburgh	W	10	—	165
Dec 1	⑩	Joey Maxim★	Cleveland	W	10	—	166
1943							
Jan 7	⑩	Jimmy Bivins★	Cleveland	L	10	—	165
Mar 31	⑩	Lloyd Marshall	Cleveland	KO'd	8	—	168
1946							
Feb 18		Al Sheridan	Cincinnati	KO	2	—	173
Mar 25		Tee Hubert	Cincinnati	W	10	—	173
Apr 1		Billy Duncan	Pittsburgh	KO	4	—	174
Apr 15		Georgie Parks	Pittsburgh	KO	6	—	174
May 13		Tee Hubert	Cincinnati	KO	4	—	170
May 20	⑩	Archie Moore★	Pittsburgh	W	10	—	171
Jun 13		Sheldon Bell	Youngstown, OH	KO	5	—	173
Jul 29	⑩	Lloyd Marshall	Cincinnati	KO	6	—	169
Sep 23		Billy Smith	Cincinnati	W	10	—	172
Nov 12		Jimmy Bivins★	Pittsburgh	W	10	—	175
1947							
Feb 17	⑩	Billy Smith	Cleveland	KO	5	—	173
Mar 10		Jimmy Bivins★	Cleveland	KO	4	—	170

Date		Opponent	Location	Result	Rounds		Weight
Apr 4		Erv Sarlin	Pittsburgh	W	10	—	176
May 5	⑩	Archie Moore★	Cincinnati	W	10	—	173
Jul 14	⑩	Fitzie Fitzpatrick	Cincinnati	KO	5	—	174
Jul 25	⑩	Elmer Ray	New York	L	10	—	174
Sep 16		Joe Matisi	Buffalo, NY	W	10	—	175
Sep 29	⑩	Lloyd Marshall	Cincinnati	KO	2	—	173
Oct 16		Al Smith	Akron, OH	KO	4	—	178
Oct 27		Clarence Jones	Huntington, WV	KO	1	—	180
Nov 3		Teddy Randolph	Buffalo	W	10	—	174
Dec 2	⑩	Fitzie Fitzpatrick	Cleveland	KO	4	—	173
1948							
Jan 13	⑩	Archie Moore★	Cleveland	KO	8	—	173
Feb 20		Sam Baroudi	Chicago	KO	10	—	176
May 7	⑩	Elmer ("Violent") Ray	Chicago	KO	9	—	175
May 20		Erv Sarlin	Buffalo	W	10	—	173
Sep 13	⑩	Jimmy Bivins★	Washington, DC	W	10	—	176
Nov 14		Walter Hafer	Cincinnati	KO	7	—	178
Dec 10	⑩	Joe Baksi	New York	KO	11	—	178
1949							
Feb 7		Johnny Haynes	Philadelphia	KO	8		179
Feb 28	⑩	Joey Maxim★	Cincinnati	W	15	—	181
Jun 22	⑩	Jersey Joe Walcott★	Chicago	W	15	Won-Vac-NBA-H	181
Aug 10	⑩	Gus Lesnevich	New York	TKO	7	Ret-NBA-H	180
Oct 14	⑩	Pat Valentino	San Francisco	KO	8	Ret-NBA-H	182
1950							
Aug 15		Freddie Beshore	Buffalo	TKO	14	Ret-NBA-H	183
Sep 27	⑩	Joe Louis★	New York	W	15	Won-Vac-World-H	184
Dec 5	⑩	Nick Barone	Cincinnati	KO	11	Ret-World-H	185
1951							
Jan 12	⑩	Lee Oma	New York	TKO	10	Ret-World-H	185
Mar 7	⑩	Jersey Joe Walcott★	Detroit	W	15	Ret-World-H	186
May 30	♛	Joey Maxim★	Chicago	W	15	Ret-World-H	182
Jul 18	⑩	Jersey Joe Walcott★	Pittsburgh	KO'd	7	Lost-World-H	182
Oct 10	⑩	Rex Layne	Pittsburgh	TKO	11	—	188
Dec 12	♛	Joey Maxim★	San Francisco	W	12	—	189
Dec 21		Joe Kahut	Portland, OR	KO	8	—	189
1952							
Jun 5	♛	Jersey Joe Walcott★	Philadelphia	L	15	For-World-H	196
Aug 8	⑩	Rex Layne	Ogden, UT	L	10	—	190
Oct 8		Bernie Reynolds	Cincinnati	KO	2	—	189
Oct 24	⑩	Cesar Brion	New York	W	10	—	186
Nov 26	⑩	Jimmy Bivins★	Chicago	W	10	—	185
Dec 15		Frank Buford	Boston	TKO	7	—	187
1953							
Jan 14		Wes Bascom	St. Louis	TKO	9	—	188
Feb 4	⑩	Tommy Harrison	Detroit	TKO	9	—	187
Apr 1		Rex Layne	San Francisco	W	10	—	187
May 12		Bill Gilliam	Toledo, OH	W	10	—	189
May 26		Larry Watson	Milwaukee	KO	5	—	188
Aug 11	⑩	Nino Valdes	Miami Beach	L	10	—	191
Sep 8	⑩	Harold Johnson★	Philadelphia	L	10	—	185
Dec 16	⑩	Coley Wallace	San Francisco	KO	10	—	190
1954							
Jan 13	⑩	Bob Satterfield	Chicago	KO	2	—	189

Date		Opponent	Location	Result	Rounds	Title	Weight
Jun 17	♛	Rocky Marciano ★	New York	L	15	For-World-H	185
Sep 17	♛	Rocky Marciano ★	New York	KO'd	8	For-World-H	192
1955							
Feb 18	⑩	Charley Norkus	New York	W	10	—	191
Apr 11		Vern Escoe	Edmonton, Alberta, Canada	KO	3	—	196
Apr 27	⑩	John Holman	Miami Beach	KO'd	9	—	193
Jun 8	⑩	John Holman	Cincinnati	W	10	—	195
Jul 13	⑩	Paul Andrews	Chicago	W	10	—	193
Aug 3	⑩	Tommy Jackson	Syracuse, NY	L	10	—	191
Aug 31	⑩	Tommy Jackson	Cleveland	L	10	—	191
Nov 14		Toxie Hall	Providence, RI	L	10	—	197
Dec 6		Toxie Hall	Rochester, NY	W	10	—	197
Dec 22		Bob Albright	San Francisco	W	10	—	196
Dec 29	⑩	Young Jack Johnson	Los Angeles	KO'd	6	—	196
1956							
Apr 21		Don Jasper	Windsor, Ontario, Canada	KO	9	—	195
May 21	⑩	Wayne Bethea	New York	L	10	—	195
Jun 19		Bob Albright	Phoenix	KO	7	—	197
Jul 13		Pat McMurtry	Tacoma, WA	L	10	—	197
Aug 13		Harry Matthews	Seattle	L	10	—	200
Oct 2		Dick Richardson	London	LD	2	—	195
1958							
Aug 28		Johnny Harper	Fairmont, WV	W	10	—	198
Sep 30		Alfredo Zuany	Juarez, Mexico	L	10	—	199
Oct 27		Donnie Fleeman	Dallas	KO'd	6	—	202
1959							
Jul 3		Dave Ashley	Cincinnati	KO	7	—	204
Jul 30		George Logan	Boise, ID	KO'd	8	—	190
Sep 1		Alvin Green	Oklahoma City	L	10	—	201

decisioned Jersey Joe Walcott in Chicago to win the National Boxing Association heavyweight title—vacant after Joe Louis's retirement. Charles defended this title three times, but it took a victory over the deposed king to gain him universal recognition as the world champion. Charles and Louis, who came out of retirement in an effort to recapture his crown, met in Yankee Stadium in 1950. Overweight and past his prime, Louis was no match for Charles, who out-pointed the Brown Bomber with relative ease. Many thought Charles could have knocked out the ex-champ, but Charles appeared to ease off in the later rounds when he had the fight well in hand.

Walcott was Charles's most threatening nemesis, and although Charles held him off in a title challenge in March 1951, Jersey Joe came back to take the crown in July. The fight was held in Forbes Field in Pittsburgh, and Charles fell in the seventh round to a knockout left hook. Charles failed in an attempt to win the title again in 1952 when Walcott outboxed him, and two tries against Walcott's successor, Rocky Marciano, were also unsuccessful.

In retirement, Charles made bad investments in a number of business ventures. He also wrestled professionally. He died in 1975, virtually penniless and after having suffered for several years from lateral sclerosis of the spine, an ailment that eventually paralyzed him from the waist down.

CURTIS COKES

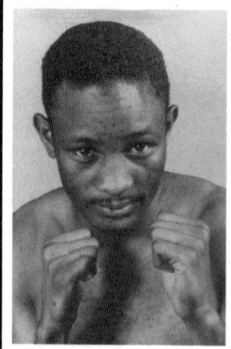

WELTERWEIGHT

Right-handed; 5'9"; 154–170 lbs.

81 bouts, 3/24/1958 to 10/5/1972

Managers: Pinkie George 1964; Doug Lord 1966–68, 1970; Tiger Reed 1969; Charlie Dietz 1972

WBA/WBC Welterweight Champ 1966–69
World Welterweight Champion 1968–69

Hall of Fame Induction: 2003

Born: 6/15/1937, Dallas, TX

Cokes was born in Dallas on June 15, 1937. He was very active in sports as a youth. Though Cokes wasn't large, he was an accomplished baseball and basketball player in high school, earning all-state honors in both sports. The Brooklyn Dodgers had a farm club in Fort Worth and held an open tryout camp there. Cokes, a shortstop, attended the tryout but was sent home because he was too small: he weighed only 126 pounds. Even though he never grew more than 5'9", Cokes played some basketball in the Dallas area for the Harlem Magicians, a professional touring team. Cokes started boxing when he was fourteen at a YMCA. After his rejection by the Dodgers, he decided to try to make it in the ring. Because the Texas Golden Gloves tournament was not racially integrated at the time, Cokes was barred. He fought in informal smokers—winning all 22 of those fights by his account—before he turned professional.

In his first pro fight on March 24, 1958, Cokes decisioned Manuel Gonzalez in Midland. He won his next eight fights, including another decision over Gonzalez to close out 1958. The next year, Gonzalez beat him in a ten-round decision, but Cokes knocked out future top-five contender Rip Randall in one round—after the two had previously fought a technical draw.

In 1961, Cokes faced Luis Rodriguez twice, fighting once to a draw and dropping a decision in the rematch. A decision loss to Hilario Morales also marred his record. He knocked Morales out in their rematch.

In 1963, he journeyed to the Big Apple to meet second-rated contender Jose Stable at Sunnyside Garden in Queens. Despite Cokes staggering Stable in the second, ninth, and tenth, Stable was able to get inside Cokes and bothered him with flurries to the body and the head.

Cokes (R) pummels Luis Rodriguez with a two-fisted attack in the fifteenth round, just before Rodriguez's corner throws in the towel. This third meeting of the fighters was a July 6, 1966, elimination bout for the vacant WBA welterweight title held in New Orleans.

IN THE RING	WON 63	LOST 14	DRAWS 3	TB 81	KO 30	W 33	WF 0	D 3	KO'd 3	L 11	LF 0	NC 1

Date	Opponent	Site	Result / Rounds		Title	Wt.
1958						
Mar 24	Manuel Gonzalez	Midland, TX	W	6	—	—
Apr 8	Gil Tapia	Dallas	W	4	—	—
Apr 28	Jimmy Leach	Dallas	W	6	—	—
May 12	Lamoine Vance	Waco, TX	W	6	—	—
May 26	Cecil Courtney	Dallas	W	6	—	—
Jun 30	Sammy Williams	Dallas	KO	6	—	—
Oct 27	Elmo Henderson	Dallas	W	6	—	—
Nov 22	Manuel Gonzalez	Lubbock, TX	W	8	—	143
Dec 1	Ruben Flores	Dallas	W	6	—	—
1959						
Jan 20	George Carson	Lubbock	KO	3	—	—
Apr 1	Henry Watson	Dallas	W	4	—	—
Apr 27	Manuel Gonzalez	Dallas	L	10	—	—
May 18	Garland ("Rip") Randall	Dallas	NC	3	—	—
Jul 27	Garland ("Rip") Randall	Dallas	KO	1	—	—
Aug 27	Reggie Williams	Baton Rouge, LA	KO	5	—	144
Sep 14	Mel Ferguson	Dallas	W	8	—	—
Dec 2	Frankie Davis	Houston	L	6	—	—
Dec 14	Aman Peck	Dallas	KO	5	—	—
1960						
Mar 1	Lovell Jenkins	Amarillo, TX	W	8	—	148
Jul 29	Pedro Ruiz	El Paso, TX	KO	3	—	—
Sep 13	Joe Hargrove	Dallas	KO	1	—	—
Oct 24	Stefan Redl	Dallas	TKO	8	—	148
1961						
Jan 16	Joe Miceli	Dallas	W	10	—	147
Feb 13	Charlie ("Tombstone") Smith	Dallas	W	10	—	145
Apr 4	Hilario Morales	Ciudad Juarez, Mexico	L	10	—	147
Jun 8	Kenny Lane	Dallas	D	10	—	141
Aug 3 ⑩	Luis Rodriguez★	Dallas	W	10	—	147
Sep 14	Manuel Gonzalez	Dallas	W	10	—	144
Dec 2 ⑩	Luis Rodriguez★	Miami	L	10	—	144
1962						
Jan 23	Carlos Macias	Houston	TKO	4	—	146
Feb 13	Ramon Rodriguez	San Antonio, TX	W	10	—	146
Apr 6	Hilario Morales	Dallas	KO	5	—	147
May 11	Rudolph Bent	Dallas	KO	8	—	147
Aug 22	Joey Limas	Albuquerque, NM	W	10	—	146
Sep 8 ⑩	Manuel Alvarez	Monterrey, Mexico	L	10	—	145
Nov 15	Hubert Jackson	Dallas	KO	1	—	147
Dec 10	Gregorio Ceniceros	Dallas	KO	2	—	145
1963						
Feb 11	Johnny Newman	Hollywood, CA	KO	2	—	147
Feb 25	Joey Parks	Wichita Falls, KS	KO	5	—	147
Apr 20 ⑩	Jose Stable	New York	L	10	—	145
May 21 ⑩	Stan Harrington	Honolulu	W	10	—	145
May 30	Flory Olguin	Albuquerque	KO	5	—	146
1964						
May 1	Stanley Hayward	Philadelphia	TKO'd	4	—	147

Date		Opponent	Location	Result	Rounds		Weight
May 12		Tony Montano	Los Angeles	W	10	—	147
Jun 9		Al Andrews	Las Vegas	W	10	—	147
Aug 10		Al Andrews	Fresno, CA	W	10	—	146
Aug 27		Eddie Pace	Los Angeles	L	10	—	144
1965							
Mar 15		Marshall Wells	Dallas	KO	12	Won-Texas-W	147
Apr 23	ⓦ	Fortunato Manca	Rome	W	10	—	149
Dec 13		Billy Collins	New Orleans	W	12	Won-South-W	150
1966							
Jul 6	ⓦ	Luis Rodriguez★	New Orleans	TKO	15	—	146
Aug 24		Manuel Gonzalez	New Orleans	W	15	Won-Vac WBA-W	149
Sep 24		Enrique Cruz	Corpus Christi, TX	KO	7	—	149
Nov 28	ⓦ	Jean Josselin	Dallas	W	15	Won-WBA/WBC-W	145
1967							
Jan 24	ⓦ	Francois Pavilla	Paris	D	10	—	146
Feb 20	ⓦ	Ted Whitfield	Dallas	KO	3	—	148
Mar 31	ⓦ	Gypsy Joe Harris	New York	L	10	—	149
May 19	ⓦ	Francois Pavilla	Dallas	TKO	10	Ret-WBA/WBC-W	145
Oct 2	ⓦ	Charlie Shipes	Oakland	TKO	8	Ret-WBA/WBC-W	145
1968							
Feb 5	ⓦ	Jean Josselin	Paris	W	10	—	—
Mar 15		Jimmy Lester	Oakland	W	10	—	154
Apr 16	ⓦ	Willie Ludick	Dallas	TKO	5	Won-World-W	145
May 26		Cecil Courtney	Dallas	W	6	—	—
Jun 15		Joe N'Gidi	Johannesburg, South Africa	TKO	4	—	150
Jun 28	ⓦ	Willie Ludick	Lourenco Marques, Mozambique	TKO	3	—	148
Jul 5		Joseph Sishi	Durban, South Africa	KO	5	—	150
Oct 21		Ramon La Cruz	New Orleans	W	15	Ret-World-W	146
1969							
Feb 10		Don Cobbs	St. Louis, MO	KO	1	—	154
Apr 18	ⓦ	Jose Napoles★	Inglewood, CA	TKO'd	13	Lost-World-W	145
Jun 29	♛	Jose Napoles★	Mexico City	TKO'd	10	For-World-W	146
1970							
Jan 29		Roberto Pena	Ft. Worth, TX	KO	5	—	160
Aug 11		Danny Perez	Dallas	KO	7	—	161
Sep 11		Fate Davis	Ft. Worth	W	10	—	158
Sep 29		Harold Richardson	Dallas	W	10	—	158
Nov 3		Billy Braggs	Milwaukee, WI	KO	6	—	158
1971							
Mar 17		Fate Davis	Akron, OH	D	10	—	158
May 24	ⓦ	Rafael Gutierrez	San Francisco	L	10	—	158
Dec 2		Carlos Salinas	Sacramento, CA	L	10	—	163
1972							
Sep 2		Elijah Makhatini	Durban	L	10	—	157
Sep 23		Joseph Hali	Port Elizabeth, South Africa	W	10	—	—
Oct 5		Ezra Mzinyane	Cape Town, South Africa	W	10	—	—

Stable earned the unanimous decision. Frustrated with the direction his career was taking, Cokes retired in October 1963.

He returned to the ring and then retired again, before staging another comeback on December 13, 1965, when he decisioned Billy Collins in New Orleans. Cokes had always been primarily a skillful boxer rather than a slugger. At the urging of his manager, Doug Lord, Cokes began to use his strong right hand more aggressively in an effort to make himself more attractive to promoters.

Cokes got his chance when Emile Griffith did not defend his welterweight title, and the WBA stripped him of the belt. The WBA then organized a four-man tournament for the title. Luis Rodriguez was seeded first, Stan Hayward second, Manuel Gonzalez third, and Cokes fourth. In his semi-final bout with Rodriguez on July 6, 1966, in New Orleans, Cokes came up with the biggest victory of his career—to that point—when he upset Rodriguez. Rodriguez got off to a strong start, but the tide turned in the eleventh round. Cokes opened a cut over Rodriguez's left eye. In the fifteenth round, Cokes drove Rodriguez into the corner and fired away with devastating combinations. The referee stopped the fight.

After Gonzalez upset Hayward, Cokes faced Gonzalez—who had been his first pro opponent and who was a good friend outside the ring—for the WBA title on August 24, 1966, at the New Orleans Municipal Auditorium. Cokes, a clever counterpuncher, kept Gonzalez at bay with his strong jab. He knocked Gonzalez down in the twelfth and kept up the pressure with stiff combinations. Cokes won an easy decision by scores of 14-1, 8-2-5, and 11-2-2.

Cokes then faced Jean Josselin at home in Dallas in a fight that would effectively unify the welterweight title. Cokes totally dominated the fight. He had a reach advantage of ten inches on Josselin and used his jab, left hook, and right uppercuts to assault his opponent. Cokes won the fifteen-round decision by a wide margin. He was now considered the world champion everywhere but California. After a couple more fights, he traveled to Oakland to meet Charlie Shipes, holder of the California version of the world welterweight title. Cokes knocked Shipes down in the fourth with a right and left to the jaw. He floored him again in the sixth with a left hook to the jaw and a hard right. In the eighth, Cokes knocked Shipes down with a right and then put him down for good with another right to the head. Cokes earned acclaim as the undisputed world champion.

Cokes won his next eight fights, including two title defenses, before he faced Jose Napoles at the Forum in Los Angeles on April 18, 1969. A crowd of 15,878—many of them Napoles's supporters from his adopted country of Mexico—did not see Cokes at his best. Napoles initiated the action and threw far more punches. After thirteen rounds, Cokes's manager, Doug Lord, told the referee to stop the fight because Cokes could barely see. In the rematch two months later in Mexico City, Napoles again dominated. Cokes could not continue after ten rounds.

Cokes moved up to middleweight but never challenged for a title. He retired once and for all after a points win over Ezra Mzinyane in Cape Town, South Africa, on October 5, 1972.

Outside the ring, Cokes has been involved in many different activities. He owned or co-owned a steakhouse, a construction company, a nightclub, and a landscaping company. While still an active boxer, he acted in the critically acclaimed boxing movie, *Fat City*. Director John Huston was so impressed by his performance that he wanted Cokes to appear in another of his films. The shooting schedule conflicted with a bout, so Cokes had to pass. He also wrote *The Complete Book of Boxing for Fighters and Fight Fans,* a book that sold more than 77,000 copies. For the last twenty years or so, Cokes has worked as a trainer. His fighters have included such notables as Quincy Taylor and Kirk Johnson.

BILLY CONN
The Pittsburgh Kid

LIGHT HEAVYWEIGHT

Right-handed; 6'1"; 135–187 lbs.
76 bouts, 6/28/1934 to 11/25/1948
Manager: Johnny Ray
Light Heavyweight Champ 1939–41
Hall of Fame Induction: 1990
Born: 10/8/1917, Pittsburgh, PA
Named: William David Conn, Jr.
Died: 5/29/1993

Best known as the contender who could have knocked off Joe Louis's heavyweight crown if he'd been less eager, Billy Conn was a light heavyweight champ with the talent to fight heavyweights on their own terms. Known as "The Pittsburgh Kid," Conn started fighting as a youth in the alleys of the East Liberty section of Pittsburgh. Idolizing another Pittsburgh fighter, Harry Greb, Conn started working in the gym at a young age under the guidance of Johnny Ray. He never fought as an amateur, but went straight into the professional ranks at age sixteen.

Conn began as a lightweight and, as he grew, advanced through the welterweight, middleweight, and light heavyweight ranks. He fought mostly in the Pittsburgh area, where he compiled an impressive record. Not a great puncher, Conn used clever boxing skills and an indomitable spirit to pile up his victories. By 1938, Conn was ranked as the ninth-best light heavyweight contender in *The Ring's* annual rankings.

Hall of Famer Georges Carpentier looks on from the referee's spot as brothers Jackie and Billy Conn (R) prepare to spar. Carpentier preceded Billy Conn by nineteen years as light heavyweight champion.

IN THE RING	WON 64	LOST 12	DRAWS 1	TB 77	KO 15	W 49	WF 0	D 1	KO'd 3	L 9	LF 0

Date	Opponent	Site	Result / Rounds		Title	Wt.
1934						
Jun 28	Dick Woodward	Fairmont, WV	L	4	—	—
Jul 20	Johnny Lewis	Charleston, SC	KO	3	—	135
Aug 30	Bob Dronan	Parkersburg, WV	W	6	—	136
Sep 27	Paddy Gray	Pittsburgh	W	4	—	137
Nov 12	Pete Leone	Wheeling, WV	TKO'd	3	—	139
1935						
Jan 29	Johnny Birek	Pittsburgh	W	6	—	143
Feb 25	Ray Eberle	Pittsburgh	L	6	—	143
Mar 13	Stanley Nagy	Wheeling	W	4	—	—
Apr 8	George Schlee	Pittsburgh	KO	1	—	144
Apr 25	Ralph Gizzy	Pittsburgh	L	4	—	143
Jun 3	Ray Eberle	Millvale, PA	W	6	—	146
Jun 10	Ralph Gizzy	Millvale	L	6	—	142
Jul 9	Teddy Movan	Millvale	L	4	—	144
Jul 29	Ray Eberle	Millvale	W	5	—	145
Aug 19	Teddy Movan	Millvale	L	4	—	147
Sep 9	George Leggins	Pittsburgh	W	4	—	147
Sep 10	Johnny Yurcini	Washington, PA	W	6	—	147
Oct 7	Johnny Yurcini	Johnstown, PA	W	6	—	149
Oct 14	Teddy Movan	Pittsburgh	D	6	—	147
Nov 18	Steve Walters	Pittsburgh	W	6	—	150
1936						
Jan 27	Johnny Yurcini	Pittsburgh	TKO	4	—	149
Feb 3	Kid Cook	Pittsburgh	W	6	—	152
Feb 17	Kid Cook	Pittsburgh	W	8	—	151
Mar 16	Steve Nickleash	Pittsburgh	W	6	—	152
Apr 13	Steve Nickleash	Pittsburgh	W	6	—	155
Apr 27	General Burrows	Pittsburgh	W	6	—	157
May 19	Dick Ambrose	Pittsburgh	W	6	—	—
May 27	Honeyboy Jones	Pittsburgh	W	8	—	156
Jun 3	Honeyboy Jones	Pittsburgh	W	10	—	155
Jun 15	General Burrows	Pittsburgh	W	8	—	154
Jul 30	Teddy Movan	Pittsburgh	W	8	—	157
Aug 10	Teddy Movan	Pittsburgh	W	8	—	155
Sep 8	Honeyboy Jones	Pittsburgh	W	10	—	151
Sep 21	Roscoe Manning	Pittsburgh	KO	5	—	156
Oct 19	Charlie Weise	Pittsburgh	W	10	—	156
Oct 22	Ralph Chong	Pittsburgh	W	10	—	154
Dec 2	Jimmy Brown	Pittsburgh	KO	9	—	158
Dec 28	⑩ Fritzie Zivic★	Pittsburgh	W	10	—	156
1937						
Mar 11	⑩ Babe Risko	Pittsburgh	W	10	—	160
May 3	Vince Dundee	Pittsburgh	W	10	—	161
May 27	⑩ Oscar Rankins	Pittsburgh	W	10	—	161
Jun 30	⑩ Teddy Yarosz★	Pittsburgh	W	12	—	161

Date		Opponent	Location	Result	Rds	Title	Wt
Aug 3		Ralph Chong	Youngstown, OH	TKO	6	—	—
Aug 13	⑩	Young Corbett III★	San Francisco	L	10	—	160
Sep 30	⑩	Teddy Yarosz★	Pittsburgh	W	15	—	162
Nov 8	⑩	Young Corbett III★	Pittsburgh	W	10	—	163
Dec 16	⑩	Solly Krieger	Pittsburgh	L	12	—	163
1938							
Jan 24		Honeyboy Jones	Pittsburgh	W	12	—	165
Apr 4		Domenic Ceccarelli	Pittsburgh	W	10	—	167
May 10		Eric Seelig	Pittsburgh	W	10	—	169
Jul 25	⑩	Teddy Yarosz★	Pittsburgh	L	12	—	160
Sep 14	⑩	Ray Actis	San Francisco	KO	8	—	169
Oct 27		Honeyboy Jones	Pittsburgh	W	10	—	167
Nov 28		Solly Krieger	Pittsburgh	W	12	—	165
1939							
Jan 6		Fred Apostoli★	New York	W	10	—	167
Feb 10		Fred Apostoli★	New York	W	15	—	167
May 12		Solly Krieger	New York	W	12	—	170
Jul 13	♛	Melio Bettina	New York	W	15	Won-Vac World-LH	170
Aug 14	⑩	Gus Dorazio	Philadelphia	KO	8	—	173
Sep 25	⑩	Melio Bettina	Pittsburgh	W	15	Ret-World-LH	171
Nov 17	⑩	Gus Lesnevich	New York	W	15	Ret-World-LH	171
1940							
Jan 10		Henry Cooper	New York	W	12	—	173
Jun 5	⑩	Gus Lesnevich	Detroit	W	15	Ret-World-LH	173
Sep 6	⑩	Bob Pastor	New York	KO	13	—	174
Oct 18		Al McCoy	Boston	W	10	—	172
Nov 29	⑩	Lee Savold	New York	W	12	—	174
1941							
Feb 27		Ira Hughes	Clarksburg, WV	KO	4	—	182
Mar 6		Dan Hassett	Washington, DC	KO	5	—	181
Apr 4		Gunnar Barlund	Chicago	TKO	8	—	178
May 26		Buddy Knox	Pittsburgh	KO	8	—	180
Jun 18	♛	Joe Louis★	New York	KO'd	13	For-World-H	174
1942							
Jan 12		Henry Cooper	Toledo, OH	W	12	—	182
Jan 28		J.D. Turner	St. Louis	W	10	—	183
Feb 13		Tony Zale★	New York	W	12	—	175
1946							
Jun 19	♛	Joe Louis★	New York	KO'd	8	For-World-H	182
1948							
Nov 15		Mike O'Dowd	Macon, GA	KO	9	—	190
Nov 25		Jackie Lyons	Dallas	KO	9	—	188

In 1939, Conn faced Melio Bettina in New York for the world light heavyweight championship—vacant since the retirement of John Henry Lewis. Conn fell behind in the first six rounds and lost the thirteenth but otherwise dominated the fight. He won the decision to take the title. Conn also won the rematch later that year and twice defended his title against Gus Lesnevich.

In 1941, Conn relinquished the light heavyweight title in order to challenge Joe Louis for the world heavyweight championship. The fight was held in New York's Polo Grounds before 54,486 fans, including 6,000 Conn supporters from Pittsburgh. Louis had been on top for four years. He was 27; Conn was 24. Conn weighed in at 174 pounds, while Louis tipped the scales at 199. Conn looked good, dancing away from Louis's punches and landing a few speedy blows when Louis was off-guard. Although Louis won the first two rounds, Conn won the third and, by the twelfth, was ahead on two cards and even on the third. With a win by decision in the making, Conn made a tactical error in the unlucky thirteenth. Instead of continuing to fight in the same style with which he had built his lead, Conn attempted to take Louis out. He launched into Louis with abandon. Conn's more offensive posture enabled Louis to penetrate, and he knocked Conn out with a right to the jaw. Louis later conceded that the fight had been one of the closest of his career.

A scheduled rematch was postponed due to family problems that demanded Conn's attention. Next, Conn broke his hand, which delayed the rematch until after the end of World War II. Before the rematch finally took place in Yankee Stadium, Louis said of Conn, "He can run but he can't hide." Louis was right. Louis won easily, knocking Conn out in the eighth. Conn fought twice more and then retired.

Conn starred in a movie about himself, called *The Pittsburgh Kid.* Much later, he and his wife were the subjects of a lengthy article by Frank Deford in *Sports Illustrated* titled "The Boxer and the Blonde."

Conn (L) connects solidly with a jab to Joe Louis's heart. Conn twice challenged the much-larger Louis for the heavyweight championship. In their first meeting, in 1941, he came remarkably close to victory.

PIPINO CUEVAS

W E L T E R W E I G H T

Right-handed; 5'8"; 133–173 lbs.

50 bouts, 11/14/1971 to 9/25/1989

Manager: Lupe Sanchez

WBA Welterweight Champion 1976–1980

Hall of Fame Induction: 2002

Born: 12/27/1957, Santo Tomis, Mexico

Named: Isidro Pipino Cuevas Gonzalez

A very popular fighter both in his native Mexico and in the United States, Pipino Cuevas won the world welterweight title when he was just eighteen years old.

Cuevas was born in the Colonia Panamericana section of Mexico City. One of eleven children, he learned to fight in his tough neighborhood, where he spurned the local gangs but fought his own individual battles. When he was thirteen, his father, a butcher, took Cuevas to a Mexico City gym to learn to fight properly and to channel his aggression more productively than in street combat. Before he finally became a full-time boxer, Cuevas worked for his father, shined shoes, and sold gum on the street.

Cuevas bypassed the apprenticeship of a lengthy amateur boxing career and turned pro at fourteen, with his first fight on November 14, 1971. He made an inauspicious debut and was knocked out in the second round. Undeterred, he compiled a seven and five record in his first twelve fights as he gained experience.

By 1974, Cuevas began to exhibit his great ability by winning all four of his fights, three of them one-round knockouts. The next year, he won the Mexican welterweight title with a tenth-round knockout of Jose Palacios, who was later a ranked contender. Cuevas relinquished the belt just seven months later, setting his sights on a world championship. Toward that end, he made his first appearance in the United States on June 2, 1976, when he faced Andy ("Hawk") Price, who had fought 28 fights to Cuevas's twenty. Price won a split decision. WBA welterweight champion

In the sixth round of his first WBA title defense, Cuevas fells Shoji Tsujimoto at Jissen Rinri Stadium in Kanazawa, Japan, on October 27, 1976.

IN THE RING	WON 35	LOST 15	DRAWS 0	TB 50	KO 31	W 4	WF 0	D 0	KO'd 6	L 9	LF 0

Date	Opponent	Site	Result / Rounds		Title	Wt.
1971						
Nov 14	Al Castro	Mexico City	KO'd	2	—	134
1972						
Jan 1	Jose Arias	Mexico City	TKO	4	—	—
Mar 4	Mario Roman	Mexico City	L	6	—	—
May 25	Rielero Rodriguez	Mexico City	TKO	2	—	—
Jun 22	Pancho Benitez/Paco Tapia	Mexico City	TKO	2	—	—
Aug 20	Juan Pablo Oropeza	Mexico City	L	8	—	—
Dec 7	Raul Martinez	Mexico City	KO	1	—	134
1973						
Mar 1	Sergio Alejo	Mexico City	TKO	4	—	133
May 13	Memo Cruz	Mexico City	L	10	—	135
Aug 4	Jose Figueroa	Mexico City	TKO	3	—	144
Oct 7	Octavio Amparan	Mexico City	TKO	7	—	133
Nov 24	Eleazar Delgado	Mexico City	L	10	—	—
1974						
May 11	Salvador Ruvalcaba	Mexico City	KO	1	—	145
Jun 12	Sugar Sanders	Mexico City	TKO	1	—	—
Aug 21	Jose Luis Pena	Mexico City	KO	1	—	—
Oct 26	Sammy Garcia	Mexico City	KO	3	—	143
1975						
Jan 25	Ruben Vasquez	Mexico City	W	10	—	145
Jul 12	Carlos Obregon	Mexico City	W	10	—	145
Sep 27	Jose Palacios	Mexico City	KO	10	Won-Mexico-W	147
1976						
Apr 3	Rafael Piamonte	Mexicali, Mexico	KO	1	—	—
Jun 2	Andy Price	Los Angeles	L	10	—	146
Jul 17 ♛	Angel Espada	Mexicali	TKO	2	Won-WBA-W	146
Oct 27	Shoji Tsujimoto	Kanazawa, Japan	TKO	6	Ret-WBA-W	145
1977						
Mar 13 ⑩	Miguel Angel Campanino	Mexico City	KO	2	Ret-WBA-W	146
Aug 6 ⑩	Clyde Gray	Los Angeles	KO	2	Ret-WBA-W	145
Nov 19 ⑩	Angel Espada	San Juan, PR	TKO	12	Ret-WBA-W	147
1978						
Mar 4 ⑩	Harold Weston	Los Angeles	TKO	10	Ret-WBA-W	146
May 20 ⑩	Billy Backus	Inglewood, CA	TKO	2	Ret-WBA-W	146
Sep 9 ⑩	Pete Ranzany	Sacramento, CA	TKO	2	Ret-WBA-W	146
1979						
Jan 29	Scott Clark	Los Angeles	TKO	2	Ret-WBA-W	146
Jul 30 ⑩	Randy Shields	Chicago	W	15	Ret-WBA-W	146
Dec 8 ⑩	Angel Espada	Los Angeles	TKO	10	Ret-WBA-W	146
1980						
Apr 6	Harold Volbrecht	Houston	KO	5	Ret-WBA-W	146
Aug 2 ⑩	Thomas Hearns	Detroit	KO'd	2	Lost-WBA-W	146
1981						
Feb 7	Bernardo Prada	Los Angeles	KO	2	—	147
Jun 25	Joergen Hansen	Houston	TKO	2	—	147
Nov 7 ⑩	Roger Stafford	Las Vegas	L	10	—	147

1983						
Jan 29 ⑩	Roberto Duran	Los Angeles	TKO'd	4	—	149
1984						
Mar 1	Mauricio Bravo	Los Angeles	TKO	1	—	150
Jul 12	Jun-Suk Hwang	Los Angeles	L	10	—	150
1985						
Mar 7	Herman Montes	Los Angeles	KO'd	3	—	152
1986						
Feb 25	Felipe Vaca	Inglewood	W	4	—	159
Mar 4	Steve Little	Sacramento	L	10	—	153
Jul 25	Louis Mateo	Chicago	TKO	3	—	155
Oct 4	Lorenzo Garcia	Salta, Argentina	L	10	—	152
Dec 19	Jorge Vaca	Guadalajara, Mexico	KO'd	2	—	155
1987						
Jul 25	Daniel Valenzuela	Mexico City	KO	6	—	173
1989						
May 29	Francisco Carballo	Tijuana, Mexico	KO	4	—	—
Jul 31	Martin Martinez	Tijuana	KO	1	—	—
Sep 25	Lupe Aquino	Tijuana	KO'd	2	—	160

Angel Espada was in attendance at the fight, and he picked Cuevas to be his next opponent, expecting that he would be a pushover.

On July 17, 1976, only six weeks after losing to Price, Cuevas entered the ring with Espada in Mexicali, Mexico, for the welterweight crown. The eighteen year old made short work of the champion and stopped him in just two rounds to win the world title. In the rematch a year later, one of Cuevas's toughest fights, he scored a technical knockout against Espada in twelve rounds and broke Espada's jaw in the bargain.

Cuevas did not shy away from defending his title. He won ten defenses by knockout against such opponents as Espada; contenders Clyde Gray, Harold

Cuevas hones his reflexes on the speed bag.

Weston, and Pete Ranzany; and former champion Billy Backus. In his only victorious title defense that actually went the distance, Cuevas emerged with a unanimous decision on July 30, 1979, over Randy Shields in front of nearly 4,500 fans at the International Amphitheater in Chicago. As usual, Cuevas was the aggressor in the fight. A head butt opened a cut above Shields's right eye in the fourth round, and though Shields jabbed to throw off Cuevas's rhythm and was never knocked down, the champ took the fight on all three cards: 73-71, 71-70 and 73-67.

The fight against Shields was an anomaly because Cuevas did not do any real damage to him with his vaunted left hook. Never fighting on the defensive, Cuevas liked to move forward, work the body, and then unleash his lethal left. He became extremely popular with Mexican fans, though he rarely smiled—even outside the ring.

After knocking out Harold Volbrecht, the confident Cuevas signed on to another defense, this time against Thomas ("Hit Man") Hearns, the Motor City Cobra, in the challenger's hometown of Detroit, on August 2, 1980. Hearns brought Cuevas's title reign to an end with a knockout in the second round.

Six months later, a capacity crowd packed the Olympic Auditorium in Los Angeles to see Cuevas fight for the first time since losing his title. Thousands more had to be turned away. Cuevas did not disappoint, knocking out Bernardo Prada in two rounds. After a decision loss to tenth-ranked contender Roger Stafford on November 7, 1981, Cuevas stayed away from the ring again, this time for over a year, before returning to face Roberto Duran on January 29, 1983. Duran proved too much for Cuevas, knocking him out in four rounds.

Cuevas fought only nine times in the next four years and won only four of those fights. Finally, after a long hiatus of almost two years, Cuevas fought three times in Tijuana in 1989. When Lupe Aquino beat him with a second-round knockout on September 25, 1989, Cuevas retired for good. Though the last nine years of his career had been a disappointment, Cuevas is remembered for his four-year title reign and his willingness to take on all challengers to his crown.

After his retirement, Cuevas purchased land for each of his brothers and sisters and a new house with a five-horse stable for his parents. He has been active in a number of business ventures in Mexico, including a string of butcher's shops, a restaurant, and a security business. He has even worked in the Mexico City government.

Cuevas enjoys a stroll with boxing writer Rose Trentman and his manager, Lupe Sanchez. Trentman later became a New York State Boxing Commissioner.

GABRIEL ("FLASH") ELORDE

JR. LIGHTWEIGHT

Left-handed; 5'6"; 118–137 lbs.

117 bouts, 6/16/1951 to 5/20/1971

Manager: Lope Sarreal

Jr. Lightweight Champion 1960–67

Hall of Fame Induction: 1993

Born: 3/22/1935, Bogo, Cebu, Philippines

Died: 1/2/1985

Gabriel ("Flash") Elorde, of the Philippines, entered the international boxing scene of the 1950s to become the world junior lightweight champion. A frequent defender of his crown, Elorde had a seven-year reign as champ. Elorde began his career in his hometown of Cebu at the age of sixteen. The next year he won the Filipino bantamweight title, the first of his many Asian and Filipino honors. Within a year, Elorde added the Oriental bantamweight crown to his ring honors. Other regional championships he acquired during his career include the Oriental featherweight, Filipino lightweight, and Oriental lightweight titles.

Elorde first caught the attention of American boxing enthusiasts when he faced world featherweight champion Sandy Saddler in an over-the-weight (non-title) match in Manila. Elorde won a ten-round decision over Saddler, earning the right

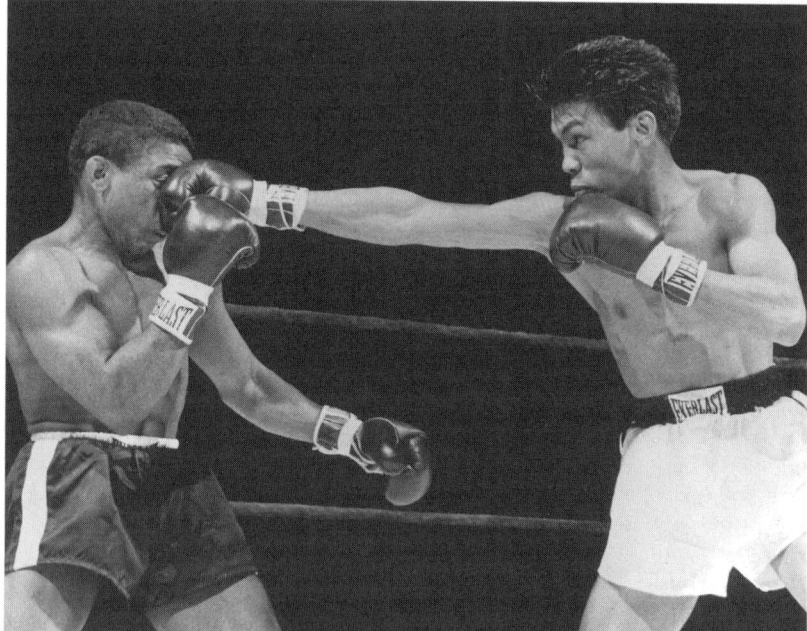

Quick-jabbing Elorde (R) connects to the face of Miguel Berrios in one of their two 1956 meetings. Berrios triumphed in both ten-round decisions. The year 1956 saw Elorde fighting entirely in the U.S.

IN THE RING	WON 87	LOST 27	DRAWS 2	TB 116	KO 33	W 53	WF 1	D 2	KO'd 4	L 23	LF 0

Date	Opponent	Site	Result / Rounds		Title	Wt.
1951						
Jun 16	Kid Gonzaga	Cebu, Philippines	KO	4	—	—
Jun 23	Young Basilian	Cebu	KO	3	—	—
Jun 30	Mike Sanchez	Cebu	W	5	—	—
Jul 14	Kid Santos	Cebu	KO	5	—	—
Jul 28	Star Mercado	Cebu	KO	1	—	—
Aug 11	Fighting Chavez	Cebu	KO	1	—	—
Aug 20	Fighting Chavez	Cebu	KO	7	—	—
Sep 8	Little Patilla	Cebu	KO	6	—	—
Sep 15	Star Flores	Cebu	W	10	—	—
Oct 16	Kid Independence	Cebu	KO'd	10	—	—
Dec 1	Lucky Strike	Cebu	KO	5	—	—
1952						
Jan 30	Tenejeros Boy	Davao, Philippines	W	8	—	—
Feb 24	Little Dundee	Davao	L	8	—	—
Mar 16	Tommy Romulo	Davao	D	10	—	—
May 3	Benny Escobar	Caloocan, Philippines	W	8	—	—
May 10	Paulito Escarlan	Caloocan	W	6	—	121
May 31	Tanny Campo	Caloocan	W	8	—	120
Jul 26	Tanny Campo	Manila	W	12	Won-Philippines-B	117
Aug 12	Little Dundee	Davao	KO	4	Ret-Philippines-B	120
Oct 18	Hiroshi Horiguchi	Tokyo	W	12	Won-Orient-B	118
Nov 18	Akiyoshi Akanuma	Tokyo	D	10	—	118
1953						
Feb 18	Willie Brown	Manila	KO	4	—	—
Mar 15	Al Cruz	Manila	W	10	—	—
May 20	Larry Bataan	Manila	L	12	For-Orient-FE	126
Jul 6	Akiyoshi Akanuma	Tokyo	W	12	Ret-Orient-B	118
Aug 8	Shigeji Kaneko	Nishinomiya, Japan	L	10	—	—
Oct 8	Noboru Tanaka	Tokyo	W	10	—	—
Nov 25	Masashi Akiyama	Tokyo	L	10	For-Japan-JL	123
1954						
Jan 21	Kiyoaki Nakanishi	Tokyo	W	10	—	127
Apr 21	Hiroshi Okawa	Tokyo	W	10	—	128
Jun 29	Shigeji Kaneko	Tokyo	L	12	For-Orient-FE	125
Aug 5	Roy Higa	Tokyo	W	10	—	—
Aug 18	Tommy Romulo	Manila	W	12	Won-Philippines-L	131
Nov 20	Katsumi Kosaka	Manila	KO	8	—	—
Nov 27	Masashi Akiyama	Manila	W	10	—	130
1955						
Jan 12	Masashi Akiyama	Tokyo	L	10	—	131
Apr 15	Severo Fuentes	Manila	W	10	—	—
Jun 15	Leo Alonzo	Manila	L	12	Lost-Philippines-L	135
Jul 20 ♛	Sandy Saddler ★	Manila	W	10	—	129
Oct 3	Shigeji Kaneko	Tokyo	L	10	—	—
1956						
Jan 18 ♛	Sandy Saddler ★	San Francisco	TKO'd	13	For-World-FE	125
Apr 23	Cleo Lane	San Francisco	KO	1	—	130

Date		Opponent	Location	Result	Rounds	Title	Weight
May 8		Chico Rosa	Stockton, CA	W	10	—	129
Jun 11		Gil Velarde	San Francisco	TKO	7	—	130
Jun 26		Cecil Schoonmaker	Stockton	KO	9	—	130
Jul 24		Dave Gallardo	San Jose, CA	W	10	—	129
Aug 22	⑩	Miguel Berrios	San Francisco	L	10	—	129
Oct 16		Luke Sandoval	San Jose	KO	2	—	129
Nov 9	⑩	Miguel Berrios	New York	L	10	—	129

1957

Date		Opponent	Location	Result	Rounds	Title	Weight
Feb 5		Hidemi Wada	Osaka, Japan	KO	5	—	130
Mar 16		Tommy Romulo	Manila	W	12	Reg-Philippines-L	130
Apr 27		Hideto Kobayashi	Nagoya, Japan	W	12	Won-Vac Orient-L	133
Jun 23		Omsap Laempapha	Bangkok	L	12	Lost-Orient-L	130
Aug 4		Salika Yontrakit	Bangkok	KO	3	—	—
Sep 24		Shigeji Kaneko	Tokyo	L	10	—	130
Oct 23		Leo Alonzo	Manila	W	12	—	131

1958

Date		Opponent	Location	Result	Rounds	Title	Weight
Mar 2		Hiroshi Okawa	Tokyo	W	12	Reg-Orient-L	133
May 3		Javellana Kid	Manila	W	12	Ret-Orient-L	129
Jun 10	⑩	Ike Chestnut	Honolulu	W	10	—	129
Sep 2		Hisao Kobayashi	Tokyo	W	12	Ret-Orient-L	132
Nov 15		Keiichi Ishikawa	Manila	TKO	6	Ret-Orient-L	132
Dec 27		Kiyoaki Nakanishi	Davao	TKO	3	—	128

1959

Date		Opponent	Location	Result	Rounds	Title	Weight
Feb 6		Takeo Sugimori	Tokyo	W	12	Ret-Orient-L	132
Feb 23	⑩	Paolo Rosi	San Francisco	L	10	—	132
Mar 31		Teddy Davis	Stockton	W	10	—	133
May 25	⑩	Sonny Leon	Caracas	W	10	—	130
Jun 15		Vicente Rivas	Caracas	L	10	—	135
Jul 29		Solomon Boysaw	Cleveland	L	10	—	134
Oct 7		Hisao Kobayashi	Tokyo	W	12	Ret-Orient-L	131
Nov 26		Isami Ikeyama	Tokyo	TKO	4	—	135
Dec 15		Nursery Kid	Manila	W	10	—	135

1960

Date		Opponent	Location	Result	Rounds	Title	Weight
Mar 16	♛	Harold Gomes	Quezon, Philippines	KO	7	Won-World-JL	130
Jul 9		Hachiro Ito	Manila	TKO	5	—	135
Aug 17	⑩	Harold Gomes	San Francisco	KO	1	Ret-World-JL	130
Oct 17		Sakuzi Shinozawa	Manila	W	12	Ret-Orient-L	135
Dec 16		Vicente Rivas	Manila	W	10	—	134

1961

Date		Opponent	Location	Result	Rounds	Title	Weight
Mar 19		Joey Lopes	Manila	W	15	Ret-World-JL	130
May 31		Giordano Campari	Manila	W	10	—	134
Sep 2		Teruo Kosaka	Manila	W	12	Ret-Orient-L	134
Dec 16	⑩	Sergio Caprari	Manila	TKO	1	Ret-World-JL	130

1962

Date		Opponent	Location	Result	Rounds	Title	Weight
Mar 10		Somkiat Katmuangyon	Manila	KO	2	Ret-Orient-L	135
Apr 30		Teruo Kosaka	Tokyo	L	12	Lost-Orient-L	133
Jun 23	⑩	Auburn Copeland	Manila	W	15	Ret-World-JL	130
Aug 4		Teruo Kosaka	Cebu	W	12	Reg-Orient-L	134
Nov 17		Isarasak Puntainorasing	Manila	TKO	3	• —	135
Dec 21		Solomon Boysaw	Manila	W	10	—	136

1963

Date		Opponent	Location	Result	Rounds	Title	Weight
Feb 16	⑩	John Bizzarro	Manila	W	15	Ret-World-JL	130
Jun 1		Tsunstomi Miyamoto	Manila	TKO	9	Ret-Orient-L	134
Aug 3	⑩	Love Allotey	Manila	W	10	—	136
Nov 16	⑩	Love Allotey	Quezon	WD	11	Ret-World-JL	130

Date		Opponent	Location	Result		Title	Wt
1964							
Feb 15	♛	Carlos Ortiz★	Manila	TKO'd	14	For-World-L	135
May 8		Tadashi Matsumoto	Manila	W	12	Ret-Orient-L	135
Jul 27	⑩	Teruo Kosaka	Tokyo	TKO	12	Ret-World-JL	130
Nov 21	⑩	Kang-Il Suh	Manila	W	12	Ret-Orient-L	135
1965							
Feb 27	⑩	Rene Barrientos	Manila	W	12	Ret-Orient-L	135
Jun 5	⑩	Teruo Kosak	Quezon	KO	15	Ret-World-JL	130
Aug 5		Frankie Narvaez	New York	W	10	—	135
Dec 4	⑩	Kang-Il Suh	Quezon	W	15	Ret-World-JL	130
1966							
Mar 19	⑩	Ismael Laguna★	Tokyo	W	10	—	135
Jun 9		Yoshiaki Numata	Tokyo	L	12	Lost-Orient-L	135
Aug 7		Percy Hayles	Quezon	W	10	—	136
Oct 22		Vicente Derado	Quezon	W	15	Ret-World-JL	130
Nov 14	♛	Carlos Ortiz★	New York	KO'd	14	For-World-L	134
1967							
Apr 25		Fujio Mikami	Honolulu	W	10	—	135
Jun 15	⑩	Yoshiaki Numata	Tokyo	L	15	Lost-World-JL	130
Oct 28		Akihisa Someya	Manila	L	10	—	135
1969							
Feb 15		Eugenio Espinoza	Quito, Ecuador	L	10	—	136
Apr 26	⑩	Jaguar Kakizama	Quezon	L	10	—	—
1970							
Apr 10		Mongai Munchai	Manila	KO	5	—	—
May 16		Isao Ichihara	Davao	KO	9	—	—
Jun 27		Kenji Iwata	Manila	W	10	—	136
Aug 28		Chico Andrade	Manila	TKO	5	—	134
Oct 31		Tatsunao Mitsuyama	Quezon	W	10	—	—
Dec 18		Isao Ichihara	Agana, Guam	L	10	—	—
1971							
Feb 14		Isao Ichihara	Quezon	KO	6	—	—
May 20		Hiroyuki Murakami	Tokyo	L	10	—	137

to face the champ for his title. The bout, which took place at the Cow Palace in San Francisco in 1956, marked Elorde's first appearance in America. The win was awarded to Saddler, despite the fact that he trailed on points, when it was stopped in the thirteenth round to prevent further damage to a cut over Elorde's eye.

For the next few years, Elorde honed his skills with fights in American, Japanese, and Pacific Rim cities. Loaded down with Asian titles, Elorde again climbed into the ring in 1960, for a chance at a world title. He faced Harold Gomes, holder of the world junior lightweight title. This weight class had been reinstituted in 1959 after not having a champion for almost 25 years. Elorde knocked Gomes out in seven rounds. In a return match, Elorde laid Gomes out in less than two minutes. Elorde proved to be a lasting champion. Fighting mostly on home turf, he successfully defended the title ten times before losing it on a decision to Yoshiaki Numata in 1967. Elorde twice attempted to take Carlos Ortiz's world lightweight title, but both times he was stopped in the fourteenth round. After losing his title to Numata, Elorde fought once more and then did not box for over a year before returning to the ring for ten more fights. Elorde built a school, an orphanage, and a church with his ring earnings. He died of lung cancer at age 49.

JEFF FENECH
Marrickville Mauler

FEATHERWEIGHT

Right-handed; 5′7½″; 116–135 lbs.

32 bouts, 10/12/1984 to 5/18/1996

Manager: Theo Onisforou

IBF Bantamweight Champ 1985–87
WBC Junior Featherweight Champ 1987–88
WBC Featherweight Champion 1988–89

Hall of Fame Induction: 2002

Born: 5/28/1964, Sydney, Australia

Named: Jeffrey Fenech

Jeff Fenech is one of a select group of fighters who have won world titles in three weight classes. Some longtime ring observers may grouse that this is easier today than in years past due to the expanded number of sanctioning bodies and weight divisions, but Fenech's masterful achievement is still worthy of great praise.

Born in Sydney, the son of Maltese immigrants, Fenech learned to fight in the streets, running with a rough crowd and spending time in a home for troubled boys. Eventually Fenech arrived at a gym run by Johnny Lewis, who became his trainer for the majority of his career. In 1984, Fenech represented his country in the Los Angeles Olympics, where he lost in the quarterfinals to Redzep Redzepovski of Yugoslavia. It was a questionable loss, as the judges' 3–2 decision in Fenech's favor was overturned by the five-member jury. After the fight, Fenech said to the media, "I've worked so hard for the chance to win Australia's first boxing gold medal at the Olympics, only to have the chance taken away by a bunch of senile old men."

Shortly after returning home from the Olympic Games, Fenech began his professional career with a second-round knockout of Bobby Williams.

Always a tough customer, here Fenech sports some swelling and a cut under his left eye.

IN THE RING	WON 28	LOST 3	DRAWS 1	TB 32	KO 21	W 6	WF 1	D 1	KO'd 3	L 0	LF 0

Date		Opponent	Site	Result / Rounds		Title	Wt.
1984							
Oct 12		Bobby Williams	Marrickville, Australia	KO	2	—	116
Oct 26		Percy Israel	Marrickville	KO	7	—	118
Nov 30		Junior Thompson	Marrickville	KO	2	Won-Australia-JB	115
Dec 15		Iliesa Manila	Suva, Fiji	KO	2	—	118
1985							
Feb 1		Wayne Mulholland	Dapto, Australia	TKO	5	—	117
Mar 4		Rolando Navarro	Sydney	TKO	4	—	116
Apr 26	♛	Satoshi Shingaki	Sydney	TKO	9	Won-IBF-B	118
Jun 14		John Matienza	Sydney	TKO	6	—	121
Jul 26		John Farrell	Brisbane, Australia	TKO	9	—	120
Aug 23		Satoshi Shingaki	Sydney	TKO	4	Ret-IBF-B	118
Nov 4		Kenny Butts	Brisbane	TKO	2	—	121
Dec 2	⑩	Jerome Coffee	Sydney	W	15	Ret-IBF-B	118
1986							
Apr 11	⑩	Daniel Zaragoza	Perth, Australia	W	10	—	123
Jul 18		Steve McCrory	Sydney	TKO	14	Ret-IBF-B	118
1987							
Apr 3		Tony Miller	Melbourne	W	12	Won-Australia-FE	125
May 8		Samart Payakaroon	Sydney	KO	4	Won-WBC-JFE	122
Jul 10	♛	Greg Richardson	Sydney	TKO	5	Ret-WBC-JFE	122
Oct 16		Carlos Zarate★	Sydney	TW	4	Ret-WBC-JFE	122
Dec 11		Osmar Avila	Sydney	KO	1	—	126
1988							
Mar 7	⑩	Victor Callejas	Sydney	TKO	10	Won-WBC-FE	126
Aug 12		Tyrone Downes	Melbourne	KO	5	Ret-WBC-FE	126
Nov 30		George Navarro	Melbourne	KO	5	Ret-WBC-FE	126
1989							
Apr 8	⑩	Marcos Villasana	Melbourne	W	12	Ret-WBC-FE	125
Nov 24	⑩	Mario Martinez	Melbourne	W	12	—	132
1991							
Jan 19		John Kalbhenn	Adelaide, Australia	TKO	4	—	133
Jun 28	♛	Azumah Nelson★	Las Vegas	D	12	For-WBC-JL	128
Sep 13		Miguel Francia	Melbourne	W	10	—	132
1992							
Feb 28	♛	Azumah Nelson★	Melbourne	TKO'd	8	For-WBC-JL	130
1993							
Jun 7	⑩	Calvin Grove	Melbourne	KO'd	7	—	131
1995							
Nov 18		Tito Tovar	Atlantic City	TKO	8	—	135
1996							
Mar 9		Mike Juarez	Melbourne	TKO	2	—	132
May 18	♛	Philip Holiday	Melbourne	KO'd	2	For-IBF-L	134

After recording five more knockouts, Fenech challenged Satoshi Shingaki for the IBF bantamweight title on April 26, 1985. Though he had only six professional fights under his belt, Fenech thoroughly dominated the champion and knocked him out in the ninth round, seizing a world championship at the age of 21. He improved his record in the rematch, downing Shingaki in only three rounds.

Fenech defended his title against top contender Jerome Coffee in a fifteen-round decision, the first fight where Fenech was forced to go the whole distance. It was also one of the first times he used his boxing skills to win a fight; his reputation was that of a raw brawler rather than a skilled ring tactician. Fenech then achieved a sort of revenge against his perceived Olympic injustice when he knocked out American Steve McCrory in the fourteenth round of a title defense on July 18, 1986. McCrory was the gold medal winner in Los Angeles in Fenech's weight class.

Fenech was now having trouble meeting the bantam weight limit, and he vacated his title to move up to super bantamweight. On May 8, 1987, he faced WBC super bantamweight champ Samart Payakaroon. Fenech had an easy time of it, knocking out Payakarun at 2:42 of the fourth round. Two doctors had to rush into the ring to extract Payakarun's tongue from his throat. The former champ revived after six minutes and spent the night in the hospital.

Fenech also successfully defended his new title, starting with a knockout victory over Greg Richardson. He then defeated aging Hall of Famer Carlos Zarate with a technical decision: the fight was stopped in the fourth round because Fenech's eye was injured by an accidental head butt.

After less than a year as champion, Fenech again vacated his title to move up another weight class. On March 7, 1988, at the Sydney Entertainment Center, Fenech fought Victor Callejas for the vacant WBC featherweight title. His right crosses knocked Callejas down in the third and eight, and Callejas was staggered many times in the fight before it was stopped in the tenth. Fenech had now become a three-division champion. After the fight, he boasted that he had broken his right hand a month earlier and had won the championship match with only one hand.

After decisioning Marcos Villasana on April 8, 1989, Fenech announced his retirement. He had broken both his hands in the Villasana fight. He returned to the ring seven months later and won a decision over Mario Martinez, but his right hand was injured again, and he was forced to undergo corrective surgery. After another absence, this one of a little over a year, Fenech returned to knock out Johnny Kalbhenn, setting the stage for one of the most memorable fights of his career.

Fenech was now given a title shot against Azumah Nelson for the WBC super featherweight title. He was bidding to become a champion in four weight classes, and for the first time in his career he fought in the United States. Indeed, it was only his second fight outside of Australia. Held on June 28, 1991, in Las Vegas on the undercard of a Mike Tyson–Razor Ruddock main event, the fight opened with Fenech as the aggressor. Nelson fought back, meeting Fenech's advances with jabs and hooks that made Fenech miss. Nelson won the first two rounds before he spent the next three fighting against the ropes. Fenech unleashed a barrage, but failed to land many clean punches. Nelson bobbed and weaved, threw uppercuts and hooks, then tried moving and jabbing in the sixth. Despite these maneuvers, Fenech stayed with Nelson, and appeared to be weakening him. In the twelfth round, Fenech scored with a right and then fired a torrent of punches that had Nelson wobbly at the end of the fight. The verdict, however, was a disappointing draw, with one judge scoring the fight even, the others splitting. Most observers believed that Fenech should have been the victor.

Before the rematch, held at the Princes Park football grounds in Melbourne, Australia, Fenech boasted, "The only way they're going to take [Nelson] home to Ghana is in a body bag." Fortunately for Nelson, however, Fenech did not make good on his prediction. Nelson knocked Fenech down three times before the fight was called in the eighth round for Fenech's first defeat.

Fenech did not fight again for fifteen months. When he did get back into the ring, Calvin Grove knocked him out in the seventh round. He required 30 stitches to repair the damage Grove had caused to his face. Fenech announced his retirement the next day. He did fight twice more, but after Philip Holiday knocked him out in the second round of an IBF lightweight title fight on May 18, 1996, Fenech retired for good.

Fenech now trains and manages fighters in addition to running his own gym. He is also active in broadcasting. Fenech's biography, *Jeff Fenech: I Love Youse All*, by Terry Smith was published in Australia in 1993.

Fenech connects with a straight left to Azumah Nelson's throat in their hard-fought draw on June 28, 1991, in Las Vegas.

GEORGE FOREMAN
Big George

HEAVYWEIGHT

Right-handed; 6'3½"; 212–267 lbs.
81 bouts, 6/23/1969 to 11/22/1997
Manager: Dick Sadler 1969–74, 1977
1968 Olympic Heavyweight Gold Medalist
Heavyweight Champion 1973–74
WBA Heavyweight Champ 1994
IBF Heavyweight Champ 1994–95
WBU Heavyweight Champ 1995–97
Hall of Fame Induction: 2003
Born: 1/10/1949, Marshall, TX
Named: George Edward Foreman

Probably no figure in the history of boxing has experienced two wholly distinct careers in the ring the way that George Foreman has. In his first career, he was a fearsome, surly, extremely powerful fighter who demolished a previously unbeaten Joe Frazier to become heavyweight champion of the world—only to lose his title to Muhammad Ali in the "Rumble in the Jungle." A few years later, Foreman walked away from boxing when he had a religious experience. In his second career—begun after a ten-year hiatus from the sport—Foreman was a cheerful, bald, pudgy pugilist whose self-deprecating humor endeared him to boxing fans around the world. He went out of his way to make himself a popular celebrity. Foreman advanced from the status of a boxing sideshow to that of a credible challenger to title-holder Evander Holyfield, and finally to a stunning second stint as heavyweight champion, after he knocked out Michael Moorer to take the crown. Along the way, he became beloved by the public and made a huge fortune from endorsements.

Foreman was born in Marshall, Texas, on January 10, 1949. He was from a large family. When Foreman was a small child, the family moved to Houston. The Foremans were poor, with barely enough food to go around. Foreman did not do well in school and dropped out as soon as he could. He got involved with a group of youth who were up to no good and soon became a mugger.

Upset with the direction his life was taking, Foreman heeded the advice of a relative and joined the Job Corps. Though Foreman liked the Job Corps, he struggled with his temper and often engaged in fights. When he was transferred to the Job Corps unit in Pleasanton, California,

Trainer Dick Sadler helps George Foreman on with his gloves in Caracas, Venezuela, where they are preparing for a title defense against Ken Norton.

IN THE RING	WON 76	LOST 5	DRAWS 0	TB 81	KO 68	W 8	WF 0	D 0	KO'd 1	L 4	LF 0

Date	Opponent	Site	Result / Rounds		Title	Wt.
1969						
Jun 23	Donald Waldheim	New York	TKO	3	—	219
Jul 1	Fred Ashew	Houston	KO	1	—	215
Jul 14	Sylvester Dullaire	Seattle	TKO	1	—	218
Aug 18	Chuck Wepner	New York	TKO	3	—	213
Sep 18	John Carroll	Seattle	KO	1	—	215
Sep 23	Cookie Wallace	Houston	KO	2	—	215
Oct 7	Vernon Clay	Houston	KO	2	—	217
Oct 31	Roberto Davila	New York	W	8	—	214
Nov 5	Leo Peterson	Scranton, PA	KO	4	—	214
Nov 18	Max Martinez	Houston	KO	2	—	215
Dec 6	Bob Hazelton	Las Vegas	KO	1	—	214
Dec 16	Levi Forte	Miami Beach	W	10	—	215
Dec 18	Gary Wilder	Seattle	KO	1	—	214
1970						
Jan 6	Charlie Polite	Houston	KO	4	—	217
Jan 26	Jack O'Halloran	New York	KO	5	—	214
Feb 16	Gregorio Peralta	New York	W	10	—	213
Mar 31	Rufus Brassell	Houston	TKO	1	—	217
Apr 17	James Woody	New York	TKO	3	—	215
Apr 29	Aaron Easting	Cleveland	TKO	4	—	212
May 16	George Johnson	Los Angeles	TKO	7	—	216
Jul 20	Roger Russell	Philadelphia	KO	1	—	220
Aug 4 ⑩	George Chuvalo	New York	TKO	3	—	218
Nov 3	Lou Bailey	Oklahoma City, OK	TKO	3	—	215
Nov 18	Boone Kirkman	New York	TKO	2	—	216
Dec 19	Mel Turnbow	Seattle	TKO	1	—	219
1971						
Feb 8	Charlie Boston	St. Paul, MN	KO	1	—	218
Apr 3	Stanford Harris	Lake Geneva, NY	KO	2	—	218
May 10 ⑩	Gregorio Peralta	Oakland	TKO	10	Won-Vac NABF-H	216
Sep 14	Vic Scott	El Paso, TX	KO	1	—	222
Sep 21	Leroy Caldwell	Beaumont, TX	KO	3	—	224
Oct 7	Ollie Wilson	San Antonio, TX	KO	2	—	219
Oct 29	Luiz Pires	New York	TKO	4	—	215
1972						
Feb 29	Murphy Goodwin	Austin, TX	KO	2	—	225
Mar 7	Clarence Boone	Beaumont	KO	2	—	224
Apr 10	Ted Gullick	Los Angeles	KO	2	—	221
May 11	Miguel Paez	Oakland	KO	2	Won-Pan Amer-H	217
Oct 10	Terry Sorrels	Salt Lake City, UT	KO	2	—	220
1973						
Jan 22 ♛	Joe Frazier★	Kingston, Jamaica	TKO	2	Won-World-H	217
Sep 1	Jose Roman	Tokyo	KO	1	Ret-World-H	219
1974						
Mar 26 ⑩	Ken Norton★	Caracas	TKO	2	Ret-World-H	224
Oct 30 ⑩	Muhammad Ali★	Kinshasa, Zaire	KO'd	8	Lost-World-H	220
1976						
Jan 24 ⑩	Ron Lyle	Las Vegas	KO	5	—	226
Jun 15 ⑩	Joe Frazier★	Uniondale, NY	KO	5	—	224

Aug 14	Scott Le Doux	Utica, NY	TKO	3	—	229
Oct 15	John Denis	Hollywood, FL	TKO	4	—	231
1977						
Jan 22	Pedro Agosto	Pensacola, FL	TKO	4	—	226
Mar 17 ⑩	Jimmy Young	San Juan, PR	L	12	—	229
1987						
Mar 9	Steve Zouski	Sacramento, CA	TKO	4	—	267
Jul 9	Charles Hostetter	Oakland	KO	3	—	247
Sep 15	Bobby Crabtree	Springfield, MO	TKO	6	—	250
Nov 21	Tim Anderson	Orlando, FL	TKO	4	—	243
Dec 18	Rocky Sekorski	Las Vegas	TKO	3	—	244
1988						
Jan 23	Tom Trimm	Orlando	TKO	1	—	243
Feb 5	Guido Trane	Las Vegas	TKO	5	—	244
Mar 19	Dwight Muhammad Qawi★	Las Vegas	TKO	7	—	235
May 21	Frank Williams	Anchorage, AK	KO	3	—	243
Jun 26	Carlos Hernandez	Atlantic City	TKO	4	—	245
Aug 25	Ladislao Mijangos	Ft. Myers, FL	TKO	2	—	255
Sep 10	Bobby Hitz	Auburn Hills, MI	KO	1	—	244
Oct 27	Tony Fulilangi	Marshall, TX	TKO	2	—	250
Dec 28	David Jaco	Bakersfield, CA	KO	1	—	251
1989						
Jan 26	Mark Young	Rochester, NY	TKO	7	—	251
Feb 16	Manoel De Almeida	Orlando	TKO	3	—	252
Apr 30	J.B. Williamson	Galveston, TX	TKO	5	—	255
Jun 1	Bert Cooper	Phoenix	TKO	2	—	253
Jul 20	Everett Martin	Tucson, AZ	W	10	—	256
1990						
Jan 15	Gerry Cooney	Atlantic City	KO	2	—	253
Apr 17	Mike Jameson	Lake Tahoe, NV	KO	4	—	260
Jun 16	Adilson Rodrigues	Las Vegas	KO	2	—	263
Jul 31	Ken Lakusta	Edmonton, Canada	KO	3	—	261
Sep 25	Terry Anderson	London	KO	1	—	259
1991						
Apr 19 ♛	Evander Holyfield	Atlantic City	L	12	For-World-H	257
Dec 7	Jimmy Ellis	Reno, NV	TKO	3	—	257
1992						
Apr 11	Alex Stewart	Las Vegas	W	10	—	259
1993						
Jan 16	Pierre Coetzer	Reno	TKO	8	—	258
Jun 7 ⑩	Tommy Morrison	Las Vegas	L	12	For-WBO-H	256
1994						
Nov 5 ♛	Michael Moorer	Las Vegas	KO	10	Won-WBA/IBF-H	250
1995						
Apr 22	Axel Schulz	Las Vegas	W	12	Ret-IBF-H, Won-Vac WBU-H	256
1996						
Nov 3	Crawford Grimsley	Chiba, Japan	W	12	Ret-WBU-H	253
1997						
Apr 26	Lou Savarese	Atlantic City	W	12	Ret-WBU-H	253
Nov 22	Shannon Briggs	Atlantic City	L	12	—	260

Foreman came under the tutelage of the camp's boxing instructor, Doc Broadus. Broadus taught Foreman the basic boxing skills to accompany his already fearsome power. Foreman went to the National Golden Gloves tournament in 1967 but lost in the first round.

After graduating from the Job Corps—where he earned a high school general equivalency degree plus training in electronics—Foreman took a job washing dishes and mopping floors at the Job Corps camp in Pleasanton, so he could continue training under Broadus. In 1968, he won the National AAU tournament to earn a spot in the Olympic Trials. Foreman won the trials and headed to Mexico City as a member of the U.S. Olympic Team. He won the gold medal in the heavyweight division and brought added attention to himself by waving a small American flag in the ring after his win. This gesture was widely considered a rebuke of Tommie Smith and John Carlos, African-American sprinters who each had raised a black-gloved fist in a Black Power salute during the playing of the National Anthem at their medal ceremony. Foreman later said, "I didn't look at it as a protest or anti-protest. It was just the way I felt at the moment."

Foreman did not turn professional immediately after the Olympics. He fought some exhibitions and trained and sparred with former heavyweight champion Sonny Liston under the direction of Dick Sadler. Foreman first fought for pay on June 23, 1969, against Don Waldheim at Madison Square Garden on the undercard of the Joe Frazier–Jerry Quarry heavyweight championship fight. Foreman knocked out Waldheim in the third round. He then kept to a busy schedule in 1969, fighting thirteen times in the final six months

During George Foreman's "first career" he revealed flashes of the charm that would endear him to the public many years later.

of the year. He won all thirteen bouts—eleven by knockout—including five KOs in the first round. None of the opponents were especially noteworthy except, perhaps, Chuck Wepner, the "Bayonne Bleeder," who later fought Ali and was the inspiration for the Rocky Balboa movie character.

On August 4, 1970, Foreman faced his most highly touted opponent to date: the veteran fighter George Chuvalo who had knocked out Jerry Quarry just the previous December. In the third round, Foreman shook Chuvalo with a left hook and then battered him along the ropes. Chuvalo kept his hands up but didn't really defend himself—prompting Hall of Fame referee Arthur Mercante to stop the fight at the 1:41 mark of the round. Foreman was only the second fighter to knock out Chuvalo; Joe Frazier had been the first. The fight attracted a crowd of 12,526 to Madison Square Garden. Foreman was guaranteed $17,500 while Chuvalo earned $50,000. Foreman finished the year ranked as the second-place contender for Frazier's heavyweight title, trailing only Ali in the annual rankings of *The Ring.*

Foreman was less active in 1971. In 1972, he knocked out all five of his opponents—all of them in the second round. Though none of them were ranked fighters, it was still an impressive achievement—impressive enough to earn Foreman a shot at the world heavyweight title against Frazier in Kingston, Jamaica, on January 22, 1973. Foreman was a 3½-1 underdog to the unbeaten Frazier. In the first round, Foreman landed two left jabs and then knocked Frazier down with a right to the face. Frazier got up but soon went down again after a barrage of Foreman rights to the head. Frazier climbed to his feet but was sent to the canvas once more as the first round ended. In the second round, a Foreman left and right to the jaw knocked Frazier down for the fourth time, but Frazier was up at the count of two. Then Foreman sent him down yet again with a pair of left hooks. Once more Frazier got up. Foreman continued the assault and knocked him down a sixth time. Mercante, the third man in the ring, stopped the fight at 1:35 of the second round. Foreman had scored a stunning upset in most impressive fashion. One lasting memory of the fight is legendary broadcaster Howard Cosell's distinctive call of "Down goes Frazier!" which was often imitated. For this bout, Foreman was guaranteed $375,000 while Frazier was guaranteed $850,000.

Foreman defended his title for the first time in Tokyo against Jose ("King") Roman. He made short work of Roman, knocking him down in the first 45 seconds with a right to the ribs. Foreman then hit Roman in the jaw when he was sitting on the canvas after this knockdown. Fortunately for Foreman, it was ruled that he could not have stopped his punch, which began as Roman was sliding down the ropes. A right to the head sent Roman down again. He was up at the count of four, but Foreman's hard right uppercut knocked Roman out for good. Foreman earned $250,000 for less than three minutes of work.

Hall of Famer Ken Norton didn't fare much better against the champ in Caracas, Venezuela, on March 26, 1974. In the second round, Foreman drove Norton into the ropes with four hard rights—prompting the referee to administer a standing eight count. Foreman again knocked Norton into the ropes. A right uppercut, a left to the jaw, another right uppercut, and a left as Norton was falling resulted in a legitimate knockdown. When the referee reached the count of nine, the fight was stopped.

In his next fight, Foreman put the title up against Ali in the "Rumble in the Jungle" in Kinshasa, Zaire. The hoopla surrounding the fight was depicted in the Academy Award–winning documentary film *When We Were Kings*. The fight was set to start at 4 am Kinshasa time so that it could be shown on closed circuit television in the eastern United States at 10 pm. Foreman was installed as a 3-1 betting favorite over the older Ali. Ali was cheered on in the Stade du 20 Mai by most of the crowd of almost 60,000 who chanted "Ali bomaye" which translates to "Ali, kill him." In the first round, Ali displayed the strategy which became known as the "rope-a-dope." Ali leaned against the ropes, protected his head, and allowed Foreman to punch his arms and ribs. Foreman wobbled Ali in the second. In the third, Ali again lay against the ropes—though he occasionally unleashed his left jab. Again in the fourth, Ali jabbed, but also spent a great deal of time against the ropes absorbing Foreman's punches. In the sixth, Ali came off the ropes and jabbed very effectively. By the seventh, a weary Foreman, whose face was beginning to look puffy, lumbered after Ali. In the eighth, Ali fired a left-right combination, which knocked Foreman out. Foreman later offered some explanations for his defeat: his trainer, Sadler, did not awaken him in time to prepare for the match or perhaps his water was drugged. Probably Ali's clever strategy had simply worked well: Foreman had punched himself out, while inflicting little damage to show for his labors.

Foreman did not re-enter the ring for quite some time after his defeat. On April 26, 1975, in Toronto he fought an odd exhibition bout of twelve total rounds against five different fighters. He entered the squared circle in earnest on January 24, 1976, against Ron Lyle at Caesars Palace casino in Las Vegas. Gil Clancy was now Foreman's trainer. In the fourth round, Lyle knocked Foreman down with a right-left combination. Foreman got up and knocked Lyle down with a right. Lyle then closed the round by knocking Foreman down again. In the fifth, Foreman pummeled Lyle with a furious attack and knocked him out. Next came a rematch with Frazier before a crowd of 10,341 at Nassau Coliseum in Uniondale, New York. The fight was relatively even for the first four rounds. In the fifth, Foreman combinations knocked Frazier down. When a right floored Frazier again, the fight was stopped.

After three consecutive knockout victories, Foreman faced Jimmy Young—fresh off a victory over Ron Lyle—at Roberto Clemente Stadium in San Juan, Puerto Rico. For the first six rounds, Young, a good technical boxer, walked from side to side, bent down, and lounged on the ropes and held. Young had the crowd behind him. A Foreman left hook high on the head in the seventh

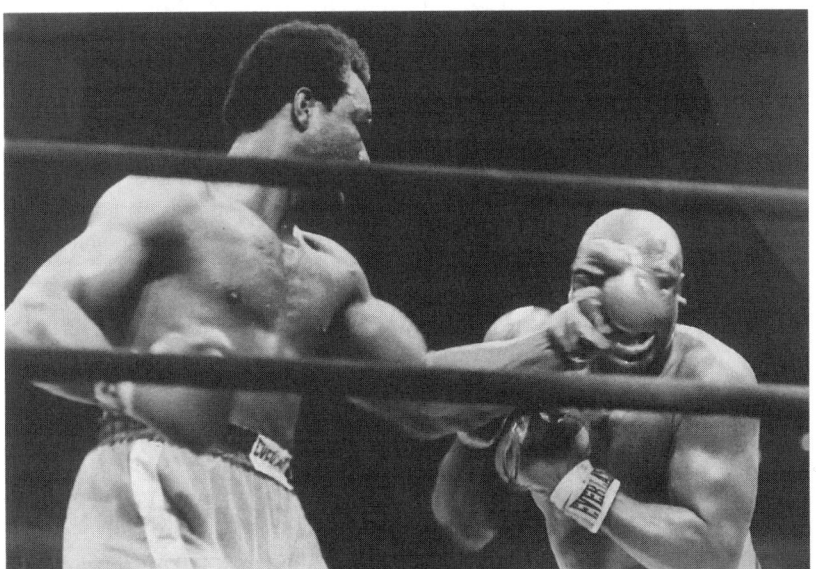

A powerful left by George Foreman (L) twists the features of Joe Frazier in their second meeting in Uniondale, Long Island, NY, on June 15, 1976. Foreman knocked Frazier out in five rounds.

caused Young to move away, but a Young left then forced Foreman to back off. Young became more aggressive and knocked Foreman down for a one count in the twelfth and final round. Young won the decision. Later, in the locker room after the fight, Foreman underwent a religious experience that changed his life.

At 29, Foreman retired from the ring. He shed most of the trappings of fame, though he retained his ranch in Marshall, Texas. He then worked as a street corner preacher. He avoided boxing and allowed himself to become obese so that he would not have the temptation to get in the ring. As his weight soared to over 300 pounds, Foreman continued his ministry.

In 1980, he established the Church of the Lord Jesus Christ in Houston and preached there. He also started the George Foreman Youth Center for underprivileged children in Houston. In order to raise money for these organizations, Foreman finally decided to get back in the ring. At first the idea was treated as a joke. Though Foreman shed some of the weight he had gained, he still weighed about 40 pounds more than he had for his last fight. He had not fought in about ten years. Also, the public was not clamoring for the return of the surly 6'4" giant. Foreman ignored the naysayers and concentrated on getting back in shape. As he honed his body, an entirely different George Foreman emerged. The new Foreman smiled and joked about his age, weight, and love of cheeseburgers. He made himself a media darling and became attractive to fans in a way that he never was as champion.

Foreman started his comeback on March 9, 1987, at the Arco Arena in Sacramento against Steve Zouski. Foreman battered the outclassed Zouski until the fight was stopped in the fourth round. Over the next two years or so, Foreman knocked out his next sixteen opponents. The best known of them was Hall of Famer Dwight Muhammad Qawi. By the time he knocked out former heavyweight contender Gerry Cooney in the second round, Foreman was such a sensation that he was invited to appear on late night television with David Letterman. On June 16, 1990, he faced a ranked opponent for the first time in his comeback: Adilson Rodrigues. Foreman knocked him out in the second round.

Ten months later, Foreman received a shot at the world heavyweight title held by Evander Holyfield at the Atlantic City Convention Center on April 19, 1991. Archie Moore and Charlie Shipes trained Foreman, while Hall of Famer Angelo Dundee served as his cut man. In the second round, Foreman hurt Holyfield with a jab and two clubbing rights. In the third, Holyfield staggered Foreman. In the fifth, Foreman stunned Holyfield with a hook to the head. In the seventh, Foreman threw a hard right to the head and fired away with 27 punches before Holyfield retaliated with eighteen unanswered blows. In the ninth, Holyfield froze Foreman with a right to the chin. The two fighters kept at each other until the end of the bout. Though Foreman put up a game performance, Holyfield won a unanimous decision. Foreman earned $12.5 million for his efforts.

Foreman won his next three fights before he dropped a decision to Tommy Morrison in a duel for the vacant WBO heavyweight title. Then, on November 5, 1994, Foreman faced WBA and IBF heavyweight champion Michael Moorer in a championship match. Foreman wore the same trunks he had worn when he lost the title to Ali twenty years before. Foreman trailed through nine rounds of the fight. In the tenth, he scored with a left and then a right. He then unleashed a short, chopping right that knocked out Moorer. Amazingly, twenty years after he lost the title Foreman had regained it at age 45.

Foreman successfully defended his title against Axel Schulz in a controversial majority decision. Technically, Foreman at this point only held the IBF title and won the vacant WBU title in the fight against Schulz. He went on to win two more fights by decision. Then after losing a majority decision to Shannon Briggs on November 22, 1997, Foreman—who no longer held any title—retired for good.

Foreman still had his church, and he had become widely known as a celebrity endorser of such products as Meineke mufflers, Thompson's water sealant, McDonald's, Dorito's, and Kentucky Fried Chicken. He was famous for naming all five of his sons "George." He worked as a commentator on HBO boxing telecasts, and he even briefly starred in his own TV sitcom, entitled—naturally—George. However, he became best known for his pitching of the George Foreman Lean Mean Fat Reducing Grilling Machine. In 1995, he appeared with the grill at a gourmet products trade show in Las Vegas. His appearance created such a stir that the manufacturer of the grill, Salton, entered into a promotional agreement with Foreman which guaranteed the champ 45 percent of the profits. Foreman took an active role in the enterprise and suggested ways to improve the product. When Foreman and Salton presented the grill on the TV shopping network QVC and in TV infomercials featuring Foreman and many of his ten children, the product took off. The grill became such a success that Foreman received endorsement checks for $4 million a month. In 1999, Salton bought Foreman's name and image for $137 million in cash and stock—$110 million in the form of cash.

In 2004, Foreman introduced the George Foreman Signature Collection of big and tall men's clothing. He also released a compact disc of his inspirational singing. These days, Foreman continues to make appearances for the grill. He has launched a line of cleaning products, and he has also written cookbooks, a children's book, and a guide to life. He lives in Houston, preaches at his church, and spends time at his ranch. Foreman's great success as a celebrity salesman should not distract boxing fans from his pugilistic accomplishments: the incredible power he displayed in beating Frazier and Norton, and his amazing feat of re-taking the heavyweight title twenty years after he had lost the championship.

George Foreman made frequent television appearances after he regained the heavyweight title. He was Jay Leno's guest in June 1995.

BOB FOSTER

LIGHT HEAVYWEIGHT

Right-handed; 6'3"; 170–188 lbs.

65 bouts, 3/27/1961 to 6/3/1978

Manager: Lou Viscusi

Light Heavyweight Champ 1968–74

Hall of Fame Induction: 1990

Born: 12/15/1938, Albuquerque, NM

Named: Robert Lloyd Foster

One of the top fighters of the late 1960s and early '70s, light heavyweight champion Bob Foster did not always receive the acclaim due him because he labored in one of boxing's more anonymous divisions. At times overshadowed by the more glamorous heavyweight fighters of the era, Foster neverthless was almost unbeatable in his weight class.

Foster first fought as an amateur in his native New Mexico, and also boxed while serving in the Air Force. He was undefeated in over one hundred amateur bouts and earned a place on the 1959 Pan American Games team. He abandoned his goal of fighting in the 1960 Olympics when the only slot offered him was as a middleweight. The light heavyweight spot on the team went to Muhammad Ali, then known as Cassius Clay.

Turning pro in 1961, Foster won his first nine fights before Doug Jones knocked him out in eight rounds in 1962. Jones was a top heavyweight contender

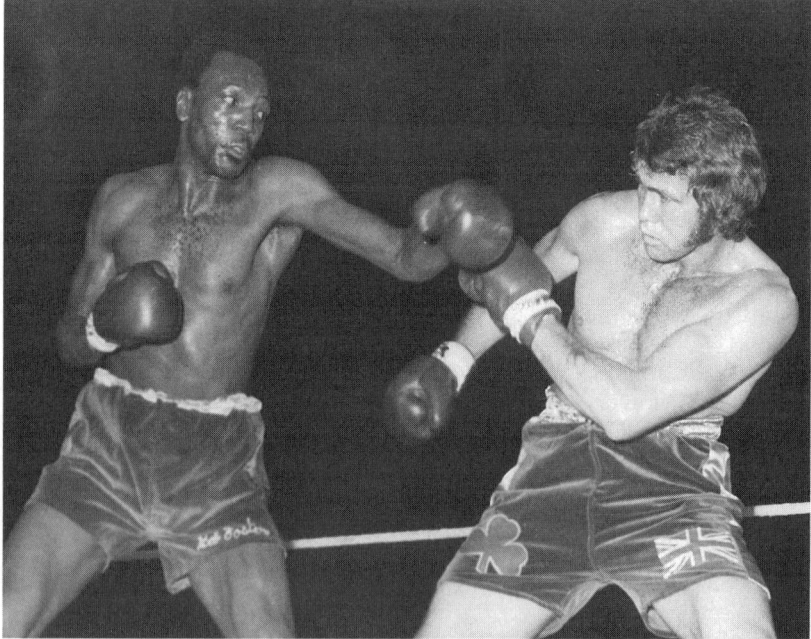

Foster's first overseas match was this fourteen-round knockout of Chris Finnegan (R) in London on September 26, 1972. Less than two months later, Foster met Ali for the NABF heavyweight title.

IN THE RING	WON 56	LOST 8	DRAWS 1	TB 65	KO 46	W 10	WF 0	D 1	KO'd 6	L 2	LF 0

Date		Opponent	Site	Result / Rounds		Title	Wt.
1961							
Mar 27		Duke Williams	Washington, DC	KO	2	—	178
Apr 3		Clarence Ryan	New York	W	4	—	176
May 8		Billy Johnson	New York	W	4	—	176
Jun 22		Ray Bryan	Montreal	KO	2	—	—
Aug 8		Floyd McCoy	Montreal	W	6	—	—
Nov 22		Ernie Knox	Norfolk, VA	KO	4	—	—
Dec 4		Clarence Floyd	Toronto	TKO	4	—	—
1962							
May 19		Billy Tisdale	New York	KO	2	—	170
Jun 27		Bert Whitehurst	New York	W	8	—	176
Oct 20	⑩	Doug Jones	New York	TKO'd	8	—	174
1963							
Feb 18		Richard Benjamin	Washington, DC	KO	1	—	189
Apr 29		Curtis Bruce	Washington, DC	KO	4	—	174
Nov 6	⑩	Mauro Mina	Lima, Peru	L	10	—	176
Dec 11		Willi Besmanoff	Norfolk	TKO	3	—	182
1964							
Feb 25		Dave Bailey	Miami	KO	1	—	181
May 8		Allen Thomas	Chicago	KO	1	—	171
Jul 10	⑩	Ernie Terrell	New York	KO'd	7	—	183
Nov 12		Don Quinn	Norfolk	KO	1	—	177
Nov 23		Norm Letcher	San Francisco	KO	1	—	176
Dec 11	⑩	Henry Hank	Norfolk	TKO	10	—	176
1965							
Jan 15		Roberto Rascon	Albuquerque, NM	KO	2	—	170
Mar 21		Dave Russell	Norfolk	TKO	6	—	176
May 24		Chuck Leslie	New Orleans	TKO	3	—	176
Jul 26		Henry Hank	New Orleans	W	12	—	170
Dec 6	⑩	Zora Folley	New Orleans	L	10	—	181
1966							
Dec 6		Leroy Green	Norfolk	KO	2	—	—
1967							
Jan 16		Jim Robinson	Washington, DC	TKO	1	—	175
Feb 27	⑩	Andres Selpa	Washington, DC	TKO	2	—	173
May 8	⑩	Eddie Cotton	Washington, DC	TKO	3	—	174
Jun 9		Henry Matthews	Roanoke, VA	TKO	2	—	175
Oct 25		Levan Roundtree	Washington, DC	KO	8	—	178
Nov 20		Eddie Vick	Providence, RI	W	10	—	178
Dec 5		Sonny Moore	Washington, DC	KO	5	—	179
1968							
May 24	♛	Dick Tiger★	New York	KO	4	Won-World-LH	173
Jul 29		Charley Polite	Springfield, MA	TKO	3	—	179
Aug 26		Eddie Vick	Albuquerque	TKO	9	—	178
Sep 9	⑩	Roger Rouse	Washington, DC	TKO	5	—	177
1969							
Jan 22		Frank DePaula	New York	TKO	1	Ret-World-LH	171
May 24	⑩	Andy Kendall	Springfield	TKO	4	Ret-World-LH	174
Jun 19		Levan Roundtree	Atlanta	TKO	4	—	179

Nov 2		Chuck Leslie	New Orleans	TKO	5	—	180
1970							
Feb 24		Bill Hardney	Orlando	TKO	4	—	177
Mar 9		Roy Wallace	Tampa	KO	6	—	177
Apr 4		Roger Rouse	Missoula, MT	TKO	4	Ret-World-LH	174
Jun 27	⑩	Mark Tessman	Baltimore	KO	10	Ret-World-LH	173
Nov 18	♛	Joe Frazier★	Detroit	KO'd	2	For-World-H	188
1971							
Mar 2		Hal Carroll	Scranton, PA	KO	4	Ret-World (WBC)-LH	174
Apr 24		Ray Anderson	Tampa	W	15	Ret-World (WBC)-LH	170
Aug 17		Vernon McIntosh	Miami	TKO	3	—	182
Oct 29		Tommy Hicks	Scranton	TKO	8	Ret-World (WBC)-LH	174
Dec 16	⑩	Brian Kelly	Oklahoma City	TKO	3	Ret-World (WBC)-LH	172
1972							
Apr 7	♛	Vicente Rondon	Miami	KO	2	Ret-World-LH	175
Jun 27	⑩	Mike Quarry	Las Vegas	KO	4	Ret-World-LH	173
Sep 26	⑩	Chris Finnegan	London	KO	14	Ret-World-LH	174
Nov 21	⑩	Muhammad Ali★	Stateline, NV	KO'd	8	For-NABF-H	180
1973							
Aug 21	⑩	Pierre Fourie	Albuquerque	W	15	Ret-World-LH	173
Dec 1	⑩	Pierre Fourie	Johannesburg	W	15	Ret-World-LH	174
1974							
Jun 17	⑩	Jorge Ahumada	Albuquerque	D	15	Ret-World-LH	174
1975							
Jun 28		Bill Hardley	Santa Fe, NM	KO	3	—	179
1976							
May 8		Al Bolden	Missoula	KO	3	—	183
Aug 28		Harold Carter	Missoula	W	10	—	185
Sep 25		Al Bolden	Spokane, WA	TKO	6	—	181
1977							
Sep 2		Bob Hazelton	Willemstad, Curacao	KO	10	—	—
1978							
Feb 9		Mustapha Wasajja	Copenhagen	TKO'd	5	—	—
Jun 3		Bob Hazelton	Wichita, KS	TKO'd	2	—	183

at that time. Foster was KO'd by heavyweight contender Ernie Terrell in 1964 and lost to another tough heavyweight, Zora Folley, the next year. By 1965, although Foster had achieved recognition as the third-rated light heavyweight in *The Ring's* annual rankings, he was having second thoughts about boxing as a career. He went to work in a munitions plant and fought only once in 1966. But by 1967, Foster was back in the ring and at the height of form. He racked up seven straight wins, six by knockout, and in 1968, got a shot at the light heavyweight title held by Nigerian dynamo Dick Tiger.

The fight with Tiger drew 11,547 fans to Madison Square Garden. Tiger hurt Foster in the first round, but Foster seized command in the third. In the next round, Foster nailed Tiger with a right uppercut followed by a left hook for a knockout, the first of Tiger's career. This sensational sequence was named the "round of the year" by *The Ring.* Foster had little trouble defending his title over the next six years, knocking out eleven of fourteen opponents. Fast, young British champion Chris Finnegan, who may have been Foster's toughest challenger, was felled in the fourteenth round of their match in 1972. After fighting to a draw with Jorge Ahumada in 1974, Foster announced his retirement, only to make a comeback attempt the next year. This effort ended with two consecutive knockout losses in 1978.

Foster's forays into the heavyweight ranks were often disappointing. In an article in the September 1968 issue of *The Ring,* Foster declared, "My goal is to be the first light heavyweight champion in history to win the heavyweight title." Foster failed to achieve this objective, suffering knockouts at the hands of Joe Frazier and Muhammad Ali, among others. He fought Frazier for the world heavyweight title in 1970 and challenged Ali for the NABF heavyweight title in 1972. That Foster reached for the heavyweight title does not detract from his solid domination of the light heavyweight division.

After retirement, Foster began a long career in law enforcement in his hometown of Albuquerque, New Mexico.

Muscles knotted with the effort, Foster digs into a heavy bag. Vulnerable against the best heavyweights of his day, Foster's record was nearly perfect when he fought against light heavyweights.

JOE FRAZIER
Smokin' Joe

HEAVYWEIGHT

Right-handed; 5'11½"; 197–229 lbs.

37 bouts, 8/16/1965 to 12/3/1981

Manager: Yancy ("Yank") Durham, Eddie Futch

1964 Olympic Heavyweight Gold Medalist

Heavyweight Champion 1970–73

Hall of Fame Induction: 1990

Born: 1/12/1944, Beaufort, SC

Named: Joseph William Frazier

Joe Frazier was a great heavyweight champion who put up the toughest resistance Muhammad Ali ever faced. As one half of the 1971 "Fight of the Century," he was the first man to defeat Ali. And only Ali and George Foreman ever beat him.

Frazier was born on a farm in Beaufort, South Carolina. After marrying at the age of fifteen, Frazier moved north, eventually settling in Philadelphia and working in a slaughterhouse. He went to a gym in an effort to lose weight and there received his first formal boxing training. He fought well as an amateur, losing only once—to huge Buster Mathis in the 1964 Olympic trials. When Mathis dropped out because of an injury, Frazier took his place and won the gold medal in the heavyweight division.

Frazier (R) bores in on Ali in the March 8, 1971, "Fight of the Century" in Madison Square Garden while shrugging off the painful effects of Ali's long jab. Frazier floored Ali in the fifteenth and won the unanimous decision.

IN THE RING	WON 32	LOST 4	DRAWS 1	TB 37	KO 27	W 5	WF 0	D 1	KO'd 3	L 1	LF 0

Date		Opponent	Site	Result / Rounds		Title	Wt.
1965							
Aug 16		Woody Goss	Philadelphia	TKO	1	—	203
Sep 20		Michael Bruce	Philadelphia	KO	3	—	—
Sep 28		Ray Staples	Philadelphia	KO	2	—	—
Nov 11		Abe Davis	Philadelphia	KO	1	—	—
1966							
Jan 17		Mel Turnbow	Philadelphia	KO	1	—	199
Mar 4		Dick Wipperman	New York	TKO	5	—	199
Apr 4		Charley Polite	Philadelphia	TKO	2	—	197
Apr 28		Don Smith	Pittsburgh	KO	3	—	200
May 19		Chuck Leslie	Los Angeles	KO	3	—	—
May 26		Memphis Jones	Los Angeles	KO	1	—	198
Jul 25		Billy Daniels	Philadelphia	TKO	6	—	202
Sep 21	⑩	Oscar Bonavena	New York	W	10	—	204
Nov 21		Eddie Machen	Los Angeles	TKO	10	—	205
1967							
Feb 21		Doug Jones	Philadelphia	KO	5	—	205
Apr 11		Jeff Davis	Miami Beach	KO	5	—	207
May 4		George Johnson	Los Angeles	W	10	—	203
Jul 19	⑩	George Chuvalo	New York	TKO	4	—	204
Oct 17		Tony Doyle	Philadelphia	TKO	2	—	204
Dec 18		Marion Connors	Boston	KO	3	—	210
1968							
Mar 4		Buster Mathis	New York	KO	11	Won-Vac NY World-H	204
Jun 24	⑩	Manuel Ramos	New York	TKO	2	Ret-NY World-H	203
Dec 10	⑩	Oscar Bonavena	Philadelphia	W	15	Ret-NY World-H	203
1969							
Apr 22		Dave Zyglewicz	Houston	KO	1	Ret-NY World-H	204
Jun 23	⑩	Jerry Quarry	New York	TKO	7	Ret-NY World-H	203
1970							
Feb 16	♛	Jimmy Ellis	New York	TKO	5	Won-Vac World-H	205
Nov 18		Bob Foster★	Detroit	KO	2	Ret-World-H	209
1971							
Mar 8	⑩	Muhammad Ali★	New York	W	15	Ret-World-H	205
1972							
Jan 15		Terry Daniels	New Orleans	TKO	4	Ret-World-H	215
May 25		Ron Stander	Omaha, NE	TKO	5	Ret-World-H	217
1973							
Jan 22	⑩	George Foreman★	Kingston, Jamaica	TKO'd	2	Lost-World-H	214
Jul 2	⑩	Joe Bugner	London	W	12	—	208
1974							
Jan 28	⑩	Muhammad Ali★	New York	L	12	For-NABF-H	209
Jun 17	⑩	Jerry Quarry	New York	TKO	5	—	212
1975							
Mar 1		Jimmy Ellis	Melbourne	TKO	9	—	200
Sep 30	♛	Muhammad Ali★	Quezon, Philippines	TKO'd	14	For-World-H	203
1976							
Jun 15	⑩	George Foreman★	Uniondale, NY	KO'd	5	—	224
1981							
Dec 3		Floyd Cummings	Chicago	D	10	—	229

Frazier turned professional the next year in Philadelphia and won his first eleven fights by knockout, four in the first round. In 1966, Frazier began to face opponents who were or had once been ranked contenders. He knocked out Billy Daniels and Eddie Machen and decisioned Oscar Bonavena. In its 1966 rankings of the top heavyweights, *The Ring* placed Frazier as the sixth-best contender. After victories over Doug Jones and Canada's "Man of Steel," George Chuvalo, in 1967, Frazier was considered the top contender for the heavyweight title. Just three years after launching his professional career, Frazier was ready to face champions on their own terms.

After Muhammad Ali was stripped of his title for refusing induction into the armed forces, the New York State Athletic Commission paired Frazier with his old amateur opponent, Buster Mathis, for its version of the world title. Madison Square Garden boxing officials Harry Markson and Teddy Brenner staged the bout as part of the opening festivities of the new Garden. Frazier and Mathis fought evenly for the first six rounds. But from the seventh round on, Frazier dominated the fight with his aggressive style and trademark left hook, then pounded Mathis to the canvas in the eleventh round for the knockout. He defended the New York title four times, conquering Bonavena, Dave Zyglewicz, Manuel Ramos, and Jerry Quarry. In 1970, Frazier unified the heavyweight championship with a fifth-round knockout of WBA champion Jimmy Ellis.

Later that year, Ali was cleared to begin fighting again. Eager to regain his championship, he challenged Frazier. Enmity brewed as the two fighters signed to fight on March 8, 1971, at Madison Square Garden. Ali bragged about his undiminished prowess and denigrated "stand-in" champion Frazier as a white man's pawn, a charge that infuriated Frazier. The bout was dubbed "The Fight of the Century," and few fights in recent times have attracted as much attention. An estimated 300 million fans watched it on closed-circuit television or via satellite, resulting in a gross of about $23 million for the promoters. The fight lived up to its billing. Ali dazzled the fans by battering Frazier with thundering combinations in the first rounds, but Frazier fought in close and worked at wearing Ali down. At times, each man appeared uncertain of how to stay on his feet and, in the eleventh, the two propped each other up in a staggering embrace. Frazier finally launched the magic punch and knocked Ali down in the fifteenth, only the third time that feat had ever been accomplished. He had plainly won the fight and proven with great spirit and courage that he was the world champion.

In 1973, Frazier lost the title to George Foreman, who knocked him down six times in two rounds. Foreman may have had the title, but the Ali–Frazier rematch was the hot ticket. The 1974 bout attracted a crowd of 20,748 to Madison Square Garden and set a non-title, indoor gate record of $1,053,688. Frazier landed more power punches, but Ali scored more frequently to win a unanimous decision. Frazier complained that Ali held him behind the head.

The two great champions met for a final clash in the Philippines, in 1975, with Ali's world title on the line. Called the "Thrilla in Manila," this fight is considered one of the greatest battles of all time. Ali scored often early in the fight, but Frazier seized control of the middle rounds and by the end of ten, the contest was even. In the twelfth, however, Ali unleashed a blistering two-handed attack which cut

Frazier's mouth and swelled his left eye nearly shut. Ali continued the onslaught until Frazier's trainer, Eddie Futch, stopped the fight after fourteen rounds.

After another knockout loss to Foreman in 1976, Frazier retired, although he did make a brief one-fight comeback five years later. In retirement, the popular Frazier has trained fighters and sung with his band, The Knockouts.

Frazier trains on the speed bag at the Concord Hotel, a Catskill Mountain resort north of New York City. Frazier was reknowned for wearing down his opponents with a determined and relentless attack.

GENE FULLMER

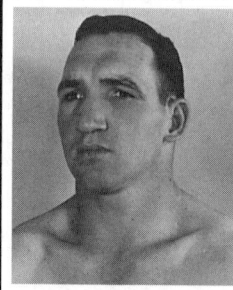

MIDDLEWEIGHT

Right-handed; 5'8"; 153–162 lbs.

64 bouts, 6/9/1951 to 8/28/1963

Manager: Marv Jensen

Middleweight Champ 1957
NBA Middlewt. Champ 1959–62

Hall of Fame Induction: 1991

Born: 7/21/1931, West Jordan, UT

The small town of West Jordan, Utah, produced boxer Gene Fullmer, whose aggressive, crowd-pleasing style twice earned him the middleweight crown. Not a particularly polished fighter, Fullmer was an all-out slugger who made up for his lack of science with raw punching power. He fought in thirteen title bouts and for the last four years of his career, fought exclusively in championship matches. Although his face bore the evidence of many blows that hit their marks, only Sugar Ray Robinson and Dick Tiger were able to knock Fullmer out.

Fullmer, reportedly named Gene after heavyweight champion Gene Tunney, started boxing at age eleven. His amateur record, which included a string of knockouts, was an impressive 70 wins with only four losses. He won four Utah

Carmen Basilio's defense is down as Fullmer (R) jabs. Fullmer beat Basilio on late-round TKOs in San Francisco in 1959 and Salt Lake City in 1960. Both fights were for the NBA middleweight title.

IN THE RING	WON 55	LOST 6	DRAWS 3	TB 64	KO 24	W 31	WF 0	D 3	KO'd 2	L 4	LF 0

Date	Opponent	Site	Result / Rounds		Title	Wt.
1951						
Jun 9	Glen Peck	Logan, UT	KO	1	—	—
Jun 16	Andy Jackson	West Jordan, UT	KO	1	—	—
Jun 23	Gary Carr	Midvale, UT	KO	3	—	—
Jul 2	Eddie Duffy	Vernal, UT	KO	1	—	—
Jul 9	Eddie Duffy	Salt Lake City	KO	2	—	155
Jul 16	Lamar Peterson	West Jordan	KO	1	—	—
Aug 1	Carlos Martinez	San Francisco	KO	1	—	167
Aug 24	Sam Healy	Hurricane, UT	KO	1	—	—
Aug 25	Buddy Sloane	Hurricane	KO	2	—	—
Sep 7	Charley Cato	West Jordan	KO	4	—	—
Sep 14	Sam Healy	Vernal	KO	4	—	—
Sep 25	Garth Panter	Salt Lake City	W	10	—	149
Oct 3	Gary Hanley	West Jordan	KO	1	—	—
Oct 10	Rudy Zadell	Pittsburgh	W	6	—	148
Oct 17	Ray Jones	Vernal	KO	1	—	—
1952						
Aug 8	Mickey Rhodes	Ogden, UT	KO	6	—	—
Sep 20	Armando Cotero	Hollywood	W	6	—	159
1954						
Feb 6	Kid Leon	West Jordan	KO	1	—	—
Apr 26	Charley Cato	Salt Lake City	KO	1	—	—
May 17	Andy Anderson	Salt Lake City	TKO	7	—	155
Jun 5	Kid Rico	Salt Lake City	TKO	1	—	153
Jul 12	Govan Small	Salt Lake City	W	10	—	157
Jul 29	Reno Abellira	West Jordan	W	10	—	153
Aug 16	Dick Wolfe	West Jordan	KO	4	—	153
Nov 8	Jackie LaBua	Brooklyn	W	10	—	154
Nov 15	Peter Muller	Brooklyn	W	10	—	155
1955						
Jan 31	Marcel Assire	Brooklyn	W	10	—	156
Feb 14	Paul Pender	Brooklyn	W	10	—	156
Mar 21	Govan Small	Salt Lake City	W	10	—	156
Apr 4	Gil Turner	Brooklyn	L	10	—	154
Jun 20	Gil Turner	Salt Lake City	W	10	—	154
Jul 26	⑩ Del Flanagan	Butte, MT	W	10	—	154
Sep 12	Al Andrews	Ogden	W	10	—	159
Sep 28	⑩ Bobby Boyd	Chicago	L	10	—	155
Nov 25	⑩ Eduardo Lausse	New York	L	10	—	156
1956						
Jan 4	⑩ Rocky Castellani	Cleveland	W	10	—	157
Feb 17	Gil Turner	New York	W	10	—	157
Apr 20	⑩ Tiger Jones	Cleveland	W	10	—	160
May 25	⑩ Charley Humez	New York	W	10	—	158
Sep 22	Moses Ward	West Jordan	KO	3	—	160
1957						
Jan 2	♛ Sugar Ray Robinson★	New York	W	15	Won-World-M	157
Jan 28	Wilf Greaves	Salt Lake City	W	10	—	160

Feb 18		Ernie Durando	Denver	W	10	—	163
May 1	⑩	Sugar Ray Robinson★	Chicago	KO'd	5	Lost-World-M	159
Jun 7	⑩	Tiger Jones	Chicago	W	10	—	161
Sep 4		Chico Veja	West Jordan	W	10	—	158
Nov 15	⑩	Neal Rivers	New York	W	10	—	159
1958							
Mar 3		Milo Savage	Salt Lake City	W	10	—	159
Jul 7		Jimmy Hegerle	West Jordan	W	10	—	160
Sep 11	⑩	Spider Webb	Salt Lake City	W	10	—	159
Nov 10		Joe Miceli	Salt Lake City	KO	2	—	159
1959							
Jan 9		Milo Savage	San Antonio, TX	W	10	—	160
Feb 20		Wilf Greaves	New York	W	10	—	161
Aug 28	⑩	Carmen Basilio★	San Francisco	TKO	14	Won-Vac NBA-M	159
Dec 4	⑩	Spider Webb	Logan	W	15	Ret-NBA-M	159
1960							
Apr 20	⑩	Joey Giardello★	Bozeman, MT	D	15	Ret-NBA-M	160
Jun 29	⑩	Carmen Basilio★	Salt Lake City	TKO	12	Ret-NBA-M	159
Dec 3	⑩	Sugar Ray Robinson★	Los Angeles	D	15	Ret-NBA-M	159
1961							
Mar 4	⑩	Sugar Ray Robinson★	Las Vegas	W	15	Ret-NBA-M	159
Aug 5	⑩	Florentino Fernandez	Ogden	W	15	Ret-NBA-M	159
Dec 9	⑩	Benny Paret	Las Vegas	KO	10	Ret-NBA-M	159
1962							
Oct 23	⑩	Dick Tiger★	San Francisco	L	15	Lost-NBA-M	160
1963							
Feb 23	♛	Dick Tiger★	Las Vegas	D	15	For-WBA-M	160
Aug 28	⑩	Dick Tiger★	Ibadan, Nigeria	TKO'd	7	For-Vac World-M	160

Golden Glove titles and five Inter-Mountain Amateur Athletic Union championships, although he lost in the Western finals of the 1948 Olympic welterweight trials. Fullmer worked as a welder in the mining industry before turning pro in 1951 in his home state. His first eleven fights were knockouts, all accomplished in four rounds or fewer.

Fullmer's first fights outside his region came in 1954 when Teddy Brenner matched him against Jackie LaBua and Peter Muller in Brooklyn. Fullmer won both fights by decision. In 1955, Fullmer decisioned future champ Paul Pender and split two decisions with Gil Turner.

Fullmer continued to work his way through the ranks, methodically dispensing with opponents until nothing stood in the way of a middleweight title shot. He was viewed as a top contender when he faced champ Sugar Ray Robinson in January 1957 in Madison Square Garden for the title. Robinson had been on top for a long time, and he was the definite favorite. Fullmer was relentless, mauling the older boxer and hanging in tight to deliver forceful body punches. With a left to the jaw and a right to the body, he knocked Robinson to the canvas in the seventh, and just three seconds were left in the count when the champ got up. The fight went the distance with neither fighter scoring another decisive punch, but Fullmer's persistent attack obviously tired Robinson, and the judges unanimously awarded Fullmer the win. Fullmer's reign as Robinson's vanquisher was short, however. In May, when Robinson took back the championship with a decisive five-round knockout in Chicago Stadium, many observers felt Fullmer's time had come and gone.

Fullmer was far from finished, however, and he took another crack at a championship in 1959 when he faced Carmen Basilio for the vacant NBA middleweight title in San Francisco's Cow Palace. Basilio and Fullmer were two of a kind: fast, hard-hitting boxers who could withstand immense punishment in the ring. Fullmer battered his opponent until the fourteenth round, when the referee called a halt after Fullmer bulled Basilio over. After the fight, Basilio exclaimed, "Fullmer kicked the hell out of me."

Fullmer successfully defended his title against both Basilio and Robinson, as well as top contenders Joey Giardello, Spider Webb, Florentino Fernandez, and Benny Paret. He met Robinson twice in title bouts, first fighting to a draw and then winning a fifteen-round decision. Dick Tiger finally ended Fullmer's winning streak in 1962 with a fifteen-round decision in Candlestick Park. Fullmer challenged Tiger twice more, in his final two professional appearances. He fought Tiger to a draw in Las Vegas in 1963 in an attempt to regain the NBA title and travelled to Nigeria that same year to battle for the vacant world middleweight crown. Tiger leveled Fullmer in seven.

Fullmer then retired to Utah, where he operated a successful mink ranch for many years. A Mormon, he reportedly donated ten percent of his considerable ring earnings to the church.

Fullmer (R) keeps the pressure on a reeling Gil Turner. Fullmer won ten-round decisions in Salt Lake City and New York, avenging Turner's victory in their first meeting in Brooklyn in 1955.

KHAOSAI GALAXY
The Thai Tyson

JUNIOR BANTAMWEIGHT

Left-handed; 5'4"; 114–121 lbs.

51 bouts, 12/17/1980 to 12/12/1991

Manager: Niwat Laosunwanawat

WBA Jr. Bantamweight Champion 1984–91

Hall of Fame Induction: 1999

Born: 5/15/1959, Napa, Petchaboon, Thailand

Named: Sura Saenkham

Also fought as: Khaosai Vangchamphoo

Although he is virtually unknown in the United States, Khaosai Galaxy is regarded by many as the greatest junior bantamweight ever and certainly the greatest boxer to emerge from Thailand. From his southpaw stance, Galaxy moved forward relentlessly, punishing his opponents with devastating left-handed body shots.

Galaxy grew up in a small rice-growing village in northeastern Thailand. When Khaosai and his twin brother Khaokor were five, their mother, an enthusiastic fight fan, gave them two pairs of boxing gloves. Sparring and training together as they grew, the young boxers both became world champions.

Galaxy started his career as a kick boxer, mastering Muay Thai, the ancient and extremely popular Thai combat sport. He made the switch to conventional boxing in 1980 and quickly found success using only his hands. He won his first several bouts before he faced Sakda Saksuree for the bantamweight championship of Thailand. Galaxy lost the fight in a ten-round decision, the only defeat of his entire career. He avenged himself upon Saksuree only six weeks later with a knockout victory in six rounds, though this time the fight was not for a belt. Finally, on January 25th of the next year, Galaxy knocked out Sakdisami Chorsirirat in seven rounds to win the Thai bantamweight title.

Galaxy won his next eleven fights by knockout, none of them lasting longer than the fifth round, and though he continued to fight exclusively in Thailand, he was becoming known as a leading junior bantamweight. Junior bantamweight was a new weight class with a 115-pound limit. The WBC crowned its first champion in 1980, with the WBA following suit in 1981. WBA junior bantamweight champion Jiro Watanabe

Song-Uhm Jae (L) managed to last ten rounds with Galaxy at Rajdamnern Stadium, in Bangkok, by covering up and easing his punishment. Galaxy was only eight months away from a title shot.

IN THE RING	WON 50	LOST 1	DRAWS 0	TB 51	KO 44	W 6	WF 0	D 0	KO'd 0	L 1	LF 0

Date	Opponent	Site	Result / Rounds		Title	Wt.
1980						
Dec 17	Pukk Sithrum	Bangkok	KO	5	—	119
Dec 31	Sansung Sithkempetch	Bangkok	KO	3	—	119
1981						
Jan 26	Prasong Sithkempetch	Bangkok	KO	1	—	118
May 13	Sakdi Porntavee	Bangkok	KO	3	—	121
Jun 10	Thaene Singchaowang	Bangkok	KO	1	—	118
Jun 24	Phichitsuk Korusayarm	Bangkok	W	10	—	117
Jul 29	Sakda Saksuree	Bangkok	L	10	For-Thai-B	117
Aug 29*	Mornsakdi Muangsurin	Bangkok	TKO	3	—	—
Sep 10*	Sakda Saksuree	Bangkok	KO	6	—	—
Oct 14	Tsuguyuki Toma	Bangkok	KO	4	—	118
1982						
Jan 25	Sakdisami Chorsirirat	Bangkok	KO	7	Won-Thai-B	117
Mar 10	Katsuyuki Ohashi	Bangkok	KO	3	—	119
Apr 14	Yuh-Ok Joo	Bangkok	KO	4	—	116
May 24	Ali Formentera	Bangkok	KO	5	—	117
Jul 10	Agus Suyanto	Bangkok	KO	4	—	116
Aug 26	Adan Uribe Perez	Bangkok	KO	4	—	115
Oct 13	Willie Jensen	Bangkok	KO	2	—	116
Nov 27	Mun-Kyun Joo	Korat, Thailand	KO	4	—	116
Dec 24	Marciano Sekiyama	Bangkok	KO	4	—	118
1983						
Feb 23	Jose Luis Soto	Bangkok	KO	2	—	117
May 10	Luis Ibanez	Bangkok	KO	3	—	117
Jun 30	Montsayarm Mahachai	Bangkok	KO	3	—	—
Aug 3	Chang-Young Park	Bangkok	W	10	—	117
Oct 12	Gil Ragas	Bangkok	TKO	7	—	116
Dec 14	Noritetsu Kato	Bangkok	TKO	5	—	117
1984						
Mar 14	Song-Uhm Jae	Bangkok	W	10	—	117
Jul 11	Val De Vera	Bangkok	TKO	7	—	116
Sep 2	Yun-Lee Moon	Bangkok	KO	2	—	117
Nov 21	Eusebio Espinal	Bangkok	KO	6	Won-Vac WBA-JB	114
1985						
Mar 6	Dong-Choon Lee	Bangkok	KO	7	Ret-WBA-JB	115
Jul 17	Rafael Orono	Bangkok	TKO	5	Ret-WBA-JB	115
Dec 23	⑩ Edgar Montserrat	Bangkok	TKO	2	Ret-WBA-JB	115
1986						
Nov 1	Israel Contreras	Willemstad, Curaçao	KO	5	Ret-WBA-JB	114
1987						
Feb 28	Ellyas Pical	Djakarta, Indonesia	TKO	14	Ret-WBA-JB	114
Jun 25	Sap-Chun Chung	Bangkok	KO	3	—	118
Oct 12	Byung-Kwan Chung	Bangkok	KO	3	Ret-WBA-JB	115

*Some boxing historians don't believe that these bouts occurred.

1988							
Jan 26	Kongtorani Payakaroon	Bangkok	W	12	Ret-WBA-JB	115
May 9	Kap-Sup Song	Bangkok	TKO	7	—	118
Sep 12	Jun Llano	Bangkok	TKO	3	—	117
Oct 9	Chang-Ho Choi	Seoul	KO	8	Ret-WBA-JB	115
1989							
Jan 15	Tae-Il Chang	Samutprakarn, Thai.	KO	2	Ret-WBA-JB	115
Apr 8	Kenji Matsumura	Yokohama, Japan	W	12	Ret-WBA-JB	114
Jul 29	Alberto Castro	Surin, Thai.	TKO	10	Ret-WBA-JB	115
Oct 31	Kenji Matsumura	Kobe, Japan	TKO	12	Ret-WBA-JB	115
1990							
Mar 29	Ari Blanca	Bangkok	KO	5	Ret-WBA-JB	115
Jul 5	Shunichi Nakajima	Chiang Mai, Thai.	KO	7	Ret-WBA-JB	115
Sep 29	Yong-Kang Kim	Suphanburi, Thai.	KO	6	Ret-WBA-JB	115
Dec 9	Ernesto Ford	Petchaboon, Thai.	KO	6	Ret-WBA-JB	115
1991							
Apr 5	Jae-Suk Park	Samut Songkram, Thai.	TKO	5	Ret-WBA-JB	115
Jul 20 ⑩	David Griman	Samutprakarn	TKO	5	Ret-WBA-JB	115
Dec 12 ⑩	Armando Castro	Bangkok	W	12	Ret-WBA-JB	115

defeated Payao Pooltarat on July 5, 1984, to unify the championship, but the WBA then stripped Watanabe of its title.

In order to fill the now-vacant WBA junior bantamweight championship, the WBA paired Galaxy with Eusebio Espinal in Bangkok on November 21, 1984. Before the fight, the previously unbeaten Espinal boasted that he would finish Galaxy with a knockout. In the fifth round, Galaxy unleashed a thundering body attack and knocked Espinal down for the eight count. He followed up in the sixth with right and left hooks to Espinal's midsection until Espinal fell to the canvas at two minutes and sixteen seconds of the round. Crowned champion, Galaxy held the WBA title until he retired.

Each of the combatants analyzed the bout in postfight interviews. Galaxy stated, "Espinal's left hooks were strong. But I found his weakness at his midsection in the third round. From the next round on, I opened up my body attacks. My fight plan worked well."

Espinal praised the victor: "Khaosai was a ferocious puncher, and he never stopped coming forward."

In 1985, Galaxy knocked out all three challengers to his title. In 1986, he fought only once, leaving Thailand for Willemstad, Curaçao, to face unbeaten Israel Contreras on November 1, 1986. Though Contreras was the aggressor in the first two rounds, Galaxy knocked him down in the third and fourth. A pair of Galaxy uppercuts and a right to the jaw in the fifth set up the finishing blow— a sharp left hook to Contreras's head. The challenger did not recover from that punch for several minutes.

Galaxy mounted another title defense on July 29, 1989, against top WBA junior bantamweight contender Alberto Castro. As his body matured, Galaxy had to work hard to make weight, and he faced Castro somewhat weakened by weight loss. In the second round, Castro, not cowed by the champ's power and reputation, countered a looping right hook with a sharp right. Galaxy went down, sprung up quickly, but was unsteady for the remainder of the round.

Behind solid lefts in the third, the experienced champion recovered some momentum. The bout was touch and go through the sixth, and Castro nearly floored Galaxy with a sixth-round right to the chin. Somehow, he managed to stay aloft on his rubbery legs. In the same round, the champ also suffered a cut over his eye. The seventh proved the turning point when Galaxy concentrated his legendary power on Castro's midsection. By the tenth, the game Colombian was beaten. At one point in that round, Castro turned his back on the champ to try to avoid the pounding to his body. After a final desperate flurry, Castro waved his arm to show the referee that he could endure no more and walked back to his corner. Khaosai Galaxy, "The Thai Tyson," was still the WBA junior bantamweight title-holder.

The Castro fight serves as a good example of Galaxy's style. An aggressive southpaw fighter with strength and the determination to come back after hitting the canvas, he overwhelmed opponents with both right and left hands and was especially effective in going to the body. He punched with incredible power, especially with his left.

After the Castro fight, Galaxy made seven more successful title defenses before retiring in the wake of an eighth defense—a twelve-round decision over Armando Castro on December 12, 1991. His last fight was attended by 11,000 fans at Bangkok's Thepsapin Stadium. Galaxy accepted gifts for 35 minutes before the fight started.

In his nineteen title defenses, Galaxy knocked out sixteen of his opponents. He scored wins over future WBA flyweight champion David Griman, three-time IBF junior bantamweight champion Ellyas Pical, two-time WBC junior flyweight champion Rafael Orono, and flyweight champion Yong-Kang Kim. A national hero in Thailand, Galaxy has stayed active in boxing since his retirement. His twin brother, Khaokor, also won the WBA bantamweight title, making them the first set of twins to both be world champions.

An intense Galaxy connects with a hard right to the chin of Yong-Kang Kim on September 29, 1990. Galaxy won with a sixth-round KO.

VICTOR GALINDEZ
El Leopardo de Morón

LIGHT HEAVYWEIGHT

Right-handed; 5'10"; 160–190 lbs.

70 bouts, 5/10/1969 to 6/14/1980

WBA Light Heavyweight Champion 1974–1978

Hall of Fame Induction: 2002

Born: 11/2/1948, Vedia, Buenos Aires, Argentina

Named: Victor Emilio Galindez

Died: 10/26/1980

One of the greatest "large" South American fighters of all time, Victor Galindez twice won the light heavyweight world championship.

As a child, Galindez worked on his uncle's farm, in a butcher shop, as a bootblack, and as a newsboy. When he was sixteen, his friends urged the imposing Galindez to try his hand at boxing. A local promoter drafted the big Argentine for one of his shows in Lujan, near Buenos Aires, and his fight career had begun.

After boxing for pay in unregulated bouts, Galindez made a foray into amateur boxing. He represented Argentina in the 1967 Pan American Games and the 1968 Olympics, where he was defeated in the first round of the tournament. He officially turned pro with a fourth-round knockout of Ramon Ruiz on May 10, 1969, in Buenos Aires. In 1970, Galindez fought ten times and compiled a 5-3-1 record, with one no contest.

On November 28, 1970, Galindez challenged for the Argentine light heavyweight title. He lost a twelve-round decision to Avenamar Peralta but won their first rematch. Two more meetings in 1971 would go to Peralta. Also that year, Galindez won two of three fights against future light heavyweight contender Jorge Ahumada.

His prospects improved in 1972. He faced Carlos Santagada on January 22. Galindez trailed after seven rounds of the ten-round battle. However, in the eighth he stopped Santagada short with a furious assault. On July 22, Galindez decisioned Juan Aguilar to win the Argentine light heavyweight title. Afterwards he declared, "I am a new fighter," and he certainly seemed to be, following up with two successful title defenses against Peralta and two wins and one draw with Aguilar.

Billy Douglas (L) faces off against Galindez on August 21, 1976, in Buenos Aires. Galindez won by decision. Douglas later managed the boxing career of his son, James ("Buster") Douglas, who will always be remembered for his huge upset knockout of Mike Tyson.

	WON	LOST	DRAWS	TB	KO	W	WF	D	KO'd	L	LF	ND
IN THE RING	**55**	**9**	**4**	70	34	21	0	4	3	6	0	2

Date	Opponent	Site	Result / Rounds		Title	Wt.
1969						
May 10	Ramon Ruiz	Buenos Aires	TKO	4	—	161
Jun 28	Ruperto Robledo	Buenos Aires	TKO	3	—	160
Aug 16	Adolfo Cejas	Azul, Argentina	D	10	—	164
1970						
Jan 17	Adolfo Cardoza	Buenos Aires	TKO	5	—	172
Mar 13	Ramon Rocha	Rosario, Argentina	TKO	9	—	169
Apr 8	Juan Aguilar	Buenos Aires	L	10	—	170
May 9	Ramon Cerrezuela	Lujan, Argentina	TKO	6	—	169
May 20	Alfredo Segura	Buenos Aires	TKO	3	—	168
Jun 24	Juan Aguilar	Buenos Aires	D	10	—	166
Jul 22	Jorge Ahumada	Buenos Aires	KO	5	—	170
Aug 14	Juan Aguilar	Mendoza, Argentina	NC	1	—	170
Sep 18	Juan Aguilar	Mendoza	L	10	—	172
Nov 28	Avenamar Peralta	Buenos Aires	L	12	For-Argentina-LH	170
1971						
Jan 9	Avenamar Peralta	Buenos Aires	W	10	—	171
Apr 7	Pedro Rimovsky	Buenos Aires	NC	1	—	173
May 24	Jorge Ahumada	Mendoza	L	10	—	169
Jun 12	Pedro Rimovsky	Buenos Aires	D	10	—	168
Jul 31	Jorge Ahumada	Buenos Aires	KO	9	—	170
Sep 11	Avenemar Peralta	Buenos Aires	TKO'd	9	—	171
Oct 30	Juan Aguilar	Buenos Aires	W	10	—	169
Dec 18	Avenemar Peralta	Buenos Aires	L	10	—	172
1972						
Jan 22	Carlos Santagada	9 de Julio, Arg.	TKO	8	—	174
May 6	Eddie Jones	Buenos Aires	W	10	—	176
Jul 22	Juan Aguilar	Buenos Aires	W	12	Won-Argentina-LH	171
Aug 19	Adolfo Cardoza	Rosario	TKO	4	—	175
Sep 2	Avenemar Peralta	Buenos Aires	W	12	Ret-Argentina-LH	172
Oct 7	Avenemar Peralta	Buenos Aires	W	12	Won-Vac-S Amer-LH	173
Nov 10	Oscar Wondryk	Venado Tuerto, Arg.	TKO	7	—	177
Dec 15	Juan Aguilar	Mendoza	D	10	—	176
1973						
Jan 29	Ruben Gonzalez	Salta, Argentina	TKO	3	—	174
Apr 14	Juan Aguilar	Buenos Aires	W	12	Ret-Argentina-LH	174
May 12	❿ Eddie Owens	Buenos Aires	TKO	3	—	174
Jul 14	Karl Zurheide	Buenos Aires	KO	2	—	174
Aug 10	Juan Aguilar	Tucuman, Argentina	KO	6	—	177
Sep 7	Raul Loyola	Buenos Aires	W	12	Ret-Argentine-LH	174
Nov 10	Raul Loyola	Buenos Aires	TKO	8	—	174
Dec 8	Eddie Duncan	Buenos Aires	KO	2	—	176
1974						
Feb 16	Ray Anderson	Balcarce, Argentina	KO	2	—	179
Apr 5	Ruben Gonzalez	Rio Cuarto, Argentina	KO	3	—	178
Jun 8	Jose Gonzalez	Buenos Aires	W	10	—	176
Jul 12	Domingo Silveyra	Jujuy, Argentina	TKO	4	—	181
Sep 1	Domingo Silveyra	San Juan, Argentina	TKO	5	—	182

Date		Opponent	Location	Result	Round	Notes	Weight
Sep 14		Angle Oquendo	Buenos Aires	W	10	—	176
Oct 5		Domingo Silveyra	Parana, Argentina	KO	4	—	178
Dec 7	⑩	Len Hutchins	Buenos Aires	TKO	13	Won-Vac WBA-LH	174
1975							
Feb 15		John Griffin	Balcarce	KO	6	—	180
Apr 7	⑩	Pierre Fourie	Johannesburg	W	15	Ret-WBA-LH	172
May 16		Ray J. Elson	Las Vegas	TKO	8	—	177
Jun 30	⑩	Jorge Ahumada	New York	W	15	Ret-WBA-LH	174
Sep 13	⑩	Pierre Fourie	Johannesburg	W	15	Ret-WBA-LH	175
1976							
Mar 28		Harald Skog	Oslo	KO	3	Ret-WBA-LH	173
Apr 8	⑩	Jesse Burnett	Copenhagen	W	10	—	174
May 22	⑩	Richie Kates	Johannesburg	KO	15	Ret-WBA-LH	174
Aug 21		Billy Douglas	Buenos Aires	W	10	—	178
Oct 5		Kosie Smith	Johannesburg	W	15	Ret-WBA-LH	175
1977							
Apr 6		Guillermo Aquirrezabala	Mendoza	KO	4	—	182
Jun 18	⑩	Richie Kates	Rome	W	15	Ret-WBA-LH	174
Sep 17	⑩	Alvaro ("Yaqui") Lopez	Rome	W	15	Ret-WBA-LH	174
Oct 19		Eddie Gregory	Turin, Italy	W	15	Ret-WBA-LH	173
1978							
Apr 8		Ramon Cerrezuela	Buenos Aires	W	10	—	179
May 6	⑩	Alvaro ("Yaqui") Lopez	Via Reggio, Italy	W	15	Ret-WBA-LH	174
Jun 16		Antonio Musaldino	Mendoza	TKO	9	—	181
Jul 8		Waldemar de Oliveira	Buenos Aires	TKO	9	—	178
Aug 19		Marcos A. Tostos	General Pico, Argentina	TKO	6	—	182
Sep 15	⑩	Mike Rossman	New Orleans	TKO'd	13	Lost-WBA-LH	174
1979							
Mar 10		Roberto Aguilar	San Miguel, Argentina	TKO	6	—	185
Apr 14	♔	Mike Rossman	New Orleans	TKO	10	Reg-WBA-LH	174
Nov 30	⑩	Marvin Johnson	New Orleans	TKO'd	11	Lost-WBA-LH	174
1980							
Jun 14		Jesse Burnett	Anaheim, CA	L	12	—	190

Starting with the Santagada fight, Galindez racked up a streak of 22 wins and a single draw before he signed for a match with Len Hutchins on December 7, 1974, in the famed Luna Park in Buenos Aires. Light Heavyweight Champion Bob Foster had just retired, and the WBA announced it would consider the winner of the Galindez–Hutchins contest its new title holder. Galindez injured his knee in a car accident a month before the fight, and then, just a week before the bout, he injured his ankle horseback riding. Both times he refused to postpone, fearing that he would never get another chance at a world title. A pre-fight meal of frogs upset his stomach immediately before the match, but he had no trouble stopping Hutchins in thirteen.

At this point in his career, Galindez was a "walk-in slugger" who left himself open to the blows of a skillful boxer. All-time great middleweight Carlos Monzon, his close friend and fellow Argentine, helped Galindez focus on boxing and counterpunching rather than just whacking his opponent. Galindez successfully defended his title in a tough fifteen-round decision against Ahumada in his first fight held in the United States, but had difficulty making weight for the June 30, 1975, match in New York.

On May 22, 1976, Galindez had one of his roughest match-ups, against top contender Richie Kates in Johannesburg, South Africa. In the third round, Kates opened a deep gash over Galindez's right eye, which bled in round after punishing round for the rest of the fight. Late in the fifteenth, Galindez uncorked a left hook to the jaw, and Kates was counted out with eleven seconds left in the fight. Galindez won the rematch as well.

In 1977, Galindez triumphed over Yaqui Lopez and future champion Eddie Gregory (who later became Eddie Mustafa Muhammad). Galindez won a narrow decision over Gregory, who might have won but for points lost on fouls. For his next title defense against Mike Rossman in New Orleans on September 15, 1978, Galindez jumped rope for over an hour in a hot hotel boiler room, again struggling to make weight. He lost the thirteen-round fight and the championship.

After protracted negotiations, he agreed to fight Rossman again in the New Orleans Superdome, on April 14, 1979. Stung by the loss of his title, Galindez had worked himself into top form. Rossman opened with left jabs, winning the first round, but Galindez countered by taking a quick step forward, shooting a lunging left jab, followed by a right. Rossman fought back with jabs over Galindez's right and also won the second and third rounds. In the fourth, the challenger unleashed a furious attack that went past the bell. When referee Stanley Christodoulou ruled that Galindez had not heard the signal, Rossman's brother leapt into the ring and swung at Galindez. The ring filled with partisans of both sides until Christodoulou regained control and the fight resumed. Rossman suffered a broken hand in the fifth, and, though Galindez had dislocated his elbow, he took control and Rossman could not continue in the ninth. After the fight, Galindez said of Rossman, "He's a chicken. I'll never give him a rematch."

He did not need to. His first defense on November 30, 1979, ended with a broken jaw and an ignominious knockout at the hands of Marvin Johnson. After surgery, Galindez fought twice more. Lightly regarded Jesse Burnett knocked him down twice and beat him in twelve rounds on June 14, 1980. Galindez announced his retirement on August 28, 1980; he had suffered two detached retinas, and his doctors advised him to quit.

Always fascinated with cars, Galindez decided to try his hand at auto racing. He obtained a racing license and rode with Antonio Lizeviche in a competition on October 26, 1980. Though warned to stay inside the car if it experienced engine trouble during the race, they exited the vehicle and another race car hit them, killing them both.

In a Rome rematch, on June 18, 1977, Galindez (L) lands a left to the body of Richie Kates. The decision win was Galindez's seventh successful title defense.

KID GAVILAN
The Cuban Hawk

WELTERWEIGHT

Right-handed; 5'10½"; 118–155 lbs.
143 bouts, 6/5/1943 to 6/18/1958
Managers: Fernando Balido, Angel Lopez, Yamil Chade
Welterweight Champion 1951–54
Hall of Fame Induction: 1990
Born: 1/6/1926, Camaguey, Cuba
Named: Gerardo Gonzalez
Died: 2/13/2003

A regular in the early days of televised boxing, with 34 TV appearances, Kid Gavilan was well known to fans for his confounding style that included playing possum, suddenly switching strategies, and slipping punches. He imported the "bolo punch," a looping uppercut that he could swing with enough power to lift an opponent off his feet.

A worker on a sugar plantation in Cuba, Gavilan competed in amateur bouts from age twelve on. When his family moved to Havana, he was spotted by a team of managers who molded his career and eventually took him to the United States. The young fighter was named after a Havana cafe owned by manager Fernando Balido and known as El Gavilan ("the hawk").

Gavilan turned professional in 1943, at the age of sixteen. After fighting for three years in Cuba, Mexico, and Puerto Rico, he had matches in New York. By 1947, Gavilan was considered one of the top welterweight contenders, although the next year held some setbacks: a loss to veteran Ike Williams by decision, and an over-the-weight match with Sugar Ray Robinson, which Gavilan also lost by decision.

In 1949 Gavilan again met Robinson, this time for the welterweight title. Once more, Robinson proved to be too much for Gavilan and won a decision after fifteen rounds—although some observers believed the victory belonged to the Kid. Gavilan waited two years to take another shot at a world championship (vacated when Robinson moved up to middleweight), when he met Johnny Bratton, who held the NBA version of the welterweight title, in Madison Square Garden. From the first round, Bratton was in trouble, and Gavilan easily won the decision to capture the undisputed title.

Gavilan successfully defended his belt against Billy Graham, although rumors surfaced that the split decision may have resulted from underworld influence. Gavilan won a rematch with Graham and also defended the title against Carmen Basilio. In 1954, he challenged Carl ("Bobo") Olson for the middleweight title. Overwhelmed by the larger man's punching power, Gavilan lost the decision. That same year, Gavilan lost the welterweight

Gavilan (L) was less than one year from the welterweight title when he decisioned ranked contender Joe Miceli in New York a few days before Christmas 1950.

title to Johnny Saxton. Saxton won a decision, even though 19 of the 21 writers at ringside gave the fight to Gavilan. The bout may have been fixed—without Gavilan's knowledge—so that his only hope of winning would have been by knockout.

Gavilan continued to fight for four more years, compiling a 10-15-1 record. A crowd-pleaser, Gavilan showed great speed in the ring, good counter-punching ability, and stamina. His bolo punch, which traced the same motion he had used with a machete in the sugar cane fields, was dreaded by many. He held his own with top fighters of his day and was never knocked out. Gavilan returned to Cuba after Castro took power. His street preaching as a Jehovah's Witness landed him in jail. In the mid-1980s he sold sausages in Miami. He died of a heart attack at age 77.

IN THE RING	WON 108	LOST 30	DRAWS 5	TB 143	KO 28	W 80	WF 0	D 5	KO'd 0	L 30	LF 0

Date	Opponent	Site	Result / Rounds		Title	Wt.
1943						
Jun 5	Antonio Diaz	Havana	W	4	—	122
Jun 12	Bartolo Molina	Havana	W	4	—	121
Aug 7	Valeriano Dustet	Havana	W	6	—	124
Sep 11	Sergio Prieto	Havana	KO	5	—	—
1944						
Oct 1	Juan Villalba	Havana	KO	9	—	—
Nov 25	Esmerido Salazar	Havana	W	10	—	—
Dec 23	Miguel Acevedo	Havana	W	10	—	132
1945						
Feb 10	Esmerido Salazar	Havana	W	10	—	130
Mar 10	Jose Pedroso	Havana	W	10	—	136
Apr 21	Santiago Sosa	Havana	KO	9	—	—
May 13	Kid Bebo	Cienfuegos, Cuba	KO	4	—	—
May 26	Julio ("Yucatan Kid") Jimenez	Havana	W	10	—	135
Jun 23	Pedro Ortega	Havana	W	10	—	132
Jul 7	Jose Pedroso	Havana	KO	4	Won-Cuba-L	134
Aug 4	Julio ("Yucatan Kid") Jimenez	Mexico City	W	10	—	—
Aug 26	Pedro Ortega	Mexico City	KO	6	—	—
Sep 22	Carlos Malacara	Mexico City	L	10	—	—
Nov 5	Carlos Malacara	Havana	W	10	—	135
Nov 17	Johnny Suarez	Havana	W	10	—	132
1946						
Jan 26	Kid Bururu	Havana	W	10	—	134
Feb 9	Kid Bururu	Havana	W	10	—	133
Mar 2	Jose R. Zorilla	Bayamon, PR	KO	4	—	—
Mar 9	Santiago Sosa	Havana	W	10	—	—
Apr 5	Tony Martinez	Mexico City	L	10	—	136
Jun 25	Chico Varona	Havana	W	10	—	—
Aug 4	Hankin Barrows	Havana	KO	7	—	—
Aug 24	Jack Larrimore	Havana	KO	3	—	146
Sep 7	Hankin Barrows	Havana	W	10	—	146
Nov 1	Johnny Ryan	New York	KO	5	—	146
Dec 2	Johnny Williams	New York	W	10	—	144
Dec 13	Johnny Williams	New York	W	10	—	144
1947						
Jan 28	Julio Pedroso	Havana	W	10	—	145
Feb 8	Jose Garcia Alvarez	Havana	W	10	—	145
Feb 22	Pablo Roca	Havana	W	10	—	145
Mar 12	Nick Moran	Havana	W	10	—	146

Apr 26		Vince Gambill	Havana	KO	2		—	144
Aug 11		Charlie Williams	Newark, NJ	W	10		—	149
Aug 18		Bobby Lee	Baltimore	W	10		—	147
Sep 2		Doug Ratford	Newark	L	10		—	144
Sep 15		Charley Millan	Baltimore	KO	1		—	142
Sep 18		Billy Justine	Philadelphia	W	8		—	143
Oct 23		Billy Nixon	Philadelphia	W	8		—	145
Nov 3		Bee Bee Wright	Baltimore	TKO	10		—	143
Dec 29		Buster Tyler	New York	D	10		—	144

1948

Jan 12	⑩	Gene Burton	New York	D	10		—	147
Jan 23		Joe Curcio	New York	TKO	2		—	146
Feb 13		Vinnie Rossano	New York	W	10		—	144
Feb 27	⑩	Ike Williams★	New York	L	10		—	141
Apr 13		Doug Ratford	Brooklyn	L	10		—	142
Apr 26	⑩	Tommy Bell	Philadelphia	W	10		—	146
May 28		Rocco Rossano	New York	KO	1		—	144
Jul 22		Roman Alvarez	New York	W	10		—	147
Aug 12		Buster Tyler	New York	W	10		—	148
Sep 23	♛	Sugar Ray Robinson★	New York	L	10		—	148
Oct 21		Vinnie Rossano	Washington, DC	TKO	6		—	148
Nov 12		Tony Pellone	New York	W	10		—	147
Dec 11		Abdul Ben Buker	Havana	W	10		—	147

1949

Jan 28	⑩	Ike Williams★	New York	W	10		—	145
Apr 1	⑩	Ike Williams★	New York	W	10		—	146
May 2		Al ("Red") Priest	Boston	W	10		—	147
Jun 7		Cliff Hart	Syracuse, NY	KO	2		—	145
Jul 11	♛	Sugar Ray Robinson★	Philadelphia	L	15	For-World-W		144
Sep 9		Rocky Castellani	New York	W	10		—	150
Oct 14	⑩	Beau Jack★	Chicago	W	10		—	148
Oct 21	⑩	Lester Felton	Detroit	L	10		—	145
Nov 21	⑩	Laurent Dauthuille	Montreal	W	10		—	151
Dec 17		Bobby Lee	Havana	W	10		—	146

1950

Feb 10	⑩	Billy Graham★	New York	L	10		—	146
Mar 6		Otis Graham	Philadelphia	W	10		—	148
Mar 20	⑩	Robert Villemain	Montreal	L	10		—	147
May 8	⑩	George Costner	Philadelphia	L	10		—	149
May 26		George Small	New York	W	10		—	151
Jun 8		Mike Koballa	Brooklyn	W	10		—	151
Jun 19		Bobby Mann	Hartford, CT	W	10		—	155
Jul 2		Sonny Horne	Brooklyn	W	10		—	151
Jul 13		Phil Burton	Omaha, NE	W	10		—	149
Aug 15		Johnny Greco	Montreal	KO	6		—	147
Oct 23		Tommy Ciarlo	New Haven, CT	D	10		—	149
Oct 30	⑩	Eugene Hairston	Scranton, PA	L	10		—	150
Nov 17	⑩	Billy Graham★	New York	W	10		—	147
Dec 4		Tony Janiro	Cleveland	W	10		—	148
Dec 22	⑩	Joe Miceli	New York	W	10		—	146

1951

Jan 26	⑩	Paddy Young	New York	W	10		—	146
Feb 19		Tommy Ciarlo	Caracas	W	10		—	151
Mar 10		Tommy Ciarlo	Havana	TKO	8		—	146
Mar 30	⑩	Eugene Hairston	New York	W	10		—	150
Apr 20		Aldo Minelli	New York	W	10		—	150
May 18	♛	Johnny Bratton	New York	W	15	Won-Vac World-W		145
Jul 16		Fitzie Pruden	Milwaukee	W	10		—	148
Aug 29	⑩	Billy Graham★	New York	W	15	Ret-World-W		145

Date		Opponent	Location	Result	Rounds	Title	Weight
Oct 4		Bobby Rosado	Havana	TKO	7	—	147
Nov 7		Tony Janiro	Detroit	TKO	4	—	149
Nov 28	⑩	Johnny Bratton	Chicago	D	10	—	149
Dec 14	⑩	Walter Cartier	New York	TKO	10	—	151
1952							
Feb 4	⑩	Bobby Dykes	Miami	W	15	Ret-World-W	147
Feb 28		Don Williams	Boston	W	10	—	149
May 19		Ralph Zannelli	Providence, RI	W	10	—	153
May 28		Fitzie Pruden	Indianapolis	TKO	6	—	150
Jul 7	⑩	Gil Turner	Philadelphia	TKO	11	Ret-World-W	146
Aug 16		Mario Diaz	Buenos Aires, Argentina	W	10	—	150
Sep 6		Rafael Merentino	Buenos Aires	TKO	9	—	151
Sep 13		Eduardo Lausse	Buenos Aires	W	10	—	151
Oct 5	⑩	Billy Graham ★	Havana	W	15	Ret-World-W	146
1953							
Jan 13		Aman Peck	Tampa	W	10	—	150
Jan 21		Vic Cardell	Washington, DC	W	10	—	152
Feb 11	⑩	Chuck Davey	Chicago	TKO	10	Ret-World-W	146
Apr 14		Livio Minelli	Cleveland	W	10	—	152
May 2	⑩	Danny Womber	Syracuse	L	10	—	151
Jun 10		Italo Scortichini	Detroit	W	10	—	151
Jul 15	⑩	Ramon Fuentes	Milwaukee	W	10	—	152
Aug 26		Ralph Jones	New York	W	10	—	154
Sep 18	⑩	Carmen Basilio ★	Syracuse	W	15	Ret-World-W	146
Nov 13	⑩	Johnny Bratton	Chicago	W	15	Ret-World-W	146
1954							
Feb 23		Johnny Cunningham	Miami Beach	W	10	—	156
Mar 8		Livio Minelli	Boston	W	10	—	153
Apr 2	♛	Carl ("Bobo") Olson ★	Chicago	L	15	For-World-M	155
Oct 20	⑩	Johnny Saxton	Philadelphia	L	15	Lost-World-W	145
1955							
Feb 4		Ernie Durando	New York	W	10	—	152
Feb 23	⑩	Hector Constance	Miami Beach	L	10	—	154
Mar 16		Bobby Dykes	Miami	L	10	—	152
Jun 2		Luigi Cemulini	Santa Clara, Cuba	KO	3	—	152
Jul 24		Cirilo Gil	Buenos Aires	W	10	—	143
Aug 13		Juan Bautista Burgues	Montevideo, Uruguay	KO	7	—	151
Sep 3	⑩	Eduardo Lausse	Buenos Aires	L	12	—	152
Dec 3		Dogomar Martinez	Montevideo	L	10	—	155
1956							
Feb 7		Peter Waterman	London	L	10	—	147
Mar 29		Germinal Ballarin	Paris	L	10	—	150
Apr 24		Peter Waterman	London	W	10	—	147
May 13		Louis Trochon	Marseilles, France	D	10	—	151
Aug 18		Jimmy Beecham	Havana	W	10	—	149
Oct 13	⑩	Tony DeMarco	Boston	L	10	—	148
Nov 13		Chico Vejar	Los Angeles	W	10	—	149
Dec 4		Walter Byars	Boston	L	10	—	148
Dec 20	⑩	Ramon Fuentes	Los Angeles	L	10	—	152
1957							
Feb 26	⑩	Vince Martinez	Newark	L	10	—	148
Apr 24		Del Flanagan	St. Paul, MN	L	10	—	147
Jun 17	⑩	Vince Martinez	Jersey City, NJ	L	10	—	147
Jul 31	⑩	Gaspar Ortega	Miami Beach	W	10	—	153
Oct 22	⑩	Gaspar Ortega	Los Angeles	L	12	—	146
Nov 20		Walter Byars	Chicago	W	10	—	151
1958							
Feb 19	⑩	Ralph Jones	Miami Beach	L	10	—	154
Apr 4	⑩	Ralph Jones	Philadelphia	W	10	—	155
Jun 18		Yama Bahama	Miami Beach	L	10	—	150

JOEY GIARDELLO

MIDDLEWEIGHT

Right-handed; 5'10"; 140–175 lbs.
133 bouts, 10/2/1948 to 11/6/1967
Manager: Anthony Ferrante
Middleweight Champion 1963–65
Hall of Fame Induction: 1993
Born: 7/16/1930, Brooklyn, NY
Named: Carmine Orlando Tilelli

An example of persistence and professionalism, Joey Giardello did not win a championship until he was 33 years old, an age at which many fighters have already retired. A self-taught brawler who built a record of wins that spanned the era from post–World War II through the 1960s, Giardello combined his dodging, dancing style with quick on-target jabs , often opening up his opponents for the knockout.

Giardello turned professional in 1948 at the age of eighteen, without the benefit of organized amateur experience. By 1952, he had won recognition as a top middleweight contender. He fought his first important matches in 1952 and 1953 with Billy Graham. In the three-fight series, the unheralded Giardello began by upsetting Graham, who was eight years older and far more experienced in the ring. In the rematch, the ringside judges initially gave Giardello the split decision, but two commissioners of the New York State Athletic Commission changed one of the judge's scores, giving the win to Graham. Giardello sued, and the case went to New York's Supreme Court. The court ruled that the commissioners did not have the authority to change the scorecard, and Giardello was acknowledged as the winner once again. His victory restored, Giardello faced Graham for a third time, with Graham taking the decision.

Giardello continued to fight top contenders over the next several years, but he did not receive a title shot until he challenged Gene Fullmer for the NBA middleweight crown in April 1960. The match took place in the Montana State University field house in Bozeman and went a bitter and bruising fifteen rounds—with each boxer protesting the other's tactics—before being declared a draw. Years later, Giardello still expressed anger about this bout, calling Fullmer "the dirtiest fighter in the book." Fullmer, who claimed Giardello had fractured his skull with a headbutt, unhesitatingly returned the charge. The score was never settled; Fullmer and Giardello never fought again.

In 1963, Giardello's moment finally arrived when he was signed to fight Dick Tiger for the world middleweight championship, which Tiger had wrested from Fullmer the year before. Giardello fought defensively and scored with jabs and hooks to win the

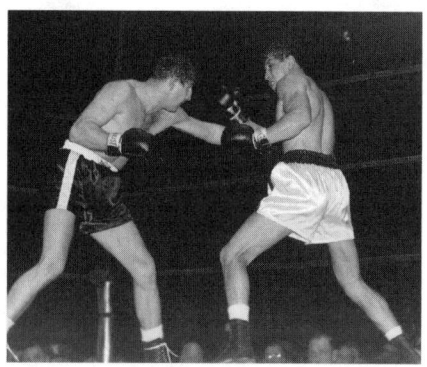

The result was in doubt long after this December 1952 Garden meeting between Billy Graham and Joey Giardello (R). After the NYSAC reversed the win by Giardello, a court reconfirmed the original decision.

fifteen-rounder in Atlantic City. Middleweight champion at last, Giardello held onto the title for two years. He defended it once, winning over Rubin Carter in 1964, then lost it in a rematch with Tiger in 1965.

Giardello fought twice in 1966 and twice in 1967 before retiring at 37. In a long, sometimes frustrating career, Giardello racked up a hundred victories.

In retirement, Giardello worked in the insurance and chemical industries. He is active in charitable work for handicapped children. He successfully sued Universal Pictures for his "false depiction" in the 1999 film *The Hurricane*.

IN THE RING	WON 101	LOST 25	DRAWS 8	TB 134	KO 33	W 68	WF 0	D 8	KO'd 4	L 21	LF 0

Date	Opponent	Site	Result / Rounds		Title	Wt.
1948						
Oct 2	Johnny Noel	Trenton, NJ	KO	2	—	154
Oct 10	Jimmy Larkin	Atlantic City	KO	1	—	154
Nov 7	Bobby Clark	Wilkes-Barre, PA	W	4	—	—
Nov 16	Jacke Cole	Trenton, NJ	KO	1	—	154
Nov 20	Johnny Brown	Reading, PA	KO	4	—	—
Dec 16	Johnny Madison	Atlantic City	KO	1	—	154
Dec 30	Willie Wigfall	Philadelphia	KO	1	—	152
1949						
Feb 24	Clyde Diggs	Philadelphia	D	6	—	153
Mar 15	Don Ennis	Reading	KO	4	—	152
Apr 7	Bill Montgomery	Philadelphia	KO	1	—	157
Apr 25	Ray Morris	Wilkes-Barre	W	4	—	153
Apr 28	Joe Aurillo	Philadelphia	W	6	—	154
May 2	Emerson Charles	Philadelphia	W	4	—	155
Jun 6	Henry Vonsavage	Philadelphia	KO	2	—	155
Jun 20	Ray Hass	Philadelphia	KO	3	—	156
Jul 13	Leroy Fleming	Washington, DC	KO	1	—	154
Nov 14	Mitchell Allen	Philadelphia	W	6	—	157
Dec 5	Jim Dockery	Philadelphia	KO	2	—	160
1950						
Jan 5	Johnny Fry	Philadelphia	W	6	—	160
Jan 16	Joe DiMartino	New Haven, CT	L	8	—	156
Jan 26	Johnny Bernardo	Philadelphia	W	8	—	157
Feb 9	Johnny Bernardo	Philadelphia	W	8	—	154
Mar 23	Armando Amanini	Brooklyn	W	8	—	156
Mar 27	Steve Sabatino	Philadelphia	KO	1	—	158
Mar 29	Johnny Brown	Allentown, PA	W	6	—	—
Apr 20	Tommy Varsos	Brooklyn	KO	1	—	157
May 4	Hurley Sanders	Brooklyn	W	8	—	158
May 17	Carey Mace	New York	KO'd	8	—	156
Aug 25	Al Berry	Scranton, PA	KO	1	—	158
Sep 26	Ted DiGiammo	Wilkes-Barre	KO	1	—	158
Oct 16	Bruce Ubaldo	Wilkes-Barre	W	8	—	—
Oct 26	Harold Green	Brooklyn	KO'd	6	—	156
Nov 27	Gene Roberts	Philadelphia	D	8	—	158
Dec 18	Leroy Allen	Philadelphia	KO	5	—	158
1951						
Jan 6	Freddie Lott	Brooklyn	W	8	—	155
Feb 10	Jan Henri	Philadelphia	W	8	—	157
Feb 22	Hal Sampson	Brooklyn	W	8	—	156

Feb 24		Tony Wolfe	Philadelphia	KO	3	—	155
Mar 15		Roy Wouters	Philadelphia	L	8	—	155
Mar 29		Primos Cutler	Philadelphia	W	8	—	156
Apr 12		Roy Wouters	Philadelphia	W	8	—	155
Apr 30	⑩	Ernie Durando	Scranton	W	10	—	154
May 25		Gus Rubicini	New York	L	8	—	155
Aug 13		Otis Graham	Philadelphia	W	8	—	154
Aug 27		Johnny Noel	Philadelphia	W	8	—	155
Sep 14		Tommy Bazzano	New York	W	6	—	156
Oct 8		Tony Amato	New York	KO	7	—	159
Nov 13	⑩	Rocky Castellani	Scranton	L	10	—	156
Dec 12		Bobby Dykes	Miami Beach	L	10	—	156
1952							
Jan 9		Sal DiMartino	Miami Beach	D	10	—	155
Mar 28		Sammy Giuliani	New York	D	8	—	159
May 5	⑩	Joe Miceli	Scranton	D	10	—	153
Jun 5		Roy Wouters	Philadelphia	W	6	—	154
Jun 23	⑩	Pierre Langlois	Brooklyn	W	10	—	156
Aug 4	⑩	Billy Graham★	Brooklyn	W	10	—	151
Sep 15		Georgie Small	Brooklyn	W	10	—	155
Oct 13		Joey Giambra	Brooklyn	W	10	—	155
Nov 11		Joey Giambra	Buffalo, NY	L	10	—	154
Dec 19	⑩	Billy Graham★	New York	W	10	—	151
1953							
Feb 2		Harold Green	Brooklyn	W	10	—	155
Mar 6	⑩	Billy Graham★	New York	L	12	—	155
Apr 7	⑩	Gil Turner	Philadelphia	W	10	—	154
May 30		Hurley Sanders	Newark, NJ	W	10	—	159
Jun 26	⑩	Ernie Durando	New York	W	10	—	156
Sep 29	⑩	Johnny Saxton	Philadelphia	L	10	—	155
Oct 26		Walter Dartier	Brooklyn	W	10	—	158
Nov 23		Tuzo Portuguez	Brooklyn	W	10	—	160
1954							
Jan 8		Garth Panter	New York	TKO	5	—	160
Feb 5		Walter Cartier	New York	TKO	1	—	157
Mar 19	⑩	Willie Troy	New York	TKO	7	—	159
May 21	⑩	Pierre Langlois	New York	L	10	—	160
Jun 11	⑩	Bobby Jones	New York	W	10	—	159
Jul 7		Billy Kilgore	Philadelphia	W	10	—	158
Sep 24		Tiger Jones	Philadelphia	W	10	—	159
1955							
Jan 25		Al Andrews	Norfolk, VA	W	10	—	162
Feb 15		Andy Mayfield	Miami Beach	KO	8	—	161
Mar 1		Peter Mueller	Milwaukee	KO	2	—	158
1956							
Feb 11		Tim Jones	Trenton, NJ	TKO	10	—	160
Mar 10		Hurley Sanders	Paterson, NJ	W	10	—	161
Mar 27		Joe Shaw	Philadelphia	W	10	—	159
May 7		Charlie Cotton	New York	L	10	—	159
May 28		Charlie Cotton	New York	L	10	—	160
Jul 2		Tony Baldoni	New York	KO	1	—	159
Jul 26		Franz Szuzina	Milwaukee	W	10	—	160
Aug 28		James Bussey	Miami Beach	TKO	9	—	161
Sep 28	⑩	Bobby Boyd	Cleveland	KO	5	—	159
Nov 15		Charlie Cotton	Milwaukee	W	10	—	159
Dec 14		Charlie Cotton	Cleveland	W	10	—	159

1957

Date		Opponent	Location	Result	Rounds	Notes	Weight
Feb 6		Randy Sandy	Chicago	W	10	—	159
Mar 27	⑩	Willie Vaugh	Kansas City, MO	D	10	—	159
May 17	⑩	Rory Calhoun	Cleveland	W	10	—	160
Jul 2		Joe Gray	Detroit	KO	6	—	160
Jul 17		Chico Vejar	Louisville, KY	W	10	—	159
Sep 27		Bobby Lane	Cleveland	KO	7	—	161
Nov 5		Wilf Greaves	Denver	W	10	—	160
Dec 27	⑩	Tiger Jones	Miami Beach	W	10	—	159

1958

Date		Opponent	Location	Result	Rounds	Notes	Weight
Feb 12		Franz Szuzina	Philadelphia	W	10	—	160
May 5	⑩	Rory Calhoun	San Francisco	W	10	—	159
Jun 11		Franz Szuzina	Washington, DC	W	10	—	160
Jun 30	⑩	Joey Giambra	San Francisco	L	10	—	161
Nov 19	⑩	Spider Webb	San Francisco	TKO'd	7	—	159

1959

Date		Opponent	Location	Result	Rounds	Notes	Weight
Jan 28	⑩	Tiger Jones	Louisville	L	10	—	162
May 6	⑩	Holley Mims	Washington, DC	W	10	—	161
Jun 16	⑩	Del Flanagan	St. Paul, MN	KO	1	—	161
Aug 11		Chico Vejar	St. Paul	W	10	—	160
Sep 30	⑩	Dick Tiger★	Chicago	L	10	—	162
Nov 4	⑩	Dick Tiger★	Cleveland	W	10	—	160

1960

Date		Opponent	Location	Result	Rounds	Notes	Weight
Apr 20	♛	Gene Fullmer★	Bozeman, MT	D	15	For-NBA-M	158
Sep 27		Clarence Hinnant	Billings, MT	TKO	3	—	164
Oct 11	⑩	Terry Downes	London	L	10	—	160
Dec 1		Peter Mueller	Cologne, Germany	L	10	—	157

1961

Date		Opponent	Location	Result	Rounds	Notes	Weight
Mar 6	⑩	Ralph Dupas	New Orleans	L	10	—	160
May 15		Wilf Greaves	Philadelphia	TKO	9	—	162
Jul 10	⑩	Henry Hank	Detroit	L	10	—	159
Sep 12	⑩	Jesse Smith	Philadelphia	W	10	—	161
Nov 6	⑩	Jesse Smith	Chicago	W	10	—	163
Dec 12		Joe DeNucci	Boston	D	10	—	161

1962

Date		Opponent	Location	Result	Rounds	Notes	Weight
Jan 30	⑩	Henry Hank	Philadelphia	W	10	—	162
Jul 9		Jimmy Beecham	St. Paul	W	10	—	162
Aug 6	⑩	George Benton	Philadelphia	L	10	—	161
Nov 12		Johnny Morris	Baltimore	W	10	—	162

1963

Date		Opponent	Location	Result	Rounds	Notes	Weight
Feb 25		Wilf Greaves	Jacksonville, FL	W	10	—	163
Mar 25		Ernie Burford	Philadelphia	W	10	—	161
Jun 24		Sugar Ray Robinson★	Philadelphia	W	10	—	160
Dec 7	♛	Dick Tiger★	Atlantic City	W	15	Won-World-M	158

1964

Date		Opponent	Location	Result	Rounds	Notes	Weight
Apr 17		Rocky Rivero	Cleveland	W	10	—	163
May 22		Rocky Rivero	Cleveland	W	10	—	164
Dec 14	⑩	Rubin Carter	Philadelphia	W	15	Ret-World-M	160

1965

Date		Opponent	Location	Result	Rounds	Notes	Weight
Apr 23		Gil Diaz	Cherry Hill, NJ	W	10	—	163
Oct 21	⑩	Dick Tiger★	New York	L	15	Lost-World-M	160

1966

Date		Opponent	Location	Result	Rounds	Notes	Weight
Sep 22		Cash White	Reading	W	10	—	168
Dec 5		Nate Collins	San Francisco	TKO'd	8	—	168

1967

Date		Opponent	Location	Result	Rounds	Notes	Weight
May 22		Jack Rodgers	Pittsburgh	L	10	—	173
Nov 6		Jack Rodgers	Philadelphia	W	10	—	168

WILFREDO GOMEZ
Bazooka

FEATHERWEIGHT

Right-handed; 5'5"; 121–142 lbs.
48 bouts, 11/16/1974 to 7/19/1989
Manager: Yamil Chade
WBC Super Bantamweight
Champion 1977–83
WBC Featherweight Champion 1984
Jr. Lightweight Champion 1985–86
Hall of Fame Induction: 1995
Born: 10/29/1956, Las Monjas, PR

Dubbed in 1994 by *The Ring* as the greatest junior featherweight (super bantamweight, in WBC parlance) of all time, Wilfredo Gomez successfully defended this title seventeen times, each time by knockout. He was a champion in three divisions, and a titleholder for nearly a decade. A skillful boxer with a repertoire of powerhouse punches, Gomez was inducted into the Hall of Fame the first year he was eligible.

A native of Puerto Rico, Gomez had an excellent amateur record that included a world amateur title won in Havana in 1974. He first fought professionally in Panama with a 1974 draw with Jacinto Fuentes. After that fight, Gomez knocked out 32 consecutive opponents, including Fuentes. A loss by knockout to Salvador

Gomez's (R) powerful right grotesquely distorts the jaw of Derrick Holmes. The referee called a halt to this August 22, 1980, match after Holmes was knocked down eight times. Holmes required surgery to repair his broken jaw.

IN THE RING	WON 44	LOST 3	DRAWS 1	TB 48	KO 42	W 2	WF 0	D 1	KO'd 3	L 0	LF 0

Date		Opponent	Site	Result / Rounds		Title	Wt.
1974							
Nov 16		Jacinto Fuentes	Panama City	D	6	—	120
Dec 21		Mario Hernandez	San Jose, Costa Rica	KO	1	—	—
1975							
Feb 16		Jorge Bernal	Panama City	TKO	1	—	119
Mar 2		Antonio DaSilva	Panama City	KO	2	—	118
May 3		Jose Jimenez	Panama City	KO	1	—	120
Jun 21		Jacinto Fuentes	Panama City	KO	2	—	119
Aug 2		Clotilde Garcia	Managua, Nicaragua	KO	3	—	—
Sep 19		Joe Guevara	San Juan, PR	TKO	6	—	120
Dec 20	⑩	Andres Hernandez	San Juan	TKO	8	—	119
1976							
Feb 20		Cornell Hall	San Juan	KO	3	—	120
Apr 5		Rick Quijano	San Juan	TKO	1	—	120
May 8		Sak Lempthong	San Juan	TKO	3	—	122
Jul 19		Albert Davila	San Juan	TKO	3	—	120
Aug 16		Tony Rocha	San Juan	TKO	2	—	120
Oct 11		Jose Medel	San Juan	KO	4	—	122
1977							
Feb 12		John Meza	San Juan	TKO	2	—	118
May 21	♛	Dong-Kyun Yum	Hato Rey, PR	KO	12	Won-WBC-JFE (SB)	121
Jul 11	⑩	Raul Tirado	Hato Rey	KO	5	Ret-WBC-JFE (SB)	122
1978							
Jan 19		Royal Kobayashi	Kitakyushu, Japan	KO	3	Ret-WBC-JFE (SB)	121
Apr 8		Juan Lopez	Bayamon, PR	TKO	7	Ret-WBC-JFE (SB)	121
Jun 2		Sakad Porntavee	Korat, Thailand	TKO	3	Ret-WBC-JFE (SB)	121
Sep 9		Leonardo Cruz	San Juan	TKO	13	Ret-WBC-JFE (SB)	122
Oct 28		Carlos Zarate★	Hato Rey	TKO	5	Ret-WBC-JFE (SB)	121
1979							
Mar 9		Nestor ("Baba") Jimenez	New York	KO	5	Ret-WBC-JFE (SB)	122
May 21		Nelson Cruz-Tamariz	New York	KO	2	—	125
Jun 16		Julio Hernandez	Hato Rey	TKO	5	Ret-WBC-JFE (SB)	122
Sep 28		Carlos Mendoza	Las Vegas	TKO	10	Ret-WBC-JFE (SB)	122
Oct 26	⑩	Nicky Perez	New York	KO	5	Ret-WBC-JFE (SB)	122
1980							
Feb 3		Ruben Valdez	Las Vegas	TKO	6	Ret-WBC-JFE (SB)	122
Apr 27		Eddie Ndukwu	San Juan	TKO	4	—	129
Aug 22		Derrik Holmes	Las Vegas	TKO	5	Ret-WBC-JFE (SB)	122
Dec 13	⑩	Jose Cervantes	Miami	KO	3	Ret-WBC-JFE (SB)	122
1981							
Jun 20		Raul Silva	San Juan	KO	3	—	128
Aug 21	♛	Salvador Sanchez★	Las Vegas	TKO'd	8	For-WBC-FE	126
1982							
Jan 9		Jose Gonzalez	San Juan	TKO	7	—	129
Feb 20		Jose Soto	San Juan	KO	2	—	125
Mar 27	⑩	Juan Meza	Atlantic City	TKO	6	Ret-WBC-JFE (SB)	121
Jun 11		Juan Lopez	Las Vegas	KO	10	Ret-WBC-JFE (SB)	121

Date		Opponent	Location	Result	Rnd	Title	Page
Aug 18	⑩	Ruberto Rubaldino	San Juan	KO	8	Ret-WBC-JFE (SB)	122
Dec 3	⑩	Lupe Pintor	New Orleans	TKO	14	Ret-WBC-JFE (SB)	121
1983							
Apr 23		Ivan Zamuco	Ponce, PR	TKO	3	—	133
Dec 14		Eladio Santana	Hato Rey	TKO	2	—	133
1984							
Mar 31	♛	Juan LaPorte	Hato Rey	W	12	Won-WBC-FE	125
Dec 8	⑩	Azumah Nelson★	San Juan	KO'd	11	Lost-WBC-FE	125
1985							
May 19	♛	Rocky Lockridge	San Juan	W	15	Won-World (WBA)-JL	129
1986							
May 24	⑩	Alfredo Layne	San Juan	TKO'd	9	Lost-World (WBA)-JL	130
1988							
Jul 30		Mario Gonzalez	Miami Beach	TKO	6	—	138
1989							
Jul 19		Mario Salazar	Hallandale, FL	TKO	2	—	142

Sanchez interrupted Gomez's nearly perfect record, and he never had to submit to the judges' ruling again until he won a decision over Juan LaPorte in 1984.

In 1977, Gomez fought the nearly invincible Dong-Kyun Yum for the WBC super bantamweight title. It was Gomez's seventeenth pro fight. In round one, Yum knocked Gomez down with a sweeping left hook. The shocked Gomez allowed Yum to control rounds two and three as well. By round four, Gomez had recovered, and he unleashed a variety of punches to seize control of the bout. In the twelfth, Gomez knocked Yum out—Yum's first knockout in 62 fights—and was the new champion. Gomez would later call this victory his greatest thrill in boxing.

In 1978, Gomez defended his title against Hall of Famer Carlos Zarate. At that time, Zarate was undefeated in 52 bouts. Zarate took the initiative in the first three rounds, although Gomez scored frequently. In the fourth, Gomez exploded, knocking Zarate down three times in a round which lasted an extra fifteen seconds. Gomez floored Zarate once more in the fifth before the contest was stopped.

Gomez's knockout string continued until he challenged Sanchez in Las Vegas in 1981 for the WBC featherweight title. In a fight called "The Battle of the Little Giants," fans saw Sanchez knock Gomez down twice before stopping him in the eighth round. A proposed rematch never took place due to Sanchez's death in an automobile accident.

LOSSES

Who's the boxer with the most losses? It's Arnold ("Kid") Sheppard, a welterweight from Cardiff, Wales. Sheppard suffered a record 154 defeats. Along the way he also won 96 fights and drew 36. In a thirteen-year career spanning the period from 1926 to 1939, the game Sheppard often fought hurt. Seldom stopped, an amazing 222 of his bouts went the full distance.

Gomez (R) sends Nestor ("Baba") Jimenez down to the canvas in a March 9, 1979, super bantamweight title defense in New York. This bout was the seventh of seventeen successful title defenses for Gomez.

After this loss, Gomez returned to the super bantamweight division where he continued unbeaten. He KO'd contenders Juan Meza, Roberto Rubaldino, and Lupe Pintor in 1982. In 1983, he relinquished his title and moved up to featherweight. In 1984, Gomez challenged Juan LaPorte for the WBC featherweight title. Gomez won a twelve-round decision to capture the title. Azumah Nelson dethroned him in Gomez's first title defense, knocking him out in eleven in San Juan in December 1984.

Gomez was undaunted by this loss, however, and five months later, won his third championship when he decisioned Rocky Lockridge for the world junior lightweight belt, a title he held for just under a year before losing it to Alfredo Layne. Three times a champion, Gomez fought once in 1988 and once in 1989 before retiring with a secure reputation as an excellent puncher with fine defensive skills. In retirement, Gomez moved to Venezuela where he struggled with drug addiction. After serving time in prison for drug offenses, he overcame his chemical dependencies and returned to boxing as a trainer and manager.

CHIQUITA GONZALEZ

JUNIOR FLYWEIGHT

Right-handed; 5′1″; 107–110 lbs.

45 bouts, 9/4/1984 to 7/15/1995

Manager: Rafael Mendoza

WBC Junior Flyweight Champion 1989–90, 1991–93
World Jr Flyweight Champ 1994–95

Hall of Fame Induction: 2006

Born: 3/25/1966, Nezahualcóyotl, Mexico

Named: Humberto Gonzalez

Though Humberto ("Chiquita") Gonzalez tipped the scales at only 108 pounds as a junior flyweight, he packed surprising power. He recorded 31 knockouts in 43 victories. Gonzalez was born in Nezahualcóyotl, Mexico, on March 25, 1966. He began boxing at a young age and turned professional after compiling an unblemished 23-0 record as an amateur. His first professional fight was a four-round decision over Jorge Ortega in Mexico City on September 4, 1984. Gonzalez continued to rack up wins. On September 26, 1987, he decisioned Jorge Cano in twelve rounds to take the Mexican junior flyweight title.

On June 25, 1989, Gonzalez fought outside Mexico for the first time when he traveled to Chonju, South Korea, where he met Yul-Woo Lee for the WBC

Chiquita Gonzalez (R) connects with a left to the jaw of Armando Diaz in their November 17, 1993, fight in Atlantic City. Benjy Jr. Esteves is the referee. Gonzalez took the ten-round decision.

IN THE RING	WON 42	LOST 3	DRAWS 0	TB 45	KO 31	W 11	WF 0	D 0	KO'd 3	L 0	LF 0

Date	Opponent	Site	Result / Rounds		Title	Wt.
1984						
Sep 4	Jorge Ortega	Mexico City	W	4	—	—
Dec 19	Narciso Perez	Mexico City	TKO	1	—	—
1985						
Feb 20	Carmelo Perez	Mexico City	TKO	1	—	—
Apr 20	Francisco Villagomez	Mexico City	TKO	1	—	—
Jun 8	Martin Alvarez	Mexico City	TKO	2	—	—
Jul 27	Otilio Gallegos	Mexico City	TKO	2	—	—
Sep 7	Eduardo Ramirez	Mexico City	KO	4	—	—
Nov 9	Javier Alvarez	Mexico City	TKO	1	—	—
Dec 14	Carlos Rezago	Mexico City	KO	5	—	—
1986						
Mar 15	Martin Perez	Mexico City	TKO	2	—	—
May 22	Sergio Medina	Nezahualcóyotl, Mexico	KO	3	—	—
Jun 18	Alcides Hernandez	Mexico City	TKO	2	—	—
Jul 14	Martin Ortega	Mexico City	KO	1	—	—
Oct 8	Agustin Macias	Mexico City	TKO	4	—	—
Dec 6	Jorge Gutierrez	Mexico City	TKO	6	—	—
1987						
Feb 22	Javier Alonso	Acapulco, Mexico	KO	1	—	—
May 9	Ruben Padilla	Mexico City	TKO	7	—	—
Jun 13	Santiago Mendez	Mexico City	TKO	8	—	—
Jul 25	Jose Manuel Diaz	Mexico City	KO	2	—	—
Sep 26	Jorge Cano	Cancun, Mexico	W	12	Won-Mexico-JFL	108
1988						
Mar 5	Jose Luis Zepeda	Tijuana, Mexico	KO	6	Ret-Mexico-JFL	108
Jun 4	Javier Varguez	Mexico City	TKO	5	Ret-Mexico-JFL	108
Oct 22	Jorge Rivera	Cozumel, Mexico	KO	4	—	—
1989						
Jun 25	Yul-Woo Lee	Chonju, South Korea	W	12	Won-WBC-JFL	106
Dec 9	Jung-Koo Chang	Taegu, South Korea	W	12	Ret-WBC-JFL	108
1990						
Mar 24	Francisco Tejedor	Mexico City	KO	3	Ret-WBC-JFL	108
Jun 4	Luis Monzote	Inglewood, CA	TKO	3	Ret-WBC-JFL	107
Jul 23	Jung-Keun Lim	Inglewood	TKO	5	Ret-WBC-JFL	107
Aug 25	Jorge Rivera	Cancun	TKO	9	Ret-WBC-JFL	108
Dec 19	Rolando Pascua	Inglewood	KO'd	6	Lost-WBC-JFL	107
1991						
Mar 15	Rey Hernandez	Ciudad Juarez, Mexico	TKO	9	—	—
Jun 3	Melchor Cob Castro	Las Vegas	W	12	Reg-WBC-JFL	108
1992						
Jan 27	Domingo Sosa	Inglewood	W	12	Ret-WBC-JFL	107
Jun 7	Kwang-Sun Kim	Seoul	TKO	12	Ret-WBC-JFL	108
Sep 14	Napa Kiatwanchai	Inglewood	KO	2	Ret-WBC-JFL	108
Dec 7	Melchor Cob Castro	Inglewood	W	12	Ret-WBC-JFL	108
1993						
Mar 13	Michael Carbajal★	Las Vegas	KO'd	7	For-WBC/IBF-JFL	107
Aug 28	Pablo Tiznado	Inglewood	W	10	—	109
Nov 17	Armando Diaz	Atlantic City	W	10	—	109

1994						
Feb 19	Michael Carbajal★	Inglewood	W	12	Won-WBC/IBF-JFL	107
Jul 8	Armando Diaz	Inglewood	TKO	3	—	110
Sep 10	Juan Domingo Cordoba	Stateline, NV	TKO	8	Ret-WBC/IBF-JFL	108
Nov 12	Michael Carbajal★	Mexico City	W	12	Ret-WBC/IBF-JFL	107
1995						
Mar 31	Jesus Zuniga	Anaheim, CA	KO	5	Ret-WBC/IBF-JFL	108
Jul 15	Saman Sorjaturong	Inglewood	TKO'd	7	Lost-WBC/IBF-JFL	107

junior flyweight title. Gonzalez earned a unanimous decision to take the crown. His first defense came six months later, again in South Korea. This time the opponent was Jung-Koo Chang. Once again, Gonzalez earned a unanimous decision. He defended his title at home with a third-round knockout of Francisco Tejedor, a future flyweight champ. Gonzalez's first fight in the United States was his title defense against Luis Monzote at the Great Western Forum in Inglewood, California. He stopped Monzote in the third to retain the belt. It appeared that Gonzalez was almost unstoppable until he faced unheralded Rolando Pascua again at the Great Western Forum on December 19, 1990. Gonzalez, who had never lost a fight before—either at the amateur or professional level—was stopped in the sixth round.

Gonzalez regained the title on June 3, 1991, in Las Vegas when he decisioned the classy boxer Melchor Cob Castro who had taken the crown from Pascua. He defended his title successfully with a decision win over previously undefeated Domingo Sosa again at the Forum. After three more successful defenses, he faced fellow Hall of Famer Michael Carbajal, the IBF junior flyweight champion. For the first time ever, the junior flyweight weight class received widespread attention due to these two great fighters. Their meeting in Las Vegas on March 13, 1993, was the first bout in which two fighters in this weight class were guaranteed $1 million each. It was also the first junior flyweight bout to headline a pay-per-view card. Fans got plenty of what they were looking for as soon as the fight began. The powerful Gonzalez attempted to brawl with Carbajal. He knocked Carbajal down in the second and fifth rounds. The second-round knockdown showcased Gonzalez's prodigious skills. Gonzalez landed a left and then a right to the body before getting out of Carbajal's range. He then switched to southpaw and threw a right-left-right combination for the knockdown. Gonzalez was leading on all three cards when Carbajal knocked him out in the seventh round with an incredibly fast left hook. *The Ring* named this action-packed bout its 1993 Fight of the Year.

In the rematch on February 19, 1994, at the Great Western Forum before 10,333—including many fans from Mexico who traveled to cheer on their countryman—Gonzalez changed his style. He credited his trainer Nacho Beristain for advising him to employ a great deal of lateral movement and footwork to confuse Carbajal, who had expected the same tactics from Gonzalez as in their first fight. Gonzalez wanted to conserve his strength so that he would be fresh in the later rounds. In contrast to the first fight, there was not much action in the first five rounds—though Gonzalez did suffer a cut, which bled profusely, over his left eye. Gonzalez believed that the cut was caused by an accidental head butt, but Carbajal thought it came from his right. Referee Lou Filippo ruled that the cut was caused by a punch. It appeared that the fight might be stopped late in the fourth round when doctors examined the cut, but they allowed the fight to continue. In the sixth, Carbajal backed Gonzalez up with a big right hand. In the seventh round, the pair started slugging away. In the eighth, despite an effective Gonzalez left-uppercut/right-uppercut combination, Carbajal won the round on two cards. Over the last four rounds Gonzalez dominated. He was awarded a unanimous decision and became the junior flyweight champion for the third time.

After a knockout title defense over Juan Domingo Cordoba, Gonzalez faced Carbajal for the third time. This time the setting was a bull ring in Mexico City, on November 12, 1994, in front of 15,000 fans and a pay-per-view television audience. This fight was a far cry from the first one. Gonzalez reemployed his boxing tactics from the second fight, but Carbajal seemed reluctant to attack the champion. Gonzalez earned a majority decision.

After another victorious title defense, Gonzalez faced Saman Sorjaturong on July 15, 1995, at the Forum in Inglewood, California. In contrast to the somnambulant third Carbajal fight, the action in this bout was such that it earned Fight of the Year honors for 1995. Gonzalez knocked Sorjaturong down twice before he was knocked out in the seventh. The three-time world champion announced his retirement at age 29. In Mexico, he has followed in the footsteps of his father as a butcher. Gonzalez owns three butcher shops and sometimes dons the white apron himself.

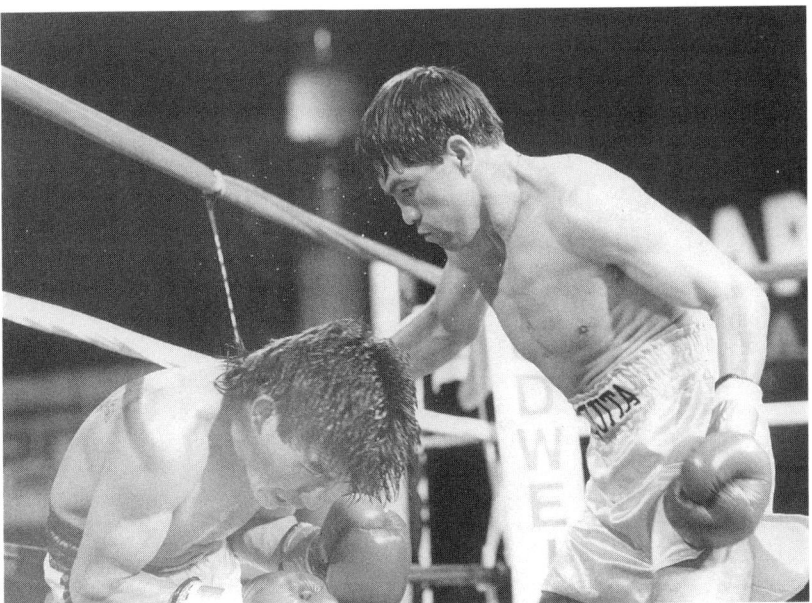

Chiquita Gonzalez (R) pounds Armando Diaz along the ropes in their November 17, 1993, fight at Caesars Palace in Atlantic City. Gonzalez took the ten-round decision.

BILLY GRAHAM

WELTERWEIGHT

Right-handed; 5'8"; 127–156 lbs.
126 bouts, 4/14/1941 to 4/1/1955
Manager: Irving Cohen
Hall of Fame Induction: 1992
Born: 9/9/1922, New York, NY
Named: William Walter Graham
Died: 1/22/1992

Though never a champion, Billy Graham won over one hundred fights and made innumerable friends in a career which lasted fourteen years. Born on the East Side of New York, Graham was encouraged to box by his father and began fighting at the local Catholic Boys' Club. Legend has it that at the age of eleven, he beat a youngster named Walker Smith, who would later become known as Sugar Ray Robinson. As a teenager, Graham was denied entrance to the Golden Gloves competition because of a heart murmur.

Graham turned professional in 1941. For the first five years of his career, he fought exclusively in the New York/New Jersey area and was undefeated in his first 58 fights. Though Graham was ranked the tenth-best lightweight in 1946 in the annual rankings by *The Ring*, he did not achieve national prominence until 1950. By then a veteran of over 90 fights, Graham fought the popular Kid Gavilan twice, with each winning a decision.

In 1951, Graham challenged Gavilan for the world welterweight title. Although experts agreed that Graham dominated the fight, Gavilan won the

Kid Gavilan (L) was ruled the winner of this August 29, 1951, title defense against Billy Graham. Ringside observers gave the bout to Graham all the way. Reportedly gangsters "got to" one of the judges.

IN THE RING	WON 102	LOST 15	DRAWS 9	TB 126	KO 26	W 76	WF 0	D 9	KO'd 0	L 15	LF 0

Date	Opponent	Site	Result / Rounds		Title	Wt.
1941						
Apr 14	Connie Savoie	New York	KO	4	—	130
May 5	Frankie Van	New York	W	4	—	128
May 19	Jimmy Kemp	New York	D	4	—	128
Jun 9	Joey Manfro	New York	D	4	—	129
Jun 24	Bobby Henry	New York	W	4	—	129
Jul 30	Joey Agro	New York	D	4	—	128
Sep 30	Bobby Henry	White Plains, NY	W	4	—	129
Oct 13	Bobby Henderson	Brooklyn	W	4	—	129
Nov 10	Bobby Henderson	New York	W	4	—	130
Nov 18	Bobby Henderson	White Plains	W	4	—	131
Nov 24	Mike Martinez	New York	KO	3	—	131
Dec 9	Louis LaSalle	White Plains	D	4	—	129
Dec 18	Al Guido	New York	W	4	—	132
1942						
Jan 19	Joe Maldonado	New York	W	4	—	130
Jan 26	Julian Malavez	New York	KO	3	—	130
Feb 2	Bobby Henry	New York	KO	2	—	131
Feb 17	Harry Diduck	Brooklyn	W	6	—	131
Feb 19	Terry Amico	Elizabeth, NJ	KO	2	—	—
Feb 24	Harry Diduck	New York	W	6	—	130
Mar 3	Al Guido	Brooklyn	W	6	—	130
Mar 23	Al Guido	New York	W	6	—	132
Apr 1	Lew Maxwell	Elizabeth	W	6	—	—
Apr 7	Davey Crawford	New York	W	6	—	131
Apr 16	Tom Sawyer	Elizabeth	KO	1	—	—
Apr 27	Al Simmons	New York	KO	1	—	132
Apr 30	Lew Maxwell	Elizabeth	W	6	—	—
May 15	Moe Weiss	New York	W	4	—	132
Jun 1	Bob Root	New York	W	6	—	133
Jun 5	Jimmy Anest	Elizabeth	W	6	—	132
Jun 9	Wallace Brown	New York	D	6	—	131
Jul 3	Bobby Henderson	Elizabeth	W	6	—	—
Jul 9	Jeff Holloway	Brooklyn	KO	5	—	135
Jul 23	Ted Christie	Newark, NJ	KO	2	—	—
Aug 1	Cedric Flournoy	New York	KO	3	—	133
Sep 14	Gus Levine	New York	W	8	—	134
Sep 19	Julian Malavez	Brooklyn	W	6	—	133
Oct 12	Johnny Rudd	New York	TKO	2	—	135
Oct 15	Thaddeus Cabey	Elizabeth	KO	3	—	—
Oct 27	Mickey LaRosa	Brooklyn	KO	5	—	135
Nov 5	Lew Maxwell	Jersey City, NJ	W	6	—	—
Nov 13	Joey Varoff	New York	D	6	—	134
1944						
Apr 13	Ralph Pacheco	Hyde Park, NY	W	6	—	—
Apr 19	Jackie Smallwood	Elizabeth	KO	1	—	140
May 4	Sammy Mammone	Hyde Park	W	6	—	142
May 10	Sammy Mammone	Elizabeth	W	6	—	140
May 31	Doug Carter	Elizabeth	W	6	—	—
Jun 26	George Johnson	New York	TKO	5	—	140

Date		Opponent	Location	Result	Rounds		Weight
Jun 28		Johnny Williams	Elizabeth	KO	4	—	140
Jul 10		Jimmy Pierce	New York	W	6	—	140
Jul 17		Julian Malavez	Newark	W	6	—	—
Jul 21		Jackie Connor	Long Branch, NJ	TKO	6	—	140
1945							
Mar 5		Tommy Mills	New York	W	6	—	137
Mar 17		Herbie Solomon	Brooklyn	W	6	—	138
Mar 31		Jeff Holloway	Brooklyn	W	8	—	138
Apr 21		Johnny Williams	Brooklyn	W	8	—	139
May 25		Joey Manfro	New York	W	6	—	137
Aug 13		Johnny Rinaldi	New York	TKO	4	—	137
Aug 27		Donnie Maes	New York	TKO	1	—	134
Sep 11		Tony Pellone	New York	L	10	—	135
Oct 8		Cabey Lewis	New York	W	10	—	134
1946							
Mar 25		Charley Milan	Baltimore	W	10	—	139
Apr 15		Pat Scanlon	New York	TKO	6	—	140
May 8		Pedro Biesca	New York	W	8	—	140
May 13		Frankie Carto	New York	KO	9	—	136
May 20		Jimmy Joyce	Baltimore	W	10	—	137
Aug 20		Vic Costa	New York	W	8	—	139
Aug 30	⑩	Tony Pellone	New York	L	10	—	139
Oct 15		Cleo Shans	New York	W	10	—	141
Oct 25		Doll Rafferty	New York	W	10	—	141
1947							
Jan 17		Ruby Kessler	New York	W	10	—	141
Mar 21	⑩	Tippy Larkin	New York	L	10	—	139
May 27		Ernie Petrone	Brooklyn	W	8	—	141
Jun 2	⑩	Aldo Minelli	New York	W	8	—	142
Sep 12		Billy Seep	Worcester, MA	KO	2	—	147
Oct 13		Pat Giordano	Rochester, NY	W	10	—	146
Oct 24		Willie Beltram	New York	W	10	—	140
Nov 21		Rocco Rossano	New York	W	10	—	142
1948							
Jan 20		Jimmy Joyce	New York	TKO	5	—	141
Feb 2		Patsy Brandino	Brooklyn	W	10	—	142
Jun 21		Patsy Brandino	New York	W	8	—	142
Jul 16		Maxie Starr	New York	W	8	—	138
Aug 26	⑩	Terry Young	New York	W	10	—	139
Dec 2		Joe Lucignano	New York	W	8	—	145
Dec 13		Billy Lee	Newark	W	8	—	143
1949							
Jan 26		Fitzie Pruden	New York	W	10	—	144
Feb 7		Eddie Thomas	London	L	10	—	142
Mar 4	⑩	Paddy DeMarco	New York	L	10	—	141
Apr 9		Mike Koballa	Brooklyn	W	8	—	145
Jun 7		Sonny Hampton	Wilkes-Barre, PA	W	10	—	—
Jul 8		Jimmy Sanders	Long Beach, NY	W	10	—	141
Sep 19		James Cox	Miami	KO	3	—	144
Oct 19		Jean Walczak	New York	W	10	—	144
Nov 23		Tony LaBua	New York	W	10	—	142
1950							
Jan 18		Tony Pellone	New York	W	10	—	144
Feb 10	⑩	Kid Gavilan★	New York	W	10	—	144
Apr 14		Phil Burton	Wilkes-Barre	W	10	—	146

Date		Opponent	Location	Result	Rounds		Weight
Apr 18		Jimmy Sanders	Cleveland	W	10	—	145
Jul 14		Tommy Bazzano	Long Beach, NY	W	10	—	145
Aug 14		Sammy Mastrean	Brooklyn	W	10	—	145
Oct 24		Kid Dussart	Toledo, OH	W	10	—	145
Nov 17	⑩	Kid Gavilan★	New York	L	10	—	145
Dec 19		Tommy Ciarlo	New York	W	8	—	146
1951							
Aug 2		Billy Jenkins	North Adams, MA	W	8	—	148
Aug 29	♛	Kid Gavilan★	New York	L	15	For-World-W	145
Oct 8		Mario Trigo	Milwaukee	D	10	—	147
Oct 22		Jimmy Brown	Holyoke, MA	KO	4	—	147
Nov 1		Johnny Cesario	Canton, OH	W	10	—	148
Nov 27		Danny Stepanovitch	Cincinnati	W	10	—	147
1952							
Feb 15		Jimmy Herring	New York	W	10	—	148
Mar 24		Mike Gillo	Holyoke	W	10	—	149
Apr 14		Art Soto	San Francisco	W	10	—	149
May 16	⑩	Rocky Castellani	New York	D	10	—	147
Aug 4	⑩	Joey Giardello★	Brooklyn	L	10	—	148
Aug 20		Carmen Basilio★	Chicago	W	10	—	148
Oct 5	♛	Kid Gavilan★	Havana, Cuba	L	15	For-World-W	146
Dec 19	⑩	Joey Giardello★	New York	L	10	—	149
1953							
Jan 29	⑩	Art Aragon	Los Angeles	W	10	—	147
Mar 6	⑩	Joey Giardello★	New York	W	12	—	149
Jun 6	⑩	Carmen Basilio★	Syracuse, NY	L	12	—	147
Jul 25	⑩	Carmen Basilio★	Syracuse	D	12	—	147
Dec 18	⑩	Paddy Young	New York	W	10	—	150
1954							
Jun 10		Charlie Simmons	Danbury, CT	TKO	6	—	155
Jul 19	·	Chris Christensen	Brooklyn	L	10	—	150
Oct 21	⑩	Ramon Fuentes	Los Angeles	L	10	—	150
1955							
Mar 4		Chico Vejar	New York	L	10	—	148
Apr 1		Chico Vejar	Syracuse	L	10	—	156

decision. Regarding the verdict, matchmaker Teddy Brenner said, "If a fighter ever won a fight, Graham won that fight. It ranks among the worst decisions I've ever seen." In Brenner's autobiography, he stated that Arthur Schwartz, one of the judges in the fight, had been pressured to give the decision to Gavilan by "certain figures." Apparently, before the fight, Irving Cohen, Graham's manager, had refused to give a percentage of Graham's contract to underworld denizen Frankie Carbo. The New York State Athletic Commission reviewed the matter in 1985 but did not change the decision.

Graham lost his rematch with Gavilan in Havana. He both won and lost to Joey Giardello and Carmen Basilio in 1952 and 1953, and retired two years later. Never a hard puncher, Graham did not record many knockouts in his career, but he was never knocked down either. A popular fighter, Graham won the respect of the entire boxing community. He worked for liquor companies after he left the ring—including 25 years with Seagram's. He was also a boxing judge and referee. Graham died of cancer at age 70.

ROCKY GRAZIANO

MIDDLEWEIGHT

Right-handed; 5'7"; 147–162 lbs.

83 bouts, 3/31/1942 to 9/17/1952

Managers: Irving Cohen,
Jack Hurley

Middleweight Champion 1947–48

Hall of Fame Induction: 1991

Born: 1/1/1922, New York, NY

Named: Thomas Rocco Barbella

Died: 5/22/90

Though Rocky Graziano often found himself embroiled in controversy during his boxing career, he emerged as one of the most popular fighters of the 1940s and early '50s. Born in New York City, Graziano overcame an impoverished, delinquent boyhood to become the middleweight champion of the world. After a stint in reform school, he entered the Metropolitan AAU boxing tournament in New York as a replacement for another fighter. Graziano won the tournament—his first organized boxing experience. Graziano served time in prison at Riker's Island and later, while in the Army, in military prison for striking an officer. He then officially began his professional

Satin-robed Graziano is at the center of a discussion. Graziano stayed in the spotlight after his ring career ended. He acted in TV shows and movies, exhibited his paintings, and wrote his autobiography.

IN THE RING	WON 67	LOST 10	DRAWS 6	TB 83	KO 52	W 14	WF 1	D 6	KO'd 3	L 7	LF 0

Date	Opponent	Site	Result / Rounds		Title	Wt.
1942						
Mar 31	Curtis Hightower	Brooklyn	KO	2	—	152
Apr 6	Mike Mastandrea	New York	KO	3	—	152
Apr 14	Kenny Blackmar	Brooklyn	KO	1	—	151
Apr 20	Godfrey Howell	New York	D	4	—	150
Apr 28	Charley Ferguson	Brooklyn	L	4	—	152
May 4	Ed Lee	New York	KO	4	—	151
May 12	Godfrey Howell	Brooklyn	KO	4	—	149
May 25	Lou Miller	New York	D	6	—	148
1943						
Jun 11	Gilbert Vasquez	Brooklyn	KO	1	—	144
Jun 16	Joe Curcio	Elizabeth, NJ	KO	4	—	—
Jun 24	Frankie Falco	Brooklyn	KO	5	—	148
Jul 8	Johnny Attelly	Brooklyn	TKO	2	—	148
Jul 22	Georgie Stevens	Brooklyn	KO	1	—	148
Jul 27	Randy Drew	Long Island City, NY	KO	1	—	149
Aug 12	Charley McPherson	Brooklyn	W	6	—	149
Aug 20	Ted Apostoli	New York	W	4	—	148
Aug 24	Tony Grey	Long Island City	KO	6	—	147
Sep 10	Joe Agosta	New York	L	6	—	149
Sep 21	Sonny Wilson	Brooklyn	W	8	—	151
Oct 5	Freddie Graham	Brooklyn	KO	1	—	150
Oct 13	Jimmy Williams	Elizabeth	TKO	2	—	151
Oct 27	Charley McPherson	Elizabeth	D	6	—	151
Nov 12	Steve Riggio	New York	L	6	—	149
Nov 30	Freddie Graham	Jersey City, NJ	W	8	—	—
Dec 6	Charley McPherson	New York	W	6	—	151
Dec 27	Milo Theodorescu	Newark, NJ	TKO	1	—	152
1944						
Jan 4	Harry Gray	Jersey City	W	8	—	152
Jan 7	Jerry Pittro	New York	TKO	1	—	153
Jan 18	Phil Enzenga	Brooklyn	TKO	5	—	154
Feb 9	Steve Riggio	New York	L	6	—	148
Feb 24	Manny Morales	Highland Park, NJ	KO	4	—	150
Mar 4	Leon Anthony	Brooklyn	KO	1	—	151
Mar 8	Harry Gary	Elizabeth	W	6	—	151
Mar 14	Ray Rovelli	Brooklyn	W	8	—	152
Apr 10	Bobby Brown	Washington, DC	KO	5	—	150
May 9	Freddie Graham	Washington, DC	KO	3	—	151

boxing career in 1942, although he had fought so-called amateur bouts for compensation before that.

By 1945, Graziano had started to make a name for himself, knocking out Billy Arnold and Bummy Davis. In 1946, the title war between Graziano and middleweight champ Tony Zale commenced. Zale ultimately got the best of Graziano but not until Graziano had worn the crown for a year. It started when Graziano challenged Zale for the championship in New York in a fight *The Ring's* International Ratings Panel called the fourth-greatest of all time. Both fighters had strong

Date		Opponent	Location	Result			
May 29		Tommy Mollis	Washington, DC	TKO	7	—	149
Jun 7		Larney Moore	Brooklyn	KO	2	—	152
Jun 27		Frankie Terry	Brooklyn	TKO	6	—	150
Jul 21		Tony Reno	Brooklyn	W	8	—	151
Aug 14		Jerry Fiorello	Long Island City	W	8	—	149
Sep 15		Frankie Terry	New York	D	8	—	151
Oct 6		Danny Kapilow	New York	D	10	—	152
Oct 24		Bernie Miller	Brooklyn	TKO	2	—	154
Nov 3	⑩	Harold Green	New York	L	10	—	150
Dec 22	⑩	Harold Green	New York	L	10	—	154
1945							
Mar 9	⑩	Billy Arnold	New York	TKO	3	—	152
Apr 17		Solomon Stewart	Washington, DC	KO	4	—	153
May 25		Al ("Bummy") Davis	New York	TKO	4	—	151
Jun 29	♛⑩	Freddie ("Red") Cochrane	New York	KO	10	—	153
Aug 24	♛⑩	Freddie ("Red") Cochrane	New York	KO	10	—	154
Sep 28	⑩	Harold Green	New York	KO	3	—	153
1946							
Jan 18		Sonny Horne	New York	W	10	—	155
Mar 29	♛	Marty Servo	New York	TKO	2	—	152
Sep 27	♛	Tony Zale★	New York	KO'd	6	For-World-M	154
1947							
Jun 10		Eddie Finazzo	Memphis, TN	TKO	1	—	159
Jun 16		Jerry Fiorello	Toledo, OH	TKO	5	—	159
Jul 16	♛	Tony Zale★	Chicago	TKO	6	Won-World-M	155
1948							
Apr 5		Sonny Horne	Washington, DC	W	10	—	160
Jun 10	⑩	Tony Zale★	Newark	KO'd	3	Lost-World-M	158
1949							
Jun 21		Bobby Claus	Wilmington, DE	KO	2	—	159
Jul 18		Joey Agosta	W. Springfield, MA	KO	2	—	159
Sep 14	⑩	Charley Fusari	New York	TKO	10	—	159
Dec 6		Sonny Horne	Cleveland	W	10	—	159
1950							
Mar 6		Joe Curcio	Miami	TKO	1	—	162
Mar 31		Tony Janiro	New York	D	10	—	159
Apr 24		Danny Williams	New Haven, CT	KO	3	—	161
May 9		Vinnie Cidone	Milwaukee	TKO	3	—	160
May 16		Henry Brimm	Buffalo, NY	KO	4	—	160
Oct 4		Gene Burton	Chicago	KO	7	—	160
Oct 16		Pete Mead	Milwaukee	KO	3	—	162
Oct 27		Tony Janiro	New York	W	10	—	158
Nov 27		Honey Johnson	Philadelphia	KO	4	—	158
1951							
Mar 19		Reuben Jones	Miami	KO	3	—	164
May 21		Johnny Greco	Montreal	KO	3	—	161
Jun 18		Freddie Lott	Baltimore	KO	5	—	162
Jul 10		Cecil Hudson	Kansas City, MO	TKO	3	—	162
Aug 6		Chuck Hunter	Boston	WD	2	—	164
Sep 19		Tony Janiro	Detroit	TKO	10	—	160
1952							
Feb 18		Eddie O'Neill	Louisville, KY	TKO	4	—	165
Mar 27		Roy Wouters	Minneapolis	TKO	1	—	164
Apr 16	♛	Sugar Ray Robinson★	Chicago	KO'd	3	For-World-M	159
Sep 17		Chuck Davey	Chicago	L	10	—	158

crowd appeal, and the fans went crazy as Zale and Graziano traded explosive punches. Zale knocked Graziano down in the first round. Then, just before the bell ended the third round, Graziano sent Zale through the ropes. Zale recovered to knock Graziano out with a left hook in the sixth.

In their rematch the next year in Chicago, Graziano got his revenge. Zale cut Graziano early and punished him severely in the third round, but Graziano recovered to knock Zale down in the sixth and then battered him at will along the ropes before the referee stopped the fight. In 1948, Zale knocked Graziano out in three to reclaim the title.

The Zale fights serve as prime examples of Graziano's style. A great slugger, Graziano was not a clever boxer. He absorbed a tremendous amount of punishment while he waited for the opening he needed to try for a knockout. His record of 52 knockouts in 83 fights is proof of his great punching ability.

Before the third Zale fight, Graziano's prison record was made public, and he temporarily lost his license to box in New York for not reporting an attempted bribe. The ban was hard on Graziano, and many observers, including noted boxing writer W.C. Heinz, believed the nine-month penalty was unduly harsh.

When Graziano then backed out of a scheduled fight in California with former champion Fred Apostoli, he drew the ire of West Coast boxing officials.

In 1952, Graziano went up against the middleweight champion Sugar Ray Robinson for one last title attempt. In the third round, Graziano floored Robinson, but Robinson quickly recovered and knocked Graziano out before the round was finished. Graziano fought just once more before retiring. He then wrote an extremely successful autobiography titled *Somebody Up There Likes Me*, which was later made into a movie starring Paul Newman. The colorful Graziano then had a lengthy career as an actor and commercial spokesman.

Defending champ Tony Zale (L) is frozen by Graziano's deadly overhand right. On July 16, 1947, Graziano took the title with a sixth-round TKO.

EMILE GRIFFITH

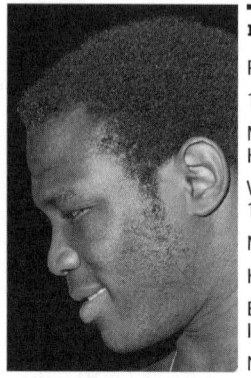

MIDDLEWEIGHT

Right-handed; 5′7½″; 144–162 lbs.

112 bouts, 6/2/1958 to 7/30/1977

Managers: Gil Clancy and Howard Albert

Welterweight Champion 1961, 1962–63, 1963–66

Mdlwt Champ 1966–67, 1967–68

Hall of Fame Induction: 1990

Born: 2/3/1938, St. Thomas, Virgin Islands

Named: Emile Alphonse Griffith

Emile Griffith held the welterweight championship three times and the middleweight championship twice. Born in the Virgin Islands, Griffith moved to New York when he was nineteen and found work as a stock boy at a millinery. Howard Albert, the owner of the millinery and later Griffith's co-manager, encouraged his employee to try boxing and sent him to Gil Clancy, who would ultimately serve as Griffith's co-manager and trainer. Under Clancy's tutelage, Griffith won the New York Golden Gloves and the Inter-City tournament in 1957. He turned professional the next year at age twenty.

Griffith quickly found success as a welterweight. He won 21 of his first 23 fights and in 1961, earned a shot at the welterweight title held by Benny ("Kid") Paret. In the fight, held at the Miami Beach Convention Hall, Paret had a slim lead until the thirteenth round when Griffith plied him with a left hook followed by a right to knock him out. Griffith lost the rematch in a split decision. He believed he had won the fight, and his opinion was shared by twelve boxing writers at ringside.

Six months later, Griffith met Paret for the third and final time in Madison

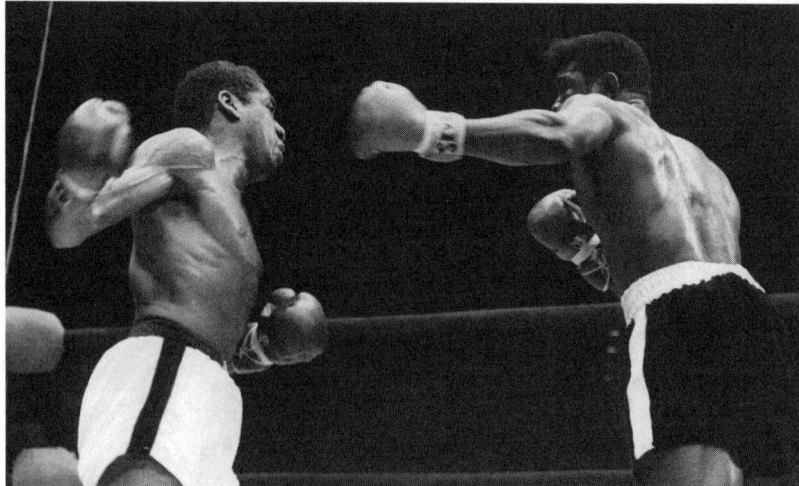

Griffith (R) retained his welterweight title in a decision over Luis Rodriguez in June 1964 at Las Vegas— the fourth and final fight of their classic series.

IN THE RING	WON 85	LOST 24	DRAWS 2	TB 112	KO 23	W 62	WF 0	D 2	KO'd 2	L 21	LF 1	NC 1

Date		Opponent	Site	Result / Rounds		Title	Wt.
1958							
Jun 2		Joe Parham	New York	W	4	—	157
Jun 23		Bobby Gibson	New York	W	4	—	149
Jul 21		Martin Leaks	New York	W	4	—	147
Oct 6		Art Cunningham	New York	W	6	—	146
Nov 17		Sergio Rios	New York	KO	3	—	147
Dec 15		Larry Jones	New York	KO	5	—	146
1959							
Jan 26		Gaylord Barnes	New York	KO	5	—	148
Feb 9		Willie Johnson	New York	KO	5	—	147
Feb 23		Barry Allison	New York	KO	5	—	147
Mar 23		Bobby Shell	New York	W	10	—	148
Apr 27		Mel Barker	New York	W	10	—	148
May 25		Willie Stevenson	New York	W	10	—	147
Aug 7		Kid Fichique	New York	W	10	—	147
Oct 26		Randy Sandy	New York	L	10	—	150
Nov 23		Ray Lancaster	New York	TKO	7	—	147
1960							
Jan 8		Roberto Pena	New York	w	10	—	146
Feb 12	⑩	Gaspar Ortega	New York	W	10	—	147
Mar 11	⑩	Denny Moyer	New York	W	10	—	150
Apr 26	⑩	Denny Moyer	Portland, OR	L	10	—	151
Jun 3	⑩	Jorge Fernandez	New York	W	10	—	147
Jul 25	⑩	Jorge Fernandez	New York	W	10	—	150
Aug 25	⑩	Florentino Fernandez	New York	W	10	—	149
Oct 22		Willie Toweel	New York	TKO	8	—	147
Dec 17	⑩	Luis Rodriguez★	New York	W	10	—	147
1961							
Apr 1	♛	Benny ("Kid") Paret	Miami Beach	KO	13	Won-World-W	145
Jun 3	⑩	Gaspar Ortega	Los Angeles	TKO	12	Ret-World-W	145
Jul 29	⑩	Yama Bahama	New York	W	10	—	150
Sep 30	⑩	Benny ("Kid") Paret	New York	L	15	Lost-World-W	147
Nov 4		Stanford Bulla	Hamilton, NY	TKO	4	—	155
Dec 23		Isaac Logart	New York	W	10	—	149
1962							
Feb 3		Johnny Torres	St. Thomas, VI	W	10	—	152
Mar 24	♛	Benny ("Kid") Paret	New York	TKO	12	Reg-World-W	144
Jul 13	⑩	Ralph DuPas	Las Vegas	W	15	Ret-World-W	145
Aug 18	⑩	Denny Moyer	Tacoma, WA	W	10	—	156
Oct 6		Don Fullmer	New York	W	10	—	151
Oct 17	⑩	Teddy Wright	Vienna	W	15	Won-Vac EBU World-JM	150
Dec 8	⑩	Jorge Fernandez	Las Vegas	TKO	9	Ret-World-W	145
1963							
Feb 3		Chris Christensen	Copenhagen	TKO	9	Ret-EBU World-JM	152
Mar 21	⑩	Luis Rodriguez★	Los Angeles	L	5	Lost-World-W	145
Jun 8	♛	Luis Rodriguez★	New York	W	15	Reg-World-W	146
Aug 10		Holly Mims	Saratoga Springs, NY	W	10	—	150
Oct 5		Jose Gonzalez	San Juan, PR	W	10	—	151
Dec 20		Rubin ("Hurricane") Carter	Pittsburgh	TKO'd	1	—	151
1964							
Feb 10	⑩	Ralph DuPas	Sydney	KO	3	—	149
Mar 11		Juan Duran	Rome	NC	7	—	154

Date		Opponent	Location	Result	Rounds	Title	Weight
Apr 14	⑩	Stan Harrington	Honolulu	KO	4	—	147
Jun 12	⑩	Luis Rodriguez★	Las Vegas	W	15	Ret-World-W	146
Sep 22	⑩	Brian Curvis	London	W	15	Ret-World-W	145
Dec 1		Dave Charnley	Wembley, England	TKO	9	—	148
1965							
Jan 21	⑩	Manuel Gonzalez	Houston	L	10	—	149
Mar 30	⑩	Jose Stable	New York	W	15	Ret-World-W	146
Jun 14	⑩	Eddie Pace	Honolulu	W	10	—	149
Aug 20	⑩	Don Fullmer	Salt Lake City	L	12	—	153
Sep 14		Gabe Terronez	Fresno, CA	KO	4	—	148
Oct 4		Harry Scott	Kensington, England	TKO	7	—	154
Dec 10	⑩	Manuel Gonzalez	New York	W	15	Ret-World-W	146
1966							
Feb 3		Johnny Brooks	Las Vegas	W	10	—	155
Apr 25	♛	Dick Tiger★	New York	W	10	Won-World-M	150
Jul 13	⑩	Joey Archer	New York	W	15	Ret-World-M	152
1967							
Jan 23	⑩	Joey Archer	New York	W	15	Ret-World-M	152
Apr 17	⑩	Nino Benvenuti★	New York	L	15	Lost-World-M	153
Sep 29	♛	Nino Benvenuti★	Flushing, NY	W	15	Reg-World-M	154
Dec 15		Remo Golfarini	Rome	KO	6	—	157
1968							
Mar 4	⑩	Nino Benvenuti★	New York	L	15	Lost-World-M	154
Jun 11		Andy Heilman	Oakland	W	12	—	157
Aug 6	⑩	Joe Harris	Philadelphia	W	12	—	157
Oct 29	⑩	Stan Hayward	Philadelphia	L	10	—	156
1969							
Feb 3	⑩	Andy Heilman	New York	W	10	—	156
May 12	⑩	Stan Hayward	New York	W	12	—	155
Jul 11		Dick DiVeronica	Syracuse, NY	TKO	7	—	152
Aug 15		Art Hernandez	Sioux Falls, SD	W	10	—	151
Oct 18	♛	Jose Napoles★	Inglewood, CA	L	15	For-World-W	144
1970							
Jan 28	⑩	Doyle Baird	Cleveland	W	10	—	161
Mar 11		Carlos Marks	New York	W	12	—	156
Jun 4	⑩	Tom Bogs	Copenhagen	W	10	—	159
Jul 15	⑩	Dick Tiger★	New York	W	10	—	157
Oct 17		Danny Perez	St. Thomas	W	10	—	—
Nov 10		Nate Collins	San Francisco	W	10	—	158
1971							
Mar 23	⑩	Rafael Gutierrez	San Francisco	W	10	—	155
Apr 10		Juan Ramos	St. Thomas	KO	2	—	—
May 3		Ernie Lopez	Las Vegas	W	10	—	154
Jul 26		Nessim Cohen	New York	W	10	—	156
Sep 25	♛	Carlos Monzon★	Buenos Aires	TKO'd	14	For-World-M	154
Dec 10		Danny McAloon	New York	W	10	—	154
1972							
Jan 31		Armando Muniz	Anaheim, CA	W	10	—	154
Feb 21		Jacques Kechichian	Paris	W	10	—	157
Mar 30	⑩	Ernie Lopez	Los Angeles	W	10	—	153
Sep 16		Joe DeNucci	Boston	W	10	—	156
Oct 11		Joe DeNucci	Boston	W	12	—	156
Dec 18	⑩	Jean Claude Bouttier	Paris	LD	7	—	159
1973							
Mar 12		Max Cohen	Paris	D	10	—	154
Jun 2	♛	Carlos Monzon★	Monte Carlo	L	15	For-World-M	157
Nov 1		Manny Gonzalez	Tampa	W	10	—	157
Nov 19	⑩	Tony Mundine	Paris	L	10	—	157

1974								
Feb 5	⑩	Tony Licata	Boston	L	12	For-Vac NABF-M	158	
May 25		Renato Garcia	Monte Carlo	W	10	—		
Oct 9	⑩	Bennie Briscoe	Philadelphia	W	10	—	160	
Nov 22	⑩	Vito Antuofermo	New York	L	10	—	158	
Dec 10	⑩	Donato Paduano	Montreal	W	10	—	157	
1975								
May 31	⑩	Jose Duran	Cali, Columbia	L	10	—	—	
Jul 23		Leo Saenz	Landover, MD	W	10	—	157	
Aug 9		Elijah Makhatini	Johannesburg	L	10	—	—	
Nov 7		Jose Chirino	Albany, NY	W	10	—	165	
1976								
Feb 9		Loucif Hamani	Paris	L	10	—	158	
Jun 26	⑩	Bennie Briscoe	Monte Carlo	D	10	—		
Sep 18	⑩	Eckhard Dagge	Berlin	L	15	For-WBC-JM	150	
Oct 24		Dino Del Cid	Cartagena, Colombia	TKO	4	—		
Dec 4		Frank Reiche	Hamburg, Germany	TKO	10	—	—	
1977								
Feb 2		Christy Elliott	New York	W	10	—	161	
Apr 15		Joel Bonnetaz	Periqueux, France	L	10	—	—	
Jul 19		Mayfield Pennington	Louisville, KY	L	10	—	159	
Jul 30	⑩	Alan Minter	Monte Carlo	L	10	—		

Square Garden in front of 7,600. Though knocked down early, Griffith controlled the fight and by the twelfth round was in such command that he blasted Paret along the ropes with multiple punches before referee Ruby Goldstein stopped him. Paret died soon after the fight as a result of this beating and residual damage done by his previous opponent, Gene Fullmer. Paret's death wore heavily on Griffith. "I would have quit," he said later, "but I didn't know how to do anything but fight."

Griffith did continue to fight, though perhaps with less of a will to finish off his opponents. He defended his welterweight title once before adding the new junior middleweight crown to his accomplishments with a win over Teddy Wright in Austria in 1962. Griffith lost the welterweight title to Luis Rodriguez in 1963 but decisioned Rodriguez the same year to win it back. Although he suffered a stunning one-round knockout at the hands of Rubin ("Hurricane") Carter in Pittsburgh late in 1963, the loss did not occur in a title fight.

Griffith defended his welterweight titles against several top contenders before going up a class in 1966 to take the world middleweight title with a decision over Dick Tiger. Nino Benvenuti beat Griffith the next year to claim the title, but in the rematch, Griffith battered Benvenuti, cutting his eye, mouth, and nose. Both judges gave Griffith the fight, with the referee calling it a draw. Griffith lost to Benvenuti in their third fight, the opener for the new Madison Square Garden.

Griffith continued to fight for nine more years, losing title bids to welterweight Jose Napoles and middleweight Carlos Monzon. A very likable fan favorite and a fixture of Madison Square Garden main events, Griffith combined speed, aggressiveness, and determination to post 85 victories in his career.

Griffith worked as a prison guard in retirement. A moving 2005 documentary film, *Ring of Fire,* reveals that the Paret ring death came after he called Griffith a derogatory term for homosexual at their weigh-in.

MARVELOUS MARVIN HAGLER

MIDDLEWEIGHT

Left-handed; 5'9½"; 155–163 lbs.

67 bouts, 5/18/1973 to 4/6/1987

Managers: Goody and Pat Petronelli

Middleweight Champion 1980–87

Hall of Fame Induction: 1993

Born: 5/23/1954, Newark, NJ

Marvelous Marvin Hagler successfully defended his middleweight title twelve times—second only to Carlos Monzon's fourteen title defenses. One of boxing's few southpaw champions, Hagler's heroic good looks were incidental to his astounding ring skills. He was a devastating puncher as well as an elegant boxer who could adapt his defense to any opponent's style.

Born in Newark, New Jersey, Hagler moved as a child with his family to Brockton, Massachusetts, the same town which produced Rocky Marciano. Hagler idolized Mickey Mantle and Willie Mays as a boy and dreamed of a baseball career until Floyd Patterson's emergence on the sports scene convinced him that he wanted to become a boxer.

In Brockton, Hagler started boxing under the direction of Goody and Pat

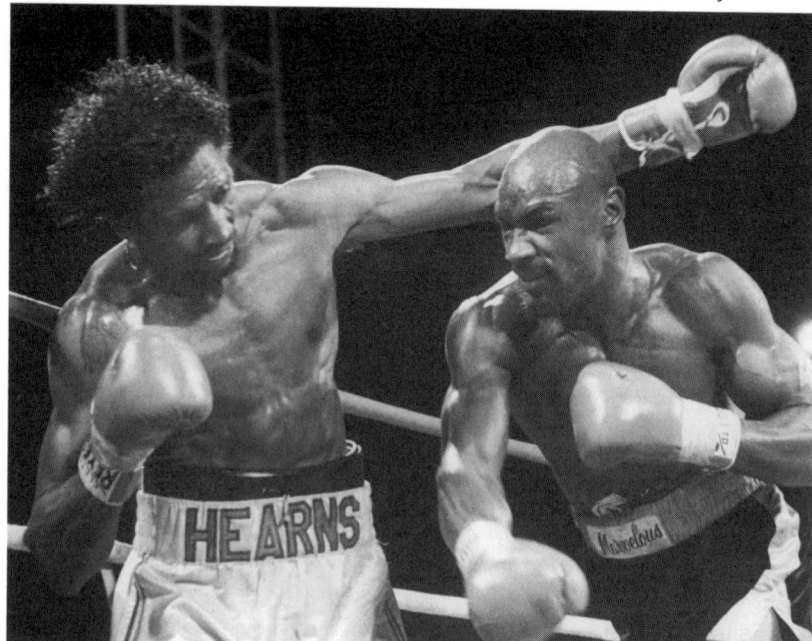

Shaved head glistening, Hagler follows through with a powerful right sending Tommy ("Hit Man") Hearns to the canvas at 2:01 of the 3rd in their April 15, 1985, bout at Caesar's Palace in Las Vegas.

IN THE RING	WON 62	LOST 3	DRAWS 2	TB 67	KO 52	W 9	WF 1	D 2	KO'd 0	L 3	LF 0

Date	Opponent	Site	Result / Rounds		Title	Wt.
1973						
May 18	Terry Ryan	Brockton, MA	TKO	2	—	160
Jul 25	Sonny Williams	Boston	W	6	—	160
Aug 8	Muhammad Smith	Boston	KO	2	—	163
Oct 6	Don Wigfall	Brockton	W	8	—	160
Oct 26	Cove Green	Brockton	TKO	4	—	161
Nov 18	Cocoa Kid	Brockton	KO	2	—	160
Dec 7	Manny Freitas	Portland, ME	TKO	1	—	161
Dec 18	James Redford	Boston	TKO	4	—	162
1974						
Feb 5	Bob Harrington	Boston	TKO	5	—	161
Apr 5	Tracy Morrison	Boston	TKO	8	—	162
May 4	Jim Redford	Brockton	TKO	2	—	157
May 30	Curtis Phillips	Portland, ME	KO	5	—	162
Jul 16	Robert Williams	Boston	TKO	3	—	159
Aug 13	Peachy Davis	New Bedford, MA	KO	1	—	160
Aug 30	Sugar Ray Seales	Boston	W	10	—	156
Oct 29	Morris Jordan	New Bedford	TKO	4	—	162
Nov 16	George Green	Brockton	KO	1	—	155
Nov 26	Sugar Ray Seales	Seattle	D	10	—	158
Dec 20	D.C. Walker	Boston	KO	2	—	159
1975						
Feb 15	Don Wigfall	Brockton	KO	5	—	158
Mar 31	Joey Blair	Boston	KO	2	—	160
Apr 14	Jimmy Owens	Boston	W	10	—	160
May 24	Jimmy Owens	Brockton	WD	6	—	160
Aug 7	Jesse Bender	Portland, ME	KO	1	—	159
Sep 30	Lamont Lovelady	Boston	TKO	7	—	161
Dec 20	Johnny Baldwin	Boston	W	10	—	160
1976						
Jan 13	⑩ Bobby Watts	Philadelphia	L	10	—	157
Feb 7	Matt Donovan	Boston	TKO	2	—	160
Mar 9	⑩ Willie Monroe	Philadelphia	L	10	—	161
Jun 2	Bob Smith	Taunton, MA	TKO	5	—	162
Aug 3	D.C. Walker	Providence, RI	TKO	6	—	160
Sep 14	Eugene Hart	Philadelphia	TKO	8	—	160
Dec 21	George Davis	Boston	TKO	6	—	162
1977						
Feb 15	Willie Monroe	Boston	TKO	12	Won-NABF-M	160
Mar 16	Reggie Ford	Boston	KO	3	—	161
Jun 10	Roy Jones	Hartford, CT	TKO	3	—	159
Aug 23	Willie Monroe	Philadelphia	TKO	2	—	159
Sep 24	Ray Phillips	Boston	TKO	7	—	158
Oct 15	Jim Henry	Providence	W	10	—	160
Nov 26	⑩ Mike Colbert	Boston	KO	12	Ret-NABF-M	160
1978						
Mar 4	Kevin Finnegan	Boston	TKO	9	—	158
Apr 7	Doug Demmings	Los Angeles	TKO	8	—	158
May 13	Kevin Finnegan	Boston	TKO	7	—	160
Aug 24	⑩ Bennie Briscoe	Philadelphia	W	10	—	159
Nov 11	Willie Warren	Boston	TKO	7	—	158

Date		Opponent	Location	Result	Round	Title	Weight
1979							
Feb 3		Ray Seales	Boston	TKO	1	—	161
Mar 12		Bob Patterson	Providence	TKO	3	—	162
May 26		Jaime Thomas	Portland, ME	KO	3	—	158
Jun 30		Norberto Cabrera	Monte Carlo	TKO	8	—	160
Nov 30	♛	Vito Antuofermo	Las Vegas	D	15	For-World-M	158
1980							
Feb 16	⑩	Loucif Hamani	Portland, ME	TKO	2	—	161
Apr 19		Bobby Watts	Portland, ME	TKO	2	—	158
May 17		Marcos Geraldo	Las Vegas	W	10	—	160
Sep 27	♛	Alan Minter	Wembley, England	TKO	3	Won-World-M	160
1981							
Jan 17	⑩	Fulgencio Obelmejias	Boston	TKO	8	Ret-World-M	159
Jun 13	⑩	Vito Antuofermo	Boston	TKO	5	Ret-World-M	160
Oct 3	⑩	Mustafa Hamsho	Rosemont, IL	TKO	11	Ret-World-M	157
1982							
Mar 7		William Lee	Atlantic City	KO	1	Ret-World-M	158
Oct 31	⑩	Fulgencio Obelmejias	San Remo, Italy	KO	5	Ret-World-M	158
1983							
Feb 11	⑩	Tony Sibson	Worcester, MA	KO	6	Ret-World-M	158
May 27	⑩	Wilford Scypion	Providence	KO	4	Ret-World-M	160
Nov 10		Roberto Duran	Las Vegas	W	15	Ret-World-M	157
1984							
Mar 30	⑩	Juan Roldan	Las Vegas	KO	10	Ret-World-M	159
Oct 19	⑩	Mustafa Hamsho	New York	KO	3	Ret-World-M	159
1985							
Apr 15	⑩	Thomas ("Hit Man") Hearns	Las Vegas	TKO	3	Ret-World-M	159
1986							
Mar 10	⑩	John Mugabi	Las Vegas	KO	11	Ret-World-M	159
1987							
Apr 6		Sugar Ray Leonard ★	Las Vegas	L	12	Lost-World-M	160

Petronelli, who remained as his co-managers for many years. He compiled a fine amateur record, including winning the 1973 national Amateur Athletic Union middleweight championship. He first fought professionally in May of that same year, with a second-round technical knockout of Terry Ryan.

Hagler won fourteen fights in a row before facing his first real test in Boston against former Olympic champion, Sugar Ray Seales. The fighters were closely matched, but Hagler won the ten-round decision. In a rematch several months later, they fought to a draw. In 1976, Hagler journeyed to Philadelphia and lost two hotly contested ten-round decisions to ranked fighters, Bobby ("Boogalou") Watts and Willie ("The Worm") Monroe.

By 1977, Hagler had earned a place as one of the top middleweight contenders in the annual rankings of *The Ring*. He took the NABF middleweight title from Monroe in 1977 and successfully defended it against contender Mike Colbert later that year.

Hagler did not receive a shot at the world middleweight title until 1979, when he fought Vito Antuofermo in Las Vegas. The bout was called a draw, angering Hagler who claimed he had won the fight. Less than a year later, Hagler took the title from new world champion, Alan Minter, in England. Hagler opened cuts around Minter's left eye and dominated the fight after the first round, forcing the referee to stop the fight in the third with Minter bleeding profusely.

Hagler showed his true mettle as champion. Every one of his fights from the victory over Minter to the end of his career was a championship bout. His first defense was against Fulgencio Obelmejias of Venezuela, a ranked fighter with an unblemished record of wins. Obelmejias was battered mercilessly by Hagler for eight rounds in Boston before the referee stopped the fight. In a rematch in San Remo, Italy, the next year, Hagler knocked out the big Venezuelan in five.

Hagler never ducked a contender and recorded knockouts in eleven of his twelve winning title defenses. His one victory by unanimous decision came over the great Roberto Duran, who although aging was still a formidable opponent. The WBC refused to recognize the bout as a title contest because it went fifteen and not twelve rounds, but Hagler was still generally acknowledged to be the champ. His victory over Thomas Hearns included an exciting first round which boxing historian Herbert Goldman labeled as one of the best first rounds of all time. The two slugged it out at a ferocious pace. Hagler won the hard-fought second round and dominated in the third when he knocked Hearns down with three vicious rights. The referee intervened and called a knockout.

In 1987, Hagler faced Sugar Ray Leonard, who was making a comeback after five years away from the ring. In one of the most ballyhooed fights ever, the gifted Leonard won a split decision, which years later Hagler still claims should have been his. Hagler resisted pressure to return to the ring and embarked instead on a film career in Europe. His mastery of punches, ability to fight as both a right- and left-hander, and his intimidating ring demeanor have not been matched in the middleweight division since his retirement.

With biceps bulging, Marvelous Marvin Hagler thrusts a right through the defenses of southpaw John ("The Beast") Mugabi. Hagler retained the middleweight crown on March 10, 1986, in Las Vegas.

MASAHIKO ("FIGHTING") HARADA

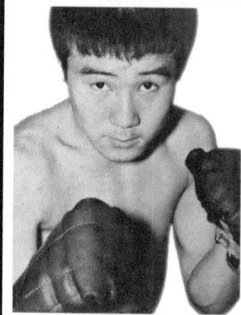

BANTAMWEIGHT

Right-handed; 5'4"; 110–127 lbs.

62 bouts, 2/21/1960 to 1/6/1970

Manager: Takeshi Sasazaki

Flyweight Champ 1962–63
Bantamweight Champ 1965–68

Hall of Fame Induction: 1995

Born: 4/5/1943, Setagaya Ward, Tokyo, Japan

Masahiko ("Fighting") Harada won championships in two weight classes—and came within a point of winning in a third—at a time when there were only ten weight divisions. He is the first fighter to win both the flyweight and bantamweight world titles. The son of a Tokyo gardener, Harada trained at home for two years before turning professional at sixteen. He dispatched 26 of the first 27 opponents and, by 1962, had earned a shot at the flyweight championship held by Pone Kingpetch of Thailand. Harada was just nineteen. The fight was held in Tokyo with 12,000 Japanese fans cheering Harada on. Displaying the aggressive style which was likened to a windmill or a typhoon, Harada knocked Kingpetch out in the eleventh round to win the title.

Harada (R) sends a sharp right to the jaw of flyweight champion Pone Kingpetch on October 10, 1962, in Tokyo. His buzzsaw attack climaxed with an eleventh-round knockout, and Harada took the title.

IN THE RING	WON 55	LOST 7	DRAWS 0	TB 62	KO 22	W 33	WF 0	D 0	KO'd 2	L 5	LF 0

Date	Opponent	Site	Result / Rounds		Title	Wt.
1960						
Feb 21	Isami Masui	Tokyo	TKO	4	—	110
Mar 2	Mitsuo Motohashi	Tokyo	W	4	—	110
Mar 27	Goro Iwamoto	Tokyo	KO	3	—	111
Apr 4	Yuichi Noguchi	Tokyo	W	4	—	112
Apr 13	Ken Morita	Tokyo	W	4	—	111
Jun 10	Masatake Ogura	Tokyo	TKO	3	—	112
Jun 26	Ken Morita	Tokyo	KO	1	—	111
Jul 18	Masaru Kodangi	Tokyo	TKO	3	—	110
Sep 1	Yukio Suzuki	Tokyo	W	4	—	111
Oct 28	Sadayoshi Yoshida	Tokyo	KO	4	—	112
Nov 7	Hachiro Arai	Tokyo	W	4	—	112
Dec 11	Yoshinori Hikita	Tokyo	KO	3	—	111
Dec 24	Hiroyuki Ebihara	Tokyo	W	6	—	111
1961						
Jan 5	Takeshi Nakamura	Tokyo	W	6	—	111
Jan 28	Riichi Tanaka	Tokyo	W	6	—	111
Mar 5	Yasuo Fujita	Tokyo	W	6	—	113
May 1	Ray Perez	Tokyo	W	10	—	112
Jun 19	Shigeru Ito	Tokyo	W	10	—	111
Jul 31	Akio Maki	Tokyo	TKO	8	—	111
Sep 9	Sombang Banbung	Tokyo	KO	5	—	112
Oct 9	Akio Maki	Osaka, Japan	W	10	—	111
Dec 10	Ryoji Shiratori	Nagoya, Japan	KO	6	—	112
1962						
Jan 12	Kozo Nagata	Tokyo	W	10	—	118
Mar 18	Tadao Kawamura	Tokyo	W	10	—	116
May 4	Baby Espinosa	Tokyo	W	10	—	115
Jun 15	Edmundo Esparza	Tokyo	L	10	—	115
Jul 23	Little Rufe	Tokyo	W	10	—	111
Oct 10	⑩ Pone Kingpetch	Tokyo	KO	11	Won-World-FL	111
1963						
Jan 12	⑩ Pone Kingpetch	Bangkok	L	15	Lost-World-FL	111
Mar 21	Tetsuro Kawai	Tokyo	W	10	—	119
May 5	Jose Cejuda	Okinawa, Japan	KO	1	—	120
Jun 19	Thira Loedjalengabo	Nagoya	TKO	6	—	121
Aug 7	Dommy Balajada	Tokyo	W	10	—	118
Sep 26	⑩ Joe Medel	Tokyo	TKO'd	6	—	118
Nov 25	Emile de Leon	Tokyo	W	10	—	126
1964						
Jan 2	Avelino Estrada	Tokyo	KO	5	—	122
Feb 14	Somsak Laemphafa	Osaka	KO	2	—	121
Jul 6	⑩ Ray Asis	Los Angeles	W	10	—	120
Sep 17	Oscar Reyes	Tokyo	W	10	—	124

Date		Opponent	Location	Result	Rounds	Title	Weight
Oct 29		Katsutoshi Aoki	Tokyo	KO	3	—	119
1965							
Jan 4		Dommy Froilan	Tokyo	TKO	6	—	124
May 17	♛	Eder Jofre ★	Nagoya	W	15	Won-World-B	118
Jul 28		Katsuo Saito	Tokyo	W	12	—	121
Nov 30	⑩	Alan Rudkin	Tokyo	W	15	Ret-World-B	117
1966							
Feb 15		Soo Kang Soo	Nagoya	W	12	—	124
Jun 1	⑩	Eder Jofre ★	Tokyo	W	15	Ret-World-B	118
Aug 1		Dio Espinosa	Sapporo, Japan	W	10	—	124
Oct 25		Antonio Herrera	Osaka	W	12	—	124
1967							
Jan 3	⑩	Joe Medel	Nagoya	W	15	Ret-World-B	117
Apr 4		Tiny Palacio	Fukuoka City, Japan	W	12	—	124
Jul 4	⑩	Bernardo Caraballo	Tokyo	W	15	Ret-World-B	118
Sep 25		Hajime Taroura	Osaka	KO	2	—	126
Nov 28		Soo Bok Kwon	Okayama, Japan	KO	8	—	126
1968							
Feb 26	⑩	Lionel Rose	Tokyo	L	15	Lost-World-B	117
Jun 5		Dwight Hawkins	Tokyo	W	10	—	126
Sep 4		Nobuo Chiba	Sano, Japan	TKO	7	—	127
Dec 4		Roy Amolong	Tokyo	KO	2	—	127
1969							
Apr 2		Alton Colter	Tokyo	L	10	—	127
Jun 5		Vil Tumulak	Nagoya	W	10	—	127
Jul 28	♛	Johnny Famechon	Sydney	L	15	For-WBC-FE	125
Oct 1		Pat Gonzales	Fukui City, Japan	KO	8	—	127
1970							
Jan 6	♛	Johnny Famechon	Tokyo	TKO'd	14	For-WBC-FE	126

Within months, Harada lost the rematch to Kingpetch in a disputed decision. The fight was held on Kingpetch's home turf, and Harada had to contend with the extremely hostile and unruly crowd that blocked his entrance to the ring. Although all three judges decided in Kingpetch's favor, the Associated Press scored the fight 72–67 for Harada.

Harada had such difficulty making the weight for the flyweight division that he moved up to bantamweight after his loss to Kingpetch and, in 1965, he challenged the unbeaten Eder Jofre of Brazil for the bantamweight championship. At the time, Jofre was considered by many ring experts to be the greatest boxer, in

DECISIONS

RINGFACT

Two Hall of Famers have won the greatest number of fights by decision. Maxie Rosenbloom was victorious in 186 fights that went to the scorecards. Willie Pep took 165 decisions. ("Newspaper decisions" are not counted in this tally.)

Nineteen-year-old, 111-pound Masahiko ("Fighting") Harada, who was ranked only tenth in his division entering the fight, is exhaltant after wresting the flyweight title from Pone Kingpetch.

any weight class. Employing his characteristic aggressive style, Harada earned a decision over Jofre to win his second title.

Australian fighter Lionel Rose came to Tokyo in 1968 to win a fifteen-round decision over Harada and take the bantamweight title. Undaunted, Harada then attempted to attain what he later called "his dream of taking the triple crown." In 1969, he met another Australian, Johnny Famechon, for the WBC featherweight championship. The two fought a close and hotly contested battle. It was initially announced that referee and sole judge Willie Pep had scored the bout a draw. However, a review of Pep's scorecard indicated that he had actually scored the bout 70 to 69 in Famechon's favor. Famechon was awarded the victory. Harada had knocked Famechon down three times and was judged by the Australian sportswriters at ringside to have beaten their countryman. Harada lost a rematch with Famechon and then retired.

In retirement, Harada had a successful career as an actor in Japan before returning to boxing as a trainer.

BEAU JACK

LIGHTWEIGHT

Right-handed; 5'6"; 126–145 lbs.
118 bouts, 4/12/1939 to 8/12/1955
Managers: Joe Caron 1940–41,
Bowman Milligan 1941–42, Chick
Wergeles 1942–51
NY World Lightweight Champion
1942–43, 1943–44
Hall of Fame Induction: 1991
Born: 4/1/1921, Augusta, GA
Named: Sidney Walker
Died: 2/9/2000

Along with Ike Williams and Bob Montgomery, the man they called Beau Jack delighted boxing fans of the 1940s and '50s with his courageous, attacking style. Barely literate and with little pretense to being anything but a good fighter, Jack came from a poor Southern background. Born Sidney Walker, Jack first started fighting as a child in Georgia. Often, he and five or more other black youths would be blindfolded and placed in a ring to fight each other in "battle royals" for the entertainment of white spectators.

When he was eighteen, Jack had a job shining shoes at the Augusta National Golf Club, the home of the Masters. Impressed with his fighting ability, golf legend Bobby Jones and others gave Jack enough money to go to Massachusetts and receive formal boxing training. He trained ardently, a habit he followed throughout his career and, a year later, turned professional in Holyoke, Massachusetts. He continued to fight in the Holyoke area until mid-1941 when he was first signed for bouts in New York.

In late 1942, Jack faced Tippy Larkin in Madison Square Garden for the vacant New York world lightweight title. Larkin landed a few good punches, but the fight was all Jack's. He knocked Larkin down in the first round, then swarmed over him with punches thrown from all angles. In the third round, Jack ended the fight with a knockout.

A titleholder at 21, Jack embarked on an ambitious schedule, fighting against three top contenders—and future Hall of Famers—in a three-month period. He won two decisions over Fritzie Zivic and one from Henry Armstrong. He then faced Bob Montgomery in the first of three title fights in Madison Square Garden, where Jack had become a regular main-event attraction. Montgomery was a

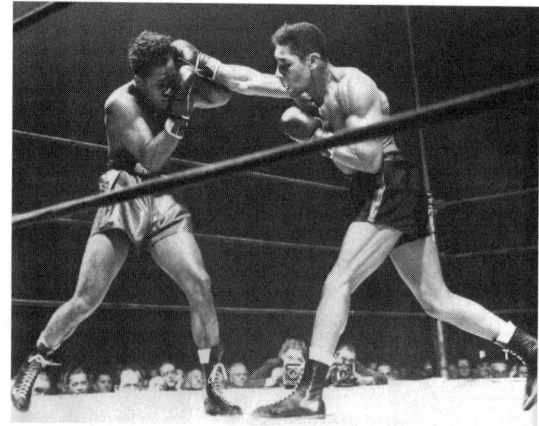

Beau Jack (R) headlines the Madison Square Garden card in this ten-round decision over contender Willie Joyce on December 14, 1945. Jack's 21 main-event bouts at the Garden drew a total of over 335,000 fans.

IN THE RING	WON 88	LOST 24	DRAWS 5	TB 118	KO 43	W 45	WF 0	D 5	KO'd 4	L 20	LF 0	ND 1

Date	Opponent	Site	Result / Rounds		Title	Wt.
1939						
April 12	Battling Henry Burns	Aiken, SC	KO	5	—	—
1940						
Feb 8	Battling Henry Burns	Aiken	W	4	—	131
Feb 15	Alvin Stevens	Aiken	KO	3	—	—
Mar 21	Silent Stafford	Aiken	W	6	—	—
Mar 27	Joe James	Aiken	KO	2	—	—
May 20	Frankie Allen	Holyoke, MA	D	4	—	—
May 27	Billy Bannick	Holyoke	KO	3	—	—
Jun 17	Jackie Parker	Holyoke	L	4	—	—
Jul 14	Joe Polowitzer	New Haven, CT	L	6	—	—
Jul 21	Joe Polowitzer	New Haven	W	6	—	—
Aug 19	Jackie Parker	Holyoke	L	4	—	—
Aug 26	Carlo Daponde	Holyoke	W	4	—	—
Sep 2	Jackie Small	Holyoke	KO	4	—	—
Sep 16	Ollie Barbour	Holyoke	KO	3	—	132
Sep 30	Tony Dupre	Holyoke	TKO	2	—	126
Oct 14	Abe Cohen	Holyoke	KO	3	—	—
Oct 21	Ritchie Jones	Holyoke	KO	3	—	—
Nov 14	Joey Stack	Holyoke	W	6	—	—
Dec 2	Jimmy Fox	Holyoke	W	6	—	—
Dec 16	Young Buff	Holyoke	KO	1	—	—
Dec 30	Mel Neary	Holyoke	KO	5	—	130
1941						
Jan 27	Joey Silva	Holyoke	L	6	—	—
Feb 10	Joe Rivers	Holyoke	TKO	4	—	—
Feb 24	Lenny Isrow	Holyoke	TKO	3	—	—
Mar 10	Nickey Jerome	Holyoke	KO	3	—	—
Mar 24	Joey Silva	Holyoke	W	6	—	—
Apr 7	Tony Iacovacci	Holyoke	KO	6	—	—
Apr 21	Bob Reilly	Holyoke	TKO	7	—	—
Apr 28	Harry Gentile	Holyoke	TKO	1	—	—
May 5	⑩ Chester Rico	Holyoke	D	8	—	—
May 19	George Salamone	Holyoke	KO	8	—	134
Jun 2	⑩ Tommy Spiegel	Holyoke	W	8	—	136
Jun 16	George Zengaras	Holyoke	W	8	—	135
Aug 5	Minnie DeMore	Brooklyn	TKO	3	—	134
Aug 14	Al Roth	Brooklyn	TKO	6	—	135
Aug 26	Guillermo Puente	New York	W	6	—	136
Sep 19	Al Reid	New York	KO	7	—	134
Oct 14	⑩ Tommy Spiegel	Brooklyn	W	8	—	135
Oct 31	Guillermo Puente	New York	W	8	—	135
Dec 1	Joe Rivers	Brooklyn	KO	3	—	136
Dec 8	Freddie Archer	New York	L	8	—	136
Dec 29	Freddie Archer	New York	L	8	—	136
1942						
Jan 5	Carmelo Fenoy	Holyoke	W	10	—	135
May 22	⑩ Bobby ("Poison") Ivy	New York	W	8	—	137
Jun 23	Guillermo Puente	New York	KO	1	—	138
Jul 3	Bobby McIntire	Fort Hamilton, KY	TKO	6	—	138

Date		Opponent	Location	Result	Rounds	Notes	Weight
Jul 7		Cosby Linson	Long Island City, NY	TKO	8	—	137
Aug 1		Ruby Garcia	Elizabeth, NJ	KO	6	—	138
Aug 18		Carmine Fatta	New York	KO	1	—	137
Aug 28		Billy Murray	New York	W	10	—	137
Sep 28		Joe Torres	Washington, DC	KO	4	—	—
Oct 2	⑩	Chester Rico	New York	W	8	—	138
Oct 12		Terry Young	New York	W	10	—	136
Nov 13	⑩	Allie Stolz	New York	TKO	7	—	132
Dec 18		Tippy Larkin	New York	KO	3	Won-Vac NY World-L	132
1943							
Feb 5	⑩	Fritzie Zivic★	New York	W	10	—	137
Mar 5	⑩	Fritzie Zivic★	New York	W	12	—	136
Apr 2		Henry Armstrong★	New York	W	10	—	135
May 21	⑩	Bob Montgomery★	New York	L	15	Lost-NY World-L	135
Jun 21		Maxie Starr	Washington, DC	KO	6	—	135
Jul 19		Johnny Hutchinson	Philadelphia	TKO	6	—	135
Oct 4		Bobby Ruffin	New York	L	10	—	140
Nov 19	♛	Bob Montgomery★	New York	W	15	Reg-NY World-L	132
1944							
Jan 7	⑩	Lulu Costantino	New York	W	10	—	139
Jan 28	⑩	Sammy Angott★	New York	D	10	—	138
Feb 15		Maxie Berger	Cleveland	W	10	—	138
Mar 3	⑩	Bob Montgomery★	New York	L	15	Lost-NY World-L	134
Mar 17	⑩	Al ("Bummy") Davis	New York	W	10	—	138
Mar 31	⑩	Juan Zurita	New York	W	10	—	136
Aug 4	♛	Bob Montgomery★	New York	W	10	—	138
1945							
Dec 14	⑩	Willie Joyce	New York	W	10	—	144
1946							
Jan 4		Morris Reif	New York	KO	4	—	143
Feb 8	⑩	Johnny Greco	New York	D	10	—	142
May 31	⑩	Johnny Greco	New York	W	10	—	141
Jul 8	⑩	Sammy Angott★	Washington, DC	TKO	7	—	142
Aug 19		Danny Kapilow	Washington, DC	W	10	—	143
Oct 22		Buster Tyler	Elizabeth	L	10	—	142
1947							
Feb 21	⑩	Tony Janiro	New York	TKO'd	4	—	141
Nov 3		Humberto Zavala	St. Louis	KO	4	—	141
Dec 16		Frankie Vigeant	Hartford, CT	W	10	—	140
Dec 29		Billy Kearns	Providence, RI	W	10	—	140
1948							
Jan 5		Jimmy Collins	New Haven	KO	2	—	140
Jan 23	⑩	Johhny Bratton	Chicago	TKO	8	—	139
Feb 20	⑩	Terry Young	New York	L	10	—	141
Apr 9	⑩	Johnny Greco	Montreal	W	10	—	139
May 24	⑩	Tony Janiro	Washington, DC	W	10	—	140
Jul 12	♛	Ike Williams★	Philadelphia	TKO'd	6	For-World-L	134
Oct 28		Eric Boon	Washington, DC	TKO	3	—	143
Nov 23		Chuck Taylor	Philadelphia	TKO	3	—	144
Dec 17		Leroy Willis	Detroit	W	10	—	139
1949							
Jan 17		Jackie Weber	Boston	W	10	—	139
Mar 28	⑩	Johnny Greco	Montreal	L	10	—	138
Jul 13		Eddie Giosa	Washington, DC	W	10	—	139
Aug 31		Johnny Gonsalves	Oakland	W	10	—	138

Date	Opponent	Location	Result	Rounds		Weight
Sep 6	Tote Martinez	Los Angeles	W	10	—	139
Sep 30	Livio Minelli	Chicago	W	10	—	139
Oct 14	⑩ Kid Gavilan ★	Chicago	L	10	—	141
Dec 16	⑩ Tuzo Portuguez	New York	L	10	—	142
1950						
Apr 3	Joey Carkido	Hartford	L	10	—	142
Apr 14	Lew Jenkins ★	Washington, DC	TKO	6	—	139
May 8	Jackie Weber	Providence	TKO	7	—	141
May 22	Johnny Potenti	Boston	W	10	—	141
Jun 28	Ronnie Harper	Indianapolis	TKO	5	—	141
Jul 8	Sonny West	Springfield, MA	ND	3	—	137
Jul 17	Bobby Timpson	Atlanta	TKO	6	—	142
Oct 4	Philip Kim	Honolulu	W	10	—	141
Nov 14	⑩ Frankie Fernandez	Honolulu	L	10	—	144
1951						
Jan 1	Fitzie Pruden	Milwaukee	L	10	—	141
Jan 18	⑩ Del Flanagan	Minneapolis	L	10	—	138
Jan 31	Emil Barao	Hartford	W	10	—	140
Mar 5	⑩ Ike Williams ★	Providence	L	10	—	137
Mar 30	Leroy Willis	New Orleans	W	10	—	142
Apr 16	⑩ Gil Turner	Philadelphia	L	10	—	145
May 21	⑩ Gil Turner	Philadelphia	TKO'd	8	—	145
1955						
Jan 20	Eddie Green	Columbia, SC	W	10	—	147
Apr 9	Ike Williams ★	Augusta, GA	D	10	—	145
Jul 4	Willie Johnson	Daytona Beach, FL	W	10	—	—
Aug 12	Ike Williams ★	Augusta	TKO'd	9	—	146

dangerous fighter, light on his feet and in possession of a full arsenal of punches. Jack was a good match for this aggressive contender and had Montgomery in trouble in the first round but, as the fight continued, Montgomery took control. By the end of fifteen, both of Jack's eyes were almost swollen shut, and his lips were puffy. Montgomery won the unanimous decision and the New York world lightweight title.

In the rematch a few months later, Jack turned the tables on Montgomery. He used great speed, bolo punch uppercuts, and a sharp jab to take the bout. Though Jack absorbed some punishment, he did not tire as he had in the first fight, and he won the unanimous decision to regain the title. In 1944, the pair fought for a third time. A crowd of 19,006 filled Madison Square Garden to see these two enemies meet again in a furious contest that at times resembled a wrestling match. Jack jabbed furiously, but Montgomery's barrage of blows was too much for him. Montgomery won the decision. In their fourth bout, Jack won a non-title rematch with the proceeds going for war bonds.

In 1948, Jack challenged Ike Williams for the world lightweight title but was knocked out in six rounds. He retired in 1951 but staged a four-fight comeback attempt in 1955. Jack's energetic, swarming style made him a fan favorite, especially in Madison Square Garden. He fought there 27 times and headlined 21 cards, many of which drew crowds of close to 20,000. After leaving the ring, Jack worked at the Fontainebleau Hotel in Miami Beach, pursuing the only other occupation he had ever had—shining shoes.

LEW JENKINS
The Sweetwater Swatter

LIGHTWEIGHT

Right-handed; 5'7"; 125–144 lbs.

114 bouts, 12/1/1935 to 4/14/1950

Managers: Benny Woodhall, Frank Bachman, Hymie Kaplan

Lightweight Champion 1940-41

Hall of Fame Induction: 1999

Born: 12/4/1916, Milburn, TX

Named: Verlin E. Jenkins

Died: 10/30/1981

Lew Jenkins was a powerful boxer whose career was hampered by drinking and carousing. Yet after he retired, Jenkins was considered a hero in the armed services.

Jenkins was the son of a travelling blacksmith and cotton picker. After his father's death, he joined the T.J. Tidwell carnival, where he earned 25 cents a day to fight men—of all sizes—in the boxing and wrestling tent.

In 1936, Jenkins joined the army but continued boxing. He won the welterweight championship of Fort Bliss, Texas, and boxed professionally while on furlough. He left the army in 1938 to box full time, reeling off seven straight knockouts in Dallas. When Jenkins married, his wife, Katie, took charge of his career. After Katie determined that they would have to move to a larger city to make a living in the ring, the couple relocated first to Chicago and then New York.

Katie created quite a stir when she and her husband appeared at the famed Stillman's Gym and asked for a locker. Lou Stillman replied that women were not allowed in the gym, but under a withering barrage of salty language from Katie, he gave in.

Once in New York, Jenkins began working under the care of experienced managers and soon racked up ten straight wins, including knockouts over highly regarded fighters like future junior welterweight champion Tippy Larkin.

The Larkin victory earned Jenkins a May 10, 1940, chance at the lightweight title held by Lou Ambers. But success led Lew and Katie to excessive drinking and revelry. While Jenkins trained fairly diligently, he was spotted the day of the fight in Toots Shor's famous bar, having a few. Still, at fight time Jenkins performed well, knocking

Katie Jenkins often worked the corner in her husband's fights.

IN THE RING	WON 70	LOST 39	DRAWS 5	TB 114	KO 48	W 21	WF 1	D 5	KO'd 12	L 27	LF 0

Date	Opponent	Site	Result / Rounds		Title	Wt.
1935						
Dec 1	Lee Mullins	Phoenix, AZ	W	4	—	—
Dec 13	Ray Corillo	Phoenix	L	4	—	—
1936						
Mar 5	Sailor Fay Koskey	Silver City, NM	W	4	—	—
Jul 28	Moon Mullins	Columbus, TX	W	8	—	—
1937						
—	Jimmy Maddox	—	D	8	—	—
—	Rudolfo Ramirez	—	KO'd	8	—	—
Apr 12	Billy Firpo	Houston	L	6	—	—
Aug 1	Ray Serrano	Houston	W	4	—	—
1938						
Jan 11	Ray Serrano	Houston	D	6	—	—
Jan 14	Kid Levy	Dallas	KO	5	—	—
Jan 28	Young Ernest	Dallas	KO	5	—	138
Feb 4	Jackie Conway	Dallas	KO	2	—	136
Feb 18	Frankie Graham	Dallas	KO	4	—	—
Mar 11	Louis Arriola	Dallas	KO	5	—	—
Mar 18	Ray Serrano	Dallas	KO	2	—	136
Apr 1	Jackie Sharkey	Dallas	KO	2	—	137
Apr 8	Lew Feldman	Dallas	W	10	—	135
Apr 28	Wesley Ramey	Dallas	L	10	—	136
May 14	Chief Evening Thunder	Dallas	KO	8	—	137
May 27	Bobby Britton	Dallas	KO'd	7	—	137
Jun 17	Chief Evening Thunder	Dallas	KO	3	—	—
Jul 22	Willard Brown	Dallas	KO	4	—	137
Jul 29	Chino Alvarez	Dallas	KO'd	8	—	133
Aug 23	Zeke Castro	Los Angeles	W	6	—	138
Sep 9	Cullen Williams	Corpus Christi,TX	KO	5	—	—
Sep 16	Jackie Griffin	Dallas	W	6	—	—
Sep 23	Carlos Malacara	Dallas	L	10	—	—
Sep 30	Don Eddy	Dallas	KO	8	—	132
Oct 6	Luis Orozco	Dallas	KO	1	—	—
Oct 20	Carl Faust	Dallas	KO	8	—	132
Nov 3	Carl Faust	Dallas	KO	8	—	133
Nov 9	Sammy Musco	Corpus Christi	D	10	—	—
Nov 17	Lew Feldman	Dallas	L	10	—	129
Dec 2	Sammy Musco	Dallas	W	10	—	133
Dec 16	Wesley Ramey	Dallas	L	10	—	131
Dec 23	Pedro Ortega	San Antonio, TX	L	8	—	—
Dec 29	Ted Tellos	Dallas	W	8	—	—
1939						
Jan 6	Joe Law	Chicago	W	6	—	—
Jan 20	Willie Joyce	Chicago	D	10	—	130
Jan 31	Sam Scully	Houston	KO	10	—	131
Feb 17	Willie Joyce	Chicago	L	8	—	130
Feb 24	Willie Joyce	Chicago	L	8	—	130
Mar 24	⑩ Pete Lello	Chicago	KO'd	7	—	130
May 6	Panchito Campos	Mexico City	KO	1	—	—

Date	Opponent	Location	Result	Rounds	Title	Weight
May 26	Jimmy Hatcher	Dallas	KO	2	—	130
Jun 19	Jorge Morelia	San Antonio	W	10	—	128
Jul 18	Bus Breese	Long Island City, NY	W	8	—	133
Aug 1	Joey Fontana	Long Island City	W	8	—	132
Aug 15	Bus Breese	Long Island City	W	8	—	132
Sep 5	Ginger Foran	Long Island City	KO	4	—	133
Sep 12	Primo Flores	Long Island City	KO	4	—	131
Oct 10	Primo Flores	New York	KO	5	—	130
Nov 21	Mike Belloise	New York	TKO	8	—	130
Dec 15	Billy Marquart	New York	KO	3	—	129

1940

Date	Opponent	Location	Result	Rounds	Title	Weight
Jan 24	Chino Alvarez	Dallas	KO	1	—	130
Mar 8	Tippy Larkin	New York	KO	1	—	134
May 10	♛ Lou Ambers★	New York	TKO	3	Won-World-L	132
Jul 17	♛ Henry Armstrong★	New York	TKO'd	6	—	135
Sep 16	⑩ Bob Montgomery★	Philadelphia	W	12	—	135
Nov 22	⑩ Pete Lello	New York	TKO	2	Ret-World-L	131
Dec 20	♛ Fritzie Zivic★	New York	D	10	—	135

1941

Date	Opponent	Location	Result	Rounds	Title	Weight
Feb 28	⑩ Lou Ambers★	New York	TKO	7	—	134
May 16	⑩ Bob Montgomery★	New York	L	10	—	135
Aug 4	Joey Zodda	Newark, NJ	KO	3	—	136
Sep 12	Cleo McNeil	Minneapolis	KO	3	—	133
Oct 6	Freddie ("Red") Cochrane	New York	L	10	—	135
Dec 19	⑩ Sammy Angott★	New York	L	15	Lost-World-L	133

1942

Date	Opponent	Location	Result	Rounds	Title	Weight
Feb 17	Marty Servo	Philadelphia	L	10	—	139
Mar 27	Mike Kaplan	Boston	L	10	—	144
May 13	Jack Byrd	Hot Springs, AK	L	10	—	138
May 25	⑩ Fritzie Zivic★	Pittsburgh	TKO'd	10	—	138
Aug 17	Cosby Linson	New Orleans	L	10	—	142
Aug 27	Carmen Notch	Detroit	L	10	—	143
Sep 22	Al Tribuani	Wilmington, DE	L	10	—	138
Nov 18	Chato Gonzalez	Las Vegas	KO	2	—	144
Dec 4	⑩ Henry Armstrong★	Portland, OR	TKO'd	8	—	143
Dec 22	John Thomas	Los Angeles	TKO'd	5	—	137

1943

Date	Opponent	Location	Result	Rounds	Title	Weight
Jul 28	Steve Rosina	Oran, Algeria	KO	2	—	—
Aug 6	Chick Broussard	Oran	W	3	—	—

1945

Date	Opponent	Location	Result	Rounds	Title	Weight
Dec 3	⑩ Jimmy Doyle	Cleveland	TKO'd	4	—	141

1946

Date	Opponent	Location	Result	Rounds	Title	Weight
Jan 15	Jerry Zullo	Salem, MA	KO	2	—	139
Jan 25	Jack Garrity	Danbury, CT	KO	1	—	139
Jan 29	Johnny Cool	Manchester, NH	WF	2	—	139
May 21	Henry Majcher	Houston	L	10	—	138
Jun 14	Lou Flyer	Dallas	KO'd	6	—	140
Sep 26	Tony Davila	Waco, TX	KO	1	—	—
Nov 20	Ted ("Mustang") Garcia	Galveston, TX	KO	9	—	136
Dec 13	Hubert Gray	Dallas	KO	10	—	138
Dec 20	Nick Castiglione	Chicago	KO	4	—	138

1948

Date	Opponent	Location	Result	Rounds	Title	Weight
Dec 10	Andres Balderas	El Paso, TX	KO	3	—	134

1949

Date	Opponent	Location	Result	Rounds	Title	Weight
Jan 17	Rene Camacho	Philadelphia	KO	2	—	133

Jan 31	Chuck Burton	Philadelphia	KO	9	—	134
Feb 28	Percy Bassett	Philadelphia	L	10	—	132
Mar 17	Santa Bucca	Philadelphia	KO	4	—	138
Mar 28	Joey Carkido	Philadelphia	KO	4	—	139
Apr 11	Bobby Timpson	Philadelphia	KO	10	—	139
May 2	Eddie Giosa	Philadelphia	L	10	—	136
Jun 6	Jimmy Collins	Philadelphia	W	8	—	138
Jun 21	Mario Marino	Allentown, PA	KO	2	—	137
Jul 1	Beppe Colasanti	Long Beach, CA	L	10	—	137
Aug 1	Lou Joyce	Allentown	W	8	—	141
Aug 17	Don Williams	Worcester, MA	W	10	—	139
Sep 1	Bob Sandberg	Milwaukee	L	10	—	139
Sep 21	Don Williams	Worcester	L	10	—	140
Sep 30	Eddie Giosa	Philadelphia	W	10	—	139
Oct 20	Ike Jenkins	Philadelphia	W	8	—	139
Nov 14	Calvin Smith	Philadelphia	L	10	—	—
Dec 5	Johnny DeFazio	Newark	KO	8	—	139
Dec 19	Iggy Vaccari	Boston	KO	9	—	139
1950						
Jan 9	Al Pennino	Newark	KO	3	—	142
Jan 25	Walter Haines	New York	L	8	—	138
Jan 31	Rafael Lastre	Toledo, OH	TKO'd	10	—	140
Mar 6	Carmen Basilio ★	Syracuse, NY	L	10	—	140
Apr 14	Beau Jack ★	Washington, DC	TKO'd	6	—	139

down Ambers several times. In the third, he floored the champ, and Ambers failed to beat the count, suffering the first knock-out defeat of his career.

As champion, Jenkins's drinking and rowdiness escalated. He eschewed training for his next fight, against Henry Armstrong. On fight day, Jenkins escaped from his locked hotel room to go on a binge with friends. His trainer, Willie Ketchum, found him and dragged him to the ring where Armstrong floored Jenkins seven times before referee Arthur Donovan stopped the fight.

A car accident preceded Jenkins's non-title rematch with Ambers. Jenkins drove into a bridge, but was unhurt. After the weigh-in, however, he got so drunk that he had to be helped into the ring. Somehow, he held on through the sixth round and then finished Ambers with a knockout in the seventh. Jenkins next suffered whiplash in a drunken motorcycle accident shortly before a fight with Freddie ("Red") Cochrane. He removed his neck brace the day of the fight, self-administering doses of whiskey during the bout. Cochrane won a ten-round decision.

On December 19, 1941, Jenkins's stormy title reign came to an end. Still suffering from his various injuries, he could do little to defend himself in the fight against Sammy Angott, who took the decision and the title.

Katie left Jenkins. He was broke. After losing nine of ten fights in 1942, he enlisted in the Coast Guard. While on duty, he fought in military-sponsored fights. Resuming his pro boxing career in 1945, he won seven of his first ten bouts but was no longer considered a contender. He reenlisted in the army and remarried while in the service, yet he was drawn back to boxing in 1949. He lost the last four bouts of his career.

Jenkins served with distinction in the Korean War, earning a Silver Star, and continued to serve until 1963. He is buried in Arlington National Cemetery.

EDER JOFRE

FEATHERWEIGHT

Right-handed; 5'4"; 116–126 lbs.
78 bouts, 3/26/1957 to 10/8/1976
Manager: Abraham Katzenelson
NBA Bantamwt. Champ 1960–61
Bantamwt. Champ 1961–65
WBC Featherwt. Champ 1973–74
Hall of Fame Induction: 1992
Born: 3/26/1936, Sao Paulo, Brazil

Although not well known to American boxing fans—he only fought three times in the United States—Eder Jofre of Brazil held three championship titles during his long career, with thirteen years separating his first from his last title victory. Jofre retired for three years late in his career before re-establishing himself not only as an international contender, but as a champion.

Jofre's father and others in his family were active in boxing and wrestling, and Jofre started boxing at a very young age. As an amateur, he represented Brazil in the 1956 Olympics, going to the quarterfinals before being eliminated.

He turned professional the next year and compiled a record of 34-0-2, earning him a chance to fight for the vacant NBA bantamweight title against Eloy Sanchez in 1960. The fight in Los Angeles was Jofre's second bout outside South America. Jofre knocked Sanchez out in the sixth with a hook-cross combination to the jaw. The next year, Jofre scored a technical knockout over Piero Rollo in Rio de Janeiro to claim the vacant world bantamweight title.

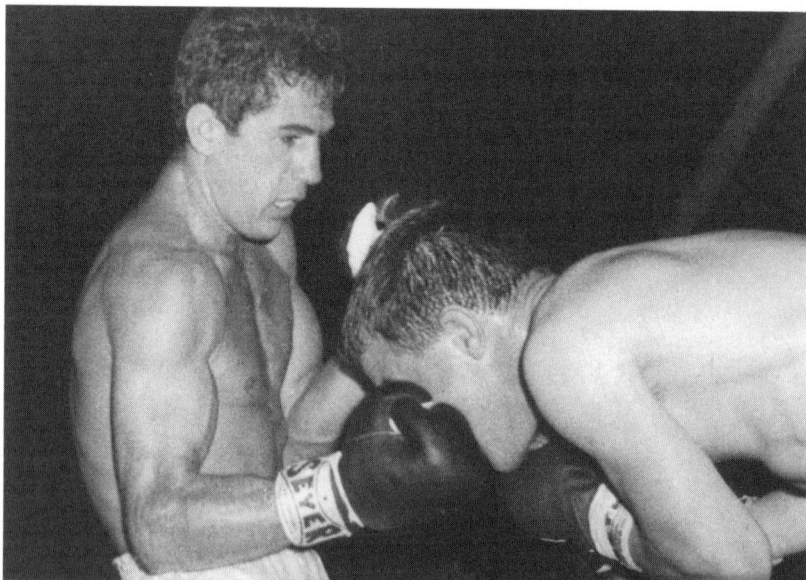

Referee Willie Pep halted this bout in the tenth round as Jofre (L) beat EBU champ Johnny Caldwell in Sao Paulo on January 18, 1962. Caldwell's manager threw in the towel to stop the slaughter.

IN THE RING	WON 72	LOST 2	DRAWS 4	TB 78	KO 50	W 22	WF 0	D 4	KO'd 0	L 2	LF 0

Date	Opponent	Site	Result / Rounds		Title	Wt.
1957						
Mar 26	Raul Lopez	Sao Paulo, Brazil	KO	3	—	—
Apr 23	Raul Lopez	Sao Paulo	TKO	5	—	—
May 5	Osvaldo Perez	Sao Paulo	TKO	1	—	—
Jun 7	Osvaldo Perez	Sao Paulo	KO	2	—	—
Jun 14	Juan Gonzalez	Sao Paulo	TKO	5	—	—
Jul 5	Raul Jamie	Sao Paulo	W	10	—	—
Jul 19	Raul Jamie	Sao Paulo	W	10	—	—
Aug 16	Ernesto Miranda	Sao Paulo	D	10	—	—
Sep 6	Ernesto Miranda	Sao Paulo	D	10	—	—
Oct 31	Luis Jimenez	Sao Paulo	TKO	8	—	—
Dec 13	Adolfo Pendas	Sao Paulo	W	10	—	—
Dec 22	Carlos Galisans	Rio de Janeiro	W	8	—	—
1958						
Jan 24	Avelino Romero	Sao Paulo	KO	2	—	—
Mar 7	Cristobal Galisans	Sao Paulo	TKO	6	—	—
Apr 13	German Escudero	Sao Paulo	KO	2	—	—
Apr 27	German Escudero	Rio de Janeiro	KO	2	—	—
May 14	Ruben Caceres	Montevideo, Uruguay	D	10	—	—
Jul 18	Juan Acebal	Sao Paulo	KO	2	—	—
Aug 9	Roberto Olmedo	Sao Paulo	KO	5	—	—
Sep 12	Jose Casas	Sao Paulo	W	10	—	—
Oct 9	Jose Casas	Sao Paulo	KO	5	—	—
Nov 14	Jose Smecca	Sao Paulo	TKO	7	—	—
Dec 12	Roberto Castro	Sao Paulo	KO	2	—	—
1959						
Mar 23	Aniceto Pereyra	Sao Paulo	W	10	—	—
Apr 20	Salustiano Suarez	Sao Paulo	KO	4	—	—
Jun 4	Leo Espinosa	Sao Paulo	W	10	—	118
Jun 28	Angel Bustos	Sao Paulo	KO	1	—	—
Jul 19	Salustiano Suarez	Sao Paulo	KO	4	—	—
Jul 31	Ruben Caceres	Sao Paulo	KO	7	—	—
Oct 9	Angel Bustos	Rio de Janeiro	KO	3	—	122
Oct 30	Gianni Zuddas	Sao Paulo	W	10	—	—
Dec 12	⑩ Danny Kid	Sao Paulo	W	10	—	120
1960						
Feb 19	⑩ Ernesto Miranda	Sao Paulo	W	15	Won-S Am-B	117
Jun 10	⑩ Ernesto Miranda	Sao Paulo	KO	3	Ret-S Am-B	116
Jul 15	Claudio Barrientos	Sao Paulo	KO	8	—	122
Aug 18	⑩ Jose Medel	Los Angeles	KO	10	—	118
Sep 30	Ricardo Moreno	Sao Paulo	TKO	6	—	122
Nov 18	⑩ Eloy Sanchez	Los Angeles	KO	6	Won-Vac NBA-B	118
Dec 16	Billy Peacock	Sao Paulo	KO	2	—	123
1961						
Mar 25	⑩ Piero Rollo	Rio de Janeiro	TKO	10	Won-Vac World-B	117
Apr 18	Sugar Ray	Sao Paulo	KO	2	—	123
Jul 26	Sadao Yaoita	Sao Paulo	KO	10	—	121
Aug 19	Ramon Arias	Caracas	KO	7	Ret-World-B	117
Dec 6	Fernando Soto	Sao Paulo	KO	8	—	—

1962							
Jan 18	♛	Johnny Caldwell	Sao Paulo	TKO	10	Ret-World-B	117
May 4	⑩	Herman Marquez	San Francisco	KO	10	Ret-World-B	117
Sep 11	⑩	Jose Medel	Sao Paulo	KO	6	Ret-World-B	117
1963							
Apr 4	⑩	Katsutoshi Aoki	Tokyo	KO	3	Ret-World-B	118
May 18		Johnny Jamito	Quezon, Philippines	TKO	12	Ret-World-B	117
1964							
Nov 27	⑩	Bernardo Caraballo	Bogota, Columbia	KO	7	Ret-World-B	117
1965							
May 17	⑩	Fighting Harada★	Nagoya, Japan	L	15	Lost-World-B	118
Nov 5	⑩	Manny Elias	Sao Paulo	D	10	—	121
1966							
Jun 1	♛	Fighting Harada★	Tokyo	L	15	For-World-B	116
1969							
Aug 27		Rudy Corona	Sao Paulo	KO	6	—	—
1970							
Jan 30		Nevio Carbi	Sao Paulo	W	10	—	123
May 29		Manny Elias	Sao Paulo	W	10	—	—
Sep 25		Roberto Wong	Sao Paulo	KO	3	—	—
Nov 7		Giovanni Girgenti	Sao Paulo	W	10	—	125
1971							
Mar 26		Jerry Stokes	Sao Paulo	KO	2	—	—
Jul 9		Domenico Chilorio	Sao Paulo	W	10	—	125
Sep 10		Terry Jumao	Sao Paulo	W	10	—	—
Oct 29		Roberto Porcel	Sao Paulo	KO	2	—	—
1972							
Mar 24		Guillermo Morales	Sao Paulo	KO	6	—	—
Apr 28		Felix Figueroa	Sao Paulo	W	10	—	—
Jun 30		Jose Bisbal	Sao Paulo	KO	2	—	—
Aug 18		Shig Fukuyama	Sao Paulo	TKO	9	—	—
Sep 29		Djiemei Belhadf	Sao Paulo	KO	3	—	—
1973							
May 5	♛	Jose Legra	Brasilia, Brazil	W	15	Won-WBC-FE	125
Jul 21		Godfrey Stevens	Sao Paulo	KO	4	—	—
Aug 25		Frankie Crawford	Bauru, Brazil	W	10	—	—
Oct 21		Vicente Saldivar	Salvador, Brazil	KO	4	Ret-WBC-FE	124
1975							
Jan 3		Filiberto Herrera	Jundiai, Brazil	W	10	—	—
1976							
Feb 24		Enzo Farinelli	Porto Alegre, Brazil	KO	4	—	—
May 1		Michael Lefevbre	Brasilia	KO	3	—	—
May 29		Pasquale Mortibelli	Sao Paulo	KO	4	—	—
Jul 2		Gitano Jimenez	Sao Paulo	W	10	—	—
Aug 13	⑩	Juan Lopez	Sao Paulo	W	10	—	—
Oct 8	⑩	Octavio Gomez	Sao Paulo	W	12	—	—

Jofre won his next ten fights, all by knockout, to maintain a firm hold on the bantamweight belt. In 1965, he traveled to Nagoya, Japan, for a title bout with the former flyweight champion, Fighting Harada. Making the weight for his title defenses had been a continual struggle for Jofre and, in Japan, he once again had trouble. Two pounds over at the weigh-in, Jofre had to go for an hour's run in order to get down to the necessary weight. The fight didn't go Jofre's way. Harada's intense, attacking style proved to be too much for him, and Harada won a split decision to take the title. Jofre complained that referee Barney Ross lost control of the fight and allowed Harada to butt and hold throughout the match. In a rematch the next year in Tokyo, Harada again won a fifteen-round decision.

After this second loss to Harada, Jofre retired. Three years later, in 1969, he was back, this time fighting as a featherweight. It may have seemed that a comeback at age 33 was doomed, but Jofre showed that he still had the classic boxing skills and punching ability which had won him the bantamweight title. He was 37 when he won a 1973 majority decision over Jose Legra to take the world featherweight title. He was stripped of the title the next year for failure to defend but continued to fight for another two years before retiring for good.

In retirement, Jofre has been active in politics in Brazil, where he continues to enjoy great popularity. He is one of the few vegetarians to hold a world title.

After campaigning for most of his career as a bantamweight, Eder Jofre moved up to featherweight and took the WBC's version of that championship from Spain's José Legra in Brasilia on May 5, 1973.

INGEMAR JOHANSSON
Ingo

H E A V Y W E I G H T

Right-handed; 6'½"; 192–207 lbs.
28 bouts, 12/5/1952 to 4/21/1963
Manager: Edwin Ahlquist
Heavyweight Champion 1959–60
Hall of Fame Induction: 2002
Born: 9/22/1932, Gothenburg, Sweden

A heavyweight champion who upset Floyd Patterson in his prime, Ingemar Johansson made a lasting impression on boxing fans with his likeable personality, unique training methods, and potent right hand.

Johansson was born in Sweden, and from the time he was a small boy he carried a potent punch. His father was a maintenance foreman, and Johansson followed the same job path after he quit school at age fifteen.

He embarked on his amateur boxing career on February 17, 1948, and won a decision over his first opponent. In all, Johansson would compile a 60-11 amateur record. As a member of the European Golden Gloves team in 1951, he knocked out American Ernest Fann in the second round of their bout. In the 1952 Olympics, Johansson represented Sweden and reached the championship match, where he faced Eddie Sanders of the United States. Unfortunately, Johansson was disqualified in the second round for "not trying." He was disgraced in the eyes of his countrymen and the entire boxing community, and the silver medal, usually awarded to the loser in the finals, was withheld from him. He finally received if from the International Olympic Committee in 1982.

Johansson began fighting for pay in exhibitions with a traveling circus, but his formal boxing career started with a fourth-round knockout of Robert Masson on December 5, 1952. Johansson won his next four fights but was then forced to temporarily hang up his gloves while he served a stint in the Swedish Navy. After his discharge, he continued to rack up victories, culminating in a September 30, 1956, win over Franco Cavicchi in thirteen rounds to claim the European heavyweight title. That year, *The Ring* ranked Johansson as the

Johansson uncorked three powerful knockdown rights in his important 9/14/1958 fight with Californian Eddie Machen. Machen failed to rise from the third, and Johansson won in 2:16 of the first round.

IN THE RING	WON 26	LOST 2	DRAWS 0	TB 28	KO 17	W 8	WF 1	D 0	KO'd 2	L 0	LF 0

Date	Opponent	Site	Result / Rounds		Title	Wt.
1952						
Dec 5	Robert Masson	Gothenburg, Sweden	KO	4	—	193
1953						
Feb 6	Emile Bentz	Gothenburg	KO	2	—	196
Mar 6	Lloyd Barnett	Gothenburg	W	6	—	198
Mar 12	Erik Jensen	Copenhagen	W	6	—	—
Dec 4	Raymond Degl'Innocenti	Gothenburg	KO	2	—	193
1954						
Nov 5	Werner Wiegand	Gothenburg	TKO	5	—	197
1955						
Jan 6	Ansel Adams	Gothenburg	W	6	—	200
Feb 13	Kurt Schiegl	Stockholm	KO	5	—	191
Mar 4	Aldo Pellegrini	Gothenburg	WF	5	—	194
Apr 3	Uber Bacilieri	Stockholm	W	8	—	195
Jun 12	Günther Nürnberg	Dortmund, Germany	KO	7	—	—
Aug 28	Hein ten Hoff	Gothenburg	TKO	1	—	195
1956						
Feb 24	Joe Bygraves	Gothenburg	W	8	—	199
Apr 15	Hans Friedrich	Stockholm	W	10	—	195
Sep 30	Franco Cavicchi	Bologna, Italy	TKO	13	Won-European-H	200
Dec 28	Peter Bates	Gothenburg	KO	2	—	204
1957						
May 19	Henry Cooper	Stockholm	TKO	5	Ret-European-H	200
Dec 13	Archie McBride	Gothenburg	W	10	—	202
1958						
Feb 21	Joe Erskine	Gothenburg	KO	13	Ret-European-H	197
Jul 13	Heinz Neuhaus	Gothenburg	TKO	4	—	197
Sep 14	⑩ Eddie Machen	Gothenburg	TKO	1	—	198
1959						
Jun 26	♛ Floyd Patterson★	New York	TKO	3	Won-World-H	196
1960						
Jun 20	⑩ Floyd Patterson★	New York	KO'd	5	Lost-World-H	194
1961						
Mar 13	♛ Floyd Patterson★	Miami	KO'd	6	For-World-H	206
1962						
Feb 9	Joe Bygraves	Gothenburg	TKO	7	—	200
Apr 15	Wim Snoek	Stockholm	KO	5	—	198
Jun 17	Dick Richardson	Gothenburg	KO	8	Reg-European-H	202
1963						
Apr 21	⑩ Brian London	Stockholm	W	12	—	207

seventh-best contender for the heavyweight championship held by Floyd Patterson.

Johansson successfully defended his European crown with knock-out victories over Henry Cooper and Joe Erskine, yet he and his advisor Edwin Ahlquist—a Swedish manager and promoter—realized that Johansson would have to do more than beat up Europe's best to earn recognition in the U.S. and a shot at the world championship. With that goal in mind, Ahlquist arranged for top contender Eddie Machen to come to Gothenburg to fight Johansson. Johansson knocked Machen down three times and finally put him out in the first round of the fight, September 14, 1958. The victory over Machen propelled Johansson to *The Ring*'s top contender spot, and Patterson agreed to meet him for a title match.

Johansson moved his operation to Grossinger's, a resort in the Catskills, where he started training rigorously for the upcoming fight. His unusual methods attracted much attention. He brought his parents, his sister, and even his fiancée with him, though women were normally not allowed in a fighter's training camp. His running schedule was far tougher than the norm—six miles a day—and he trained at night because the fight was to take place at night. Johansson refused to use his fearsome right hand in sparring, and he rounded out his training with swimming and dancing.

Johansson was a heavy underdog as the day of the fight—June 26, 1959—approached, and many ridiculed his training regimen. In front of 19,000 fans in Yankee Stadium, the battle began quietly, with little action in the first round. In the second, Patterson scored with lefts to Johansson's face, but in the third spectators witnessed one of the most action-packed rounds in heavyweight championship history. Patterson threw two jabs to the face. Johansson responded with a left jab and then a right that knocked Patterson down for a nine count. Another right and left sent Patterson tumbling again. The champion got up, but another Johansson right, hitting behind the ear, toppled him to the canvas for a third time. An uppercut knocked Patterson down for a count of six, and a swinging right connected for the fifth knockdown of the round, while a left and right combination floored the now bleeding Patterson yet again. The champ gamely rose to his feet only to be met by a looping right that put him down for the seventh time. At this point, referee Ruby Goldstein stopped the fight.

The first Patterson match showed Johansson at his boxing best, a skillful fighter who looked for openings to fire his right hand, a pounding weapon that earned nicknames like "Hammer of Thor," "Toonder and Lightning," and "Ingo's Bingo."

Referee Ruby Goldstein has seen enough after Floyd Patterson suffers his seventh third-round knockdown. The first of the three Patterson–Johansson fights ended with Ingemar Johansson becoming the first European Heavyweight Champion of the World in 25 years.

The Associated Press named Johansson its Athlete of the Year for 1959, an honor rarely bestowed on a boxer.

Johansson's rematch with Patterson took place at the Polo Grounds on June 20, 1960, in front of 32,000 fans, and the belt changed hands again. This time Patterson led through the first four rounds, then put Johansson down for a nine count in the fifth, followed immediately by a knockout— both falls on powerful left hooks. The brawling fighters met for a third time, on March 13, 1961, at Convention Hall in Miami Beach. This time Johansson knocked Patterson down twice in the first round, but Patterson pulled off a win when Ingo failed to beat the count in the sixth.

After these two defeats, Johansson returned to Europe. He would never fight again in the United States—a choice that he would later regret. He did regain the European heavyweight title when he knocked out Dick Richardson in June of 1962, yet after barely decisioning Brian London in a fight where he was literally saved by the bell, on April 21, 1963, Johansson knew it was time to retire.

Johansson has led an active life outside of the ring. While still in boxing, he appeared on television with Dinah Shore and joined her in a duet. He also acted in a television production of Hemingway's *The Killers,* and worked as a boxing correspondent for Swedish TV. In July 1959, at the peak of Johansson's fame, rocker Johnny Lion released a song entitled "Ingemar Johansson" on the B-side of his single, "Haunted Heart." Johansson also starred in a 1960 suspense film, *48 Hours to Live,* in which a scientist is held hostage on a secluded island by nuclear weapon–seeking terrorists. Johansson has owned a fishing boat, a restaurant, and a motel, and was involved in the construction business both in Europe and the United States. He also was an importer of fish and prefabricated houses to the U.S.

Though not a typical boxer, for a short period Johansson held that elusive and imposing title: "Heavyweight Champion of the World."

With palm trees as a background, Johansson holds a public workout at Miami Beach before his third and final fight with Floyd Patterson.

HAROLD JOHNSON

LIGHT HEAVYWEIGHT

Right-handed; 5'10"; 161-184 lbs.
87 bouts, 1946 to 3/30/1971
Manager: Pat Olivieri
NBA Lt. Heavywt. Champ 1961–62
Light Heavywt. Champ 1962–63
Hall of Fame Induction: 1993
Born: 8/9/1928, Manayunk, PA

Appreciated by the connoisseurs of boxing if not by casual fans, Harold Johnson was one of the best technical boxers of all time. As a measure of Johnson's greatness, he was either champion or a ranked contender every year except one from 1951 to 1964.

Although Johnson's father, Phil, had been a professional fighter, the young Johnson did not learn to box at home. He ran away to join the navy at age fifteen and while there, had one amateur bout and boxed an exhibition with Hall of Famer Billy Conn. With this minimal amateur experience, Johnson turned professional upon his discharge from the navy in 1946.

Johnson reeled off 24 straight wins at the start of his career before losing a decision in ten rounds to Archie Moore. Jersey Joe Walcott put Johnson out in three rounds in 1950, one of the few times Johnson was knocked out. At times fighting heavyweight as well as light heavyweight opponents, Johnson won most of his bouts. By 1951, he was recognized by *The Ring* as one of the top contenders in the light heavyweight division.

Moore continued to be the man to beat, as far as Johnson was concerned. In a four-month period in late 1951 and early 1952, Johnson and Moore fought three times. Each fight went ten rounds; Johnson lost two and won one. He suffered one more loss in 1952, to Bob Satterfield, whom he later KO'd in two. The year 1953 yielded only wins for Johnson.

In 1954, Johnson faced Moore, who by then had become light heavyweight champion for the fifth time. With Moore's title at stake, Johnson battled hard. He knocked

Harold Johnson had a total of nine fights against other Hall of Famers. He battled Archie Moore five times.

Moore down in the tenth and was winning the fight through the thirteenth. In the fourteenth, Moore charged out of his corner to hit Johnson with a hard right. Then he unleashed a barrage of punches with both hands before knocking Johnson down with a crushing left hook. Johnson made it to his feet but was so groggy, referee Ruby Goldstein stopped the fight.

A mystery surrounding a 1955 fight in Philadelphia caused a slowdown in Johnson's career. In the second round, Johnson inexplicably fell to the canvas, giving the fight to opponent Julio Mederos. Although barbiturates were found in Johnson's urine, he claimed ignorance of the source and blamed his condition on an adulterated orange he had been given before the fight. Johnson passed a

IN THE RING	WON 76	LOST 11	DRAWS 0	TB 87	KO 32	W 44	WF 0	D 0	KO'd 5	L 6	LF 0

Date	Opponent	Site	Result / Rounds		Title	Wt.
1946						
Jul 30	Joe Riley	Wilmington, DE	KO	2	—	—
Aug 20	Charley Lester	Wilmington,	KO	2	—	—
Sep 25	Jack Simon	Allentown, PA	KO	4	—	—
Oct 25	Randy Ingram	Philadelphia	KO	4	—	161
1947						
Jan 10	Frank Lowry	Philadelphia	KO	2	—	166
Jan 24	Chappie Manning	Reading, PA	W	6	—	—
Feb 10	Jimmy Holden	Allentown	KO	4	—	—
Feb 17	Joe Van Loan	Philadelphia	KO	2	—	169
Mar 10	Tony Gillo	Philadelphia	W	6	—	167
Apr 28	Leon Szymurski	Philadelphia	KO	3	—	168
May 26	Fred Lester	Philadelphia	KO	8	—	166
Jul 8	Tommy Ruth	Philadelphia	KO	6	—	168
Aug 4	Al Pinel	Philadelphia	W	6	—	166
Oct 6	Eddie Beazley	Philadelphia	KO	1	—	168
Nov 6	Jimmy Moore	Atlantic City	KO	5	—	170
Nov 24	Herbie Katz	Philadelphia	KO	1	—	172
Dec 11	Kid Wolfe	Atlantic City	W	8	—	173
1948						
Mar 1	Kenny Harris	Philadelphia	W	8	—	167
Mar 29	Kenny Harris	Philadelphia	W	10	—	170
May 13	Vernon Williams	Atlantic City	W	8	—	170
Sep 28	Augustino Guedes	Philadelphia	KO	3	—	176
Nov 9	Jim Holden	Allentown	W	8	—	176
Dec 14	Willie Brown	Philadelphia	KO	7	—	173
1949						
Feb 24	Arturo Godoy	Philadelphia	W	10	—	178
Apr 26	⑩ Archie Moore★	Philadelphia	L	10	—	172
Jun 16	⑩ Henry Hall	Milwaukee	W	10	—	173
Jul 25	⑩ Henry Hall	Milwaukee	W	10	—	169
Oct 26	⑩ Jimmy Bivins★	Philadelphia	W	10	—	177
Dec 7	⑩ Bert Lytell	Dayton, OH	W	10	—	171
1950						
Feb 8	⑩ Jersey Joe Walcott★	Philadelphia	KO'd	3	—	180
Dec 18	Harry Daniels	Philadelphia	KO	2	—	170

1951							
Jan 22		Dusty Wilkerson	Philadelphia	KO	4	—	174
Feb 9		Chuck Hunter	New York	W	8	—	168
Jun 18		Elkins Brothers	Philadelphia	KO	10	—	178
Jul 23		Chubby Wright	Philadelphia	W	10	—	175
Sep 24	⑩	Archie Moore★	Philadelphia	L	10	—	174
Dec 10	⑩	Archie Moore★	Milwaukee	W	10	—	171
1952							
Jan 29	⑩	Archie Moore★	Toledo, OH	L	10	—	170
Mar 17	⑩	Clarence Henry	Philadelphia	W	10	—	178
Aug 6	⑩	Bob Satterfield	Chicago	L	10	—	175
Sep 16		Leonard Morrow	Toledo	TKO	3	—	173
Oct 6	⑩	Bob Satterfield	Philadelphia	KO	2	—	175
Nov 24		Nino Valdes	Brooklyn	W	10	—	176
1953							
Jan 16	⑩	Jimmy Slade	New York	W	10	—	175
Mar 21		Bill Gilliam	Toledo	W	10	—	176
May 11		Toxie Hall	Miami	W	10	—	176
Sep 8	⑩	Ezzard Charles★	Philadelphia	W	10	—	177
Nov 7		Henry Hall	Milwaukee	W	10	—	174
Nov 19		Chubby Wright	Hershey, PA	W	10	—	177
1954							
Jan 29	⑩	Jimmy Slade	New York	W	10	—	178
Feb 15		Charlie Williams	Miami	KO	8	—	174
Mar 17	⑩	Paul Andrews	Chicago	W	10	—	176
Aug 11	♛	Archie Moore★	New York	TKO'd	14	For-World-LH	172
Oct 8	⑩	Billy Smith	Philadelphia	KO'd	2	—	174
Dec 7		Julio Mederos	Miami Beach	W	10	—	175
Dec 22	⑩	Marty Marshall	Detroit	W	10	—	174
1955							
Feb 11	⑩	Paul Andrews	New York	KO	6	—	175
May 6		Julio Mederos	Philadelphia	TKO'd	2	—	179
1956							
Dec 8		Bert Whitehurst	Portland, ME	W	10	—	179
1957							
Mar 12		Bob Satterfield	Miami Beach	W	10	—	180
May 31	⑩	Clarence Hinnant	New York	KO	1	—	176
Sep 20	⑩	Wayne Bethea	Philadelphia	W	10	—	181
Dec 17		Sid Peaks	Toledo	KO	5	—	179
1958							
Jan 17		Bert Whitehurst	Syracuse, NY	W	10	—	176
Apr 15		Oliver Wilson	Hartford, CT	KO	2	—	180
Dec 3		Howard King	Chicago	W	10	—	180
Dec 15		Rudy Watkins	Philadelphia	KO	6	—	179
1959							
Aug 4		Johnny York	Pittsfield, IL	TKO	6	—	182
Nov 11	⑩	Sonny Ray	Chicago	TKO	10	—	175
1960							
May 4		Clarence Floyd	Philadelphia	W	10	—	178
1961							
Feb 7		Jesse Bowdry	Miami Beach	TKO	9	Won-Vac NBA-LH	172
Apr 24	⑩	Von Clay	Philadelphia	KO	2	Ret-NBA-LH	174
Jul 1	⑩	Eddie Machen	Atlantic City	W	10	—	181
Aug 29	⑩	Eddie Cotton	Seattle	W	15	Ret-NBA-LH	173

1962							
May 12	⑩	Doug Jones	Philadelphia	W	15	Won-Vac World-LH	171
Jun 23	⑩	Gustav Scholz	Berlin	W	15	Ret-World-LH	172
1963							
Mar 19		Tommy Merrill	Scranton, PA	KO	9	—	184
Jun 1	⑩	Willie Pastrano★	Las Vegas	L	15	Lost-World-LH	173
Dec 6	⑩	Henry Hank	Philadelphia	W	10	—	176
1964							
Apr 20		Hank Casey	Santa Monica, CA	KO	8	—	176
1966							
Jan 7		Johnny Persol	New York	L	10	—	176
Dec 6		Pekka Kokkonen	Vienna	W	10	—	181
1967							
May 1		Herschel Jacobs	New Orleans	W	10	—	177
Aug 7	⑩	Eddie Jones	New Orleans	W	10	—	176
1968							
Mar 2	⑩	Lothan Stengel	Frankfurt, Germany	W	10	—	170
Jun 11		Johnny Alford	Miami Beach	W	10	—	179
1971							
Mar 30		Herschel Jacobs	New York	TKO'd	3	—	177

lie detector test clearing his name, but the uproar resulted in a three-month suspension of boxing in Pennsylvania, by order of the governor.

Following this incident, Johnson found it more difficult to gain bouts. Moore was reluctant to fight him again, and it was not until 1961, after Moore had forfeited his crown for inactivity, that Johnson finally got another chance at a light heavyweight title. He knocked out Jesse Bowdry in Miami Beach to win the vacant NBA title. Muhammad Ali, on the undercard that night, was reportedly very impressed with Johnson.

Johnson unified the title when he decisioned Doug Jones in convincing fashion in 1962. He held the undisputed world championship for one year before losing on a decision to a last-minute replacement, Willie Pastrano. Johnson continued to fight for five years and even made a brief comeback in 1971 at 42. Though never a great favorite of the fans, Johnson earned the respect of those inside boxing. Asked why he never put Johnson in a nationally televised fight, matchmaker Teddy Brenner said cryptically, "Harold Johnson represents perfection in the art of boxing, and there is no room in this world for perfection." In retirement, Johnson has worked in contracting.

Johnson was recognized as champ by the NBA in 1961. The following year he gained universal recognition.

ISMAEL LAGUNA
El Tigre Colonense

L I G H T W E I G H T

Right-handed; 5'9"; 116–139 lbs.

75 bouts, 1/8/1961 to 9/13/1971

Manager: Hector ("Tato") Valdes

Lightweight Champion 1965, 1970

Hall of Fame Induction: 2001

Born: 6/28/1943, Colon, Panama

Named: Ismael Laguna Meneses

One of the top lightweights of the 1960s, Ismael Laguna twice reigned as world lightweight champion. A twin and one of ten children in his family, Laguna idolized the boxers who trained at a local gym, and he would spend his time there after school. The boxers, for their part, took a liking to Laguna and taught him the rudiments of boxing. After competing as an amateur, he turned pro as a bantamweight on January 8, 1961, knocking out Antonio Morgan in the second round.

Fighting exclusively in Colon and Panama City, Laguna won his first 27 bouts, nineteen of them with knock-out victories. Along the way, he captured the Panamanian featherweight title with a knockout over Pedro Ortiz. Laguna suffered his first defeat in Bogata, Columbia, a decision on June 8, 1963, that went to Antonio Herrera. He returned to Panama to knock Herrera out in the rematch on Laguna's home turf. The following year, Laguna lost a decision to Hall of Famer Vicente Saldivar, who would soon be the featherweight champion, but nevertheless rose to the top-contender spot in *The Ring* rankings.

Given his five-foot, nine-inch frame, it was not difficult for Laguna to advance to the lightweight division. On April 10, 1965, he received his first title shot against lightweight champ Carlos Ortiz, a Hall of Famer. Before 18,000 fans in Panama City, the fight opened with Laguna aggressively taking charge, throwing swift jabs and punishing shots to the body. Ortiz made an attempt to slow Laguna down, rushing inside, but Laguna countered with swift punches and out-boxed

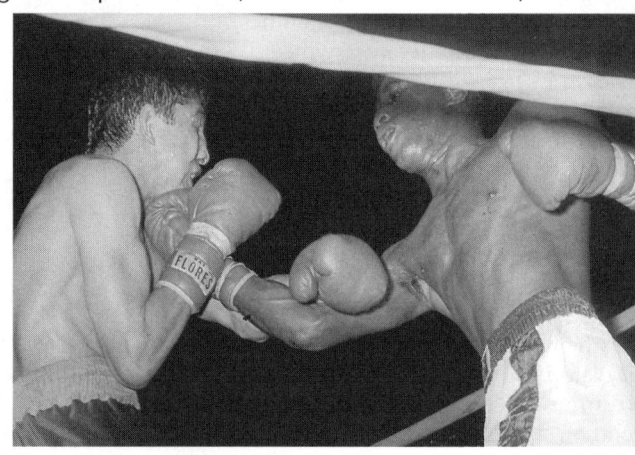

Laguna (R) regains his world lightweight title with a March 3, 1970, TKO victory over Armando ("Mando") Ramos in Los Angeles. Laguna's uppercut is an effective weapon.

IN THE RING	WON 65	LOST 9	DRAWS 1	TB 75	KO 37	W 28	WF 0	D 1	KO'd 0	L 9	LF 0

Date	Opponent	Site	Result / Rounds		Title	Wt.
1961						
Jan 8	Antonio Morgan	Colon, Panama	KO	2	—	—
Jan 22	Eduardo Frutos	Colon	W	4	—	118
Mar 5	Javier Valle	Panama City	W	4	—	116
Mar 26	Carlos Real	Panama City	W	4	—	117
Apr 16	Jose Pacheco	Panama City	TKO	3	—	118
Apr 30	Ernest Campbell	Panama City	W	6	—	116
May 21	Battling Escudero	Colon	KO	2	—	117
Jun 4	Killer Solomon	Colon	KO	7	—	—
Jun 25	Claudio Martinez	Colon	KO	4	—	116
Aug 27	Enrique Hitchman	Panama City	W	10	—	118
Oct 15	Euro Partides	Panama City	KO	4	—	118
Dec 1	Hector Hicks	Colon	KO	5	—	—
1962						
Jan 14	Eloy Sanchez	Colon	KO	3	—	118
Mar 2	Castor Castillo	Maracaibo, Venezuela	W	10	—	—
Apr 15	Nelson Estrada	Panama City	KO	7	—	117
Jun 3	Jorge Uzcategui	Colon	KO	2	—	—
Jun 10	Agustin Carmona	Panama City	KO	6	—	119
Jun 24	Carlos Celis	Panama City	KO	3	—	123
Jul 29	Jorge Salazar	Panama City	KO	6	—	—
Sep 16	Pedro Ortiz	Panama City	TKO	7	Won-Panama-FE	123
Oct 28	Beresford Francis	Colon	KO	5	—	123
Nov 18	Enrique Hitchman	Colon	KO	2	—	121
Dec 16	Tony Herrera	Panama City	KO	2	—	124
1963						
Jan 20	Bobby Gray	Colon	KO	9	—	125
Feb 22	Juan Ramirez	Panama City	W	10	—	124
Mar 17 ⑩	Auburn Copeland	Panama City	W	10	—	125
May 21	Filiberto Nava	Panama City	KO	3	—	127
Jun 8 ⑩	Antonio Herrera	Bogota	L	10	—	127
Jul 21 ⑩	Don Johnson	Panama City	KO	3	—	126
Aug 24	Eduardo ("Lalo") Guerrero	Panama City	W	10	—	126
Sep 15 ⑩	Antonio Herrera	Panama City	TKO	7	—	126
Nov 18 ⑩	Rafiu King	Paris	W	10	—	127
1964						
Jan 26	Pedro Miranda	Colon	KO	4	—	—
Feb 21	Orispo Dos Santos	Sao Paulo, Brazil	KO	7	—	128
Mar 9	Angel Robinson Garcia	Paris	W	10	—	130
Jun 1 ⑩	Vicente Saldivar★	Tijuana, Mexico	L	10	—	125
Jul 6	Kid Anahuac	Los Angeles	KO	8	—	130
Aug 2 ⑩	Vicente Derado	Panama City	W	10	—	132
Oct 25	Percy Hayles	Panama City	TKO	7	—	134
Dec 19	Sebastiao Nascimento	Panama City	W	10	—	132
1965						
Apr 10 ♛	Carlos Ortiz★	Panama City	W	15	Won-World-L	132
Jun 20	Raul Soriano	Panama City	KO	8	—	136
Jul 17 ⑩	Nicolino Loche	Buenos Aires	D	10	—	136
Nov 13 ⑩	Carlos Ortiz★	San Juan, PR	L	15	Lost-World-L	133

1966							
Feb 19	♛	Carlos Hernandez	Panama City	TKO	8	—	133
Mar 19	♛	Gabriel ("Flash") Elorde★	Manila	L	10	—	134
Jul 28		Al Grant	Los Angeles	W	10	—	135
Oct 2		Percy Hayles	Kingston, Jamaica	KO	6	—	135
Dec 3		Daniel Guanin	Panama City	KO	8	—	135
1967							
Mar 10	⑩	Frankie Narvaez	New York	W	10	—	134
Apr 2		Vicente Rivas	Panama City	KO	5	—	135
Jun 3		Alfredo Urbina	Panama City	W	10	—	136
Aug 16	♛	Carlos Ortiz★	New York	L	15	For-World-L	135
Oct 28	⑩	Paul Armstead	Panama City	W	10	—	133
1968							
Feb 26		Ray Adigun	Paris	W	10	—	136
Apr 15		Bud Anderson	Philadelphia	TKO	10	—	135
Apr 29	⑩	Frankie Narvaez	San Juan	W	10	—	136
Jul 17		Victor Melendez	New York	W	10	—	136
Aug 20	⑩	Lloyd Marshall	New York	TKO	9	—	136
Oct 7		Gabe LaMarca	Scranton, PA	KO	7	—	136
Oct 22		Grady Ponder	Miami Beach	W	10	—	137
Nov 15		Ramon Blanco	New York	W	10	—	136
1969							
Mar 1		Curly Aguirre	Panama City	KO	4	—	—
Mar 31		Maurice Tavant	Paris	W	10	—	—
May 24		Eugenio Espinosa	Quito, Ecuador	L	10	—	135
Jul 5		Eugenio Espinosa	Panama City	W	10	—	135
Jul 14		Gennaro Soto	New York	W	10	—	136
1970							
Jan 10		Jose Luis Vallejo	Colon	KO	3	—	—
Mar 3	♛	Armando ("Mando") Ramos	Los Angeles	TKO	9	Reg-World-L	135
Jun 6		Ishimatsu Suzuki	Panama City	TKO	13	Ret-World-L	135
Sep 26	⑩	Ken Buchanan★	San Juan	L	15	Lost-World-L	134
1971							
Mar 6		Lloyd Marshall	Panama City	W	10	—	137
Apr 3	⑩	Chango Carmona	Panama City	W	10	—	135
Jun 22		Eddie Linder	Miami Beach	L	10	—	139
Sep 13	♛	Ken Buchanan★	New York	L	15	For-World-L	135

the champion. In the seventh round, Laguna's hard-hitting combinations opened a gash in Ortiz's mouth and split open his left eye. Ortiz came back in the ninth, hammering his opponent with a left to the head, a right to his mid-section, and another right that sent Laguna reeling into the ropes. Yet the attack did not faze Laguna, and he came back with both fists flying to end the Ortiz rally. For the rest of the bout, Laguna was clearly in command and he won a majority decision, with referee Jersey Joe Walcott's card showing 143-132, one judge's card showing 149-137, and the other judge inexplicably scoring the battle 145-145. The latter judge escaped the arena with police protection, and Laguna was the champion.

In the rematch seven months later in San Juan, Ortiz capitalized on his superior strength and nearly ended the fight in both the twelfth and thirteenth rounds, but Laguna toughed it out and lasted for the full fifteen rounds. The decision, however, went to Ortiz, and he recaptured his championship title. On August 16, 1967, the two came together for another match, this time meeting in Shea Stadium in New York. Laguna eluded the bull-like rushes of Ortiz, but he failed to mount a strong attack, and the belt stayed with the champion in a fifteen-round decision.

Laguna won fourteen of his next fifteen fights, earning him another shot at the lightweight title, which was now held by Mando Ramos. Fifteen thousand fans packed the Los Angeles Sports Arena, Ramos's home turf. Laguna went on the attack and opened cuts over both of Ramos's eyes, and by the ninth round, Ramos could not continue. Laguna was again the champion.

Laguna successfully defended his title against Ishimatsu Suzuki, then faced Hall of Famer Ken Buchanan. Though he was favored, Laguna found he had his hands full with Buchanan. The latter scored well in the twelfth round especially, and the split decision went to Buchanan. A year later, on September 13, 1971, in Madison Square Garden, the two fighters came together once more. Laguna changed his plan of attack, attempting to brawl with Buchanan, but lost another fifteen-round decision to the champion. Faced with defeat, Laguna retired.

Laguna was a complete fighter, possessed of a strong jab and a knock-out punch, and combining great boxing skill with impressive resilience. Described as a "tall, immaculate boxer," he knocked out almost half of his opponents and was not once knocked to the canvas during his 75 fights.

In retirement, Laguna resided in Panama City, where he remained an extremely popular figure. Unlike many boxers, he had not squandered his ring earnings. He moved on to promote some fights, until weakened by sickle cell anemia.

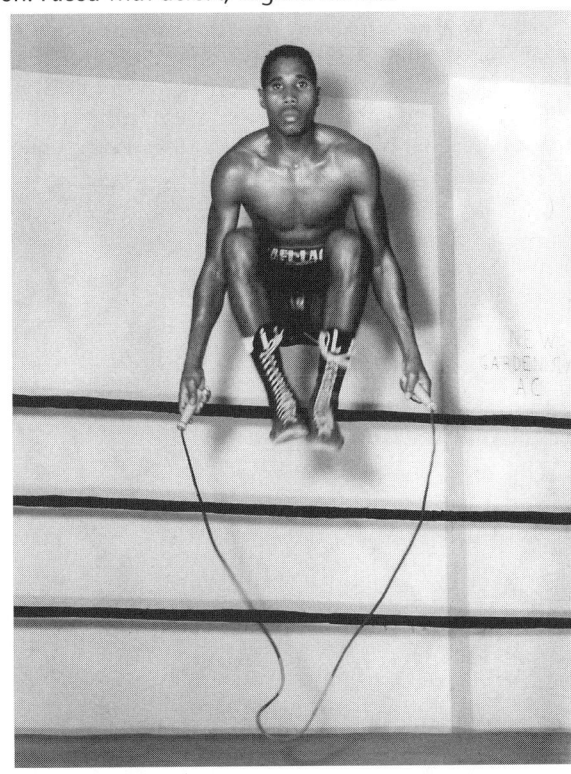

Laguna shows amazing leg spring in this high-flying jump rope demonstration.

JAKE LAMOTTA
The Bronx Bull

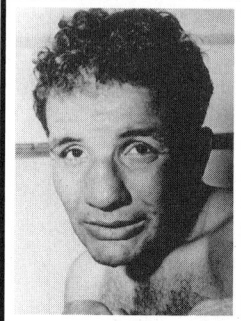

MIDDLEWEIGHT

Right-handed; 5'8"; 154–175 lbs.

106 bouts, 3/3/1941 to 4/14/1954

Managers: Mike Capriano, Joey LaMotta

Middleweight Champion 1949–51

Hall of Fame Induction: 1990

Born: 7/10/1921, Bronx, NY

Named: Giacobe LaMotta

Jake LaMotta, perennial opponent of Sugar Ray Robinson, was a tough, cagey fighter. He fought with a brutal will to win and was a master of playing possum in the ring. LaMotta's fame was given an extra dimension by the Academy Award–winning movie, *Raging Bull*, in which the fighter was portrayed by Robert DeNiro.

Born in New York, LaMotta was a street fighter who ran afoul of the law as a youth and spent some time in reform school. He began boxing in his teens, fought as an amateur for two years, then turned pro at the age of eighteen. He quickly made a name for himself and by 1942, was ranked by *The Ring* as the sixth-best middleweight contender. That year he fought Sugar Ray Robinson in the first of their six match-ups. LaMotta lost the ten-round decision, but in 1943, he became the first to beat the then-undefeated Robinson. LaMotta also battled Hall of Famer Fritzie Zivic four times in seven months in 1943 and 1944, losing only once.

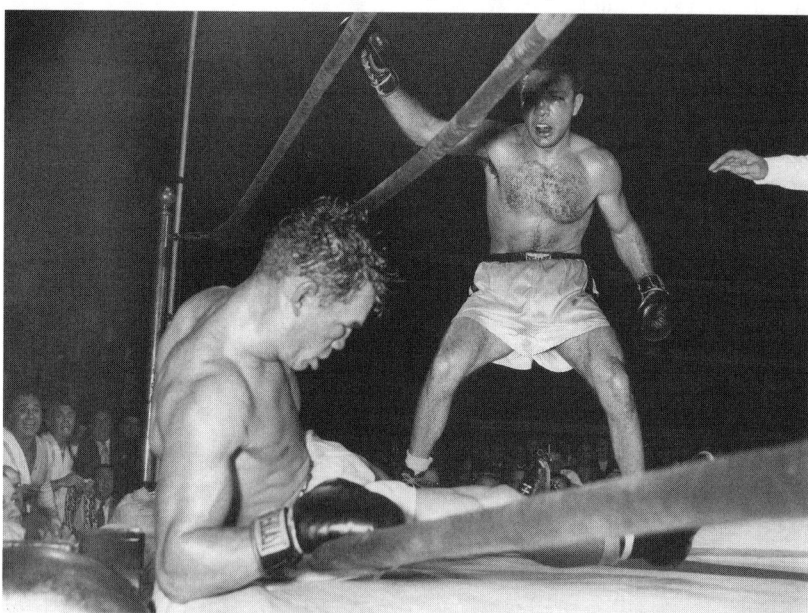

Battered and swollen, LaMotta (R) summons his last reserves to knock out Laurent Dauthuille with a mere thirteen seconds remaining before the final bell in this September 1950 Motor City meeting.

IN THE RING	WON 83	LOST 19	DRAWS 4	TB 106	KO 30	W 53	WF 0	D 4	KO'd 4	L 15	LF 0

Date	Opponent	Site	Result / Rounds		Title	Wt.
1941						
Mar 3	Charley Mackley	New York	W	4	—	167
Mar 14	Tony Gillo	Bridgeport, CT	W	6	—	—
Apr 1	Johnny Morris	White Plains, NY	TKO	4	—	174
Apr 8	Joe Fredericks	White Plains	KO	1	—	168
Apr 15	Stanley Goicz	White Plains	W	4	—	171
Apr 22	Lorne McCarthy	White Plains	W	4	—	170
Apr 26	Monroe Crewe	Brooklyn	W	4	—	169
May 20	Johnny Cihlar	Brooklyn	W	4	—	170
May 27	Johnny Morris	New York	W	4	—	167
Jun 9	Lorenzo Strickland	Woodhaven, NY	W	4	—	166
Jun 16	Lorenzo Strickland	New York	W	6	—	166
Jun 23	Johnny Morris	New York	KO	3	—	164
Jul 15	Joe Baynes	Long Island City, NY	W	6	—	166
Aug 5	Joe Shikula	Long Island City	D	6	—	166
Aug 11	Cliff Koerkle	New York	W	6	—	166
Sep 24	Jimmy Reeves	Cleveland	L	10	—	167
Oct 7	Lorenzo Strickland	White Plains	W	8	—	167
Oct 20	Jimmy Reeves	Cleveland	L	10	—	166
Nov 14	Jimmy Casa	New York	W	6	—	162
Dec 22	Nate Bolden	Chicago	L	10	—	164
1942						
Jan 27	Frankie Jamison	New York	W	8	—	162
Mar 3	Frankie Jamison	New York	W	8	—	163
Mar 18	Lorenzo Strickland	New York	W	10	—	161
Apr 7	Lou Schwartz	New York	KO	9	—	160
Apr 21	Buddy O'Dell	New York	W	10	—	158
May 12	⑩ Jose Basora	New York	D	10	—	159
Jun 2	Vic Dellicurti	New York	W	10	—	157
Jun 16	⑩ Jose Basora	New York	L	10	—	158
Jul 28	Lorenzo Strickland	New York	W	8	—	160
Aug 28	⑩ Jimmy Edgar	New York	W	10	—	160
Sep 8	Vic Dellicurti	New York	W	10	—	158
Oct 2	⑩ Sugar Ray Robinson★	New York	L	10	—	157
Oct 20	Wild Bill McDowell	New York	TKO	5	—	162
Nov 6	Henry Chmielewski	Boston	W	10	—	165
1943						
Jan 2	⑩ Jimmy Edgar	Detroit	W	10	—	161
Jan 15	⑩ Jackie Wilson	New York	W	10	—	161
Jan 22	Charley Hayes	Detroit	TKO	6	—	160
Feb 5	⑩ Sugar Ray Robinson★	Detroit	W	10	—	160
Feb 26	⑩ Sugar Ray Robinson★	Detroit	L	10	—	160
Mar 19	Jimmy Reeves	Detroit	KO	6	—	159
Mar 30	Ossie Harris	Pittsburgh	W	10	—	161
May 12	Tony Ferrara	Cincinnati	KO	6	—	160
Jun 10	⑩ Fritzie Zivic★	Pittsburgh	W	10	—	155
Jul 12	⑩ Fritzie Zivic★	Pittsburgh	L	15	—	157
Sep 17	⑩ Jose Basora	Detroit	W	10	—	162
Oct 11	Johnny Walker	Philadelphia	TKO	2	—	164
Nov 12	⑩ Fritzie Zivic★	New York	W	10	—	161

1944

Jan 14	⑩	Fritzie Zivic★	Detroit	W	10	—	159
Jan 28		Ossie Harris	Detroit	W	10	—	158
Feb 25		Ossie Harris	Detroit	W	10	—	162
Mar 17	⑩	Coley Welch	Boston	W	10	—	163
Mar 31		Sgt. Lou Woods	Chicago	W	10	—	162
Apr 21	⑩	Lloyd Marshall	Cleveland	L	10	—	160
Sep 29	⑩	George Kochan	Detroit	W	10	—	162
Nov 3	⑩	George Kochan	Detroit	TKO	9	—	161

1945

Feb 23	⑩	Sugar Ray Robinson★	New York	L	10	—	157
Mar 19		Lou Schwartz	Norfolk, VA	KO	1	—	161
Mar 28		George Costner	Chicago	KO	6	—	157
Apr 19	⑩	Vic Dellicurti	New York	W	10	—	163
Apr 27	⑩	Bert Lytell	Boston	W	10	—	160
Jul 6		Tommy Bell	New York	W	10	—	161
Aug 10	⑩	Jose Basora	New York	TKO	9	—	159
Sep 17		George Kochan	New York	KO	9	—	162
Sep 26	⑩	Sugar Ray Robinson★	Chicago	L	12	—	159
Nov 13		Coolidge Miller	New York	KO	3	—	165
Nov 23		Walter Woods	Boston	KO	8	—	164
Dec 7		Charley Parham	Chicago	TKO	6	—	159

1946

Jan 11	⑩	Tommy Bell	New York	W	10	—	161
Mar 29		Marcus Lockman	Boston	W	10	—	163
May 24		Joe Reddick	Boston	W	10	—	162
Jun 13	⑩	Jimmy Edgar	Detroit	D	10	—	156
Aug 7	⑩	Holman Williams	Detroit	W	10	—	162
Sep 12		Bob Satterfield	Chicago	KO	7	—	167
Oct 25		O'Neill Bell	Detroit	KO	2	—	159
Dec 6		Anton Raadik	Chicago	W	10	—	162

1947

Mar 14	⑩	Tommy Bell	New York	W	10	—	161
Jun 6	⑩	Tony Janiro	New York	W	10	—	154
Sep 3		Cecil Hudson	Chicago	L	10	—	165
Nov 14	⑩	Billy Fox	New York	TKO'd	4	—	167

1948

Jun 1		Ken Stribling	Washington, DC	TKO	5	—	164
Sep 7		Burl Charity	New York	TKO	6	—	166
Oct 1		Johnny Colan	New York	TKO	10	—	165
Oct 18		Vern Lester	Brooklyn	W	10	—	165
Dec 3		Tommy Yarosz	New York	W	10	—	164

1949

Feb 21	⑩	Laurent Dauthuille	Montreal	L	10	—	161
Mar 25	⑩	Robert Villemain	New York	W	12	—	160
Apr 18		O'Neill Bell	Detroit	KO	4	—	167
May 18		Joey DeJohn	Syracuse, NY	TKO	8	—	162
Jun 16	♛	Marcel Cerdan★	Detroit	TKO	10	Won-World-M	158
Dec 9	⑩	Robert Villemain	New York	L	10	—	165

1950

Feb 3		Dick Wagner	Detroit	TKO	9	—	170
Mar 28		Chuck Hunter	Cleveland	TKO	6	—	168
May 4		Joe Taylor	Syracuse	W	10	—	169
Jul 12	⑩	Tiberio Mitri	New York	W	15	Ret-World-M	159
Sep 13	⑩	Laurent Dauthuille	Detroit	KO	15	Ret-World-M	159

1951							
Feb 14		Sugar Ray Robinson★	Chicago	TKO'd	13	Lost-World-M	160
Jun 27	⑩	Bob Murphy	New York	TKO'd	7	—	175
1952							
Jan 28	⑩	Norman Hayes	Boston	L	10	—	169
Mar 5		Eugene Hairston	Detroit	D	10	—	168
Apr 9	⑩	Norman Hayes	Detroit	W	10	—	167
May 21		Eugene Hairston	Detroit	W	10	—	168
Jun 11	⑩	Bob Murphy	Detroit	W	10	—	169
Dec 31	⑩	Danny Nardico	Coral Gables, FL	TKO'd	8	—	173
1954							
Mar 11		Johnny Pretzie	W. Palm Beach, FL	KO	4	—	169
Apr 3		Al McCoy	Charlotte, NC	KO	1	—	168
Apr 14		Billy Kilgore	Miami Beach	L	10	—	167

LaMotta lost two decisions to Robinson in 1945. He continued to box well but was not given a chance at the middleweight title. Later, LaMotta testified before a U.S. Senate Anti-Monopoly Subcommittee that he was denied a title fight because he refused to become involved with mobsters. In the same hearings, however, LaMotta said he took a dive in a 1947 fight with Billy Fox in return for a promise that he could fight for the title.

In 1949, LaMotta finally got his chance at the middleweight title, against Marcel Cerdan. The match was held at Briggs Stadium in Detroit before 22,183 fans. After he wrestled Cerdan to the canvas in the first round, injuring Cerdan's left shoulder, LaMotta easily controlled the fight. He was given the victory when Cerdan failed to answer the bell for the tenth round. The chance of a rematch, first delayed by a claim of injury by LaMotta, was lost forever when Cerdan was killed in a plane crash.

LaMotta had two amazing fights left in his career. In 1950, he scored a fifteenth-round knockout of Laurent Dauthuille. Dauthuille, who dominated through most of the bout, fell victim in the twelfth round to LaMotta's trick of feigning serious injury. When Dauthuille came in close, LaMotta unleashed a flurry of blows. LaMotta, still behind in the fifteenth, gathered the strength for one last foray. He knocked Dauthuille out with thirteen seconds to go in the fight.

Actor Robert DeNiro (L) played Jake LaMotta (R) in the acclaimed biographical movie Raging Bull.

LaMotta lost his final fight with Robinson, held on Valentine's Day 1951 in Chicago Stadium. The two seemed fairly well matched in the early going, but as time went on, Robinson's pummeling of LaMotta became painful to watch. That LaMotta could still stand amazed the ringside experts. With LaMotta still on his feet but Robinson clearly the winner, the fight was stopped in the thirteenth round. LaMotta fought for another three years before turning to acting and other pursuits.

SUGAR RAY LEONARD

WELTERWEIGHT

Right-handed; 5'10"; 141–168 lbs.
40 bouts, 2/5/1977 to 3/1/1997
Manager: Angelo Dundee
1976 Olympic Light Welterweight Gold Medalist
WBC Welterweight Champion 1979–80, 1980–81
World Wltrwt Champ 1981–82
WBA Junior Midwt Champ 1981
WBC Midwt Champ 1987
WBC Light Hvywt Champ 1988
WBC Super Midwt Champ 1988–90
Hall of Fame Induction: 1997
Born: 5/17/1956, Wilmington, NC
Named: Ray Charles Leonard

Sugar Ray Leonard first captured the public's imagination with an electrifying gold medal performance in the 1976 Olympics, and his popular appeal has never diminished. Fast, powerful, and stylish in the ring, Leonard has proven to be one of the greatest boxers of the modern era. His stellar career brought him world championships in five weight classes, over $100 million in earnings, and fame that spread far beyond boxing.

Leonard was thirteen years old when he started training at a recreation center in Palmer Park, Maryland, under the guidance of Janks Morton and Dave Jacobs. In 1972, at just sixteen, Leonard advanced to the quarterfinals of the Olympic trials. Other amateur honors

Two young future Hall of Famers contested the welterweight championship on November 30, 1979, in Las Vegas. Challenger Leonard (R), 23 years old, defeated titleholder Wilfred Benitez, only 21.

IN THE RING	WON 36	LOST 3	DRAWS 1	TB 40	KO 25	W 11	WF 0	D 1	KO'd 1	L 2	LF 0

Date		Opponent	Site	Result / Rounds		Title	Wt.
1977							
Feb 5		Luis Vega	Baltimore	W	6	—	141
May 14		Willie Rodriguez	Baltimore	W	6	—	141
Jun 10		Vinnie DeBarros	Hartford, CT	TKO	3	—	142
Sep 24		Frank Santore	Baltimore	KO	5	—	142
Nov 5		Agustin Estrada	Las Vegas	KO	5	—	145
Dec 17		Hector Diaz	Washington	KO	2	—	145
1978							
Feb 4		Rocky Ramon	Baltimore	W	8	—	143
Mar 1		Art McKnight	Dayton, OH	TKO	7	—	145
Mar 19		Javier Muniz	New Haven, CT	KO	1	—	144
Apr 13		Bobby Haymon	Landover, MD	TKO	3	—	147
May 13		Randy Milton	Utica, NY	TKO	8	—	—
Jun 3		Rafael Rodriguez	Baltimore	W	10	—	147
Jul 18		Dick Ecklund	Boston	W	10	—	146
Sep 9	⑩	Floyd Mayweather	Providence, RI	TKO	9	—	146
Oct 6	⑩	Randy Shields	Baltimore	W	10	—	147
Nov 3		Bernardo Prada	Portland, ME	W	10	—	146
Dec 9	⑩	Armando Muniz	Springfield, MA	TKO	6	—	149
1979							
Jan 11	⑩	Johnny Gant	Landover	TKO	8	—	146
Feb 11		Fernand Marcotte	Miami Beach	TKO	8	—	149
Mar 24		Daniel Gonzalez	Tucson, AZ	KO	1	—	147
Apr 21	⑩	Adolfo Viruet	Las Vegas	W	10	—	145
May 20		Marcos Geraldo	New Orleans	W	10	—	153
Jun 24	⑩	Tony Chiaverini	Las Vegas	TKO	4	—	151
Aug 12	⑩	Pete Ranzany	Las Vegas	TKO	4	Won-NABF-W	147
Sep 28	⑩	Andy Price	Las Vegas	KO	1	Ret-NABF-W	146
Nov 30	♛	Wilfred Benitez★	Las Vegas	TKO	15	Won-WBC-W	146
1980							
Mar 31	⑩	Davey ("Boy") Green	Landover	KO	4	Ret-WBC-W	147
Jun 20	⑩	Roberto Duran	Montreal	L	15	Lost-WBC-W	145
Nov 25	♛	Roberto Duran	New Orleans	TKO	8	Reg-WBC-W	146
1981							
Mar 28		Larry Bonds	Syracuse, NY	TKO	10	Ret-WBC-W	145
Jun 25	♛	Ayub Kalule	Houston	KO	9	Won-WBA-JM	153
Sep 16	♛	Thomas ("Hit Man") Hearns	Las Vegas	TKO	14	Won-World-W	146
1982							
Feb 15	⑩	Bruce Finch	Reno, NV	TKO	3	Ret-World-W	146
1984							
May 11		Kevin Howard	Worcester, MA	TKO	9	—	149
1987							
Apr 6	♛	Marvelous Marvin Hagler★	Las Vegas	W	12	Won-WBC-M	160
1988							
Nov 7	♛	Don Lalonde	Las Vegas	TKO	9	Won-WBC-SM & LH	167

1989							
Jun 12	⑩	Thomas ("Hit Man") Hearns	Las Vegas	D	12	Ret-WBC-SM	160
Dec 7	♛	Roberto Duran	Las Vegas	W	12	Ret-WBC-SM	168
1991							
Feb 9	♛	Terry Norris★	New York	L	12	For-WBC-JM	154
1997							
Mar 1	⑩	Hector ("Macho") Camacho	Atlantic City	TKO'd	5	For-IBC-M	159

followed as Leonard won the national junior lightweight title in 1972; national Golden Gloves titles in 1973, 1974, and 1975; AAU championships in 1974 and 1975; the North American junior welterweight title in 1974 and 1975; and the Pan American Games championship in 1975.

Leonard capped his amateur career by striking gold in the 1976 Olympics in the light welterweight division. As part of the U.S. team that produced four other gold medal winners (Leon Spinks, Michael Spinks, Howard Davis, and Leo Randolph), Leonard tore through five opponents before winning the top honors with a decision over Andres Aldama of Cuba. The national television audience saw

Trading canvas for hardwood for one evening, Leonard drives past Pernell ("Sweet Pea") Whitaker in a charity basketball game held at Norfolk State University in Norfolk, Virginia, on August 29, 1990. Whitaker's team came out on top.

Leonard (L) floored Thomas ("Hit Man") Hearns in Las Vegas in their 1981 welterweight unification bout. The referee halted the contest in the fourteenth round and declared Leonard the winner.

Leonard as a charismatic, personable young man who, as ABC-TV's Howard Cosell reported, went into the ring with a picture of his girlfriend taped to his shoe.

Initially, Leonard hoped his Olympic stardom would lead to commercial endorsements and enough money to go to college and also to help care for his ailing parents. When no endorsement offers arrived, he decided to turn professional. Morton and Jacobs stayed with him, and Maryland attorney Mike Trainer also came on the scene. Partly on the advice of Ali and Cosell, Trainer and Leonard hired Angelo Dundee as manager.

CBS televised Leonard's pro debut on February 5, 1977, against Luis ("the Bull") Vega. The fight drew a record crowd of 10,170 to the Baltimore Civic Center. Leonard's win by decision earned him $40,000 (a then-record paycheck for a pro debut), while Vega took home just $650. By the end of 1978, Leonard had won all seventeen of his fights, including three victories over ranked opponents. *The Ring* rated him the third-best welterweight contender.

In 1979, Leonard beat an impressive lineup of ranked contenders and was given a shot at the WBC welterweight title held by Wilfred Benitez. For this much-anticipated bout, Benitez penned a contract for $1 million and Leonard $1.2 million. Although Benitez evaded more blows than any of Leonard's previous opponents, Leonard downed the champ with a jab in the third. Benitez fought gamely and well until late in the last round when Leonard knocked him down with a left uppercut, then followed with a devastating combination that convinced referee Carlos Padilla to stop the fight. Just six seconds short of the final bell, Leonard had won his first world title.

Despite his speed and power, some considered Leonard a bit of a hot dog who liked to play to the crowd and imitate the Ali shuffle. His first fight with Roberto Duran made it clear, however, that Leonard was as tough as they come. On June 20, 1980, he faced former lightweight champion Duran—one of the most aggressive and fearsome fighters ever.

Rankled by an exchange of pre-fight insults with Duran, Leonard entered the ring angry and tried to slug it out in the early going. He fired effective combinations, but Duran was able to work inside to counteract Leonard's speed. The fight went the full fifteen rounds, many of them scored even, but Duran won the unanimous decision with scores of 6-4-5, 6-5-4, and 3-2-10.

Five months later Leonard faced Duran again at the Superdome in New Orleans. Leonard peppered Duran's head with swift jabs. When Duran tried to bull him into the ropes, Leonard eluded his charges and responded with rights to the head and uppercuts to the body. While Duran won a couple of rounds, Leonard remained firmly in control. As the fight went on, Leonard taunted the faltering Duran. With sixteen seconds to go in the eighth, Duran threw up his hands and said to the referee, "No mas" (no more), and thus gave up the fight and the championship.

On June 25, 1981, Leonard took a world title in a second weight class when he knocked out WBA world junior middleweight champ (and previously undefeated) Ayub Kalule in the ninth round. Next Leonard, the WBC welterweight champ, faced WBA champ Thomas ("Hit Man") Hearns in a unification bout. The fighters traded punches in the early rounds with Leonard developing a swelling under one eye. In the sixth, Leonard unleashed a flurry of punches, breaking through Hearns's defense. From the eighth through the twelfth, Hearns outboxed Leonard and worked on his eye, which was beginning to close. In the thirteenth round, Leonard caught Hearns with a right to the temple and then pummeled him with 24 unanswered blows. Hearns went through the ropes, but the referee ruled that Leonard had pushed him so it was not judged a knockdown. Behind on all three judges' scorecards, Leonard finished off Hearns in the fourteenth, when the referee stopped the fight and granted him a TKO victory.

On November 9, 1982, Leonard announced that his June 1982 surgery for a detached retina had convinced him to hang up his gloves. Nevertheless, he came back in 1984 to fight unheralded Kevin Howard. Howard knocked him down, but Leonard recovered to score a TKO in the ninth. Dissatisfied with his performance, Leonard again said he was retiring.

He returned from this second retirement to fight long-time middleweight champion Marvelous Marvin Hagler, whom Leonard believed could be vulnerable. Held on April 6, 1987, at Caesar's Palace in Las Vegas, the fight drew 15,336 and earned Leonard approximately $12 million. Though he had fought only once in the past five years, Leonard looked fresh, and his gritty performance earned him a split-decision victory in a match *The Ring* called the Fight of the Year and

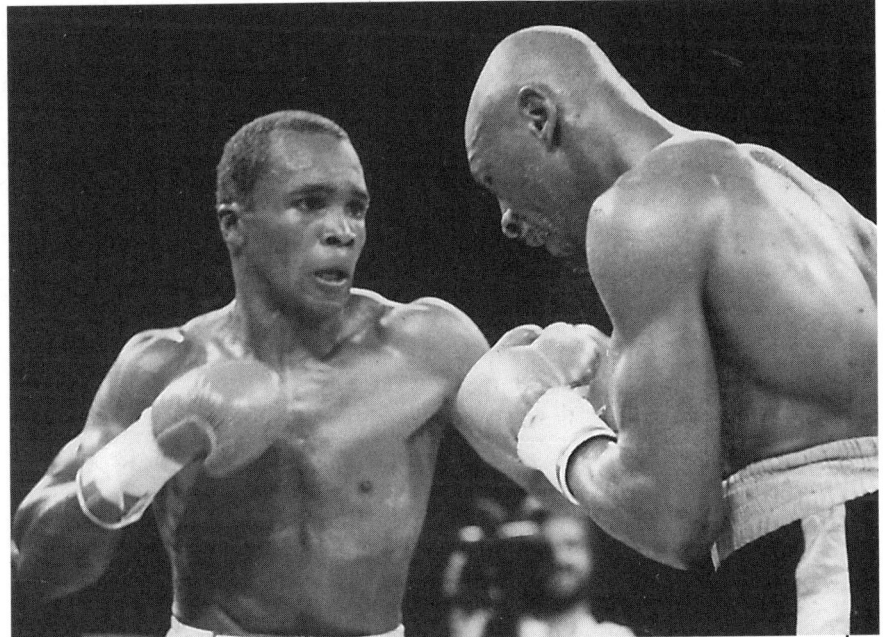

Two legends of modern boxing squared off when Leonard (L) met Marvelous Marvin Hagler for the WBC middleweight crown. In a thrilling, closely contested match in Las Vegas on April 6, 1987, Leonard took the split decision.

the Upset of the Year. Leonard then retired with the middleweight title.

A year and a half later, Leonard boxed again, facing WBC light heavyweight champ Don Lalonde at the super middleweight limit of 168. Lalonde agreed to the weight so that the fight could be for both the super middleweight and light heavyweight titles. Knocked down early, Leonard recovered to stop Lalonde in the ninth. He followed that fight with a controversial draw with Hearns (in which Hearns scored two knockdowns) and a win-by-decision over Duran in a rubber match. Leonard then trimmed down to fight for the WBC super welterweight title held by Terry Norris, but Norris totally dominated the fight to win easily by decision.

Although it appeared that Leonard had retired for good after the February 1991 Norris fight, he returned to the ring on March 1, 1997, at the age of 40 against Hector ("Macho") Camacho. Leonard, hindered by a torn calf muscle, could not handle the younger Camacho, who knocked him down in the fifth shortly before the fight was stopped.

Despite his checkered comeback attempts, Leonard compiled an outstanding lifetime record. He is revered as a great fighter and perhaps the best non-heavyweight since Sugar Ray Robinson. With boxing as a springboard, Leonard has become a well-known sports figure, earning such honors as *Sports Illustrated* Sportsman of the Year. In retirement Leonard has endorsed products and worked as a boxing commentator and actor.

CHARLES ("SONNY") LISTON

HEAVYWEIGHT

Right-handed; 6'1"; 198–226 lbs.

54 bouts, 9/2/1953 to 6/29/1970

Managers: Joseph ("Pep") Barone, George Katz, Jack Nilon, Dick Sadler

Heavyweight Champion 1962–64

Hall of Fame Induction: 1991

Born: 5/8/1932, St. Francis County, AR

Named: Charles L. Liston

Died: 12/30/1970

One of the triumvirate of great heavyweight champions of the early 1960s, Sonny Liston blasted Floyd Patterson off the throne only to be tossed out himself by a sassy young kid named Cassius Clay. Liston, an ex-convict with a cold stare that made him the bane of weigh-ins, was scary in the ring and unreadable in private life. The twists in Liston's career were influenced as much by his reputation as a bad man as by his formidable boxing skills.

Liston was born in rural Arkansas into an enormous family of 24 brothers and sisters. At about the age of thirteen, he fled his grindingly poor environment and moved to St. Louis to join his mother. St. Louis street life bred in Liston a propensity for crime. After a conviction for armed robbery, he was sentenced to two concurrent five-year terms in the Missouri State Penitentiary. While in prison, Liston began to participate, for the first time, in a formal boxing program under the direction of the prison chaplain. Paroled in 1952, he started fighting on the

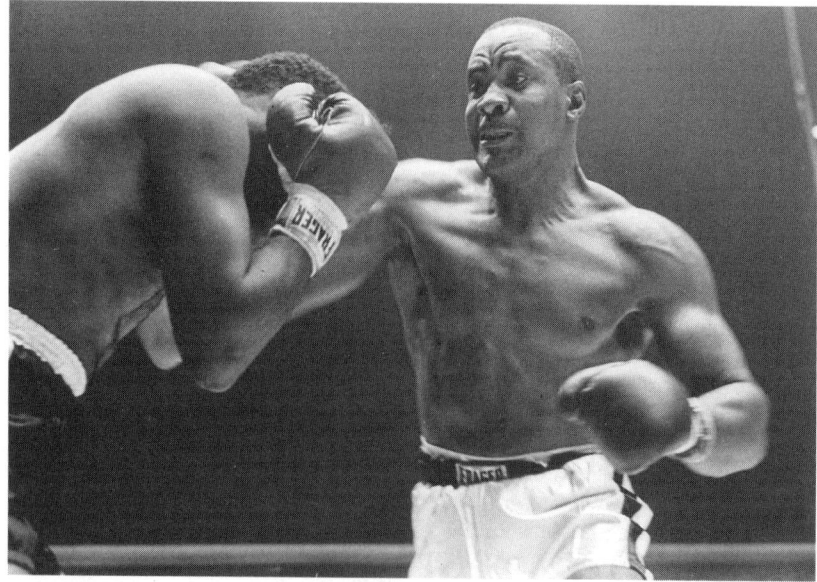

In a reprise of the fight a year earlier in which he took the title from Floyd Patterson, fearsome Sonny Liston pummels Patterson with a right hook en route to a first-round KO July 22, 1963, in Las Vegas.

IN THE RING	WON 50	LOST 4	DRAWS 0	TB 54	KO 39	W 11	WF 0	D 0	KO'd 3	L 1	LF 0

Date	Opponent	Site	Result / Rounds		Title	Wt.
1953						
Sep 2	Don Smith	St. Louis	TKO	1	—	200
Sep 17	Ponce De Leon	St. Louis	W	4	—	200
Nov 21	Benjamin Thomas	St. Louis	W	6	—	198
1954						
Jan 24	Martin Lee	St. Louis	TKO	6	—	201
Mar 31	Stanley Howlett	St. Louis	W	6	—	203
Jun 24	John Summerlin	Detroit	W	8	—	206
Aug 10	John Summerlin	Detroit	W	8	—	201
Sep 7 ⑩	Marty Marshall	Detroit	L	8	—	204
1955						
Mar 1	Neil Welch	St. Louis	W	8	—	202
Apr 21 ⑩	Marty Marshall	St. Louis	TKO	6	—	202
May 5	Emil Brtko	Pittsburgh	TKO	5	—	202
May 25	Calvin Butler	St. Louis	TKO	2	—	206
Sep 13	John Gray	Indianapolis	TKO	6	—	212
Dec 13	Larry Watson	St. Louis	TKO	4	—	209
1956						
Mar 6	Marty Marshall	Pittsburgh	W	10	—	203
1958						
Jan 29	Bill Hunter	Chicago	KO	2	—	210
Mar 11	Benjamin Wise	Chicago	KO	4	—	210
Apr 3	Bert Whitehurst	St. Louis	W	10	—	205
May 14	Julio Mederos	Chicago	TKO	3	—	204
Aug 6 ⑩	Wayne Bethea	Chicago	TKO	1	—	206
Oct 7	Frankie Daniels	Miami Beach	KO	1	—	212
Oct 24	Bert Whitehurst	St. Louis	W	10	—	212
Nov 18	Ernie Cab	Miami Beach	TKO	8	—	211
1959						
Feb 18 ⑩	Mike De John	Miami Beach	TKO	6	—	210
Apr 15	Cleveland Williams	Miami Beach	TKO	3	—	212
Aug 5	Geraldo Valdez	Chicago	KO	3	—	211
Dec 9	Willi Besmanoff	Cleveland	TKO	7	—	210
1960						
Feb 23	Howard King	Miami Beach	TKO	8	—	212
Mar 21	Cleveland Williams	Houston	TKO	2	—	212
Apr 25 ⑩	Roy Harris	Houston	TKO	1	—	212
Jul 18 ⑩	Zora Folley	Denver	KO	3	—	212
Sep 7 ⑩	Eddie Machen	Seattle	W	12	—	211
1961						
Mar 8	Howard King	Miami Beach	KO	3	—	219
Dec 4	Albert Westphal	Philadelphia	KO	1	—	212
1962						
Sep 25 ♛	Floyd Patterson ★	Chicago	KO	1	Won-World-H	214
1963						
Jul 22 ⑩	Floyd Patterson ★	Las Vegas	KO	1	Ret-World-H	215
1964						
Feb 25 ⑩	Cassius Clay ★	Miami Beach	TKO'd	7	Lost-World-H	218

1965							
May 25	♛	Muhammad Ali★	Lewiston, ME	KO'd	1	For-World-H	218
1966							
Jun 29		Gerhard Zech	Stockholm	KO	7	—	221
Aug 19		Amos Johnson	Gothenburg, Sweden	KO	3	—	218
1967							
Mar 30		Dave Bailey	Gothenburg	KO	1	—	221
Apr 28		Elmer Rush	Stockholm	TKO	6	—	223
1968							
Mar 16		Bill McMurray	Reno, NV	KO	4	—	223
May 23		Billy Joiner	Los Angeles	TKO	8	—	222
Jul 6		Henry Clark	San Francisco	TKO	7	—	219
Oct 14		Sonny Moore	Phoenix	KO	3	—	221
Nov 3		Willie Earls	Juarez, Mexico	KO	2	—	223
Nov 12		Roger Rischer	Pittsburgh	KO	3	—	219
Dec 10		Amos Lincoln	Baltimore	KO	2	—	215
1969							
Mar 28		Billy Joiner	St. Louis	W	10	—	219
May 19		George Johnson	Las Vegas	TKO	7	—	217
Sep 23		Sonny Moore	Houston	KO	3	—	226
Dec 6	ⓝ	Leotis Martin	Las Vegas	KO'd	9	For-Vac NABF-H	219
1970							
Jun 29		Chuck Wepner	Jersey City, NJ	TKO	10	—	219

amateur level. He was an extremely talented boxer and won the 1953 National Golden Gloves title.

Liston turned professional later in 1953, winning fourteen of his first fifteen fights. His budding career was derailed when he got into a fight with a St. Louis policeman and was again sent to prison. It is believed that Liston may have been the victim of police harassment. Upon his release, Liston continued his climb up the rungs of the heavyweight ladder. In 1958, *The Ring* ranked him as the ninth-best contender for the heavyweight title. By 1960, the venerable boxing publication ranked him the number one challenger.

Heavyweight champ Floyd Patterson was in no hurry to sign for a title match against Liston. Liston's incredibly strong jab, great left hook, strong right, and good boxing skills had destroyed many worthy opponents. In addition, it was generally acknowledged in the boxing world that Liston had underworld connections, and Patterson's manager, Cus D'Amato, would not let his fighter take on anyone that was mob controlled.

Then a U.S. Senate committee investigating organized crime in boxing subpoenaed Liston to testify about his criminal contacts. On December 13, 1960, Liston stated before the committee that he had no information about Philadelphia racketeer Frank ("Blinky") Palermo. It was alleged that Palermo and gangster Frankie Carbo were Liston's "behind the scenes" managers. Palermo refused to testify about his association with boxing.

After Liston switched to a more reputable manager, Patterson agreed to meet Liston in Chicago's Comiskey Park in 1962. The end for Patterson was abrupt. Liston, who seldom allowed anyone to go the distance, hammered Patterson with two left hooks and a right to knock him out in the first round. Less than a year later, Patterson was back for the rematch and Liston did it again: a first-round knockout reaffirmed him as the world's top heavyweight.

Then along came the brash-talking Cassius Clay, a pretty fighter who was Liston's opposite in too many ways to count. Some observers said the world-weary Liston was confused by Clay. Clay quipped where Liston stared, he danced where Liston stood firm. As the fight, held in February 1964 in Miami Beach, developed, Clay proved too fast for Liston. He slammed at the champ with lightning punches, then slipped out of the way. During the fifth round, Clay's vision was impaired when some ointment Liston's handlers had applied to Liston's cuts, and perhaps to his shoulders or gloves, got into Clay's eyes. Although Clay begged his cornermen to cut off his gloves, they urged him to keep fighting. In the sixth, Clay's eyes began to clear, and he dominated the fight again. When the bell rang to start round seven, Liston did not come out, claiming an injured shoulder. Questions about the reasons for Liston's poor performance were never answered.

The circumstances of Liston's rematch with Clay in Lewiston, Maine, the next year are equally murky. Clay, by then known as Muhammad Ali, knocked Liston down in the first round. Ali was slow in retreating to a neutral corner for the count, and Liston stayed down for some time. Referee Jersey Joe Walcott motioned for the fighters to continue after Liston got up. Then Nat Fleischer, editor of *The Ring,* shouted to Walcott that the fight should be stopped because Liston had been down for too long. The fight ended there. Once again, rumors of a fix were never substantiated.

Liston continued to fight for another six years. He was knocked out by Leotis Martin in his second-to-last fight, a bid for the vacant NABF heavyweight title. His seventeen-year career ended in 1970 when he died in his home in Las Vegas under suspicious circumstances. Officially, the cause of death was listed as lung congestion and heart failure. Unofficially, the death appeared to be the result of a heroin overdose, and some police officials and Liston associates believed that Liston was murdered.

A nimble, big man, Liston once demonstrated his jump rope skills on the Ed Sullivan show. Here he turns a headstand, wearing his "anti-foul" protector.

NICOLINO LOCCHE
El Intocable (The Untouchable)

JUNIOR WELTERWEIGHT

Right-handed; 5'6"; 131–145 lbs.

136 bouts, 12/11/1958 to 8/7/1976

Manager: Francisco Bermudez

WBA Junior Welterweight
Champion 1968–72

Hall of Fame Induction: 2003

Born: 9/2/1939, Tunuyán,
Mendoza, Argentina

Died: 9/7/2005

Nicolino Locche was born in Tunuyán, Argentina, on September 2, 1939, one of six children. By the time Locche was twelve, he was boxing in exhibitions at local clubs and military bases. He had a fine amateur record, losing only five of 122 bouts before he turned professional. Locche's first foray into the pro ranks took place on December 11, 1958, when he knocked out Luis Garcia in the second round. Over the course of his career, Locche would score knockouts in just over ten percent of his fights.

Despite Locche's defensive style, he soon became a real drawing card. On June 29, 1963, he went fifteen rounds for the first time and decisioned Sebastian Nascimento to win the South American lightweight title. The next year, he fought a draw with world lightweight champion Ismael Laguna in a non-title fight. On April 7, 1966, Locche earned another non-title draw with new world champion Carlos Ortiz. Though *The Ring* rated Locche as the top lightweight contender, he seemingly could not get a title shot.

Locche moved up to junior welterweight. On December 12, 1968, he finally got a chance to fight for a world title. He went to Tokyo to face champion Paul Fujii. Locche built up an early lead as he scored with left jabs to the head and had no trouble evading the wild punches of Fujii. In the fourth, Fujii's right eye became very swollen. A thoroughly beaten Fujii failed to answer the bell for the tenth round, giving Locche a well-deserved championship.

Locche successfully defended the title in his first four tries, the last a fifteen-round decision over Hall of Famer Antonio Cervantes. His reign ended on March 10, 1972, when Alfonso ("Peppermint") Frazer won a fifteen-round decision. He then fought sporadically, finally retiring in 1976. The great defensive stylist died of heart failure on September 7, 2005.

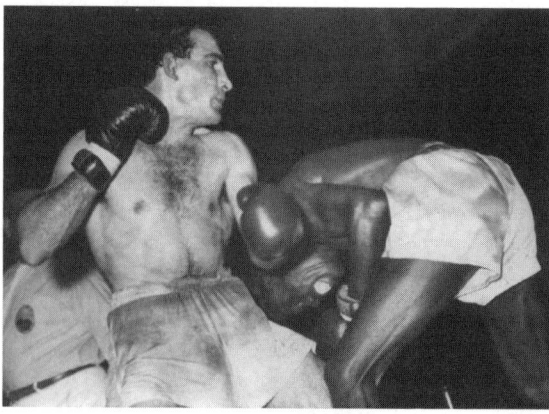

Joe ("Old Bones") Brown dodges the attack of Nicolino Locche (L). Locche took the decision before a huge Luna Park (Buenos Aires) crowd.

IN THE RING	WON 117	LOST 4	DRAWS 14	TB 136	KO 14	W 103	WF 0	D 14	KO'd 1	L 3	LF 0	NC 1

Date	Opponent	Site	Result / Rounds		Title	Wt.
1958						
Dec 11	Luis Garcia	Mendoza, Argentina	KO	2	—	134
1959						
Jan 9	Rodolfo Catalini	Mendoza	W	8	—	133
Jan 30	Eduardo Zalazar	Mendoza	W	10	—	134
Feb 27	Leandro Ahumada	Mendoza	NC	9	—	134
Mar 6	Rodolfo Catalini	Mendoza	KO	4	—	132
Apr 3	Leandro Ahumada	Mendoza	W	10	—	132
Jul 29	Juan Ramirez	Buenos Aires	W	8	—	133
Aug 8	Pedro Videla	Buenos Aires	W	8	—	136
Oct 16	Juan Campos	Mendoza	D	10	—	134
Nov 6	Vicente Derado	Mendoza	L	10	—	134
Dec 11	Ricardo Jofre	Mendoza	D	10	—	133
1960						
Jan 8	Hector Tula	Mendoza	TKO	5	—	132
Jan 22	Vicente Derado	Mendoza	D	10	—	133
Feb 26	Jaime Gine	Mendoza	W	10	—	133
Mar 25	Juan Campos	Mendoza	W	10	—	135
Jun 11	Jaime Gine	Buenos Aires	D	10	—	133
Jul 30	Pedro Beneli	Buenos Aires	W	10	—	134
Sep 17	Manuel Alvarez	Buenos Aires	D	10	—	134
Nov 4	Rogelio Andre	Mendoza	W	10	—	133
1961						
Jan 20	Vicente Derado	Mendoza	W	10	—	135
Jan 27	Juan Campos	Cordoba, Argentina	D	10	—	135
Mar 10	Antonio Repollo	Mendoza	W	10	—	133
May 12	Julio Catalini	Mendoza	TKO	10	Won-Mendoza Prov.-L	134
Jun 9	Guillermo Cano	Mendoza	W	12	Ret-Mendoza Prov.-L	132
Sep 1	Juan Flores	Mendoza	KO	5	—	133
Sep 29	Ubaldino Escobar	Mendoza	W	10	—	133
Oct 10	Ubaldino Escobar	Mendoza	W	10	—	133
Nov 4	Jaime Gine	Buenos Aires	W	12	Won-Argentina-L	131
Dec 1	Pedro Beneli	Mendoza	W	10	—	—
Dec 16	Vicente Derado	Buenos Aires	W	10	—	135
1962						
Jan 25	Nuncio Canistra	Palmira, Argentina	TKO	9	—	133
Mar 30	Fernando Azocar	Mendoza	W	10	—	135
Apr 24	Abelardo Sire	Mendoza	W	10	—	133
May 16	Horacio Rivero	Mendoza	TKO	2	—	134
Jun 5	Eulogio Caballero	Mendoza	W	10	—	133
Jul 6	Humberto Barbatto	Mendoza	W	10	—	136
Aug 24	Hugo Juarez	Mendoza	W	10	—	131
Sep 29	Pedro Beneli	Buenos Aires	W	10	—	132
Oct 20	Manuel Alvarez	Buenos Aires	W	12	Ret-Argentina-L	133
Dec 14	Tristan Falfan	Cordoba	KO	6	—	135
Dec 28	Tony Padron	Mendoza	W	10	—	135
1963						
Feb 1	Pedro Beneli	Mendoza	W	10	—	135

Feb 22	Gregorio Cintas	Salta, Argentina	D	10		—	135
Mar 23	Javier Gomez	Buenos Aires	W	10		—	135
Apr 26	Rodolfo Catalini	Mendoza	W	10		—	136
May 24	Gregorio Cinta	Mendoza	W	10		—	135
Jun 8	Eulogio Caballero	Montevideo, Uruguay	W	10		—	136
Jun 29	Sebastian Nascimento	Buenos Aires	W	15	Won-South America-L		133
Jul 20	Rodolfo Espinosa	Mar Del Plata, Argentina	W	10		—	—
Aug 10	Joe Brown	Buenos Aires	W	10		—	135
Sep 13	Adan Gomez	Mendoza	W	10		—	136
Sep 27	Carlos Cappella	Tucuman, Argentina	D	10		—	136
Oct 11	Tristan Falfan	Cordoba	D	10		—	138
Dec 14	Raul Villalba	Buenos Aires	W	10		—	134

1964

Jan 31	Pedro Beneli	Tucuman	W	10		—	134
Feb 14	Julio Palavecino	Mar Del Plata	D	10		—	136
Feb 28	Raul Villalba	Mar Del Plata	W	10		—	136
Apr 18	Julio Palavecino	Buenos Aires	W	10		—	135
Jun 19	Carlos Cappella	Mendoza	W	10		—	—
Jul 10	Carlos Clemente	Mendoza	W	10		—	135
Aug 8	Abel Laudonio	Buenos Aires	W	10		—	134
Aug 21	Deolidio Sosa	Rosario, Argentina	W	10		—	—
Sep 4	Julio Palavecino	Mendoza	W	10		—	—
Sep 19	Gualberto Gutierrez	Montevideo	D	10		—	—
Oct 9	Humberto Barbatto	Bahia Blanca, Argentina	W	10		—	—
Nov 14	Abel Laudonio	Buenos Aires	L	12	Lost-Argentina-L		135
Dec 18	Pedro Beneli	Cordoba	W	10		—	—

1965

Jan 26	Adan Gomez	Santa Fe, Argentina	W	10		—	134
Mar 20	Hugo Rambaldi	Buenos Aires	W	10		—	136
Apr 10	Abel Laudonio	Buenos Aires	W	12	Ret-S Am-L & Reg-Arg-L		135
Apr 30	Juan Salinas	Rio Cuarto, Argentina	TKO	8		—	—
Jul 17 ⑩	Ismael Laguna★	Buenos Aires	D	10		—	135
Aug 6	Leonardo Peralta	Resistencia, Argentina	W	10		—	—
Sep 16	Raul Villalba	Mendoza	W	10		—	136
Dec 18	Hugo Rambaldi	Buenos Aires	W	12	Ret-Argentina-L		133

1966

Jan 21	Omar Gottifredi	Mendoza	W	10		—	136
Apr 7 ♛	Carlos Ortiz★	Buenos Aires	D	10		—	138
Aug 19	Omar Salvo	Rio Gallegos, Argentina	W	10		—	141
Sep 10 ♛	Sandro Lopopolo	Buenos Aires	W	10		—	138
Oct 7	Omar Gottifredi	Mendoza	W	10		—	138
Dec 30	Omar Salvo	Mendoza	W	10		—	142

1967

Jan 13	Everaldo Costa	Mendoza	W	10		—	141
Apr 7	Ubaldino Escobar	Mendoza	W	10		—	140
Apr 21	Ruben Loayza	Mendoza	W	10		—	143
May 13	L.C. Morgan	Buenos Aires	W	10		—	139
Jun 2	Adan Gomez	Bahia Blanca	W	10		—	141
Jul 7	Jose Acha-Paz	Mendoza	TKO	6		—	141
Jul 22	Carlos Clemente	Tandil, Argentina	W	10		—	144
Aug 4	Osvaldo Piazza	Cipolletti, Argentina	W	10		—	145
Aug 19	Eddie Perkins	Buenos Aires	W	10		—	140
Sep 1	Ramon Gomez	Bahia Blanca	TKO	10		—	142

Sep 24	Osvaldo Piazza	Cordoba	W	10	—	143
Oct 4	Abel Cachazu	Buenos Aires	W	10	—	142
Oct 18	Leonardo Peralta	San Rafael, Argentina	W	10	—	145
Nov 10	Abel Cachazu	Mendoza	W	10	—	143
Nov 24	Adan Gomez	San Juan, Argentina	W	10	—	140
Dec 2	Vicente Derado	Buenos Aires	TKO	6	—	138

1968

Apr 10	Alfredo Urbina	Mar Del Plata	W	10	—	139
Apr 20	Juan Gomez	Mar Del Plata	W	10	—	145
May 11	Alfredo Urbina	Buenos Aires	W	10	—	138
Jun 8	Abel Cachazu	Buenos Aires	W	10	—	140
Jul 14	Juan Aranda	Mendoza	W	10	—	140
Aug 2	Tito Del Barco	Cordoba	W	10	—	140
Aug 26	Hilario Suarez	San Francisco, Argentina	W	10	—	—
Sep 13	Orlando Ribeiro	Mendoza	W	10	—	140
Oct 12	Anibal Di Lella	Mar Del Plata	TD	8	—	143
Dec 12 ♛	Takeshi ("Paul") Fuji	Tokyo	TKO	10	Won-WBA-JW	138

1969

Apr 3		Manuel Hernandez	Mendoza	W	10	—	141
May 3	⑩	Carlos Hernandez	Buenos Aires	W	15	Ret-WBA-JW	139
Aug 2	⑩	German Gastelbondo	Buenos Aires	W	10	—	140
Aug 22		Angel Roman	Cordoba	W	10	—	143
Oct 11	⑩	Joao Henrique	Buenos Aires	W	15	Ret-WBA-JW	139

1970

Apr 3		Martin Juarez	Rosario	W	10	—	144
Apr 18		Marcelino Acevedo	Tandil	TKO	9	—	143
May 16	⑩	Adolph Pruitt	Buenos Aires	W	15	Ret-WBA-JW	139

1971

Feb 14		Juan Carlos Peralta	San Juan	W	10	—	143
Mar 10		Adan Gomez	La Falda, Argentina	W	10	—	143
Apr 3		Domingo Barrera Corpas	Buenos Aires	W	15	Ret-WBA-JW	140
Oct 29		Angel Roman	Salta	W	10	—	142
Nov 13		Tony Ortiz	Buenos Aires	W	10	—	141
Dec 11		Antonio Cervantes★	Buenos Aires	W	15	Ret-WBA-JW	139

1972

Feb 4		Juan Carlos Peralta	San Juan, Argentina	W	10	—	143
Feb 16		Nicolas Arkuszyn	Cruz Del Eje, Argentina	W	10	—	140
Mar 10	⑩	Alfonso ("Peppermint") Frazer	Panama City, Panama	L	15	Lost-WBA-JW	139
Nov 18		Gerardo Ferrat	Buenos Aires	W	10	—	141
Dec 16		Rey Mercado	Buenos Aires	W	10	—	141

1973

Jan 25		Pedro Adigue	Buenos Aires	W	10	—	141
Feb 9		Benny Huertas	Mendoza	W	10	—	140
Mar 17 ♛		Antonio Cervantes★	Maracay, Venezuela	TKO'd	10	For-WBA-JW	139

1975

Aug 9	Javier Ayala	Buenos Aires	W	10	—	141
Sep 13	Omar Zarza	Venado Tuerto, Argentina	W	10	—	143
Oct 18	Jimmy Heair	Buenos Aires	W	10	—	139
Dec 19	Rogelio Zarza	Rio Cuarto, Argentina	W	10	—	141

1976

Jan 17	Emiliano Villa	Buenos Aires	W	10	—	141
May 8	Lorenzo Trujillo	Buenos Aires	W	10	—	141
Aug 7	Ricardo Molina	Bariloche, Argentina	W	10	—	143

DUILIO LOI
King of Milano

JUNIOR WELTERWEIGHT

Left-handed; 5'4½"; 135–147 lbs.

126 bouts, 11/1/1948 to 12/15/1962

Manager: Steve Klaus

Junior Welterweight Champion 1960–62, 1962

Hall of Fame Induction: 2005

Born: 4/19/1929, Trieste, Italy

Duilio Loi became the second world champion in the junior welterweight division after that weight class was revived in 1959. Born in Trieste, Italy, on April 19, 1929, Loi fought most of his career in his native country. He turned professional on November 1, 1948, when he earned a six-round decision over Nino Frangioni. On July 18, 1951, Loi won the vacant Italian lightweight championship when he scored a twelve-round decision over Gianni Uboldi.

On August 18, 1952, Loi attempted to take the European lightweight title, but he suffered the first loss of his career when Jorgen Johansen bested him in a fifteen-round decision. Loi won the rematch and the European title on February 6, 1954. He successfully defended the title twice that year and journeyed to Australia where he won two fights. His eye on the world championship, Loi fought in the United States for the first time. In a fight that was nationally televised on NBC on January 14, 1955, he won a ten-round decision over Glen Flanagan. Loi took the initiative in the first two rounds, with three lefts to the face and a right to the jaw in the first and a chopping right to the face in the second. The action lagged in the middle of the fight, but Loi came on towards the end.

Family considerations forced Loi to return to Italy after that one contest. He successfully defended his European title six times from 1955 thru 1958. He also won 40 non-title fights in those years without a defeat. From 1955 to 1957, *The Ring* ranked him as the top lightweight contender, but he did not receive a chance at the crown. In his only bout of 1959, Loi floored Emilio Marconi twice to win the European welterweight title in a fifteen-round decision.

Just when it appeared that Loi's career would end without him ever fighting for a world championship, the resurrection of the junior welterweight division—the ideal class for a fighter of

Fighting as junior welterweights, Duilio Loi (L) and Carlos Ortiz met three times. Loi won two of the contests.

IN THE RING	WON 115	LOST 3	DRAWS 8	TB 126	KO 26	W 88	WF 1	D 8	KO'd 0	L 3	LF 0

Date	Opponent	Site	Result / Rounds		Title	Wt.
1948						
Nov 1	Nino Frangioni	Genoa, Italy	W	6	—	—
1949						
Feb 12	George Georgescu	Genoa	W	6	—	—
Mar 12	Gaetano De Lucia	Genoa	W	6	—	—
Apr 12	Ruggero Grilli	Milan	W	6	—	—
Apr 24	Giulio Di Rocco	Genoa	W	6	—	—
Oct 5	Bruno Bisterzo	Milan	W	8	—	—
Nov 23	Jean Berthelier	Milan	W	6	—	—
Nov 30	Oreste Baiocco	Cagliari, Italy	TKO	8	—	—
Dec 16	Young Robert	La-Chaux-de-Fonds, France	W	10	—	—
1950						
Jan 31	Vittorio Costa	Cagliari	W	8	—	—
Mar 4	Vittorio Costa	Bologna, Italy	W	8	—	—
Mar 15	Pedro Martinez	Milan	KO	2	—	—
Mar 22	Nicola Funari	Milan	W	8	—	—
Apr 15	Jan Nicolaas	Milan	W	10	—	—
May 8	Djiali Bouaziz	Gallarate, Italy	W	8	—	—
May 17	Giuseppe DeJoanni	Milan	W	8	—	—
Jul 14	Gianluigi Uboldi	Milan	W	8	—	—
Sep 13	Allan Tanner	Bologna	D	10	—	—
Nov 8	Luigi Malè	Milan	D	12	For-Italy-L	—
Dec 14	Frank Hermal	Milan	W	10	—	—
1951						
Feb 21	Karl Machart	Milan	W	10	—	—
Mar 6	Jean Castellanos	Monza, Italy	W	10	—	—
Mar 14	Raul Guillaume	Milan	TKO	5	—	—
Mar 31	Roland Guilbert	Modena, Italy	W	8	—	—
Apr 14	Leon Bourlet	Milan	W	8	—	—
Jun 9	Morlay Kamara	Cagliari	W	10	—	—
Jul 6	Ray Lewis	Genoa	W	10	—	—
Jul 18	Gianluigi Uboldi	Milan	W	12	Won-Italy-L	—
Sep 1	Leyton Lewis	Varese, Italy	TKO	2	—	—
Oct 9	Ray Lewis	Cagliari	TKO	2	—	—
Oct 26	Svend Wad	Geneva, Italy	W	10	—	—
Dec 10	Tommy Barnham	London	W	10	—	137
Dec 26	Emilio Orozco	Milan	TKO	6	—	—
1952						
Jan 12	Karl Pinsdorf	Genoa	W	10	—	—
Apr 2	Emilio Marconi	Cagliari	W	12	Ret-Italy-L	—
Apr 12	Charles Colpin	Genoa	TKO	6	—	—
Jun 4	Agustin Argote	Milan	W	10	—	—
Aug 18 ⑩	Jorgen Johansen	Copenhagen, Denmark	L	15	For-Europe-L	—
Nov 12	Alois Brand	Cagliari	W	10	—	—
Nov 26	Serge Ceustermans	Milan	W	10	—	—
Dec 17	Francis Bonnardel	Milan	W	10	—	—
1953						
Jan 28	Ernesto Formenti	Milan	TKO	9	Ret-Italy-L	—
Feb 20	Giuseppe De Joanni	Genoa	W	10	—	—

Date	Opponent	Location	Result	Rounds	Title	Weight
Apr 2	Allan Tanner	Milan	W	10	—	—
May 8	Jean Labalette	Geneva	W	10	—	—
Jun 20	Ernesto Formenti	Milan	TKO	10	—	—
Jun 27	Franco Antonini	Foligno, Italy	D	10	—	—
Jul 11	Mario Rosellini	La Spezia, Italy	KO	2	—	—
Sep 13	Emilio Marconi	Grosetto, Italy	D	12	Ret-Italy-L	—
Oct 21	Valde Fusaro	Milan	W	10	—	—
Nov 4	Sandy Manuel	Milan	W	10	—	—
Nov 15	Jo Janssens	Milan	W	10	—	—

1954

Date	Opponent	Location	Result	Rounds	Title	Weight
Feb 6	Jorgen Johanssen	Milan	W	15	Won-Europe-L	—
Mar 3	Franco Antonini	Genoa	W	10	—	—
Mar 18	Giuseppe De Joanni	Rome	W	10	—	—
May 13	Bruno Visintin	Milan	W	15	Ret-Europe-L	134
Jun 23	Mario Ciccarelli	Milan	W	10	—	—
Jul 16	Jacques Herbillon	Milan	W	15	Ret-Europe-L	134
Sep 10	Ivor Germain	Melbourne	TKO	9	—	137
Oct 1	Mario Trigo	Melbourne	W	12	—	137
Nov 8	Agustin Argote	Sydney	W	12	—	141

1955

Date	Opponent	Location	Result	Rounds	Title	Weight
Jan 14	Glen Flanagan	Miami	W	10	—	139
Feb 19	⑩ Ray Famechon	Milan	W	10	—	135
Mar 30	Guy Gracia	Milan	W	10	—	—
Apr 30	Alby Tissong	Trieste, Italy	W	10	—	135
May 22	Luis Carrara	Milan	W	10	—	—
Jun 8	Morley Kamara	Florence, Italy	W	10	—	—
Jul 2	Giancarlo Garbelli	Milan	W	15	Ret-Europe-L	—
Jul 30	Frank Hermal	St. Vincent, Italy	TKO	3	—	—
Sep 13	Boswell St Louis	Milan	TKO	5	—	—
Oct 15	Joe Lucy	Milan	W	10	—	—
Oct 29	Werner Handkte	Milan	W	10	—	—
Nov 26	Serafin Ferrer	Milan	W	15	Ret-Europe-L	134
Dec 26	Gordon Goodman	Milan	KO	6	—	139

1956

Date	Opponent	Location	Result	Rounds	Title	Weight
Jan 21	⑩ Orlando Zulueta	Milan	W	10	—	137
Apr 7	Manolo Garcia	Milan	W	10	—	—
Apr 21	Ben Buker II	Tunis, Tunisia	W	10	—	—
May 12	Jose Hernandez	Milan	D	15	Ret-Europe-L	134
Jun 23	Fred Galiana	Milan	KO	6	—	136
Jul 11	Piet Van Klaveren	Milan	TKO	6	—	—
Jul 21	Karl Friedrick	Bologna	W	10	—	—
Sep 15	Fernand Nollet	Milan	W	10	—	—
Sep 23	Albert Mueller	Forli, Italy	TKO	3	—	139
Oct 13	Maurice Auzel	Milan	W	10	—	—
Nov 10	Saveur Chiocca	Milan	W	10	—	—
Dec 3	Felix Chiocca	Paris	W	10	—	136
Dec 26	Jose Hernandez	Milan	W	15	Ret-Europe-L	133

1957

Date	Opponent	Location	Result	Rounds	Title	Weight
Feb 2	Bobby Ros	Milan	WF	5	—	137
Apr 3	Karl Heinz Bick	Milan	TKO	10	—	138
Apr 27	Hoacine Khalfi	Milan	W	10	—	—
May 29	Rudi Langer	Milan	W	10	—	—
Jun 2	Francisco ("Chico") Santos	Lecco, Italy	KO	6	—	—
Jun 9	Ahcene Attar	Cagliari	W	10	—	—
Jun 26	Piet van Klaveren	Milan	TKO	6	—	138

Date	Opponent	Location	Result	Rounds	Title	Weight
Jul 12	Ernst Zetzmann	Milan	W	8	—	—
Jul 27	Jack Subero	Genoa	W	10	—	132
Sep 7	Stefano Bellotti	Rome	W	10	—	—
Sep 25	Idrissa Dione	Milan	W	10	—	138
Oct 29	Marcel Dupre	Milan	W	10	—	—
Dec 26	Felix Chiocca	Milan	W	15	Ret-Europe-L	132
1958						
Feb 8	Manfred Neuke	Basile, Italy	D	10	—	—
Mar 1	Wallace ("Bud") Smith	Milan	TKO	9	—	137
Apr 27	Al Nevarez	Milan	W	10	—	137
Jul 7	Charles Douglas	Naples, Italy	W	10	—	—
Sep 5	Mario Vecchiatto	Milan	D	15	Ret-Europe-L	135
Dec 13	Conny Rudhoff	Turin, Italy	W	10	—	141
1959						
Apr 19	Emilio Marconi	Milan	W	15	Won-Europe-W	143
1960						
Feb 13	Bruno Visintin	Milan	W	15	Ret-Europe-W	141
Mar 16	Tommy Molloy	Milan	TKO	5	—	—
Mar 31	Giacomo Nervi	Rome	W	10	—	—
Jun 15	♛ Carlos Ortiz★	San Francisco	L	15	For-World-JW	140
Sep 1	♛ Carlos Ortiz★	Milan	W	15	Won-World-JW	139
Nov 25	Maurice Auzel	Rome	W	15	Ret-Europe-W	145
1961						
May 10	⑩ Carlos Ortiz★	Milan	W	15	Ret-World-JW	138
Aug 5	Christian Christensen	St. Vincent	W	15	Ret-Europe-W	145
Oct 21	Eddie Perkins	Milan	D	15	Ret-World-JW	138
Dec 6	Ephifane Akono	Rome	TKO	8	—	145
Dec 20	Gale Kerwin	Milan	TKO	7	—	141
1962						
Feb 9	James ("J.D.") Ellis	Rome	W	10	—	143
Mar 27	Billy Collins	Milan	W	10	—	142
Apr 13	Willie Stevenson	Rome	W	10	—	143
Apr 29	Roger Harvey	Milan	TKO	8	—	145
May 26	Ike Vaughn	Milan	KO	5	—	145
Jul 15	Fortunato Manca	Cagliari	W	15	Ret-Europe-W	145
Sep 14	⑩ Eddie Perkins	Milan	L	15	Lost-World-JW	140
Dec 15	♛ Eddie Perkins	Milan	W	15	Reg-World-JW	137

his size—provided him an opportunity. On June 15, 1960, Loi traveled to San Francisco to face junior welterweight champion Carlos Ortiz. In a hotly contested fight, Ortiz earned a split decision to retain the title. The crowd booed the decision in what was only the second defeat of Loi's career.

In the rematch before a record crowd of 65,000 at San Siro Stadium in Milan, Loi came back in the late rounds to win a majority decision to take the title. A fine boxer/puncher, Loi relied on his left hook more than most boxers. In his third meeting with Ortiz, he again scored a fifteen-round decision victory.

Loi next defended his title against Eddie Perkins on October 21, 1961, in a lackluster fight in Milan. In the rematch on September 14, 1962, again in Milan, Perkins took the title in a unanimous decision. The pair met for a third time on December 15, 1962, in Milan. Loi won the rubber match and recaptured the title in a close fifteen-round fight. The next month he announced his retirement.

Loi was never knocked out in his career and lost only three times. In retirement, he serves as president of an Italian organization of retired boxers.

JOE LOUIS
The Brown Bomber

HEAVYWEIGHT

Right-handed; 6'1½"; 181–218 lbs.

70 bouts, 7/4/1934 to 10/26/1951

Managers: Julian Black and John Roxborough 1934–49, Marshall Miles 1950–51

Heavyweight Champion 1937–49

Hall of Fame Induction: 1990

Born: 5/13/1914, Lafayette, AL

Named: Joseph Louis Barrow

Died: 4/12/1981

Joe Louis dominated the sport of boxing from the 1930s into the 1950s. He was arguably the best heavyweight champion ever and, in an era when blacks were still riding in the back of the bus, was widely respected as an individual. Fans didn't just like Louis, they loved him. He was also a hero to a generation of younger boxers, some of whom faced him in his post-championship years.

Born in Alabama, Louis moved to Detroit as a child and first became involved in boxing there at Brewster's Gym. In his first amateur bout, Louis was knocked down seven times. He was seldom knocked down again. He won the 1934 National AAU light heavyweight title and ended his amateur career that year with a record of 53 wins and three losses.

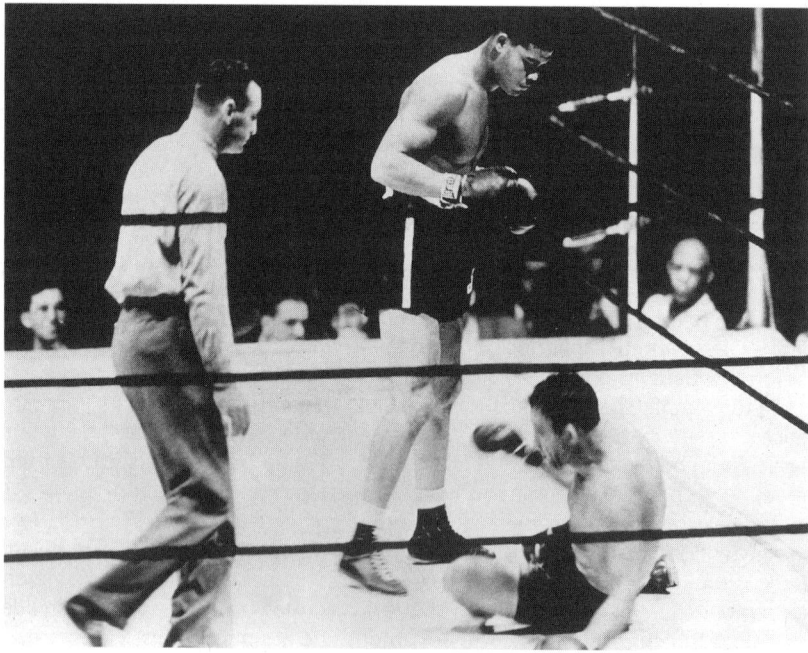

Twenty-two-year-old Louis hands Hall of Famer Jack Sharkey his final defeat with a third-round knockout on August 18, 1936, in New York. This was the first fight for Louis after his loss to Schmeling.

IN THE RING	WON 68	LOST 3	DRAWS 0	TB 71	KO 54	W 13	WF 1	D 0	KO'd 2	L 1	LF 0

Date	Opponent	Site	Result / Rounds		Title	Wt.
1934						
Jul 4	Jack Kracken	Chicago	TKO	1	—	181
Jul 12	Willie Davies	Chicago	TKO	3	—	190
Jul 30	Larry Udell	Chicago	TKO	2	—	190
Aug 13	Jack Kranz	Chicago	W	8	—	188
Aug 27	Buck Everett	Chicago	KO	2	—	187
Sep 11	Alex Borchuk	Detroit	TKO	4	—	191
Sep 26	Adolph Wiater	Chicago	W	10	—	188
Oct 24	Art Sykes	Chicago	KO	8	—	190
Oct 31	Jack O'Dowd	Detroit	KO	2	—	—
Nov 14	Stanley Poreda	Chicago	KO	1	—	193
Nov 30	Charley Massera	Chicago	KO	3	—	188
Dec 14	⑩ Lee Ramage	Chicago	TKO	8	—	192
1935						
Jan 4	⑩ Patsy Perroni	Detroit	W	10	—	195
Jan 11	Hans Birkie	Pittsburgh	TKO	10	—	194
Feb 21	⑩ Lee Ramage	Los Angeles	TKO	2	—	196
Mar 8	Donald ("Red") Barry	San Francisco	TKO	3	—	200
Mar 29	⑩ Natie Brown	Detroit	W	10	—	196
Apr 12	Roy Lazer	Chicago	TKO	3	—	196
Apr 22*	Biff Bennett	Dayton, OH	KO	1	—	198
Apr 25*	Roscoe Toles	Flint, MI	KO	6	—	200
May 3*	Willie Davies	Peoria, IL	KO	2	—	199
May 7*	Gene Stanton	Kalamazoo, MI	KO	3	—	202
Jun 25	⑩ Primo Carnera	New York	TKO	6	—	196
Aug 7	King Levinsky	Chicago	TKO	1	—	198
Sep 24	⑩ Max Baer★	New York	KO	4	—	198
Dec 14	Paolino Uzcudun	New York	TKO	4	—	200
1936						
Jan 17	⑩ Charley Retzlaff	Chicago	KO	1	—	199
Jun 19	⑩ Max Schmeling★	New York	KO'd	12	—	198
Aug 18	Jack Sharkey★	New York	KO	3	—	199
Sep 22	⑩ Al Ettore	Philadelphia	KO	5	—	203
Oct 9	Jorge Brescia	New York	KO	3	—	202
Dec 14	Eddie Simms	Cleveland	TKO	1	—	202
1937						
Jan 11*	Steve Ketchel	Buffalo, NY	KO	2	—	209
Jan 29	⑩ Bob Pastor	New York	W	10	—	203
Feb 17	Natie Brown	Kansas City, MO	TKO	4	—	206
Jun 22	♛ James J. Braddock★	Chicago	KO	8	Won-World-H	197
Aug 30	⑩ Tommy Farr	New York	W	15	Ret-World-H	197
1938						
Feb 23	⑩ Nathan Mann	New York	KO	3	Ret-World-H	200
Apr 1	Harry Thomas	Chicago	KO	5	Ret-World-H	202
Jun 22	⑩ Max Schmeling★	New York	KO	1	Ret-World-H	198
1939						
Jan 25	♛ John Henry Lewis★	New York	KO	1	Ret-World-H	200
Apr 17	Jack Roper	Los Angeles	KO	1	Ret-World-H	201
Jun 28	⑩ Tony Galento	New York	TKO	4	Ret-World-H	200

Some boxing historians believe these bouts were exhibition matches.

Date		Opponent	Location	Result	Rnd		Rec
Sep 20	⑩	Bob Pastor	Detroit	KO	11	Ret-World-H	200
1940							
Feb 9	⑩	Arturo Godoy	New York	W	15	Ret-World-H	203
Mar 29	⑩	Johnny Paychek	New York	KO	2	Ret-World-H	201
Jun 20	⑩	Arturo Godoy	New York	TKO	8	Ret-World-H	199
Dec 16		Al McCoy	Boston	TKO	6	Ret-World-H	202
1941							
Jan 31	⑩	Red Burman	New York	KO	5	Ret-World-H	202
Feb 17		Gus Dorazio	Philadelphia	KO	2	Ret-World-H	203
Mar 21	⑩	Abe Simon	Detroit	TKO	13	Ret-World-H	202
Apr 8		Tony Musto	St. Louis	TKO	9	Ret-World-H	203
May 23	⑩	Buddy Baer	Washington, DC	WD	7	Ret-World-H	201
Jun 18	⑩	Billy Conn★	New York	KO	13	Ret-World-H	199
Sep 29	⑩	Lou Nova	New York	TKO	6	Ret-World-H	202
1942							
Jan 9	⑩	Buddy Baer	New York	KO	1	Ret-World-H	206
Mar 27	⑩	Abe Simon	New York	KO	6	Ret-World-H	207
1946							
Jun 19	⑩	Billy Conn★	New York	KO	8	Ret-World-H	207
Sep 18	⑩	Tami Mauriello	New York	KO	1	Ret-World-H	211
1947							
Dec 5	⑩	Jersey Joe Walcott★	New York	W	15	Ret-World-H	211
1948							
Jun 25	⑩	Jersey Joe Walcott★	New York	KO	11	Ret-World-H	213
1950							
Sep 27	♛	Ezzard Charles★	New York	L	15	For-World-H	218
Nov 29		Cesar Brion	New York	W	10	—	216
1951							
Jan 3		Freddie Beshore	Detroit	TKO	4	—	210
Feb 7		Omelio Agramonte	Miami	W	10	—	209
Feb 23		Andy Walker	San Francisco	TKO	10	—	207
May 2		Omelio Agramonte	Detroit	W	10	—	208
Jun 15	⑩	Lee Savold	New York	KO	6	—	211
Aug 1		Cesar Brion	San Francisco	W	10	—	207
Aug 15		Jimmy Bivins★	Baltimore	W	10	—	203
Oct 26	⑩	Rocky Marciano★	New York	KO'd	8	—	212

Louis's first professional fight was a one-round knock-out win. He followed that victory with seventeen more in less than a year. After his first year as a pro, Louis was rated the ninth top contender for the heavyweight title by *The Ring* in its annual rankings. In 1935, he knocked out former champions Primo Carnera and Max Baer to vault to the status of top contender.

Louis suffered his first defeat when he faced another former champion, Max Schmeling of Germany, in Yankee Stadium before a crowd of 60,000. Louis was knocked down in the fourth round and, though he did inflict damage on Schmeling, trailed throughout the fight. Schmeling caught Louis with two overhand rights in the twelfth and knocked him out.

In 1937, Louis met champion James J. Braddock for the heavyweight title in Comiskey Park in Chicago. Braddock knocked Louis down early on but, as the fight continued, Louis dominated. A crushing straight right to Braddock's head finished the champion off in the eighth.

Louis had become the first black heavyweight champion since Jack Johnson and as such was a tremendous source of pride for black Americans. Promoter Mike

Jacobs and Louis's managers, Julian Black and John Roxborough, made sure that Louis did not do anything in public which would lower him in the critical eyes of white America. For instance, Louis was directed not to smile after defeating a white opponent. Whatever he felt inside, Louis allowed himself to be guided in this way, perhaps because he already possessed an uncommon sense of dignity. When some called Louis "a credit to his race," sportswriter Jimmy Cannon commented, "Yes, Louis is a credit to his race—the human race."

Sugar Ray Robinson (LC) and Joe Louis (RC) share a laugh in their Army uniforms on August 29, 1943, at Mitchell Field, New York.

In 1938, Louis got a chance to avenge his loss to Schmeling in Yankee Stadium in front of a colossal crowd of 75,000. He sent them home early with a one-round knockout of Schmeling, whom German leaders had put forward as an Aryan figurehead. Louis, who was seen as a standard-bearer for all Americans, had met

Max Schmeling hears the count of ten in the first round of his June 22, 1938, return match with Louis. The reigning champ is placidly victorious in the fourth defense of his heavyweight title.

President Franklin D. Roosevelt at the White House before the fight, which indicated the importance assigned to the match.

Louis continued to defend his title successfully. Though some of his opponents were disparaged as members of the "Bum of the Month Club," Louis handled them all. In June of 1941, he fought one of his most memorable fights against former light heavyweight champion Billy Conn. Fighting before another large crowd of 54,487 in the Polo Grounds, Conn gave a Louis a good battle and was leading after twelve rounds. Louis's corner told Louis that he needed a knockout to win. The champ rose to the occasion and knocked Conn out with a flurry of punches in the thirteenth round.

Louis fought twice in 1942 and donated his purses to the war effort. He then enlisted in the Army and fought 96 exhibitions before some two million GIs in the United States, North Africa, and Europe. Louis received the Legion of Merit for his work in this regard and further endeared himself to the American public with his comment that the United States would win the war because "we're on God's side."

After the war, Louis fought the long-awaited rematch with Conn and knocked him out in the eighth round. The next year, Louis fought the tough Jersey Joe

Louis stands over Hall of Famer Billy Conn who slipped to the canvas in the first round of their June 18, 1941, bout. In the thirteenth round, Louis, behind on the scorecards, knocked out Conn.

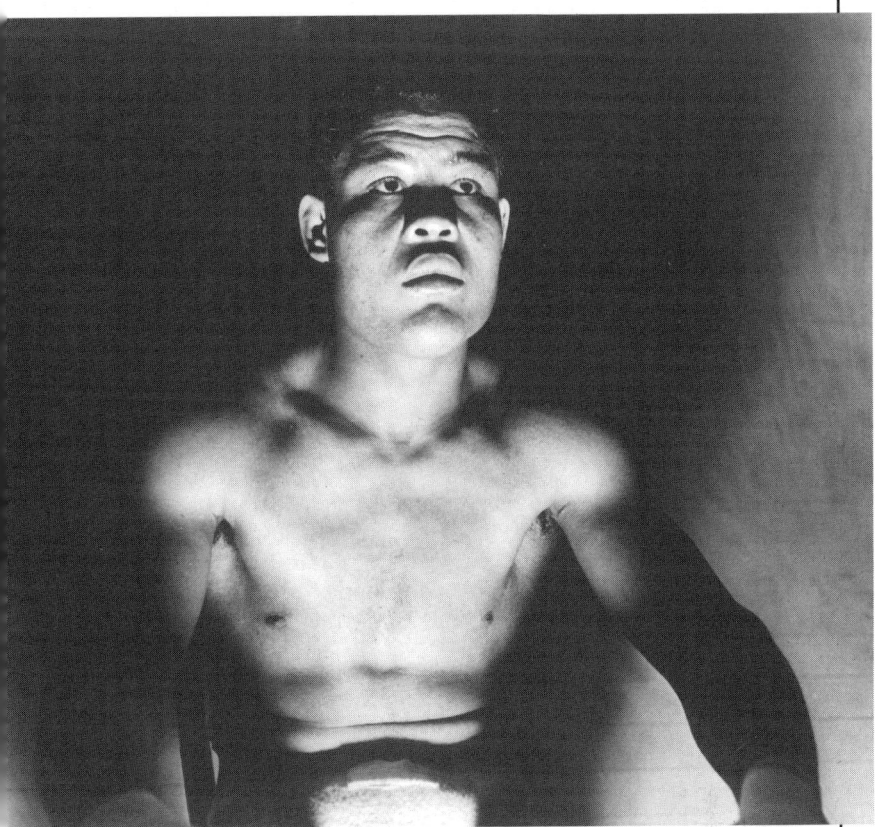

Despite his long career, Louis was only knocked to the canvas a total of ten times. Accomplishing this feat were Schmeling (2), Braddock, Galento, Buddy Baer, Jersey Joe Walcott (3), and Marciano (2).

Walcott, struggling to come in under 212 pounds as the contract specified. In Madison Square Garden before 18,194, Louis retained the title though he was knocked down in the first and fourth rounds. He won a split decision which many believed should have gone to Walcott. Louis knocked Walcott out in the rematch and, soon thereafter, announced his retirement.

In 1950, Louis made a comeback and lost by decision to Ezzard Charles in his bid to regain the championship. He then won eight fights in a row before facing the up-and-coming Rocky Marciano, who knocked him out in the eighth round. Louis then retired for good. Ring experts point to his great left jab, left hook, and powerful right, as well as his solid boxing skills, to rank Louis at or near the top of the all-time list of heavyweights. After retiring, he struggled to settle longstanding Internal Revenue Service problems by working in various businesses. He also worked as a wrestler, a wrestling referee, and as a greeter for a Las Vegas hotel. For the rest of his life, he maintained an association with the fight game and remained much admired by both the boxing community and the general public.

ROCKY MARCIANO
The Brockton Blockbuster

H E A V Y W E I G H T

Right-handed; 5'11"; 178–192 lbs.

49 bouts, 3/17/1947 to 9/21/1955

Managers: Gene Caggiano, Al Weill

Heavyweight Champion 1952–56

Hall of Fame Induction: 1990

Born: 9/1/1923, Brockton, MA

Named: Rocco Francis Marchegiano

Died: 8/31/1969

Rocky Marciano fought 49 times as a professional and never lost once. To date, he is the only heavyweight champion of the world to retire undefeated. Easy-going and gentle outside the ring, Marciano could be a hellish opponent. He offered a stolid resistance to whatever came his way, and the blockbuster punches that made him famous were some of the most dangerous ever thrown.

Marciano was born in Brockton, Massachusetts, just outside Boston. According to legend, he told his father he would one day be heavyweight champ of the world, but the young Marciano also dreamed of becoming a catcher in major league baseball. Although an uncle showed him the rudiments of boxing, Marciano didn't apply himself seriously until he did a stint in the Army. After leaving

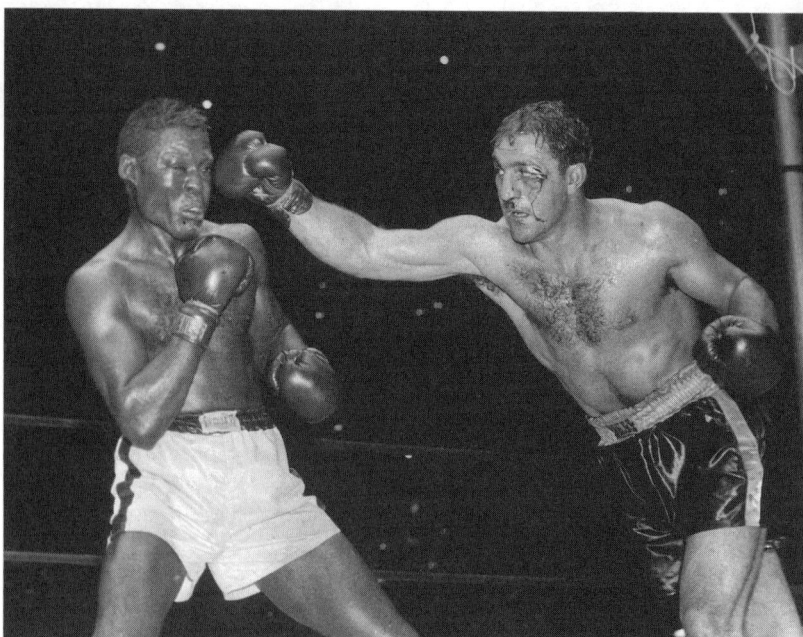

Blood trailing down his face, Marciano (R) unleashes "Susie Q" (his powerful right-hand punch) at Ezzard Charles in the first of his two successful 1954 title defenses.

the service, Marciano boxed as an amateur and won top honors in a New England Golden Gloves tournament.

As a novice, Marciano displayed great power but little control. In training, he sometimes swung his punches with so much momentum he fell down. He was a crude slugger that few expected to go very far. He was also considered too short, too light, and lacking the necessary reach to contend with heavyweights. Marciano's reach was only 68" (for comparison, Muhammad Ali's reach was 82"),

IN THE RING	WON 49	LOST 0	DRAWS 0	TB 49	KO 43	W 6	WF 0	D 0	KO'd 0	L 0	LF 0

Date	Opponent	Site	Result / Rounds		Title	Wt.
1947						
Mar 17	Lee Epperson	Holyoke, MA	KO	3	—	192
1948						
Jul 12	Harry Bilzarian	Providence, RI	TKO	1	—	185
Jul 19	John Edwards	Providence	KO	1	—	186
Aug 9	Bobby Quinn	Providence	KO	3	—	183
Aug 23	Eddie Ross	Providence	KO	1	—	184
Aug 30	Jimmy Weeks	Providence	TKO	1	—	184
Sep 13	Jerry Jackson	Providence	TKO	1	—	183
Sep 20	Bill Hardeman	Providence	KO	1	—	182
Sep 30	Gil Cardione	Washington, DC	KO	1	—	179
Oct 4	Bob Jefferson	Providence	TKO	2	—	178
Nov 29	Pat Connolly	Providence	TKO	1	—	185
Dec 14	Gilley Ferron	Philadelphia	TKO	2	—	180
1949						
Mar 21	Johnny Pretzie	Providence	TKO	5	—	183
Mar 28	Artie Donato	Providence	KO	1	—	182
Apr 11	James Walls	Providence	KO	3	—	183
May 2	Jimmy Evans	Providence	TKO	3	—	183
May 23	Don Mogard	Providence	W	10	—	181
Jul 18	Harry Haft	Providence	KO	3	—	184
Aug 16	Pete Louthis	New Bedford, MA	KO	3	—	184
Sep 26	Tommy Di Giorgio	Providence	KO	4	—	179
Oct 10	Ted Lowry	Providence	W	10	—	180
Nov 7	Joe Dominic	Providence	KO	2	—	185
Dec 2	Pat Richards	New York	TKO	2	—	181
Dec 19	Phil Muscato	Providence	TKO	5	—	183
Dec 30	Carmine Vingo	New York	KO	6	—	180
1950						
Mar 24 ⑩	Roland La Starza	New York	W	10	—	183
Jun 5	Eldridge Eatman	Providence	TKO	3	—	189
Jul 10	Gino Buonvino	Boston	TKO	10	—	188
Sep 18	Johnny Shkor	Providence	KO	6	—	190
Nov 13	Ted Lowry	Providence	W	10	—	186
Dec 18	Bill Willson	Providence	KO	1	—	190
1951						
Jan 29	Keene Simmons	Providence	TKO	8	—	191
Mar 20	Harold Mitchell	Hartford, CT	TKO	2	—	186
Mar 26	Art Henri	Providence	TKO	9	—	186

Apr 30		Red Applegate	Providence	W	10	—	185
Jul 12	ⓞ	Rex Layne	New York	KO	6	—	185
Aug 27		Fred Beshore	Boston	TKO	4	—	187
Oct 26	ⓞ	Joe Louis★	New York	KO	8	—	187
1952							
Feb 13		Lee Savold	Philadelphia	KO	6	—	186
Apr 21		Gino Buonvino	Providence	KO	2	—	189
May 12		Bernie Reynolds	Providence	KO	3	—	186
Jul 28	ⓞ	Harry Matthews	New York	KO	2	—	187
Sep 23	♛	Jersey Joe Walcott★	Philadelphia	KO	13	Won-World-H	184
1953							
May 15	ⓞ	Jersey Joe Walcott★	Chicago	KO	1	Ret-World-H	184
Sep 24	ⓞ	Roland La Starza	New York	TKO	11	Ret-World-H	185
1954							
Jun 19	ⓞ	Ezzard Charles★	New York	W	15	Ret-World-H	187
Sep 17	ⓞ	Ezzard Charles★	New York	KO	8	Ret-World-H	187
1955							
May 16	ⓞ	Don Cockell	San Francisco	TKO	9	Ret-World-H	189
Sep 21	ⓞ	Archie Moore★	New York	KO	9	Ret-World-H	188

one of the smallest of any heavyweight champion, which forced him to fight his opponents at close range. But Trainer Charley Goldman saw the potential in Marciano and taught him to fight from a crouch that made him very difficult to hit. Marciano spent countless hours training to perfect the lessons taught him by Goldman.

Marciano turned professional in 1947 with a third-round knockout of Lee Epperson. He went on to record sixteen consecutive knockouts, nine in the first round. Indeed, a look at Marciano's career record shows that few fighters ever went the distance with him. By 1950, Marciano was ranked tenth among heavyweight contenders in the annual rankings by *The Ring*. In 1951, his name became a household word when he fought Joe Louis, who had come out of retirement. Louis was old but still a master of the ring. Marciano had the edge in the close fight and in the eighth, knocked Louis down with a left hook to the jaw. He followed that up with a flurry of punches and ended the fight with a powerful right to the jaw.

In 1952, Marciano took the world heavyweight title from Jersey Joe Walcott, a fierce defender of his crown. The memorable battle was held at Philadelphia's Municipal Stadium before 40,379 fans. Walcott opened up by knocking Marciano down in the first round. From then on, it was a bloody contest. Both fighters inflicted significant damage, including multiple cuts. After twelve rounds, Walcott was ahead on the cards of both judges and the referee. The only way Marciano could win was by knockout. In the thirteenth, Marciano plunged a crushing right into Walcott's jaw. "Susie Q," Marciano's pet name for his piston-like right, had done her job. Walcott was out and Marciano was the new world champion. A rematch with Walcott ended much more abruptly, with a one-round knockout confirming Marciano's right to the title.

Marciano twice defended his title against former champ Ezzard Charles, winning both bouts. In 1955, he entered the ring against light heavyweight champion Archie Moore, a master boxer and ring veteran whose age hadn't caught up with him. Moore knocked Marciano down in the second, but Marciano recovered and knocked Moore out in the ninth. After this fight, Marciano retired. He left behind an unblemished record and the memory of his powerful punching ability. Well-liked, Marciano also left behind many friends. He died in a plane crash in 1969, en route to a personal appearance in Des Moines, Iowa.

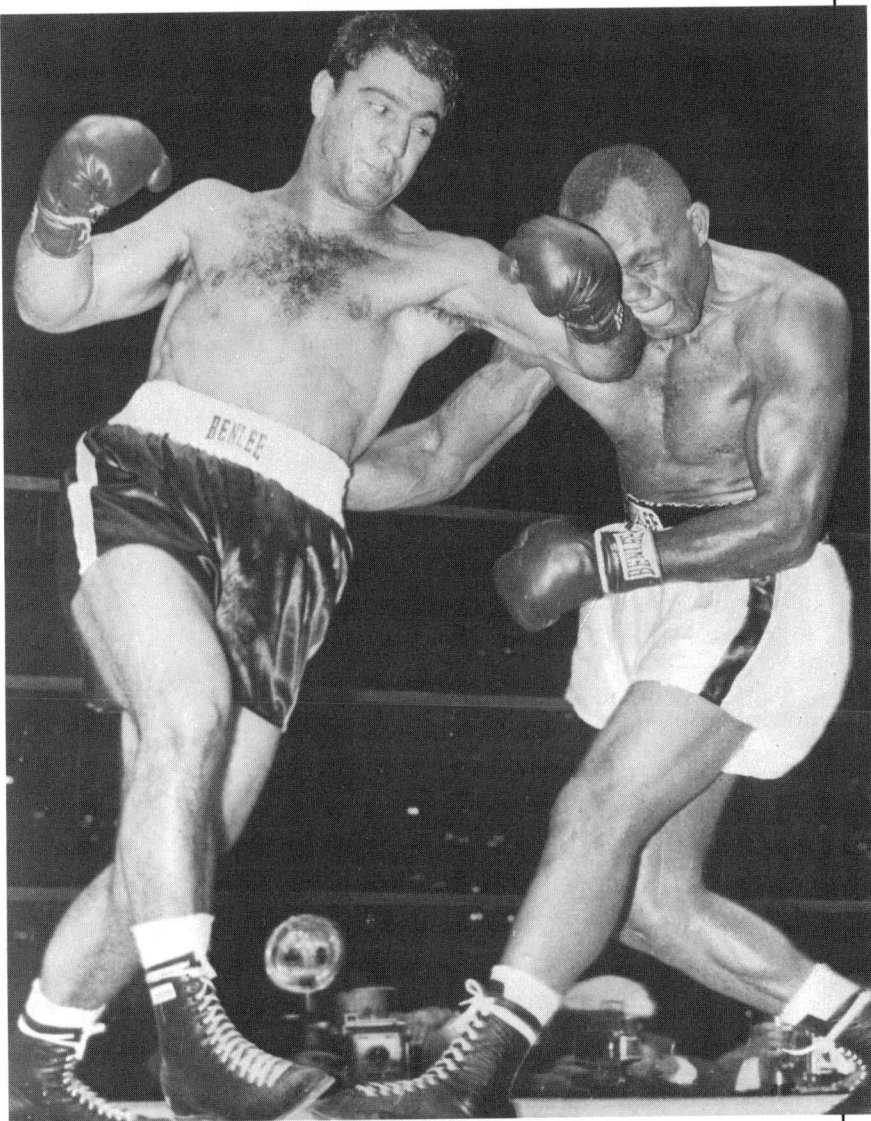

Marciano (L) crushes Jersey Joe Walcott with a left and a trailing forearm. With Walcott ahead on the cards, Marciano took him out in the thirteenth round on September 23, 1952.

JOEY MAXIM

LIGHT HEAVYWEIGHT

Right-handed; 6'1"; 169–192 lbs.
115 bouts, 1/13/1941 to 5/17/1958
Manager: Jack ("Doc") Kearns
Light Heavyweight Champ 1950–52
Hall of Fame Induction: 1994
Born: 3/28/1922, Cleveland, OH
Named: Giuseppe Antonio Berardinelli
Died: 6/2/2001

Joey Maxim used solid boxing skills to win 82 fights and the world light heavyweight championship in the span of a seventeen-year career. Maxim teamed with Jack Dempsey's former trainer, Jack ("Doc") Kearns, to face the best fighters of his era, and he was the first man to beat Floyd Patterson.

Maxim began boxing professionally in Cleveland at eighteen. Never a strong puncher, he did not record a knockout until his tenth fight. Maxim was sternly tested in 1942 when he twice lost decisions to future Hall of Famer Ezzard Charles. The next year, he suffered the only knockout of his career—a first-rounder at the hands of Curtis Sheppard.

Building up his record, Maxim won the first of three fights with the venerable Jersey Joe Walcott. Three years later, in 1949, he decisioned Gus Lesnevich to win the American light heavyweight title. At the close of that year, *The Ring* ranked Maxim as the top contender for the light heavyweight championship held by Freddie Mills. In 1950, Maxim travelled to England to face Mills in a fight held before a capacity crowd at Earl's Court Arena in London. The favored Mills struck early but without enough power to knock

Joey Maxim's most troublesome career opponent was Ezzard Charles. He met Charles five times between 1942 and 1951 and lost all five decisions.

IN THE RING	WON 82	LOST 29	DRAWS 4	TB 115	KO 21	W 61	WF 0	D 4	KO'd 1	L 27	LF 1

Date	Opponent	Site	Result / Rounds		Title	Wt.
1941						
Jan 13	Bob Berry	Cleveland	W	4	—	169
Jan 27	Frank McBride	Chicago	W	8	—	170
Feb 17	Orlando Trotter	Chicago	L	8	—	169
Apr 29	Bob Berry	Cleveland	W	6	—	—
Jul 11	Tony Paoli	Cleveland	W	10	—	—
Jul 28	Johnny Trotter	Chicago	W	8	—	171
Sep 13	Lee Oma	Youngstown, OH	W	8	—	—
Sep 15	Nate Bolden	Chicago	W	10	—	180
Oct 6	Bill Peterson	Chicago	W	10	—	178
Oct 27	Oliver Shanks	Chicago	TKO	5	—	178
Dec 1	⑩ Red Burman	Cleveland	W	10	—	178
1942						
Jan 16	⑩ Booker Beckwith	Chicago	L	10	—	181
Mar 11	⑩ Herbie Katz	Cleveland	KO	6	—	181
Mar 23	⑩ Lou Brooks	Baltimore	W	10	—	180
Apr 20	Frank Green	Chicago	KO	2	—	178
May 11	Charles Roth	Chicago	LF	2	—	178
Jun 1	Charles Roth	Chicago	KO	4	—	179
Jun 22	⑩ Jimmy Bivins★	Cleveland	L	10	—	178
Jul 10	⑩ Lou Brooks	Wilmington, DE	W	10	—	179
Jul 27	Curtis Sheppard	Pittsburgh	W	10	—	183
Aug 10	Altus Allen	Chicago	L	10	—	180
Aug 27	Jack Marshall	Chicago	KO	8	—	184
Sep 22	Shelton Bell	Pittsburgh	W	10	—	180
Oct 5	Hubert Hood	Chicago	W	8	—	190
Oct 13	Larry Lane	Akron, OH	W	10	—	190
Oct 27	⑩ Ezzard Charles★	Pittsburgh	L	10	—	181
Dec 1	⑩ Ezzard Charles★	Cleveland	L	10	—	184
1943						
Jan 18	Clarence Brown	Chicago	W	10	—	182
Feb 15	Clarence Brown	Chicago	W	10	—	188
Mar 10	⑩ Curtis Sheppard	Cleveland	KO'd	1	—	181
Mar 31	⑩ Curtis Sheppard	Cleveland	W	10	—	182
Apr 26	Al Jordan	Chicago	W	10	—	183
Aug 9	⑩ Nate Bolden	Chicago	W	10	—	175
Oct 29	⑩ Buddy Scott	Chicago	W	10	—	182
Dec 1	Claudio Villar	Cleveland	KO	6	—	182
1944						
Jan 31	Georgie Parks	Washington, DC	W	10	—	182
Apr 28	Buddy Walker	Detroit	W	10	—	181
May 29	⑩ Bob Garner	Chicago	W	10	—	187
Jun 26	Frank Androff	Chicago	W	10	—	189
Jul 27	⑩ Lloyd Marshall	Cleveland	L	10	—	187
Dec 19	Johnny Flynn	Cleveland	L	10	—	183
1945						
Feb 2	Johnny Flanagan	Chicago	W	8	—	183
Apr 16	Clarence Brown	Detroit	W	10	—	188
Nov 26	Cleo Everett	Detroit	W	10	—	185

1946

Date		Opponent	Location	Result	Rounds	Notes	Weight
Mar 4		Howard Williams	Detroit	W	10	—	186
Mar 11		John Thomas	New York	L	10	—	185
Mar 27		Ralph DeJohn	Buffalo, NY	TKO	1	—	185
Apr 1		Buddy Walker	Baltimore	W	10	—	186
Apr 9	⑩	Phil Muscato	Buffalo	L	10	—	186
May 7		Charley Eagle	Buffalo	D	10	—	182
May 14	⑩	Phil Muscato	Buffalo	W	12	—	180
Aug 2	⑩	Phil Muscato	Rochester, NY	W	10	—	184
Aug 14		Henry Cooper	Chicago	W	10	—	—
Aug 28	⑩	Jersey Joe Walcott★	Camden, NJ	W	10	—	180
Oct 10		Clarence Jones	Akron	W	10	—	184
Oct 16		Bearcat Jones	Toledo, OH	KO	5	—	184
Nov 12		Jim Ritchie	St. Louis	D	10	—	179
Dec 3		Jimmy Webb	Houston	KO	6	—	182
Dec 12		Al Velez	El Paso, TX	W	10	—	180
Dec 17		Jack Marshall	Houston	W	10	—	180

1947

Date		Opponent	Location	Result	Rounds	Notes	Weight
Jan 6	⑩	Jersey Joe Walcott★	Philadelphia	L	10	—	181
Jan 28		Marty Clark	Miami	TKO	7	—	185
May 12		Charlie Roth	Louisville, KY	KO	4	—	186
Jun 23	⑩	Jersey Joe Walcott★	Los Angeles	L	10	—	182
Sep 8		Clarence Jones	Wheeling, WV	KO	5	—	186
Sep 17		John Thomas	Cleveland	W	10	—	185
Nov 12	⑩	Bob Foxworth	Chicago	W	10	—	183
Dec 8	⑩	Billy Thompson	Philadelphia	W	10	—	179

1948

Date		Opponent	Location	Result	Rounds	Notes	Weight
Jan 9		Olle Tandberg	New York	W	10	—	179
Feb 2		Bob Sikes	Little Rock, AR	W	10	—	179
Feb 13		Tony Bosnich	San Francisco	W	10	—	179
Mar 22	⑩	Pat Valentino	San Francisco	D	10	—	178
Apr 27		Louis Berlier	Houston	W	10	—	185
May 7		Francisco de la Cruz	El Paso	W	10	—	189
May 27		Roy Hawkins	Tacoma, WA	W	10	—	182
Jun 7	⑩	Pat Valentino	San Francisco	D	10	—	180
Jun 22	⑩	Joe Kahut	Portland, OR	W	10	—	181
Jun 29		Bill Petersen	Seattle	W	10	—	182
Sep 28		Bill Petersen	Portland, OR	W	10	—	186
Oct 19	⑩	Joe Kahut	Portland, OR	L	15	—	183
Nov 12		Bob Satterfield	Chicago	W	10	—	181
Dec 7		Jimmy Bivins★	Cleveland	W	10	—	182

1949

Date		Opponent	Location	Result	Rounds	Notes	Weight
Feb 28	⑩	Ezzard Charles★	Cincinnati	L	15	—	184
May 23	⑩	Gus Lesnevich	Cincinnati	W	15	Won-Vac Amer-LH	174
Oct 25	⑩	Joe Kahut	Cincinnati	TKO	5	—	182
Nov 30		Pat McCafferty	Wichita, KS	TKO	4	—	181
Dec 9		Bill Petersen	Grand Rapids, MI	W	10	—	183

1950

Date		Opponent	Location	Result	Rounds	Notes	Weight
Jan 24	♔	Freddie Mills	London	KO	10	Won-World-LH	174
Apr 19		Joe Dawson	Omaha, NE	KO	2	—	182
May 12		Bill Petersen	Memphis, TN	KO	6	—	185
Sep 25		Johnny Swanson	Huntington, WV	KO	3	—	179
Oct 10		Bill Petersen	Salt Lake City	W	10	—	186

Date		Opponent	Location	Result	Rounds	Title	Weight
Nov 22		Big Boy Brown	Moline, IL	W	10	—	184
Dec 11	⑩	Dave Whitlock	San Francisco	KO	4	—	183
1951							
Jan 27		Hubert Hood	Indianapolis	KO	3	—	182
May 30	♛	Ezzard Charles★	Chicago	L	15	For-World-H	181
Aug 22	⑩	Bob Murphy	New York	W	15	Ret-World-LH	173
Dec 12	⑩	Ezzard Charles★	San Francisco	L	12	—	178
1952							
Mar 6		Ted Lowry	St. Paul, MN	W	10	—	184
Jun 25		Sugar Ray Robinson★	New York	TKO	14	Ret-World-LH	173
Dec 17	⑩	Archie Moore★	St. Louis	L	15	Lost-World-LH	174
1953							
Mar 4	⑩	Danny Nardico	Miami	W	10	—	183
Jun 24	♛	Archie Moore★	Ogden, UT	L	15	For-World-LH	175
1954							
Jan 27	♛	Archie Moore★	Miami	L	15	For-World-LH	174
Jun 7	⑩	Floyd Patterson★	Brooklyn	W	8	—	177
Nov 24	⑩	Paul Andrews	Chicago	W	10	—	189
1955							
Apr 13	⑩	Carl ("Bobo") Olson★	San Francisco	L	10	—	175
Jun 28	⑩	Willie Pastrano★	New Orleans	L	10	—	183
1956							
Sep 29		Edgardo Jose Romero	Vancouver, B.C.	W	10	—	191
1957							
Jan 25	⑩	Eddie Machen	Miami Beach	L	10	—	192
May 3	⑩	Eddie Machen	Louisville	L	10	—	189
Jun 18		Carl ("Bobo") Olson★	Portland, OR	L	10	—	188
1958							
Apr 11		Heinz Neuhaus	Stuttgart, Germany	L	10	—	190
Apr 27		Mino Bozzano	Milan, Italy	L	10	—	190
May 17		Ulli Ritter	Mannheim, Germany	L	10	—	186

out the challenger. Surprising many observers, Maxim knocked Mills out in the tenth round with a left to the jaw and a right cross to the chin.

In 1951, Maxim attempted to move up in class with a challenge to Ezzard Charles, who was by then the heavyweight champion. In this, their fourth meeting, Maxim lost the decision. The next year brought Maxim two of his most important fights. The first took place in June in Yankee Stadium before 48,000 sweltering fans on a night when the temperature exceeded 100°F. Maxim was defending his title against Sugar Ray Robinson, a two-time champion who was attempting to win a belt in a third weight class. Robinson fought all-out and was ahead on the judges' cards when he failed to answer the bell for the fourteenth round. The exhausted Robinson had apparently not paced himself for going the distance with Maxim. Maxim had fought a sound fight and received credit for a knockout.

Six months later Maxim lost his title to Archie Moore on a decision. He met Moore two more times but came away defeated. One of the final victories of his career was an eight-round decision over a young Floyd Patterson. After winning just one of his last nine fights, Maxim retired in 1958 and worked at a variety of jobs: cabdriver, restauranteur and stand-up comic. He died of complications from a stroke at age 79.

MIKE MCCALLUM
The Bodysnatcher

LIGHT HEAVYWEIGHT

Right-handed; 5'11½"; 150–181 lbs.

55 bouts, 2/19/1981 to 2/22/97

Managers: Emmanuel Steward, Lou Duva, Shelly Finkel

WBA Jr Middleweight Champ 1984–88

WBA Middleweight Champ 1989–91

WBC Light Hvywt Champ 1994–95

Hall of Fame Induction: 2003

Born: 12/7/1956, Kingston, Jamaica

Named: Mike McKenzie McCallum

Mike McCallum won three world titles—ranging from junior middleweight to light heavyweight—in a sixteen-year professional career. McCallum was born in Kingston, Jamaica, on December 7, 1956. Once, when he was fifteen, another boy drew a knife on him in the street. McCallum responded by firing off some left jabs that drew blood from his assailant. Someone from the local gym saw him and was impressed. McCallum began to train at the gym and three months later won an All-Island boxing title.

McCallum had a distinguished amateur career. He finished fifth in the 1974 World Championships at 147 pounds and finished second in the 1975 North American Championships. He went to the 1976 Olympics in Montreal and finished in a tie for fifth—making it to the quarterfinals. He kept his amateur standing after the Olympics. He won the Central American Championships in 1976–1978, the National Golden Gloves in 1977 and 1979, and the 1978 British Commonwealth Games—still as a welterweight—and finished second in the 1979 Pan American Games after losing to Cuban Andres Aldama in the gold medal match. McCallum was primed to avenge this defeat in the 1980 Olympics in Moscow. Jamaica did not follow the United States–led boycott of those Games. However, about ten days before the Olympics began, McCallum became ill with appendicitis—ending his Olympic hopes.

McCallum waited until February 19, 1981, to turn pro. He knocked out Rigoberto Lopez in four rounds in Las Vegas. Then McCallum fought a series of fights in Tampa for matchmaker Phil Alessi. McCallum knocked out all eight of his Tampa opponents and knocked out two other opponents in 1981 as well.

Mike McCallum (R) digs with a right to Sean Mannion's solar plexus in their October 19, 1984, Madison Square Garden bout for the vacant WBA junior middleweight title. He took the fifteen-round decision.

IN THE RING	WON 49	LOST 5	DRAWS 1	TB 55	KO 36	W 13	WF 0	D 1	KO'd 0	L 5	LF 0

Date	Opponent	Site	Result / Rounds		Title	Wt.
1981						
Feb 19	Rigoberto Lopez	Las Vegas	TKO	4	—	156
Mar 3	Rocky Fabrizio	Tampa	TKO	1	—	157
Mar 20	Rick Sheppard	Tampa	TKO	5	—	157
Apr 2	Shelby Wikerson	Tampa	TKO	5	—	151
Apr 24	Danny Chapman	New York	TKO	4	—	155
Apr 30	Charles Smith	Tampa	TKO	3	—	154
Jun 10	Freddy Cheech	Tampa	TKO	3	—	157
Jul 19	Bruce Strauss	Youngstown, OH	TKO	2	—	159
Aug 27	Tirso Roque	Tampa	TKO	3	—	154
Sep 8	Ed Harris	Tampa	KO	1	—	150
Oct 8	Jimmy Heair	Tampa	TKO	2	—	150
1982						
Jan 22	Greg Young	New York	TKO	5	—	154
Mar 26	Gilberto Armonte	Kingston, Jamaica	TKO	1	—	156
Apr 30	Reggie Ford	New York	KO	4	—	155
Jun 11	Kevin Perry	New York	W	10	—	155
Oct 22	Carlos Betancourt	New York	TKO	3	—	158
Nov 13	Ayub Kalule	Atlantic City	TKO	7	—	154
1983						
Apr 26	Tony Suero	Atlantic City	TKO	3	—	156
Aug 31	Jose Vallejo	Atlantic City	TKO	5	—	155
Oct 25	Manuel Jimenez	Atlantic City	W	10	—	156
1984						
Mar 10	Hasim Razzaq	Detroit	KO	1	—	153
Oct 19	Sean Mannion	New York	W	15	Won-Vac WBA-JM	153
Dec 1	Luigi Minchillo	Milan	TKO	14	Ret-WBA-JM	153
1985						
Jun 15	Marcos Martinez	Las Vegas	TKO	2	—	160
Jul 28	⑩ David Braxton	Miami	TKO	8	Ret-WBA-JM	154
1986						
May 2	Jim Shavers	Atlantic City	KO	6	—	163
Aug 23	⑩ Julian Jackson	Miami Beach	KO	2	Ret-WBA-JM	152
Sep 15	Irvin Hines	Paris	KO	4	—	162
Oct 25	Said Skouma	Paris	KO	9	Ret-WBA-JM	154
1987						
Mar 21	Leroy Hester	Kingston	KO	1	—	165
Apr 19	Milton McCrory	Phoenix	TKO	10	Ret-WBA-JM	153
Jul 18	Donald Curry	Las Vegas	KO	5	Ret-WBA-JM	153
1988						
Mar 5	⑩ Sumbu Kalambay	Pesaro, Italy	L	12	For-Vac WBA-M	158
Jun 27	David McCluskey	New York	TKO	2	—	168
Dec 22	Randy Smith	Vincennes, France	W	10	—	171
1989						
Jan 9	Ralph Moncrief	Nogent Sur Marne, France	TKO	5	—	170
May 10	Herol Graham	London	W	12	Won-Vac WBA-M	159
1990						
Feb 3	Steve Collins	Boston	W	12	Ret-WBA-M	159
Apr 14	⑩ Michael Watson	Wembley, England	KO	11	Ret-WBA-M	159

1991						
Feb 19	Frank Minton	Kansas City, MO	TKO	4	—	168
Mar 29	⑩ Sumbu Kalambay	Monte Carlo, Monaco	W	12	Ret-WBA-M	159
Aug 29	Carlos Cruzat	Reno, NV	W	10	—	168
Oct 10	Nicky Walker	Las Vegas	TKO	5	—	167
Dec 13	♛ James Toney	Atlantic City	D	12	For-IBF-M	157
1992						
May 21	Fermin Chirino	Las Vegas	W	10	—	167
Aug 29	♛ James Toney	Reno	L	12	For-IBF-M	158
1993						
Mar 25	Ramzi Hassan	Amiens, France	W	10	—	180
Aug 14	Glenn Thomas	London	W	10	—	175
1994						
Mar 4	Randall Yonker	Las Vegas	TKO	5	—	175
Jul 23	♛ Jeff Harding	Bismarck, ND	W	12	Won-WBC-LH	174
1995						
Feb 25	Carl Jones	Millwall, England	TKO	7	Ret-WBC-LH	174
Jun 16	Fabrice Tiozzo	Lyon, France	L	12	Lost-WBC-LH	174
1996						
Jun 22	Ali Saidi	Dortmund, Germany	W	10	—	—
Nov 22	⑩ Roy Jones Jr	Tampa	L	12	For-Interim WBC/IBF-LH	175
1997						
Feb 22	♛ James Toney	Uncasville, CT	L	12	For-WBU-C	181

On October 19, 1984, the still-undefeated McCallum got a crack at the vacant WBA junior middleweight title when he faced Sean Mannion. Mannion, an over-matched fighter who could not handle McCallum. For the first three rounds, McCallum trained his jab on Mannion—employing his superior reach. As the fight went on, McCallum drilled Mannion with combinations to the head and body. By the twelfth round, Mannion's nose was bleeding, and his eyes were puffy. McCallum, who made $30,000 for the fight, won a unanimous decision by the lopsided scores of 150-134, 149-136, and 149-123.

McCallum continued his winning ways by knocking out Luigi Minchillo in the fourteenth round in his first title defense. His next defense was against his former sparring partner, David Braxton, on July 28, 1985, in Miami. Though McCallum was nicknamed "The Bodysnatcher" because of his great ability to work the body, he concentrated on the head in this bout. McCallum battered Braxton in the fourth round and cut him near the bridge of his nose. In the fifth, McCallum inflicted a deep cut over Braxton's left eye. This cut led to the stoppage of the fight in the eighth round. In his next title defense, McCallum impressively stopped Julian Jackson of the Virgin Islands in the second round. It was the first time that two fighters from the West Indies had opposed each other in a world championship bout.

McCallum had one of the most important fights of his career when he faced Donald Curry, a former welterweight champion, on July 18, 1987, at Caesars Palace. Curry, a 2-1 favorite, got off to a good start and actually wobbled McCallum in the second. After four rounds, Curry was ahead on all three cards. In the fifth, McCallum unleashed a powerful left hook to the head, which knocked out Curry. McCallum, a technically proficient boxer, was a master at setting up a fighter for a knockout. This time, McCallum used right uppercuts to the body to set up the finishing blow.

After the Curry fight, McCallum relinquished the junior middleweight title and moved up to middleweight. In his first fight in that class, he faced WBA middleweight champ Sumbu Kalambay. Kalambay outboxed McCallum and showed great speed and counterpunching ability to win a twelve-round decision. McCallum received another opportunity to fight for the title when he faced Herol Graham for the then-vacant WBA middleweight title in London on May 10, 1989. Graham employed an awkward style, which it made it tough for "The Bodysnatcher." However, McCallum's superior punching power carried the day as he took a split decision. Graham was penalized a point in the eighth round for wrestling McCallum off balance. That point, as it turned out, cost him a draw.

McCallum successfully defended his title three times, including a decision over Kalambay. The WBA then stripped McCallum of the title. It was reported that McCallum refused to fork over a second $50,000 payment to Barney Eastwood, the promoter of contender Steve Collins, after he had already paid an initial $75,000. The payments were to secure McCallum the right to bypass a mandatory title defense against Collins and free himself to fight IBF middleweight champion James ("Lights Out") Toney.

At any rate, the Toney fight took place and was a fine exhibition of boxing. The bout went the full twelve rounds. The fighters continually traded punches. In the eighth, Toney shook McCallum with a right-left-right combination, but McCallum answered with short rights and lefts of his own. In the twelfth, Toney tried to knock out McCallum; a left hook caused McCallum's knees to buckle. McCallum fired back with combinations. The fight was scored a draw. The decision drew some boos from the crowd, which believed Toney had won. In the rematch on August 29, 1992, in Reno, Toney won a majority decision in a lackluster fight. Hall of Fame trainer Eddie Futch, who now trained McCallum, disputed the scoring.

On July 23, 1994, the 37-year-old McCallum captured the WBC light heavyweight title with a decision over Jeff Harding. He successfully defended the title once before losing this belt by decision to Fabrice Tiozzo. Over one year later, an almost 40-year-old McCallum lost a decision to Roy Jones Jr. After he lost the decision in a rematch with Toney on February 22, 1997, McCallum retired. In retirement, McCallum has been a successful trainer based in Las Vegas. In 2005, the American Foundation of the University of the West Indies named McCallum as one of thirteen "Caribbean Luminaries" of the year.

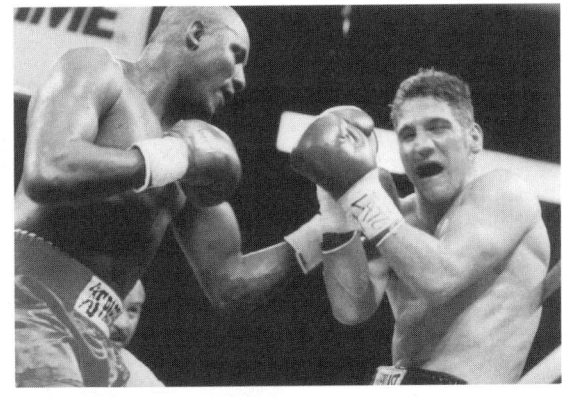

Mike McCallum (L) punishes Randall Yonker along the ropes before referee Joe Cortez stepped in to stop this fight with just five seconds left in the fifth round. McCallum was TKO victor on March 4, 1994, at the MGM Grand in Las Vegas.

BARRY McGUIGAN
The Clones Cyclone

F E A T H E R W E I G H T

Right-handed; 5′6″; 124–131 lbs.

35 bouts, 5/10/1981 to 5/31/1989

Manager: Barney Eastwood

WBA Featherweight Champion 1985–86

Hall of Fame Induction: 2005

Born: 2/28/1961, Monaghan, Ireland

Named: Finbar Patrick McGuigan

It was said that a Barry McGuigan fight was the only force strong enough to unify, at least temporarily, the warring factions in Northern Ireland. McGuigan was a charismatic, crowd-pleasing fighter from Clones in the Republic of Ireland, located just accross the border from Northern Ireland. He often fought in Northern Ireland, and many of his fans lived in that troubled part of Great Britain. A Catholic himself, McGuigan even crossed traditional religious boundaries by marrying a Protestant woman. He never chose sides in the bitter Irish sectarian disputes.

McGuigan was born on February 28, 1961. He first became interested in boxing when he and some other boys found a pair of boxing gloves in a vacant house. Soon he was going to a gym on a regular basis. By the time he was twelve years old, he was seriously training to be a boxer. He did roadwork during a break in his schoolday and then came home to work out in the gym his father had built for him. Unlike many boxers, McGuigan did not come from an impoverished background. His parents operated a grocery store, and his father was a singer of some renown. Later, he would sometimes climb into the ring before his son's fights and sing "Danny Boy."

McGuigan had a successful amateur boxing career. He won a gold medal in the 1978 Commonwealth Games in Edmonton, Alberta, Canada. He then fought in the Olympics in 1980 but was upset in the third round by Zambia's Winfred Kabunda. McGuigan turned professional on May 10, 1981, with a second-round knockout of Selvin Bell in Dublin. He spurned the management offer from Hall of Famer Mickey Duff and signed with wealthy Irish businessman Barney Eastwood. Surprisingly, McGuigan suffered a decision loss in his third fight to Peter Eubank. He bounced back in his next bout to defeat former

McGuigan's knockdown of WBA Featherweight Champ Eusebio Pedroza (center) was the turning point in their June 8, 1985, bout. McGuigan took the title by unanimous decision.

IN THE RING	WON **32**	LOST **3**	DRAWS **0**	TB 35	KO 28	W 4	WF 0	D 0	KO'd 1	L 2	LF 0

Date	Opponent	Site	Result / Rounds		Title	Wt.
1981						
May 10	Selvin Bell	Dublin, Ireland	TKO	2	—	126
Jun 21	Gary Lucas	Wembley, England	TKO	4	—	129
Aug 3	Peter Eubank	Brighton, England	L	8	—	128
Sep 22	Jean-Marc Renard	Belfast, Northern Ireland	W	8	—	128
Oct 26	Terry Pizarro	Belfast	TKO	4	—	124
Dec 8	Peter Eubank	Belfast	TKO	8	—	127
1982						
Jan 27	Jose Luis De La Sagra	Belfast	W	8	—	127
Feb 8	Ian Murray	London	TKO	3	—	128
Feb 23	Angel Oliver	Belfast	TKO	3	—	128
Mar 23	Angelo Licata	Belfast	TKO	2	—	129
Apr 22	Gary Lucas	Enniskillen, Northern Ireland	KO	1	—	129
Jun 14	Young Ali	London	KO	6	—	126
Oct 5	Jimmy Duncan	Belfast	TKO	5	—	126
Nov 9	Paul Huggins	Belfast	TKO	5	—	125
1983						
Apr 12	Vernon Penprase	Belfast	TKO	2	Won-Vac UK-FE	126
May 22	Sammy Meck	Navan, Ireland	TKO	6	—	127
Jul 9	Lavon McGowan	Chicago	KO	1	—	128
Oct 5	Ruben Herasme	Belfast	KO	2	—	127
Nov 16	Valerio Nati	Belfast	KO	6	Won-Europe-FE	126
1984						
Jan 26	Charm Chiteule	Belfast	TKO	10	—	126
Apr 4	Jose Caba	Belfast	TKO	7	—	124
Jun 5	Esteban Eguia	Kensington, England	KO	3	Ret-Europe-FE	124
Jun 30	Paul DeVorce	Belfast	TKO	5	—	126
Oct 13	Felipe Orozco	Belfast	TKO	2	—	127
Dec 19	Clyde Ruan	Belfast	KO	5	Ret-Europe-FE	125
1985						
Feb 23 ⑩	Juan Laporte	Belfast	W	10	—	126
Mar 26	Farid Gallouze	Wembley	TKO	2	Ret-Europe-FE	124
Jun 8	Eusebio Pedroza	London	W	15	Won-WBA-FE	125
Sep 28 ⑩	Bernard Taylor	Belfast	TKO	8	Ret-WBA-FE	125
1986						
Feb 15	Danilo Cabrera	Dublin	TKO	14	Ret-WBA-FE	125
Jun 23 ⑩	Steve Cruz	Las Vegas	L	15	Lost-WBA-FE	126
1988						
Apr 20	Nicky Perez	London	TKO	4	—	131
Jun 25	Francisco Tomas Da Cruz	Luton, England	TKO	4	—	131
Dec 1	Julio Cesar Miranda	London	TKO	8	—	131
1989						
May 31	Jim McDonnell	Manchester, England	TKO'd	4	—	130

European junior lightweight champion Jean-Marc Renard who had knocked him to the canvas. The Renard fight was McGuigan's first pro contest in Belfast, Northern Ireland. He would fight a total of eighteen times in Belfast.

McGuigan continued his winning ways. On December 8, 1981, he avenged his loss to Eubank when he won by technical knockout in the eighth round. On June 14, 1982, he knocked out Young Ali in the sixth round. Ali lapsed into a coma after the fight and later died. McGuigan was badly shaken by Ali's death and seriously considered retiring. To the delight of his fans, he kept fighting.

McGuigan angered some of his Irish supporters when he applied for British citizenship so that he could fight for British and European titles. He won the vacant British featherweight title when he knocked out Vernon Penprase in two rounds on April 12, 1983. The Penprase fight marked the first of many battles for McGuigan in Belfast's King's Hall. Later that same year on November 16, McGuigan added the vacant European featherweight title to his laurels when he knocked out Valerio Nati in the sixth round. He successfully defended this title three times with knockouts of Esteban Eguia, Clyde Ruan, and Farid Gallouze.

McGuigan served notice to the world fight community that he was a world-class contender when he fought the very tough, former WBC featherweight champion Juan Laporte on February 23, 1985, before 7,000 in Belfast. McGuigan mixed his punches well. He employed his quickness to avoid most of Laporte's jabs. In the middle of the fifth round, McGuigan was startled by a short right but answered with a strong left hook, his signature punch, later in the round. In the last round of the fight, a McGuigan right shook Laporte. The referee, who was the only judge in the bout, gave McGuigan the decision, 99-97.

After a mandatory European title defense against an overmatched Farid Gallouze, McGuigan met Hall of Famer Eusebio Pedroza with the latter's WBA featherweight title at stake. Pedroza was defending his title for the twentieth time. More than ever the popular slogan "Let McGuigan do the fighting" was apt as 12,000 McGuigan fans from both Northern Ireland and the Republic of Ireland traveled across the Irish Sea to watch McGuigan's shot at the title at the Queens Park Rangers Football Stadium in London on June 8, 1985. The crowd totaled more than 25,000. Unknown to them, McGuigan's manager, Eastwood, almost did not let the fight go on because Pedroza weighed in before Eastwood and McGuigan arrived. Pedroza's weight was announced at the featherweight limit of 126, and Eastwood insisted on seeing Pedroza get weighed. When his request was refused, Eastwood led McGuigan away from the scale but minutes later, he returned with McGuigan and allowed McGuigan to get weighed. Before the fight, McGuigan's father, Pat, stirred the crowd with his rendition of "Danny Boy."

McGuigan initiated most of the action, primarily with his left jab, since an elbow injury prevented him from relying on his patented left hook to the liver. Pedroza used the entire twenty-foot ring as he spent much of the fight backpedaling. At times, McGuigan pinned Pedroza in a corner where he unleashed left jabs and rights. In the second round, Pedroza's left cheek was swollen. He later suffered a cut over the left eyebrow. In the seventh, McGuigan powered a right cross to the jaw. As Pedroza started to go down, McGuigan followed with a left hook to the head. Pedroza was back up at the count of three. Pedroza fought back bravely in the eighth. Late in the ninth, McGuigan staggered Pedroza with a right to the head and battered him with both hands until the bell sounded. McGuigan continued his domination for the rest of the fight and won the unanimous decision by scores of 148-138, 149-139, and 147-140. The new champion was hailed in every corner of the Emerald Isle.

McGuigan's first title defense was against a previously unbeaten southpaw, Bernard Taylor, in Belfast's King's Hall before an enthusiastic sellout crowd of 7,000. This was the first

McGuigan (R) rocks Argentinean lightweight Julio Cesar Miranda with a right. The bout was stopped a little over a minute into the eighth round with McGuigan the victor by TKO.

world title fight in Belfast in 36 years. McGuigan was bothered by Taylor's awkward style. Taylor won the early rounds with his counterpunching, but by the sixth McGuigan had taken control and was firing away with shots to the head and body. In the eighth, McGuigan worked the body so effectively that Taylor could not defend himself. Taylor did not answer the bell for the ninth round.

After knocking out Danilo Cabrera, McGuigan traveled to the United States to take part in the heavily promoted "Triple Hitter" card on June 23, 1986, at Caesars Palace in Las Vegas. McGuigan was to face unheralded Steve Cruz. Also on the card were Thomas Hearns and Roberto Duran. Those two, along with McGuigan, comprised the "triple hitters." The three went on a lengthy pre-fight promotional tour to New York, Boston, Washington, Miami, St. Louis, and Chicago. The night of the outdoor fight was extremely hot, hitting 109°— which severely bothered the heavily favored McGuigan, already suffering from a training injury to his ankle. Cruz got off to a good start, though McGuigan came back and by the fourteenth round seemed to be in control. Cruz may have taken the fight in the last round. A left hook to the head followed by a right knocked McGuigan down. He got up only to be floored again by a right hand. Cruz won a unanimous decision 143-142, 143-139, and 142-141.

The loss triggered a round of lawsuits between McGuigan and Eastwood. McGuigan argued that Eastwood had agreed to pay him $250,000 in addition to his purse if he lost, since he had not wanted to fight in Las Vegas. Eastwood countersued, keeping McGuigan out of the ring. Eastwood ultimately paid McGuigan the $250,000 and no longer managed "The Clones Cyclone."

McGuigan returned to the ring on April 20, 1988, when he knocked out Nicky Perez in four. His comeback ended on May 31, 1989, when Jim McDonnell stopped him in the fourth round. In retirement, McGuigan has engaged in a variety of post-boxing activities including race-car driving, announcing, singing, organizing a union for boxers, and training actor Daniel Day-Lewis for his role in the movie The Boxer.

BOB MONTGOMERY
The Bobcat

LIGHTWEIGHT

Right-handed; 5'8"; 133–143 lbs.

97 bouts, 10/23/1938 to 3/27/1950

Managers: Frankie Thomas 1938–44, Joe Gramby 1944–47

NY World Lightweight Champ 1943, 1944–47

Hall of Fame Induction: 1995

Born: 2/10/1919, Sumter, SC

Died: 8/25/1998

One of the top lightweights in an era which included Hall of Famers Beau Jack and Ike Williams, Bob Montgomery won acclaim for his aggressive, take-no-prisoners approach. His intense boxing style led sportswriter Johnny Webster of the *Philadelphia Inquirer* to dub Montgomery the "Bobcat" because of Montgomery's way of continually moving forward and pawing an opponent until he got him.

Born in South Carolina, Montgomery followed a brother to Philadelphia at the age of fifteen and shortly thereafter began boxing. Montgomery quickly came under the tutelage of Joe Gramby, who would eventually become Philadelphia's most influential black manager. Fighting primarily in the Philadelphia area in the late 1930s and early '40s, Montgomery quickly achieved designation as *The Ring*'s top lightweight contender for the year 1941. Never one to shy away from a tough fight, Montgomery split two non-title bouts with lightweight champ Lew Jenkins and lost two non-title bouts by decision to Sammy Angott.

In May 1943, Montgomery challenged Hall of Famer Beau Jack for the New York world lightweight title. Montgomery dominated the Madison Square Garden

The lightweight title was disputed during Montgomery's tenure. While he held the NY world belt, Angott, Zurita, and Williams were the NBA champs.

fight, effectively countering Jack's furious attacks with skillful combinations. This first meeting began a memorable series with Jack. The pair would duel three more times. In the title rematch in November, Jack upset the heavily favored Montgomery before another large crowd in the Garden to reclaim the crown. They met again in 1944 in Madison Square Garden, where Montgomery withstood a frantic effort by Jack in the tenth, eleventh, and twelfth rounds. Montgomery won on

IN THE RING	WON 75	LOST 19	DRAWS 3	TB 97	KO 37	W 38	WF 0	D 3	KO'd 3	L 16	LF 0

Date	Opponent	Site	Result / Rounds		Title	Wt.
1938						
Oct 23	Young Johnny Buff	Atlantic City	KO	2	—	—
Oct 27	Pat Patucci	Atlantic City	KO	2	—	137
Nov 4	Eddie Stewart	Philadelphia	TKO	2	—	134
Nov 10	Joe Beltrante	Atlantic City	KO	3	—	136
Nov 17	Red Rossi	Atlantic City	KO	2	—	137
Dec 8	Jackie Sheppard	Atlantic City	W	8	—	138
1939						
Jan 19	Harvey Jacobs	Atlantic City	KO	1	—	138
Feb 2	Charley Burns	Atlantic City	W	8	—	139
Feb 23	Jay Macedon	Atlantic City	W	8	—	140
Mar 9	Billy Miller	Atlantic City	TKO	2	—	138
Mar 16	Frankie Saia	Philadelphia	KO	4	—	139
Mar 30	Benny Berman	Atlantic City	W	8	—	142
Apr 13	Young Raspi	Atlantic City	TKO	6	—	140
Apr 20	Eddie Guerra	Atlantic City	W	8	—	142
May 1	George Zengaras	Philadelphia	D	10	—	137
May 23	Norment Quarles	Philadelphia	KO	4	—	—
Jun 15	Charley Burns	Atlantic City	KO	2	—	136
Jun 21	Tommy Rawson	Philadelphia	KO	1	—	134
Jul 3	Frankie Wallace	Philadelphia	W	10	—	131
Aug 14	Jimmy Murray	Philadelphia	KO	3	—	134
Aug 24	Ray Ingram	Atlantic City	W	10	—	135
Oct 5	Charles Gilley	Atlantic City	KO	6	—	135
Oct 23	Mike Evans	Philadelphia	W	10	Won-PA-L	132
Nov 10	Tommy Spiegel	Philadelphia	L	10	—	135
Nov 17	Mike Evans	Philadelphia	KO	1	—	138
1940						
Jan 29	Al Nettlow	Philadelphia	D	10	—	136
Mar 11	Al Nettlow	Philadelphia	W	10	—	136
Jun 3	Al Nettlow	Philadelphia	W	12	—	136
Jul 5	Jimmy Vaughn	Atlantic City	KO	2	—	139
Sep 16	♛ Lew Jenkins★	Philadelphia	L	10	—	136
Nov 7	Norment Quarles	Atlantic City	D	10	—	137
Nov 25	♛ Sammy Angott	Philadelphia	L	10	—	138
1941						
Jan 29	Julie Kogon	Brooklyn	W	8	—	138
Feb 7	Al Nettlow	New York	W	8	—	139
Mar 3	George Zengaras	Philadelphia	TKO	3	—	142
Apr 28	Nick Peters	Philadelphia	TKO	3	—	138
May 16	♛ Lew Jenkins★	New York	W	10	—	136

Date		Opponent	Location	Result	Round	Notes	Weight
Jun 16		Manuel Villa II	Baltimore	KO	1	—	139
Jun 30		Wishy Jones	Washington, DC	TKO	6	—	136
Jul 3		Frankie Wallace	Atlantic City	KO	3	—	137
Jul 14		Luther ("Slugger") White	Baltimore	W	10	—	134
Sep 8		Mike Kaplan	Philadelphia	W	10	—	136
Oct 10		Davey Day	Chicago	KO	1	—	137
Oct 24		Julie Kogon	Chicago	W	10	—	137
Oct 30		Frankie Wallace	Williamsport, PA	TKO	5	—	138
Dec 8		Jimmy Garrison	Philadelphia	TKO	4	—	137
1942							
Jan 5		Mayon Padlo	Philadelphia	KO	8	—	139
Mar 6	♛	Sammy Angott★	New York	L	12	—	135
Apr 20	⑩	Joey Peralta	Philadelphia	W	10	—	137
May 8		Carmen Notch	Toledo, OH	W	10	—	135
Jul 7	♛	Sammy Angott★	Philadelphia	L	12	—	137
Aug 13	⑩	Bobby Ruffin	New York	W	10	—	135
Oct 6	⑩	Maxie Shapiro	Philadelphia	L	10	—	135
Dec 1	⑩	Maxie Shapiro	Philadelphia	W	10	—	135
1943							
Jan 8	⑩	Chester Rico	New York	TKO	8	—	134
Feb 22	⑩	Lulu Costantino	Philadelphia	W	10	—	134
Apr 5		Roman Alvarez	Philadelphia	KO	4	—	137
Apr 30		Gene Johnson	Scranton, PA	W	10	—	136
May 3		Henry Vasquez	Holyoke, MA	W	8	—	135
May 21	♕	Beau Jack★	New York	W	15	Won-NY World-L	134
Jul 4		Al Reasoner	New Orleans	KO	6	—	139
Jul 30	⑩	Frankie Wills	Washington, DC	W	10	—	137
Aug 23	⑩	Fritzie Zivic★	Philadelphia	W	10	—	136
Oct 25		Petey Scalzo	Philadelphia	TKO	6	—	137
Nov 19	⑩	Beau Jack★	New York	L	15	Lost-NY World-L	133
1944							
Jan 7	⑩	Joey Peralta	Detroit	W	10	—	137
Jan 25	⑩	Ike Williams★	Philadelphia	KO	12	—	137
Feb 18	⑩	Al ("Bummy") Davis	New York	KO'd	1	—	137
Mar 3	♛	Beau Jack★	New York	W	15	Reg-NY World-L	135
Apr 28	⑩	Joey Peralta	Chicago	W	10	—	140
Aug 4	⑩	Beau Jack★	New York	L	10	—	137
1945							
Feb 13		Cecil Hudson	Los Angeles	W	10	—	140
Mar 20		Genaro Rojo	Los Angeles	TKO	8	—	139
May 8	⑩	Nick Moran	Los Angeles	L	10	—	140
Jul 9	⑩	Nick Moran	Philadelphia	W	10	—	135
1946							
Feb 3		Bill Parsons	New Orleans	W	10	—	143
Feb 15		Leo Rodak	Chicago	W	10	—	138
Mar 8	⑩	Tony Pellone	New York	W	10	—	139
Mar 21		Ernie Petrone	New Haven, CT	KO	4	—	137
Jun 28	⑩	Allie Stolz	New York	KO	13	Ret-NY World-L	134
Jul 29		George LaRover	Springfield, MA	W	10	—	136
Aug 19		Wesley Mouzon	Philadelphia	KO'd	2	—	137
Nov 26		Wesley Mouzon	Philadelphia	TKO	8	Ret-NY World-L	135
1947							
Jan 20		Eddie Giosa	Philadelphia	TKO	5	—	138
Feb 7	⑩	Tony Pellone	Detroit	L	10	—	140

Feb 25		Joey Barnum	Los Angeles	TKO	7	—	138
Mar 31	⑩	Jesse Flores	San Francisco	KO	3	—	138
May 12		George LaRover	Philadelphia	W	10	—	140
Jun 2		Julie Kogon	New Haven	W	10	—	137
Jun 9		Frankie Cordino	Springfield	W	10	—	136
Aug 4	♛	Ike Williams★	Philadelphia	TKO'd	6	For-Vac World-L	133
Nov 24		Livio Minelli	Philadelphia	L	10	—	142
Dec 22		Joey Angelo	Boston	L	10	—	136
1950						
Feb 3		Aldo Minelli	Washington, DC	L	10	—	145
Feb 27		Johnny Greco	Montreal	L	10	—	142
Mar 9		Don Williams	Worcester, MA	L	10	—	142
Mar 27		Eddie Giosa	Philadelphia	L	10	—	143

a split decision and once again relieved Jack of the title. In yet another tough battle, Jack prevailed on points in a non-title ten-rounder.

Montgomery's two fights with Ike Williams are also memorable for their ferocity. Montgomery may have had a personal grudge against Williams. In any case, in their first fight, a non-title contest in 1944, he administered a terrific beating to Williams, punishing him for twelve rounds before knocking him out. The two met again in 1947. Williams, by then holder of the NBA lightweight crown, put his title on the line, while Montgomery followed suit with his New York title. For five rounds, the two combatants engaged in an extremely hard-fought, even battle. In the sixth, Williams knocked Montgomery down twice, and the referee stopped the fight. This bout was ranked as one of the twenty greatest fights of all time in a 1981 poll by *The Ring*.

After that, Montgomery fought six more bouts and lost them all. However, those late-career losses do not detract from his reputation as one of the best lightweights of all time. In 1971 Montgomery promoted boxing events at the Blue Horizon in Philadelphia. He died at age 79.

Early in his career, Montgomery fought a grueling schedule. He had nineteen fights in 1939, all in Philadelphia or Atlantic City.

CARLOS MONZON
Escopeta (Gun)

MIDDLEWEIGHT

Right-handed; 5'11½"; 151–166 lbs.

100 bouts, 2/6/1963 to 7/30/1977

Managers: Amilcar Brusa, Rodolfo Sabbatini

Middleweight Champion 1970–77

Hall of Fame Induction: 1990

Born: 8/7/1942, Santa Fe, Argentina

Named: Carlos Roque Monzon

Died: 1/8/1995

The greatest middleweight champion of the 1970s and possibly one of the greatest middleweights of all time, Carlos Monzon dominated the division as few had before him. Monzon beat all comers and, with time, overcame critics' complaints that he did not face particularly tough competition.

Born in Argentina, Monzon started his professional career in 1963. He fought an average of once a month in the early stages of his career and posted a record of 29-3-6, with one no-contest, before capturing the Argentine middleweight title in 1966. The next year, he added the South American middleweight title. By 1968, Monzon had achieved sufficient international stature to be ranked eighth in the rankings compiled by *The Ring*.

In 1970, Monzon faced Hall of Famer Nino Benvenuti in a challenge for the world middleweight title. Monzon took the championship in convincing fashion, knocking out Benvenuti in the twelfth round with a right to the head. Monzon also won the rematch, stopping Benvenuti in the third round.

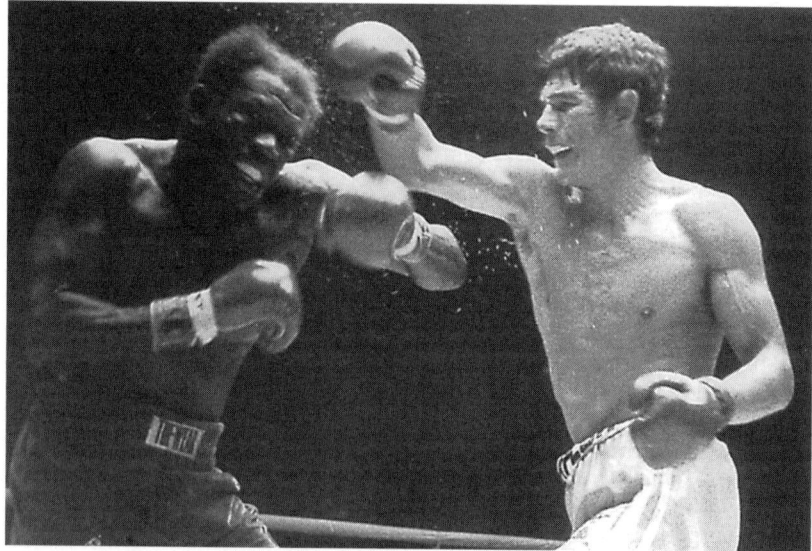

Veteran boxer Emile Griffith, who had lost the middleweight title three years earlier to Nino Benvenuti, recoils from a Monzon (R) right hook on September 25, 1971, in Buenos Aires. Griffith went in fourteen.

IN THE RING	WON 87	LOST 3	DRAWS 9	TB 100	KO 59	W 28	WF 0	D 9	KO'd 0	L 3	LF 0	NC 1

Date	Opponent	Site	Result / Rounds		Title	Wt.
1963						
Feb 6	Ramon Montenegro	Rafaela, Argentina	KO	2	—	—
Mar 13	Albino Veron	Vila, Argentina	NC	1	—	—
Apr 9	Albino Veron	Santa Fe, Argentina	TKO	2	—	155
Apr 26	Mario Suarez	Posadas, Argentina	TKO	7	—	153
May 3	Raul Rivas	Posadas	TKO	5	—	151
May 31	Jose N. Rodriguez	Parana, Argentina	KO	5	—	—
Jul 17	Andres Cejas	Buenos Aires	TKO	4	—	158
Aug 9	Lisandro Guzman	Cordoba, Argentina	TKO	3	—	158
Aug 28	Antonio Aguilar	Buenos Aires	L	10	—	158
Oct 18	Benito Sanchez	Reconquista, Argentina	KO	8	—	—
Dec 6	Rene Sosa	Parana	KO	6	—	157
1964						
Jan 17	Roberto Carabajal	Parana	KO	8	—	157
Jun 13	Angel Coria	Mar Del Plata, Argentina	W	8	—	—
Jun 28	Felipe Cambeiro	Rio de Janeiro	L	8	—	159
Jul 10	Roberto Carabajal	Tostado, Argentina	W	10	—	—
Jul 24	Walter Villa	Ceres, Argentina	KO	9	—	—
Aug 14	Juan Diaz	Villa Angela, Argentina	TKO	9	—	—
Sep 4	Americo Vaca	Parana	KO	3	—	159
Sep 25	Francisco Olea	Tostado	TKO	9	—	—
Oct 9	Alberto Massi	Cordoba	L	10	—	160
Oct 28	Francisco Gelabert	Buenos Aires	TKO	4	—	160
Nov 18	Celedonio Lima	Buenos Aires	D	10	—	158
1965						
Jan 8	Andres Selpa	Mar Del Plata	D	10	—	161
Mar 11	Andres Selpa	Santa Fe	W	10	—	154
Apr 9	Emilio Ale-Ali	Tucuman, Argentina	D	10	—	158
May 19	Anibal Cordoba	Buenos Aires	W	10	—	158
Jul 14	Alberto Redondo	Buenos Aires	TKO	8	—	159
Aug 1	Felipe Cambeiro	Sao Paulo, Brazil	W	8	—	157
Aug 14	Manoel Severino	Rio de Janeiro	D	8	—	158
Aug 28	Manoel Severino	Rio de Janeiro	D	8	—	157
Oct 6	Gregorio Gomez	Buenos Aires	W	10	—	157
Nov 17	Celedonio Lima	Buenos Aires	KO	5	—	159
Dec 8	Antonio Aguilar	Buenos Aires	W	10	—	157
Dec 29	Carlos Salinas	Buenos Aires	W	10	—	158
1966						
Feb 4	Ramon Rocha	Santa Fe	W	10	Won-Argentina State-M	156
Feb 17	Norberto Juncos	Santa Fe	TKO	7	—	157
Apr 29	Ismael Hamze	San Nicolas, Argentina	TKO	9	—	158
Jun 3	Marcos Bustos	Rio Gallegos, Argentina	D	10	—	159
Jul 8	Benito Sanchez	San Pereyra, Argentina	KO	4	—	—
Sep 3	Jorge Fernandez	Buenos Aires	W	12	Won-Argentina-M	157
Oct 1	Angel Coria	Mar Del Plata	W	10	—	161
Nov 18	Luis Pereyra	Santa Fe	TKO	2	—	160
Dec 2	Alberto Massi	Santa Fe	TKO	8	—	161
Dec 23	Marcelo Farias	San Cristobal, Argentina	KO	3	—	—

1967

Date		Opponent	Location	Result	Rnd	Notes	Wt
Jan 13		Carlos Salinas	Santa Fe	KO	8	—	159
Jan 27		Eudoro Robledo	Charata, Argentina	TKO	4	—	163
Feb 15		Alberto Massi	San Francisco, Argentina	W	10	—	—
Mar 9		Osvaldo Marino	Santa Fe	TKO	7	—	158
Mar 25		Angel Coria	Mar Del Plata	KO	6	—	161
Apr 9		Benito Sanchez	Santa Elena, Argentina	TKO	3	—	—
May 6		Bennie Briscoe	Buenos Aires	D	10	—	157
Jun 10		Jorge Fernandez	Buenos Aires	W	12	Won-S Am-M	157
Jul 29		Antonio Aguilar	Buenos Aires	KO	9	—	160
Aug 16		Tito Marshall	Buenos Aires	W	10	—	158
Sep 8		Ramon Rocha	Rosario, Argentina	W	10	—	160
Oct 6		Carlos Estrada	Trelew, Argentina	TKO	7	—	—
Oct 20		Ramon Rocha	San Juan, Argentina	TKO	7	—	—
Nov 18		Tito Marshall	Buenos Aires	W	10	—	159

1968

Date		Opponent	Location	Result	Rnd	Notes	Wt
Apr 15		Juan Aguilar	Mendoza, Argentina	D	10	—	159
May 17		Alberto Massi	Cordoba	W	10	—	160
Jun 19		Juan Aguilar	Buenos Aires	W	10	—	158
Jul 5		Benito Sanchez	Chaco, Argentina	KO	4	—	159
Aug 14		Doug Huntley	Buenos Aires	KO	4	—	159
Oct 23		Charlie Austin	Buenos Aires	W	10	—	160
Dec 7		Johnny Brooks	Buenos Aires	W	10	—	160
Dec 20		Emilio Ale-Ali	Mendoza	W	10	—	159

1969

Date		Opponent	Location	Result	Rnd	Notes	Wt
Jan 10		Ruben Orrico	Santa Fe	KO	9	Ret-S Am-M	159
Mar 14		Mario Taborda	Chaco	KO	3	—	162
Apr 25		Carlos Salinas	Parana	D	10	—	161
Jun 6		Carlos Salinas	Parana	TKO	7	—	161
Jul 5		Harold Richardson	Buenos Aires	TKO	3	—	159
Aug 9		Tom Bethea	Buenos Aires	W	10	—	159
Sep 5		Emilio Ale-Ali	Tucuman	TKO	7	—	161
Sep 27		Manoel Severino	Buenos Aires	KO	6	Ret-S Am-M	159
Dec 12		Carlos Estrada	Santa Fe	KO	2	—	162

1970

Date		Opponent	Location	Result	Rnd	Notes	Wt
Feb 2		Antonio Aguilar	Rosario	KO	6	Ret-Argentina-M	159
Mar 7		Juan Aguilar	Santa Fe	TKO	9	—	164
Apr 17		Adolfo Cardozo	Buenos Aires	TKO	3	—	166
Jul 18		Eddie Pace	Buenos Aires	W	10	—	160
Sep 19		Candy Rosa	Buenos Aires	KO	4	—	162
Nov 7	♛	Nino Benvenuti★	Rome	KO	12	Won-World-M	159
Dec 20		Charley Austin	Buenos Aires	KO	2	—	161

1971

Date		Opponent	Location	Result	Rnd	Notes	Wt
Feb 19		Domingo Guerrero	Salta, Argentina	TKO	2	—	161
Mar 6		Roy Lee	Santa Fe	TKO	2	—	162
May 7	⑩	Nino Benvenuti★	Monte Carlo	TKO	3	Ret-World-M	159
Sep 25	⑩	Emile Griffith★	Buenos Aires	TKO	14	Ret-World-M	159
Dec 4	⑩	Fraser Scott	Buenos Aires	TKO	3	—	161

1972

Date		Opponent	Location	Result	Rnd	Notes	Wt
Mar 4	⑩	Denny Moyer	Rome	TKO	5	Ret-World-M	159
Jun 17	⑩	Jean-Claude Bouttier	Paris	TKO	13	Ret-World-M	159
Aug 19		Tom Bogs	Copenhagen	TKO	5	Ret-World-M	159
Nov 11	⑩	Bennie Briscoe	Buenos Aires	W	15	Ret-World-M	158

1973

Date		Opponent	Location	Result	Rnd	Notes	Wt
May 5		Lee Roy Dale	Rome	KO	5	—	164
Jun 2	⑩	Emile Griffith★	Monte Carlo	W	15	Ret-World-M	159

Sep 29	⑩	Jean-Claude Bouttier	Paris	W	15	Ret-World-M	159
1974							
Feb 9	⑩	Jose Napoles ★	Paris	TKO	7	Ret-World-M	159
Oct 5	⑩	Tony Mundine	Buenos Aires	KO	7	Ret-World (WBA)-M	160
1975							
Jun 30	⑩	Tony Licata	New York	TKO	10	Ret-World (WBA)-M	159
Dec 13	⑩	Gratien Tonna	Paris	KO	5	Ret-World (WBA)-M	159
1976							
Jun 26	♛	Rodrigo Valdez	Monte Carlo	W	15	Ret-World-M	159
1977							
Jul 30	⑩	Rodrigo Valdez	Monte Carlo	W	15	Ret-World-M	159

Monzon successfully defended his belt a record fourteen times. He vanquished such notables as Emile Griffith, Jose Napoles, and Rodrigo Valdez.

Monzon's two fights with Valdez at the end of his career validated his strength as a champion. Valdez held the WBC title, which Monzon had forfeited in 1974. Monzon won the first fight, although Valdez believed he deserved the decision. In the rematch, Valdez knocked down Monzon in the second round, but the tenacious 35-year-old champion rose from the canvas to win a unanimous decision. Monzon then retired from the ring, with fourteen of his last sixteen fights having been successful title defenses.

Monzon was never knocked out at any time in his career and never even lost a fight after 1964. In analyzing his greatness, boxing experts have pointed to his superior height and reach as compared to most middleweights, as well as his great boxing intelligence, superior power, and possession of a complete arsenal of punches.

Monzon's extraordinary competence did not extend to his life outside the squared circle. In 1988, Monzon was convicted of murdering his estranged lover and sentenced to eleven years in prison. Then, in 1995, while returning to prison after a furlough for good behavior, Monzon was killed when the car he was driving ran off a country road.

Carlos Monzon (R) throws a quick combination at dazed Tony Licata while retaining his WBA middle-weight crown. The ten-round knockout took place in Madison Square Garden on June 30, 1975.

ARCHIE MOORE
The Old Mongoose

LIGHT HEAVYWEIGHT

Right-handed; 5'11"; 155–206 lbs.

219 bouts, 7/14/1936 to 3/15/1963

Managers: Kid Bandy, George Wilsman, Cal Thompson, Felix Thurman, Jack Richardson, Jimmy Johnston, Charley Johnston, Jack ("Doc") Kearns

Light Heavyweight Champ 1952–62 *(NBA withdrew recognition in 1960)*

Hall of Fame Induction: 1990

Born: 12/13/1913, (disputed) Benoit, MS

Named: Archibald Lee Wright

Died: 12/9/1998

Archie Moore recorded more knockouts than anyone else in the long history of boxing, with 130 lights-out punches. His career lasted 27 years, and it seemed as if "The Old Mongoose" would never stop fighting. Respected by both fans and his boxing colleagues, he stayed active through the pre-war, post-war, and television ages.

Born in Mississippi around 1913, Moore moved to St. Louis as a youth. He was convicted of stealing money from a streetcar and served two years in reform school, where he learned to box. Moore then joined the Civilian Conservation Corps and boxed in amateur tournaments while off duty. He had turned professional by 1936, fighting as a middleweight. He boxed in the St. Louis area for a year, then moved to San Diego. Seeking tougher competition, he went to Australia in 1940. On his return, he sported a record of 41-4-3, which caught the boxing world's attention. That year, *The Ring* ranked Moore as the fourth-best middleweight contender.

By 1945, Moore had moved up to light heavyweight and held the position of top contender. *The Ring* considered him one of the top light heavyweights in every year from 1945 to 1951. But though he fought steadily, Moore was passed over for a championship bout. Willing to go anywhere to get a fight, Moore toured South America in 1951. In many ways, his plight was similar to that of Charley Burley. Black and not managed properly, both fighters were arguably too good to get top fights.

In 1952, at an age when most fighters had long retired, Moore finally received a shot at the light heavyweight title, then held by Joey Maxim. Fighting before a crowd of 12,610 in his hometown of St. Louis, Moore attacked Maxim relentlessly. Although Maxim stayed in the fight for the full fifteen rounds, Moore

Four days after his 39th birthday, Moore finally got a shot at the light heavyweight title. Although he didn't score a knockout, Moore (R) battered champion Joey Maxim for fifteen rounds and took the decision.

IN THE RING	WON 184	LOST 24	DRAWS 10	TB 219	KO 130	W 54	WF 0	D 10*	KO'd 7	L 15	LF 2	NC 1

*includes 1 Technical Draw

Date	Opponent	Site	Result / Rounds		Title	Wt.
1936						
Jul 14	Murray Allen	Quincy, IL	W	6	—	—
Aug	Sammy Christian	Quincy	D	6	—	—
Sep 30	Murray Allen	Keokuk, IA	KO	3	—	—
Oct 9	Sammy Jackson	St. Louis	W	5	—	—
Dec 8	Sammy Jackson	St. Louis	D	5	—	—
1937						
Jan 5	Dynamite Payne	St. Louis	KO	1	—	—
Jan 18	Johnny Davis	Quincy	KO	3	—	—
Jan 29	Sammy Jackson	Quincy	D	8	—	155
Feb 2	Joe Huff	St. Louis	KO	2	—	—
Mar 23	Ham Pounder	Ponce City, AR	KO	2	—	—
Apr 9	Charley Dawson	Indianapolis	KO	5	—	—
Apr 23	Karl Martin	Indianapolis	KO	1	—	—
—	Franky Hatfield	—	KO	1	—	—
—	Al Dublinsky	—	KO	1	—	—
Aug 19	Deacon Logan	St Louis	KO	3	—	—
Sep 1	Billy Adams	Cincinnati	L	8	—	—
Sep 9	Sam Slaughter	Indianapolis	W	10	—	—
Sep 17	Charley Dawson	St. Louis	TKO	5	—	—
Nov 16	Sammy Christian	St Louis	W	5	—	—
Dec 1	Sammy Jackson	Jackson, MO	KO	8	—	—
1938						
Jan 7	Carl Lautenschlager	St. Louis	KO	2	—	—
May 20	Jimmy Brent	San Diego	KO	1	—	—
May 27	Ray Vargas	San Diego	TKO	3	—	160
Jun 24	Johnny ("Bandit") Romero	San Diego	L	10	—	160
Jul 22	Johnny Sykes	San Diego	KO	1	—	161
Aug 5	Lorenzo Pedro	San Diego	W	10	—	158
Sep 02	Johnny ("Bandit") Romero	San Diego	KO	8	—	161
Sep 16	Frank Rowsey	San Diego	TKO	3	—	162
Sep 27	Tom Henry	Los Angeles	KO	4	—	—
Oct 1	Bob Yannes	San Diego	KO	2	—	—
Nov 22	Ray Lyle	St. Louis	KO	2	—	160
Dec 7	Bob Turner	St. Louis	KO	2	—	160
1939						
Jan 20	Jack Moran	St. Louis	KO	1	—	—
Mar 2	Domenic Ceccarelli	St. Louis	KO	1	—	—
Mar 16	Marty Simmons	St. Louis	W	10	—	155
Apr 1	Marty Simmons	Minneapolis	W	10	—	—
Apr 20 ⑩	Teddy Yarosz★	St. Louis	L	10	—	158
Jul 21	Jack Coggins	San Diego	NC	8	—	—
Sep 1	Jack Coggins	San Diego	W	10	—	—
Sep 22	Bobby Seaman	San Diego	KO	7	—	158
Nov 13	Freddy Dixon	Phoenix	TD	8	—	—
Nov 27	Billy Day	Phoenix	KO	8	—	—
Dec 7	Honeyboy Jones	San Diego	W	10	—	—
Dec 29	Shorty Hogue	San Diego	L	6	—	158
1940						
Mar 30	Jack McNamee	Melbourne	KO	4	—	—
Apr 18 ⑩	Ron Richards	Sydney	KO	10	—	158

Date		Opponent	Location	Result	Rounds	Title	Weight
May 9		Atilio Sabatino	Sydney	KO	5	—	—
May 12		Joe Delaney	Adelaide, Australia	KO	7	—	—
Jun 2		Frank Lindsay	Hobart, Tasmania	KO	4	—	—
Jun 27		Fred Henneberry	Sydney	KO	7	—	—
Jul 11	⑩	Ron Richards	Sydney	W	12	—	159
Oct 18		Pancho Ramirez	San Diego	KO	5	—	—
Dec 5		Shorty Hogue	San Diego	L	6	—	—
1941							
Jan 17		Clay Rowan	San Diego	KO	1	—	—
Jan 31		Shorty Hogue	San Diego	L	10	—	—
Feb 20		Eddie Booker	San Diego	D	10	—	161
1942							
Jan 28		Bobby Britt	Phoenix	KO	3	—	165
Feb 27		Guero Martinez	San Diego	KO	2	—	161
Mar 17		Jimmy Casino	San Francisco	KO	5	—	170
Oct 30		Shorty Hogue	San Diego	KO	2	—	158
Nov 6		Tabby Romero	San Diego	KO	2	—	159
Nov 27	⑩	Jack Chase	San Diego	W	10	—	158
Dec 11	⑩	Eddie Booker	San Diego	D	12	For-CA-M	158
1943							
May 8	⑩	Jack Chase	San Diego	W	15	Won-CA-M	159
Jul 1		Willard Hogue	San Diego	TKO	5	—	160
Jul 28		Eddie Cerda	San Diego	KO	3	—	157
Aug 2	⑩	Jack Chase	San Francisco	L	15	Lost-CA-M	158
Aug 16		Aaron Wade	San Francisco	L	10	—	160
Nov 5		Kid Hermosillo	San Diego	KO	5	—	155
Nov 26	⑩	Jack Chase	Hollywood	W	10	—	158
1944							
Jan 7		Amado Rodriguez	San Diego	KO	1	—	163
Jan 21		Eddie Booker	Hollywood	KO'd	8	—	160
Mar 24		Roman Starr	Hollywood	TKO	2	—	166
Apr 21	⑩	Charley Burley★	Hollywood	L	10	—	161
May 19		Kenny La Salle	San Diego	W	10	—	166
Aug 11		Louis Mays	San Diego	KO	3	—	171
Aug 18		Jimmy Hayden	San Diego	KO	5	—	170
Sep 1		Battling Monroe	San Diego	KO	6	—	171
Dec 18	⑩	Nate Bolden	New York	W	10	—	172
1945							
Jan 11		Joey Jones	Boston	KO	1	—	176
Jan 29		Bob Jacobs	New York	KO	9	—	166
Feb 12		Nap Mitchell	Boston	KO	6	—	178
Apr 2	⑩	Nate Bolden	Baltimore	W	10	—	167
Apr 23		Teddy Randolph	Baltimore	KO	9	—	168
May 21	⑩	Lloyd Marshall	Cleveland	W	10	—	167
Jun 18		George Kochan	Baltimore	KO	6	—	164
Jun 26	⑩	Lloyd Marshall	Cleveland	TKO	10	—	162
Aug 22	⑩	Jimmy Bivins★	Cleveland	TKO'd	6	—	168
Sep 17	⑩	Cocoa Kid	Baltimore	KO	8	—	165
Oct 22	⑩	Holman Williams	Baltimore	L	10	—	172
Nov 12		Odell Riley	Detroit	KO	6	—	174
Nov 26	⑩	Holman Williams	Baltimore	TKO	11	—	169
Dec 13		Colion Chaney	St. Louis	KO	5	—	170
1946							
Jan 28	⑩	Curtis Sheppard	Baltimore	W	12	—	172
Feb 5		Georgie Parks	Washington, DC	TKO	1	—	170
May 2		Verne Escoe	Orange, NJ	TKO	7	—	175

Date		Opponent	Location	Result	Rounds		No.
May 20	⑩	Ezzard Charles★	Pittsburgh	L	10	—	174
Aug 19		Buddy Walker	Baltimore	KO	4	—	173
Sep 9		Shamus O'Brien	Baltimore	KO	2	—	174
Oct 23	⑩	Billy Smith	Oakland	D	12	For-CA-M	171
Nov 6	⑩	Jack Chase	Oakland	D	10	—	171
1947							
Mar 18	⑩	Jack Chase	Los Angeles	KO	9	Won-CA-M	173
Apr 11		Rusty Payne	San Diego	W	10	—	176
May 5	⑩	Ezzard Charles★	Cincinnati	L	10	—	172
Jun 16	⑩	Curtis Sheppard	Washington, DC	W	10	—	175
Jul 14		Bert Lytell	Baltimore	W	10	—	173
Jul 30		Bobby Zander	Oakland	W	12	Ret-CA-M	171
Sep 8		Jimmy Bivins★	Baltimore	KO	9	—	174
Nov 10		George Fitch	Baltimore	KO	6	—	182
1948							
Jan 13	⑩	Ezzard Charles★	Cleveland	KO'd	8	—	173
Apr 12		Dusty Wilkerson	Baltimore	KO	7	—	179
Apr 19	⑩	Doc Williams	Newark, NJ	KO	7	—	173
May 5	⑩	Oakland Billy Smith	Cincinnati	W	10	—	176
Jun 2	⑩	Leonard Morrow	Oakland	KO'd	1	Lost-CA-M	175
Jun 28	⑩	Jimmy Bivins★	Baltimore	W	10	—	172
Aug 2		Ted Lowry	Baltimore	W	10	—	174
Sep 20	⑩	Oakland Billy Smith	Baltimore	KO	4	—	177
Oct 15	⑩	Henry Hall	New Orleans	L	10	—	—
Nov 1		Lloyd Gibson	Washington, DC	LD	4	—	173
Nov 15	⑩	Henry Hall	Baltimore	W	10	—	174
Dec 6		Bob Amos	Washington, DC	W	10	—	174
Dec 27	⑩	Doc Williams	Baltimore	KO	7	—	175
1949							
Jan 10		Alabama Kid	Toledo, OH	KO	4	—	175
Jan 31		Bob Satterfield	Toledo	KO	3	—	167
Mar 4		Alabama Kid	Columbus, OH	KO	3	—	174
Mar 23		Dusty Wilkerson	Philadelphia	KO	6	—	173
Apr 11	⑩	Jimmy Bivins★	Toledo	KO	8	—	172
Apr 26	⑩	Harold Johnson★	Philadelphia	W	10	—	172
Jun 13		Clinton Bacon	Indianapolis	LD	6	—	172
Jun 27		Bob Sikes	Indianapolis	KO	3	—	173
Jul 29		Esco Greenwood	North Adams, MA	KO	2	—	177
Oct 4		Bob Amos	Toledo	W	10	—	177
Oct 24		Phil Muscato	Toledo	TKO	6	—	181
Dec 6	⑩	Doc Williams	Hartford, CT	KO	8	—	175
Dec 13	⑩	Leonard Morrow	Toledo	KO	10	—	173
1950							
Jan 31	⑩	Bert Lytell	Toledo	W	10	—	175
Jul 31		Vernon Williams	Chicago	KO	2	—	182
1951							
Jan 2		Oakland Billy Smith	Portland, OR	TKO	8	—	182
Jan 28		John Thomas	Panama City	KO	1	—	179
Feb 21		Jimmy Bivins★	New York	TKO	9	—	176
Mar 13		Abel Cestac	Toledo	W	10	—	180
Apr 26		Herman Harris	Flint, MI	TKO	4	—	179
May 14		Art Henri	Baltimore	TKO	4	—	181
Jun 9		Abel Cestac	Buenos Aires	TKO	10	—	177
Jun 23		Karel Sys	Buenos Aires	D	10	—	177
Jul 8		Alberto Lovell	Buenos Aires	KO	1	—	175
Jul 15		Vicente Quiroz	Montevideo, Uruguay	KO	6	—	—

Date		Opponent	Location	Result	Rounds	Title	Weight
Jul 26		Vicente Carabajal	Cordoba, Argentina	TKO	3	—	—
Jul 28		Americo Capitanelli	Tucuman, Argentina	TKO	3	—	—
Aug 5		Rafael Miranda	Tucuman	TKO	4	—	—
Aug 17		Alfredo Lagay	Bahia Blanca, Argentina	KO	3	—	179
Sep 5		Embrell Davison	Detroit	KO	1	—	175
Sep 24	⑩	Harold Johnson★	Philadelphia	W	10	—	174
Oct 29		Chubby Wright	St. Louis	TKO	7	—	180
Dec 10	⑩	Harold Johnson★	Milwaukee	L	10	—	178
1952							
Jan 29	⑩	Harold Johnson★	Toledo	W	10	—	175
Feb 27	⑩	Jimmy Slade	St. Louis	W	10	—	180
May 19	⑩	Bob Dunlap	San Francisco	KO	6	—	183
Jun 26	⑩	Clarence Henry	Baltimore	W	10	—	176
Jul 25		Clint Bacon	Denver	TKO	4	—	181
Dec 17	♛	Joey Maxim★	St. Louis	W	15	Won-World-LH	172
1953							
Jan 27		Toxie Hall	Toledo	KO	4	—	179
Feb 16		Leonard Dugan	San Francisco	TKO	8	—	179
Mar 3		Sonny Andrews	Sacramento, CA	KO	5	—	182
Mar 11	⑩	Nino Valdes	St. Louis	W	10	—	180
Mar 17		Al Spaulding	Spokane, WA	KO	3	—	180
Mar 30		Frank Buford	San Diego	TKO	9	—	180
Jun 24	⑩	Joey Maxim★	Ogden, UT	W	15	Ret-World-LH	173
Aug 22		Reinaldo Ansaloni	Buenos Aires	TKO	4	—	180
Sep 12		Dogomar Martinez	Buenos Aires	W	10	—	180
1954							
Jan 27	⑩	Joey Maxim★	Miami	W	15	Ret-World-LH	175
Mar 9	⑩	Bob Baker	Miami	TKO	9	—	190
Jun 7		Bert Witehurst	New York	KO	6	—	189
Aug 11	⑩	Harold Johnson★	New York	TKO	14	Ret-World-LH	173
1955							
May 2	⑩	Nino Valdes	Las Vegas	W	15	—	196
Jun 22	⑩	Carl ("Bobo") Olson★	New York	KO	3	Ret-World-LH	175
Sep 21	♛	Rocky Marciano★	New York	KO'd	9	For-World-H	188
1956							
Feb 20		Howard King	San Francisco	W	10	—	197
Feb 27		Bob Dunlap	San Diego	KO	1	—	196
Mar 17		Frankie Daniels	Hollywood	W	10	—	194
Mar 27		Howard King	Hollywood	W	10	—	191
Apr 10		Willie Bean	Richmond, VA	TKO	5	—	196
Apr 16		George Parmentier	Seattle	TKO	3	—	193
Apr 26		Sonny Andrews	Edmonton, Alb.	KO	4	—	190
Apr 30		Gene Thompson	Tucson, AZ	TKO	3	—	189
Jun 5	⑩	Yolande Pompey	London	TKO	10	Ret-World-LH	174
Jul 25		James Parker	Toronto	TKO	9	—	186
Sep 8		Roy Shire	Ogden	TKO	3	—	191
Nov 30	⑩	Floyd Patterson★	Chicago	KO'd	5	For-Vac World-H	187
1957							
May 1		Hans Kalbfell	Essen, Germany	W	10	—	206
Jun 2		Alain Cherville	Stuttgart, Germany	TKO	6	—	189
Sep 20	⑩	Tony Anthony	Los Angeles	TKO	7	Ret-World-LH	175
Oct 31		Bob Mitchell	Vancouver, B.C.	TKO	5	—	193
Nov 5		Eddie Cotton	Seattle	W	10	—	192
Nov 29		Roger Rischer	Portland, OR	KO	4	—	199
1958							
Jan 18		Luis Ignacio	Sao Paulo, Brazil	W	10	—	190

Date		Opponent	Location	Result	Round		Weight
Feb 1		Julio Neves	Rio de Janeiro	KO	3	—	189
Mar 4		Bert Withehurst	San Bernardino, CA	TKO	10	—	196
Mar 10		Bob Albright	Vancouver	TKO	7	—	201
May 2		Willi Besmanoff	Louisville, KY	W	10	—	196
May 17		Howard King	San Diego	W	10	—	195
May 26		Charlie Norkus	San Francisco	W	10	—	196
Jun 9		Howard King	Sacramento	W	10	—	196
Aug 4		Howard King	Reno, NV	D	10	—	189
Dec 10	⑩	Yvon Durelle	Montreal	KO	11	Ret-World-LH	173
1959							
Mar 9		Sterling Davis	Odessa, TX	TKO	3	—	192
Aug 12	⑩	Yvon Durelle	Montreal	KO	3	Ret-World-LH	174
1960							
May 25		Willi Besmanoff	Indianapolis	TKO	10	—	206
Sep 13		George Abinet	Dallas	TKO	3	—	195
Oct 29	⑩	Giulio Rinaldi	Rome	L	10	—	190
Nov 28		Buddy Turman	Dallas	W	10	—	189
1961							
Mar 25		Buddy Turman	Manila	W	10	—	201
May 12		Clifford Gray	Nogales, Mexico	KO	4	—	185
Jun 10	⑩	Giulio Rinaldi	New York	W	15	Ret-World-LH	174
Oct 23		Pete Rademacher	Baltimore	TKO	6	—	198
1962							
Mar 30	⑩	Alejandro Lavorante	Los Angeles	TKO	10	—	197
May 7		Howard King	Tijuana, Mexico	KO	1	—	199
May 28	⑩	Willie Pastrano★	Los Angeles	D	10	—	201
Nov 15	⑩	Cassius Clay★	Los Angeles	TKO'd	4	—	191
1963							
Mar 15		Mike DiBiase	Phoenix	TKO	3	—	206

dominated him with his powerful punching and easily won the unanimous decision. He held the light heavyweight title for the next nine years.

In 1955, Moore attempted to move up to the heavyweight title by fighting the undefeated Rocky Marciano in Yankee Stadium. Moore knocked Marciano down in the second round with a right, but he was up at the count of two. Marciano knocked Moore down in the sixth, eighth, and ninth rounds, the last time for the knockout. After Marciano's retirement, Moore fought Floyd Patterson for the title but fell in five.

In 1958, Moore engaged in a memorable defense of his light heavyweight title against Yvon Durelle in Montreal's Forum. Managed by Hall of Famer Jack Kearns since the victory over Maxim, Moore was a strong favorite. However, Durelle knocked Moore down three times in the first round and again in the fifth. But from then on, Moore used his left to weaken Durelle, knocking him down in the seventh and finishing him off with a short right in the eleventh.

Moore continued to fight, even after the NBA stripped him of his belt for failure to defend the light heavyweight title. Then, in 1962, he met with Muhammad Ali—then known as Cassius Clay—who had briefly trained with him but had disagreed with Moore's instructions. Ali knocked him out in the fourth round. Moore's date of birth is disputed, but his age in the Ali fight hovered somewhere around 50. After fighting just once more, The Old Mongoose retired. He remained active in boxing as a trainer, embarked on a film career, and worked with youth.

JOSE NAPOLES
Mantequilla (Butter)

WELTERWEIGHT

Right-handed; 5'7½"; 127–153 lbs.

85 bouts, 8/2/1958 to 12/6/1975

Managers: Cuco Conde, Alfredo Cruz

Welterwt Champ 1969–70, 1971–75

Hall of Fame Induction: 1990

Named: Jose Angel Napoles

Born: 4/13/1940, Santiago de Cuba, Oriente, Cuba

Jose Napoles earned the nickname "Mantequilla" (Spanish for "butter") because of his smooth style. A native of Cuba, Napoles began fighting as a small boy in the Santiago slums under the tutelage of his three uncles. He worked odd jobs in Havana gyms so that he could watch fighters train. As an amateur, Napoles compiled an astonishing 114-1 record. He turned pro in 1958 and won his first time out, with a one-punch knockout. Early in his career, fighting exclusively in Havana, Napoles battled as a featherweight and as a lightweight.

Napoles fled Cuba soon after Fidel Castro banned professional boxing there.

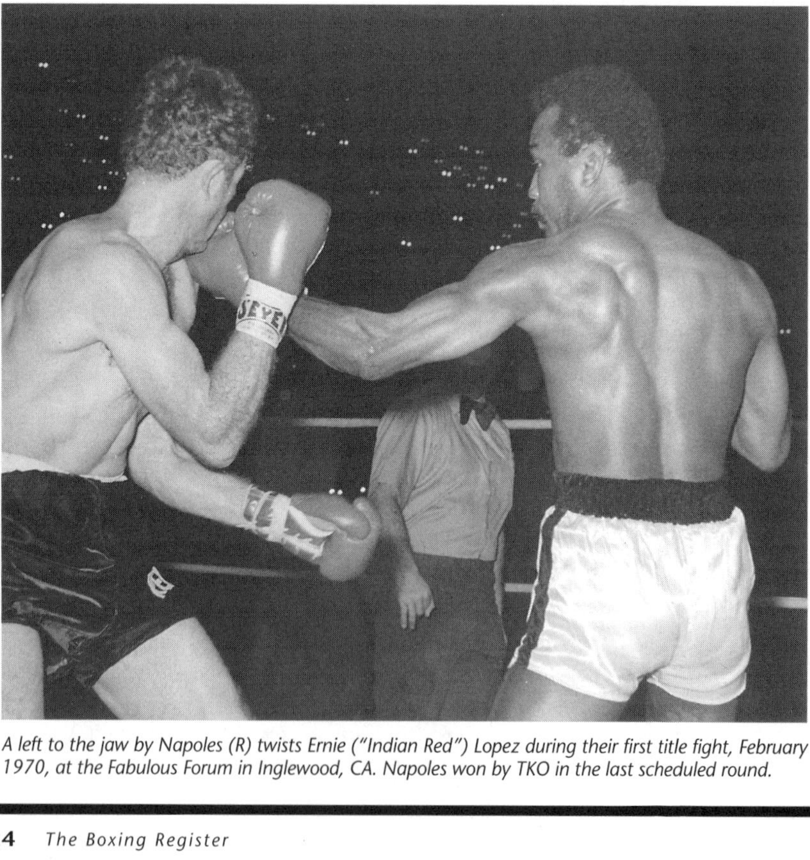

A left to the jaw by Napoles (R) twists Ernie ("Indian Red") Lopez during their first title fight, February 1970, at the Fabulous Forum in Inglewood, CA. Napoles won by TKO in the last scheduled round.

IN THE RING	WON **78***	LOST **7**	DRAWS **0**	TB 85	KO 55	W 22	WF 1*	D 0	KO'd 4	L 3	LF 0

*includes 1 Technical Win

Date	Opponent	Site	Result / Rounds		Title	Wt.
1958						
Aug 2	Julio Rojas	Havana, Cuba	KO	1	—	—
Oct 11	Eurispides Guerra	Havana	KO	4	—	—
Nov 29	Felix Pomares	Havana	TKO	2	—	—
1959						
Feb 21	Armando Castillo	Havana	W	4	—	—
May 16	Juan Bacallao	Havana	TKO	4	—	—
Jul 11	Cloroaldo Hernandez	Havana	TKO	3	—	—
Jul 25	Cristobal Gonzalez	Havana	W	10	—	—
Aug 22	Hilton Smith	Havana	L	10	—	127
Oct 3	Chris Gonzalez	Havana	W	8	—	—
Nov 28	Ramon ("Bobby') Cervantes	Havana	TKO	1	—	—
1960						
Jan 2	Isaac Espinosa	Havana	W	10	—	131
Feb 20	Diwaldo Ventosa	Havana	W	10	—	133
May 21	Angel Garcia	Havana	W	10	—	132
Jul 2	Leslie Grant	Havana	W	10	—	—
Oct 15	Tony Padron	Havana	W	10	—	—
Nov 26	Rolando Morales	Havana	W	10	—	—
1961						
Jan 28	Guillermo Valdez	Havana	W	10	—	—
Mar 19	Rolando Morales	Havana	W	10	—	133
Mar 29	Enrique Carabeo	Havana	TKO	9	—	—
1962						
Jul 21	Enrique Camarena	Mexico City	KO	2	—	134
Aug 25	Kid Anahuac	Mexico City	KO	9	—	135
Sep 29	Bobby Cervantes	Mexico City	TKO	2	—	135
Nov 10	Tony Perez	Los Mochis, Mexico	W	10	—	—
1963						
Jan 5	Tony Perez	Hermosillo, Mexico	L	10	—	—
Feb 9	Jorge Gutierrez	Mexico City	TKO	7	—	133
Mar 30	Baby Vasquez	Mexico City	W	10	—	134
Apr 27	⑩ Alfredo Urbina	Mexico City	L	10	—	135
May 27	Raul Soriano	Tijuana, Mexico	KO	4	—	135
Aug 19	Pulga Serrano	Tijuana	TKO	10	—	—
Oct 23	Francisco Cancio	Mexico City	KO	1	—	136
Nov 16	Tony Perez	Mexico City	TKO	3	—	135
Nov 30	L.C. Morgan	Caracas	KO	7	—	—
1964						
Mar 1	Taketeru Yoshimoto	Tokyo	KO	1	—	—
Apr 25	⑩ Alfredo Urbina	Mexico City	TKO	1	—	135
Jun 22	⑩ Carlos Hernandez	Caracas	TKO	7	—	—
Aug 15	Eduardo Moreno	Culiacan, Mexico	TKO	5	—	—
Nov 14	⑩ Alfredo Urbina	Mexico City	KO	3	—	—
1965						
Jan 1	Carlos Rios	Laguna, Mexico	TKO	7	—	140
Feb 28	L.C. Morgan	Monterrey, Mexico	KO	3	—	143
Mar 25	⑩ Giordano Campari	Caracas	TKO	2	—	—
Aug 3	⑩ Eddie Perkins	Juarez, Mexico	W	10	—	140

Dec 11	⑩ Adolph Pruitt	Mexico City	TKO	3	—	—

1966

Feb 12	⑩ Johnny Santos	Mexico City	KO	3	—	138
Apr 17	Al Grant	Reynosa, Mexico	TKO	4	—	—
Jul 27	Humberto Trottman	Juarez	TKO	2	—	140
Aug 22	L.C. Morgan	Reynosa	TKO'd	4	—	138
Oct 30	Jimmy Fields	San Luis Potosi, Mexico	TKO	10	—	—
Dec 17	⑩ Eugenio Espinoza	Mexico City	TKO	6	—	140

1967

Jun 4	Johnny Brooks	Merida, Mexico	KO	7	—	—
Jul 10	L.C. Morgan	Tijuana	TKO	2	—	—
Sep 11	Johnny De Peiza	Juarez	TKO	10	—	140
Dec 3	Charlie Watson	Merida	KO	5	—	—

1968

Feb 18	Mike Cruz	Tampico, Mexico	TKO	4	—	137
Apr 29	Herbie Lee	Tijuana	TKO	4	—	139
Jun 2	Peter Cobblah	Mexico City	W	10	—	141
Jun 14	Leroy Roberts	Los Angeles	TKO	1	—	145
Jul 15	Eddie Pace	Tijuana	W	10	—	144
Nov 4	Des Rea	Inglewood, CA	TKO	5	—	144
Dec 22	Lennox Beckles	Mexico City	KO	1	—	148

1969

Feb 15	Fate Davis	Mexico City	TKO	7	—	144
Apr 18	♛ Curtis Cokes★	Inglewood	TKO	13	Won-World-W	143
Jun 29	⑩ Curtis Cokes★	Mexico City	TKO	10	Ret-World-W	145
Oct 12	⑩ Emile Griffith★	Inglewood	W	15	Ret-World-W	144

1970

Feb 15	⑩ Ernie ("Indian Red") Lopez	Inglewood	TKO	15	Ret-World-W	145
Aug 14	Fighting Mack	Inglewood	KO	3	—	150
Oct 5	Pete Toro	New York	TKO	9	—	150
Dec 3	⑩ Billy Backus	Syracuse, NY	TKO'd	4	Lost-World-W	144

1971

Mar 27	Manuel Gonzalez	Mexico City	KO	6	—	148
Jun 4	♛ Billy Backus	Inglewood	TKO	8	Reg-World-W	146
Jul 31	David Melendez	Mexico City	TKO	5	—	150
Aug 23	⑩ Jean Josselin	Inglewood	KO	5	—	152
Oct 17	Esteban Osuna	Mexico City	W	10	—	150
Dec 14	⑩ Hedgemon Lewis	Los Angeles	W	15	Ret-World-W	145

1972

Mar 28	Ralph Charles	Wembley, England	KO	7	Ret-World-W	146
Jun 10	⑩ Adolph Pruitt	Monterrey	KO	2	Ret-World-W	146
Aug 5	Edmundo Leite	Mexico City	TKO	2	—	147

1973

Feb 28	⑩ Ernie Lopez	Los Angeles	KO	7	Ret-World-W	146
Jun 23	⑩ Roger Menetrey	Grenoble, France	W	15	Ret-World-W	146
Sep 22	⑩ Clyde Gray	Toronto	W	15	Ret-World-W	147

1974

Feb 9	♛ Carlos Monzon★	Monte Carlo	KO'd	7	For-World-M	153
Aug 3	⑩ Hedgemon Lewis	Mexico City	TKO	9	Ret-World-W	145
Dec 14	⑩ Horacio Saldano	Mexico City	KO	3	Ret-World-W	146

1975

Mar 30	⑩ Armando Muniz	Acapulco, Mexico	TW	12	Ret-World-W	147
Jul 12	⑩ Armando Muniz	Mexico City	W	15	Ret-World (WBC)-W	146
Dec 6	⑩ John Stracey	Mexico City	TKO'd	6	Lost-World (WBC)-W	147

Napoles explained, "I have no interest in politics. I wanted to make a decent living for my wife and son, so I went to Mexico City and resumed my boxing career."

By 1962, Napoles was considered the tenth-best junior welterweight in *The Ring*'s annual rankings. In 1967, Napoles moved up to welterweight. He earned a title shot in 1969 against Curtis Cokes in the Fabulous Forum in Inglewood, California. Napoles knocked Cokes out in thirteen rounds to win the championship. The battered Cokes had a cut mouth and bloody nose, and both eyes were almost swollen shut. In their rematch two months later in Mexico City, Napoles knocked out Cokes in the tenth.

Napoles defended this belt three times, winning a decision over Emile Griffith, and a TKO over Ernie Lopez before losing to Billy Backus, of Canastota, New York. That fight, which took place in Syracuse, New York, late in 1970, was stopped because of serious cuts around Napoles's eyes. Napoles won the rematch in June 1971 with an eighth-round TKO. Having regained the title, Napoles defended it six times before attempting to move up to middleweight.

In 1974, Napoles challenged Hall of Famer Carlos Monzon for the middleweight crown. However, Monzon proved to be too much for Napoles, who was stopped in seven rounds. Still welterweight champ, Napoles defended this title four more times, in each case against a top-ten contender, until he lost to John Stracey on a sixth-round TKO in December 1975. Napoles retired after the Stracey fight. Although susceptible to cuts, Napoles was a stylish boxer who possessed a wide array of left-hand punches, a fine right uppercut, and great speed.

Courageous Billy Backus (R) traded punches with Napoles in their June 4, 1971, rematch. The ringside physician stopped the bout in the eighth after an examination of Backus's bruised face.

AZUMAH NELSON
The Professor

JUNIOR LIGHTWEIGHT

Right-handed; 5'5"; 126–134 lbs.

46 bouts, 12/1/1979 to 7/11/1998

WBC Featherweight Champ. 1984–88
WBC Junior Lightweight Champion
1988–94, 1995–97

Hall of Fame Induction: 2004

Born: 9/19/1958, Accra, Ghana

A national hero in his home country of Ghana, Nelson was born on September 19, 1958, in Accra, Ghana. His father was a tailor and his mother was a trader in fabrics and jewelry. When Nelson was five years old, his father took him to watch his first prizefight. The youngster was instantly captivated by the sport and boasted to his father that he could beat the winners on the spot! When Nelson first boxed a neighborhood boy a couple of years later, he was in for a rude awakening. The other boy had received boxing training. Nelson could not hit him and could not avoid being hit. Later, Floyd Robertson, a trainer of five world champions from Ghana, became Nelson's trainer. Some of Robertson's training methods were unusually harsh. If one of his charges was hit by a punch that Robertson believed should not have landed, he caned the battered fighter. Nelson blossomed under Robertson and compiled a fine amateur record of 50-2.

Nelson turned pro with a decision in eight rounds over Billy Kwame on December 1, 1979. In only his third pro fight, he knocked out Henry Saddler to win the Ghanaian featherweight title. In his tenth fight, he knocked out Brian Roberts to win the British Commonwealth featherweight title.

When Hall of Fame matchmaker Mickey Duff asked the inexperienced Nelson if he wanted to step in as a last minute replacement opponent for Hall of Famer and WBC featherweight champion Salvador Sanchez, Nelson readily agreed although he had only thirteen pro fights under his belt. The bout was only a few weeks away, so Nelson had very little time to prepare. The fight was held in Madison Square Garden on July 21, 1982. Nelson gave a great accounting of himself, although he did not win the fight—Sanchez stopped him in the fifteenth round. However, Nelson

On September 26, 1981, Azumah Nelson (L) parries with Brian Roberts in Accra, Ghana, on the way to a fifth-round TKO victory the vacant Commonwealth featherweight title.

		IN THE RING	WON **39**	LOST **5**	DRAWS **2**	TB **46**	KO **28**	W **11**	WF **0**	D **2**	KO'd **1**	L **4**	LF **0**

Date		Opponent	Site	Result / Rounds		Title	Wt.
1979							
Dec 1		Billy Kwame	Accra, Ghana	W	8	—	—
1980							
Feb 2		Nii Nuer	Accra	KO	3	—	—
Mar 3		Henry Saddler	Accra	KO	9	Won-Ghana-FE	—
Apr 17		Henry Optoki	Accra	KO	8	—	—
Jul 4		David Capo	Accra	W	10	—	—
Dec 13		Joe Skipper	Accra	TKO	10	Won-Africa-FE	—
1981							
Feb 24		Bossou Aziza	Lome, Togo	W	10	—	—
May 2		Don George	Accra	KO	5	—	—
Aug 18		Miguel Ruiz	Bakersfield, CA	TKO	3	—	131
Sep 26		Brian Roberts	Accra	TKO	5	Won-Vac Brit Com-FE	124
Dec 4		Kabiru Akindele	Freetown, Ivory Coast	KO	6	Ret-Brit Com-FE	—
1982							
Feb 28		Charm Chiteule	Lusaka, Zambia	KO	10	Ret-Brit Com/Africa-FE	—
Jun 26		Mukaila Bukare	Accra	TKO	6	—	—
Jul 21	♛	Salvador Sanchez★	New York	TKO'd	15	For-WBC-FE	124
Oct 31		Irving Mitchell	McAfee, NJ	KO	5	—	126
1983							
Feb 12		Ricky Wallace	Cleveland	W	10	—	126
Aug 17		Alvin Fowler	Las Vegas	TKO	2	—	127
Sep 23		Alberto Collazo	Richfield, OH	TKO	2	—	127
Nov 23		Kabiru Akindele	Lagos, Nigeria	KO	9	Ret-Brit Com-FE	126
1984							
Mar 9		Hector Cortez	Las Vegas	W	10	—	127
Dec 8	♛	Wilfredo Gomez★	San Juan, PR	KO	11	Won-WBC-FE	125
1985							
Sep 6		Juvenal Ordenes	Miami	TKO	5	Ret-WBC-FE	126
Oct 12		Pat Cowdell	Birmingham, England	KO	1	Ret-WBC-FE	125
1986							
Feb 25		Marcos Villasana	Inglewood, CA	W	12	Ret-WBC-FE	125
Jun 22		Danilo Cabrera	San Juan	KO	10	Ret-WBC-FE	125
Dec 13		Aaron Duribe	Accra	KO	6	—	—
1987							
Mar 7		Mauro Gutierrez	Las Vegas	KO	6	Ret-WBC-FE	124
Aug 29		Marcos Villasana	Los Angeles	W	12	Ret-WBC-FE	125
1988							
Feb 29		Mario Martinez	Inglewood	W	12	Won-Vac WBC-JL	129
Jun 25		Lupe Suarez	Atlantic City	TKO	9	Ret-WBC-JL	125
Dec 10		Sydney Dal Rovere	Accra	TKO	3	Ret-WBC-JL	128
1989							
Feb 25		Mario Martinez	Las Vegas	TKO	12	Ret-WBC-JL	129
Nov 5		Jim McDonnell	Kensington, England	TKO	12	Ret-WBC-JL	130
1990							
May 19	♛	Pernell Whitaker	Las Vegas	L	12	For-WBC/IBF-L	134
Oct 13		Juan Laporte	Sydney	W	12	Ret-WBC-JL	129
1991							
Mar 16		Daniel Mustapha	Zaragoza, Spain	TKO	4	—	—

Jun 28	Jeff Fenech★	Las Vegas	D	12	Ret-WBC-JL	129
1992						
Mar 1	Jeff Fenech★	Melbourne	TKO	8	Ret-WBC-JL	129
Nov 7	Calvin Grove	Stateline, NV	W	12	Ret-WBC-JL	129
1993						
Feb 20	Gabriel Ruelas	Mexico City	W	12	Ret-WBC-JL	128
Sep 10	James Leija	San Antonio, TX	D	12	Ret-WBC-JL	128
1994						
May 7	James Leija	Las Vegas	L	12	Lost-WBC-JL	129
1995						
Dec 1	Gabriel Ruelas	Indio, CA	TKO	5	Reg-WBC-JL	130
1996						
Jun 1	James Leija	Las Vegas	TKO	6	Ret-WBC-JL	130
1997						
Mar 22	Genaro Hernandez	Corpus Christi, TX	L	12	Lost-WBC-JL	129
1998						
Jul 11	James Leija	San Antonio	L	12	For-Vac-IBA-L	132

was ahead on one judge's card entering that round and had staggered Sanchez in the thirteenth. Though Nelson was knocked down twice and suffered a cut lip and a badly swollen right eye, he favorably impressed onlookers.

Nelson won his next six bouts—with five of them contested in the United States—before he received another shot at the WBC featherweight title, then held by Hall of Famer Wilfredo Gomez. This time Nelson knocked Gomez down in the eleventh. He then finished Gomez off with one or two seconds left in the round, using a combination that knocked him out. Nelson then defended his title six times, including an impressive first-round knockout of Pat Cowdell. After that, Nelson moved up in weight class to super featherweight.

On February 29, 1988, Nelson faced Mario Martinez in the Forum for the vacant WBC super featherweight belt. This fight was not one for the ages. It was relatively actionless. Most believed that Martinez displayed more life in the bout than his opponent. In fact, Martinez knocked Nelson down with a left hook in the tenth. Nevertheless, Nelson received a split decision, winning 115-113 on two cards while losing 114-113 on the other. The announcement of the decision brought not only a chorus of boos from the rowdy spectators, but also a shower of beer, drenching those at ringside, including promoter Don King.

Nelson successfully defended his title four times in the next year and a half. Included in those four bouts was a knock-out victory in the rematch with Martinez as well as a knockout of Jim McDonnell. Then Nelson attempted to add the WBC and IBF lightweight titles to his collection when he squared off against the great stylist Pernell ("Sweet Pea") Whitaker on May 19, 1990, in Las Vegas. Unfortunately, as Nelson was preparing for the fight, he received word that his wife—ill with cancer—had been rushed to the hospital. She died a week after the fight. Nelson lost a decision to the highly skilled Whitaker.

However, he still retained the super featherweight title. He decisioned the tough Juan Laporte in a title fight and then fought Hall of Famer Jeff Fenech to a controversial draw on the undercard of the Mike Tyson–Razor Ruddock fight. Fenech seemed to have the better of the action, which ended with Nelson wobbly. In the rematch, Nelson knocked Fenech down three times, before the fight was stopped in the eighth round.

Nelson defended his title with decisions against Calvin Grove and Gabriel Ruelas before beginning a four-fight series with James Leija. In their first fight in San Antonio, the pair fought to a draw. In the rematch, the 35-year-old Nelson looked like he might have reached the end of the line when Leija won a unanimous decision to take the title, which Nelson had clung to for seven years.

Nelson got a chance to win back the title from Ruelas, however, in his next fight. He shook off the effects of age and floored Ruelas in both the first (with a right counterpunch) and in the fourth (with a left hook to the body and a right to the head). In the fifth, he completely overwhelmed Ruelas, and the referee stopped the contest.

After 1993, Nelson was fighting just once a year. He defended his title against Leija on June 1, 1996, at the Boulder Station Casino in Las Vegas. As was usual at his fights, drums beat incessantly in the background. In the first round, Nelson knocked Leija down with a powerful right. Leija arose at the count of nine just before the bell rang to end the round. Nelson continued his attack in the second, though Leija came back in the third and fourth, and snapped off a series of rights in the fifth. Later in that round, a left hook from Nelson opened a gash on Leija's eyelid. Nelson took total command in the sixth, and referee Richard Steele stopped the fight at the 1:58 mark.

That was the last victory of Nelson's career. The following March, Genaro Hernandez won a split decision over Nelson to snatch his title. Then Nelson closed his career with a decision loss to Leija in a match for the lightly regarded IBA lightweight title. Nelson broke his left hand in the fifth round and essentially fought with one hand for the rest of the match. He retired soon after the loss and vowed not to attempt a comeback. He was true to his word. He returned to Ghana, where he had maintained a home during his career. Nelson was a fine boxer who could also slug with both hands. He threw punches from a variety of angles and was an adept counterpuncher. He also had a very cerebral style and was able to adapt to the tactics of his opponent. In recognition of this adaptability, he came to be known as "The Professor."

Since his retirement, Nelson has been involved in a variety of businesses including a teak plantation, real estate, a cookware company, and a ceramic tile factory. He is also active in charitable and environmental affairs in Ghana. In 2004, the Ghanaian Ministry of Environment and Science named Nelson environmental ambassador.

Azumah Nelson was once called "The Best Boxer Nobody Knows" by Timothy W. Smith, boxing writer for The New York Times.

TERRY NORRIS
Terrible Terry

JUNIOR MIDDLEWEIGHT

Right-handed; 5'9"; 146–159 lbs.
56 bouts, 8/2/1986 to 11/30/1998
Manager: Joe Sayatovich
WBC Junior Middleweight Champion 1990–93, 1994, 1995–97
IBF Jr Middleweight Champ 1995–97
Hall of Fame Induction: 2005
Born: 6/17/1967, Lubbock, TX
Named: Terry Wayne Norris

"Terrible" Terry Norris formed part of one of boxing's few world champion brother combinations with his brother Orlin Jr., a cruiserweight champion. Norris was born on June 17, 1967, in Lubbock, Texas. He became interested in boxing when he was nine years old. For a time, however, it seemed that Norris was headed for a career in baseball. He dreamed of playing for the Houston Astros. He was a fine player in high school and received some scholarship offers. However, after he took part in a brawl—triggered by derogatory racial comments—some of the colleges backed away from their earlier offers. The incident left a bad taste in Norris's mouth, and he soon gave up baseball.

When he was eighteen, Norris followed in his brother's footsteps and went to train at the First Fighter Squadron, a ranch and training facility owned by Joe Sayatovich, who became his manager. Unlike some boxers, Norris did not have a lengthy amateur career. He turned pro on August 2, 1986, with a first-round knockout of Jose Luis Cordova in San Jose. Norris won his next eleven fights before he lost to Derrick Kelly by a close, but unanimous decision. The next year, Norris captured the NABF junior middleweight title when he stopped Steve Little in the sixth round.

On July 30, 1989, Norris challenged Julian Jackson for the latter's WBA junior middleweight title. Though Norris performed well in the first round and actually hurt Jackson, the champion rebounded in the second round and scored a technical knockout over him. Less than a year later, Norris fought for the WBC super welterweight title against John ("The Beast") Mugabi. Like the Jackson fight, this bout did not last long. The result was different, however, as Norris knocked out Mugabi in the first round.

Despite his status as a world champion, Norris was not very well known ex-

Always fit, Terry Norris fought at the junior middleweight level for his entire professional career.

	WON **47**	LOST **9**	DRAWS **0**	TB 56	KO 31	W 16	WF 0	D 0	KO'd 4	L 2	LF 3

Date	Opponent	Site	Result / Rounds		Title	Wt.
1986						
Aug 2	Jose Luis Cordova	San Jose, CA	KO	1	—	148
Aug 13	Carlos Gutierrez	Inglewood, CA	W	4	—	149
Sep 25	George Murphy	Inglewood	W	4	—	151
Oct 7	Daryl Colquitt	Inglewood	TKO	4	—	150
Nov 21	Carlos Gutierrez	Reseda, CA	W	4	—	148
Dec 3	Lang McGowan	Inglewood	W	4	—	149
1987						
Feb 5	Gilbert Baptist	Riverside, CA	W	4	—	149
Feb 26	Richard Green	San Diego	TKO	1	—	149
Mar 16	Tino Leon	Inglewood	TKO	1	—	154
Mar 26	Mauro Veronica	Los Angeles	TKO	2	—	151
Apr 3	Sergio ("Nieto") Ramos	Las Vegas	TKO	1	—	155
May 27	Nathan Dryer	Las Vegas	TKO	3	—	152
Aug 13	Derrick Kelly	Inglewood	L	10	—	146
Sep 4	Edward Neblett	Las Vegas	TKO	6	—	153
Nov 25	Joseph Walker	Las Vegas	LF	1	—	152
1988						
Jan 21	Roman Nunez	San Diego	TKO	1	—	152
Feb 3	Richard Aguirre	Riverside, CA	TKO	3	—	152
Mar 28	Clayton Hires	Inglewood	TKO	2	—	154
Aug 12	Quincy Taylor	Las Vegas	W	10	—	154
Oct 18	Gilbert Baptist	San Diego	W	10	—	152
Dec 9	Steve Little	Las Vegas	TKO	6	Won-Vac NABF-JM	151
1989						
Mar 28	Buster Drayton	Las Vegas	W	12	Ret-NABF-JM	151
May 23	Ralph Ward	Atlantic City	W	10	—	155
Jul 30	Julian Jackson	Atlantic City	TKO'd	2	For-WBA-JM	152
Sep 21	Nathan Dryer	San Diego	TKO	4	—	151
Oct 18	Jorge Vaca	Tijuana, Mexico	W	10	—	153
Nov 21	Tony Montgomery	Santa Monica, CA	W	12	Ret-NABF-JM	150
1990						
Mar 31 ♛	John Mugabi	Tampa	KO	1	Won-WBC-JM	153
Jul 13	Rene Jacquot	Annecy, France	W	12	Ret-WBC-JM	152
1991						
Feb 9	Sugar Ray Leonard★	New York	W	12	Ret-WBC-JM	152
Jun 1	Donald Curry	Palm Springs, CA	KO	8	Ret-WBC-JM	151
Aug 17	Brett Lally	San Diego	TKO	1	Ret-WBC-JM	153
Dec 13	Jorge Castro	Paris	W	12	Ret-WBC-JM	151
1992						
Feb 22	Carl Daniels	San Diego	TKO	9	Ret-WBC-JM	152
May 9	Meldrick Taylor	Las Vegas	TKO	4	Ret-WBC-JM	149
Dec 13	Pat Lawlor	Las Vegas	TKO	3		154
1993						
Feb 20	Maurice Blocker	Mexico City	TKO	2	Ret-WBC-JM	154
Jun 19	Troy Waters	San Diego	TKO	3	Ret-WBC-JM	154
Sep 10	Joe Gatti	San Antonio, TX	TKO	1	Ret-WBC-JM	153
Dec 18	Simon Brown	Puebla, Mexico	KO'd	4	Lost-WBC-JM	151

1994							
Mar 18		Armando Campas	Las Vegas	KO	4	—	154
May 7	♛	Simon Brown	Las Vegas	W	12	Reg-WBC-JM	153
Nov 12		Luis Santana	Mexico City	LF	5	Lost-WBC-JM	151
1995							
Apr 8	♛	Luis Santana	Las Vegas	LF	3	For-WBC-JM	153
Aug 19	♛	Luis Santana	Las Vegas	TKO	2	Reg-WBC-JM	152
Sep 16		David Gonzales	Las Vegas	TKO	9	Ret-WBC-JM	151
Dec 16	♛	Paul Vaden	Philadelphia	W	12	Won-WBC/IBF-JM	151
1996							
Jan 27		Jorge Luis Vado	Phoenix	TKO	2	Ret-WBC/IBF-JM	152
Feb 24		Vincent Pettway	Richmond, VA	TKO	8	Ret-WBC/IBF-JM	150
Sep 7		Alex Rios	Las Vegas	TKO	5	Ret-WBC/IBF-JM	153
1997							
Jan 11		Nick Rupa	Nashville, TN	TKO	10	Ret-WBC/IBF-JM	154
Aug 8		Joaquin Velazquez	Kansas City, MO	KO	2	—	155
Sep 10		Andreas Arellano	Las Vegas	KO	2	—	159
Dec 6		Keith Mullings	Atlantic City	TKO'd	9	Lost-WBC-JM	154
1998							
Sep 25	♛	Dana Rosenblatt	Ledyard, CT	L	12	For-IBA-M	156
Nov 30	♛	Laurent Boudouani	Versailles, France	TKO'd	9	For-WBA-JM	154

cept by boxing cognoscenti. He hoped to change that in his second WBC title defense—against world-famous Hall of Famer Sugar Ray Leonard, who was in the midst of one of his comebacks. Leonard, who had last fought as a super middleweight over a year before, shed fourteen pounds to make the super welterweight limit. The fight was held on February 9, 1991, in Madison Square Garden. Norris knocked Leonard down in the second and seventh rounds en route to a unanimous decision.

In his next title defense, Norris faced former welterweight and super welterweight champion Donald Curry. Curry had the advantage at long range where he used his jab to land blows and blocked Norris's punches with his elbows and gloves. When Norris could fight in close, he had a clear edge and employed chopping punches to wear Curry down. Curry shook Norris in the sixth with a left hook to the head. In the seventh, Norris was credited with a knockdown—though many onlookers believed it was a push. In the eighth, Norris pounded Curry with two rights, sending him to the canvas. Norris made sure that he was down by hitting Curry with a questionably legal right as Curry's trunks brushed the mat. Curry was counted out and announced his retirement after the fight.

Norris successfully defended his super welterweight title seven more times before Simon Brown stopped him in the fourth round in Puebla, Mexico, on December 18, 1993. Before the fight, Norris declared himself "the greatest fighter" in the world and characterized Brown as a stepping-stone to a middleweight title. Brown was inspired by Norris's boasts. He used short, powerful rights and combinations to dethrone Norris. He knocked him down in the first round, sent him sprawling to his corner at the end of the second, and put him down for a final time at 1:06 of the fourth round.

Norris regained the title by unanimous decision in the rematch in Las Vegas on May 7, 1994. A fine technical boxer who could punch, Norris controlled the fight with his boxing skills. His next two fights, however, could only be characterized as bizarre. On November 12, 1994, he faced Luis Santana in Mexico City. Norris appeared to be in control of the match. In the fifth round, it seemed that he was close to ending the fight and he did—but not in the way that was expected. When Santana was caught against the ropes with his back to Norris, Norris hit him in the back of the head. Santana had to leave the ring on a stretcher but won a disqualification, as Norris was penalized for throwing an illegal rabbit punch. In the rematch on April 8, 1995, Norris knocked Santana down in the second and third rounds. When the bell sounded to end the third round, the referee separated the fighters and warned Santana for the second time for hitting below the belt. Norris did not return to his corner. When the referee finished warning Santana and stepped away—this was well after the bell had rung—Norris hit Santana on the chin and knocked him out. Again, Santana left the ring on a stretcher, and again Santana was the victor because of Norris's disqualification.

Finally, in their third fight, Norris legally knocked out Santana in the second round to regain the super welterweight championship. He added the IBF version of the title when he decisioned Paul Vaden on December 16, 1995. Norris was stripped of the IBF title when he refused to defend it against mandatory challenger Raul Marquez. Norris's WBC title reign came to an end when Keith Mullings scored a TKO in the ninth round on December 6, 1997. Norris fought twice more. After Laurent Boudouani knocked him out in the ninth round of their WBA super welterweight title fight on November 30, 1998, Norris retired.

During his ring career Norris displayed fine athleticism with great speed and power. He was a skillful counter-puncher and dazzled opponents with his double left lead and other combinations.

More than two years after his retirement, Norris wanted to make a comeback but was denied a license on medical grounds by the Nevada Athletic Commission. It appeared that Norris's speech was slurred.

Norris later made news when he sued Hall of Fame promoter Don King. Norris alleged that he had entered into a contract with King, which provided him with only "illusory" compensation because of lies King and Norris's manager, Sayatovich, had told Norris. King settled with Norris and agreed to pay him $7.5 million. This huge settlement was the final major victory in Norris's unusual ring career.

Norris retired to San Diego. In 2005, with the support of many San Diego businesses, he established the Terrible T's Youth Boxing Foundation.

Terry Norris fields questions at a Las Vegas news conference before an upcoming bout at the MGM Grand.

KEN NORTON

H E A V Y W E I G H T

Right-handed; 6'3"; 201–225 lbs.
50 bouts, 11/14/1967 to 5/11/1981
Manager: Bob Biron
WBC Heavyweight Champion 1978
Hall of Fame Induction: 1992
Born: 8/9/1943, Jacksonville, IL
Named: Kenneth Howard Norton

Ken Norton's name is inextricably linked to that of Muhammad Ali. Norton fought Ali three times and handed "The Greatest" the second defeat of his career, the result of a jaw-fracturing punch in the first round. Asked in a 1992 interview what he thought he would be most remembered for, Norton replied, "Fighting Ali." Nevertheless, Norton was a key player in the heavyweight wars of the 1960s and '70s. He was an aggressive fighter who could move with a confusing fluidity and who commanded a dangerous repertoire of punches.

Unlike many fighters, Norton did not grow up boxing or dreaming of becoming a fighter. He played football, basketball, and track in high school and received

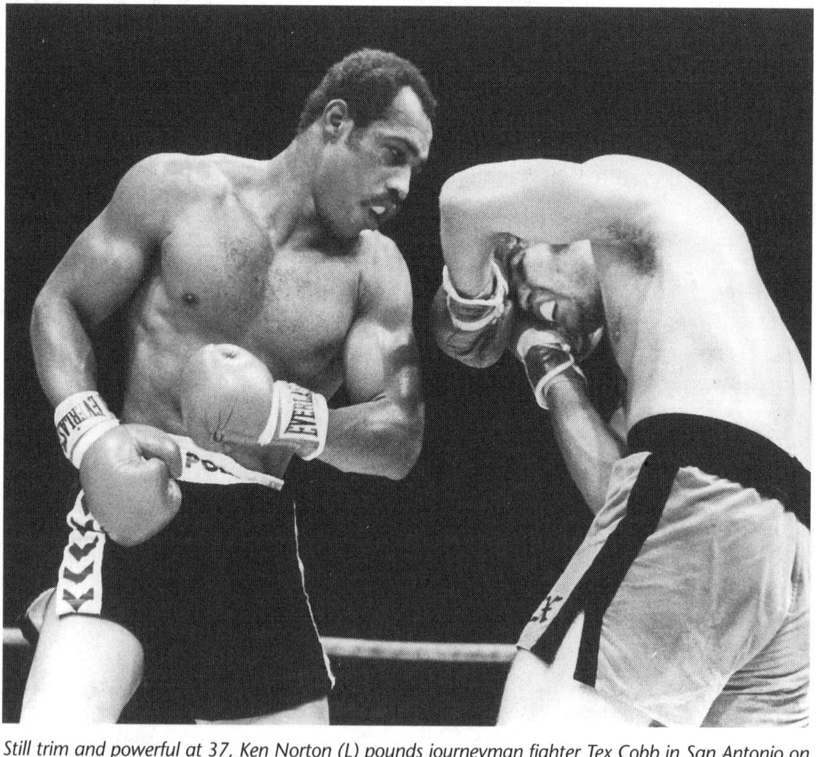

Still trim and powerful at 37, Ken Norton (L) pounds journeyman fighter Tex Cobb in San Antonio on November 7, 1980. Norton took the ten-round decision. This proved to be his next-to-last fight.

IN THE RING	WON 42	LOST 7	DRAWS 1	TB 50	KO 33	W 9	WF 0	D 1	KO'd 4	L 3	LF 0

Date	Opponent	Site	Result / Rounds		Title	Wt
1967						
Nov 14	Grady Brazell	San Diego	KO	9	—	201
1968						
Jan 16	Sam Wyatt	San Diego	W	6	—	202
Feb 6	Harold Dutra	Sacramento, CA	KO	3	—	210
Mar 26	Jimmy Gilmore	San Diego	KO	7	—	205
Jul 23	Wayne Kindred	San Diego	TKO	6	—	203
Dec 5	Cornell Nolan	Los Angeles	KO	6	—	207
1969						
Feb 11	Joe Hemphill	Woodland Hills, CA	TKO	3	—	206
Feb 20	Wayne Kindred	Los Angeles	KO	9	—	205
Mar 31	Pedro Sanchez	San Diego	TKO	2	—	203
May 29	Bill McMurray	Los Angeles	TKO	7	—	202
Jul 25	Gary Bates	San Diego	KO	8	—	204
Oct 21	Julius Garcia	San Diego	KO	3	—	210
1970						
Feb 4	Aaron Eastling	Las Vegas	KO	2	—	207
Mar 13	Stamford Harris	San Diego	KO	3	—	205
Apr 7	Bob Mashburn	Cleveland	KO	4	—	205
May 8	Ray Ellis	San Diego	KO	2	—	205
Jul 2	⑩ Jose Luis Garcia	Los Angeles	KO'd	8	—	207
Aug 29	Cookie Wallace	San Diego	KO	4	—	209
Sep 26	Chuck Leslie	Woodland Hills	W	10	—	205
Oct 16	Roby Harris	San Diego	KO	2	—	205
1971						
Apr 24	Steve Carter	Woodland Hills	TKO	3	—	208
Jun 12	Vic Brown	Santa Monica, CA	KO	5	—	211
Aug 19	Chuck Haynes	Santa Monica	KO	10	—	207
Sep 30	James Woody	San Diego	W	10	—	209
1972						
Feb 17	Charlie Harris	San Diego	KO	3	—	216
Mar 17	Jack O'Halloran	San Diego	W	10	—	212
Jun 5	Herschel Jacobs	San Diego	W	10	—	206
Jun 30	James Woody	San Diego	TKO	7	—	209
Nov 21	Henry Clark	Stateline, NV	KO	9	—	209
Dec 13	Charlie Reno	San Diego	W	10	—	208
1973						
Mar 31	⑩ Muhammad Ali★	San Diego	W	12	Won-NABF-H	210
Sep 10	⑩ Muhammad Ali★	Los Angeles	L	12	Lost-NABF-H	205
1974						
Mar 26	♛ George Foreman★	Caracas	TKO'd	2	For-World-H	212
Jun 25	Boone Kirkman	Seattle	TKO	8	—	218
1975						
Mar 4	Reco Brooks	Oklahoma City	KO	1	—	224
Mar 24	⑩ Jerry Quarry	New York	TKO	5	Won-NABF-H	218
Aug 14	Jose Luis Garcia	St Paul, MN	TKO	5	—	218

1976							
Jan 3		Pedro Lovell	Las Vegas	KO	5	—	220
Apr 30		Ron Stander	Landover, MD	KO	5	—	224
Jul 10		Larry Middleton	San Diego	TKO	10	—	220
Sep 28	♛ Muhammad Ali★	New York	L	15	For-World-H	217
1977							
May 11	⑩ Duane Bobick	New York	TKO	1	—	222
Sep 14		Lorenzo Zanon	Las Vegas	TKO	5	—	223
Nov 5	⑩ Jimmy Young	Las Vegas	W	15	—	215
1978							
Jun 8	⑩ Larry Holmes	Las Vegas	L	15	Lost-WBC-H	220
Nov 10		Randy Stephens	Las Vegas	KO	4	—	220
1979							
Mar 23	⑩ Earnie Shavers	Las Vegas	TKO'd	1	—	225
Sep 19	⑩ Scott Le Doux	Bloomington, MN	D	10	—	223
1980							
Nov 7		Randall ("Tex") Cobb	San Antonio, TX	W	10	—	218
1981							
May 11	⑩ Gerry Cooney	New York	TKO'd	1	—	218

a scholarship to Northeast Missouri State, which he attended for two years. It wasn't until Norton joined the Marine Corps that he began boxing. In the marines, Norton compiled a 24-2 amateur record and won the All-Marine heavyweight title three times. He also won a title in the Pan American Games trials.

Norton turned pro in 1967 at the relatively advanced age of 24 with a knockout of Grady Brazell. He fought primarily in the Southern California area and won his first sixteen fights before suffering a knockout loss to Jose Luis Garcia, the first ranked contender he ever faced. This was a loss he avenged five years later. By 1972, Norton appeared in the number nine slot in The Ring's annual ranking of top contenders.

In March 1973, Norton faced Ali for the NABF heavyweight title in a fight broadcast on national television from the San Diego Sports Arena. Ali had failed to train adequately for the match and had trouble avoiding Norton's advances. Norton, who was in top form, broke Ali's jaw in the first round. Although Ali went the distance, the injury took its toll, and Norton won on a split decision. Ali won the rematch in Los Angeles in September with a blistering final round. Again the result was a split decision. Norton then faced George Foreman in March 1974 in Caracas for the heavyweight championship. Foreman won easily, knocking Norton out in the second round.

Norton beat Jerry Quarry in New York in 1975 with a fifth-round TKO to take the NABF heavyweight title. Seeking a world title, Norton again faced Ali, acknowledged as champion once more after a win over Foreman. The fight was held in Yankee Stadium in 1976 in front of 30,296 fans. Norton led early on, but Ali recovered and won a unanimous decision, though Norton clearly believed that he had won the fight.

Norton was awarded the WBC heavyweight title when Leon Spinks refused to honor an agreement to defend his title against Norton. Norton defended his awarded championship against Larry Holmes and lost a close decision in a very exciting bout.

Norton's pressing style combined with a hook to the body and a right upper-cut to the head made him a formidable foe. But after losing to Earnie Shavers and Gerry Cooney in one-round knockouts, he retired.

Norton, whose undeniable good looks were affected very little by boxing, had a brief acting career. His son, Ken Norton, Jr., grew up to become a linebacker with the San Francisco 49ers and the Dallas Cowboys and has played in three Super Bowls.

Norton (R) jolts Jerry Quarry, a heavyweight who also faced Ali and Frazier, with a straight left to the jaw. Norton won the NABF heavyweight title with a fifth-round TKO on March 24, 1975, in New York.

RUBEN OLIVARES

El Puas

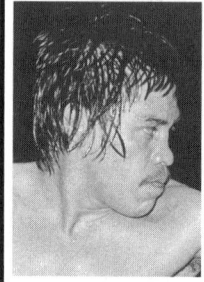

FEATHERWEIGHT

Right-handed; 5'5½"; 112–135 lbs.

104 bouts, 1/4/1965 to 3/12/1988

Manager: Pancho Rosales

Bantamwt Champ 1969–70, 1971–72
WBA Featherweight Champion 1974
WBC Featherweight Champion 1975

Hall of Fame Induction: 1991

Born: 1/14/1947, Mexico City, Mexico

Considered by many to be the best bantamweight of all time, Ruben Olivares twice won the world bantamweight title and twice won versions of the world featherweight title. Olivares started his career in his native Mexico with an impressive record. He knocked out his first 23 opponents and 54 of his first 57 opponents. In the other three bouts, Olivares took one decision, one win on a foul, and one draw. Overall, Olivares recorded 78 knockouts in his fourteen-year career.

Olivares captured the world bantamweight title at the Fabulous Forum in Inglewood, California, knocking out Lionel Rose in the fifth round in August 1969. In 1970, also at the Forum, Olivares suffered his first loss when Chucho Castillo scored a technical knockout in the fourteenth round to take the title. The next year Olivares again fought Castillo at the Forum before a crowd of 18,456. The

Olivares (L) knocks champion Lionel Rose of Australia into a glassy-eyed daze in the fifth round to seize the world bantamweight championship on August 22, 1969, in the Fabulous Forum in Inglewood, CA.

IN THE RING	WON 88	LOST 13	DRAWS 3	TB 104	KO 78	W 9	WF 1	D 3	KO'd 9	L 4	LF 0

Date	Opponent	Site	Result / Rounds		Title	Wt.
1965						
Jan 4	Isidro Sotelo	Cuernavaca, Mexico	KO	1	—	—
Jan 18	Freddy Garcia	Cuernavaca	KO	1	—	—
Feb 1	Geronimo Cisneros	Mexico City	TKO	3	—	—
Feb 16	Francisco Silva	Gomez Palacio, Mexico	TKO	6	—	113
Apr 1	Tony Gallegos	Gomez Palacio	KO	4	—	112
Aug 14	Nemesio Zenil	Mexico City	TKO	2	—	112
Sep 8	Jorge Ruiz	Torreon, Mexico	TKO	8	—	—
Oct 20	Mateo Jaimes	Mexico City	TKO	5	—	112
Nov 24	Pablo Martinez	Mexico City	TKO	2	—	—
1966						
Jan 17	Reynaldo De La Cerda	Mexico City	TKO	3	—	112
Feb 16	Eduardo Alvarado	Mexico City	TKO	2	—	112
Mar 12	Gallito Camacho	Mexico City	TKO	1	—	114
Apr 4	Juan Molina	Mexico City	TKO	2	—	112
May 19	Emetrio Campas	Tampico, Mexico	TKO	4	—	113
Jun 12	Alfonso Cazares	Mexico City	TKO	2	—	112
Jun 23	German Guzman	Tampico	TKO	4	—	113
Jul 10	Gerardo Lujano	Mexico City	TKO	5	—	113
Aug 7	Oscar Rivas	Tampico	TKO	3	—	—
Sep 1	Ramiro Garcia	Mexico City	KO	9	—	112
Sep 30	Monito Aguilar	Tampico	TKO	3	—	—
Oct 18	Rafael Macias	Mexico City	TKO	5	—	112
Dec 17	Daniel Gutierrez	Mexico City	TKO	10	—	112
1967						
Feb 5	Antonio Leal	Mexico City	KO	1	—	114
Mar 8	Felipe Gonzalez	Mexicali, Mexico	W	10	—	115
Jun 7	Julio Guerrero	Mexico City	KO	4	—	114
Jul 14	Angel Hernandez	Leon, Mexico	KO	5	—	116
Jul 29	German Bastidas	Mexico City	D	10	—	—
Sep 6	Grillo Aguilar	Poza Rica, Mexico	KO	5	—	113
Sep 20	Gustavo Sosa	Puebla, Mexico	TKO	3	—	115
Oct 14	Ushiwakamaru Harada	Mexico City	TKO	2	—	—
Nov 3	Chamaco Castillo	Veracruz, Mexico	TKO	5	—	117
Nov 19	Felipe Gonzalez	La Paz, Mexico	TKO	6	—	—
1968						
Jan 28	German Bastidas	Mexico City	TKO	5	—	—
Mar 3	Pornchai Popraigam	La Paz	TKO	9	—	117
Mar 30 ⑩	Salvatore Burruni	Mexico City	TKO	3	—	118
Apr 27	Manuel Arnal	Mexico City	WF	6	—	—
May 20	Kid Gavilan	Puebla	KO	4	—	120
Jun 8 ⑩	Octavio Gomez	Mexico City	KO	5	—	116
Jun 25	Enrique Yepes	Jalapa, Mexico	KO	5	—	119
Jul 11	Gary Garber	Torreon	TKO	3	—	118
Aug 10	Tiny Palacio	Mexico City	KO	6	—	118
Aug 28	Bernabe Fernandez	Inglewood, CA	TKO	3	—	119
Sep 15	Antoine Porcel	Mexico City	KO	1	—	115
Oct 11	Wally Brooks	Mexico City	KO	1	—	—
Nov 23	Jose Medel	Monterrey, Mexico	KO	8	—	117

1969

Date		Opponent	Location	Result	Rd	Notes	Wt
Jan 26	⑩	Kazuyoshi Kanazawa	Mexico City	TKO	2	—	118
Feb 23		Jose Bisbal	Mexico City	KO	3	—	117
Mar 9		Carlos Zayas	Tuxtla Gutierrez, Mexico	TKO	7	—	118
Mar 17		Ernie De La Cruz	Inglewood	TKO	9	—	121
May 6		Frank Adame	Nogales, Mexico	KO	2	—	120
May 23	⑩	Takao Sakurai	Inglewood	KO	6	—	117
Jun 29		Nene Jun	Mexico City	TKO	1	—	120
Aug 22	♛	Lionel Rose	Inglewood	KO	5	Won-World-B	118
Oct 27		Shigeyoshi Oki	Juarez, Mexico	KO	3	—	122
Dec 12	⑩	Alan Rudkin	Inglewood	KO	2	Ret-World-B	117

1970

Date		Opponent	Location	Result	Rd	Notes	Wt
Feb 22		Angel Hernandez	Acambaro, Mexico	KO	3	—	122
Mar 18		Romy Ruelas	San Antonio, TX	TKO	6	—	122
Apr 18	⑩	Chucho Castillo	Inglewood	W	15	Ret-World-B	117
Jul 22		Shuji Chiyoda	Chicago	W	10	—	124
Aug 14		Jose Arranz	Inglewood	TKO	3	—	123
Sep 11		Guillermo Rodriguez	Acapulco	KO	5	—	125
Oct 16	⑩	Chucho Castillo	Inglewood	TKO'd	14	Lost-World-B	118

1971

Date		Opponent	Location	Result	Rd	Notes	Wt
Mar 4		Chung-Sul Park	Guadalajara, Mexico	KO	6	—	118
Apr 3	♛	Chucho Castillo	Inglewood	W	15	Reg-World-B	118
May 19		Tsujio Mineyama	Tijuana, Mexico	TKO	3	—	125
Jun 7		Yambito Blanco	Managua, Nicaragua	KO	5	—	125
Jul 11	⑩	Efren Torres	Guadalajara	TKO	4	—	120
Aug 23		Valentin Galeano	Inglewood	TKO	9	—	120
Oct 25		Kazuyoshi Kanazawa	Nagoya, Japan	TKO	14	Ret-World-B	117
Dec 14	⑩	Jesus Pimentel	Inglewood	TKO	11	Ret-World-B	118

1972

Date		Opponent	Location	Result	Rd	Notes	Wt
Mar 19	⑩	Rafael Herrera	Mexico City	KO'd	8	Lost-World-B	117
Aug 19		Godfrey Stevens	Monterrey	W	10	—	124
Nov 14	⑩	Rafael Herrera	Inglewood	L	10	—	121

1973

Date		Opponent	Location	Result	Rd	Notes	Wt
Apr 28		Walter Seeley	Inglewood	TKO	2	—	126
Jun 23	⑩	Bobby Chacon★	Inglewood	TKO	9	Won-Vac NABF-FE	126
Sep 4	⑩	Art Hafey	Monterrey	TKO'd	5	—	126
Dec 2		Francisco Durango	Matamoros, Mexico	W	10	—	—

1974

Date		Opponent	Location	Result	Rd	Notes	Wt
Mar 4	⑩	Art Hafey	Inglewood	W	12	Ret-NABF-FE	126
May 14		Adrian Zapanta	Juarez	KO	2	—	123
Jul 9		Zensuke Utagawa	Inglewood	KO	7	Won-Vac WBA-FE	125
Aug 31		Enrique Garcia	Monterrey	TKO	5	—	126
Oct 6		Carlos Mendoza	Juarez	TKO	6	—	129
Nov 23		Alexis Arguello★	Inglewood	KO'd	13	Lost-WBA-FE	125

1975

Date		Opponent	Location	Result	Rd	Notes	Wt
Apr 7		Benjamin Ortiz	Tijuana	KO	6	—	127
Jun 20	♛	Bobby Chacon★	Inglewood	TKO	2	Won-WBC-FE	125
Sep 20	⑩	David Kotey	Inglewood	L	15	Lost-WBC-FE	126
Dec 4	⑩	Danny Lopez	Inglewood	KO'd	7	—	127

1976

Date		Opponent	Location	Result	Rd	Notes	Wt
Jun 2		Pajet Lupikanete	Los Angeles	KO	1	—	128
Jul 30		Fernando Cabanela	Los Angeles	W	10	—	125
Nov 19	⑩	Jose Cervantes	Los Angeles	KO'd	6	—	122

1977

Date		Opponent	Location	Result	Rd	Notes	Wt
Aug 20	⑩	Bobby Chacon★	Inglewood	L	10	—	130
Dec 6		Ricky Gutierrez	San Antonio	W	10	—	128

1978						
Apr 28	Jose Luis Ramirez	Obregon, Mexico	TKO	2	—	128
Oct 18	Shig Fukuyama	Houston	KO	2	—	127
Nov 20	Isaac Vega	Houston	TKO	3	—	126
1979						
Apr 22	Guillermo Morales	Tuxtla Gutierrez	D	10	—	—
Jun 30	Adrian Zapanta	Albuquerque, NM	KO	2	—	—
Jul 21 ♛	Eusebio Pedroza★	Houston	TKO'd	12	For-WBA-FE	125
1980						
Mar 7	Carlos Serrano	Chicago	KO	5	—	126
Apr 25	Sergio Reyes	Nuevo Laredo, Mexico	TKO	7	—	—
Aug 24	Rafael Gandarilla	McAllen, TX	TKO'd	9	—	128
1981						
Nov 24	Margarito Marquez	Houston	L	10	—	129
1986						
Feb 25*	Roman Almaguer	Inglewood	D	4	—	133
1988						
Mar 12*	Ignacio Madrid	Mexico City	KO'd	4	—	135

Some official records do not include these four-round bouts.

fight started slowly with little action until Castillo rocked Olivares in the sixth. Olivares then started to take charge. He mixed left hooks and right crosses to win easily by unanimous decision and regain his bantamweight title.

Olivares retained the belt for about a year before losing it to challenger Rafael Herrera, who knocked him out in the eighth round. Shortly thereafter, Olivares moved up to the featherweight division, where he quickly found success. Again fighting at the Forum, he faced Zensuke Utagawa of Japan for the vacant WBA featherweight title. Olivares dominated the entire fight, pounding Utagawa with close shots to the body. In the seventh, Olivares knocked Utagawa down three times. Utagawa got up twice but could not recover from the third knockdown, and Olivares was the champion.

In his first defense of the title, Olivares lost the belt to Hall of Famer Alexis Arguello on a thirteenth-round knockout. Seven months later, Olivares won the WBC version of the featherweight belt with an impressive victory over Bobby Chacon, stopping him in two rounds. Olivares failed to defend the title successfully, losing a decision to David Kotey in his next fight.

Olivares fought for another five years and suffered six of his thirteen career defeats during this period. After a five-year layoff, he made two brief comeback attempts, but failed to secure a win. The hard-partying Olivares will be remembered as a superb knock-out artist and the greatest draw ever to Inglewood's Fabulous Forum.

Promoter George Parnassus and Olivares after he regained the title from Castillo in April 1971.

BOBO OLSON
The Hawaiian Swede

M I D D L E W E I G H T

Right handed; 5'10½"; 135–178 lbs.
117 bouts, 8/19/1944 to 11/22/1966
Managers: Sid Flaherty, Herbert Campos
World Middleweight Champ 1953-55
Hall of Fame Induction: 2000
Born: 7/11/1928, Honolulu, HI
Named: Carl Elmer Olson
Died: 1/16/2002

Carl ("Bobo") Olson's colorful career ensured his lasting fame. His father was a Swedish immigrant who went to Hawaii during World War I, and Olson was nicknamed "The Hawaiian Swede."

Olson learned fighting on the streets of Honolulu, sometimes brawling with grown men. His parents broke up when he was only twelve, and he found work on a dairy farm and at odd jobs. As news of his fighting prowess spread, the young Olson participated in amateur bouts and bootleg fights against servicemen, some of whom had been professionals before enlisting.

Olson's first professional bout took place on August 19, 1944, when the sixteen-year-old knocked out Bob Correa in just two rounds. Sid Flaherty, a boxing manager who was serving in Hawaii as a sergeant in the army, was impressed enough with Olson's performance to sign him to a contract, and he took Olson with him to San Francisco after the war.

Olson won eight fights in 1946 before he lost his California State Boxing Commission license for being underage. He returned to Hawaii and came under the management of Herbert Campos. The next four years, Olson fought in Hawaii, Manila, and Australia, where he won 30 of 33 fights. His toughest opponent was Australian Dave Sands, a highly regarded middleweight title contender, who held the British Empire middleweight title. Sands knocked Olson down in the first round, but Olson battled back and lasted the full twelve rounds before losing a close decision on March 20, 1950. Just seven months later, on October 26, 1950, Olson traveled

During WWII, the teenaged Bobo Olson took part in many bootleg bouts, most against professionals competing with a special military exemption stationed in Hawaii. He picked up a lot of experience from these bouts, along with his two trademark tattoos.

IN THE RING	WON 99	LOST 16	DRAWS 2	TB 117	KO 49	W 50	WF 0	D 2	KO'd 7	L 9	LF 0

Date	Opponent	Site	Result / Rounds		Title	Wt.
1944						
Aug 19	Bob Correa	Honolulu	TKO	2	—	135
Aug 28	Ben Ramos	Honolulu	TKO	4	—	128
Sep 10	Young Pancho	Honolulu	W	4	—	138
1945						
Nov 23	Art Robinson	San Francisco	KO	4	—	163
Dec 10	Bobby Jones	San Francisco	KO	2	—	159
1946						
Jan 7	Obie Wooten	San Francisco	KO	1	—	159
Jan 14	Vepe Watson	San Francisco	KO	1	—	160
Jan 28	Pedro Jimenez	San Francisco	KO	4	—	160
Feb 4	Chuck Ross	San Francisco	W	6	—	158
Feb 25	Delaware Bradby	San Francisco	KO	3	—	160
— —*	Lavelle Perrin	San Francisco	KO	3	—	—
— —*	Lloyd Wagner	San Francisco	KO	3	—	—
— —*	Jackie Downlee	San Francisco	KO	2	—	—
Jul 19	Ernie ("Trader") Horne	Honolulu	TKO	2	—	163
Jul 26	Johnny Boski	Honolulu	KO	4	—	166
Aug 19	Johnny Boski	Honolulu	KO	3	—	162
Sep 9	Jackie Ryan	Honolulu	TKO	6	—	156
Oct 7	Wayne Powell	Honolulu	TKO	4	—	157
Dec 2	Wayne Powell	Honolulu	TKO	4	—	161
1947						
Jan 28	Gil Mojica	Honolulu	W	10	—	162
Mar 21	Candy McDaniels	Honolulu	W	10	—	158
May 2	Leroy Wade	Honolulu	TKO	5	—	160
Jun 20	Paul Lewis	Honolulu	W	10	—	157
Jul 4	George Duke	Honolulu	L	10	—	158
Aug 19	George Duke	Honolulu	W	10	—	158
Nov 22	Boy Brooks	Manila	L	10	—	155
Dec 17	Nai Som Pong	Manila	TKO	3	—	—
1948						
Jan 17	Boy Brooks	Manila	W	12	—	153
Apr 7	Flashy Sebastian	Manila	KO	7	—	—
May 11	Bobby Castro	Honolulu	W	8	—	155
Jul 20	Charley Cato	Honolulu	W	8	—	159
Oct 12	Boy Brooks	Honolulu	TKO	3	—	160
Oct 26	Kenny Watkins	Honolulu	W	10	—	160
Dec 14	Johnny Boski	Honolulu	KO	1	—	163
1949						
Jan 11	Paulie Perkins	Honolulu	KO	2	—	161
Mar 15	Anton Raadik	Honolulu	KO	7	—	159
Jun 3	Tommy Yarosz	Honolulu	W	10	—	163
Jul 26	Milo Savage	Honolulu	W	10	—	162
Aug 23	Art Hardy	Honolulu	KO	3	—	164
Nov 22	Johnny Duke	Honolulu	W	10	—	163
Dec 13	Earl Turner	Honolulu	W	10	—	152
1950						
Feb 22	Don Lee	Honolulu	W	10	—	165

Some historians believe that these bouts did not occur.

Date		Opponent	Location	Result	Rds	Note	Weight
Mar 20	⑩	Dave Sands	Sydney	L	12	—	162
Apr 25		Roy Miller	Honolulu	KO	5	—	164
May 22		Otis Graham	Honolulu	W	10	—	159
Sep 5		Henry Brimm	Honolulu	W	10	—	164
Oct 26	♚	Sugar Ray Robinson★	Philadelphia	KO'd	12	For-Penn World-M	159
1951							
Mar 20		Art Soto	Honolulu	W	10	—	162
May 7		Lloyd Marshall	Honolulu	KO	5	—	167
Jul 9		Chuck Hunter	San Francisco	W	10	—	166
Jul 27		Charlie Cato	Richmond, CA	KO	3	—	165
Aug 27		Bobby Jones	San Francisco	W	10	—	160
Oct 3	⑩	Dave Sands	Chicago	L	10	—	163
1952							
Feb 12		Woody Harper	Sacramento, CA	W	10	—	162
Feb 15		Tommy Harrison	Hollywood	W	10	—	162
Mar 13	♚	Sugar Ray Robinson★	San Francisco	L	15	For-World-M	159
May 6		Woody Harper	Richmond	KO	7	—	161
May 19	⑩	Walter Cartier	Brooklyn	KO	5	—	163
Jun 6		Jimmy Beau	New York	W	10	—	161
Jul 12	⑩	Robert Villemain	San Francisco	W	10	—	164
Aug 27	⑩	Eugene Hairston	New York	KO	7	—	160
Nov 20	⑩	Lee Sala	San Francisco	KO	2	—	163
Dec 18	⑩	Norman Hayes	San Francisco	W	10	—	163
1953							
Feb 7	⑩	Norman Hayes	Boston	W	10	—	162
Mar 16		Garth Panter	Butte, MT	W	10	—	165
Jun 19	⑩	Paddy Young	New York	W	15	Won-Amer-M	159
Oct 21	⑩	Randy Turpin★	New York	W	15	Won-Vac-World-M	159
1954							
Jan 23		Joe Rindone	San Francisco	KO	5	—	165
Apr 2	♚	Kid Gavilan★	Chicago	W	15	Ret-World-M	159
Jun 15		Jesse Turner	Honolulu	TKO	8	—	166
Jul 7		Pedro Gonzales	Oakland	KO	4	—	167
Aug 20	⑩	Rocky Castellani	San Francisco	W	15	Ret-World-M	160
Nov 3		Garth Panter	Richmond, VA	KO	8	—	166
Dec 15	⑩	Pierre Langlois	San Francisco	TKO	11	Ret-World-M	159
1955							
Feb 16	⑩	Ralph ("Tiger") Jones	Chicago	W	10	—	168
Mar 12		Willie Vaughn	Hollywood	W	10	—	168
Apr 13	⑩	Joey Maxim★	San Francisco	W	10	—	169
Jun 22	♚	Archie Moore★	New York	KO'd	3	For-World-LH	170
Aug 13		Jimmy Martinez	Portland, OR	W	10	—	165
Aug 26		Joey Giambra	San Francisco	W	10	—	166
Dec 9	⑩	Sugar Ray Robinson★	Chicago	KO'd	2	Lost-World-M	159
1956							
May 18	♚	Sugar Ray Robinson★	Los Angeles	KO'd	4	For-World-M	160
1957							
Jun 18		Joey Maxim★	Portland, OR	W	10	—	187
Aug 17	⑩	Pat McMurtry	Portland, OR	KO'd	2	—	185
1958							
Oct 28		Don Grant	Oakland	TKO	7	—	173
Nov 25		Paddy Young	Oakland	KO	6	—	170
Dec 16		Tommy Villa	Fresno, CA	TKO	5	—	175
1959							
Mar 30		Rory Calhoun	San Francisco	W	10	—	174

Date		Opponent	Location	Result	Rounds		Weight
Aug 25		George Kartalian	Fresno, CA	KO	5	—	176
1960							
Apr 7		Roque Maravilla	Portland, OR	KO	7	—	173
May 5		Al Sparks	Vancouver, BC	KO	5	—	178
Jun 6	⑩	Mike Holt	Johannesburg	W	10	—	176
Aug 31	⑩	Doug Jones	Chicago	KO'd	6	—	179
1961							
Jan 19		Bobby Daniels	Spokane, WA	W	10	—	177
Feb 16		Floyd Buchanan	Victoria, B.C., Can	KO	3	—	—
Aug 14		Roque Maravilla	Oakland	W	10	—	177
Sep 11		Sixto Rodriguez	San Francisco	L	10	—	178
Oct 23		Sixto Rodriguez	San Francisco	W	10	—	178
Nov 14		Leroy Smith aka Yancy D	Honolulu	KO	8	—	177
1962							
Jan 12		Al Williams	Honolulu	W	10	—	175
Jan 19		Artie Dixon	Honolulu	W	10	—	177
Apr 3		Pete Rademacher	Honolulu	L	10	—	181
Jun 3		Lennart Risberg	Stockholm	KO	6	—	177
Dec 14	⑩	Giulio Rinaldi	Rome	D	10	—	178
1963							
Jan 25		Al Williams	Eugene, OR	TKO	5	—	175
Apr 30		Sonny Ray	Honolulu	KO	8	—	178
May 14		Jesse Bowdry	Honolulu	W	10	—	178
Oct 21		Jose Menno	San Francisco	W	10	—	176
Dec 9		Hank Casey	San Francisco	D	10	—	176
1964							
Mar 27	⑩	Wayne Thornton	San Francisco	W	10	—	176
Jun 19	⑩	Johnny Persol	New York	L	10	—	176
Aug 28	⑩	Wayne Thornton	New York	W	10	—	177
Nov 27	⑩	Jose Torres ★	New York	KO'd	1	—	176
1965							
Jun 24		Andy Kendall	Reno, NV	W	10	—	176
Sep 23		Fred Roots	Reno	KO	3	—	175
1966							
Jul 11		Piero Del Papa	San Francisco	W	10	—	177
Nov 22	⑩	Don Fullmer	Oakland	L	10	—	175

to Philadelphia to challenge Sugar Ray Robinson for his Pennsylvania world middleweight title. Robinson, far more experienced than his opponent, knocked Olson out with a combination that ended in a left to the stomach in the twelfth round. About eighteen months later, Olson again faced Robinson, this time for the world middleweight championship in San Francisco. He gave Robinson a good battle in the first ten rounds, but Robinson fought back in the last five and won a narrow decision, though he had to be helped from the ring.

When Robinson retired and his title was declared vacant, two Europeans and two Americans were chosen for a four-man tournament to crown the new champ. Olson decisioned Paddy Young to face Randy Turpin for the title on October 21, 1953, in front of 19,000 fans in Madison Square Garden. Turpin got off to a good start, stunning Olson in the first and winning the first three rounds convincingly. Olson took charge after that and sent Turpin down in the tenth for a nine count. Olson won the title and wept with joy when the decision was announced. He was declared *The Ring*'s Fighter of the Year for 1953.

The next year saw more of the same with successful title defenses against Hall of Famer and welterweight champion Kid Gavilan, Rocky Castellani, and Pierre Langlois. Olson won non-title bouts against Joe Rindone, Jesse Turner, Pedro Gonzales, and Garth Panter. His great year earned him another major pugilistic award: the Boxing Writers Association of America's Edward J Neil Trophy for Fighter of the Year.

In 1955, Olson easily decisioned former light heavyweight champion Joey Maxim at the Cow Palace in San Francisco, and decided to aim for the heavyweight championship held by Rocky Marciano. He needed the light heavyweight title first, and so Olson signed to face champion Archie Moore on June 22 in the Polo Grounds. He won the first two rounds and opened cuts on Moore's face, but in the third, Moore put him down for the count with a right to the jaw. Olson earned $125,000 for the fight but did not see a penny of the winnings because of tax problems.

Olson was about to lose his middleweight title. On December 9, 1955, in Chicago Stadium, Robinson, having emerged from his brief retirement, knocked Olson out in the second round with a left hook. In the rematch, Olson unleashed a solid attack to Robinson's body for three rounds, but fell victim to a Robinson combination in the fourth and was knocked out.

Olson (L) sends a driving right just over the shoulder of Bobby Jones. Jones, holder of both the California welterweight and middleweight titles, dropped a ten-round decision to Olson in San Francisco on August 27, 1951.

At the same time, Olson's personal life came under heavy scrutiny when *Confidential* magazine revealed that he had two wives, Helen and Jane, and ten children between them. Both women knew about the arrangement, but they weren't happy with it. Helen filed for divorce, delivering another financial blow to Olson, though it allowed him to legally marry Jane.

Olson briefly retired after his last loss at Robinson's hands, but returned to the ring on June 18, 1957, with a decision over Maxim. He attempted to move up to heavyweight, but was knocked out in two rounds by Pat McMurtry. On June 6, 1960, Olson decisioned highly regarded light heavyweight contender Mike Holt. Unfortunately, Doug Jones knocked Olson out in his next fight. Olson returned to *The Ring*'s rankings in 1962 as the fifth place light heavyweight contender with a knockout over Lennart Risberg and a draw against Giulio Rinaldi.

In 1964, Olson sandwiched two wins over formidable light heavyweight Wayne Thornton around a loss to contender Johnny Persol. He was then pitted against Hall of Famer Jose Torres for an opportunity to fight for the title held by Willie Pastrano. Olson was knocked out in the first round, ending his title hopes for good. He fought four more times before retiring after a loss to Don Fullmer.

After leaving the ring, Olson worked in California as recreation director for the pre-apprentice program of the Operating Engineers Union. He also worked in public relations for the Teamsters Union and made numerous personal appearances.

A shot to the body staggers Kid Gavilan (L) to the ropes. Gavilan stepped up in weight to challenge Olson for the middleweight crown, but he couldn't withstand the champ's powerful right. Olson took the fifteen-round decision in Chicago on April 2, 1954.

CARLOS ORTIZ

LIGHTWEIGHT

Right-handed; 5'7"; 132–145 lbs.

70 bouts, 2/14/1955 to 9/20/1972

Manager: Bill Daly

Jr Welterweight Champ 1959–60
Lightwt Champ 1962–65, 1965–68

Hall of Fame Induction: 1991

Born: 9/9/1936, Ponce, PR

Born in Puerto Rico, Carlos Ortiz first learned to fight on the streets of New York, where his family moved when he was eight. Battling neighborhood toughs who taunted him because of his ethnic heritage, Ortiz developed physical skills, as well as a will to win, which would later help him in the ring. He started boxing as an amateur at the Madison Square Boys Club. Turning professional at the age of eighteen, he won his first 20 fights.

In 1959, Ortiz fought crafty Kenny Lane for the vacant world junior welterweight title. Ortiz had lost to Lane the year before in a ten-round decision in Miami Beach, but this time he avenged the defeat, stopping Lane in the second round. The junior welterweight crown had not been contested in thirteen years and had limited value, but Ortiz defended it three times in 1960. He KO'd

Ortiz (L) keeps Kenny Lane at bay with a jab. He beat Lane on points to keep his lightweight title on April 11, 1964. The two fighters twice met earlier as junior welterweights, splitting the results.

IN THE RING	WON 61	LOST 7	DRAWS 1	TB 70	KO 30	W 31	WF 0	D 1	KO'd 1	L 6	LF 0	NC 1

Date	Opponent	Site	Result / Rounds		Title	Wt.
1955						
Feb 14	Harry Bell	New York	KO	1	—	136
Feb 28	Morris Hodnett	New York	KO	1	—	135
May 13	Danny Roberts	New York	KO	3	—	133
May 30	Juan Pacheco	New York	KO	2	—	133
Jun 24	Jimmy DeMura	Syracuse, NY	W	6	—	133
Aug 10	Tony DeCola	New York	W	6	—	137
Aug 22	Armand Bush	New York	W	6	—	136
Sep 19	Hector Rodriguez	New York	KO	2	—	132
Oct 3	Leroy Graham	New York	KO	2	—	136
Oct 29	Al Duarte	Boston	KO	4	—	—
Nov 12	Lem Miller	Boston	W	8	—	—
Dec 10	Charley Titone	Paterson, NJ	KO	2	—	133
1956						
Jan 9	Ray Portilla	New York	W	8	—	135
Feb 17	Ray Portilla	New York	W	8	—	139
May 25	Johnny Gorman	New York	W	6	—	138
Jul 30	Tommy Salem	New York	W	10	—	135
Oct 27	Mickey Northrup	Hollywood	W	10	—	136
Dec 15	Phil Kim	Hollywood	TKO	9	—	139
Dec 31	Gale Kerwin	New York	W	10	—	135
1957						
Jan 23	Bobby Rogers	Chicago	W	10	—	136
Mar 2	Lou Filippo	Hollywood	NC	9	—	138
Apr 9	Lou Filippo	Hollywood	KO	7	—	137
May 7	Ike Vaughn	Miami Beach	W	10	—	138
May 29	Felix Chiocca	Chicago	W	10	—	134
Sep 23	Harry Bell	New York	W	10	—	137
1958						
Feb 28	Tommy Tibbs	New York	W	10	—	135
May 9	⑩ Joe Lopes	Hollywood	W	10	—	135
Jun 27	⑩ Johnny Busso	New York	L	10	—	137
Sep 19	⑩ Johnny Busso	New York	W	10	—	137
Oct 28	⑩ Dave Charnley	London	W	10	—	135
Dec 31	⑩ Kenny Lane	Miami Beach	L	10	—	135
1959						
Apr 13	⑩ Len Matthews	Philadelphia	TKO	6	—	136
Jun 12	⑩ Kenny Lane	New York	TKO	2	Won-Vac World-JW	139
1960						
Feb 4	⑩ Battling Torres	Los Angeles	KO	10	Ret-World-JW	137
Jun 15	⑩ Duilio Loi★	San Francisco	W	15	Ret-World-JW	137
Sep 1	⑩ Duilio Loi★	Milan	L	15	Lost-World-JW	138
1961						
Feb 2	⑩ Cisco Andrade	Los Angeles	W	10	—	137
May 10	♛ Duilio Loi★	Milan	L	15	For-World-JW	136
Sep 2	⑩ Doug Vaillant	Miami Beach	W	10	—	139
Nov 18	⑩ Paolo Rosi	New York	W	10	—	136

1962							
Apr 21	♛	Joe Brown★	Las Vegas	W	15	Won-World-L	134
Aug 1	⑩	Arthur Persley	Manila	W	10	—	137
Nov 7	⑩	Kazuo Takayama	Tokyo	W	10	—	136
Dec 3	⑩	Teruo Kosaka	Tokyo	KO	5	Ret-World-L	134
1963							
Apr 7	⑩	Doug Vaillant	San Juan, PR	TKO	13	Ret-World-L	134
Sep 18		Pete Acera	Honolulu	KO	7	—	138
Oct 22		Maurice Cullen	London	W	10	—	138
1964							
Feb 15		Flash Elorde★	Manila	TKO	14	Ret-World-L	135
Apr 11	⑩	Kenny Lane	San Juan	W	15	Ret-World-L	135
Dec 14		Dick Divola	Boston	KO	1	—	140
1965							
Apr 10	⑩	Ismael Laguna★	Panama City	L	15	Lost-World-L	134
Nov 13	♛	Ismael Laguna★	San Juan	W	15	Reg-World-L	135
1966							
Apr 6	⑩	Nicolino Locche★	Buenos Aires	D	10	—	138
Jun 20	⑩	Johnny Bizzarro	Pittsburgh	TKO	12	Ret-World-L	135
Oct 22	⑩	Sugar Ramos★	Mexico City	TKO	5	Ret-World-L	134
Nov 28		Flash Elorde★	New York	KO	14	Ret-World-L	135
1967							
Jul 1	⑩	Sugar Ramos★	San Juan	TKO	4	Ret-World-L	135
Aug 16	⑩	Ismael Laguna★	New York	W	15	Ret-World-L	135
1968							
Jun 29	⑩	Carlos Teo Cruz	Santo Domingo, D.R.	L	15	Lost-World-L	135
1969							
Nov 21		Edmundo Fur Tado Leite	New York	W	10	—	144
1971							
Dec 1		Jimmy Ligons	Las Vegas	KO	3	—	141
1972							
Jan 8		Bill Whittenburg	Miami	KO	7	—	145
Jan 20		Terry Rondeau	Portland, ME	TKO	4	—	139
Jan 31		Ivelaw Eastman	Waltham, MA	TKO	2	—	144
Feb 19		Leo DiFiore	San Juan	KO	2	—	—
Mar 20		Junior Varney	Ponce, PR	KO	2	—	—
May 1		Greg Potter	Los Angeles	W	10	—	142
Jun 3		Gerardo Ferrat	Chicago	KO	3	—	140
Aug 1		Johnny Copeland	Oklahoma City	KO	3	—	140
Sep 20	⑩	Ken Buchanan★	New York	TKO'd	6	—	139

Battling Torres in Los Angeles and won a fifteen-round decision over Italian Duilio Loi. Months later, Ortiz lost the belt to Loi on a controversial decision in Loi's hometown of Milan. Ortiz faced Loi in Milan again in 1961 and again lost a fifteen-round decision.

But for Ortiz, a much more worthy goal was the lightweight title. In 1962, he got his chance, facing Joe ("Old Bones") Brown in a nationally televised match in Las Vegas. Ortiz devised a strategy for the fight which involved peppering Brown with left jabs and avoiding a slugfest with the seasoned veteran. The strategy worked to perfection, and Ortiz won a lopsided decision.

He maintained the lightweight championship until 1965 when he lost a decision to Ismael Laguna. Ortiz regained the title six months later, with a

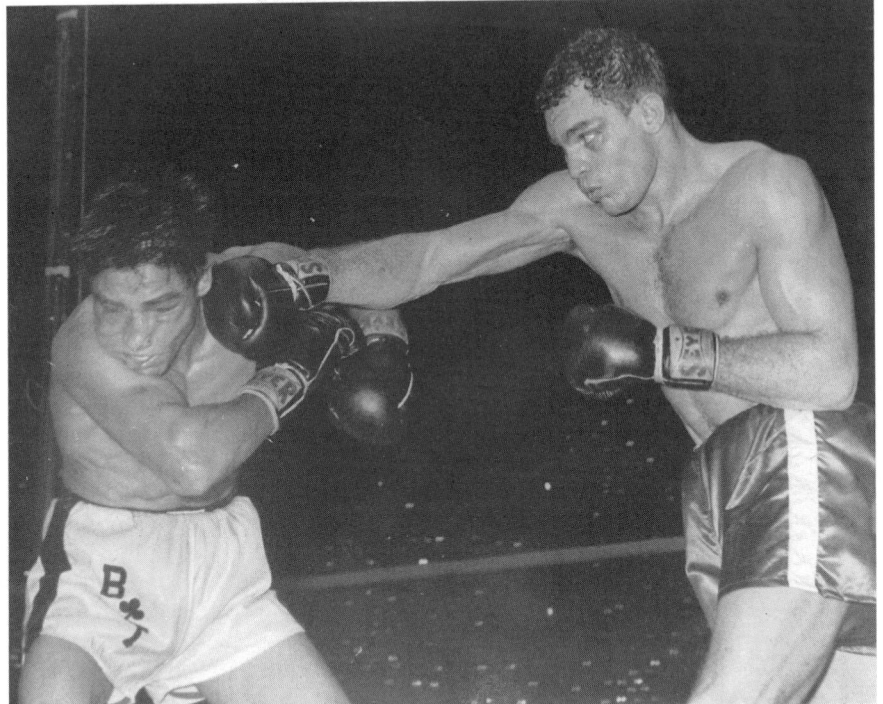

Ortiz (R) scorches Battling Torres with an overhand right in his first title defense on February 4, 1960. Ortiz was the first junior welterweight champion (140-pound limit) to campaign in thirteen years.

decision over Laguna and held it until 1968 when he lost a controversial split decision to Carlos Teo Cruz in Cruz's native Dominican Republic. Ortiz retired briefly, then made a comeback in 1971 and 1972, which ended in defeat at the hands of former champion lightweight Ken Buchanan.

FIXES

The Sweet Science has often been tainted by talk of fixed fights. While the vast majority of bouts are on the level, some matches have certainly been rigged for the benefit of gamblers.

• In Tom Sharkey's nine-round win over Jim Corbett, the Corbett corner-man who jumped in the ring causing a loss by foul was apparently a plant on the Sharkey camp's payroll.

• Was he bribed? Wild West legend Wyatt Earp was refereeing a Tom Sharkey–Bob Fitzsimmons bout in 1896 and disqualified a legitimate knock-out punch by Fitzsimmons, giving the victory to Tom Sharkey as a win by foul.

• Jake LaMotta admitted to having taken a dive, in exchange for a future title shot opportunity, in his four-round TKO loss to Billy Fox.

RINGFACT

MANUEL ORTIZ

BANTAMWEIGHT

Right-handed; 5'4"; 110–137 lbs.

128 bouts, 2/25/1938 to 12/10/1955

Managers: Noel Johnson 1938–41, Tommy Farmer and Johnny Rogers 1941–51

Bantamweight Champion 1942–47, 1947–50

Hall of Fame Induction: 1996

Born: 7/2/1916, Corona, CA

Died: 5/31/1970

Twice bantamweight champ, Manuel Ortiz defended his title more times than any other champion except Joe Louis. Born in California, Ortiz left school for work after one year of high school. At nineteen, he attended an amateur boxing match. When one of the scheduled fighters failed to appear, Ortiz's friends persuaded him to enter the ring. He knocked down his opponent on the way to a victory. Thus encouraged, Ortiz began training for an amateur career. He won the Southern California amateur flyweight title, the California Golden Gloves, and a national amateur title.

Although his professional debut was a loss, Ortiz improved under the direction of Noel Johnson. Within two years, he compiled a 17-9 record, with a knockout win over Jackie Jurich, and a fourth-place flyweight ranking from *The Ring*.

In 1941, Ortiz hired manager Tommy Farmer. Farmer coached Ortiz, seconded him, lived with him during training, and cooked his meals. Moving up to bantamweight, Ortiz was rated second-best contender for the title held by Lou Salica. In August 1942, a fight with Salica—and the title—went to Ortiz but because the bout lasted only twelve rounds, it was not recognized by New York. Ortiz settled this matter in a rematch the next year, with an eleventh-round knockout.

In a non-title bout in Paris on November 14, 1949, Ortiz (L) has Theo Medina in trouble. Ortiz took the ten-round decision.

IN THE RING	WON 96	LOST 29	DRAWS 3	TB 128	KO 49	W 47	WF 0	D 3	KO'd 1	L 28	LF 0

Date		Opponent	Site	Result / Rounds		Title	Wt.
1938							
Feb 25	⑩	Benny Goldberg	Hollywood	L	4	—	—
Mar 11		Tony Navarro	Hollywood	W	4	—	—
Mar 25		Frenchy Savidan	Hollywood	W	4	—	—
Apr 14		Serio Mendoza	Hollywood	W	4	—	—
May 3		General Padilla	Los Angeles	KO	4	—	—
May 17		Santos Lugo	Los Angeles	KO	4	—	—
Jun 3		Sammy LaPorte	Hollywood	W	4	—	—
Jun 24		Frenchy Savidan	Hollywood	W	4	—	—
Jul 5		Pablo Dano	Los Angeles	L	6	—	116
Aug 5	⑩	Benny Goldberg	Hollywood	L	4	—	—
Aug15		Tony Navarro	El Centro, CA	KO	3	—	—
Sep 30		Richie Lemos	Hollywood	W	6	—	—
Oct 21		Richie Lemos	Hollywood	W	10	—	115
Nov 8	⑩	David Young	Los Angeles	L	10	—	115
Nov	⑩	Benny Goldberg	Hollywood	L	10	—	115
Dec 6		Bernie Reyes	Los Angeles	W	10	—	120
1939							
Jan 2	⑩	Small Montana	Stockton, CA	L	10	—	114
Feb 15		Ken Martinez	El Centro	KO	3	—	115
Mar 14	⑩	Jackie Jurich	San Jose	TKO	7	—	115
Apr 11		Tommy Cobb	San Jose	W	10	—	115
May		Sammy LaPorte	El Centro	KO	7	—	—
Jun 9	⑩	Jackie Jurich	Hollywood	L	10	—	110
Aug		Bobby Leyvas	Yuma, AZ	L	10	—	—
Sep 15	⑩	Lou Salica	Hollywood	L	10	—	116
Oct 17		Donnie Maes	San Jose, CA	L	10	—	114
Oct 24		Horace Mann	San Jose	W	10	—	114
Dec 5		Cyril Joseph	San Jose	KO	5	—	117
Dec 14		Elwood Romero	Sacramento, CA	W	10	—	115
1940							
Jan 30	♛	Little Dado	Stockton	D	10	—	115
Mar 22		Andy Vasquez	Hollywood	TKO	5	—	116
Apr 5	⑩	Jackie Jurich	Hollywood	KO	9	—	112
Apr 20		Panchito Villa	Mexico City	W	10	—	—
May 18		Panchito Villa	Mexico City	L	10	—	—
Oct 9		Panchito Villa	Mexico City	KO	7	—	—
1941							
Jan 10	⑩	Rush Dalma	Hollywood	KO	3	—	116
Feb		Jose Robleto	Calexito, CA	TKO	6	—	—
Mar 14	⑩	Lupe Cardoza	Sacramento	KO	9	—	117
Apr 4	⑩	Carlos Chavez	Hollywood	D	10	—	117
May 9	⑩	Carlos Chavez	Hollywood	W	10	—	118
May 20		Jesus Llanes	El Centro	W	10	—	—
Jun 6		Lou Transparenti	Hollywood	KO	7	—	118
Aug 8	⑩	Tony Olivera	Hollywood	L	10	—	116
Nov 7		Donnie Maes	Hollywood	W	10	—	121
Nov 21		Johnny Grady	San Diego	W	10	—	—
1942							
Jan 2	⑩	Tony Olivera	Hollywood	W	10	Won-CA State-B	117

Date		Opponent	Location	Result	Rounds	Title	Weight
Mar 6		Little Pancho	Hollywood	TKO	7	—	120
May 8	⑩	Kenny Lindsay	Hollywood	KO	6	—	119
May 30	⑩	Leonardo Lopez	Tijuana, Mexico	W	10	—	121
Jul 3		Elwood Romero	Hollywood	TKO	6	—	118
Aug 7	♛	Lou Salica	Hollywood	W	12	Won-World-B	116
Sep 25		Bobby Carroll	San Diego	KO	5	—	121
Oct 9		Nat Corum	Portland, OR	W	10	—	121
Oct 30		Nat Corum	Hollywood	KO	6	—	120

1943

Date		Opponent	Location	Result	Rounds	Title	Weight
Jan 1		Kenny Lindsay	Portland, OR	W	10	Ret-World-B	117
Jan 27		Georgie Freitas	Oakland	TKO	10	Ret-World-B	117
Mar 10	⑩	Lou Salica	Oakland	TKO	11	Ret-World-B	117
Apr 2		Pedro Ramirez	Hollywood	KO	6	—	119
Apr 16		Jose Robleto	San Diego	W	10	—	123
Apr 28		Lupe Cardoza	Fort Worth, TX	KO	6	Ret-World-B	118
May 26		Jose Robleto	Long Beach, CA	W	15	Ret-World-B	118
Jun 25	⑩	Tony Olivera	Hollywood	TKO	7	—	120
Jul 12		Jose Robleto	Seattle	TKO	7	Ret-World-B	117
Aug 13	⑩	Leonardo Lopez	Hollywood	W	10	—	119
Sep 4		Filio Gonzalez	Mexico City	KO	5	—	
Oct 1	⑩	Leonardo Lopez	Hollywood	KO	4	Ret-World-B	117
Nov 23	⑩	Benny Goldberg	Los Angeles	W	15	Ret-World-B	117

1944

Date		Opponent	Location	Result	Rounds	Title	Weight
Mar 14	⑩	Ernesto Aguilar	Los Angeles	W	15	Ret-World-B	118
Apr 4	⑩	Tony Olivera	Los Angeles	W	15	Ret-World-B	117
May 19		Pee Wee Lewis	Hollywood	TKO	9	—	124
Jun 29	⑩	Larry Bolvin	Boston	W	10	—	125
Jul 17		Willie Pep★	Boston, MA	L	10	—	127
Aug 29	⑩	Enrique Bolanos	Los Angeles	TKO	6	—	123
Sep 12	⑩	Luis Castillo	Los Angeles	TKO	4	Ret-World-B	118
Sep 30	⑩	Carlos Chavez	Hollywood	W	10	—	123
Nov 14	⑩	Luis Castillo	Los Angeles	TKO	9	Ret-World-B	117
Nov 22	⑩	Lorenzo Safora	Oakland	W	10	—	121

1945

Date		Opponent	Location	Result	Rounds	Title	Weight
Jan 12		Jose ("Baby") Gonzalez	Hollywood	W	10	—	123
Jan 26		Bert White	San Diego	KO	7	—	123
Nov 2		Horace Leftwich	San Diego	W	10	—	124
Nov 12		Jose Andreas	Dallas	W	10	—	122
Nov 20		Proctor Heinold	San Antonio, TX	W	10	—	124

1946

Date		Opponent	Location	Result	Rounds	Title	Weight
Feb 15		Eli Golindo	Hollywood	KO	4	—	123
Feb 25	⑩	Luis Castillo	San Francisco	KO	13	Ret-World-B	117
Mar 19	⑩	Carlos Chavez	Los Angeles	D	15	For-Calif-FE	122
Apr 22		Horace Leftwich	San Francisco	W	10	—	122
May 18		Kenny Lindsay	Hollywood	TKO	5	Ret-World-B	118
Jun 10		Jackie Jurich	San Francisco	KO	11	Ret-World-B	117
Jul 12	⑩	David Young	Honolulu	KO	7	—	122
Oct 22	⑩	Carlos Chavez	Los Angeles	L	12	For-Calif-FE	125

1947

Date		Opponent	Location	Result	Rounds	Title	Weight
Jan 6	⑩	Harold Dade	San Francisco	L	15	Lost-World-B	117
Mar 11	♛	Harold Dade	Los Angeles	W	15	Reg-World-B	117
May 30	⑩	David Young	Honolulu	W	15	Ret-World-B	118
Oct 15		Manny Ortega	El Paso, TX	TKO'd	8	—	122
Dec 20	⑩	Tirso Del Rosario	Manila, Philippines	W	15	Ret-World-B	118

1948

Date		Opponent	Location	Result	Rounds	Title	Weight
Apr 27		Joey Dolan	Portland, OR	TKO	6	—	123

Date		Opponent	Location	Result	Rds	Notes	Wt
May 25	⊛	Henry Davis	Honolulu	W	10	—	125
Jul 4	⊛	Memo Valero	Mexicali, Mexico	TKO	8	Ret-World-B	117
Sep 28		Lauro Salas	Los Angeles	L	10	—	133
Oct 29		Buddy Jacklich	Hollywood	KO	8	—	129
Dec 14		Maxie Docusen	Los Angeles	L	10	—	126
1949							
Jan 1		Jose Cardenas	Mexicali	W	10	—	122
Mar 1		Dado Marino	Honolulu	W	15	Ret-World-B	118
Mar 29	⊛	Henry Davis	Honolulu	L	10	—	124
Apr 26	⊛	Lauro Salas	Los Angeles	W	10	—	121
May 15		Baby Mickey	Sonora, Mexico	KO	5	—	—
May 20		Pinky Peralta	Mexico City	KO	5	—	—
Jun 25		Roberto Coaury	Veracruz, Mexico	L	10	—	—
Jun 29		Roberto Carvajal	Merida, Mexico	W	10	—	—
Jul 16	⊛	Memo Valero	Mexico City	KO	7	—	125
Jul 23		Tony Vasquez	Tampico, Mexico	KO	4	—	—
Aug 29		Jimmy Cooper	Washington, DC	L	10	—	129
Oct 3	⊛	Ronnie Clayton	Manchester, England	L	10	—	125
Oct 26	⊛	Jackie Paterson	Glasgow, Scotland	W	10	—	124
Nov 14	⊛	Theo Medina	Paris	W	10	—	122
1950							
Mar 7		Harold Dade	Los Angeles	W	10	—	132
May 31	⊛	Vic Toweel	Johannesburg	L	15	Lost-World-B	117
Nov 10		Jackie McCoy	Hollywood	W	10	—	131
Dec 5	⊛	Eddie Chavez	San Jose	L	10	—	130
1951							
Jan 26	⊛	Lauro Salas	Hollywood	L	10	—	129
Mar 3		Bonnie Espinosa	Manila	KO	8	—	125
Jun 2		Tirso del Rosario	Manila	L	10	—	125
Jul 17		Jackie Graves	Los Angeles	L	10	—	137
Sep 3	⊛	Eddie Chavez	Santa Clara, CA	L	10	—	136
1953							
Mar 6		Manuel Hernandez	Mexicali	TKO	6	—	—
1955							
Jun 10		Manuel Hernandez	Ensenada, Mexico	KO	4	—	—
Jul 22		Memo Valero	Mexicali	KO	3	—	132
Aug 16		Papelero Sanchez	Mexicali	KO	3	—	124
Dec 10		Enrique Esqueda	Mexico City	L	10	—	—

He defended his title eight times in 1943 and four times in 1944. That year, he also won a decision over Larry Bolvin and lost another to Hall of Famer Willie Pep. After a reduced schedule in 1945 because of military service, Ortiz successfully defended his title three more times in 1946. At the beginning of 1947, Harold Dade beat Ortiz to take the bantamweight title. Two months later, Ortiz recovered it by decision. That year he also suffered the only knockout of his career, dished out by Manny Ortega.

Ortiz defended his crown far less frequently during his second reign, fighting only four title challengers in three years, before facing Vic Toweel in 1950. Twelve years younger than Ortiz and fighting in his hometown of Johannesburg, South Africa, Toweel took the title in a fifteen-round decision.

Ortiz continued to fight for five more years before hanging up his gloves at 42. In retirement, he owned a farm, a ranch, and a nightclub, but when these ventures failed, he worked at a series of odd jobs until his death from a liver ailment on May 31, 1970.

CARLOS PALOMINO

W E L T E R W E I G H T

Right-handed; 5'8 ½"; 146–152 lbs.

38 bouts, 9/14/1972 to 5/30/1998

Manager: Jackie McCoy

WBC Welterweight Champion 1976–79

Hall of Fame Induction: 2004

Born: 8/10/1949, San Luis, Mexico

Carlos Palomino was one of a group of great welterweights in the late 1970s and early '80s, which also included Pipino Cuevas, Wilfred Benitez, Sugar Ray Leonard, Roberto Duran, and Thomas Hearns. Palomino was born in San Luis, Mexico, on August 10, 1949. At the age of ten, Palomino moved to Santa Ana, California, with his large family, which came to include eleven children. He did not know any English when he came to the United States but learned quickly from a tutor and from the other kids on the playground. While in high school, he worked in construction jobs after school.

Upon graduation, Palomino got a job as a welder. He started to work out at the Stanton Athletic Club to stay in shape, but he did not have any intention of becoming a boxer at that time. A trainer, Noe Cruz, was impressed with Palomino, however, and began to work with him. Palomino won four amateur bouts. He then was drafted into the United States Army and served his country as a boxer. He was the All-Army welterweight champion in 1971 and 1972. He won other amateur titles and capped off his amateur career with a victory over Sugar Ray Seales in the 1972 national AAU championship. Seales went on to the Olympics and won the United States' only boxing gold medal in the Munich Games.

Palomino elected to turn professional while continuing his education. He attended Orange Coast College and then transferred to Long Beach State, where he earned a degree in physical education and recreation. Palomino's first pro fight was a four-round decision victory over Javier Martinez on September 14, 1972. Palomino also won the rematch. He earned a draw in his next bout but won his next five straight. He was then sidelined for over a year after he suffered a shoulder injury in his victory over Tommy Coulson. Fighting almost exclusively in Los Angeles, Palomino compiled a record of 10-1-2 over his next thirteen fights. Hedgemon Lewis was his most prominent opponent during this period. Palomino fought to a draw with

A proud and determined competitor, Palomino (R) has the distinction of never suffering a knockout in his professional boxing career.

IN THE RING	WON 31	LOST 4	DRAWS 3	TB 38	KO 19	W 12	WF 0	D 3	KO'd 0	L 4	LF 0

Date	Opponent	Site	Result / Rounds		Title	Wt.
1972						
Sep 14	Javier Martinez	Los Angeles	W	4	—	146
Oct 5	Javier Martinez	Los Angeles	W	4	—	147
Nov 16	Ted Liggett	Los Angeles	D	4	—	147
1973						
Jan 19	Tim Walker	San Bernardino, CA	W	6	—	149
Feb 1	Ramon Solitario	Los Angeles	KO	3	—	146
Mar 1	Rosario Zavala	Los Angeles	W	6	—	152
Mar 29	Lalo Barriente	Los Angeles	W	6	—	149
Apr 2	Tommy Coulson	Los Angeles	W	6	—	147
1974						
May 3	David Arellano	San Diego	W	8	—	146
May 23	Juan Garza	Los Angeles	KO	3	—	149
Jun 14	David Arellano	San Diego	KO	9	—	148
Aug 2	Andy Price	San Diego	L	10	—	146
Oct 10	Nelson Ruiz	Los Angeles	KO	6	—	146
Oct 24	Jose Miranda	Los Angeles	KO	6	—	146
Dec 20	Tommy Howard	Los Angeles	W	10	—	149
1975						
Feb 13	Zovek Barajas	Los Angeles	D	10	—	147
Mar 27	Zovek Barajas	Los Angeles	TKO	9	—	148
May 23	Roger Buckskin	Los Angeles	W	10	—	148
Jul 19	Johnny Pinedo	Los Angeles	KO	2	—	148
Oct 25	Eddie Alexander	Los Angeles	TKO	5	—	147
Nov 22	Hedgemon Lewis	Los Angeles	D	10	—	147
1976						
Feb 12	Mike Avans	Los Angeles	W	10	—	149
Apr 29	Toshiharu Nambu	Los Angeles	TKO	2	—	149
Jun 22	♛ John Stracey	Wembley, England	TKO	12	Won-WBC-W	145
1977						
Jan 22	⑩ Armando Muniz	Los Angeles	TKO	15	Ret-WBC-W	146
Jun 14	⑩ Dave ("Boy") Green	Wembley	KO	11	Ret-WBC-W	147
Sep 13	⑩ Everaldo Costa Azevedo	Los Angeles	W	15	Ret-WBC-W	147
Dec 10	⑩ Jose Palacios	Los Angeles	KO	13	Ret-WBC-W	147
1978						
Feb 11	Ryu Sorimachi	Las Vegas	KO	7	Ret-WBC-W	147
Mar 18	Mimoun Mohatar	Las Vegas	TKO	9	Ret-WBC-W	147
May 27	⑩ Armando Muniz	Los Angeles	W	15	Ret-WBC-W	147
1979						
Jan 14	♛ Wilfred Benitez★	San Juan, PR	L	15	Lost-WBC-W	146
Jun 22	Roberto Duran	New York	L	10	—	145
1997						
Jan 10	Ismael Diaz	Hollywood, CA	KO	8	—	147
May 9	Wilbur Garst	Hollywood	KO	2	—	149
Jun 8	Rene Arredondo	Hollywood	KO	1	—	148
Oct 26	Eric Vazquez	Bakersfield, CA	KO	9	—	147
1998						
May 30	Wilfredo Rivera	Los Angeles	L	10	—	148

Lewis. A second-round knockout of Toshiharu Nambu led to a shot at the welterweight title held by John H. Stracey.

Palomino met Stracey at Wembley Empire Pool in England in front of a crowd of 8,000 on June 22, 1976. In the early rounds, champion and challenger went toe to toe. Palomino proved to be the stronger. Stracey fired ineffective jabs and left himself open for Palomino's attacks. In the twelfth round, a Palomino hook sent Stracey to the canvas. He came to his feet but another left sent him down again. He got up once more but slumped helplessly against the ropes as Palomino peppered him with blows—until the referee stopped the fight. Palomino earned $10,000 for his efforts.

Palomino's first title defense was delayed until January 22, 1977, because he chipped a bone in his right hand while training for the fight with Armando Muniz. Palomino stopped Muniz in the fifteenth round. For his next defense he journeyed back to Wembley to face Dave ("Boy") Green, his former sparring partner. In a hard-hitting fight, Palomino emerged victorious. He fired a great left hook in the eleventh that knocked Green out. It was the first time in 109 amateur fights and 24 professional fights that Green had been knocked down. The blow had such an effect that 45 minutes later Green did not know what had happened. Palomino closed out a busy 1977 with title defenses against Everaldo Costa Azevedo and Jose Palacios.

In 1978, Palomino successfully defended his title three times. In the last defense—a decision over Muniz—Palomino broke his left hand. As a result, he did not fight again until January 14, 1979, when he traveled to San Juan to face Hall of Famer Wilfred Benitez in Hiram Bithorn Stadium. The twenty-year-old Benitez outboxed Palomino to earn a split-decision victory. Palomino was well compensated for the bout, making $465,000.

Palomino next faced all-time great Roberto Duran on the undercard of the Larry Holmes–Mike Weaver heavyweight championship bout in New York. Duran out-boxed Palomino to win a ten-round decision. Palomino admitted after the fight that he was not the fighter he had been five years before. He announced his retirement and concentrated on becoming an actor. Soon, he appeared in episodes of the television shows *Taxi* and *The White Shadow*. He also was in two extremely popular commercials for Lite Beer from Miller. He worked seriously at his craft, taking acting and voice lessons. Palomino appeared in many movies, television shows, and plays over the years. He also stayed involved with boxing as a member of the California State Athletic Commission.

He was shaken when his younger brother, Paul, died in the tragic 1980 plane crash that claimed the lives of many of the United States' top amateur boxers. To an extent, Palomino blamed himself for Paul's death because he had advised his brother to remain an amateur rather than turn professional.

In his retirement from pugilism, Palomino stayed in shape through long distance running. He ran in many marathons. After his father's death in 1996, Palomino felt a need to return to the ring. First, he just sparred. Then he decided to make a full-fledged comeback at the unlikely age of 47. He won his first four fights by knockout. He stepped up in class to face ranked welterweight Wilfredo Rivera on May 30, 1998. Rivera won a ten-round decision as he primarily worked the body. Palomino's trademark left hook bloodied Rivera's mouth in the tenth round. Palomino retired after the fight and renewed his commitment to acting. During the last several years, his silver screen appearances include roles in: *Detonator* (1998), *If . . . Dog . . . Rabbit* (1999), *Price of Glory* (2000), and *American Crime* (2004). Recent television parts have included the title role in "The Boxer"—an episode of *Star Trek Voyager*—and Mr. Sanchez in an episode of the comedy *Sibling Rivalry*.

WORLD WELTERWEIGHT CHAMPIONSHIP

CARLOS 15 RDS. MANDO

PALOMINO vs MUNIZ

KO'd John Stracey to win title

WORLD CHAMPION   NO. 3 CONTENDER

Bruising KO Puncher. Predicts he'll win crown

PETE **RANZANI**   No.6 10 Rds. **VS** Welterweight   ABEL **CORDOBA** KO Artist

Sat. Jan. 22 6:30 PM OLYMPIC AUD.

TICKET PRICES:
RINGSIDE $30.00
LOWER & UPPER BALCONY $15.00
GENERAL ADMISSION $10.00

TICKETS ON SALE: OLYMPIC AUD.,
1801 S. Grand, RI 9-5171 MISSION
JEWELERS, 256 S. Broadway
628-7796, NACHO HUIZAR, Tijuana,

OSTIONERIA MI HACIENDA, 5949
Whittier Bl.; TICKETRON AGENCIES,
MONTGOMERY WARD, BROADWAY
SEARS, PH. 670-3315

WORLD'S WELTERWEIGHT CHAMPIONSHIP

CARLOS   15 Rounds   JOSE

PALOMINO vs PALACIOS

WORLD CHAMPION   TOP CHALLENGER - MEXICO

SAT. DEC. 10 7:00 P.M. OLYMPIC AUD

PLUS GREAT ALL STAR CARD

RESERVED TICKETS
RINGSIDE $30.00
LOWER BAL. $20.00
UPPER BAL. $15.00
CLUB CIRCLE $15.00

TICKETS ON SALE: OLYMPIC AUD., 1801 S. Grand Ave., Los Angeles, RI 9-5171
MISSION JEWELERS   TICKETRON OUTLETS   LIBERIAS Y DISCOTECA MEXICO
256 S. Broadway, L.A.   MAY CO., SEARS, WARDS   314 E. 4th St., Santa Ana 714-547-7663

PROMOTER: AILEEN EATON   MATCHMAKER: DON CHARGIN

Over a dozen of Palomino's bouts—including these two welterweight title defenses—were held at Los Angeles's Olympic Auditorium. Hall of Famer Don Chargin was the matchmaker and Hall of Famer Aileen Eaton was the promoter at this famed fistic venue.

LASZLO PAPP
Laci Bacsi (Uncle Laci)

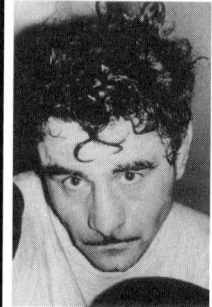

MIDDLEWEIGHT

Left-handed; 5'5½"; 157-166 lbs.

29 bouts, 5/19/1957 to 10/9/1964

1948 Olympic Middleweight Gold Medalist

1952, 1956 Olympic Light Middleweight Gold Medalist

Hall of Fame Induction: 2001

Born: 3/25/1926, Angyaföld, Hungary

Died: 10/16/2003

Laszlo Papp had one of the most unusual careers of any fighter in the International Boxing Hall of Fame.

As a youth in Hungary, Papp initially preferred soccer, track, and wrestling to boxing. After much cajoling, his friends persuaded him to join them at the Budapest Railwayman's Club to learn the sport. Papp quickly displayed a natural flair for fighting. Club officials decided to keep him under wraps by restricting him to fights in the outlying provinces. On October 6, 1945, a tournament was held at Budapest's Sports Hall to select a team to represent Hungary in an upcoming series of matches against Austria. Papp was asked to step in at the last minute to fill a cancellation, and he knocked out his opponent in the second round to earn a place on the Hungarian national team. Papp easily won his bout in Austria, starting a long career of international triumphs.

Papp had 50 amateur boxing wins (47 by knockout) before he represented Hungary as a middleweight at the 1948 London Olympics. He won all five of his matches and the gold medal.

American medalists usually turn pro shortly after their Olympic victories, to cash in on their fame. Because Papp's native Hungary was, at that time, a part of the Soviet-ruled

Boxing Illustrated *correspondent Jose Alvarez congratulates Papp after his 1963 eighth-round knockout of Luis Folledo in Madrid.*

IN THE RING	WON 27	LOST 0	DRAWS 2	TB 29	KO 15	W 12	WF 0	D 2	KO'd 0	L 0	LF 0

Date	Opponent	Site	Result / Rounds		Title	Wt.
1957						
May 19	Alois Brand	Cologne, Germany	W	4	—	—
Jun 15	Herbert Sowa	Dortmund, Germany	W	4	—	—
Jun 28	Gerhard Moll	Hamburg, Germany	W	6	—	—
1958						
Oct 17	Hugo Koehler	Vienna	KO	6	—	—
Dec 15	Francois Anewy	Paris	KO	3	—	—
1959						
Feb 9	Andre Drille	Paris	W	10	—	—
Mar 16	Jean Ruellet	Vienna	W	10	—	—
Apr 13	Germinal Ballarin	Paris	D	10	—	—
Sep 10	Bill Tate	Vienna	KO	3	—	—
1960						
Feb 10	Lou Perry	Vienna	W	10	—	—
Sep 23	Erich Walter	Vienna	KO	9	—	—
Oct 1	Mohammed Boudib	Agram, Yugoslavia	KO	7	—	—
Dec 26	Giancarlo Garbelli	Milan, Italy	D	10	—	162
1961						
Feb 20	Sauveur Chiocca	Paris	W	10	—	—
Apr 8	Moussa Sangare	Vienna	W	10	—	166
Sep 10	Peter Mueller	Cologne	TKO	8	—	—
Oct 13	Peter Mueller	Vienna	TKO	4	—	—
Dec 2	Michel Francois	Frankfurt	KO	2	—	—
1962						
Mar 21	Ralph ("Tiger") Jones	Vienna	W	10	—	159
May 16	Christian Christensen	Vienna	TKO	7	Won-Eur-M	157
Nov 19	Hippolyte Annex	Paris	TKO	9	Ret-Eur-M	157
1963						
Feb 6	George Aldridge	Vienna	KO	15	Ret-Eur-M	159
Mar 30	Peter Mueller	Dortmund	TKO	4	Ret-Eur-M	157
May 17	Randy Sandy	Vienna	W	10	—	158
Jun 14	Eddie Cotton	Cologne	KO	7	—	158
Dec 6	⑩ Luis Folledo	Madrid	TKO	8	Ret-Eur-M	157
1964						
Mar 13	Harry Scott	Vienna	W	10	—	158
Jul 2	Christian Christensen	Copenhagen	KO	4	Ret-Eur-M	158
Oct 9	⑩ Mick Leahy	Vienna	W	15	Ret-Eur-M	158

Eastern Bloc, he wasn't permitted to compete professionally. Relegated to the ranks of amateur pugilism, Papp continued to accumulate honors, including two victories at the European amateur championships and three wins at the World Student Games.

But Papp made his greatest impact on the boxing scene in the Olympic Games. He slimmed down one weight class and earned two more gold medals as a light middleweight in 1952 and 1956. Times were difficult in Hungary in the early 1950s. Opportunities to train were difficult to secure, and jobs—required even for Olympic-grade athletes—were scarce. Fortunately, Papp found employment that helped build up his strength and endurance. At work, his duties included carrying heavy packages up and down stairs.

In the semifinals of the latter competition, Papp decisioned Zbiginiew Pietrykowski, who had stopped him short of the three-round amateur limit for the first time in his career earlier that year in Warsaw. He also decisioned future light heavyweight champion and Hall of Famer Jose Torres in the finals. The short-lived Hungarian revolt against Soviet occupation took place just before the Hungarian team left for the 1956 Olympics in Melbourne, Australia. Papp was a devoted Roman Catholic and was deeply saddened by the death and suffering resulting from the repression of the Hungarian revolt. His belief was that his participation in the 1956 Olympics, at a time when his nation was experiencing such trauma, would help turn the world's attention to Hungary's plight. Though a third of the Hungarian team defected to the West after the Games, Papp was among the athletes who returned to their homeland.

Papp stood alone as the first Olympic boxer to win three gold medals. Since then, Cubans Teofilo Stevenson (in 1972, 1976, and 1980) and Felix Savon (in 1992, 1996, and 2000) have matched this Herculean feat, but it has never been surpassed. After winning three gold medals, Papp wished to test his skill against professional boxers, who were naturally barred from Olympic competition. In an unprecedented move, Hungary allowed Papp to compete professionally. Through his ring earnings, or perhaps from a more direct government grant, Papp acquired the use of a

Hoisted onto his supporters' shoulders like the heroes of old, Papp joyously celebrates his victory over Christian Christensen in Vienna on May 16, 1962, to take the European middleweight title.

villa on the Danube and an expensive car. His wife and son were allowed to travel much more frequently than most Hungarians, shuttling between Budapest and Vienna, where Papp trained.

In the ring, Papp met his first professional opponent on May 19, 1957, winning a four-round decision over Alois Brand in Cologne, Germany. At 31, Papp was considered old for the sport, especially since he was just making his debut. He won his next six fights, including a wild brawl with Andre Drille who knocked Papp down twice before succumbing to the Hungarian. Papp floored Drille five times to win the ten-round decision. On April 13, 1959, Papp faced Germinal Ballarin in Paris. Although most observers believed that he won seven of ten rounds, the fight was called a draw. Of greater consequence was a broken hand that Papp suffered during the fight. He did not fight again for five months. The next year, Papp defeated American Lou Perry, but he broke his left hand again, this time so severely that he required surgery. Though he was out of action for another seven months, he won his first two fights before recording a draw against Giancarlo Garbelli in Milan, though this may have been the result of hometown scoring.

On March 21, 1962, Papp faced his first well-known American opponent, Ralph ("Tiger") Jones, a former middleweight contender who had once beaten Sugar Ray Robinson. Papp knocked Jones down three times to win an easy decision. In his next fight, at the Vienna City Hall on May 16, Papp fought European champion Christian Christensen for the latter's title. Each man was cut in the second round, yet Papp held the advantage in the first three, scoring with right hooks. Indeed, his right hook was an effective weapon for the left-handed Papp, who was able to lead with both hands and was an effective boxer/puncher. Christensen won the fourth round, but in the fifth Papp floored him with a hard right hook, and in the seventh another blow opened a cut near Christensen's eye. At the end of the round, the referee stopped the fight at the orders of the ringside doctor. Papp was champion.

The next year, he won all five of his fights, including a knockout victory over ranked contender Luis Folledo. He advanced to the fourth contender spot for 1963 and held the position in 1964, defeating ranked contender Mick Leahy.

In 1964, there was some concern that Papp would be forced to abandon his career to coach the Hungarian Olympic team, but he was allowed to continue fighting. In early 1965, it appeared that he might at last receive a title shot against middleweight champion Joey Giardello. Earlier rumored fights against champions Paul Pender and Dick Tiger had fallen through. Before a date was set for the Giardello match, Papp was ordered back to Hungary. Officially, it was announced that his "professional career would not be compatible with our [Hungary's] socialist principles." Speculation as to the reasons for the decision ranged from envy at his financial success and anger at his refusal to coach the '64 Olympic team to worry that, at 38, he might not remain undefeated for much longer. Papp regretted the decision, stating, "I'm very sorry about all this. I was hoping they would change their minds, but the ruling was definite—I am not supposed to box as a professional anymore."

In retirement, Papp served for many years as coach of the Hungarian boxing team. He died after a long illness at age 77.

WILLIE PASTRANO
Willie The Wisp

LIGHT HEAVYWEIGHT

Right handed; 5'11¾"; 122–191 lbs.

84 bouts, 9/10/1951 to 3/30/1965

Managers: Whitey Esneault, Angelo Dundee

Light Heavyweight Champ 1963–65

Hall of Fame Induction: 2001

Born: 11/27/1935, New Orleans, LA

Named: Wilfred Raleigh Pastrano

Died: 12/6/1997

Willie Pastrano was perhaps the foremost practitioner of the busy jabbing, constant-motion "New Orleans–style" of fighting. Pastrano was obese as a youngster and was mercilessly taunted and beaten by neighborhood kids. He was known as "Fat-meat" for weighing 200 pounds at age ten. When he came home in tears, his father forced him to fight his tormenters. Ralph Dupas, Pastrano's friend and future world junior middleweight champ, took him to Whitey Esneault's boxing gym to get him in shape and teach him how to fight. By the time he was thirteen, Pastrano had slimmed down to featherweight size. At fourteen, he was knocked down in a street fight and vowed to give up fighting if he were ever knocked down again.

Pastrano turned pro at the age of fifteen with a four-round decision over Domingo Rivera in New Orleans on September 10, 1951. After five wins and a draw with Alvin Pellegrini, Esneault sent Pastrano to Angelo Dundee to train in Miami Beach. Fighting almost exclusively in New Orleans and Miami Beach, he compiled a 21-4-3 record through 1953, but in 1954 he won all seven of his fights, including decisions over the tough Jackie LaBua and Bobby Dykes.

Though Pastrano was light for the division, Dundee usually matched him with heavyweights, where the purses were larger. In 1955, Pastrano had another banner year, winning decisions over Hall of Famer Joey Maxim, ranked light heavyweight Chuck Spieser, and former ranked heavyweight Rex Layne. 1956 saw more of the same, with decisions over Spieser, future heavyweight contender Pat McMurtry, and former contender Charlie Norkus. The next year he met Roy ("Cut and Shoot") Harris,

Hall of Famer Angelo Dundee (R) started training Pastrano at Miami Beach in the summer of 1952.

IN THE RING	WON 63	LOST 13	DRAWS 8	TB 84	KO 14	W 49	WF 0	D 8	KO'd 2	L 11	LF 0

Date	Opponent	Site	Result / Rounds		Title	Wt.
1951						
Sep 10	Domingo Rivera	New Orleans	W	4	—	127
Sep 17	Frank Speed	New Orleans	W	4	—	122
Oct 1	Jimmy Connino	New Orleans	W	4	—	129
Oct 22	Domingo Rivera	New Orleans	W	4	—	—
1952						
Apr 1	Alvin Boudreaux	New Orleans	W	4	—	144
Apr 21	Alvin Pellegrini	New Orleans	D	4	—	143
Jul 1	Buzz Brown	Miami Beach	KO	2	—	—
Jul 8	John Chaney	Miami Beach	W	6	—	—
Jul 22	Al McCoy	Miami Beach	KO	2	—	—
Jul 28	Jim Carter	Pensacola, FL	KO	4	—	—
Aug 5	Sonny Luciano	Miami Beach	W	8	—	—
Aug 19	Sonny Luciano	Miami Beach	W	8	—	—
Sep 8	Johnny Capitano	New Orleans	W	6	—	139
Oct 6	Alvin Pellegrini	New Orleans	L	6	—	147
Oct 14	Lonnie Rylant	New Orleans	KO	3	—	144
Nov 17	Alvin Pellegrini	New Orleans	W	6	—	144
Nov 24	Alvin Boudreaux	New Orleans	KO	2	—	147
Dec 15	Alvin Pellegrini	New Orleans	D	8	—	145
1953						
Jan 26	Alfredo LaGrutta	New Orleans	W	8	—	146
Feb 24	Emerson Butcher	New Orleans	W	8	—	148
Mar 3	Chic Boucher	Miami Beach	KO	3	—	145
Mar 16	Roger Trevino	New Orleans	W	8	—	147
Apr 6	Chato Hernandez	New Orleans	W	8	—	147
May 25	Johnny Cesario	New Orleans	L	8	—	148
Jul 14	Del Flanagan	Miami Beach	L	8	—	154
Sep 22	Elmer Beltz	Miami Beach	D	10	—	158
Oct 5	Elmer Beltz	New Orleans	W	8	—	154
Nov 30	Italo Scortichini	New Orleans	L	10	—	156
1954						
Mar 29	Jimmy Martinez	New Orleans	W	10	—	157
Apr 12	Jacques Royer-Crecy	New Orleans	W	10	—	158
Jun 18	Tommy Hatcher	Mobile, AL	KO	1	—	—
Aug 9	Tommy Bazzano	New Orleans	KO	8	—	161
Aug 24	Jimmy Martinez	Miami Beach	W	10	—	161
Sep 14	Jackie LaBua	Miami Beach	W	10	—	162
Nov 23	Bobby Dykes	Miami Beach	W	10	—	166
1955						
Mar 1	Tony Johnson	Miami Beach	W	10	—	167
Mar 23	Al Andrews	Chicago	W	10	—	164
Apr 22	Willie Troy	Chicago	D	10	—	166
Jun 28	⑩ Joey Maxim★	New Orleans	W	10	—	176
Jul 27	⑩ Chuck Spieser	Chicago	W	10	—	175
Oct 3	Paddy Young	New Orleans	W	10	—	175
Nov 18	Joey Rowan	New York	W	10	—	181
Dec 19	⑩ Rex Layne	New Orleans	W	10	—	185

1956

Date		Opponent	Location	Result	Rounds		Weight
Jan 27	⑩	Chuck Spieser	Miami Beach	D	10	—	182
Apr 4		Johnny Arthur	New Orleans	W	10	—	188
May 30	⑩	Chuck Spieser	New Orleans	W	10	—	182
Aug 24		Pat McMurtry	Tacoma, WA	W	10	—	186
Dec 26		Charlie Norkus	Miami Beach	W	10	—	189

1957

Date		Opponent	Location	Result	Rounds		Weight
Feb 20		John Holman	Louisville, KY	W	10	—	187
May 14		Neal Welch	Miami Beach	W	10	—	192
Jun 11		Roy Harris	Houston	L	10	—	187
Sep 10		George Peyton	Miami Beach	KO	8	—	191
Oct 22		Dick Richardson	London	W	10	—	188
Nov 27	⑩	Willie Besmanoff	Miami Beach	W	10	—	190

1958

Date		Opponent	Location	Result	Rounds		Weight
Feb 25	⑩	Brian London	London	W	10	—	187
Apr 21		Joe Bygraves	Leicester, England	W	10	—	187
Jun 15		Franco Cavicchi	Bologna, Italy	W	10	—	189
Aug 25		Tommy Thompson	Colombus, OH	KO	4	—	188
Sep 30	⑩	Brian London	London	TKO'd	5	—	187

1959

Date		Opponent	Location	Result	Rounds		Weight
Feb 24		Joe Erskine	London	L	10	—	185
Jul 24		Alonzo Johnson	Louisville	L	10	—	187
Aug 30		Tom Davis	Knoxville, TN	KO	4	—	185
Dec 7		Charley Pavlis	Tampa, FL	W	10	—	180

1960

Date		Opponent	Location	Result	Rounds		Weight
Jan 20		Jerry Luedee	Miami Beach	W	10	—	177
Apr 9		George Kartalian	Augusta, GA	KO	6	—	177
May 6		Alonzo Johnson	Louisville	W	10	—	178
Jun 1	⑩	Sonny Ray	Chicago	W	10	—	175
Sep 16	⑩	Chic Calderwood	Glasgow, Scotland	L	10	—	177
Dec 27	⑩	Jesse Bowdry	Miami Beach	L	10	—	180

1961

Date		Opponent	Location	Result	Rounds		Weight
Aug 6		Lennart Risberg	Stockholm	D	12	—	178

1962

Date		Opponent	Location	Result	Rounds		Weight
May 1		Tom McNeeley	Boston	W	10	—	185
May 28	⑩	Archie Moore★	Los Angeles	D	10	—	185
Jun 25		Billy Ryan	New Orleans	W	10	—	181
Sep 8		Rodolfo Diaz	Miami Beach	W	10	—	184

1963

Date		Opponent	Location	Result	Rounds		Weight
Feb 9	⑩	Wayne Thornton	New York	L	10	—	176
Mar 23	⑩	Wayne Thornton	New York	D	10	—	175
May 4	⑩	Wayne Thornton	Las Vegas	W	10	—	177
Jun 1	♛	Harold Johnson★	Las Vegas	W	15	Won-World-LH	174
Aug 31		Ollie Wilson	Jacksonville, FL	W	10	—	180
Sep 20	⑩	Gregorio Peralta	Miami Beach	L	10	—	179
Nov 30		Mike Holt	Johannesburg	W	10	—	178

1964

Date		Opponent	Location	Result	Rounds		Weight
Apr 10	⑩	Gregorio Peralta	New Orleans	KO	6	Ret-World-LH	174
Nov 30	⑩	Terry Downes	Manchester, England	KO	11	Ret-World-LH	174

1965

Date		Opponent	Location	Result	Rounds		Weight
Mar 30	⑩	Jose Torres★	New York	KO'd	10	Lost-World-LH	174

with a strong possibility that the winner of the fight would get a title shot against heavyweight champ Floyd Patterson. Pastrano clearly lost the decision.

In 1958, for the first time in his career, Pastrano was stopped within the distance by Brian London, whom he had previously defeated. The referee stopped the fight after five rounds because of a cut on Pastrano's eyelid. He won only six of his next ten fights.

While in Louisville for a fight, Pastrano sparred with a young amateur named Cassius Clay. Afterwards, he told Dundee he would only fight Clay again if he was paid for it. "Angie, this kid's got it. I know it," said Pastrano. Some credit Pastrano with helping Ali develop his distinctive style.

Dundee and Pastrano now decided that he should fight at his more natural weight class of light heavyweight. After stripping Archie Moore of its title, the NBA set up a tournament in which Hall of Famer Harold Johnson would face the winner of a Pastrano–Jesse Bowdry fight for the championship. Pastrano lost a unanimous decision to Bowdry on December 27, 1960, in Miami Beach. Pastrano fought only once in the next sixteen months. In 1962, he fought Archie Moore to a draw.

Light heavyweight champion Johnson now turned to Pastrano after fights with Mauro Mina and Henry Hank fell through because of injuries. Pastrano was reluctant, but when offered $21,500, he agreed to the match, held at the Las Vegas Convention Center on June 1, 1963. Pastrano, a five-to-one underdog, used jabs and occasional rights while moving from side to side to pile up points, sometimes switching to right jabs from a southpaw stance to confuse Johnson. Pastrano won a narrow decision to become the champion.

Pastrano successfully defended his title twice before facing Jose Torres on March 30, 1965, in Madison Square Garden. Torres attacked him from the start and

bloodied his nose in the first round, then knocked him down in the sixth. Referee Johnny Lobiano wouldn't allow a dazed Pastrano to answer the bell in the tenth, and true to his word so long ago, he never fought again.

Retirement was not kind to Pastrano, and he developed a serious heroin habit that he finally managed to kick in 1969. Finally, he returned to New Orleans and worked in a youth boxing program, managing a few fighters. Pastrano died of cancer in New Orleans on December 6, 1997.

Pastrano's (R) first New York fight was against Joey Rowan on November 18, 1955. His eyes swollen to slits, Pastrano connects with a solid right.

FLOYD PATTERSON

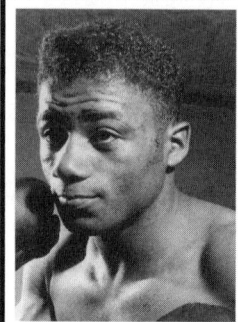

HEAVYWEIGHT

Right-handed; 6'; 163–200 lbs.
64 bouts, 9/12/1952 to 9/20/1972
Manager: Cus D'Amato, Dan Florio
1952 Olympic Middleweight
Gold Medalist
Hvywt. Champ 1956-59, 1960-62
Hall of Fame Induction: 1991
Born: 1/4/1935, Waco, NC
Died: May 11, 2006

Floyd Patterson's pleasant face and demeanor belied the ferocity he showed in the ring. A quiet tiger, Patterson was seldom the favorite in his bouts with other past and future champions, but he was the youngest heavyweight yet to win the title, and he wore the crown twice. He was also among the lightest of the modern heavyweight champions, never topping 200 pounds.

Patterson was born into a large family in North Carolina, but he grew up in one of New York's toughest black ghettos. He got into trouble early in life and spent some time in reform school, where he first learned to box. He was discovered by manager Cus D'Amato, who helped build him into championship material. (D'Amato would later present Mike Tyson to the boxing world.) Patterson trained

Keeping his left held high, Patterson (L) goes at aging Archie Moore with a straight right. Patterson took the title with a fifth-round KO in this 1956 matchup to replace retired champ Rocky Marciano.

Date	Opponent	Site	Result / Rounds		Title	Wt.
1952						
Sep 12	Eddie Godbold	New York	TKO	4	—	164
Oct 6	Sammy Walker	Brooklyn	TKO	2	—	166
Oct 21	Lester Johnson	New York	TKO	3	—	165
Dec 19	Lalu Sabotin	Brooklyn	TKO	5	—	167
1953						
Jan 28	Chester Mieszala	Chicago	TKO	5	—	163
Apr 3	Dick Wagner	Brooklyn	W	8	—	166
Jun 1	Gordon Wallace	Brooklyn	TKO	3	—	165
Oct 19	Wes Bascom	Brooklyn	W	8	—	166
Dec 14	Dick Wagner	Brooklyn	TKO	5	—	167
1954						
Feb 15	Yvon Durelle	Brooklyn	W	8	—	167
Mar 30	Sam Brown	Washington, DC	TKO	2	—	167
May 10	Jesse Turner	Brooklyn	W	8	—	167
Jun 7	⑩ Joey Maxim★	Brooklyn	L	8	—	165
Jul 12	Jacques Royer-Crecy	New York	TKO	7	—	168
Aug 2	Tommy Harrison	Brooklyn	TKO	1	—	164
Sep 14	Alvin Williams	Brooklyn	W	8	—	169
Oct 11	Ferdinand Esau	New York	W	8	—	169
Oct 22	Joe Gannon	New York	W	8	—	170
Nov 19	⑩ Jimmy Slade	New York	W	8	—	169
1955						
Jan 7	⑩ Willie Troy	New York	TKO	5	—	166
Jan 17	Don Grant	Brooklyn	TKO	5	—	168
Mar 17	Ferdinand Esau	Oakland	TKO	10	—	174
Jun 23	Yvon Durelle	Newcastle, DE	TKO	5	—	170
Jul 6	Archie McBride	New York	KO	7	—	170
Sep 8	Alvin Williams	Moncton, N.B.	TKO	8	—	177
Sep 29	⑩ Dave Whitlock	San Francisco	TKO	3	—	175
Oct 13	Calvin Brad	Los Angeles	KO	1	—	175
Dec 8	⑩ Jimmy Slade	Los Angeles	TKO	7	—	178
1956						
Mar 12	Jimmy Walls	New Britain, CT	TKO	2	—	183
Apr 10	Alvin Williams	Kansas City, MO	KO	3	—	183
Jun 8	⑩ Tommy Jackson	New York	W	12	—	178
Nov 30	⑩ Archie Moore★	Chicago	KO	5	Won-Vac World-H	182
1957						
Jul 29	⑩ Tommy Jackson	New York	TKO	10	Ret-World-H	184
Aug 22	Pete Rademacher	Seattle	KO	6	Ret-World-H	187
1958						
Aug 18	⑩ Roy Harris	Los Angeles	TKO	13	Ret-World-H	184
1959						
May 1	⑩ Brian London	London	KO	11	Ret-World-H	182
Jun 26	⑩ Ingemar Johansson★	New York	TKO'd	3	Lost-World-H	182
1960						
Jun 20	♛ Ingemar Johansson★	New York	KO	5	Reg-World-H	190
1961						
Mar 13	⑩ Ingemar Johansson★	Miami Beach	KO	6	Ret-World-H	194

Dec 4		Tom McNeeley	Toronto	KO	4	Ret-World-H	188
1962							
Sep 25	ⓦ	Sonny Liston★	Chicago	KO'd	1	Lost-World-H	189
1963							
Jul 22	♛	Sonny Liston★	Las Vegas	KO'd	1	For-World-H	194
1964							
Jan 6		Dante Amonti	Stockholm	TKO	8	—	192
Jul 5	ⓦ	Eddie Machen	Stockholm	W	12	—	192
Dec 12		Charles Powell	San Juan, PR	KO	6	—	197
1965							
Feb 1	ⓦ	George Chuvalo	New York	W	12	—	197
May 14		Tod Herring	Stockholm	TKO	3	—	196
Nov 22	♛	Muhammad Ali★	Las Vegas	TKO'd	12	For-World-H	196
1966							
Sep 29		Henry Cooper	London	KO	4	—	193
1967							
Feb 13		Willie Johnson	Miami Beach	KO	3	—	200
Mar 30		Bill McMurray	Pittsburgh	KO	1	—	197
Jun 9	ⓦ	Jerry Quarry	Los Angeles	D	10	—	194
Oct 28	ⓦ	Jerry Quarry	Los Angeles	L	12	—	195
1968							
Sep 14	♛	Jimmy Ellis	Stockholm	L	15	For-WBA-H	188
1970							
Sep 15		Charlie Green	New York	KO	10	—	186
1971							
Jan 16		Levi Forte	Miami Beach	TKO	2	—	192
Mar 29		Roger Russell	Philadelphia	TKO	9	—	190
May 26		Terry Daniels	Cleveland	W	10	—	190
Jul 17		Charley Polite	Erie, PA	W	10	—	190
Aug 21		Vic Brown	Buffalo, NY	W	10	—	189
Nov 23		Charlie Harris	Portland, OR	KO	6	—	195
1972							
Feb 11	ⓦ	Oscar Bonavena	New York	W	10	—	191
Jul 14		Pedro Agosto	New York	TKO	6	—	193
Sep 20	ⓦ	Muhammad Ali★	New York	TKO'd	7	For-NABF-H	188

and fought in D'Amato's Gramercy Park Gym and compiled a fine amateur record. In 1952, he won a gold medal in the 165-pound class at the Olympic Games in Helsinki.

Patterson then turned professional, fighting as a light heavyweight. He won his first twelve bouts before losing a decision to Hall of Famer Joey Maxim, then went on to win another 23 straight fights. By 1956, he was picked for a shot at the world heavyweight title (which Rocky Marciano had vacated upon his retirement) in a bout with veteran fighter Archie Moore. Moore was older and slower, but he was also a master of the ring who had beaten the best men of his time, and the odds were heavily in his favor. But Patterson had trained hard and he made short work of Moore, knocking him out in the fifth round. At 21, Patterson had become heavyweight champion of the world.

Patterson is often criticized for the string of second-rate challengers he accepted, but D'Amato refused to match him with any fighter controlled by promoter James Norris and his corrupt International Boxing Club. Patterson therefore found few worthy opponents, and D'Amato was forced to import fighters for private bouts with Patterson to keep him sharp. When Swedish champion Ingemar Johansson appeared on the scene in 1959, a genuine championship fight was in the offing. This time, Patterson was the favorite, but after two hard-fought rounds, Johansson caught Patterson with a powerful right cross that put the champ down in the third. Patterson got up and was knocked down again a half-dozen times before referee Ruby Goldstein called an end to the fight.

A year later, Patterson was back, looking to regain the title. Patterson shook off the effects of a Johansson right in round two and, in the fifth, he knocked Johansson down with a sweeping left hook. Johansson got up only to meet a second left hook that put him down for good. Patterson thus became the first man to regain the heavyweight championship. The two fought a third time, in March 1961, in a wild melee in which Patterson was knocked down twice and Johansson once in the first round. Patterson triumphed with a sixth-round knockout. Patterson KO'd Tom McNeeley in December 1961 in a title bout, then faced a boxer many said he had been avoiding: Sonny Liston. Here D'Amato, who was criticized for being overly protective of his fighter, and Patterson parted ways.

The match with Liston was one of the shortest title fights on record. Within two minutes, Patterson was sprawled on the canvas and Liston was champ. In the rematch, Liston again took Patterson out in one round. Patterson had two more shots at the title but lost both, to Muhammad Ali and Jimmy Ellis. After a second loss to Ali in 1972, Patterson retired. His distinctive peek-a-boo style—keeping his gloves high in front of his face—had led him to win 55 fights and two world championships. In retirement, Patterson remained active in boxing. His adopted son, Tracy Patterson, had a very successful career in the ring, partly under his father's management. In 1995, Governor George Pataki appointed Patterson chairman of the New York State Athletic Commission. He died in 2006 after battling Alzheimer's disease and prostate cancer.

Floyd Patterson vigorously works the heavy bag.

EUSEBIO PEDROZA
El Alacrán (The Scorpion)

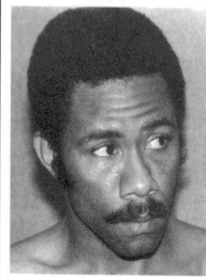

FEATHERWEIGHT

Left handed; 5'9"; 117–137 lbs.

50 bouts, 12/1/1973 to 11/21/1992

Manager: Santiago Del Rio

WBA Featherweight Champion 1978–85

Hall of Fame Induction: 1999

Born: 3/2/1953, Panama City, Panama

One of the top featherweight fighters of the 1970s and '80s, Eusebio Pedroza held his WBA featherweight championship title from 1978 to 1985, successfully defending it an impressive nineteen times.

Pedroza grew up in the poor Maranon neighborhood of Panama City. He boxed professionally by age twenty, winning his first bout with a knock-out victory over Julio Garcia. Competing as a bantamweight, he won fourteen of his first fifteen fights.

Pedroza received a title shot against WBA bantamweight champion Alfonso Zamora in Mexicali, Mexico, April 3, 1976. Zamora, champion and 1972 Olympic silver medalist at only 22, stood undefeated and had won all his 24 fights by knockout. Although at 5'9" Pedroza was seven inches taller than his opponent and faster, he could not defeat Zamora. The champ knocked Pedroza out in the second round with his much-vaunted left hook.

Pedroza (R) unleases a combination to the head of then-undefeated Bernard Taylor in their October 16, 1982, meeting in Charlotte, NC. Just starting his third year as a pro, Taylor took champion Pedroza to a fifteen-round draw.

By 1978, Pedroza had moved up to featherweight, and on April 15, 1978, he again went up against a champion, this time WBA featherweight title-holder Cecilio Lastra. The Lastra–Pedroza matchup was held in Panama City, before more than 12,000 Pedroza fans; he did not disappoint them. Pedroza beat Lastra onto the canvas in the third round, closed his eye later in the same round, and floored him twice in the thirteenth, ending the fight and winning the title.

IN THE RING	WON 42	LOST 6	DRAWS 1	TB 50	KO 26	W 15	WF 0	D 1	KO'd 3	L 3	LF 0	NC 1

Date	Opponent	Site	Result / Rounds		Title	Wt.
1973						
Dec 1	Julio Garcia	Panama City	TKO	4	—	120
Dec 22	Jose Santana	Panama City	W	4	—	122
1974						
Feb 8	Jorge Bernal	Panama City	W	6	—	121
Mar 1	Loitolier Chacon Plata	Panama City	TKO	1	—	121
Mar 30	Jacinto Fuentes	Panama City	KO	1	—	117
May 4	Ricardo Vega	Panama City	TKO	2	—	117
Jun 14	Ernesto Davis	Panama City	KO	1	—	120
Jul 20	Vicente Worrel	Panama City	KO	1	—	119
Sep 14	Senen Rios	Panama City	TKO	6	—	120
1975						
Jan 15	Alfonso Perez	Panama City	TKO'd	3	—	124
Feb 22	Ernesto Mathias	Panama City	TW	8	—	120
Mar 21	Benicio Sosa	David, Panama	W	10	—	118
Apr 26	Marcos Britton	Panama City	KO	4	—	120
Jul 19	Guillermo Almengot	Panama City	TKO	7	—	122
Nov 5	Orlando Amores	Panama City	TKO	9	—	119
1976						
Apr 3 ♛	Alfonso Zamora	Mexicali, Mexico	KO'd	2	For-World-B	118
Jun 12	Pablo Jimenez	Panama City	W	10	—	125
Jul 11	Oscar Reyes Arnal	Caracas	TKO'd	6	—	127
1977						
Apr 2	Jose Santana	Panama City	W	10	—	126
May 14	Reynaldo Hidalgo	Panama City	TKO	9	—	126
Nov 26	Rodolfo Francis	Panama City	TKO	7	—	126
1978						
Apr 15 ⑩	Cecilio Lastra	Panama City	TKO	13	Won WBA-FE	125
Jul 2	Ernesto Herrera	Panama City	TKO	12	Ret-WBA-FE	126
Nov 27	Enrique Solis	San Juan, PR	W	15	Ret-WBA-FE	126
1979						
Jan 9	Royal Kobayashi	Tokyo	TKO	14	Ret-WBA-FE	126
Apr 7 ⑩	Hector Carrasquilla	Panama City	TKO	11	Ret-WBA-FE	126
Jul 21	Ruben Olivares★	Houston	TKO	12	Ret-WBA-FE	126
Nov 17	Johnny Aba	Port Moresby, New Guinea	TKO	11	Ret-WBA-FE	126
1980						
Jan 22	Spider Nemoto	Tokyo	W	15	Ret-WBA-FE	126
Mar 29	Juan Malvarez	Panama City	KO	9	Ret-WBA-FE	125
Jul 20	Sa-Wang Kim	Seoul	KO	8	Ret-WBA-FE	126
Oct 4 ⑩	Rocky Lockridge	McAfee, NJ	W	15	Ret-WBA-FE	126
1981						
Jan 17	Raul Silva	Panama City	TKO	4	—	129
Feb 14	Pat Ford	Panama City	KO	13	Ret-WBA-FE	125
Aug 1 ⑩	Carlos Pinango	Caracas	KO	7	Ret-WBA-FE	126

Dec 5	Bashew Sibaca	Panama City	KO	5	Ret-WBA-FE	126
1982						
Jan 24 ⑩	Juan Laporte	Atlantic City	W	15	Ret-WBA-FE	125
Jul 17	Rudy Alpizar	Panama City	NC	2	—	130
Oct 16 ⑩	Bernard Taylor	Charlotte, NC	D	15	Ret-World-FE	126
1983						
Apr 24 ⑩	Rocky Lockridge	San Remo, Italy	W	15	Ret-World-FE	126
Oct 22 ⑩	Jose Caba	St. Vincent, Italy	W	15	Ret-World-FE	126
1984						
May 27	Angel Levy	Maracaibo, Venezuela	W	15	Ret-World-FE	126
Jun 23	Gerald Hayes	Panama City	TKO	10	—	132
1985						
Feb 2	Jorge Lujan	Panama City	W	15	Ret-World-FE	126
Jun 8 ⑩	Barry McGuigan★	London	L	15	Lost-World-FE	126
1986						
Aug 9	Edgar Castro	Panama City	L	10	—	132
1991						
Oct 25	Tomas Rodriguez	Miami	W	8	—	136
Dec 15	Jorge Romero	Miami	W	10	—	134
1992						
Mar 14	Tomas Quinones	Antibes, France	TKO	3	—	135
Nov 21	Mauro Gutierrez	Detroit	L	10	—	137

Though Pedroza faced a wide variety of fighters in his lengthy title reign, he never received the opportunity to unify the title against WBC champions like Danny "Little Red" Lopez and Hall of Famer Salvador Sanchez, both of whom garnered more widespread acclaim than did Pedroza.

Pedroza sported a reach of 68 inches, far more than most of his featherweight competitors. He had a fine jab and good boxing skills, and unlike many tall fighters, Pedroza also performed well on the inside. He became known for his bolo punches and his ability to wear down an opponent with a blistering body attack. Often, he was also criticized as a dirty fighter.

Though his first title defense was a twelve-round knock-out victory over Ernesto Herrera in his hometown of Panama City, Pedroza's title fights took him around the world. In 1979, he retained his championship in four title matches, including a knock-out victory over Hall of Famer Ruben Olivares, an all-time great slightly past his prime.

The next year saw four more title defenses, the final one against undefeated future junior lightweight champ Rocky Lockridge, October 4, 1980, at the Playboy Club in McAfee, New Jersey. Lockridge dominated the first six rounds getting the champ on the ropes in the fifth and twice stunning the champion with rights and hooks. By the seventh, Pedroza began to take command with his left jab. The ninth and tenth saw Pedroza fire effective shots to the body and follow with hard, short counters to the chest and head. The champ came away with a split decision; the rematch two years later went to Pedroza by decision. Televised on CBS, the fight brought Pedroza to the attention of U.S. boxing fans.

On January 24, 1982, Pedroza fought one of the most controversial battles of his career against Juan Laporte in Atlantic City. Laporte jumped out to a fast start, winning the first three rounds with right-hand leads and hooks, and staggered Pedroza twice. Yet by the ninth, Laporte appeared to be tiring. Pedroza used every weapon in his arsenal, fighting after the bell, using his elbows inside, frequently hitting Laporte below the belt and using illegal kidney punches, as well as his famed bolo punch and an effective uppercut. Despite two points deducted by the referee, he won the decision by a narrow margin on all three cards. Laporte later called Pedroza, "the dirtiest fighter I ever fought." Laporte's manager Howie Albert filed protests with both the WBA and the New Jersey State Athletic Commission, alleging that Pedroza was using drugs or stimulants, in addition to committing at least 34 fouls. The WBA upheld the original decision in the fight, and Pedroza kept his title.

Pedroza remained champion until June 8, 1985, when he faced Barry McGuigan in London. McGuigan won a solid, unanimous decision and knocked Pedroza down in the seventh round. The next year, Pedroza retired after losing a decision to Edgar Castro. Pedroza became a well-known political figure in Panama, serving in Congress and as boxing coordinator at the National Sports Institute. After the U.S. invasion of Panama, he ended his retirement and fought four times in 1991 and 1992 before retiring again. In retirement, Pedroza worked for the government as chief of General Services. He now owns a pig farm.

Juan Laporte lost a split decision to Pedroza (R) in a tough 1982 Atlantic City title brawl that was punctuated with complaints from LaPorte's corner about low blows and other rough stuff.

WILLIE PEP
Will o' the Wisp

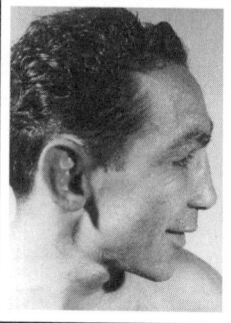

FEATHERWEIGHT

Right-handed; 5'5½"; 105–139 lbs.

242 bouts, 7/3/1940 to 3/16/1966

Manager: Lou Viscusi

Featherweight Champion 1942–48, 1948–50

Hall of Fame Induction: 1990

Born: 9/19/1922, Middletown, CT

Named: Guiglermo Papaleo

Willie Pep is one of the biggest winners in the history of boxing. In 242 contests, Pep emerged victorious 230 times. Fighting as a featherweight, Pep developed a ring artistry that veteran boxing observers still admire. His style of boxing has been likened to tap dancing with gloves on. He once won a round without even throwing a punch because his tactical movements kept his opponent completely off-balance.

Pep rose through the amateur ranks in his home state of Connecticut, winning that state's amateur flyweight championship in 1938 and the Connecticut State Amateur Bantamweight Championship in 1939. He turned professional the following year. After winning over 50 fights in a little over two years, Pep challenged Chalky Wright for the New York version of the world featherweight championship. Pep did not hurt Wright but scored often enough to win the decision. At twenty, Pep was the youngest champion to win a title in 40 years.

Pep continued to win and became the sole claimant to the world featherweight title when he won a decision over NBA titleholder Phil Terranova in 1945. Pep's

Pat Marcune (R) is in trouble as Pep intently probes for weaknesses. On June 5, 1953, in New York, Marcune fell in ten on a TKO. Today, Pep is a frequent visitor to the International Boxing Hall of Fame.

IN THE RING	WON 230	LOST 11	DRAWS 1	TB 242	KO 65	W 165	WF 0	D 1	KO'd 6	L 5	LF 0

Date	Opponent	Site	Result / Rounds		Title	Wt.
1940						
Jul 3	James McGovern	Hartford, CT	W	4	—	105
Jul 25	Joey Marcus	Hartford	W	4	—	—
Aug 8	Joey Wasnick	New Haven, CT	KO	3	—	—
Aug 29	Tommy Burns	Hartford	KO	1	—	—
Sep 5	Joey Marcus	New Britain, CT	W	6	—	—
Sep 19	Jack Moore	Hartford	W	6	—	—
Oct 3	Jimmy Riche	Waterbury, CT	TKO	3	—	—
Oct 24	Jimmy McAllister	New Haven	W	6	—	—
Nov 22	Carlo Daponde	New Britain	TKO	6	—	—
Nov 29	Frank Topazio	New Britain	TKO	5	—	—
Dec 6	Jim Mutane	New Britain	KO	2	—	—
1941						
Jan 28	Augie Almeida	New Haven	TKO	6	—	126
Feb 3	Joe Echevarria	Holyoke, MA	W	6	—	—
Feb 10	Don Lyons	Holyoke	KO	2	—	—
Feb 17	Ruby Garcia	Holyoke	W	6	—	—
Mar 3	Ruby Garcia	Holyoke	W	6	—	—
Mar 25	Marty Shapiro	Hartford	W	6	—	—
Mar 31	Joey Gatto	Holyoke	KO	2	—	127
Apr 14	Henry Vasquez	Holyoke	W	6	—	—
Apr 22	Joey Silva	Hartford	W	6	—	—
May 6	Lou Puglese	Hartford	KO	2	—	—
May 12	Johnny Cockfield	Holyoke	W	6	—	—
Jun 24	Eddie De Angelis	Hartford	TKO	3	—	—
Jul 16	Jimmy Gilligan	Hartford	W	8	—	128
Aug 1	Harry Hintlian	Manchester, CT	W	6	—	—
Aug 5	Paul Frechette	Hartford	TKO	3	—	—
Aug 12	Eddie Flores	Thompsonville, MI	KO	1	—	—
Sep 26	Jackie Harris	New Haven	TKO	1	—	—
Oct 10	Carlos Manzano	New Haven	W	8	—	—
Oct 22	Connie Savoie	Hartford	KO	2	—	—
Nov 7	Billie Spencer	Los Angeles	W	4	—	126
Nov 24	Dave Crawford	Holyoke	W	8	—	—
Dec 12	Ruby Garcia	New York	W	4	—	126
1942						
Jan 8	Joey Rivers	Fall River, MA	KO	4	—	129
Jan 16	Sammy Parrota	New York	W	4	—	126
Jan 27	Abie Kaufman	Hartford	W	8	—	126
Feb 10	Angelo Callura	Hartford	W	8	—	126
Feb 24	Willie Roache	Hartford	W	8	—	127
Mar 18	Johnny Compo	New Haven	W	8	—	127
Apr 14	Spider Armstrong	Hartford	KO	4	—	127
May 4	Curley Nichols	New Haven	W	8	—	127
May 12	Aaron Seltzer	Hartford	W	8	—	128
May 26	Joey Iannotti	Hartford	W	8	—	127
Jun 23	Joey Archibald	Hartford	W	10	—	128
Jul 21	Abe Denner	Hartford	W	12	—	125
Aug 1	Joey Silva	Waterbury	TKO	7	—	128
Aug 10	⑩ Pedro Hernandez	Hartford	W	10	—	128
Aug 20	Nat Litfin	West Haven, CT	W	10	—	128
Sep 1	⑩ Bobby ("Poison") Ivy	Hartford	TKO	10	—	127
Sep 10	Frank Franconeri	New York	TKO	1	—	130
Sep 22	Vince Dell'Orto	Hartford	W	10	—	126
Oct 5	Bobby McIntire	Holyoke	W	10	—	129

Date		Opponent	Location	Result	Rounds		Weight
Oct 16		Joey Archibald	Providence, RI	W	10	—	128
Oct 27		George Zengaras	Hartford	W	10	—	130
Nov 20	♔	Albert ("Chalky") Wright★	New York	W	15	Won-World-FE	125
Dec 14		Jose Aponte Torres	Washington, DC	KO	7	—	—
Dec 21		Joey Silva	Jacksonville, FL	TKO	9	—	128
1943							
Jan 4		Vince Dell'Orto	New Orleans	W	10	—	129
Jan 19		Bill Speary	Hartford	W	10	—	129
Jan 29	⑩	Allie Stolz	New York	W	10	—	127
Feb 11		Davey Crawford	Boston	W	10	—	129
Feb 15		Bill Speary	Baltimore	W	10	—	129
Mar 2		Lou Transparenti	Hartford	KO	6	—	129
Mar 19	⑩	Sammy Angott★	New York	L	10	—	130
Mar 29		Bobby McIntire	Detroit	W	10	—	129
Apr 9	⑩	Sal Bartolo	Boston	W	10	—	127
Apr 19		Angel Aviles	Tampa, FL	W	10	—	128
Apr 26	⑩	Jackie Wilson	Pittsburgh	W	12	—	128
Jun 8	⑩	Sal Bartolo	Boston	W	15	Ret-World-FE	126
1944							
Apr 4		Leo Francis	Hartford	W	10	—	133
Apr 20		Harold ("Snooks") Lacey	New Haven	W	10	—	129
May 1		Jackie Leamus	Philadelphia	W	10	—	126
May 19		Frankie Rubino	Chicago	W	10	—	126
May 23		Joey Bagnato	Buffalo, NY	KO	2	—	128
Jun 6		Julie Kogon	Hartford	W	10	—	127
Jul 7	⑩	Willie Joyce	Chicago	W	10	—	127
Jul 17	⑩	Manuel Ortiz★	Boston	W	10	—	127
Aug 4		Lulu Costantino	Waterbury	W	10	—	128
Aug 29		Joey Peralta	Springfield, MA	W	10	—	128
Sep 19	⑩	Cabey Lewis	Hartford	KO	8	—	127
Sep 29	⑩	Albert ("Chalky") Wright★	New York	W	15	Ret-World-FE	125
Oct 25		Jackie Leamus	Montreal	W	10	—	127
Nov 14	⑩	Cabey Lewis	Hartford	W	10	—	125
Nov 27		Pedro Hernandez	Washington, DC	W	10	—	128
Dec 5	⑩	Albert ("Chalky") Wright★	Cleveland	W	10	—	128
1945							
Jan 23		Ralph Walton	Hartford	W	10	—	127
Feb 5	⑩	Willie Roache	New Haven	W	10	—	127
Feb 19	⑩	Phil Terranova	New York	W	15	Ret-World-FE	124
Oct 30		Paulie Jackson	Hartford	W	8	—	130
Nov 5		Mike Martyk	Buffalo	TKO	5	—	129
Nov 26		Eddie Giosa	Boston	W	10	—	130
Dec 5		Harold Gibson	Lewiston, ME	W	10	—	128
Dec 13		Jimmy McAllister	Baltimore	D	10	—	128
1946							
Jan 15		Johnny Virgo	Buffalo	KO	2	—	129
Feb 13		Jimmy Joyce	Buffalo	W	10	—	128
Mar 1		Jimmy McAllister	New York	KO	2	—	129
Mar 26	⑩	Jackie Wilson	Kansas City, MO	W	10	—	128
Apr 8		Georgie Knox	Providence	KO	3	—	130
May 6		Ernie Petrone	New Haven	W	10	—	128
May 13		Joey Angelo	Providence	W	10	—	128
May 22		Jose Aponte Torres	St. Louis	W	10	—	129
May 27		Jimmy Joyce	Minneapolis	W	8	—	127
Jun 7	⑩	Sal Bartolo	New York	KO	12	Ret-World-FE	126
Jul 10		Harold Gibson	Buffalo	TKO	7	—	127
Jul 25	⑩	Jackie Graves	Minneapolis	TKO	8	—	126
Aug 26		Doll Rafferty	Milwaukee	KO	6	—	131
Sep 4		Walter Kolby	Buffalo	TKO	5	—	131
Sep 17		Maurice LaChance	Hartford	KO	3	—	129
Nov 1		Paulie Jackson	Minneapolis	W	10	—	131

Nov 15		Tomas Beato	Waterbury	KO	2	—	128
Nov 27	⑩	Albert ("Chalky") Wright★	Milwaukee	KO	3	—	130
1947							
Jun 17		Victor Flores	Hartford	W	10	—	130
Jul 1		Joey Fortuna	Albany, NY	KO	5	—	130
Jul 8		Leo LeBrun	Norwalk, CT	W	8	—	128
Jul 11		Jean Barriere	North Adams, MA	KO	4	—	130
Jul 15		Paulie Jackson	New Bedford, MA	W	10	—	129
Jul 23		Humberto Sierra	Hartford	W	10	—	129
Aug 22	⑩	Jock Leslie	Flint, MI	TKO	12	Ret-World-FE	125
Oct 21		Jean Barriere	Portland, ME	KO	1	—	129
Oct 27		Archie Wilmer	Philadelphia	W	10	—	130
Dec 22		Alvaro Estrada	Lewiston, NY	W	10	—	128
Dec 30		Maurice LaChance	Manchester	TKO	8	—	132
1948							
Jan 6		Pedro Biesca	Hartford	W	10	—	129
Jan 12		Jimmy McAllister	St. Louis	W	10	—	128
Jan 19		Joey Angelo	Boston	W	10	—	135
Feb 24		Humberto Sierra	Miami	TKO	10	Ret-World-FE	125
May 7		Leroy Willis	Detroit	W	10	—	131
May 19		Cabey Lewis	Milwaukee	W	10	—	129
Jun 17	⑩	Miguel Acevedo	Minneapolis	W	10	—	129
Jun 25		Luther Burgess	Flint	W	10	—	128
Jul 28		Young Junior	Utica, NY	KO	1	—	131
Aug 3		Teddy Davis	Hartford	W	10	—	128
Aug 17		Teddy Davis	Hartford	W	10	—	127
Sep 2		Johnny Dell	Waterbury	TKO	8	—	129
Sep 10	⑩	Paddy DeMarco	New York	W	10	—	128
Oct 12		Chuck Burton	Jersey City, NJ	W	8	—	132
Oct 19		John LaRusso	Hartford	W	10	—	127
Oct 29	⑩	Sandy Saddler★	New York	KO'd	4	Lost-World-FE	125
Dec 20		Hermie Freeman	Boston	W	10	—	130
1949							
Jan 17		Teddy Davis	St. Louis	W	10	—	129
Feb 11	♛	Sandy Saddler★	New York	W	15	Reg-World-FE	126
Jun 6		Luis Ramos	New Haven	W	10	—	131
Jun 14		Al Pennino	Pittsfield, MA	W	10	—	131
Jun 20		John LaRusso	Springfield	W	10	—	129
Jul 12		Jean Mougin	Syracuse, NY	W	10	—	128
Sep 20		Eddie Compo	Waterbury	TKO	7	Ret-World-FE	126
Dec 12		Harold Dade	St. Louis	W	10	—	130
1950							
Jan 16	⑩	Charley Riley	St. Louis	KO	5	Ret-World-FE	123
Feb 6		Roy Andrews	Boston	W	10	—	130
Feb 22		Jimmy Warren	Miami	W	10	—	129
Mar 17	⑩	Ray Famechon	New York	W	15	Ret-World-FE	124
May 15		Art Llanos	Hartford	KO	2	—	130
Jun 1		Terry Young	Milwaukee	W	10	—	129
Jun 26		Bobby Timpson	Hartford	W	10	—	127
Jul 25		Bobby Bell	Washington, DC	W	10	—	130
Aug 2		Proctor Heinold	Scranton, PA	W	10	—	131
Sep 8	⑩	Sandy Saddler★	Bronx, NY	TKO'd	8	Lost-World-FE	124
1951							
Jan 30		Tommy Baker	Hartford	TKO	4	—	135
Feb 26		Billy Hogan	Sarasota, FL	TKO	2	—	128
Mar 5		Carlos Chavez	New Orleans	W	10	—	127
Mar 26		Pat Iacobucci	Miami	W	10	—	127
Apr 17		Neftali Ortiz	St. Louis	TKO	5	—	126
Apr 27		Eddie Chavez	San Francisco	W	10	—	127
Jun 4		Jesus Compos	Baltimore	W	10	—	131
Sep 4		Corky Gonzales	New Orleans	W	10	—	129

Date		Opponent	Location	Result	Rounds		Weight
Sep 26	♛	Sandy Saddler★	New York	TKO'd	9	For-World-FE	125

1952

Date		Opponent	Location	Result	Rounds		Weight
Apr 29		Santiago Gonzales	Tampa	W	10	—	131
May 5		Kenny Leach	Columbus, GA	W	10	—	130
May 10		Buddy Baggett	Aiken, SC	KO	5	—	—
May 21		Claude Hammond	Miami Beach	W	10	—	129
Jun 30	⑩	Tommy Collins	Boston	TKO'd	6	—	126
Sep 3		Billy Lima	Pensacola, FL	W	10	—	127
Sep 11		Bobby Woods	Vancouver, B.C.	W	10	—	130
Oct 1		Armand Savoie	Chicago	W	10	—	129
Oct 20		Billy Lima	Jacksonville	W	10	—	129
Nov 5		Manny Castro	Miami Beach	TKO	5	—	128
Nov 19		Fabela Chavez	St. Louis	W	10	—	129
Dec 5		Jorge Sanchez	West Palm Beach, FL	W	10	—	127

1953

Date		Opponent	Location	Result	Rounds		Weight
Jan 19		Billy Lauderdale	Nassau, Bahamas	W	10	—	127
Jan 27		Davey Mitchell	Miami Beach	W	10	—	130
Feb 10		Jose Alvarez	San Antonio, TX	W	10	—	129
Mar 31		Joey Gambino	Tampa	W	10	—	131
Apr 7		Noel Paquette	Miami Beach	W	10	—	129
May 13		Jackie Blair	Dallas	W	10	—	129
Jun 5		Pat Marcune	New York	TKO	10	—	127
Nov 21		Sonny Luciano	Charlotte, NC	W	10	—	130
Dec 4		Davey Allen	West Palm Beach	W	10	—	129
Dec 8		Billy Lima	Houston	KO	2	—	129
Dec 15		Tony Longo	Miami Beach	W	10	—	129

1954

Date		Opponent	Location	Result	Rounds		Weight
Jan 19		David Seabrooke	Jacksonville	W	10	—	128
Feb 26	⑩	Lulu Perez	New York	TKO'd	2	—	127
Jul 24		Mike Turcotte	Mobile, AL	W	10	—	131
Aug 18		Til LeBlanc	Moncton, N.B., Canada	W	10	—	129
Nov 1		Mario Colon	Daytona Beach, FL	W	10	—	128

1955

Date		Opponent	Location	Result	Rounds		Weight
Mar 11		Myrel Olmstead	Bennington, VT	W	10	—	129
Mar 22		Charley Titone	Holyoke	W	10	—	130
Mar 30		Gil Cadilli	San Francisco	L	10	—	128
May 18		Gil Cadilli	Detroit	W	10	—	128
Jun 1		Joey Cam	Boston	TKO	4	—	129
Jun 14		Mickey Mars	Miami Beach	TKO	7	—	128
Jul 12		Hector Rodriguez	Bridgeport, CT	W	10	—	130
Sep 13		Jimmy Ithia	Hartford	TKO	6	—	129
Sep 27		Pappy Gault	Holyoke	W	10	—	129
Oct 10		Charley Titone	Brockton, MA	W	10	—	129
Nov 29		Henry ("Pappy") Gault	Tampa	W	10	—	127
Dec 13		Lee Carter	Houston	TKO	4	—	127
Dec 28		Andy Arel	Miami Beach	W	10	—	128

1956

Date		Opponent	Location	Result	Rounds		Weight
Mar 13		Kid Campeche	Tampa	W	10	—	127
Mar 27		James ("Buddy") Baggett	Beaumont, TX	W	10	—	127
Apr 17		Jackie Blair	Hartford	W	10	—	130
May 22		Manuel Armenteros	San Antonio	TKO	7	—	128
Jun 19		Russ Tague	Miami Beach	W	10	—	130
Jul 4		Hector Bacquette	Lawton, OK	KO	4	—	—

1957

Date		Opponent	Location	Result	Rounds		Weight
Apr 23		Cesar Morales	Ft. Lauderdale, FL	W	10	—	—
May 10		Manny Castro	Florence, SC	W	10	—	128
Jul 16		Manny Castro	El Paso, TX	W	10	—	122
Jul 23		Russ Tague	Houston	W	10	—	131
Dec 17		Jimmy Connors	Boston	W	10	—	131

1958

Date		Opponent	Location	Result	Rounds		Weight
Jan 14		Tommy Tibbs	Boston	L	10	—	129

Mar 31	Prince Johnson	Holyoke	W	10	—	130
Apr 8	George Stephany	Bristol, CT	W	10	—	129
Apr 14	Cleo Ortiz	Providence	W	10	—	129
Apr 29	Jimmy Kelly	Boston	W	10	—	129
May 20	Bobby Singleton	Boston	W	10	—	130
Jun 23	Pat McCoy	New Bedford, MA	W	10	—	129
Jul 1	Bobby Soares	Athol, MA	W	10	—	127
Jul 17	Bobby Bell	Norwood, MA	W	10	—	128
Aug 4	Luis Carmona	Presque Isle, ME	W	10	—	128
Aug 9	Jesse Rodrigues	Painesville, OH	W	10	—	129
Aug 26	Al Duarte	North Adams, MA	W	10	—	129
Sep 20	♛ Hogan ("Kid") Bassey	Boston	TKO'd	9	—	129
1959						
Jan 26	⑩ Victor ("Sonny") Leon	Caracas	L	10	—	133
1965						
Mar 12	Hal McKeever	Miami	W	8	—	137
Apr 26	Jackie Lennon	Philadelphia	W	6	—	137
May 21	Johnny Gilmore	Norwalk	W	6	—	134
Jul 26	Benny Randell	Quebec City, Mon.	W	10	—	—
Sep 28	Johnny Gilmore	Philadelphia	W	6	—	137
Oct 1	Willie Little	Johnstown, PA	KO	3	—	136
Oct 4	Tommy Haden	Providence	TKO	3	—	136
Oct 14	Sergio Musquiz	Phoenix	KO	5	—	139
Oct 25	Ray Coleman	Tucson, AZ	TKO	5	—	132
1966						
Mar 16	Calvin Woodland	Richmond, VA	L	6	—	—

career was temporarily derailed when he suffered serious injuries in a plane crash in 1947. Pep defied those who said he would never fight again by winning a ten-round decision over Victor Flores barely five months after the accident.

Though he had lost a non-title bout to the heavier Sammy Angott, Pep continued to be unbeaten at the featherweight level until he faced Sandy Saddler in 1948 at Madison Square Garden. Saddler gave Pep more trouble than any other opponent in his 26-year career. In this first of their four title bouts over the years, Saddler knocked Pep out in the fourth round, and questions arose because Pep had performed so badly. In the rematch at Madison Square Garden in 1949, Pep took many punches but boxed a clever fight and won a decision over Saddler to regain his championship. With cuts over each eye and on both cheeks, Pep felt he was vindicated of the allegations concerning the first fight. In 1981, *The Ring* rated the rematch one of the ten greatest bouts of all time.

Pep and Saddler met for a third time in Yankee Stadium in 1950 before 38,781 fans. Saddler cut Pep early and knocked him down in the third round. Pep won the next three rounds but Saddler battered Pep in the seventh, and Pep failed to answer the bell for the eighth, claiming a dislocated shoulder. These two warriors met for a last time in 1951 at New York's Polo Grounds. The crowd of 13,786 witnessed a wild melee complete with heeling, gouging, tripping, butting, pushing, shoving, and wrestling. Nat Fleischer labeled the bout "a disgraceful brawl." Pep suffered a technical knockout when he retired after the ninth round. Pep continued to box until 1959 and made a comeback in 1965 at the age of 42.

In retirement, Pep served his home state of Connecticut as the boxing and wrestling inspector. He has married six times.

PASCUAL PEREZ
El Terrier, El León Mendocino

FLYWEIGHT

Right-handed; 5′; 104–112 lbs.

92 bouts, 12/5/1952 to 3/15/1964

Manager: Lazaro Koci

1948 Olympic Flywt. Gold Medalist

Flyweight Champion 1954–60

Hall of Fame Induction: 1995

Born: 3/4/1926, Tupungate, Mendoza, Argentina

Died: 1/22/1977

Considered by many to be the finest flyweight in the modern era of boxing, Pascual Perez did not follow the usual path to stardom as a boxer. After a strong amateur career, Perez took time off and did not fight professionally until he was 26.

Born in Argentina, Perez grew up working in his family's vineyard. Despite his family's opposition to his boxing, Perez, inspired by his idol, Argentine heavyweight Luis Angel Firpo, became a top amateur. He won the flyweight gold medal in the 1948 Olympic Games but then dropped out of boxing and worked as a janitor in government civil service. Finally, in 1952, in an effort to earn more money, he fought and won his first professional fight.

Perez then reeled off 22 straight wins—21 by knockout—and within a year proved he was the best flyweight in Argentina. In July 1954, world flyweight

Chin tucked low, globetrotting champion Perez (R) won on points over Dommy Ursua in his December 15, 1958, title defense in Manila. President Juan Peron of Argentina keenly followed Perez's career.

IN THE RING	WON 84	LOST 7	DRAWS 1	TB 92	KO 57	W 27	WF 0	D 1	KO'd 3	L 4	LF 0

Date	Opponent	Site	Result / Rounds		Title	Wt.
1952						
Dec 5	Jose Ciorino	Gerli, Argentina	TKO	4	—	—
Dec 19	Jorge Flores	San Fernando, Argentina	KO	3	—	—
1953						
Jan 3	Ramon Stronatti	Mendoza, Argentina	TKO	2	—	—
Feb 20	Mario Ahumada	Mendoza	TKO	3	—	—
Mar 16	Miguel Carrasco	Mendoza	KO	5	—	—
Mar 30	Juan Godoy	Buenos Aires	KO	4	—	—
Nov 11	Marcelo Quiroga	Buenos Aires	TKO	4	Won-Argentina-FL	104
Nov 25	Eduardo Lliuzzi	Buenos Aires	TKO	1	—	—
Dec 23	Hernan Rojas	Mendoza	KO	2	—	—
Dec 30	Roberto Romero	Uspallata, Argentina	KO	2	—	—
1954						
Jan 8	Nestor Rojas	Catamarca, Argentina	TKO	2	Ret-Argentina-FL	—
Jan 19	Jose Luna	Tucuman, Argentina	TKO	2	—	—
Jan 29	Antonio Zapata	Catamarca	TKO	5	—	—
Feb 6	Marcelo Quiroga	Buenos Aires	TKO	4	—	—
Feb 12	Nestor Rojas	Tandil, Argentina	KO	3	—	—
Feb 24	Nicolas Paez	Buenos Aires	KO	1	—	—
Mar 12	Pablo Sosa	Catamarca	KO	6	—	—
Mar 24	Pablo Sosa	Buenos Aires	KO	2	—	—
Apr 22	Juan Bishop	Buenos Aires	W	10	—	—
May 19	Vicente Bruno	Buenos Aires	TKO	3	—	—
Jun 5	Domingo Sandoval	Comodoro Rivadavia, Arg.	KO	4	—	—
Jun 12	Pablo Sosa	Comodoro Rivadavia	TKO	8	—	—
Jun 25	Marcelo Quiroga	La Plata, Argentina	KO	4	—	—
Jul 24 ♛	Yoshio Shirai	Buenos Aires	D	10	—	108
Nov 26 ♛	Yoshio Shirai	Tokyo	W	15	Won-World-FL	107
1955						
Apr 13	Alberto Barenghi	Buenos Aires	KO	3	—	108
May 30 ⑩	Yoshio Shirai	Tokyo	KO	5	Ret-World-FL	108
Aug 26	Alberto Palomeque	Catamarca	KO	4	—	—
Oct 22 ⑩	Danny Kidd	Buenos Aires	W	10	—	106
1956						
Jan 11 ⑩	Leo Espinosa	Buenos Aires	W	15	Ret-World-FL	107
Feb 10	Antonio Gomez	Mar Del Plata, Argentina	W	10	—	106
Mar 21	Antonio Gomez	Buenos Aires	TKO	8	—	108
Mar 31	Marcelo Quiroga	Mendoza	W	10	—	104
Jun 8	Ricardo Valdez	Bahia Blanca, Argentina	TKO	6	—	108
Jun 15	Pablo Sosa	Martinez, Argentina	KO	4	—	—
Jun 30 ⑩	Oscar Suarez	Montevideo, Uruguay	TKO	11	Ret-World-FL	108
Aug 3	Ricardo Valdez	Tandil	KO	5	—	108
Aug 25	Hector Almaraz	Rosario, Argentina	KO	3	—	106
Sep 6	Conrado Moreira	Sao Paulo, Brazil	W	10	—	107
Sep 28	Hernan Rojas	Asuncion, Paraguay	TKO	8	—	—
Dec 12	Conrado Moreira	Buenos Aires	W	10	—	108
1957						
Mar 30 ⑩	Dai Dower	Buenos Aires	KO	1	Ret-World-FL	107
Jul 12	Luis Jimenez	Babilonia, Argentina	W	10	—	108
Aug 2	Urbieta Sosa	Santa Fe, Argentina	TKO	4	—	—

Date		Opponent	Location	Result	Rounds	Notes	
Aug 17		Pablo Sosa	Tandil	KO	3	—	107
Sep 13		Conrado Moreira	La Plata	W	10	—	103
Dec 7	Ⓝ	Young Martin	Buenos Aires	KO	3	Ret-World-FL	108
1958							
Mar 22		Ricardo Valdez	Moron, Argentina	KO	8	—	106
Apr 19	Ⓝ	Ramon Arias	Caracas	W	15	Ret-World-FL	105
Aug 9		Tito Ragone	Ciudad Trujillo, D.R.	W	10	—	110
Nov 22		Tito Ragone	Willemstad, Curacao	W	10	—	
Dec 15	Ⓝ	Dommy Ursua	Manila	W	15	Ret-World-FL	109
1959							
Jan 16	Ⓝ	Sadao Yaoita	Tokyo	L	10	—	110
Feb 18	Ⓝ	Kenji Yonekura	Tokyo	W	10	—	111
Aug 10	Ⓝ	Kenji Yonekura	Tokyo	W	15	Ret-World-FL	107
Nov 5	Ⓝ	Sadao Yaoita	Osaka, Japan	KO	13	Ret-World-FL	107
1960							
Apr 16	Ⓝ	Pone Kingpetch	Bangkok	L	15	Lost-World-FL	112
Sep 22	♛	Pone Kingpetch	Los Angeles	TKO'd	8	For-World-FL	110
1961							
Mar 18		Hugo Villarreal	Avellaneda, Argentina	TKO	4	—	—
Apr 1		Juan Moreira	Quilmes, Argentina	W	10	—	—
Apr 9		Pablo Sosa	San Pedro, Argentina	KO	3	—	—
May 13		Juan Montevero	General Roca, Argentina	TKO	6	—	—
May 19		Francisco Bahamondez	Cipolletti, Argentina	TKO	3	—	—
Jul 8		Hugo Villarreal	Punta Alta, Argentina	KO	3	—	—
Jul 15		Juan Montevero	Rio Gallegos, Argentina	KO	5	—	—
Jul 29		Wladimiro Torres	Rio Gallegos	KO	8	—	—
Aug 19		Simon Rios	Trelew, Argentina	KO	6	—	—
Sep 5		Wladimiro Torres	Bolivar, Argentina	KO	3	—	—
Oct 12		Jose Diaz	Esquel, Argentina	KO	7	—	—
Oct 21		Alberto Garcia	Rosario	TKO	6	—	—
Dec 22		Rodolfo Trivis	Cordoba, Argentina	W	10	—	—
1962							
Jan 27		Demetrio Acosta	Nueve de Julio, Argentina	KO	2	—	—
Feb 23		Ursino Bernal	Balcarce, Argentina	W	10	—	—
Mar 2		Rodolfo Trivis	Miramar, Argentina	W	10	—	—
Apr 21		Ursino Bernal	Tucuman	TKO	6	—	—
Apr 27		Juan Moreira	Salta, Argentina	KO	3	—	—
May 2		Martin Luque	Santiago del Estero, Arg.	TKO	5	—	—
May 19		Cirilo Avellaneda	Formosa, Argentina	KO	5	—	—
Jun 9		Rodolfo Trivis	Tucuman	W	10	—	—
Jun 15		Martin Luque	Jujuy, Argentina	KO	5	—	—
Dec 8		Juan Moreira	Cordoba	TKO	9	—	108
1963							
Jan 25		Cirilo Avellaneda	Villa Dolores, Argentina	W	10	—	—
Feb 1		Miguel Herrera	San Luis, Argentina	W	10	—	—
Feb 16		Rodolfo Trivis	Montevideo	W	10	—	—
Apr 5		Juan Moreira	Villa Dolores	W	10	—	—
Apr 12		Cirilo Avellaneda	Bahia Blanca	KO	7	—	—
Apr 30	Ⓝ	Leo Zulueta	Manila	L	10	—	112
Jun 16		Manuel Moreno	Panama City	W	10	—	111
Jul 26	Ⓝ	Bernardo Caraballo	Bogota, Colombia	L	10	—	112
Aug 9		Adolfo Osses	Guayaquil, Ecuador	W	10	—	—
Oct 19	Ⓝ	Efren Torres	Guadalajara, Mexico	TKO'd	3	—	109
1964							
Mar 15		Eugenio Hurtado	Panama City	TKO'd	6	—	107

champion Yoshio Shirai of Japan came to Buenos Aires to test Perez's mettle in a non-title fight. The two fought to a draw, setting the stage for a title fight four months later in Tokyo. Shirai was seven inches taller than the challenger, whom fight experts gave little chance of dethroning the champion. However, Perez fought inside and battered Shirai to earn a fifteen-round decision. Called "El Terrier" in his home country, Perez was known for the tremendous drive contained within his 5' frame. He returned to Argentina a conquering hero.

Perez knocked Shirai out in their rematch and commenced to defend his title against all comers. He defeated top-ten contenders Leo Espinoza and Oscar Suarez in 1956, and Dai Dower and Young Martin in 1957. He triumphed in title bouts in Caracas and Manila in 1958 and fought exclusively in Japan in 1959, defending his title twice against top Japanese contenders. The end for the diminutive Argentine came in 1960 when he faced Pone Kingpetch in Bangkok. Although Kingpetch was ten years younger and eight inches taller, El Terrier put up a valiant effort but lost a split decision. The fight ended with both men cut around the eyes.

Perez made his only appearance in the United States when he faced Kingpetch in a rematch in Los Angeles. Perez could not mount an effective attack against Kingpetch, and the referee stopped the fight in the eighth round. Though past his prime, Perez continued to fight until he was 38, campaigning successfully against secondary competition.

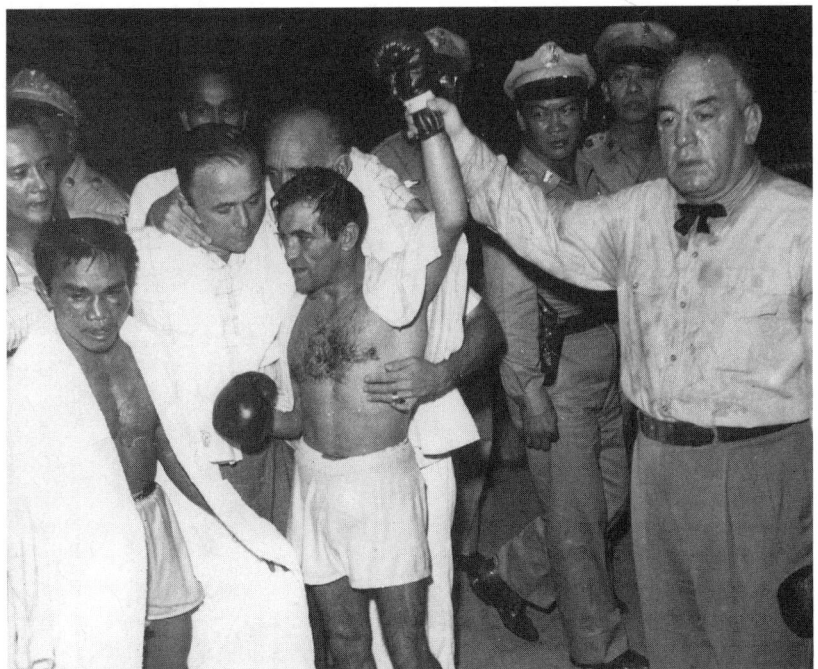

An exhausted Pascual Perez (R) wins the unanimous decison over Dommy Ursua in their 1958 bout. His left eye badly swollen, Ursua suffered the defeat in Rizal Memorial Football Stadium, Manila's soccer venue.

AARON PRYOR
The Hawk

JUNIOR WELTERWEIGHT

Right-handed; 5'6½"; 134–154 lbs.
40 bouts, 11/12/1976 to 12/4/1990
Manager: Buddy LaRosa
WBA Junior Welterwt Champ 1980–83
IBF Junior Welterwt Champ 1984–85
Hall of Fame Induction: 1996
Born: 10/20/1955, Cincinnati, OH

One of the most thrilling fighters of the late 1970s and early '80s, Aaron Pryor compiled an outstanding 39-1 record in a career known as much for personal turmoil as for brilliant performance. Born in Cincinnati, Pryor was one of seven children in a poor family. He spent much of his time on the streets but, by age thirteen, he had found his way to a gym and learned to box. As an amateur, he won 204 of 220 fights and two national Golden Gloves titles. Representing the U.S. 21 times in international competition, he only lost once—in the finals of the 1975 Pan-American Games.

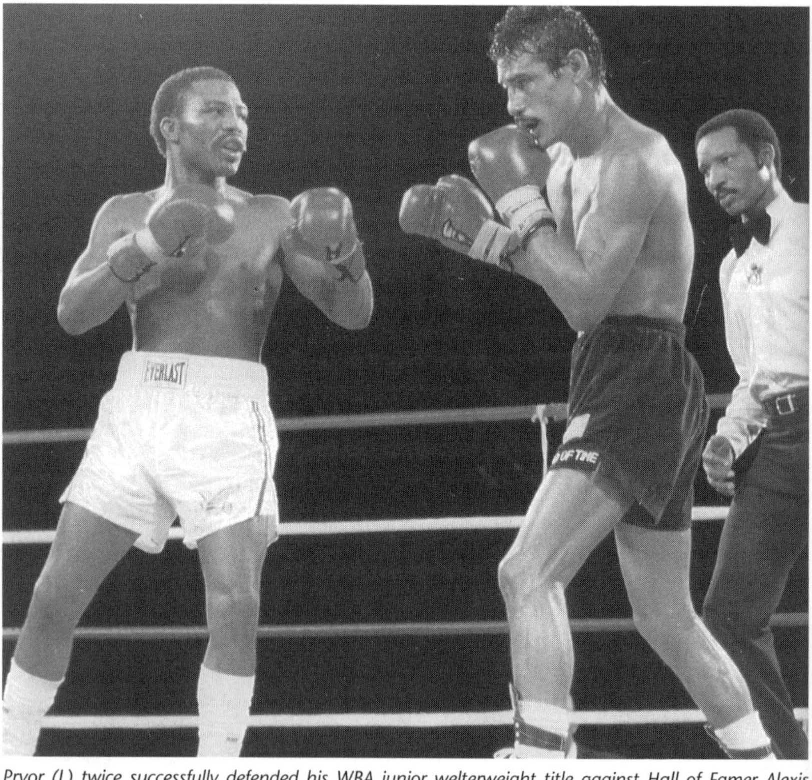

Pryor (L) twice successfully defended his WBA junior welterweight title against Hall of Famer Alexis Arguello. Both bouts ended in knockout wins, but Pryor suffered lasting eye damage in one of the fights.

IN THE RING	WON **39**	LOST **1**	DRAWS **0**	TB 40	KO 35	W 4	WF 0	D 0	KO'd 1	L 0	LF 0

Date	Opponent	Site	Result / Rounds		Title	Wt.
1976						
Nov 12	Larry Smith	Cincinnati	TKO	2	—	137
1977						
Feb 1	Larry Moore	Cincinnati	TKO	4	—	139
Feb 24	Harvey Wilson	Cincinnati	TKO	1	—	139
Mar 12	Nicky Wills	Lincoln Heights, OH	KO	1	—	139
Mar 26	Isaac Vega	Cincinnati	KO	2	—	141
May 7	Jose Resto	Cincinnati	W	8	—	140
Sep 3	Melvin Young	Covington, KY	TKO	4	—	140
Oct 7	Johnny Summerhays	Cincinnati	W	8	—	139
Nov 4	Angel Cintron	Cincinnati	KO	3	—	141
1978						
Jan 16	Roberto Tijerina	Cincinnati	KO	2	—	136
Mar 1	Ron Pettigrew	Dayton, OH	TKO	5	—	140
Mar 10	Alfred Franklin	Cincinnati	TKO	3	—	136
May 3	Scotty Foreman	Miami Beach	TKO	6	—	138
Jul 18	Marion Thomas	Dayton	KO	8	—	139
1979						
Mar 16	Johnny Copeland	Cincinnati	KO	7	—	139
Apr 13	Norman Goins	Cincinnati	KO	9	—	140
Apr 27	Freddie Harris	Dayton	KO	3	—	137
May 11	Al Ford	Cincinnati	TKO	4	—	140
Jun 23	Jose Fernandez	Cincinnati	KO	1	—	141
Oct 20	Alfonso Frazer	Cincinnati	TKO	5	—	136
1980						
Feb 24	Juan Garcia	Las Vegas	KO	1	—	138
Mar 16	⑩ Julio Valdez	Miami	TKO	4	—	136
Apr 13	Leonidas Asprilla	Kansas City, MO	TKO	10	—	134
Jun 20	Carl Crowley	Cincinnati	KO	1	—	143
Aug 2	♛ Antonio Cervantes★	Cincinnati	KO	4	Won-WBA-JW	138
Nov 1	Danny Myers	Dayton	TKO	3	—	138
Nov 22	Gaetan Hart	Cincinnati	TKO	6	Ret-WBA-JW	138
1981						
Jun 27	⑩ Lennox Blackmoore	Las Vegas	TKO	2	Ret-WBA-JW	140
Nov 14	⑩ Dujuan Johnson	Cleveland	TKO	7	Ret-WBA-JW	139
1982						
Mar 21	⑩ Miguel Montilla	Atlantic City	TKO	12	Ret-WBA-JW	139
Jul 4	Akio Kameda	Cincinnati	TKO	6	Ret-WBA-JW	139
Nov 12	Alexis Arguello★	Miami	TKO	14	Ret-WBA-JW	140
1983						
Apr 2	⑩ Sang-Hyun Kim	Atlantic City	TKO	3	Ret-WBA-JW	140
Sep 9	Alexis Arguello★	Las Vegas	KO	10	Ret-WBA-JW	140
1984						
Jun 22	Nick Furlano	Toronto	W	15	Ret-IBF-JW	139
1985						
Mar 2	⑩ Gary Hinton	Atlantic City	W	15	Ret-IBF-JW	140

1987						
Aug 8	Bobby Joe Young	Sunrise, FL	KO'd	7	—	148
1988						
Dec 15	Herminio Morales	Rochester, NY	KO	3	—	146
1990						
May 16	Darryl Jones	Madison, WI	KO	3	—	154
Dec 4	Roger Choate	Norman, OK	TKO	7	—	148

Despite his excellent amateur record, Pryor never fought in the Olympics. When the 1976 trials were held in Cincinnati, he was favored in his weight class, but lost by decision to Howard Davis, who eventually took the gold medal. Davis beat Pryor again in the box-off at the Olympic training camp in Vermont, but some observers believe Pryor was denied an Olympic shot because of official concern about his behavior outside the ring.

As a result, Pryor was unable to use the 1976 Olympics as a springboard to a professional career as did Davis, Sugar Ray Leonard, and Leon and Michael Spinks. Pryor turned professional on November 12, 1976, knocking out former kick boxer Larry Smith in the second round to earn $400. By contrast, Davis earned $250,000 for his first pro fight.

Still, defeating one opponent after another, Pryor was bound to be noticed. Fighting mostly in Cincinnati under manager Buddy LaRosa, he gained a reputation as a hard hitter who went after opponents with reckless abandon. By mid-1980, he had scored knockouts in 22 of his first 24 fights and applied the same treatment to Antonio ("Kid Pambele") Cervantes to take the WBA junior welterweight championship. In an attempt to unify the title, promoter Harold Smith lined up a fight for Pryor with the WBC junior welterweight titleholder, Saoul Mamby. Before this match came off, however, Pryor's wife shot him during a domestic dispute.

The resulting delay, coupled with some legal difficulties involving promoter Smith, ended hopes of a unification bout. A falling-out with LaRosa then cost Pryor a fight with Roberto Duran, which would have paid him $750,000.

Pryor defended his title five times by knockout before he entered "The Ring of Fire" with Alexis Arguello in 1982 for the most memorable fight of his career. Having held the featherweight, junior lightweight, and lightweight titles, Arguello was aiming to be the first fighter in history to win four world titles in four weight classes.

From the opening bell in Miami's Orange Bowl, Pryor was on the attack. He threw 130 punches in the first round. In the second, Arguello twice caught Pryor with strong rights. In the view of Arguello's agent, Bill Miller, the second punch "would have decapitated anybody else," but Pryor was barely fazed. After thirteen rounds, Pryor was ahead on two cards and Arguello on one. In the fourteenth, Pryor snapped Arguello's head back with a hook, then sent him to the ropes with a series of furious blows. Defenseless, Arguello took 23 more punches before the fight was stopped. On the canvas for four minutes, Arguello collapsed again on the way to his dressing room.

Pryor defended his crown eight times, readily dominating his weight class. But after beating Arguello in their rematch, he announced his retirement and relinquished his title.

Missing the ring and also needing to fund a serious drug habit, Pryor came back less than a year later. He won a few fights and was awarded the IBF's junior welterweight championship, but by 1985 had lost the crown because of inactivity.

Plagued by a worsening drug addiction and a detached retina which eventually led to severe vision loss in one eye, Pryor came back again two years later for the only loss of his career, to Bobby Joe Young. Although Pryor should not have been licensed because of his vision problem, he fought three more times before retiring for good in 1990.

In 1991, Pryor was imprisoned after pleading guilty to a reduced charge of drug abuse. Drained of all his earnings by crack addiction, Pryor left prison to live

Alexis Arguello (L) is counted out in the tenth round on September 9, 1983, in his second defeat at the hands of triumphant Aaron Pryor.

on the streets, often going days without food or sleep. After nearly dying from bleeding ulcers, he began to turn his life around. He now works training fighters in Cincinnati and is a deacon in a local church. On June 5, 2003, Pryor married Frankie Lynn Wagnes at the Courtyard of Champions Amphitheater at the Boxing Hall of Fame. In spite of all his problems outside the ring, fight fans remember Pryor for his ceaseless attack and a capacity to take the best punches an opponent could throw.

DWIGHT MUHAMMAD QAWI
Camden Buzzsaw

CRUISERWEIGHT

Right-handed; 5'6¾"; 169–232 lbs.

53 bouts, 4/19/1978 to 11/25/1998

Managers: Wesley Mouzon, Quenzell McCall, Rock Newman

WBC Light Heavywt Champ 1981–83
WBA Cruiserweight Champion 1985–86

Hall of Fame Induction: 2004

Born: 1/5/1953, Baltimore, MD

Named: Dwight Braxton

Qawi was born Dwight Braxton in Baltimore, Maryland, on January 5, 1953. He moved to Camden, New Jersey, as a small boy. Qawi was one of thirteen children in a single parent household. He frequently got into trouble on the streets of Camden and served time in reform schools. When Qawi was nineteen, he attempted to rob a liquor store. He was arrested, convicted of armed robbery, and sentenced to Rahway State Prison. Qawi served five and one-half years before he was released. In prison, Qawi received his high school GED, took advantage of vocational training, and began to box.

Upon Qawi's release from prison, his friend Ike Hammonds took him to Joe Frazier's gym in Philadelphia. There he sparred with such veteran boxers as Benny Briscoe, Willie ("The Worm") Monroe, and Bougaloo Watts. Qawi had no amateur career. He turned professional on April 19, 1978, when he fought a draw with Leonard Langley. After a win and a loss, Qawi won his next twelve fights.

Qawi faced the sternest test, to date, in the form of Mike Rossman, a former light heavyweight champion. Though he was only 5'6¾" tall, he outjabbed the 6'0" Rossman. Qawi repeatedly threw overhand rights—landing over Rossman's left. Qawi next unleashed a barrage of hooks. In the seventh round, he backed Rossman into the ropes with an overhand right and then knocked him out with a left hook.

In his next bout, Qawi returned to Rahway to fight James Scott. Though Scott was a convicted murderer and an inmate at Rahway, he had become a ranked fighter and was somewhat of a sensation, fighting behind bars. Qawi and Scott had been imprisoned at the same time and had sparred together, but the two were not friends. Qawi relied on

Qawi initially fought under the name Dwight Braxton. By the time he stopped Eddie Davis at Atlantic City on November 20, 1982, he was billed under his Muslim name, Dwight Muhammad Qawi.

IN THE RING	WON 41	LOST 11	DRAWS 1	TB 53	KO 25	W 16	WF 0	D 1	KO'd 2	L 9	LF 0

Date	Opponent	Site	Result / Rounds		Title	Wt.
1978						
Apr 19	Leonard Langley	Washington, DC	D	6	—	173
Jun 3	Lou Benson, Jr.	Baltimore	W	6	—	169
Nov 2	Johnny Davis	New York	L	6	—	174
1979						
May 25	Lou Butler	Baltimore	W	6	—	172
Jul 3	Lou Butler	Atlantic City	W	8	—	175
Sep 26	Donald ("Biff") Cline	Baltimore	TKO	1	—	173
Nov 14	Johnny Wilburn	Baltimore	W	8	—	174
1980						
Feb 4	Theunis Kok	Durban, South Africa	KO	10	—	175
Mar 29	Cornell Chavis	Atlantic City	TKO	1	—	178
May 8	Leonard Langley	Atlantic City	TKO	2	—	174
Jun 5	Charlie Smith	Atlantic City	TKO	4	—	174
Aug 14	Rick Jester	Chicago	TKO	3	—	175
Nov 6	Tony Mesoraca	Atlantic City	TKO	6	—	172
1981						
Jan 8	Johnny Davis	Atlantic City	W	10	—	174
Mar 5	Al Bolden	Philadelphia	W	10	—	176
May 31	Mike Rossman	Atlantic City	TKO	7	—	172
Sep 5 ⑩	James Scott	Rahway, NJ	W	10	—	175
Dec 19 ♛	Matthew Saad Muhammad★	Atlantic City	TKO	10	Won-WBC-LH	174
1982						
Mar 21 ⑩	Jerry Martin	Las Vegas	KO	6	Ret-WBC-LH	175
Aug 7 ⑩	Matthew Saad Muhammad★	Philadelphia	TKO	6	Ret-WBC-LH	174
Nov 20 ⑩	Eddie Davis	Atlantic City	TKO	11	Ret-WBC-LH	174
1983						
Mar 18 ♛	Michael Spinks★	Atlantic City	L	15	Lost-WBC-LH, For-WBA-LH	174
Sep 17 ⑩	Johnny Davis	Atlantic City	W	10	—	177
1984						
Mar 21	Vic Valentino aka Pat Cuillo	Atlantic City	W	10	—	180
Dec 12	Stanley Ross	Atlantic City	W	10	—	187
1985						
Feb 27	Michael Greer	Atlantic City	W	10	—	193
Jul 27 ♛	Piet Crous	Sun City, South Africa	KO	11	Won-WBA-C	189
1986						
Jan 8	Ric Enis	Atlantic City	KO	1	—	194
Mar 22	Leon Spinks	Reno, NV	TKO	6	Ret-WBA-C	189
Jul 12 ⑩	Evander Holyfield	Atlanta	L	15	Lost-WBA-C	189
1987						
Feb 6	Narcisco ("Sixto") Maldonado	Atlantic City	KO	4	—	207
May 15	Ossie Ocasio	Las Vegas	L	10	—	195
Aug 15	Lee Roy Murphy	St. Tropez, France	TKO	6	—	191
Dec 5 ♛	Evander Holyfield	Atlantic City	KO'd	4	For-WBA/IBF-C	190
1988						
Mar 19	George Foreman★	Las Vegas	TKO'd	7	—	220
Nov 24	Olian Alexander	Philadelphia	TKO	3	—	193
1989						
Feb 15	Tyrone Booze	Philadelphia	W	10	—	196

Apr 18		Andre McCall	Scranton, PA	W	12	—	194
May 22		Everett Martin	Atlantic City	W	10	—	198
Nov 28	⑩	Robert Daniels	Paris	L	12	For-Vac WBA-C	188
1990							
Mar 16		Mike Hunter	Newark, NJ	L	12	—	194
1991							
Mar 2		Bert Gravely	Atlantic City	KO	3	—	197
Apr 20		Tommy Richardson	Atlantic City	KO	1	—	196
Jun 11		James Salerno	Miami	W	10	—	198
Jul 23		Ed Taylor aka Young Joe Louis	Atlantic City	TKO	4	—	198
Nov 7		Ricky Parkey	Washington, DC	TKO	8	—	193
1992							
Apr 7		Ric Lainhart	Atlantic City	KO	1	—	199
May 8	⑩	Arthur Williams	Las Vegas	L	10	—	196
Jul 18		Dave Fiddler	Las Vegas	TKO	2	—	198
Oct 13	⑩	Nate Miller	Philadelphia	L	10	—	194
1997							
May 8		Earl Clark	Paterson, NJ	W	6	—	215
Jun 27		Tyrone Demby	Atlantic City	TKO	2	—	220
1998							
Nov 25		Tony LaRosa	Rosemont, IL	L	8	—	232

his left jab, in part because he had cut his right hand two weeks earlier while peeling potatoes. Qawi got ahead early, though he seemed to tire in later rounds. Nevertheless he won a unanimous decision in the ten-round fight. He did not find it pleasant to be back at Rahway. He left without taking a shower and told reporters, "I'm getting claustrophobia. I want out of here."

The victory over Scott set up a bout with Matthew Saad Muhammad, the WBC light heavyweight champion, in Atlantic City on December 19, 1981. The shorter Qawi employed a low, crouching style, which enabled him to concentrate on the champion's midsection while still allowing him to throw overhand rights to the head. Qawi worked best inside, while Muhammad scored from long range. Muhammad stunned Qawi briefly in the seventh, but Qawi administered most of the punishment. In the tenth, Qawi knocked Muhammad down with a strong right. Muhammad's cut man jumped into the ring waving a towel before the fight could resume, and referee Arthur Mercante stopped the fight. After only eighteen fights, Qawi was a world champion.

In his first title defense, Qawi knocked out Jerry Martin. He then met Saad Muhammad again in a fight dubbed "The Liberty Brawl" in Philadelphia at the Spectrum on August 7, 1982. Qawi dominated the fight. He fought from a deep crouch, bobbing and weaving. In the first round, he landed overhand rights and leaping left hooks on the much taller Muhammad. In the second, a left hook and a straight right caused Muhammad's legs to buckle. In the third, another left hook sent Muhammad to the canvas. Finally, in the sixth round, referee Carlos Padilla stopped the bout.

Qawi then knocked out Eddie Davis in a title defense before he faced Hall of Famer and WBA light heavyweight champion Michael Spinks in Atlantic City on March 18, 1983. The two fighters had a lengthy history—having sparred about 120 rounds at Joe Frazier's gym in 1980. Qawi was the shortest light heavyweight champion in history; Spinks, at 6'2½", was one of the tallest. Qawi entered the fight with a bad head cold. The fight was a tactical match. Spinks scored with his jab and sidestepped away from Qawi. Qawi knocked Spinks down in the eighth, but Spinks claimed that Qawi stepped on his foot. In the end, Spinks was impressive enough to earn a unanimous decision.

Qawi then moved up to cruiserweight. On July 27, 1985, he journeyed to Sun City, South Africa, to meet WBA cruiserweight champion Piet Crous. Qawi's manager, Rock Newman, refused to make the trip to South Africa because of its oppressive apartheid laws. The fight was fairly even for the first eight rounds. In the ninth, Qawi landed a big right to the head—sending Crous into the ropes. Qawi continued to apply pressure, but Crous stayed on his feet. In the tenth, Qawi connected with heavy rights upstairs. In the eleventh, he unloaded with a series of rights to the head, which floored Crous. He got up at the count of eight. A left-right combination knocked the champion down again. This time he was counted out. At 32, Qawi was a world champion for the second time.

In his first defense of the cruiserweight belt, Qawi avenged his loss to Spinks by knocking out Spinks's brother, Leon, in the sixth round. He then met up-and-coming Evander Holyfield in Holyfield's home turf of Atlanta. Holyfield started fast and won the first three rounds. By the fourth round, the seasoned Qawi had the inexperienced Holyfield missing, while he connected to Holyfield's face. In the eighth, Qawi landed the best punch of the fight, a right to the head. In the ninth round, Qawi began to tire. He countered effectively in rounds eleven through thirteen. However, Holyfield seemed to grow stronger as the exciting fight wore on. Holyfield was awarded a split decision. In their rematch, seventeen months later, Holyfield knocked Qawi out in the fourth round—the first time he had been stopped short of the distance.

Qawi's next fight was against George Foreman, on the comeback trail. In the sixth round Foreman knocked Qawi into the ropes. In the seventh, Foreman found his range and peppered him at will, until referee Carlos Padilla stopped the bout.

After a loss to Mike ("The Bounty") Hunter, Qawi fought only sporadically. He retired after he dropped a decision to Tony LaRosa on November 25, 1998.

In retirement, Qawi revealed that he had long battled addictions to drugs and alcohol. Late in his career, Qawi received treatment at The Lighthouse rehabilitation facility. He defeated his demons around 1992. He now works as a drug and alcohol counselor at The Lighthouse.

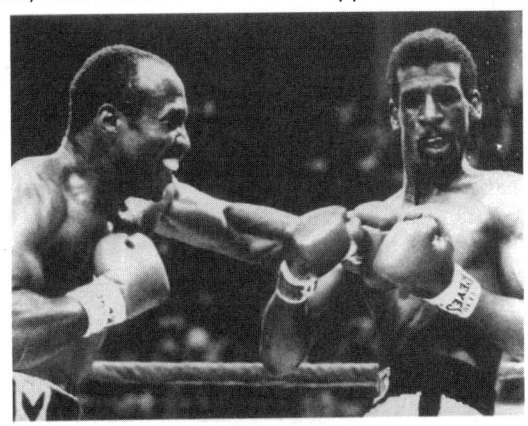

Qawi (L) twists WBA light heavyweight title holder Michael Spinks with a left hook. Spinks came back later in the fight to win on points and unify the light heavyweight championship.

SUGAR RAMOS

FEATHERWEIGHT

Right handed; 5'4½"; 124–138 lbs.

66 bouts, 10/5/1957 to 4/25/1972

Manager: Cuco Conde

Featherweight Champion 1963–64

Hall of Fame Induction: 2001

Born: 12/2/1941, Matanzas, Cuba

Named: Ultiminio Ramos Zaqueira

Ultiminio ("Sugar") Ramos was a fine, strong, intense fighter with a big right hand. Unfortunately he is also remembered as Davey Moore's opponent in the fight that led to Moore's untimely death.

Ramos was born into a very large, very poor family. One of 22 children, he began boxing at an early age and turned professional at fifteen, with a knock-out victory over Rene Arce on October 5, 1957. Ramos won nineteen of his first twenty fights, with only a single draw against featherweight title contender Ike Chestnut marring his otherwise perfect record. Tragically, one opponent, José ("Tigre") Blanco, died after a Ramos knockout. Blanco's mother did not blame Ramos for her son's death, however, and she urged him to continue boxing.

Ramos did just that. On February 27, 1960, he went twelve rounds for the first time when he decisioned Orlando Castillo to take the Cuban featherweight title. He had promised Blanco's mother a championship belt, and so he presented her with his featherweight title belt. He then knocked out his opponents in his five remaining fights in 1960 and advanced to the second contender spot in *The Ring*. When Fidel Castro banned all professional sports, including boxing, in 1961, Ramos left Cuba for Mexico. That year, he suffered his first defeat on a disqualification after four rounds to Rafael Camacho.

In 1962, Ramos made his first trip to the United States, knocking out Eddie Garcia in an L.A. bout. He decisioned one of the top featherweights, Rafiu King, and also knocked out the highly regarded Jose Luis Cruz in just two rounds.

Now ranked as top contender, Ramos had earned a shot at Davey Moore's featherweight title. A crowd of 26,000 attended the triple-header of championship bouts at Dodger Stadium on March 21, 1963: welterweight champ Emile Griffith faced number-one contender Luis Rodriguez,

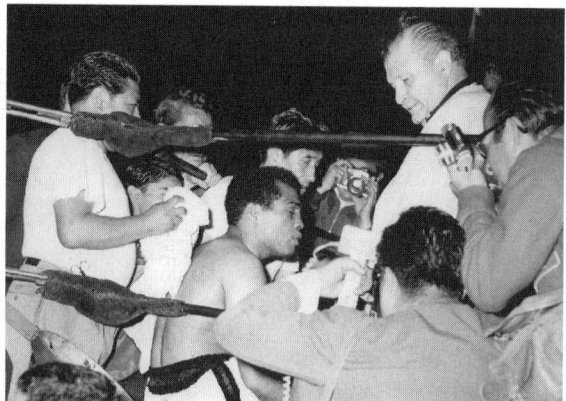

Ramos sits in his corner, dazed, after suffering a serious cut over his left eye. Referee Billy Conn stopped his October 22, 1966, challenge for the lightweight championship and declared Carlos Ortiz the winner by TKO.

IN THE RING	WON 55	LOST 7	DRAWS 4	TB 66	KO 40	W 14	WF 1	D 4	KO'd 4	L 2	LF 1

Date	Opponent	Site	Result / Rounds		Title	Wt.
1957						
Oct 5	Rene Arce	Havana, Cuba	KO	2	—	—
Nov 30	Inocencio Cartas	Havana	KO	3	—	—
1958						
Jan 11	Juan Machado	Havana	KO	2	—	—
Feb 7	Carlos Suarez	Ranchuelo, Cuba	KO	3	—	—
Apr 12	Felix Pomares	Havana	KO	2	—	—
May 24	Humberto De La Rosa	Havana	KO	4	—	—
Jul 5	Hector Medina	Havana	KO	3	—	—
Jul 19	Manuel Perdomo	Havana	W	6	—	125
Aug 9	Wilfredo Gonzalez	Ciunfuegos, Cuba	KO	2	—	—
Sep 20	Al Castillo	Havana	KO	5	—	—
Oct 11	Augusto Narvalle	Havana	WF	6	—	—
Nov 8	Jose ("Tigre") Blanco	Havana	KO	8	—	—
Dec 4	Antonio Coria	Havana	KO	4	—	—
1959						
Feb 14	Orlando Castillo	Havana	KO	10	—	—
Mar 28	Wally Livingston	Havana	KO	10	—	128
May 9	Angel Guerrero	Havana	KO	4	—	127
Jun 29	Victor Leon	Caracas	W	10	—	—
Aug 1	Johnny Bean	Havana	KO	3	—	—
Oct 31	⑩ Ike Chestnut	Caracas	D	10	—	—
Nov 20	Francisco Barraez	Matanzas, Cuba	W	10	—	—
1960						
Feb 27	Orlando Castillo	Havana	W	12	Won Cuban-FE	124
Apr 1	Tony Padron	Caracas	KO	4	—	—
May 28	Vernon Lynch	Havana	TKO	7	—	127
Aug 17	Tony Padron	Havana	KO	8	—	—
Aug 28	Jesus Santamaria	Colon, Panama	KO	9	—	127
Dec 30	Sergio Gomez	Havana	KO	9	—	—
1961						
Jan 23	Jesus Santamaria	Panama City	KO	6	—	128
Feb 8	Edwin Sykes	Panama City	KO	4	—	127
Apr 22	Juan Ramirez	Mexico City	TD	7	—	128
May 8	⑩ Felix Cervantes	Tijuana, Mexico	KO	3	—	126
May 27	Ramon ("Bobby") Cervantes	Guadalajara, Mexico	KO	4	—	132
Jun 17	Alfredo Urbina	Mexico City	W	10	—	131
Sep 2	Alfredo Urbina	Mexico City	D	10	—	132
Sep 30	Kid Anahuac	Guadalajara	W	10	—	131
Dec 13	Rafael Camacho	Puebla, Mexico	LF	4	—	131
1962						
Jan 12	Eddie Garcia	Los Angeles	KO	9	—	131
Mar 26	⑩ Rafiu King	Paris	W	10	—	130
May 11	⑩ Danny Valdez	Los Angeles	TKO	7	—	126
Jul 15	Baby Vasquez	Mexico City	W	10	—	133
Sep 3	Baby Vasquez	Tijuana	KO	10	—	135
Oct 20	Eloy Sanchez	Mexico City	KO	3	—	127
Dec 30	⑩ Jose Luis Cruz	Mexico City	KO	2	—	—

1963							
Mar 21	♛	Davey Moore	Los Angeles	TKO	10	Won-World-FE	125
Jul 13	Ⓦ	Rafiu King	Mexico City	W	15	Ret-World-FE	125
Oct 12		Sammy McSpadden	London	TKO	2	—	135
Nov 9		Kid Anahuac	Los Mochis, Mexico	KO	8	—	—
1964							
Jan 10	Ⓦ	Vicente Derado	Los Angeles	W	10	—	132
Feb 28	Ⓦ	Mitsunori Seki	Tokyo	TKO	6	Ret-World-FE	126
May 9	Ⓦ	Floyd Robertson	Accra, Ghana	W	15	Ret-World-FE	125
Sep 26	Ⓦ	Vicente Saldivar★	Mexico City	TKO'd	12	Lost-World-FE	124
1965							
Apr 17		Antonio Rosales	Acapulco, Mexico	W	10	—	127
Jun 4		Delfino Rosales	Ciudad Juarez, Mexico	KO	1	—	—
Aug 24		Raul Soriano	Tijuana	KO	6	—	—
Dec 11		Raul Soriano	Mexico City	KO	2	—	133
1966							
Feb 12		Antonio Herrera	Mexico City	W	10	—	133
Oct 22	♛	Carlos Ortiz★	Mexico City	KO'd	5	For-World-L	134
1967							
Jul 1	♛	Carlos Ortiz★	San Juan, PR	TKO'd	4	For-World-L	135
1969							
Jun 29		Rudy Gonzalez	Mexico City	KO	2	—	137
Sep 30	Ⓦ	Chango Carmona	Tijuana	TKO	7	—	136
Dec 14	Ⓦ	German Gastelbondo	Vera Cruz, Mexico	KO	1	—	—
1970							
Mar 26		Raul Rojas	Los Angeles	W	10	—	135
Aug 7	Ⓦ	Mando Ramos	Los Angeles	L	10	—	137
1971							
Jan 10		Antonio Amaya	Monterrey, Mexico	L	10	—	131
Oct 15	Ⓦ	Jimmy Robertson	Los Angeles	D	10	—	136
1972							
Mar 24		Lyle Randolph	Chicago	KO	7	—	—
Apr 25		Cesar Sinda	Inglewood, CA	TKO'd	10	—	138

Battling Torres and Roberto Cruz vied for the vacant junior welterweight crown, and Ramos faced Moore. Moore dominated the first two rounds, but as the fight wore on, Ramos took command, sending Moore to the ropes in the tenth. A quick series of lefts and rights drove Moore to the centerfield side of the ring, and then a left hook knocked him down, his head landing against the lowest of the three ring ropes. Moore got up at the count of three, but by the end of the round a Ramos right had Moore draped over the ropes. Before the start of the eleventh, Moore's manager, Willie Ketchum, told the referee that Moore could not continue.

Ramos was champion. Moore talked with reporters for about 40 minutes after the fight, then slipped into unconsciousness. He never woke again and died on March 23. When Ramos heard of Moore's death, he wept. An investigation revealed that Moore's death was caused by his head hitting the bottom rope. Calls came for the banning of the entire sport, including Bob Dylan's song, "Who Killed Davey Moore?".

Ramos continued his boxing career. He decisioned Rafiu King in his first title defense and then traveled to Tokyo to face Mitsunori Seki, the top contender, on February 28, 1964, at Kuramae Sumo Stadium. Ramos was in command from the start, opening a cut over Seki's eye in the fifth. In the sixth, Ramos felled Seki with a right to the jaw, and the contender took an eight count. When the action resumed, Ramos unleashed a flurry of lefts and rights, which put Seki down again. His manager, Iwao Wakamatsu, afraid of a repeat of the Moore incident, screamed for the ref to stop the fight.

In his next match, Ramos flew to Africa to face another contender, Floyd Robertson of Ghana, at the Accra Sports Stadium. Ramos initially won a split decision, with Ramon Velazquez, chairman of the Mexican Boxing Commission, and Ed Lassman, president of the WBA, giving the fight to Ramos, and referee Jack Hart giving the nod to Robertson. After the decision was announced, the crowd reacted angrily, and the Ghana Boxing Authority declared the bout "no contest," and then awarded the victory to Robertson. The WBA and the rest of the boxing world stuck by the original decision, and Ramos retained his title.

The Ghana fight was Ramos's last successful defense. In his next bout, he faced Hall of Famer Vicente Saldivar in Mexico City on September 26, 1964. Both fighters went at each other with reckless fury and, by the seventh round, Ramos's face was covered in blood. He could not answer the bell for the twelfth.

A little more than two years later, Ramos challenged Hall of Famer Carlos Ortiz for the world lightweight title in Mexico City, a locale where Ramos was a fan favorite. A deep cut in Ramos's left eyelid, which would require 22 stitches to close, caused referee Billy Conn to stop the fight in the fifth. Unhappy with Conn's decision, a portion of the crowd rioted and twenty minutes later Mexican Boxing Commission Chairman Velazquez ordered Ortiz to return to the ring and resume fighting. Ortiz refused. Velazquez then declared Ramos the lightweight champion, but as with the Ghana decision, the boxing community at large did not recognize the hometown decision. In the rematch the next year, Ortiz proved his dominance by knocking Ramos out in four rounds. Following his defeat, Ramos announced his retirement.

After several failed business ventures, Ramos returned to the ring. He won the first four fights of his comeback before dropping a ten-round split decision to Mando Ramos in a spirited battle before a sellout crowd of 10,400. That bout was considered one of the greatest fights ever hosted at the Olympic Auditorium.

After a heartbreaker, in which referee John Thomas stopped Ramos's fight with Cesar Sinda in the final moments—with Ramos ahead on all three cards—Ramos left boxing for good.

Referee George Latka brings a halt to the tragic Ramos vs. Davey Moore bout in the tenth round. After a left hook sent Moore down to the bottom rope, he rose and continued to fight. A subsequent flurry by Ramos forced Moore through the ropes and ended the fight.

SUGAR RAY ROBINSON

M I D D L E W E I G H T

Right-handed; 5'11"; 134–165 lbs.

202 bouts, 10/4/1940 to 11/10/1965

Manager: George Gainford

Welterweight Champion 1946–51
Middleweight Champion 1951,
1951–52, 1955–57, 1958–60

Hall of Fame Induction: 1990

Born: 5/3/1921, Detroit, MI

Named: Walker Smith, Jr.

Died: 4/12/1989

The real Ray Robinson has faded into boxing obscurity, while the boy who subbed for him in an amateur bout became one of the sweetest fighters in history. Walker Smith, who adopted the name Sugar Ray Robinson, won the world middleweight title on five separate occasions—a record that is likely to stand for a long time.

Born in Detroit, Robinson was first exposed to boxing in his teens at the same Brewster Gym where Joe Louis had learned to fight. Robinson later moved to New York and started fighting in amateur bouts there. He won the New York Golden Gloves featherweight title in 1940 and turned pro that year at age twenty.

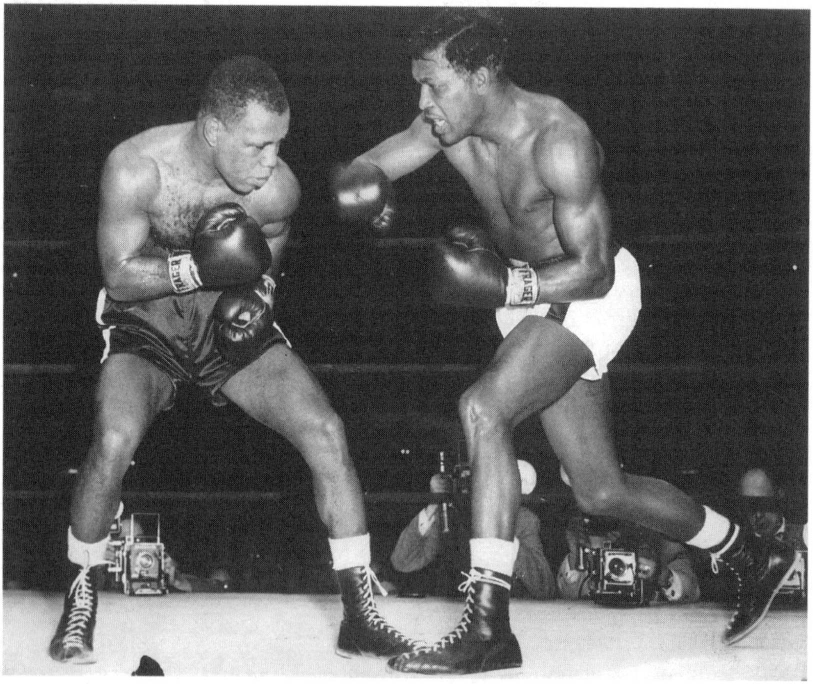

Robinson (R) suffered a defeat in a ten-round contest in Chicago on January 19, 1955, at the hands of Ralph ("Tiger") Jones. This was just the third bout after Robinson's return from his 1952 retirement.

IN THE RING	WON 173	LOST 19	DRAWS 6	TB 200	KO 108	W 65	WF 0	D 6	KO'd 1	L 18	LF 0	NC 2

Date		Opponent	Site	Result / Rounds		Title	Wt.
1940							
Oct 4		Joe Echevarria	New York	TKO	2	—	134
Oct 8		Silent Stafford	Savannah, GA	KO	2	—	—
Oct 22		Mitsos Grispos	Bronx	W	6	—	135
Nov 11		Bobby Woods	Philadelphia	KO	1	—	135
Dec 9		Norment Quarles	Philadelphia	TKO	4	—	135
Dec 13		Oliver White	New York	TKO	3	—	134
1941							
Jan 4		Henry LaBarba	Brooklyn	TKO	1	—	136
Jan 13		Frankie Wallace	Philadelphia	KO	1	—	136
Jan 31		George Zengaras	New York	W	6	—	135
Feb 8		Benny Cartagena	Brooklyn	TKO	1	—	135
Feb 21		Bobby McIntire	New York	W	6	—	135
Feb 27		Gene Spencer	Detroit	TKO	5	—	135
Mar 3		Jimmy Tygh	Philadelphia	KO	8	—	135
Apr 14		Jimmy Tygh	Philadelphia	TKO	1	—	138
Apr 24		Charley Burns	Atlantic City	KO	1	—	138
Apr 30		Joe Ghnouly	Washington, DC	TKO	3	—	134
May 10		Vic Troise	Brooklyn	TKO	1	—	139
May 19		Nick Castiglione	Philadelphia	KO	1	—	135
Jun 16		Mike Evans	Philadelphia	KO	2	—	137
Jul 2	⑩	Pete Lello	New York	TKO	4	—	137
Jul 21	⑩	Sammy Angott★	Philadelphia	W	10	—	136
Aug 27		Carl Guggino	Long Island City, NY	TKO	3	—	139
Aug 29		Maurice Arnault	Atlantic City	KO	1	—	140
Sep 19		Maxie Shapiro	New York	TKO	3	—	135
Sep 25		Marty Servo	Philadelphia	W	10	—	141
Oct 31	⑩	Fritzie Zivic★	New York	W	10	—	139
1942							
Jan 16	⑩	Fritzie Zivic★	New York	TKO	10	—	141
Feb 20		Maxie Berger	New York	TKO	2	—	144
Mar 20	⑩	Norman Rubio	New York	TKO	8	—	143
Apr 17		Harvey Dubs	Detroit	TKO	6	—	145
Apr 30		Dick Banner	Minneapolis	KO	2	—	146
May 28		Marty Servo	New York	W	10	—	144
Jul 31	♛	Sammy Angott★	New York	W	10	—	144
Aug 21		Reuben Shank	New York	KO	2	—	144
Aug 27	⑩	Tony Motisi	Chicago	KO	1	—	144
Oct 2	⑩	Jake LaMotta★	New York	W	10	—	145
Oct 19	⑩	Izzy Jannazzo	Philadelphia	W	10	—	143
Nov 6		Vic Dellicurti	New York	W	10	—	144
Dec 1	⑩	Izzy Jannazzo	Cleveland	TKO	8	—	145
Dec 14		Al Nettlow	Philadelphia	TKO	3	—	144
1943							
Feb 5	⑩	Jake LaMotta★	Detroit	L	10	—	144
Feb 19	⑩	Jackie Wilson	New York	W	10	—	142
Feb 26	⑩	Jake LaMotta★	Detroit	W	10	—	145
Apr 30		Freddie Cabral	Boston	KO	1	—	148
Jul 1	⑩	Ralph Zannelli	Boston	W	10	—	147

Date		Opponent	Location	Result	Rounds	Notes	Weight
Aug 27	⑩	Henry Armstrong ★	New York	W	10	—	145
1944							
Oct 13	⑩	Izzy Jannazzo	Boston	TKO	2	—	148
Oct 27		Sgt. Lou Woods	Chicago	TKO	9	—	147
Nov 17	⑩	Vic Dellicurti	Detroit	W	10	—	149
Dec 12		Richard ("Sheik") Rangel	Philadelphia	TKO	2	—	146
Dec 22		Georgie Martin	Boston	TKO	7	—	148
1945							
Jan 10		Billy Furrone	Washington, DC	TKO	2	—	148
Jan 16		Tommy Bell	Cleveland	W	10	—	145
Feb 14		George Costner	Chicago	KO	1	—	147
Feb 24	⑩	Jake LaMotta ★	New York	W	10	—	148
May 14	⑩	Jose Basora	Philadelphia	D	10	—	149
Jun 15	⑩	Jimmy McDaniels	New York	KO	2	—	145
Sep 18		Jimmy Mandell	Buffalo, NY	TKO	5	—	151
Sep 26	⑩	Jake LaMotta ★	Chicago	W	12	—	150
Dec 4	⑩	Vic Dellicurti	Boston	W	10	—	148
1946							
Jan 14		Dave Clark	Pittsburgh	TKO	2	—	148
Feb 5		Tony Riccio	Elizabeth, NJ	TKO	4	—	147
Feb 15		O'Neill Bell	Detroit	KO	2	—	147
Feb 26		Cliff Beckett	St. Louis	KO	4	—	147
Mar 4	⑩	Sammy Angott ★	Pittsburgh	W	10	—	147
Mar 14		Izzy Jannazzo	Baltimore	W	10	—	149
Mar 21		Freddy Flores	New York	KO	5	—	150
Jun 12		Freddy Wilson	Worcester, MA	KO	2	—	156
Jun 25		Norman Rubio	Union City, NJ	W	10	—	147
Jul 12		Joe Curcio	New York	KO	1	—	149
Aug 15		Vinnie Vines	Albany, NY	KO	6	—	151
Sep 25		Sidney Miller	Elizabeth	KO	3	—	149
Oct 7		Ossie Harris	Pittsburgh	W	10	—	152
Nov 1		Cecil Hudson	Detroit	KO	6	—	146
Nov 6		Artie Levine	Cleveland	KO	10	—	150
Dec 20	⑩	Tommy Bell	New York	W	15	Won-Vac World-W	146
1947							
Mar 27		Bernie Miller	Miami	TKO	3	—	153
Apr 3		Fred Wilson	Akron, OH	KO	3	—	153
Apr 8		Eddie Finazzo	Kansas City, MO	TKO	4	—	155
May 16	⑩	Georgie Abrams	New York	W	10	—	150
Jun 24	⑩	Jimmy Doyle	Cleveland	TKO	8	Ret-World-W	146
Aug 21		Sammy Secreet	Akron	KO	1	—	152
Aug 29		Flashy Sebastian	New York	KO	1	—	152
Oct 28	⑩	Jackie Wilson	Los Angeles	TKO	7	—	151
Dec 10		Billy Nixon	Elizabeth	TKO	6	—	151
Dec 19		Chuck Taylor	Detroit	TKO	6	Ret-World-W	146
1948							
Mar 4		Ossie Harris	Toledo, OH	W	10	—	152
Mar 16		Henry Brimm	Buffalo	W	10	—	152
Jun 28	⑩	Bernard Docusen	Chicago	W	15	Ret-World-W	146
Sep 23	⑩	Kid Gavilan ★	New York	W	10	—	150
Nov 15		Bobby Lee	Philadelphia	W	10	—	154
1949							
Feb 10		Gene Buffalo	Wilkes-Barre, PA	KO	1	—	151
Feb 15		Henry Brimm	Buffalo	D	10	—	153

Date		Opponent	Location	Result	Rounds	Notes	Weight
Mar 25		Bobby Lee	Chicago	W	10	—	154
Apr 11		Don Lee	Omaha, NE	W	10	—	155
Apr 20		Earl Turner	Oakland, NE	TKO	8	—	153
Jun 7		Freddie Flores	New Bedford, MA	TKO	3	—	151
Jun 20		Cecil Hudson	Providence, RI	TKO	5	—	153
Jul 11	⑩	Kid Gavilan★	Philadelphia	W	15	Ret-World-W	147
Aug 24	⑩	Steve Belloise	New York	TKO	7	—	153
Sep 9		Benny Evans	Omaha	TKO	5	—	154
Sep 12		Charley Dotson	Houston	KO	3	—	152
Nov 9		Don Lee	Denver	W	10	—	155
Nov 13		Vern Lester	New Orleans	KO	5	—	150

1950

Date		Opponent	Location	Result	Rounds	Notes	Weight
Jan 30		George LaRover	New Haven, CT	TKO	4	—	153
Feb 13		Al Mobley	Miami	TKO	6	—	153
Feb 22		Aaron Wade	Savannah	KO	3	—	156
Feb 27		Jean Walzack	St. Louis	W	10	—	157
Mar 22	⑩	George Costner	Philadelphia	KO	1	—	154
Apr 21		Cliff Beckett	Columbus, OH	TKO	3	—	155
Apr 28	⑩	Ray Barnes	Detroit	W	10	—	156
Jun 5	⑩	Robert Villemain	Philadelphia	W	15	Won-Vac PA World-M	155
Aug 9	⑩	Charley Fusari	Jersey City, NJ	W	15	Ret-World-W	147
Aug 25		Jose Basora	Scranton, PA	KO	1	Ret-PA World-M	154
Sep 4		Billy Brown	New York	W	10	—	156
Oct 16		Joe Rindone	Boston	KO	6	—	159
Oct 26		Carl ("Bobo") Olson★	Philadelphia	KO	12	Ret-PA World-M	158
Nov 8		Bobby Dykes	Chicago	W	10	—	157
Nov 27		Jean Stock	Paris	TKO	2	—	156
Dec 9		Luc Van Dam	Brussels	KO	4	—	156
Dec 16		Jean Walzack	Geneva	W	10	—	156
Dec 22	⑩	Robert Villemain	Paris	TKO	9	—	155
Dec 25		Hans Stretz	Frankfurt, Germany	KO	6	—	157

1951

Date		Opponent	Location	Result	Rounds	Notes	Weight
Feb 14	♛	Jake LaMotta★	Chicago	TKO	13	Won-World-M	155
Apr 5		Holly Mims	Miami	W	10	—	159
Apr 9		Don Ellis	Oklahoma City	KO	1	—	157
May 21		Kid Marcel	Paris	TKO	5	—	160
May 26		Jean Wanes	Zurich, Switzerland	W	10	—	162
Jun 10		Jan de Bruin	Antwerp, Belgium	TKO	8	—	160
Jun 16		Jean Walzack	Liege, Belgium	TKO	6	—	154
Jun 24		Gerhard Hecht	Berlin	NC	2	—	157
Jul 1		Cyrille Delannoit	Turin, Italy	TKO	3	—	160
Jul 10	⑩	Randy Turpin★	London	L	15	Lost-World-M	154
Sep 12	♛	Randy Turpin★	New York	TKO	10	Reg-World-M	157

1952

Date		Opponent	Location	Result	Rounds	Notes	Weight
Mar 13	⑩	Carl ("Bobo") Olson★	San Francisco	W	15	Ret-World-M	157
Apr 16	⑩	Rocky Graziano★	Chicago	KO	3	Ret-World-M	157
Jun 25	♛	Joey Maxim★	New York	TKO'd	14	For-World-LH	157

1955

Date		Opponent	Location	Result	Rounds	Notes	Weight
Jan 5		Joe Rindone	Detroit	KO	6	—	159
Jan 19	⑩	Ralph ("Tiger") Jones	Chicago	L	10	—	159
Mar 29		Johnny Lombardo	Cincinnati	W	10	—	162
Apr 14		Ted Olla	Milwaukee	TKO	3	—	163
May 4		Garth Panter	Detroit	W	10	—	163
Jul 22	⑩	Rocky Castellani	San Francisco	W	10	—	159

Dec 9	♛ Carl ("Bobo") Olson★	Chicago	KO	2	Reg-World-M	159

1956

May 18	⓪ Carl ("Bobo") Olson★	Los Angeles	KO	4	Ret-World-M	159
Nov 10	Bob Provizzi	New Haven	W	10	—	165

1957

Jan 2	⓪ Gene Fullmer★	New York	L	15	Lost-World-M	160
May 1	♛ Gene Fullmer★	Chicago	KO	5	Reg-World-M	159
Sep 23	⓪ Carmen Basilio★	New York	L	15	Lost-World-M	160

1958

Mar 25	♛ Carmen Basilio★	Chicago	W	15	Reg-World-M	159

1959

Dec 14	Bob Young	Boston	TKO	2	—	161

1960

Jan 22	⓪ Paul Pender	Boston	L	15	Lost-World-M	159
Apr 2	Tony Baldoni	Baltimore	KO	1	—	165
Jun 10	♛ Paul Pender	Boston	L	15	For-World-M	158
Dec 3	♛ Gene Fullmer★	Los Angeles	D	15	For-NBA-M	158

1961

Mar 4	♛ Gene Fullmer★	Las Vegas	L	15	For-NBA-M	159
Sep 25	Wilf Greaves	Detroit	W	10	—	160
Oct 21	⓪ Denny Moyer	New York	W	10	—	159
Nov 20	Al Hauser	Providence	TKO	6	—	162
Dec 8	Wilf Greaves	Pittsburgh	KO	8	—	161

1962

Feb 17	⓪ Denny Moyer	New York	L	10	—	159
Apr 27	Bobby Lee	Port of Spain, Trinidad	KO	2	—	168
Jul 9	Phil Moyer	Los Angeles	L	10	—	160
Sep 25	⓪ Terry Downes	London	L	10	—	159
Oct 17	Diego Infantes	Vienna	KO	2	—	160
Nov 10	Georges Estatoff	Lyons, France	TKO	6	—	164

1963

Jan 30	⓪ Ralph Dupas	Miami Beach	W	10	—	162
Feb 25	Bernie Reynolds	Santo Domingo, D.R.	KO	4	—	—
Mar 11	Billy Thornton	Lewiston, ME	KO	3	—	161
May 5	Maurice Robinet	Sherbrooke, Que.	KO	3	—	161
Jun 24	⓪ Joey Giardello★	Philadelphia	L	10	—	158
Oct 14	Armand Vanucci	Paris	W	10	—	159
Nov 9	Fabio Bettini	Lyons	D	10	—	162
Nov 16	Emile Saerens	Brussels	KO	8	—	160
Nov 29	Andre Davier	Grenoble, France	W	10	—	158
Dec 9	Armand Vanucci	Paris	W	10	—	160

1964

May 19	Gaylord Barnes	Portland, OR	W	10	—	162
Jul 8	Clarence Riley	Pittsfield, MA	TKO	6	—	161
Jul 27	Art Hernandez	Omaha	D	10	—	162
Sep 3	Mick Leahy	Paisley, Scotland	L	10	—	163
Sep 28	Yolande Leveque	Paris	W	10	—	161
Oct 12	Johnny Angel	London	TKO	6	—	162
Oct 24	Jackie Cailleau	Nice, France	W	10	—	161
Nov 7	Jean Baptiste Rolland	Calen, France	W	10	—	162
Nov 14	Jean Beltritti	Marseilles, France	W	10	—	163
Nov 27	Fabio Bettini	Rome	D	10	—	159

1965

Date		Opponent	Location	Result	Round		Weight
Mar 6		Jimmy Beecham	Kingston, NY	KO	2	—	165
Apr 4		Earl Basting	Savannah	KO	1	—	161
Apr 28		Gary ("Rocky") Randell	Norfolk, VA	KO	3	—	163
May 24		Memo Ayon	Tijuana, Mexico	L	10	—	160
Jun 1	⑩	Stan Harrington	Honolulu	L	10	—	159
Jun 24		Harvey McCullough	Richmond, VA	W	10	—	—
Jul 12		Ferd Hernandez	Las Vegas	L	10	—	160
Jul 27		Harvey McCullough	Richmond	W	10	—	161
Aug 10	⑩	Stan Harrington	Honolulu	L	10	—	159
Sep 15		Neil Morrison	Norfolk	NC	2	—	162
Sep 23		Harvey McCullough	Philadelphia	W	10	—	162
Oct 1		Peter Schmidt	Johnstown, PA	W	10	—	159
Oct 20		Rudolph Bent	Steubenville, OH	TKO	3	—	161
Nov 10	⑩	Joey Archer	Pittsburgh	L	10	—	160

Robinson made his debut at Madison Square Garden with a quick two-round victory. He rapidly moved through the welterweight ranks, and the next year, he defeated Sammy Angott and Fritzie Zivic. *The Ring* already ranked him as the top welterweight contender by 1941. The next few years brought victories over Angott, Zivic, Jackie Wilson, Henry Armstrong, and—beginning a long and bitter rivalry—Jake LaMotta.

By 1946, Robinson had gained the admiration of ring devotees for his lightning speed, impeccable timing, solid punching power, and graceful style. That year, Robinson faced Tommy Bell for the vacant welterweight title. He outpointed Bell to take the belt. He defended the welterweight title five times through 1950, one with a win over the tough Kid Gavilan, and meanwhile annexed Pennsylvania's world middleweight title with a victory over Robert Villemain.

Now solidly in middleweight territory, Robinson met his old foe LaMotta in a challenge for the middleweight crown. He and LaMotta had fought five times up to then, with Robinson winning four of their fierce battles. On Valentine's Day in 1951, Robinson faced LaMotta for the sixth time in Chicago Stadium in front of 14,802 fans. It was an ugly, brutal fight from which neither man came away unscathed. After eight rounds of mutual battering, LaMotta led on two cards and Robinson on one. Robinson took control in the ninth. By the twelfth, he had complete command of the fight. LaMotta was bloody and staggering when the referee stopped the fight with one minute left in the thirteenth round.

Robinson took his newly won title to Europe, where he was upset by Randy Turpin, who won the championship in London on a decision. In a rematch back in the United States, Robinson stopped Turpin in the tenth round to reclaim the title. He then defended his middleweight crown twice in 1952, with a fifteen-round decision over Bobo Olson in March and a three-round KO of Rocky Graziano in April.

Robinson now wanted to join the light heavies and in 1952, on a blistering hot day in Yankee Stadium, he challenged Joey Maxim for the light heavyweight title. Robinson seized the fight early, scoring at will and dancing away from Maxim's offensive thrusts. The first nine rounds were almost all Robinson.

The popular Robinson lived extravagantly in the 1950s and early '60s. At times his entourage included a voice coach, drama instructor, barber, golf pro, masseur, secretary, trainers, and a dwarf mascot.

Maxim took the tenth. Robinson won the eleventh and the twelfth, but he was visibly wilting in the intense heat. He flagged in the thirteenth and could not answer the bell for the fourteenth round. Officially, the loss was recorded as a knockout, the first and only KO of Robinson's career.

Robinson then retired but was back in January 1955. By December, he had reclaimed the middleweight title by knocking out Olson in two rounds. Robinson lost the title in 1957 to Gene Fullmer, but he won it back for the fourth time with a knockout in their rematch. That same year Robinson faced Hall of Famer Carmen Basilio in Yankee Stadium before 35,000 fans. The aging Robinson came into the match as the underdog. He got off to a good start and won the first four rounds, cutting Basilio's eye and nose. Basilio pressed forward and won four of the next five rounds. The two great champions battled toe-to-toe for the rest of the fight. When the result was announced, Basilio was the winner by a split decision. In the rematch, Robinson, though fighting a virus, dominated the fight and closed Basilio's left eye. An exhausted Robinson won the decision and the championship for the fifth time.

He lost the title in 1960 to Paul Pender by decision and was defeated in their rematch as well. After two failed attempts to win the NBA middleweight title from Fullmer, the 40-year-old Robinson received no more opportunities for title fights. He finally retired from the ring at the age of 44. In retirement, Robinson had some acting roles, ran a popular Harlem nightclub, and established the Sugar Ray Robinson Youth Foundation. He suffered from Alzheimer's Disease in his last years and ultimately died from it.

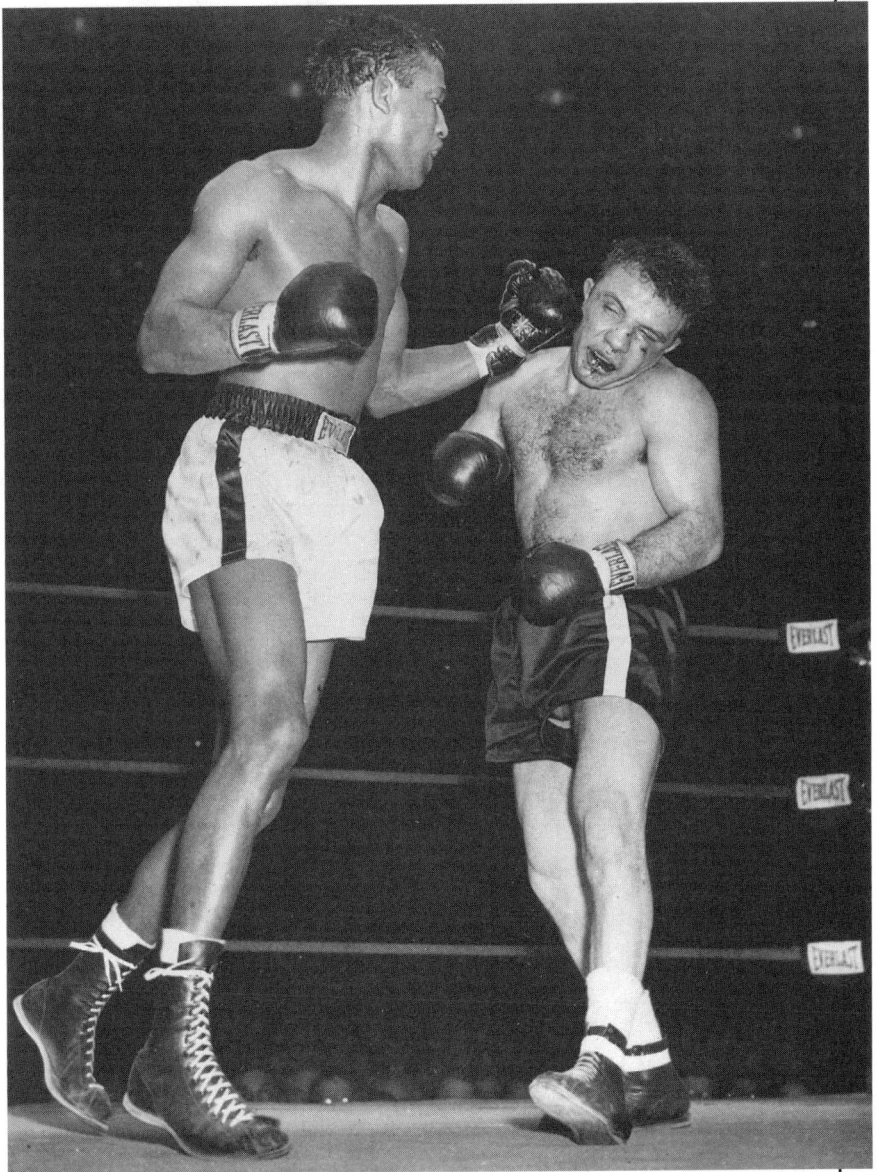

It was called the "St. Valentine's Day Massacre" after Robinson (L) battered the determined and courageous Jake LaMotta for nearly thirteen rounds to take the middleweight title in Chicago on February 14, 1951.

LUIS RODRIGUEZ
El Feo

W E L T E R W E I G H T

Right-handed; 5'8"; 144–168 lbs.

121 bouts, 6/2/1956 to 4/12/1972

Managers: Ernesto Corrales and Angelo Dundee

Welterweight Champion 1963

Hall of Fame Induction: 1997

Born: 6/17/1937, Camaguey, Cuba

Named: Luis Manuel Rodriguez

Died: 7/1/1996

Luis Rodriguez was a top welterweight of the 1960s, along with his frequent rival and fellow Hall of Famer, Emile Griffith. Rodriguez and Griffith fought four times, each bout going to the scorecards. Rodriguez won the only unanimous decision in the series; Griffith took the rest on splits.

Born in Camaguey, Cuba, the city that had produced Kid Gavilan, Rodriguez grew up in poverty and, while still a boy, had to work selling newspapers and shining shoes. Rodriguez learned to box and won a Cuban national Golden Gloves title, knocking out ten consecutive opponents. His first pro fight was a three-round knockout on June 2, 1956. Except for one bout that was stopped by rain, Rodriguez won all of his first 35 fights. Manager Ernesto Corrales took him to Florida and signed him with Angelo Dundee as co-manager. Rodriguez then decisioned a series of strong opponents and earned *The Ring*'s ranking as the top contender for the welterweight crown in 1959.

Despite his top-contender status in 1959, 1960, and 1962 (he was fourth in 1961), Rodriguez did not get a chance to fight for the title. Still, "El Feo," or "The Ugly One," as Rodriguez was called, continued to achieve great success. On December 17, 1960, he met Griffith in Madison Square Garden in a non-title contest. Griffith was awarded a split decision, possibly because of his status as champion.

Over the next two years, Rodriguez won fourteen of fifteen fights, and on March 21, 1963, he finally fought Griffith for the title in Dodger Stadium in Los Angeles before 26,142 fans. In a close fight, Rodriguez took the unanimous decision. The rematch in the Garden two months later was another close battle. The official decision was split in favor of Griffith, but most writers at ringside believed that Rodriguez had won.

In his final bout with Griffith, Rodriguez lost another hotly

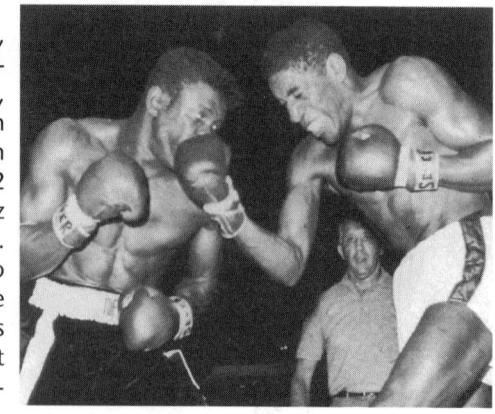

Rodriguez faced Hall of Famer Emile Griffith (L) four times. The two fighters were so closely matched, Griffith once commented that both deserved to be champion.

IN THE RING	WON 107	LOST 13	DRAWS 0	TB 121	KO 49	W 57	WF 1	D 0	KO'd 3	L 10	LF 0	NC 1

Date	Opponent	Site	Result / Rounds		Title	Wt.
1956						
Jun 2	Lazaro Hernandez Kessell	Havana, Cuba	KO	3	—	—
Jul 21	Vicente Reyes	Havana	W	4	—	—
Oct 20	Julian Yanes	Havana	W	4	—	—
Nov 28	Pablo Cardenas	Havana	KO	2	—	—
Dec 15	Jose Hernandez	Havana	NC	2	—	—
1957						
Jan 12	Jose Hernandez	Havana	KO	5	—	—
Feb 16	Guillermo Diaz	Havana	W	6	—	144
Mar 23	Vicente Reyes	Havana	W	6	—	—
May 18	Vicente Reyes	Havana	W	6	—	—
Jun 22	Antonio Salas	Havana	W	8	—	144
Jul 20	Guillermo Diaz	Havana	WF	6	—	142
Sep 28	Gomeo Brennan	Havana	W	8	—	—
Nov 15	Rolando Rodriguez	Havana	W	8	—	—
1958						
Feb 8	Benny Paret	Havana	W	10	—	—
Mar 29	Rolando Rodriguez	Havana	KO	4	—	—
Apr 19	Tony Armenteros	Havana	W	10	—	—
Jul 26	Charley Scott	Havana	KO	9	—	144
Aug 9	Benny Paret	Havana	W	10	—	—
Sep 20	Kid Fichique	Havana	W	12	Won-Cuba-W	144
Nov 22	Juan Padilla	Havana	W	10	—	—
1959						
Feb 21	Joe Miceli	Havana	KO	5	—	145
May 9	Cecil Shorts	Havana	KO	9	—	144
Jun 17	⑩ Virgil Akins	Miami Beach	W	10	—	147
Aug 26	⑩ Rudell Stitch	Louisville, KY	W	10	—	147
Oct 3	Larry Baker	Havana	W	10	—	145
Oct 21	⑩ Isaac Logart	Miami Beach	W	10	—	145
Dec 23	⑩ Garnet ("Sugar") Hart	Miami Beach	W	10	—	146
1960						
Feb 10	Carl Hubbard	Miami Beach	KO	4	—	148
Mar 2	Chico Vejar	Miami Beach	W	10	—	149
Apr 7	Alvaro Gutierrez	Los Angeles	TKO	4	—	146
May 26	Alfredo Cota	Los Angeles	KO	2	—	145
Jul 6	Virgil Akins	Louisville	W	10	—	147
Aug 17	Basil Campbell	Havana	KO	5	—	147
Oct 24	Mel Collins	Tampa, FL	W	10	—	147
Nov 16	Yama Bahama	Miami Beach	W	10	—	147
Nov 28	⑩ Johnny Gonsalves	Oakland, CA	W	10	—	144
Dec 17	⑩ Emile Griffith★	New York	L	10	—	148
1961						
Feb 21	Lyle Mackin	Oakland	TKO	5	—	147
Mar 22	Johnny Gonsalves	Oakland	W	10	—	146
Apr 15	Alvaro Gutierrez	Mexico City	KO	5	—	146
May 13	Alfredo Cota	Guadalajara, Mexico	KO	4	—	147
Aug 3	⑩ Curtis Cokes★	Dallas	L	10	—	145
Sep 13	Guy Sumlin	Miami Beach	KO	5	—	148

Date		Opponent	Location	Result	Round		Weight
Oct 24		Jose Gonzalez	Miami Beach	TKO	7	—	152
Dec 2	⑩	Curtis Cokes★	Miami Beach	W	10	—	149
1962							
Jan 27	⑩	Federico Thompson	New York	W	10	—	150
Mar 17		Ricardo Falech	Miami Beach	TKO	3	—	147
May 4	⑩	Yama Bahama	New York	TKO	3	—	151
Jun 30		Gene Armstrong	New York	TKO	8	—	150
Aug 29		Ernie Burford	Miami Beach	KO	7	—	151
Nov 6		Santiago Gutierrez	San Antonio, TX	KO	3	—	148
Dec 12		Mel Collins	Miami Beach	W	10	—	152
1963							
Jan 19	⑩	Joey Giambra	Miami Beach	W	10	—	150
Mar 21	♛	Emile Griffith★	Los Angeles	W	15	Won-World-W	146
Jun 8	⑩	Emile Griffith★	New York	L	15	Lost-World-W	146
Aug 17	⑩	Denny Moyer	Miami Beach	KO	9	—	151
Oct 18		Wilbert McClure	New York	W	10	—	150
Dec 27		Wilbert McClure	Miami Beach	W	10	—	151
1964							
Mar 20		Holly Mims	New York	W	10	—	151
Apr 3		Jesse Smith	Miami Beach	W	10	—	151
Jun 12	♛	Emile Griffith★	Las Vegas	L	15	For-World-W	146
Nov 14		L.C. Morgan	Mexico City	KO	2	—	148
1965							
Feb 13	⑩	Rubin ("Hurricane") Carter	New York	W	10	—	151
Mar 26		Johnny Smith	Los Angeles	KO	10	—	149
Apr 21		Garland Randall	Tampa	W	10	—	147
Jul 16		Memo Ayon	Los Angeles	TKO	3	—	150
Jul 26		Jose Asumpcion	Las Vegas	W	10	—	150
Aug 3		Charley Austin	Phoenix	W	10	—	152
Aug 26	⑩	Rubin ("Hurricane") Carter	Los Angeles	W	10	—	150
Oct 4		Johnny Morris	Philadelphia	TKO	2	—	150
Nov 16		Cecil Mott	Miami Beach	KO	4	—	151
Dec 2	⑩	Eddie Pace	Los Angeles	W	10	—	150
Dec 21		Joe Louis Murphy	Albuquerque, NM	KO	4	—	149
1966							
Jan 18		Fred McWilliams	Phoenix	TKO	9	—	152
Jan 25		Joey Limas	Albuquerque	TKO	4	—	149
Mar 7		George Benton	Albuquerque	TKO	9	—	151
Apr 11		Percy Manning	Philadelphia	L	10	—	151
May 7		Tommy Caldwell	San Juan, PR	TKO	2	—	150
Jul 6	⑩	Curtis Cokes★	New Orleans	TKO'd	15	—	146
Sep 24		Ruben Orrico	Rosario, Argentina	TKO	4	—	—
Nov 8		Juarez de Lima	Rosario	KO	3	—	149
1967							
Jan 21		Manuel Alvarez	Mar del Plata, Argentina	KO	8	—	—
Feb 7		Esteban Osuna	Rosario	W	10	—	—
Mar 20		Bennie Briscoe	San Juan	W	10	—	152
Jun 4		Rocky Rivero	San Juan	W	10	—	154
Jun 17		Jimmy Lester	Oakland	W	10	—	151
Sep 7	⑩	Ferd Hernandez	Oakland	W	10	—	151
Sep 29		Phil Robinson	Caracas	KO	3	—	—
Nov 6		Percy Manning	Caracas	TKO	1	—	152
Nov 16		Marvin McFarland	Maracaibo, Venezuela	W	10	—	152
Dec 15		Bennie Briscoe	New York	W	10	—	152

1968						
Feb 6	Charley Austin	Miami Beach	TKO	6	—	154
Mar 26	Carl Moore	Miami Beach	W	10	—	154
May 7	Teddy Wright	Miami Beach	W	10	—	156
Jun 3	Vicente Rondon	San Juan	L	10	—	154
Jul 18	Vicente Rondon	San Juan	W	10	—	154
Sep 4	Rudy Rodriguez	Key West, FL	TKO	4	—	152
Nov 15	⑩ Joe Shaw	New York	W	10	—	153
1969						
Jan 21	Dub Huntley	Miami Beach	W	10	—	157
Feb 20	Robert ("Songbird") Williams	Tampa	KO	7	—	155
Mar 31	Rafael Gutierrez	San Diego	TKO	6	—	156
Jul 8	Eddie Owens	Miami Beach	KO	7	—	158
Aug 12	David Beckles	Miami Beach	TKO	2	—	158
Sep 23	Tom Bethea	Miami Beach	W	10	—	159
Nov 22	♛ Nino Benvenuti★	Rome	KO'd	11	For-World-M	156
1970						
Feb 10	Porter Rolle	Miami Beach	KO	4	—	162
Mar 17	Joe Cokes	Miami Beach	TKO	4	—	161
Apr 14	Willie Warren	Miami Beach	W	10	—	159
Jun 16	Kirkland ("Baby Boy") Rolle	Miami	KO	5	—	162
Jul 31	Jose Gonzalez	San Juan	L	10	—	—
Aug 20	⑩ Fraser Scott	Seattle	W	10	—	158
Sep 24	Jose Gonzalez	Miami Beach	W	12	—	161
Dec 1	J.C. Ponder	Miami Beach	KO	5	—	167
1971						
Jan 26	⑩ Bobby Cassidy	Miami Beach	W	10	—	164
Apr 7	Tony Mundine	Melbourne	KO	1	—	161
May 25	⑩ Bunny Sterling	London	L	10	—	159
Aug 3	⑩ Rafael Gutierrez	San Francisco	KO'd	6	—	163
Nov 1	Mike Padgett	Greenwood, SC	KO	2	—	—
Nov 30	Dave Hilton	Miami Beach	W	10	—	168
1972						
Mar 16	Mike Lancaster	Seattle	L	10	—	161
Apr 12	Donato Paduano	Montreal	L	10	—	163

contested split decision. Rodriguez was the second-ranked welterweight contender in 1966. When he moved up to middleweight, *The Ring* considered him that division's top contender in 1967, second in 1968, and third in 1969.

On November 22, 1969, in Rome, Rodriguez went after Nino Benvenuti's middleweight crown. Rodriguez outboxed Benvenuti for ten rounds, but fell to a knock-out left hook in the eleventh. Rodriguez remained a highly rated contender for the next year, but he began losing as often as he won, and he retired at the age of 34. He had won over a hundred fights.

In retirement the affable Rodriguez trained amateur boxers for the City of Miami. He died in 1996 at the age of 59.

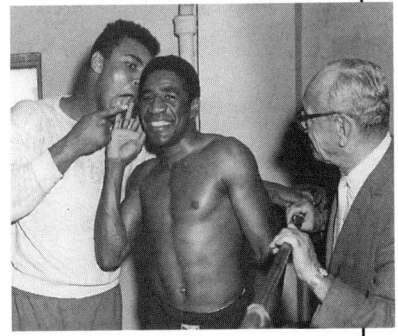

In the presence of Philadelphia boxing promoter Herman Taylor (R), Cassius Clay offers the good-natured Rodriguez some counsel at Miami Beach's Fifth Street Gym.

EDWIN ROSARIO
El Chapo

JUNIOR WELTERWEIGHT

Right-handed; 5'6", 119–149 lbs.

53 bouts, 3/3/1979 to 9/25/1997

Manager: Jimmy Jacobs

WBC Lightweight Champ 1983–84
WBA Lightweight Champ 1986–87, 1989–90
WBA Jr Welterweight Champ 1991–92

Hall of Fame Induction: 2006

Born: 3/15/1963, Toa Baja, PR

Died: 1/12/1997

In Edwin Rosario's short and troubled life, he won four world boxing championships. Rosario was born on March 15, 1963, in Toa Baja, Puerto Rico. He played Little League baseball until he was eight years old and followed his older brother, who had a successful professional boxing career himself, into the gym. Right from the start, Rosario came under the watchful eye of trainer Manny Siaca, who also trained lightweight champion Esteban DeJesus. As an amateur, Rosario became a Puerto Rican Golden Gloves titleholder.

Rosario turned pro when he was only fifteen and knocked out Jorge Ortega in the second round on March 3, 1979. Later a ninth-round technical knockout of Javier Flores on August 22, 1980, in Las Vegas, attracted the attention of manager Jim Jacobs. After Wilfredo Gomez knocked out Derrik Holmes in a nationally televised super bantamweight title fight in five rounds, the network showed Rosario–Flores, which it had taped earlier that evening. Viewing at home, Jacobs was amazed: "I watched one round of fighting and I couldn't believe any human could fight this way at seventeen years of age. At seventeen, this fighter had technical skills that world champions didn't show me." Midway through the fight, Hall of Fame trainer and manager Cus D'Amato called Jacobs to rave about Rosario's performance. Jacobs's management partner, Bill Cayton, was also very impressed. Cayton and Jacobs purchased Rosario's contract from Siaca—who remained Rosario's trainer—for $80,000.

Rosario continued his success in the Cayton/Jacobs stable. On May 30, 1982, Rosario put together

Rosario (R) started his professional career with an impressive record of fifteen straight knockouts. Tony Tris was his twelfth victim.

IN THE RING	**WON 47**	**LOST 6**	**DRAWS 0**	*TB* 53	*KO* 41	*W* 6	*WF* 0	*D* 0	*KO'd* 5	*L* 1	*LF* 0	

Date	Opponent	Site	Result / Rounds		Title	Wt.
1979						
Mar 3	Jorge Ortega	Santo Domingo, D.R.	KO	2	—	—
Mar 3	Juan Caro	Santo Domingo	KO	1	—	—
Mar 27	Enrique Maldonado	Santo Domingo	KO	3	—	—
May 12	Julio Miranda	Santo Domingo	KO	4	—	—
Jul 20	Jose Villegas	San Diego	KO	5	—	119
Aug 1	James Sowell	Los Angeles	KO	2	—	126
Sep 22	Pancho Muletta	San Juan, PR	KO	2	—	119
1980						
Feb 18	Leopoldo Frias	San Juan	KO	2	—	121
Mar 10	Pascual Polanco	San Juan	KO	4	—	120
Jul 7	Jose Luis Lara	Bloomington, MN	KO	2	—	124
Aug 22	Javier Flores	Las Vegas	KO	9	—	122
1981						
Apr 10	Tony Tris	New York	KO	4	—	128
May 23	Jose Resendez	Las Vegas	KO	6	—	124
Jun 25	Refugio Rojas	New York	KO	2	—	129
Jul 18	Rodrigo Aguirre	Tampa	KO	9	—	130
Sep 16	James Martinez	Las Vegas	W	10	—	127
Nov 13	Roberto Garcia	Las Vegas	KO	2	—	130
Dec 10	Ernesto Herrera	Tampa	KO	3	—	133
1982						
Jan 30	Ezzard Adams	Las Vegas	TKO	3	—	131
Mar 21	Dennis Quimayousie	Las Vegas	KO	1	—	131
May 30	Edwin Viruet	Las Vegas	TKO	3	—	134
1983						
May 1 ⑩	Jose Luis Ramirez	San Juan	W	12	Won-Vac WBC-L	134
1984						
Mar 17 ⑩	Roberto Elizondo	San Juan	TKO	1	Ret-WBC-L	134
Jun 23 ⑩	Howard Davis, Jr.	Hato Rey, PR	W	12	Ret-WBC-L	133
Nov 3 ⑩	Jose Luis Ramirez	San Juan	TKO'd	4	Lost-WBC-L	135
1985						
Mar 13	Eduardo Valdez	Atlantic City	TKO	3	—	138
Apr 15	Alberto Ramos	New York	TKO	2	—	136
Jun 16	Frankie Randall	London	W	10	—	132
Dec 27	Roque Montoya	Latham, NY	TKO	7	—	138
1986						
Jun 13 ♛	Hector ("Macho") Camacho	New York	L	12	For-WBC-L	134
Sep 26 ♛	Livingstone Bramble	Miami Beach	KO	2	Won-WBA-L	135
1987						
Mar 7	Roger Brown	Las Vegas	KO	2	—	139
Aug 11	Juan Nazario	Chicago	KO	8	Ret-WBA-L	134
Nov 21 ⑩	Julio Cesar Chavez	Las Vegas	TKO'd	11	Lost-WBA-L	135
1988						
Jun 2	Ramiro Lozano	New York	KO	3	—	139
Jul 31	Javier Cerna	New York	KO	1	—	140
Aug 11	Rafael Gandarilla	New York	TKO	3	—	138
Sep 3	Felipe Angulo	Atlantic City	TKO	2	—	138
Oct 27	Juan Minaya	New York	KO	4	—	141

1989							
Feb 9		Jesus Gallardo	New York	TKO	8	—	141
Mar 16		Larry Benson	New York	TKO	5	—	139
Jul 9	⑩	Anthony Jones	Atlantic City	TKO	6	Won-WBA-L	135
1990							
Apr 4	⑩	Juan Nazario	New York	TKO'd	8	Lost-WBA-L	134
Aug 23		Dwayne Swift	Callicoon, NY	W	10	—	142
1991							
Jun 14	⑩	Loreto Garza	Sacramento, CA	TKO	3	Won-WBA-JW	139
1992							
Apr 10		Akinobu Hiranaka	Naucalpan, Mexico	TKO'd	1	Lost-WBA-JW	140
Aug 8		George Kellmann	San Juan	TKO	5	—	147
1993							
Jan 30		Frankie Randall	Memphis, TN	TKO'd	7	—	146
1997							
May 22		Maurice Roberson	Bayamon, PR	TKO	4	—	149
Jun 7		Calvin Moody	Miami	TKO	3	—	146
Jul 17		Roger Flores	Bayamon	W	12	—	143
Aug 23		Sangford Ricks	New York	KO	8	—	144
Sep 25		Harold Bennett	Bayamon	KO	2	—	143

a very impressive performance—stopping Edwin Viruet at 1:37 of the third round. Viruet was a tough competitor who had lasted fifteen rounds with Roberto Duran in a lightweight title bout and who had drawn with WBC junior welterweight champion Saoul Mamby. Rosario knocked Viruet down in the second with a right to the side of the head. He finished him in the third with a right to the jaw. Viruet got to his feet by the count of ten and then began wandering dazedly around the ring before referee Harry Krause stopped the fight. It was the first time in over 40 fights that Viruet had been vanquished short of the distance.

At this time the comparisons to Roberto Duran and Wilfredo Gomez seemed very apt, and it appeared that Rosario would soon be a world champion. Unfortunately, while sparring he suffered a wrist injury which required surgery. Rosario returned to the ring when he met Jose Luis Ramirez for the vacant WBC lightweight title in San Juan on May 1, 1983. Rosario re-injured his wrist early in the fight. Though he did not display his characteristic knock-out power, he managed to box well enough to earn a twelve-round decision and the title.

After several months of healing, he returned to the ring and defended his title with a one-round knockout of Roberto Elizondo. In his next fight, he faced 1976 U.S. Olympic gold medalist Howard Davis at the Roberto Clemente Coliseum in Hato Rey, Puerto Rico. It was an action-packed see-saw bout. With the fight almost over, Rosario landed a left hook to the chin, dropping Davis. He got up as the referee completed the eight count and the bell sounded to end the fight. Rosario won a narrow split decision. Without the knockdown at the end, Rosario most likely would not have won. Rosario earned $250,000 for his efforts.

For his next title defense, Rosario met Jose Luis Ramirez in a rematch at Hiram Bithorn Stadium in San Juan. Rosario was very strong at the start. He knocked Ramirez down with a right for a three-count in the first round and dominated for the rest of the stanza. In the second, Rosario again knocked Ramirez down with a right hand for a count of six. In the third the tide turned. The southpaw Ramirez stunned Rosario with a left to the jaw and a big left hook. Ramirez continued in control in the fourth and initiated an onslaught that left Rosario out on his feet when the referee stopped the fight at 2:52 of the fourth round. It was the first defeat of Rosario's career.

Rosario won his next four fights to gain another chance at the title then held by Hector ("Macho") Camacho. By the time of this bout, Rosario had parted company with longtime trainer Manny Siaca. He was now coached by Lalo Medina. Camacho resisted the urge to go toe to toe with Rosario and fought a tactical fight, sticking and moving. In the fifth round, Rosario staggered Camacho with a left hook to the head. He then assaulted Camacho with both hands and opened a cut over his left eye. Rosario hurt Camacho again in the eleventh. However, Camacho impressed the judges with his skills. In a verdict that was met with boos when it was announced, Camacho won a split decision.

Rosario received another title shot about three months later when he met WBA lightweight titleholder Livingstone Bramble in Miami Beach. In the second round, the underdog Rosario hurt Bramble with an uppercut to the head and staggered him with a right and a left hook to the head, opening a cut above Bramble's eye. Rosario then unleashed a flurry of punches to the head to which Bramble mounted no defense. Finally, Rosario fired a right to the jaw, sending Bramble to the canvas and ending the fight. Rosario was once again a world champion.

He easily defended his title against Juan Nazario with an eighth-round knockout. He then faced Julio Cesar Chavez, the WBC super featherweight champion. Chavez won every round on the Associated Press's scorecard before the fight was stopped in the eleventh round when Rosario was bleeding heavily from several cuts to the nose, mouth, and right eye. In addition, his left eye was totally closed.

Rosario won his next seven fights to get a shot at the vacant WBA lightweight title against Anthony Jones on July 9, 1989, at the Showboat Hotel and Casino in Atlantic City. Jones won three of the early rounds. In the sixth, Rosario knocked Jones down with a straight right to the chin. When Jones got up, Rosario floored him again. The fight was stopped, and Rosario was a champion for the third time.

Rosario finally ended his feud with Manny Siaca and again employed his longtime mentor as a trainer. Rosario moved up to junior welterweight and faced Loreto Garza, the WBA champion, on June 14, 1991. He shocked Garza when he knocked him down with a straight right not ten seconds into the contest. He flattened him again late in the first round. Rosario scored two more knockdowns in the third. The referee stopped the bout after the fourth knockdown of the fight, and Rosario was the WBA junior welterweight champ.

The four-time titleholder did not have a long tenure. He was stopped by Akinobu Hiranaka in the first round of his only title defense. After a win over George Kellmann and a loss to Frankie Randall, Rosario stopped fighting for four years as he struggled with drug addiction. His habit cost him his marriage, homes, cars, and a year spent in jail in San Juan. He then came back and won five fights in 1997 before he died of acute pulmonary edema, which apparently resulted from a drug overdose. Though Rosario didn't achieve all that was expected of him at the start of his career, he did win four world titles and impressed the boxing world with his counterpunching, explosive right hand, and great technical skill.

MATTHEW SAAD MUHAMMAD

LIGHT HEAVYWEIGHT

Right-handed; 5'11"; 172–187 lbs.
58 bouts, 1/14/1974 to 3/21/1992
Manager: Bilal Muhammad
WBC Light Hvywt Champ 1979–81
Hall of Fame Induction: 1998
Born: 6/16/54, Jenkintown, PA
Named: Maxwell Antonio Loach
Also fought as: Matthew Franklin

In a sport that is filled with stories of athletes who rose from humble beginnings to become world champions, few can rival the history of Matthew Saad Muhammad.

Born Maxwell Antonio Loach near Philadelphia, Saad Muhammad was orphaned as a very young child. He and his older brother lived with his aunt who, when she could not afford to care for both children, told Saad Muhammad's brother to lose him. His brother took him to the Benjamin Franklin Parkway and ran away. The lost child was taken to a Catholic shelter where the nuns named him Matthew after the saint and Franklin after the place where he was found.

In and out of reform school as a youth, Saad Muhammad's life took a turn when he saw Muhammad Ali sparring in a local Philadelphia gym. He decided to become a fighter. Saad Muhammad turned professional in 1974, fighting as Matthew Franklin. Three years later, Saad Muhammad lost a decision to Eddie Gregory who later, as Eddie Mustafa Muhammad, became WBA light heavyweight champion. Saad Muhammad knocked Gregory down in the first round

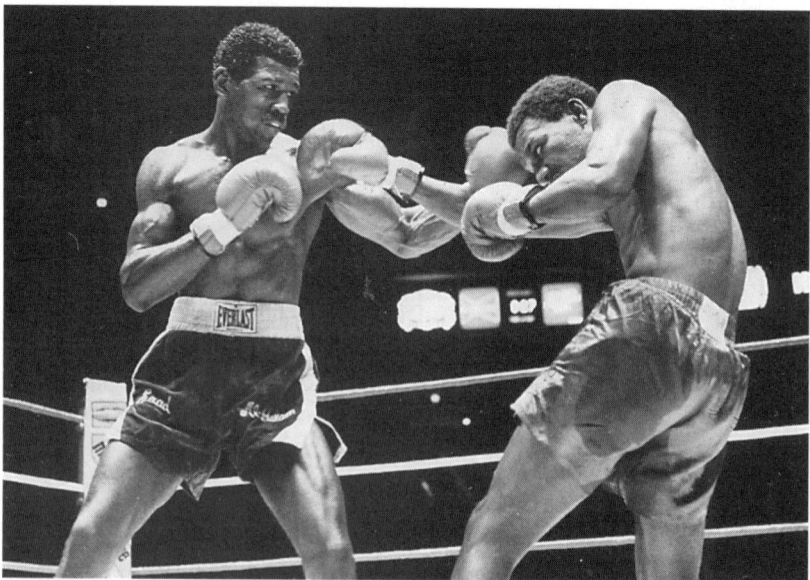

Saad Muhammad (L) connects with a left jab as he racks up points on the way to a ten-round decision over Larry Davis on September 9, 1983, in New York.

IN THE RING	WON 39	LOST 16	DRAWS 3	TB 58	KO 29	W 10	WF 0	D 3	KO'd 8	L 8	LF 0

Date	Opponent	Site	Result / Rounds		Title	Wt.
1974						
Jan 14	Billy Early	Philadelphia	KO	2	—	—
Feb 25	Bele Apolosa	Paris	W	4	—	—
Mar 11	Roy Ingram	Philadelphia	W	4	—	—
May 22	Joe Middleton	Philadelphia	KO	5	—	—
Jul 15	Joe Jones	Philadelphia	KO	3	—	—
Sep 10	Lloyd Richardson	Philadelphia	TKO	4	—	—
Oct 22	Joe Middleton	Alexandria, VA	KO	2	—	—
Dec 10	Wayne Magee	Philadelphia	L	6	—	—
1975						
Feb 25	Vandell Woods	Philadelphia	KO	6	—	174
Jul 24	Roosevelt Brown	Philadelphia	TKO	4	—	173
Oct 21	Wayne Magee	Philadelphia	D	6	—	—
1976						
Feb 13	Harold Carter	Baltimore	W	10	—	—
May 21	Mate Parlov	Milan	W	8	—	—
Jul 17	Marvin Camel	Stockton, CA	W	10	—	174
Sep 15	Bobby Walker	Scranton, PA	TKO	4	—	177
Oct 23	Marvin Camel	Missoula, MT	L	10	—	175
Dec 3	Mate Parlov	Trieste, Italy	D	10	—	—
1977						
Mar 11	Eddie Gregory	Philadelphia	L	10	—	176
Apr 21	Joe Maye	Wilmington, DE	W	10	—	175
Jun 23	Ed Turner	Philadelphia	TKO	6	—	175
Jul 26	⑩ Marvin Johnson	Philadelphia	KO	12	Won-Vac-NABF-LH	175
Sep 17	Billy Douglas	Philadelphia	KO	6	Ret-NABF-LH	175
Nov 1	Lee Royster	Philadelphia	W	10	—	178
1978						
Feb 10	⑩ Richie Kates	Philadelphia	TKO	6	Ret-NABF-LH	175
Jun 19	Dale Grant	Philadelphia	TKO	5	—	178
Aug 16	Fred Bright	Newark, NJ	KO	8	—	—
Oct 24	⑩ Yaqui Lopez	Philadelphia	TKO	11	Ret-NABF-LH	175
1979						
Apr 22	⑩ Marvin Johnson	Indianapolis	TKO	8	Won-WBC-LH	175
Aug 18	⑩ John Conteh	Atlantic City	W	15	Ret-WBC-LH	172
1980						
Mar 29	⑩ John Conteh	Atlantic City	TKO	4	Ret-WBC-LH	175
May 13	Louis Pergaud	Halifax, N.S., Canada	KO	5	Ret-WBC-LH	174
Jul 13	⑩ Yaqui Lopez	McAfee, NJ	TKO	14	Ret-WBC-LH	174
Nov 28	⑩ Lottie Mwale	San Diego	KO	4	Ret-WBC-LH	175
1981						
Feb 28	Vonzell Johnson	Atlantic City	TKO	11	Ret-WBC-LH	174
Apr 25	⑩ Murray Sutherland	Atlantic City	KO	9	Ret-WBC-LH	175
Sep 26	⑩ Jerry Martin	Atlantic City	TKO	11	Ret-WBC-LH	172
Dec 19	Dwight Braxton	Atlantic City	TKO'd	10	Lost-WBC-LH	174
1982						
Apr 17	Pete McIntyre	Atlantic City	TKO	2	—	174
Aug 7	♛ Dwight Braxton	Philadelphia	KO'd	6	For-WBC-LH	175

1983							
Mar 23		Eric Winbush	Atlantic City	TKO'd	3	—	176
Sep 9		Larry Davis	New York	TKO	10	—	172
1984							
Feb 11	⑩	Willie Edwards	Detroit	TKO'd	11	For-NABF-LH	175
1986							
Jan 10		Chris Wells	Hallendale, FL	TKO	6	—	187
Feb 21		Uriah Grant	Fort Lauderdale, FL	L	10	—	176
Nov 15		Tomas Polo-Ruiz	Port of Spain, Trinidad	W	10	—	—
1987							
Jan 30		Pat Strachan	Nassau, Bahamas	L	10	—	—
Jun 26		James Coakley	Nassau	KO	3	—	—
Dec 4		Bobby Thomas	Weirton, WV	W	10	—	175
1988							
Mar 8		Lee Harris	Mechanicsville, VA	TKO	1	—	176
Oct 21		Frank Swindell	Newark	TKO'd	1	—	179
1989							
Oct 24		Kevin Wagstaff	Brisbane, Australia	D	8	—	178
1990							
Feb 16		Markus Bott	Hamburg, Germany	TKO'd	3	—	—
1991							
Feb 26		Ed Mack	Philadelphia	L	8	—	174
May 9		Anton Josipovic	Novisad, Yugoslavia	L	8	—	—
Aug 15		Govonor Chavers	Marbella, Spain	KO	1	—	—
Oct 5		Michael Green	Woodbridge, VA	L	8	—	176
Oct 29		Andrew Maynard	Washington, DC	TKO'd	3	—	176
1992							
Mar 21		Jason Waller	Fredericksburg, VA	KO'd	2	—	186

but then fought cautiously the whole remainder of the bout. After this defeat, Saad Muhammad vowed that he would no longer be a defensive fighter.

In 1977, Saad Muhammad faced Marvin Johnson for the vacant North American Boxing Federation light heavyweight championship in Philadelphia at the Spectrum. He knocked Johnson out in the twelfth round. He then successfully defended this regional title three times before facing Johnson for the WBC light heavyweight title in Johnson's hometown of Indianapolis on April 22, 1979. A sparse crowd of 7,000 witnessed what ESPN boxing commentator Al Bernstein called "one of the most incredible brawls any light heavyweights ever staged." Both fighters were hurt from the first round on. In the early going, southpaw Johnson pressed the action, with Saad Muhammad counterpunching. By the fifth round, Johnson had a bloody nose and a cut under his right eye, while Saad Muhammad had cuts under both eyes. In the seventh, Saad Muhammad scored with fifteen unanswered punches to leave Johnson wobbly at the bell. In the eighth round, Johnson opened a gash over Saad Muhammad's left eye. Knowing the action could be stopped at any time, Saad Muhammad unleashed a barrage of punches that finally knocked Johnson down. Although Johnson got up at the count of nine, the referee stopped the fight. *The Ring* later named the eighth round its Round of the Year.

In his very next fight, Saad Muhammad, who adopted his Muslim name after winning the light heavyweight title, won a decision over former champion

John Conteh. Another bloody and damaging brawl, the fight aroused controversy over the use of a substance by Saad Muhammad's cut man, Adolph Ritaccio. Some of the substance applied to Saad Muhammad's cuts apparently got on his gloves and then affected Conteh's vision. The WBC suspended Ritaccio for one year and ordered a rematch. Saad Muhammad won the 1980 encounter with a fourth-round TKO.

On July 13, 1980, Saad Muhammad fought Yaqui Lopez, whom he had previously beaten in an NABF title defense, in a bout televised from the Playboy Club in McAfee, New Jersey. Through seven rounds neither fighter gave an inch. In the eighth, Lopez caught Saad Muhammad with a hook to the chin, then issued two dozen shots to the head. Saad Muhammad rallied and staggered Lopez before the end of the round. In the fourteenth, he dropped Lopez four times before the referee stopped the fight, which *The Ring* later named Fight of the Year.

Saad Muhammad defended his title four more times, all by knockout, before meeting Dwight Braxton (later, Dwight Muhammad Qawi) in Atlantic City on December 19, 1981. Saad Muhammad was pummeled by Braxton before the referee stopped the fight in the tenth. In the rematch (dubbed "the Liberty Brawl") in Philadelphia, Saad Muhammad was battered and bloody by the second round and was knocked down in the third. Braxton scored a technical knockout in the sixth.

Saad Muhammad continued to fight for another ten years, finally hanging up his gloves in 1992. During his later career, he owned a limousine service and a seafood restaurant. He also worked as a model and was offered the movie role in "Rocky III" that eventually went to Mr. T. Saad Muhammad recently served as an instructor at a fantasy boxing camp organized by Gleason's Gym of Brooklyn.

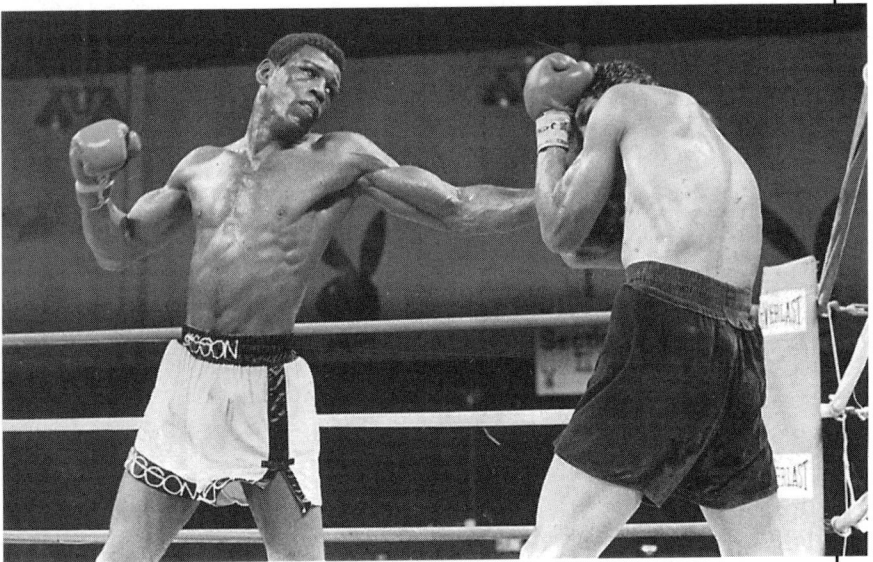

As he did in many fights, Saad Muhammad (L) had to rally to defeat excellent light heavyweight Yaqui Lopez on July 13, 1980, in a tough, nationally-televised bout.

SANDY SADDLER

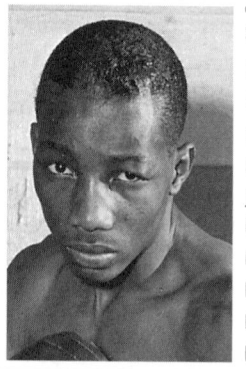

FEATHERWEIGHT

Right-handed; 5'8½"; 115–134 lbs.
162 bouts, 3/7/1944 to 4/14/1956
Manager: Charley Johnston
Featherweight Champion 1948–49
Jr. Lightweight Champion 1949–51
Featherweight Champion 1950–57
Hall of Fame Induction: 1990
Born: 6/23/1926, Boston, MA
Named: Joseph Saddler
Died: 9/18/2001

One of the top featherweights of all time, Sandy Saddler is best remembered for his four brawls with Willie Pep. Few opponents ever fought as viciously or with as much determination as did Saddler and Pep. And few fighters ever worked as hard as Saddler in his quest to be champion. Tall for his weight and possessing a 70" reach, Saddler was a strong puncher. Over the course of his career, he knocked out 103 opponents.

Saddler was born in Boston of West Indian parents and grew up in Harlem, where he learned to box. After about 50 amateur bouts, he turned professional in 1944 at age seventeen when a last-minute substitute was needed for a scheduled

On December 14, 1948, several weeks after Saddler (L) seized the featherweight championship from Willie Pep, editor Nat Fleischer presented Saddler with The Ring belt to commemorate his achievement.

IN THE RING	WON 144	LOST 16	DRAWS 2	TB 162	KO 103	W 41	WF 0	D 2	KO'd 1	L 14	LF 1

Date	Opponent	Site	Result / Rounds		Title	Wt.
1944						
Mar 7	Earl Roys	Hartford, CT	W	8	—	117
Mar 21	Jock Leslie	Hartford	KO'd	3	—	118
Mar 27	Al King	Holyoke, MA	KO	2	—	—
Apr 17	Joe Landry	Holyoke	KO	1	—	—
May 8	Jose Aponte Torres	Trenton, NJ	W	6	—	115
May 15	Jose Aponte Torres	Holyoke	W	6	—	—
May 23	Domingo Diaz	Jersey City, NJ	W	6	—	—
Jun 13	Jose Aponte Torres	Union City, PA	W	8	—	—
Jun 15	Lou Alter	Fort Hamilton, NY	L	6	—	119
Jun 23	Lou Alter	New York	D	4	—	116
Jul 11	Clyde English	Dexter, NY	W	6	—	118
Jul 18	Benny Saladino	Brooklyn	KO	3	—	120
Jul 25	Al Pennino	Brooklyn	W	6	—	—
Aug 8	Georgie Knox	Brooklyn	KO	3	—	118
Aug 18	Clifford Smith	New York	W	6	—	117
Nov 11	Manuel Torres	Brooklyn	W	6	—	124
Nov 13	Ken Tompkins	Newark, NJ	KO	1	—	119
Nov 24	Manuel Torres	New York	KO	5	—	127
Nov 28	Percy Lewis	Jersey City	KO	1	—	123
Dec 12	Tony Oshiro	Jersey City	KO	2	—	124
Dec 16	Earl Mintz	Brooklyn	KO	2	—	125
Dec 26	Midget Mayo	Newark	KO	3	—	—
1945						
Jan 13	Tony Oshiro	Brooklyn	W	6	—	125
Jan 15	Mickey Johnson	Newark	KO	1	—	125
Jan 22	Joey Puig	New York	KO	1	—	120
Jan 26	Benny May	New Brunswick, NJ	W	6	—	—
Feb 19	Joey Gatto	New York	KO	1	—	125
Mar 10	Harold Gibson	Brooklyn	W	6	—	123
Mar 19	Joe Montiero	New York	KO	4	—	124
Mar 22	Georgie Knox	Camden, NJ	KO	4	—	126
Apr 2	Jimmy Allen	Newark	KO	1	—	126
Apr 19	Willie Anderson	Detroit	KO	5	—	—
Apr 30	Chilindrina Valencia	Detroit	KO	9	—	120
Jun 18	Caswell Harris	Baltimore	KO	3	—	—
Jun 25	Bobby Washington	Allentown, PA	KO	2	—	124
Jun 29	Leo Methot	New York	KO	1	—	126
Jul 23	Herbert ("Biff") Jones	Baltimore	KO	3	—	—
Jul 24	Joe Montiero	Brooklyn	KO	5	—	125
Jul 30	Luis Rivera	New York	KO	4	—	126
Aug 16	Louis Langley	Brooklyn	KO	1	—	125
Aug 20	Bobby English	Providence, RI	KO	3	—	122
Aug 27	Earl Mintz	Providence	KO	1	—	123
Sep 21	Richie Myashiro	New York	W	6	—	120
Dec 3	Benny Daniels	Holyoke	W	6	—	—
Dec 14	Joe Montiero	Boston	W	8	—	131
Dec 21	Filiberto Osario	New York	W	6	—	127

1946

Jan 17	Arvey Bowie	Orange, NJ	KO	1		—	129
Feb 18	Bobby McQuillar	Detroit	L	10		—	126
Apr 8	Ralph LaSalle	New York	KO	1		—	128
Apr 11	Johnny Wolgast	Atlantic City	W	8		—	129
Apr 25	Pedro Firpo	Atlantic City	W	8		—	127
Jun 13	Cedric Flournoy	Detroit	KO	4		—	—
Jul 10	George Cooper	Brooklyn	KO	7		—	129
Jul 23	⑩ Phil Terranova	Detroit	L	10		—	125
Aug 5	Dominic Amoroso	Providence	KO	2		—	130
Aug 22	Pedro Firpo	Brooklyn	W	10		—	122
Oct 10	Jose ("Joe") Rodriguez	Atlantic City	KO	3		—	130
Nov 12	Art Price	Detroit	W	10		—	128
Dec 9	Clyde English	Holyoke	KO	3		—	—
Dec 26	Luis Marquez	Jamaica, NY	KO	2		—	131
Dec 30	Leonard Caesar	Newark	KO	2		—	—

1947

Jan 20	George ("Dusty") Brown	Holyoke	KO	4		—	132
Jan 27	Humberto Zavala	New York	KO	7		—	128
Feb 7	Larry Thomas	Asbury Park, NJ	KO	2		—	132
Mar 8	Leonardo Lopez	Mexico City	KO	2		—	124
Mar 29	Carlos Malacara	Mexico City	W	10		—	130
Apr 14	⑩ Cabey Lewis	New York	W	10		—	128
May 2	Joe Brown★	New Orleans	KO	3		—	131
May 9	Melvin Bartholomew	New Orleans	W	10		—	130
Jun 3	Jimmy Carter★	Washington, DC	D	10		—	130
Jul 26	⑩ Oscar Calles	Caracas	KO	5		—	—
Aug 14	Leslie Harris	Atlantic City	KO	5		—	127
Aug 29	⑩ Miguel Acevedo	New York	KO	7		—	130
Sep 17	Angelo Ambrosano	Jamaica	KO	2		—	127
Oct 3	⑩ Humberto Sierra	Minneapolis	L	10		—	125
Oct 13	Al Pennino	New York	KO	4		—	130
Oct 26	Lino Garcia	Caracas	KO	5		—	—
Nov 9	Emilio Sanchez	Caracas	KO	5		—	—
Dec 5	Lino Garcia	Havana, Cuba	KO	3		—	128
Dec 13	Orlando Zulueta	Havana	W	10		—	127

1948

Feb 2	Charley Noel	Holyoke	W	10		—	129
Feb 9	Joey Angelo	New York	W	10		—	129
Mar 5	Archie Wilmer	New York	W	8		—	129
Mar 8	Thompson Harmon	Holyoke	TKO	8		—	129
Mar 23	Bobby Timpson	Hartford	W	10		—	128
Apr 10	Luis Monagas	Caracas	KO	3		—	—
Apr 17	Jose Diaz	Caracas	KO	8		—	—
Apr 26	Young Tanner	Oranjestad, Aruba	KO	5		—	127
May 24	Harry LaSane	Holyoke	W	10		—	129
Jun 29	⑩ Chico Rosa	Honolulu	L	10		—	124
Aug 16	Kid Zefine	Panama City	TKO	2		—	126
Aug 23	Aguilino Allen	Panama City	TKO	2		—	126
Oct 11	Willie Roache	New Haven, CT	TKO	3		—	128
Oct 29	♛ Willie Pep★	New York	KO	4		Won-World-FE	124
Nov 19	Tomas Beato	Bridgeport, CT	TKO	2		—	126
Nov 29	Dennis Pat Brady	Boston	W	10		—	129
Dec 7	Eddie Giosa	Cleveland	KO	2		—	129

Date		Opponent	Location	Result		Notes	Weight
Dec 17	⑩	Terry Young	New York	TKO	10	—	128

1949

Date		Opponent	Location	Result		Notes	Weight
Jan 17		Young Finnegan	Panama City	KO	5	—	127
Feb 11	⑩	Willie Pep★	New York	L	15	Lost-World-FE	124
Mar 21		Felix Ramirez	Newark	W	10	—	130
Apr 18		Ermano Bonetti	Philadelphia	KO	2	—	130
Jun 2		Jim Keery	London	KO	4	—	129
Jun 23		Luis Ramos	New York	KO	5	—	128
Jul 15		Chief Gordon House	New York	TKO	5	—	127
Aug 2		Chuck Burton	Pittsfield, MA	KO	5	—	130
Aug 8		Johnny Rowe	Brooklyn	KO	8	—	127
Aug 24		Alfredo Escobar	Los Angeles	TKO	9	—	128
Sep 2		Harold Dade	Chicago	W	10	—	127
Sep 20		Proctor Heinold	Schenectady, NY	KO	2	—	129
Oct 28	⑩	Paddy DeMarco	New York	TKO	9	—	129
Nov 7		Leroy Willis	Toledo, OH	W	10	—	130
Dec 6		Orlando Zulueta	Cleveland	W	10	Won-Vac Ohio World-JL	127

1950

Date		Opponent	Location	Result		Notes	Weight
Jan 16		Paulie Jackson	Caracas	KO	1	—	131
Jan 22		Pedro Firpo	Caracas	KO	1	—	131
Feb 6		Chuck Burton	Holyoke	KO	1	—	129
Feb 20		Luis Ramos	Toronto	TKO	3	—	129
Apr 10		Reuben Davis	Newark	TKO	7	—	131
Apr 18	⑩	Lauro Salas	Cleveland	TKO	9	Ret-Ohio World-JL	130
Apr 29		Jesse Underwood	Waterbury, CT	W	10	—	126
May 25	⑩	Miguel Acevedo	Minneapolis	TKO	6	—	129
Jun 19		Johnny Forte	Toronto	KO	3	—	129
Jun 30		Leroy Willis	Long Beach, NY	TKO	2	—	131
Sep 8	♛	Willie Pep★	Bronx, NY	TKO	8	Reg-World-FE	124
Oct 12		Harry LaSane	St. Louis	W	10	—	131
Nov 1	⑩	Charley Riley	St. Louis	W	10	—	128
Dec 6	⑩	Del Flanagan	Detroit	L	10	—	128

1951

Date		Opponent	Location	Result		Notes	Weight
Jan 23		Jesse Underwood	Buffalo, NY	W	10	—	130
Feb 28		Diego Sosa	Havana	KO	2	Ret-Ohio/Cuba World-JL	127
Mar 27	⑩	Lauro Salas	Los Angeles	TKO	6	—	130
Apr 3		Freddie Herman	Los Angeles	TKO	5	—	130
May 5		Harry LaSane	Hershey, PA	W	10	—	130
Jun 2		Alfredo Prada	Buenos Aires	KO	4	—	132
Jun 16		Oscar Flores	Buenos Aires	KO	1	—	134
Jun 22		Mario Salinas	Santiago, Chile	KO	5	—	131
Jun 30		Angel Olivieri	Buenos Aires	KO	5	—	132
Aug 20		Hermie Freeman	Philadelphia	TKO	5	—	130
Aug 27	⑩	Paddy DeMarco	Milwaukee	L	10	—	128
Sep 26	⑩	Willie Pep★	New York	TKO	9	Ret-World-FE	125
Dec 7	⑩	Paddy DeMarco	New York	L	10	—	130

1952

Date		Opponent	Location	Result		Notes	Weight
Jan 14	⑩	George Araujo	Boston	L	10	—	132
Mar 3		Armand Savoie	Montreal	LD	4	—	130
Mar 17	⑩	Tommy Collins	Boston	TKO	5	—	130

1954

Date		Opponent	Location	Result		Notes	Weight
Jan 15	⑩	Bill Bossio	New York	TKO	9	—	130
Mar 4		Charlie Slaughter	Akron, OH	TKO	4	—	130
Apr 1		Augie Salazar	Boston	TKO	7	—	133

May 17		Hoacine Khalfi	New York	L	10	—	132
Jul 5		Libby Manzo	New York	KO	10	—	131
Aug 30		Jackie Blair	Caracas	TKO	1	—	129
Sep 27	⑩	Baby Neff Ortiz	Caracas	TKO	3	—	123
Oct 25	⑩	Ray Famechon	Paris	TKO	6	—	128
Dec 10		Bobby Woods	Spokane, WA	W	10	—	129
1955							
Jan 17		Lulu Perez	Boston	KO	4	—	131
Feb 25	⑩	Teddy Davis	New York	W	15	Ret-World-FE	124
Apr 5		Kenny Davis	Butte, MT	TKO	5	—	129
May 24	⑩	Joe Lopes	Sacramento, CA	L	10	—	130
Jul 8		Shigeji Kaneko	Tokyo	TKO	6	—	131
Jul 20	⑩	Flash Elorde ★	Manila	L	10	—	129
Dec 12		Dave Gallardo	San Francisco	TKO	7	—	131
1956							
Jan 18	⑩	Flash Elorde ★	San Francisco	TKO	13	Ret-World-FE	126
Feb 13		Curley Monroe	Providence	TKO	3	—	132
Apr 14	⑩	Larry Boardman	Boston	L	10	—	130

bout. Though he won that fight, Saddler lost his second bout by knockout to the more experienced Jock Leslie. This was the only time Saddler was knocked out in his 162-fight career.

Saddler started as a bantamweight, then quickly moved up to featherweight and earned recognition in 1946 as the seventh-best featherweight contender in the annual rankings by *The Ring*. With his phenomenal string of knockouts, Saddler probably deserved a title shot long before Pep finally agreed to fight him, but in October 1948, the stage was set for the first of their four encounters for the featherweight championship. Saddler dominated the fight. He cut Pep in the first round, knocked him down twice in the third, and finally knocked him out in the fourth. In the rematch the next year, Pep was at the top of his form and regained the championship with an outstanding display of boxing skill. Pep was badly battered—he received eleven stitches after the bout—but Saddler lost the unanimous decision.

In December 1949, Saddler won a decision over Orlando Zulueta in Cleveland

WHEN TO QUIT

A perennial problem for successful fighters is knowing when to hang up the gloves and find a day job. Several great boxers would have enjoyed perfect records if they had known when to quit. James J. Jeffries was coaxed out of his undefeated retirement to stand as a "white hope" against the first African-American heavyweight champion, Jack Johnson. Jeffries, out of shape after a six-year layoff, was KO'd in fifteen rounds. Michael Spinks's only career defeat was against Mike Tyson, with Spinks re-entering the ring after a 12-month hiatus. Spinks weighed in at a career-high 212 for his last bout.

Terry Young (R) could duck, but he couldn't hide. In his eighteenth bout of the year, Saddler beat Young by a TKO in ten on December 17, 1948. Saddler was a rough-and-tumble fighter who gave no quarter.

to take the vacant world junior lightweight title. He held this title for two years, successfully defending it twice. In September 1950, Saddler was back in Pep's face for another go at the featherweight title. The match was a rouser, with each fighter flying at the other with a relentless will to inflict damage. Saddler knocked Pep down in the third with a left hook, then peppered him with body punches. As the match went on, it developed into a no-holds-barred brawl. Saddler won when an exhausted Pep could not answer the bell for the eighth round. Saddler had reclaimed his title, but Pep wanted a rematch and the two met again a year later. Their fourth meeting was the grimmest of all and involved even more wrestling, gouging, tripping, and other illegal maneuvers than any of their earlier fights. Saddler won with the TKO in the ninth round. As a result of their actions in this bout, both fighters were suspended briefly by the New York State Athletic commission.

Saddler spent the next two years in the Army and was allowed to retain his featherweight championship. When he returned to the ring, he re-established his hold on the title by beating contenders Teddy Davis in 1955 and Flash Elorde in 1956. He retained the title until announcing his retirement in 1957 after suffering serious eye injuries in an auto accident.

In retirement Saddler was a successful trainer. He succumbed to Alzheimer's disease at age 75.

VICENTE SALDIVAR
Zurdo de Oro (Lefty of Gold)

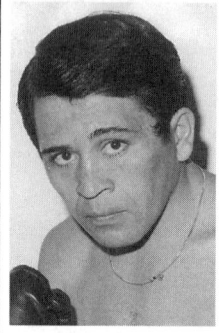

FEATHERWEIGHT

Left-handed; 5'3"; 124–132 lbs.
41 bouts, 2/18/1961 to 10/20/1973
Manager: Adolpho Perez
Featherweight Champion 1964–67
WBC Featherweight Champion 1970
Hall of Fame Induction: 1999
Born: 5/3/1943, Mexico City, Mexico
Named: Vicente Samuel Saldivar Garcia
Died: 7/18/1985

Vicente Saldivar retired as featherweight champion at 24, only to return to the ring and regain the title by the time he was 27.

Born in one of the poorest sections of Mexico City, Saldivar learned to fight on the streets. He was introduced to organized boxing by his father, who was an avid fight fan. Although Saldivar wanted to box, his first priority was helping to support his family, and he became an apprentice printer. But he soon met boxing referee Ernesto Arcos, who gave the eager Saldivar boxing instruction. After learning the rudiments from Arcos, Saldivar came under the tutelage of trainer Jose Merino. Though only seventeen, Saldivar was chosen to represent Mexico in the 1960 Olympic Games. He did not fare well at the games, but he gained valuable ring experience and learned from the top boxers he observed.

On February 18, 1961, Saldivar began his professional career with a first-round

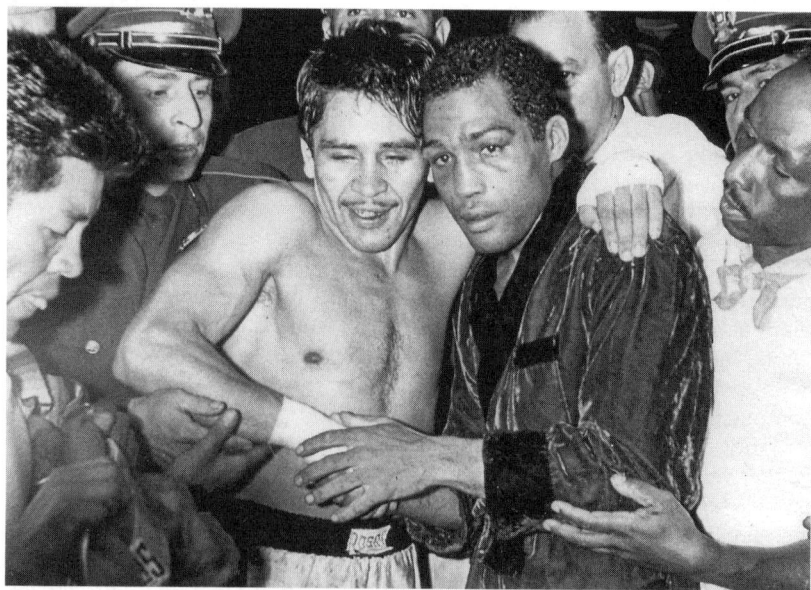

Saldivar (L) is all smiles after taking the featherweight crown from Sugar Ramos in Mexico City on September 26, 1964.

IN THE RING	WON 38	LOST 3	DRAWS 0	TB 41	KO 27	W 10	WF 1	D 0	KO'd 2	L 0	LF 1

Date		Opponent	Site	Result / Rounds		Title	Wt.
1961							
Feb 18		Baby Palacios	Oaxaca, Mexico	KO	1	—	125
Mar 22		Frijol Gonzalez	Oaxaca	KO	4	—	—
Apr 16		Eduardo Meza	Oaxaca	KO	3	—	132
May 20		Babe Lopez	Leon, Mexico	KO	3	—	—
Oct 14		Jose Luis Mora	Huachinango, Mexico	W	10	—	126
Dec 3		Juan Rodriguez	Leon	TKO	6	—	128
1962							
Jan 6		Ernesto Beltran	Acapulco, Mexico	KO	6	—	127
Feb 8		Rosendo Martinez	Huachinango	TKO	5	—	128
Mar 18		Juan Zavala	Tuxtla, Mexico	KO	10	—	—
Apr 4	⑩	Jorge Salazar	Matamoros, Mexico	KO	4	—	—
May 2		Gennaro Gonzalez	Mexico City	WF	8	—	—
Jun 27		Indio Fernandez	Mexico City	TKO	6	—	—
Aug 22		Alberto Soto	Mexico City	TKO	2	—	—
Oct 11		Luis Hernandez	Los Mochis, Mexico	KO	1	—	—
Nov 17		Jose Lopez	Monterrey, Mexico	W	10	—	—
Dec 16	⑩	Jorge Salazar	Matamoros	KO	5	—	—
Dec 29		Baby Luis (Emiro Durgel)	Mexico City	LF	7	—	—
1963							
Mar 16		Luis Hernandez	Los Mochis	KO	2	—	—
Apr 19		Dwight Hawkins	Monterrey	KO	5	—	—
Jun 12		Baby Luis (Emiro Durgel)	Mexico City	TKO	8	—	124
Jul 13		Eloy Sanchez	Mexico City	KO	1	—	—
Sep 22		Beresford Francis	Mexico City	TKO	2	—	126
Dec 16		Felix Gutierrez	Cuernavaca, Mexico	TKO	3	—	—
1964							
Feb 8		Juan Ramirez	Mexico City	TKO	2	Won-Mex-FE	126
Apr 4		Eduardo Guerrero	Mexico City	W	12	Ret-Mex-FE	123
Jun 1	⑩	Ismael Laguna★	Tijuana, Mexico	W	10	—	126
Sep 26	♛	Ultiminio ("Sugar") Ramos★	Mexico City	TKO	12	Won-World-FE	125
Dec 6		Delfino Rosales	Leon	TKO	11	Ret-Mex-FE	126
1965							
Feb 13		Eduardo Torres	Guadalajara, Mexico	KO	4	—	—
May 7	⑩	Raul Rojas	Los Angeles	TKO	15	Ret-World-FE	124
Sep 7	⑩	Howard Winstone	London	W	15	Ret-World-FE	125
1966							
Feb 12	⑩	Floyd Robertson	Mexico City	KO	2	Ret-World-FE	123
Aug 7	⑩	Mitsunori Seki	Mexico City	W	15	Ret-World-FE	124
1967							
Jan 29	⑩	Mitsunori Seki	Mexico City	TKO	7	Ret-World-FE	124
Jun 15	⑩	Howard Winstone	Cardiff, Wales	W	15	Ret-World-FE	125
Oct 14	⑩	Howard Winstone	Mexico City	TKO	12	Ret-World-FE	125
1969							
Jul 18	⑩	Jose Legra	Inglewood, CA	W	10	—	127
1970							
May 9	♛	Johnny Famechon	Rome	W	15	Reg-WBC-FE	126
Dec 11	⑩	Kuniaki Shibata	Tijuana	TKO'd	13	Lost-WBC-FE	125

1971							
Jul 15	⑩	Frankie Crawford	Los Angeles	W	10	—	128
1973							
Oct 20	♛	Eder Jofre★	Salvador, Brazil	KO'd	4	For-WBC-FE	125

knockout of Baby Palacios in Oaxaca, Mexico. Saldivar defeated his first sixteen opponents, thirteen of them by knockout, before losing to Baby Luis on December 29, 1962, on a disqualification. He defeated his next six opponents, all by knockouts, including a Baby Luis rematch. Saldivar's impressive record earned him a shot at the Mexican featherweight title against Juan Ramirez, whom he knocked out in the second round to win the crown. After defending his championship once, Saldivar faced his first world title contender in Hall of Famer Ismael Laguna on June 1, 1964, in Tijuana. Laguna was *The Ring*'s top-ranked contender in 1964, yet Saldivar earned a decision in ten rounds and the right to challenge world featherweight champion Sugar Ramos.

The title fight was held in Mexico City on September 26, 1964. Ramos and Saldivar gave the fans a good show, going at each other with reckless abandon. As the fight wore on, Ramos's face was covered in blood, but the champion fought on through the pain. By the twelfth round, however, Ramos could not answer the bell, and the 21-year-old Saldivar was the new world champion. The title fight served as a showcase for Saldivar's style. He fought as a southpaw and had tremendous power in both his right and left hands. He was able to box at a furious pace, an ability he believed he owed to an abnormally slow heart rate.

Saldivar was a busy champion. Soon after knocking out Delfino Rosales, he traveled to the United States for the first time and faced Raul Rojas at Memorial Coliseum in Los Angeles on May 7, 1965. After a quick start, he rocked Rojas in the sixth round with a left to the head. Throwing off the blow, Rojas was able to win the next round; Saldivar cut Rojas above the eye in the eighth; Rojas retaliated by cutting Saldivar's cheek in the ninth. Finally, Saldivar took control of the fight. In the fifteenth round, he pummeled Rojas with rights and lefts to the head and body before the referee stopped the fight with only ten seconds to go.

For his next defense, Saldivar met European featherweight champ Howard Winstone in London. Winstone outboxed Saldivar in the early going, but the champion came back strong to retain his title. This was only the first of three meetings between Saldivar and Winstone. On June 15, 1967, at Ninian Stadium in Cardiff, Wales, under the eyes of 30,000 fans, the two met again. Winstone opened quickly with jabs and rights, while Saldivar often missed his clever opponent. Saldivar worked the body in the middle of the fight, but Winstone continued to score with jabs. Finally, Saldivar's heavy body punches began to weaken Winstone. Saldivar was then able to move his attack to the head, and in the fourteenth he knocked Winstone down. He retained control in the fifteenth and won a close decision. After his third victory over Winstone in a twelve-round knockout in Mexico City on October 14, 1967, the 24-year-old Saldivar announced his retirement. Standing in the center of the ring, Zurdo de Oro (Lefty of Gold), as he was known in his native country, shocked his fans when he told them, "I have made more money as a boxer than I can ever spend. I am tired of always training and never having any fun while I am still young. . . . This was my last fight." Many in the crowd wept.

However, like many boxers who retire early, Saldivar could not stay away for long. On July 18, 1969, he won a ten-round decision over Jose Legra. Legra had defeated Winstone to win the vacant WBC featherweight title, then lost the title to Johnny Famechon. On May 9, 1970, Saldivar met Famechon at the Palazza dello Sport in Rome, before a crowd of about 16,000, for a chance to regain the WBC title and general recognition as world champion. Saldivar took to the attack. Although he suffered a badly puffed eye, he continued to be the aggressor. Saldivar won a clear-cut decision by scores of 71-68, 72-68, and 73-70.

Saldivar's second reign as champion was short lived. In his very next fight, he was knocked out by Kuniaki Shibata in the thirteenth round—the first time Saldivar had been stopped short of the distance. In this bout, Saldivar was plagued by serious cuts around his eyes. After decisioning Frankie Crawford seven months after his loss, Saldivar did not fight for over two years. He then faced Hall of Famer Eder Jofre in another bid for the featherweight title. Saldivar was knocked out by Jofre in four rounds. He retired for good at the age of 30, and trained boxers in Mexico until he suffered a fatal heart attack at the age of 42.

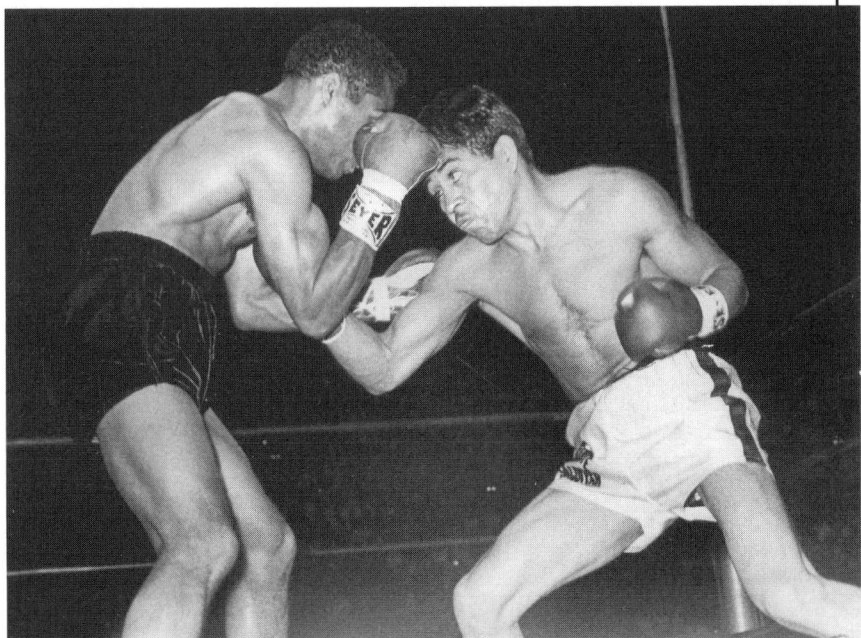

Raul Rojas (L) fails to block a Saldivar shot in Saldivar's first title defense, and his first fight outside Mexico, in Los Angeles on May 7, 1965.

SALVADOR SANCHEZ
Chava

FEATHERWEIGHT

Right-handed; 5'7"; 117–129 lbs.

46 bouts, 5/4/1975 to 7/21/1982

Manager: Cristobal Rosas

WBC Featherwt. Champ 1980–82

Hall of Fame Induction: 1991

Born: 1/26/1959, Santiago Tianguistenco, Mexico

Died: 8/12/1982

Thoughts about the career of Salvador Sanchez must invariably turn to the tragic and early end of his life. Sanchez was only 23 years old when he died after his Porsche collided with a pickup truck in Mexico. Nevertheless, Sanchez had a brilliant seven-year career that culminated in a championship.

Sanchez began his career in 1975 at the age of sixteen and won his first eighteen fights before losing to Antonio Becerra in a bid to obtain the vacant Mexican bantamweight title. He first rose to international prominence in 1979, when he appeared in the eighth position in *The Ring*'s world rankings for featherweights.

In 1980, Sanchez challenged the colorful WBC featherweight champion, Danny ("Little Red") Lopez for his belt. Sanchez thrashed the champion from the

In his fifth defense of the WBC featherweight belt at Caesars in Las Vegas, Sanchez (L) feints with his left and prepares to unload on Roberto Castanon with his right. Sanchez won by 10th-round TKO.

IN THE RING	WON 44	LOST 1	DRAWS 1	TB 46	KO 32	W 12	WF 0	D 1	KO'd 0	L 1	LF 0

Date	Opponent	Site	Result / Rounds		Title	Wt.
1975						
May 4	Al Gardeno	Veracruz, Mexico	KO	3	—	—
May 25	Miguel Ortiz	Misantla, Mexico	KO	3	—	—
Aug 10	Victor Martinez	Misantla	KO	2	—	—
Oct 19	Cesar Lopez	Misantla	KO	4	—	—
Nov 25	Candido Sandoval	Mexico City	TKO	7	—	—
Dec 11	Fidel Trejo	Mexico City	W	8	—	—
1976						
Jan 24	Juan Granados	Mexico City	TKO	3	—	117
Feb 25	Javier Solis	Mexico City	TKO	7	—	—
Mar 31	Serafin Pacheco	Mexico City	TKO	4	—	—
Apr 24	Jose Chavez	Mexico City	TKO	7	—	118
May 26	Fidel Trejo	Mexico City	KO	6	—	—
Jul 5	Pedro Sandoval	Mexico City	TKO	9	—	121
Aug 11	Joel Valdez	Mexico City	TKO	9	—	—
Oct 31	Saul Montana	Nuevo Laredo, Mexico	TKO	9	—	118
Dec 25	Antonio Leon	Mexico City	TKO	10	—	119
1977						
Feb 5	Raul Lopez	Mexicali, Mexico	TKO	10	—	—
Mar 12	Daniel Felizardo	Mexico City	KO	5	—	118
May 21	Rosalio Badillo	Mexico City	TKO	5	—	—
Sep 9	Antonio Becerra	Mazatlan, Mexico	L	12	For-Vac Mexico-B	118
Nov 11	Jose Soto	Los Mochis, Mexico	W	10	—	—
Dec 5	Eliseo Cosme	Mexico City	W	10	—	—
1978						
Apr 15	Juan Escobar	Los Angeles	D	10	—	128
Jul 1	Jose Sanchez	Mexico City	W	10	—	—
Aug 13	Hector Cortez	Mazatlan	TKO	7	—	—
Sep 26	Francisco Ponce	Houston	KO	2	—	129
Nov 21	Edwin Alarcon	San Antonio, TX	TKO	9	—	—
Dec 16	Jose Santana	Mexico City	TKO	2	—	126
1979						
Feb 3	Carlos Mimila	Mexico City	KO	3	—	129
Mar 13	James Martinez	San Antonio	W	10	—	126
May 19	Salvador Torres	Mexico City	TKO	7	—	126
Jun 17	Fel Clemente	San Antonio	W	12	—	126
Jul 22	Rosalio Muro	San Luis Potosi, Mexico	KO	3	—	125
Aug 7	Felix Trinidad	Houston	KO	5	—	127
Sep 25	⑩ Richard Rozelle	Los Angeles	TKO	3	—	128
Dec 15	Rafael Gandarilla	Guadalajara, Mexico	TKO	5	—	—
1980						
Feb 2	♛ Danny Lopez	Phoenix	TKO	13	Won-WBC-FE	125
Apr 12	⑩ Ruben Castillo	Tucson, AZ	W	15	Ret-WBC-FE	126
Jun 21	⑩ Danny Lopez	Las Vegas	TKO	14	Ret-WBC-FE	126

Sep 13	⑩	Patrick Ford	San Antonio	W	15	Ret-WBC-FE	126
Dec 13	⑩	Juan LaPorte	El Paso, TX	W	15	Ret-WBC-FE	126
1981							
Mar 22	⑩	Roberto Castanon	Las Vegas	TKO	10	Ret-WBC-FE	126
Jul 11	⑩	Nicky Perez	Los Angeles	W	10	—	129
Aug 21		Wilfredo Gomez★	Las Vegas	TKO	8	Ret-WBC-FE	126
Dec 12	⑩	Pat Cowdell	Houston	W	15	Ret-WBC-FE	126
1982							
May 8		Rocky Garcia	Dallas	W	15	Ret-WBC-FE	126
Jul 21	⑩	Azumah Nelson★	New York	TKO	15	Ret-WBC-FE	126

sixth to the thirteenth round, when the referee called for an end to the slaughter. Nine of Sanchez's last ten fights were title defenses, including a victory over Hall of Famer Wilfredo Gomez. Sanchez dominated the previously unbeaten Gomez and then knocked him out in the eighth.

In an interview shortly before his death, Sanchez spoke of his wish to move up to lightweight and fight Alexis Arguello. He expressed no particular desire to

Sanchez (L) holds off Hall of Famer and junior featherweight champ Wilfredo Gomez, who put on four extra pounds and challenged for Sanchez's belt. It was Sanchez by an eighth-round TKO.

In his ninth defense in just a little over two years since winning the WBC featherweight title, Sanchez faced Azumah Nelson, a tough customer from Ghana, on July 21, 1982, in Madison Square Garden. Sanchez floored Nelson (R) in the fifteenth round and won by TKO. Twenty-two days later, Sanchez died in an accident north of Mexico City. His sports car crashed into a heavily laden truck.

unify the featherweight title though, as he considered his WBC belt to have the widest recognition.

Although Sanchez recorded 32 knockouts in his 46 fights, he was not considered a big puncher. His primary skill was as a boxer and an observant tactician. As Sanchez said, "The KO's come through undermining my opponents." Sanchez greatly admired the ring artistry of Jose Napoles, Ruben Olivares, and Sugar Ray Leonard.

PAPERWEIGHTS

Many fight fans assume that the bantamweight division was the lightest contested division until the flyweight class was introduced in England in 1909. In fact, the 105-pound division was contested in America as the "paperweight" class from the 1890s through at least 1910. The term "flyweight" wasn't generally accepted for 105-pounders in the U.S. until the New York State Athletic Commission adopted new standards in 1920. Johnny Coulon was the last well-known paperweight champ, winning the title by besting Kid Murphy in Peoria, Illinois, in 1908. Coulon successfully defended the title three times before moving up to bantamweight.

RINGFACT

MAX SCHMELING
The Black Uhlan

H E A V Y W E I G H T

Right-handed; 6'1"; 175–196 lbs.

70 bouts, 8/2/1924 to 10/31/1948

Managers: Arthur Bulow 1924–28, Joe Jacobs 1928–38

Heavyweight Champion 1930–32

Hall of Fame Induction: 1992

Born: 9/28/1905, Klein-Luckaw, Brandenburg, Germany

Named: Maximillian Adolph Otto Siegfried Schmeling

Died: 2/2/2005

At one time a very hated man in the United States, Max Schmeling was an excellent boxer and sportsman who proved himself worthy of the world heavyweight championship. Schmeling was held up by Nazi Germany as an example of Aryan supremacy. His fights became symbolic of a much greater struggle, but Schmeling, the man, was simply a good fighter who wanted to reach the top. He neither sought nor rejected the role which he filled for the German propaganda machine.

Schmeling turned professional in his native Germany in 1924. Initially fighting as a light heavyweight, he won the German light heavyweight title in 1926 with a one-round knockout of Max Diekmann (who had handed Schmeling his first defeat two years earlier). In the next couple of years, Schmeling took the European light heavyweight and German heavyweight titles. In late 1928, Schmeling began fighting in the United States and became known to American audiences. A strong puncher with both hands and the owner of an especially

Franklin Roosevelt meets Max Schmeling on June 1, 1930, after watching a training session in Kingston, NY. FDR was then governor of New York. Schmeling was preparing for his title fight with Sharkey.

IN THE RING	WON 56	LOST 10	DRAWS 4	TB 70	KO 39	W 14	WF 3	D 4	KO'd 5	L 5	LF 0

Date	Opponent	Site	Result / Rounds		Title	Wt.
1924						
Aug 2	Hans Czapp	Dusseldorf, Germany	KO	6	—	—
Sep 20	Willy Louis	Duisburg, Germany	KO	1	—	—
Sep 22	Pietrus Van Der Veer	Dusseldorf	KO	3	—	—
Oct 4	Rocky Knight	Cologne, Germany	W	8	—	—
Oct 10	Max Diekmann	Berlin	TKO'd	4	—	—
Oct 31	Fred Hammer	Cologne	KO	3	—	—
Dec 4	Hans Breuer	Cologne	KO	2	—	—
Dec 7	Battling Marthar	Dusseldorf	KO	3	—	—
Dec 17	Helmuth Hartig	Berlin	KO	1	—	—
Dec 26	Jimmy Lygget	Cologne	WD	4	—	—
1925						
Jan 18	Johnny Kloudts	Cologne	KO	2	—	—
Jan 20	Joe Mehling	Berlin	W	6	—	—
Mar 1	Leon Randol	Cologne	KO	4	—	—
Mar 15	Alf Baker	Cologne	KO	3	—	—
Apr 3	Jimmy Lygget	Berlin	D	8	—	—
Apr 28	Fred Hammer	Bonn, Germany	W	8	—	—
May 9	Jack Taylor	Cologne	L	10	—	—
Jun 14	Leon Randol	Brussels	D	10	—	—
Sep 1	Larry Gains	Cologne	KO'd	2	—	—
Nov 8	Rene Compere	Cologne	W	8	—	—
1926						
Feb 12	Max Diekmann	Berlin	D	8	—	—
Mar 19	Willy Louis	Cologne	KO	1	—	—
Jul 13	August Vongehr	Berlin	KO	1	—	—
Aug 24	Max Diekmann	Berlin	KO	1	Won-Germany-LH	—
Oct 1	Hermann Van't Hoff	Berlin	WD	8	—	—
1927						
Jan 13	Jack Stanley	Berlin	KO	8	—	175
Jan 23	Louis Wilms	Breslau, Poland	KO	8	—	—
Feb 4	Joe Mehling	Dresden, Germany	KO	3	—	—
Mar 12	Leon Sebilo	Dortmund, Germany	KO	2	—	—
Apr 8	Francis Charles	Berlin	KO	8	—	—
Apr 26	Stanley Glen	Hamburg, Germany	KO	1	—	—
May 7	Robert Larsen	Frankfurt, Germany	W	10	—	—
May 17	Raoul Paillaux	Frankfurt	KO	3	—	—
Jun 19	Fernand Delarge	Dortmund	KO	14	Won-Europe-LH	—
Jul 13	Jack Taylor	Hamburg	W	10	—	—
Aug 7	Willem Westbroeck	Essen, Germany	KO	1	—	—
Sep 2	Robert Larsen	Berlin	KO	3	—	—
Oct 2	Louis Clement	Dortmund	KO	6	—	—
Nov 6	Hein Domogergen	Leipzig, Germany	KO	7	Ret-Europe-LH	—
Dec 2	Gypsie Daniels	Berlin	W	10	—	—
1928						
Jan 6	Michele Bonaglia	Berlin	KO	1	Ret-Europe-LH	—
Feb 25	Gypsie Daniels	Frankfurt	KO'd	1	—	—
Mar 11	Ted Moore	Dortmund	W	10	—	—

Date		Opponent	Location	Result	Rounds	Title	Weight
Apr 4		Franz Diener	Berlin	W	15	Won-Germany-H	188
Nov 23		Joe Monte	New York	KO	8	—	183
1929							
Jan 4		Joe Sekyra	New York	W	10	—	181
Jan 22		Pietro Corri	Newark, NJ	KO	1	—	183
Feb 1	⑩	Johnny Risko	New York	TKO	9	—	185
Jun 27	⑩	Paolino Uzcudun	New York	W	15	—	187
1930							
Jun 12	⑩	Jack Sharkey★	New York	WF	4	Won-Vac World-H	188
1931							
Jul 3	⑩	Young Stribling★	Cleveland	TKO	15	Ret-World-H	189
1932							
Jun 21	⑩	Jack Sharkey★	Long Island, NY	L	15	Lost-World-H	188
Sep 26		Mickey Walker★	Long Island	TKO	8	—	188
1933							
Jun 8	⑩	Max Baer★	New York	TKO'd	10	—	189
1934							
Feb 13	⑩	Steve Hamas	Philadelphia	L	12	—	189
May 12		Paulino Uzcudun	Barcelona	D	12	—	187
Aug 26		Walter Neusel	Hamburg	TKO	9	—	193
1935							
Mar 10	⑩	Steve Hamas	Hamburg	KO	9	—	189
Jul 7		Paolino Uzcudun	Berlin	W	12	—	191
1936							
Jun 19	⑩	Joe Louis★	New York	KO	12	—	192
1937							
Dec 14		Harry Thomas	New York	KO	8	—	196
1938							
Jan 30		Ben Foord	Hamburg	W	12	—	192
Apr 16		Steve Dudad	Hamburg	KO	5	—	194
Jun 22	♛	Joe Louis★	New York	KO'd	1	For-World-H	193
1939							
Jul 2		Adolf Heuser	Stuttgart, Germany	KO	1	Won-Europe-H	193
1947							
Sep 28		Werner Vollmer	Frankfurt	KO	7	—	194
Dec 7		Hans-Joachim Draegenstein	Hamburg	W	10	—	192
1948							
May 23		Walter Neusel	Hamburg	L	10	—	191
Oct 2		Hans-Joachim Draegenstein	Kiel, Germany	KO	9	—	—
Oct 31		Reifdel Vogt	Berlin	L	10	—	194

destructive short right hook, Schmeling was the second-ranked heavyweight contender in *The Ring*'s annual rankings in 1929.

In 1930, Schmeling met Jack Sharkey in Yankee Stadium for the vacant heavyweight title. More than 80,000 fans were curious to see who would succeed Gene Tunney, who had given up the crown two years earlier. The first three rounds were fast and furious. In the fourth, Schmeling momentarily stunned Sharkey, but Sharkey retaliated with a left to the body, knocking Schmeling down. Schmeling claimed that he had been fouled by a low blow. The officials supported his contention and awarded him the title. This was the only time the heavyweight crown had changed hands on a foul, and the manner in which he won the championship did not make Schmeling particularly popular in the U.S.

Schmeling defended his title against Young Stribling in 1931. American fans were anxious to get the title back from Europe, and knockout artist Stribling was their hope. Schmeling hammered at Stribling for fourteen rounds and finally finished him in the fifteenth. By now, Sharkey was fidgeting for a rematch. The two intervening years had been enough to turn the tables, and Sharkey won a fifteen-round decision to take the title.

Schmeling continued to box. He demolished Mickey Walker in a fight that had fans calling for it to be stopped, then was himself the victim of a vicious battering by Max Baer. In 1936, Schmeling fought young Joe Louis, then unbeaten. Schmeling knocked Louis down in the fourth round, the first time anyone had ever floored the Brown Bomber, and dropped Louis to his knees for the ten-count in the twelfth. Schmeling was again in line for the championship and signed for a match with the current champion James J. Braddock. The fight never took place because American boxing officials did not want to risk losing the heavyweight title to Europe.

But when Joe Louis became champion, a match was allowed in 1938. The contest was fraught with social and political implications. Louis became America's flagbearer against all that was evil in Adolf Hitler's reign. Schmeling was publicized by the German government as an example of the superiority of the German "race" and way of life. (Stories later surfaced that Schmeling had hid Jewish youths in his hotel during Kristallnacht and had helped Jews escape Germany during the war.) Louis made short work of Schmeling, knocking him out with such fury in the first round that Schmeling screamed. The Nazis quickly cut the radio broadcast in Germany. Schmeling, who served as a paratrooper in the German military, continued to box after World War II until 1948, before beginning a long period of employment with Coca-Cola in Germany.

This sequence shows Jack Sharkey (R) landing the low blow to Schmeling that caused a disqualification by foul. Schmeling became champion—the only time the heavyweight title changed hands on a foul.

MICHAEL SPINKS
The Spinks Jinx

HEAVYWEIGHT

Right-handed; 6'2½"; 165–212 lbs.
32 bouts, 4/17/1977 to 6/27/1988
Manager: Butch Lewis
1976 Olympic Middlewt. Gold Medalist
WBA Light Heavywt. Champ 1981–83
Light Heavyweight Champion 1983–85
Heavyweight Champion 1985–88
Hall of Fame Induction: 1994
Born: 7/13/1956, St. Louis, MO

Michael Spinks accomplished what no other light heavyweight champion had ever been able to achieve. Spinks became the first light heavyweight champ to move up in class and grab the heavyweight crown when he defeated Larry Holmes in 1985. Light heavyweights on the Hall of Fame roster such as Tommy Loughran, Bob Foster, Archie Moore, and Billy Conn had all failed in bids to win the heavyweight title. Though sometimes overshadowed by his older brother Leon, heavyweight champion in 1978, Michael was a top-shelf fighter who lost only one fight in his nine-year career.

Born in St. Louis, Spinks gained national prominence when he represented the United States in the 1976 Olympics as a middleweight. Spinks was one of five Americans to win gold medals at the Montreal games, along with brother Leon, Sugar Ray Leonard, Howard Davis, and Leo Randolph. Spinks did not immediately turn pro but worked for a time in a chemical plant. Convinced in 1977 by flamboyant promoter Butch Lewis to join the pro ranks, Spinks quickly found success in the light heavyweight division.

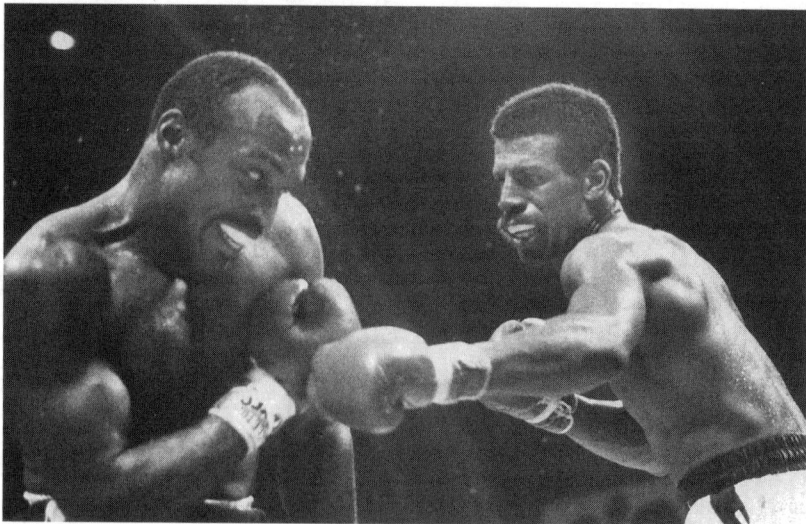

En route to a fifteen-round victory to unify the light heavyweight title, Spinks (R) goes after formidable Dwight Muhammad Qawi (originally Dwight Braxton), the WBC champ. They fought in Atlantic City.

IN THE RING	WON **31**	LOST **1**	DRAWS **0**	TB **32**	KO 21	W 10	WF 0	D 0	KO'd 1	L 0	LF 0

Date	Opponent	Site	Result / Rounds		Title	Wt.
1977						
Apr 17	Eddie Benson	Las Vegas	KO	1	—	165
May 9	Luis Rodriguez	St. Louis	W	6	—	165
Jun 1	Joe Borden	Montreal	KO	2	—	167
Aug 23	Jasper Brisbane	Philadelphia	TKO	1	—	166
Sep 13	Ray Elson	Los Angeles	KO	1	—	168
Oct 21	Gary Summerhays	Las Vegas	W	8	—	169
1978						
Feb 15	Tom Bethea	Las Vegas	W	8	—	170
Dec 15	Eddie Phillips	White Plains, NY	TKO	4	—	170
1979						
Nov 24	Marc Hans	Bloomington, MN	TKO	1	—	180
1980						
Feb 1	Johnny Wilburn	Louisville, KY	W	8	—	175
Feb 4	Ramon Ronquillo	Atlantic City	TKO	6	—	174
May 4	Murray Sutherland	Kiamesha Lake, MI	W	10	—	179
Aug 2	David Conteh	Baton Rouge, LA	TKO	9	—	177
Oct 18	⑩ Yaqui Lopez	Atlantic City	TKO	7	—	176
1981						
Jan 24	Willie Taylor	Philadelphia	TKO	8	—	176
Mar 28	⑩ Marvin Johnson	Atlantic City	KO	4	—	176
Jul 18	♛ Mustafa Muhammad	Las Vegas	W	15	Won-WBA-LH	175
Nov 7	Vonzell Johnson	Atlantic City	TKO	7	Ret-WBA-LH	173
1982						
Feb 13	Mustapha Wasajja	Atlantic City	KO	6	Ret-WBA-LH	173
Apr 11	⑩ Murray Sutherland	Atlantic City	KO	8	Ret-WBA-LH	172
Jun 12	⑩ Jerry Celestine	Atlantic City	TKO	8	Ret-WBA-LH	173
Sep 18	⑩ John Davis	Atlantic City	TKO	9	Ret-WBA-LH	173
1983						
Mar 18	♛ Dwight Braxton★	Atlantic City	W	15	Won-Vac World-LH	173
Nov 25	⑩ Oscar Rivadeneyra	Vancouver, B.C.	TKO	10	Ret-World-LH	173
1984						
Feb 25	⑩ Eddie Davis	Atlantic City	W	12	Ret-World-LH	175
1985						
Feb 23	⑩ David Sears	Atlantic City	TKO	3	Ret-World-LH	170
Jun 6	⑩ Jim MacDonald	Las Vegas	TKO	8	Ret-World-LH	175
Sep 21	♛ Larry Holmes	Las Vegas	W	15	Won-World (IBF)-H	200
1986						
Apr 19	⑩ Larry Holmes	Las Vegas	W	15	Ret-World (IBF)-H	205
Sep 6	Steffan Tangstad	Las Vegas	TKO	4	Ret-World (IBF)-H	201
1987						
Jun 15	Gerry Cooney	Atlantic City	TKO	5	—	208
1988						
Jun 27	♛ Mike Tyson	Atlantic City	KO'd	1	Lost-World-H	212

Spinks won his first sixteen fights, which included victories over the well–regarded David Conteh as well as ranked contenders Yaqui Lopez and Marvin Johnson. The record put Spinks in line for a championship bout with WBA title

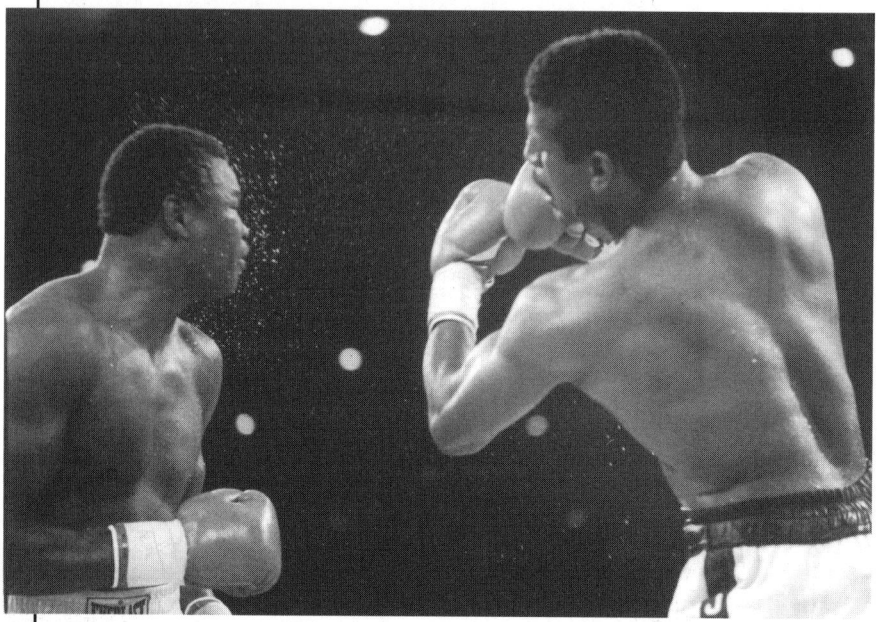

Spinks twice beat heavyweight great Larry Holmes. The first victory gave Spinks the title. In their April 19, 1986, rematch, he connects with a left hook to Holmes's jaw, on the way to another decision.

holder Eddie Mustafa Muhammad in July 1981 in Las Vegas. Muhammad was a powerful but graceless fighter, dangerous in his unpredictability. He was unquestionably the most formidable opponent Spinks had faced to date. Spinks fell behind early, shaken by Muhammad's flailing attacks, but from the fifth round on Spinks dominated the bout. He used his superior control to cut the champion over both eyes, and he knocked Muhammad down in the twelfth. Spinks's arsenal of uppercuts, overhand lefts, and body shots earned him the unanimous decision.

Spinks was in championship territory now, and fourteen of the remaining fifteen fights in his career were title defenses or challenges. In the period from November 1981 to September 1982, he defended the light heavyweight title five times, vanquishing all comers with knockouts in nine or fewer rounds. Tough Jerry Celestine went down in eight in Atlantic City, reduced to helplessness by Spinks's insistent attack.

In 1983, Spinks unified the light heavyweight title with a fifteen-round decision over Dwight Braxton (who later changed his name to Dwight Muhammad Qawi). He defended the title four times through June 1985. Building on this success, Spinks seized the opportunity to challenge the undefeated heavyweight champion Larry Holmes. Holmes was aging, but he had destroyed every contender that had come his way in seven years and was expected to retain his crown. But Spinks outmaneuvered the champ and won a fifteen-round decision at the Riviera Hotel in Las Vegas. He kept Holmes from initiating the action with his vaunted jab, and he avoided battling the larger man inside. He used a variety of tactics to score enough to win the fight without allowing Holmes to hurt him.

Holmes demanded a rematch, and the two met again in April 1986 in Las Vegas. Intent on taking Spinks out early, Holmes was all over the smaller man in the first rounds, but Spinks again used his excellent ring skills to stay out of serious trouble. It wasn't until the fourteenth round that Holmes caught him with a strong right, slamming him into the ropes. Spinks sagged but did not fall. He came back in the fifteenth to box expertly, and the judges awarded him the decision. Boxing's warring governing bodies then intervened, and both the WBA and WBC stripped Spinks of his titles for granting Holmes a rematch in violation of their rules. Holmes later went on to meet defeat at the hands of Mike Tyson.

Spinks took out ferocious Gerry Cooney in a non-title bout and then went up against Tyson to see who really was the world champion. As it turned out, it was Tyson all the way as Iron Mike destroyed Spinks in under two minutes. Spinks then retired, having gone further than any light heavyweight in boxing history.

Giant Gerry Cooney (R) hunches his shoulders as he struggles to defend himself from a Spinks on-slaught. Spinks won in five on June 15, 1987, at Atlantic City. This bout was Spinks's last win.

DICK TIGER

LIGHT HEAVYWEIGHT

Right-handed; 5'8"; 158–169 lbs.

81 bouts, 1952 to 7/15/1970

Manager: Jersey Jones

WBA Middlewt. Champ 1962–63
Middlewt. Champ 1963, 1965–66
Light Heavywt. Champ 1966–68

Hall of Fame Induction: 1991

Born: 8/14/1929, Amaigbo,
Orlu, Nigeria

Named: Richard Ihetu

Died: 12/14/1971

Dick Tiger earned wide admiration not only for his considerable boxing skills—as evidenced by world championship victories in two weight classes—but also for his gentlemanly demeanor and his efforts on behalf of the impoverished Biafran people in his home country of Nigeria.

Tiger started fighting professionally in Nigeria at the age of 23 and built up a good record there for three years before Jack Farnsworth, an English insurance salesman and creator of the Nigerian Boxing Board of Control, sent him to Liverpool to train under Peter Benencko. Tiger had difficulty adjusting to life in England and to the style of British fighters and lost his first four fights after the move. Before long, however, he found his footing and won the British Empire middleweight title in 1958, defeating Pat McAteer.

In 1959, Tiger began to campaign extensively in the United States where he experienced both success and popularity, with a 11-2-1 record. In October 1962, he was given a chance at the NBA crown held by Hall of Famer Gene Fullmer. In Candlestick Park in San Francisco, Tiger scored a convincing fifteen-round decision over Fullmer, whose eyes were seriously cut and bleeding from Tiger's well-placed shots.

Later that year the New York State Athletic Commission, European Boxing

Tiger enlisted in the Biafran army after war broke out in Nigeria. In the ring, he held the middle- and light heavyweight titles.

IN THE RING	WON 59	LOST 19	DRAWS 3	TB 81	KO 26	W 33	WF 0	D 3	KO'd 2	L 17	LF 0

Date	Opponent	Site	Result / Rounds		Title	Wt.
1952						
—	Simon Eme	Aba, Nigeria	KO	2	—	—
—	Lion Ring	Nigeria	TKO	6	—	—
—	Simon Eme	Nigeria	W	8	—	—
—	John Ama	Nigeria	KO	2	—	—
—	Robert Nwanne	Nigeria	KO	2	—	—
—	Peter Okptra	Nigeria	KO	8	—	—
Sep	Koko Kid	Port Hardcourt, Nigeria	W	8	—	—
Oct	Easy Dynamite	Port Hardcourt	KO	3	—	—
Dec 13	Tommy West	Aba	L	10	—	—
1953						
Jan 30	Blackie Power	Lagos	W	8	—	—
May 5	Tommy West	Lagos	TKO'd	7	For-Nigeria-M	—
1954						
Jan 29	Tommy West	Lagos	L	6	—	—
Jun 12	Mighty Joe	Aba	W	6	—	—
Jul 18	Super Human Power	Aba	W	8	—	—
1955						
Jan 31	Raheem ("Roy") Fargbemy	Lagos	W	6	—	—
Aug 31	Bolaji Johnson	Lagos	W	6	—	—
Dec 8	Alan Dean	Liverpool, England	L	6	—	162
1956						
Jan 27	Gerry McNally	Blackpool, England	L	8	—	161
Mar 2	Jimmy Lynas	Blackpool	L	8	—	162
Mar 22	George Roe	Liverpool	L	8	—	159
May 3	Dennis Rowley	Liverpool	KO	1	—	164
May 10	Alan Dean	Liverpool	W	8	—	163
May 28	Wally Scott	West Hartlepool, England	TKO	4	—	162
Jul 2	Jimmy Lynas	West Hartlepool	W	8	—	162
Oct 18	Alan Dean	Liverpool	L	6	—	165
Nov 9	Alan Dean	Blackpool	W	8	—	162
1957						
Apr 29	Johnny Read	London	TKO	2	—	165
May 14	Terry Downes	London	TKO	5	—	162
Jun 4	Marius Dori	London	TKO	7	—	160
Jul 15	Willie Armstrong	West Hartlepool	L	8	—	167
Jul 25	Alan Dean	Liverpool	W	8	—	164
Sep 9	Phil Edwards	Cardiff, Wales	W	10	—	163
Oct 21	Jean Poison	Cardiff	W	10	—	—
Nov 11	Pat McAteer	Cardiff	D	10	—	—
Nov 29	Paddy Delargy	Birmingham, England	TKO	6	—	163
1958						
Jan 13	Jean Ruellet	Hull, England	W	8	—	162
Feb 3	Jimmy Lynas	Manchester, England	TKO	7	—	162
Feb 25	Johnny Read	London	TKO	6	—	163
Mar 27	Pat McAteer	Liverpool	KO	9	Won-Brit Emp-M	158
May 1	Billy Ellaway	Liverpool	TKO	2	—	—

Date		Opponent	Location	Result	Rounds	Notes	
Jun 24	⓾	Spider Webb	London	L	10	—	161
Oct 14	⓾	Yolande Pompey	London	W	10	—	163
1959							
Mar 19		Randy Sandy	Liverpool	L	10	—	161
May 12		Randy Sandy	London	W	10	—	161
Jun 5	⓾	Rory Calhoun	New York	D	10	—	163
Jul 17	⓾	Rory Calhoun	Syracuse, NY	L	10	—	162
Sep 2	⓾	Gene Armstrong	Camden, NJ	W	10	—	162
Sep 30	⓾	Joey Giardello★	Chicago	W	10	—	160
Nov 4	⓾	Joey Giardello★	Cleveland	L	10	—	161
Dec 30	⓾	Holly Mims	Chicago	W	10	—	160
1960							
Feb 24		Gene Armstrong	Chicago	W	10	—	160
Apr 1		Victor Zalazar	Boston	W	10	—	161
Jun 22		Wilf Greaves	Edmonton, Alb.	L	15	Lost-Brit Emp-M	—
Nov 30		Wilf Greaves	Edmonton	TKO	9	Reg-Brit Emp-M	159
1961							
Feb 18		Gene Armstrong	New York	TKO	9	—	158
Apr 15		Spider Webb	New York	TKO	6	—	160
May 15	⓾	Hank Casey	New Orleans	W	10	—	161
Dec 16		Bill Pickett	New York	W	10	—	160
1962							
Jan 20	⓾	Floro Fernandez	Miami Beach	TKO	6	—	160
Mar 31	⓾	Henry Hank	New York	W	10	—	160
Oct 23	♛	Gene Fullmer★	San Francisco	W	15	Won-NBA-M	159
1963							
Feb 23	⓾	Gene Fullmer★	Las Vegas	D	15	Ret-NBA-M	160
Aug 10	⓾	Gene Fullmer★	Ibadan, Nigeria	TKO	7	Won-Vac World-M	159
Dec 7	⓾	Joey Giardello★	Atlantic City	L	15	Lost-World-M	159
1964							
Jul 31		Jose Gonzalez	New York	TKO	6	—	163
Sep 11		Don Fullmer	Cleveland	W	10	—	164
Oct 16	⓾	Joey Archer	New York	L	10	—	160
1965							
Mar 12		Rocky Rivero	New York	TKO	6	—	169
May 20	⓾	Rubin Carter	New York	W	10	—	163
Oct 21	♛	Joey Giardello★	New York	W	15	Reg-World-M	158
1966							
Feb 18		Peter Mueller	Dortmund, Germany	KO	3	—	162
Apr 25	♛	Emile Griffith★	New York	L	15	Lost-World-M	160
Dec 16	♛	Jose Torres★	New York	W	15	Won-World-LH	167
1967							
Feb 5		Abraham Tomica	Port Harcourt	TKO	5	—	—
May 16	⓾	Jose Torres★	New York	W	15	Ret-World-LH	167
Nov 17	⓾	Roger Rouse	Las Vegas	TKO	12	Ret-World-LH	168
1968							
May 24	⓾	Bob Foster★	New York	KO'd	4	Lost-World-LH	168
Oct 25		Frank DePaula	New York	W	10	—	167
1969							
May 26	⓾	Nino Benvenuti★	New York	W	10	—	166
Nov 14	⓾	Andy Kendall	New York	W	10	—	168
1970							
Jul 15	⓾	Emile Griffith★	New York	L	10	—	167

Tiger cut up Gene Fullmer (R) and stripped him of his WBA middleweight title on October 23, 1962. These two rivals battled three times in less than a year. Tiger won two; one fight was called a draw.

Union, and the British Boxing Board of Control all recognized Tiger as middleweight champion. *The Ring* further honored Tiger by naming him its Fighter of the Year for 1962.

In 1963, Tiger lost the title to Hall of Famer Joey Giardello but regained it in a return match decision in 1965. He was again named *The Ring*'s Fighter of the Year. At age 36, Tiger faced a stern challenge from welterweight champion Emile Griffith. The younger Griffith fought brilliantly, outboxing Tiger to win a decision.

Tiger continued fighting, in part to gain aid for the people of Biafra. He moved up in class and outpointed Jose Torres to win the light heavyweight title in 1966. He retained the title until 1968 when he faced the great Bob Foster, who was nine years younger, seven inches taller, and had a reach advantage of eight inches. Foster did what no other fighter had accomplished up until then: he knocked Tiger out in the fourth round, a session *The Ring* later called the most exciting round of 1968.

Tiger continued to fight for two more years to recoup from the confiscation of his property by the Nigerian government. He retired in 1971 and went to live in his beloved Biafra, where he died of cancer less than six months later. His old rival Fullmer called Tiger "a great competitor and champion and, most important, a gentleman."

JOSE TORRES
Chegui

LIGHT HEAVYWEIGHT

Right-handed; 5'10"; 158–182 lbs.

45 bouts, 5/24/1958 to 7/14/1969

Manager: Cus D'Amato

1956 Olympic Light Middleweight Silver Medalist

Light Heavyweight Champ 1965–66

Hall of Fame Induction: 1997

Born: 5/3/1936, Playa Ponce, Puerto Rico

Named: Jose Luis Torres

Today Jose Torres is almost as well known as a boxing writer and administrator as for his considerable achievements in the ring. However, his other successes will never obscure his greatness as a fighter.

Growing up in Puerto Rico, Torres was a street fighter. When he was sixteen, he was accused of stealing a car. Although he was cleared in court, Torres volunteered to join the U.S. Army to turn his life around. He joined the boxing team where his natural talent was developed by army trainers.

Torres won the Caribbean army title in 1954. After transferring to Fort Meade in Maryland in 1955, Torres continued to claim amateur crowns including the Maryland State AAU title, the Second Army championship, and the All-Army and All-Service titles. Torres represented the U.S. in the 1956 Olympics in the light middleweight division. He took a silver medal in the finals in Melbourne, losing a 3-2 decision to Hungary's Laszlo Papp.

Torres (L) was 17-0-1 on April 1, 1961, when he faced Bobby Barnes in Paterson, NJ's Plaza Ballroom. He triumphed with a third-round KO.

IN THE RING	WON 41	LOST 3	DRAWS 1	TB 45	KO 29	W 12	WF 0	D 1	KO'd 1	L 2	LF 0

Date	Opponent	Site	Result / Rounds		Title	Wt.
1958						
May 24	Gene Hamilton	Brooklyn	KO	1	—	163
Jun 7	Walter Irby	Brooklyn	W	6	—	162
Jun 21	Joe Salvato	Brooklyn	KO	4	—	164
Jul 5	Wes Lowery	Brooklyn	W	6	—	161
Aug 18	Benny Doyle	Los Angeles	KO	1	—	164
Sep 29	Otis Woodard	New York	KO	5	—	160
Oct 13	Frankie Anselm	New York	KO	9	—	158
Nov 3	Burke Emery	New York	TKO	5	—	164
Dec 4	Ike Jenkins	New York	KO	5	—	159
1959						
Feb 26	Eddie Wright	New York	KO	5	—	163
Mar 19	Leroy Oliphant	New York	TKO	3	—	162
Apr 23	Joe Shaw	New York	KO	5	—	164
Jun 27	Al Andrews	New York	KO	6	—	164
Sep 26	⑩ Benny Paret	San Juan, PR	D	10	—	159
1960						
Jan 30	Randy Sandy	Elizabeth, NJ	W	10	—	162
Mar 15	Tony Dupas	Buffalo, NY	W	10	—	159
Jun 11	Randy Sandy	New York	W	10	—	161
1961						
Feb 17	Gene Hamilton	San Juan	KO	4	—	—
Apr 1	Bobby Barnes	Paterson, NJ	TKO	3	—	164
May 23	Bob Young	Boston	TKO	5	—	164
Jun 5	Mel Collins	Boston	KO	7	—	164
Jun 27	Ike White	Boston	TKO	3	—	159
Oct 31	Georgie Price	Houston	KO	2	—	164
Nov 28	Tony Montano	Houston	KO	4	—	161
1962						
Apr 10	Jimmy Watkins	Utica, NY	KO	7	—	158
Jul 27	Dulio Nunez	San Juan	KO	7	Won-PR-M	160
Dec 14	Al Hauser	Boston	KO	3	—	166
1963						
May 26	Florentino Fernandez	San Juan	KO'd	5	—	161
Oct 9	Don Fullmer	Teaneck, NJ	W	10	—	161
1964						
Jan 3	Jose Gonzalez	New York	W	10	Ret-PR-M	161
Apr 21	Walker Simmons	New York	TKO	8	—	171
May 15	Wilbert McClure	New York	W	10	—	161
Jun 22	Frankie Olevera	New Bedford, MA	KO	5	—	164
Jul 20	Walker Simmons	New Bedford	TKO	6	—	173
Sep 4	Gomeo Brennan	Miami Beach	W	10	—	167
Nov 27	⑩ Carl ("Bobo") Olson★	New York	KO	1	—	170
1965						
Mar 30	♛ Willie Pastrano★	New York	TKO	9	Won-World-LH	171
Jul 31	Tom McNeeley	San Juan	W	10	—	182
1966						
May 21	⑩ Wayne Thornton	Flushing, NY	W	15	Ret-World-LH	175
Aug 15	⑩ Eddie Cotton	Las Vegas	W	15	Ret-World-LH	173

Date		Opponent	Location	Result	Rounds	Title	Weight
Oct 15		Chic Calderwood	San Juan	KO	2	Ret-World-LH	175
Dec 16	⑩	Dick Tiger★	New York	L	15	Lost-World-LH	175
1967							
May 16	♛	Dick Tiger★	New York	L	15	For-World-LH	173
1968							
Apr 1	⑩	Bob Dunlop	Sydney	TKO	6	—	175
1969							
Jul 14		Charlie Green	New York	KO	2	—	176

Torres left the Army and turned professional in 1958 with a first-round knockout of Gene Hamilton. Fighting under the tutelage of Hall of Famer Cus D'Amato, Torres mastered the distinctive peekaboo style of fighting—hands held high to shield the face—similar to another of D'Amato's protégés, Floyd Patterson. Fighting as a middleweight, Torres won his first thirteen bouts before fighting to a draw with future welterweight champ Benny ("Kid") Paret. He won another string of thirteen before Florentino Fernandez knocked him out in five rounds in San Juan in 1963.

Although Torres had a record of 26-1-1 to this point, he had very little to show for it financially until he gained the sponsorship of Brooklyn real estate dealer Cain Young. Young got Torres a fight with the third-ranked light heavyweight Carl ("Bobo") Olson by guaranteeing Olson $10,000. Though still a comparatively light 170 pounds, Torres moved up a weight class and faced Olson at Madison Square Garden on November 27, 1964. (Torres had never fought in the Garden because of D'Amato's opposition to the corrupt International Boxing Club, controllers of the arena for over a decade.) In a one-round knockout, Torres devastated Olson with a four-punch combination—a left hook to the kidney followed by a right cross, left hook, and a right uppercut, all to the jaw. *The Ring* rated this as the Round of the Year for 1964.

The victory over Olson gave Torres a shot at the light heavyweight title held by Willie Pastrano. Held in Madison Square Garden on March 30, 1965, the fight drew 18,112 fans and a gate of $239,956. A large contingent of Puerto Rican fans rooted for Torres, who attacked Pastrano with fiery aggression. He bloodied Pastrano's nose in the first

Torres (L) confers with his derby-hatted trainer, Hall of Famer Cus D'Amato (C).

round and, in the sixth, slammed the champion with a left hook to the body that took him to the canvas—the first time Pastrano had ever been floored. *The Ring* would later label this round the best of 1965. Pastrano held on through nine but could not answer the bell for the tenth. Torres was the new champion, and his friend, novelist Norman Mailer, hosted a victory party whose guests included James Baldwin, George Plimpton, and Senator Jacob Javits.

Torres successfully defended the title three times in 1966. On December 16, 1966, Torres's title reign came to an end when Hall of Famer Dick Tiger defeated him in a close decision. Five months later, Tiger won a decision in a rematch. Torres only fought twice more. When Charlie Green knocked him down in the first round of their July 14, 1969, fight, Torres decided it was time to retire. He knocked Green out in two, but he never fought again, thus ending his career with a victory.

Mailer and fellow writers Pete Hamill and Budd Schulberg encouraged Torres to pursue writing. He authored boxing books *Sting Like a Bee,* about Muhammad Ali, and *Fire and Fear,* a study of Mike Tyson, and has written numerous articles for newspapers and magazines. Torres campaigned for Senators Robert Kennedy and George McGovern and has worked on issues affecting Puerto Rico.

Torres served five years as chairman of the New York State Athletic Commission, from 1983 to 1988. He was also president of the World Boxing Organization (WBO) from 1993 to 1995. The eloquent Torres appeared as an announcer on Spanish language telecasts of the USA Network's *Tuesday Night Fights.*

Torres dispatched Al Hauser in three rounds in their December 14, 1962, Boston match-up. That gave Torres ten consecutive knock-out victories.

RANDY TURPIN
The Leamington Licker

MIDDLEWEIGHT

Right-handed; 5′9½″; 156–176 lbs.
75 bouts, 9/17/1946 to 9/1/1964
Manager: George Middleton
Middleweight Champion 1951
Hall of Fame Induction: 2001
Born: 6/7/1928, Leamington, Warwickshire, England
Named: Randolph Adolphus Turpin
Died: 5/17/1966

Randy Turpin's triumphant 64-day reign as the middleweight champion of the world is somewhat tarnished by his tragic life outside the ring.

Turpin's father, Lionel, was a native of British Guiana. Wounded and exposed to mustard gas while serving in World War I, he was sent to convalesce in England where he met and married the daughter of a bare-knuckle fighter. Randy Turpin was born just a few months before his father's death.

Turpin and his brothers became well known as fighters, his brother Dick winning the Lonsdale Belt as the British middleweight champion and Jackie Turpin boxing professionally as a featherweight. Randy was dubbed "Leamington Licker," or simply "Licker," because he could lick anyone in a fight.

Turpin won three British junior titles. In 1945, he won the ABA welterweight title, and he secured the ABA middleweight title the next year. In what was perhaps his most memorable amateur fight, he knocked out Harold Anspach of the United States boxing team to help England defeat the Americans five to three in a special tournament. Around this time, Turpin served as a cook in the Royal Navy. While on leave, he ingested a poisonous substance and had to have his stomach pumped. He was charged with attempted suicide, though the case was soon dropped. Already, his tortured personal life was impacting his boxing career.

Turpin turned professional on September 17, 1946, with a first-round knockout of Gordon Griffiths, and he rolled on to an 18-0-1 record before losing a decision to Albert Finch on April 26, 1948. Some blamed this loss, and a knockout at the hands of Jean Stock five months later, on tumult between Turpin and his wife. Arrested later for assaulting her, Turpin was not convicted.

After the British Boxing Board of Control rescinded its rule prohibiting blacks from fighting for its titles, Dick Turpin won the middleweight championship. Although Randy was qualified to fight for the title, the brothers had vowed never to face each other in the ring. When Finch dethroned Dick, Turpin got his chance not only to try for the title, but also to avenge his own

The three fighting Turpin brothers (L to R): Randy, Jackie, and Dick.

IN THE RING	WON 66	LOST 8	DRAWS 1	TB 75	KO 45	W 17	WF 4	D 1	KO'd 5	L 3	LF 0

Date	Opponent	Site	Result / Rounds		Title	Wt.
1946						
Sep 17	Gordon Griffiths	London	TKO	1	—	160
Nov 19	Des Jones	London	W	6	—	—
Dec 26	Bill Blything	Birmingham, England	KO	1	—	—
1947						
Jan 14	Jimmy Davis	London	KO	4	—	157
Jan 24	Dai James	Birmingham	KO	3	—	—
Feb 18	Johnny Best	London	TKO	1	—	159
Mar 18	Bert Hyland	London	KO	1	—	161
Apr 1	Frank Dolan	London	TKO	2	—	161
Apr 15	Tommy Davies	London	KO	2	—	162
Apr 28	Bert Sanders	London	W	6	—	—
May 12	Ron Coopers	Oxford, England	TKO	4	—	—
May 27	Jury VII	London	W	6	—	158
Jun 3	Mark Hart	London	W	6	—	—
Jun 23	Leon Fouquet	Coventry, England	KO	1	—	156
Sep 9	Jimmy Ingle	Coventry	TKO	3	—	—
Oct 20	Mark Hart	London	D	6	—	—
1948						
Jan 26	Freddie Price	Coventry	KO	1	—	—
Feb 17	Gerry McCready	London	TKO	1	—	—
Mar 16	Vince Hawkins	London	W	8	—	—
Apr 26	Albert Finch	London	L	8	—	—
Jun 28	Alby Hollister	Birmingham	W	8	—	—
Sep 21	Jean Stock	London	TKO'd	5	—	—
1949						
Feb 7	Jackie Jones	Coventry	TKO	5	—	—
Feb 21	Doug Miller	London	W	8	—	—
Mar 25	Mickey Laurent	Manchester, England	TKO	3	—	—
May 3	William Poli	London	WF	4	—	160
Jun 20 ⑩	Cyrille Delannoit	Birmingham	TKO	8	—	—
Aug 22	Jean Wanes	Manchester	TKO	3	—	—
Sep 19	Roy Wouters	Coventry	TKO	5	—	—
Nov 15	Pete Mead	London	TKO	5	—	160
1950						
Jan 31	Gilbert Stock	London	W	8	—	162
Mar 6	Richard Armah	Croydon, England	TKO	6	—	161
Apr 24	Gus Degouve	Nottingham, England	W	8	—	161
Sep 5	Eli Elandon	Watford, England	KO	2	—	—
Oct 17	Albert Finch	London	KO	5	Won-British-M	158
Nov 13	Jose Alamo	Abergavenny, Wales	KO	2	—	—
Dec 12 ⑩	Tommy Yarosz	London	WF	8	—	163
1951						
Jan 22	Eduardo Lopez	Birmingham	KO	1	—	163
Feb 27	Luc Van Dam	London	KO	1	Won-Vac Eur-M	159
Mar 19	Jean Stock	Leicester, England	TKO	5	—	163
Apr 16	Billy Brown	Birmingham	KO	2	—	164
May 7	Jan DeBruin	Coventry	KO	6	—	159
Jun 5	Jackie Keough	London	TKO	7	—	160

Date		Opponent	Location	Result	Rounds	Title	Weight
Jul 10	♛	Sugar Ray Robinson★	London	W	15	Won-World-M	158
Sep 12	⑩	Sugar Ray Robinson★	New York	TKO'd	10	Lost-World-M	159
1952							
Feb 12		Alex Buxton	London	TKO	7	—	163
Apr 22		Jacques Hairabedjian	London	KO	3	—	164
Jun 10	⑩	Don Cockell	London	TKO	11	Won-Vac Comwlth-LH	162
Oct 21	⑩	George Angelo	London	W	15	Won-Vac Comwlth-M	157
1953							
Jan 19		Victor d'Haes	Birmingham	KO	7	—	160
Feb 16		Duggie Miller	Leicester	W	10	—	161
Mar 17		Walter Cartier	London	WF	2	—	160
Jun 9		Charles Humez	London	W	15	Ret-Eur-M	160
Oct 21	⑩	Carl ("Bobo") Olson★	New York	L	15	For-Vac-World-M	157
1954							
Mar 30		Olle Bengtsson	London	W	10	—	162
May 2	⑩	Tiberio Mitri	Rome	TKO'd	1	Lost-Eur-M	158
1955							
Feb 15		Ray Schmitt	Birmingham	WF	8	—	171
Mar 8		Jose Gonzalez	London	KO	7	—	171
Apr 26		Alex Buxton	London	KO	2	Ret-Commonwealth-LH	171
Sep 19		Ed Polly Smith	Birmingham	W	10	—	177
Oct 18		Gordon Wallace	London	KO'd	4	—	—
1956							
Apr 17		Sandro D'Ottavio	Birmingham	TKO	6	—	174
Jun 18		Jacques Bro	Birmingham	KO	5	—	175
Sep 21	⑩	Hans Stretz	Hamburg, Ger.	L	10	—	175
Nov 26		Alex Buxton	Leicester	TKO	5	Won-Vac British-LH	173
1957							
Jun 11		Arthur Howard	Leicester	W	15	Ret-British-LH	172
Sep 17		Ahmed Boulgroune	London	TKO	9	—	171
Oct 28		Sergio Burchi	Birmingham	TKO	2	—	172
Nov 25		Uwe Janssen	Leicester	TKO	8	—	—
1958							
Feb 1		Wim Snoek	Birmingham	W	10	—	—
Apr 21		Eddie Wright	Leicester	TKO	7	—	176
Jul 22		Redvers Sangoe	Oswestry, Eng.	TKO	4	—	—
Sep 9	⑩	Yolande Pompey	Birmingham	KO'd	2	—	175
1963							
Mar 19		Eddie Marcano	Wisbech, Eng.	KO	6	—	—
1964							
Sep 1		Charles Seguna	Valetta, Malta	TKO	2	—	—

previous loss, as well as his brother's. On October 17, 1950, he knocked out Finch in five rounds, and four months later, he added the European middleweight title to his collection with a first-round knockout of Luc Van Dam. Four more knockout victories followed, setting the stage for Turpin's greatest triumph.

Sugar Ray Robinson, the middleweight champion of the world (with only one loss in 135 fights), was touring Europe. On July 10, 1951, Robinson put his title on the line against Turpin before 18,000 fans at Earl's Court Arena in London. Robinson was the heavy favorite, yet Turpin's unorthodox, spread-legged stance confused the champ, and Turpin scored with a strong left and outmuscled Ray in the clinches. He won the decision in a fight that ranks with the biggest upsets of all time.

Unfortunately, Turpin did not fare well in the rematch, held 64 days later at the Polo Grounds. Robinson felled Turpin in the tenth with a right to the jaw. By the end of the round, Robinson had his battered opponent pinned against the ropes. Referee Ruby Goldstein stopped the fight with eight seconds remaining. The ring death of George Flores in a bout eleven days earlier may have colored the referee's decision, but most observers supported Goldstein's call.

Turpin returned to England and knocked out Don Cockell in the eleventh round to win the vacant British Empire light heavyweight title. He followed up with a decision over George Angelo for the Empire middleweight title. Turpin next outpointed Charlie Humez in London in a bout to select the European to meet an American contender for the now-vacant middleweight title.

Turpin came to the United States to face Carl ("Bobo") Olson in Madison Square Garden on October 21, 1953. He had not trained properly for the fight, reportedly distracted by arguments with his brother Dick and separation from his girlfriend. Turpin won the first three rounds, but it was Olson who came away with the title in a fifteen-round decision. Before he could return to Britain, Turpin was arrested on an assault charge brought by a 24-year-old woman. Authorities dropped the criminal case, but his accuser forced Turpin into a settlement in civil court.

Back in the ring, Turpin lost the European middleweight title to Tiberio Mitri in a first-round knockout. He then moved up to light heavyweight and won the British title. Despite his success, he retired after a second-round knock-out loss to Yolande Pompey on September 9, 1958, fighting only twice more, five and six years later.

In retirement, the embittered Turpin realized that he had frittered away most of his ring earnings and owed significant back taxes to the British government. Turpin found work in his manager's scrap yard. Later, he and his second wife operated a small transport café. Eventually, he filed for bankruptcy.

On May 14, 1966, Turpin received a final demand from the tax authorities for a settlement. His café also faced condemnation to make room for a garage. On May 17, Turpin took his seventeen-month-old daughter, Carmen, to an attic bedroom, shot her, and then shot and killed himself. Carmen survived.

Randy Turpin (L) floors Don Cockell in the third round of their June 10, 1952, London battle for the British Light Heavyweight title. Turpin won in the eleventh, when the referee stopped the fight.

JERSEY JOE WALCOTT

HEAVYWEIGHT

Right-handed; 6'; 158–201 lbs.

71 bouts, 9/9/1930 to 5/15/1953

Managers: Sonny Banks,
Felix Bocchicchio 1945–53

Heavyweight Champion 1951–52

Hall of Fame Induction: 1990

Born: 1/31/1914, Merchantville, NJ

Named: Arnold Raymond Cream

Died: 2/25/1994

Jersey Joe Walcott was 33 years old before he was given a chance to fight for the heavyweight championship. It took four more years before he attained his goal. On a slow rise through the professional ranks, Walcott literally outlived the color bar that kept many black boxers of the 1930s and '40s from meeting their full potential. He was a master of defense as well as a fearless attacker, and he never ducked a challenge.

Born Arnold Cream, Walcott took his name in honor of his idol, the great Joe Walcott of Barbados. He was sixteen when he fought in his first professional bout in his native New Jersey. Early in his career, Walcott trained briefly with Jack Blackburn and was scheduled to accompany him to Chicago when Blackburn was assigned to train Joe Louis. Walcott's career might have been different

Tommy Gomez crumbles as Walcott (R) stands ready to hand out more punishment. The third round of their August 1946 fight proved to be the last. Walcott was about a year away from his first title shot.

IN THE RING	WON 51	LOST 18	DRAWS 2	TB 71	KO 32	W 18	WF 1	D 2	KO'd 6	L 12	LF 0

Date	Opponent	Site	Result / Rounds		Title	Wt.
1930						
Sep 9	Frank ("Cowboy") Willis	Vineland, NJ	KO	1	—	165
Oct 10	Jimmy O'Toole	Camden, NJ	TKO	4	—	165
Oct 24	Frankie Matthews	Camden	TKO	4	—	165
1931						
Apr 20	Carl Mays	Atlantic City	KO	2	—	158
1933						
May 5	Bob Norris	Camden	KO	1	—	—
Jul 28	Henry Taylor	Camden	TKO	1	—	176
Nov 16	Henry Taylor	Philadelphia	L	6	—	179
1935						
May 21	Al Lang	Camden	KO	1	—	—
Aug 26	Lew Alva	Camden	KO	3	—	180
Oct 1	Pat Roland	Camden	TKO	4	—	181
Oct 29	Joe King	Camden	KO	1	—	180
Nov 26	Roxie Allen	Camden	KO	7	—	183
1936						
Jan 21	⑩ Al Ettore	Camden	TKO'd	8	—	188
Mar 16	Willie Reddish	Philadelphia	W	10	—	189
Apr 28	Joe Colucci	Camden	KO	4	—	—
Jun 4	Billy Ketchell	Camden	D	10	—	182
Jun 16	Lou Lepage	Coney Island, NY	KO	3	—	188
Jun 22	Phil Johnson	Philadelphia	KO	3	—	188
Jul 14	Billy Ketchell	Camden	D	10	—	188
Aug 1	Young Passarella	Camden	W	8	—	—
Sep 1	Billy Ketchell	Camden	L	10	—	187
1937						
May 22	⑩ Tiger Jack Fox	New York	KO'd	8	—	184
Sep 3	Joe Lipps	Atlantic City	KO	2	—	183
Sep 25	Elmer Ray	New York	KO	3	—	185
Oct 9	George Brothers	New York	L	8	—	184
1938						
Jan 10	Fred Fiducia	Philadelphia	W	8	—	187
Jan 20	Jim Whitest	Philadelphia	W	8	—	187
Mar 25	Art Sykes	Philadelphia	KO	4	—	187
Apr 12	Lorenzo Pack	Camden	KO	4	—	196
May 10	⑩ Tiger Jack Fox	Camden	L	10	—	185
Jun 14	Roy Lazer	Fairview, NJ	L	8	—	188
Dec 23	Bob Tow	Camden	W	8	—	190
1939						
Aug 14	Al Boros	Newark, NJ	W	8	—	191
Nov 18	Curtis Sheppard	New York	W	8	—	192
1940						
Jan 19	Tiger Red Lewis	Philadelphia	KO	6	—	192
Feb 12	⑩ Abe Simon	Newark	KO'd	6	—	192

1944							
Jun 7		Felix Del Paoli	Batesville, NJ	W	8	—	—
Jun 28		Ellis Singleton	Batesville	KO	3	—	—

1945							
Jan 11		Jackie Saunders	Camden	TKO	2	—	188
Jan 25		Johnny ("Skippy") Allen	Camden	L	8	—	191
Feb 22		Austin Johnson	Camden	W	6	—	189
Mar 15		Johnny ("Skippy") Allen	Camden	W	8	—	192
Aug 2	⑩	Joe Baksi	Camden	W	10	—	188
Sep 20		Johnny Denson	Camden	KO	2	—	192
Oct 23		Steve Dudas	Paterson, NJ	KO	5	—	193
Nov 12	⑩	Lee Q. Murray	Baltimore	WF	9	—	189
Dec 10	⑩	Curtis Sheppard	Baltimore	KO	10	—	192

1946							
Jan 30		Johnny ("Skippy") Allen	Camden	KO	3	—	192
Feb 25	⑩	Jimmy Bivins★	Cleveland	W	10	—	196
Mar 20		Al Blake	Camden	KO	4	—	192
May 24	⑩	Lee Oma	New York	W	10	—	192
Aug 16		Tommy Gomez	New York	TKO	3	—	191
Aug 28	⑩	Joey Maxim★	Camden	L	10	—	192
Nov 15	⑩	Elmer Ray	New York	L	10	—	191

1947							
Jan 6	⑩	Joey Maxim★	Philadelphia	W	10	—	191
Apr 3	⑩	Elmer Ray	Miami	W	10	—	192
Jun 23	⑩	Joey Maxim★	Los Angeles	W	10	—	192
Dec 5	♛	Joe Louis★	New York	L	15	For-World-H	194

1948							
Jun 25	♛	Joe Louis★	New York	KO'd	11	For-World-H	194

1949							
Jun 22	⑩	Ezzard Charles★	Chicago	L	15	For-Vac NBA-H	195
Aug 14		Olle Tandberg	Stockholm	KO	5	—	194

1950							
Feb 8	⑩	Harold Johnson★	Philadelphia	KO	3	—	197
Mar 3	⑩	Omelio Agramonte	New York	KO	7	—	198
Mar 13		Johnny Shkor	Philadelphia	KO	1	—	197
May 28		Hein ten Hoff	Mannheim, Germany	W	10	—	201
Nov 24	⑩	Rex Layne	New York	L	10	—	200

1951							
Mar 7	♛	Ezzard Charles★	Detroit	L	15	For-World-H	194
Jul 18	♛	Ezzard Charles★	Pittsburgh	KO	7	Won-World-H	194

1952							
Jun 5	⑩	Ezzard Charles★	Philadelphia	W	15	Ret-World-H	196
Sep 23	⑩	Rocky Marciano★	Philadelphia	KO'd	13	Lost-World-H	196

1953							
May 15	♛	Rocky Marciano★	Chicago	KO'd	1	For-World-H	197

had he gone, but he was stricken with typhoid fever and never made the trip.

Walcott fought as a second-tier attraction for several years. He had the responsibility of supporting his mother and siblings, but pay for a fair-to-middling black boxer was often skimpy. Sometimes Walcott simply could not afford to box, and he held down a variety of jobs or subsisted on welfare. He married and over the years fathered six children. By 1940, Walcott was fighting only twice a year, and

Ezzard Charles (L) and Walcott met three times for the unified heavyweight title. March 7, 1951—Charles successfully defended his crown. July 18, 1951—Walcott won the title. June 5, 1952—Walcott kept the belt.

his career seemed to be winding down.

in 1945, perhaps because of the loss of fighters during World War II or perhaps because color had become less important, doors started to open for Walcott. He began to be signed for bouts with better opposition and, for the first time, he earned a place in *The Ring*'s annual top ten ratings.

In 1947, Walcott was put up against Joe Louis for the heavyweight championship of the world. The fight was held in Madison Square Garden. Walcott knocked Louis down twice and nearly closed his left eye. At the end of fifteen, referee Ruby Goldstein indicated that Walcott had won, but two judges scored the fight in favor of Louis, and Jersey Joe lost the split decision. He got another chance a year later, but Louis was better prepared and knocked Walcott out in the eleventh round. Walcott's first two tries to take the title from Ezzard Charles also failed. However, in July 1951, in Pittsburgh's Forbes Field, Walcott knocked Charles out with a thunderous left hook. At the age of 37, Walcott was the champion. After winning the rematch with Charles, Walcott lost the title in September 1952 to Rocky Marciano, who bounded up from a first-round knockdown to drop Walcott in the thirteenth. After Marciano knocked him out in the first round of the rematch in 1953, Walcott retired.

After leaving the ring, Walcott worked as a boxing and wrestling referee, as a sheriff in New Jersey, as chairman of the New Jersey State Athletic Commission, and as a director of special projects for New Jersey Governor Brendan Byrne. Assessing Walcott's career, esteemed trainer Eddie Futch called him "one of the finest technicians in heavyweight boxing history."

IKE WILLIAMS

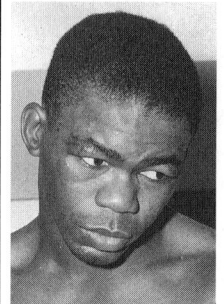

LIGHTWEIGHT

Right-handed; 5'9½"; 128–155 lbs.
155 bouts, 3/15/1940 to 8/12/1955
Managers: Connie McCarthy 1940–46,
Frank ("Blinky") Palermo 1946–55
NBA Lightweight Champion 1945–47
Lightweight Champion 1947–51
Hall of Fame Induction: 1990
Born: 8/2/1923, Brunswick, GA
Named: Isiah Williams
Died: 9/5/1994

Lightweight champion for six years, Ike Williams was known as a relentless fighter who also demonstrated grace and finesse in the ring. He started boxing as an amateur in 1938 and made his professional debut in 1940. He won the NBA lightweight championship in Mexico City in 1945 when he knocked out Juan Zurita in the second round.

Williams's career was sidetracked after his victory over Zurita when he had a dispute with his manager, Connie McCarthy, and decided to go out on his own. The then-powerful Managers Guild blackballed Williams for his action.

The boycott was effective and Williams had great difficulty securing fights, until he agreed to be managed by Frank ("Blinky") Palermo. Palermo straightened out Williams's problems with the guild and got him a rematch with Bob Montgomery, who then held the New York version of the lightweight title. Williams fought masterfully and knocked Montgomery out in the sixth.

For much of the time he owned the title, Williams engaged in over-the-weight non-title matches where his strong jab, formidable straight right, and a fine defense served him well. Williams held the lightweight title until 1951 when Jimmy Carter soundly defeated him in Madison Square Garden.

According to testimony Williams gave to the Kefauver committee during the Senate's investigation of organized crime's ties to boxing, Palermo often suggested that Williams throw fights. Although he testified that he had never taken a dive, he did admit to the committee that he carried Enrique Bolanos and had put forth less than his best effort at other times. Williams said he sometimes never saw a penny of his purses.

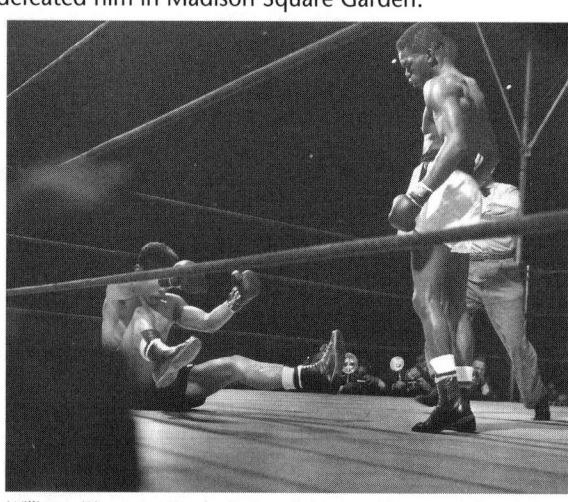

Williams (R) puts contender Enrique Bolanos on the canvas, but this successful lightweight title defense went the full fifteen rounds. The bout took place on May 25, 1948.

IN THE RING	WON 126	LOST 24	DRAWS 5	TB 155	KO 60	W 66	WF 0	D 5	KO'd 6	L 18	LF 0

Date	Opponent	Site	Result / Rounds		Title	Wt.
1940						
Mar 15	Carmine Fatta	New Brunswick, NJ	W	4	—	—
Mar 29	Billy George	New Brunswick	W	4	—	—
Apr 1	Patsy Gall	Hazleton, PA	D	6	—	—
May 10	Billy Hildebrand	Morristown, NJ	L	6	—	—
Jun 14	Billy Hildebrand	Mt. Freedom, NJ	TKO	6	—	132
Jul 19	Joe Romero	Mt. Freedom	KO	2	—	128
Sep 9	Pete Kelly	Trenton, NJ	KO	2	—	—
Nov 11	Tony Maglione	Trenton	L	8	—	—
1941						
Jan 6	Tommy Fontana	Trenton	W	8	—	131
Feb 19	Carl Zullo	Perth Amboy, NJ	TKO	2	—	—
Mar 5	Joey Zodda	Perth Amboy	L	6	—	—
Mar 19	Joe Genovese	Perth Amboy	W	5	—	—
Apr 9	Johnny Rudolph	Perth Amboy	W	6	—	—
Apr 14	Hugh Civatte	Trenton	KO	3	—	—
Oct 1	Freddie Archer	Perth Amboy	L	8	—	132
Oct 27	Benny Williams	Newark, NJ	D	6	—	—
Nov 3	Vince DeLia	Newark	W	6	—	—
Dec 16	Eddie Dowe	Perth Amboy	W	6	—	—
1942						
Jan 26	Eddie Dowe	Newark	W	6	—	—
Mar 26	Pedro Firpo	Atlantic City	W	8	—	135
Apr 10	Angelo Panatellas	Atlantic City	KO	5	—	135
Apr 24	Willie Roache	Perth Amboy	W	8	—	133
May 7	Abie Kaufman	Atlantic City	W	8	—	135
Jun 29	Ivan Christie	Newark	KO	5	—	—
Jul 29	Angelo Maglione	Trenton	KO	3	—	131
Aug 13	Jan Ruby Garcia	Atlantic City	W	8	—	—
Sep 10	Charley Davis	Elizabeth, NJ	W	8	—	135
Oct 20	Gene Burton	White Plains, NY	KO	4	—	131
Dec 7	Bob Gunther	Trenton	W	8	—	131
Dec 21	Sammy Daniels	Baltimore	W	6	—	134
1943						
Jan 29	Jerry Moore	New York	W	6	—	131
Feb 22	Sammy Daniels	Philadelphia	KO	2	—	134
Feb 23	Bobby McQuillar	Cleveland	KO	3	—	134
Mar 8	Bill Speary	Philadelphia	KO	2	—	133
Apr 2	Rudy Giscombe	New York	TKO	3	—	132
Apr 5	Ruby Garcia	Philadelphia	W	8	—	130
Apr 21	Joe Genovese	Cleveland	TKO	4	—	133
May 7	⑩ Maurice LaChance	Boston	W	8	—	131
May 17	Ray Brown	Philadelphia	W	10	—	131
Jul 19	Jimmy Hatcher	Philadelphia	TKO	6	—	130
Aug 24	Tommy Jessup	Hartford, CT	TKO	5	—	131
Aug 31	Johnny Bellus	Hartford	W	10	—	131
Sep 13	Jerry Moore	W. Springfield, MA	W	10	—	131
Oct 1	⑩ Maurice LaChance	Boston	TKO	4	—	131
Oct 22	Ed Perry	New Orleans	KO	2	—	133
Oct 29	Gene Johnson	New Orleans	W	10	—	133
Nov 8	Johnny Hutchinson	Philadelphia	KO	3	—	131
Nov 29	Willie Cheatum	New Britain, CT	W	8	—	133
Dec 13	Mayon Padlo	Philadelphia	W	10	—	134

1944

Date		Opponent	Location	Result	Rnd		Weight
Jan 25	⑩	Bob Montgomery★	Philadelphia	KO'd	12	—	131
Feb 28		Ellis Phillips	Philadelphia	TKO	1	—	138
Mar 13		Leo Francis	Trenton	W	8	—	138
Mar 27	⑩	Joey Peralta	Philadelphia	TKO	9	—	134
Apr 10		Leroy Saunders	Holyoke, MA	KO	5	—	138
Apr 17		Mike Delia	Philadelphia	KO	1	—	135
May 16	⑩	Luther ("Slugger") White	Philadelphia	W	10	—	135
Jun 7	⑩	Sammy Angott★	Philadelphia	W	10	—	134
Jun 23		Cleo Shans	New York	TKO	10	—	136
Jul 10		Joey Pirrone	Philadelphia	KO	1	—	136
Jul 20		Julie Kogon	New York	W	10	—	134
Aug 29		Jimmy Hatcher	Washington, DC	W	10	—	136
Sep 6	⑩	Sammy Angott★	Philadelphia	W	10	—	136
Sep 19		Freddie Dawson	Philadelphia	KO	4	—	135
Oct 18		Johnny Green	Buffalo, NY	KO	2	—	138
Nov 2		Ruby Garcia	Baltimore	TKO	7	—	132
Nov 13		Willie Joyce	Philadelphia	L	10	—	134
Dec 5	⑩	Lulu Costantino	Cleveland	W	10	—	136
Dec 12		Dave Castilloux	Buffalo	TKO	5	—	135

1945

Date		Opponent	Location	Result	Rnd		Weight
Jan 8	⑩	Willie Joyce	Philadelphia	W	12	—	133
Jan 22		Mike Berger	Philadelphia	KO	4	—	133
Mar 2	⑩	Willie Joyce	New York	L	12	—	133
Mar 26		Dorsey Lay	Philadelphia	KO	3	—	134
Apr 18	♛	Juan Zurita	Mexico City	KO	2	Won-NBA-L	131
Jun 8	⑩	Willie Joyce	New York	L	10	—	137
Aug 14		Charley Smith	Union City, NJ	W	10	—	137
Aug 28		Gene Burton	Philadelphia	W	10	—	134
Sep 7	⑩	Nick Moran	New York	W	10	—	134
Sep 19	⑩	Sammy Angott★	Pittsburgh	TKO'd	6	—	136
Nov 26		Wesley Mouzon	Philadelphia	D	10	—	135

1946

Date		Opponent	Location	Result	Rnd		Weight
Jan 8		Charley ("Petey") Smith	Trenton	W	10	—	137
Jan 20	⑩	Johnny Bratton	New Orleans	W	10	—	139
Jan 28	⑩	Freddie Dawson	Philadelphia	D	10	—	134
Feb 14		Cleo Shans	Orange, NJ	W	10	—	137
Feb 22		Ace Miller	Detroit	W	10	—	137
Mar 11		Eddie Giosa	Philadelphia	TKO	4	—	136
Apr 8		Eddie Giosa	Philadelphia	TKO	1	—	136
Apr 30	⑩	Enrique Bolanos	Los Angeles	TKO	8	Ret-NBA-L	134
Jun 12	⑩	Bobby Ruffin	Brooklyn	TKO	5	—	138
Aug 6		Ivan Christie	Norwalk, CT	KO	2	—	138
Sep 4	⑩	Ronnie James	Cardiff, Wales	KO	9	Ret-NBA-L	134

1947

Date		Opponent	Location	Result	Rnd		Weight
Jan 27	⑩	Gene Burton	Chicago	L	10	—	139
Apr 14		Frankie Conti	Allentown, PA	TKO	7	—	137
Apr 25		Willie Russell	Columbus, OH	W	10	—	139
May 9	⑩	Ralph Zannelli	Boston	W	10	—	139
May 26		Juste Fontaine	Philadelphia	TKO	4	—	135
Jun 20	⑩	Tippy Larkin	New York	KO	4	—	136
Aug 4	♛	Bob Montgomery★	Philadelphia	KO	6	Won-Vac World-L	133
Sep 29		Doll Rafferty	Philadelphia	KO	4	—	140
Oct 10		Talmadge Bussey	Detroit	TKO	9	—	139
Dec 12	⑩	Tony Pellone	New York	W	10	—	139

1948

Date		Opponent	Location	Result	Rnd		Weight
Jan 13		Doug Carter	Camden, NJ	W	10	—	138
Jan 26	⑩	Freddie Dawson	Philadelphia	W	10	—	136
Feb 9		Livio Minelli	Philadelphia	W	10	—	137

Date		Opponent	Location	Result	Rnd	Note	No.
Feb 27	⑩	Kid Gavilan★	New York	W	10	—	136
May 5		Rudy Cruz	Hartford	W	10	—	140
May 25	⑩	Enrique Bolanos	Los Angeles	W	15	Ret-World-L	135
Jul 12	⑩	Beau Jack★	Philadelphia	TKO	6	Ret-World-L	134
Sep 23	⑩	Jesse Flores	New York	KO	10	Ret-World-L	134
Nov 8		Buddy Garcia	Philadelphia	KO	1	—	140
Nov 18		Billy Nixon	Philadelphia	TKO	4	—	139
1949							
Jan 17	⑩	Johnny Bratton	Philadelphia	W	10	—	138
Jan 28	⑩	Kid Gavilan★	New York	L	10	—	140
Apr 1	⑩	Kid Gavilan★	New York	L	10	—	136
Apr 23		Vince Turpin	Cleveland	TKO	6	—	140
Jun 21		Irvin Steen	Los Angeles	W	10	—	141
Jul 21	⑩	Enrique Bolanos	Los Angeles	TKO	4	Ret-World-L	135
Aug 3		Benny Walker	Oakland	W	10	—	140
Sep 30		Doug Ratford	Philadelphia	W	10	—	139
Oct 24		Al Mobley	Trenton	W	10	—	141
Nov 14		Jean Walzack	Philadelphia	W	10	—	140
Dec 5	⑩	Freddie Dawson	Philadelphia	W	15	Ret-World-L	135
1950							
Jan 20	⑩	Johnny Bratton	Chicago	TKO	8	—	143
Feb 17	⑩	Sonny Boy West	New York	KO	8	—	141
Feb 27	⑩	John L. Davis	Seattle	W	10	—	143
Jun 2	⑩	Lester Felton	Detroit	W	10	—	144
Jul 12	⑩	George Costner	Philadelphia	L	10	—	143
Aug 7	⑩	Charley Salas	Washington, DC	L	10	—	139
Sep 26	⑩	Charley Salas	Washington, DC	W	10	—	142
Oct 2	⑩	Joe Miceli	Milwaukee	L	10	—	142
Nov 23	⑩	Joe Miceli	Milwaukee	W	10	—	146
Dec 12		Dave Marsh	Akron, OH	TKO	9	—	137
Dec 18	⑩	Rudy Cruz	Philadelphia	W	10	—	144
1951							
Jan 5		Jose Maria Gatica	New York	TKO	1	—	140
Jan 22		Ralph Zannelli	Providence, RI	KO	5	—	143
Jan 31		Vic Cardell	Detroit	TKO	9	—	143
Feb 19	⑩	Joe Miceli	Philadelphia	L	10	—	141
Mar 5		Beau Jack★	Providence	W	10	—	142
Apr 11		Fitzie Pruden	Chicago	W	10	—	145
May 25	⑩	Jimmy Carter★	New York	TKO'd	14	Lost-World-L	135
Aug 2		Don Williams	Worcester, MA	L	10	—	146
Sep 10	⑩	Gil Turner	Philadelphia	TKO'd	10	—	144
1952							
Mar 17		Johnny Cunningham	Baltimore	KO	5	—	142
Mar 26	⑩	Chuck Davey	Chicago	TKO'd	5	—	145
Nov 24		Pat Manzi	Syracuse, NY	TKO	7	—	148
1953							
Jan 12	⑩	Carmen Basilio★	Syracuse	L	10	—	148
Mar 9		Claude Hammond	Trenton	W	10	—	150
Mar 28		Vic Cardell	Philadelphia	W	10	—	152
Apr 20		Billy Andy	Trenton	W	10	—	151
May 10		Billy Andy	Erie, PA	W	10	—	152
Jun 8		George Johnson	Trenton	TKO'd	8	—	147
Sep 17		Dom Zimbardo	Newark	TKO	2	—	150
Nov 9		Jed Black	Fort Wayne, IN	L	10	—	151
1954							
Jul 2		Rafael Lastre	Havana, Cuba	L	10	—	148
1955							
Apr 9		Beau Jack★	Augusta, GA	D	10	—	155
Aug 12		Beau Jack★	Augusta	TKO	9	—	154

ALBERT ("CHALKY") WRIGHT

FEATHERWEIGHT

Right-handed; 5'7¹/₂"; 124–139 lbs.

220 bouts, 2/23/1928 to 3/9/1948

Manager: Eddie Walker

Featherweight Champ 1941–42

Hall of Fame Induction: 1997

Born: 2/10/1912 (disputed), Durango, CO

Named: Albert Garfield Wright

Died: 8/12/1957

A small, plucky fighter whose career started in the 1920s, Chalky Wright persevered for thirteen years and over 140 fights before he won a championship belt.

Most sources list Wright's birthplace as Durango, Colorado. Officially, his date of birth is February 10, 1912, but many believe that he was much older. When Wright's father abandoned his mother shortly after the boy was born, she moved her young family to the Los Angeles area. As a young man, Wright turned to prizefighting more for survival than glory, and in his first bout in 1926, he decisioned Nilo Balles.

Fighting exclusively in California against unranked opponents, Wright racked up a record of 48-7-11 in his first five years of fighting. In the next five years he fought less frequently and, for a time, worked as a chauffeur for the glamorous comedic actress Mae West. Wright posted a dismal 0-6 record against ranked fighters, including Freddie Miller and Henry Armstrong. However, Armstrong was impressed with Wright's boxing style and hired him as a sparring partner to help him sharpen up for a fight with Barney Ross. Wright performed so well in these sparring sessions that manager Eddie Walker added Wright to his stable. Wright started winning again and in 1938 was ranked as the sixth-best featherweight by The Ring.

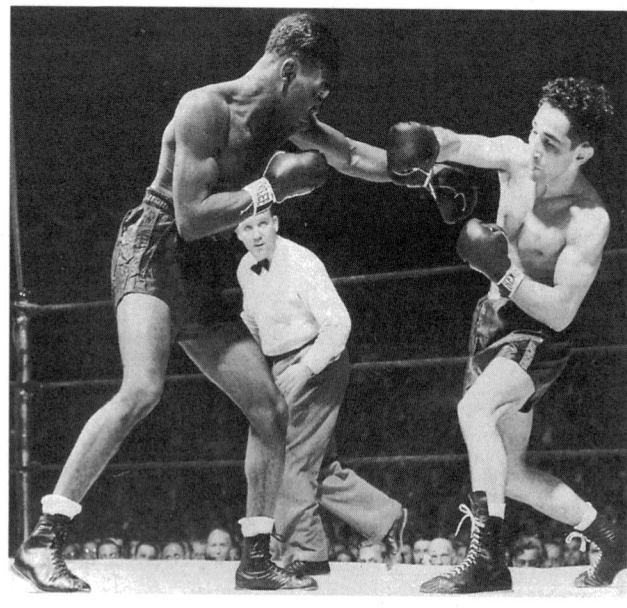

Wright (L) relinquished his world featherweight title to the legendary Willie Pep in a fifteen-round decision in Madison Square Garden on November 20, 1942.

IN THE RING	WON 160	LOST 43	DRAWS 16	TB 220	KO 81	W 79	WF 0	D 16	KO'd 7	L 36	LF 0	NC 1

Date	Opponent	Site	Result / Rounds		Title	Wt.
1928						
Feb 23	Nilo Balles	San Bernardino, CA	W	4	—	—
Apr 12	Nilo Balles	San Bernardino	KO	3	—	—
May 3	Val Martin	San Bernardino	W	4	—	—
May 31	Victor Acosta	San Bernardino	KO	2	—	—
Jul 12	Young Valentino	San Bernardino	D	4	—	—
Jul 26	Ray Davis	San Bernardino	L	4	—	—
Aug 23	Joe Hernandez	San Bernardino	L	4	—	—
Sep 13	Joe Hernandez	San Bernardino	D	4	—	—
Nov 22	Ray Davis	San Bernardino	W	4	—	—
Dec 13	Louie Contreras	San Bernardino	D	6	—	—
Dec 20	Ray Davis	San Bernardino	W	6	—	—
1929						
Jan 17	Patsy Callope	San Bernardino	KO	2	—	—
Feb 7	Joey Velardi	San Bernardino	L	6	—	—
Mar 14	Tony Opodoca	Pasadena, CA	W	4	—	—
Mar 28	Paul Hardy	San Bernardino	KO	3	—	—
Apr 9	Harry Wallinger	Los Angeles	D	4	—	—
Apr 18	Johnny Mason	San Bernardino	W	6	—	—
May 2	Ray Billobas	San Bernardino	D	6	—	—
Jul 5	Frisco Lenda	El Centro, CA	L	4	—	—
Sep 12	Pal Shoaf	San Bernardino	W	4	—	—
Oct 7	Kid Avelino	Los Angeles	W	4	—	—
Oct 10	Harry Purdue	San Bernardino	W	4	—	—
Oct 24	Harry Barrere	San Bernardino	W	6	—	—
Nov 11	Ray Cervantes	Los Angeles	W	4	—	—
1930						
Apr 24	Canto Robleto	Pasadena	L	8	—	—
May 8	Clayton Gouyd	Pasadena	W	6	—	—
Jun 12	Jimmy Mack	Pasadena	W	6	—	—
Jun 17	Frisco Lenda	San Bernardino	W	6	—	—
Jun 26	Ray Navarro	Pasadena	KO	5	—	—
Jul 5	Frisco Lenda	El Centro	L	4	—	—
Jul 10	Carlos Chipres	Pasadena	KO	2	—	—
Jul 21	Sammy Seaman	Los Angeles	D	6	—	—
Aug 12	Sid Torres	Los Angeles	W	6	—	—
Sep 16	Manuel Trevino	Los Angeles	KO	3	—	—
Oct 7	Kid Avelino	Los Angeles	W	6	—	—
Oct 21	Martin Cane	Los Angeles	KO	4	—	—
Oct 24	Mose Bailey	San Diego	D	6	—	—
Nov 7	Johnny Lee	San Diego	KO	3	—	—
Nov 10	Ray Cervantes	Los Angeles	W	4	—	—
Nov 14	Jerry Duffy	San Diego	W	6	—	—
Nov 18	Ray Cervantes	Los Angeles	W	6	—	—
Dec 12	Ramon Montoya	San Diego	L	10	—	—
1931						
Jan 13	Huerta Evans	Los Angeles	L	6	—	—
Feb 13	Ray Butler	San Diego	W	10	—	—
Mar 10	Ernie Chacon	Los Angeles	W	4	—	—
Mar 31	Mike Cordova	Los Angeles	W	4	—	—
May 1	Claude Roberts	San Diego	W	6	—	—
Jun 12	Rod Alcantera	Ventura, CA	KO	1	—	128
Jul 4	Martin Zuniga	Pismo Beach, CA	L	6	—	—

Aug 6	Martin Zuniga	Sacramento, CA	D	6	—	—
Aug 11	Baby Jack Dempsey	Los Angeles	KO	2	—	—
Sep 15	Mike Cordova	Los Angeles	W	6	—	—
Oct 8	Huerta Evans	San Bernardino	W	8	—	—
Oct 29	Huerta Evans	San Bernardino	D	10	—	—
Nov 24	Clemente Avila	Los Angeles	W	6	—	—
1932						
Jan 12	Tony Tassi	Los Angeles	KO	4	—	126
Feb 8	Ramon Montoya	San Diego	W	6	—	—
Feb 16	Marty Zuniga	Los Angeles	D	6	—	127
Apr 29	Al Greenfield	San Diego	W	6	—	—
May 3	Willie Davies	Los Angeles	W	4	—	134
May 18	Jose Pimental	San Francisco	KO	2	—	130
Jun 7	Huerta Evans	Los Angeles	KO	5	—	130
Jul 12	Al Greenfield	Los Angeles	W	4	—	130
Aug 26	Johnny Minella	San Diego	W	6	—	—
Sep 2	Mose Bailey	San Diego	D	6	—	—
Oct 11	Jess Macy	Los Angeles	KO	1	—	—
Oct 19	Kid Ponce	Long Beach, CA	KO	2	—	120
Nov 15	Baby Jack Dempsey	Los Angeles	KO	1	—	—
Nov 22	Al Greenfield	Los Angeles	W	4	—	128
Dec 15	Benny Garcia	Ventura, CA	W	6	—	—
1933						
Jan 6	Pedro Villanueva	Ventura	W	6	—	—
Jan 20	Newsboy Brown	—	L	10	—	—
Apr 11	Mickey Cohen	Los Angeles	KO	3	—	127
May 3	Whitey Neal	Portland, OR	W	6	—	128
Aug 22	Whitey Neal	Portland, OR	W	6	—	128
Sep 1	Huerta Evans	San Francisco	KO	4	—	128
Sep 5	Willie Jabura	Los Angeles	KO	3	—	123
Sep 19	Allan Foston	Portland, OR	D	8	—	127
Oct 17	⑩ Eddie Shea	Los Angeles	KO'd	1	For-CA-130 lbs	127
1934						
Jan 30	Bobby Gray	Seattle	W	6	—	128
Feb 20	Augie Soliz	Seattle	KO	5	—	130
Apr 17	Jimmy Alvarado	Los Angeles	KO	2	—	132
May 1	Albert Ladou	Los Angeles	W	4	—	129
May 25	Frankie Venegas	El Centro	KO	5	—	—
Jun 8	♛ Freddie Miller★	El Centro	L	10	—	—
Jun 29	Perfecto Lopez	Ventura	W	6	—	—
Oct 8	Mose Butch	Pittsburgh	L	10	—	123
Nov 17	Lew Monte	Brooklyn	L	6	—	126
1935						
Feb 2	⑩ Baby Arizmendi★	Mexico City	KO'd	4	—	132
Feb 16	Chico Cisneros	Mexico City	L	10	—	—
Apr 6	Mark Diaz	Sacramento	KO	4	—	—
May 10	⑩ Pablo Dano	Watsonville, CA	KO'd	2	—	125
1936						
Mar 28	Claude Varner	Vancouver, B.C., Can	W	10	—	126
Apr 10	Young Corpuz	Aberdeen, WA	W	10	—	130
Apr 17	Buzz Brown	Butte, MT	W	10	—	126
Apr 28	Willie Davis	Portland, OR	TKO	7	—	128
May 21	Eddie Spina	Tacoma, WA	W	10	—	—
Jul 16	Eddie Spina	Portland, OR	W	6	—	—
Aug 20	Cecil Payne	Tacoma	D	6	—	129
Sep 29	Doug Wirth	Portland, OR	KO	1	—	—
1937						
Jan 15	Jimmy McClain	Bremerton, WA	KO	2	—	—
Apr 14	Kid Ray	Tacoma	W	6	—	129
May 18	Sonny Valdez	Los Angeles	W	6	—	—

Date	Opponent	Location	Result	Rounds	Notes	Weight
Jun 14	Bobby Gray	Los Angeles	KO	5	—	—
Jul 21	Norbert Meehan	Oakland, CA	KO	5	—	—
Aug 17	Georgie Hansford	Los Angeles	D	10	—	—
Sep 7	Georgie Hansford	Los Angeles	W	10	—	125
Oct 5	Baby Arizmendi★	Los Angeles	L	10	—	125
Oct 19	Babe Santella	Los Angeles	KO	1	—	129
Nov 30	Bus Breese	Los Angeles	W	10	—	—

1938

Date	Opponent	Location	Result	Rounds	Notes	Weight
Feb 1	♛ Henry Armstrong★	Los Angeles	TKO'd	3	—	128
Aug 17	Al Reid	New York	KO	4	—	125
Nov 7	Cristobal Jaramillo	New York	W	8	—	128
Nov 25	Vince Dell'Orto	New York	W	6	—	125
Dec 5	Pete De Grasse	New York	KO	5	—	129
Dec 26	Joey Ferrando	New York	L	8	—	127

1939

Date	Opponent	Location	Result	Rounds	Notes	Weight
Jan 3	Tommy Speigel	Brooklyn	W	10	—	127
Jan 14	Johnny Rohrig	Brooklyn	W	8	—	128
Jan 31	Lew Feldman	Brooklyn	L	8	—	128
Feb 14	Johnny Bellus	New York	L	8	—	126
Mar 10	Joe DeJesus	New York	KO	2	—	129
Mar 21	Red Guggino	Brooklyn	W	8	—	129
Apr 27	Dan McAllister	Liverpool, England	KO	5	—	129
May 25	George Daly	London	W	8	—	129
Jun 8	⑩ Kid Tanner	Liverpool	KO	7	—	126
Aug 8	Teddy Baldwin	Garfield, NJ	W	8	—	—
Aug 21	Billy Bullock	Baltimore	KO	5	—	—
Sep 18	Lew Feldman	Baltimore	L	10	—	—
Dec 1	Young Rightmire	New York	W	6	—	127

1940

Date	Opponent	Location	Result	Rounds	Notes	Weight
Jan 16	Sammy Julian	Brooklyn	W	8	—	128
Jan 29	Paul Junior	Portland, ME	L	10	—	130
Feb 19	Frankie Gilmore	Baltimore	W	10	—	—
Feb 22	Mike Martinez	Baltimore	KO	3	—	130
Mar 11	Charley Gomer	Baltimore	KO	4	—	130
Apr 1	⑩ Tommy Speigel	Baltimore	W	10	—	129
Apr 29	⑩ Cocoa Kid	Baltimore	L	10	—	130
Jun 24	Saverio Turiello	Baltimore	W	10	—	—
Jul 15	Joey Silva	Baltimore	KO	7	—	125
Aug 12	Paul Junior	Philadelphia	KO	5	—	128
Sep 9	Joey Ferrando	Baltimore	KO	4	—	127
Oct 7	Teddy Baldwin	Philadelphia	KO	4	—	127
Dec 9	⑩ Pete Leto	Baltimore	L	10	—	127

1941

Date	Opponent	Location	Result	Rounds	Notes	Weight
Jan 6	Johnny Williams	New York	KO	5	—	127
Jan 14	Norment Quarles	Jersey City, NJ	W	8	—	127
Feb 4	Norman Rahn	Jersey City	KO	2	—	128
Feb 19	Frank Terranova	Allentown, PA	KO	6	—	130
Feb 24	Maurice Arnault	Baltimore	KO	2	—	129
Mar 6	Texas Lee Harper	Washington, DC	KO	3	—	128
Mar 17	Charles Schnaupoff	Wilkes-Barre, PA	KO	5	—	126
May 1	Charley Varre	New York	W	8	—	128
May 22	⑩ Sal Bartolo	New York	W	8	—	127
May 29	Norment Quarles	Atlantic City	W	8	—	—
Jun 3	Guillermo Puentes	Long Island City, NY	KO	5	—	128
Jun 17	Lloyd Pine	Wilkes-Barre	KO	2	—	127
Jun 24	Bobby McIntire	Long Island City	KO	5	—	127
Jul 17	⑩ Jackie Wilson	Baltimore	W	10	—	131
Aug 5	Paco Villa	Long Island City	KO	6	—	126
Sep 11	♛ Joey Archibald	Washington, DC	KO	11	Won-World-FE	124
Oct 2	Joey Peralta	Wilkes-Barre	L	10	—	126

Date		Opponent	Location	Result	Rounds		Weight
Oct 31		Ray Lunny	San Francisco	W	10	—	126
Nov 28		Jorge Morelia	San Diego	KO	6	—	131
1942							
Jan 13	⑩	Bobby Ruffin	New York	L	10	—	128
Feb 3	⑩	Richie Lemos	Los Angeles	KO	6	—	127
Feb 19		Ritchie Fontaine	Oakland	W	10	—	130
Mar 24		Jorge Morelia	Los Angeles	KO	6	—	130
Apr 6		Vern Bybee	San Francisco	L	10	—	130
May 7	⑩	Lulu Constantino	New York	W	8	—	128
Jun 19	⑩	Harry Jeffra	Baltimore	TKO	10	Ret-World-FE	124
Jul 13		Lou Transparenti	Baltimore	KO	4	—	130
Aug 6	⑩	Allie Stoltz	New York	L	10	—	128
Aug 15		Tommy ("Curley") St. Angelo	Springfield, MA	KO	2	—	—
Aug 27		Joey Marinelli	Detroit	KO	2	—	130
Sep 25	⑩	Lulu Constantino	New York	W	15	Ret-World-FE	125
Oct 13		Carlos ("No No") Cuebas	Hartford, CT	KO	4	—	129
Oct 20		Henry Vasquez	New Haven, CT	KO	8	—	130
Nov 20		Willie Pep★	New York	L	15	Lost-World-FE	125
1943							
Jan 15	⑩	Joey Peralta	New York	W	10	—	130
Feb 15		Morris Parker	Newark, NJ	KO	4	—	131
Feb 23	⑩	Joey Peralta	St. Louis	W	10	—	130
Mar 10		Joey Pirrone	Cleveland	KO	3	—	131
May 17		Frankie Carto	Baltimore	KO	8	—	130
May 25		Billy Pinti	Brooklyn	KO	4	—	130
Jun 4	⑩	Phil Terranova	New York	KO	5	—	125
Jul 3		Kid National	Havana, Cuba	KO	8	—	127
Jul 21	⑩	Lulu Constantino	Cleveland	L	10	—	129
Aug 9		Angel Avila	Washington, DC	KO	7	—	130
Oct 26		Patsy Spataro	Brooklyn	TKO	2	—	132
Nov 8		Billy Banks	Philadephia	KO	5	—	131
Nov 19		Al Reasoner	New Orleans	KO	2	—	132
1944							
Jan 25		Baby Al Brown	Panama City	KO	5	—	131
Feb 10		Alberto Carlos	Panama City	KO	6	—	132
Mar 5		Young Finnegan	Panama City	D	10	—	131
May 1		Clyde English	Scranton, PA	KO	7	—	133
May 22		Sammy Daniels	Baltimore	KO	8	—	132
Jun 5		Vince Dell'Orto	Washington, DC	KO	3	—	133
Jul 10		Ruby Garcia	Houston	KO	8	—	139
Jul 17		Johnny Cockfield	Norfolk, VA	KO	5	—	131
Sep 29	♛	Willie Pep★	New York	L	15	For-World-FE	125
Dec 5	♛	Willie Pep★	Cleveland	L	10	—	132
1945							
Feb 5	⑩	Willie Joyce	Philadelphia	L	10	—	132
Apr 9		Jackie Wilson	Baltimore	NC	7	—	133
Apr 17	⑩	Willie Joyce	Los Angeles	W	10	—	132
Jul 31		Henry Jordan	Brooklyn	KO	6	—	133
Aug 28	⑩	Enrique Bolanos	Los Angeles	W	10	—	133
Sep 21		Humberto Zavala	New York	W	10	—	132
Oct 5	⑩	Bobby Ruffin	Detroit	W	10	—	129
Nov 2		Leroy Willis	Detroit	W	10	—	132
Dec 14		Johnny Bratton	New Orleans	W	10	—	134
1946							
Jan 25		Pedro Firpo	New York	W	10	—	134
Feb 19	⑩	Enrique Bolanos	Los Angeles	L	10	—	133
Mar 5		Georgie Hansford	Milwaukee	KO	4	—	136

Mar 27		Frankie Moore	Oakland	KO'd	1	—	134
Apr 17		Frankie Moore	Oakland	L	10	—	135
Aug 27		Johnny Dell	New York	L	10	—	134
Oct 15	⑩	Enrique Bolanos	Los Angeles	L	10	—	131
Nov 27	♛	Willie Pep ★	Milwaukee	KO'd	3	—	132
1947							
May 19		Frankie Saucedo	Juarez, Mexico	D	10	—	—
Jun 24		Larry Cisneros	Albuquerque, NM	L	10	—	136
1948							
Mar 9		Ernie Hunick	Salt Lake City	TKO'd	3	—	135

Wright finally got a chance to fight for the featherweight title against champion Joey Archibald on September 11, 1941, in Washington, DC's Griffith Stadium. Wright started quickly and dominated the fight. He knocked Archibald down twice before finishing him off with a left hook to the body and a right to the jaw in the eleventh.

After successfully defending his title twice, Wright lost the championship to the undefeated Willie Pep at Madison Square Garden on November 20, 1942. Yet even after Wright lost the title, he impressed schooled observers as a consummate boxer. Reporter Stanley Woodward, after he watched Wright's five-round knockout of Phil Terranova, wrote in the June 6, 1943, *New York Tribune*:

"It was the first time we ever had seen Chalky and we came away convinced that he is the greatest boxer and smartest operator and the most efficient puncher of his time. . . . Every move he makes is the perfect illustration for a treatise on how to box. He walks out flatfooted, conserving his ancient legs. He blocks nonchalantly and slips punches by moving his head just enough. When he hits he doesn't miss. The one-two with which he knocked down the outclassed Terranova in the second round was the most perfect punch seen in the Garden since Joe Louis was a civilian."

In a 1944 rematch following Pep's discharge from the Navy, Wright got in some shots, but Pep's incredible defensive skills prevailed. (This bout is also noteworthy in that it was the first televised fight sponsored by The Gillette Safety Razor Company.) Two months later, Wright again lost to Pep. Although he continued to fight for four more years, Wright was definitely past his prime. He won only one of his last ten fights and suffered a knock-out loss to Pep. After Ernie Hunick knocked him out in three rounds, Wright announced his retirement.

The fact that he was unable to defeat Hall of Famer Willie Pep should not detract from Wright's accomplishments. He took on all comers, including lightweights and welterweights. He possessed a fine left hook and a strong right. He could box on the outside or mix it up in close. Distinguished boxing historian Hank Kaplan described Wright as "a good all-around boxer-puncher."

In retirement Wright lost most of his ring earnings gambling. He was working in a bakery when he moved back to his mother's house after a dispute with his wife. On August 12, 1957, his mother came home to find Wright slumped in the bathtub, dead after a fall.

TONY ZALE
The Man of Steel

MIDDLEWEIGHT

Right-handed; 5'8"; 154–164 lbs.

87 bouts, 6/11/1934 to 9/21/1948

Managers: Harry Shall 1934–36, John Zale 1936–37, Sam Pian and Art Winch 1937–48

NBA Middlewt. Champ 1940–41 Middlewt. Champ 1941–47, 1948

Hall of Fame Induction: 1991

Born: 5/29/1913, Gary, IN

Named: Anthony Florian Zaleski

Died: 3/21/1997

Tony Zale has been called the greatest comeback fighter in the history of boxing. Few, if any, have equaled Zale's ability to withstand a tremendous beating and then rebound to take charge of a fight which appeared to be totally lost.

Zale grew up under the haze of steel town Gary, Indiana. He and his brothers had been active in amateur boxing, but Zale did not turn to fighting in earnest until he was about to graduate from high school and saw the steel mills looming as his most likely place of employment. "I didn't want those mills," recalled Zale later in his career.

Zale did work in the mills but only as a day job while he compiled a solid amateur record of 87-8 before making his professional debut in 1934. He boxed

Rocky Graziano crashes to the canvas after a pile driver body punch and a left hook by Zale. This fight, the first of three battles between these two well-matched warriors, took place in September 1946.

in the Chicago area for five years and was recognized as the tenth-best middle-weight contender in *The Ring*'s annual rankings of 1939. Under the guidance of the managerial team of Art Winch and Sam Pian, Zale had his first major fight, a non-title bout with NBA middleweight champion Al Hostak. The unheralded Zale surprised Hostak and took the decision. Six months later, the two squared off for the title with Zale winning by knockout in thirteen. In 1941, Zale unified the middleweight championship with a decision over the New York champion, Georgie Abrams. After a rather lackluster loss to the light heavyweight Billy Conn, Zale joined the navy for the duration of World War II.

IN THE RING	WON 67	LOST 18	DRAWS 2	TB 87	KO 45	W 22	WF 0	D 2	KO'd 5	L 13	LF 0

Date	Opponent	Site	Result / Rounds		Title	Wt.
1934						
Jun 11	Eddie Allen	Chicago	W	4	—	—
Jun 15	Johnny Simpson	Chicago	W	4	—	—
Jun 21	Bobby Millsap	Chicago	KO	1	—	—
Jun 25	Johnny Liston	Chicago	KO	3	—	—
Jul 2	Ossie Jefferson	Chicago	KO	3	—	—
Jul 9	Lou Bartell	Chicago	W	4	—	159
Jul 16	Einar Hedquist	Chicago	KO	4	—	—
Jul 30	Bobby Millsap	Chicago	W	4	—	—
Aug 6	Bruce Wade	Peoria, IL	KO	3	—	165
Aug 13	Billy Hood	Chicago	L	6	—	—
Aug 15	George ("Billy") Black	Chicago	L	6	—	—
Aug 27	Wilbur Stokes	Chicago	W	8	—	—
Sep 3	Mickey Misko	Chicago	L	8	—	161
Sep 17	Mickey Misko	Chicago	KO	4	—	—
Oct 8	Young Jack Blackburn	Chicago	W	8	—	165
Oct 22	Frankie Misko	Chicago	KO	6	—	159
Oct 28	Jackie Schwartz	Milwaukee	KO	4	—	159
Nov 5	Jack Chavez	Chicago	W	8	—	—
Nov 26	Kid Leonard	Peoria	L	10	—	157
Dec 17	Jack Gibbons	Chicago	L	10	—	160
Dec 28	Joey Bazzone	Chicago	L	6	—	160
1935						
Feb 25	Young Jack Blackburn	Chicago	W	6	—	161
Mar 11	Max Elling	Chicago	W	8	—	154
Mar 27	Frank Glover	Cincinnati	KO'd	9	—	159
May 6	Johnny Phagan	Chicago	TKO'd	6	—	157
Jul 2	Dave Clark	Chicago	L	5	—	159
1936						
Apr 13	Jack Moran	Chicago	D	5	—	—
1937						
Jul 26	Elby Johnson	Chicago	W	4	—	160
Aug 17	Emanuel Davila	Chicago	L	4	—	—
Sep 17	Elby Johnson	Chicago	TKO	3	—	—
Oct 11	Billy Brown	Chicago	KO	1	—	159
Oct 18	Bobby Gerry	Chicago	KO	2	—	—
Nov 1	Nate Bolden	Chicago	L	5	—	160
Nov 10	Leon Jackson	Gary, IN	W	6	—	—
Nov 22	Nate Bolden	Chicago	W	6	—	160

1938

Date		Opponent	Location	Result	Rounds	Notes	Weight
Jan 3		Nate Bolden	Chicago	W	8	—	162
Jan 24		Henry Schaft	Chicago	W	8	—	159
Feb 21		Jimmy Clark	Chicago	KO'd	1	—	160
Mar 28		King Wyatt	Chicago	W	8	—	159
May 16		Bobby LaMonte	Chicago	TKO	5	—	—
Jun 13		Jimmy Clark	Chicago	TKO	8	—	156
Jul 18		Billy Celebron	Chicago	D	10	—	156
Aug 22		Billy Celebron	Chicago	L	10	—	158
Oct 10		Tony Cisco	Chicago	W	10	—	157
Oct 31		Jimmy Clark	Chicago	TKO	2	—	159
Nov 18		Enzo Iannozzi	Chicago	W	6	—	158

1939

Date		Opponent	Location	Result	Rounds	Notes	Weight
Jan 2	⑩	Nate Bolden	Chicago	L	10	—	160
May 1		Johnny Shaw	Chicago	KO	5	—	160
May 23		Babe Orgovan	New York	W	6	—	161
Aug 14		Milton Shivers	Chicago	KO	3	—	163
Oct 6		Sherman Edwards	Chicago	TKO	3	—	—
Nov 3		Al Wardlow	Youngstown, OH	KO	3	—	158
Nov 11		Eddie Meleski	Chicago	KO	1	—	159
Dec 12		Babe Orgovan	Chicago	KO	3	—	—

1940

Date		Opponent	Location	Result	Rounds	Notes	Weight
Jan 29	♛	Al Hostak	Chicago	W	10	—	162
Feb 29		Enzo Iannozzi	Youngstown	KO	4	—	162
Mar 29	⑩	Ben Brown	Chicago	KO	3	—	159
Jun 12		Baby Kid Chocolate	Youngstown	KO	4	—	157
Jul 19	♛	Al Hostak	Seattle	TKO	13	Won-NBA-M	158
Aug 21	⑩	Billy Soose	Chicago	L	10	—	161
Nov 19		Fred Apostoli ★	Seattle	W	10	—	161

1941

Date		Opponent	Location	Result	Rounds	Notes	Weight
Jan 1		Tony Cianciola	Milwaukee	TKO	7	—	162
Jan 10		Steve Mamakos	Chicago	W	10	—	163
Feb 21		Steve Mamakos	Chicago	KO	14	Ret-NBA-M	159
May 28	⑩	Al Hostak	Chicago	KO	2	Ret-NBA-M	158
Jul 23		Ossie Harris	Chicago	KO	1	—	161
Aug 16		Billy Pryor	Milwaukee	KO	9	—	163
Nov 28	⑩	Georgie Abrams	New York	W	15	Won-Vac World-M	158

1942

Date		Opponent	Location	Result	Rounds	Notes	Weight
Feb 13	⑩	Billy Conn ★	New York	L	12	—	164

1946

Date		Opponent	Location	Result	Rounds	Notes	Weight
Jan 7		Bobby Giles	Kansas City, MO	KO	4	—	162
Jan 17		Tony Gillo	Norfolk, VA	KO	5	—	162
Feb 7		Oscar Boyd	Des Moines, IA	KO	3	—	159
Feb 26		Bobby Claus	Houston	KO	4	—	162
Apr 12		Ira Hughes	Houston	KO	2	—	162
May 2		Eddie Rossi	Memphis, TN	KO	4	—	160
Sep 27	⑩	Rocky Graziano ★	New York	KO	6	Ret-World-M	160

1947

Date		Opponent	Location	Result	Rounds	Notes	Weight
Feb 3		Deacon Logan	Omaha, NE	TKO	6	—	162
Feb 12		Len Wadsworth	Wichita, KS	KO	3	—	162
Mar 20		Tommy Charles	Memphis	KO	4	—	162
Apr 1		Al Timmons	Kansas City, KS	KO	5	—	162
May 8		Cliff Beckett	Youngstown	KO	6	—	161
Jul 16	⑩	Rocky Graziano ★	Chicago	TKO'd	6	Lost-World-M	159

1948

Date		Opponent	Location	Result	Rounds	Notes	Weight
Jan 23		Al Turner	Grand Rapids, MI	KO	5	—	161
Mar 8		Bobby Claus	Little Rock, AR	KO	4	—	160
Mar 19		Lou Woods	Toledo, OH	KO	3	—	160
Jun 10	♛	Rocky Graziano ★	Newark, NJ	KO	3	Reg-World-M	158
Sep 21	⑩	Marcel Cerdan ★	Jersey City, NJ	TKO'd	12	Lost-World-M	159

On his return from the war, Zale, still viewed as the world champion, engaged in a series of career-defining battles: three all-out struggles with Hall of Famer Rocky Graziano. The two first met in Yankee Stadium before a crowd of 39,827. Most observers expected Zale to fall to Graziano, who was nine years younger. In one of the most brutal battles on record, the fighters went at each other as if their killer instincts had been released. Zale dropped Graziano in the first round but was knocked down in the second. Graziano then battered and cut Zale until Zale was so groggy from punches at the end of the fifth, he mistook his opponent's corner for his own. Fans yelled for referee Ruby Goldstein to stop the fight, but the veteran official allowed it to continue. Then, astoundingly, Zale came out for the sixth round as if it were the first. In under two minutes, Graziano was on the canvas, victim of a Zale knockout.

There was a rematch in 1947 and a rubber match in 1948, both as vicious and unrelenting as the initial battle. Graziano, although bleeding from several cuts, won the first by battering Zale to insensibility by the sixth round. Zale took the second with a third-round knockout to reclaim his title.

Within three months, 35-year-old Zale faced Marcel Cerdan in a title defense. He was knocked out in twelve rounds. After this fight, the great battler retired. Zale briefly returned to the ring to play himself in the movie version of Graziano's autobiography, *Somebody Up There Likes Me*.

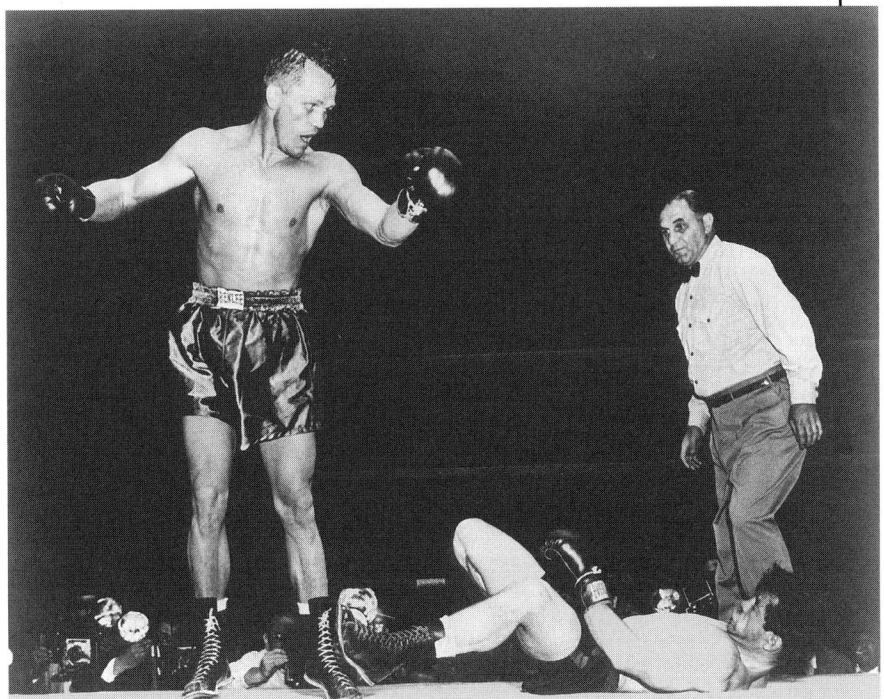

Gaunt Tony Zale (L) knocks out Rocky Graziano in the third round of their third meeting on June 10, 1948, in Newark, NJ. Over 21,000 fans witnessed the fight, held in Ruppert Stadium.

DANIEL ZARAGOZA
The Mouse

JUNIOR FEATHERWEIGHT

Left-handed; 5'7"; 117–126 lbs.

66 bouts, 10/17/1980 to 9/6/1997

WBC Bantamweight Champion 1985

WBC Junior Featherweight Champion 1988–90, 1991–92, 1995–97

Hall of Fame Induction: 2004

Born: 12/11/1957, Mexico City, Mexico

Daniel Zaragoza fought in twenty world title fights in a career that spanned seventeen years. Zaragoza, born on December 11, 1957, in Mexico City, came from a fighting family. His father, Agustin Zaragoza, boxed under the nom de ring Zurita II. In a thirteen-year career, Agustin fought nearly 500 times. The money the senior Zaragoza earned helped to feed his large family, which eventually numbered twelve children. Mr. Zaragoza taught all five of his sons to box. Agustin Zaragoza Jr., Daniel Zaragoza's brother, won a bronze medal as a middleweight in the 1968 Mexico City Olympics. Daniel Zaragoza took up boxing in earnest when he nineteen. He was a bronze medalist in the 1977 Mexican Golden Gloves and won the title the next year. He then set his sights on the 1980 Olympics and participated in various international competitions. He won gold medals in competitions in Moscow and Mexico City and won a Latin American amateur title. He lost in the quarterfinals of the Pan American Games. Unfortunately, Zaragoza did not realize his dream of winning an Olympic medal either. He was upset in the quarterfinals by Michael Anthony of Ghana.

Zaragoza rebounded from his Olympic disappointment and turned professional on October 17, 1980, when he knocked out Ernesto Gutierrez in four rounds. He faced fairly stiff competition right from the start of his career but proved equal to the task—winning his first fourteen fights. He racked up his first loss to Harold Petty in Las Vegas on July 29, 1982, in an all-southpaw match. In his next fight, Zaragoza decisioned Jorge Ramirez, a contender ranked by the WBC, to win the Mexican bantamweight title. The Mexican title served as a springboard to a North American Boxing Federation (NABF) title shot with Petty. Once again,

Daniel Zaragoza (L) absorbs a solid right to the ribcage while he delivers a left uppercut to Hector Acero Sanchez. The pair twice fought for Sanchez's WBC junior featherweight title. The first battle was a draw.

IN THE RING	WON 55*	LOST 8	DRAWS 3	TB 66	KO 27	W 26*	WF 2	D 3	KO'd 3	L 5	LF 0

*includes 1 Technical Win

Date	Opponent	Site	Result / Rounds		Title	Wt.
1980						
Oct 17	Ernesto Gutierrez	Poza Rica, Mexico	KO	4	—	117
Dec 19	Porfirio Urrutia	Tampico, Mexico	TKO	3	—	117
1981						
Feb 21	Joel ("Chato") Segura	Merida, Mexico	TKO	7	—	119
Mar 29	Jesus Maravilla	Villahermosa, Mexico	TKO	2	—	118
May 15	Jose Zapata	Villahermosa	W	10	—	119
Jun 27	Roque Guillen	Tuxtla, Mexico	TKO	3	—	119
Jul 22	Alonzo Gonzalez	Los Angeles	W	10	—	117
Aug 28	Rayito Gonzalez	Campeche, Mexico	TKO	4	—	119
Sep 16	Javier Marquez	Mexicali, Mexico	TKO	8	—	121
Oct 30	Julio ("Rubia") Avendano	Acapulco, Mexico	TKO	4	—	123
Nov 21	Mario Chavez	Mexicali	W	10	—	120
1982						
Feb 12	Miguel Juarez	Acapulco	W	10	—	118
Mar 5	Francisco ("Paco") Mayo	Acapulco	TKO	5	—	119
Apr 23	Ramon Concha	Acapulco	TKO	2	—	118
Jul 29	Harold Petty	Las Vegas	L	10	—	118
Sep 4	Jorge Ramirez	Guadalajara, Mexico	W	12	Won-Mexico-B	118
Nov 29	Jesus ("Chuyin") Lopez	Tijuana, Mexico	W	12	Ret-Mexico-B	118
1983						
Jan 29	Lorenzo Ramirez	Los Angeles	W	10	—	118
Mar 18	Rigoberto Estrada	Juarez, Mexico	W	12	Ret-Mexico-B	117
May 27	Jesus Lopez	Juarez	W	12	Ret-Mexico-B	118
Aug 8	⑩ Harold Petty	Houston	L	12	For-NABF-B	117
Sep 26	Martin Torres	Tijuana	TKO	5	Ret-Mexico-B	118
Oct 29	Rodolfo Martinez	Jalisco, Mexico	TKO	11	Ret-Mexico-B	118
Dec 16	Rigoberto Estrada	Juarez	W	12	Ret-Mexico-B	118
1984						
Feb 18	Javier Marquez	Mexicali	KO	5	—	119
Mar 16	Patrick Young	Mexicali	KO	4	—	119
May 21	Mario Gomez	Tijuana	TKO	3	Ret-Mexico-B	118
Sep 21	Jorge Ramirez	Juarez	WF	11	Ret-Mexico-B	118
Nov 30	Jorge Ramirez	La Paz, Mexico	W	12	Ret-Mexico-B	118
1985						
May 4	⑩ Freddie Jackson	Oranjestad, Aruba	WF	7	Won-Vac WBC-B	117
Aug 9	⑩ Miguel ("Happy") Lora	Miami	L	12	Lost-WBC-B	118
1986						
Apr 11	⑩ Jeff Fenech★	Perth, Australia	L	10	—	121
Jul 4	Antonio Gonzalez	Tijuana	W	10	—	124
Aug 29	Raul Negrete	Tijuana	TW	7	—	123
Dec 6	Mike Ayala	San Antonio, TX	KO	7	Won-NABF-JFE	122
1987						
Apr 3	Aaron Lopez	San Antonio	W	12	Ret-NABF-JFE	121
Jun 28	Ramiro Adames	Houston	TKO	5	—	124
Jul 31	Darryl Thigpen	San Antonio	W	12	Ret-NABF-JFE	121
Dec 17	Noe Gonzalez	Naucalpan, Mexico	TKO	7	—	124

1988							
Feb 29		Carlos Zarate★	Inglewood, CA	KO	10	Won-Vac WBC-JFE	121
May 29	ⓦ	Seung Hoon Lee	Yeosu, South Korea	D	12	Ret-WBC-JFE	122
Nov 26		Valerio Nati	Forli, Italy	KO	5	Ret-WBC-JFE	122
1989							
Jun 22	ⓦ	Paul Banke	Inglewood	W	12	Ret-WBC-JFE	122
Aug 31		Frankie Duarte	Inglewood	TKO	10	Ret-WBC-JFE	121
Dec 1		Chan Yong Park	Inchon; South Korea	W	12	Ret-WBC-JFE	121
1990							
Apr 23	ⓦ	Paul Banke	Inglewood	TKO'd	9	Lost-WBC-JFE	122
1991							
Apr 5		Moi Hernandez	Piedras Niegras, Mexico	W	10	—	124
Jun 14	♛	Kiyoshi Hatanaka	Nagoya, Japan	W	12	Reg-WBC-JFE	121
Aug 24		Chun Huh	Seoul	W	12	Ret-WBC-JFE	122
Dec 9		Paul Banke	Los Angeles	W	12	Ret-WBC-JFE	122
1992							
Mar 20		Thierry Jacob	Calais, France	L	12	Lost-WBC-JFE	122
Dec 5	♛	Tracy Harris Patterson	Berck Sur Mer, France	D	12	For-WBC-JFE	122
1993							
Sep 25	♛	Tracy Harris Patterson	Poughkeepsie, NY	TKO'd	7	For-WBC-JFE	122
Dec 4		Alejandro Batista	Miami	TKO	3	—	123
1994							
Jun 11		Juan Francisco Soto	Inglewood	W	10	—	126
Jul 1		Wilfredo Urbina	Tlalnepantla, Mexico	TKO	5	—	—
Aug 11		Nino Ruiz	Mexico City	TKO	4	—	—
Oct 22		Wilfredo Vargas	Miami	TKO	7	—	126
1995							
Feb 11		Jose Sanabria	Miami	W	10	—	125
Jun 2	♛	Hector Acero Sanchez	Ledyard, CT	D	12	For-WBC-JFE	122
Nov 6	♛	Hector Acero Sanchez	Inglewood	W	12	Reg-WBC-JFE	122
1996							
Mar 3		Joichiro Tatsuyoshi	Yokohama, Japan	TKO	11	Ret-WBC-JFE	122
Jul 20		Tsuyoshi Harada	Osaka	TKO	7	Ret-WBC-JFE	122
1997							
Jan 11		Wayne McCullough	Boston	W	12	Ret-WBC-JFE	121
Apr 14		Joichiro Tatsuyoshi	Osaka	W	12	Ret-WBC-JFE	121
Sep 6		Erik Morales	El Paso, TX	KO'd	11	Lost-WBC-JFE	122

Petty came away with the decision. Zaragoza continued to defend his Mexican title, though he nearly lost it in a rematch with Ramirez. Ramirez appeared to be winning the fight when he was disqualified for butting Zaragoza in the eleventh.

A disqualification also figured in Zaragoza's first world title fight. Zaragoza won the WBC bantamweight championship on May 4, 1985, in a match for the vacant title when Freddie Jackson fouled him in the seventh and was disqualified. He did not hold the title for long. Miguel ("Happy") Lora used a devastating right hand to earn a unanimous twelve-round decision over Zaragoza. Zaragoza also lost his next bout as Hall of Famer Jeff Fenech decisioned him.

Zaragoza moved up to super bantamweight and won the NABF title in that weight class when he knocked out Mike Ayala on December 6, 1986. On February 29, 1988, he fought for the vacant WBC super bantamweight title against Hall of Famer Carlos Zarate—a fellow Mexican, who was at the end of his career.

A crowd of 8,442 saw Zaragoza completely dominate the bout as he drew a bead on Zarate's head with a succession of straight lefts. When Zaragoza staggered Zarate with a right to the cheek, the referee stopped the fight at the 2:54 mark of the tenth round.

Zaragoza defended the title five times in less than two years, including a split-decision victory over Paul Banke. In the rematch, Banke won when the fight had to be stopped in the ninth round because Zaragoza suffered severe cuts. Throughout his career, cuts would be a major problem for Zaragoza, whose face was lined with scars from his many ring battles. Zaragoza regained the title on June 14, 1991, when he journeyed to Japan to win a split decision over Kiyoshi Hatanaka. He won the rubber match of his series with Banke before losing the title on a decision to Thierry Jacob.

Zaragoza did not find it as easy to regain the title a second time. He fought a draw for the title with champion Tracy Harris Patterson and then was knocked out by Patterson in the rematch. He fought another draw two years later when matched with champion Hector Acero Sanchez—though many onlookers thought Zaragoza had done enough to win. In a rematch on November 6, 1995, at the Forum before 4,170, Zaragoza suffered a cut over the right eye in the second round, another in the middle of his hairline in the fourth, and a third on the right side of his forehead in the tenth. The veteran warrior seemed indifferent to his wounds. He was the aggressor throughout and scored with lefts to the head. Zaragoza won a unanimous decision, 115-112, 116-112, and 114-113.

Zaragoza defended his title four more times, including a split-decision victory over highly regarded Wayne Mc-Cullough. He lost the championship for the last time to Erik Morales. In this fight, the 39-year-old Zaragoza was cut as usual. Morales then knocked him down in the tenth and finished him off with a right to the midsection in the eleventh. Zaragoza retired after the loss.

Though a good boxer, Zaragoza was not a smooth ring stylist. However, he could think on his feet and change his mode of attack in the middle of a fight. He was not an incredibly hard hitter and cut easily, but nonetheless was a great fighter worthy of induction into the International Boxing Hall of Fame.

When Daniel Zaragoza (R) and Hector Acero Sanchez faced off for the second time, on November 6, 1995, for Sanchez's WBC junior featherweight title, Zaragoza took the twelve-round decision.

CARLOS ZARATE
Pepito

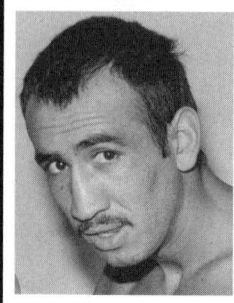

BANTAMWEIGHT

Right-handed; 5'8"; 111–127 lbs.

70 bouts, 2/2/1970 to 2/29/1988

Manager: Arturo ("Cuyo") Hernandez

WBC Bantamweight Champion 1976–79

Hall of Fame Induction: 1994

Born: 5/23/1951, Tepito, Mexico

One of the top fighters of the 1970s, bantamweight Carlos Zarate is most notable for his record of knock-out wins. Of his first 52 fights, an amazing 51 ended in knock-out victories. And all but nine of the knockouts occurred in five rounds or less.

Born in Tepito, Mexico, Zarate became a professional boxer at the age of eighteen. He fought exclusively in his homeland for the first four years of his career, building up a strong record of knockouts, many in the second round. In 1972, only one fighter went more than two rounds with Zarate.

In 1976, Zarate challenged Rodolfo Martinez at the Fabulous Forum in Inglewood, California, for the WBC bantamweight title. Zarate had a pattern of approaching his opponent carefully at first, then relentlessly stalking him until the perfect moment occurred to launch a knock-out punch. He used this technique on Martinez, whom he knocked down in the fifth round and KO'd in the ninth to win the title.

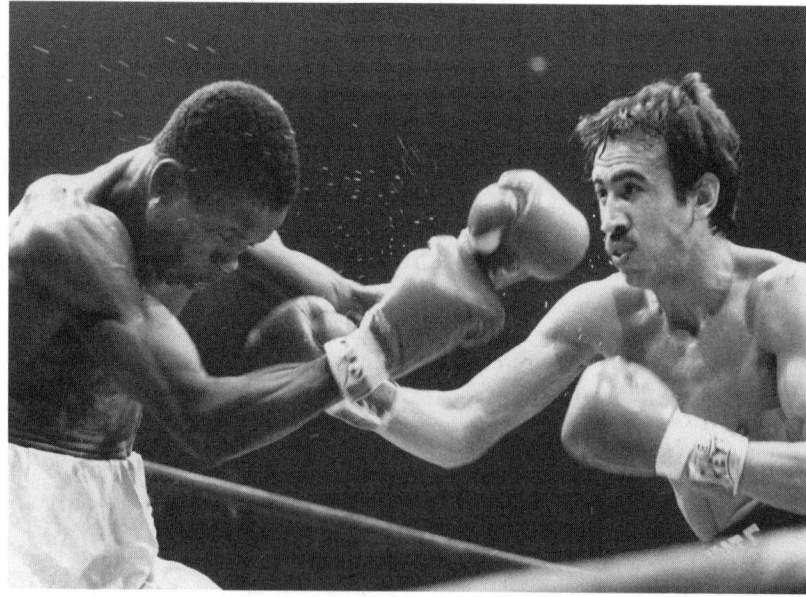

Back in the ring after his first loss, Carlos Zarate (R) keeps his WBC bantamweight title with a three-round shellacking of Mensah Kpalongo (from Togo, West Africa) on March 10, 1979, in Inglewood, CA.

IN THE RING	WON 66	LOST 4	DRAWS 0	TB 70	KO 63	W 3	WF 0	D 0	KO'd 2	L 1	LF 1

Date	Opponent	Site	Result / Rounds		Title	Wt.
1970						
Feb 2	Luis Castaneda	Cuernavaca, Mexico	KO	3	—	111
Mar 2	Jose Pavon	Cuernavaca	KO	1	—	—
Apr 1	Costenito Sotelo	Villahermosa, Mexico	KO	2	—	—
Nov 17	Nuno Temix	Villahermosa	TKO	3	—	—
Dec 18	Alfredo Perez	Acapulco	KO	2	—	116
1971						
Feb 15	Antonio Lucas	Cuernavaca	KO	3	—	—
Mar 20	Fermin Ramos	Toluca, Mexico	KO	2	—	—
May 5	Ramon Pinedo	Cuernavaca	KO	2	—	—
Aug 7	Julio Martinez	Morelia, Mexico	KO	2	—	—
Nov 26	Victor Nava	Acapulco	KO	3	—	—
1972						
Jan 28	Emiliano Mayoral	Acapulco	TKO	3	—	—
Feb 7	Jose Gonzalez	Tampico, Mexico	KO	2	—	—
Mar 19	Jose Morales	Mexico City	TKO	2	—	115
Aug 19	Jesus Escobedo	Monterrey, Mexico	KO	2	—	116
Oct 8	Arturo Patino	Ciudad Madero, Mexico	KO	2	—	113
Oct 31	Armando Carrasco	Villahermosa	KO	2	—	116
Dec 3	Juan Perez	La Paz, Mexico	TKO	2	—	—
1973						
Jun 2	Juan Perez	La Paz	KO	2	—	118
Jul 12	Francisco Pino	Cuernavaca	KO	2	—	—
Aug 21	Al Torres	Tijuana, Mexico	TKO	5	—	—
Oct 2	Antonio Castaneda	Tijuana	TKO	9	—	117
Nov 1	Eduardo Miranda	Tijuana	KO	5	—	—
Dec 11	Sixto Perez	Tijuana	KO	2	—	—
1974						
Jan 30	Victor Ramirez	Mexico City	W	10	—	118
Feb 22	Carlos Armenta	Matamoros, Mexico	KO	1	—	—
Apr 9	Alfonso Ibarra	Tijuana	KO	2	—	117
May 3	Chamaco Limon	Monterrey	KO	3	—	117
May 25	Juan Ordonez	Mexico City	KO	3	—	119
Aug 3	Magallo Lozada	Mexico City	TKO	5	—	119
Oct 27	Francisco Cruz	Mexicali, Mexico	TKO	2	—	118
Nov 23	James Martinez	Los Angeles	TKO	7	—	118
1975						
Feb 4	Alberto Cabanig	Ciudad Victoria, Mexico	TKO	4	—	—
Mar 14	Joe Guevara	Inglewood, CA	TKO	4	—	117
Jun 20	Orlando Amoros	Inglewood	KO	3	—	118
Aug 16	Jose Sanchez	Mexico City	TKO	3	—	118
Sep 20	Benicio Sosa	Inglewood	TKO	4	—	119
Oct 11	Jorge Torres	Guadalajara, Mexico	TKO	9	—	118
Dec 7	Nestor Jimenez	Mexicali	KO	2	—	—
1976						
Mar 27	Cesar Deciga	Monterrey	TKO	4	—	—
May 8 ♛	Rodolfo Martinez	Inglewood	KO	9	Won-WBC-B	116

Jun 26		Felix Illanos	Mexicali	KO	2	—	—
Aug 2		Antonio Paredes	Chihuahua, Mexico	TKO	2	—	—
Aug 28	Ⓦ	Paul Ferreri	Inglewood	TKO	12	Ret-WBC-B	117
Nov 13		Waruinge Nakayama	Culiacan, Mexico	KO	4	Ret-WBC-B	118
1977							
Feb 5		Fernando Cabanela	Mexico City	TKO	3	Ret-WBC-B	118
Apr 23	♛	Alfonso Zamora	Inglewood	TKO	4	—	119
Oct 29		Danilo Batista	Los Angeles	TKO	6	Ret-WBC-B	116
Dec 2		Juan Rodriguez	Madrid	TKO	5	Ret-WBC-B	117
1978							
Feb 25	Ⓦ	Albert Davila	Inglewood	TKO	8	Ret-WBC-B	118
Apr 22		Andres Hernandez	San Juan, PR	TKO	13	Ret-WBC-B	118
Jun 9		Emilio Hernandez	Las Vegas	KO	4	Ret-WBC-B	118
Sep 30		Rudy Gonzalez	Matamoros	KO	4	—	121
Oct 28	♛	Wilfredo Gomez★	Hato Rey, PR	TKO'd	5	For-WBC-JFE (SB)	122
1979							
Mar 10		Mensah Kpalongo	Inglewood	KO	3	Ret-WBC-B	118
May 1		Celso Chairez	Houston	TKO	5	—	—
Jun 3	Ⓦ	Lupe Pintor	Las Vegas	L	15	Lost-WBC-B	117
1986							
Feb 25		Adam Garcia	Inglewood	W	4	—	127
Apr 12		Jose De La Dora	Zacapu, Mexico	KO	3	—	—
May 5		Hector Napoles	Torreon, Mexico	KO	2	—	—
May 23		Jesus Muniz	Chicago	W	10	—	123
Jul 19		Alejandro Garcia	Juarez, Mexico	KO	2	—	—
Sep 13		Gerardo Esparza	Zapopan, Mexico	KO	5	—	—
Nov 21		Eddie Rodriguez	San Jose, CA	TKO	3	—	126
Dec 13		Alex Galvan	Fresno, CA	TKO	7	—	125
1987							
Feb 20		Francis Childs	San Jose	KO	4	—	124
May 5		John Boyd	Los Angeles	TKO	5	—	126
Jun 19		Tony Montoya	San Jose	KO	3	—	126
Aug 15		Richard Savage	Mexico City	TKO	5	—	—
Oct 16	♛	Jeff Fenech★	Sydney	TL	4	For-WBC-JFE (SB)	122
1988							
Feb 29		Daniel Zaragoza	Inglewood	TKO'd	10	For-WBC-JFE (SB)	122

Though not sanctioned as a title fight, the greatest ring victory Zarate scored came when he stopped undefeated WBA bantamweight champion Alfonso Zamora in four rounds in 1977. Zarate dominated Zamora, knocking him down three times.

Zarate tried to move up in class and win the WBC junior featherweight title but was defeated in five rounds by Hall of Famer Wilfredo Gomez. Later, it was revealed that Zarate had climbed into the ring against Gomez while suffering from the flu.

After losing a controversial decision to his former stable mate Lupe Pintor in 1979, Zarate asked the WBC to reverse the decision. Jose Sulaiman, President of the WBC, agreed that the decision appeared to be incorrect but would not change it.

Zarate then left the fight game, only to make a comeback after almost seven years of inactivity. He continued to build on his stupendous record, winning twelve fights in a row, but his last two fights were losses. He failed in a WBC junior featherweight title bid against Jeff Fenech in Sydney in 1987. His last fight was in February, 1988, against Daniel Zaragoza, again for the WBC junior featherweight crown. Zaragoza scored a technical knockout in the tenth round. Zarate then hung up the gloves again.

An intense Carlos Zarate (R) pounds Paul Ferreri. Zarate ended his first title defense with a twelfth-round TKO on August 28, 1976, in the Fabulous Forum. This bout was Zarate's 43rd consecutive win.

FRITZIE ZIVIC
The Croat Comet

WELTERWEIGHT

Right-handed; 5'9"; 133–159 lbs.

234 bouts, 10/5/1931 to 1/17/1949

Managers: Luke Carney 1931–42, Louis Stokan 1942–49

Welterweight Champ 1940–41

Hall of Fame Induction: 1993

Born: 5/8/1913, Pittsburgh, PA

Named: Ferdinand Zivic

Died: 5/16/1984

Carrying the dubious distinction of being one of the most openly dirty fighters in the history of boxing, Fritzie Zivic was also one of the most popular. His bouts set attendance records at Madison Square Garden, and a Zivic fight was almost always guaranteed to set the crowd roaring. One of five boxing brothers from Pittsburgh, Zivic turned professional as a featherweight in 1931. He generally met with success but, in 1935 and 1936, lost eight fights in a row, a sour streak that might have discouraged a less-dedicated fighter. Nevertheless, in 1936 *The Ring* ranked Zivic as one of the top contenders for the welterweight title.

In his rise to the top, Zivic faced such notables as fellow Pittsburghers Billy Conn and Charley Burley, losing his only meeting with Conn and two out of three to Burley. He beat tough Sammy Angott in 1940, which won him a shot at the

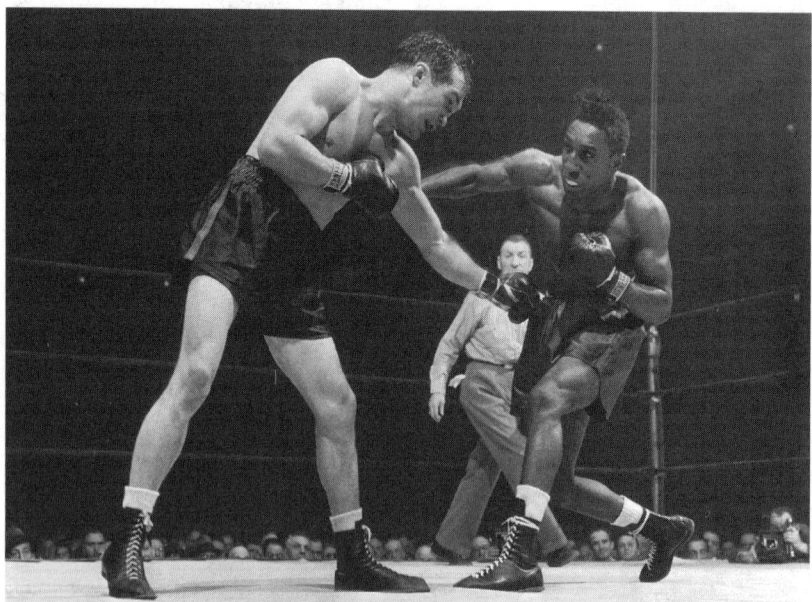

Zivic's (L) punch looks south of the border as Billy Arnold swings a roundhouse right. Zivic took the eight-round decision in 1945. After losing his crown in 1941, Zivic never had another title shot.

IN THE RING	WON 159	LOST 65	DRAWS 9	TB 234	KO 81	W 77	WF 1	D 9	KO'd 4	L 61	LF 0	ND 1

Date	Opponent	Site	Result / Rounds		Title	Wt.
1931						
Oct 5	Al Rettinger	Pittsburgh	TKO	1	—	—
Nov 16	Steve Senich	Pittsburgh	L	6	—	—
1932						
Jan 1	Paddy Gilmore	Pittsburgh	KO	4	—	—
Mar 4	Elmer Kozak	Pittsburgh	TKO	4	—	—
Jun 9	Young Lowstetter	Millvale, PA	W	6	—	—
Jun 22	Steve Senich	North Braddock, PA	L	6	—	—
Sep 26	Jim Dorsey	Pittsburgh	KO	4	—	—
Oct 14	Terry Waner	Pittsburgh	TKO	3	—	—
Nov 18	Jerry Clements	Pittsburgh	L	6	—	134
Dec 13	Billy Criggin	Pittsburgh	W	4	—	—
1933						
Jan 30	George Schlee	Pittsburgh	TKO	2	—	—
Feb 8	Steve Senich	Pittsburgh	KO	2	—	—
Mar 24	U.S. Carpenter	Pittsburgh	KO	4	—	—
Apr 10	Eddie Brannon	Pittsburgh	KO	6	—	135
Apr 28	Patsy Hennigan	Pittsburgh	W	6	—	135
Jun 26	Don Asto	Pittsburgh	W	6	—	134
Jul 10	Don Asto	Pittsburgh	KO	3	—	133
Aug 7	Joey Greb	Millvale	W	10	—	134
Oct 12	Joe Pimental	Pasadena, CA	KO	4	—	—
Nov 3	Gus Vagas	San Francisco	KO	2	—	138
Nov 23	Don Miller	Pasadena	KO	3	—	141
Dec 4	Homer Foster	Pico, CA	D	4	—	—
Dec 15	Vincent Martinez	Hollywood	W	4	—	140
Dec 27	Rudy Ayon	Pico	W	4	—	142
1934						
Jan 5	Luis Carranza	Los Angeles	W	6	—	143
Jan 23	Baby Sal Sorio	Los Angeles	KO	2	—	143
Jan 30	Lloyd Smith	Los Angeles	D	6	—	—
Feb 22	Perfecto Lopez	Los Angeles	W	6	—	—
Apr	Phil Rios	Los Angeles	W	6	—	—
May 8	Lloyd Smith	Los Angeles	D	6	—	—
Jul 2	Eddie Ran	Pittsburgh	W	10	—	139
Jul 25	Joe Firpo	Lake Conneaut, PA	W	8	—	—
Sep 27	Harry Carlton	Pittsburgh	W	8	—	—
Oct 25	Laddie Tonelli	Chicago	KO'd	3	—	141
1935						
Feb 4	⑩ Jimmy Leto	Holyoke, MA	L	10	—	136
Feb 18	Johnny Jadick	Washington, DC	L	10	—	139
Mar 4	K.O. Pete Castillo	Holyoke	W	10	—	139
Mar 25	Dominic Mancini	Pittsburgh	D	10	—	143
Apr 2	Dominic Mancini	Pittsburgh	KO	11	—	140
Apr 16	Marty Gornick	Steubenville, OH	KO	5	—	—
Apr 29	Freddie Chenowyth	Chicago	W	8	—	140
May 6	Sammy Chivas	Chicago	KO	3	—	143
May 21	Eddie Adams	Kent, OH	KO	8	—	147
Jul 1	⑩ Lou Ambers★	Pittsburgh	L	10	—	138

Date		Opponent	Location	Result	Rounds		Weight
Jul 15		Jackie McFarland	Millvale	W	10	—	141
Aug 1		Mike Barto	Millvale	W	12	—	141
Aug 8	⑩	Joey Ferrando	Jersey City, NJ	L	10	—	139
Sep 30		Tony Herrera	Pittsburgh	L	10	—	—
Oct 4		George Salvadore	New York	L	6	—	143
Dec 16		Billy Celebron	Chicago	L	10	—	144
1936							
Jan 13	⑩	Eddie Cool	Pittsburgh	L	10	—	139
Jan 27	⑩	Joey Ferrando	New York	L	8	—	140
Feb 24		Chuck Woods	Pittsburgh	L	10	—	144
Apr 17		Young Gene Buffalo	Atlantic City	L	10	—	145
May 22		Billy Celebron	St. Louis	KO	1	—	133
Jun 9		Tony Falco	Pittsburgh	KO	8	—	144
Jun 27		Al Manfredo	St. Louis	W	10	—	146
Jul 2		Lou Jallos	Steubenville	W	10	—	—
Jul 6		Laddie Tonelli	Pittsburgh	KO	4	—	146
Jul 22		Mickey Duris	Johnstown, PA	W	12	—	144
Jul 30		Laddie Tonelli	Pittsburgh	TKO	6	—	145
Aug 12	⑩	Cleo Locatelli	Brooklyn	L	10	—	146
Sep 28		Jackie McFarland	Canton, OH	W	10	—	146
Oct 5		Johnny Durso	Pittsburgh	KO	2	—	143
Oct 16		Chuck Woods	St. Louis	KO	6	—	—
Nov 9		Gaston LeCadre	Pittsburgh	W	10	—	146
Dec 2	⑩	Harry Dublinsky	Pittsburgh	KO	6	—	146
Dec 28		Billy Conn★	Pittsburgh	L	10	—	149
1937							
Feb 11		Johnny Jadick	Pittsburgh	KO	6	—	147
Mar 1		Bobby Pacho	Pittsburgh	W	10	—	145
Apr 6		Chuck Woods	Detroit	W	10	—	146
May 21		Tony Petroskey	Muskegon, MI	W	10	—	146
Oct 27		Frankie Portland	Clarksburg, WV	KO	2	—	144
Nov 18		Jimmy Reilly	McKeesport, PA	KO	1	—	146
Dec 25		Tommy Bland	Pittsburgh	L	10	—	146
1938							
Jan 1		Harold Brown	Chicago	W	10	—	146
Feb 14		Frankie Blair	Pittsburgh	W	10	—	148
Mar 7		Tommy Bland	Pittsburgh	TKO	8	—	150
Mar 21	⑩	Charley Burley★	Pittsburgh	W	10	—	148
Apr 12		Remo Fernandez	Detroit	W	10	—	147
May 29		Petey Mike	Brooklyn	KO	1	—	148
Jun 13	⑩	Charley Burley★	Pittsburgh	L	10	—	148
Jun 20		Ercole Buratti	Pittsburgh	KO	4	—	146
Jul 9		Eddie Conley	Walnut Beach, PA	KO	6	—	148
Jul 12		Phil Furr	Pittsburgh	TKO	3	—	145
Aug 2		Joe Lemieux	Newark, NJ	TKO	4	—	146
Aug 12		Joe Pennino	Coney Island, NY	W	8	—	146
Aug 22		Steve Kahley	Newark	KO	3	—	147
Aug 26		Mickey Paul	Long Beach, NY	KO	3	—	147
Sep 13		Bobby Pacho	Newark	W	10	—	148
Oct 3		Paul Cortlyn	Newark	KO	4	—	150
Oct 10		Jay Macedon	Newark	TKO	5	—	147
Oct 27		Salvy Saban	Pittsburgh	W	10	—	147
Nov 15		Frankie Blair	Brooklyn	W	8	—	150
Nov 21		Al Hamilton	Columbus, OH	KO	5	—	148

Date		Opponent	Location	Result	Rounds		Notes	Weight
Dec 7		Vincent Pimpinella	Pittsburgh	W	10	—		148
Dec 26		Howell King	Toledo, OH	ND-D	10	—		148

1939

Date		Opponent	Location	Result	Rounds		Notes	Weight
Jan 5		Al Costello	Columbus	KO	2	—		—
Jan 20		Jackie Burke	St. Louis	W	10	—		148
Feb 10		Eddie Booker	New York	W	8	—		136
Feb 15		Charlie Bell	Columbus	KO	3	—		145
Mar 20		Nick Pastore	Miami	KO	9	—		147
Mar 29		Bobby Britton	Miami	W	10	—		145
Apr 20		Tiger Kid Walker	St. Louis	KO	1	—		146
May 9		Kenny LaSalle	Houston	L	10	—		146
May 16		Al Traino	Rochester, NY	W	10	—		144
Jun 5		Kenny LaSalle	Pittsburgh	W	10	—		146
Jul 11		Jackie Burke	St. Louis	W	10	—		146
Jul 17	⑩	Charley Burley★	Pittsburgh	L	10	—		145
Sep 5		Pete DeRuzza	Pittsburgh	KO	6	—		148
Sep 12		Ralph Gizzy	Pittsburgh	KO	2	—		148
Oct 24		Kid Azteca	Houston	W	10	—		145
Oct 30		Milo Theodorescu	Pittsburgh	W	10	—		146
Nov 18		Billy Lancaster	Brooklyn	TKO	7	—		144
Dec 9		Wicky Harkins	Philadelphia	KO	9	—		—
Dec 27	⑩	Milt Aron	Chicago	KO'd	8	—		146

1940

Date		Opponent	Location	Result	Rounds		Notes	Weight
Jan 22	⑩	Mike Kaplan	Philadelphia	W	10	—		144
Feb 16		Remo Fernandez	Cleveland	TKO	7	—		—
Mar 4		Saverio Turiello	Philadelphia	KO	1	—		143
Mar 14		Johnny Barbara	Chicago	W	10	—		147
Apr 8		Johnny Barbara	Philadelphia	L	10	—		146
May 3		Mansfield Driskell	Detroit	W	10	—		149
May 7		Johnny Barbara	Philadelphia	L	10	—		146
May 21		Ossie Harris	Pittsburgh	KO	3	—		148
Jun 24		Johnny Rinaldi	Pittsburgh	KO	1	—		143
Jul 8		Ossie Harris	Pittsburgh	W	10	—		149
Jul 22		Leonard Bennett	Chicago	KO	4	—		150
Aug 5		Kenny LaSalle	Pittsburgh	W	10	—		147
Aug 28	⑩	Sammy Angott★	Pittsburgh	W	10	—		143
Oct 4	♛	Henry Armstrong★	New York	W	15	Won-World-W		145
Nov 15		Al Davis	New York	WD	2	—		147
Nov 26		Ronnie Beaudin	Buffalo, NY	KO	2	—		149
Dec 20		Lew Jenkins★	New York	D	10	—		142

1941

Date		Opponent	Location	Result	Rounds		Notes	Weight
Jan 17	⑩	Henry Armstrong★	New York	TKO	12	Ret-World-W		145
Mar 17		Saverio Turiello	Pittsburgh	W	10	—		149
Mar 20		Felix Garcia	Baltimore	KO	2	—		150
Apr 4		Dick Demeray	Minneapolis	KO	4	—		150
Apr 18	⑩	Mike Kaplan	Boston	L	10	—		148
May 2	⑩	Tony Marteliano	New York	W	10	—		149
Jul 2		Al Davis	New York	TKO	10	—		149
Jul 14		Johnny Barbara	Philadelphia	W	12	—		150
Jul 29	⑩	Freddie ("Red") Cochrane	Newark	L	15	Lost-World-W		145
Sep 15		Milt Aron	Pittsburgh	KO	5	—		147
Oct 31	⑩	Sugar Ray Robinson★	New York	L	10	—		145
Nov 26		Phil Furr	Washington, DC	W	10	—		149
Dec 1		Harry Weekly	Cleveland	TKO	9	—		143
Dec 12		Young Kid McCoy	New York	D	10	—		148

1942

Date		Opponent	Location	Result	Rounds		Weight
Jan 16	⑩	Sugar Ray Robinson★	New York	TKO'd	10	—	148
Feb 8		Raul Carabantes	Pittsburgh	W	10	—	148
Feb 27	⑩	Tony Motisi	Chicago	L	10	—	148
Mar 9	⑩	Izzy Jannazzo	Pittsburgh	TKO	5	—	151
Mar 30		Bill McDowell	Newark	TKO	6	—	147
Apr 13		Maxie Berger	Pittsburgh	W	10	—	149
Apr 23		Reuben Shank	Minneapolis	L	10	—	149
May 25	⑩	Lew Jenkins★	Pittsburgh	TKO	10	—	144
Jun 4		Reuben Shank	Minneapolis	W	10	—	148
Jun 22		Bobby Britton	Wilkes-Barre, PA	TKO	4	—	150
Jun 29	⑩	Norman Rubio	Newark	L	10	—	149
Jul 27	⑩	Norman Rubio	Pittsburgh	TKO	9	—	148
Aug 13		Garvey Young	New York	TKO	6	—	148
Sep 10		Freddie ("Red") Cochrane	New York	W	10	—	147
Sep 21		Johnny Walker	Philadelphia	W	10	—	146
Oct 13		Tito Taylor	Milwaukee	W	10	—	149
Oct 26	⑩	Henry Armstrong★	San Francisco	L	10	—	146
Nov 16	⑩	Richard ("Sheik") Rangel	San Francisco	L	10	—	149
Dec 15		Carmen Notch	Pittsburgh	W	10	—	150

1943

Date		Opponent	Location	Result	Rounds		Weight
Feb 5	♛	Beau Jack★	New York	L	10	—	145
Feb 16		Mayon Padlo	Pittsburgh	W	10	—	149
Mar 5	♛	Beau Jack★	New York	L	12	—	147
Apr 30		Johnny Roszina	Milwaukee	TKO	8	—	150
Jun 10	⑩	Jake LaMotta★	Pittsburgh	L	10	—	151
Jul 12	⑩	Jake LaMotta★	Pittsburgh	W	15	—	151
Aug 9		Young Kid McCoy	Pittsburgh	TKO	4	—	149
Aug 23	♛	Bob Montgomery★	Philadelphia	L	10	—	144
Sep 10		Vinnie Vines	New York	KO	1	—	151
Oct 15	⑩	Jose Basora	Detroit	L	10	—	150
Oct 29		Bobby Richardson	Chicago	W	10	—	149
Nov 12	⑩	Jake LaMotta★	New York	L	10	—	149
Dec 20	⑩	Ralph Zannelli	Boston	L	10	—	152

1944

Date		Opponent	Location	Result	Rounds		Weight
Jan 3		Ossie Harris	Pittsburgh	KO	10	—	152
Jan 14	⑩	Jake LaMotta★	Detroit	L	10	—	151
Mar 27		Harry Teaney	Milwaukee	W	10	—	149
Mar 29	⑩	Freddie Archer	Elizabeth, NJ	L	10	—	147
Jun 26	⑩	Tommy Bell	Pittsburgh	L	10	—	150
Aug 1		Pete DeRuzza	Houston	TKO	8	—	152
Sep 12		Felix Morales	San Antonio, TX	KO	2	—	152
Sep 26		Artie Dorrell	Galveston, TX	KO	7	—	152
Oct 16		Tommy Roman	Shreveport, LA	L	10	—	152
Oct 18		Pat Saia	Dallas	TKO	8	—	151
Nov 14		Chick Hirst	Houston	KO	5	—	152
Nov 29		Manuel Villa	Dallas	KO	6	—	156
Dec 12		Kid Azteca	San Antonio	W	10	—	151

1945

Date		Opponent	Location	Result	Rounds		Weight
Jan 5	⑩	Billy Arnold	New York	W	8	—	153
Feb 22		Kid Estrada	Camp Maxey, TX	KO	2	—	—
Mar 6		Bill McDowell	Galveston	W	10	—	152
Mar 22		Ben Evans	Galveston	KO	8	—	152
Apr 3		Manuel Villa	San Antonio	KO	8	—	152
May 7		Kid Azteca	San Antonio	W	10	—	155

Date		Opponent	Location	Result	Rounds		Weight
May 8		Pat Saia	Beaumont, TX	W	10	—	—
Jun 12		Baby Zavala	San Antonio	KO	4	—	152
Jun 22		Harold Green	New York	L	10	—	151
Jul 3		Reuben Shank	Pittsburgh	L	10	—	153
Jul 10		Ossie Harris	Pittsburgh	L	10	—	160
Jul 16		Bill McDowell	New Orleans	L	10	—	149
Sep 12		Paul Altman	Houston	L	10	—	152
Sep 18		Billy Deeg	Oklahoma City	W	10	—	150
Oct 20		Joe Reddick	Brooklyn	L	10	—	152
Nov 2	⑩	Freddie Archer	New York	L	10	—	153
Nov 13		Joe Curcio	Elizabeth, NJ	L	10	—	152
Dec 10		Cecil Hudson	New York	L	10	—	150
1946							
Jan 15	⑩	Al ("Red") Priest	Boston	L	10	—	151
Feb 1		O'Neill Bell	Detroit	L	10	—	149
Feb 25		Aaron Perry	Washington, DC	L	10	—	150
Mar 19		Levi Southall	Kansas City, MO	W	10	—	149
Mar 26		Tony Elizondo	San Antonio	L	10	—	147
Apr 5		Manuel Villa	El Paso, TX	D	10	—	—
Apr 12		Lincoln Stanley	Portland, OR	W	10	—	149
Apr 18		Don Lee	Hollywood	W	10	—	148
Apr 29		Howard Bleyhl	Omaha, NE	L	10	—	147
May 1		Joey Martinez	Wichita, KS	TKO	8	—	147
May 14	⑩	Jackie Wilson	Hollywood	L	10	—	144
May 27		Tommy Lemmon	Milwaukee	L	10	—	147
Oct 29		Russell Wilhite	Memphis, TN	TKO	5	—	146
Nov 12		Al Mobley	Trenton, NJ	L	8	—	146
Nov 18		Jimmy McGriff	Washington, DC	D	10	—	148
Dec 2		Ralph Zannelli	Providence, RI	L	10	—	148
Dec 6		Pete Mead	Grand Rapids, MI	L	10	—	150
Dec 10		Bobby Britton	Memphis	W	10	—	150
1947							
Jan 8		Clyde Gordon	Miami	L	10	—	146
Feb 15		Kid Azteca	Mexico City	KO'd	5	—	—
1948							
Oct 28		Eddie Steele	Macon, GA	D	10	—	150
1949							
Jan 12		Al Reid	Macon	W	10	—	146
Jan 17		Eddie Steele	Augusta, GA	W	10	—	146

welterweight championship held by Henry Armstrong. In a well-attended fight in Madison Square Garden, Zivic upset the heavily favored Armstrong. It was a close bout. Zivic withstood Armstrong's body blows and targeted his opponent's eyes, vulnerable from previous batterings, nearly closing them in the final rounds. In the last round, Zivic knocked down the exhausted Armstrong just before the ending bell.

Zivic won the rematch with Armstrong with a TKO in twelve but lost his title to Red Cochrane in 1941. Though he continued to fight for eight years, he never received another chance to fight for the title. Zivic's reputation for hitting low while hitting high to distract the referee, grinding his laces into cuts or just worrying ring wounds until they became serious seemed to enhance rather than diminish his appeal as a ring hero. He was well liked by the sporting world and later enjoyed a reputation as an entertaining after-dinner speaker.

BOXING AT THE
MOVIES

Since the beginning of motion pictures, the sport of boxing has been one of the cinema's favorite subjects. In 1894, Thomas Edison set up a kinetograph in his West Orange, New Jersey, laboratory and then filmed heavyweight champion James J. Corbett in an exhibition match. Since then, boxing has been featured in documentaries, dramas, and comedies—both full-length movies and shorts—and many real-life boxers have starred in films about non-boxing subjects.

In many ways, this marriage of pugilism and cinema is a match made in heaven. The inherent drama of flying fists in "mano a mano" combat coupled with the small and easy-to-film ring make boxing a natural for the big screen. Of course, boxing's often-sordid reputation is another draw for filmmakers, who have made many pictures about fixed fights and broken fighters. The colorful lives of many real-life boxers are readily transferable to film. John L. Sullivan, James Braddock, Jake LaMotta, Joe Louis, and Muhammad Ali all led fascinating lives, and possessed a ready-made fan base that flocked to movies about their heroes.

While most boxing movies are fictional, the earliest significant ring films were recordings of actual fights. Even though boxing was illegal in many jurisdictions, showing filmed matches, legally held elsewhere, was not. Thus, in the first decade of the 1900s boxing films took the place of live legal matches in some parts of the country. These screen displays of boxing helped maintain popular interest in the sport and provided a source of additional revenue for the boxing community. Before long, however, moralist opponents to boxing and parties motivated by racism formed a coalition with groups such as the United Society of Christian Endeavor, the Anti-Saloon League of America, and the California Federation of Women's Clubs to lobby state legislatures to ban movie house showings of the 1910 Jack Johnson–James Jeffries fight. Among their concerns was the fear that blacks would riot against whites if they witnessed Johnson's victory.

Soon, at least fifteen states and the District of Columbia passed laws prohibiting the showing of all films of prizefights. In 1912, Congress passed a law banning the transportation of fight films in interstate commerce for the purpose of public exhibition. The next ten years saw many violations of the new law, and enforcement was spotty at best. In 1927, a federal judge instructed a jury that transportation of a film was different from the actual screening of a film, which was regulated by state—not federal—law. Finally, in 1940, Congress repealed its earlier law outlawing the interstate shipment of boxing films.

It is, however, the fictionalized biographies of boxers, rather than films of actual fights, that have etched the deepest mark in cinematic history. One of the most successful boxing biographies was *Gentleman Jim,* a 1942 movie about James J. Corbett, starring Errol Flynn. Great pains were taken to film realistic fight scenes, with Hall of Famer Freddie Steele doubling for Flynn.

Wallace Beery and Jackie Cooper in The Champ *(1931).*

Three years later, John L. Sullivan was the focus of *The Great John L.,* which starred Greg McClure and featured Rory Calhoun as Corbett. Another accomplished boxing film was the now-seldom-seen *Joe Louis Story* (1953), which starred Coley Wallace. A movie with an almost-all-black cast, it avoided the patronizing depiction of African Americans typical of that era. Footage of some of Louis's actual fights was interwoven with staged segments. Then there was the 1957 film *Monkey on My Back,* a dramatization of Hall of Famer Barney Ross's life. The movie covered Ross's boxing career, WWII heroics, and fight against drug addiction.

Hall of Famer Rocky Graziano's autobiography of his rise from the New York slums to the world middleweight championship was captured on film in *Somebody Up There Likes Me* (1956). James Dean was originally slated to play the part of Graziano, but the role went to Paul Newman, instead, who gave a fine performance in an early starring role. Sal Mineo and Steve McQueen also appeared in the film.

Perhaps the greatest boxing movie of all time and one of the best sports films ever is *Raging Bull* (1980), directed by Martin Scorsese. Based on Hall of Famer Jake LaMotta's autobiography, the graphically violent film led to Robert DeNiro's best actor Academy Award for his portrayal of LaMotta.

More recently, Denzel Washington starred as boxer Rubin ("Hurricane") Carter in *The Hurricane* (1999), the story of the middleweight who spent years in prison for a crime he did not commit. In 2001, the movie *Ali* was released to favorable reviews and garnered an Oscar nomination for Will Smith's portrayal of Muhammad Ali and for Jon Voight's supporting role as Howard Cosell. (Voight also starred in two earlier boxing films, *The All American Boy* in 1973 and the 1979 version of *The Champ.*) Other fine boxing movies include *Body and Soul, The Harder They Fall, The Set-Up, Fat City,* the original *Kid Galahad,* and *The Milky Way.*

Though few of them emerged as great actors, actual boxers have appeared in many movies throughout the years. Muhammad Ali starred as himself in the often-fanciful story of his life up until 1977, *The Greatest,* and appeared in the 1981 version of *Body and Soul.* He also had a brief role in *Requiem for a Heavyweight* (1962), an excellent film starring Anthony Quinn as the over-the-hill boxer Mountain Rivera. After he fails to lose a fight to a boxer played by Ali, Rivera is forced to humiliate himself to save the life of his manager, played by Jackie Gleason. Mickey Rooney turned in a fine performance as Rivera's trainer, while Jack Dempsey, Barney Ross, Arthur Mercante, and Willie Pep all appeared in the movie as well.

Hall of Famer Max Baer had a successful acting career that included a starring role in *The Prizefighter and the Lady* (1933) with Myrna Loy. In the film's climactic scene, Baer rose from the canvas to fight a draw with Primo Carnera, who played himself. Carnera refused to be defeated on film, though in real life Baer knocked him out in their 1934 championship fight. Dempsey, James J. Jeffries, and former heavyweight champion Jess Willard all played themselves in the movie.

Billy Conn, Joe Louis, Maxie Rosenbloom, Tony Zale, Archie Moore, Joe Frazier, Jersey Joe Walcott, Jose Torres, and Sugar Ray Robinson are among the numerous fighters who dabbled in film at some point in their careers.

Like Paul Newman in *Somebody Up There Likes Me,* actors' careers have been jump-started by roles in boxing movies. In *Golden Boy* (1939), based on a play by Clifford Odets, William Holden had his first major role as an excellent but impoverished violinist who enters the ring to make some money. A talented boxer, Holden's character worries about injuring his hands and ending the violin career his father always wanted for him. The 1949 film *Champion* launched Kirk Douglas. Douglas earned an Academy Award nomination for his portrayal of a boxer who climbs to the top of the middleweight ranks only to become a tool of a crime syndicate.

Any list of career-making boxing movies would be incomplete without *Rocky,* the story of a Philadelphia club fighter who gets a shot at the world championship held by Apollo Creed (Carl Weathers). *Rocky* won Oscars for best picture, best director, and best editing, spawned four sequels, and made its leading actor and screenwriter, Sylvester Stallone, into a world-famous superstar.

Other famous names that starred in boxing movies include some of Hollywood's best and brightest stars, like John Garfield, James Cagney, Robert Taylor, Tony Curtis, James Earl Jones, Humphrey Bogart, Danny Kaye, Elvis Presley, Douglas Fairbanks Jr., Barbra Streisand, and Robert Ryan.

Rocky and *Raging Bull* were not the only boxing films to capture Academy Awards. In 1996, *When We Were Kings* won best documentary feature for its account of the famous "Rumble in the Jungle" in 1974, the fight where Ali reclaimed his

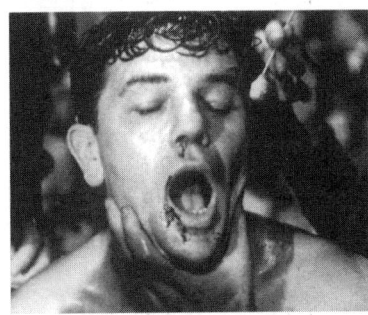

heavyweight championship by knocking out George Foreman. *Here Comes Mr. Jordan*, a 1941 flight of fancy about a boxer who dies before his time and is temporarily returned to earth to win the heavyweight championship, won for best original story and best screenplay. An earlier movie, *The Champ* (1931), won for best original story as well, and garnered its star, Wallace Beery, a statue for best actor.

John Garfield in Body and Soul *(1947).*

More recently, the film *Million Dollar Baby* won four Academy Awards in 2004. Based on short stories collected in the book *Rope Burns* by Jerry Boyd (pen name F.X. Toole), *Million Dollar Baby* told of a hard-boiled veteran trainer who takes a female boxer under his wing. Clint Eastwood both directed and starred in the movie and earned an Oscar for Best Director. Hilary Swank played the boxer and received an Academy Award for Best Performance by an Actress in a Leading Role. Morgan Freeman played Eastwood's assistant and friend and won a Best Supporting Actor Academy Award. The movie itself won the coveted Best Picture Academy Award.

Boxing was again the subject of a respected film treatment in 2005. *Cinderella Man*, the story of Hall of Famer James J. Braddock, was very well-received. Russell Crowe starred as Braddock. The movie earned three Academy Award nominations for Best Achievement in Editing, Best Achievement in Makeup, and Best Supporting Actor—Paul Giamatti who played the part of Braddock's manager, Joe Gould.

Perhaps emboldened by the success of *Million Dollar Baby* and *Cinderella Man*, noted director Spike Lee is currently seeking financing for a movie based on a screenplay he wrote with Hall of Famer Budd Schulberg concerning the lives of heavyweight champions Joe Louis and Max Schmeling.

From the early raw footage of real bouts to the masterful Academy Award–winning boxing dramas, no other sport has been so regularly, faithfully, and powerfully depicted in American cinema.

THE
NON-COMBATANTS
Boxing's Supporting Cast

THE ATTENTION OF MOST boxing fans is, of course, focused on the combatants in the ring, but the sport could never have achieved its success and visibility without a host of behind-the-scenes personalities. The International Boxing Hall of Fame honors the contributions of such individuals in a section titled "Non-Participants." These inductees include promoters, matchmakers, managers, trainers, patrons, referees, writers, and broadcasters. In contrast to the Hall's other inductees, non-combatant members do not have to be retired before they are honored.

The stories of these important figures in boxing, some of whom started their careers as fighters, are integral to the rich history of the sport.

THOMAS S. ANDREWS
Writer and Publisher

A successful boxing promoter in Milwaukee, Thomas S. Andrews made his greatest contributions to the sport through his writing and publishing efforts. Andrews's books were invaluable resources for boxing devotees and participants in the early decades of the twentieth century. He edited and published *T.S. Andrews' World Sporting Annual* from 1903 through 1938. This publication, which covered all sports but featured boxing, included complete lists of champions, cumulative records, and other boxing information. Andrews also wrote a record book of boxing from its earliest beginnings. Titled *Ring Battles of the Centuries,* it was first published in 1914. Andrews was involved with other aspects of boxing as well. When the National Boxing Association (NBA) was organized in 1904, he was elected the first secretary-treasurer. He was also the first matchmaker at the Olympic Auditorium in Los Angeles. He died in 1941 at the age of 72. Hall of Fame Induction: 1992.

RAY ARCEL
Trainer

One of the most respected men in the history of boxing, Ray Arcel trained a record twenty world champions. Born in Terre Haute, Indiana, on August 30, in 1899, Arcel grew up in a tough New York City neighborhood.

He learned his trade from Frank ("Doc") Bagley, who once managed Gene Tunney, and from Dai Dolling, who handled Harry Wills, Jack Britton, and Johnny Dundee. In 1923, Arcel developed his first champion, flyweight Frankie Genaro. In 1925, he helped bantamweight Charley Phil Rosenberg lose 37 pounds in three months in preparation for a winning title fight. From 1925 to 1934, Arcel worked in partnership with a fellow Hall of Famer, trainer Whitey Bimstein. Among the champions Arcel and Bimstein handled were Jackie ("Kid") Berg, Lou Brouillard, and Sixto Escobar. Arcel also worked with Barney Ross, and managed and trained his early idol, Benny Leonard, in a comeback try.

Arcel first handled a heavyweight champion when he trained James J. Braddock for his bout with Joe Louis, which Braddock lost. Over the next several years, Arcel trained fourteen Louis opponents before producing one who could beat the Brown Bomber. In 1950, Arcel and Ezzard Charles—who won a decision over Louis—ended the parade which had come to be called "The Meat Wagon." During this period, Arcel also guided many fighters in lower weight classes to championships. The list includes Tony Marino, Ceferino Garcia, Billy Soose, and Tony Zale.

In the early fifties, Arcel apparently ran afoul of organized crime after arranging fights for the ABC television network. The matches competed with other network television fights run by the International Boxing Club (IBC), reputed to have underworld ties. In September 1953, in front of a Boston hotel, Arcel was struck on the head with a lead pipe. Many believed that the assault was related to his work in television. Arcel recovered but dropped out of boxing soon after the incident.

Not until the early seventies did Arcel return. He trained Peppermint Frazier for a title bid, then began an eight-year association with Roberto Duran, seeing Duran to a win in his first meeting with Sugar Ray Leonard. Arcel broke with Duran following the second match with Leonard in 1980, when Duran uttered his famous "no mas" and quit the fight.

Arcel capped his career with three years of work with Larry Holmes, training him for his title defense against Gerry Cooney in 1982. For that fight, Arcel teamed with Eddie Futch. He then retired but continued to follow boxing and to comment on the sport until his death on March 6, 1994. Arcel trained over 2,000 boxers and won the admiration and respect of his fighters, his peers, and the media. Hall of Fame Induction: 1991.

BOB ARUM
Promoter

There was nothing in the first 35 years of Bob Arum's life that hinted at his future as one of boxing's greatest promoters and a Hall of Fame inductee. Born in Brooklyn on December 8, 1931, Arum was the son of orthodox Jewish parents. He graduated from New York University in 1953 and then studied law at Harvard, where he graduated cum laude in 1956. Arum served in the tax division of the United States Department of Justice under Attorney Generals Robert F. Kennedy and Robert Morgenthau from 1961 to 1965. In 1962, he was assigned to investigate allegations that part of the proceeds of the Sonny Liston–Floyd Patterson fight in Chicago were sneaked out of the country to avoid taxes. Thus, through a criminal investigation, Arum first became acquainted with many of boxing's leading figures.

Arum's next brush with the boxing world came when he recommended to a client that he hire a black commentator to support flagging ticket sales for the Ernie Terrell–George Chuvalo heavyweight bout. The client hired football great Jim Brown, and it was Brown who introduced Arum to Muhammad Ali. This additional contact with boxing inspired Arum to found a fight promotion company, Main Bouts, Inc. Surprisingly, he had never even seen a boxing match until he promoted Ali–Chuvalo in March 1966. He promoted many more Ali fights, including bouts against Henry Cooper, Brian London, Karl Mildenberger, Cleveland Williams, and Terrell. When Ali lost his boxing license for refusing to enter the army, Arum assisted with his legal defense.

In 1970, Arum formed Top Rank, Inc., and to this day he continues to promote under the Top Rank banner. Though initially known for his association with Ali, he branched out to promote many other contests in all weight classes. Arum has promoted over 1,000 cards, including 27 fights featuring Ali, 20 with Marvelous Marvin Hagler, and 14 with George Foreman. Indeed, some of the best-known and highest-grossing fights of the last 35 years have been promoted by Arum, including Hagler–Sugar Ray Leonard, Hagler–Thomas Hearns, Leonard–Roberto Duran I, Foreman–Evander Holyfield, Foreman–Moorer, Ali–Joe Frazier II, and both Ali–Leon Spinks bouts. More recently, Arum promoted fan favorite and multiple-title-holder Oscar De La Hoya.

Arum has long appreciated the role of pay-per-view, closed circuit, and cable television in the sport and is savvy at using these media to his advantage. In 1980, he initiated a long-running and profitable association between ESPN and Top Rank.

"My essential strength as a promoter," Arum told *KO Magazine*, "is that I'm a good administrator. I'm also able to run a promotion in a dispassionate manner. And there's no great trick in selling a fight to a network or cable system. What really calls on one's ability is the big closed-circuit and pay-per-view fights. That's what I specialize in."

In recent years, Arum has taken a stance in favor of open scoring. Although some boxing enthusiasts like the suspense inherent in the present system, he believes that fairer scoring will be achieved if judges' cards were displayed as a bout progressed.

In his long career, Arum has had his share of legal battles, many of them with his rival Don King. At the racketeering trial of former International Boxing Federation president Bob Lee, Arum admitted that he made improper payments to encourage the IBF to sanction one of his fights.

Still one of the top promoters, he currently promotes Floyd Mayweather, Jr., Jose Luis Castillo, Martin Castillo, Miguel Cotto, Erik Morales, and Hasim Rahman. Hall of Fame Induction: 1999.

JARVIS ASTAIRE
Promoter and Manager

Few members of the International Boxing Hall of Fame have been involved in as many enterprises as Jarvis Astaire. Astaire was born in England on October 6, 1923. His father made a good living making women's hats. Astaire started in pharmaceuticals and the surgical instrument business at the age of nineteen. At about the same time, he promoted his first professional boxing tournament. Astaire then went into the men's outfitting business before selling that venture. With a partner, Astaire began investing in real estate. Astaire and his partner also purchased Mappin and Webb, a retail purveyor of jewelry dating back to 1774, before selling that concern. Astaire branched out into merchant banking, bookmaking shops (legal in England), golf driving ranges, pool halls, racehorses, and professional wrestling. He even made a name for himself in show business as both the business manager of actor Dustin Hoffman and as a movie producer.

In boxing, Astaire became one of the most prominent figures in the sport in England. He managed former world middleweight champion Terry Downes and other pugilists. In the 1960s Astaire served as the co-promoter of the Muhammad Ali–Henry Cooper and Ali–Karl Mildenberger heavyweight championship fights. Through his company, Viewsport, Astaire showed many fights on closed circuit television in England. Viewsport also aired English soccer games and the Super Bowl. Astaire also served as a director of Wembley PLC, which owned Wembley Stadium, perhaps the world's preeminent soccer venue.

In all his dealings, Astaire was a refined, debonair gentleman, the likes of which are not often found in the fight game. Astaire appeared as if he would be more at home at a high society charity event than in a sweaty boxing gym. In fact, Astaire received an Order of the British Empire for his many charitable activities in the New Year's honors list of 2004. Hall of Fame Induction: 2006.

GIUSEPPE BALLARATI
Publisher and Historian

While virtually unknown in the United States, Giuseppe Ballarati established a reputation as the preeminent boxing historian and publisher in continental Europe. Born in Italy in 1919, Ballarati began his career in boxing as a fighter in 1937. He fought for a time as a bantamweight, then eventually turned to managing fighters. Although he worked with many contenders, none of his charges ever won a world title.

However, it is not for fighting or managing that Ballarati is a Hall of Famer. Ballarati compiled *La Bibbia del Pugilato*, a compendium of boxing records and statistics akin to *The Ring Record Book,* first published in 1962 and subsequently published annually for the next three decades. He also published a series of books about the sport's all-time greats, which translates to *Champions of the Past.*

A boxing purist, Ballarati was extremely concerned about the proliferation of sanctioning bodies. Hall of Fame Induction: 1999.

GEORGE BENTON
Trainer

Using the knowledge he gained during his twenty years as a professional boxer, George Benton became one of the sport's top trainers. Born on May 15, 1933, in Philadelphia, Benton became interested in boxing at an early age. He frequented a gym run by Joe Rose, and at the age of twelve or thirteen was left in charge of the gym when Rose was away. He was an active amateur boxer at age fourteen and turned professional at sixteen, establishing a record of 30-2-1 before joining the army at 23. The highlight of Benton's early career was a victory over future middleweight contender Holly Mims in 1952. He resumed his career after leaving the army and in 1962 was rated by *The Ring* as the third-best middleweight contender. That year he decisioned Hall of Famer Joey Giardello.

Known as a stylish, clever boxer with a strong punch, Benton never fought for a middleweight title. In part, this was because the champions avoided him, but he also lost key fights to Willie Dockery in 1958 and to Rubin ("Hurricane") Carter in 1963—bouts which could have been a springboard to capturing the title. Benton continued fighting until 1970. In addition to his victory over Giardello, he defeated Freddie Little and Jimmy Ellis, who both held world titles at one time, and compiled a record of 61-13-1, with 36 knockouts. Benton was still an active fighter when he was shot on a Philadelphia street by a man who had a beef with one of Benton's brothers.

Unable to fight again, Benton spent a short time as a numbers writer. He then worked with a few fighters before being hired by Joe Frazier to train fighters in his gym when Eddie Futch was unavailable. Benton added to his ring knowledge—especially the psychological aspects of training—by working with Futch.

Benton came to prominence as a trainer when his fighter, Leon Spinks, upset Muhammad Ali to win the heavyweight title. Benton counseled Spinks to stay on top of Ali and jab at his left shoulder to prevent Ali from throwing his own jab in the later rounds. However, after Spinks won the championship, his camp froze Benton out until shortly before the Spinks–Ali rematch. Because he wasn't permitted to speak with Spinks after each round, Benton left the arena in disgust before the end of the fight in which Ali was victorious.

In the '80s, Benton began working for managers Shelly Finkel and Lou Duva. After the 1984 Olympics, he and Duva took control of the professional careers of U.S. Olympic team members Evander Holyfield, Meldrick Taylor, and Pernell ("Sweetpea") Whitaker. The three went on to become champions and household names in boxing. When Holyfield took the heavyweight title from Buster Douglas, Benton was working the corner.

Hall of Famer Duva and Benton managed and trained seventeen champions before Benton, dubbed "The Professor" for his knowledge and teaching ability, broke with the Duva family Main Events, Inc. enterprise. After his departure from Main Events, Benton worked with fighters, including Mike McCallum, Rocky Lockridge, and Michael Moorer.

Benton graciously acknowledged Lou Duva's role in his success in his Hall of Fame induction speech. A two-time recipient of the John F.X. Condon Award for the Trainer of the Year, Benton is now in semiretirement. Hall of Fame Induction: 2001.

WHITEY BIMSTEIN
Trainer and Cut Man

One of the legendary trainers, seconds, and cut men in boxing history, Morris ("Whitey") Bimstein worked either with or against virtually every well-known fighter from the 1920s until the 1960s. He was born on the Lower East Side of Manhattan. Bimstein hadn't much enthusiasm for education and quit after he graduated from grammar school in 1910. After his father moved the family to the Bronx to get Bimstein away from his tough crowd of friends, Bimstein took boxing lessons from a priest, Father Ryan, at a Bronx church named St. Jerome's.

Bimstein boxed professionally under the name Johnny White and had about 70 fights. He hated training, disdained roadwork, and overindulged on hot dogs and other unhealthy foods. When it dawned on him that not only wasn't he making any money but he was getting hit as well, Bimstein hung up his gloves. He then served in the U.S. Navy during World War I as a boxing instructor. After leaving the Navy, Bimstein decided to learn to become a trainer and cut man. He hung around gyms and made himself useful in various ways: drying fighters after workouts, carrying their bags, buying tape and bandages, or doing whatever was needed. As he performed these menial tasks, Bimstein gained the knowledge and experience he needed to train a fighter and work in his corner.

In 1925, Bimstein formed a partnership with fellow Hall of Famer Ray Arcel. For nine years the two worked together training fighters. Sometimes two prizefighters in their stable were matched against one another. Then Arcel and Bimstein would flip a coin to decide who would work in which fighter's corner. In addition to becoming a fine trainer, Bimstein became known as an incredibly gifted cut man. He learned this craft from trainer Doc Bagley. Bimstein became known as a magician with the swabs—which could be seen protruding from his mouth while he worked in a corner—and with various ointments and chemical substances he used on his fighters. Countless times, he was able to keep a fight from being stopped due to excessive bleeding or a closed eye.

Some of the fighters who benefited from Bimstein's expertise were Gene Tunney, Harry Greb, Georges Carpentier, Benny Leonard, Lou Ambers, James J. Braddock, Barney Ross, Billy Graham, Bobo Olson, Ingemar Johansson, and Fred Apostoli. The total number of fighters with whom he worked is staggering. Bimstein was in Tunney's corner when he first beat Jack Dempsey for the heavyweight title and was in Braddock's corner when Braddock defeated Max Baer to triumph in his unlikely run at the heavyweight title. He also was in Johansson's corner when he beat Floyd Patterson to take the heavyweight crown.

Bimstein ended his partnership with Arcel in 1934 because of the financial pressures of the Depression, but he continued to be in demand as a trainer and second. On September 23, 1937, at the famed Carnival of Champions promotion by Mike Jacobs at the Polo Grounds, Bimstein was in the corner for four of the fighters: Ambers, Ross, Apostoli, and Sixto Escobar. After World War II, he entered into another training partnership with Freddie Brown. While the pair had a large stable of fighters, Bimstein continued to be in wide demand as a second and cut man. He worked in Rocky Marciano's corner when Marciano suffered a split nose during a title fight with Ezzard Charles. Perhaps his greatest achievement in a corner was patching up his charge, Rocky Graziano, between the third and fourth round of the second Graziano–Tony Zale fight. In the minute between rounds, Bimstein lanced and drained Graziano's closed right eye and then went to work on Graziano's upper left eyelid, which was split open. The physician in attendance at ringside allowed the fight to continue because he was so impressed with the work Bimstein did. Graziano went on to record a knockout in the sixth round.

Bimstein always had his fighters' welfare in mind and was known to help many a down-on-his-luck ex-pug. Notwithstanding his concern for his boxers, Bimstein employed some unorthodox methods as a second, such as pricking a fighter with a pin to get him going. Once, when Apostoli came back to his corner during a fight with Melio Bettina and claimed he had no energy, Bimstein hit him in the head. The punch had the desired effect as Apostoli went on to defeat Bettina.

Bimstein was a favorite of writers such as A.J. Liebling who profiled Bimstein in *The New Yorker*. He continued to serve as a trainer and corner man until health problems related to diabetes prevented him from working. He died in 1969 in New York at the age of 72. Hall of Fame Induction: 2006.

JACK BLACKBURN
Trainer

Jack Blackburn had a fine career as a fighter but is honored in the Hall of Fame for his even greater achievement as the trainer of Joe Louis. Born in Versailles, Kentucky, in 1883, Blackburn was the son of a minister. He moved with his family to Terre Haute, Indiana, where he first began boxing, then headed to Pittsburgh and Philadelphia to continue his ring career. He was quick, had a fine jab and a powerful left hook, and though he weighed only 135 pounds, often fought much larger men. He made good showings against such greats as Joe Gans and Sam Langford (who outweighed him by 45 pounds), and he gave Philadelphia Jack O'Brien all he could handle in a no-decision bout in 1908.

In January 1909, Blackburn's career was derailed when he went on a shooting spree in Philadelphia. In the midst of an argument, he killed three people, including his wife. He was convicted of manslaughter and sentenced to ten to fifteen years in prison. Blackburn, who gave boxing lessons to the warden and his children, was released on good behavior after four years and eight months.

Blackburn returned to professional boxing, taking on opponents such as Ed ("Gunboat") Smith and Harry Greb. He retired from fighting in 1923 after losing by knockout to Panama Joe Gans and Ray Pelkey. Blackburn posted an official career record of 38-3-12 with 50 no-decisions. He claimed to have fought 385 times.

Blackburn then became a trainer and guided weak puncher Sammy Mandell to the lightweight title in 1926. He also trained Bud Taylor, who won the bantamweight title in 1927, and worked briefly with Jersey Joe Walcott in Philadelphia.

Blackburn at first expressed skepticism about Joe Louis, predicting that a black heavyweight would not have many opportunities. Nevertheless, Blackburn worked tirelessly with Louis, schooling him on every aspect of fighting, such as balance, stepping forward when throwing a punch, and hitting with accuracy. According to Hall of Fame trainer Eddie Futch, Blackburn changed Louis from a "box and move" type to a more aggressive fighter. Though Blackburn was tough on Louis, the two grew close and called each other "Chappie." Louis later said, "Chappie made a fighter out of me. He was my closest friend."

Blackburn had problems with drinking and with arthritis during the time he trained Louis. His health deteriorated and, in 1942, he died. Hall of Fame Induction: 1992.

WILLIAM A. BRADY
Manager and Promoter

A showman of the stage and the ring, William A. Brady managed two heavy-weight champions, James J. Corbett and James J. Jeffries. Brady was born in San Francisco on June 19, 1863. While still a boy, he went to work as a candy seller for the Union Pacific. His success in attracting passengers to buy his wares led him to try a career in the theater, first as an actor, then as a stage manager, and eventually as a producer in New York City.

Brady first hired up-and-coming heavyweight James J. Corbett as an actor but quickly took on the job of managing Corbett's fighting career. After seeing him box an exhibition with John L. Sullivan, Brady was convinced that his charge had a very promising future. He commissioned Charles T. Vincent to write a play about a genteel prizefighter called "Gentleman Jack," in which Corbett was to have the starring role. To generate more publicity for Corbett, Brady pitted him against three opponents on the same night. Corbett knocked out the first two and outboxed the third.

Brady arranged a Corbett–Sullivan bout, littering New York with posters that heralded the appearance of the "new champion Corbett" at the New York Garden the week after the fight. Corbett did in fact defeat Sullivan, and "Gentleman Jack" was a big hit at the box office. After Bob Fitzsimmons defeated Corbett, Brady amicably ended his association with the deposed champion.

Two years later, Brady returned to boxing as the manager of Corbett's former sparring partner, James J. Jeffries. Brady leased the Bauer Pavilion at Coney Island to stage a championship bout between Jeffries and Fitzsimmons. Jeffries won, and Brady had his second world champion. But Brady's efforts to parlay Jeffries' victory into a theatrical tour did not prove as big a hit as his earlier venture with Corbett.

Brady was very successful in the theater, producing more than 260 plays. He also participated in the nascent motion picture industry and, with Thomas Edison, staged an 1884 Corbett–Peter Cortney bout that was filmed for the Kineograph Company and widely distributed. From 1915 to 1922, Brady was head of the National Association of the Motion Picture Industry. In 1937, his daughter, Alice Brady, won an Academy Award for best supporting actress for her role in *Old Chicago*.

Brady died of heart failure on January 6, 1950. Hall of Fame Induction: 1998.

UMBERTO BRANCHINI
Manager

One of the greatest boxing managers of continental Europe, Umberto Branchini managed eleven world champions and 43 European champions in a career that spanned over 50 years. Branchini was born on July 17, 1914, in Modena, Italy. His family was very prominent in horse racing in Italy, and Branchini was also enormously interested in that sport. He was known as "The Cardinal" for his competence, ring knowledge, and good nature. In boxing, a sport with more than its share of dishonest characters, Branchini was much admired for his honesty and integrity. Though based in Italy, Branchini managed and sometimes trained and seconded boxers from all over the world. His career was at its zenith in the 1960s and '70s. Champions he managed included light heavyweight

Miguel Angel Cuello, super welterweight Rocky Mattioli, flyweight Chartchai Chionoi, and heavyweight Francesco Damiani. One of Branchini's more colorful fighters was the Basque heavyweight Jose Manuel Ibar Azpiazu who was known as Urtain—El Tigre de Cestona. Urtain was a hero in Spain's Basque country, entering the ring after excelling in the regionally popular strongman sport of rock lifting.

Branchini also promoted boxing matches in Italy. Title bouts he promoted included: Rocky Lockridge–Kamel Bou-Ali (WBA junior lightweight title) and Daniel Zaragoza–Valerio Nati (WBC super bantamweight title).

Branchini died in March 1997. Hall of Fame Induction: 2004.

TEDDY BRENNER
Matchmaker

Teddy Brenner made matches based on two guidelines: Would he buy a ticket, and was the public interested? This standard did not always endear him to managers who wanted their fighters to go up against easy competition, but it made for hundreds of exciting fights that fans willingly paid to see. Surviving boxing's power struggles and unsavory influences, Brenner arranged matches not only for greats such as Muhammad Ali and Sugar Ray Robinson, but also for tyros in whom he saw championship potential.

Born in New York, Brenner got his start in boxing after World War II, arranging fights in New Brunswick, New Jersey, for his close friend Irving Cohen. In 1947, Brenner began his off-and-on association with Madison Square Garden, working as an assistant matchmaker. When the Garden lost its booking rights in a dispute with the Boxing Managers' Guild, Brenner moved to Laurel Gardens in Newark, New Jersey, as a promoter. When the International Boxing Club (IBC) took over promotion at Madison Square Garden, Brenner returned there to work as assistant matchmaker to Al Weill. He booked preliminary matches at the Garden and cards at St. Nicholas Arena, also in New York. In 1950, Brenner left the IBC, alleging Weill had ordered him to make a match for a fixed fight.

Brenner ran operations at the Coney Island Velodrome and also worked for the Long Beach Stadium in New York. In 1952, he became the matchmaker for the Eastern Parkway Arena in Brooklyn, site of the Dumont television network's broadcasts of Monday night fights. This arena became famous as the "House of Upsets" because of Brenner's good, even matches. It was here that Brenner gave Floyd Patterson and Gene Fullmer their first national exposure. Fifty-seven of the 156 television bouts made by Brenner at Eastern Parkway were later booked by the IBC as return matches in Madison Square Garden.

By 1955, Eastern Parkway was struggling with declining television ratings, and Brenner moved to St. Nicholas Arena for four years. In 1959, with the breakup of the IBC, Brenner moved back to Madison Square Garden, where he stayed as matchmaker for fourteen years. His bookings included Muhammad Ali's first fights in New York, the first fights in the new Madison Square Garden, the first Ali–Frazier meeting, Roberto Duran's first bout in the United States, and George Foreman's first fights.

In 1973, when Harry Markson retired, Brenner assumed the presidency of Madison Square Garden Boxing, Inc. His boss, Sonny Werblin, fired him in 1978 because Werblin wanted to do business with Don King. In 1980, Brenner joined Bob Arum's Top Rank, Inc., where he stayed as an advisor after retiring from full-time matchmaking. He died January 7, 2000 at age 82. Hall of Fame Induction: 1993.

LESTER BROMBERG
Writer

Lester Bromberg was one of the nation's finest boxing writers, but boxing played only a part in his long and successful career in journalism. Born in Brooklyn on March 12, 1909, Bromberg reported for the *Brooklyn Eagle* after graduating from high school, assigned to the city news beat. He next joined the *New York Post*, where he was scholastic sports editor for three years before moving to the *New York World Telegram*. There, he covered high school athletics for another seven years before he became the paper's boxing writer. By the early 1950s, Bromberg was one of only three full-time boxing writers in New York, and his lengthy career spanned countless world title bouts, beginning with the second Louis–Schmeling fight in 1938. After 35 years at the *World Telegram*, he moved his columns to the *New York Post*.

In addition to writing his regular columns, Bromberg wrote two books on boxing, *World's Champs* in 1958 and *Boxing's Unforgettable Fights* in 1962. He also wrote articles on the sport for numerous publications like *Sport* and *The Saturday Evening Post*. Boxing historian Herbert G. Goldman said, "The late Mr. Bromberg, who covered the fight game extensively for many, many years, was so knee-deep in the business and happenings of boxing that he was probably one of the last of the real day-to-day information diggers among the boxing journalists." Well regarded in the fighting world, Bromberg also achieved legendary status as a gourmand, once consuming a 113-ounce steak in a single sitting! In retirement, Bromberg continued to write freelance articles on boxing. He died February 21, 1989. Hall of Fame Induction: 2001.

JIMMY CANNON
Journalist

Jimmy Cannon was one of the most respected sports columnists in the United States in the post-World War II period, writing with a distinctive flair and an abiding respect for the athletes he covered.

Cannon was born in 1910 in Greenwich Village. He left school in ninth grade for a job as a copy boy with the *New York Daily News*, and he remained a newspaperman for the rest of his life. Writing dispatches on the Lindbergh kidnapping trial, Cannon attracted the attention of Damon Runyon, who advised him to write sports and helped him get a job with a Hearst newspaper. Like Runyon, Cannon was attracted to the bookies, gamblers, and talent agents who frequented New York's nightspots. In his reports from the front as a correspondent for *Stars and Stripes* during the war, Cannon developed his signature style—what David Remnick described in *King of the World* as "florid, sentimental prose with an underpinning of hard-bitten wisdom, and urban style that he had picked up in candy stores and nightclubs and from Runyon, Ben Hecht, and Westbrook Pegler."

After the war, Cannon became a sports columnist for the *New York Post*, under the title "Jimmy Cannon Says." He frequently wrote about boxing, and penned the memorable line that Joe Louis was "a credit to his race: the human race." He often wrote columns entitled "Nobody Asked Me, But…" in which he would string together a series of seemingly random observations, a style of writing still popular among news columnists today.

In 1959, Cannon moved to the New York *Journal American,* but he also wrote for *PM* and his column was syndicated by King Features and Hearst—the first $1,000-a-week columnist. Cannon wrote often about corruption in the boxing world, though he treated the individual athletes with great regard. He did not appreciate the new type of sportswriter who emerged in the '50s and '60s, an irreverent breed who looked at stories beyond the game, dubbing them "chipmunks," because they were always chattering away in the press box.

Cannon was a distinctive presence wherever he went, his bushy black eyebrows, thick-rimmed glasses, wide-brimmed hats, plaid jackets, and striped ties marking him out in a crowd. He was extremely dedicated to his column, and though he suffered a stroke in 1971, he continued to write until his death in 1973. In addition to the International Boxing Hall of Fame, Cannon is a member of the National Sportscasters and Sportswriters Association Hall of Fame. Hall of Fame Induction: 2002.

BILL CAYTON
Film Historian and Manager

Boxing historians and boxing fans in general owe a debt of gratitude to Bill Cayton for his incomparable collection of fight films, which have been shown on television for more than 50 years. William D'Arcy Cayton was born in New York City on June 6, 1918. He graduated from the University of Maryland with a degree in engineering. Upon graduation, he worked at DuPont on the development of polymers. As part of his job, he transformed dry, technical reports into interesting, readable material. He then obtained a position with the Newell-Emmett Advertising Agency in New York. He also started his own company—Cayton Chemical and Engineering—to produce and market an acrylic deck surfacing he had developed. Cayton found that he really liked marketing and advertising better than other aspects of business, so, in 1945, he founded an advertising agency, Cayton, Inc.

In 1948 one of his clients, Chesebrough Manufacturing, needed a new marketing campaign for its product, Vaseline Hair Tonic. Cayton reasoned that the product was geared to men and men liked sports. This was in the infancy of television when boxing dominated televised sports coverage. Cayton pitched the idea for a weekly program of historic fight films to be called *The Greatest Fights of the Century.* Chesebrough liked the concept and bought the show. Initially, Cayton leased the films. Later, he bought all the film rights from the promoters of virtually all famous fighters. *The Greatest Fights of the Century* was a fifteen-minute program, which led to another show, *Knockout.* Created for the Gillette Company, *Knockout* featured two-minute highlights of bouts ending in knockouts. Gillette licensed world telecasts of the show for twenty years. In the end, *Knockout* was seen in 78 countries. Cayton continued to acquire films not only of old fights, but also of modern ones that had been promoted by the Twentieth Century Sporting Club and the International Boxing Club. He even bought rights to the first boxing film ever made—a sparring session between Mike Leonard and Jack Cushing that Thomas Edison filmed in 1894.

In 1952, Cayton formed Big Fights, Inc., to produce a series known as *The Full Fights as Fought,* in which fighters provided commentary about themselves in the ring. In 1961, Cayton joined forces with Hall of Famer Jimmy Jacobs, a collector of boxing films himself. The two worked together to buy, restore, and market fight films. In the 1970s, networks and promoters began to realize the value of the rights to fight films and were less willing to sell them to Cayton. By that time, he had already amassed an incredible film library. Cayton used the footage to produce documentaries, such as *a.k.a. Cassius Clay* and *Jack Johnson*. In the 1970s, Cayton and Jacobs turned to managing fighters. The first fighter whose career they directed was Hall of Famer Wilfred Benitez. The pair also represented champion Edwin Rosario. Their partnership became well known when the pair managed heavyweight titleholder Mike Tyson until 1988. After the death of Jacobs in 1988, Cayton continued as a manager, guiding the careers of such fighters as Tommy Morrison, Vinny Pazienza, and Michael Grant. In 1998, Cayton sold his collection of fight films to ESPN, and they are often seen on the ESPN Classic network. Under the terms of the sale, Cayton retained the rights to show the films in museums. As a result, the films are made available to the International Boxing Hall of Fame. Cayton died of lung cancer on October 4, 2003. Hall of Fame Induction: 2005.

JOHN GRAHAM CHAMBERS
Author of Queensberry Rules

Although not often heralded, John Graham Chambers made an important contribution to the development of boxing when he devised the Marquess of Queensberry Rules on which the modern sport is based. Born in Carmarthenshire, Wales, in 1843, Chambers attended Magdalene College at Cambridge where he met John Sholto Douglas, the eighth Marquess of Queensberry. The two shared an interest in boxing. An accomplished oarsman, Chambers rowed for Cambridge and went on to coach the Cambridge crew. In 1866, he founded the Amateur Athletic Club and later played a key role in organizing Britain's Amateur Athletic Association. In 1867, Chambers created a set of twelve rules to govern boxing, which established the mandatory use of gloves, the ten-count for a knockout, and three-minute rounds. Douglas agreed to sponsor the regulations which led to them being known as the Queensberry Rules. Hall of Fame Induction: 1990.

DON CHARGIN
Promoter

From "Wonder Boy" to elder statesman, Don Chargin's long boxing career has covered every aspect of the sport. Born June 5, 1928, he first became interested in boxing when his father took him to a Manuel Ortiz fight in 1940. In high school, Chargin became captain of the boxing team before an injury forced him from the squad his senior year. His coach kept him involved in boxing as an unofficial assistant. After graduation, Chargin worked at a variety of odd jobs and spent his free time at gyms, working as a second, trainer, or in whatever role was available.

On Labor Day 1950, the 22-year-old Chargin—who had been turned down repeatedly for a promoter's license because of his age—staged his first boxing promotion at the Washington Baseball Park in Santa Clara. A good crowd turned out for the event, a match between local attraction Eddie Chavez and Hall of Famer Manuel Ortiz, which ended in a ten-round victory for Chavez. Chargin was inspired by the $16,000 he netted for the card and went on to promote fights in Oakland, Stockton, Fresno, Richmond, Merced, and San Jose. Scant financial success in these ventures led him to briefly abandon promoting and turn to managing. He directed the ring career of flyweight contender Keeny Teran, who lost a shot at Flash Elorde's title when he was arrested on a narcotics charge.

With his father's encouragement, Chargin returned to promoting in the late fifties, primarily in Oakland and at his Bonanza Club in Sacramento. His promotions in Oakland's Auditorium included bouts between Bobo Olson and Don Grant, Olson and Paddy Young, and Joey Gambia and Chico Vejar.

When the Coliseum Arena opened next to the Oakland–Alameda County Coliseum, Chargin staged the first pro boxing event there. The main event was an Andy Heilman–Jimmy Lester middleweight bout. At different stages of Chargin's long career, he promoted bouts featuring all three generations of the fighting Lester family, including Jimmy Lester's father, Top Row Allen, and Jimmy's son, Jimmy Lester Jr. The late '60s saw Chargin host two WBA heavyweight title elimination fights at the Coliseum Arena: Thad Spencer–Jerry Quarry and Quarry–Jimmy Ellis.

Though his promotional base was in northern California, Chargin was a long-time matchmaker for Hall of Famer Aileen Eaton at the Olympic Auditorium in Los Angeles. In 1970, Chargin pitted Hall of Famer Ismael Laguna against Mando Ramos for the latter's lightweight title. He also staged Sugar Ramos against Mando Ramos on August 7, 1970, at the Olympic, the toughest fight Chargin ever witnessed. During the '70s, he booked bouts at the L.A. Sports Arena, including Danny ("Little Red") Lopez–Bobby Chacon.

Chargin remained active in boxing, promoting in Northern California with such notables as Tony Lopez and Loreto Garza, and staging a 1995 bout at the ARCO Arena between heavyweight great Lennox Lewis and Lionel Butler. In 2001, Chargin promoted the Willie Jorrin and Oscar Larrios match for the WBC super bantamweight championship in Sacramento. Don Chargin Productions is a joint effort of Don and his wife Lorraine. Together they won the 2001 James J. Walker Award for Long and Meritorious Service to Boxing. Recently Don also served at a consultant for Oscar de la Hoya's Golden Boy Promotions. Hall of Fame Induction: 2001.

STANLEY CHRISTODOULOU
Referee

One of the preeminent referees of the last forty years, Stanley Christodoulou has refereed in over 100 world championship bouts. He also is a well-respected boxing judge. Christodoulou has refereed bouts in all of boxing's seventeen weight classes. Born in Johannesburg, South Africa, on January 31, 1946, Christodoulou, the son of immigrants from Cyprus, often engaged in fights with other neighborhood youths while growing up. Listening to radio broadcasts of bouts involving such greats as Floyd Patterson, Sonny Liston, and Muhammad Ali fostered his interest in boxing. Christodoulou began his career as a boxer and won all twelve of his fights before a broken knuckle ended his career.

In 1963, George Owen-Davies, chairman of the Transvaal Boxing Board, observed Christodoulou closely watching fights and asked him if he would like to help out. The next day, Christodoulou applied for a license as a judge. In 1965, he refereed for the first time. Christodoulou made a name for himself in South Africa as a referee and was chosen to be the "third man in the ring" for the world bantamweight title fight held on November 3, 1973, in Johannesburg's Rand Stadium between Arnold Taylor and Romeo Anaya. In a tough, brutal bout, Christodoulou won accolades for his ability to maintain control of the fight, which Taylor eventually won on a knockout in the fourteenth round.

Another turning point in Christodoulou's career came when he was the referee for the

Victor Galindez–Richie Kates light heavyweight championship fight on May 22, 1976, again in Rand Stadium. In the third round, Galindez and Kates bumped heads, which opened a gash above Galindez's right eye. After the gash, Christodoulou stopped the fight and sent Galindez to his corner. Photographers and other onlookers stormed the ring in the belief that the fight was over. However, Christodoulou had not stopped the fight. He had a doctor examine Galindez. When the doctor pronounced Galindez fit to continue, the fight resumed after a six-minute delay. A bloody battle followed, and Galindez finally knocked Kates out with one second left in the fifteenth round.

Some of the more notable of all of the great fights that Christodoulou has worked are the first fight between Aaron Pryor and Alexis Arguello, Marvelous Marvin Hagler–Roberto Duran, Barry McGuigan–Eusebio Perez, Thomas Hearns–Pipino Cuevas, and Mike Weaver–James ("Quick") Tillis. Additionally, he has served as a judge for such notable heavyweight title fights as Evander Holyfield–Michael Moorer, Holyfield–Lennox Lewis, and John Ruiz–Roy Jones, Jr. Christodoulou is noted for his ability to keep control of the action even in trying circumstances—including the time when Soon Yun Chung's cornerman attempted to stab him with a pair of scissors.

Besides his work in the ring and at ringside, Christodoulou has logged many years as a boxing administrator. He served as executive director of the South Africa Boxing Board for almost 30 years. He has served as South Africa's representative to the World Boxing Association (WBA) and has advised boxing federations of other African nations. Hall of Fame Induction: 2004.

RALPH CITRO
Statistician and Cut Man

Ralph Citro first got his start in boxing as a twelve-year old back in 1938, when he walked into a YMCA gym in Youngstown Ohio. Since then Citro has been an amateur fighter, trainer, gym owner, manager, matchmaker, cut man, statistician, and record keeper.

Boxing as an amateur after a WWII stint in the marines, Citro compiled an 18-3 record before he hung up his gloves, explaining, "If I can't beat Willie Pep and Sandy Saddler, I might as well give it up." Citro stayed involved in boxing as a trainer in a Camden, New Jersey, gym while he worked for the Post Office in Blackwood. In 1958, he opened Blackwood Gym, where he trained and managed fighters while also selling insurance. Around this time, Hall of Famer Jersey Joe Walcott—then fight promoter at the Camden Convention Hall—asked for Citro's help as a trainer. Though Citro trained several fighters, including Walcott's son, and worked for a while as a matchmaker, his venture with Walcott proved unsuccessful.

Citro began work as a cut man, so impressing boxer Gaten Hart with his corner work at a bout in Canada that he was hired by the fighter. According to Citro, Hart averaged 43 stitches per fight, so a cut man was extremely important. When Hart defeated contender Ralph Racine, keeping him from a title shot against Hilmer Kenty, Citro kept Hart in the fight despite two bleeding eyes and a bloody nose. Emanuel Steward, who handled Kenty for the Kronk stable in Detroit, was so impressed with Citro's work that he hired him to work as cut man with fighters like Kenty and Thomas Hearns. By his own estimate, Citro has worked 125 title bouts; he was in the corner for both of Hearns's bouts with Sugar Ray Leonard and worked for sixteen of Riddick Bowe's fights, including his heavyweight championship triumph over Evander Holyfield.

In 1981, Citro began Computer Boxing Update, a database of boxing records for use by commissions, matchmakers, promoters, managers, and the media. He maintained the Update for thirteen years, publishing ten annual volumes before his retirement in 1993. Computer Boxing Update continues today as *The Boxing Record Book* by Fight Fax, Inc.

Citro, however, did not retire from the field of boxing. From 1993 to 2000 he served as director of the International Boxing Research Organization, a group devoted to maintaining the accuracy of historical boxing records. He also wrote a book, *So You Want to be a Cornerman*, as a guide for aspiring seconds. In recognition of his varied contributions to the sport, the Boxing Writers Association of America named Citro as the 1992 recipient of the James J. Walker Award for Long and Meritorious Service to Boxing. He died on October 2, 2004 at the age of 78. Hall of Fame Induction: 2001.

GIL CLANCY
Trainer and Manager

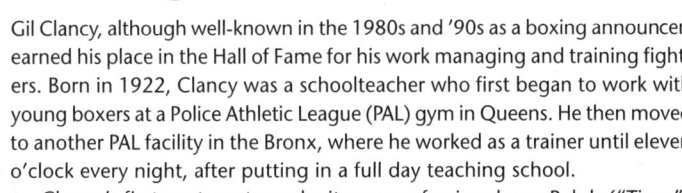

Gil Clancy, although well-known in the 1980s and '90s as a boxing announcer, earned his place in the Hall of Fame for his work managing and training fighters. Born in 1922, Clancy was a schoolteacher who first began to work with young boxers at a Police Athletic League (PAL) gym in Queens. He then moved to another PAL facility in the Bronx, where he worked as a trainer until eleven o'clock every night, after putting in a full day teaching school.

Clancy's first protege to make it as a professional was Ralph ("Tiger") Jones, who, although he never became a champion, won over 50 fights in a twelve-year career and defeated Hall of Famers Sugar Ray Robinson, Kid Gavilan, and Joey Giardello. Clancy also trained and managed Emile Griffith, the great welter- and middleweight, for his whole career. Middleweight champion Rodrigo Valdez and heavyweight contender Jerry Quarry thrived under Clancy's guidance. He also trained George Foreman.

In 1978, Clancy worked for three years as the matchmaker for Madison Square Garden. He then turned his attention to announcing and became highly successful as a boxing analyst for CBS and other networks, including HBO. In the 1990s, Clancy came out of retirement to work with Oscar de la Hoya. The Boxing Writers Association honored Clancy in 1967 and again in 1973 with the Al Buck Memorial Award given to the manager of the year. Hall of Fame Induction: 1993.

JAMES W. COFFROTH
Promoter

James W. Coffroth was the first large-scale boxing promoter. Born in California in 1872, Coffroth worked as a clerk in the Surrogate Court in San Francisco, but he had a great interest in boxing and would often travel east to see important matches. He became friendly with New York promoter Jim Kennedy, and the two began to promote fights on the West Coast. Coffroth was able to secure a permit to stage boxing events in San Francisco from Abe Ruef, the local political power broker.

Their first fight of national interest was a heavyweight championship match between James J. Jeffries and Gus Ruhlin in 1901. The bout ended when Ruhlin's man-ager threw in the sponge between the fifth and sixth rounds, the first time in American boxing history a fight had ended that way. It went into the books as a fifth-round knockout and established a precedent for scoring rules. When Kennedy died in 1903, Coffroth went on to promote events in California for another twelve years.

Other notable fights promoted by Coffroth include Corbett–Jeffries, Bob Fitzsimmons–George Gardner, Battling Nelson–Joe Gans, and Stanley Ketchel–Jack Johnson. Coffroth instituted the practice of paying fighters a percentage of the gate receipts. He was also aware of the value of publicity and held frequent press conferences.

As competition grew and the political climate changed, Coffroth lost his permits for bouts in San Francisco and moved his operations to the nearby towns of Colma and Daly City. Coffroth lost out to rival Tex Rickard on the mammoth Jeffries–Johnson fight. In sealed bids, Coffroth bid $100,000. Rival Tex Rickard bid $120,000 in gold.

Coffroth made most of his money in horse racing and continued operating tracks long after he retired from boxing promotion. He died in 1943. Hall of Fame Induction: 1991.

IRVING COHEN
Manager

Irving Cohen managed over 500 fighters in a career spanning more than 30 years. Born on January 2, 1904, in Vilna, Russia, Cohen left home for the land of opportunity. Though Cohen boxed as an amateur, he didn't immediately find a career in the sport, and even worked as a lingerie salesman before becoming a fight manager. Calm, quiet, and distinguished, the 5'6" Cohen did not fit the stereotype of the loud, insensitive, cigar-chomping manager.

Cohen's first promising fighter was Sammy Garcia, who came to him in 1935. When Garcia began to attract attention, Cohen was instructed to meet with Jimmy Doyle, a New York racketeer involved in boxing. When Cohen met Doyle and his associates at the office of Hall of Famer James J. Johnston, Doyle threatened to throw Cohen out the window if he refused to relinquish control of Garcia. Cohen replied steadily, "Jimmy, if I go out that window, you're coming with me." The racketeer backed off.

Cohen skillfully and carefully guided his best fighter, Graziano, to the top—not an easy task given Rocky's disinterest in training. Cohen brought Graziano along slowly and, for a while, even had him live with his own family.

Besides Graziano, Cohen also managed Hall of Famer Billy Graham. When Sugar Ray Robinson vacated the welterweight title in 1951 to move up to middleweight, Graham and Kid Gavilan were the two top contenders. The corrupt International Boxing Club controlled much of the sport at this time, and IBC president James D. Norris and mobster Frankie Carbo—the power behind Norris—allegedly met with Cohen to discuss a championship matchup. They offered Cohen's fighter a title shot if they could have a piece of Graham. Cohen told Graham and Graham's father about the offer. But the Grahams nixed it, largely because of their loyalty to and admiration for Cohen.

Gavilan and Graham finally met in Madison Square Garden on August 29, 1951. An anonymous phone call to Cohen on the day of the fight led him to believe that Graham could only win by knockout, since the referees and judges were "committed" to picking Gavilan. The caller told Cohen which officials would be assigned to the contest. An upset Cohen went to the offices of the New York State Athletic Commission to lodge a complaint, but his fears were dismissed by the commission. Gavilan won a split decision in a fight that many thought should have belonged to Graham. Teddy Brenner, a protege of Cohen, re-counted a deathbed confession from one of the judges, avowing that the fight was fixed.

Cohen also promoted fights at New York-area clubs such as the St. Nicholas Arena and

Sunnyside Garden, and managed the famous Stillman's Gym in its final years. When diagnosed with glaucoma in the mid-'60s, Cohen heeded his doctor's advice to slow down and retired. He died on June 25, 1991, in Scottsdale, Arizona. Hall of Fame Induction: 2002.

CUS D'AMATO
Manager

Cus D'Amato earned a reputation as one of the most forthright and honest men in boxing. He guided Floyd Patterson and Jose Torres to world titles and was instrumental in launching Mike Tyson's career. Top trainers Teddy Atlas, Kevin Rooney, and Joe Fariello all learned their trade from D'Amato.

Born in 1908 in New York, D'Amato grew up as one of five brothers and learned to fight in the streets. At the age of 22, he opened the Empire Sporting Club with Jack Barrow at the Gramercy Gym. The purpose of the club was to develop young boxers. D'Amato was devoted to the gym and actually lived there for years. He was very attentive to his boxers, and his belief in his young stars was important to their success. He built the neophyte Patterson into an Olympic gold medal winner and then world heavyweight champion, and he later guided Jose Torres to the light heavyweight championship. Both Torres and Patterson continued responsible careers after boxing, Torres as a writer and member of the New York State Athletic Commission, Patterson as head of the New York State Athletic Commission.

Once Patterson won the championship, D'Amato carefully selected his opponents with an eye towards both maximizing revenues for his fighter and thwarting the International Boxing Club (IBC). Although it meant bypassing many top challengers, D'Amato refused to match his fighter in any bout promoted by the powerful but corrupt IBC. The IBC was eventually found to be in violation of anti-trust laws and was dissolved. However, D'Amato's stance had the unintended effect of decreasing interest in boxing because Patterson fought infrequently and did not face many top contenders.

After Patterson's and Torres's careers had ended, D'Amato worked in relative obscurity for some years, surfacing briefly as a possible trainer for Wilt Chamberlain when the basketball great considered going into the ring. D'Amato then moved to Catskill, New York, where he opened a gym. He began to work with Mike Tyson who was in a nearby reform school. D'Amato did much to develop Tyson into a top heavyweight contender, but he died in 1985 before Tyson became the youngest world heavyweight titleholder in history. Hall of Fame Induction: 1995.

JEFF DICKSON
Promoter

Although he was an American, Jeff Dickson made his mark as a boxing promoter in Paris and throughout Europe. Born in Natchez, Mississippi, in 1896, Dickson found a job as a newsboy at age seven. He continued in journalism as a war photographer, travelling to Europe in 1917. When World War I ended the next year, Dickson was stationed in Paris as part of the Signal Corps. For a fee, Dickson staged "war" pictures of American soldiers still in Paris who had seen no action before the armistice, complete with trenches dug by himself, actors in rented German uniforms, and action shots of "combat"—a very profitable scheme.

After his demobilization, Dickson remained in France, becoming a newsreel cameraman and travelling throughout Europe. He became friendly with the owner of the Salle Wagram—the major fight venue of Paris—and began lending him money. When the business failed, Dickson took it over and, after promoting fight cards there, moved to the larger Palais des Sports in 1924.

At the Palais des Sports and throughout Europe at venues in London, Berlin, Brussels, Rome, Barcelona, and Oslo, Dickson used his unique public relations sense to stage boxing matches. He also staged skating events, six-day bicycle races, bullfights, hockey, basketball, tennis, wrestling matches, animal shows, and other extravaganzas. To promote a fight between Primo Carnera and Paulino Uzcudun, this master of publicity won the hearts of the Spanish public by staging a bullfight—with himself as matador! His victory over the bull led the Spanish press to support a fight they and the public had originally opposed because it was promoted by a foreigner. An amazing 85,000 people attended the fight, confirming not only Dickson's skills, but the public appeal of Carnera, whom Dickson afterwards took to London to fight British heavyweight Reggie Meen.

Dickson's unusual approach to running a promotion also extended to the way he managed his arenas. He had no objection to riots after unpopular decisions. In fact, he had a special retractable net installed around the ring, in case angry fans at the Palais des Sports threw bottles or other debris from the balconies. Although Dickson, like all good promoters, was a hard-nosed businessman, each year during the Christmas season he invited about 20,000 poor and orphaned children to a free festival, where athletes, actors, and comedians entertained, and candy, food, and toys were given away to all comers.

Dickson realized that a successful promotion needed good fighters. To that end, he had scouts comb European gyms for promising young boxers to bring into his fold. After the appropriate training, he would match these novices with proven fighters to see if they showed promise.

Dickson regularly visited New York, but Paris remained his home, and he lived there until the day before the Germans captured the city during World War II. He then returned to the United States and re-enlisted in the U.S. Army. Dickson was killed in action when his plane was shot down during an Army Air Corps bombing raid over Germany. Hall of Fame Induction: 2000.

ARTHUR DONOVAN
Referee

Arthur Donovan refereed fourteen heavyweight championship fights from 1933 to 1946. The son of Professor Mike Donovan, the noted American middleweight champion and boxing instructor, Donovan was born on August 13, 1891, and grew up around boxers. Gentleman Jim Corbett actually befriended the youngster when he came for a visit. Against his father's wishes, Donovan boxed professionally for a time, under an assumed name.

When his father retired as boxing instructor at the New York Athletic Club, Donovan took the job and held it for exactly 50 years to the minute. He also served two tours in the military, and after World War I, tried unsuccessfully to revive his boxing career. In 1923, James Farley, New York State Athletic Commissioner, urged Donovan to become a referee. Donovan agreed and was immediately called for important fights. He became a favorite of fans, who often asked him for autographs. He officiated at twenty

Joe Louis fights, including both Schmeling bouts. After retiring as a referee, Donovan continued in his instructor's job, which he had never left. He died on September 1, 1980.

Donovan's son, Art, is a well-known television personality and was enshrined in the Pro Football Hall of Fame after a career with the Baltimore Colts. Hall of Fame Induction: 1993.

MICKEY DUFF
Promoter and Manager

Mickey Duff was a dominant force in British boxing for nearly 50 years, and his influence on the sport spread across the globe. Born Monek Prager on June 7, 1929, near Krakow, Poland, Duff was the son, grandson, and great-grandson of rabbis. He was exposed to the ugliness of anti-Semitism at a young age when he saw his grandfather beaten by thugs. In 1938, Duff and his parents moved to London's East End.

To avoid the air raids during the war, Duff was sent to a Jewish hostel in Gateshead, where he received his first formal exposure to boxing. He reached the finals of the London schoolboys' boxing tournament, but his family did not approve of his participation. At the young age of twelve, Duff argued with his father and vowed never to speak to him again, but he adopted the name "Mickey Duff" to avoid embarrassing his family. "Mickey" was an anglicized version of his given name, while "Duff" was a character played by James Cagney in the motion picture *Cash and Carry*.

Duff entered professional boxing at the age of fifteen and amassed a 55-8-6 record in four years, before deciding that he would have more success outside the ring. He served briefly as a trainer and cut man but made his real mark as a matchmaker, quickly displaying a skill for choosing the right fighter for a match based on talent and character. Though he started out at small venues, by 1960 Duff was working for London promoter Harry Levene and booking fights in Wembley, Manchester, Glasgow, and Cardiff. He later worked for another promoter in Royal Albert Hall and served as matchmaker/director for the Anglo-American Sporting Clubs of the London Hilton and Manchester Piccadilly hotels. Duff matched Sugar Ray Robinson at his first event for the Hilton.

As his influence and reputation continued to grow, Duff became an independent manager and promoter, involved in fistic events all over the world, though he focused his attention in England. There, he replaced Hall of Famer Jack Solomons as the country's premier promoter. The first world champion with whom he worked was Terry Downes. Over the course of his career, he was involved with eighteen more champions or former champs. These included Howard Winstone, John Conteh, Barry McGuigan, Lloyd Honeyghan, and Cornelius Boza-Edwards. Additionally, Duff set up Mike Tyson's first eighteen bouts at the request of Tyson handler Jim Jacobs.

Duff's influence began to wane, and Frank Warren replaced him as England's top boxing figure. Duff decried what he saw as the negative influence of such prominent promoters as Warren, Don King, and Bob Arum on the sport he loved, and he retired from boxing in 1999 after his fighter, Billy Schwer, was defeated in a bid for the world lightweight title. At about the same time, he wrote his autobiography, entitled *Twenty and Out*. The title referred to the number of world champions he would have handled, had Schwer been victorious. A promoter and manager with first-hand experience in the ring, Duff was a major figure in the boxing world for the last half of the twentieth century. He is now a popular public speaker. Hall of Fame Induction: 1999.

ANGELO DUNDEE
Trainer

Angelo Dundee is best known for his work as the trainer of Muhammad Ali. Born in Philadelphia in 1923, Dundee was originally named Angelo Mirena, Jr. He changed his name to Dundee after his older brother Joe adopted it in honor of Hall of Famer Johnny Dundee. In the army in World War II, Dundee boxed a couple of times and worked as a corner man in service bouts.

After the war, Dundee moved to New York to do corner work for his brother Chris, who was then a fight manager. He also spent a great deal of time in Stillman's Gym, watching the action and learning from great trainers such as Charley Goldman, Ray Arcel, Bill Gore, Whitey Bimstein, and Chickie Ferrara. In 1950, Dundee took over the management of his first fighter, Bill Bossio, and in 1952, he was hired as chief second and cut man for Carmen Basilio, who won both the welterweight and middleweight titles. He later became Basilio's trainer.

During the 1950s, Dundee built up a stable of fighters, although Basilio was his only champion. Then in 1960, Dundee was hired to train a fighter who would change his life: Cassius Clay, later known as Muhammad Ali. Dundee enjoyed working with the superbly talented boxer, even if Ali at times resisted his advice, and he remained in the Ali camp for over twenty years. Ali credited Dundee not only with getting him through some crisis points in key fights, but with having faith in him after Ali lost to Joe Frazier and Ken Norton.

At the same time he was training Ali, Dundee handled other champions. On March 21, 1963, two of his charges won world titles on the same card in Los Angeles. Ultiminio ("Sugar") Ramos knocked out Davey Moore to win the featherweight title, and Luis Rodriguez decisioned Emile Griffith to win the welterweight title. Two other fighters in the Dundee stable, Ralph Dupas and Willie Pastrano, won titles in 1963 in the junior middleweight and light heavyweight divisions.

Dundee also trained Jose Napoles, who won the welterweight title in 1969. Napoles lost the title when Billy Backus stopped him on cuts in 1970. On the night of the Backus fight, Dundee was with Ali and his services as the best cut man in boxing were not available to Napoles. Napoles won the rematch with Dundee back in his corner.

As Ali's career wound down, Dundee took on a new high-profile fighter, Sugar Ray Leonard. Under Dundee's direction, Leonard became an outstanding fighter and perhaps the most popular boxer of the post-Ali era. Other champions trained or managed by Dundee include Pinklon Thomas, Slobodan Kacar, Jimmy Ellis, and Michael Nunn. Most recently, Dundee worked with the 46-year-old George Foreman in his 1994 comeback win over Michael Moorer for the heavyweight championship.

In 2001, Dundee served as a technical advisor for the film *Ali*. A few years later, he trained Russell Crowe for his starring role in *Cinderella Man*—the dramatized movie biography of long-shot heavyweight champion James J. Braddock. Dundee also appeared in that movie, playing a corner man. After they worked together, Crowe and Dundee became good friends.

Howard Cosell said of Dundee, "If I had a son who wanted to be a fighter, the only man I would entrust him to would be Angelo Dundee." The Boxing Writers Association of America voted Dundee its Manager of the Year Award in both 1968 and 1979. The same organization awarded him its Long and Meritorious Service Award in 1996. Hall of Fame Induction: 1992.

CHRIS DUNDEE
Manager and Promoter

Although he was never a professional fighter, Chris Dundee's life was boxing. He managed approximately 300 fighters, promoted hundreds of bouts, and ran a famous gym. Born in Philadelphia in 1908, Dundee began life with the name Cristofo Mirena. Like his brothers Angelo, who became a top trainer, and Joe, a club fighter, he adopted the name used by Hall of Famer Johnny Dundee.

In 1928, Dundee started managing fighters. He shepherded Midget Wolgast to the world flyweight title in 1930, and Ken Overlin to the New York version of the world middleweight title in 1941.

Starting in 1932, Dundee also acted as a boxing promoter, putting on shows in the Norfolk, Washington, and Baltimore areas. In 1950, with the completion of the Miami Beach Convention Hall, Dundee moved his base of operations there and promoted boxing and wrestling at that venue for 27 years. He succeeded in putting on a large number of cards annually, even as promoters in similar-sized cities were going out of business. Some of the important bouts he promoted included the Harold Johnson–Jesse Bowdry light heavyweight championship fight, the world welterweight title fight in which Emile Griffith first defeated Benny ("Kid") Paret, and the famous world heavyweight title fight in which Muhammad Ali defeated Sonny Liston.

After relinquishing his exclusive hold on the Miami Beach hall, Dundee worked for British promoter Chris Wilson. For approximately 30 years, Dundee also owned and operated the famous Fifth Street Gym in Miami Beach, where Ali and many other prominent fighters trained. He died on November 16, 1998. Hall of Fame Induction: 1994.

DON DUNPHY
Broadcaster

Don Dunphy enjoyed a long career behind the mike calling fights at ringside for radio and then television audiences. In his 40-year career, Dunphy called the blow-by-blow of over 2,000 fights, with over 200 of them for titles, including 50 heavyweight championships.

Born in New York in 1908, Dunphy went to Manhattan College, where he was a college correspondent for a number of New York newspapers. After graduating, Dunphy worked for a time at the New York Coliseum, broadcasting hockey and wrestling from the site. He also hosted a daily sports show, for no pay, on radio station WHOM, and worked at WINS as a spotter for football broadcasts before getting air time himself, mostly doing ticker tape re-creations. He worked Newark Bears minor league baseball games and, in 1936, assisted at broadcasts of Cornell University football games. In 1937, Dunphy became the sports director at WINS, a job he held for the next ten years. He also hosted a popular boxing talk show on WINS on Saturday afternoons.

In 1939, Dunphy ventured into local fight broadcasts, and in 1941, he auditioned for radio sponsor Gillette Safety Razor Company by calling the Gus Lesnevich–Anton Christoforidis fight at Madison Square Garden. He got the job, and his next broadcast was the first Joe Louis–Billy Conn fight. Dunphy called fights on radio for Gillette for nineteen years.

In 1960, Dunphy moved over to television and called fights on the ABC network for four years. He also worked fights for WOR-TV and continued to call many championship fights on radio. By the 1970s and early '80s, Dunphy had retired from network television, but he was still very much in demand on closed-circuit telecasts, calling such fights as Ali–Frazier I, and Ali–Foreman. His final complete blow-by-blow of a major fight was the first Sugar Ray Leonard–Thomas Hearns fight in 1981.

Dunphy worked with color man Bill Corum for many years. He was also paired with such celebrity broadcasting partners as Muhammad Ali, Pearl Bailey, Flip Wilson, and Ryan O'Neal. Throughout his career, Dunphy broadcast New York Yankee games, the Cotton Bowl, track events, bowling, basketball, and horse racing. Dunphy died July 22, 1998. Hall of Fame Induction: 1993.

DAN DUVA
Promoter

Dan Duva was part of one of the few father/son combinations inducted into the International Boxing Hall of Fame. He made his mark as a boxing promoter in a life that ended much too early due to cancer when he was only 44. The son of Hall of Fame trainer and manager Lou Duva, Dan was around boxing his whole life. He was born on November 7, 1951, in New Jersey. Despite his father's occupation, it was not guaranteed that Duva would stay in the "family business." He graduated from Rutgers University in 1973 and then attended Seton Hall University Law School. After graduating in 1976, he joined the law firm of Cerreto & LaPenna in Newark, New Jersey. Duva had dabbled in boxing promotion since 1973. In 1977, he and his father formed the promotional company Main Events. Initially, Main Events staged small shows at a club in Totowa, New Jersey, known as Ice World, where monthly Main Events shows were televised. Such future champions as Rocky Lockridge, Livingstone Bramble, Bobby Czyz, Johnny ("Bump City") Bumphus, Vinny Pazienza, and Pinklon Thomas fought at Ice World.

In 1981, Main Events grew from a small regional promoter to a major player in the sport when it landed the promotional rights to the Sugar Ray Leonard–Thomas Hearns bout. The fight grossed $40 million—at that time the biggest grossing fight in boxing history.

Main Events focused on finding young fighters who were somewhat well known due to their success in the amateur ranks. Duva and Main Events signed some of the leading amateur fighters in the country after the United States decided to boycott the 1980 Olympics held in Moscow. In 1984, this plan came to fruition when Main Events signed Olympic stars Pernell ("Sweet Pea") Whitaker, Evander Holyfield, Mark Breland, and Meldrick Taylor. All of these fighters became champions. Main Events has promoted or co-promoted over 100 world championship bouts. Some of the more notable fighters who fought on Main Events cards include Lennox Lewis, George Foreman, Michael Moorer, Alexis Arguello, Aaron Pryor, and Mike McCallum.

Though Duva was an influential figure in boxing, he retained an unassuming, "nice guy" manner which earned him a great deal of respect in a boxing community inured to the flashier styles of other promoters.

Unfortunately, Duva developed brain cancer and underwent surgery in 1994. The cancer recurred in 1995, and Duva died on January 30, 1996. Main Events is now run by Dan's wife, Kathy. Hall of Fame Induction: 2003.

LOU DUVA
Trainer and Manager

Lou Duva has been a boxer, manager, trainer, matchmaker, and promoter, but his career did not really take off until he was almost 60. Born in New York on May 28, 1922, Duva moved to Paterson, New Jersey, as a child. His older brother Carl introduced Duva to boxing when he was only ten. At fifteen, Duva boxed for five dollars a fight before dropping out of school to join the Civilian Conservation Corps. After working with the Corps in Oregon, Duva returned home and won the New Jersey Diamond Gloves welterweight championship.

During World War II, Duva taught boxing at Camp Hood, Texas. After the war, he went to Florida where he worked in his parents' restaurant and boxed on the side. Back in New Jersey, he started a trucking business, but whenever he had the opportunity, Duva went to Stillman's Gym in New York to be around boxing. He later worked as a bail bondsman before becoming president of the local Teamsters union. During this time, he promoted many small boxing shows in the Paterson area. His most significant promotion was the Joey Giardello–Dick Tiger middleweight championship in 1963.

In 1977, Lou's son Dan, a law school graduate, organized the family's boxing operations as a promotional company called Main Events. Duva served as manager, with his son as promoter and matchmaker. When Main Events linked up with rock promoter Shelly Finkel, who excelled at recruiting talent, it became a major player in the sport. In 1981, Main Events won promotional rights to the Sugar Ray Leonard–Thomas Hearns bout that grossed $34 million.

Duva sought more talented boxers to join the Main Events stable, sometimes serving as manager, sometimes as trainer. He also signed top amateur fighters such as 1984 Olympians Pernell Whitaker, Mark Breland, and Evander Holyfield. Duva worked the corner for these fighters and other stars of the 1980s and 1990s, including Bobby Czyz, Livingstone Bramble, Darrin Van Horn, Meldrick Taylor, and Michael Moorer. On February 4, 1989, Duva was in Las Vegas when Breland won the WBA welterweight title by knocking out Seung-Soon Lee. The very next day, Duva was ringside in Atlantic City when Van Horn won the IBF junior middleweight title over Robert Hines. Duva reached the pinnacle of his career when Holyfield knocked out James "Buster" Douglas to win the world heavyweight championship. In 1996, Lou suffered the loss of his son Dan to a brain tumor. Dino, Dan's younger brother, took over as Main Events president.

Duva is known for fierce devotion to his fighters which, combined with his pugnacious demeanor, has resulted in some unorthodox activities in the ring. He once charged at a referee with whom he disagreed. He almost attacked Don King after the latter shouted "something rude" at Duva following Mike Tyson's knockout of Duva's charge, Tyrell Biggs.

Duva was part of the melee that took place after Andrew Golota, Duva's fighter, was disqualified in his first fight with Riddick Bowe. Duva, who had suffered a heart attack more than fifteen years before, had to be carried out of the ring on a stretcher. In 1999, Lou Duva, along with son Dino and daughter Donna Brooks, departed Main Events after a dispute with Dan's widow, Kathy Duva. Now Lou concentrates on his work as a trainer while Dino and Donna each organize their own boxing promotions. Duva loves to mix with boxing fans and is always a willing signer of autographs. Hall of Fame Induction: 1998.

AILEEN EATON
Promoter

Aileen Eaton, the only female member of the International Boxing Hall of Fame, staged top boxing promotions at the Olympic Auditorium in Los Angeles for almost 40 years.

Eaton, born Aileen Goldstein in Vancouver, British Columbia, on February 5, 1909, did not originally intend to pursue a career ringside. A widowed mother of two in need of a job to support her children, Eaton left law school and entered the world of boxing as a private secretary to Frank A. Garbutt, president of the Los Angeles Athletic Club, which owned the Olympic Auditorium. In 1942, Garbutt asked Eaton to find out why boxing promotions at the Olympic lost money. When she reported back that the current promoter was incompetent, Garbutt told her to find a new one. She selected Cal Eaton, an inspector for the California State Athletic Commission. Eaton soon joined Cal's staff and learned the fine arts of publicity, advertising, and matchmaking. She ultimately married Cal, and served as his copromoter.

The first fight card Eaton helped promote drew 2,212 fans on July 21, 1942, to watch Jack Chase decision Big Boy Hogue in the main event. While Cal Eaton was officially the promoter, Aileen quickly became closely involved in all aspects of boxing promotions at the Olympic.

Eaton staged weekly shows at the Olympic from 1942 to 1980. While it was not unusual for a fight club to hold regular weekly events in the '40s, by the '70s such regularity was rare. By some accounts, the Olympic was the only one of around 400 1940s venues still holding weekly fight cards into the late '70s. After Cal died in 1966, Eaton functioned as the Olympic's sole promoter, assisted by two Hall of Fame matchmakers, George Parnassus beginning in 1957, and then Don Chargin.

Eaton's promotional achievements are almost too numerous to list. She staged over 2,500 cards, 10,000 fights, and 100 title fights. In addition to regular bouts at the Olympic, she staged promotions at other L.A. sites, like Dodger Stadium, the Los Angeles Sports Arena, and the Coliseum. She promoted the championship triple-header in Dodger Stadium on March 21, 1963, in which Sugar Ramos faced champion Davey Moore for the featherweight title, welterweight title-holder Emile Griffith fought number-one contender Luis Rodriquez, and Battling Torres and Roberto Cruz vied for the vacant junior welterweight crown in front of 26,000 fans. Another notable Eaton promotion was the Lauro Salas upset of heavily favored Jimmy Carter for the lightweight title, a bout held at the Olympic on May 14, 1952. Eaton also promoted contests with Sugar Ray Robinson, George Foreman, Joe Frazier, Carmen Basilio, Floyd Patterson, Archie Moore, Manuel Ortiz, Ike Williams, Mando Ramos, Art Aragon, Danny Lopez, Carlos Palomino, and Muhammad Ali. Additionally, Eaton had a hand in the Las Vegas promotion of the Sugar Ray Leonard–Wilfred Benitez fight. Eaton credited herself with giving Muhammad Ali the idea for his "I am the greatest" shtick.

Aileen Eaton's sons, Mike and Gene LeBell, gained fame as professional wrestlers. Gene won two consecutive national Judo championships and worked as a stunt man in over 1,000 movies and TV shows. Eaton stopped promoting fights at the Olympic in 1980, and two years later she was appointed as a commissioner of the California State Athletic Commission, the first person with boxing industry experience ever appointed to that organization. Eaton died on November 7, 1987. Hall of Fame Induction: 2002.

PIERCE EGAN
Historian

All students of boxing history owe a debt of gratitude to Pierce Egan, the first boxing historian. He was the most popular and successful of English sports journalists, and the public eagerly sought out his vivid descriptions of bare-knuckle bouts in the London *Weekly Dispatch*.

Egan was born in England, probably in 1772. He began publishing his magnum opus, *Boxiana*, in 1812. A history of boxing containing biograph-ical sketches of fighters, round-by-round descriptions of fights, and other information about the sport and its participants, the work was issued in monthly paperbound sections and sold by subscription. By 1813, enough material had been issued to create the first book-length volume, and, by 1829, Egan published *Boxiana* as a five-volume set with an additional volume contributed by Jon Bee (John Babcock). Egan's work is often cited by writers discussing the early days of fisticuffs.

Egan also wrote plays, songs, novels, epigrams, and a dictionary of slang; he also appeared on stage as an actor. His knowledge of London's seamier elements lent richness to his reports of criminal trials. His 1821 bestseller, *Life in London*, is said to have inspired and influenced Charles Dickens. Egan died in 1849. Hall of Fame Induction: 1991.

JACK FISKE
Journalist

For decades, Jack Fiske was one of the nation's most respected boxing writers and was especially highly regarded on the West Coast. Fiske covered boxing for more than 40 years. Though it is rare today for boxing to receive such regular coverage, Fiske wrote a twice-weekly column on boxing for the *San Francisco Chronicle* for many years until November 27, 1987, when the paper discontinued it.

Although he spent his professional career in San Francisco, Fiske was born Jacob Finkelstein in New York City in 1917. He graduated from the Univer-sity of Alabama. He then headed to California, first to Los Angeles before finding a home at the *Chronicle*.

Fiske's columns dealt with more than just the "big fights" of the day, and appealed to both San Franciscans and a national audience of boxing enthusiasts. A typical column might include a prediction for an upcoming world championship fight, inside dope on why a fight was scheduled for a certain time for television, and a mention of an up-and-coming local fighter. In his final column, Fiske decried what he believed was the current trend in boxing: making the fighters secondary to ring announcers, television commenta-tors, promoters, "showboat" referees, and ring card girls. He also bemoaned the refusal of boxing commissions to enforce their own rules.

Fiske rated the following as the most exciting fights he had ever seen: Bobby Chacon–Bazooka Limon IV, George Foreman–Ron Lyle, Larry Holmes–Ken Norton, Rory Calhoun–Spider Webb, Sugar Ray Leonard–Thomas Hearns I, and Michael Carbajal–Chiquita Gonzalez. Fiske was also an avid collector of boxing material. A portion of his collection of cartoons, art, and photographs was displayed in a show on boxing at the Center for the Arts at Yerba Buena Gardens in the San Francisco area.

The boxing community recognized Fiske's greatness and dedication to the sport. In

1987, he received the prestigious James J. Walker Award for Long and Meritorious Service to Boxing. His colleague at the *San Francisco Chronicle,* Dwight Chapin, described Fiske as an excellent reporter and a "master of concise, pull-no-punches writing." Hall of Fame referee Arthur Mercante called Fiske "a brilliant writer" while Hall of Fame trainer Angelo Dundee added, "He was one of the great columnists of our time. He was so good for boxing."

Fiske died January 24, 2006, in Redwood City, California, after a long battle with Parkinson's disease. He was 88. Hall of Fame Induction: 2003.

NAT FLEISCHER
Writer and Publisher

Nathaniel S. Fleischer is best known for founding *The Ring* magazine in 1922. He published this "bible of boxing" until his death in 1972. Born in New York on November 3, 1887, Fleischer grew up participating in a variety of sports including boxing. He graduated from City College of New York in 1908, then worked for the *New York Press* while pursuing studies at New York University. He left NYU after causing an explosion in the chemistry lab.

Fleischer eventually became sports editor of the *Press* and, when the newspaper merged with the *Morning Sun,* Fleischer became sports editor of the reconstituted *Sun Press.* As the paper's owner, Frank A. Munsey, bought a succession of newspapers, Fleischer became sports editor of each until 1929, when he left to devote full attention to his magazine. *The Ring* quickly became the authoritative voice on boxing.

The magazine's annual rankings of fighters were highly influential. When Fleischer first came up with the idea, he asked Tex Rickard to make the selections. After Rickard's death, Jack Dempsey made the choices for a year. Ultimately, Fleischer decided that *The Ring* staff and correspondents were best qualified to rank fighters. Fleischer also used the magazine to speak out on matters such as corruption or the influence of television. Fleischer became a kind of moral voice for boxing, advocating more extensive physical examinations for fighters, padded rings, and a halt to fights where one of the combatants had been seriously cut.

Fleischer strongly believed that titles should be won and lost in the squared circle. Although he denigrated Muhammad Ali's abilities at times and referred to him as Cassius Clay long after he had changed his name, Fleischer continued to list Ali as champion after he had been stripped of his title for refusing induction into the armed services.

In addition to the magazine, Fleischer published *Nat Fleischer's Ring Record Book and Boxing Encyclopedia* annually, beginning in 1941. The record book continued to be published until 1987. Fleischer also wrote many books about boxing, including *Black Dynamite*, a series on great African-American boxers; a history of the heavyweight championship; an autobiography; a history of wrestling; and several technical boxing manuals.

Fleischer refereed and judged a great many title bouts, including Pone Kingpetch–Pascual Perez, Carlos Ortiz–Flash Elorde, and Muhammad Ali–Karl Mildenberger.

Fleischer was one of the founders of the Boxing Writers Association and twice received its James J. Walker Award for Long and Meritorious Service to Boxing. The organization named the Nathaniel S. Fleischer Award after him to honor fine boxing writing. Fleischer also established a (no longer extant) museum and hall of fame in the offices of *The Ring.* Throughout his life, Fleischer fought for what he believed was best for the sport of boxing. He died on June 25, 1972. Hall of Fame Induction: 1990.

RICHARD K. FOX
Writer and Publisher

Second only to his frequent nemesis, John L. Sullivan, Richard K. Fox did more than anyone to popularize boxing in the late nineteenth century. Fox gave the sport extensive coverage in his tabloid, *The National Police Gazette,* and helped to organize key ring contests. Born in Belfast, Ireland, in 1846, Fox came to the United States in 1874 with less than five dollars in his pocket.

Within two years, he had taken over the financially troubled *Police Gazette* and expanded its quota of sensational, lurid tales of crime, sex, and scandal. He built up the distribution network until the *Gazette* was available nationally and in 26 countries around the world.

By the 1880s, the *Gazette* had a circulation of 150,000. In addition to accounts of murders and pictures of showgirls, the paper contained news of sporting events. When sales of issues covering the 1880 Joe Goss–Paddy Ryan fight leaped to 400,000, Fox decided to make the *Gazette* the "leading prize ring authority in America."

Fox's role in boxing grew after his first meeting with John L. Sullivan. According to legend, the two encountered each other at Harry Hill's saloon in New York. Sullivan supposedly insulted Fox by refusing to come to his table, and Fox seemed to bear a long grudge. His paper gave considerable column inches to Sullivan and his exploits but often portrayed the champion in a negative light.

Fox backed a succession of challengers to the "Boston Strongboy," among them Paddy Ryan, Tug Wilson, Herbert Slade, and Jake Kilrain. He named champions in several weight classes and bestowed upon them the *Police Gazette* Diamond Belt. Fox backed his champion, Kilrain, against Sullivan in the last bare-knuckle heavyweight championship bout, which Sullivan won.

Although the *Police Gazette* declined in the twentieth century, when Fox died in 1922 he was a wealthy man, leaving an estate of over $1.5 million. The colorful Fox, known for his Prince Albert coat and top hat, contributed greatly to the growth of boxing by publicizing fighters and bouts, backing fighters financially, and helping to establish standardized weight classes. His successes also helped spur the development of regular sports sections in daily newspapers. Hall of Fame Induction: 1997.

DEWEY FRAGETTA
Booking Agent

Though Dewey Fragetta served in a variety of capacities in an almost-five-decade-long boxing career, his place in boxing history was secured by his role as a booking agent. Fragetta was born in Utica, New York, in 1909. He became interested in boxing and wrestling as a teenager. His idols were the fighter Bushy Graham, a bantamweight champion, and the grappler Joe Malacevici. In 1928, he joined the *Utica Observer-Dispatch* and worked in the sports department covering bowling and boxing. Boxing held much more interest for Fragetta, who began promoting amateur bouts for a church in addition to writing about the sport. He later struck up an association with his hero, Graham, and in time became his manager. Under Fragetta's management, Graham fought Hall of Famer Fidel LaBarba. Fragetta managed other fighters, and in 1933, he opened an office in New York City.

Not content to serve as a manager, Fragetta developed a business where he served as the New York representative for promoters from all over the United States. When a promoter from another state needed some fighters for a card he was staging, he would contact Fragetta. With his great knowledge of New York fighters and his connections in the fight game, Fragetta would provide the needed boxers by arranging the details with the fighter and/or his manager and then making sure that the fighter arrived for the fight. In the early years of his booking business, Fragetta concentrated on booking fighters in the United States. World War II halted his business for the duration as he served in the United States Army until his discharge as a lieutenant.

After the war, when Fragetta again began booking fights, he turned more and more to the international market because of the reduction in the number of domestic boxing cards due to televised boxing. However, Fragetta did play a part in bringing boxing to television. In the early 1950s, he joined with Hall of Famer Ray Arcel to stage boxing shows on Saturday nights on ABC.

Fragetta continued to work primarily as a booking agent. In time, 90 percent of his business was in foreign countries. He placed fighters on cards in Venezuela, Italy, Australia, England, France, South Africa, Japan, the Philippines, and Peru. He prided himself on maintaining good long-term relationships with promoters and managers, and he frequently helped arrange publicity and television contracts for fights. Many great boxers fought in matches which Fragetta planned, including Joe Frazier, Bob Foster, Carlos Monzon, Emile Griffith, Carlos Ortiz, and Flash Elorde. Fragetta was very proud of helping to stage what was perhaps the first interracial bout in South Africa—between Foster and Pierre Fourie. Another of Fragetta's great achievements was the booking of bouts on the same night in South Africa, South America, Europe, Asia, and the United States.

Fragetta also published a monthly series of notes on boxing known as "Fistic Facts of Interest," which he sent to clients, potential clients, and sportswriters. In his unique career, he played a part in approximately 8,000 bouts before his death in 1977. Hall of Fame Induction: 2003.

DON FRASER
Publicist and Promoter

A legend in West Coast boxing circles, Don Fraser served as a writer, editor, publicist, matchmaker, promoter, and athletic commission official in a more than 40-year career in the sport. Fraser was born on January 28, 1927, in Blythe, California, and grew up in Los Angeles. He got his start in boxing in high school when he worked as a "behind the scenes second" for weekly amateur matches at the Southwest Arena in Los Angeles. Following graduation from Manual Arts High School, he served in the U.S. Army and attended Los Angeles City College. He left the army when his stint was over and became the California correspondent for *The Ring,* also serving as editor of *Knockout* magazine—a respected West Coast boxing periodical—from 1950 to 1955. In this role, Fraser came into contact with important California boxing figures. Despite his youth, he had an eye for a good story and for interesting up-and-coming fighters.

In 1956, Fraser embarked on a new chapter in his boxing career when he became public relations director for Legion Stadium in Hollywood. Early in his tenure, he handled publicity and marketing for the middleweight title fight held in that venue between Bobo Olson and Sugar Ray Robinson. The fight was a sellout. In 1959, Fraser moved to the

Olympic Auditorium as public relations director where he worked under Hall of Famers Aileen Eaton and George Parnassus. Fraser handled the publicity for the fight card at the massive Los Angeles Coliseum that featured a bantamweight title bout between Jose Becerra and Alphonse Halimi and a junior welterweight title bout between Carlos Ortiz and Battling Torres. The card drew 31,000—a great success at a site that had not previously hosted boxing matches. During this period, Fraser reportedly gave a young Muhammad Ali a button that read "I am the Greatest" and told him about the self-promotional antics of wrestler Gorgeous George and boxer Art Aragon.

In 1967, Jack Kent Cooke hired Fraser as the director of boxing and public relations at his new arena—the Fabulous Forum—built to house the Los Angeles Lakers and Kings, both owned by Cooke. In addition to contributing his usual public relations expertise, Fraser served as the promoter at the Forum for fourteen years. He produced many sellout events. The crowning achievement of his tenure was the promotion of the second Ali–Ken Norton match at the Forum, which set a California record for largest gate receipts for a fight. He also promoted the Ruben Olivares–Bobby Chacon WBC featherweight title fight in 1975. Fraser remained at the Forum until Governor Jerry Brown appointed him Executive Officer of the California State Athletic Commission in 1981. While Fraser did a fine job in this post, he longed to return to promoting fights. In 1983, he left the CSAC to become the head boxing promoter for the Olympic Auditorium.

Fraser left the Olympic the next year and considered exiting the sport. However, in 1985, the Marriot Hotel in Irvine, California, hired Fraser as promoter for its new concept of providing dinner with boxing matches. He had a very successful run at this small venue for seven years before he retired and turned the promotion over to his assistant. Fraser continues to live in California. Hall of Fame Induction: 2005.

EDDIE FUTCH
Trainer and Manager

One of the finest trainers in boxing history, Eddie Futch was in the winning corner each of the first two times Muhammad Ali was defeated. Born in Hillsboro, Mississippi, in 1911, Futch moved to Detroit as a child and grew up in the rough Black Bottom neighborhood. Although only 5'7", Futch starred on a crack semi-pro basketball team which travelled to such cities as Chicago and Pittsburgh to play.

When lack of funds kept Futch from going to college, he turned to boxing. He won the Detroit Athletic Association championship as a lightweight in 1932 and the Detroit Golden Gloves in 1933. Futch worked at the same gym as the young Joe Louis, who liked to spar with Futch because of the smaller man's speed and cleverness.

Futch's plans for a pro career ended when doctors discovered that he had a heart murmur. He began training amateur fighters in his spare time and, in the 1940s, started to develop pro fighters. He then left boxing for several years but returned in the early 1950s. Futch's first champion was Don Jordan, who won the welterweight title in 1958. Even with this success, Futch needed to work other jobs, including a long stint with the post office. Futch trained Hall of Famer Bob Foster and helped him to the world light heavyweight championship.

In 1966, Futch began training Joe Frazier, helping him to develop his bob-and-weave, which made the compact fighter even more difficult to hit. Under his guidance, Frazier won the heavyweight title during Muhammad Ali's enforced exile. When Frazier met Ali in the

"Fight of the Century," Futch instructed Frazier to back Ali into the ropes and work the body before moving to the head. He also instructed Frazier to make Ali throw right uppercuts which would leave him open to a left hook. Following Futch's instructions, Frazier won the fight over the previously unbeaten Ali. After the death of Yank Durham, Frazier's manager, Futch took over his managerial duties as well. Futch made the decision not to send the battered Frazier out for the fifteenth round in the "Thrilla in Manila."

Futch also handled Ken Norton for many years and was in his corner when Norton beat Ali. Futch's strategy of having Norton jab every time Ali jabbed, left Ali open to attack and led to Norton's victory. Futch also worked with Larry Holmes, Alexis Arguello, and Michael Spinks. When Spinks fought Holmes, Futch declined to work in either corner. Futch was the recipient of the James J. Walker Award for Long and Meritorious Service to Boxing in 1982. He also won the Al Buck Award as Manager of the Year in 1975 and the John Condon Award as Trainer of the Year in 1991. Active well into his eighties, Futch recently trained Riddick Bowe and Wayne McCullough. By the time he finally announced his retirement in January 1998, Futch had helped 22 fighters earn world titles. Futch died on October 10, 2001. Hall of Fame Induction: 1994.

BILL GALLO
Cartoonist and Journalist

While an accomplished sportswriter, Bill Gallo is best known for his work as a sports cartoonist with the *New York Daily News*. Born December 28, 1922, Gallo learned about the newspaper business and boxing from his father, Francisco ("Frank") Gallo, a reporter and editor for the Spanish language newspaper *La Prensa*. Gallo had to grow up quickly when his father died, leaving the eleven-year-old to finish school while working to support his family.

Following high school graduation in 1941, Gallo became a copyboy at the *Daily News*, but his career was cut short by the war. In 1942, he enlisted in the marines, where he saw plenty of action in the Pacific Theater, including the invasion of Iwo Jima. Back in New York after the war, Gallo became an apprentice in the art department of the *Daily News*, and attended the Cartoonists and Illustrators School at Columbia University at the same time.

During the 1950s, Gallo worked under the *Daily News* sports cartoonist, Leo O'Mealia, replacing him when O'Mealia died in 1960. In describing his own style, Gallo stated, "I've always tried to make it easy on the reader, whether I'm writing or drawing. Make it simple and natural on his eyes so he doesn't have to strain and wonder, 'Who is this? What is that?'"

Despite his 60 years in the newspaper business—with time out for military service—Gallo shows no signs of quitting, and his column appears weekly in the *Daily News*. To date he has drawn over 14,000 cartoons. His drawings have also appeared in *The Sporting News* and several have a place in the National Baseball Hall of Fame and Museum in Cooperstown, New York. Gallo has also written a regular column for the *Daily News*, and while he is not afraid to criticize sports and athletes—in both his cartoons and his column—he has earned the respect of those he covers.

Gallo has received numerous other honors. He has won ten Reuben Awards from the National Cartoonists Society as Best Sports Cartoonist of the Year, and in 1999, he earned the Milt Caniff Lifetime Achievement Award. In 1981, he received the James J. Walker Award for Long and Meritorious Service to Boxing from the Boxing Writers Association of America, and in 2001 he was inducted into the National Black Sports and Entertainment Hall of Fame for his role in helping black athletes, one of only three Caucasians selected for this honor. In 2000, he published a book showcasing his cartoons, entitled *Drawing a Crowd: Bill Gallo's Greatest Sports Moments*. Hall of Fame Induction: 2001.

CHARLEY GOLDMAN
Trainer

The man who shaped Rocky Marciano into a champion, Charley Goldman also trained four other world champions and, in his younger days, had a successful career as a fighter himself. Born Israel Goldman in Warsaw, Poland, in 1888, Goldman grew up in the tough Red Hook section of Brooklyn and learned to fight in the streets. He left school in the fourth grade and began fighting in the back of bars to earn spending money. He turned professional at the age of fifteen.

Goldman fought mostly as a bantamweight. He idolized Terry McGovern and started wearing his trademark derby hat in imitation of McGovern. He fought bantamweight champion Johnny Coulon in a no-decision bout in 1912. Goldman retired in 1914 with a recorded tally of 36-6-11 and 84 no-decision bouts. Goldman claimed that he actually fought about 400 times.

Goldman quickly found success as a trainer. In 1914, he trained Al McCoy, who won the middleweight title. With the passage of the Walker Law legalizing boxing in 1920, Goldman teamed with manager Al Weill. After five years, Goldman left boxing and moved to Newburgh, New York, to open a roadhouse, although Weill still occasionally sent him fighters to train.

In the mid-1930s, Goldman returned to New York and training fulltime. Although he often worked with Weill's boxers, he also handled other fighters. He worked with such champions as lightweight Lou Ambers, welterweight Marty Servo, and featherweight Joey Archibald. But in the late 1940s and '50s, Goldman gained his greatest fame training Rocky Marciano. When Goldman first saw him, Marciano had a strong punch but a crude style. Employing his philosophy of improving upon but not changing a fighter's basic style, Goldman strengthened Marciano's defense, left jab, and left hook. Marciano worked tirelessly to implement Goldman's instructions, and, of course, won the world championship.

Goldman was well liked and respected by the trainers, sportswriters, and others who frequented Stillman's Gym. For many years, he spent about six hours a day at Stillman's and then went to a C.Y.O. gym to work with very young fighters. He died of a heart attack in 1968. Hall of Fame Induction: 1992.

RUBY GOLDSTEIN
Referee

Famed referee Ruby Goldstein also had a distinguished career as a fighter. Born on the East Side of New York in 1907, Goldstein learned to box at the Henry Street Settlement House and started boxing in amateur tournaments at the age of sixteen. He turned pro in 1925 with a second-round knockout of Al Vano. He was nicknamed "the Jewel of the Ghetto."

Goldstein won his first 23 fights before Ace Hudkins knocked him out, and he compiled an early record of 50 wins in 55 bouts. However, after losing five fights by knockout, including one to Hall of Famer Jimmy McLarnin, Goldstein realized that he didn't have what it took to become a champion. Nevertheless, he continued to fight until 1937, retiring after winning a decision over Kid Bon Bon.

After leaving the ring, Goldstein remained on the fringes of boxing, and he also managed a pool hall. He started to referee while in the Army during World War II. He served as referee when Joe Louis fought exhibitions at military installations.

After his discharge, Goldstein continued to officiate. His first heavyweight title fight was the first Joe Louis–Jersey Joe Walcott match. Goldstein scored the fight for Walcott, while the two judges scored the fight in Louis's favor. Many observers thought that Walcott had won. When Louis was asked about Goldstein's scoring, he replied, "I know Ruby. He calls 'em like he sees 'em."

Louis's comment helped build Goldstein's reputation and, from then on, he officiated at many important fights, including the first Zale–Graziano match and the Robinson–Maxim light heavyweight championship fight (where the 104° heat conquered Goldstein in the tenth round and Robinson in the fourteenth). Goldstein officiated for the Emile Griffith–Benny ("Kid") Paret fight in which Paret was killed in the ring. That event bothered Goldstein greatly, and he retired after working one more fight.

Goldstein worked for longtime employer Schenley Distillers and wrote a column for *The Ring,* before retiring to Miami Beach. He died on April 22, 1984. Hall of Fame Induction: 1994.

MURRAY GOODMAN
Publicist

Murray Goodman had a long and varied career, but he is perhaps best known for his work as a boxing publicist. Born in Petricov, Russia, on January 1, 1914, Goodman immigrated to the United States at the age of eight. At twelve he began working for the Hearst Service as an office boy. By age seventeen he had his own byline with another news group, Universal Service, with whom he stayed until 1937—writing a nationally syndicated column as the Service's sports editor for the last five years of his tenure.

After the demise of Universal Service, Goodman became manager and publicist to the well-known "Clown Prince of Baseball," Al Schacht, with whom he worked for eight years, including collaboration on two books. During his time with Schacht, Goodman also served as the sports and publicity director for the Infantile Paralysis (Polio) Fund of New York.

Goodman next served briefly as publicity director for the Jumping Brook Resort in Neptune, New Jersey, where he arranged for heavyweight contender Tami Mauriello to train, and then as the promotion and tournament director of the short-lived and long-forgotten World Professional (Tennis) League.

Goodman then began a direct association with boxing when he was hired by the Tournament of Champions promotional organization to handle publicity for Marcel Cerdan before the Cerdan–Tony Zale middleweight championship fight. The Tournament of Champions later became the International Boxing Club and dominated the world of fight promotion in the late 1940s and '50s from its base of operations at the old Madison Square Garden. Goodman handled publicity for both Garden fights and IBC's national promotions held outside of New York.

Around 1960, Goodman left the IBC, working for the Yonkers Raceway before briefly becoming the public relations director for the New York Titans (later the Jets) of the American Football League. He also promoted the Dick Tiger–Joey Giardello middleweight title fight.

Goodman next headed to the sports division of the advertising and public relations division of Richard Kerr, Inc., where he helped publicize many major fights through the late '60s and early '70s. He and his son Bobby then opened Murray Goodman Associates, creating publicity for the two greatest promoters of recent times, Hall of Famers Don King and Bob Arum.

In his long career, Goodman publicized fights involving such notables as Joe Louis, Sugar Ray Robinson, Marcel Cerdan, Muhammad Ali, Rocky Graziano, Kid Gavilan, Sugar Ray Leonard, Bob Foster, Ken Norton, and Larry Holmes. In 1969, he received the James J. Walker Award for Long and Meritorious Service to Boxing from the Boxing Writers Association of America. He is credited with originating the S. Rae Hickok Professional Athlete of the Year Award, sponsored by the Hickok Manufacturing Company, and awarded annually from 1950 to 1976. Goodman wrote seventeen books—none of them about boxing—before his death on March 8, 1996. Hall of Fame Induction: 1999.

REG GUTTERIDGE
Broadcaster and Journalist

Over the last half century, Reg Gutteridge has been one of the best known figures in British and international boxing circles and is also heir to the legacy of one of Britain's greatest boxing families. His grandfather, Arthur Gutteridge, was a professional fighter who was on the card at the opening of the National Sporting Club at Covent Garden in 1898 and reportedly gave boxing lessons to Rudyard Kipling. Reg's father, Dick Gutteridge, and his uncle, Jack Gutteridge, were identical twins, both well known in boxing circles as amateur fighters, club and school coaches, professional trainers, and seconds. They were known as the "Trainers of Champions."

It was, perhaps, inevitable that Gutteridge would follow in his family's boxing tradition. He has spent his life covering boxing, both as a writer and a broadcaster. Born in Islington, England, in 1924, his father let him hold the boxers' robes at Bethnal Green when he was only ten. Gutteridge even fought a few times as an amateur, but it was soon apparent to him that a life inside the ring was not his best career opportunity. In 1938, Gutteridge left school and got a job as a messenger with the London *Evening News*. He served in the British Army during WWII, and lost half his left leg in 1944 to a land mine in Normandy.

After the war, Gutteridge returned to the *Evening News*, where he became the paper's boxing correspondent, a position he held until the paper merged with another publication in 1980. Gutteridge has also written numerous columns and articles for boxing publications in Great Britain and the United States, and has authored or coauthored several books about boxing, including *Boxing: The Great Ones, Mike Tyson: The Release of Power, The Big Punchers,* and his autobiography, *Uppercuts and Dazes.*

For decades, Gutteridge also has been a boxing broadcaster for British radio and television. In 1991, the Boxing Writers Association of America awarded him the Sam Taub Award for Excellence in Broadcasting Journalism.

Gutteridge found that he actually preferred his longstanding BBC television duties to print journalism. "I enjoyed the TV work; writing for a newspaper is much harder. Before you start you look at a blank page, and it's like a desert."

Throughout his long career, Gutteridge has traveled the globe and has developed close relationships with some of the fighters he has covered. He once lured Muhammad Ali to the set of the British edition of *This is Your Life*, and Ali let Gutteridge interview him between rounds of his 1973 fight with Rudi Lubbers. When Gutteridge was hospitalized with blood poisoning, he awoke to find Ali praying at his bedside.

Besides his induction into the International Boxing Hall of Fame, Gutteridge has received another great honor: In 1995, Queen Elizabeth II awarded Gutteridge an Order of the British Empire for his service to boxing. Hall of Fame Induction: 2002.

W.C. HEINZ
Writer

Not "just" a sportswriter, W.C. Heinz was a successful reporter, columnist, war correspondent, freelance writer, biographer, and novelist. Even with his many varied interests, both personal and professional, Heinz always was extremely interested in boxing and returned to it frequently in both his fiction and non-fiction writing. Wilfred Charles Heinz was born on January 11, 1915, in Mount Vernon, New York. Heinz became interested in sports as a youth and played hockey through high school. He also was a voracious reader. When he received the *Omnibus of Sport*, an anthology of sportswriting, for Christmas in 1932, Heinz found something that combined his two main interests: sports and good writing. Heinz graduated from Middlebury College in 1937 where he served as the sports editor of the college newspaper.

After college, he worked at the *New York Sun,* first as a messenger boy and then as a copy boy. In 1939, he was promoted to cub reporter and occasionally contributed pieces about skiing and basketball. During World War II, Heinz became the junior war correspondent for the *Sun* in 1943, spending a month and a half on an escort carrier on antisubmarine duty, then moving to England to cover the Allied invasion of Europe. From then until the end of the war, he moved with the troops—often putting himself in danger. When the paper's senior war correspondent was captured by the German army, Heinz replaced him. As a war correspondent, Heinz became a polished writer and developed a distinctive style.

Upon his return to the United States after the end of the war in Europe, Heinz began to cover sports full-time although the *Sun* offered him the post of the newspaper's Washington correspondent. His work was admired by such luminaries as Hall of Famer Damon Runyon. Heinz became a master of the "conversation piece," a novelistic technique where long sequences of dialog were reported without comments by the writer. In 1948, he was rewarded with his own column, "The Sports Scene." Heinz wrote five columns a week about all sports, but concentrated mostly on boxing.

When the *Sun* folded in 1950, Heinz became a freelance magazine writer. Three of his articles from his freelance period were included in the anthology, *The Best American Sports Writing of the Century.* No other writer had more than two selections. One of Heinz's entries was "Brownsville Bum," a portrait of boxer Bummy Davis written for *True* magazine. Heinz wrote for such periodicals as *Collier's, Cosmopolitan, The Saturday Evening Post, Sport, Argosy, True, Esquire,* and *Look.* He also contributed pieces to *The Ring* early in his freelance career. Heinz frequently profiled boxers in his articles, including such Hall of Famers as Carmen Basilio, Rocky Marciano, Joe Louis, Ingemar Johansson, Archie Moore, Beau Jack, Floyd Patterson, Sugar Ray Robinson, and Ezzard Charles. Heinz believed that boxing was the purest form of competition and likened it to a work of art.

In 1958, he published his first novel, *The Professional,* the story of Eddie Brown, a middleweight who was modeled on Hall of Famer Billy Graham. The book received good reviews, including one from Ernest Hemingway who called it "the only good novel I've ever read about a fighter and an excellent first novel in its own right." Heinz continued to write for magazines but gained even more acclaim, with Vince Lombardi, when he wrote the very successful book *Run to Daylight* (which covered a week's preparation for a game with the Detroit Lions). Heinz roomed with Lombardi at the Green Bay Packers training camp as he gathered material for the book. Heinz also wrote an adaptation of the book for television—produced by his friend, Howard Cosell. At about the same time, he wrote another novel, *The Surgeon,* based on a thoracic surgeon he had written about for *Life* magazine.

For *The Saturday Evening Post,* Heinz wrote "Great Day at Trickem Fork," an article about the famous Selma civil rights march. In 1968, he co-wrote *M*A*S*H** which later became a movie and an extremely popular long-running television show. Heinz's shorter works have been collected in three book-length volumes: *American Mirror, Once They Heard the Cheers,* and *What a Time It Was.* In the introduction to the third work, Jeff MacGregor stated that, in terms of boxing writers, "There is W.C. Heinz. There is A.J. Liebling. There is everyone else." In the foreword to the same volume, David Halberstam credits Heinz with helping to change journalism by giving it a more natural style that employed some of the conventions of fiction. Heinz has also edited anthologies of boxing and baseball, including the recent, *Sports Illustrated Classics: The Book of Boxing,* an updated version of his *Fireside Book of Boxing.* A collection of his wartime writing, *When We Were One: Stories of World War II,* was recently published as well. Heinz was inducted into the National Sportscasters and Sportswriters Hall of Fame in 2001. He currently lives in Vermont. Hall of Fame Induction: 2004.

JOE HUMPHREYS
Announcer

The first ring announcer to be inducted into the International Boxing Hall of Fame, Joe Humphreys earned this honor by announcing tens of thousands of fights in a career that lasted from 1890 until his death in 1936.

Born on New York City's Lower East Side on October 19, 1872, Humphreys was orphaned at the age of ten and received only limited schooling. He became involved in boxing as a mascot of the Nonpareil Athletic Club. Known as "Joe the Beaut" for his good looks and fine singing voice, Humphreys first announced a fight at a benefit for an injured boxer. Humphreys sang on the program and impressed the crowd with his booming voice and commanding presence.

As a reward for his work in the political campaign of Big Tim Sullivan of Tammany Hall in the late 1890s, Humphreys received the announcing assignment at the Broadway Athletic Club. Early in his career, Humphreys worked without a microphone. He also served as public address announcer for the New York Yankees but quit when owner Frank Farrell wanted him to use a megaphone. "I myself am the loudspeaker," Humphreys said indignantly.

Humphreys had the unique ability to know how to handle a fight crowd that was about to turn into an unruly mob. His announcement of "Quiet, please, quiet" instantly commanded a crowd's attention. In Yankee Stadium on May 20, 1927, prior to the Jack Sharkey–Jim Maloney bout, Humphreys quelled a disturbance over the previous bout by asking the crowd to pray for Charles Lindbergh, who had just embarked on his historic transatlantic flight earlier that day.

Some of the most noteworthy fights Humphreys introduced were the Jack Dempsey–

Georges Carpentier "Battle of the Century" at Boyle's Thirty Acres in New Jersey, Dempsey–Luis Firpo, and the second Dempsey–Gene Tunney fight. Humphreys was also co-manager of Hall of Famer Terry McGovern. Humphreys died of a heart attack on July 11, 1936, in Fairhaven, New Jersey. Hall of Fame Induction: 1997.

SAM ICHINOSE
Promoter

Sam Ichinose, the greatest boxing promoter in Hawaiian history, was born on November 12, 1907. He dropped out of Lahainaluna High School after his fumble in the football game against traditional rival Maui High School led to a Maui touchdown and defeat for his team. He then considered a career in boxing but lost his first and only amateur bout. When professional boxing was legalized in Hawaii in 1929, Ichinose decided to work in the fight game and began his new career by managing a fighter named Freddie Gomez. Ichinose dubbed Gomez "Mexicali Rose" because of his Irish and Mexican heritage. Ichinose's experience with Gomez led him to other fighters, and by 1952, he was promoting fights in Japan, Indonesia, and Europe in addition to his home base of Hawaii where—with partner Ralph Yempuku—he promoted under the Boxing Enterprises banner. He often went to the continental United States to publicize his fighters, where his penchant for displaying a hang-dog expression when talking to sportswriters led to his nickname "Sad Sam."

In his lengthy career, Ichinose was instrumental in Ben Villaflor's rise to the world junior lightweight championship. He also managed Dado Marino to the world flyweight championship and worked with Hall of Famer Bobo Olson.

In 1981, the year of his retirement, Ichinose tried to obtain a license for Muhammad Ali to fight in Hawaii, but the Hawaii Boxing Commission refused his application. In addition to his career in boxing, he owned Sad Sam's Bar, which remained in business for over three decades. Ichinose served a two-year term in the Territorial House of Representatives, and was both a city and county supervisor. Ichinose is also a member of the Hawaii Sports Hall of Fame. He died on January 24, 1993. Hall of Fame Induction: 2000.

JIMMY JACOBS
Manager and Film Historian

Jimmy Jacobs is primarily known to boxing for his vast collection of fight films, but he was also a fight manager and, as a young man, a handball champion. Born in St. Louis in 1930, Jacobs grew up in Los Angeles, and while he excelled in baseball, football, and basketball, his primary sport was handball. He was a six-time national singles handball champion and a six-time national doubles champion. Handball experts credit him with first using the ceiling shot.

Jacobs was also a boxing enthusiast, and in his travels to other countries to give handball exhibitions, he began to acquire films of old fights which were no longer available in this country. In 1961, Jacobs joined forces with another collector, Hall of Famer Bill Cayton, to restore and preserve the films. Their corporation, Big Fights, Inc., produced over 1,000 boxing features with the old films as a base. Three of their productions were nominated for Academy Awards.

In addition to his film collecting, Jacobs also managed fighters with Cayton. The pair handled three world champions: Wilfred Benitez, Edwin Rosario, and Mike Tyson. As a manager, Jacobs was content to let the trainer determine the fight strategy and training regimen.

Jacobs died on March 23, 1988, after a long struggle with leukemia. He was hailed in both the boxing and handball worlds for his successes and fine character. Along with his spot in the Boxing Hall of Fame, Jacobs is an inductee of the Handball Hall of Fame. Hall of Fame Induction: 1993.

MIKE JACOBS
Promoter

Following in the footsteps of Tex Rickard, Mike Jacobs ruled as the dominant boxing promoter of the 1930s and '40s. Born in New York City in 1880, Jacobs came from a poor family and went to work as a boy, selling newspapers and candy on Coney Island excursion boats. Noticing that ticket purchases for the boats were often confusing to prospective passengers, Jacobs began scalping boat tickets. He then bought concession rights on all the boats docked at the Battery, sold train tickets to recent immigrants, and eventually ran his own ferryboats.

Jacobs then became the premier ticket scalper in New York, buying and selling theater, opera, or sports events tickets. He began backing events himself—any sort of venture he believed would profit in the end—including charity balls, bike races, and circuses.

Jacobs met Rickard at the Gans–Nelson fight in 1906, Rickard's first promotion, and helped Rickard become active in the New York area. Jacobs profited from Rickard's ventures, both from ticket sales and from investing in Rickard's promotions.

After Rickard's death in 1929, Jacobs focused his money-making talents elsewhere until sportswriters Damon Runyon, Ed Frayne, and Bill Farnsworth of the Hearst newspaper chain arranged for him to stage Hearst's annual Milk Fund boxing benefit at the Bronx Coliseum. In 1933, the three reporters and Jacobs formed the Twentieth Century Sporting Club to promote boxing. Jacobs used the Hippodrome in New York as his primary venue. The Club's initial bout was staged in January 1934 between Barney Ross and Billy Petrolle.

In 1935, Jacobs signed the young heavyweight Joe Louis to an exclusive contract. Louis's first bout in Yankee Stadium grossed $328,655, while his fight with Max Baer grossed over $1 million. Jacobs's link to Louis, the biggest attraction in boxing, solidified his position as a top promoter. This was borne out when he staged the Tournament of Champions on September 23, 1937, in Yankee Stadium, in which four world championship bouts were fought. Following on this success, Madison Square Garden leased the arena and the outdoor Madison Square Garden Bowl to the Twentieth Century Sporting Club.

Jacobs now had complete control of boxing in New York. In 1938, his relationship with the Garden changed from tenant-landlord to a partnership. At about that time, Jacobs became the sole shareholder of the Twentieth Century Sporting Club, paying off Runyon and forcing the other two partners out. Through the rest of the 1930s and into the postwar period, Jacobs was unmatched as a promoter, reaching his peak with the second Louis–Billy Conn fight, which brought in almost two million dollars. Every fight that Louis fought as a champion was promoted by Jacobs. In his heyday, the stretch on Manhattan's 49th Street between Broadway and Eighth Avenue was known as "Jacob's Beach."

Jacobs suffered a cerebral hemorrhage in 1946 but remained in charge of the organization with his relative Sol Strauss operating the club on a day-to-day basis. When Louis decided to retire and then go into business with the group that became the International Boxing Club, the Twentieth Century Sporting Club ceased to function. Jacobs remained in ill health and died in January 1953. Hall of Fame Induction: 1990.

JAMES J. JOHNSTON
Promoter and Manager

Known as the "Boy Bandit," James J. Johnston was a top manager and promoter for many years, as well as one of the more colorful figures in boxing history. Born in Liverpool, England, on November 28, 1875, Johnston was twelve when his parents moved to Hell's Kitchen in New York City. Although his parents were Irish, his English accent led him into many fights in that Irish neighborhood. Johnston quit school at thirteen and went to work with his father at an iron foundry.

Johnston toyed with professional boxing but had limited success and moved on to helping Billy Newman operate fight clubs in New York. When Charles Harvey, a fight manager specializing in importing fighters from England, asked Johnston to become his assistant, he gladly accepted. Together, Harvey and Johnston brought over noteworthy fighters like Hall of Famers Owen Moran, Jim Driscoll, and Ted ("Kid") Lewis. Harvey's stable grew so large, he had trouble getting matches for all his fighters, so Johnston devised a plan whereby each fighter was paired with a promoter in need of a card. This arrangement worked well until the fighters began to make side deals among themselves that resulted in less than scintillating bouts.

While still working for Harvey, Johnston promoted fights at St. Nicholas Rink, later St. Nicholas Arena, in the years before WWI. He frequently used Harvey's fighters, which led other managers to complain of favoritism, but Johnston was more concerned with ticket sales than fairness. He staged midget boxing matches and brought in a suffragette speaker, which was sure to draw hecklers. Johnston's other stunts included having a white man with yellow face paint masquerade as a Chinese champion, and another man pose as a gypsy fighter. These tactics seem tawdry today, but Johnston won great acclaim in boxing circles of the time.

After his success at St. Nicholas Rink, Johnston was invited to promote at Madison Square Garden in 1914, and for brief periods before and after World War I, he promoted at both the Rink and the Garden. Although he no longer was associated with Harvey, he continued to manage some fighters, including George Rodel—whom he falsely claimed was a veteran of the Boer War—and Lewis. He also continued to use shady tactics in and out of the ring. He planted the idea that Rodel had a weak heart in the mind of Jess Willard, whose last bout had resulted in his opponent's accidental death. Willard's fear of killing Rodel made him lose the newspaper decision.

Johnston became promoter/manager at Tex Rickard's "New" Madison Square Garden from 1933 to 1937, where he promoted three heavyweight title fights in which the belt changed hands: Primo Carnera–Jack Sharkey, Carnera–Max Baer, and Baer–James J. Braddock. Johnston lost control of the heavyweight division to Mike Jacobs when the latter matched Braddock against Joe Louis in Chicago, and later lost out to Jacobs at the Garden as well.

Still, Johnston continued to manage fighters—he goaded Joe Louis into a rematch against his charge, Bob Pastor, even after Pastor did little but run from Louis in their first fight—and spent countless hours during World War II speaking at veterans' hospitals. The Boxing Writers Association of America awarded him the James J. Walker Award for Long and Meritorious Service to Boxing in 1945. He died of heart failure on May 7, 1946, just after attending a fight at St. Nicholas Arena. Marcus Griffin authored a fine early biography of Johnston in 1933—to which Damon Runyon contributed a foreword—entitled *Wise Guy: James J. Johnston: A Rhapsody in Fistics*. Hall of Fame Induction: 1999.

JERSEY JONES
Publicist and Writer

During a career in boxing that spanned more than 60 years, Willis ("Jersey") Jones served as a fighter, trainer, manager, promoter, publicist, and writer. Born in Brooklyn, New York, on October 24, 1898, Jones grew up in West Orange, New Jersey. His career as a boxer started at a smoker in West Orange on October 5, 1912. Jones fought as an amateur, as a professional, and as a member of the United States Marine Corps in World War I. He compiled a combined record of 58-4. Jones worked as a sportswriter before the war and, after it, served as the sports editor of the *New York Globe* before that paper's demise. He then promoted boxing in Bayonne, New Jersey; West New York, New Jersey; Syracuse, New York; and Montreal. He also trained fighters.

It was as a publicity man that Jones achieved his greatest notice. He worked publicity at 40 training camps for fights involving Mike Jacobs's promotions, including sixteen fights for Joe Louis. Jones handled publicity for Billy Conn's camp before his first fight with Louis. In addition to boxing, Jones was in charge of publicity for the New York Rangers in the National Hockey League, and helped them rise to prominence over the more established but now defunct New York Americans. Besides hockey, Jones dabbled in other sports. He promoted roller derby, indoor soccer, and tennis at Madison Square Garden, and bike racing at velodromes in Coney Island and New Jersey.

In 1946, Jones joined the staff of *The Ring* and remained there until his retirement in 1970. Even after his official retirement, Jones contributed historical articles to "The Bible of Boxing" until his death on December 18, 1973. Because of its appreciation of Jones, *The Ring* relaxed its rule that prevented one of its staff from managing or training a fighter and allowed Jones to have a hand in the management of two world champions, Hogan Bassey and Hall of Famer Dick Tiger. Hall of Fame Induction: 2005.

HANK KAPLAN
Historian

Many consider Hank Kaplan the foremost boxing historian in the world today. Boxing fans, magazines, writers, and even the International Boxing Hall of Fame itself rely on Kaplan's encyclopedic boxing knowledge and incredible storehouse of boxing books, photographs, and memorabilia.

Kaplan was born in Brooklyn, the first child of an immigrant couple from Lithuania. Kaplan's father, a tailor, died of tuberculosis when Kaplan was ten, and Kaplan, his mother, and his three siblings were so poor that they had trouble getting enough food to eat. Since Kaplan's mother could not provide adequate support for her family, Kaplan—along with his brother and sisters— was placed in an orphanage, the Hebrew Orphans Asylum. Kaplan later called the orphanage "the greatest thing that ever happened to us." While at a summer camp run by the orphanage, Kaplan got his first exposure to boxing when a much smaller boy gave him a bloody nose in a fight. From that moment on Kaplan was fascinated with the art and science of boxing.

As a teenager, Kaplan attended school while he worked several jobs until he dropped out so that he could work full-time. He eventually earned a GED and attended college at the University of Miami. Kaplan also boxed, and even won his only professional bout.

When World War II began, Kaplan tried to enlist in the U.S. Navy but was turned down. He then joined the U.S. Coast Guard, following the example of Jack Dempsey. After basic training, Kaplan was sent to the chemical warfare school. He was then stationed in Miami where he taught sailors to recognize and to protect themselves from chemical agent attacks. After the war Kaplan settled in Miami, where he joined the Public Health Service. The unit in which he worked ultimately became the Centers for Disease Control. Kaplan worked as a quarantine officer. He also traveled internationally for the Public Health Service.

Though his days were spent in the service of his country, Kaplan continued to pursue his avocation, boxing. In the 1950s, he became an informal press agent for promoter Chris Dundee and trainer Angelo Dundee, who were based in Miami Beach. Through his association with the Dundees, Kaplan became acquainted with Muhammad Ali. Ali would often ask Kaplan for his analysis of the strengths and weaknesses of upcoming opponents.

Kaplan served as a technical advisor for the Rocky Marciano–Ali computer bout, which used a then-sophisticated computer program to plot how a bout between the two great champions, in their primes, would have unfolded. Marciano (wearing a wig to mask his age) and Ali were filmed sparring in approximately 70 one-minute segments, which were subsequently assembled—according to the computer's direction—to make a filmed record of the battle. (The combatants received instruction that punches to the head were to be "pulled.") The fight was shown on closed circuit television on January 20, 1970. (Marcino won with a 13th-round knockout!)

Kaplan's varied roles in boxing have also included editor of *Boxing World* and *World Wide Boxing Digest,* writer of boxing articles for publications located around the world, manager, cornerman, and promoter in the Fort Lauderdale area. Through all these various endeavors Kaplan kept adding to his boxing knowledge and the books, photos, clippings, and memorabilia which are considered the largest private boxing library in the world. *Sports Illustrated* hired him as a consultant on boxing for more than twenty years. Kaplan helped found the World Boxing Historians Association and the International Boxing Research Organization. In 2002, the Boxing Writers Association of America named Kaplan the winner of its annual James J. Walker Award for Long and Meritorious Service to Boxing. Hall of Fame Induction: 2006.

JACK KEARNS
Manager

Best known as heavyweight champion Jack Dempsey's manager, Jack ("Doc") Kearns spent over 60 years in boxing. Kearns and Dempsey, both rough-and-tumble characters with a great zest for life, were partners for six years.

Born in 1882, Kearns grew up in the state of Washington. When he was fourteen, he joined the Alaska Yukon gold rush by stowing away on a freighter. The young Kearns did not strike it rich and on returning home worked as a ranch hand. He also accepted pay in return for helping to smuggle Chinese immigrants into the United States. He gravitated toward boxing and first fought professionally in Billings, Montana, in 1900. Kearns later claimed to have had over 60 professional bouts.

Kearns spent a year in prison for fighting in a street brawl. He operated a bar and a boxing club in Spokane. But San Francisco, then the boxing center of the nation, was the place to be, and Kearns eventually found his way there. He thrived in the active boxing world and quickly started managing and promoting fights. Harry Wills was prominent among the boxers he managed.

In 1917, Kearns and Dempsey met. Though Kearns claimed Dempsey came to his aid in a bar fight, others said that Kearns had seen him fight in New York and was impressed with his crude power. Kearns guided Dempsey to the championship in 1919 with a victory over Jess Willard. He was a master of publicity and was largely responsible for making possible the first million-dollar gate in boxing history when Dempsey fought Georges Carpentier. Kearns's managerial acumen also allowed Dempsey to receive $300,000 for a fight in Shelby, Montana, which virtually bankrupted the town.

Dempsey split with Kearns after the Dempsey–Firpo fight in 1923. Dempsey and his new wife, actress Estelle Taylor, believed that Kearns had been mishandling the fighter's funds. The parting was acrimonious and involved multiple lawsuits.

Although Kearns's greatest success was with Dempsey, he remained active as a fight manager until his death on July 17, 1963. Among the other fighters he managed were Hall of Famers Joey Maxim, Archie Moore, and Mickey Walker. He spent five years in the employ of the International Boxing Club, setting matches. When asked to testify before the Kefauver committee, which was investigating ties between organized crime and boxing, Kearns positively impressed the panel of senators and did not prove to be directly linked to the mob figures who heavily influenced the International Boxing Club. Kearns has also been credited with staging the first fight in Las Vegas—a 1955 bout between Moore and Nino Valdes. Hall of Fame Induction: 1990.

DON KING
Promoter

Don King has been involved in every aspect of promotion, from setting up world championship bouts in far-flung locales to selling broadcast rights to major television networks and pay-per-view channels. With persistence and energy, King has taken an innovative approach to boxing promotion for over 30 years.

King grew up in Cleveland, where as a young man he became involved in running gambling operations. At age 23 and again twelve years later, King was involved in homicides connected to the gambling business. He was convicted in the second incident and served more than four years in prison, where he read voraciously, devouring the classics and works of philosophy. For a time, King also owned a nightclub in Cleveland called the New Corner Tavern, where such musicians as Erroll Garner, B.B. King, and Lloyd Price performed.

King first became involved in boxing promotion in 1972 when, with Don Elbaum, he organized a boxing benefit for the black-owned Forest City Hospital in Cleveland. King got Muhammad Ali to box ten exhibition rounds with an assortment of fighters and Cleveland radio personalities. The evening's festivities, which also included a concert featuring Marvin Gaye, Lou Rawls, and Wilson Pickett, brought in $81,000.

King went on to promote several fighters, including heavyweight Earnie Shavers. His first widespread public acclaim came with the "Rumble in the Jungle" heavyweight championship fight matching George Foreman and Muhammad Ali in Kinshasa, Zaire, on October 30, 1974. The fight was the first to offer a $10 million purse—guaranteed by the Zairian government.

Working independently, King then promoted Ali's championship defense against Chuck Wepner in Cleveland. With Bob Arum, King promoted Ali's third fight with Joe Frazier, "The Thrilla in Manila," on October 1, 1975. He then went on to assemble a series of big-name fights, including many featuring Larry Holmes. "The Last Hurrah," Ali's failed 1980 comeback attempt against Holmes in Las Vegas, was a King production that brought in the first $6 million live gate. Other notable King promotions include Sugar Ray Leonard–Roberto Duran I (co-promoted with Bob Arum), in which Leonard was the first fighter ever guaranteed a $10 million purse, and the "Grand Slam of Boxing," featuring four world championship fights headlined by Julio Cesar Chavez. The latter show drew a paid attendance of 132,274 to Mexico City's Estadio Azteca.

King has promoted a total of over 500 championship fights. He has owned and operated his own cable and pay-per-view television networks and was involved in promoting singer Michael Jackson's "Victory Tour." He promoted Mike Tyson's first comeback fight, on August 19, 1995, which generated over $90 million worldwide and set a U.S. pay-per-view record. King's November 1996 show pitting Tyson against Evander Holyfield brought in $14 million—the highest-ever revenues from a live gate. Tyson–Holyfield II topped the previous pay-per-view record with approximately 1.9 million buys.

A man of apparent contrasts, King has donated millions to charitable organizations. His unparalleled influence over boxing has led to money disputes with some fighters and further appearances in court. Named by *Sports Illustrated* as one of the "most influential sports figures of the past 40 years," King's activities led him to be named "Promoter of the Century" by the WBA and the "Greatest Promoter of All Time" by the IBF and WBC. In 1997, the NAACP awarded King its prestigious President's Award. Only two years before, acclaimed writer Jack Newfield documented King's history in the revealing book *Only in America: The Life and Crimes of Don King*.

Age 65 at the time of his induction into the Hall of Fame, Don King's strong personality, distinctive "electric" stand-up hair, and flowery speech peppered with the catchphrase "Only in America" have made him a well-known figure throughout the world.

Among King's recent promotional coups was the "2001 Middleweight World Championship Series" which led to the crowning of Bernard Hopkins as the first undisputed middleweight champ since Marvelous Marvin Hagler. Hall of Fame Induction: 1997.

TITO LECTOURE
Promoter

The only South American promoter in the International Boxing Hall of Fame, Juan Carlos ("Tito") Lectoure gained worldwide recognition—in a career spanning 31 years—for both himself and his primary venue, the storied Luna Park in Buenos Aires, Argentina.

Luna Park was opened in 1932 by Lectoure's uncle—the first Argentine lightweight champion, Jose Lectoure—and Ismael Pace. The original arena lacked even a roof, but it was remodelled into a fully enclosed stadium, seating about 25,000. Inspired by his uncle, Lectoure decided to become a boxer himself, and he sparred with Archie Moore when "The Old

Mongoose" was training for a fight at Luna Park.

Though he served in the army and attended college, Lectoure's true calling was boxing, and early on he became involved in the operations of Luna Park. After Pace and Jose Lectoure died within five years of each other in the 1950s, Tito's aunt put the nineteen-year-old Lectoure in charge of the arena. At first he worked under the tutelage of Luna Park's official promoter, Juan Manual Morales, but soon staged his first personally promoted card on September 14, 1956. It was an auspicious date—September 14 is "Boxer Day" to Argentine fight fans, celebrating Luis Firpo's 1923 match against Jack Dempsey.

Lectoure staged an incredible two fights per week at Luna Park, on Wednesdays and Saturdays, for 31 years, a total of 2,976 cards. The Wednesday night fights were a special challenge, since they were televised. In addition to managing all the boxing events at Luna Park, Lectoure was responsible for securing the services of every other show at the arena, including circuses, ice shows, and even the Harlem Globetrotters. He also operated the spacious Luna Park Gymnasium, where 100 fighters could train at one time.

Lectoure's impact on the world of boxing extended beyond Argentina. In 1966, he staged his first world title bout at Luna Park, pitting WBA flyweight champion Horacio Accavallo against former champ Hiryoki Ebihara in a sold-out fight. He promoted five world title fights at his arena for Nicolino Locche, who was perhaps Lectoure's favorite boxer. By the end of his career, he had sponsored 24 world title fights at Luna Park. Perhaps the highlight of those two dozen bouts was the Carlos Monzon–Emile Griffith middleweight championship match in 1971, which set a South American box office record and was televised in the United States on ABC's *Wide World of Sports*. Twelve Argentine fighters became world champions while working under Lectoure's promotion. In addition, Hall of Famers Archie Moore, Sandy Saddler, Kid Gavilan, Joe Brown, Carlos Ortiz, Ismael Laguna, Eder Jofre, and Antonio Cervantes fought at Luna Park.

Lectoure, a shrewd promoter with a knack for finding matches that were attractive to the paying public, was involved as a promoter or co-promoter in another 100 world title fights at other venues. Highly respected for his business acumen, boxing knowledge, and character, Lectoure left boxing in 1987. The last bout that he promoted was a welterweight fight between Arce Rossi and Ramón Abeldaño on October 17, 1987. Next Lectoure turned his promotional skills to the arts. Luna Park hosted events with the likes of Luciano Pavarotti, the Bolshoi Ballet, and a great array of plays and concerts. He died March 1, 2002, in Buenos Aires. Hall of Fame Induction: 2000.

A.J. LIEBLING
Writer

One of boxing's greatest chroniclers, A.J. Liebling wrote about the sport with a brilliance and wit that may never be surpassed. In a series of essays for *The New Yorker*, Liebling interpreted boxing's mayhem and beauty for a wide audience. Liebling spent many an hour at ringside, but his best writing sprang from his connections behind the scenes. He knew the players and could reflect their voices with spellbinding realism. He wrote about boxing with a wry honesty that neither glamorized nor vilified its violence.

Born in New York, Liebling went to Dartmouth College before being expelled for not attending chapel. He then attended and graduated from the Columbia School of Journalism and went to work at *The New York Times*, which fired him for an alleged lack of attention to detail. He then worked for newspapers in Providence, Rhode Island, lived in Paris where he studied medieval history, and worked for five years for *The New York World Telegram*.

In 1935, Liebling began a 28-year association with *The New Yorker*, which lasted until his death in 1963. He wrote on a number of subjects including politics, war, food, horse racing, and the media. His essays on boxing appeared in *The New Yorker* from 1951 until his death and have been collected in two books, *The Sweet Science* and *A Neutral Corner*. Hall of Fame Induction: 1992.

LORD LONSDALE
Patron

As the first president of the National Sporting Club, which governed boxing in England from 1891 to 1929, Hugh Cecil Lowtner, the fifth Earl of Lonsdale, helped establish the club as the major force in English boxing. He donated the original Lonsdale belts presented to English champions.

Lonsdale's great wealth allowed him to live a life of leisure and luxury. He had a genuine love for and knowledge of boxing. He was taught to box by Hall of Famer Jem Mace. In an era when boxing was not considered respectable, Lonsdale was one of the few aristocrats to take an interest in seeing that bouts took place fairly under proper rules. He appeared in court to assist boxers prosecuted for ring fatalities. He also had a role in the development of the original Queensberry Rules and the padded boxing glove.

When he became president of the National Sporting Club, Lonsdale expanded his efforts to legitimize boxing. Starting in 1909, the National Sporting Club began awarding the Lonsdale Belt, named after its patron. It was originally presented to the champion in each British weight division, and the holder could keep the belt if it was won and then defended two times. The belt was first won by Freddie Welsh in 1909 for winning the British lightweight title. Heavyweight Henry Cooper was the first person to win three Lonsdale Belts outright. The belt is still won today and awarded by the British Boxing Board of Control, although to keep it a boxer must win and defend it three times. Hall of Fame Induction: 1990.

HARRY MARKSON
Publicist and Promoter

Harry Markson was involved in the promotion of boxing matches for 40 years, from the time of Joe Louis to the time of Muhammad Ali. Born in Kingston, New York, Markson graduated from Union College and worked as a sportswriter for the *Bronx Home News*. In 1933, he became a part-time publicity man for Madison Square Garden. Four years later, he became publicity director for promoter Mike Jacobs and his Twentieth Century Sporting Club. At that time, Jacobs was the premier promoter in boxing, handling Joe Louis's fights and other major New York bouts.

In 1948, Jacobs made Markson managing director of the Twentieth Century Sporting Club. When the International Boxing Club (IBC), controlled by James Norris, replaced Jacobs and Twentieth Century as the promotional entity at Madison Square Garden, Markson took a top position with the IBC. An anti-trust ruling eventually forced Norris to untangle himself from a web of interlocking entities, and Markson became the top executive in charge of boxing for the Madison Square Garden Corporation. In 1968, he became president of Madison Square Garden Boxing, Inc. He held that position until 1973, when he retired to a consulting position.

Although Norris and his organization were associated with organized crime figures, Markson managed to avoid their influence. He helped schedule the two championship fights which opened the new Madison Square Garden: Joe Frazier–Buster Mathis and Emile Griffith–Nino Benvenuti. He also played a key role in the staging of Ali–Frazier I at Madison Square Garden in 1971.

In 1963, Markson received the James J. Walker Award of the Boxing Writers Association for Long and Meritorious Service to Boxing. A lover of classical music, Markson brought an air of refinement to an often crude game. He died November 10, 1998, at the age of 92. Hall of Fame Induction: 1992.

ARTHUR MERCANTE
Referee

Arthur Mercante refereed 145 world championship fights in a career that started in 1954. Born in Brockton, Massachusetts, in 1920, Mercante has lived in New York state since he was eight. He boxed as an amateur and made the Golden Gloves finals in 1938. He attended New York University and was a member of the varsity football and swimming teams. After graduating in 1942, Mercante served four years in the navy under Gene Tunney as a recruit trainer and physical rehabilitation specialist. One of Mercante's duties was to referee in service bouts.

After World War II, Mercante coached and officiated boxing at the amateur level. In 1954, he became licensed as a professional referee. His first world title fight was the second Johansson–Patterson heavyweight title bout on June 20, 1960. Other notable matches he has handled include Paret–Thompson, Ali–Frazier I, Frazier–Foreman I, and Ali–Norton III.

Mercante showed his toughness in the ring when he officiated the Ernie Terrell–Bob Foster fight in 1964. During the fight, Terrell slugged him with a punch intended for Foster. Mercante shook off the blow and continued in the ring until he stopped the fight to protect the battered Foster. Terrell was upset that the fight was stopped because he wanted to win by a knockout, but his manager told him he shouldn't complain since his best shot hadn't even hurt the referee.

Despite his philosophy that a referee should be largely invisible in the ring, Mercante earned a well-deserved reputation for fairness and safety conciousness. Angelo Dundee recently stated, "Whenever Mercante was in the ring you were guaranteed a well-refereed bout. He kept the action *going!*"

Mercante has occasionally served as a color commentator on fight broadcasts and has been paired with such well-known announcers as Chris Schenkel, Al Michaels, and Howard Cosell. Mercante finally retired on September 29, 2001, at the age of 81, after refereeing Richardo Lopez's eighth-round knockout of Zolani Petelo in their Madison Square Garden title bout. For many years, Mercante also worked for the Hempstead, New York, Department of Parks and Recreation. Even after retirement as a referee, Mercante still occasionally served as a boxing judge. In 2006, he published his autobiography, *Inside the Ropes*. Mercante's son Arthur Jr. is also a prominent referee. Hall of Fame Induction: 1995.

DAN MORGAN
Manager

One of the most colorful characters in boxing, Dan Morgan always had an opinion or an amusing anecdote to offer about any fight or any fighter. Born in New York on July 3, 1873, Morgan began boxing as an amateur at the Chelsea A.C. Gym and turned professional in 1894. After Phil Kelley knocked him out in the fifteenth round of a fight at Brooklyn's Pelican Club, Morgan hung up his gloves and became a manager.

In 1904, Morgan opened what he claimed was the first fight manager's office in New York City and also served as his own press agent. During a newspaper campaign to drum up interest in one of his fighters, Morgan prepared a 15,000-word publicity brochure. He presented this treatise to Tad Dorgan, well-known writer, humorist, and cartoonist—then sports editor of *The New York Journal*—who, stunned at the length of the article, asked, "Shall I call you 'One-Word Morgan' or simply 'Dumb Dan'?" Morgan replied, "Keep my bum's name in the paper and you can call me anything you want." Dorgan ran the entire brochure in his paper and even added eight cartoons, and the ironic nickname "Dumb Dan" stuck with Morgan—the price of his publicity success and loquaciousness.

Among the hundreds of fighters managed by Morgan were world middleweight champion Al McCoy and Hall of Famers Battling Levinsky and Jack Britton. Morgan gave up managing McCoy in disgust after the light-hitting titleholder—derisively known as the "Cheese Champion"—ran off a series of newspaper losses in non-title, no-decision bouts. Great light heavyweight Levinsky's real name was Barney Lebrowitz. He initially fought as Barney Williams, but his career took off after Morgan bestowed upon him the more euphonic "Battling Levinsky." Morgan's favorite fighter was Britton; he marveled at the durable welterweight's willingness to test his skills in the ring over 300 times. Morgan managed fighters until 1925, when the strain led his doctor to recommend retirement.

In retirement, Morgan continued to advise and coach both amateur and professional boxers, including Max Schmeling. Under Morgan's tutelage, Schmeling defeated Joe Louis with a knockout in their first meeting. Morgan also claimed to have helped James J. Braddock defeat Max Baer for the heavyweight championship by placing an attractive blond at ringside and drawing Baer's attention to her, distracting him and allowing Braddock to triumph. He also kept up his work in publicity, helping to win public attention for fights promoted by Mike Jacobs and Jim Norris. Yet Morgan regarded most of the fighters he encountered at this latter stage of his career as vastly inferior to the previous generation of greats from the days of his youth. In particular, he had limited respect for the boxing skills of longtime boxing champ Joe Louis. On different occasions, Morgan believed that both Sam Langford and Jack Dempsey would have defeated Louis if the fighters had met in the primes of their careers.

Morgan made countless appearances at banquets and dinners and visited veterans' hospitals, where he told stories about boxing and even staged boxing shows for the patients. As a result of this charitable work, Morgan received the Boxing Writers Association of America's James J. Walker Award for Long and Meritorious Service to Boxing in 1948. In 1953, he published his memoirs titled *Dumb Dan* with the writing assistance of boxing journalist John McCallum. He died on July 7, 1955, at the age of 82. Hall of Fame Induction: 2000.

WILLIAM MULDOON
Trainer and Official

A trainer of championship boxers, William Muldoon was a powerful athlete in his own right and later became the head of the first modern boxing commission. Born in Belfast, New York, in 1845, Muldoon fought for the North in the Civil War. As a youth, he was a wrestler of some renown, and he continued to wrestle in the army. He competed in the "Greco-Roman" wrestling style of the day—which barred holds below the waist. After the war, Muldoon became a bouncer and then a policeman in New York City. Known as "The Solid Man" and "The Iron Duke," he wrestled in both professional and amateur matches, defeating the police department champion as well as English wrestler Edwin Bibby.

Muldoon served six years on the police force, then quit to open a bar which was popular with boxers and wrestlers as well as bankers and financiers. He toured the country with boxing champion John L. Sullivan, and the two posed, wrestled, boxed, and performed feats of strength in exhibitions. He also acted in stage plays, including the role of Charles the Wrestler in *As You Like It*.

A great believer in physical fitness, Muldoon opened the Muldoon Hygienic Institute in Purchase, New York. Here, he trained Sullivan for his famous fight with Jake Kilrain, whipping the overweight, out-of-shape Sullivan into fighting trim. Supposedly, Muldoon had to threaten the champ with a baseball bat to get him to follow the training regimen and wrestled Sullivan into submission when he wanted to go out for a drink. Sullivan entered the ring in excellent condition and won the Kilrain fight. Muldoon also trained Kid McCoy and Jack Dempsey, "The Nonpareil."

After the Walker Law legalized boxing in New York State in 1920, Muldoon was appointed to chair the New York State Athletic Commission. In this role, Muldoon attempted to bar known gamblers from attending fights, established a no-smoking rule for bouts, and pushed for improved sanitary conditions for boxers. Muldoon was opposed to mixed-race bouts and was voted out of the chairmanship after he refused to approve a fight between heavyweight champion Jack Dempsey and the great black fighter Harry Wills. Nevertheless, Muldoon remained on the commission until 1929.

Muldoon later joined with Gene Tunney to award the Tunney-Muldoon Trophy to world heavyweight champions. He died of cancer in 1933, at the age of 88, having been associated with boxing since its bare-knuckle days. Hall of Fame Induction: 1996.

HARRY MULLAN
Editor and Writer

A writer and historian of boxing in the tradition of Pierce Egan and Gilbert Odd, Harry Mullan gained a reputation as an honest, insightful, accurate, and prolific reporter and writer. Mullan was born in County Derry, Ireland, on April 22, 1946. Mullan grew up in Portstewart and, after college, he sought a career as a boxing writer. The great Odd befriended him and became his mentor, encouraging him to write boxing articles for English and Irish publications on a freelance basis.

In 1974, Mullan joined *Boxing News*, the world's oldest publication devoted to boxing. In 1977, he became the editor of the weekly British publication and served as its editor for approximately twenty years. His writing was not limited to the pages of *Boxing News,* however. He also worked for the London newspapers *The Sunday Times* and the *Independent on Sunday,* and the Irish publication *Sportfirst.* He also wrote many books on boxing, including *The Illustrated History of Boxing, The Ultimate Encyclopedia of Boxing, Heroes and Hardmen: The Story of Britain's World Boxing Champions,* and *Fighting Words.* In addition, he co-authored *Barry McGuigan: The Untold Story* and served as a commentator, covering fights on radio and television.

Mullan truly loved boxing but fearlessly criticized the sport and its participants when he felt that it was proper to do so. He died on May 21, 1999, after battling cancer for four years. Hall of Fame Induction: 2005.

BARNEY NAGLER
Writer

Enormously well-liked and well-respected by his peers, Barney Nagler received many honors in his more than 50-year career as a sportswriter. Nagler was born in Brooklyn, New York, on August 24, 1911. He majored in journalism at New York University and got his first taste of the newspaper business reading football copy on Saturday afternoons for the *New York Post.* After a series of stints at various papers, he landed a job at the *Bronx Home News* in 1934. In 1937, he began sportswriting full time when he succeeded Hall of Famer Harry Markson as the *Home News*'s boxing writer.

Nagler came into his own when he became a sports columnist for the *New York Telegraph* in 1950. Although he wrote about other sports, he concentrated primarily on boxing and horse racing. He continued with the *Telegraph* until it ceased publication in 1972. In addition to his writing, Nagler worked in television and radio. He wrote for "Bill Stern's Colgate Sports Newsreel" on national radio. He also served as a producer for televised sports on NBC and ABC in the '50s and '60s. Among other assignments, he worked on segments for *Wide World of Sports* and the 1964 Winter Olympics.

After leaving the *Telegraph,* Nagler became a columnist for *The Daily Racing Form*— though Nagler feared that many of the readers of the paper only read it for the horse racing data and did not read his column. Nagler served as president of the New York Boxing Writers Association twelve times between 1960 and 1980 and as president of the Boxing Writers Association of America from 1984 to 1989. The latter organization made Nagler the first recipient of the Nat Fleischer Memorial Award for Excellence in Boxing Journalism in 1972 and awarded him the James J. Walker Award for Long and Meritorious Service to Boxing in 1973. He also received significant awards for his reporting on horse racing.

Although he was based in New York his whole career, Nagler traveled widely and covered fights all over the world. He was at ringside for 41 of Muhammad Ali's fights. He was one of the few writers to develop a close friendship with New York Yankees owner George Steinbrenner, who paid some of Nagler's medical bills when Nagler suffered from cancer.

Besides his newspaper work, Nagler displayed his elegant writing style in several books he wrote or co-wrote including *Only the Ring was Square* with Hall of Famer Teddy Brenner, and *Brown Bomber: The Pilgrimage of Joe Louis.* Of lasting importance is Nagler's exposé of the corruption in boxing of the 1950s: *James J. Norris and The Decline of Boxing.*

Nagler was known for providing young writers with helpful advice. Nagler died in 1996. Hall of Fame Induction: 2004.

GILBERT ODD
Writer

The premier modern British boxing writer, Gilbert Odd contributed much to the sport as a reporter, historian, and record keeper. Born in England in 1902, Odd developed a great fascination for boxing as a boy. After a short amateur boxing career, he became a ringside correspondent at the age of eighteen for the British weekly boxing publication, *Boxing*. In 1941, he started a ten-year stint as the editor of *Boxing*, by then called *Boxing News*.

In 1944, Odd joined with G.W. Whiting to publish *The Boxers Annual*, a compendium of both amateur and professional records. Odd also launched another record book, known as *Boxing News Authors' and Record Book*. After leaving his position as editor, Odd continued to write hundreds of articles on boxing and became known as the top boxing historian in England. In addition to many articles, Odd has written over a dozen books, including *Ali—The Fighting Prophet* (1975), *The Fighting Blacksmith* (1976), *The Encyclopedia of Boxing* (1983), and *Kings of the Ring* (1985).

Odd served as a member of the British Boxing Board of Control from 1961 to 1969 and is a founding member of the Boxing Writers Club. Odd has also broadcast boxing on radio and television, and he is the only journalist to be made an honorary member of the National Sporting Club. He died on May 12, 1996. Hall of Fame Induction: 1995.

TOM O'ROURKE
Manager

One of boxing's greatest managers, Tom O'Rourke was at the pinnacle of his success at the end of the nineteenth and the beginning of the twentieth centuries. Born in Boston on May 13, 1856, O'Rourke enjoyed fighting as a youth, but his great talent as an athlete was rowing. Professionally, he turned his attention to boxing, managing his first fighter, Jack Havlin, in a bloody battle against Ike Weir, "The Belfast Spider," on July 20, 1887—a bout that ended in a draw after 61 grueling rounds.

It was not until 1889 that a truly great fighter came under O'Rourke's stewardship—Hall of Famer George Dixon. After seeing Dixon match the much heavier Paddy Kelly in a fifteen-round draw at Boston's Cribb Club, O'Rourke was so impressed that he immediately became Dixon's manager. He took Dixon to England at a time when American fighters did not often campaign overseas. Under his guidance, Dixon became the bantamweight champion in 1891, and then the featherweight titleholder in 1892, when he took part in the three-day Carnival of Champions at New Orleans' Olympia Club. It was a significant match for another reason: Dixon was allowed to take part in a mixed-race bout, a rarity for the South at that time, and a tribute to O'Rourke's managerial skills. Dixon remained the featherweight champ until 1900.

O'Rourke managed another Hall of Famer, the original Joe Walcott, who became welterweight champion under O'Rourke's direction. O'Rourke took Walcott and Dixon on a "meet all comers" tour, bringing along his own ring, slightly smaller than the standard size, thus giving his own fighters an advantage in controlling the bout. The highly regarded Sailor Tom Sharkey fought under O'Rourke's banner when he lost to heavyweight champion James J. Jeffries in 1899.

In addition to managing fighters, O'Rourke operated boxing clubs in New York, including the Lenox Club, the National Sporting Club, and the Broadway. He also ran the Delavan Hotel in the same city. During the second decade of the twentieth century, O'Rourke managed the career of German-American heavyweight Al Palzer. The big, powerful puncher's career was abruptly ended when he was shot and killed by his father. O'Rourke continued to maintain an active role in boxing through the '20s. In 1923 he helped stage title bouts at the Polo Grounds: Hall of Famers Johnny Kilbane and Johnny Dundee, each against Eugene Criqui for the feather-weight belt; and Pancho Villa versus Jimmy Wilde for the flyweight title. O'Rourke was then appointed by the New York State Athletic Commission to the position of boxing judge. He also served as a NYSAC Inspector.

One June 19, 1936, O'Rourke collapsed with a fatal heart attack in Max Schmeling's dressing room at Yankee Stadium, just before Schmeling's first fight against Joe Louis. Active in boxing for almost 50 years, the canny O'Rourke left an indelible mark on the sport's history. Hall of Fame Induction: 1999.

DAN PARKER
Sports Editor and Columnist

Damon Runyon called Dan Parker "the most constantly brilliant of all sportswriters." In his 38 years as a columnist for *The New York Daily Mirror* and, at the very end of his career, *The New York Journal-American*, Parker was a frequent crusader against corruption in boxing and other sports. He is credited with doing the most in print to expose the crooked International Boxing Club, which in the 1950s had a stranglehold on boxing promotion.

Parker, whose bulk was memorable (he stood 6'4" tall and weighed over 200 pounds), wrote about every sport from baseball to horse racing. He was noted for his humor as well as his compassion for losers or the unlucky, but he was relentless in his exposure of payoffs and fixes. At one time, he discovered that wrestling promoters were printing up cards based on the "winners" of matches that hadn't taken place yet. Parker reported the winners' names in advance of the matches, infuriating the promoters.

Parker showed not only a strong moral sense but great courage in writing about the underworld connections to boxing. His columns helped spark the investigations that resulted in the breakup of the IBC and the conviction of mobster Frankie Carbo and others. Apparently impervious to threats, Parker wrote as his conscience directed. "There's always been larceny in boxing," Parker told a *Newsweek* interviewer in 1964, "and when I've seen it, I've written it."

Parker was born in Waterbury, Connecticut, in 1893. After graduating from high school, he worked first as a reporter, then city editor and sportswriter at *The Waterbury American*. He joined the staff of the Hearst chain's *Daily Mirror* in 1924 and within two years launched his column. He wrote for the *Mirror* until it folded in 1963 and, although the rest of the staff moved on, remained in the paper's defunct newsroom for another year filing columns for the *Journal-American*. He also wrote for *The Ring*, *The Saturday Evening Post*, and *Sport*.

Parker was honored by his peers several times during his career. He won the Headliners' Award for sportswriting in 1949; received the New York Newspaper Guild's Page One award in 1951, 1956, and 1961; and the National Sportscasters and Sportswriters award in 1960. He was inducted into the National Sportscasters and Sportswriters Hall of Fame. In memory of his friend and fellow sportswriter, Parker established the Damon Runyon fund for cancer research. Parker died in 1967. Hall of Fame Induction: 1996.

GEORGE PARNASSUS
Promoter

George Parnassus was one of the top promoters in boxing history. He expanded the range of boxing venues and saw the value in promoting fighters in the smaller weight classes. Born in Methone, Greece, in 1897, Parnassus followed his brother to the United States in 1916 and first found work as a waiter and dishwasher. Eventually, he and his brother saved enough money to purchase a restaurant in Phoenix, Arizona. The restaurant happened to be located across the street from a fight gym. Legend has it that the fighters began running up unpaid bills at the restaurant, and Parnassus began managing them to settle the debts.

As a manager, Parnassus had great success with Mexican boxers, such as lightweight champ Juan Zurita, Enrique Bolanos, bantamweight champ Raton Macias, and Jose Beccera. In the late 1950s, Parnassus moved from managing to matchmaking and promoting. In 1957, he became the matchmaker for the Olympic Auditorium in Los Angeles. Parnassus's shrewd matchmaking ability helped save the Olympic from financial ruin.

Parnassus excelled in matching fighters in smaller weight classes when his rivals were concentrating on the heavyweights. He promoted a bantamweight title bout between Jose Beccera and Alphonse Halimi and a junior welterweight championship match between Carlos Ortiz and Battling Torres on the same card at the massive Los Angeles Coliseum, which had not previously been used for boxing. The event was a huge success and gave Parnassus a well-deserved reputation as one of the greatest promoters in the world.

In the 1960s, Parnassus staged fights in such diverse locales as Wales, Mexico, Japan, Thailand, Argentina, Italy, and England. During this period, Parnassus helped establish and finance the World Boxing Council (WBC). Starting in 1966, Parnassus staged successful bouts in Jack Kent Cooke's new venue, The Fabulous Forum in Los Angeles. Ruben Olivares and Jose Napoles were his top draws during this period.

Throughout his career, Parnassus always aimed for top quality shows. He declared, "The thing is not to be the richest promoter in the world, but to be the best." His honesty and fairness were highly valued in professional boxing. Parnassus died of a heart attack in 1975. Hall of Fame Induction: 1991.

J RUSSELL PELTZ
Promoter

One of the most sucessful regional promoters of the past 35 years, J Russell Peltz has put together innumerable great fight cards, and his name has become synonymous with boxing in Philadelphia. Peltz was born on December 9, 1946, in Philadelphia. He went to Temple University in that city to study journalism. While at Temple, he worked at the *Philadelphia Bulletin,* first on a part-time, then later on a full-time basis. Unlike many college students who are in debt when they graduate, Peltz had saved several thousands of dollars by the time of his graduation. He used this money to finance his first boxing promotion in September 1969, at the Blue Horizon, an aging Philadelphia ballroom that he would later make famous. Middleweight Bennie Briscoe was the headliner, and the promotion netted a profit of approximately $1,500. Dubbed "the Boy Wonder," Peltz promoted about fifteen cards from September 1969 through May 1970, while he continued to work one night a week at the *Bulletin*.

In the summer of 1970, Peltz left the paper and devoted his full attention to boxing. He encouraged his brother-in-law to purchase Briscoe's contract because he realized Briscoe was a skilled, crowd-pleasing Philadelphia middleweight who had a solid future ahead of him. Peltz knew that there was a group of good young middleweights in Philadelphia, and they all would have to eventually fight Briscoe—making for many potentially great middleweight match-ups. Peltz promoted 31 of Briscoe's fights. These promotions helped Peltz establish his place in Philadelphia boxing.

After a few years of promoting in smaller venues like the Blue Horizon, Peltz was named director of boxing at the Spectrum, home of the Philadelphia 76ers and the Philadelphia Flyers. He worked at the Spectrum from 1973 to 1980. Peltz promoted a total of 73 cards there, many of them successful, high profile fight nights that included such notable boxers as Hall of Famers Marvelous Marvin Hagler, Jeff Chandler, and Matthew Saad Muhammad. After seven years, Peltz left the Spectrum to resume his career as an independent promoter. In the early '80s, he frequently promoted fights at The Sands in Atlantic City, New Jersey. In 1982, three bouts promoted by Peltz and shown on NBC television were named "Fight of the Month" by *The Ring*.

Peltz soon returned to the place of his first promotion, the Blue Horizon. His sold-out shows—which were often seen on television on USA Network and on ESPN2—made the Blue Horizon famous and were known for their high quality. Peltz also served as a boxing consultant for ESPN2. Peltz left the Blue Horizon in 2001 in part because of his dissatisfaction with maintenance and upkeep at the club. He promoted fights at other sites in Philadelphia and elsewhere. After the Blue Horizon received a much-needed facelift, Peltz again promoted there.

Peltz has a great love for boxing and has amassed an impressive collection of boxing memorabilia. He was an annual attendee at the International Boxing Hall of Fame's induction ceremonies even before his own induction. In addition to the IBHOF's honor, the Boxing Writers Association of America awarded Peltz the James J. Walker Award for Long and Meritorious Service to Boxing in 1999. Hall of Fame Induction: 2004.

MARQUESS OF QUEENSBERRY
Patron

Although his association with boxing was rather tangential, John Sholto Douglas, the ninth Marquess of Queensbury, gained lasting fame when he sponsored the rules compiled by his friend John Graham Chambers. Douglas became acquainted with Chambers at Magdalene College at Cambridge, and in 1867 he agreed to lend the new rules his name and patronage. The Queensbery Rules, as they came to be known, did much to establish universally recognized standards of fairness by which boxing matches could be conducted. The rules, the basis for the boxing regulations of today, included the establishment of three-minute rounds with one-minute rest periods between rounds. They also ushered out the bare-knuckle era by mandating the use of boxing gloves.

An avid boxing enthusiast, Douglas was born in 1844, succeeded to his hereditary title in 1858, and died in 1900. Hall of Fame Induction: 1990.

GEORGE ("TEX") RICKARD
Promoter

George ("Tex") Rickard led boxing into the era of million-dollar gates, huge crowds, and fights at Madison Square Garden. Born in Missouri in 1871, Rickard left school at age nine and, while still a youngster, worked cattle drives from Texas to Montana. At 21, he became a town marshal in Henrietta, Texas. He also tried cattle ranching in Brazil. In 1894, he went to Alaska and discovered gold, although he later remarked that he sold his claim for too low a price. When the Klondike gold rush started, Rickard ran a hotel in Dawson known as the Northern. He made a sizable fortune before going broke in the boom-and-bust economy. He opened another version of the Northern in Nome and stayed in Alaska for the next twelve years.

Rickard followed gold prospectors to Nevada, where he opened another hotel called the Northern, before boxing caught his fancy. Local business leaders wanted to stage a boxing match to publicize the growing community. Rickard had recently attended a boxing match in New York, so he was given the task of making the arrangements. He tried unsuccessfully to sign Terry McGovern and Jimmy Britt—the two fighters he had seen in New York, but then landed Joe Gans and Battling Nelson for $30,000. The gate receipts from the fight, held on Labor Day 1906, were $69,715, the largest ever for a boxing match.

Although Rickard was no boxing expert, he saw the earning potential of the sport. Backed by Montana mining interests, Rickard outbid James Coffroth among others for the right to promote the James J. Jeffries–Jack Johnson fight. The fight was held in Reno on July 4, 1910. Rickard helped recoup the money paid to the fighters by selling the film rights for $101,000. The fight drew 15,760 fans who paid $270,775 to see the spectacle.

Rickard believed in getting top attractions, publicizing them, and charging high prices for the tickets. When he shifted his base of operations to New York following the passage of the Walker Law which legalized boxing in the state, Rickard made successful overtures to the upper strata of society. He was also skillful in dealing with politicians to facilitate the promotion of his fights.

At the urging of Jack Dempsey's manager, Jack ("Doc") Kearns, Rickard agreed to promote the Jess Willard–Dempsey championship fight in Toledo, Ohio, in 1919. Although that match was not one of Rickard's most successful promotions, it set the stage for another Dempsey fight held at Boyle's Thirty Acres near Jersey City on July 2, 1921. Rickard matched heavyweight champion Dempsey with light heavyweight champion Georges Carpentier. Although Dempsey outweighed Carpentier by about twenty pounds, Rickard raised interest in the fight to never-before-seen levels. He played on the fact that Carpentier had been a French war hero in World War I, while Dempsey had avoided military service. Dempsey won the fight easily, but the real story was the gate. More than 80,000 fans paid a record $1,789,238. Five years later, in a Rickard promotion, 120,757 paid $1,895,733 to watch Gene Tunney upset Dempsey. The rematch held in Soldier Field in Chicago drew 104,943 with a gate of $2,658,660.

Rickard developed Madison Square Garden into a top boxing venue. With help from Nat Fleischer and others in site selection and financing, Rickard built a new Madison Square Garden at 49th Street and Eighth Avenue, which became known as "The House That Tex Built." The New York Rangers hockey team was named after Rickard as a wordplay on

"Texas Rangers." Rickard built another famed sports arena in Boston. Originally dubbed the "Boston Madison Square Garden," the name was shortened to Boston Garden shortly after its November 1928 opening. The facility served as home to the Boston Bruins and Celtics for nearly 70 years.

Rickard also helped Nat Fleischer start *The Ring* magazine and compiled the first annual top-ten-contender ratings for the magazine. At the time of his death on January 6, 1929, Rickard was planning on expanding his base of operations to Florida and England.

Rickard was no saint. He once told Dempsey to carry an opponent for a few rounds, and he refused to promote a match between black heavyweight Harry Wills and Dempsey. However, he brought boxing into the modern era with his large-scale promotions. Hall of Fame Induction: 1990.

IRVING RUDD
Publicist

 One of the last, great, old-time press agents, Irving Rudd had nothing but disdain for the new-school, public relations flacks, who conducted business from a cushy seat in a fancy restaurant and never saw the inside of a gym. Rudd's boxing career stretched across much of twentieth century boxing. He worked for three of the century's premier promoters: Mike Jacobs, Don King, and Bob Arum, and he worked with champs from Louis to Leonard. Born in Brooklyn on October 13, 1917, Rudd became an enthusiastic sports fan—especially of the Dodgers. In 1933, working as a reporter for his high school newspaper, he interviewed Hall of Famer Max Baer, who was in town to promote his movie, *The Prizefighter and the Lady*. Baer took a liking to Rudd, and invited him to spend a week with him in Baltimore, his next tour stop. The following year, Rudd spent several weekends at Baer's training camp in Asbury Park, New Jersey, and it is Baer whom Rudd credits for getting him into boxing.

After high school, Rudd worked as a bookkeeper at the Fulton Fish Market, but a day's trip to Stillman's Gym proved propitious: Big Al Douglas, owner of the Harlem fight club called the Rockland Palace, offered Rudd work as a press agent for $18 a week. Rudd quickly accepted and thrived in his new position. He worked at several such small boxing venues in the years that followed, including the Eastern Parkway Arena, the Ridgewood Grove Arena, and the Queensboro Arena. He also assisted Hall of Fame promoter Mike ("Uncle Mike") Jacobs.

With smaller fighting clubs quickly losing audiences to the allure of television, Rudd left boxing to work for the Dodgers as promotions director, staying until their 1958 move to Los Angeles. Rudd next went to work for the Yonkers Raceway. His most famous publicity stunt there involved repainting its sign incorrectly to spell "Racewya," drawing much attention. He remained at the track until 1969, when he became the public relations director of New York's Off Track Betting Corporation.

In 1976, Rudd returned to boxing, drumming up publicity for the Muhammad Ali–Ken Norton championship fight at Yankee Stadium. He then worked for Don King during the time of the scandal-ridden U.S. Boxing Championships. Not long after, he moved to Bob Arum's Top Rank, Inc., where he developed a close friendship with Thomas Hearns. Rudd pulled off an outrageous publicity coup during his promotion of the Marvelous Marvin Hagler–Hearns fight. He succeeded in convincing the IRS that Hagler and Hearns would be ideal spokesmen for a huge public service TV campaign to "file early." For weeks before their scheduled showdown the two combatants appeared in living rooms throughout the country. In his lengthy career, Rudd was involved in over 100 title fights and over 2,000 fights in all. He was awarded the Boxing Writers Association of America's James J. Walker Award for Long and Meritorious Service to Boxing in 1985.

Rudd, also known as "Unswerving Irving" and the "Happy Rabbit" continued with Top Rank, Inc., until his retirement in 1991. Credited with a unique ability to serve both his employer and the press, he was always available for the media, and often gave them great quotes. When someone said to him that broadcaster Howard Cosell was his own worst enemy, Rudd responded, "Not while I'm alive." He recounted his many contacts with the colorful figures of sports in his book—co-written with Stan Fischler—*The Sporting Life: The Duke and Jackie, Pee Wee, Razor, Phil, Ali, Mushky Jackson and Me*. Rudd died on June 2, 2000. Hall of Fame Induction: 1999.

DAMON RUNYON
Writer

Perhaps best known for his depictions of gamblers, bookies, and gangsters—characters who came to be known as "Runyonesque" (the musical *Guys and Dolls* is based on one of his short stories)—Damon Runyon was also a first-rate sportswriter. In his long career, he covered boxing, baseball, and horse racing, along with many other sports, and was involved in boxing as a manager and promoter.

Born Alfred Damon Runyan on October 4, 1884, in Manhattan, Kansas, where his father was the publisher of the *Manhattan Enterprise*, Runyan's name was changed accidently to Runyon when it appeared that way in a byline. After his mother fell sick with consumption, the family moved to Colorado, where she died when Runyon was only seven. His sisters were sent to live with their grandmother, but Runyon remained under the nominal care of his father. While he received very little in the way of parental guidance and was a troublemaker at school, he did develop a strong interest in writing and had a poem published in the Pueblo *Chieftain*. The next year, at twelve years old, he got a job as a reporter at the Pueblo *Evening Express*.

During the Spanish-American War, Runyon served as a bugler, primarily in the Philippines. After leaving the military, he worked for various Colorado newspapers before moving to the *Denver Post* in 1905. Fired the very next year, he moved to another Denver paper, *The Rocky Mountain News*. In addition to his newspaper work, Runyon wrote verses and short stories that appeared in national magazines.

In 1910, Runyon traveled to New York, where he soon found a job as a sportswriter for the *American*, and dropped the "Alfred" from his byline. Runyon covered baseball's New York Giants from 1911 to 1920 and began to know the city and its colorful characters. In covering games, he often wrote about personalities and subjects only tangentially related to the game itself. He did not keep a scorecard, and the paper ran a play-by-play account next to his report. Over time, especially after becoming a columnist, Runyon changed his schedule so that he came home at dawn, slept until noon, worked in the afternoon and early evening, and then went to restaurants and clubs for the rest of the night. In addition to sportswriting, Runyon also reported on courtroom trials and covered the U.S. Army's pursuit of the infamous bandit Pancho Villa in Mexico. He also traveled to Europe during World War I to gather news from the front.

When Jack Dempsey arrived on the New York scene, he looked up Runyon on the advice of a mutual friend. Runyon reported some of his fights, including his triumph over Jess Willard for the heavyweight title. During the course of his career, Runyon covered many fights, and he also managed some fighters, though not very successfully. His involvement in setting up matches for Mrs. Hearst's Milk Fund charity boxing benefits in the '20s led him to a partnership with sportswriters Ed Frayne and Bill Farnsworth, and Hall of Fame promoter Mike Jacobs in the Twentieth Century Sporting Club. Jacobs bought out Runyon and took sole control of the promotional enterprise about ten years later.

Besides his newspaper work, Runyon published many short stories, the majority of which dealt with the colorful characters he saw in New York. At least a half dozen of these stories were eventually made into movies, including *Little Miss Marker,* which made a star of Shirley Temple, and *Guys and Dolls.*

In 1938, Runyon developed throat cancer. An operation in 1944 left him unable to speak, and for the remainder of his life, Runyon communicated by writing notes. He died on December 10, 1946. The Damon Runyon Memorial Fund for Cancer Research was established by his close friend, columnist Walter Winchell. Now known as the Damon Runyon Memorial Cancer Foundation, the organization has raised over $135 million to combat the disease.

In addition to the International Boxing Hall of Fame, Runyon is a member of the National Sportscasters and Sportswriters Association Hall of Fame. In 1967, the Baseball Writers' Association of America posthumously awarded him the J.G. Taylor Spink Award, given by the National Baseball Hall of Fame for meritorious contributions to baseball writing. Hall of Fame Induction: 2002.

RODOLFO SABBATINI
Promoter

After initially making a name for himself as a sportswriter in his home country of Italy, Rodolfo Sabbatini turned to boxing promotion. From the mid-1960s until his death on December 12, 1985, Sabbatini was one of the top promoters in Europe. Initially, Sabbatini only staged bouts in Italy. As he became more prominent in the sport, he promoted fights throughout Europe, Latin America, and the United States—often in conjunction with a local promoter in the foreign country. At times Sabbatini served as the European associate of Bob Arum of Top Rank, Inc.

During his illustrious career, Sabbatini staged over 1,000 shows. More than 150 of his cards involved world, European, or national titles. Some of the greats who fought on Sabbatini productions include Hall of Famers Nino Benvenuti, Carlos Monzon, and Victor Galindez. Sabbatini handled Monzon's interests in Europe. Perhaps Sabbatini's greatest promotional achievement occured on December 1, 1967. He staged the fight between European light middleweight champion Sandro Mazzinghi and Jo Gonzalez at the Palaeur in Rome. The 18,000-seat venue was packed, and the streets were crowded with boxing fans who couldn't get a ticket. Sabbatini also promoted a San Remo, Italy, bout in which Marvelous Marvin Hagler met Fulgencio Obelmejias for the middleweight title. The last world title bout Sabbatini promoted was the IBF light heavyweight match between Slobodan Kacar and Eddie Mustafa Muhammad. Boxing journalist Jerry Izenberg—contrasting Sabbatini's business dealings with the erratic machinations of some boxing commissions—wrote that the Italian promoter "may be the only logical man in boxing." Hall of Fame Induction: 2006.

LOPE SARREAL
Promoter

Considered by many the greatest promoter in the history of Asian boxing, Lope Sarreal promoted fights not only in his native Philippines but also in Japan, Thailand, and South Korea. In his lengthy career, he promoted more than twenty world champions. Sarreal was born on September 25, 1905, in Imus, Cavite, Philippines. Sarreal was involved in boxing for virtually his entire adult life. He is perhaps best known for promoting Hall of Famer Gabriel ("Flash") Elorde who became his son-in-law. Elorde's son and Sarreal's grandson, Gabriel ("Bebot") Elorde, is currently a promoter in the Philippines. Also, Lope Sarreal Jr. has long followed in his father's footsteps as a promoter.

Other prominent champions with whom Sarreal was involved include flyweight Masao Ohba, super lightweight Saensak Muangsirin, and super featherweight Ricardo Arrendondo. More than anyone, Sarreal opened Asia to professional boxing. He died on March 14, 1995. To commemorate the one hundredth anniversary of his birth, Bebot Elorde promoted four World Boxing Foundation title bouts in Paranaque City, Philippines. Hall of Fame Induction: 2005.

BUDD SCHULBERG
Writer

One of the few members of the International Boxing Hall of Fame who is actually best-known for his achievements outside boxing, Budd Schulberg is an Academy Award–winning screenwriter as well as a very successful and critically acclaimed novelist. In addition to these achievements, Schulberg is a recipient of the Boxing Writers Association of America's A.J. Liebling Award for Outstanding Boxing Writing.

Budd Wilson Schulberg was born in New York City on March 27, 1914. His father, B.P. Schulberg, was a pioneer in the motion picture business with Paramount Pictures, first in New York and later in Hollywood. The elder Schulberg was an avid boxing fan and took his then six-year-old son to Madison Square Garden to see Hall of Famer Benny Leonard fight. Like his father, Budd Schulberg quickly came to love the sport. Schulberg moved to Hollywood when the movie industry became established there.

Encouraged by his mother, Schulberg wrote poems and short stories at a young age and got his start in the movie industry when he was seventeen, working as a publicist at Paramount. After graduating from Dartmouth, Schulberg returned to Paramount and worked as a screenwriter. While at Paramount, he continued to write short stories, which appeared in *Liberty, Collier's,* and *The Saturday Evening Post.* Schulberg then wrote *What Makes Sammy Run,* a best-selling novel, which was awarded the National Critics' Choice as the Best First Novel of the Year in 1941. During World War II, he served in the Navy as a lieutenant, junior grade, as part of John Ford's documentary unit. He wrote narration for Ford's movie, *December 7th,* which won an Academy Award in 1944 for best short subject. After the war, Schulberg was an assistant at the Nuremberg Trials in charge of photographic evidence.

In 1947, Schulberg was asked to appear before the House Un-American Activities Committee as part of the Committee's investigation of supposed communists in the movie industry. He had been a member of the Communist Party in the late 1930s. He answered the Committee's questions. His cooperation led several friends to sever all contact with him.

Schulberg drew on his love of boxing when he wrote *The Harder They Fall* in 1947, a novel about corruption in professional boxing. It was later made into a movie starring Humphrey Bogart and Rod Steiger. Boxing even figured in *On the Waterfront,* the screenplay for which he won an Academy Award. In this famous film that explored corruption in a dockworker's union, Marlon Brando played an ex-fighter who spoke some of the most famous words ever uttered in a movie, "I coulda been a contendah." Brando's character was forced to take a dive, then served as a mob enforcer until he ultimately turned against his corrupt employers.

Schulberg continued to write frequently about boxing. He served as *Sports Illustrated*'s boxing editor in the early days of that magazine when boxing was featured very prominently in its pages. He also wrote a biography of Muhammad Ali in 1972 entitled *Loser and Still Champion.* Schulberg has covered fights and fighters for such publications as *Playboy, Esquire,* and *Newsday.* A collection of his boxing writing, *Sparring with Hemingway,* was published in 1995. Boxing has been such an important part of his life that Hall of Famer Fidel LaBarba and West Coast fan favorite Art Aragon served as best men at his marriage to actress Geraldine Brooks.

Schulberg lives in Quoque, Long Island, New York. He continues to be active in his nineties and still loves boxing. Hall of Fame Induction: 2003

GEORGE SILER
Referee

A well-known and respected referee in the early days of American boxing, George Siler officiated at a time when the Marquess of Queensberry Rules were first introduced and boxing was evolving from bare-knuckle to gloved fisticuffs. Born in 1846, Siler officiated at the James J. Corbett–Bob Fitzsimmons heavyweight championship fight in 1897. Corbett admonished Siler for counting too slowly when he knocked Fitzsimmons down in the sixth round. Later, Siler counted Corbett out after Fitzsimmons floored him.

Siler also refereed such important fights as Fitzsimmons–James J. Jeffries, Fitzsimmons–Peter Maher, and Tom Sharkey–Jeffries. As the third man in the Joe Gans–Battling Nelson bout, Siler gave the fight to Gans after Nelson landed several low blows in the 42nd round. Siler had a reputation for honesty in an era when not all officials shared that virtue. He was also very knowledgeable about the sport and wrote about it as a newspaper correspondent. Siler died in 1908. Hall of Fame Induction: 1995.

SAM SILVERMAN
Promoter

Sam Silverman promoted over 10,000 fights in New England in his 40 years in boxing. He was a colorful figure in the fight game, a rotund man with finely tailored suits, white-on-white shirts, an ever-present cigar, and a new Cadillac every year. He always maintained a good relationship with the press, realizing the role the news media played in helping his promotions.

Silverman was born on December 25, 1909, and attended Boston University as a journalism major. Short of funds, he dropped out of school and turned to boxing. His lack of success in the ring led him to try his hand at managing, then matchmaking, and finally, promoting. Though Silverman's operation was centered in Boston, he staged matches throughout New England. Many of his promotions involved "name" fighters, but Silverman put on financially viable shows in many areas with only local boxers. In the mid-1930s, he promoted shows in an average of eleven different cities per week. In the '60s, Silverman staged weekly shows in Worcester, Lowell, and Framingham, Massachusetts; Bangor, Portland, and Lewiston, Maine; Providence, Rhode Island; and Boston, where he was known as "Subway Sam." Fight fans could take the subway to bouts all over the city, to venues like Boston Garden, the Boston Arena, the Mechanics Building, Fenway Park, the Rollaway Arena in Revere, and even to the elite Harvard Club, where Silverman was quoted as complaining about the vichyssoise served in the Club dining room: "I thought you said this was a class joint. The damn chef gives us cold soup."

Silverman was involved in the promotion of about 25 championship matches, including Sugar Ray Robinson–Paul Pender and Tony DeMarco–Carmen Basilio. Further, Silverman promoted 32 of Rocky Marciano's 49 fights. Though liked by many, he also had his share of enemies. He fought off knife-wielding assailants in London, escaped injury from a bullet through his window, and avoided a dynamite explosion in the basement of his building when he and his family were out. The fearless Silverman took on the powerful and corrupt International Boxing Club, and sued the promotional behemoth for $9,000,000, alleging that it was a monopoly. He ultimately settled for $150,000.

Silverman was so singularly devoted to boxing, that he had only disdain for other sports. He called the Celtics a "bunch of giraffes," the Bruins "foreigners playing a foreign game," and said of the Red Sox, they "put you to sleep." While boxing's fortunes waxed and waned, he remained active as a promoter. Into the 1970s, he staged regular cards in Boston, Portland, and Peabody, Massachusetts. On July 8, 1977, Silverman drove fighter Al Romano home from Geneva, New York, after a small boxing card. After dropping Romano off at his house, Silverman was continuing to his own home when his car went off the road in Cambridge and crashed. Silverman died the next day. Over two decades later, he is still remembered as one of the top regional promoters of the twentieth century, a man who held an unshakable commitment to boxing. Hall of Fame Induction: 2002.

JACK SOLOMONS
Promoter

The foremost promoter in the history of British boxing, Jack Solomons brought top American fighters to England in the post-World War II period, when boxing enthusiasm in that country was at its peak. Solomons spent close to 50 years in the sport, during which he staged 26 title fights.

Born into a family of fish marketers, Solomons's first import to Britain was live carp. He became involved in boxing in the 1930s as the manager of Eric Boone and as operator of the Devonshire Club, a boxing venue for up-and-coming London talent. He also worked as a matchmaker for the leading promoters before venturing into his own shows. His first big promotion was the Bruce Woodcock–Jack London British heavyweight title fight.

In 1946, when he brought American world light heavyweight champion Gus Lesnevich to England to face Freddie Mills, he opened the door to many more transatlantic matches. A connection with Hall of Famer Mike Jacobs, then the preeminent American promoter, helped to provide Solomons with the best American talent. Solomons quickly became the most important man in British boxing. He had the best fighters, and he created an air of theatrical excitement around his fights that greatly advanced the sport's popularity. The Sugar Ray Robinson–Randy Turpin middleweight title fight in 1951 was perhaps Solomons's most memorable production. The program cover for this bout showed not the fighters, but Solomons's bow-tie clad, cigar-chomping countenance.

Competition and the growth of television gradually reduced Solomons's influence, but he continued to stage many important bouts until his death in 1979. He brought Muhammad Ali (then known as Cassius Clay) to England in 1963 to fight Henry Cooper, and he opened the private World Sporting Club and staged many promotions through its auspices. Hall of Fame Induction: 1995.

EMANUEL STEWARD
Trainer and Manager

One of the most successful trainers and managers active in boxing today, Emanuel Steward turned the basement of an obscure Detroit community center into a top training ground for boxers. Under Steward's leadership, the famous Kronk Center Gym continues to produce champion-level fighters, although the facility is now threatened with closure because of Detroit's budgetary woes.

Steward was born in West Virginia in 1944. His interest in boxing began at age eight, when he was given a pair of Jack Dempsey boxing gloves. He grew up fighting other boys, sometimes in illegal smokers that his father ran to entertain adults. When his parents separated, Steward moved with his mother to Detroit. He continued fighting, both in the streets and in organized competition. At age twelve, he began training at Brewster's Gym, the same gym where Joe Louis got his start. Steward wasn't a hard hitter, but he compiled an amateur record of 94-3 and won a 1963 National Golden Gloves title. Steward then coached amateur boxers for three years while working at a variety of jobs, until he gave up boxing altogether while studying to become an electrician.

In 1969, Steward's father asked him to look after his half-brother, James, who was fifteen. Steward took his brother to a local gym named after a Detroit city councilman, John Kronk, and soon guided James to a Detroit Golden Gloves title. He became a part-time coach at Kronk and, in 1971, seven of his charges won Golden Gloves championships. The next year, although Steward had become a master electrician at Detroit Edison where he supervised 200 employees, he left that career to work full-time in the amateur program at the gym, while holding other part-time jobs.

Steward took his first fighter into the professional ranks when Thomas Hearns debuted in 1977. Steward has since developed such great boxers as Mike McCallum, Dennis Andries, Hilmer Kenty, Jimmy Paul, Duane Thomas, and Michael Moorer.

As a trainer and manager, Steward preaches balance and even weight distribution for his fighters. He believes in varied but strenuous training sessions—often held in hot, humid conditions—and he insists on total control of his fighters leading up to a fight. He oversees his fighters' diets to keep their energy levels high. He gets to know his boxers well and motivates each of them accordingly.

Recently, Steward has trained champions Lennox Lewis, Evander Holyfield, Oscar de la Hoya, and Prince Naseem Hamed. Also recently, Steward has served as an insightful commentator on HBO's successful late-night series *Boxing After Dark*. Hall of Fame Induction: 1996.

BERT RANDOLPH SUGAR
Writer and Commentator

One of the most colorful figures in a sport that has had more than its share, Bert Randolph Sugar's fame transcends boxing: he is a celebrated figure throughout the sports world. Sugar is known for his quick quips, the incredible number of books he has written, and, of course, for his trademark fedora and ever-present cigar. In fact, the hat and cigar preceded Sugar into the Hall of Fame: they were on display in boxing's shrine in Canastota, New York, even before Sugar was inducted.

Sugar was born on June 7, 1937, in Washington, D.C. He grew up in nearby Richmond, Virginia. He loved sports from an early age and attempted to make his mark in football, rugby, baseball, and boxing. Sugar achieved only modest success in these endeavors and later dubbed himself "the great white hopeless." Sugar attended Harvard University for a year before he transferred to the University of Maryland. He earned a law degree from the University of Michigan and passed the District of Columbia bar exam. He later remarked that it was the only bar that he ever passed! Sugar practiced law briefly, but soon realized that he really wanted to be a sportswriter. While pursuing that goal, he moved to New York and worked in the advertising industry for about ten years. He is credited with originating the well-known jingle "N-E-S-T-L-E-S, Nestles makes the very best . . . chocolate."

Sugar eventually left advertising to become a writer and editor of *Boxing Illustrated*—a magazine that evolved from the merger of *Ringside News* and *Boxing Illustrated/Wrestling News*. When that publication was sold, he left to become editor-in-chief of *Argosy,* a men's adventure and fiction magazine. He briefly returned to advertising before returning to sports in 1977 as the editor-in-chief of *The Ring*—known as "The Bible of Boxing." *The Ring* had lost some of its luster in a ratings scandal before Sugar came on board, so he immediately attempted to garner respect for the venerable publication. In 1979, Sugar, basketball great Dave DeBusschere, and Chicago White Sox executive Nick Kladis purchased the bankrupt *Ring.* Sugar ran the day-to-day operations of the magazine and became the guardian of the magazine's rich archives, which thoroughly document boxing history. However, the magazine did not become profitable, and after five years he was forced out. He sued his partners for breach of contract and eventually settled the suit for an undisclosed amount of money and the ownership of two wrestling magazines and *Boxing Illustrated,* which *The Ring* had acquired. Sugar remained in charge at *Boxing Illustrated* until the 1990s. He later published *Fight Game,* another boxing magazine.

In addition to his work in boxing magazines, Sugar has written or edited over 80 books on subjects such as baseball, card collecting, football, television sports, gambling, and, of course, boxing. Some of his more notable boxing books include *Sting Like a Bee: The Muhammad Ali Story,* written with Hall of Famer Jose Torres; *Boxing's Greatest Fights; The 100 Greatest Boxers of All Time;* and *Bert Sugar on Boxing,* a collection of his writing on the sport.

The extroverted, loquacious Sugar frequently appears on television, radio, and Internet web sites to comment on boxing and other subjects. He also has appeared in several movies. Sugar received the Boxing Writers Association of America's Nat Fleischer Award in 1990 for Excellence in Boxing Journalism. Hall of Fame Induction: 2005

SAM TAUB
Broadcaster

Considered the first great boxing broadcaster, Sam Taub was associated with the sport for over 60 years. A longtime sports writer and editor for the *New York Morning Telegraph,* Taub pioneered live, blow-by-blow announcing of boxing matches on radio. At the end of his career, Taub estimated that he had seen almost 12,000 fights and had broadcast 7,500.

He started working the *Friday Night Fights* on the NBC Radio Network in 1924, first with Angelo Palange and later with broadcasting legend Bill Stein.

Taub's voice became well known in broadcasts from many New York City boxing venues, including Madison Square Garden. At the height of his activity, Taub broadcast six boxing or wrestling shows a week. He was replaced at NBC by Don Dunphy in 1941. The last fight Taub called was the second Rocky Graziano–Tony Zale fight in 1947.

Taub also hosted *The Hour of Champions* on New York radio station WHN. The show aired for 24 years, and featured interviews with sports personalities. Taub also wrote for *The Ring* from the magazine's earliest days, and for decades, until his death in 1979, he contributed a column called "Up and Down Old Broadway."

In 1958, the Boxing Writers Association awarded Taub the James J. Walker Award for Long and Meritorious Service to Boxing. In 1978, the same group created The Sam Taub Award for Excellence in Broadcast Journalism. Taub was the first recipient. Hall of Fame Induction: 1994.

HERMAN TAYLOR
Promoter

Herman ("Muggsy") Taylor, born in Philadelphia on May 1, 1887, was one of the top promoters in boxing history. As a young man, Taylor got a job with promoter Jack McGuigan, distributing placards about upcoming fights, setting up the ring and seating, selling concessions, even sweeping floors. The experience affected him for the rest of his life.

Taylor actually fought twice as a flyweight and retired 2-0, but his boxing future was on the business side of the sport. In 1912, he purchased the Broadway Athletic Club and, in 1916, he formed a partnership with Bobby Gunnis.

The pair, dubbed the "Boy Promoters," were the first to bring fights to Philadelphia's major stadiums. (Years later Taylor promoted the first fight at the Spectrum when, in 1967, Joe Frazier knocked out Tony Doyle in two rounds.)

In 1926, Taylor and Gunnis did much of the behind-the-scenes work for Tex Rickard's first Jack Dempsey–Gene Tunney heavyweight championship match, a fight which 120,757 fans paid $1,895,733 to see. The final Taylor and Gunnis promotion took place in 1936 when Joe Louis knocked out Philadelphian Al Ettore in five rounds before 55,000 people at Municipal Stadium. Gunnis suffered a heart attack and died a week before the fight.

On his own, Taylor continued to stage entertaining and profitable fights. He co-promoted the Joe Louis–Tony Galento heavyweight championship match, Sugar Ray Robinson bouts, Louis–Gus Dorazio, and the Ike Williams–Bob Montgomery battles.

In 1952, Taylor staged three championship fights in Philadelphia. In the first on June 5, Jersey Joe Walcott defeated Ezzard Charles in a heavyweight championship match. On July 7, Kid Gavilan knocked out Gil Turner to retain the welterweight crown, and on

September 23, Rocky Marciano won the heavyweight championship by knocking out Walcott in the thirteenth.

Taylor lost his license for a time in the early sixties amid hints that a match on one of his cards was fixed. He rebounded, however, to stage the Harold Johnson–Doug Jones light heavyweight title fight in 1962 and continued to promote fights through 1975. Even at the time of his death on June 27, 1980, it was said the 93-year-old promoter was still looking to promote another fight. Hall of Fame Induction: 1998.

LOU VISCUSI
Manager

Lou Viscusi managed three world champions and Hall of Famers in a long career as a manager and promoter. Born in Schenectady, New York, on June 15, 1909, Viscusi grew up in Tampa, Florida. He got into boxing at an early age and was already a manager by nineteen. In 1929, he left Tampa with a couple of his fighters in tow—Patsy Alvarez and Young Grenado—and journeyed to New York. Because the fighters had not brought their birth certificates with them, they could not be licensed in New York. Frustrated, Viscusi accepted an invitation to have Grenado train with Louis ("Kid") Kaplan in Hartford, Connecticut. There Grenado would be allowed to box; Viscusi quickly established a base of operations in the Nutmeg State. For approximately eighteen years, Viscusi both managed fighters and promoted bouts at the Hartford Auditorium, a former trolley barn. In addition to boxing, Viscusi also promoted wrestling, ice shows, circuses, and semi-pro football.

"Mr. Lou," as he was known throughout New England, managed hundreds of fighters. He guided the careers of welterweight Del Flanagan, heavyweight Roy ("Cut and Shoot") Harris, middleweight Tony Licata, welterweight Manny Gonzalez, and heavyweight Cleveland Williams, but was best remembered for aiding three Hall of Famers to world championships: featherweight Willie Pep, lightweight Joe ("Old Bones") Brown, and light heavyweight Bob Foster. Viscusi often teamed with trainer Bill Gore—Viscusi dealing with the business affairs of their fighters while Gore handled the training. Late in Bob Foster's career, Viscusi's health forced him to sell Foster's management contract to Yancey ("Yank") Durham. Viscusi died on August 10, 1997.

In Sugar Ray Robinson's autobiography, Robinson writes that he custom ordered his trademark pink Cadillac to be painted the exact hue that would match a fuchsia necktie that Lou Viscusi had given him! Hall of Fame Induction: 2004.

JAMES J. WALKER
Politician

James J. ("Jimmy") Walker, the famous New York City mayor of the Roaring Twenties, was a career politician who made an invaluable contribution to the development of boxing. In his days as minority leader of the New York State Senate, he sponsored the Walker Law, which legalized boxing in the state and provided a model for its regulation by state athletic commissions.

Walker was a native New Yorker, born in 1881. He trained as a lawyer and was elected to the state Assembly in 1909. In 1915, he was elected to the state Senate, eventually becoming minority leader in 1921. He introduced the bill that would legalize boxing in 1920. In 1925, Walker was elected mayor of New York.

He was a popular leader even though he had come to symbolize the free-wheeling life of speakeasies and Tammany Hall improprieties. Shortly after his reelection in 1929, rumors of corruption surfaced, and Walker was investigated by a committee of the state legislature. Evidence of graft was uncovered and, in 1932, Governor Franklin D. Roosevelt summoned Walker to Albany to explain his actions. Shortly thereafter, Walker resigned as mayor.

Walker had a great fondness for boxing and was often seen at ringside at major New York fights. He was a regularly featured speaker at the Boxing Writers Association annual dinners and, in 1940, received that organization's award for long and meritorious service to boxing. The award was renamed the James J. Walker Memorial Award after Walker's death in 1946. The writers group had earlier honored Walker with its Edward J. Neil Memorial Award for Outstanding Contributions to Boxing.

Walker's life story was made into a movie starring former professional boxer and legendary comedian, Bob Hope. Hall of Fame Induction: 1992.

AL WEILL
Manager

Weill was born on December 28, 1893, in Gebwiler, Alsace-Lorraine, France, with the given name Armond. He immigrated to the United States at the age of thirteen with his father. Weill left school as soon as he was legally able.

Weill roomed with a fighter. One night he accompanied his roommate to his bout and served as his second. He fell in love with the sport. He served as an assistant to John ("The Barber") Reisler, a leading manager in the World War I era. When professional boxing as we know it was legalized in New York—with the passage of the Walker Law—Weill quickly registered as a manager. For quite a few years, Weill earned a living in boxing by managing a great number of rather ordinary fighters. He was vigilant in searching for fights for his charges.

Weill's knowledge of boxers and their styles led Mike Jacobs of the Twentieth Century Sporting Club to employ him as his matchmaker in 1931 and again from 1937 to 1938. Weill also spent a brief period as a promoter in the New York area.

However, it was as a manager that Weill earned his place in the International Boxing Hall of Fame. He managed Hall of Famer Lou Ambers when he won the lightweight championship, Joey Archibald when he won the featherweight championship, and Marty Servo when he won the welterweight championship.

Dubbed the "Vest" and the "Weskit King" for his penchant for wearing vests, Weill gained even more fame for his management of a powerful, if initially awkward, heavyweight who came to his attention early in the fighter's career: Rocky Marciano. Although Weill did not initially predict greatness for Marciano or immediately take over his management, he encouraged Marciano to move his operations to Providence where Weill had strong connections. Soon, Weill took a more direct interest in the future champion.

At about the same time, Weill was named matchmaker of the International Boxing Club. This powerful job put Weill in contact with the most important promoters and figures in the sport. He used these connections to further Marciano's career. Because the New York State Athletic Commission rules prevented someone from serving as both a matchmaker and a manager, Weill's stepson, Marty Weill, technically served as Marciano's manager for three years. Later, when forced to choose between serving as a matchmaker or as Marciano's manager, Weill cast his lot with Marciano.

When Marciano defeated Jersey Joe Walcott to take the world heavyweight championship on September 23, 1952, Weill had reached the pinnacle of his profession. The pair remained together until Marciano's retirement. Weill stayed in boxing for a few years but failed in his attempt to lure Marciano back into the ring. He then retired from the sport and moved to Florida. Weill died on October 20, 1969. Hall of Fame Induction: 2003.

STANLEY WESTON
Magazine Publisher

Stanley Weston was involved in the publication of boxing magazines from the time he was a teenager until his death at the age of 83—with time out for military service. Weston was born in New York on September 25, 1919. When he was ten years old, his father gave him an old copy of *The Ring*. Weston was fascinated with the stories but especially with the pictures. Over time he built up quite a magazine collection.

When Weston was thirteen, he moved with his family to Long Beach, New York. There a meeting with a neighbor changed his life. One day Weston was playing football on a lawn near where he lived. The owner came out of the house, grabbed the football and ordered the boys to leave. After sizing the boys up, the man changed his mind and offered the boys a dollar each to take care of his lawn, wash his car, and clean up his property. With their wages, the man gave each boy a new copy of the August 1933 issue of *The Ring*. The neighbor was Nat Fleischer, the owner of *The Ring*. Weston talked with Fleischer who was impressed with the youngster's knowledge of and interest in boxing. In 1935, Fleischer hired him to hand color 100 black-and-white boxing photos, which were to be hung in Jack Dempsey's restaurant.

When Weston graduated from high school in 1937, Fleischer offered him a summer job at his magazine. Weston jumped at the chance and performed a variety of duties and errands for $20 per week. He stayed on when the summer was over and for many years thereafter. In 1939, Fleischer asked the young man to paint a cover for the magazine. Weston's depiction of Hall of Famer Billy Conn appeared on the cover of the December 1939 issue and was the first of 57 striking covers he would paint between 1939 and 1951.

In 1941 Weston was drafted into the Army where he served until his discharge as a major in 1945. He returned to the magazine in December 1945, but he left *The Ring* in 1951 to take a position with Joe Weider Publications. One week later, the United States Air Force recalled him to active duty in the Korean War.

After his discharge, Weston started his own magazine, *Boxing and Wrestling*. This venture came at a cost. Weston's mentor, Fleischer, felt betrayed and, according to Weston, used his influence to hamper Weston's access to press releases, publicity photographs, and fight tickets. Despite these obstacles, Weston succeeded and started another magazine, *Boxing Illustrated,* in 1958. He left that magazine in 1964, after a dispute with his financial backers. Some of the other boxing magazines Weston started include *Boxing International, World Boxing, Boxing Pictorial, KO, Knockout,* and *Boxing 90*.

Weston's involvement with *The Ring* was not over, however. Fleischer died in 1972. *The Ring* went through some difficult periods, actually ceasing publication in 1989. Weston bought the magazine. Weston owned *The Ring* until 1992 when he sold it to London Publishing Company. Weston remained as the publisher until 1997. Weston also wrote books about boxing, including *The Ring: Boxing in the 20th Century,* which he co-authored with Steve Farhood. Weston died on April 12, 2002. Hall of Fame Induction: 2006.

Heavyweight Cha

Sonny Liston

HEROES AND HISTORY
The International Boxing Hall of Fame

ALI WAS THERE. He took an early morning jog through the streets of the village. Archie Moore, Jersey Joe Walcott, Carmen Basilio, Jake LaMotta, Sandy Saddler, Jose Napoles, Emile Griffith, Bob Foster, Billy Conn, Kid Gavilan, Ike Williams, and Willie Pep—they were all there, too.

The occasion that brought these boxing greats—and the memories of so many others—together was the first induction weekend, June 8, 9, and 10, 1990, at the International Boxing Hall of Fame in Canastota, New York. Forty-six boxers, from the earliest bare-knuckle brawlers to modern heroes like Muhammad Ali and Joe Frazier, were chosen by a panel of over 100 boxing writers and historians to become the first members of the Hall of Fame. In addition, seven men who contributed outside the ring to boxing's growth through the years were also honored. The inimitable promoter Tex Rickard, Nat Fleischer of *The Ring* magazine, and manager of champions, Jack Kearns, topped this list.

On the second weekend of each successive June, more inductees have been installed, increasing the membership in the Hall to over 325.

BOXING ARRIVES BY CANAL BOAT

Canastota has a rich boxing heritage which makes it an ideal home for the International Boxing Hall of Fame. This small central New York town (population: 5,000) is located about twenty miles east of Syracuse on the New York State Thruway. It was once a thriving stop on the Erie Canal, which linked it to New York City and Buffalo. When the canal builders and barge crews brought bare-knuckle fighting and boxing news to the town, the locals took up the sport enthusiastically. In 1895, the first projection of a motion picture film, with a device known as the Biograph, took place in Canastota. Appropriately, the film showed boxers sparring.

In the twentieth century, boxing gyms and clubs flourished in Canastota, and an active amateur program continues there today. For many years, the American Legion sponsored amateur boxing teams, and high schools in the Canastota area competed in boxing until the late 1940s. In addition to its own boxing tradition, Canastota is close to Syracuse, a major boxing venue for many years. More recently, the nearby Turning Stone Casino, owned by the Oneida Indian Nation, has begun hosting high profile, nationally televised professional boxing matches. Their handsome facility hosted the much hyped bout between the daughters of Muhammad Ali and Joe Frazier. A boxing program at Turning Stone is sometimes a Friday night feature of the annual Induction Weekend.

A TOWN'S DETERMINATION

Canastota is most proud, however, of the two champions its boxing environment eventually produced: native sons Carmen Basilio, welter- and middleweight champion in the late 1950s, and Basilio's nephew Billy Backus, welterweight champ in 1970 and '71.

In August 1982, two American Legionnaires and

longtime Canastota residents, Joe Bonaventura and Farrell Miller, were particularly struck by an article written by Mike Milmoe, editor of the *Canastota Bee-Journal*, on the 25th anniversary of Basilio's victory over Sugar Ray Robinson for the middleweight title. Something ought to be done, thought Bonaventura and Miller, to commemorate the accomplishments of the boy who once worked in the onion fields just outside of town and grew up to become a world champion. That the Canastota area had also produced another champion in Backus, as well as strong welterweight contender Dickie DiVeronica—ranked eighth-best in his weight division in the early 1960s—redoubled the sense that the town had something to crow about.

A movement was started to raise $30,000 in donations from local businesses to construct a showcase featuring memorabilia from the careers of Basilio and Backus. The showcase, a brick structure with tall picture windows and overhanging roof, was built directly across the street from the future site of the Hall of Fame. It was dedicated in August 1984.

This success gave impetus to the group that had already established itself as the Boxing Hall of Fame, Inc., to plan and build a shrine for the sport and its stars from around the world. *The Ring* had at one time inducted members into a Hall of Fame

The bronze statue of Carmen Basilio (left) is one of three life-size boxer sculptures on display at the Hall of Fame. Basilio was the proud recipient of this commemorative championship belt (above), presented by The Ring magazine.

located in its offices. However, that hall never established an existence independent of the magazine and did not survive changes in the publication's ownership and offices.

Many Canastota residents put their energies behind the effort to establish a new Hall of Fame, and local boxing enthusiast Edward Brophy became the Hall's executive director. The Hall's founders secured two state grants for $50,000 for a feasibility study and other preliminary work. Twenty-five area residents pledged $1,000 each, and the village and township councils approved small annual appropriations. A location near the Thruway, and agreements from collectors to donate boxing

The huge fist of Ken Norton dominates this display of plaster fist casts from the Hall of Fame's unique collection. Emile Griffith's, Joey Giardello's, and Ruben Olivares's fists are displayed in the foreground.

memorabilia to the museum were lined up, and four years later, the 2,000 square-foot facility opened its doors to the public. The Hall has seen two major expansions since its opening, and further plans, including a new library facility, are in the works. The village continues to actively support the Hall, and many residents have contributed a decade or more of service. Don Ackerman has served as the Board of Director's president for the past twenty years. Charter board members Mike Milmoe and Paul Basilio (Carmen's brother) have each served 22 years. The efforts of many townsfolk have been instrumental in the Hall's success.

INSIDE THE HALL

Once you walk through the doors of the International Boxing Hall of Fame, as the authors of *The Volvo Guide to Halls of Fame* found, "you are immediately thrown into the colorful and unforgiving world of flesh and flash." Exhibits include the "Wall of Fame," where each inductee is represented with a plaque including a photo and brief biography, and boxing fans will glory in the Hall's collection of ring accoutrements. Championship belts, plaster casts of famous fists, and the robes, trunks, and gloves of storied fighters are prominently displayed. The mystique of Joe Louis's trademark purple trunks or the gloves Rocky Marciano wore when he fought Jersey Joe Walcott is inescapable.

The Hall owes its unique collection of fist casts to Dr. Walter H. Jacobs, a dentist who applied his knowledge of plaster casting to making lifelike models of the hands of the great ring heroes of his day. Jacobs created exact likenesses of fists belonging to champions Jack Dempsey, Jack Johnson, Benny Leonard, and many others. The mammoth fist of former heavyweight champion Primo Carnera dwarfs all the other fists on display. The collection grows each year as living honorees join in fist-casting on the induction weekends.

Other displays in the Hall include tickets and programs from famous fights, and historic copies of *The Ring*. In addition, a collection of equipment Harold Johnson used in training shows the different gloves and protective devices used in preparing for a fight. An exhibit of the tools used by cut men gives the boxing fan a rare opportunity to see firsthand what a cornerman uses to control cuts. In addition to these and other exhibits, videotapes of great fights and fighters are shown on monitors located throughout the museum.

The Hall of Fame also boasts an extensive boxing library, available for use by the general public by appointment. The library's holdings include annual editions of *The Ring Record Book,* biographies and autobiographies of boxing figures, and many other books dealing with the sport. Of special interest to the boxing enthusiast is the collection of boxing magazines and programs, most notably the complete bound volumes of *The Ring*. The museum also has a gift shop, replete with boxing collectibles.

THE VOTE

Members of the Hall of Fame fall into five categories: Modern, Old-Timer, Pioneer, Non-Participant, and Observer, and are chosen by a vote of 150 boxing experts, historians, and writers. (*The Boxing Register* groups the last two categories as Non-Combatants.) The voters hail from all parts of the globe, including Australia, South Africa, Italy and other parts of Europe, Canada, Argentina, Japan, and the United States. In order to be placed on the ballot, individuals must first clear a pre-screening committee of boxing historians. Modern fighters are additionally required to have been retired for five years. Non-participants can

Tickets, posters, and programs of historic fights are on display.

Each June, the Hall of Fame Induction Weekend brings together an amazing cast of boxing immortals. This photo shows part of the inaugural class of inductees from 1990. Front row: Sandy Saddler, Ike Williams, Kid Gavilan, Willie Pep, Jake LaMotta, Carmen Basilio. Back row: Billy Conn, Jose Napoles, Jersey Joe Walcott, Muhammad Ali, Emile Griffith, Bob Foster, Archie Moore.

be elected to the Hall of Fame even if they are still active, assuming they have achieved enough in their careers to merit selection.

The current ballots contain 45 modern-day fighters and from 15 to 40 names in the other categories. The board of directors of the Hall of Fame determines how many people are to be inducted each year. At present, approximately three Moderns, three Old-Timers, two "Non-Participants," two "Observers," and one Pioneer are to be elected each year. The candidates who accrue the most votes are those who become inductees. Ballots are mailed out on November 1 each year with the announcement of the new class of inductees coming in mid-January.

THE FESTIVITIES

The high point of the year at the International Boxing Hall of Fame is the Hall of Fame Weekend in June, when new members are inducted. Famous boxers, past and present, pour into town. The atmosphere is casual, and members of the public are

quite likely to be able to talk with and get autographs from some of the sport's heroes.

Besides the induction ceremony itself, the weekend features many other boxing-related activities, such as live boxing, a golf tournament where fans can play golf with the boxing greats, a cocktail party, a banquet, and a parade of champions through the town. In addition, the public can attend ringside lectures given by fighters and other prominent figures in the sport. For those interested in boxing memorabilia, a large boxing collectibles show is held in the Canastota High School gym.

As an added attraction, a celebrity serves as Grand Marshal of the parade. Female boxing champion Christy Martin, basketball coach Jim Boeheim and celebrities from the entertainment world such as Mr. T, John Amos, Sherman Hemsley, Danny Aiello, Bo Derek, Al Lewis, Tony Sirico, Tony Orlando, and Ryan O'Neal have each taken a turn.

In 2005, Hollywood stars Russell Crowe and Daniel Day-Lewis enjoyed the Hall of Fame Weekend festivities.

That the Hall of Fame Weekend is so well run and that the events come off without a hitch is a tribute to Executive Director Brophy, his staff, and his army of volunteers. Forty committee chairpersons begin planning the June event the previous November. In the last month before the event, they are helped by about 150 local volunteers and 100 organizations which help with the various events. The Hall of Fame Weekend is well publicized and draws thousands of boxing fans to Canastota each year.

Though it is still relatively young, the International Boxing Hall of Fame has firmly established itself as the worldwide center for boxing history.

International
Boxing Hall of Fame

1 Hall of Fame Drive, Canastota, NY 13032

PHONE (315) 697-7095   FAX (315) 697-5356
WEBSITE http://www.ibhof.com

OPEN DAILY: 9 a.m.– 5 p.m.

DIRECTIONS: Adjacent to the New York State Thruway, Exit 34

Anderson, Dave. *In the Corner: Boxing's Greatest Trainers Talk about Their Art.* New York: William Morrow & Company, 1991.

Andre, Sam, and Nat Fleischer. *A Pictorial History of Boxing: From the Bare-Knuckle Days to the Present.* New York: Carol Publishing Group, 1989.

Armstrong, Henry. *Gloves, Glory and God: An Autobiography.* Westwood, NJ: Fleming H. Revell, 1957.

Arnold, Peter. *All Time Greats of Boxing.* Edison, NJ: Book Sales, 1993.

Ashe, Arthur R. Jr. *A Hard Road to Glory: A History of the African-American Athlete.* 4 vols. New York: Amistad Press, 1988.

Astor, Gerald. *". . . and a credit to his race": The Hard Life and Times of Joseph Louis Barrow, a.k.a. Joe Louis.* New York: Saturday Review Press, 1974.

Baker, Mark Allen. *Complete Guide to Boxing Collectibles.* Iola, WI: Krause Publications, 1995.

Bordman, Gerald Martin. *The Oxford Companion to American Theatre.* Oxford: Oxford U. Press, 1992.

Brenner, Teddy, and Barney Nagler. *Only the Ring was Square.* Englewood Cliffs, NJ: Prentice-Hall, 1981.

Breslin, Jimmy. *Damon Runyon: A Life.* New York: Ticknor & Fields, 1991.

Bromberg, Lester. *Boxing's Unforgettable Fights.* New York: Ronald Press, 1962.

Cannon, Jack, and Tom Cannon. *Nobody Asked Me, But... (The World of Jimmy Cannon).* New York: Holt, Rinehart, and Winston, 1978.

Cantwell, Robert. *The Real McCoy: The Life and Times of Norman Selby.* Princeton, NJ: Auerbach Publishers, 1971.

Castleman, H., and W. J. Podrazik. *Watching TV: Four Decades of American Television.* New York: McGraw-Hill, 1982.

Clark, Tom. *The World of Damon Runyon.* New York: Harper & Row, 1978.

Collins, Nigel. *Boxing Babylon: Behind the Shadowy World of the Prize Ring.* New York: Carol Publishing Group, 1990.

Corbett, Jim. *My Life and Fights.* London: John Ousely, 1910.

Cornell, Phil. *Drawing a Crowd: Bill Gallo's Greatest Sports Moments.* New York: Jonathan David, 2000.

Cosell, Howard. *Cosell.* Chicago: Playboy Press, 1973.

Cosell, Howard. *I Never Played the Game.* New York: William Morrow & Company, 1985.

Cramer, Richard Ben. *Joe DiMaggio: The Hero's Life.* New York: Simon & Schuster, 2000.

De Cristofaro, S. *Boxing's Greatest Middleweights.* Rochester, NY (26 Everett Dr., Rochester 14624): S. De Cristofaro, 1982.

Deghy, Guy. *Noble and Manly: The History of the National Sporting Club.* London: Hutchinson, 1956.

Dempsey, Jack, and Barbara P. Dempsey. *Dempsey.* New York: HarperCollins, 1977.

Dibble, Roy F. *John L. Sullivan: an Intimate Narrative.* Boston: Little, Brown, and Company, 1925.

Dickson, Paul, and Robert Skole. *The Volvo Guide to Halls of Fame: The Traveler's Handbook of North America's Most Inspiring and Entertaining Attractions.* Washington, DC: Living Planet Press, 1995.

Donovan, Arthur J. Jr. *Fatso: Football When Men Were Really Men.* New York: William Morrow & Company, 1988.

Dundee, Angelo, and Mike Winters. *Only Talk Winning.* Chicago: Contemporary Books, 1985.

Durant, John. *The Heavyweight Champions.* London: Arco Publications, 1961.

Fleischer, Nat. *50 Years at Ringside.* New York: Greenwood Press, 1969.

Fleischer, Nat. *Black Dynamite.* 5 vols. New York: Ring Athletic Library, 1938–47.

Fleischer, Nat. *The Heavyweight Championship: An Informal History of Heavyweight Boxing from 1719 to the Present Day.* London: Putnam, 1949.

Fleischer, Nat. *Jack Dempsey.* New Rochelle, N.Y.: Arlington House, 1972.

Fleischer, Nat. *The Michigan Assassin: The Saga of Stanley Ketchel.* New York: Ring Book Shop, 1946.

Fleischer, Nat, Bert Sugar, and Herbert G. Goldman, et al., eds. *The Ring Record Book & Boxing Encyclopedia.* 46 vols. 1941–1967. New York: Ring Book Shop and others.

Foreman, George, and Joel Engel. *By George: The Autobiography of George Foreman.* New York: Villard Books, 1995.

Fried, Ronald K. *Corner Men: Great Boxing Trainers.* New York: Four Walls Eight Windows, 1991.

Fullerton, Hugh. *Two Fisted Jeff.* Chicago: Consolidated Book Publishers, 1929.

Gallico, Paul. *Farewell to Sport.* New York: A.A. Knopf, 1938.

Gipe, George. *The Great American Sports Book.* New York: Doubleday & Company, 1978.

Goldstein, Ruby, and Frank Graham. *Third Man in the Ring.* Westport, CT: Greenwood Publishing Group, 1986.

Golesworthy, Maurice. *Encyclopaedia of Boxing.* London: Robert Hale, 1988.

Gorn, Elliot J. *Manly Art: Bare-Knuckle Prize Fighting in America.* Ithaca, NY: Cornell University Press, 1986.

Graziano, Rocky, and Rowland Barber. *Somebody Up There Likes Me: The Story of My Life Until Today.* New York: Simon and Schuster, 1955.

Harding, John. *Lonsdale's Belt: The Story of Boxing's Greatest Prize.* London: Robson Books, 1994.

Hassan, John. *1998 ESPN Information Please Sports Almanac.* New York: Warner Books, 1997.

Hauser, Thomas. *Muhammad Ali: His Life & Times.* New York: Simon & Schuster, 1991.

Heinz, W. C. *What a Time It Was.* Cambridge, MA: Da Capo, 2001.

Heller, Peter. *In This Corner!* New York: Simon & Schuster, 1973.

Isenberg, Michael. *John L. Sullivan and His America.* Urbana, IL: U. of Illinois Press, 1994.

Johnston, Alexander. *Ten—and Out! The Complete Story of the Prize Ring in America.* New York: I. Washburn, 1927.

Kahn, Roger. *A Flame of Pure Fire: Jack Dempsey and the Roaring '20s.* New York: Harcourt Brace & Co., c1999.

Kearns, Jack, and Oscar Fraley. *The Million Dollar Gate.* New York: Macmillan, 1966.

Lardner, Rex. *The Legendary Champions.* New York: American Heritage Press, 1972.

Liebling, A. J. *A Neutral Corner: Boxing Essays.* New York: Simon & Schuster, 1992.

Liebling, A. J. *The Sweet Science.* Westport, CT: Greenwood Publishing Group, 1973.

Louis, Joe, Edna Rust, and Art Rust Jr. *Joe Louis: My Life.* New York: Harcourt Brace Jovanovich, 1978.

McCallum, John. *Encyclopedia of World Boxing Champions.* Radnor, PA: Chilton Book Company, 1975.

McCallum, John. *The World Heavyweight Boxing Championship.* Radnor, PA: Chilton, 1974.

McIlvanney, Hugh. *McIlvanney On Boxing: An Anthology.* London: Mainstream Publishing, 1996.

McNeil, Alex. *Total Television.* New York: Viking Penguin, 1980.

Mead, Chris. *Champion: Joe Louis, Black Hero in White America.* New York: Scribner, 1985.

Menke, Frank G. *The Encyclopedia of Sports.* 6th ed. New York: A. S. Barnes, 1978.

Miles, Henry Downes. *Pugilistica: The History of British Boxing.* 3 vols. Edinburgh: John Grant, 1906.

Moore, Archie. *Any Boy Can: The Archie Moore Story.* Englewood Cliffs, NJ: Prentice-Hall, 1971.

Mullan, Harry. *The Great Book of Boxing.* New York: Crescent Books, 1987.

Mullan, Harry. *The Illustrated History of Boxing.* New York: Crescent Books, 1987.

Mullan, Harry. *The Ultimate Encyclopedia of Boxing.* Edison, NJ: Chartwell Books, 1996.

Nagler, Barney. *James Norris and the Decline of Boxing.* Indianapolis: Bobbs Merrill Co., 1964.

Nelson, Battling. *Life, Battles, and Career of Battling Nelson, Lightweight Champion of the World.* self published, 1908.

Newfield, Jack. *Only in America: The Life and Crimes of Don King.* New York: William Morrow & Company, 1995.

Odd, Gilbert E. *Boxing: The Great Champions.* London: Hamlyn, 1974.

Odd, Gilbert E. *Encyclopedia of Boxing.* Edison, NJ: Book Sales, 1989.

Odd, Gilbert E. *The Fighting Blacksmith: A Biography of Bob Fitzsimmons.* London: Pelham, 1976.

Patterson, Floyd, and Milton Gross. *Victory Over Myself.* London: Pelham Books, 1962.

Pepe, Phil. *Come Out Smokin': Joe Frazier, The Champ Nobody Knew.* New York: Coward McCann & Geoghegan, 1972.

Porter, David L., ed. *Biographical Dictionary of American Sports: Basketball and Other Indoor Sports.* Westport, CT: Greenwood Publishing Group, 1989.

Reid, J.C. *Bucks and Bruisers: Pierce Egan and Regency England.* London: Routledge & Kegan Paul, 1971.

Remnick, David. *King of the World.* New York: Random House, 1998.

Robinson, Sugar Ray, and Dave Anderson. *Sugar Ray.* New York: Viking Press, 1970.

Ross, Barney. *No Man Stands Alone: The True Story of Barney Ross.* Philadelphia: Lippincott, 1957.

Sammons, Jeffrey T. *Beyond the Ring: The Role of Boxing in American Society.* Champaign, IL: U. of Illinois Press, 1988.

Skehan, Everett M. *Rocky Marciano: Biography of a First Son.* Boston: Houghton Mifflin, 1977.

Sugar, Bert Randolph. *The 100 Greatest Boxers of All Time.* New York: Bonanza Books, 1984.

Sugar, Bert Randolph. *One Hundred Years of Boxing: A Pictorial History of Modern Boxing, 1882-1982.* New York: Smithmark Publishers, 1982.

Sugar, Bert Randolph, and The Editors of Ring Magazine. *The Great Fights: A Pictorial History of Boxing's Greatest Bouts.* New York: Gallery Books, 1981.

Sullivan, Russell. *Rocky Marciano: The Rock of His Times.* Urbana, IL: University of Illinois Press, 2002.

Suster, Gerald. *Champions of the Ring: The Lives and Times of Boxing's Heavyweight Heroes.* Jersey City, NJ: Parkwest Publications, 1994.

Torres, Jose. *Fire & Fear: The Inside Story of Mike Tyson.* New York: Warner, 1989.

Variety Obituaries, Vol. 1-10. New York: Garland, 1988.

Vecchione, Joseph J., ed. *The New York Times Book of Sports Legends.* New York: Times Books, 1991.

Walsh, Peter. *Men of Steel: The Lives and Times of Boxing's Middleweight Champions.* London: Robson Books, 1993.

Ward, Geoffrey C. *Unforgivable Blackness: The Rise and Fall of Jack Johnson.* New York: A.A. Knopf, 2004.

Weston, Stanley, and Steven Farhood. *The Ring: Chronicle of Boxing.* London: Hamlyn, 1993.

Wignall, Trevor C. *The Story of Boxing.* New York: Brentano's, 1924.

Wiley, Ralph. *Serenity: A Book about Fighters, Why They Fight & How It Feels to Be One.* New York: Henry Holt & Company, 1989.

Young, A.S. ("Doc"). *Sonny Liston: The Champion Nobody Wanted.* Chicago: Johnson Publishing Co., 1963.

INTERNET SOURCES

3615, Boxing Avenue
www.boxing-records.com

ABCNews.com
www.abcnews.go.com

Amazon.com
www.amazon.com

American Legends
www.americanlegends.com/
interviews/budd_schulberg.html

Belfast Telegraph Digital
www.belfasttelegraph.co.uk

BillyConn.net
www.billyconn.net

BoxingTalk
www.boxingtalk.com

The Boxing Times
www.boxingtimes.com

BoxRec.com
www.boxrec.com

CBS SportsLine.com
www.cbs.sportsline.com

CourierPostonline.com
www.courierpostonline.com

Cyber Boxing Zone
www.cyberboxingzone.com

ESPN
www.espn.go.com

Fightnews.com
www.fightnews.com

Guardian Unlimited
www.guardian.co.uk

HBO
www.hbo.com

International Boxing Hall of Fame
www.ibhof.com

Irish-Boxing.com
www.irish-boxing.com

Jews in Sports
www.jewsinsports.com

Latino Legends in Sports
www.latinosportslegends.com

Leonardo.it
www.leonardo.it

MaxBoxing.com
www.maxboxing.com

Miami New Times
www.miaminewtimes.com

National Baseball Hall of Fame and
Museum
www.baseballhalloffame.org

NewspaperArchive.com
www.newspaperarchive.com

NSSA Hall of Fame
www.nssahalloffame.com

Pocono Record
www.poconorecord.com

Ring Talk
www.ringtalk.com

Schneider Publishing Company
www.schneiderpublishing.com

SecondsOut.com
www.secondsout.com

Spartacus International
www.spartacus.schoolnet.co.uk

TigerBoxing
www.tigerboxing.com

Travel & Sports, Puerto Rico
MasterGuide
www.travelandsports.com

Upcomingmovies.com
www.movies.yahoo.com/mv/
upcoming/

USA Today
www.usatoday.com

Harold Johnson (L) makes the obligatory trip to a photography studio for publicity photos.

PHOTO CREDITS

Photographs, etchings, drawings and other illustrations used in this book are from the collections of *The Ring* magazine (including the Stanley Weston Collection), The International Boxing Hall of Fame, Sports Legends Photos, Inc., and from the private collections of the authors.

The photograph of Dan Parker is from UPI/CORBIS–BETTMAN.

Andrew Gillis of Cascadilla Photography took photographs of the International Boxing Hall of Fame expressly for this book.

Other individual photographers and studios, where known, are listed below:

20th Century Sporting Club:
Jenkins

Ace Photographers:
Joe Brown

Sam Andre:
Jenkins in corner

Bill Apter:
Chandler vs. Murata, Dunphy, Dan Duva, Lou Duva, Fiske, Futch, Gallo, Gomez, Goodman, Markson, Sugar Ray Leonard, McCallum, McCallum vs. Mannion, Pedroza vs. LaPorte, Pryor, Rudd, Sanchez, Sanchez vs. Nelson (2), Spinks vs. Braxton

D. Arnow:
Benny Leonard

H.A. Atwell, Chicago:
Fields (shirt)

Al Bello:
Mercante, Norris

Box Photo:
Broulliard (full length)

Scott K. Brown:
Sugar Ray Leonard Basketball

Les Clark:
Lennox Lewis

Brent Cook:
Gonzalez

David Corona:
Ortiz vs. Torres

Cosmopolitan, N.Y.:
Wright

Louis Dummett:
Saddler & Fleischer

Theo Ehret:
Ali vs. Norton, Arguello, Foster vs. Quarry, Griffith, Laguna vs. Ramos, Napoles, Napoles vs. Backus, Napoles vs. Lopez, Olivares, Olivares & Parnassus,

Olivares vs. Rose, Parnassus, Saldivar, Carlos Zarate, Zarate vs. Ferreri

Fotocronache Olympia:
Benvenuti vs. Griffith

Gunther:
Griffith vs. Rodriguez, Liston handstand, Liston vs. Patterson, Ortiz vs. Lane

Will Hart:
A. Nelson (short hair)

David Jones:
Chris Dundee

King:
Foreman vs. Frazier

J. Lash:
McCallum vs. Yonker

Jim Laurie:
Hagler vs. Hearns

Jason Ross Lavin:
Duff, Gonzalez vs. Diaz (2)

Arturo LeConte:
Norton vs. Quarry, Rosario, Rosario vs. Tris

Esaul Lopez:
Locche

Ray Monaco:
LaMotta & DeNiro

Frank Monell:
Basilio vs. Saxton

A.C. McManus:
Spinks vs. Cooney

NBC:
Qawi

J.J. O'Brien, N.Y.:
Fitzsimmons (photo montage)

Omega Fotocronache:
Branchini

Pat Orr:
Christodoulou, Zaragoza (3)

Pacemaker Press International:
McGuigan vs. Pedroza

Charlotte Peters:
Benton, Pedroza, Pedroza vs. Taylor

Duncan Raban:
McGuigan

Ken Regan:
Schulberg

P.A. Reuter:
Tiger

Bert Roberts:
Wills

D. Rowe:
Buchanan vs. Cullen

Osvaldo Salas:
Giardello vs. Graham

N.J. Sax:
Saad Muhammad vs. Lopez

Russ Scott:
Pep vs. Leslie

M. Smith:
Robinson

Paul Thompson:
Dillon

Underwood & Underwood:
Willard

U.S. Navy:
Apostoli (uniform)

Von Romerheim Studio:
Kid Chocolate

D.L. Waite:
Benitez vs. Hope, Hagler vs. Mugabi, Sanchez vs. Castanon, Sanchez vs. Gomez, Spinks vs. Holmes

Harry E. Winkler:
Yarosz

John Wood:
Jack Dempsey ("The Nonpareil")

INDEX

Canzoneri, Tony, 56, 66–67, **82–83**, 155, 178, 179, 189, 205, 210–211, 225, 307

Carbajal, Danny, 330, 332

Carbajal, Michael, 330–333, 420–421

Carbo, Frankie, 258–259, 264, 425, 478

Cardona, Prudencio, 342

Cardona, Ricardo, 342

Carey, Ed, 136

Carnera, Primo, 62, 63, 173, 215, 256–257, 489

Carney, Jem, 20, 180–181

Carpentier, Georges, 84–85, 109, *130*, 143, 167, 171

   v. Dempsey, *84*, 85, 103–104

   as referee, *362*

Carr, Red, 218

Carter, Benny, 95

Carter, Jack, 22, 43

Carter, Jimmy, 316, **334–337**, 658

Carter, Rubin ("Hurricane"), 411, 433

Carter, Wilfred ("Whizbang"), 308

Casanova, Baby, 116

Casino, Jimmy, 221

Casson, Dr. Ira, 261

Castanon, Roberto, *630*

Castellani, Rocky, 548

Castillo, Chucho, 346, 540, 543

Castillo, Orlando, 596

Castro, Albert, 400–401

Castro, Armando, 401

Castro, Edgar, 577

Castro, Melchor Cob, 333, 420

Cauliflower ears, *216*

Caunt, Ben, 34, 46

Cavagnoli, Carlo, 174

Cavicchi, Franco, 454

Cayton, Bill, 612, **701–702**

Celestine, Jerry, 640

Cerdan, Marcel, 338–341, 469, 671

Cervantes, Antonio 294, 296, **342–345**, 483, 590

Chacon, Bobby, 346–349, 543

Chacon, Valerie, 346, 349

Chambers, Arthur, 21, 27, 29

Chambers, John Graham, 12–13, **702**

Chandler, Jeff, 350–353

Chaney, George ("K.O."), 115, 226, 246

Chang, Jung-Koo, 420

Chapman, Red, 66, *66*, 67

Chargin, Don, *561*, **702–703**

Charles, Ezzard, 311, 322, **354–357**, *494*, 496, 498, 501, 657, *657*

   v. Louis, *354*, 357, 493

Charnley, Dave, *317*

Chavez, Jesus, 260

Chavez, Julio Cesar, 260, 615

Chestnut, Ike, 596

Chip, George, 96, 130

Chmielewski, Henry, 77

Chorsirirat, Sakdisami, 398

Choynski, Joe, 86–87, 89, 144, 147, 182, 183, 201, 216, 236

Christensen, Christian, *564*, 565

Christie, Gus, 130

Christodoulou, Stanley, 405, **703–704**

Christoforidis, Anton, 308, 311

Churchill, Frank, 234

Chuvalo, George, 381, 392

Citro, Ralph, 704–705

Clabby, Jimmy, 96, *96*, 128, *152*

Clamp, Bill, 33

Clancy, Gil, 383, 430, **705**

Clark, Elky, 158

Clark, Johnny, 21

Clarke, Jeff, 161

Clay, Cassius. *See* Ali, Muhammad

Clayton, Jack, 17

Cleveland, Captain, 196

Cobb, Tex, *536*

Coburn, Joe, 35

Cochrane, Freddie ("Red"), 449, 685

Cockell, Don, 653, *653*

Cocoa Kid, 151

Coffee, Jerome, 376

Coffroth, James W., 55, **705–706**

Cohen, Irving, 425, **706–707**

Cokes, Curtis, 358–361, 527

Colbert, Mike, 436

Colima, Babe, 58

Collins, Billy, 360

Collins, Tom, 14

Collyer, Sam, 27

Colpoys, Al, 218

Conn, Billy, 255, 279, **362–365**, 458, *596*, 599, 669, 680, *762*

   v. Louis, 364–365, *365*, 492, *492*

Conn, Jackie, *362*

Connelly, William, 14

Conteh, David, 639

Conteh, John, 619

Contreras, Israel, 400

Cooney, Gerry, 384, 539, 641, *641*

Cooper, Gypsy, 26

Cooper, Henry, 269, 455

Cooper, Joe, 118

Corbett, James J., 45, **88–89**, 141, 145, *166*, 195, 212, 217, 223, 553

   v. Choynski, 86–87, 88

   v. Fitzsimmons, 89, *120*, 120–121

Corbett, Young, 198

Corbett, Young II, *186*, 187

Corbett, Young III, 90–91, 119, 189, 279

Cordero, Jose ("Pepe"), 50

Cordoba, Juan Domingo, 421

Cordova, Jose Luis, 532

Corrales, Ernesto, 608

Correa, Bob, 544

Corri, Eugene, 207

Eagan, Joe, 218

Earp, Wyatt, 120, 217, 553

Eastwood, Barney, 506, 508, 509

Eaton, Aileen, *561*, 714

Edwards, Billy, 21, **27**

Edwards, Frankie, 206

Edward VII, King of England, 139

Egan, Pierce, 18, 26, 36, **715**

Ekwert, Whitey, 235

Elizondo, Hector, 614

Ellis, Jimmy, 392, 573

Ellis, William, 34

Elorde, Gabriel ("Flash"), **370–373**, 625

Epperson, Lee, 496

Erlanger, A. L., 137

Erne, Frank, 124, 163, 187

Erskine, Joe, 455

Ertle, Johnny, 247

Escalera, Alfredo, 283

Escobar, Sixto, 116–117

Esneault, Whitey, 566

Espada, Angel, 368

Espinal, Eusebio, 400

Espinal, Ignacia, *329*

Espinoza, Leo, 587

Espinoza, Pedro, 332

Esteves, Benjy Jr., *418*

Eubank, Peter, 506, 508

European Boxing Union (EBU), 48

Eustache, Robert, 84

Evans, Samuel. *See* Young Dutch Sam

F

Famechon, Johnny, 441, 629

Farmer, Tommy, 554

Farnsworth, Jack, 642

Farren, Shep, 246

Fawcett, Will, 27

Fearns, Duggan, 32

Feeney, George, 321

Feldman, Lew, 155

Fenech, Jeff, **374–377**, 530–531, 674, 679

Fernandez, Florentino, 648

Ferns, Jim ("Rube"), 108, 237

Ferrer, Jose, 341

Ferreri, Paul, *679*

Fewterel, William, 31

Fields, Jackie, 77, 90–91, **118–119**

Figg, James, 12, **28**

Filippo, Lou, 421

Finch, Albert, 650, 652

Fink, Louis, 244

Finnegan, Chris, *386*, 388

Firley, Jack, 39

Firpo, Luis Angel, 104, *105*, 245, *248*, 249, 584

Fiske, Jack, **715–716**

Fitzgerald, Squire, 36

Fitzmaurice, Bill, 19

Fitzpatrick, Sam, *162*

Fitzsimmons, Bob, 87, 89, 101, **120–121**, 144, 147, 201, 212, 213, 217, 553

Fitzsimmons, Floyd, 249

Flaherty, Sid, 544

Flanagan, Glen, 484

Flanagan, Steve, 136

Fleischer, Nat, 50, 139, 270, 479, 583, *620*, **716**

Flood, John, 44

Flores, Elino, 234

Flores, Javier, 352

Flores, Jose, 612

Flores, Victor, 583

Flowers, Tiger, 98, **122–123**, 133, 239

Flynn, Jim, 80, 103, 106–107

Flynn, Porky, 166

Foley, Larry, 35, 134, 140

Folledo, Luis, 565

Folley, Zora, 388

Force, Harry, *100*

Foreman, George, **378–385**, 538

v. Ali, *266*, 271, 378, 382–383

v. Frazier, 378, 382, *383*, 392, 393

Foster, Bob, **386–389**, 645, *762*

Foster, Pop, 188

Foutts, Ray, 254

Fox, Billy, 469, 553

Fox, Richard K., 45, 48–49, 194, **717**

Fox, Tiger Jack, 77

Fragetta, Dewey, **717–718**

Frangoni, Nino, 484

Fraser, Don, **718–719**

Frazer, Alfonso ("Peppermint"), 342, *342*, 483

Frazier, Billy, 180, 181

Frazier, Joe, 389, **390–393**

v. Ali, 270, 390, *390*, 392–393

v. Foreman, 378, 382, *383*, 392, 393

Frush, Danny, 115, 157

Fuentes, Jacinto, 414

Fujii, Paul, 483

Fuller, Sammy, 307

Fulljames, George, 100

Fullmer, Don, 549

Fullmer, Gene, 293, **394–397**, 410, 433, 606, 642

Fulton, Fred, 249

Futch, Eddie, 393, 505, **719–720**

on Burley, 325

on Walcott, 657

G

Galaxy, Khaosai, **398–401**

Galento, Tony, *62*

Galindez, Victor, **402–405**

Gallico, Paul, 215

Gallo, Bill, **720–721**

Gallouze, Farid, 508

Ganigan, Andy, 283

Gans, Baby Joe, 220

Gans, Joe, **124–125**, 135, 160, 187, 198–199

Gans, Panama Joe, 122

Garbelli, Giancarlo, 565

Garcia, Bobby, 150

Garcia, Ceferino, *210*, 220, 279, 289

Garcia, Constancio ("Rocky"), 328

Garcia, Eddie, 596

Garcia, Jose Luis, 538

Garcia, Julio, 574

Garcia, Luis, 480

Gardner, George, 121

Gardner, Jim, 216

Gardner, Orville ("Awful"), 38

Garza, Loreto, 615

Gavilan, Kid, 290, *334*, **406–409**, 422, *422*, 425, 548, *549*, 605, *762*

Genaro, Frankie, 126–127, 158, 234, 235, 253

Giardello, Joey, 410–413, 425, 565, 645

Gibbons, Mike, 128–129, 185

Gibbons, Tommy, 104, *128*, **130–131**, 132

Gibson, Billy, *230*

Gilmore, Harry, 64

Gimbel, Bernard, 122

Giminez, Carlos, 345

Gine, Jamie, 480

Glassman, Phil, 66, 226

Glick, Joe, *82*

Glover, Mike, 74

Goddard, Joe, 87

Godfrey, George, 140

Goldman, Charley, 496, **721**

Goldman, Nate, 227

Goldman, Sammy, 210

Goldstein, Abe, 177, 234

Goldstein, Ruby, 433, 456, 459, 573, 653, 657, 671, *671*, **721–722**

Goldstein, Sammy, 176

Gomes, Harold, 373

Gomez, Tarcisio, 326

Gomez, Tommy, *654*

Gomez, Wilfredo, 414–417, 530, 632, *632*, 678

Gonzales, Pedro, 548

Gonzalez, Betulio, *326*, 328

Gonzalez, Humberto ("Chiquita"), *330*, 332–333, **418–421**

Gonzalez, Manuel, 358, 361

Goodman, Jack, 137

Goodman, Murray, 722–723

Goodrich, Jimmy, 178, 202

Gore, Bill, 316

Gorman, Jim, 64

Gorring, Walter, 224

Goss, Joe, 29, 44

Gould, Joe, 72, 73

Graham, Billy, 290, 406, 410, *410*, **422–425**

Graham, Herol, 505

Gramby, Joe, 510

Grassi, Auguste, 94

Graziano, Rocky, 257, **426–429**, 605, *668*, 671, *671*

Greb, Harry, *122*, 122–123, 129, 130, **132–133**, 167, 172, 238, *238*

v. Tunney, 132–133, 231, *232*

Green, Charlie, 649

Green, Dave ("Boy"), 560

Greene, Abe J., 49

Greenlee, Gus, 169

Gregorio, Vidal, 78–79

Gregory, Eddie. *See* Muhammad, Eddie Mustafa

Gregory, Jim, 15

Griffin, Corn, 72

Griffin, Hank, 144

Griffin, Jim, 207, 251

Griffith, Emile, 296, **430–433**, *514*, 517, 527, 608, *608*, 611, 645, *762*

v. Benvenuti, 298, 301, *301*, 433

Griffith, Tuffy, 72

Griffiths, Gordon, 650

Griffo, Young, 134–135, 162, 181

Grigsby, Will, 332

Griman, David, 401

Grove, Calvin, 377, 531

Gully, John, 39

Gummer, Tom, *170*

Gutierrez, Ernesto, 672

Gutierrez, Luis, 154

Gutteridge, Reg, 723–724

Guttridge, George, 34

■H■

Hagler, Marvelous Marvin, **434–437**, 474–475, *475*

Hague, Ian, *160*

Haley, Patsy, *68*, *70*, 133, *204*

Hamill, Pete, 649

Hamilton, Gene, 648

Hammonds, Ike, 592

Hamsho, Mustafa, 297

Hank, Henry, 569

Hanley, Joe, 46

Hanlon, Eddie, 198

Harada, Masahiko ("Fighting"), **438–441**, 452–453

Harding, Jeff, 505

Hardwick, Harold, 97

Harnatty, Ned, 194

Harris, Harry, 65, **136–137**

Harris, Morris, 142

Harris, Roy ("Cut and Shoot"), 569

Harris, Sam, 136, 246

Harry the Coalheaver, 36

Hart, Jack, 599

Hart, Marvin, 80, 147

Harvey, Charley, 196

Harvey, Len, *168*

Hatanaka, Kiyoshi, 675

Hauser, Al, *649*

Hayward, Stan, 361

Hearns, Thomas ("Hit Man"), 369, *434*, 437, *473*, 474, 475

National Boxing Association (NBA), 49–50

National Sporting Club, 48

Navarro, Ruben, 321, *321*

Nazario, Juan, 615

Neat, Bill, 43

Neil, Al, 108

Neil, Frankie, 196

Nelson, Azumah, 376–377, *377*, 417, **528–531**, *633*

Nelson, Battling, 61, *124*, 125, 185, *196*, 197, **198–199**, 240, 250, *250*, 251

Newman, Rock, 595

New York State Athletic Commission (NYSAC), 49

Niderost, Joe, 276, 278

Nixon, Richard, *337*

Norfolk, Kid, 122

Norkus, Charlie, 569

Norris, James, 258–259, 572

Norris, Orlin Jr., 532

Norris, Terry, 475, **532–535**

Norton, Al, *106*

Norton, Ken, 382, **536–539**

v. Ali, *271*, 536, 538

Norton, Ken Jr., 539

Nosworthy, William, 25

Numata, Yoshiaki, 373

Nuñiz, Alicia, *257*

O'Brien, Philadelphia Jack, 80, 108, 121, 152, 161, **200–201**, *234*

O'Connell, Bill, 136

O'Keefe, Pat, 202

O'Neill, "KO" Becky, 350, 352

O'Neill, Willie, 350, 352

O'Rourke, Sam, 19

O'Rourke, Tom, 108, 110, 236

O'Rourke, Tom, **739–740**

O'Sullivan, Jack, *132*

O'Toole, Tommy, 196

Obelmejias, Fulgencio, 437

Odd, Gilbert, **739**

Oguma, Shoji, 328–329

Olin, Bob, 169, 208

Olivares, Ruben, 280, 283, 346, 348–349, **540–543**, 576

Oliver, Stephen ("Death"), 32

Olson, Bobo 406, **544–549**, 605, 606, 648, 653

Orme, Harry, 34

Orono, Rafael, 401

Ortega, Jorge, 418

Ortega, Manny, 557

Ortega, Rodolfo, 329

Ortiz, Carlos, 317, 321, 373, 483, *484*, 487, **550–553**, *596*, 599

v. Laguna, 462, 464–465, 552–553

Ortiz, Manuel, **554–557**

Ortiz, Pedro, 462

Overlin, Ken, 220, 278

Padden, Billy, 242

Paddock, Tom, 46

Paddu, Antonio, 321

Padilla, Carlos, 474, 594

Paduano, Donato, 321

Painter, Ned, 43

Palacios, Baby, 628

Palacios, Jose, 366, 560

Palermo, Billy, 264

Palermo, Frank ("Blinky"), 259, 478, 658

Palmer, Tom ("Pedlar"), 137, 186

Palomino, Carlos, *294*, 296, **558–561**

Palomino, Paul, 560

Pancho, Kid, 58

Panter, Garth, 548

Papke, Billy, 152, **202–203**

Papke, Billy Jr., 203

Papke, Edna, 203

Papp, Laszlo, **562–565**, 646

Paret, Benny ("Kid"), 430, 648

Park, Chan-Hee, 329

Parker, Dan, 176, 215

Parker, Dan, **740**

Parnassus, George, 50, *543*, **741**

Pascua, Rolando, 420

Pastor, Bob, 311

Pastrana, Mauricio, 333

Pastrano, Willie, 461, **566–569**, 648–649

Patchett, Sailor, 78

Patterson, Floyd, 498, 523, **570–573**

v. Johansson, 454, *456*, 456–457, 573

v. Liston, 476, *476*, 478–479, 573

Patterson, Tracy, 573, 675

Paul, Tommy, 58, 192

Payakaroon, Samart, 376

Payne, Rusty, 311

Peakes, Nipper, 134

Pearce, Henry ("Hen"), 16, **39**

Pedroza, Eusebio, *506*, 508–509, **574–577**

Pelkey, Arthur, 244

Pellegrini, Alvin, 566

Peltz, J. Russell, 352, **741–742**

Pender, Paul, 293, 396, 606

Pendleton, Nat, 70

Penprase, Vernon, 508

Pep, Willie, 272, 440, 557, **578–583**, *662*, 667, *762*

v. Saddler, 583, 620, 624, 625

as referee, 441, *450*

Peralta, Avenamar, 402

Perez, Luis, 116

Perez, Nicky, 509

Perez, Pascual, **584–587**

Perez, Victor, 127

Perkins, Eddie, 483, 487

Perrins, Isaac, 32

Perry, Bill, 42

Perry, Lou, 565

Petrolle, Billy, 69, 189, **204–205**

Petronelli, Goody and Pat, 434, 436

Petty, Harold, 672

Phelps, Lloyd, 168

Pian, Sam, 669

Pical, Ellyas, 401

Pietrykowski, Zbiginiew, 564

Pintor, Lupe, 417, 679

Pirrone, Paul, 278

Pitardi, Vincenzo, 318

Pladner, Emile ("Spider"), 127

Poesy, Jean, 113

Ponce, Joe, 346

Pool, Vincente, 326

Poulson, Harry, 42

Povich, Shirley, 325

Powers, Tom, 236

Prada, Bernardo, 369

Price, Andy ("Hawk"), 366

Price, Tom, 29

Pryor, Aaron, 283, 345, **588–591**

Q

Qawi, Dwight Muhammad, 384, **592–595**, 619, *638*, 640

Quarry, Jerry, 261, 270, 392, 538, *539*

Queensberry, Marquess of (John Sholto Douglas), 13, 702, **742**

Queensberry Rules, 13, 88, 89, 702, 742

R

Raft, George, 208

Ramirez, Jorge, 672, 674

Ramirez, Jose Luis, 614–615, 628

Ramos, Armando ("Mando"), *462*, 465, 599

Ramos, Manuel, 392

Ramos, Sugar, 596–599, *626*, 628

Ran, Eddie, *204*

Randal, Rip, 358

Randall, Frankie, 615

Randall, Jack, 40

Randolph, Leo, 638

Ray, Johnny, 362

Reagan, Johnny, 60

Redmond, Frank, 14

Redzepovski, Redzep, 374

Reilly, Pete, 69, 98, *98*, 192

Renard, Jean-Marc, 507

Rice, Bandsman, 84

Richardson, Dick, 457

Richardson, Greg, 376

Richmond, Bill, 12, 22, 37, **41**

Rickard, George ("Tex"), 55, 71, 85, 97, 125, 135, 226–227, *230*, **743–744**

Dempsey's fights and, 103–104, 232, 245, 249

Rickens, Joe, 47

Rinaldi, Giulio, 549

Rindone, Joe, 548

Risberg, Lennart, 549

Risko, Babe, 220, 254–255, 278

Risko, Johnny, 71

Ritaccio, Adolph, 619

Ritchie, Willie, 206–207, 241, 251

Rivera, Domingo, 566

Rivera, Wilfredo, 560–561

Rivero, Jesus, 326

Rivers, Mexican Joe, *206*, 250–251

Roberts, Brian, 528, *528*

Roberts, Jimmy, 70

Roberts, Ted, 242

Robertson, Floyd, 528, 599

Robinson, Floyd, *244*

Robinson, George, 47

Robinson, Sugar Ray, 272, 394, 396–397, 406, 422, 429, 466, 469, *491*, 501, **600–607**, 652–653

v. Basilio, 290, *290*, 291, 293, 606

v. Olson, 547, 548, 549, 605, 606

Rocap, Billy, 138, 247

Roche, Billy, 190

Roche, Spider, 276

Rocks, Jim, 147

Rodak, Leo, 193, 272

Rodel, George ("The Boer"), 191

Rodrigues, Adilson, 384

Rodriguez, Luis, 358, *358*, 361, *430*, 433, **608–611**

Rojas, Raul, 628, *629*

Roman, Jose ("King"), 382

Rooke, George, 23

Rooke, Jack, 29

Rooney, Kevin, *283*

Roosevelt, Franklin D., 492, *634*

Roosevelt, Theodore, 23, 55, 183

Root, Jack, 183

Rosa, José Antonio, 346

Rosales, Delfino, 628

Rosario, Edwin, 612–615

Rose, Lionel, 441, 540, *540*

Rosenberg, Archie, 68

Rosenberg, Charlie Phil, 126, 225

Rosenbloom, Slapsie Maxie, 63, 123, 169, **208–209**, *218*, 219, 223, 239, 440

Ross, Barney, 69, 83, 188, 189, 205, **210–211**, 287, 662

as referee, 453

Ross, Joe, 112

Rossman, Mike, 405, 592

Roupp, Lucien, 338

Routis, Andre, 68–69, 82

Rowan, Joey, *569*

Roxborough, John, 491

Rubaldino, Roberto, 417

Rudd, Irving, 744–745

Ruelas, Gabriel, 531

Ruffalo, Patsy, 118

Ruhlin, Gus, 144, 145, 182, 217

Ruiz, Pedrito, 174

Ruiz, Ramon, 402

Runyon, Damon, 73, 167, **745–746**

Ruppert, Jacob, 71

Ryan, Bill, 15

"I really enjoyed this book!" —*Jake LaMotta*

"Arthur Mercante, takes you on a fascinating journey behind the scenes of some of boxing's biggest superstars . . . If you want to get a real taste of boxing give yourself a treat and read *Inside the Ropes!*" —*Sugar Ray Leonard*

"One of the good guys in boxing, one of the most knowledgeable and certainly one of the greatest referees ever, has written a terrific book about what he knows best."

—*Tony Danza*

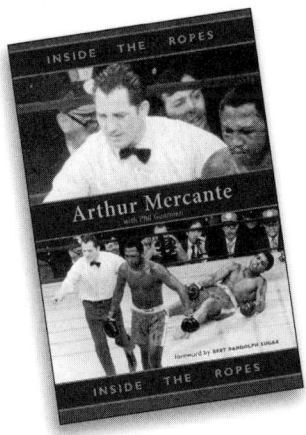

Arthur Mercante's
INSIDE THE ROPES

REFEREE AND ELDER STATESMAN of boxing Arthur Mercante gives behind-the-scenes glimpses into his world, and into the lives and careers of the greatest boxers of all time. From Jack Dempsey to Muhammad Ali, to George Foreman and Marvin Hagler, Mercante has known them all. He has officiated more championship fights than any other referee, and his blow-by-blow accounts are peppered with inside details.

BUT MERCANTE SHARES PRIVATE MOMENTS as well. Making a commercial with Rocky Graziano, giving Sugar Ray Leonard a serious pep-talk in the dressing room before a bout, discovering to his surprise that Mike Tyson is a fan of his, these are the stories behind the glamour and the grit!

Hardcover • ISBN 1-59013-126-6 • 256 pages • $22.95